IMMIGRATION & NATIONALITY LAW HANDBOOK

2008–09 EDITION

AILA TITLES OF INTEREST

AILA'S OCCUPATIONAL GUIDEBOOKS

Immigration Options for Artists and Entertainers

Immigration Options for Physicians

*Immigration Options for Nurses
& Allied Health Care Professionals*

Immigration Options for Religious Workers

Immigration Options for Academics and Researchers

Immigration Options for Investors and Entrepreneurs

STATUTES, REGULATIONS, AGENCY MATERIALS & CASE LAW

Immigration & Nationality Act (INA)

Immigration Regulations (CFR)

*Agency Interpretations of Immigration Policy
(Cables, Memos, and Liaison Minutes)*

AILA's Immigration Case Summaries

CORE CURRICULUM

Navigating the Fundamentals of Immigration Law

Immigration Law for Paralegals*

*AILA's Guide to Technology and Legal Research for the
Immigration Lawyer*

CD PRODUCTS & TOOLBOX SERIES

AILA's Immigration Practice Toolbox

AILA's Litigation Toolbox

FOR YOUR CLIENTS

Client Brochures (10 Titles)

*U.S. Tax Guides for Foreign Persons and Those Who Pay Them,
4 volumes—
(H-1Bs, L-1s, J-1s, B-1s)**

ONLINE RESEARCH TOOLS

AILALink Online

AILA'S FOCUS SERIES

EB-2 & EB-3 Degree Equivalency
by Ronald Wada

Waivers Under the INA
by Julie Ferguson

Private Bills & Pardons in Immigration
by Anna Gallagher

TREATISES & PRIMERS

Kurzban's Immigration Law Sourcebook
by Ira J. Kurzban

Professionals: A Matter of Degree
by Martin J. Lawler

AILA's Asylum Primer
by Regina Germain

*Immigration Consequences
of Criminal Activity*
by Mary E. Kramer

Essentials of Removal and Relief
by Joseph A. Vail

Essentials of Immigration Law
by Richard A. Boswell

Litigating Immigration Cases in Federal Court
by Robert Pauw

OTHER TITLES

*AILA's Guide to Worksite Enforcement
and Corporate Compliance*

David Stanton Manual on Labor Certification

*AILA's Global Immigration Guide:
A Country-by-Country Survey*

Immigration & Nationality Law Handbook

The Visa Processing Guide

Ethics in a Brave New World

*Immigration Practice Under NAFTA
and Other Free Trade Agreements*

GOVERNMENT REPRINTS

BIA Practice Manual

Immigration Judge Benchbook

Citizenship Laws of the World

CBP Inspector's Field Manual

Affirmative Asylum Procedures Manual

USCIS Adjudicator's Field Manual

EOIR Immigration Practice Manual

Tables of Contents and other information about these publications
can be found at *www.ailapubs.org*. Orders may be placed at that site or
by calling 1-800-982-2839.

*An AILA-distributed title

Immigration & Nationality Law
Handbook
2008–09 EDITION

Editor-in-Chief
Richard J. Link

Assistant Editors
Tatia L. Gordon-Troy
Danielle Polen

Senior Editors

Gregory P. Adams
Dan H. Berger
Jan H. Brown
Leigh Polk Cole
James P. Eyster II
Carl Falstrom
Ester Greenfield

Nancy-Jo Merritt
Steven A. Morley
Allen Orr, Jr.
John L. Pinnix
Rita Kushner Sostrin
William A. Stock
T. Douglas Stump

Associate Editors

Romy Kapoor
Rodney A. Malpert
Cyrus D. Mehta
Dev B. Viswanath

Website for Corrections and Updates

Corrections and other updates to AILA publications
can be found online at: ***www.aila.org/BookUpdates.***

If you have any corrections or updates to the information in this book, please let us know by
sending a note to the address below, or e-mail us at ***books@aila.org***.

This publication is designed to provide accurate and authoritative information in regard to the
subject matter covered. It is distributed with the understanding that the publisher is not
engaged in rendering legal, accounting, or other professional service. If legal advice or other
expert assistance is required, the services of a competent professional should be sought.

*—from a Declaration of Principles jointly adopted by a committee of the American Bar
Association and a committee of publishers*

Printed in the United States of America

ISBN 978-1-57370-245-4
Stock No. 52-45

TABLE OF CONTENTS

Practice and Ethics

Business and Employment

PERM and Labor Certification

Litigating in State and Federal Courts and Other Tribunals

Admissibility and Waivers

Temporary Visa Categories

Consular Issues

Asylum, Withholding, and CAT Relief

Removal and Relief

Protection for Women and Children

Family Immigration

Worksite Enforcement and Corporate Compliance

State and Local Law Enforcement

PREFACE

With the failure of Congress to enact comprehensive immigration reform legislation in the past year, and sweeping changes in the immigration laws seemingly on hold for a while, immigration law practitioners can take advantage of the lull by consolidating or deepening their knowledge of existing areas of immigration law, or even venture into new territories. This year's *Immigration & Nationality Law Handbook* is an indispensable resource in this regard, as it collects a wealth of information and practical advice from some of the foremost authorities in their fields.

As it does every year, the *Handbook* contains several extremely useful articles on law practice management, including a contribution this year from Jay Foonberg, the renowned author of *How to Get and Keep Good Clients* and *How to Start and Build a Law Practice*. You'll find expert analysis and guidance as well on the substantive law, including the intricacies of labor certification applications and PERM, the various family– and employment-based paths to immigrant and nonimmigrant visas, protected statuses, admissibility, waivers, and litigation issues, among other topics. Practitioners looking to expand their practice these days may need to ensure they have a sufficient understanding of the defenses available to the targets of increased enforcement efforts by ICE. This edition of the *Handbook* contains several timely articles around this theme.

The articles in this *Handbook* were written by panelists from the advanced and masters track sessions at the 2008 AILA annual conference, with contributions by several other authors writing on topics of current interest. Beginning practitioners and others seeking an understanding of the basic concepts underlying particular areas of immigration law also should obtain this book's conference companion, *Navigating the Fundamentals of Immigration Law: Guidance and Tips for Successful Practice*. AILA offers that tome, updated by panelists from the fundamentals track sessions, and Richard Boswell's *Essentials of Immigration Law*, to complement the more advanced-level and specialized articles contained in this *Handbook*.

Thanks go out to all the contributing authors for finding time on top of their busy work day—especially during a time of year when so many of them are deep in the throes of H-1B filings—to make this book happen. Special thanks are owed to the editors of the articles—Greg Adams, Dan Berger, Jan Brown, Leigh Cole, Jason Eyster, Carl Falstrom, Ester Greenfield, Romy Kapoor, Rod Malpert, Cyrus Mehta, Nancy-Jo Merritt, Steve Morley, Allen Orr, Jack Pinnix, Rita Sostrin, Bill Stock, Doug Stump, and Dev Viswanath. These colleagues of yours volunteer their time to ensure the articles you read are of the highest quality. Thanks also to my colleagues at AILA's Conferences department, especially Michelle Gergerian, Grace Akers, and Barry Collins, for organizing the lineup of authors. Special thanks go to the stellar staff of AILA Publications—Tatia L. Gordon-Troy, Danielle Polen, Kathy Jo Frazier, Kristine L. Tungol, and Mark Ryscavage—for their editorial assistance and production work on this year's *Handbook*.

Richard J. Link
AILA Legal Editor
June 2008

ABOUT AILA

The American Immigration Lawyers Association (AILA) is a national bar association of more than 11,000 attorneys who practice immigration law and/or work as teaching professionals. AILA member attorneys represent tens of thousands of U.S. families who have applied for permanent residence for their spouses, children, and other close relatives for lawful entry and residence in the United States. AILA members also represent thousands of U.S. businesses and industries who sponsor highly skilled foreign workers seeking to enter the United States on a temporary or permanent basis. In addition, AILA members represent foreign students, entertainers, athletes, and asylum-seekers, often on a pro bono basis. Founded in 1946, AILA is a nonpartisan, not-for-profit organization that provides its members with continuing legal education, publications, information, professional services, and expertise through its 36 chapters and over 50 national committees. AILA is an affiliated organization of the American Bar Association and is represented in the ABA House of Delegates.

American Immigration Lawyers Association
1331 G Street, NW
Washington, D.C. 20005
Tel: (202) 507-7600
Fax: (202) 783-7853
www.aila.org

ABOUT THE EDITORS

GREGORY P. ADAMS *(senior editor)* is a partner in the Cincinnati office of Dinsmore & Shohl LLP, where he manages the firm's immigration practice team. Mr. Adams has served as chair of the AILA Connecticut and Ohio Chapters, has co-authored "Foreign Students and Educational Visitors," a chapter in R. Rapp, *Education Law*, and has authored numerous articles for AILA publications. Mr. Adams has been an editor of AILA's *Immigration & Nationality Law Handbook* since 1993. He is listed in *The International Who's Who of Corporate Immigration Lawyers* and *The Best Lawyers in America*. He is a graduate of Middlebury College in Middlebury, VT, and Suffolk University Law School in Boston.

DAN H. BERGER *(senior editor)* is a graduate of Harvard College and Cornell Law School. He won the 1995 AILF Edward L. Dubroff Legal Writing Contest for an article on INS policies toward international adoptions. He is chair of the AILA Board of Publications, and has served on the AILA Vermont Service Center Liaison Committee for several years. He developed his interest in immigration in college, where he studied immigration history and taught English as a Second Language classes for adult refugees. He now specializes in serving academic clients for the firm of Curran & Berger in Northampton, MA.

JAN H. BROWN *(senior editor)* is a principal in the Law Offices of Jan H. Brown, P.C., centered in New York. He has been practicing immigration and nationality law since 1979. Mr. Brown has frequently lectured and written on the subject of U.S. immigration law. He is the co-chair of the Immigration and Nationality Law Committee of the New York State Bar Association's International Law and Practice Section and the vice-chair of the AILA New York Chapter.

LEIGH POLK COLE *(senior editor)* is a shareholder and director of Dinse, Knapp & McAndrew, P.C., in Burlington, VT. Her immigration practice consists of representing U.S. educational and health care institutions and companies employing foreign nationals in the United States. She received a B.A. from Cornell University in 1985 in government and international trade policy, and a J.D. from Albany Law School of Union University in 1991, where she served as editor-in-chief of the *Albany Law Review*. She serves on the AILA Committee on Healthcare Professionals (Non-Physicians).

JAMES P. EYSTER *(senior editor)*, an assistant clinical professor at Ave Maria School of Law, has practiced immigration law in Ann Arbor for 10 years. Prior to that, he served first as executive director of the Princeton-in-Asia Foundation and then in the same capacity for the University of Michigan's Southeast Asia Business Program, for which he edited the *Journal of Asian Business*. He is a graduate of Princeton University and Fordham Law School, where he served as editor-in-chief of the *Fordham International Law Journal*. Mr. Eyster is listed in *Who's Who in American Law*.

CARL FALSTROM *(senior editor)* is of counsel to McGlinchey Stafford PLLC in New Orleans. He received his bachelor's degree from the University of Chicago and his law degree from the University of California, Hastings College of the Law. Mr. Falstrom is a former AILA Northern California Chapter chair and has served on a number of AILA liaison, program, and other committees.

TATIA L. GORDON-TROY *(assistant editor)* is director of AILA Publications and managing editor of AILA's bi-monthly journal, *Immigration Law Today*. Ms. Gordon-Troy has been with AILA for eight years. A 1995 graduate of the University of Baltimore School of Law and member of the Maryland bar, Ms. Gordon-Troy practiced in the areas of employment, family, and administrative law as an associate with the Baltimore firm of Gohn, Hankey & Stichel prior to joining the staff of AILA. In a past life, she was deputy editor of several monthly law newsletters published by *The Daily Record* in Baltimore and served as press secretary to U.S. Representative Elijah E. Cummings (D-MD).

ESTER GREENFIELD *(senior editor)* is a director at MacDonald, Hoague & Bayless in Seattle. She is a past chair of the AILA Washington State Chapter and has taught immigration law and an immigration clinic as an adjunct professor at Seattle University. She has served on local and national AILA Department of Labor liaison committees. She was co-editor-in-chief of AILA's *David Stanton Manual on Labor Certification* (3d Ed. 2005), and co-editor of AILA's *Department of Labor Directory for Immigration Lawyers* (2002–03 Eds.). Ms. Greenfield is listed in *The Best Lawyers in America* and *The International Who's Who of Corporate Immigration Lawyers*.

ROMY K. KAPOOR *(associate editor)* was the program chair for the AILA 2006 Annual Conference. He is an elected director of AILA's Board of Governors and member of the DOL Liaison Committee. Mr. Kapoor is the founder of Kapoor & Associates, with offices in Atlanta and Orlando. He has spoken extensively on business– and family-based immigration topics for AILA and the State Bars of Georgia and Florida. Mr. Kapoor was named a Georgia Super Lawyer in 2006, 2007, and 2008.

RICHARD J. LINK *(editor-in-chief)* is a legal editor at AILA Publications. Mr. Link received a B.A. in Language Studies from the University of California, Santa Cruz (1986), and a J.D. from the University of California, Davis School of Law (1990), where he served as senior research editor of the *U.C. Davis Law Review*. The bulk of Mr. Link's career has been spent in various editorial capacities for legal publishers.

RODNEY MALPERT *(associate editor)* is a partner at Fragomen, Del Rey, Bernsen & Loewy, LLP in Phoenix. Formerly, he taught immigration law at Southern Methodist Law School. He has also been on the Board of Directors of the American Council on International Personnel. Mr. Malpert is frequently sought for commentary, being interviewed for publications such as *CNN Money Magazine*, *Business Week*, and various newspapers. He publishes two looseleaf treatises: *Business Immigration Law: Strategies for Employing Foreign Nationals*, and *Business Immigration Law: Forms and Filings*. He is a 1986 graduate of Cornell University Law School.

CYRUS D. MEHTA *(associate editor)*, a graduate of Columbia Law School, is the managing member of Cyrus D. Mehta & Associates, PLLC in New York City. The firm represents corporations and individuals from around the world in a variety of areas. Mr. Mehta has received an AV rating from Martindale-Hubbell and is listed in *Chambers USA*, *The International Who's Who of Corporate Immigration Lawyers*, *The Best Lawyers in America*, and *Super Lawyers*. He is past chair of the American Immigration Law Foundation's Board of Trustees. He is a frequent speaker and writer on various immigration-related issues.

NANCY-JO MERRITT *(senior editor)*, a director in the Phoenix office of Fennemore Craig, P.C., has more than three decades of practice in the field of immigration law. Her practice is broad-based and includes the representation of domestic and international companies regarding visa and work authorization issues for foreign national employees. She also assists employers with federal compliance issues in the contexts of mergers and acquisitions and government audits. Ms. Merritt has bachelor's (1964) and master's (1974) degrees in English from Arizona State University and a law degree from the same institution (1978).

STEVEN A. MORLEY *(senior editor)* is a partner in the Philadelphia-based law firm of Morley, Surin & Griffin, where he concentrates in all facets of immigration law and criminal defense. He has served as an officer and chair of the AILA Philadelphia Chapter and as chair of the Criminal Justice Section of the Philadelphia Bar Association. Mr. Morley is a frequent regional and national lecturer on immigration law. He has successfully argued matters before the U.S. Third Circuit Court of Appeals and before the U.S. Supreme Court in the decision of *Mitchell v. United States*, extending the Fifth Amendment right to remain silent to sentencing proceedings. Mr. Morley is an honors graduate of the University of Wisconsin Law School.

ALLEN ORR, JR. *(senior editor)* is an immigration associate in the international practice group at Baker & McKenzie. He entered private practice in 1998, and has represented numerous companies and individuals in immigration visa and compliance matters. He managed an I-9 compliance audit for a Fortune 100 company, which involved review and analysis of 250,000 employees' immigration records, and assisted employers in settling civil and criminal investigations. He received his J.D. from Howard University in 1998.

JOHN L. PINNIX *(senior editor)* is a past president of AILA (2002–2003) and a founding member of AILA's Carolinas Chapter. He attained B.A. and M.A. degrees in History at the University of North Carolina at Greensboro and his J.D. at the Wake Forest University School of Law. He has served as an adjunct professor at North Carolina Central University School of Law and as a senior lecturing fellow at Duke University School of Law. He also is an adjunct professor at the Elon University School of Law. Mr. Pinnix is a principal in the Raleigh law firm Allen and Pinnix, P.A., and is a North Carolina board-certified immigration specialist.

DANIELLE M. POLEN *(assistant editor)* serves as associate director of publications for AILA. Prior to joining AILA, she spent eight years as chief legislative correspondent for *Interpreter Releases*, a weekly information service on immigration, nationality, and related matters. Ms. Polen also has practiced immigration law, clerked for the Honorable Marvin H. Morse at the Executive Office for Immigration Review, and served as an adjunct professor in the Shepherd College legal research and writing program. She is a graduate of the George Washington University's National Law Center and the University of Texas at El Paso, and is a member of the District of Columbia Bar.

WILLIAM "BILL" STOCK *(senior editor)* is a founding partner of Klasko, Rulon, Stock & Seltzer, LLP. He handles all aspects of immigration law, including assisting companies and individuals in obtaining employment– and family-based visas; resolving citizenship issues and obtaining naturalization; and defending clients in ICE and DOL enforcement proceedings. Mr. Stock, who is an adjunct faculty member at Villanova University School of Law, is the immediate past chair of AILA's Philadelphia Chapter, is a past member of the AILA Board of Governors, and has received AILA's Joseph Minsky Young Lawyer Award. In 2003, he was selected for inclusion in *Best Lawyers in America*. He is a member of editorial boards for Matthew Bender and AILA and has authored many articles on immigration law topics.

T. DOUGLAS STUMP *(senior editor)* maintains a practice focused on employment-based immigration law, complex deportation, litigation, and family immigration matters. Mr. Stump is on the AILA Board of Governors, ICE Liaison Committee, and USCIS Service Center Operations, Nomination, and Benefits Policy Committees. He chaired the AILA Texas Chapter, the AAO Liaison Committee, and the TSC Liaison Committee. He is recognized in *Best Lawyers in America* and in *Super Lawyers* as one of Oklahoma's Top 50 Super Lawyers.

DEV BANAD VISWANATH *(associate editor)* is the principal attorney of the Banad Law Offices, P.C., with offices located in Manhattan and Queens, NY. Mr. Viswanath obtained his undergraduate degree in Psychology and Philosophy from Boston University and his J.D. from Pace University School of Law in White Plains, NY. He has also obtained a certificate of concentration in international law. He has been honored by his peers with the Adolf Homberger Outstanding Humanitarian Award. Mr. Viswanath has worked in the field of immigration law since 2002. He has represented individuals and corporations from all over the world in various stages of the immigration and nationality process, including consular processing, citizenship, permanent residence, and nonimmigrant visa petitions. Mr. Viswanath currently is of counsel to the Law Offices of Michael Phulwani, P.C. and to Baron, Mundie, and Shelkin, P.C. Additionally, he is the general counsel to International Television Broadcasting, Inc. (ITV) and Asian FM radio network.

TABLE OF AUTHORS

STRUCTURING THE ROLE OF THE PARALEGAL: TOOLS, TRAINING, AND SUPERVISION

*by Joan S. Claxton, Andrew B. Greenfield, Helen L. Jugović, and Alberta M. Poland**

INTRODUCTION

Immigration attorneys have long debated what type of case is best for a beginning paralegal, and how to teach "enough" immigration law to a new paralegal so that he or she can meet a firm's business needs during the various stages of his or her career. Most of us have discovered gaps in training or quality control, and asked ourselves how those problems can be avoided in the future while still maintaining efficiency. Structuring the role of the paralegal is challenging and time consuming. But properly doing so can have great benefits at times, like when your paralegal comes up with a strategy that saves the day or proposes a client relations idea that you never considered.

In law practice management, we talk about being both lawyer and businessperson. In terms of paralegal development, we must also balance the role of *educator* with real-world legal/business needs. Achieving this necessary balance requires planning and the integration of tools, training programs, and supervisory practices with respect to our paralegals. Training cannot be just a long-winded lecture, off-hand instruction,[1] or merely placing a book on fundamentals in the paralegal's hands. Training teaches how and when to use the appropriate tools, and how to conform the tools to match the limits of the paralegal role. Tools like templates, checklists, and best practices models are key training and business efficiency aids, and they assist attorney supervision by facilitating review of both work product and conduct.

TRAINING: AN ONGOING PROCESS

The verb "train" is defined in *Webster's Dictionary* as "to direct the growth of (a plant) by bending, pruning and tying ... to form by instruction, discipline, or drill ... to teach so as to make fit, qualified or proficient ... to make prepared for a test of skill ..." Training is perhaps the most important thing you can do to ensure that your paralegals are properly fulfilling their role. One need not resort to bending, pruning, or tying to train paralegals, but rather one should teach to make proficient. Training consists of three basic elements: explain, practice, and review. Training can be complex and formal education, or it can be as simple as correcting an error and explaining what the correct answer/process/procedure is and why. Feedback is training and also serves to demonstrate your support of the importance of the role of the paralegal in your practice. Training should not end after the paralegal's first week. It must be an on-going

* **Joan S. Claxton** is an attorney with Hammond Claxton, P.C. and a member of the Maryland and District of Columbia bars. She is a graduate of the American University Washington College of Law and the George Washington University Paralegal Certificate Program. Ms. Claxton has a unique perspective on the role of paralegals and nonlawyer support staff due to her extensive experience as both paralegal and supervising attorney across a range of legal environments, from sole practitioners and small immigration firms to large international multipractice firms.

Andrew B. Greenfield is managing partner of Fragomen, Del Rey, Bernsen & Loewy, LLP's Washington, D.C. office. He has served as vice chair of AILA's Washington, D.C. chapter as well as on AILA's Vermont Service Center Liaison Committee. He received his bachelor's degree with honors from the University of Pennsylvania and his J.D. from the George Washington University Law School.

Helen L. Jugović joined the immigration law division of McKinney & Justice, P.A. in February 2008. Heading up the firm's second office in Wilmington, NC, she counsels both individuals and businesses in all aspects of immigration law, including citizenship, employment-based immigration, and removal defense, in English and Spanish. Since 2007, she has served as the AILA Carolinas Chapter ICE Liaison.

Alberta M. Poland is director of special projects with Fragomen, Del Rey, Bernsen & Loewy, LLP. She began her career with Fragomen in 1974 as a corporate paralegal. She then served in a number of administrative/management capacities for the firm until assuming her current role. Alberta is involved primarily in corporate compliance, training, client relations, and best practices. She is a frequent speaker on I-9 and labor certification application compliance issues. Alberta holds a bachelor's degree in political science from The Pennsylvania State University, a master's degree in history from the University of Massachusetts, and an MBA degree in management from New York University.

---

[1] Bear in mind that no two immigration cases are exactly alike, and your paralegals may have a very different take than you do on instructions like "It's a straightforward case" or "It's similar to the other case."

process throughout the paralegal's career with the firm.

Paralegals joining a practice need training in three basic areas: immigration law and procedures, which includes ethics; computer applications and tools used by the practice; and general training on how to function within the office. Following are some suggestions that can be implemented in a practice of any size.

Immigration Law and Procedures

Orientation and Overview

It is essential to provide the new paralegal with an overview of the law and procedures so they develop an understanding of the forest before dealing with the trees. If they understand the context within which cases are prepared, they will have a far better comprehension of what will be required of them. This overview, or "Immigration 101," can be provided in one to two hours, one-on-one, or it can be conducted seminar style. The overview should include how the law, regulations, and other legal authority interrelate; the role of the federal agencies; basic immigration concepts; and a summary of the nonimmigrant and immigrant visa categories your practice deals with.

Related Tools

- Consider using beginner continuing legal education materials as a reference as you develop your orientation overview, rather than creating your training program and overview from scratch. This can eliminate gaps in training, starting with a proper overview, and focus the initial training on the basics.

- At a minimum, have a checklist for your verbal overview.

- See Appendix A for sample overview tools and training schedules.

Training on Specific Cases

Once you have presented a general overview, you can begin to instruct your paralegal on how to prepare a particular case type (*e.g.*, an L-1A visa petition). The authors recommend assigning the paralegal a hypothetical case file to review and organize, and then to draft a basic immigration package, including client correspondence letters. Using hypothetical rather than actual cases may take longer than letting the new paralegal sink or swim, but it is less stressful, which provides a better learning environment. Once you develop hypothetical case studies and exercises, you can use them over and over again.

Related Tools

- See Appendix B for a business immigration hypothetical—a great training tool. Notice how it leaves out certain items so that the focus is on efficient training and orientation, but still provides the big picture on a specific type of case. A hypothetical also can function as a testing tool, identifying potential "drop outs" early on, when the focus is on developing a skill quickly and not on a client case.

- See Appendix C for a naturalization template, geared toward allowing the paralegal to see the variations he or she may encounter on a "confirmation of filing" communication to a client, and allowing for proper customization. Many times, the paralegal can just jump in and customize the letter using common sense. However, clear strategy memos and supervision are required to ensure the right language from a template is used, as in the case of memos regarding visa renewal instructions for approved H-1B extensions, where the best place of renewal may vary based on the employee's nationality and other factors, or memos advising on advance parole/travel eligibility, where the advice may vary a great deal depending on whether the adjustment applicant would be subject to the inadmissibility bars upon departure.

Ethics and Role Training

It is also crucial that you instill in your new and existing paralegals their ethical obligations and responsibility to protect client privacy and confidentiality, and to avoid the unauthorized practice of law. As a supervising attorney, you assume responsibility for both the work and the conduct of your paralegals and nonlawyer staff.[2] Thus, paralegal training should include guidance on the kinds of activities, with an emphasis on communications, that may and may not be performed without direct attorney involvement.

Related Tools

- Employee handbook (*see* Appendix D)
- Confidentiality agreement, read and signed by paralegal (*see* Appendix E)
- Properly drafted retainer agreement or engagement letter clearly identifying the supervisory

---

[2] *Model Code of Prof'l Responsibility* EC 3-6.

role of the attorney and the nature of the work the paralegal will perform

- Template letters and e-mail communications, directing clients to contact attorney with X-type questions or issues, but paralegal with Y-type questions or issues, or Z-type documents

- Periodic distribution of paralegal role/ethics articles or excerpts to your staff, noting any differences in your policy or practice on relevant sections of the article[3]

- Pay for and encourage your paralegals to attend AILA paralegal conferences and audio seminars. In addition to training and education, by providing this development opportunity to paralegals, you recognize their accomplishments, boost morale, facilitate employee retention, and give junior paralegals something to look forward to.

Computer Applications

You must train your paralegals in the use of all software applications, particularly if you use specialized case management, document management, or billing systems. Live training is the best way to show your paralegals how to use your systems the way you want them to. Sending them to a class or providing them with an on-line tutorial or a manual is better than nothing, but live training by one of your experienced staff is far more effective. You do not need a full-time trainer. You can identify those staff members who have demonstrated proficiency and ask them to mentor the new hire. This is a morale builder for the trainer, and recognizes his or her experience and professionalism.[4]

Workflow tools and models, and case management applications such as LawLogix, INSZoom, and ImmigrationTracker, allow paralegals to prepare forms and supporting documents efficiently and accurately.[5] Because so much time has been invested by software developers specific to the immigration law workflow, these applications must be seen as high-value training tools. However, attorneys must customize applications and/or train paralegals to ignore unimportant bells and whistles (and vigilantly adhere to the important ones) in order to maximize the profit/efficiency potential that case management software is supposed to provide. The true value of case preparation and management tools will be determined by how solid your training program is, and whether your office culture and policy demands that everyone actively engage in using the system properly.

Do not assume that everyone on your staff knows everything about off-the-shelf applications like Word and Excel. It is important to train your new hires in how you use these in your practice. Style, formatting, use of macros, and the structure of directories need to be included in applications training.

A few weeks after the paralegal has had an opportunity to work with the various applications, have a review session. Probably as much as half of what is taught in the initial training will be forgotten, particularly if it is not used immediately. Once the paralegal has had a chance to actually use the application, the follow-up training will be more meaningful and provide an efficient means for dealing with any difficulties the paralegal has encountered. Don't try to cover too much at first. Teach the more complex use of the applications in successive trainings.

Practice Pointer

Attend technology trainings yourself. Proper supervision is impossible unless you understand and use your case management system and other technology. Every six months, offer refresher sessions on technology, especially if you have had significant turnover.

Office Procedures

Your new paralegal may have recently graduated from college with no or little experience working in an office. Things as simple as how to make a file copy may have to be demonstrated. Give your new paralegal a tour of your office. Show him or her where supplies are kept and how to handle mail, overnight courier, and messenger services. Train your paralegals in proper telephone etiquette, appropriate dress, and demeanor. You want your paralegal staff to act in a professional manner that reflects your practice.

Paralegals joining your office who already have immigration experience still need training. You need

---

[3] *E.g.*, M. Mancini, "Ethical Considerations for Immigration Attorneys Regarding Employment of Paralegals," *Immigration & Nationality Law Handbook* 44 (AILA 2006–07 Ed.).

[4] It is critical to allow your senior paralegal the time to prepare for training and a reduced caseload to allow for training. Failing to reduce the trainer's caseload can lead to shortcuts and poor mentoring relationships.

[5] For a thorough review of major case management applications and other technologies, see Jones, *et al.*, "Technology for the Immigration Practitioner," *Immigration & Nationality Law Handbook* 11 (AILA 2006–07 Ed.). *See also AILA's Guide to Technology and Legal Research for the Immigration Practitioner* (3d Ed.).

to introduce them to the specific ways in which your office functions. Assess their knowledge and skills. They may not be as experienced as their resume suggests. You may have to do some retraining in some basic areas of immigration practice.

Finally, be a mentor. Mentoring should be an attitude of enabling your paralegal staff to learn and grow. Consider the qualities of the mentors in the field who inspired and taught you throughout the years. Paralegals often are transitional individuals who may only stay on for one to three years. A good mentor will facilitate quick training, maximizing profitability, while giving the time and effort to the personal and professional development of his or her staff.[6]

SUPERVISION: A CRITICAL PART OF THE BALANCE

The use of the case processing tools and models described in this article not only provides excellent training for paralegals, but also can be of invaluable assistance in supervising the work and conduct of your paralegals. As a practical matter, attorneys delegate a wide variety of tasks to paralegals, but the attorney assumes ultimate responsibility for the delegated tasks and must continue to exercise independent professional judgment with respect to all aspects of the representation of a client.[7] Additionally, the attorney must ensure that the paralegal has the adequate education, training, and experience to handle the task being assigned. Failure to properly delegate tasks to or to adequately supervise a paralegal can result in serious consequences, including

---

[6] Ask yourself whom you have mentored, and whom you currently mentor in a devoted manner. Do you make time for paralegal questions, or is it never a good time to go over cases? Are you hot and cold as a manager depending on your day or your mood? Have you written recommendation letters for paralegals who move on in the field? How many of your paralegals have stayed on for more than two years, or continued on to law school? Over a period of years, have you kept up with what your former paralegals have gone on to accomplish? Paralegals have their own network system, and your current and former paralegals can be as valuable a source of information and contacts as your attorney network.

[7] "Provided the lawyer maintains responsibility for the work product, a lawyer may delegate to a paralegal any task normally performed by the lawyer except those tasks proscribed to a nonlawyer by statute, court rule, administrative rule or regulation, controlling authority, the applicable rule of professional conduct of the jurisdiction in which the lawyer practices, or these Guidelines." ABA Model Guidelines for the Utilization of Paralegal Services, guideline 2 (2004).

criminal and/or civil liability, and suspension or expulsion from the practice of immigration law.

Obligation to Supervise

A detailed discussion of the ethical obligations of attorneys inherent in the employment of paralegals and other nonlawyer staff is beyond the purview of this article.[8] At a minimum, however, *all* attorneys should ensure that they are familiar with their local rules of professional conduct and, specifically, the rules imposing obligations on supervising attorneys.

The American Bar Association (ABA) Model Rules of Professional Conduct (Model Rules)[9] and its predecessor, the ABA Model Code of Professional Responsibility (Model Code), impose clear obligations on attorneys who supervise the conduct and work of nonlawyer staff. While the Model Code encourages attorneys to delegate tasks to paralegals so that legal services can be rendered more economically and efficiently, delegation is only proper if the attorney "maintains a direct relationship with his client, supervises the delegated work, and has complete professional responsibility for the work product."[10] Rule 5.3 of the Model Rules provides that attorneys are ultimately responsible for all work performed by their paralegals and vicariously liable for any ethical misconduct by those paralegals.

Therefore, it behooves all supervising attorneys not only to be aware of *what* their paralegals are doing, but also of *how* their paralegals perform their duties. You must not only monitor the end product of your paralegals' work to ensure that it is timely and competently performed and substantively correct, but you also must make reasonable efforts to ensure that the paralegals' conduct is professional and compatible with your professional obligations as an attorney.

Establishing the Paralegal-Client Relationship

Shortly after you meet with or confer with a prospective client, you should formalize the attorney-client relationship with a retainer agreement or en-

---

[8] For two recent, detailed articles on the subject, see J. Chehrazi *et al.*, "Why 'Walk the Line'? Effective, Efficient, and Ethical Practices for Immigration Paralegals," *Immigration & Nationality Law Handbook* 67 (AILA 2006-07 Ed.), and M. Mancini, *supra* note 3.

[9] The Model Rules were adopted by the ABA House of Delegates in 1983 and were revised in 2002. They serve as models for the ethics rules of most states.

[10] *Model Code of Prof'l Responsibility*, EC 3-6.

gagement letter. This important document sets forth the ground rules for the relationship between the client and you and your staff. At a minimum, it describes the legal services to be provided and the fees for those services. However, it also provides an opportunity for you to inform the client that paralegals will work on the client's case, to describe the nature of the work the paralegals will perform, and to identify and establish the role of the paralegals in providing legal services. Additionally, it is an opportunity to communicate to both the client and the paralegal the expectation that all client confidences and secrets will be preserved and that you will take reasonable measures to prevent conflicts of interest resulting from a paralegal's past or concurrent employment, relationships, or interests.[11] The retainer agreement, therefore, is an important opportunity for you to inform the client of your supervisory responsibility for the paralegals' work and conduct and also to reinforce the paralegal's understanding of his or her role. A copy of the retainer agreement or engagement letter should be in the client file and provided to the paralegal or available for the paralegal's review to ensure he or she is aware of the nature of the relationship with the client.

Case Preparation and Filing

You must diligently review all work before it is sent to the client or filed with the appropriate government agency. Not only must you ensure that the work product of your paralegal is well prepared and professionally presented, but you must ensure that the information contained therein is accurate and has a basis in law or fact. For example, if a client provides information about his or her employment history or immigration history that is material to the immigration benefit they are seeking, you are responsible for ensuring that your paralegal accurately and truthfully presents this information in the application or petition. The consequences if you fail to do so can be severe. Section 274C(a)(5) of the Immigration and Nationality Act (INA) provides *criminal* penalties for any person who prepares or files an application for benefits or any document "with knowledge or in reckless disregard of the fact that such application or document was falsely made." The definition of "falsely made" is statutorily broad and encompasses the preparation or provision of an application or document with knowledge or in reckless disregard of the fact that the application or document contains a false, fictitious, or fraudulent statement or material representation, has no basis in law or fact, or otherwise fails to state a fact that is material to the purpose for which it was submitted.[12]

Access and reference to the client's information and documents is critical to your ability to review forms and documents before they are sent to the client, and again before the case is filed, to ensure that the information contained therein is accurate and provides a lawful basis for the benefit sought. You should reference these materials when reviewing petitions and applications before sending them to the client for signature and before filing with the government.

Related Tools

- Intake questionnaires and document checklists can be completed by the client to obtain all relevant personal, employment, and family information, as well as a basic immigration history. These can be provided to the client in person at an initial consultation, sent to the client as e-mail attachments, or completed through an Internet-based case management application. The completed intake forms are a valuable reference source for the reviewing attorney.

- A prefiling review checklist, like the sample at Appendix F, which requires the attorney to acknowledge that all form fields are completed, all forms are signed and dated as required, properly made-out, signed checks for all correct fees are enclosed, correct number of copies are enclosed, and the correct filing address is used, can go a long way to ensure that all outgoing work product meets the standard imposed by INA §274C(a)(5).

Paralegal Communications with Clients and Others

Immigration paralegals often function as a liaison between the attorney, the client, and various government agencies. A well-trained and experienced immigration paralegal usually has frequent and regular contact with clients and the government and a high level of independence or autonomy in the performance of his or her duties. Good immigration paralegals often build a rapport with the client, the company contact or human resources person, or government contacts with whom they regularly communicate via e-mail or telephone. Because of this relationship, clients may raise legal questions or issues in their communications with paralegals, or

---

[11] *Model Rules of Prof'l Conduct* R. 1.6, 1.7.

[12] INA §274C(f).

seek advice on case strategy. The use of template e-mail communications and adherence to the practice of copying an attorney on substantive e-mails with clients can keep the paralegal from inadvertently giving legal advice.[13] Paralegals always should take care to communicate that any legal advice provided comes from the attorney. You should instruct your paralegal to copy you on all substantive client e-mail communications so you can be aware if your paralegal directly or inadvertently provides legal advice. If you have any concerns, you can join the communications and affirm or clarify the information or advice.

Case Monitoring Practices

Every immigration attorney's nightmare involves overlooking the expiration date of a client's nonimmigrant status, missing the filing date for an appeal or response to a request for evidence, or attempting to file a PERM application on the 181st day after recruitment began. We all worry about how to keep up with all of the expiration dates, time lines, and time periods, and most of us task our paralegals with monitoring these important dates. Case monitoring is one of the most valuable tasks immigration paralegals can perform, but you must take steps to ensure that they have the proper tools and training to accomplish this adequately.

Related Tools

- Case management software is the ideal means by which to handle this function, but you must ensure all important dates are entered, set reminder notifications at appropriate intervals to alert you or your paralegals of important dates, and calendar in periodic audits of expirations.

- If your practice is smaller and you choose not to use a software management system, you must ensure that your office "tickler" system adequately tracks expiration dates and that you have practices in place to assist your paralegal in monitoring the system.

- Staff meetings or one-on-one meetings to review case status and expiration date reports should be a regular office practice.

- See Appendix G for a checklist of quality control concepts and methods.

CONCLUSION

Like developing your law practice, structuring the paralegal role, and developing and maintaining the necessary tools, training, and supervisory/management skills and aids, cannot be done overnight. It is an ongoing process. The continuous updating of these tools, regular evaluation of your training programs and results, and objective self-evaluation of your skills as business manager, attorney, and teacher over time will lead to success and help you to find the balance between these roles.

---

[13] Paralegals must disclose their status as such. *Model Code of Professional Ethics and Responsibility and Guidelines for Enforcement*, EC 1.7(a)–(c) (The National Federation of Paralegal Associations, Inc.); *Code of Ethics and Professional Responsibility*, canon 5 (National Association of Legal Assistants, Inc.).

APPENDIX A
SAMPLE TRAINING SCHEDULE

Introduction to the firm

- Welcome! Coffee and introductions
- Human resources (I-9 forms; employee handbook, benefits, etc.)
- Set up desk, list of passwords, employee ID, keys

Meeting with your supervising attorney

- Open-door policy
- Outline of training schedule
- Attorney discussion: Confidentiality
- Attorney discussion: What is legal advice?

Meeting with Senior Paralegal A:

- Overview of approaching client communications
  - When you first get a file; folders and organization
  - Attorney review of e-mails, letters, and any client communications before sending
  - Copy attorneys or supervising paralegal on communications
  - Copies of communications to file
  - Filing system/folders
  - Senior paralegal discussion: Confidentiality
  - Senior paralegal discussion: What is legal advice?
- Frequently Used Programs:
  - Central directory and network concepts
  - E-mail/calendar (*e.g.,* Outlook)
  - Calendar
  - Word processing (*e.g.,* Word, WordPerfect)
  - Browser (*e.g.,* Internet Explorer, Firefox)
  - Case management (*e.g.,* LawLogix)
  - Time and billing (*e.g.,* Timeslips)
- Time and Billing
  - Keeping time each day; entering time into software program (*e.g.,* Timeslips) each time you perform a task, and in any event, by end of day
  - Each day's entries for one client should be combined for that client.
  - Conversion chart (parts of an hour)
  - When to charge to firm or general

  - Training time: if it takes longer than you think it should for one case, record your real time and we will adjust bill later (do not worry)

LUNCH

Meeting with Paralegal B

- Case management software (*e.g.,* LawLogix) training (in person; one hour max)
  - The dual purposes (1) creating forms and (2) tracking cases on a daily, monthly, and annual basis
  - Case management
    - Intake of a case, drafting reminders, case notes
    - Creating forms
    - Using system to communicate what has been done on the case, and what remains to be done; update it so that if the case was transferred from you to another paralegal, or a client called for an immediate status update, you would be able to provide the client with the most current information possible.
    - Failing to follow rules can result in malpractice.
  - Plan for future trainings, etc.

Working the first case

Meet with attorney to discuss case strategies and ask any questions, etc.

Meeting with paralegal

  - Reviewing a family-based adjustment of status case file
  - Working with prototypes and reviewing workflow for a family-based case (use adjustment of status binder)
  - Preparing the case and forms

Reading (if time left over)

  - Chapter 12 of *Immigration Procedures Handbook* (on family-based adjustments)

APPENDIX B

SAMPLE BUSINESS IMMIGRATION HYPOTHETICAL

ABCD Ltd. (ABCD) is a British company headquartered in London that designs, engineers, and manufactures engine components for high-performance automobiles. ABCD has set up a U.S. subsidiary, ABCD USA, and established engineering operations in Los Angeles and Wilmington, NC and a sales office in Los Angeles. ABCD USA has been operating for more than one year and its operations have exceeded expectations.

Due to its increased business, ABCD has an urgent need to expand its U.S. workforce. ABCD has decided to hire a new employee to direct the U.S. sales and marketing efforts. ABCD recently hired John Walker, a British citizen who has a degree in business, to work out of the Los Angeles office as sales and marketing manager to direct and oversee ABCD USA's sales and marketing staff. Mr. Walker has completed his training at ABCD and is now ready to come to the U.S. to take up the position in Los Angeles. ABCD needs Mr. Walker in the U.S. as soon as possible.

ABCD has hired us to handle Mr. Walker's transfer to ABCD USA. We have provided ABCD with our employer intake questionnaire and Mr. Walker with our employee intake questionnaire. You have been given the ABCD Ltd. immigration case file, which contains the completed questionnaires, company information about ABCD and ABCD USA, Mr. Walker's curriculum vitae, his educational credentials, and a copy of the biographical page of his passport.

You will use this information to prepare a draft H-1B package for John Walker. You must enter the information into[software application or case management system] under "Training Module" and prepare the forms for this case. You will also prepare the supporting documents and correspondence for this case using the templates in "Docs/Toolbox/Training Case/H-1B."

APPENDIX C

CASE-SPECIFIC PROTOTYPE LETTER

[Date]

[Client name & address]

Re: Confirmation of Filing

Naturalization Application (U.S. Citizenship)

Dear Mr./Ms. Client:

Please find enclosed a copy of the Naturalization Application that we filed on your behalf on July 24, 2007. Congratulations on taking this step toward becoming a U.S. citizen.

Please safeguard your copy of the application, and bring it with you on the day of your naturalization interview (in case the USCIS officer has any questions).

We strongly recommend that you bring updated information regarding your *[any missing documents, e.g., if filed taxes late and OK to file N-400 per attorney, you will tell client here to remember to bring that info with him or her to interview]*

Overview of the Application Process

In the next one to three months, USCIS should issue an N-400 receipt notice for your case. We will send the receipt notice to you. It will have a receipt number that you can use to follow the status of your case online.

Under current USCIS procedures, a few weeks, and sometimes several months, after the receipt notice is issued, an appointment notice for fingerprinting/biometrics will be issued. We will send you the notice with instructions.

Over the next 6 to 24 months, USCIS should schedule you for a naturalization interview. You will be tested on English language (oral and written) and U.S. history/civics. Please review carefully the questions we sent you previously, and try to remain current regarding local information (*e.g.,* mayoral or gubernatorial elections).

[If Spanish exemption or elderly, refer to template language re diff type of exam]

If the interview is successful, you may be given the oath of allegiance and sworn in as a U.S. citizen on the same day. If the USCIS workload is too heavy, you will be scheduled for this ceremony on a different day.

Sometimes USCIS requests additional evidence or information regarding a case, or there are administrative delays in processing. We can help resolve these issues if and when they arise.

We will keep you informed regarding your case. Likewise, we ask that you contact us immediately and send us copies of **all correspondence** that you receive from USCIS. Sometimes USCIS fails to notify attorneys of important information.

Finally, if you need to **travel internationally** for an extended period of time, your U.S. **address**

changes, or you are **cited for a traffic or any other offense** while your application is pending, please contact us as soon as possible.

[Check file for client if has teenage kids who are LPRs to remind re auto citz]

If you have any questions, please contact us by phone, fax, or e-mail at _____.

With kind regards, I am
Respectfully yours,

[Attorney name]
[Attorney initials/Paralegal initials]
Enclosures

APPENDIX D

SAMPLE EMPLOYEE HANDBOOK TABLE OF CONTENTS[14]

Introduction and Overview

Purpose

Equal Employment/Discrimination-Free Workplace

Equal Employment Opportunity Guidelines

Anti-Harassment Policy

Sexual Harassment Policy

Discrimination/Harassment Complaint Procedure

Employment Policies

Employment on an At-Will Basis

Business Hours

Payroll Classifications

Emergency Closings/Late Openings

Holidays

Mileage/Expense Reimbursement

Lunch

Outside Employment

Pay Periods

Smoking Policy

Jury Duty

Personnel Records

Problem Resolution

Performance Evaluations

Drug-Free Workplace

Responding to Customer Inquiries & Problems

Inspection of Company Property

Network and Electronic Resources

Confidential and Proprietary Information

Rules of Conduct

Insurance and Benefits Summary

Vacation

Health and Dental Insurance

Simple IRA, 401 K or similar

Acknowledgement of Receipt of Employee Handbook

APPENDIX E

SAMPLE CONFIDENTIALITY AGREEMENT[15]

The legal profession is governed by a strict code of ethics. An area of specific concern is keeping all client information **confidential**.

All employees must use extreme caution to ensure that client information in our possession does not become available to unauthorized third parties. To maintain all client information in strict confidence, avoid:

- Discussing client affairs with a third party unless the client authorizes such communication. Note oral authorizations in a memo and place it in the client's file.

- Disclosing confidential information to unauthorized client personnel.

- Discussing client affairs in public places.

- Talking unnecessarily about client affairs anywhere, including in our own offices or homes.

Employees who violate these rules will be subject to disciplinary measures, up to and including discharge.

I understand and agree to abide by the above policies.

_____

Employee Signature, Date

---

[14] Sample courtesy of Tonia Furniss-Roe of McKinney & Justice, PA.

[15] Courtesy of Gerard M. Chapman of Chapman Law Firm, in Greensboro, NC.

APPENDIX F-1

PEER REVIEW FILING CHECKLIST

Case type: _____

Petitioner/Applicant: _____

Beneficiary: _____

To be completed by peer-reviewer:

❑ All fields completed in all forms?

❑ All forms signed and dated by employer?

❑ All forms signed and dated by attorney?

❑ Correct filing fee?

❑ Premium processing fee?

❑ Fraud detection fee?

❑ Check signed?

❑ Correct number of copies for USCIS?

❑ Correct filing address on FedEx form?

❑ Return FedEx mailer (if premium)?

To be completed by Case Manager:

Number of copies needed:_____

Method of delivery:
❑ Overnight ❑ 2nd day

Send file copies to client by FedEx:
❑ Overnight ❑ 2nd day

Case Prepared by _____ Date _____

Mailing Reviewed by _____ Date _____

To be completed by Admin Staff:

❑ File copy sent to company _____
(date and initial)

❑ File copy sent to foreign national
_____ (date and initial)

APPENDIX F-2

I-130 PETITION REVIEW CHECKLIST[16]

❑ Form G-28, Notice of attorney rep

❑ I-693 Medical examination (Sealed)

❑ Color photographs of sponsor & alien

❑ Cover letter with check attached

❑ Form I-130 or approval letter
Filing Fee for I-130 of $___

---

[16] Courtesy of McKinney & Justice, of Greensboro, NC.

❑ Form I-485
Filing Fee for I-485 of $___

❑ Form Supp. A to I-485 (for illegal entry only
$1,000 fee)
Filing Fee for I-765 of $___

❑ Form G-325A, Biographic info 4 pages for peti-
tioner and 4 pages for beneficiary
Fingerprinting Fee of $____
Filing fee for I-131 of $____

❑ Evidence of U.S. citizenship or LPR (birth certificate, Nat. Cert., LPR Card, etc.)
Filing fee for 245(i) of $____

❑ Alien birth certificate (plus translation)
Filing Fee for I-102 of $____

❑ Evidence of family relationship (usually marriage
certificate)

❑ Divorce/Death record for past marriages

❑ Copy of last I-94 (if applicable)

❑ Copy of last visa (if applicable)

❑ I-864, Affidavit of support for sponsor

❑ Sponsor's tax records for the past three years and
evidence of current employment (job letter showing date of hire, position, rate of pay, and whether
job is temporary or permanent; pay stubs)

❑ I-864 if joint sponsor (if applicable)(joint sponsor
is needed only if sponsor does not make enough
money or is short the three-year tax requirement)

❑ Contract between sponsor and household member (this form is used if someone else in the same
house, including the alien, can provide tax returns to make up for the sponsor not having
enough money)

❑ I-765 Application for employment

❑ I-131 Application for travel

APPENDIX G

SUGGESTED METHODS FOR IMPROVING QUALITY CONTROL, SUPERVISION, AND EFFICIENCY

1. **Map out your stages of review for drafts and finalizations.** Then, evaluate whether any stages of review could or should be combined, or sepa-rated, to improve quality control and efficiency.

   a. Example 1: Are paralegals responsible for bringing drafts to your desk in final form, including confirming that not only are cli-ents' names spelled correctly, but that their biographical information is consistent with what is on the birth and marriage certificate, etc.?

   i. If so, at what stage do you look at "raw" information to confirm that this is being done consistently? It's easy for a client to find a typo, but hard for a client to realize that his birth certificate does not match up to the name on his passport and transcripts.

   ii. Possible fix: Have paralegals rubber-band draft cases on top of hard copy files for review, so you can spot check from time to time; also helps you see whether files are well organized, and to look at the case as a whole.

  b. If you work for a small firm and do not have time or staff to map out stages of review for each type of case, focus your efforts on one type of case that you do regularly.

   i. Establishing a framework for one case will set the pace for future cases.

   ii. If you proceed without a core framework, your office may never find the time or resources to convert to a proper framework.

2. **Quality control for client provided information.** If clients are responsible for entering their information into a web-based case management system like LawLogix, who performs quality control on that information? Clients often enter their own information incorrectly. Are paralegals fact-checking, and then attorneys performing a second-stage review?

  a. If a client told you at intake that she was working as a hairdresser on her B-2 visa, who will make sure that the G-325 for the marriage-based adjustment contains her unauthorized self-employment history?

  b. At what stage is the intake information received from clients compared against other client-provided information?

  c. What is the most efficient way to do this in your office, based on how you perform intake, how cases are prepared, and your review and supervision system?

3. **Templates and transmittal letters to clients**

  a. Does each template letter for sending client drafts actually specify that drafts should be

reviewed by the client? It is easy to send forms for signature, without making it clear to the client what is a draft and what is a finalization.

  b. Templates are key to quality control. Who is in charge of updating yours? Who reviews and approves new templates?

4. **Use visual aids to plan quality control and supervision.** Prepare a workflow chart or diagram so that you and your staff can visualize better the various stages of review, supervision, and quality control. It helps to have the workflow diagram during initial training sessions, when outlining paralegal responsibilities. When there is a failure in your system, go back to the workflow chart and see at what level/stage the change should be made.

5. **Plan financially for quality control and supervision.** When revising and updating your fee schedule each quarter, take it as an opportunity to consider the levels of review and current number of transmittals and submissions that go into each type of case.

  a. If the National Visa Center adds a stage to consular processing cases, have you increased the number of times a case is reviewed? Have you adjusted your fees accordingly for the increased expense of an additional transmittal, and the time taken to review an additional stage?

  b. Has e-filing become available on a new type of petition, such that you need to adjust your fees and also change your workflow for quality control/supervision?

6. **Delegate appropriately.** It is easy to delegate managerial functions *ad hoc*. Set aside time to take proper law practice management decisions. If a new associate is ready to start signing off on cases and managing paralegals, try to articulate (for your and his or her benefit) the quality control and supervision methods you employ so that you both are consistent internally.

7. **Paralegal training.** What systems do you have in place to help paralegals be consistent in terms of procedure? Monthly meetings? Telephonic or monthly continuing legal education courses? Do you do on-the-job training (*e.g.,* discussing the rules for affidavits of support while working on a specific case with a paralegal)? Make a checklist for your law practice regarding training. Ask

for paralegal input. Consider time, costs, and benefits of each training method.

8. **Quality control for service providers.** Consider your approach toward monitoring quality control for credentials evaluators, translators, experts, etc. How do quality and customer service issues identified by paralegals and staff reach you?

9. **Evaluations of paralegals, staff, and self.** Consider your performance evaluations as an opportunity to identify needs in your law practice regarding supervision and quality control. If your staff (or you) score low on organization, what procedures can you implement to improve organizational methods over time?

Stay focused. There are only so many hours in a day. Limit the number of changes you make in your law practice so that they can be implemented, evaluated, and seen as part of the firm culture over time.

THE NINE STEPS (SEVEN HABITS AND TWO RULES) TO A SUCCESSFUL LAW PRACTICE

by Jay Foonberg[*]

Successful lawyers were not born that way. They became successful by adopting the habits that other successful lawyers adopted and by not adopting the habits of nonsuccessful lawyers.

The seven habits are based on studies done by the American Bar Association, and the two rules are rules superimposed by me based on 40 years of successful law practice preceded by three years of a successful certified public accountant practice.

Although many lawyers do not realize it, many of the successful habits of successful lawyers are the result of ethics duties and obligations imposed on us as lawyers, stemming from the relationship of fiduciary and beneficiary and the obligations set forth in the Restatement of Agency.

As one bar counsel opined, "Good Ethics Translates into Good Income." Bar counsel have long realized that more than half of all ethics complaints are the result of not observing one or more of the seven habits, and easily could have been avoided.

---

* **Jay Foonberg** has served in the American Bar Association (ABA) House of Delegates; he is on the Advisory Council for the ABA Commission on Evaluation of the Rules of Professional Conduct, and he was a founder of the ABA Law Practice Management Section. His book, *How to Start and Build a Law Practice* (5th Ed.), is the book that is most frequently stolen from law libraries in the United States and it has earned more than $1 million for the ABA, and has been their best seller every year since 1977. Mr. Foonberg is the author of three other important books, all available from the ABA: *How to Get and Keep Good Clients* (3rd Ed.); *Finding the Right Lawyer*; and *The ABA Guide to Lawyer Trust Accounts*. A much sought-after speaker, Mr. Foonberg has led seminars and taught client relations, malpractice prevention, ethics, and client development in every one of the 50 states and as far afield as Europe, South America, and Asia in English, Spanish, and Portuguese. Mr. Foonberg earned his J.D. from UCLA Law School and has received the prestigious Harrison Tweed Award, CLE's highest honor. He lives and practices in Beverly Hills.

This article excerpts two chapters from the author's *How to Get and Keep Good Clients* (3rd Ed.) © 2007. Mr. Foonberg's books and audio CDs contain literally hundreds of suggestions to demonstrate good ethics and attain good results. Individual chapters are available for download at *http://foonberglaw.com*.

More than 80 percent of malpractice claims have no merit.

Accordingly, the benefits of adopting the seven habits and the two rules include:

- Compliance with ethics requirements
- Reduction and elimination of nonmeritorious ethics complaints
- Reduction and elimination of nonmeritorious malpractice complaints
- More time for family, self, and community
- Higher income

Included in this article is discussion of practices that are both good ethics and good practice.

Topics covered will include:

- How and when to timely return telephone calls
- How to timely do the work
- How to listen to the client and obtain maximum information
- How to conduct a client interview
- How to keep the client informed of the progress of the legal matter
- How to preserve client confidences
- How to demonstrate interest and concern
- How to maintain time records
- How to get paid

OFFICE CONFIDENTIALITY AS A MARKETING TOOL

This part of the article will give you specific marketing techniques, which can both increase your practice and improve your confidentiality procedures.

Violating attorney-client confidences is not only unethical, it's harmful to practice growth and client relations.

Clients want an ethical lawyer. The American Bar Association's study, the Legal Needs of the

American Public, proves conclusively that ethics are high on the list of factors, which result in being recommended to other clients. If a client or potential client believes that you violate attorney-client confidences they'll leave you or won't recommend others to you.

Lawyers don't normally intentionally violate the confidentiality of the attorney-client relationship. The result of violating confidences or allowing staff personnel to violate confidences could be disbarment, loss of the client whose confidences are violated and loss of referrals from clients and others who perceive you to be unethical.

The practice of law includes a T & C Factor. T & C stands for Trust and Confidence. Clients bring you their darkest secrets. They tell you things they can't confide to their spouse. They admit embarrassing and even heinous acts. They admit to doing what they shouldn't have done. They trust you not to reveal their confidences.

Clients do not normally want the public to know that they are about to file bankruptcy or that they intend to get a divorce or that they have been charged with a crime. Often a breach of the confidential relationship is not only prejudicial to their position in the community but is also prejudicial to their legal case.

Some law offices are unknowingly riddled with breaches in protecting the confidential relationship. This chapter is designed to help you find and plug and prevent the leaks in your own office.

Rather than repeat the common mistakes lawyers make, a check list type of self administered test may help reveal some of your deficiencies. As a lawyer you should answer correctly all of the 58 questions. You do not need a key to score this test. You'll instinctively know whether you've answered correctly.

The results of this test can be used to both plug existing leaks and to prevent future leaks of information. After you have improved your office management procedures, you can use the improved procedures as a tool to help market the practice. Every person in the firm should affirmatively tell clients and potential clients of the strict procedures the firm uses to protect the confidences of a client. This will enhance the firm's reputation for ethics and improve the firm image and reputation in the community. As firm personnel do (or refrain from doing) these procedures in the presence of a client or potential client, you should expressly communicate to the client what you are doing to protect their confidence. For example, when you bring a client into your office and close the door behind you, you could say something like: "Let me close the door. Now we'll have some privacy and no one can accidentally overhear what you say or even know that you're here."

1. Do you have a written statement of the attorney-client privilege and the protection of client confidences in your office manual or which you give to all attorneys and all non-attorneys in the firm at time of hiring? _____

2. Do you have a written acknowledgement of receipt of the previous statement in which the attorneys and staff acknowledge that violation of client confidence is cause for discharge? _____

3. Does your receptionist repeat who's calling and why they are calling in the oral or visual presence of clients or strangers who are within hearing range? _____

4. Does your secretary repeat who's calling and why they are calling in the presence of clients or others within hearing range? _____

5. Does your receptionist open mail, do "light typing," word processing, or filing in an area where clients can see other clients' names? _____

6. Does your receptionist affirmatively cover up client papers in the presence of clients so that clients know that you protect attorney-client confidences? _____

7. When your client goes from reception area to your office do they pass secretarial, paralegal, or word processing work stations where they can see file folders or screens or items with client names? _____

8. When the client goes from the reception area to your office passing secretaries, paralegals, word processors, screens, etc., do the staff people cover up client papers in the presence of the client, so that clients know you protect confidences? _____

9. When someone in your firm is assembling a complex pleading or contract and has papers, exhibits, and information spread all over the conference table or library, do they cover up the papers before going to lunch or out on a break, or home for the evening? _____

10. When you bring your client into your office or conference room do you close the door to give the client the feeling of privacy and protection of the confidential nature of the attorney-client relationship? _____

11. Do you allow clients to go unescorted from the reception area to your office or conference room allowing them to look at computer screens, file cabinets and files on desks with client names and matters? ____

12. Do you escort the client to and from the reception area to be sure that the client doesn't wander into an area where there are confidential matters which can be seen or heard? ____

13. Is (are) your conference room(s) near the front of the office so visitors can be met without their passing through firm work areas? ____

14. Do you use only numbers or codes instead of client names on file covers and documents to protect confidentiality? ____

15. Do your secretaries, word processors, paralegals, etc., cover their documents or close file folders when they go to lunch or on break so that a client passing by won't see any client names? ____

16 When you see clients in your personal office do you remove or cover up all documents with clients' names or at least close all files which the client could see? ____

17. Do you restrict access to the files and file area to only those who have a need to know the contents of the files? ____

18. Have you considered meeting clients in your conference room instead of your private office, explaining to them that you meet clients in the conference room instead of your office because you have a lot of client files and papers in your office and you want to preserve attorney-client confidences for all clients including the client you are seeing? ____

19. Does your support staff (paralegals, secretaries, clerks, etc.) have a place where they can interview or work with vendors in privacy out of the presence of other office staff? ____

20. Do you or others in your office use speaker phones in offices with open doors where clients passing by or in another office can hear the receptionist or your secretary telling you who's calling and why they're calling or can hear your conversation with a client? ____

21. Are your word processing or billing equipment screens facing the client areas where the clients passing by can see what's on the screen? ____

22. When you get an emergency client call, when you are in conference with another client, do you tell the caller, "I'm in a conference with another client and I can't discuss a client's confidential matters in the presence of another client. I'll call you back in 30 minutes." Or alternatively, do you say, "I'm in conference with another client, please hold on while I go to another room so I can discuss your case." Alternatively, do you leave the room to take the call?

23. Do you really know what happens to the papers you put in the waste basket? Have you ever stayed or had someone stay and observe the process of waste paper removal to see the access points where a stranger or adverse party or private investigator or competitor or police officer could go through the trash looking for information which could prejudice your client's case? ____

24. Do you have a paper shredder for destruction of files with very sensitive client information? ____

25. Do you have telephone procedures for handling telephone information requests? For example, when a voice over the phone asks for a client's address or phone number, do you tell the caller, "I'm sorry, but we don't give out any client information over the phone, please send us a letter asking for the information, and *if* the person is a client, we'll forward your letter onto them and they can respond." Or if the caller says it's an emergency, do you inform the caller that you can't reveal whether or not the person is a client, but *if* the person is, you'll try to pass the message on for the person to call the caller? ____

26. When a client tells you that they believe their telephones may be "bugged" in some manner by a spouse or competitor or government authority, do you classify them as paranoids undeserving of your legal talent or do you take reasonable steps to avoid telephone conversations which, if the phones really are bugged, could be damaging to the client? ____

27. Is your receptionist instructed not to allow unidentified maintenance and repair people into the office unless escorted by someone from the firm? ____

28. When someone shows up at your office with a tool kit or a tool belt claiming they are there to "fix the phone" or some piece of equipment, do you ask for identification? ____

29. Do you assign someone to watch repair and maintenance people while they are working to be sure they do not look at files? ____

30. When you receive a call from a person who claims that they are a lawyer and that your client wants their file sent to the lawyer do you insist, when feasible, on a letter signed by the client authorizing the release of the file and the information in it to a specific person, and another from the recipient acknowledging they will accept the file from you? ____

31. Does your administrator have a private area to interview vendors or job applicants where they cannot overhear office discussion or see client files? ____

32. When attorneys and staff discuss client matters do they do so behind closed doors where other clients or office personnel not involved in the case cannot overhear the conversation? ____

33. When you send a bill which contains great detail as to the work done, do you mark it "personal and confidential" or similar notation, or address it to an individual to prevent unauthorized access to its confidential information by the wrong person accidentally opening it at the client's home or business? ____

34. Are your attorneys and staff prohibited, in writing in the staff manuals or otherwise, from discussing client matters in public places such as restrooms, elevators, hallways and restaurants? ____

35. Do you and your attorneys and staff violate attorney-client confidences by telling third parties who your clients are or were, and what legal matters you were or are handling for them, without first getting client permission? ____

36. Would you tell Client "A" how you helped or got a good result for Client "B" without masking the identity of Client "B"? ____

37. Do you keep telephone messages in a location where others can see who called and why they called? ____

38. Do you have signs stating "Respect Client Confidences" in your elevators, rest rooms and common areas? ____

39. Do you have a separate exit for people who want to enter or leave your office without meeting people in the reception room who might recognize them? ____

40. Do you tell your clients that you have a separate exit for the foregoing reason and that you will be happy to escort them in and out of this exit? ____

41. Have you ever suggested meeting a client out of your office so that other clients won't accidentally see them or recognize them? ____

42. Do you have security procedures to prevent unauthorized people from accessing your computer information? ____

43. Do you have a security system to prevent unauthorized access to your computer files? ____

44. Does your telephone system have a privacy system to prevent others from listening in to the conversation? ____

45. Do you have an agreement in writing with your landlord that they will take reasonable steps to instruct their employees and the contract cleaning personnel that all information in your office including the Information In waste baskets is to be considered confidential and is not to be given to third parties who ask for it? ____

46. Do you discuss client names and cases at home with your spouse at the breakfast or dinner table in front of your children so they can tell their friends who can tell their parents so it can get back to the client? ____

47. Do you discuss client legal problems on the telephone at home in front of your spouse and children? ____

48. Have you and each person in the office instructed their children and other household members not to repeat any office information they accidentally (or intentionally) overhear or see? ____

49. When the case is over and you put the client's file into a public warehouse, do you get an agreement with the warehouse that they acknowledge that the contents of the files are confidential and that they won't allow access to the files to anyone unless that person is designated by you in writing? ____

50. When you get mail to sign, is the letter accompanied by the mailing envelope or mailing label as a double check against sending your client's mail to another client? ____

51. Does your secretary or mail room have a procedure to double check that copies of mail and email are matched to envelopes or mailing labels

to prevent sending copies to the wrong people? ____

52. Does your mail room or bookkeeping section match invoices against envelopes or mailing labels to prevent sending the bills to the wrong clients, thus revealing both the identity of the client but also the nature of the work being done? ____

53. Did this test bring some of your deficiencies to light? ____

54. Do you intend, as the result of this test to put a special section in your personnel manual? ____

55. Would you consider photocopying this list and using it as the basis for an addition to your office manual? ____

56. Would you consider modifying the questions in this test to become part of your personnel testing and screening? ____

57. Do you have a DVD or tape on the subject of "confidentiality" that can be shown to all new hires as part of their indoctrination program? ____

58. Do you have a paragraph for emails and faxes indicating that the information contained is confidential with procedures to prevent accidental dissemination of information? ____

Almost all of the foregoing questions are rhetorical in that the correct answers to the questions are suggested in the questions themselves. Score three points for every correct answer giving you a possible 174 points. A score of 100 would be barely passing.

Remember, protecting client confidences is an easily observable representation of your ethical concerns. Clients and others are likely to recommend you to others and use you for repeat business if they perceive that you go to great lengths to preserve their confidences. Failure to protect confidences is easily observable and will cost you clients and repeat business.

HOW TO AVOID LOSING CLIENTS AND FEES WHEN YOU HAVE CONFLICTS OF INTEREST

It's easier and cheaper to stay out of trouble than to get out of trouble.

This is an article on how to get clients and cases ethically. It would be a counter-productive effort to get the clients and cases into your office and then have to give up or lose the client and have to disgorge the fee because you mishandled the situation.

This article can help you ethically keep both the client and the fee.

Newer lawyers have difficulty recognizing the conflicts problem and even experienced lawyers sometimes don't know "how to handle it" even if they recognize it.

This article originated with my book, *How to Start and Build a Law Practice*. I am repeating much of it here because it is worth the extra few minutes required for any lawyer to review the basics of recognizing the problem, and worth any lawyer's time to consider my solutions to the problem.

Recognizing the existence of a conflict. A lawyer is a fiduciary and a client is a beneficiary. The duty of loyalty owed to the client by the lawyer is absolute and total. Anything which does or might impair that duty of total loyalty is a conflict and must be dealt with.

All lawyers, especially new lawyers, are prone to problems involving conflicts of interest for the following reasons:

1. They don't recognize the problem when they see it.
2. They don't know how to handle this problem when they recognize it.
3. They are afraid to broach this subject for fear of frightening the client away and losing a fee.
4. They don't realize they can still do the work and gain a fee if the conflict problem is handled properly.

I. The importance of recognizing and solving conflicts of interest at the beginning:

A. *To You as the Lawyer:* If you don't recognize and solve the problem:
   1. You may have to withdraw from the case.
   2. You may not be able to collect any fees due you.
   3. You may have to refund any fees previously paid you.
   4. Depending on the extent of the problem, you may be disciplined—or disbarred for your stupidity.

B. *To the Client:* The client will have to obtain a new lawyer and waste a lot of time and energy locating and educating the new lawyer. This delay might even prejudice the case.

II. How to Recognize the Conflict Problem:

A. *Simple Conflicts.* These are conflicts between you and the client. To the extent that lawyers are compensated by clients and clients compensate them, there is always a theoretical conflict between the client and the lawyer. This theoretical conflict comes close to being actual when the lawyer is compensated by "a piece of the action" or other economic interests beyond an earned fee. This problem, however, is normally treated by Bar associations under the category of unreasonable or excessive fees rather than conflict of interest.

These simple conflicts also can arise when you have two clients unrelated to each other, such as:

1. Client A wants you to collect $5,000 from X and Client B wants to collect $8,000 from the same X. X only has, or is ever likely to have, $2,000. Who would get it? Client A or Client B or both A and B in some ratio?

2. Client A wants you to argue as a lawyer for a debtor that involuntary repossessions are unconstitutional; Client B wants you to argue to in the same or a different court in a different matter that involuntary repossessions are constitutional. Do you take both cases on the theory that the court makes the law and not the lawyer?

B. *Complex Conflicts:* These are the more common situations and arise out of the fact that multiple parties want to use only one lawyer, typically to save fees. The most common situations are:

1. *Partnerships:* Each partner and the partnership are independent entities and there are conflicts and potential conflicts in the situation.

2. *Corporations:* Each incorporator, each director, each officer, each employee and the corporation are independent and/or could have conflicting interests, depending on the capacity in which they will be acting

3. *Divorce:* Husband and wife have conflicting interests. In theory, the court represents the children. In some jurisdictions, another lawyer is appointed to represent the children.

4. *Multiple defendants* or potential defendants in criminal cases. The defendants may later wish to turn on one another or try to get immunity or other favorable treatment in exchange for testimony.

5. *Auto Accident Cases:*

(a) Insufficient insurance or assets. There may not be sufficient insurance or assets to cover all the injured parties. For example, suppose that the defendant has a $25,000-$50,000 policy and there are four seriously injured parties in your client's car. Suppose that the claims of each are reasonably worth $30,000 or more. Suppose further that the defendant is an indigent who can successfully go bankrupt on a personal injury judgment debt. Suppose further that the insurance company is willing to pay the entire $50,000. If you take all four cases, how do you divide up the insurance money? Can you take all four cases? Which client(s) do you keep or reject? If you advise one or more people to get independent counsel (probably the lesser-value cases), should you explain why? Would an explanation be a conflict with the clients you keep?

(b) Passenger or driver. Can you represent both the driver and the passengers? Is there a possibility of suing the driver/owner for negligent operation or maintenance of the vehicle, or under a guest statue?

(c) Hidden Conflicts. A lawyer is a fiduciary and a client is a beneficiary. The lawyer has a duty of total loyalty to a client. Anything which could affect 100% loyalty is a conflict whether it is a financial or personal relationship with a client or a financial or personal relationship with a non-client or former client.

6. *Other Conflict of Interest Situations:* Obviously, there is an infinite number of possible conflict of interest situations. Anytime you have, or may have, more

than one client in a matter you should ask yourself, "Do I have a conflict of interest situation here?" If you are not sure, call another lawyer and get that person's opinion or call the local Bar Association and get the name of a member of the ethics committee. Some ethics committees will answer only requests of the Bar Association itself, as opposed to individual members of the Bar Association. Some ethics committee members will respond only to written questions for fear of misunderstanding of the facts.

You should get another lawyer's opinion for the protection of both yourself and the client. The opinion of another experienced lawyer can help you decide whether you have a conflict. The fact that you were sufficiently concerned over the possibility of a conflict that you took steps to get another opinion(s) would probably be of help to you in the event of a subsequent problem.

III. *How to handle the problem.* Be honest, be forthright and put everything in writing!

The Code of Professional Responsibility does *not* totally prohibit your representing clients when there is, or might be, a conflict of interest. The lawyer may represent more than one party provided the client understands the conflict and waives it. If you can't solve the conflict problem, you're better off losing the client before you do the work than after you do the work and end up not getting paid.

All ethics questions are fact specific and are subject to local ethics rules. There is no substitute for periodically reading and re-reading the local rules.

IV. Periodically read and re-read the local rules and cases.

The increased size of law firms has caused many changes in the rules. As firms grow in size there will be more changes.

A RISK IS STILL A RISK

and the fundamentals still apply ... as time goes by

by John L. Pinnix[*]

INTRODUCTION

Today, a perfect storm, driven by an economy teetering on recession, post-9/11 national security concerns, and re-invigorated restrictionists, has transformed our practices. More lawyers serve fewer corporate clients. After a brief period of reasonably efficient and reliable adjudication, PERM has now become an increasingly treacherous and dilatory process. We face unrealistically meager quotas in the H-1B, H-2B, EB-2, and EB-3 categories. As old hands are rediscovering their family-practice roots, attorneys are encountering unconscionable delays never intended by the legislators of yore who created our pitifully antiqued family quota system. The new practice frontiers are in areas such as border issues, national security, and employer/workplace compliance. Technology has made us better able to serve our clients; yet despite our being available 24/7, we often can't get the simplest response from U.S. Citizenship and Immigration Services (USCIS). USCIS's promise of reducing processing backlogs now appears to be most illusory. Fundamental liberties are suspended in the name of national security. Frustrated clients are increasingly—and fortunately thus far figuratively—tempted to kill the messenger. To sustain lifestyles unimaginable to any previous generation, we are tempted, or sometimes feel forced, to chase incredible billable hours.

Immigration attorneys, once almost immune to the pervasive jokes told at the expense of other lawyers on talk shows, at social functions, and within their own families, now face a reality that is no joke.

AILA Past President Palma Yanni noted in an *Immigration Law Today* (ILT)[1] article that a former Florida AILA member was "sentenced to more than eight years in prison after being convicted of fraud and conspiracy in the filing of thousands of religious worker and multinational executive petitions." Another AILA member was convicted in Virginia in connection with filing phony labor certifications, and members in Washington, D.C. and Maryland have faced similar charges.[2] More recently, a California immigration attorney was sentenced to two years in federal prison for filing fraudulent employment visa applications on behalf of his own firm's employees.[3]

A veteran AILA Carolinas Chapter member was convicted for arranging a sham marriage, and "filing legal papers with authorities falsely claiming that another immigrant was gay and would be persecuted if sent back to Egypt." The "clients" were working as government informants. Also convicted, on related charges, was the attorney's then 27-year-old daughter, who worked as her paralegal.

Times are changing. Yanni added that in the District of Columbia, immigration matters now "receive the lion's share of complaints against attorneys." She went on to say: "In a distressing corollary, AILA members increasingly find themselves filing complaints against other members for ineffective

---

[*] **John L. (Jack) Pinnix** is a past president of AILA (2002–2003) and a founding member of AILA's Carolinas Chapter. He attained B.A. and M.A. degrees in History at the University of North Carolina at Greensboro and his J.D. at the Wake Forest University School of Law. He has served as an adjunct professor at North Carolina Central University School of Law and as a senior lecturing fellow at Duke University School of Law. He is currently an adjunct professor at the Elon University School of Law. Mr. Pinnix is a principal in the Raleigh law firm Allen and Pinnix, P.A., and is a North Carolina board-certified immigration specialist. He would like thank **Daniel Horne**, a senior associate at the San Francisco immigration boutique of Jackson & Hertogs LLP, and **Reid F. Trautz**, Director of Practice & Professionalism at AILA, for their assistance in updating this article. This article revisits the author's "Risk Management for the Immigration Practitioner" in *Ethics in a Brave New World: Professional Responsibility, Personal Accountability and Risk Management for Immigration Practitioners* (AILA 2004), a book of which Mr. Pinnix was editor-in-chief.

---

[1] 22 *Immigration Law Today* 6 (Nov./Dec. 2003).

[2] Department of Justice News Release, (Mar. 7, 2003), *available at www.oig.dol.gov/public/media/sgksentenced.html*.

[3] U.S. Immigration and Customs Enforcement News Release, "Two Attorneys at Immigration Law Firm Sentenced for Roles in Visa Fraud Scheme" (Mar. 10, 2008), *available at www.ice.gov/pi/news/newsreleases/articles/080310losangeles.htm*.

21

assistance of counsel under the *Matter of Lozada*[4] rubric. The BIA has left us little choice."

Yet, should this prove to be, in King Richard III's words, "the winter of our discontent,"[5] it would be irresponsible to simply damn the system and not make every effort to wrest control of our own destinies. We must acknowledge that at least some of the fault is, after all, in ourselves and not in our stars.

In a changing world, AILA has sought to respond to its members' needs for mentoring and to provide tools addressing a wide range of professional development issues. Even with powerful tools, such as InfoNet, the Mentor Directory, and the Message Center, the challenge can be daunting. In 1994, AILA had 3,700 members; in just 14 years, our rolls have grown by over 7,000 and now exceed 11,000. A comprehensive member survey conducted in late 2006 indicated that 22 percent of our membership is under the age of 35; 28 percent of respondents have been in practice less than five years. In 1998, AILA's Board of Governors passed a resolution urging each chapter to establish an ethics committee and to hold an annual continuing legal education event devoted to ethics. In her ILT article, Palma Yanni wrote that "ethics must be more than an annual event; it must be ingrained in every action we take each day we represent a client."

Every stage of a case has the potential to frustrate the most otherwise reasonable and virtuous client seeking nothing more than lawful status and family reunification. Even without the quota backlogs, governmental processing delays can destroy families.

No less formidable and demanding is the human resources (HR) director, whose own job is on the line because no one anticipated there would be a four-month delay in securing an advance parole for a key scientist, who has a desperate need to travel abroad—tomorrow.

In identifying basic rules for risk management, there are some constants, whether an attorney's area of practice emphasis is business, family, or defense.

The fact patterns giving rise to ethical dilemmas vary: the family practitioner may belatedly learn that a marriage is dubious; the attorney trying a removal case may learn that the testimony on which she was

hinging her case is suspect; and the business immigration attorney may learn that the employee has a criminal conviction undisclosed to the employer. Though mindful of Mark Twain's warning against all generalities, "including this one," there are nevertheless basic, fundamental precautions every immigration attorney can implement that will vastly reduce his or her exposure.

As in other practice areas, there are distinctions between questionable ethical conduct, malpractice, conflicts of interest, and issues of professionalism and confidentiality that face attorneys handling immigration issues. From obstruction of justice, to subordination of perjury, to harboring, immigration attorneys' exposure has never been limited to civil liability or professional sanctions. However, starting with the Illegal Immigration Reform and Immigrant Responsibility Act of 1996 (IIRAIRA),[6] and continuing to the USA Patriot Act,[7] the bars have been raised. For instance, IIRAIRA §213 removes any doubt that it is unlawful for any individual to knowingly and willfully fail to disclose, conceal, or cover up the fact that he or she has, on behalf of any person and for a fee or other remuneration, prepared or assisted in preparing an application for immigration benefits that was falsely made.[8]

While the distinctions between malpractice and other conduct are easily made by malpractice carriers, and are of understandably keen interest to the would-be claimant (who wants to be known as the "insured") on learning that the suit he or she is facing may be actionable, but is not, at least for the purpose of the coverage, "malpractice," the actual distinction may be more academic to the attorney than the issues at hand. A negligence suit, bar griev-

---

[4] 19 I&N Dec. 637 (BIA 1988), *aff'd* 857 F.2d 10 (1st Cir. 1988).

[5] William Shakespeare (1564-1616), "King Richard III," Act 1 scene 1.

[6] Pub. L. No. 104-208, div. C, 110 Stat. 3009, 3009-546 to 3009-724).

[7] Uniting and Strengthening America by Providing Appropriate Tools Required to Intercept and Obstruct Terrorism Act of 2001, Pub. L. No. 107-56, 115 Stat. 272.; *see* R. Juceam, "International Security, Civil Liberties, and Human Rights After 9/11–An Outline," *Ethics in a Brave New World, Professional Responsibility, Personal Accountability and Risk Management for Immigration Practitioners* 98 (AILA 2004), *available from* AILA Publications, *www.ailapubs.org*, (800) 982-2839.

[8] *See* INS Memorandum, P. Virtue, "Criminal Penalties for Preparation of Falsely Made Applications for Immigration Benefits Added by Sections 213 & 214 of the Illegal Immigration Reform and Immigrant Responsibility Act of 1996 (IIRAIRA)" (Sept. 3, 1997), *published on* AILA InfoNet at Doc. No. 99091790 (*posted* Sept. 17, 1997).

ance, criminal indictment, or sometimes even the loss of a single client can impact the attorney's firm, other clients, and family for the remainder of his or her professional career. Whether these harms are "ethical" considerations as such may be irrelevant to the attorney facing them at the time.

The tactics for risk prevention suggested by this article go beyond modifying conduct that will allow an underwriter a better night's sleep. They address practices that may avoid an uncovered suit, professional grievance, or the wrath of a disgruntled client. They are not intended to be in any way exhaustive, but are rather a professional reality check.

FIVE "EASY" PIECES

The real world practice of immigration law is fraught with situational ethical dilemmas.

Consider: Either the petitioner or beneficiary may initiate contact with an attorney for assistance in securing a family-based "green card" for the beneficiary. It is rare indeed for a husband and wife to have independent representation at the outset of an immediate relative case. When there is a falling out among the relatives, the sponsoring uncle regrets signing an I-864 for the troubled teenage niece he has never met. Or, on the eve of the 90-day window to remove conditional status, the husband and wife that you have represented for years separately call you and blurt out confidences that make your continued representation of either virtually impossible.

In the business area, with regard to who selects and meets with counsel, who signs the retainer agreement, or who pays the fees, an immigration attorney often *de facto* represents both the petitioning employer and the beneficiary employee. By extension this representation often includes derivative beneficiaries. Although the employer may initially think of the attorney as the worker's representative, or the worker may think of the attorney solely as the company's lawyer, the parties soon will be sharing with the attorney confidences necessary to process the application or petition. The course of action the attorney charts will necessarily have legal implications for all of the parties.

As desirable as independent representation for each party may be (for both family– and business-based cases), it is usually not sought by the client, not only for financial reasons, but also simply to facilitate processing.

Further, consider the following altogether possible scenarios:

1. You are the new in-house immigration attorney for Walnut Cove Software, Inc. Fred Software, grandson of the founder and vice president for development, instructs you to process an H-1B for Mark Smith, who is described as an Iranian computer whiz.

   Mark attained a B.S. from Nevada State University in December 2006 and worked for Software on practical training from December 2006 to December 2007. In December 2007, after speaking with your predecessor, he filed a change of status to B-2, which was approved on February 18, 2008.

   Fred tells you it is extremely important to file another change of status to H-1B for receipt on April 1, to insure that Mark's chances will be maximized should the 65,000 cap once again be reached on the first day of filing.

   Mark brings his academic credentials by your office and says if you need anything else he can be reached at his office on the 14th floor.

   "What?" you ask, "You can't be working!"

   "Well," says Mark, "the project reached a critical stage and I just couldn't stay away. But I'm not working, I'm just volunteering."

   "By the way, Mr. Software said to remind you to file an extension of my B-2; it runs out on August 18, and I obviously can't go back to Iran until my October 1 H-1B start date."

2. Fred Mertz, a Canadian entrepreneur, consults with you regarding a possible investment. Fred tells you, "Forget about filing anything for my wife Ethel. She has worked in the Boston office of Consolidated Aluminum Toothpick for years and they think she is an American." The following day the loonie overtakes the U.S. dollar and you do not hear from Fred again.

   Six weeks later, Consolidated Aluminum Toothpick contacts you and asks you to represent the company. Your first task will be to supervise the audit of their 2,500 employees' I-9s.

3. Jose Melez entered the United States without inspection on July 4, 1997. He came to join Rosa, his childhood sweetheart; they married and now have four U.S. citizen children. The youngest, George, has a serious heart defect. Soon after he arrived, Jose's priest found him a "sponsor" and you timely file a labor certification that grandfathered Jose under INA §245(i). When the I-140/485 is ripe for adju-

dication, the service center transfers the file to your district office for an interview. Although you occasionally speak by phone, you haven't actually seen Jose in a couple of years. Because Jose has been out of town you arrange to meet the couple outside the district office an hour before the scheduled interview for final preparation.

"This is the happiest day of my life," Jose exclaims. "I only wished my mother had lived to see it." You respond that you are sorry, since you didn't know she had died. "Yes," says Jose, "I just got back from her funeral in Juarez." "I was so afraid for him every moment he was away," Rosa added, "it's harder and harder to come in without papers." "Now what do we need to do to get ready for the interview?" they ask together.

4. You have represented Bret Bolivar for years, beginning with his Nicaraguan Adjustment and Central American Relief Act (NACARA) application. At long last you accompany him to his naturalization interview. When he is given a date for the swearing-in ceremony, he says his brother Bart is coming in from a neighboring state for the happy occasion and the family wants you to represent Bart, since his "identical" NACARA case is languishing. Bart makes an appointment to meet with you, the day before Bret's ceremony. Your new legal assistant does an intake and reports that much of the case appears to be similar, since Bret and Bart are identical twins. But she says Bart is awaiting his birth certificate; all he brought with him is a matricula consular and Mexican military card. He isn't sure how to get his birth certificate from the authorities in Monterrey.

5. Your oldest and most valued client is World-Wide Widgets and Software. Three months ago an I-140/I-485 was filed at the California Service Center on behalf of Widget employee Walter Worker. Last week Walter's wife Wanda called you at your home demanding to know when the adjustment would be completed, "because Walter wants to leave the employment of World-Wide Widgets and accept a position with their competitor Norfolk and Western Widgets."

Later the same evening Walter calls you, apologizes for Wanda's "insolence," and begs you not to mention the call to World-Wide's HR; but "by the way, do you think the ad-

justment will occur before my divorce from Wanda becomes final?"

The next day, the HR director at World-Wide Widgets instructs you to *quietly* delay all immigration work pending a decision regarding a buy-out offer. A possible Canadian purchaser wants to move "corporate" to Winnipeg and manufacturing to Oaxaca. Reacting to the failure of Congress to meet the need for H-1Bs, the company will fulfill high-tech functions through virtual offices abroad.

You are told, "We may need to refile a couple of labor certifications for a few jobs that will be transferred to West Virginia; we should know where we stand within three to four months."

That evening Walter Worker, knowing nothing about the director's call, e-mails you to remind you that his daughter Wyonia turns 21 in eight months.

WARNING SIGNS

"Danger, Danger, Will Robinson!"

As they say, "it doesn't take a rocket scientist …" There are often early warning signs that foreshadow later meltdowns in business cases. Every attorney has legitimate reasons to give him- or herself a pass for lack of 20/20 hindsight sometimes, but the seasoned practitioner often can avoid heartburn by taking the time to face and address troubling issues or facts as soon as they are identified. The following examples include the business immigration attorney's equivalent to the family immigration attorney's classic "bed-check" problems.

Your Contact is Limited to the Employee

At the least, this situation creates the potential that the parties are not reading from the same page of music. If problems arise later in the case, they may be harder to resolve. Is the employer willing to raise the offered wage if dictated by the wage survey? Is the employer willing and able to hold the job open until the start of the next fiscal year? Does the employer understand when a new or amended petition is required? And, in one critical area of the business immigration practice, limiting contact to the employee is entirely impermissible: labor certifications.

This rule of risk management was true even before the final rule that provides that employers are solely responsible for all PERM-related expenses and that costs may not be passed on to the worker, directly or indirectly, in whole or in part.[9] The rule likely will result in not only a degree of "creative lawyering," but among some applicants a testing of ethical limits.

The Employer is Willing to "Sponsor" the Worker; "I'll Sign Whatever You Prepare for Me"

In going down this road, the practitioner must distinguish between helpful assistance and making false statements to the government. It is one thing to help the employer prepare a visa petition within the purview and intent of the applicable law in such a way as to facilitate an approval. It is quite another to impermissibly help create accommodation positions or mischaracterize a position in a way that bears faint resemblance to the actual terms and conditions of employment.

The Beneficiary Awaiting Employment Authorization Can Never Be Reached at Home During the Day

Scenarios such as your staff encountering the worker at the "future" jobsite prior to the approval of the petition suggest several issues and ethical dilemmas. Tempting though it may be, "Don't Ask, Don't Tell" does not discharge the attorney's responsibility to the client, nor may it satisfy the attorney's duty to USCIS. You must confront the issue, and you can only do this by knowing the facts. Were false documents used to secure the employment?

Did the employment begin before or after the filing of a change or extension of nonimmigrant status or before or after the filing of the ETA-750 or I-485? Can the matter be cured by exiting the United States and re-entering (of course, without resuming unauthorized employment)? Will the I-485 be covered by INA §§245(i) or (k)? Has the employee lied to you, and, if so, are you willing to continue the representation?

Opportunities to Expand Your Client Base or Profit Center

You receive the following e-mail:

Dear Sir: We are an international professional concern with offices in Rangoon, Nairobi, Milan, and Bratislava.

We are looking for U.S. counsel to assist us in providing immigration assistance for up to 250 professionals during the upcoming year.

---

[9] 72 Fed. Reg. 27903 (May 17, 2007).

Please provide your fee schedule for qualified referrals. Initially we have several pre-screened computer programmers who need to come to the United States for final placement interviews. To qualify for B visas, they need a sponsor who is a U.S. citizen stating that they will be visiting him or her.

Air tickets, hotel accommodation, food and any other expenses will be solely on the workers' account. Kindly contact us if you can help with these cases.

The author trusts that passing on this opportunity is a no-brainer for any immigration lawyer reading this article. But what about a U.S.-based solicitation promising you a very substantial fee for referring your client for some opportunity? Even if referral fees are permitted by your bar, is your due diligence to your client compromised or co-opted by the fee, especially if you do little, if any, legal work?

The Hired Gun Syndrome

Something about your couple doesn't seem exactly right. But what the heck, they want to retain you right now and your firm's payroll is due tomorrow. After all, you tell yourself, everyone is entitled to representation, and integral to America's greatness is that we are a pluralistic society. Besides, you are loath to have some USCIS examiner expect your clients to conform to a 1950s Ozzie and Harriet stereotype. So, maybe there is a good reason this couple hasn't told their parents about their marriage. Maybe there is a good reason neither the husband or wife have a bank account. Maybe there is a good reason that a Ph.D. candidate with a fundamentalist religious background married a 19-year-old U.S. citizen high school dropout with two felony drug convictions. Maybe there is a good reason that the 42-year-old wife's 6– and 9-year-olds haven't met their 26-year-old stepdad. But if there is a good reason, and there may well be one, you should satisfy yourself about the legitimacy of the relationship before even thinking about sending the file over the government's transom. Who are you to judge? It's only your license.

SERVICING AND MAINTAINING CLIENTS

Know when to hold them, know when to fold them.

Never lose sight of the basics. This begins with an absolute duty to have and maintain the professional competence required to handle your client's case. Model Rule of Professional Conduct 1.1 requires that "a lawyer shall provide competent representation for a client. Competent representation requires legal knowledge, skill, thoroughness, and preparation reasonably necessary for the representation."

Everyone has to begin somewhere, and any licensed attorney can lawfully accept an immigration case. But immigration law is a complex area of practice, not a field for the dabbler.

Nearly 30 years ago, John P. Boyd, a former Immigration and Naturalization Service district director and then a Seattle attorney, told a West Coast symposium, "[T]he general practitioner, unfamiliar with immigration procedures, confronted with an immigration problem for the first time, may not realize the potential danger and far-reaching consequences inherent in what appears to be a simple matter. It is only after a practitioner has experienced firsthand a debacle affecting the lives of his clients that he fully realizes the necessity for a specialist."[10] This is even more true today.

The Basics 101

In addition to the duty to possess the requisite professional competence, the other basics are: (1) you have the duty to diligently and timely pursue the case; (2) your client is entitled to your full and undivided loyalty; conflicts of interests are impermissible, and the client's confidences are sacrosanct; (3) the acts and omissions of your staff are inseparable from you; and (4) if you are scratching your head and formulating exceptions to the preceding tenets, you are outside of the basics and may already have a problem.

To minimally comply with the basic requirements of professionalism and ethics, you must comply with the following:

- maintain and use an up-to-date professional library;

- track deadlines through multiple tickler systems;

- routinely do conflict checks;

- have a written retainer agreement or engagement letter for every client;

- train your staff and oversee their work product at every stage of the case;

- maintain professional liability insurance; and

- oversee appropriate termination of representation, including maintenance, or disposing, of the

client's records pursuant to the governing bar rules.

An Ounce of Prevention

There are no "silver bullets," but a high percentage of problems can be avoided or minimized by the attorney who routinely follows basic procedures that should be second nature to an entry-level lawyer. Unfortunately, the harried professional may suppress his or her better, natural instincts or delegate without adequate supervision of his or her paraprofessional staff.

The actual capital outlay for these procedures is usually minimal. While their administration can at times be time-consuming, this too is nominal in comparison with defending a suit or bar grievance.

According to Lawyers Mutual Liability Insurance Company, a North Carolina professional liability insurer, in order of frequency, the most common complaints about attorneys are that they:

- did not return the client's telephone calls;

- did not attend to the client's case;

- did not explain the process to the client;

- did not predict the outcome of the case correctly;

- did not do what the client asked; and

- had a conflict of interest.

Only a tiny fraction of Lawyers Mutual's policyholders are immigration attorneys, but these complaints have clear relevance to the practitioner handling immigration issues. Some of the complaints are remediable by discipline and common courtesy.

Each of the following complaints is addressed by the Model Rules:

Returning Telephone Calls

Returning telephone calls often goes along with explaining the process. Both the attorney and the staff should return telephone calls promptly.[11] The perception that the attorney has failed to explain the process is a related problem that can be met by maintaining lines of communication—*i.e.,* returning the client's calls. Of course, the attorney should explain the case clearly before accepting representation and throughout the process as mid-course corrections are required, or when governmental delays im-

---

[10] "Immigration and Nationality Law: The Client Who Seeks Permanent Residency Status," *Campbell Law Observer* 5 (Dec. 26, 1980).

[11] "A lawyer shall keep a client reasonably informed about the status of a matter and promptly comply with reasonable requests for information." *Model Rules Prof'l Conduct* R. 1.4.

pact the original timetable of the client's case.[12] Today's client is inundated by provocative anecdotes in the media. There is almost endless material on the Internet regarding virtually every subject, including immigration. Clients often do not understand that this material can be posted by anyone and that much of it is speculation and otherwise lacks critical analysis. Even accurate information is dangerous if it is not correctly interpreted in the context of an individual's case.

Absent clairvoyance, it is not always possible to know if even a well-educated and seemingly sophisticated client understands your explanation of processes that even most nonimmigration attorneys find hard to grasp. Invariably the attorney will make judgment calls. Those who service clients on a flat-fee basis will be accused, on occasion, of streamlining the process so that the attorney is free to proceed to handle another matter; while those charging by the hour will be accused of "churning" the account to add to their billable hours.

There is no universal answer to address this area of professional risk; but clearly the better you and your staff know the individual client, the better position you are in to gauge his or her understanding of the process, or at least the client's comfort level or informed consent vis–à–vis your course of action.

Also, do not underestimate the power of returning all client calls promptly. Returning client calls in a prompt manner is a sign of respect. It shows the client you value their legal matter and their business. Respect, in turn, builds trust between the client and your office. Clients who trust their lawyer are more loyal, make fewer disciplinary complaints, and refer more clients.

Attending to the Case

According to the American Bar Association (ABA), failure to "attend to a case" is one of the most frequent reasons for complaints to lawyer discipline tribunals.[13] In many instances, it is clear what

---

[12] "A lawyer shall explain the matter to the extent reasonably necessary to permit the client to make informed decisions." *Id.*

[13] *ABA/BNA Lawyers' Manual on Professional Conduct*, "Lawyer Client Relationship," at 31:402 (Nov. 26, 1996). Model Rule 1.3 requires that "a lawyer shall act with reasonable diligence and promptness in representing a client." And the attorney has the ethical obligation of diligence to "carry through to conclusion all matters undertaken for a client." *ABA/BNA Manual, supra*, at 01:109.

must be done to properly attend to a case. If you have been retained to file an appeal or a response to a request for evidence, or attend a USCIS interview, there is a knowable date by which you must perform. However, what about other, hazier deadlines? What about failure to notify USCIS to expedite adjudication on a case because a child is rapidly approaching the "age out" date? What about filing a cap-subject H-1B petition after the quota has already closed? What about filing a labor certification so late into a foreign national's H-1B or L-1 status that they will have to leave the country before they are eligible for adjustment of status? Attorneys should bear in mind that a complex immigration system creates many *de facto* deadlines for action, aside from the more obvious *de jure* deadlines. Be sure to have a workflow system that helps to track each case and that anticipates both "hard" and "hazy" deadlines.

Correctly Predicting the Outcome of the Case

The dynamics of immigration law have made the "prediction" of the outcome of a matter sometimes problematical, even for the seasoned practitioner. Over 50 immigration bills have been signed into law since 1986. Some are breathtaking in scope, others are niche bills, but nevertheless of critical importance to the niches affected. In many instances, the implementing regulations have not been promulgated, and the attorney has been fortunate if the agency provided any policy guidance, however informal. USCIS service centers are in meltdown, the appellate boards are years overdue in issuing decisions, the agencies are underfunded, and PERM is far from user-friendly. Under these conditions, the attorney who attempts to predict the outcome of a case is on a fool's errand. This is, of course, intolerable, given that the course of the client's life and fortune may often literally depend on the attorney's advice.

Under these conditions the attorney who guarantees results or makes predications regarding processing times without qualification and periodic professional reevaluation has abdicated his or her ethical and professional duty to the client. The temptation to overpromise is not always as easy to avoid as one might think. Many clients are determined to hear only good news, and the most optimistic spin on their chances for success. It can be a real challenge trying to educate certain clients that just because certain theories may succeed is no guarantee they will succeed—particularly if they have heard a rumor (invariably on the Internet, but sometimes from coworkers) that they simply need to do "x" to secure a fast immigration application approval. Sober risk assessment is not always compromised by over-optimistic clients. If a practitioner has once succeeded on a dicey legal theory, he or she might get overconfident of that theory's chances for success in all instances, without realizing that any given immigration application, no matter how weak, might have some ambient chance of approval due to mistakes made by overburdened USCIS adjudicators.

Did Not Do What the Client Asked

Sometimes there may be no panacea to complaints that the attorney "did not do what I asked." If the complaint is substantive rather than a matter of perception, the attorney only may be able to explain to the client why the attorney cannot, or will not, do what the client asked. Perhaps it is unlawful, unethical, or just unwise. A legal sage once observed that "sometimes the best advice you can give your client is not to make a damn fool of himself." Even if you can lawfully and ethically proceed, a course of action may be tactically inappropriate in your professional estimation. When the client insists on substituting his or her judgment for yours, you need to evaluate whether you want to terminate your relationship with that client. You need to consult not only your own retainer agreement, but the applicable rules of professional conduct. In some jurisdictions, withdrawal historically has not been permitted without "good cause."

Some rules now expressly allow withdrawal without cause or without client consent, subject to the authority of courts to require continued representation, and provided the withdrawal can be accomplished without material prejudice to the client. In addition to "good cause" and the requirement that withdrawal can be accomplished without material prejudice to the client, Model Rule 1.16 lists situations under which an attorney may withdraw. These circumstances include: the client persists in actions the lawyer reasonably believes are criminal or fraudulent; the client has used the lawyer's services to perpetrate fraud; the client insists on an objective that the lawyer considers repugnant or imprudent; or the representation has been rendered unreasonably difficult by the client. The retainer agreement of the author's firm requires the client to acknowledge that "it is essential that [the] Client advise [the] Attorneys of the true facts pertaining to this case, that the information provided on the Questionnaire submitted to [the] Attorneys is true and accurate to the best of [the] Client's knowledge and that [the] Client promptly notify [the] Attorneys of any changes or

corrections." Breach of this provision permits immediate termination of representation by the firm, and the firm rarely fails to exercise this option.

Had a Conflict of Interest

Applicable rules of professional conduct often address conflict situations arising in the context of litigation, or scenarios uncommon to an immigration practice. But common sense and good practice policy dictate that representation should be declined at the outset if there is a conflict of interest. If a conflict is later identified, the client should be promptly notified and the issue of continued representation should be resolved immediately.

The New York City Bar Association has held the following to be the *minimum* components of an effective conflicts-of-interest checking system.[14]

All law firms, even solo practitioners, must maintain "records," whether written or electronic.

The records should be maintained in a way that allows them to be quickly and easily checked for conflicts.

To qualify as a "record," the document must be one that the law firm is able to systematically and accurately check for information when it is considering a new engagement.

The records of prior engagements must be made at or near the time of the engagement.

The records should be made within days, not weeks, of the initial engagement, so that they may be checked before commencing a new engagement.

The records should be updated periodically as additional parties or other relevant information that might create a conflict of interest is acquired.

The records should be organized in a way that permits efficient access to the information they contain.

List clients and former clients alphabetically, and list engagements undertaken for each client in chronological order under each name.

Maintain a list of adverse parties, cross-referenced to the client and matter in which the adverse parties were involved.

Certain information, at a minimum, should be maintained in the system:

- Client names
- Adverse party names

---

[14] NYC Bar Ass'n Formal Op. 2003-03.

- Description of engagement

HELP IN THE TIME OF TROUBLE

The regulations only partially address discipline of attorneys and nonattorney representatives. They do not provide guidance on some of the most serious ethical issues. Generally, the ethics rules applicable to immigration attorneys are the rules of ethics for the state in which the lawyer is licensed to practice. In addition, most states have statutes regulating businesses and professions. State and federal laws regarding fraud apply to all lawyers, irrespective of their area of practice.

The attorney may encounter a legal or ethical issue that cannot be resolved after diligent research (and, if applicable, after consultation with other firm members). A filing deadline may be at hand, or sometimes more intimidating, the vice president for human resources absolutely needs to know an answer before the start of the next business day in Bonn. Where do you turn?

AILA Practice & Professionalism Center

The Practice & Professionalism Center (PPC) has a number of resources to help immigration lawyers resolve ethical matters.

By virtue of their membership, AILA attorneys have access to the AILA Mentor Program. This is an invaluable resource for evaluating and coping with ethical issues. The AILA mentor is a practicing immigration attorney with at least five years of experience in the area of practice. There are mentors for the specific area designated as "Ethics and Professional Responsibility," as well as for virtually every area of immigration practice. The mentor does not charge any fee for a brief consultation, not to exceed 15 minutes. The attorney seeking consultation must ask the AILA mentor for assistance directly. Use of this system by legal assistants and secretaries is not permitted; the calling attorney should research the issue before calling the mentor. Current mentors and the guidelines for the program may be found on the PPC pages of InfoNet.[15]

There are numerous articles written by experienced AILA members focusing on ethics and immigration practice. Furthermore, there are sample forms and agreements available through the PPC and in AILA publications such as the *Immigration Practice Toolbox*.

The PPC plans and produces topical seminars at national and chapter conferences, as well as articles in *Immigration Law Today*, *AILA Dispatch*, and conference publications.

You can also contact the director of the PPC, Reid Trautz, to discuss your ethics issues. See the PPC pages on InfoNet for more information.

Practice Pointer: Invaluable though a volunteer mentor can be, some issues will necessitate formal association of outside counsel. When this occurs, the practitioner will need to decide from the outset whether the outside counsel is representing the original client or the attorney.

The Bar

Many state bars have counselors who will advise attorneys on ethical issues. Because these bar counselors may not be familiar with immigration issues, the querying attorney will have to explain the areas of concern carefully. A less than full understanding of the problem could hopelessly skew the opinion, thereby rendering it worthless.

Note: Before utilizing this resource, the attorney should be familiar with the parameters of the service and be sure that the query will not have any unintended collateral consequences.

Attorneys will normally seek an opinion from the bar in their home state. Attorneys needing assistance in other jurisdictions can start with the state's court or bar webpage. For example, a freely accessible archive of detailed ethics opinions can be found at the website of the Los Angeles County Bar Association.[16] The New York City Bar maintains a similar online ethics opinions archive.[17]

A description profiling the services provided by each state bar is contained in the *Martindale-Hubbell Law Directory*; a directory of state bar associations is published in the ABA's annual leadership directory, and referrals also may be obtained through the National Organization of Bar Counsel, Inc., 515 Fifth Street, N.W., Building A, Room 127, Washington, DC 20001; (202) 638-1501; fax: (202) 638-0862; or e-mail: *barcounsel@aol.com*.

---

[15] *www.aila.org* (Practice & Professionalism link).

[16] Los Angeles County Bar Association, Professional Responsibility and Ethics Committee, Ethics Opinions, *available at www.lacba.org/showpage.cfm?pageid=427*.

[17] New York State Bar Association, Index of Formal Opinions, 1986–2005, *available at www.abcny.org/Ethics/index.htm*.

The ABA's ETHICSearch service permits attorneys to call, write, fax or e-mail descriptions of situations posing ethical problems. Attorneys will receive citations to the authorities, including applicable ABA ethics rules, ethics opinions issued by the ABA as well as by state and local bars, and other relevant research materials, such as case law, law review articles, and treatise materials. Most inquiries are handled on a same-day basis, and expedited same-day service can be arranged.

There is no charge for an ETHICSearch query. Further information may be obtained by calling ETHICSearch at (312) 988-5323 or writing to ETHICSearch, Center for Professional Responsibility, American Bar Association, 541 North Fairbanks Court, Chicago, IL 60611-3314. ETHICSearch can be faxed at (312) 988-5491; the e-mail address is *ethicsearch@staff.abanet.org*.

Professional Liability Insurers

Many professional liability insurers have proactive risk management programs to assist their policy holders. Just as with bar counselors, the policy holder may have to carefully explain the areas of concern if the company does not specialize in the immigration coverage area. Even if the carrier cannot resolve the problem at hand, prompt consultation with the company may be necessary under the terms of the policy.

Practice Pointer: The author encourages every attorney to maintain adequate professional liability coverage, and encourages the attorney to periodically review the terms of the policy, keeping in mind any changed circumstances and understanding that not every potentially actionable occurrence is covered.

The Government

AILA's formal liaison and other initiatives directed toward the Department of State, Department of Labor, the Executive Office for Immigration Review, U.S. Immigration and Customs Enforcement, U.S. Customs and Border Protection, USCIS, and the Social Security Administration at every level are extraordinarily valuable tools in ascertaining and influencing immigration policy for our clients.

This aside, to paraphrase the venerable punch line: "The government is here to help you." This is all too often true in the real world, at the "retail level."

With sincere respect to the thousands of dedicated public servants—and leaving issues of motive and intent aside—the agencies charged with the administration of U.S. immigration laws are frequently neither competent nor equipped to give advice on which you can rely.

Whatever advice is available is necessarily myopic: U.S. consuls do not know or understand the regulations the USCIS service centers follow. USCIS "consumer" publications and its website are replete with errors, and USCIS hotlines constantly give erroneous advice, some of which, if followed, actually could render the recipient inadmissible or removable.

If you get an answer you like, how can you ensure that USCIS will later honor it? If you receive an answer you do not like, do you follow it? If you do not follow it, after you have notice of the government's position, you may have incurred additional exposure.

If our immigration laws were in any way user-friendly, and if the advice of the government could be readily obtained or confidentially relied on, the business community, with its eye on the bottom line, would not be utilizing the services of immigration attorneys.

The World Wide Web

Check out *www.legalethics.com*. Assume that your client is looking at it, too.

Substance Abuse and Mental Health

Immigration practice is a stressful occupation, and attorneys are not immune from alcoholism, drug addiction, and mental health problems that affect every segment of our society.

The ABA states that "while ten percent of the general population has problems with alcohol abuse, anywhere from fifteen to eighteen percent of the lawyer population battles the same problem. Because many lawyers and judges are overachievers who carry enormous workload, the tendency to 'escape' from daily problems through the use of drugs and alcohol is prevalent in the legal community. Also, the daily pressures placed on these men and women can lead to inordinate amounts of stress and mental illness. Recent reports have also shown that a majority of disciplinary problems involve chemical dependency or emotional stress."[18]

In 1988, the ABA created the Commission on Lawyer Assistance Programs (CoLAP) "to advance the legal community's knowledge of impairments facing

---

[18] *www.abanet.org/legalservices/colap/*.

lawyers and its response to those issues."[19] According to the ABA, every state has now developed "lawyer assistance programs or committees focused on quality of life issues. These programs employ the use of intervention peer counseling, and referral to 12-Step Programs to assist in the lawyer's recovery process."[20]

Judge Carl Horn III eloquently addresses stress avoidance and other lifestyle issues in his book *LawyerLife—Finding a Life and a Higher Calling in the Practice of Law.*[21] "Stop to smell the roses" is but a part of the message shared by Judge Horn, but it is a message often neglected by busy attorneys. Neglected at our own peril![22]

CONCLUSION

Always do right.
This will gratify some people,
And astonish the rest.
—Mark Twain

Representing foreign nationals has always posed potential ethical challenges to the attorney. These have included cultural, educational, and linguistical barriers, as well as a misunderstanding of the role lawyers play in the immigration process and the American legal system. Sometimes just as challenging is the client who expects legal counsel to be creative and resourceful and may not care about or understand the constraints the law places on an immigration practitioner.

It is the immigration attorney's calling and responsibility to reconcile these differences and balance the interest of each client. An immigration practice requires identifying and drawing on a commonality of professionalism and ethical precepts, the same precepts that ideally are part of the professional fiber of every person practicing our profession. These precepts should be nurtured, cultivated, and preserved. Now more than ever, immigration attorneys have the unique responsibility not only to further the interest of their clients, but to educate the public as to the contributions of all immigrants to our nation, and to lead the fight to protect the fundamental due process rights guaranteed by our Constitution.

It is said that Carroll W. Weathers, who practiced real estate law in Raleigh for 17 years before serving as the Dean of the Wake Forest University School of Law for another 20 years, wished for his students that "to the end, their lives may be lived in the service of others, and they may find the satisfaction that comes from a noble purpose, high ideals and exemplary living."[23] Dean Weathers, blind and retired, continued to teach legal ethics at Wake Forest until his death at age 82. It is doubtful that Carroll Weathers ever handled an immigration matter, but he fervently believed in legal ethics and that an attorney "occupies a preferred station of leadership, possesses exceptional influence, and it not only is his privilege but his duty to use his influence and position on behalf of a better social order, and live as a worthy example to others." Such should be the highest aspiration of an immigration attorney.

---

[19] *Id.*

[20] *Id.*

[21] A key chapter of Judge Horn's book is reprinted as "Professional and Personal Fulfillment, Twelve Steps Toward Fulfillment in the Practice of Law," *Ethics in a Brave New World: Professional Responsibility, Personal Accountability and Risk Management for Immigration Practitioners* (AILA 2004).

[22] *See also* W. Miller & R. Muñoz, *Controlling Your Drinking: Tools to Make Moderation Work for You* (2005).

[23] "What Would Dean Weathers Do?" *North Carolina Lawyer* (Sept./Oct. 1999).

You Are Not Alone: Creative Practices in Managing People

by Davis C. Bae, Steven Garfinkel, and Linda Rahal[*]

Remember the courses in law school where your professors provided practical advice on managing your legal support staff? It is unlikely that you do remember because few law schools offer a practicum that covers the management of people. Too often, people-management issues are learned through trial and error. Well-meaning employers often find that when managing people, good intention is not enough and can often backfire.

This article provides some innovative yet practical ideas on how to create a workplace that promotes internal integrity while also being effective and profitable. The suggestions found in this article are actually used by the authors in their respective practices. In reviewing the best policies in our practices, we found that the ideas fall in four distinct categories: staff development, financial compensation, nonfi-

---

[*] **Davis C. Bae** is the founder and managing attorney of the Bae Law Group. Mr. Bae's practice focuses on comprehensive immigration planning for multinational and fast-growth corporations. He regularly speaks to professional associations and companies on a variety of immigration issues including corporate changes, human resources, legal advocacy, foreign recruitment, and employee retention. Mr. Bae lectures on practice management issues and teaches the course "Issues in Small & Solo Practice" at the University of Washington School of Law.

Steven Garfinkel is the founder and managing partner of Garfinkel Immigration Law Firm in Charlotte, N.C. Mr. Garfinkel graduated from Wake Forest University (1981) and the Wake Forest School of Law (1984). He has been practicing business immigration law since 1984. Mr. Garfinkel is a past chair of the Carolinas Chapter of AILA and is a North Carolina Board Certified Immigration Specialist (and current chair of the Specialization Committee). He is listed in *The International Who's Who of Corporate Immigration Lawyers* and *The Best Lawyers in America* and has spoken at the past six AILA annual conferences.

Linda Rahal is chief operating officer of Trow & Rahal. She has been with the firm since its inception in 1993 and has practiced immigration and nationality law as an attorney since 1992. Ms. Rahal has taught several courses on immigration law and conducts seminars for clients and outside organizations. She is listed in *The Best Lawyers in America*, *Washingtonian Magazine's* "Top Lawyers," *The International Who's Who of Corporate Immigration Lawyers,* and the *Martindale-Hubbell Bar Register of Preeminent Lawyers*. She is a frequent speaker on Immigration Law Updates at Society for Human Resource Management events.

nancial compensation and organizational infrastructure. And in managing staff—whether attorneys or paralegals—it is important to provide them with growth, opportunity, appreciation, and learning.

GIVE THEM A G.O.A.L.: GROWTH, OPPORTUNITY, APPRECIATION, AND LEARNING

When discussing growth, opportunity, appreciation, and learning, it is important to distinguish attorneys from your other legal staff. While some of the suggestions below are specific to attorneys and others to paralegals, most apply well to all types of employees, including administrative staff and other nonlegal employees.

Growth

Assuming that we try to find the best people for staff positions in our businesses, it can also be assumed that these people want positions that allow for growth and promotion.

For young attorneys, the difficulty is that immigration firms tend to be boutique operations that do not have a clear history of providing equity to attorneys. While not all attorneys seek equity, it is natural for any person to want a defined path to achieve it. Seek the advice of business advisors or other people experienced with equity to learn the best way to develop a plan that creates incentive for attorneys through equity plans. Many attorneys avoid equity discussions in fear that a young lawyer may try to "walk away" with their business. But a reasonable and clear path to equity allows for frank and open discussion of career opportunity, which will increase productivity, communication, and loyalty.

While paralegals and nonlegal employees do not have the option of equity, it is equally important for those essential employees to know how their responsibilities are intended to expand. Without a clear professional development path, these employees may feel their jobs have ceilings even if none actually exist. Paralegals can develop into managers of other staff and become involved in marketing and the administration of the firm's infrastructure. Administrative staff has the option of general office manager duties, billing, accounting, marketing, or even moving to the legal side and becoming paralegals. Having advancement or horizontal options for your paralegals and nonlegal staff provides a great incentive for these essential staff members to stay, rather than seek other opportunities where there are greater chances of advancement.

Opportunity

When discussing immigration staff, we must pay particular attention to the paralegal. We in the practice of immigration law are able to leverage the work of paralegals efficiently and effectively. While one must always keep in mind the ethical and legal limitations placed on paralegals, we should realize that paralegals can do most of the work required in the preparation, filing, and follow-up on a family or employment-based visa petition (short of giving legal advice). Below are some tips regarding the best use of paralegals.

Consider having supervising paralegals take on positions of leadership within the firm.

Paralegals are on the front lines, working closely not only with clients but with your case management system and other computer programs. Furthermore, paralegals with years of experience develop good ideas and habits and often know the laws and practical tasks better then young attorneys. One way to cultivate paralegal knowledge and insight is to allow them to participate in executive level/team leader meetings with attorneys.

Giving supervising paralegals other roles and responsibilities will increase their participation in the firm and contribute to a greater sense of teambuilding or "firmness." Paralegals can also be involved in training new paralegals and even entry-level attorneys, as well as in the orientation of new employees. They can even take part in the interview process of hiring new legal staff. Consider having senior paralegals provide training for more junior staff in the areas of the practice they know best. Often, with some guidance paralegals can do a better job than attorneys, as they tend to know the practical aspects of areas like consular processing, assembling adjustments, filing LCAs, and working with J-1 sponsor organizations. There are numerous tasks that must be handled by the firm, and, depending on the size and staffing of the firm, many duties, such as tracking of attendance at CLEs, can be handled effectively by paralegals. Ideas for quality control and marketing can be discussed by the paralegals and presented to firm leaders.

Have paralegals participate in both in-person and telephonic client conferences.

There are a number of reasons you should have a paralegal accompany a lawyer when a new client comes into your office for an initial consultation (or to sit in with an attorney during a conference call regarding a new matter). Although you may be one of a very small number of attorneys who take copious notes and relay all relevant information from the consultation to the paralegal, it is more likely that some information does not get recorded and transmitted. Further, many of us would like the client to view the paralegal as a main point of contact with the firm, and establishing the relationship early will make this easier to achieve. Finally, it is generally good practice not to meet with clients one on one, but rather to have another person present. Having a paralegal present will provide another person's point of view if the lawyer is ever questioned about information provided during the client meeting.

If you have corporate clients and assign your work to paralegals based on client accounts, consider taking the paralegal assigned to the corporate account to client visits. Paralegals often develop excellent relationships with the employees of the corporate clients. These employees are future referral sources!

Give paralegals responsibility—let them engage in substantial client contact.

Again, while understanding fully that paralegals may not give legal advice, most of the day-to-day work required on client matters can be performed by paralegals. Although this may vary by personality type, you will find that the majority of paralegals will have a much higher level of job satisfaction if they are doing more than simply filling out forms. Allowing them to meet with clients and communicate with clients gives them greater job satisfaction. They will take on a new level of ownership with clients and refer to companies or individual clients as "my clients."

Appreciation

Solicit input from others. (You might think you know everything, but you don't!)

Many immigration attorneys, paralegals, and other support staff enjoy the practice of immigration law but move between firms. A smart employer routinely asks new employees who have come from other immigration law firms (or practice groups within large firms) to share insights gathered at prior firms. Do not assume that you know everything and be open to new ideas. "My way or the highway" is usually the wrong way!

In addition to learning what substantive knowledge your employees have, it is important to learn about their talents and passions that are not related to the practice of law. Keep an inventory of skills with each new employee so you can evaluate how best to use their talents. Frequently, the skills they bring with them to your firm are things that they are passionate about. Skills such as event planning, graphic design, marketing and editing, and multicultural experiences, are all highly relevant to any immigration law firm.

Give public praise.

Too often, employers fail to praise the great work of employees in a public setting. Public praise to other employees, clients, and vendors is a highly effective way of showing appreciation for the work of the staff member. Do not forget to praise others when they deserve it. However, public praise can backfire if employers are perceived to play favorites.

Public praise can be done through staff meeting announcements, awards, and the posting of thank-you cards and complimentary e-mails on bulletin boards. Be sure that the praise is specific, in order to give effective substance in the compliment and describe the achievement being praised.

Learning

Have paralegals attend conferences and government liaison meetings.

As noted above, you may think that you take copious notes and relay all relevant information. However, the author has found that over many years of practice, all important notes do not get written down at chapter and liaison meetings and conferences Attending these meetings (1) gets the paralegals out of the office; (2) makes them feel like they are not just "pushing paper;" and (3) allows them to meet other attorneys and paralegals and government employees. And going to conferences is fun! Going to a new city with coworkers is a chance to form bonds and cut loose. Again, happy employees are productive employees, and paralegals are cheaper than lawyers!

An alternative way to provide training is to enable legal staff to listen to teleconferences. Often this is easier to arrange than attending a full-day conference, for a teleconference only takes an hour or so from their day and provides topic-specific information.

Invest in paralegal and attorney education in nonlegal education.

Too often firms will hire employees or vendors with specific skills and become unhappy with the results when they are not a good fit. So it is better to train your existing "A" players in skills that the firm needs rather than try to hire unknown commodities. The best people tend to want to learn and improve. Web development, computer systems administration, financial skills, marketing, and presentation development are all subjects that can be learned. Many of these courses are available at community colleges and other professional training organizations. You might also consider investing in your longer-term paralegals and nonlegal staff by providing them leadership and management training. Providing this type of training helps create a smoother transition between positions if there is an advancement path in the firm to supervising staff. It also helps staff members see and identify with the management perspective of the firm. At some point you may want to hire a vendor to handle these duties, but until then it may be more financially sensible to invest in your existing staff, thus giving them a better sense that the firm is invested in their personal success.

QUALITY OF WORK/LIFE: NONFINANCIAL COMPENSATION

Not all compensation needs to be salary. People who are drawn to the field of immigration law are frequently driven more by quality of life and the "feel good" nature of the subject matter than the bottom line in their paycheck. The following solutions create great incentive for staff without necessarily increasing your payroll.

Create a sabbatical policy.

One of the more successful incentive plans used by many law firms is a sabbatical policy. For example, a firm might provide every employee the opportunity for two months of paid leave after five years of full-time employment. Typically, most firms can handle supporting an individual's caseload for two months without hiring additional staff. Should you have a successful sabbatical policy, it will be uncommon to lose employees after their third year of employment, which is frequently when their work is most productive. In addition, they return with greater enthusiasm for their work and appreciation for their employer.

Embrace pro bono work.

Jim Collins, author of *Good to Great*, points out that companies who embrace community service outperform those that don't at a rate of three to one. This is especially true in a field like immigration law, where many of us are drawn by the opportunity to help people with key life issues. By embracing pro bono activities, the firm shows its commitment to the community, but more importantly it supports the values of its employees. While asylum, refugee, and VAWA cases are obvious choices, opportunities also include Habitat for Humanity, animal shelters, and homeless advocacy. To involve the staff, also consider asking them what pro bono activity they may want to engage in as a group. This will create cohesion and energy, which will then provide more enthusiastic employees and likely be reflected in your firm's bottom line.

Provide a solid benefits package.

Benefits are important to employees, especially those with families. Providing a solid benefits package for employees shows them that you care. Traditional benefits include health insurance, disability insurance, and 401(k) plans with matching by the firm. Other benefits may include cafeteria plans, flexible spending plans, tuition reimbursement, and parking plans. A good benefits package can be the icing on the cake for hiring new employees!

Consider flexible job schedules.

Implementing a policy of rotating Friday afternoons off for staff will not significantly impact your firm's productivity. It will (1) be loved by your staff; (2) allow a staff member to get an early start on a weekend away; and (3) seem like a big deal to your employees.

Alternatively, accommodate your staff's needs for flexible schedules. In large urban areas, the commute is a major issue, often influencing whether people take a job with a new employer or leave an employer to seek employment closer to home. To keep valuable employees who struggle with commuting, you might consider letting them work from home in the morning and then commute in later in the day when traffic is lighter. For example, why not accommodate a paralegal's desire to start at 7:30 am so he or she can leave a bit early to spend time with family? You might also let them work from home one or two days per week. A little flexibility will go a long way to get some real bang for your buck!

SALARY AND BENEFITS— FINANCIAL COMPENSATION

Although many in the Human Resources world talk about nonmonetary motivators, the authors have found over the years that money is the best motivator. What is not in dispute is that in the end, your employees will need to seek a reasonable wage for their services. Before opening your pocketbooks, however, consider that there are effective ways to use financial compensation to your advantage.

Consider giving bonuses more than once a year.

Depending on a firm's cash flow, giving bonuses more than once per year (or even after an H-1B or adjustment of status filing crunch) may be just what the doctor ordered to keep morale and productivity up.

Have clear standards for raises and bonuses.

Too many employers give raises based simply on tenure with a company. This results in a culture of entitlement with reward expectations no longer being related to exceptional work. Remember, it is not your responsibility to give raises; it is the responsibility of your employees to earn them. To give incentives related to performance, consider the following scale at a review:

- Exceptional performance: 7–10 percent
- Slightly above average: 3–6 percent
- Meeting expectations: no raise—2 percent cost of living increase.

While nonfinancial compensation may be the desert which keeps positions interesting, financial compensation is the meat and potatoes needed to keep your employment relationships healthy.

FIRM MANAGEMENT— CREATING POLICIES AND INFRASTRUCTURE THAT WORKS

Create sound policies that reinforce your goals and values as a group. Without strong controls, a firm can quickly find itself in distress, which results in issues of ethics and financial solvency.

Create a strong office handbook and procedures manual.

Part of a great work environment is having policies and procedures that allow employees certainty that they are excelling in their positions and also interacting appropriately within the organization. An employment handbook, if well-drafted, enhances staff knowledge and creates an even playing field for all employees.

Additionally, a strong office procedures manual captures the institutional knowledge that can be lost if not recorded on an annual basis. Issues such as billing, client conduct, case tracking, client communication protocols, filing systems, and firm resources can all be laid out so employees have certainty about the integrity and sophistication of the employer.

PERFORMANCE REVIEWS

Feedback, both positive and constructive, is valuable to the employment relationship. Creating a comprehensive performance-review system that provides a dialogue is extremely valuable. Consider instituting at least twice-yearly evaluations that include both an assessment of performance and a definition of improvement or development goals. Be sure to have the employees do a self-assessment and take part in their own development goal setting. You might be surprised by what they want to do or where they think they need work!

Be slow to hire, quick to fire.

When hiring a new employee, it is far better to wait to make the right hire than to rush to fill a position. Do a thorough check of references, have multiple levels of interviews with other members of your staff, and drill down on questions that truly reflect a person's capacity to succeed at your firm. If possible, hire them on a contract basis to see them in action prior to making them a permanent employee. After any evaluation period, be sure to do a full review by seeking the input of all employees who are in contact with the candidate.

When terminating an employee, make decisions quickly and decisively. Because a bad employee can ruin a workplace, it is essential for staff integrity that you hold employees accountable for their actions. Your staff will blame you, not the difficult employee, if you allow someone who fails to meet accepted standards to continue working at the firm. While it is acceptable to tolerate an employee who is coachable for specific skills such as grammar, legal knowledge and communication, there are some basic violations that cannot be tolerated—hostility to clients, dishonesty, and a bad attitude. These traits can divide staff and spread like a virus through your entire organization.

Switch to the Metric System!

Great metrics allow a business owner to anticipate issues before they arise and to gather valuable information on their business that isn't reflected in the bottom line. Some metrics that could be reviewed include case processing speed, client satisfaction, and employee stress.

A manager should establish the goals of the business and the kind of information needed to measure whether those goals are being achieved. However, the metrics should be created collaboratively with your staff, as they are the people who compile and can actively use the data. Good metrics will allow your staff to track their own progress and the progress of the entire organization.

Develop clear job duties that reflect the spirit as well as the responsibilities of a position.

Firms that are just starting out will have loosely defined job descriptions that, in many ways, serve more as guides than clear definitions of responsibility. For example, attorneys are more than just legal decision makers; they are also quality assurance experts and relationship managers. Paralegals are your highly skilled production experts. Your receptionist is the gatekeeper of your firm's brand and often the director of first impression for clients. By addressing the spirit of a role, the employee can feel more confident about taking creative steps to advance the organization and perform better.

Have firm outings quarterly, firm retreats annually.

You've all heard that you spend more waking time with your employees than you do with your families. Why not plan outings where employees and families can meet and mingle and have some fun? Whether it is a ball game (minor league baseball games are relatively cheap and easy), outdoor concerts, potluck dinners or team-building activities, a regularly scheduled outing will boost morale and productivity.

Firm retreats are not just for lawyers anymore. Take all of your staff away for a day and talk about the firm's strengths, weaknesses, and opportunities. You'll be surprised at the information you get and the ideas people will share. One accounting firm conducts a brainstorming day where management sits down with staff and receives feedback on what can be improved. Often this serves to help identify the firm's improvement goals for the next six–12 months.

Develop the firm's infrastructure.

Often, lawyers as well as other professionals know what they need to do, but they don't feel that they have the time to keep both the business development and practice going, as well as develop the firm infrastructure. So, how can infrastructure be developed? The law firm administrator or human resources person responsible can develop the job descriptions, performance systems, and related infrastructure documents. Duties can be split among the partners or managing attorneys. And paralegals and attorneys can complete a first draft of their job descriptions.

If your staff is already overworked and cannot seem to accomplish these tasks, consider hiring a business consultant or organizational coach to review your organizational structure and advise you on implementing the infrastructure. Often these consultants or coaches will develop the job descriptions, performance review system, employee handbook, and related infrastructure documentation for your firm. The investment will be worth it on many levels.

CONCLUSION

There is no magic formula for managing people, and each of the authors of this article has different styles and beliefs. The hardest part of managing people is that each person is unique and driven by different motivations. As an employer, it is essential to first know yourself and your values, which then translate to the culture you wish to create for your business. Then hire and motivate people based upon that culture. A business that lives out the right values will be a success.

BEST PRACTICES FOR FOIA REQUESTS

by Amy L. Peck[*]

The Freedom of Information Act[1] (FOIA) as we knew it changed radically with the separation of the Immigration and Naturalization Service (INS) into separate agencies. Historically, FOIA requests were sent to local INS district offices that housed FOIA officers. Processing times varied regionally, with some offices responding within the statutory 20 days and others taking months.

When the U.S. Department of Homeland Security (DHS) was formed, INS became Customs and Border Protection (CBP), Immigration and Customs Enforcement (ICE), and U.S. Citizenship and Immigration Services (USCIS). Shortly after reorganization in 2003, USCIS made a decision to centralize FOIA requests through the National Records Center (NRC). The NRC was not equipped for the increase in FOIA requests and backlogs started forming almost immediately. Coupled with this, the agencies, which had been accustomed to FOIA being a one-stop shop, suddenly began exerting control over their respective portions of the "A" file or pertinent alien information. Separate FOIAs to each agency had to be filed, with each agency doing its own file review and redaction. The problems quickly surfaced, the most obvious being that there was only one "A" file that contained information claimed by three different agencies. Documentation claimed by ICE would need to go through an ICE FOIA review, documentation claimed by USCIS would require that agency's oversight, and CBP insisted on its own review. The impracticalities of this system caused its ultimate failure, and FOIA responses slowed to a trickle. The Privacy Office, which traditionally had control over FOIA, was given only "dotted line" authority over the agencies, which meant that while they retained authority over the function, they couldn't force the agencies into cooperating with each other and could comment on policy only.

In 2005, the agencies entered into a shared services agreement, with USCIS agreeing to process FOIA requests for all agencies through a centralized request at the NRC. This agreement did not resolve all problems because each agency still insisted on doing its own redaction and review, slowing the response time considerably. Finally, in late 2006, the agencies agreed to certain review criteria and drafted a redaction policy guideline that can be utilized for all documents without the need for each agency to review its own records.

Currently there is a backlog of approximately 61,000 FOIA requests. Processing times are nine to 12 months under the First In/First Out (FIFO) system. The NRC is able to process approximately 120,000 requests per year, which is about the number of requests received each year.

Steps have been taken recently by the Privacy Office and the respective agencies to improve FOIA, which remains a moving target—procedurally speaking. The NRC has hired 60 processors recently, and is in the process of hiring an additional 88 processors. Once the processors are trained, the backlog is expected to be reduced in two years at the worst, which would be September of 2010.

The most recent information given by the Privacy Office suggests that the best FOIA practices will follow these guidelines.

1. Keep your FOIA request as simple as possible to qualify for "Simple Track" processing

A new "Simple Track" FOIA processing line was recently created to shorten processing times for easy requests. Simple Track will be eliminated once the backlog is reduced. Processing times for Simple Track can be as little as four to eight weeks. Requests that ask for specific documentation (*e.g.,* a copy of the I-130 petition) instead of the entire "A" file contents will be placed in Simple Track. Simple Track should be requested in the cover letter of the FOIA request if you believe the case qualifies.

---

[*] **Amy L. Peck** is in private practice with Peck Law Firm in Omaha, practicing exclusively in immigration law. She is the past chair of the AILA Iowa-Nebraska Chapter, and previously served as treasurer. She served on the AILA Board of Governors and AILA Membership Committee. She is the immediate past chair of AILA's ICE Liaison Committee. Ms. Peck is currently chair of AILA's DHS/FOIA Privacy Office Liaison Committee.

A previous version of this article appeared in *Immigration & Nationality Law Handbook* 235 (AILA 2007–08 Ed.).

[1] 5 USC §552(a)(6)(E)(i).

2. Request "Fast Track" or "Third Track" processing if you are in front of the Executive Office of Immigration Review (EOIR)

On February 28, 2007, USCIS announced a new track for FOIA requests involving cases in front of the immigration judge (IJ).[2] Current procedures require the filing of a G-639 (or other written request) for access to the "A" file of an alien in proceedings. This new "third" track still requires the submittal of a FOIA or other written request but results in expedited or accelerated access to the file if the requester also provides one of the following:

- A Notice to Appear (Form I-862);

- Order to Show Cause (Form I-122);

- Notice of Referral to IJ *with a hearing date*; or

- A written notice of continuation of scheduled hearing before the IJ.

The request should be sent to the main FOIA address:

U.S. Citizenship and Immigration Services
National Records Center, FOIA/PA Office
P. O. Box 648010
Lee's Summit, MO 64064-8010
Phone: (816) 350-5570
Fax: (816) 350-5785
uscis.foia@dhs.gov

You have the option of scanning the request and supplementary documents and e-mailing it to the above e-mail address.

Notably, this procedure does not apply to cases before the Board of Immigration Appeals (BIA) or for motions to reopen. For cases pending before the IJ with FOIAs already submitted under the old system, you may notify the NRC of the pending case and it should then be placed in the third track.

3. Send Border Patrol requests to CBP

CBP began its own FOIA review for Border Patrol records in June 2007. It will be a good idea to check the website prior to submittal to confirm the current mailing address. FOIA requests can be made on Form G-639, as they are with USCIS FOIA requests, or can be made in writing. Currently the CBP FOIA address is:

FOIA Officer
1300 Pennsylvania Avenue, N.W.
Mint Annex

Washington, D.C. 20229
Acting FOIA Officer/Requester Service Center
Contact: Mark Hanson
Phone: (202) 572-8720
Fax: (202) 572-8755
E-mail: *shari.suzuki@dhs.gov*

4. Check DHS website for FOIA information

DHS has recently put FOIA information on its website. Each month, more FOIA information is being added to the DHS website.

The current website with all of the FOIA contact information is:

www.dhs.gov/xfoia/Copy_of_editorial_0318.shtm #uscis.

DHS also has a website that directs requests to the proper agency handling that type of request. This website is currently:

www.dhs.gov/xfoia/editorial_0847.shtm.

An explanation of FOIA procedures, including how to submit a FOIA request is found at:

www.dhs.gov/xfoia/editorial_0316.shtm.

5. Appeal Fugitive Disentitlement Doctrine decisions

USCIS may refuse to process a FOIA request on the ground that the requester or the party on whose behalf the request was made was a "fugitive from justice" because he or she has a final removal order, or for some other unstated reason. Without citing any authority, USCIS says that "Persons who have fled the jurisdiction of the United States are not entitled to enforcement of the FOIA's access provisions." Therefore, USCIS "declines" to process such requests "until such time as your client ceases to be a fugitive."

There is no authority for this so-called doctrine. The FOIA statute does not authorize agencies to "decline" or refuse requests based on the requester's purported status or conduct. Further, the FOIA statute and regulations require agencies to either "grant" or "deny" requests. Declining to process is not an authorized response.[3] It is instructive that in the letters "declining" on this basis, USCIS does not inform such requesters of their appeal rights, which is required when an agency denies a FOIA request in whole or in part.

---

[2] *See* 72 Fed. Reg. 9017 (Feb. 28, 2007).

[3] *See* 5 USC §552(b)(1)–(9) (FOIA exemptions); 6 CFR §5.6(c).

Moreover, the fugitive disentitlement doctrine is a federal court equitable doctrine. It has been imposed on rare occasions by a federal court if the plaintiff or petitioner fled the court's jurisdiction after filing suit. Understandably, a court would hesitate to exercise its jurisdiction to assist a person who had fled the court's jurisdiction. Here, USCIS attempts to apply this court-relief doctrine to its FOIA processing, without authority, and in an inappropriate context. Appeal the decision and assert your rights.

6. Request an expedite if you qualify

The FOIA requires that each agency provide for expedited processing of requests for records in cases in which the requester demonstrates *a compelling need*, and in other cases the agency determines. The regulations must ensure that a determination of whether to provide expedited processing must be made and notice provided to the requester within 10 days after the date of the request.[4]

DHS's FOIA regulations on the expediting process, at 6 CFR §5.5(d), *reqire* FOIA requests be expedited where the lack of expedited treatment could reasonably be expected to pose *an imminent threat to the life or physical safety* of an individual. The regulations also require DHS to inform the requester within 10 calendar days of its receipt of a request for expedited processing, whether it will grant the expedite request, and notify the requester of the decision.

Putting aside the question of whether the DHS regulation's criteria for expediting is unlawfully more restrictive than the FOIA statute's criteria, the regulation as written does not preclude USCIS from expediting FOIA requests in other circumstances. As USCIS is not complying with the statutory deadlines to respond to FOIA requests, it would be reasonable and proper for USCIS to establish and apply additional criteria for expediting FOIA requests. Those criteria could include, *as the FOIA statute itself says*, circumstances where the requester demonstrates *a compelling need* for the information requested.

Compelling circumstances, for example, could include cases in proceedings; cases where an individual is in detention or facing detention and a key document is, or may be in, the file; cases where a key record in government possession is needed for a petition (such as where there is an age-out); cases on appeal where there is a brief deadline; cases where there

is any government filing deadline; and similar instances.

Argue your case if you have a compelling case, but don't abuse the system and ask for expedites unnecessarily.

7. Use a Certification of Identity when requesting information that involves a third party

The government's redaction policy requires third party information contained in an "A" file to be redacted. Any requested information that may contain a third party's name or biographical information should be accompanied by a Certification of Identity. A signed Certification of Identity by the third party allows the FOIA office to release the signatory's information without redaction.

An example of when this may be useful is if your client is listed as a dependent of a beneficiary of an I-130 petition. Obtaining the signature of the petitioner will allow the I-130 petition to be released without redaction. Sometimes the FOIA office will release documents in this example without redaction, but a signed Certificate of Identity will ensure a complete document is released. [Note: There may be better examples of this.]

8. Online case status checks will be implemented soon, along with e-filing

The Privacy Office has indicated that on-line FOIA status checks will be possible with a system similar to the USCIS Case Status System. USCIS hopes to implement on-line case status checks by May 2008. The FOIA receipt number given when you file the request will be used to check the status of your case, along with current processing times.

The website for the status checks reportedly will be at *www.uscis.gov* in the FOIA section.

USCIS also is working on e-filing of FOIA requests, and hopes to have this system completed by September 2008.

---

[4] 5 USC §552(a)(6)(E)(ii).

KEEPING YOUR CLIENTS WITHOUT LOSING YOUR LICENSE

*by Maria Fuster Glinsmann and Roy J. Watson, Jr.**

Another possible title to this article would have been "Making It Safely to Retirement in Countryside Acres by Avoiding the Common Ethical Landmines Littered Across the Game Board of Life." Never has the practice of immigration law been more perilous, with some of the most contradictory and confusing dilemmas arising in the field of business immigration law.

As immigration lawyers, we are faced with a constantly shifting landscape of sweeping changes to the laws, and little or no guidance. We interact with government agencies that are not properly funded by Congress to perform their mandates. We face a host of hostile government agencies that continue to issue "new" rules, often accompanied by severe sanctions, but again—no guidance as to the standards, notice, or a process that one can follow. We have the Department of Labor (DOL) announcing substantial increases in "oversight," with a dramatic increase in staff. These DOL staff increases are not designed to process cases within faster time frames pursuant to

---

* **Maria Fuster Glinsmann** is a principal in the law firm of Glinsmann & Glinsmann, Chartered. She received her J.D. from the Georgetown University Law Center (1993) after graduating with a Bachelor of Science, cum laude, from the University of Maryland, College of Business Administration. She is admitted to practice law in Maryland and the District of Columbia, and is a member of the bar of the Supreme Court. Ms. Glinsmann is an active member of AILA and the Bar Association of Montgomery County (BAMC), Maryland. She was awarded Outstanding Section Chair for her leadership of the Immigration Section (2000–01). She has served on the faculty for the Law School for the Public (Maryland Public Television) on the topic of New Developments in Immigration.

Roy J. Watson, Jr. is a former Chair of the American Immigration Lawyers Association's (AILA's) New England Chapter. Over the past 32 years he has served on numerous national (ABA) and local (Boston and Massachusetts Bar Associations) Immigration Law Committees and International Law Sections. A regular writer and speaker on (business) immigration law for national (ALI-ABA, AILA) and local bar associations, Mr. Watson is a graduate of Brandeis University (B.A. Economics,) Boston College Law School (J.D.) and Harvard University's Kennedy School of Government (MPA). Mr. Watson is fully licensed as both a firefighter and an EMT and proudly serves on two fire departments.

the original cornerstone of justification for the PERM program, but instead, new staff will be dedicated to search for errors in the process. And, just when you thought it was safe to go to your office and work on that case, there are more and more state bar associations that have begun to focus ever more vigorously on attorney misconduct.

As Linus would say, "Where is my blanket?!"

Contrary to hostile and often mistaken public opinion, lawyers are held to extraordinarily high standards as a condition of practice. We as lawyers must ask ourselves not only whether the considered action is in fact a violation of the rules of practice, but we also have to ask ourselves whether the otherwise lawful actions are prohibited because they give an "appearance of impropriety." For our profession, it is not enough to be legally right; we must also "appear" to be right. For our profession, the mere accusation of impropriety can devastate a reputation that took years to establish.

The concerns are as challenging to the seasoned practitioner as they are to the newest of practitioners. In some cases, the newer practitioners may have the advantage of having had a more recent review of the current standards. Too often, the seasoned practitioner relies on rules and guidance that are no longer valid. As any good attorney will tell you, "Never assume."

Therefore, the lesson to take away from this article is to set yourself and your practice of law up to steer well clear of the landmines. It is always better to take extra time to review processes and procedures and discover problems in advance of a conflict, than to learn that the rules have changed after a complaint or other inquiry has begun.

KNOW THE RULES. KEEP THEM HANDY. KEEP THEM FRESH.

All attorneys are licensed to practice by one or more states. Accordingly, each attorney should check his or her own state's rules. This is especially true for immigration practitioners who may not have occasion to stay as current on "local" changes, believing that they may not apply to an immigration law practice. Many states have revised their rules, and it behooves all attorneys to spend time reading and reviewing

43

these rules on a regular basis. Most, if not all, states have their rules of practice available online. The American Bar Association (ABA) provides an easy web link to the various state rules: *www.abanet.org/cpr/links.html.* These should be checked—regularly—for every jurisdiction in which an attorney is admitted, even if there is a well-worn, heavily underlined copy of said rules on the attorney's desk or within easy reach. Most bar associations also provide numerous other avenues for obtaining ethics information. These will include publication of ethics manuals, posting of decisions as well as "call in" hours.

Practice Pointer: Build a network of colleagues that you can call on and use as a sounding board for fleshing out possible ethical dilemmas. Using your network of colleagues to help work through difficult issues will help keep your ethics limits clear and sharp. It will also help you know when you are in the murky "gray area" and when often the "right" answer cannot be ascertained.

Practice Pointer: Get to know your local Bar Counsel and the process for obtaining advice from him or her. Document this advice. Bar Counsel can often give you current cases to review that are on point with your issue. Do not wait until you get a grievance filed against you to get to know your local Bar Counsel.

The American Bar Association (ABA) has available a wide range of supporting information that begins with the Model Rules of Professional Conduct[1] (Model Rules) which—although not binding unless they have been specifically adopted by your jurisdiction—nevertheless often form the basis or framework for many of the state's rules and will provide the main point of reference for the guidance in this article. The ABA is a great resource providing a central starting point for access to the Model Rules, decisions, ethics opinions, publications, and more in the area of ethics.

By practicing before the Board of Immigration Appeals (BIA), Executive Office for Immigration Review (EOIR) and U.S. Citizenship and Immigration Services (USCIS), we are subject to a parallel set of Rules of Professional Conduct that appear in Title 8 of the Code of Federal Regulations (8 CFR Parts 1003 and 1292). They include provisions specifying grounds for disciplinary action, requirements for receiving and investigating complaints, and procedures for conducting hearings. The rules also authorize the BIA to suspend im-

mediately a practitioner who has been subject to disbarment, suspension, or resignation with an admission of misconduct as imposed by a federal or state court, or who has been convicted of a serious crime, pending a summary proceeding and final sanction. The Rules of Professional Conduct are *available at www.usdoj.gov/eoir/vll/fedreg/2000_2001/ fr27jn00R.pdf.*

Finally, the American Immigration Lawyers Association[2] (AILA) has a number of extremely helpful resources to provide as much support and guidance as possible. During her tenure as AILA's President, Palma Yanni oversaw the publication of an excellent resource, *Ethics in a Brave New World*,[3] which was distributed without charge to every member of the association. Further, AILA maintains a section on the members' website where many helpful articles are posted, including all of the articles from *Ethics in a Brave New World*. AILA also maintains a Message Board on its website where members may post questions or concerns on a full range of immigration questions, including ethics. While one should always be somewhat skeptical about any responses or advice one gets from such an open forum, this Message Board is generally monitored by experienced practitioners who will often step in if advice is inaccurate or could be damaging. The Ethics & Best Practices forum is moderated by Reid Trautz and often serves as a "sanity check" or a safe place to ask.

BE AWARE OF THE COMMON ETHICAL LANDMINES

There are certain issues which regularly arise that are common to all areas of practice. Keeping in mind that *all* of these issues are governed by the law(s) of your specific jurisdiction(s), the following should be carefully considered.

WHO IS MY CLIENT?

When does someone become a client?

Prospective Client. This seems like a fairly simple issue. Clearly, your client is the person who hires you! What a silly question. Ah, but questions in law are never simple. Most jurisdictions apply a fairly

---

[1] *www.abanet.org/cpr/mrpc/mrpc_toc.html.*

[2] *www.aila.org.*

[3] J. Pinnix and C.L. Calder eds., *Ethics in a Brave New World: Professional Responsibility, Personal Accountability, and Risk Management for Immigration Practitioners* (AILA 2004).

low standard for when a person may "assume" that you are offering "legal advice, counsel or service," and consequentially, when you legally "become" his or her attorney. Model Rule 1.18 calls for certain rights to flow to the *"Prospective Client."*[4] Some states have created a very high standard for legally obligating an attorney to treat an individual as a client. Why is this significant? Primarily because once a person "becomes" your client, the entire range of ethical rules applies, with all of the affirmative obligations and duties of care that one must follow in all dealings. It may, in some cases, impose an obligation to take action or give notice, even though the attorney does not realize that an attorney-client relationship exists.

Dual Representation. As authors, we had some vigorous discussion on what is required in dual representation cases. Be aware that the situations that undoubtedly will arise during the representation of more than one client will put you squarely and clearly in the murky "gray" area. We will defer to other AILA articles[5] for the discussion of the issue of "dual or joint" representation. Bruce Hake's comprehensive article entitled *"Dual Representation in Immigration Practice"*[6] provides a clear outline of the issues, regardless of whether you agree with the author's conclusions.

Initial Consultation. Consider for a moment a new potential client who comes in to consult with you. Perhaps you charge a consultation fee, or perhaps the case is so hopeless, you simply advise the person of how unable anyone will be to help, and decide not to even charge for the consultation. Absent further action, most states would impute that this person can very well assume that you have become his or her attorney.

This could result in some awkward moments, especially if, for example, in spite of your clear and unambiguous statement that "trying to sneak out of the country and then sneak back in will *not* avoid a 10-year bar," your prospective client is subsequently caught while trying to sneak out of the United States and insists that he or she was only following the advice of his or her attorney! While the example is intended to be extreme, the fact remains that many people with whom you meet (and decide NOT to represent) may very well leave your office with a belief that you have magically become "their" attorney.

Practice Pointer: Set up case management systems to routinely and contemporaneously record your communications and recommendations to clients. If you ever have to defend yourself against claims by that client, you will have an ac-

---

[4] *Client-Lawyer Relationship,* Rule 1.18 Duties to Prospective Client

(a) A person who discusses with a lawyer the possibility of forming a client-lawyer relationship with respect to a matter is a prospective client.

(b) **Even when no client-lawyer relationship ensues**, a lawyer who has had discussions with a prospective client shall not use or reveal information learned in the consultation, except as Rule 1.9 would permit with respect to information of a former client.

(c) A lawyer subject to paragraph (b) shall not represent a client with interests materially adverse to those of a prospective client in the same or a substantially related matter if the lawyer received information from the prospective client that could be significantly harmful to that person in the matter, except as provided in paragraph (d). If a lawyer is disqualified from representation under this paragraph, no lawyer in a firm with which that lawyer is associated may knowingly undertake or continue representation in such a matter, except as provided in paragraph (d).

(d) When the lawyer has received disqualifying information as defined in paragraph (c), representation is permissible if:

(1) both the affected client and the prospective client have given informed consent, confirmed in writing; or

(2) the lawyer who received the information took reasonable measures to avoid exposure to more disqualifying information than was reasonably necessary to determine whether to represent the prospective client; and

(i) the disqualified lawyer is timely screened from any participation in the matter and is apportioned no part of the fee therefrom; and

(ii) written notice is promptly given to the prospective client.

(Emphasis added.)

[5] These AILA articles cover the issue of dual representation: R.E. Juceam, D. Sabagh, & R.C. Bacon, "A Roundtable on Ethical Considerations and Professional Risks in Investment Immigration," *Immigration Options for Investors & Entrepreneurs* (AILA 2006); C. Mehta, "Finding the 'Golden Mean' in Dual Representation," *Immigration & Nationality Law Handbook* 29 (AILA 2005–06 Ed.); M. Maggio, updated by A.B. Goldfarb, "Basic Ethical Issues in Labor Certification Cases," *David Stanton Manual on Labor Certification* 223 (AILA 3rd Ed. 2005); Flynn and Patel, "Dual Representation: Employers, Employees and Ethics," Vol. II *Immigration & Nationality Law Handbook* 1 (AILA 1994–95 Ed.).

[6] B. Hake, "Dual Representation in Immigration Practice," *Ethics in a Brave New World: Professional Responsibility, Personal Accountability, and Risk Management for Immigration Practitioners* (AILA 2004).

curate record of your recommendations. Defending yourself against claims by your client is an exception to the rule regarding confidentiality.

Documenting the Declined or Terminated Representation. Many firms employ the practice of issuing some kind of "non-engagement letter" that specifically states that the law firm does *not* represent the person. Model Rule 1.16, styled *"Declining Or Terminating Representation,"* governs this issue.[7] Other firms ask the individual to sign a similar statement at the conclusion of the interview. While this may seem a "best practice," it could also raise an issue of whether such a waiver is enforceable. It would seem that the best practice would be to send a letter that sets forth in clear, but general terms the fact that you and/or your firm have not been retained to represent the prospective client. Notwithstanding the fact that you do not represent the individual, and you have made that emphatically clear, you still owe that person certain "rights," the most obvious being one of confidentiality.

Telephone Calls from Prospective Clients. Query: Do the same issues and concerns apply when you simply have a telephone conversation with someone and he or she never comes into your office? The prudent practitioner would say, "Yes." This could make it a little more challenging to send such a letter, as one-time callers may not be comfortable giving you the necessary contact information. Also, in the age of the internet, I have begun to see several firms that put a disclaimer at the bottom of all emails, and some of the larger firms have a pop-up window that also provides a disclaimer whenever you attempt to send an email by clicking directly off the website.

Practice Pointer: When prospective clients call your firm, collect their address and send them a template thank-you letter that describes your law firm's conditions for becoming a client. You can use alternate versions of the follow-up letter depending on whether the prospective client scheduled an appointment with you, was referred out to another attorney, or chose not to schedule an appointment. Whether or not this prospective client scheduled an appointment, this letter can serve to outline your law firm's requirements for becoming a "client" of the firm *i.e.,* an initial consultation. Decide for yourself whether you feel comfortable,

as a matter of standard practice, to take telephone calls from persons who have not provided contact information to you or your staff.

LANDFILL, NOT A LANDMINE. DOCUMENT COLLECTION, DOCUMENT RETENTION AND DOCUMENT DESTRUCTION.

If you have been practicing for more than a few years, you will have discovered that document collection, retention and destruction is a problem that could literally fill a landfill. Consider the following with regard to documents.

Originals vs. Copies. The practice of immigration is, by its very nature, a "document-driven" practice. The law was changed a number of years ago to allow the filing of copies,[8] but that is conditioned on being able to produce the original document. There is a split of opinion among practitioners as to whether or not the attorney should retain all original documents until the end of the process, or whether the client should retain the originals. Either way, the immigration attorney's files will often contain a considerable amount of paper that has been obtained, collected, and retained at the request of the client. In most jurisdictions, all of these documents have been "paid for" by the client, and therefore are viewed as rightful property of the client.

The issue of original document retention is most often discussed and considered by states and the rules that govern the practice in the context of trial preparation. While this could certainly apply in the context of a removal proceeding, the issue of who should retain documents, and for how long is a very real and sometimes troublesome issue for all immigration practitioners. This is especially so, given that

---

[7] *Client-Lawyer Relationship,* Rule 1.16, Declining or Terminating Representation.

[8] Copies may be submitted instead of original documents except for the labor certification. 8 CFR §204.5(g)(1). Section 204.5(g)(1) states "General. Specific requirements for initial supporting documents for the various employment-based immigrant classifications are set forth in this section. In general, **ordinary legible photocopies of such documents (except for labor certifications from the Department of Labor) will be acceptable for initial filing and approval**. However, at the discretion of the director, **original documents may be required in individual cases**. Evidence relating to qualifying experience or training shall be in the form of letter(s) from current or former employer(s) or trainer(s) and shall include the name, address, and title of the writer, and a specific description of the duties performed by the alien or of the training received. If such evidence is unavailable, other documentation relating to the alien's experience or training will be considered." (Emphasis added.)

we often ask for a variety of "personal" or "family" documents to prepare and file an application.

Practice Pointer: Consider adopting a law practice management policy of NOT keeping client originals. Advise your client in writing at the outset of the representation that you are not keeping originals (with limited exceptions, such as the labor certification) and that it is thus the client's responsibility to safeguard their own originals. During the representation, make legible copies of documents. For documents that you will use repeatedly at various stages of the representation *i.e.,* birth certificates, translations, passport biographic pages, employment authorization documents, I-94 cards, use scanner technology to scan photo quality versions of these documents into your case management system. This advice goes for agency correspondence as well. Electronic access to these high-quality copies will give you legible copies every time and will save you and your client the need for collecting these documents over and over again in representations that can span many years.

Recognizing the need to be able to produce the document, is it prudent for the attorney to retain *all* original documents? It is certainly open to debate, but retaining original documents can be very problematic, especially years after the case has closed and there is either a request to produce the original by the client, or perhaps the firm has decided that enough decades have passed and it is time to consider shredding the old files.

Some firms engage in the unfortunate practice of withholding the return of documents unless and until fees are paid. We are aware of NO jurisdiction that allows this. When a client requests the return of an original document or copies of forms prepared by the firm, the firm must turn over those documents. While some states still allow firms to retain certain writings that are described as the "work product" of the attorney, most jurisdictions require the firm to provide copies of all documents. What if the documents (given the prohibitive cost of rent) are stored "off site," and there is a substantial cost to retrieve the file(s)?

Practice Pointer: At each stage of the representation *i.e.,* execution of the fee agreement or engagement letter, initial filing of applications for benefits, receipt of request for evidence, response to request for evidence and approval, adopt the practice of providing the client with a complete copy of the filing or correspondence received, as the case may be. Document the timely delivery of this copy to the client with a short cover letter to the client encouraging them to review the documents for accuracy and use a method of delivery that can be confirmed easily and/or automatically, such as Federal Express or Priority Mail. Link the automated email generated as a result of the successful deliver to the client matter in your case management system. You will be accomplishing at least two worthwhile ethics objectives. First, you'll be fulfilling the obligation to "promptly communicate" with your client on the status of his or her matter, as required by Model Rule 1.4.[9] Second, by timely providing the client with copies of materials relevant to his or her matter, you'll be relieving yourself of any claim that you are holding documents that the client does not have.

Practice Pointer: Charge your legal fees and expenses at the outset of the representation and keep the funds in a qualified Attorney Trust Account (also known as an IOLTA). You will never have to worry about holding your client's file hostage for nonpayment.

Returning Original Documents to the Client. We are not aware of any jurisdiction that does not require the return of original documents when asked, irrespective of any dispute on charges or fees. Most jurisdictions require the attorney to produce not only original documents, but also copies of any and all files requested, including (in many jurisdictions) what used to be protected, the so called "attorney

---

[9] Client-Lawyer Relationship, Rule 1.4 Communication

(a) A lawyer shall:

(1) promptly inform the client of any decision or circumstance with respect to which the client's informed consent, as defined in Rule 1.0(e), is required by these Rules;

(2) reasonably consult with the client about the means by which the client's objectives are to be accomplished;

(3) keep the client reasonably informed about the status of the matter;

(4) promptly comply with reasonable requests for information; and

(5) consult with the client about any relevant limitation on the lawyer's conduct when the lawyer knows that the client expects assistance not permitted by the Rules of Professional Conduct or other law.

(b) A lawyer shall explain a matter to the extent reasonably necessary to permit the client to make informed decisions regarding the representation.

work product." The general rule is that the client, by paying the fee, has paid for the work product. That said, there is in most jurisdictions allowance made for costs of reproduction, and where appropriate, reasonable costs for retrieval of files that are stored off site. Most jurisdictions recognize that there may be a cost to retrieve and copy documents, especially where it may be a large file. In those situations, the firm may certainly charge a "reasonable" fee for such a request, but this should not be viewed as an opportunity to recover more fees. Most jurisdictions view this as absolutely no more than actual cost, and even then there may be questions raised. A good practice would be to provide this information to the client at the beginning of any case or matter. It could be incorporated into the firm's fee/retainer agreement or it could also be set forth on a separate information sheet provided to the client as part of the retainer process.

Practice Pointer: In your fee/engagement agreement explain your policy about providing the client copies of the activity on their matter throughout the course of the representation. List a flat fee to provide future copies within your document retention period.

Retention/Destruction of Records. In the perfect world, we would all keep all documents and all records forever. However, as costs rise for both space physically located in the firm as well as for off-site storage, many firms are looking at destroying some of their "older" files. How long must you retain files? You need to check with your individual state on that. Some have fixed limits, while others leave it up to the discretion of the firm. All require you to take reasonable steps to safeguard confidential information. An increasing number of jurisdictions have included specific requirements for notification to clients as well as specific steps to insure that all reasonable efforts were used to notify the client.

Because there is no Model Rule that covers retention and destruction of documents, we refer to the ABA's Informal Opinion 1384, "*Disposition of a Lawyer's Closed or Dormant Files Relating to Representation of or Services to Clients*," May 14, 1977.

- The Model Rules do not set forth particular rules or guidelines on the subject. This Committee had not previously issued an opinion that deals directly with the subject.

- The Committee did not identify a specific time period during which a lawyer must preserve all

files and beyond which he or she is free to destroy all files.

- Good common sense should provide answers to most questions that arise.

Although the ABA opinion is "informal" and not binding, this opinion outlines the procedural burdens you need to consider in designing your law firm's retention program including:

- The duty to inspect and screen the client files before destruction.

- The duty to protect client confidences.

- The duty to maintain an index of destroyed files.

- The duty to notify clients prior to destruction.

The same ethics opinion recognizes that client files need not be kept forever. ABA Informal Opinion 1384 states in relevant part,

"All lawyers are aware of the continuing economic burden of storing retired and inactive files....A lawyer does not have a general duty to preserve all of his files permanently. Mounting and substantial storage costs can affect the cost of legal services, and the public interest is not served by unnecessary and avoidable additions to the cost of legal services."

Practice Pointer: Our earlier practice pointer of placing the burden of storing originals on your client and providing the client (or clients) promptly with copies is starting to look wise and a lot less expensive than needing to rent a storage facility until the day you die. By having a policy in place that dictates that you are not to keep originals, you will also avoid the occasional accusation by the disorganized client that can't find his or her originals and believes that you may have kept it.

BREAKING UP IS HARD TO DO: DISENGAGEMENT AND TERMINATION LETTERS

There are times when you may find yourself in a situation where it is no longer reasonable or appropriate for your firm to continue to represent a client. While each jurisdiction addresses this issue, it is advisable for all firms to have an unambiguous notice that makes clear to the client(s) that your firm no longer represents the client and that the client cannot and should not rely on the firm in any way. This is especially true in immigration where the consequences of missing a deadline or taking (or failing to take) a specific action could have profoundly negative consequences to a client. It is important that the client understands that your firm will no longer assume responsibility for any of these services. There are firms that routinely send such letters, even to clients who have themselves sent written notification of the retention of a new/other firm as part of a request for documents.

THE FOUR WORST WORDS FOR A LAWYER TO HEAR: "OH, BY THE WAY...."

Candid Communications. We all encourage our clients to be "completely candid" with us in discussing their immigration matters. This is primarily motivated by our own self interest. No one likes "surprises!" If a client has an issue that would otherwise bar them from obtaining a benefit or prevent them from seeking relief, you do not want to find this out *after* you have filed the application. In many situations, the client does not understand the full significance or consequence of the information. It is our job and our responsibility to make sure that we have asked all of the proper questions necessary to elicit the critical information. If you have a complete set of facts, then you can give reliable advice and reliable expectations. Consider that a "successful representation" can be one that ends early because, given the facts, there was no solution under current law, *i.e.,* INA §245i.

Anecdote: Fortunately, I learned this lesson early on in my career when I was meeting with a corporate executive, his wife, and two children. Although the question of prior criminal activity was on my checklist, I thought it would be insulting to ask such an accomplished and successful individual if he had ever been arrested or committed any crimes. Fortunately for me, the client carefully reviewed all of my drafts, and brought the matter to my attention! We were able to satisfactorily address the issue, but I often wonder what would have happened had he not read the draft and alerted me.

Practice Pointer: Over the years our Client Intake Form has become shorter and some questions more open ended. For instance, we used to ask a litany of questions to ascertain whether clients were inadmissible "Have you ever been arrested? Have you ever been convicted of a crime?" Now our intake form asks the more general question "Have you ever been fingerprinted for any reason?" The answer to this question will bring up a variety of scenarios in which your client may have had contact with law enforcement and that

discussion between client and attorney can give the attorney a clearer picture of the facts.

Obligation to Investigate. There are also other situations where the clients somehow believe that if they can "fool" you, they can fool the government. These situations are often difficult. You certainly do not want to appear distrusting of your client, but you also do not want to have this information first appear during an interview. We are advocates for our clients, but that does not mean we can or should turn a "blind eye" to inconsistencies or other facts that should put a reasonable person on notice that there may be a problem. The lawyer should not play the role of Inquisitor, but he or she also should not sit idly by in the face of obvious conflict or fraud. If you or your staff has a "reasonable belief" that a client is not being truthful about important facts or inconsistencies, you may have an ethical obligation to investigate further. Discovering that a client has lied to a tribunal is a difficult balancing act between confidentiality (Rule 1.6[10]) and candor toward a tribunal (Rule 3.3[11]).

---

[10] *Client-Lawyer Relationship,* Rule 1.6 Confidentiality Of Information

(a) **A lawyer shall not reveal information** relating to the representation of a client unless the client gives informed consent, the disclosure is impliedly authorized in order to carry out the representation or the disclosure is permitted by paragraph (b).

(b) **A lawyer may reveal information** relating to the representation of a client to the extent the lawyer reasonably believes necessary:

(1) to prevent reasonably certain death or substantial bodily harm;

(2) to prevent the client from committing a crime or fraud that is reasonably certain to result in substantial injury to the financial interests or property of another and in furtherance of which the client has used or is using the lawyer's services;

(3) to prevent, mitigate or rectify substantial injury to the financial interests or property of another that is reasonably certain to result or has resulted from the client's commission of a crime or fraud in furtherance of which the client has used the lawyer's services;

(4) to secure legal advice about the lawyer's compliance with these Rules;

(5) to establish a claim or defense on behalf of the lawyer in a controversy between the lawyer and the client, to establish a defense to a criminal charge or civil claim against the lawyer based upon conduct in which the client was involved, or to respond to allegations in any proceeding concerning the lawyer's representation of the client; or

(6) to comply with other law or a court order.

continued

Adverse Information. What should one do when the client volunteers information that is inconsistent or contrary to the success of the client's case? Once the client has advised you of this set of "bad" facts that are fatal to the client's case, the client turns around and immediately assures you that "No one else knows this!" Variations on this all-too-common theme include any combination of disclosures that involve unauthorized employment, false or defective skills or degrees, and revelations regarding unambiguous fraud as to the payment of wages or fees. This kind of situation and many others like it carry with them a very high risk of loss, and the question may end up being, "Which would you rather lose, your client or your license to practice?" Once again, you must carefully examine your own regulations to understand exactly what burdens and obligations of disclosure are placed upon you.

Practice Pointer: I always picture my clients, particularly the new ones, as wearing Immigra-

tion and Customs Enforcement (ICE) enforcement jackets. When they suggest "no one will ever know" I promptly advise them of how good my license looks hanging on the wall of my conference room. If that doesn't convince them, I share my wise mother's advice that the truth can always be proven and that falsities are impossible to prove.

Practice Pointer: I like to tell myself and my staff that the clients who are prone to give you or the government false information are actually the ones who need us the most. This type of client can be reformed and if they can't be reformed, its best to terminate the attorney-client relationship.

Some situations are easy. We are aware of no jurisdiction that allows an attorney to commit perjury or affirmatively misrepresent facts that he or she knows to be false. Thus, if your client tells you that his or her Bachelor's degree was "earned" through a "rigorous ten hour program," you need to carefully explain to your client that now is the perfect time to re-draft that PERM application to take out the degree requirement. Similarly, discovering unauthorized employment is often a situation that can be resolved by sending the client out for a consular appointment instead of filing a change of status application.

Other situations are much trickier. How about a client that discloses at the successful end of the representation that they have six other children in their home country, but they didn't want to tell you because they would not have been able to meet the poverty guidelines? How about the discovery of fabricated pay stubs for a client that you represented at an employment-based adjustment interview? These are situations that we have had and they test the tension between the various competing rules of professional conduct. There isn't a magic answer. The goal is to avoid these situations by putting the fear of God or ICE into your client so that this does not happen. If it does happen, you have to find a way to undo the damage without damaging your client and/or your reputation.

Anecdote: Here is an example of a timely retraction[12] of a client's misrepresentation. During an

---

(Emphasis added.)

[11] *Advocate,* Rule 3.3 Candor Toward The Tribunal

(a) A lawyer shall not knowingly:

(1) make a false statement of fact or law to a tribunal or fail to correct a false statement of material fact or law previously made to the tribunal by the lawyer;

(2) fail to disclose to the tribunal legal authority in the controlling jurisdiction known to the lawyer to be directly adverse to the position of the client and not disclosed by opposing counsel; or

(3) offer evidence that the lawyer knows to be false. If a lawyer, the lawyer's client, or a witness called by the lawyer, has offered material evidence and the lawyer comes to know of its falsity, the lawyer shall take reasonable remedial measures, including, if necessary, disclosure to the tribunal. A lawyer may refuse to offer evidence, other than the testimony of a defendant in a criminal matter, that the lawyer reasonably believes is false.

(b) A lawyer who represents a client in an adjudicative proceeding and who knows that a person intends to engage, is engaging or has engaged in criminal or fraudulent conduct related to the proceeding shall take reasonable remedial measures, including, if necessary, disclosure to the tribunal.

(c) The duties stated in paragraphs (a) and (b) continue to the conclusion of the proceeding, and apply even if compliance requires disclosure of information otherwise protected by Rule 1.6.

(d) In an ex parte proceeding, a lawyer shall inform the tribunal of all material facts known to the lawyer that will enable the tribunal to make an informed decision, whether or not the facts are adverse.

---

[12] 9 FAM 40.63 N4.6 Timely Retraction (TL:VISA-313; 08-27-2001). A timely retraction will serve to purge a misrepresentation and remove it from further consideration as a ground for INA 212(a)(6)(C)(i) ineligibility. Whether a retraction is timely depends on the circumstances of the par-
continued

adjustment interview, the applicant provided pay stubs that purported to show that she was currently employed with the petitioning employer in the sponsored position. The District Adjudications Officer issued a Form I-72 at the interview requesting additional evidence of employment with the petitioning employer. The attorney made contact with the petitioning employer to obtain the requested documentation and learned that the pay stubs were a fabrication and the employee in fact was working in a similar position with another employer. Ironically, if the applicant/client had simply disclosed that she was in fact working for another employer in a similar position, the attorney would have prepared evidence of her portability. Upon learning that the pay stubs provided were completely fabricated, the attorney considered terminating the representation. A client's lack of candor makes one question any and all statements. Because of the longstanding relationship with the petitioning employer and the belief that this type of client needs the representation the most, the attorney chose to continue the representation and attempt to undo the damage. The attorney worked with the client to prepare evidence of her eligibility under the portability provisions of AC21 for lengthy applications and the attorney submitted a statement by the applicant/client to USCIS. The applicant's statement explicitly withdrew the submission of the pay stubs provided at the interview. The statement further requested that USCIS not consider or rely on the pay stubs provided at the interview in rendering its decision. The statement did not explain the reason for the withdrawal of the documentation provided, as any explanation would have been fatal. The adjustment was approved and the misrepresentation retracted.

You are, of course, permitted to assist "a client in determining the proper scope and application of the law, and representing a client in a "good-faith argument for an extension, modification, or reversal of existing law" is entirely appropriate conduct.[13] A lawyer, however, shall not knowingly counsel or assist a client in furtherance of criminal or fraudulent means, or in litigating frivolous claims. Model Rule 1.16(a) provides that a lawyer shall not repre-

sent a client where the representation will lead to a violation of the rules or other law. Rules 3.3 and 3.5 specify particular illegal and unethical conduct from which an attorney must refrain. An attorney shall not knowingly "make a false statement…to a tribunal,"[14] or "offer evidence that the lawyer knows to be false."[15] What if the client reveals such false information to the lawyer years after the completion of the case? Comment 13 to Rule 3.3[16] states that the conclusion of the proceeding is a reasonable definite point for the termination of the obligation.

MANAGING STAFF ON ETHICAL ISSUES

Nearly all states, organizations representing lawyers and paralegals, and courts have stated that a paralegal should not perform any substantive legal work unless that work is properly supervised by an attorney. Model Rule 5.3[17] requires that your staff's

---

[14] ABA Model Rules of Professional Conduct Rule 3.3(a)(1).

[15] ABA Model Rules of Professional Conduct Rule 3.3(a)(3).

[16] ABA Model Rules of Professional Conduct Rule 3.3, Comment 13. **Duration of Obligation.** [13] A practical time limit on the obligation to rectify false evidence or false statements of law and fact has to be established. The conclusion of the proceeding is a reasonably definite point for the termination of the obligation. A proceeding has concluded within the meaning of this Rule when a final judgment in the proceeding has been affirmed on appeal or the time for review has passed.

[17] *Law Firms And Associations,* Rule 5.3 Responsibilities Regarding Nonlawyer Assistants

With respect to a nonlawyer employed or retained by or associated with a lawyer:

(a) a partner, and a lawyer who individually or together with other lawyers possesses comparable managerial authority in a law firm shall make reasonable efforts to ensure that the firm has in effect measures giving reasonable assurance that the person's conduct is compatible with the professional obligations of the lawyer;

(b) a lawyer having direct supervisory authority over the nonlawyer shall make reasonable efforts to ensure that the person's conduct is compatible with the professional obligations of the lawyer; and

(c) a lawyer shall be responsible for conduct of such a person that would be a violation of the Rules of Professional Conduct if engaged in by a lawyer if:

(1) the lawyer orders or, with the knowledge of the specific conduct, ratifies the conduct involved; or

(2) the lawyer is a partner or has comparable managerial authority in the law firm in which the person is employed, or has direct supervisory authority over the person, and knows of the conduct at a time when its consequences can be avoided or mitigated but fails to take reasonable remedial action.

---

ticular case. In general, it should be made at the first opportunity.

[13] ABA Model Rules of Professional Conduct Rule 3.1.

conduct be supervised by an attorney, that their behavior be compatible with the rules that govern the
attorney, and that, as the attorney, you take reasonable efforts to ensure this compatibility. Today,
many immigration law firms typically staff one to
three paralegals per attorney. These ratios create a
challenge for the immigration practitioner to bring
all staff into the fold and keep them there.

Practice Pointer: Develop a law firm Office Procedures Manual and have each employee keep a
personal copy. Prepare an outline of ethical obligations for staff. Provide training and examples of
situations that may arise. Have new staff acknowledge their commitment of their ethical obligations.
As difficult ethical situations arise in your workload, provide written instruction for staff and use
the opportunity to refresh and remind all your staff
about ethical obligations. Update the official manual periodically using the real life examples that
came up in your practice.

Practice Pointer: Utilize a case management system that takes the "corporate memory" burden
off any particular staff member and puts it into a
system with checks and balances.

CONCLUSION

There are many challenges that immigration lawyers face in zealously representing clients before the
various government authorities authorized to grant
our clients benefits. The foregoing ethical challenges
are common to us as business immigration lawyers.
If you can anticipate and avoid these challenges, you
and your clients will enjoy many successful outcomes together. You will have served many well-
deserving clients, some of whom you reformed
along the way. You will arrive at the "Countryside
Acres" point in the game with your head high and
your license squarely hung on the wall.

INVESTORS AND ENTREPRENEURS: INBOUND AND OUTBOUND

*by Linda W. Lau and Tina Bay**

INTRODUCTION

When advising individuals on immigration matters, U.S. immigration law practitioners are tasked with identifying options that suit each individual's background, resources, and needs. The fifth employment-based preference (EB-5) immigrant visa category[1] is a natural consideration when the person seeking advice has funds available for investment and wishes to acquire U.S. permanent resident status. For such individuals, the EB-5 category often appears to be the simplest way to secure immigration status in the United States because the basic requirements for EB-5 eligibility are succinct at the surface: to obtain conditional resident status for two years and ultimately become a permanent resident, invest $1 million in a commercial enterprise in the United States that will create 10 new full-time positions for authorized U.S. workers by the end of two years.[2]

Moreover, there are several points of attraction. For example, the commercial enterprise invested in can be any active for-profit operation established after November 29, 1990, which allows entrepreneurs great flexibility in selecting their investments.

Those who have already been in the United States for many years as nonimmigrant E-2 treaty investors,[3] but wish to pursue long-term residency, are able to make their initial E-2 investment count as part of the requisite EB-5 capital. Another positive is that if the investment is made in a "targeted employment area," the requisite amount is decreased to $500,000.[4] Additionally, if the investment is made in a regional center project that involves multiple foreign investors aggregated to revive a target employment area, the job creation requirement is relaxed to include indirect positions, not just direct positions reflected on the company's payroll.[5] Also with regional centers, an investor can deposit his or her funds into a variety of prepackaged projects, such as the renovation of warehouses, lending of funds to commercial entities, operation of dairy farms, and commercial development endeavors, thus avoiding the struggles involved in setting up a business independently.

As a practical matter, approval of petition for EB-5 classification can be obtained based on a convincing business plan when no business activities have actually been commenced for the investment enterprise. For investors with dependents, another advantage is that the investor's spouse and children under 21 are automatically included in the EB-5 petition (Form I-526, Immigrant Petition by Alien Entrepreneur) submitted to U.S. Citizenship and Immigration Services (USCIS).[6] Above all, there is the prospect of ultimately obtaining a U.S. permanent resident card with all of its attendant benefits.

DRAWBACKS OF THE EB-5 OPTION

High-Risk Investment

The conceptual appeal of an EB-5 strategy can quickly dissipate, however, in light of practical burdens that an investor must shoulder to fulfill the statutory requirements. Assuming that a targeted employment area is not involved, $1 million is a

---

* **Linda W. Lau** is principal of the Global Immigration Law Group, a Los Angeles-based firm specializing in U.S. and global immigration strategies for professionals, corporations, and high-net-worth individuals. She has been practicing immigration law for 20 years and served as chair and member of the Executive Committee of AILA's Southern California Chapter from 2002 to 2006. Ms. Lau has extensive experience in handling EB-5 cases and is a frequent speaker on the topic of investment-based immigration to the United States. She is the sole appointed U.S. agent coordinator of the Canadian and UK immigrant investor programs for HSBC Capital (Canada), the global immigration headquarters of HSBC worldwide, and has assisted high-net-worth individuals in obtaining residency in the UK and Canada through investment. Ms. Lau earned her J.D. from University of California, Los Angeles School of Law, her Master's from the University of Michigan, Ann Arbor, and her B.A. from the University of California at Berkeley. She is a member of the State Bar of California and admitted as a solicitor of England and Wales. Ms. Lau credits her associate, **Tina Bay**, Esq., with co-authoring this article.

[1] Immigration and Nationality Act (INA) §203(b)(5). For an overview of EB-5 requirements, *see* S. Yale-Loehr *et al.*, "EB-5 Immigrant Investors," in this volume.

[2] INA §203(b)(5).

[3] INA §101(a)(15)(E)(ii).

[4] INA §203(b)(5)(C)(ii); 8 CFR §204.6(f)(2).

[5] 8 CFR §204.6(m).

[6] INA §216A(a)(1).

substantial sum to invest in any enterprise. There is no guarantee of return, and the investor is left to research and select a business opportunity and completely assume the risk of failure. In addition, EB-5 investors are saddled with the burden of running the business they invest in. Immigration regulations require the EB-5 investor to be "engaged in" the management of the enterprise, as opposed to maintaining a purely passive role with regard to the investment.[7] Although this requirement appears to be softened by the fact that limited partnerships are a permissible business structure,[8] truly passive investments are clearly not allowed. This poses a problem for investors who would prefer not to be involved in business operations due to language and cultural barriers, for example. Even without the engagement requirement, most investors would have to be actively monitoring the enterprise in order to have some assurance of a return on their investment, and to see that the business creates and sustains the requisite 10 jobs. In the case of a regional center investment, an investor may request financial information on a particular project by contacting the regional center directly, but would not have the opportunity to closely control the business operations. Moreover, the return on regional center investments is low, usually ranging from 0 to 6 percent, depending on the profitability of the business. In pursuing the EB-5 route, an investor must not only put forth substantial capital, but assume an enormous risk of loss and the tremendous stress of entrepreneurship.

Restrictions on Investment Funds

Another difficulty with EB-5 is that the $1 million investment must be an equity investment in the form of tangible property, which means a loan from the investor to the enterprise cannot qualify, nor can intangible assets such as patents or specialized trade knowledge.[9] This can result in investors having to invest large sums of hard cash for the sake of EB-5 eligibility, even where other financing and capital investment arrangements may make better business sense.

Assuming the requisite capital can be furnished, the EB-5 investor also must provide detailed records showing that the source of investment funds is lawful,[10] such as all personal and business tax returns filed worldwide for the last five years. Investors must withstand the scrutiny of USCIS officers, who in a post-9/11 world are not inclined to give them the benefit of the doubt, and who are free to demand extensive source-of-funds documentation at their discretion. This may prove a challenge for those who lack strong documentation of their earnings and accumulated wealth, especially if the earnings activities date back more than five years. Even when the investment money was a gift from the investor's family member, which is permissible, the investor may at times be required to provide proof of gift-tax reporting and needs to demonstrate where the donor obtained the gifted funds. Similarly, when the investment funds were earned by the investor's spouse but used by the investor for investment purposes, the investor must establish the source of funds derived through the spouse. It should be noted that fund transfers from the joint account of a husband and wife might not even be considered a valid source of funds if the law of the place governing the marital assets does not recognize community property.

Job Creation Requirement

Another drawback of the EB-5 option is the job creation requirement. As the EB-5 visa category is made available expressly for "employment creation,"[11] proof of job creation is paramount. EB-5 investors must show at the outset of their investment that the enterprise being invested in will generate no less than 10 full time (35 hour-per-week[12]) positions within two years. When the business enterprise is a start-up with only a few workers, making representations about job creation may require a degree of foretelling beyond the investor's ability. An EB-5 investor who is granted conditional resident status for two years based on an I-526 approval may lose that status if, before the end of the two years, the 10 full-time positions in fact have not materialized.[13] This may come about despite an investor's hard work and best efforts in a declining economy.

Investors in regional centers are not necessarily safer in this regard. While such investors have the advantage of being credited with indirect job creation, this fact provides little long-term security. First, most investors in approved regional centers have never had the opportunity to review the economic analysis report of the regional center to understand how the indirect jobs are to come into existence.

---

[7] 8 CFR §204.6(j)(5).

[8] INA §203(b)(5)(A).

[9] 8 CFR §204.6(e), defining "Capital" and "Invest."

[10] 8 CFR 204.6(j)(3).

[11] INA §203(b)(5).

[12] 8 CFR §204.6(e), defining "Full-time employment."

[13] 8 CFR §216.6(a)(4)(iv).

Second, all predictions concerning indirect job creation are often revisited by USCIS examiners at the two-year mark. This means that although USCIS deems a regional center job count projection reasonable at the I-526 stage and approves the project, it will not adjudicate the actual sufficiency of the job count until the end of the conditional period. EB-5 investors will be required, per some USCIS adjudicators, to prove the jobs have indeed been created in order to be eligible for the removal of conditions on their residency.[14] While this is not a serious problem currently, the issue has been challenged previously, and the absence of clear law or policy regarding this stage of EB-5 adjudication pits regional center investors against an uncertain future. For example, it is entirely possible for an examiner to conclude that indirect jobs generated by businesses within the approved regional center do not count despite being actual and numerous, because these jobs were at one time located within the designated region, though not in the same project, before the investment.

Protracted Procedure

A final disadvantage of the EB-5 option is that it forces investors to meander through a two-step petition process with USCIS that is labor intensive and time consuming. The investor must initially file a Form I-526. For investors who are already in the United States and wish to adjust to permanent resident status, concurrent filing of the Form I-526 and I-485 (Application to Register Permanent Residence or Adjust Status) is not allowed. The current processing time for an I-526 is about six months,[15] not accounting for delays due to turning around a request for evidence by USCIS. Once the I-526 is approved, the additional processing time involved in consular processing cases is approximately nine months from the time USCIS sends the immigrant visa petition to the National Visa Center (NVC) for processing to the time that the post receives the file from the NVC and schedules the applicant for an interview. When adjustment of status is sought, the current processing time is about six months,[16] assuming no setbacks in the security check processes

conducted by the Federal Bureau of Investigation and other federal government agencies. Security check delays can occur in both consular processing and adjustment of status cases, although with respect to adjustment of status, USCIS in February 2008 announced that it will adjudicate I-485 applications when an FBI name check request has been pending for more than 180 days if the application is outside of normal processing times and is otherwise approvable.[17] Overall, the processing time from the filing of the I-526 petition to the issuance of an immigrant visa or permanent resident card generally ranges between 16 and 24 months.

If successful, an EB-5 investor will acquire lawful immigration status at the end of the I-526 and immigrant visa/adjustment of status process. However, the status acquired is a two-year "conditional permanent resident" status,[18] which is not the long-term status that most EB-5 investors initially set out to obtain. To have the conditions on residency removed and become a true permanent resident, the investor must file yet another petition with USCIS within 90 days of the conditional period's expiration.[19] Filing this petition (Form I-829, Petition by Entrepreneur to Remove Conditions) entails a new round of record sifting and document gathering that can easily exceed the burden carried at the I-526 stage. Processing time for I-829 petitions is currently listed as six months,[20] but generally extends to one year because requests for evidence are issued in most cases. Additionally, a common problem experienced in I-829 cases is delay or failure by USCIS in issuing receipt notices to EB-5 investors. An I-829 receipt notice automatically extends an EB-5 investor's lawful resident status and allows the investor to leave and re-enter the United States while the I-829 petition is pending.[21] Lack of a receipt notice naturally hinders an investor's ability to travel outside the United States while awaiting the adjudication of the I-829 petition. Also, it is difficult to track the status of pending I-829 application if for some reason the I-829 receipt notice was lost. Further, since all I-829 records are input into the Marriage Fraud Act Amendment System (MFAS) and not the claims

---

[14] *Id.*

[15] *See https://egov.uscis.gov/cris/jsps/Processtimes.jsp?SeviceCenter=CSC* [sic] (California Service Center processing dates); *https://egov.uscis.gov/cris/jsps/Processtimes.jsp?SeviceCenter=TSC* [sic] (Texas Service Center processing dates).

[16] *Id.*

[17] *See* USCIS Questions & Answers, "Background Check Policy Update" (Feb. 28, 2008), *available at www.uscis.gov/files/article/NameCheckQA_28Feb08.pdf.*

[18] INA §216A(a)(1), 8 CFR §216.2(a).

[19] 8 CFR §216.2(b).

[20] *See* webpages cited *supra* note 15.

[21] 8 CFR §216.6(a)(1).

system for other types of immigrant petitions, USCIS will not issue a duplicate receipt notice.

The timeframe from I-526 filing to I-829 approval—that is, the process an EB-5 investor must endure to obtain permanent resident status—will likely be five years. Throughout that period, the children of the investor likely have become rooted in American culture, heightening the adverse affect on the investor's family in the event of an I-829 denial. Add to the morass expensive attorney's fees paid twice over and a drastic fee hike in July 2007 for I-526 petitions (from $480 to $1,435) and I-829 petitions (from $475 to $2,850 for I-829 petitions).[22] Also consider the fact that during the conditional period, EB-5 investors are taxed by the U.S. government on their worldwide income. All in all, the EB-5 scheme imposes such onerous requirements that many investors decline it—and immigration lawyers are left questioning its utility.

WHEN OTHER U.S. IMMIGRATION OPTIONS ARE UNAVAILABLE

Often while it is not the most desirable option for many, EB-5 may be the only available option for many investors seeking to enter or acquire status in the United States. For example, they cannot qualify as treaty investors under the E-2[23] nonimmigrant visa category because they are not nationals of an E-2 treaty country. Perhaps the L-1[24] temporary visa category does not apply because they have not worked in an executive or managerial capacity at a multinational company for one out of the last three years. The H-1B[25] specialty occupation worker category may not be an option due to the absence of a bachelor's degree or willing U.S. sponsor. With respect to permanent residence strategies, the employment-based second preference (EB-2)[26] route could be foreclosed for lack of an advanced degree, adequate experience, or a U.S. employer. Or, an EB-1C[27] petition may be unworkable because the investor does not maintain a business operation overseas and would not work as a manager in a related U.S. business. The analysis of foreclosed options could continue.

What are immigration practitioners to do when the field is whittled down to a single EB-5 option that is fraught with troublesome issues? Advise investors to press on with an EB-5 petition despite their misgivings? Or alternatively, avalanche them with caveats, let them lay their U.S. immigration hopes to rest, and wish them well? Perhaps immigration lawyers would do well at this juncture to pause and turn their sights to the horizon. This means thinking outbound (away from the United States) and ask whether the investor's needs would be better met through a non-U.S. immigration program. This is an entirely appropriate question, as the primary role of immigration lawyers is not to market the U.S. immigration program but to advocate for their clients by equipping them with the best immigration strategies possible. It is also a logical question. Because investors have the resources and thus the means to be globally mobile, there is little reason why an investor's immigration options should be seen as limited to the United States.

EVALUATING THE INVESTOR'S NEEDS

Where inbound U.S. options appear unfeasible for an investor, the immigration lawyer should consider further probing the investor's needs. A deeper evaluation may generate a greater range of possibilities that were not a part of the investor's initial inquiry. What if, for example, the investor is an INA §245(i)-qualified individual who is in the midst of removal proceedings? The initial strategy might be to have that individual file an I-526 petition as a stepping stone to adjusting status in immigration court.[28] Yet, if the high investment amount and other considerations make the I-526 route difficult, the investor may be willing to explore the possibility of simply relocating outside the United States.

Immigration lawyers would do well to ask potential EB-5 investors why they wish to establish themselves in the United States. For some investors, an abundance of relatives and strong family ties in the United States makes this country the most desirable destination. They may or may not be open to relocating elsewhere. Some investors might want to relocate to the United States mainly because they wish to escape threats of kidnapping, politically-motivated threats, or terrorism in their countries of origin. For such individuals, obtaining residency or

---

[22] USCIS Form G-1055, Fee Schedule, *available at* *www.uscis.gov/files/nativedocuments/G-1055.pdf.*

[23] INA §101(a)(15)(E)(ii).

[24] INA §101(a)(15)(L).

[25] INA §101(a)(15)(H)(i)(b).

[26] INA §203(b)(2).

[27] INA §203(b)(1)(C).

[28] *See* INA §245(i).

citizenship in a country other than the United States may well serve their goals. The same could apply to high-profile investors, who may wish to have other passport or residency options on hand in case they need to retreat to a safe haven. Similarly, investors who wish to rise above strict visa requirements applicable to their home countries, resulting from geopolitical unrest and terrorism, for example, could have their needs met through non-U.S. programs.

There are numerous other reasons why investors might seek residence or citizenship outside their present home. Some individuals are motivated by taxation issues—other countries may offer friendlier regimes with lower rates—or the desire to shield their children from home country military service requirements. Some are looking to start a new chapter of their lives in a country that offers a better quality of life for their families. Others simply desire greater personal liberty by having more options to accommodate their personal or business activities. Acquiring a second or third country passport may serve the end of increasing visa-free travel privileges. Perhaps the thought of immigrating to another country is motivated by the hope of retiring in safer and more stable surroundings. Many individuals move to pursue an education, make a career change, or participate in a charitable cause. In the above scenarios, non-U.S. options might better suit the investor's needs and should be discussed.

OTHER INVESTMENT-BASED RESIDENCY AND CITIZENSHIP PROGRAMS

Following is a nonexhaustive summary of some of the alternatives available to investors seeking a second country of residence or citizenship. The author is by no means an expert on the programs mentioned, but offers broad-stroke vignettes with the aim of encouraging U.S. immigration lawyers to think globally.

Canada Immigrant Investor Program[29]

Canada operates an immigrant investor program that offers permanent residency to qualified individuals in exchange for an investment of C$400,000 into Canada's economy for a five-year period. The program does not apply to the province of Quebec, which has its own business immigration scheme. Under the federal program, the investment is made

---

[29] Detailed information on this program can be accessed via the Citizenship and Immigration Canada website. *See* www.cic.gc.ca/english/immigrate/business/investors/index.asp.

with the Canadian government rather than into a business designated and run by the investor. The investment is government-guaranteed: upon remitting the required funds, investors are issued a promissory note from the Canadian government by which they can reclaim their C$400,000 investment after five years. Once an immigrant investor application is approved, the Canadian government issues a permanent resident visa to the investor, who will then be eligible to live, work, and study anywhere in Canada, and to receive most social benefits available to Canadian citizens.

The investor's spouse or common-law partner and children under the age of 22 can be included in the immigrant investor application, though all applicants must pass background and medical checks before being issued immigration benefits. Investors applying from the United States may submit their immigrant investor applications to the Canadian consulate in Buffalo, and presently can expect a total processing time of 12 to 14 months.

To qualify for the Canada immigrant investor program, an investor must have at least C$800,000 in net worth (the fair market value of all of the assets of the investor and spouse or common-law partner, minus the fair market value of all of their liabilities), and satisfy a two-year business experience requirement. In short, documentation must be provided showing the investor has either managed or owned a qualifying business for at least two out of the last five years. Operations earning passive investment income cannot be a "qualifying business," which is defined using specified numerical metrics.

The Canadian government maintains a list of approved facilitators—government-insured financial institutions through which investors are encouraged to make their investment. One such institution is Hong Kong Shanghai Bank Corporation (Capital) Canada (HSBC), with which the authors are familiar due to our firm's role as the sole U.S. agent coordinator for the HSBC Immigrant Investor Program. Under HSBC's program, immigrant investors can choose from three financing options:

- The investor applicant takes a C$400,000 loan and pays interest to HSBC of C$120,000. This interest amount is the total interest of the loan over the five-year period, and is collected in full at the beginning of the loan period. No monthly payments are made by the investor applicant, and the total cost to the investor applicant is therefore limited to the C$120,000.

- The investor applicant deposits C$200,000 with HSBC and takes a C$200,000 loan. The investor applicant receives no interest payments during the five-year investment period, and at the end of the investment period receives approximately C$100,000 back.

- The investor applicant provides to HSBC the full C$400,000 from his or her own resources, and after landing in Canada, HSBC provides the investor applicant with a C$300,000 personal line of credit at the prime rate of interest (currently 6.25 percent/year). After the five-year investment period expires, the investor applicant receives back the C$400,000, less any balance owing on the line of credit.

After obtaining permanent resident status, an investor and dependents can maintain such status by demonstrating they have been physically present in Canada for at least two years within a five-year period. They may eventually apply for citizenship if they can demonstrate that they have lived in Canada for at least three out of the past four years. A Canadian passport would allow visa-free travel throughout many parts of the world.

United Kingdom Immigrant Investor Program[30]

The United Kingdom (UK) permits investors to enter and settle in the country for an initial period of 24 months, which can be extended for three additional years if investment and physical presence requirements are met. At the end of the aggregate five-year period, investors may be eligible to apply for permanent residency, technically termed "indefinite leave to remain." The UK tax regime includes special provisions for high-net-worth individuals classed as "UK resident, non-domicile." UK citizenship can be sought as soon as one year after obtaining indefinite leave to remain, provided presence and other criteria are satisfied. Due to the UK's membership in the European Union, a UK passport might be an attractive end goal for investors who wish to enjoy easy access to the whole of Europe.

To obtain permission to enter the UK as an investor, an individual must show that he or she has at least £1 million of his or her own money under his or her control in the UK. Alternatively, the individual can show that he or she owns personal assets exceeding £2 million in value, taking into account any personal liabilities, and has at least £1 million of his or her own money under his or her control in the UK through financing. The required investment amount is a minimum of £750,000, which must be invested for at least five years in UK government bonds, share capital, or loan capital in active and trading UK-registered companies. The rest of the investor's funds may take the form of cash in a UK bank account, net equity in a property in the UK, or a private investment in a UK company. Unlike Canada, the UK immigrant investor program does not include a business experience requirement. Persons seeking to enter the UK as investors must intend to make the UK their main home by spending more time in the UK than elsewhere.

The £2 million personal asset requirement could be satisfied by assets located anywhere in the world. The investor applicant can prove that his or her personal assets have £2milliom net worth by having such assets appraised and evaluated by a reputable appraisal firm. With respect to the £1 million requirement, the authors know from their experience as the sole U.S. agent coordinator for HSBC's UK Immigrant Investor Program that HSBC can help investor applicants by financing the amount for a nonrefundable fee of £170,000.

An investor's spouse, civil partner, and unmarried children under the age of 18 can be included in the visa application. Parents or grandparents may be included as dependents under certain circumstances. In all scenarios, investors must show they are able to support themselves and any dependents without taking any employment other than self-employment. Currently, the initial entry application under the UK immigrant investor program takes approximately four to six months to process.

Australia Business Investor Visa[31]

Australia operates a comprehensive business skills visa program that, among other things, offers immigration benefits for qualified individuals who will invest A$1,500,000 for four years in an approved Australian state or territory government bond. The investor may be sponsored by the state or territory if the particular state or territory wishes to encourage the investment activity, but sponsorship is not required. Like the UK program, Australia's im-

[30] Details on this program can be found at the UK Border and Immigration Agency website. *See www.bia.homeoffice.gov.uk/workingintheuk/investors/eligibility/.*

[31] Further specifics on this subject are available at the website of Australia's Department of Immigration and Citizenship. *See www.immi.gov.au/skilled/business/index.htm.*

migrant investor scheme involves a two-staged approach to acquiring permanent residence. First, an investor applies for a provisional visa that is valid for four years, premised on a designated investment. After the designated investment has been maintained for four years, the investor may be eligible to apply for a permanent residence visa as long as he or she has been present in Australia for two out of the four years prior to applying. Permanent resident status lasts five years, after which the investor can either apply for a resident return visa or apply for citizenship. Citizenship may be sought earlier—as quickly as 12 months into permanent residency—provided physical presence criteria are met.

Requirements for obtaining the initial business investor visa include an age limit: the investor must be less than 45 years old if not sponsored by an Australian state or territory, or less than 55 years old if sponsorship exists. Applicants also need to demonstrate a vocational level of English if not sponsored. With respect to business experience, investors are required to show that they have at least three years of experience managing a qualifying business or investment, and an overall successful record of eligible investment activity and management skill. At least one of the years of management experience must fall within the five-year period immediately preceding application. Additionally, for the two fiscal years immediately before application, the net value of the investor's and spouse's combined assets must be at least A\$2,250,000. Finally, investors must intend to develop and maintain an ownership interest in a business in Australia after the designated investment in a government bond has matured, and remain continually involved in the management of that business.

The spouse, dependent children, and other dependent relatives living with the investor may be included in the visa application. Family members accompanying the investor to Australia may avail themselves of work and study rights.

New Zealand Active Investor Migrant Policy[32]

As of November 2007, New Zealand has an "Active Investor Migrant Policy" designed to attract financial capital and business experience to the country. The policy extends residency benefits to three categories of investors: global investors, profes-

sional investors, and general (active) investors. Global and professional investors, who must invest a higher minimum amount, are given priority, with applicants in the general (active) investor category sifted using a point-based selection system. For all three categories, the investor must demonstrate four years of business experience through the ownership or management of a lawful business enterprise with at least five full-time employees, and an annual turnover of NZ\$1 million.

The global investor category is for individuals who invest NZ\$20 million in New Zealand for at least four years. At least NZ\$5 million of the funds must be in active investment, which can be met by deploying NZ\$100,000 or more to establish a new business enterprise in New Zealand or directly investing NZ\$200,000 or more in an existing New Zealand business. The professional investor category is for those investing NZ\$10 million, including at least NZ\$2 million in active investment, in New Zealand. Professional investors cannot be more than 64 years old. Persons who invest at least NZ\$2.5 million and possess an additional NZ\$1 million for settlement funds can qualify to apply for residence under the general (active) investor category, provided they accumulate sufficient points based on criteria such as age, English-language ability, and business experience. The maximum age for applicants in this category is 54.

Family members who may be included in an investor's application are a partner, whether by marriage, civil union, or de facto relationship, and unmarried dependent children up to 24 years old. The children need not live with the investor as long as they rely mainly on the investor for financial support.

Under New Zealand's policy, permanent resident status is acquired in a manner similar to the U.S. EB-5 conditional residence scheme. Investors are initially granted a two-year period of residence. Before the two years expires, an investor must provide evidence to Immigration New Zealand that he or she retained acceptable investments in the country during the two years and met the minimum physical presence requirements for each year—73 days for global investors, 109 for professional investors, and 146 for general (active) investors. Presence requirements do not apply to family members. If the investor satisfies Immigration New Zealand, he or she and the family members included in the application are eligible for a returning resident's visa that is valid for up to two years. At the end of the second two years, the investor is required to show that he or

---

[32] Program details are accessible through Immigration New Zealand's website. *See www.immigration.govt.nz/migrant/ stream/invest/activeinvestor/.*

she met investment and presence requirements over the entire four-year period. If successful, the investor and family members may obtain an indefinite returning resident's visa. Citizenship can be sought once permanent residence is held for five years and presence requirements are satisfied.

Hong Kong Special Administrative Region (Hong Kong) Capital Investment Entrant Scheme[33]

Hong Kong encourages capital investment within its borders by offering entry permits to investors who invest at least HK$6.5 million in either Hong Kong real estate or certain financial assets. These assets include shares of companies listed on the Hong Kong Stock Exchange and traded in Hong Kong dollars, convertible bonds issued by the Hong Kong government, and certificates of deposit denominated in Hong Kong Dollars and issued by authorized institutions. Investors are not required to establish or participate in the running of a business. To be eligible for migration under the Capital Investment Entrant Scheme, an investor must have net assets of at least HK$6.5 million to which he or she had uninterrupted control throughout the two years preceding application. The investor's spouse and unmarried dependent children under 18 may be included in the application.

Once an investor's application is approved and he or she can demonstrate that the investment has been made, the investor and dependents will be granted permission to stay in Hong Kong for two years. During that time, the investor will be subject to portfolio maintenance requirements designed to ensure the investor does not reduce his or her investment commitment. Following the initial two-year period, the investor may seek further extensions of two years as long as he or she continues to satisfy all eligibility criteria. After seven years of continuous ordinary residence in Hong Kong, the investor and dependents are eligible to apply for the right of abode (permanent resident status) in Hong Kong.

Hong Kong's immigrant investor scheme is not available to nationals of Afghanistan, Albania, Cuba, and the Democratic People's Republic of Korea (North Korea). Also, due to foreign exchange control rules, Chinese nationals are ineligible to apply unless they have first obtained permanent resident status in another country. Despite the restriction on investors from China, the greatest number of applications came from Chinese nationals.

Singapore Global Investors Programme[34]

Singapore's Economic Development Board operates a "Global Investors Programme," which allows individuals to apply for permanent residence on the basis of investing in a Singapore-based business. To qualify for the program, an individual must show he or she has a substantial business track record, entrepreneurial background, and an investment plan. The individual is required to invest a minimum amount of either S$1 million, S$1.5 million, or S$2 million in a new business startup, expansion of an existing business, an approved Singapore-incorporated venture capital fund, or Singapore-incorporated foundation or trust that focuses on economic development. The investor's spouse and unmarried children 21 years old and younger can be included in the application for entry permit (permanent residence application).

Singapore's tax regime favors business development, for example by setting the corporate income tax rate at a low 20 percent and not taxing dividends. There is no capital gains tax. Additionally, Singapore taxes on a territorial basis and thus only income that is derived in Singapore, or derived overseas but received in Singapore, is taxed. Businesspersons residing in Singapore can avail themselves of benefits such as deductions, rebates, loss carryovers, and foreign tax credits.

United Arab Emirates Establishments Residence Permit[35]

The United Arab Emirates (UAE), which features the burgeoning economy of Dubai, offers residency benefits to investors through its Free Zone program. An investor can apply for an "establishments residence permit" upon establishing a business presence in one of the government-designated Free Zones and obtaining a license. Free Zones permit 100 percent foreign ownership of a business enterprise and grant full exemption from import and export taxes. Businesses enjoy a 15-year corporate tax exemption that can be renewed for another 15 years, and there are no personal income taxes.

---

[33] Program parameters are accessible at the Hong Kong Special Administrative Region Immigration Department website. *See www.immd.gov.hk/ehtml/hkvisas_13.htm.*

[34] Details on this program are posted by the Singapore Economic Development Board at *www.edb.gov.sg/edb/sg/en_uk/index/our_services/for_individuals/permanent_residence.html.*

[35] *See* the UAE's website, *www.government.ae/gov/en/biz/index.jsp.*

Investors can either register a new business in the form of a Free Zone Establishment or Free Zone Company, or establish branch of an existing company based in the UAE or abroad. The independent Free Zone Authority issues the appropriate operating license, which is then used to apply for a residence permit through the particular emirate's immigration department.

Republic of South Africa[36]

The Republic of South Africa makes permanent residence available to investors who intend to establish or invest in a business in South Africa. To apply for permanent residence as a businessperson/investor, an individual must provide an accountant certification stating that at least R2,500,000 has been invested as part of the book value of the business. In addition, the investor must demonstrate either a business track record proving entrepreneurial skills, that the business being invested in will employ at least five South African citizens or permanent residents, or that the business will contribute to the geographical spread of economic activity. In lieu of showing one of these three things, the investor may show either that the business involves a transfer of technology not previously generally available in South Africa, that the business has export potential, or that the business is in one of eight particular sectors, such as agro-processing or transport.

The spouse and dependent children of the investor are also eligible to receive permanent resident permits. Should a permanent resident holder leave South Africa for more than three years, the individual's permanent residence permit may be withdrawn.

The Gambia Special Investment Certificate[37] (Passport Program)

The Gambia confers "special investment" status on persons who invest the equivalent of at least US$100,000 in fixed assets in The Gambia's domestic economy. The investment must be made outside designated free zones and must be in a government-identified priority sector, which currently includes agriculture, manufacturing, communication, and mineral exploitation. Upon meeting investment criteria, investors are issued a "special investment cer-

tificate" that gives residence rights and numerous economic incentives. The incentives last for five years and include an exemption from withholding tax and exemptions from customs duties and sales taxes on capital equipment and machinery.

The Gambia's program has been used by nationals of China as a means of obtaining foreign permanent residence for the purpose of migrating to Hong Kong under its Capital Investment Entrant Scheme.

Federation of St. Kitts and Nevis Citizenship-by-Investment Program[38]

Many investors seeking to obtain a foreign passport look to the "Citizenship-by-Investment" program of the Federation of St. Kitts and Nevis. Established in 1984, it is the longest-standing immigrant investor program in the world that leads to full citizenship and a passport. To qualify under the program, an individual must either invest a minimum of US$350,000 in a government-approved real estate project, or make a contribution to the Sugar Industry Diversity Foundation (SIDF), a public charity addressing problems arising from the closure of the sugar industry in the Federation. The real estate option requires payment of additional government registration fees in the amount of US$35,000 for the principal applicant and US$15,000 per dependent family member. There is also a US$3,500 due diligence fee for each adult included in the application. Additionally, the real estate must be held for at least five years. Dependents include a spouse and children under 18.

If the SIDF option is chosen, the requisite investment amount is either US$200,000 for a single applicant, US$250,000 for an applicant with up to three dependents, US$300,000 for an applicant with up to five dependents, or US$400,000 for an applicant with six or more dependents. The SIDF investment amounts include government due diligence fees. Under the SIDF option, the requisite funds must be held in escrow before an investor is eligible to apply, and are released on approval of the application and issuance of the citizenship certificate.

The government of St. Kitts and Nevis will conduct due diligence background checks confirming the source of investment money. Assuming the background check proceeds smoothly, processing time for

---

[36] See the immigration policy document published by the South African Department of Home Affairs, *available at* http://home-affairs.pwv.gov.za/immigration_policy_doc.asp.

[37] Further information on this program can be found at The Gambia Investment Promotion and Free Zones Agency's website, *www.gipfza.gm/IPA_Information.asp.*

[38] Details are available at the website of the Ministry of Finance of the Government of St. Kitts and Nevis. *See www.skbfinancialservices.com/citizenship.php.*

a Citizenship-by-Investment application is currently three months. Applicants are not required to physically travel to the country to be interviewed prior to before being approved for citizenship. Once an application is approved, a passport can issue within one week. Passport validity is ten years for adults and five years for minors (under 18). Passports can be renewed at any St. Kitts embassy or consulate.

Commonwealth of Dominica Economic Citizenship Program[39] (Passport Program)

Dominica also operates a program that offers citizenship in exchange for an economic contribution to the country. The program is comprised of two investment options, the "Family Option" and the "Single Option." Under the Family Option, an investor pays US$100,000 to qualify him- or herself, a spouse, and two children under 18 for citizenship. An additional US$15,000 per child is required for children who have turned 18 but are not yet 21 years of age. Also, a cash contribution of US$25,000 is required for any additional child under 21. Under the Single Option, where the investor is the sole applicant for citizenship, the investor makes a cash investment of US$75,000.

Investment moneys are applied toward public sector projects identified for financing, such as the building of schools, renovation of hospitals, and promotion of the offshore sector. Investor-applicants must be over 21 years of age, and have a basic knowledge of the English language. All investors are required to undergo an interview in Dominica by a government appointed committee or committee members. The interview is conducted in English, and no translators are permitted. If an applicant cannot travel to Dominica for the interview, he or she must pay for the airfare, hotel, and per diem expenses of interview panel members. The interview requirement cannot be waived.

Passports applications can be submitted once citizenship is granted. Advantages of Dominica citizenship include freedom from capital gains tax, estate tax, and death tax.

CONCLUSION

There is a magnificently diverse array of options for investors, and immigration lawyers should not be daunted by the idea of crafting global solutions for their investor clients. One need not be an expert in order to help investors identify outbound immigration options. In fashioning strategies, U.S. practitioners can collaborate with qualified and experienced professionals in the United States and around the world. The key is to maintain an attitude that seeks the best for the client. The call is for U.S. immigration law practitioners to embrace outbound immigration investor options as a part of their service paradigm.

---

[39] The author references information provided directly by the Financial Services Unit of the Commonwealth of Dominica.

EB-5 IMMIGRANT INVESTORS

by Stephen Yale-Loehr, Carolyn S. Lee, and Lindsay Schoonmaker[*]

OVERVIEW

Congress created the fifth employment-based preference (EB-5) immigrant visa category in 1990 for immigrants seeking to enter to engage in a commercial enterprise that will benefit the U.S. economy and create at least 10 full-time jobs.[1] The basic amount required to invest is $1 million, although that amount may be $500,000 if the investment is made in a "targeted employment area."[2] Of the approximately 10,000 numbers available for this preference each year, 3,000 are reserved for entrepreneurs who invest in targeted employment areas.[3] A separate allocation of 3,000 visas is set aside for entrepreneurs who immigrate through a regional center pilot program discussed below.

The statutory requirements of the EB-5 visa category are onerous. At most only about 1,000 people a year have immigrated in this category, just one-tenth of the visas available.[4] In FY 2005, only 346 people,

including derivatives, immigrated in this category.[5] In 2006, however, the number increased to 749.[6]

The former Immigration and Naturalization Service (INS) (now U.S. Citizenship and Immigration Services (USCIS)) made it even harder to qualify in this category by issuing four precedent decisions in 1998 that significantly restricted eligibility for EB-5 status.[7] Since then, the Administrative Appeals Office (AAO) has issued numerous nonprecedent decisions that further tighten the screws on EB-5 cases.[8]

In 2002, Congress enacted a law designed to help certain stranded immigrant investors hurt by the 1998 decisions.[9] Those provisions are discussed in detail

---

[*] Updated from an article by Mr. Yale-Loehr and Ms. Lee published at *Immigration & Nationality Law Handbook* 109 (2007–08 Ed.). Copyright © 2008 Stephen Yale-Loehr. All rights reserved.

Stephen Yale-Loehr is co-author of *Immigration Law and Procedure*, the leading immigration law treatise, published by LexisNexis/Matthew Bender. He also teaches immigration law and asylum law at Cornell Law School, and is of counsel at Miller Mayer LLP in Ithaca, NY. Mr. Yale-Loehr is a member of AILA's Investor Committee and Business Committee, and used to be the co-editor of *Interpreter Releases* and the executive editor of *Immigration Briefings*. He graduated from Cornell Law School in 1981 *cum laude*, where he was editor-in-chief of the *Cornell International Law Journal*.

Carolyn S. Lee is a partner at Miller Mayer LLP. She graduated *cum laude* from Williams College in 1993 and received her J.D. from Cornell Law School in 1999, where she graduated with a specialization in International Legal Affairs.

Lindsay Schoonmaker, a graduate of Cornell University, is a research assistant at Miller Mayer, LLP.

[1] INA §203(b)(5), 8 USC §1153(b)(5). For a detailed treatment of the EB-5 immigrant investor category, see 3 C. Gordon, S. Mailman, & S. Yale-Loehr, *Immigration Law and Procedure* §39.07 (rev. ed. 2008).

[2] INA §203(b)(5)(C)(ii), 8 USC §1153(b)(5)(C)(ii).

[3] INA §203(b)(5)(B)(i), 8 USC §1153(b)(5)(B)(i).

[4] Office of Immigration Statistics, U.S. Dep't of Homeland Security, 2006 Yearbook of Immigration Statistics 20 (2007)

(Table 6), *at* www.dhs.gov/xlibrary/assets/statistics/yearbook/2006/OIS_2006_Yearbook.pdf (last visited Feb. 21, 2008) [hereinafter 2006 Yearbook of Immigration Statistics].

[5] *Id.*

[6] *Id.*

[7] *Matter of Soffici*, 22 I&N Dec. 158, 19 Immigr. Rep. B2-25 (Assoc. Comm'r, Examinations 1998); *Matter of Izummi*, 22 I&N Dec. 169, 19 Immigr. Rep. B2-32 (Assoc. Comm'r, Examinations 1998); *Matter of Hsiung*, 22 I&N Dec. 201, 19 Immigr. Rep. B2-106 (Assoc. Comm'r, Examinations 1998); *Matter of Ho*, 22 I&N Dec. 206, 19 Immigr. Rep. B2-99 (Assoc. Comm'r, Examinations 1998).

[8] *See generally* H. Joe, R. Oh, S. Smalley, & S. Yale-Loehr, "More AAO EB-5 Decisions," 7 *Bender's Immigration Bulletin* 251 (Mar. 1, 2002); 6 *Bender's Immigration Bulletin* 945 (Sept. 15, 2001) (summaries of four AAO EB-5 decisions); L. Stone, W. Mason, B. Stern Wasser, & S. Yale-Loehr, "Immigrant Investors Strike Out Again at AAO," 6 *Bender's Immigration Bulletin* 709 (July 15, 2001); S. Park & S. Yale-Loehr, "More Bad News from the AAO for Immigrant Investors," 6 *Bender's Immigration Bulletin* 309 (Mar. 15, 2001); L. Stone, R. Oh, & S. Yale-Loehr, "Recent AAO Decisions Continue Trend of Limiting Immigrant Investor Visas," 5 *Bender's Immigration Bulletin* 1031 (Dec. 15, 2000); B. Palmer, "Recent EB-5 Denials," 4 *Bender's Immigration Bulletin* 1139 (Dec. 1, 1999); 4 *Bender's Immigration Bulletin* 810 (Aug. 15, 1999) (summaries of four AAO EB-5 denials). Some AAO EB-5 decisions are available at www.uscis.gov/uscis-ext-templating/uscis/jspoverride/errFrameset.jsp (last visited Feb. 26, 2008).

[9] 21st Century Department of Justice Appropriations Authorization Act, Pub. L. No. 107-273, 116 Stat. 1758 (2002). The immigrant investor provisions are in §§11031–37. The conference committee report is H.R. Conf. Rep. No. 107-685 (2002).

continued

below. As of the end of March 2008, regulations to implement the 2002 law have not been published.[10]

In 2003, Congress asked the U.S. Government Accountability Office (GAO) to study the EB-5 program.[11] The GAO report concluded that the program has been under-used for a variety of reasons, including the rigorous application process and the failure to issue regulations implementing the 2002 law.[12] The report found that even though few people have used the EB-5 category, EB-5 participants have invested an estimated $1 billion in a variety of U.S. businesses.[13]

STATUTORY REQUIREMENTS

The Regular Program

Immigration and Nationality Act (INA) §203(b)(5)[14] provides a yearly maximum of approximately 10,000 visas for applicants to invest in a new commercial enterprise employing at least 10 full-time U.S. workers. To qualify under the EB-5 category, the new enterprise must: (1) be one in which the person has invested (or is in the process of investing) at least $1 million (or at least $500,000 if investing in a "targeted employment area," discussed below) after November 29, 1990; (2) benefit the U.S. economy; and (3) create full-time employment for at least 10 U.S. workers. Moreover, the investor must have at least a policy-making role in the enterprise.

The Pilot Program

To encourage immigration through the EB-5 category, Congress created a temporary pilot program in 1993.[15] The Immigrant Investor Pilot Program ("pilot program") directs the attorney general and secretary of state to set aside 3,000 visas each year for people who invest in "designated regional centers." The pilot program has been renewed several times, and is currently due to expire September 30, 2008.[16] Efforts are underway in Congress to renew the pilot program. It is unclear what will happen to pending cases if the pilot program is not renewed.

The pilot program does not require that the immigrant investor's enterprise itself employ 10 U.S. workers. Instead, it is enough if 10 or more jobs will be created directly or indirectly as a result of the investment.[17] This program also differs from the regular EB-5 provisions in that it permits private and governmental agencies to be certified as regional centers if they meet certain criteria.[18] (*See* Appendix, "Designated Regional Centers," *infra*).

See further discussion of the pilot program in "Regional Centers," *infra*.

Qualified Immigrants

Outside of the investment and employment requisites, the statute does not specifically address who may be a qualified applicant. USCIS appears to preclude corporate or other nonindividual investors from this category. However, two or more individuals may join to make an EB-5 investment. A single new commercial enterprise may be used for investor/employment-creation classification by more than one investor, provided that: (1) each petitioning investor has invested (or is actively in the process of investing) the required amount; and (2) the creation of at least 10 qualifying full-time jobs may be attributable to each investor.[19] In fact, a new commercial enterprise may be used for investor/employment-creation classification even though there are several owners of the enterprise, including persons not seeking classification, if: (1) the source(s) of all capital invested is (are) identified; and (2) all invested capi-

---

[10] USCIS has published interim field guidance pending publication of the regulations. Memorandum from William R. Yates, BCIS Acting Assoc. Dir. for Operations, to all BCIS offices, "Amendments Affecting Adjudication of Petitions for Alien Entrepreneur (EB-5)," File No. HQ40/6.1.3 (June 10, 2003), *reprinted in* 8 *Bender's Immigration Bulletin* 1179 (July 1, 2003), *published on* AILA InfoNet at Doc. No. 03061744 (*posted* June 17, 2003) [hereinafter Yates Memo].

[11] Basic Pilot Program Extension and Expansion Act of 2003, Pub. L. No. 108-156, §5, 117 Stat. 1944.

[12] U.S. Government Accountability Office, No. GAO-05-256, "Immigrant Investors: Small Number of Participants Attributed to Pending Regulations and Other Factors" (Apr. 2005), *available at www.gao.gov/new.items/d05256.pdf* (last visited Feb. 29, 2008).

[13] *Id.* at 1.

[14] 8 USC §1153(b)(5).

[15] Departments of Commerce, Justice, and State, the Judiciary, and Related Agencies Appropriations Act of 1993, Pub. L. No. 102-395, §610, 106 Stat. 1828; S. Rep. No. 102-918 (1992).

[16] Basic Pilot Program Extension and Expansion Act of 2003, *supra* note 11, §4(b) (extending EB-5 pilot program five years to Sept. 30, 2008).

[17] 21st Century Department of Justice Appropriations Authorization Act, *supra* note 9, §11037(a)(3).

[18] 8 CFR §204.6(m)(3).

[19] 8 CFR §204.6(g)(1).

tal has been derived by lawful means.[20] The lawful source of funds issue is discussed in more detail in "Legal Acquisition of Capital," *infra*.

The New Commercial Enterprise

There are two basic requirements for showing a new commercial enterprise. First, the enterprise must be "new," *i.e.*, formed after November 29, 1990.[21] However, an enterprise formed before this date may qualify if an investor "restructures"[22] or "expands"[23] an existing business. Second, it must be a "commercial" enterprise. Any for-profit entity formed for the ongoing conduct of lawful business may serve as a commercial enterprise. This includes sole proprietorships, partnerships (whether limited or general),[24] holding companies, joint ventures, corporations, business trusts, or other entities publicly or privately owned.[25] This definition would even include a holding company and its wholly owned subsidiaries, if each such subsidiary is engaged in a for-profit activity formed for the ongoing conduct of a lawful business. However, the term "new commercial enterprise" does not include noncommercial activity, such as owning and operating a personal residence or nonprofit enterprise.[26]

Creating an Original Business—According to a 1998 precedent decision, an EB-5 petitioner had to have a hand in the creation of the enterprise and must be present at the enterprise's inception.[27] This posed particular problems for people investing in partnerships. The partnership will usually be created and then the general partner will seek individuals to invest as limited partners. Under the legacy INS's interpretation, such investors could not qualify for EB-5 classification because they were not partners at the establishment of the original partnership. In

2002, Congress eliminated the "establishment" requirement for EB-5 investors.[28] Instead of proving that they have "established" a commercial enterprise themselves, investors now need only show that they have "invested" in a commercial enterprise.

Restructuring? an Existing Business—By reorganizing or restructuring an existing business, an investor may create a "new commercial enterprise" and therefore qualify for a visa. The statute and regulations provide little insight into what degree of restructuring or reorganization must be done to establish a new enterprise. The AAO has held that simply changing the legal form of the enterprise does not satisfy this requirement.[29] There is only one known case where the AAO agreed the business was sufficiently restructured or reorganized.[30]

Regardless of the forms used to create a new enterprise, the focus of the law is on the creation of at least 10 new employment opportunities. Investments creating a new enterprise but failing to create 10 new jobs will also fail to qualify for EB-5 classification.

Expanding an Existing Business—An investor also can create a new enterprise by expanding an existing business. Only an expansion resulting in an increase of at least 40 percent in the net worth of the business or in the number of employees of the business will satisfy the visa requirements.[31] This could require the investor to create more than 10 new jobs to qualify for a visa if the pre-expansion number of employees was more than 25. The larger the business that the investor expands, the more onerous his or her burden to qualify for a visa under this standard. However, an investor need not show that his or her investment alone caused the 40 percent increase.[32]

---

[20] *Id.*

[21] *See, e.g., Matter of [name not provided]*, EAC-91-184-50136, 12 Immigr. Rep. B2-51 (AAU Aug. 12, 1993) (denying petition as investment made before Nov. 29, 1990; investor's documentation of "expanded business" deemed insufficient). *See also* Yates Memo, *supra* note 10, at ¶2.

[22] 8 CFR §204.6(h)(2).

[23] 8 CFR §204.6(h)(3).

[24] The 21st Century Department of Justice Appropriations Authorization Act, *supra* note 9, clarifies that a "commercial enterprise" may include a limited partnership. *Id.* §11036(b)(3).

[25] 8 CFR §204.6(e) (definition of commercial enterprise).

[26] *Id.*

[27] *Matter of Izummi*, 22 I&N Dec. 169, 198, 19 Immigr. Rep. B2-32 (Assoc. Comm'r, Examinations 1998).

[28] 21st Century Department of Justice Appropriations Authorization Act, *supra* note 9, §11036(a)(2). *See also* Yates Memo, *supra* note 10, at ¶1.

[29] *Matter of Soffici*, 22 I&N Dec. 158, 166, 19 Immigr. Rep. B2-25 (Assoc. Comm'r, Examinations 1998) ("A few cosmetic changes to the decor and a new marketing strategy for success do not constitute the kind of restructuring contemplated by the regulations, nor does a simple change in ownership.").

[30] *Matter of [name redacted]* (AAO July 11, 2001) (approved case involved the "restructuring" of a horse breeding business into a new business for horse breeding and training).

[31] 8 CFR §204.6(h)(3). *See also* Yates Memo, *supra* note 10, at ¶2.

[32] Memorandum from T. Alexander Aleinikoff, INS General Counsel, to Louis D. Crochetti, Jr., Acting Assoc. Comm'r for Examinations, "Whether a Pool of Alien Immigrant In-
continued

The AAO has insisted that proof of expansion of the company requires audited financial statements concerning the company's former net worth at the time of investment.[33]

Pooling Arrangements—The regulations specifically allow immigrant investors to pool their investments with others seeking EB-5 status.[34] Each investor must invest the applicable statutory amount. All of the new jobs created by the new commercial enterprise will be allocated among those within the pool seeking permanent investor visas.[35]

The AAO has injected a restriction on pooling investments by requiring the petitioner to show that *every* investor in the partnership identify the source of their funds and prove that they were derived by lawful means.[36]

"Engaging" in a New Commercial Enterprise

The statute requires an EB-5 applicant to enter the United States to engage in a new commercial enterprise.[37] To qualify, an investor must maintain more than a purely passive role in the new enterprise upon which the petition is based. The regulations require an EB-5 immigrant to be involved in the management of the new commercial enterprise.[38] The petitioner must either be involved in the day-to-day managerial control of the commercial enterprise or manage it through policy formulation. The regulations state that if the EB-5 petitioner is a corporate officer or board member, or, in the case of a limited partnership, is a limited partner under the provisions of the Uniform Limited Partnership Act (ULPA), he or she satisfies the requirement of engaging in the management of the new commercial enterprise.[39] The AAO, however, has found that merely calling the investor a limited partner pursuant to the ULPA in a partnership agreement does not automatically mean that the person is involved in the management of the new commercial enterprise.[40]

"Investing" or "Actively in the Process of Investing" "Capital"

The statute requires an EB-5 petitioner to have invested or be in the process of investing. Although the statute explicitly states that an EB-5 petitioner may be "in the process" of investing the required capital,[41] USCIS effectively requires the entire capital amount to be already invested and at risk in the commercial enterprise at the time the I-526 petition is filed. This interpretation appears to contravene the statute, but shows USCIS's desire to have the full amount committed and immediately available for use in job-creation.

The term "invest" means to contribute capital. A contribution of capital in exchange for a note, bond, convertible debt, obligation, or any other debt arrangement between the entrepreneur and the new commercial enterprise does not constitute a contribution of capital and will not constitute an investment.[42]

The regulations define "capital" as cash and cash equivalents, equipment, inventory, and other tangible property.[43] According to USCIS, retained earnings cannot count as "capital."[44]

---

vestors Can Create a New Commercial Enterprise by Expanding an Existing Business by at Least 40%," HQ 204.27-C (Jan. 31, 1995), *reprinted in* 73 *Interpreter Releases* 1625 (Nov. 18, 1996).

[33] *Matter of [name not provided]*, WAC-99-010-50117 (AAO Dec. 15, 2000).

[34] 8 CFR §204.6(g).

[35] *See generally* 8 CFR §204.6(g); H.R. Klasko, "Pooled Investment Arrangements: Unraveling the Controversy," 2 *Immigration & Nationality Law Handbook* 107 (1998–99 ed.) [hereinafter Klasko]; A.J. Vazquez-Azpiri, "The Role of Commercial Organizations in the EB-5 Employment Process," 2 *Bender's Immigration Bulletin* 813 (Oct. 15, 1997).

[36] *See, e.g., Matter of [name not provided]*, WAC-98-106-51072, slip op. at 20 (AAO July 6, 2000); *Matter of [name not provided]*, WAC-98-106-51583, slip. op. at 22 (AAO Sept. 11, 2000). This requirement is discussed further *infra*.

[37] INA §203(b)(5)(A), 8 USC §1153(b)(5)(A).

[38] 8 CFR §204.6(j)(5).

[39] *Id. See also* 73 *Interpreter Releases* 48, 55 (Jan. 10, 1996).

[40] *See, e.g., Matter of [name not provided]*, WAC-98-111-53508, slip op. at 23 (AAO Mar. 20, 2000) ("Despite the superficial language in the limited partnership agreement referring to the ULPA and to 8 CFR §204.6(j)(5)(iii), it is clear that the petitioner here does not in fact have the rights normally granted to limited partners under the ULPA.").

[41] INA §203(b)(5)(A)(i), 8 USC §1153(b)(5)(A)(i). *See also* 8 CFR §204.6(j)(2) (allowing an investor to be "actively in the process of investing the required amount of capital"). Indeed, even the regulations governing removal of an EB-5 investor's conditional resident status two years later acknowledge that an investor may not have invested all of his or her money by then. The regulations simply require an investor to provide evidence that the alien "invested or was actively in the process of investing the requisite capital." 8 CFR §216.6(a)(4)(ii).

[42] *See* 8 CFR §204.6(e) (definition of "invest").

[43] *Id.* (definition of "capital").

[44] Letter from Efren Hernandez, Chief, USCIS Business and Trade Branch, to Stephen Yale-Loehr, File No. HOOPRD 70/6.2.8 (June 4, 2004), *available at www.usa-continued*

Capital does not include loans by the petitioner or other parties.[45] Indebtedness secured by assets owned by the entrepreneur may be considered capital, provided the investor is personally and primarily liable for the debts and the assets of the enterprise upon which the petition is based are not used to secure any of the indebtedness.[46]

Indebtedness typically consists of a promissory note signed by the petitioner that specifies a payment schedule to the new commercial enterprise. Absent fraud, a signed promissory note that is secured by the petitioner's personal assets constitutes a contribution of capital by the petitioner.[47] The issuer of the promissory note, *i.e.*, the investor, is considered to be "at risk" if the petitioner is clearly obligated to make all the required payments on the note and there are no "escape" clauses. The investor cannot receive any bond, note, or other debt arrangement from the enterprise for the capital contributed to it. This includes any stock redeemable at the holder's request. All capital is valued at fair market value in U.S. dollars at the time it is given.[48]

Debt arrangements are extremely complicated. A prudent practitioner must do careful research and analysis to determine current USCIS positions and policies on this issue.[49]

Benefiting the U.S. Economy

The statute requires that investments "benefit the U.S. economy" to qualify the investor for an EB-5

visa or status.[50] The statute provides no guidance on which investments benefit the economy. This silence means USCIS adjudicators are left to their subjective interpretations of the investment and its relative benefits when reviewing the petition. Arguably, the petitioner has benefited the economy by merely meeting the employment and investment requirements of the visa classification. However, because the statute specifically identifies the "benefit" element as distinct from other components of the visa, it appears that the applicant must independently show that the enterprise, in the conduct of its business, will benefit the U.S. economy. Therefore, a consulting firm exclusively serving customers abroad with no return benefit to the U.S. economy (other than employing the requisite number of workers) might not support an EB-5 petition. In contrast, showing that the new enterprise provides goods or services to U.S. markets should satisfy this requirement.

Federal regulation of foreign investments is extensive. Some regulations restrict foreign investments in aviation, banking, shipping, communications, land use, energy resources, and government contracting. Additionally, Congress has imposed several disclosure and data requirements on foreign investments.[51] An investment may not be deemed beneficial to the U.S. economy if it runs afoul of any statutory limitation on foreign investment.

Creating or Saving Jobs

To qualify for EB-5 status, an investment normally must create full-time employment for at least 10 U.S. citizens, lawful permanent residents, or other immigrants lawfully authorized to be employed in the United States.[52] Neither the investor nor the investor's spouse and children count toward the 10-employee minimum.[53] Nonimmigrants are also excluded from the count. The "other immigrants" provision means that conditional residents, temporary residents, asylees, refugees, and recipients of suspension of deportation or cancellation of removal may all be considered employees for EB-5 purposes.

---

immigration.com/litigation.htm (last visited Feb. 29, 2008). *See also Kenkhuis v. INS*, No. 3:01-CV-2224-N, 2003 U.S. Dist. LEXIS 3334, at *6 (N.D. Tex. Mar. 6, 2003) ("[t]he definition of 'invest' . . . requires an infusion of new capital, not merely a retention of profits of the enterprise"); *De Jong v. INS*, No. 6:94 CV 850 (E.D. Tex. Jan. 17, 1997).

[45] *Matter of Soffici*, 22 I&N Dec. 158, 19 Immigr. Rep. B2-25 (Assoc. Comm'r, Examinations 1998).

[46] 8 CFR §204.6(e) (definition of "capital").

[47] *Matter of Hsiung*, 22 I&N Dec. 201, 19 Immigr. Rep. B2-106 (Assoc. Comm'r, Examinations 1998).

[48] *Matter of Izummi*, 22 I&N Dec. 169, 192–93, 19 Immigr. Rep. B2-32 (Assoc. Comm'r, Examinations 1998) (finding that investor failed to show how bank accounts in Japan were in trust or otherwise secured the note, as required by 8 CFR §204.6(e), and that the note was not readily enforceable and was in any event not now worth its face value payable over six years).

[49] *See generally* W. Cook, "Somewhere, Over the Rainbow . . . Lies the EB-5 Pot of Gold," 3 *Bender's Immigration Bulletin* 1205 (Dec. 1, 1998); Klasko, *supra* note 35.

---

[50] INA §203(b)(5)(A)(ii), 8 USC §1153(b)(5)(A)(ii).

[51] For a comprehensive summary of the regulations, see Marans, Williams, Griffin, & Pattison, *Manual of Foreign Investment in the United States* (3d ed. 2004); *United States Law of Trade and Investment* (B. Kozolchyk & J. Molloy eds., 2000).

[52] INA §203(b)(5)(A)(ii), 8 USC §1153(b)(5)(A)(ii).

[53] *Id.*

The regulations define an "employee" for EB-5 purposes as an individual who (1) provides services or labor for the new commercial enterprise and (2) receives wages or other remuneration directly from the new commercial enterprise.[54] This definition excludes independent contractors.[55]

The EB-5 pilot program does not require the investment to directly create 10 U.S. jobs. Instead, pilot program investments only require an indirect creation of jobs.[56]

The Types of Jobs—The jobs created must be full-time. This means employment of a qualified employee in a position that requires a minimum of 35 working hours per week, regardless of who fills the position.[57] Job-sharing arrangements, where two or more qualifying employees share a full-time position, will also serve as full-time employment if the hourly requirement per week is met.[58] Job-sharing does not include combinations of part-time positions even if when combined such positions meet the hourly requirement per week.[59]

When the Jobs Must Exist—The law is unclear about when new jobs must exist. The statutory language is prospective and therefore does not require jobs to exist at the time of initial investment or before the I-526 petition is filed. USCIS does not require retention of employees until a reasonable time after conditional visa issuance. In fact, a petitioner may support a petition with a comprehensive business plan demonstrating a need for at least 10 employees within the next two years. The business plan need only indicate the approximate dates during the following two years when the employees will be hired. The temporary vacancy of a position during the two-year conditional period does not disqualify an investor, as long as good-faith attempts to re-staff the position are made.

Where the Jobs Must Be Located—When enacting the EB-5 program, Congress took an affirmative step toward creating jobs in the geographic areas that need them most. The statute sets aside 3,000 of the approximately 10,000 EB-5 visas available annually for foreign citizens who invest in "targeted employment areas."[60] The statute defines a "targeted employment area" as a rural area or an area that has experienced high unemployment of at least 150 percent of the national average.[61] An area not within a metropolitan statistical area (as designated by the Office of Management and Budget) or the outer boundary of any city or town having a population of 20,000 or more is considered a rural area.[62] Each state notifies USCIS which state agency will apply these guidelines, and determines targeted employment areas for that state.[63]

Troubled Businesses—Special rules govern investments in "troubled" businesses. A troubled business is one that has been in existence for at least two years, has incurred a net loss for accounting purposes during the 12– or 24-month period before the petition was filed, and the loss for such period is at least equal to 20 percent of the business's net worth before the loss.[64] To establish an investment in a troubled business, the petitioner must show that the number of existing employees will be maintained at no less than the pre-investment level for at least two years. Thus, this provision includes a significant incentive in that it does not require the creation of 10 new jobs. Instead, it requires only that the business maintain the number of existing employees during the conditional status period.[65] As a caveat, if the troubled business does not remain afloat for two years after the investment, the investor might lose his or her conditional residency status.

EB-5 PROCEDURES: INITIAL EVIDENCE

The regular EB-5 program and the pilot program have similar requirements to begin the process. The distinction between the two processes is that the former requires the petitioner to submit all of the described evidence; the latter requires the designated regional center to certify that the investor has met its criteria.

---

[54] 8 CFR §204.6(e) (definition of " qualifying employee").

[55] *Id.*

[56] See 8 CFR §204.6(m)(7)(ii).

[57] 21st Century Department of Justice Appropriations Authorization Act, *supra* note 9, §11031(f). *See also* Yates Memo, *supra* note 10, at ¶ 4.

[58] 8 CFR §204.6(e) (definition of "full-time employment").

[59] *Id.*

[60] INA §203(b)(5)(B), 8 USC §1153(b)(5)(B).

[61] INA §203(b)(5)(B)(ii), 8 USC §1153(b)(5)(B)(ii).

[62] INA §203(b)(5)(B)(iii), 8 USC §1153(b)(5)(B)(iii).

[63] Several states have websites that can help determine whether a particular area in the state qualifies as a "targeted employment area" for EB-5 purposes. *See, e.g., www.labor.ca.gov/ calBIS/cbfederalvisaprog.pdf* (last updated May 2007) (last visited Feb. 29, 2008).

[64] 8 CFR §204.6(e) (definition of "troubled business").

[65] 8 CFR §§204.6(h)(3), 204.6(j)(4)(ii).

In either case the investor files for EB-5 classification using Form I-526. The petition must be signed by the investor, not someone acting on his or her behalf. If the EB-5 commercial enterprise will primarily do business in a location within the ordinary jurisdiction of the Vermont or Texas Service Centers, the petition is filed with the Texas Service Center; otherwise it is filed with the California Service Center.[66]

Initial Evidence for the Regular EB-5 Program

The following paragraphs detail the evidence that should be submitted with an I-526 petition for EB-5 classification under the regular program.

The New Commercial Enterprise—To qualify for EB-5 classification an investor must show that an investment has been made in a qualified commercial enterprise. The applicant should include:

- An organizational document for the new enterprise, including articles of incorporation, certificates of merger and consolidation, or partnership agreements;

- A business license or authorization to transact business in a state or city, if applicable; and

- For investments in an existing business, proof that the required amount of capital was transferred to the business after November 29, 1990, and that the investment has increased the net worth or number of employees by 40 percent or more.[67]

Capitalization—To show that the petitioner has invested (or is actively in the process of investing) the required amount of capital, the petition must be accompanied by evidence that the petitioner has placed the required amount of capital "at risk." A mere intention to invest will not demonstrate that the petitioner is actively in the process of investing. The investor must show actual commitment of the required amount of capital. Such evidence may include:

- Bank statements showing deposits in the U.S. account of the enterprise;

- Evidence of assets purchased for use in the enterprise;

- Evidence of property transferred from abroad;

- Evidence of funds invested in the enterprise in exchange for stock, except for stock redeemable at the holder's request; or

- Evidence of debts secured by the investor's assets and for which the investor is personally and primarily liable.[68]

The AAO has held that merely putting cash into the corporate account of a business does not show that the capital is "at risk" for the purpose of generating a return.[69] The AAO has also held that the full amount of the required capital must be expended by the enterprise directly toward job creation; otherwise that capital is not at risk of loss.[70] Based on these statements, it is difficult to know what a petitioner must do to show that the money is truly at risk.

Legal Acquisition of Capital[71]—The regulations require filing the following types of documentation to establish that capital used in the new enterprise was acquired by legitimate means:

- Foreign business registration records;

- Personal and business tax returns, or other tax returns of any kind filed anywhere in the world within the previous five years;

- Documents identifying any other source of money; or

- Certified copies of all pending governmental civil or criminal actions and proceedings, or any private civil actions involving money judgments against the investor within the past 15 years.[72]

Although the regulations list these requirements in the disjunctive, meaning that submission of any one type of document should suffice, the AAO requires investors to submit tax returns for the previ-

---

[66] *See* 63 Fed. Reg. 67135 (Dec. 4, 1998).

[67] 8 CFR §204.6(j)(1).

[68] 8 CFR §204.6(j)(2).

[69] *See Matter of [name not provided]*, file no. redacted (AAO July 7, 2000).

[70] *See, e.g., Matter of [name redacted]*, WAC-98-194-50913 (AAO Aug. 16, 2002). For a good discussion of the immigration agency's overly restrictive interpretation of the "at risk" requirement, see L. Stone, "Immigrant Investment in Local Clusters: Part II," 80 *Interpreter Releases* 937, 941–45 (July 14, 2003) [hereinafter Stone].

[71] For an in-depth discussion of the requirement that an investor's capital be from a lawful source, see Stone, *supra* note 70, at 946–50; S. Yale-Loehr & C. Repole, "Show Me the Money: Proving Lawful Source of Funds for EB-5 Immigrant Investors," at *www.millermayer.com/new/eb5funds.html* (last visited Feb. 29, 2008); L. Stone & S. Yale-Loehr, "Evidence of Source of Capital in Immigrant Investor Cases," 6 *Bender's Immigration Bulletin* 972 (Oct. 1, 2001).

[72] 8 CFR §204.6(j)(3).

ous five years.[73] This interpretation makes it harder for investors to qualify for EB-5 status, and appears to violate the regulations.

The regulations further define "capital" as only those assets acquired through lawful means.[74] The AAO has held that money earned or assets acquired while in the United States in an unlawful status are not considered lawful means to acquire capital.[75] This interpretation goes far beyond Congress' original concern to prevent drug smugglers or other criminals to use their ill-gotten gains to be able to obtain permanent residents status in the United States through the EB-5 category.

Earned income is generally the most straightforward source of funds, but it is necessary to document exactly how the money was earned and to provide tax returns documenting that all due taxes were paid in full. An example of a more complex earned income scenario our office handled involves a French academic with 20 years of tax-exempt public sector service. The French academic provided tax returns, an accountant's letter explaining the tax-exempt income, and income receipts accounting for five years of earned income.

Gift money usually requires more complex documentation of source of funds, as the donor must document lawful obtainment of funds, as well as provide tax returns. Additionally, all gift taxes due, as applicable, must be paid on the gift by the donor and/or investor.

"Old money" also presents challenges in documenting how funds obtained by inheritance were lawfully obtained.[76]

The importance of tracing funds is present in all of the above scenarios. Filings involving the sticky issues of gifting, disposition of a trust, inheritance, and other complex fact patterns must be accompanied by full documentation of the history of the funds and objective confirmation that all taxes have been paid on the acquisition and disposition of the funds.

Creating Employment—To show that a new commercial enterprise will create at least 10 full-time positions for qualified employees, the petition must be accompanied by:

- Photocopies of relevant tax records, Forms I-9, or similar documents for 10 qualifying employees; or

- A comprehensive business plan showing the need for at least 10 qualifying employees, and when the employees will be hired.[77] The plan should include a description of the business; the business' objectives; a market analysis including names of competing businesses and their relative strengths and weaknesses; a comparison of the competition's products and pricing structures; a description of the target market and prospective customers; a description of any manufacturing or production processes, materials required and supply sources; details of any contracts executed; marketing strategy including pricing, advertising, and servicing; organizational structure; and sales, cost and income projections and details of the bases therefore. In addition, specifically with respect to employment, the business plan must set forth the company's personnel experience, staffing requirements, job descriptions for all positions, and a timetable for hiring.[78]

Troubled Business—To show that a new enterprise, established through capital investment in a troubled business, meets the statutory requirement, the petition must show that the number of existing employees will be maintained at no less than the pre-investment level for a period of at least two years. The applicant should include photocopies of the I-9 forms, tax records or payroll documents, and a comprehensive business plan.[79]

Managerial Capacity of the Investor—An EB-5 immigrant must be involved in the management of a new commercial enterprise to qualify for a visa. The petitioner must either be involved in the day-to-day managerial control of the enterprise, or manage it

---

[73] *See, e.g., Matter of [name not provided]*, file no. redacted, slip op. at 12 (AAO July 7, 2000) ("In addition, the petitioner has not submitted his corporate and personal tax records for at least the five years preceding filing the petition as required by 8 CFR §204.6(j)(3).").

[74] *See* 8 CFR §204.6(e) (definition of "capital).

[75] *See, e.g., Matter of [name not provided]*, file no. redacted, slip. op. at 12 (AAO July 7, 2000); *Matter of [name not provided]*, file no. redacted, slip. op. at 12 (AAO July 11, 2000); *Matter of [name not provided]*, WAC-98-106-51583, slip. op. at 22 (AAO Sept. 11, 2000).

[76] *See, e.g., Matter of [name not provided]*, file no. WAC-00-070-52366, slip. op. at 3–6 (AAO Apr. 21, 2005) (petitioner failed to adequately document transfer of money from family trust to her).

[77] 8 CFR §204.6(j)(4)(i).

[78] *Matter of Ho*, 22 I&N Dec. 206, 19 Immigr. Rep. B2-99 (Assoc. Comm'r, Examinations 1998).

[79] 8 CFR §204.6(j)(4)(ii).

through policy formulation. These requirements may be evidenced by:

- A comprehensive job description for the position occupied by the investor. The petitioner's title should also be indicated;

- Evidence that the petitioner is a corporate officer or on the board of directors; or

- Evidence that the petitioner is involved in direct management activities or policymaking activities of a general or limited partnership. A limited partner must also show that he has rights, powers and duties commensurate with those normally granted under the Uniform Limited Partnership Act (ULPA).[80] The AAO, however, has found that merely calling the investor a limited partner pursuant to the ULPA in a partnership agreement does not automatically mean that the person is involved in the management of the new commercial enterprise.[81]

Designation of a High Unemployment Area—The state government may designate a particular geographic or political subdivision as an area of high unemployment (at least 150 percent of the national average rate). Evidence of such designation may be provided with Form I-526. Such evidence should include:

- Boundaries of the subdivision;

- The date of the designation; and

- The methods by which the statistics were gathered.[82]

Creation of Employment in a Targeted Employment Area—To show that the new commercial enterprise has created, or will create, employment in a targeted employment area, the petition must be accompanied by:

- For a rural area, evidence that the new commercial enterprise is not located within any standard metropolitan statistical area, or within any city or town having a population of 20,000 or more; or

- For a high unemployment area, evidence that the metropolitan statistical area, or the county in which a city or town with a population of 20,000 or more is located, in which the new commercial enterprise is principally doing business has experienced an average unemployment rate of 150 percent of the national average rate; or a letter from the state in which the new commercial enterprise is located which certifies that the area has been designated as a high unemployment area.[83]

Regional Centers

An investment under the EB-5 pilot program must be made in a commercial enterprise located within a "regional center," defined as "any economic unit, public or private, which is involved with the promotion of economic growth, including increased export sales, improved regional productivity, job creation, or increased domestic capital investment."[84]

A center seeking USCIS approval must submit a proposal showing how it plans to focus on a geographical region within the United States and to achieve the required growth by the means specified.[85]

The proposal must show "in verifiable detail how jobs will be created indirectly through increased exports," as well as the amount and source of capital committed and the promotional efforts made and planned.[86] The Appendix at the end of this article contains a list of designated regional centers. However, only about 17 of the approved regional centers are actually functioning. Another dozen or more applications for regional center designation are pending.

USCIS is backlogged in reviewing applications for regional center designation under the pilot program. Many applications for regional center designation have remained pending for over a year. In 2000, the INS issued five decisions on regional center applications, denying or remanding all of them.[87] The decisions set forth restrictive new requirements to qualify as a regional center.[88]

---

[80] 8 CFR §204.6(j)(5).

[81] *See* 8 CFR §204.6(j)(5); *Matter of [name not provided]*, WAC-98-111-53508, slip op. at 23 (AAO Mar. 20, 2000) ("Despite the superficial language in the limited partnership agreement referring to the ULPA and to 8 C.F.R. §204.6(j)(5)(iii), it is clear that the petitioner here does not in fact have the rights normally granted to limited partners under the ULPA.").

[82] 8 CFR §204.6(i).

[83] 8 CFR §204.6(j)(6).

[84] 21st Century Department of Justice Appropriations Authorization Act, *supra* note 9, §11037(a)(2); 8 CFR §204.6(e) (definition of "regional center").

[85] 8 CFR §204.6(m)(3).

[86] *Id.*

[87] *See generally* L. Stone, "INS Decisions Cloud Future of Investor Pilot Program," 6 *Bender's Immigration Bulletin* 233 (Mar. 1, 2001).

[88] *Id.*

To counteract this trend, in 2002 Congress amended the EB-5 regional center designation provisions.[89] Under the 2002 law, USCIS should approve applications for EB-5 regional center status as long as the applications are based on a general prediction concerning: (1) the kinds of commercial enterprises that will receive capital from investor; (2) the jobs that will be created directly or indirectly as a result of the investment of capital; and (3) the other positive economic impacts that will result from the investment of capital.[90]

USCIS is currently stepping up its review of new regional center applications and increasing oversight of existing regional centers to ensure that the EB-5 program grows in a responsible way.[91] For example, in June 2007, Maurice Berez, Program Manager for the USCIS Foreign Trader, Investor & Regional Center Program, sent an advisory letter to the Metropolitan Milwaukee Association of Commerce (MMAC), a regional center in Wisconsin.[92] The letter outlines 17 types of information that approved regional centers must track to keep their regional center designation.

The reporting requirements set forth in the MMAC letter mirror recent regional center decisions, which are growing ever longer and more detailed. In essence, USCIS is exercising greater oversight of regional centers in all aspects of the EB-5 process: (1) granting or denying regional center status; (2) maintaining regional center status; and (3) monitoring compliance through immigrant investors' I-526 and I-829 petitions filed through regional centers.

Assuming a regional center application has been approved, an applicant seeking EB-5 status under the pilot program must make the qualifying investment (*i.e.*, the amount required under the regular program)

within an approved regional center. However, the requirement of creating at least 10 new jobs is met by a showing that as a result of the new enterprise, such jobs will be created directly or indirectly.[93]

To file an I-526 form under the pilot program, attach a copy of the INS or USCIS letter designating the regional center. The petitioner's new commercial enterprise must be within the area specified in that letter. If the commercial enterprise is involved directly or indirectly in lending money to job-creating businesses, it may only lend money to businesses located within targeted employment areas to take advantage of the lesser capital requirement ($500,000).[94] The businesses receiving the loans must be within the geographic limits of the regional center if the enterprise is to qualify under the pilot program. Otherwise the enterprise is not promoting economic growth through "improved regional activity" as required by the regulations.[95]

In 2003 Congress gave USCIS discretion to "give priority" to EB-5 petitions filed through a regional center.[96] USCIS exercises this authority judiciously, and specific criteria must be met before USCIS will expedite an I-526 petition filed through a regional center.

EB-5 PROCEDURES: REMOVING THE CONDITIONS

Assuming USCIS approves an investor's I-526 petition under either the regular or pilot program, he or she becomes a conditional resident for two years following the approval of an adjustment application or admission under an immigrant visa.[97] The procedure to remove the conditions is analogous to that followed by people who obtain conditional residence through marriage to a U.S. citizen or lawful permanent resident.[98] An immigrant investor's petition to remove the conditions should be filed on Form I-829 with the relevant service center.[99] It must be accompanied by evidence that the individual invested or was in the process of investing the required capital, and that the investment created or will create 10 full-

---

[89] 21st Century Department of Justice Appropriations Authorization Act, *supra* note 9, §11037.

[90] *Id.* §11037(a)(3). For a good analysis of the kinds of economic benefits EB-5 regional centers could potentially create, see L. Stone, "Immigrant Investment in Local Clusters: Part I," 80 *Interpreter Releases* 837 (June 16, 2003).

[91] *See* Stephen Yale-Loehr & Lindsay Schoonmaker, "USCIS Increases Oversight of EB-5 Regional Centers," 12 *Bender's Immigration Bulletin* 1713 (Dec. 1, 2007), *reprinted at* www.millermayer.com/new/eb5_reg_ctrs.html (last visited Feb. 28, 2008).

[92] *See* letter from Maurice R. Berez, Program Manager, USCIS Foreign Trader, Investor & Regional Center Program, to Metropolitan Milwaukee Association of Commerce (June 12, 2007), *published on* AILA InfoNet at Doc. No. 07061360) (*posted* June 13, 2007).

[93] 8 CFR §§204.6(j)(4)(iii), 204.6(m)(7).

[94] *Matter of Izummi*, 22 I&N Dec. 169, 19 Immigr. Rep. B2-32 (Assoc. Comm'r, Examinations 1998).

[95] *Id.*

[96] Basic Pilot Program Extension and Expansion Act of 2003, *supra* note 11, §4(a)(2).

[97] *See* INA §216A, 8 USC §1186b; 8 CFR §216.6.

[98] *See* INA §216, 8 USC §1186a.

[99] 8 CFR §§216.6, 1216.6.

time jobs. These jobs may be filled by eligible U.S. workers with payroll records, relevant tax documentation, and Forms I-9.[100] The individual also must show that he or she "sustained the actions" required for removal of conditions during the person's residence in the United States. An entrepreneur will have met this requirement if he or she has "substantially met" the capital investment requirement and has continuously maintained this investment during the conditional period.[101]

Failure to File Form I-829

An immigrant investor in conditional resident status must submit Form I-829 to the appropriate service center within the 90-day period immediately preceding the second anniversary of his or her admission to the United States as a conditional permanent resident.[102] Failure to do so will result in automatic termination of the conditional resident's status and initiation of removal proceedings.[103]

Working with a Regional Center to Prepare Form I-829

If an immigrant investor has an approved I-526 petition by investing in a regional center, it is important to work with the regional center well in advance to prepare the I-829 documentation. The regional center should provide each immigrant investor with verification of employment for the employees hired because of the immigrant investor's investment, as well as documentary proof of the immigrant investor's complete deposit of funds.

Adjudication of Form I-829 by a Service Center

Initial Review of Form I-829—An immigration service center may (1) approve an I-829 petition without review, (2) issue a request for further evidence,

or (3) refer it for an adjudication (with or without the interview) by a district office.[104]

Approval of Form I-829 by the USCIS Service Center—A service center may approve an I-829 petition if the petition establishes the requirements for removing the conditions outlined above. If approved, the service center director will remove the conditions on the conditional resident's status as of the second anniversary of his or her admission as a conditional resident.[105] The approval notice will instruct the conditional resident to report to the appropriate district office for processing for a new permanent resident card (Form I-551). At the district office, the conditional resident will surrender any permanent resident card previously issued and receive interim documents valid for 12 months in the form of either a temporary I-551 stamp in his or her unexpired foreign passport, or a Form I-94 containing a temporary I-551 stamp and his or her photograph.[106]

Request for Further Evidence—A service center may also issue a request for further evidence (RFE). An RFE must be based on a determination by the service center director that the conditional resident must provide further documentation or answer certain questions in writing.[107] If the questions cannot be answered in writing, the petition must be referred for an interview. An RFE will not be issued if the petition is clearly deniable on grounds other than those for which the RFE might be issued. A conditional resident has up to 12 weeks to respond to an RFE.[108] Upon receipt of the RFE, the service center director must either approve or refer the Form I-829 petition to the district office.[109]

An RFE may be issued for many reasons. One issue that sometimes arises in I-829 adjudications is whether the proper number of jobs has been created. The regulations state that an investor must submit evidence that he or she created or can be expected to create 10 jobs "within a reasonable time."[110] Asked to define that phrase, USCIS responded:

> USCIS cannot articulate a bright line rule to define what constitutes a "reasonable period of

---

[100] *See* 8 CFR §216.6(a)(4)(iv).

[101] 8 CFR §§216.6(a)(4), 1216.6(a)(4).

[102] 8 CFR §§216.6(a)(1), 1216.6(a)(1).

[103] 8 CFR §§216.6(a)(5), 1216.6(a)(5); Memorandum from Michael A. Pearson, INS Executive Associate Comm'r, to all INS field offices, "EB-5 Field Memorandum No. 9: Form I-829 Processing" (Mar. 3, 2000), *published on* AILA InfoNet at Doc. No. 00060702 (*posted* June 7, 2000) (amending INS Adjudicators Field Manual §25.2) [hereinafter I-829 Memo]. *See also* L. Stone, "Removal of the Conditions on Permanent Residence for Immigrant Investors," *Immigration & Nationality Law Handbook* 329 (AILA 2005–06 Ed.).

[104] *Id.*

[105] 8 CFR §§216.6(d)(1), 1216.6(d)(1).

[106] I-829 Memo, *supra* note 103.

[107] *Id.*

[108] 8 CFR §103.2(b)(8).

[109] I-829 Memo, *supra* note 103.

[110] 8 CFR §216.6(a)(4)(iv).

time" as such period will depend on the factors of each individual case. USCIS will consider all appropriate evidence that would (a) clearly justify not having completed the job creation by the end of the two years of conditional residence (e.g., the nature of the investment, the industry involved, etc.) and (b) show that the full number of requisite new jobs will be created within a clear, defined and credible period of time.[111]

Determination That Referral to District Office is Appropriate—A service center will refer the petition to a district director if the initial review of the petition or the response to a request for additional evidence reveals that (1) the requirements for removal of conditions have not been met and the case should be denied without an interview, or (2) an interview is necessary to approve or deny the petition.[112]

Adjudication of Form I-829 by the District Office

Approval of Form I-829 by the District Director—A district office may approve an I-829 petition if it is satisfied that the petition satisfies the requirements for removing the condition outlined above.[113]

Denial of Form I-829 by the District Director—A district director must deny an I-829 petition if the petition does not establish the requirements for removing the condition. There is no appeal from this decision. The conditional resident may seek review of the district director's decision in removal proceedings.[114]

Status of Conditional Residents While I-829 is Pending

Immigrant investors remain in valid status while their I-829 petition is pending. Their status is supposed to be extended automatically in one-year increments until USCIS acts on the petition. During that time they are authorized to travel.[115] Practitioners have complained, however, that many offices are unaware of this procedure. Extending conditional resident status, obtaining re-entry permits, and proving authorization to travel can be particularly difficult for spouses and children of EB-5 investors.

USCIS issued a memo in January 2005 intended to help conditional residents with pending or denied I-829 petitions that might benefit from the 2002 law discussed below.[116] The memo instructs USCIS adjudicators to extend conditional resident status for affected EB-5 petitioners. The memo also instructs agency officials to assist pending I-829 petitioners with travel and parole requests.[117]

Conditional permanent residents with pending I-829 petitions should travel with an attorney "pocket letter" describing their status, with a copy of the January 2005 memo validating their claims.

TERMINATION OF EB-5 STATUS

The statute provides three separate grounds for terminating an EB-5 investor's status during the two-year conditional period.[118] Immigrant status will be terminated if USCIS determines that:

- The investment in the new commercial enterprise was to evade the immigration laws of the United States.[119] This provision requires termination only if the investment of the enterprise was "solely" to evade immigration laws. This suggests that if the investment was made with legitimate intentions, in addition to an intention to fraudulently procure permanent resident status, termination would not be proper under this ground;

- The investor failed to invest (or was not in the process of investing) the requisite capital, or failed to sustain the investments during the two-year conditional period;[120] or

- The individual was otherwise not conforming to the requirements of the employment-creation status provisions of INA §203(b)(5).[121] This catch-all provision is dangerous because it does not define the conduct giving rise to termination of status. USCIS could potentially apply this provision broadly to terminate the investor status

---

[111] AILA-USCIS liaison meeting minutes (Apr. 2, 2008), at 10, *published on* AILA InfoNet at Doc. No. 08040235 (*posted* Apr. 2, 2008).

[112] I-829 Memo, *supra* note 103.

[113] *Id.*

[114] 8 CFR §§216.6(d)(2), 1216.6(d)(2); I-829 Memo, *supra* note 103.

[115] I-829 Memo, *supra* note 103.

[116] Memorandum from William R. Yates, USCIS Assoc. Director for Operations, to all USCIS offices, "Extension of Status for Conditional Residents with Pending or Denied Form I-829 Petitions Subject to Public Law 107-273 (Jan. 18, 2005), *published on* AILA InfoNet at Doc. No. 05012167 (*posted* Jan. 21, 2005), *reprinted in* 10 *Bender's Immigration Bulletin* 236 (Feb. 15, 2005).

[117] *Id.*

[118] INA §216A(b), 8 USC §1186b(b).

[119] INA §216A(b)(1)(A), 8 USC §1186b(b)(1)(A).

[120] INA §216A(b)(1)(B), 8 USC §1186b(b)(1)(B).

[121] INA §216A(b)(1)(C), 8 USC §1186b(b)(1)(C).

of an applicant for any infraction of the section. Fortunately, however, it does not appear that USCIS has ever invoked this provision to terminate the status of an immigrant investor.

An EB-5 investor admitted under the pilot program is also subject to the same conditions and restrictions.

DETERRING FRAUDULENT INVESTMENTS

In enacting the EB-5 program, Congress expressed concern about the possibility of fraudulent investments. To deter such fraud, establishing a commercial enterprise for the purpose of "evading any provision of the immigration laws" is a felony punishable by up to five years imprisonment.[122] One reason Congress provided for two-year conditional permanent residency status for EB-5 investors is to aid in this deterrence. This two-year continuum for business activity and investment requires a significant investment and is a strong deterrent to fraud. Nonetheless, should fraud be discovered by USCIS before the two-year conditional period ends, the investor's status will be terminated.[123] So far it appears that USCIS has not prosecuted any EB-5 investors for fraud.[124]

EB-5 PETITIONS: THEORY vs. REALITY

The statutory and regulatory provisions discussed above are onerous.[125] For this reason, immigration through the EB-5 category has never approached the maximum of about 10,000 a year. Yet the legacy INS radically restricted the EB-5 program even further in 1998 by issuing four precedent AAO decisions that made it even harder to obtain EB-5 status.[126]

A complete discussion of the four precedent decisions is beyond the scope of this article. Below is a summary of the changes created by the four decisions.[127] The post-1998 requirements are listed first; prior law or policy is listed in italics.[128]

Post-1998: Promissory note valued at fair market value.

Pre-1998: Promissory note valued at face value.

Post-1998: Promissory note must generally be paid after two years.

Pre-1998: No limit on term of promissory note.

Post-1998: Security for promissory note needs to be perfected under the UCC.

Pre-1998: Security does not need to meet UCC perfected security interest requirements.

Post-1998: Bank accounts cannot be used as security.

Pre-1998: Bank accounts can be used as security.

Post-1998: Reduce the fair market value of promissory note by "considerable expense and effort" to execute on foreign assets.

Pre-1998: Promissory note valued at face value.

Post-1998: No redemption provisions can be agreed to before end of conditional residence

---

[122] INA §275(d), 8 USC §1325(d).

[123] INA §216A(b)(1), 8 USC §1186b(b)(1).

[124] For an interesting case, rife with intrigue, fraud, and shady dealings surrounding two EB-5 promoters, see *United States v. O'Connor*, 158 F. Supp. 2d 697 (E.D. Va. 2001). Individual EB-5 investors appear to have been victims, not perpetrators, of the fraud. *See also* Serova v. Teplen, No. 05 CIV.6748 (HB), 2006 U.S. Dist. LEXIS 5781 (S.D.N.Y. Feb. 16, 2006) (EB-5 investor claims her attorney failed to represent her adequately, in part by failing to disclose that he also represented the company in which she invested).

[125] For current information on litigation and other developments surrounding EB-5 provisions, see the EB-5 Litigation Document webpage at *www.usa-immigration.com/litigation .htm* (last visited Feb. 29, 2008).

---

[126] *Matter of Soffici*, 22 I&N Dec. 158, 19 Immigr. Rep. B2-25 (Assoc. Comm'r, Examinations 1998); *Matter of Izummi*, 22 I&N Dec. 169, 19 Immigr. Rep. B2-32 (Assoc. Comm'r, Examinations 1998); *Matter of Hsiung*, 22 I&N Dec. 201, 19 Immigr. Rep. B2-106 (Assoc. Comm'r, Examinations 1998); *Matter of Ho*, 22 I&N Dec. 206, 19 Immigr. Rep. B2-99 (Assoc. Comm'r, Examinations 1998). *See generally* W. Cook, "Somewhere, Over the Rainbow ... Lies the EB-5 Pot of Gold," 3 *Bender's Immigration Bulletin* 1205 (Dec. 1, 1998).

[127] Note that the requirements established by these cases may be applied retroactively, even if they contravene practices established by earlier unpublished decisions or other guidance. *See Golden Rainbow Freedom Fund v. Ashcroft*, 24 Fed. Appx. 698, 2001 U.S. App. LEXIS 25482 (9th Cir. Nov. 26, 2001). *See also R.L. Inv. Ltd. Partners v. INS*, 86 F. Supp. 2d 1014 (D. Haw. 2000), *aff'd*, 273 F.3d 874 (9th Cir. 2001). *But see Chang v. United States*, 327 F.3d 911 (9th Cir. 2003) (ruling that retroactive application of the newly established requirements is impermissible if the applicant was granted conditional residency before the new requirements came into effect); *Sang Geun An v. United States*, No. C03-3184P (W.D. Wash. Feb. 16, 2005) (following *Chang*).

[128] Thanks to H. Ronald Klasko, who drafted this list of changes and allowed them to be reprinted here.

and before conclusion of payments on promissory note.

Pre-1998: Redemption provisions can be agreed to so long as redemption does not occur until after promissory note has been paid in full.

Post-1998: Third party guarantees to investor prohibited.

Pre-1998: Third party guarantee allowed unless backed by government obligation.

Post-1998: Amounts attributable to expenses to start new commercial enterprise must be deducted from capital contribution.

Pre-1998: Start-up costs and expenses included in amount of capital contribution.

Post-1998: New ownership and new corporation are not sufficient to establish new commercial enterprise.

Pre-1998: Restructuring or reorganization sufficient to establish new commercial enterprise.

Post-1998: All of the activities must benefit the targeted geographical area to count indirect employment.

Pre-1998: The qualifying investment must be within the approved regional center; there is no separate requirement to prove benefit solely to the regional center.

Below is a summary of additional restrictive interpretations created by the AAO in nonprecedent decisions:

Post-1998: Money earned or assets acquired while in the United States in an unlawful status are not considered lawful means to acquire capital.

Pre-1998: Drug smugglers or other criminals cannot use their ill-gotten gains to obtain permanent resident status in the United States through the EB-5 category; nothing specified about others illegally in the United States.

Post-1998: All investors in the partnership must identify the source of their funds to prove that they were derived by lawful means.

Pre-1998: Only the petitioning investor must identify the source of his or her funds in the partnership to prove that they were derived by lawful means.

Post-1998: Merely injecting cash into the corporate account of a business does not show that the capital is "at risk" for the purpose of generating a return.

Pre-1998: Injecting cash into a corporate account could show that the capital is "at risk" for the purpose of generating a return.

2002 AMENDMENTS

Investors who were hurt by the changes the immigration agency made in 1998 lobbied Congress for relief. Eventually, in 2002 Congress enacted changes to the EB-5 program as part of a Justice Department authorization bill.[129] To qualify under the new law, an investor must have filed a petition for EB-5 classification (Form I-526) and had it approved between January 1, 1995 and August 31, 1998.[130] The law took effect November 2, 2002.

Section 11031(c) of the 2002 law sets forth procedures to determine whether investors can have their conditions removed. The government must decide three things: whether (1) the I-829 petition contains any material misrepresentations; (2) the investment created or saved 10 jobs; and (3) the investor has substantially complied with the investment requirement ($1 million or $500,000).[131] Investments in regional centers or in troubled businesses count.[132] The law gives investors a choice of three dates by which to measure their compliance: (1) the date the I-829 petition was filed; (2) six months after the I-829 petition was filed; or (3) the date the government makes its determination under the new law.[133]

If the investor meets the jobs and investment requirements and has not made a material misrepresentation, the government will remove the conditional resident status and the investor and family members will become permanent residents as of the second anniversary of the date they became condi-

---

[129] 21st Century Department of Justice Appropriations Authorization Act, *supra* note 9, §§11031–37. *See generally* S. Yale-Loehr, "Congress Helps Stranded Immigrant Investors," 7 *Bender's Immigration Bulletin* 1306 (Nov. 1, 2002), and at *www.millermayer.com/new/bibeb5bill.html* (last visited Feb. 29, 2008).

[130] 21st Century Department of Justice Appropriations Authorization Act, *supra* note 9, §§11031(b)(1), 11032(b).

[131] *Id.* §11031(c)(1)(A).

[132] *Id.* §11031(c)(1)(B), (C).

[133] *Id.* §11031(c)(1)(D).

tional residents.[134] If the government finds against an investor on any of the three grounds, the government must notify the investor, and provide the investor with an opportunity to submit evidence to rebut the adverse determination.[135] If the investor loses on the jobs or investment requirement, the government will continue the investor's conditional resident status for additional two years.[136] During that time the investor can try to meet those requirements.

If the government finds that the investor made a material misrepresentation, the government will terminate the investor's conditional resident status.[137] The investor can appeal to the Board of Immigration Appeals and then seek judicial review.[138] During administrative or judicial review proceedings the investor and his or her family members remain in conditional resident status.[139]

Most investors are unlikely to persuade the government that they fully met the capital investment and jobs creation requirement. The new law gives them an additional two years to make another investment. During that time they can combine investments made earlier with new investments to show that altogether they invested the total amount required.[140] This includes investments in limited partnerships.[141]

An investor must file another I-829 during the 90 days preceding the new two-year anniversary.[142] Failure to file will normally terminate a conditional resident's status.[143] There is a good cause exception.[144]

Assuming an investor files another I-829 petition, the government has 90 days to decide three things: whether (1) the I-829 petition has any material misrepresentations; (2) the investment created or saved 10 jobs; and (3) the investor has substantially complied with the investment requirement ($1 million or $500,000).[145] The investor can aggregate money in-

vested before and jobs created or saved from the initial investment.[146] Investments in regional centers or in troubled businesses count.[147]

If the investor meets the job creation and investment requirements and has not made a material misrepresentation, the government will remove the conditional resident status of the investor and family members. They will become permanent residents as of the second anniversary of the date their conditional resident status was continued.[148] If the government finds against an investor on any of the three grounds, the government must notify the investor, who may attempt to rebut the adverse facts.[149] If the investor loses, the government will terminate the investor's conditional resident status.[150]

Section 11032 of the 2002 law provides similar procedures for EB-5 investors whose I-526 petitions were approved, but who never became conditional residents because the INS never acted on their adjustment of status applications or because they remained overseas. This section defines an eligible individual as an investor who filed an I-526 petition that was approved between January 1, 1995, and August 31, 1998, and who then timely filed an adjustment of status application or applied for an immigrant visa overseas. Investors are not eligible if they are inadmissible or deportable on any ground.[151]

If INS revoked the I-526 petition on the ground that the investor failed to meet the capital investment requirement, that revocation is to be disregarded.[152] If the adjustment of status application or immigrant visa application overseas was not pending on November 2, 2002, the date of enactment, it is to be treated as reopened if: (i) it is not pending because the government claims the investor never complied with the capital investment requirement; or (ii) the investor left the United States without advance parole.[153] If an investor applied for adjustment of status in the United States but is now overseas, the government will estab-

[134] *Id.* §11031(c)(1)(E).

[135] *Id.* §11031(c)(1)(F)(i).

[136] *Id.* §11031(c)(1)(F)(ii).

[137] *Id.* §11031(c)(1)(F)(iii).

[138] *Id.* §11031(c)(1)(F)(iv).

[139] *Id.*

[140] *Id.* §11031(c)(2)(A).

[141] *Id.*

[142] *Id.* §11031(c)(2)(C)(i).

[143] *Id.* §11031(c)(2)(D).

[144] *Id.* §11031(c)(2)(C)(ii).

[145] *Id.* §11031(c)(2)(E).

[146] *Id.*

[147] *Id.*

[148] *Id.* §11031(c)(2)(F).

[149] *Id.* §11031(c)(2)(G)(i).

[150] *Id.* §11031(c)(2)(G)(ii).

[151] *Id.* §11032(b).

[152] *Id.* §11032(c)(1).

[153] *Id.* §11032(c)(2)(A).

lish a process to let the investor return to the United States if necessary to obtain adjustment.[154]

The government was supposed to approve adjustment of status applications for eligible investors by May 1, 2003, 180 days after enactment.[155] However, that has not happened yet, because USCIS has not yet published regulations to implement the 2002 law. The investors will eventually be in conditional resident status. Such investors must file an I-829 petition within two years of becoming a conditional resident.[156] The determinations and process are similar for both §11031 and §11032 investors. For example, the government must credit the investor with funds invested and jobs created or saved both before and after November 2, 2002, the date of enactment.[157] This section gives investors a choice of two dates by which to measure their compliance: (1) the date they filed their adjustment of status application; or (2) the date the government decides the I-829 petition.[158]

Finally, the new law states that a noncitizen who was admitted on a conditional basis by virtue of being the child of an EB-5 investor will still be considered a child for purposes of the new law, even if he or she turns 21 or marries.[159]

ETHICAL CONSIDERATIONS[160]

It is important for an attorney to consider the ethical considerations before beginning to represent a client in the complex EB-5 category. The American Bar Association's (ABA) Model Rules of Professional Conduct's first rule states: "A lawyer shall provide competent representation to a client. Competent representation requires the legal knowledge, skill, thoroughness and preparation reasonably necessary for the representation."[161] Therefore, repre-

senting an immigrant investor client without a good base of EB-5 knowledge could be considered a breach of ethical rules.

If an attorney feels inadequate to represent a client in an EB-5 matter, he or she may comply with competence rules by consulting with an EB-5 expert or by bifurcating representation between EB-5 and non–EB-5 related counsel. In a joint-counsel scenario, most jurisdictions require that the client be made aware of any joint representation and that the fees be split to reflect the proportional amount of work that each law firm is providing.

Finally, there is an ethical consideration concerning the referral fees that many regional centers offer to someone who recommends an investor to the regional center. Accepting such fees may involve a conflict of interest, since an attorney's representation of a client may be materially impaired by the prospect of a pecuniary gain from a regional center. An attorney has a duty of undivided loyalty to a client.

CONCLUSION

Qualifying a person for EB-5 status is one of the most complicated subspecialties in immigration law. A sophisticated knowledge of corporate, tax, investment, and immigration law is required. Moreover, the four 1998 precedent AAO decisions and subsequent nonprecedent decisions have made it even harder to obtain approvals of EB-5 petitions. Investors must discard normal investment opportunities in favor of investments structured to meet the unrealistic requirements of the precedent decisions. Attorneys, in turn, must proceed at their peril in advising clients. In many cases it may be more practicable for investors to come to the United States through other visa categories such as the E-2 investor, L-1 intracompany transferee, or EB-1-3 multinational executive or manager routes.

Nevertheless, things may be looking up for the EB-5 category. In January 2005 USCIS established a new Investor and Regional Center Unit (IRCU) at USCIS headquarters. The IRCU, since renamed the Foreign Trader, Investor and Regional Center Program, provides oversight for EB-5 policy and regulatory development, field guidance, and training. According to USCIS, establishing the IRCU will "strengthen and protect the integrity of the [EB-5] program while promoting the intent of Congress to

---

[154] *Id.* §11032(c)(2)(B).

[155] *Id.* §11032(a).

[156] *Id.* §11032(e).

[157] *Id.* §11032(e)(2).

[158] *Id.* §11032(e)(3).

[159] *Id.* §§11031(e), 11032(f).

[160] *See* C. Lee, "Ethical and Practical Considerations in EB-5 Representation," *available at www.ilw.com/articles/2007, 1120-lee.shtm,* and *at www.millermayer.com/new/eb5 ethics.html, reprinted in* 13 Bender's Immigration Bulletin 332 (Mar. 15, 2008).

[161] *See generally* Model Rules of Professional Conduct R. 1.1. The New York Disciplinary Rules of the Code of Professional Responsibility, the California Rules of Professional Conduct, *continued*

and the Maine Code of Professional Responsibility are not based on the ABA Model Rules of Professional Conduct.

encourage investment and increase employment within the United States."[162] Indeed, while only 129 individuals were admitted as EB-5 conditional residents in FY 2004, 749 individuals obtained conditional resident status in FY 2006.[163]

These changes may mark a major leap forward in USCIS policy toward the EB-5 visa category.[164] The changes hold the promise of making the EB-5 process more user-friendly in terms of processing times and responsiveness to investors' concerns. USCIS officials now say that they want to meet the needs of the business community so that the EB-5 category can be more effectively used. Many issues are still not resolved, however, and the sunset of the Pilot Program is quickly approaching. Hopefully, it will be renewed. Time will tell whether the EB-5 program continues with its current success.

---

[162] USCIS Memorandum, William R. Yates, USCIS Assoc. Dir. for Operations, to all USCIS offices, "Establishment of an Investor and Regional Center Unit," File No. HQPRD 70/6.2.8 (Jan. 19, 2005), *published on* AILA InfoNet at Doc. No. 05012663 (*posted* Jan. 26, 2005), *reprinted in* 10 *Bender's Immigration Bulletin* 195 (Feb. 15, 2005).

[163] *See* 2006 Yearbook of Immigration Statistics, *supra* note 4, at 20 (Table 6).

[164] *See generally* S. Mailman & S. Yale-Loehr, "Immigrant Investor Green Cards: Rise of the Phoenix?," *N.Y.L.J.*, Apr. 25, 2005, at 3, *reprinted in* 10 Bender's Immigration Bulletin 801 (May 15, 2005), and at *www.millermayer.com/EB5NYLJ0405. html* (last visited Feb. 28, 2008).

APPENDIX:
DESIGNATED REGIONAL CENTERS[165]

Approved and Active Regional Centers

Alabama:
Alabama Center for Foreign Investment, LLC
100 North Union Street, Suite 682
Montgomery, AL 36104
www.acfi-alabama.com/alabama.html

California:
California Consortium for Agricultural Export[166]
333 S. Grand Ave., 25th Floor
Los Angeles, CA 90071
www.ccax.com/

CMB Export LLC
Corona Professional Center
400 S. Ramona Avenue, Suite 212AA
Corona, CA 91719
www.cmbeb5visa.com/

Southeast Los Angeles Regional Center[167]
David B. Brearley, Esq.
c/o Lincoln Stone
Stone & Grzegorek LLP
800 Wilshire Boulevard, Suite 900
Los Angeles, CA 90017

Los Angeles Film Regional Center
c/o Thomas Rosenfeld
CanAm Enterprises, LLC
32 Court Street, Suite 1501
Brooklyn, NY 11201

District of Columbia:
Capitol Area Regional Center[168]
1801 K Street, NW, Suite 201-L
Washington, DC 20006
www.eb5dc.com/

Iowa:
Iowa Department of Economic Development[169]
200 East Grand Avenue
Des Moines, IA 50309
www.extension.iastate.edu/ag/staff/info/ianewfarmfamily.pdf

Kansas:
Kansas Biofuel Regional Center, LLC
3250 Wilshire Blvd., Suite #1700
Los Angeles, CA 90010

Louisiana:
City of New Orleans Office of Planning and Development[170]
1340 Poydras Street, Suite 1000
New Orleans, LA 70112
www.nobleoutreach.com/

Pennsylvania:
Philadelphia Industrial Development Corporation[171]
2600 Centre Square West
1500 Market Street
Philadelphia, PA 19102-2126
www.canamenterprises.com

Pennsylvania Department of Community & Economic Development Regional Center
Harrisburg, PA 17120
www.newPA.com

South Dakota:
South Dakota International Business Institute[172]
711 East Wells Avenue
Pierre, SD 57501-3369
www.sd-exports.org/eb-5/

Texas (& Texas/Oklahoma):
Global Century Development Group I, LP
11205 Bellaire Blvd., Suite B-33
Houston, TX 77072-2545

---

[165] Memorandum from Jacquelyn A. Bednarz, Acting INS Ass't Comm'r for Programs, "Designation of Regional Centers Under the Immigrant Investor Pilot Program," HQ 7C/6.2.5 (July 31, 1998); USCIS Memorandum, "Active Approved EB-5 Regional Centers" (Oct. 2007), *published on* AILA InfoNet at Doc. No. 07110870 (*posted* Nov. 8, 2007).

[166] Approved Feb. 27, 2002. *Available at www.ccax.com/ pdf/CCAERegionalCenterApproval.pdf* (last visited Feb. 29, 2008). Redesignation and amendment approved Mar. 19, 2007 (copy on file with authors).

[167] Approved Apr. 4, 2008 (copy on file with authors).

[168] Approved Nov. 25, 2005. *Available at www.eb5dc.com/ resources/CARc+approval+letter.pdf* (last visited Mar. 3, 2008).

[169] Approved Dec. 10, 2004. *Available at www.usa-immigration.com/litigation.htm* (last visited Feb. 29, 2008).

[170] Redesignation and amendment approved Feb. 16, 2007 (copy on file with authors).

[171] Approved Feb. 28, 2003. *Available at www.canamenterprises.com/pdfs/INS-approval-notice.pdf* (last visited Feb. 29, 2008). Amended Apr. 23, 2004. Amendment available at *www.usa-immigration.com/ litigation.htm* (last visited Feb. 29, 2008).

[172] Approved Apr. 8, 2004. *Available at www.usa-immigration.com/litigation.htm* (last visited Feb. 29, 2008). Amended Dec. 2006. Amendment available at *www.sd-exports.org/dairy2002/notification_letter_page1.htm* (last visited Feb. 29, 2008).

Southwest Biofuels Regional Center, LLC
3250 Wilshire Blvd., Suite #1700
Los Angeles, CA 90010

Vermont:
Vermont Agency of Commerce and Community Development[173]
National Life Building
Montpellier, VT 05620-0501
www.eb5greencard.com/

Washington:
The Gateway Freedom Fund
(a/k/a Golden Rainbow Freedom Fund)
c/o American Life Inc, 3223 3rd Ave South
Seattle, WA 98134
www.amlife.us/visa.html

Whatcom Opportunities Regional Center[174]
1305 11th Street, Suite 304
Bellingham, WA 98825
www.worc.biz/

Wisconsin:
Metropolitan Milwaukee Association of Commerce
756 N. Milwaukee Street
Milwaukee, WI 53202
www.mmac.org

Seeking Redesignation

Hawaii:
State of Hawaii, Department of Business,
Economic Development & Tourism
P.O. Box 2359
Honolulu, HI 96804

Nevada:
Unibex Global Corporation
1201 Eleanor Avenue
Las Vegas, NV 89106

Washington:
Aero-Space Port International Group
512 Strander Boulevard
Tukwila, WA 98188
www.aspigroup.com/

Not Active or Seeking Voluntary Termination

Arizona:
GV Development
7525 W. Highway 68

P.O. Box 10430
Golden Valley, AZ 86413-2430

California:
Alameda Trade Center
c/o Lowe Enterprises Commercial Group
1818 East 7th Street, Suite 200
Los Angeles, CA 90021

CKS Western Inc. World Trade Center
620 W. Graham Drive
Lake Elsinore, CA 92530

Empirical Entertainment
6255 Sunset Boulevard, Suite 2000
Hollywood, CA 90028

Redevelopment Agency of the City of Vernon[175]
4305 Santa Fe Avenue
Vernon, CA 90058

Trading Partners International of California LLC
2677 N. Main Street, Suite 930
Santa Ana, CA 92705

West Rand Gold Trust
P.O. Box 2222
Ridgecrest, CA 93556

Colorado:
Pueblo Economic Development Corporation
P.O. Box 5807
Pueblo, CO 81002

Florida:
Miami Chinese Community Center, Ltd.
331 NE 18th Street
Miami, FL 33132

Georgia:
Atlanta International Center for Academic [sic] and Athletics
1131 Alpharetta Street
Roswell, GA 30075

Legacy Project
1100 Spring Street, Suite 600
Atlanta, GA 30309

Michigan:
Danou Enterprises
World Trade Center Detroit/Windsor
1251 Fort Street
Trenton, MI 48183

---

[173] Redesignation and amendment approved Mar. 19, 2007 (copy on file with authors).

[174] Approved Oct. 13, 2006 (copy on file with authors).

[175] Approved Dec. 27, 2005. *Available at www.usa-immigration.com/litigation.htm* (last visited Feb. 29, 2008).

New York:
North Country Alliance
One Lincoln Boulevard
Rouses Point, NY 12979

South Carolina:
American Export Partners
180 East Bay Street, Suite 300
Charleston, SC 29401-2123
World Trade Center/Greenville-Spartenburg Inc.
315 Old Boiling Springs Road
Greer, SC 29650

Texas:
North Texas Commission
P.O. Box 610246
DFW Airport, TX 75261

Washington:
Beacon U.S. Studios Inc.
5610 Sanderling Way
Blaine, WA 98230

Matrix International, LLC
P.O. Box 22891
Seattle, WA 98122

Washington, D.C.:
Abacus, LLC
740 6thh St., NW, Suite 302
Washington, DC 20001-3798

KEEPING IT IN THE FAMILY: THE IMPACT OF CORPORATE RESTRUCTURING ON INTRACOMPANY TRANSFERS

*by Jerome G. Grzeca, Teri A. Simmons, and Molly J. Smiltneek**

International companies often transfer their highest level executives and managers and other key employees to the United States as L-1 intracompany transfers. However, when these very companies are considering a merger, acquisition, or internal reorganization, the decisions are rarely made with immigration implications in mind. This article will review the various ways of ensuring that valuable intracompany transfers stay "in the family," and that a corporate blanket transfer program remains valid in light of corporate restructuring.

ELIGIBILITY CRITERIA

Specific organizational requirements must be met to allow a company to transfer its international employees to the United States. Additionally, the qualifying relationship between the petitioning entity and its parent, branch, subsidiary and affiliate *must* be preserved in order for employees in the United States in L classification to remain in valid status.[1] If, in light of corporate restructuring, a qualifying

relationship no longer exists, the foreign national and the company must explore other nonimmigrant visa options. On the other hand, if the corporate restructure merely modifies the qualifying relationship, it may be necessary to notify the government of this change via an amended L-1 petition or by amending the list of entities on an approved L blanket approval. Or there may be no obligation to affirmatively notify the government of the change until an extension is sought.

Generally, the regulations require the petitioner to file an amended petition whenever there are changes in approved relationships, additional qualifying organizations under a blanket petition, or a change in capacity of employment.[2] Guidance from the legacy Immigration and Naturalization Service (INS) attempted to clarify that "an amended petition must be filed when there is a material change in the terms and conditions of employment or the beneficiary's eligibility."[3] While the INS, and subsequently U.S. Citizenship and Immigration Services (USCIS), maintains that minor or immaterial changes may be addressed at the time of extension, little guidance has been provided clarifying the threshold for notifying the government of changes in corporate structure in an amendment rather than merely through extension. However, it is clear that if the change in the qualifying relationship does not affect L-1 eligibility, there is no need to notify the government until extension is sought. For example, if the employing entity abroad is no longer doing business or no longer has a qualifying relationship with the U.S. petitioner, but the U.S. employer is still a continuing, qualifying part of the multinational organization and proof of that has already been filed with USCIS (such as by including an organizational chart in the original petition that listed an additional entity abroad, or by proving that the parent company is located abroad in the original filing), there is no

---

* **Jerome G. Grzeca** is the founding partner of Grzeca Law Group, S.C., and has practiced business immigration law for over 19 years, in both Washington, D.C. and Milwaukee. He is listed in *The Best Lawyers in America*. Currently, he is a director of AILA's Board of Governors, a member of AILA's DOS Liaison Committee, business subcommittee chair of the Annual Conference Planning Committee, and a member of AILA's Strategic Planning Committee.

Teri A. Simmons is a partner with Arnall Golden Gregory LLP, where she directs the international and immigration practice group. Ms. Simmons has been practicing immigration law since 1989. From 1999 to 2001, she served as AILA's Atlanta's Chapter chair. She has also served on the national board of AILA. Currently, she is a member of the national liaison committees for Customs and Border Protection and for immigrant investors. Ms. Simmons has spoken as an expert on immigration matters both in the United States and abroad for AILA, state bar associations, and for the Department of State.

Molly J. Smiltneek is an associate attorney and case manager at the Grzeca Law Group, S.C. She serves as the New Member Division liaison of the Wisconsin State Chapter of AILA. She is a graduate of the University of Wisconsin–Madison and Marquette University Law School.

[1] 8 CFR §214.2(*l*)(1)(ii)(G).

[2] 8 CFR §214.2(*l*)(7)(i)(C).

[3] *See* legacy Immigration and Naturalization Service (INS) Memorandum CO 2141-C (Oct. 22, 1992), *reproduced in* 69 *Interpreter Releases* 1431, 1449–50 (Nov. 9, 1992).

need to amend the petition to notify the government of this change.

TIMING

Unfortunately, immigration attorneys are often the last to hear about a corporate restructuring. As there is no regulatory grace period for notifying the government of material changes in the qualifying corporate relationship, this hypothetically could have devastating effects on the validity of an employee's L classification and the company's blanket approval. In reality, however, Service Centers historically have been relatively lenient in allowing belated amendments. That being said, it is imperative that amendments be filed as quickly after the effective date of the corporate restructure, date of sale, or date of closing as possible.

While immaterial changes should be brought to USCIS's attention only at the time of extension, immigration status must be maintained in order for a change or extension of status to be granted.[4] In particular, if an L-1 employee's duties change from specialized knowledge to managerial or executive in nature due to a change in corporate relationship or otherwise, that change must be reported to USCIS at the time of the change.[5] The notification timing requirements of other material changes to ensure maintenance of status are not so clear. Therefore, a conservative approach requires that an amendment reflecting the material change to an L petition be filed before any attempt to extend status is sought. A more aggressive approach, often brought about by necessity and lack of knowledge of the material change until it is time to extend status, would allow an amendment and extension to be sought at the same time.

BLANKET APPROVALS

Blanket L approval provides a useful tool for international organizations to quickly transfer executive, managerial, or specialized knowledge personnel to the United States. However, corporate restructuring often results in fundamental organizational changes to the corporate relationships among the entities listed on the blanket approval. For example, new entities may become qualifying entities while others may no longer be affiliated with the petitioning entity approved for the blanket approval. Furthermore, a new acquiring parent company may not possess a blanket approval while the acquired subsidiary has an approval with indefinite validity. With proper planning and strategic use of a blanket L approval, either through amendment or a new petition, companies should be able to continue to transfer employees seamlessly within the new corporate family.

If it has not already done so, the completion of a corporate restructuring may be the perfect time for a qualifying organization to pursue a blanket approval. From a practical standpoint, the names and ownership structure of all parents, branches, subsidiaries and affiliates are likely to be readily available. These logistical details are the cornerstone of any blanket approval petition and may be difficult for large conglomerates to gather after the fact.

A company should consider amending its existing document as soon as the intention to restructure or create new corporate relationships is announced. The documents reflecting the new relationships of entities on the blanket approval should be submitted as soon as the relationships have been formed or terminated. This is usually evidenced by the actual transfer of stock or the closing date of the sale. Acting with speed and diligence prior to, and immediately after, the sale will allow new transfers to take place under the blanket approval without having to file individual petitions and possibly pay USCIS the $1,000 premium processing fee.

Amending an existing blanket approval following a corporate restructuring may involve new issues that must be resolved, but it also may provide new opportunities for the organization as a whole. An amendment is required whenever there are changes in the corporate structure or positions that may qualify for L classification under the blanket. It is important for a company's blanket petition to accurately reflect the current list of qualifying entities in order to facilitate rapid transfer by employees when required. The last thing any immigration attorney wants to tell his or her corporate client is that it may not transfer the Vice President of its new subsidiary to the United States in two weeks because it failed to list that subsidiary on the company's blanket approval.

A merger or acquisition, in particular, may qualify a previously ineligible petitioner to apply for blanket approval. If, cumulatively, the petitioner and other qualifying organizations meet the requirements for blanket L approval, the newly formed or modified

---

[4] 8 CFR §§214.1(c)(4), 248.1(b).

[5] 8 CFR §214.2(*l*)(15).

corporate family may be ripe for a blanket L petition.[6] A merger or acquisition may provide a corporate family with a new petitioner that has an office in the United States and has been doing business for over a year,[7] or the new family may cumulatively have the three or more domestic and foreign branches, subsidiaries, or affiliates required to apply for blanket approval.[8] Finally, a merger or acquisition may push a corporate family over the threshold of 10 approved L petitions in the last year, annual sales of at least $25 million, or a U.S. workforce of at least 1,000 employees.[9]

It is important to note that the petitioner under a blanket petition need not be a U.S. entity. Instead, it must have an office in the United States that has been doing business for one year or more.[10] Nor is it required that the actual parent company be the holder of the L blanket approval. If a U.S. corporation with a blanket approval is acquired or owned by a foreign entity, it may hold a blanket approval permitting intracompany transfers within the whole corporate family. Additionally, a foreign entity with a branch in the United States may be eligible for blanket approval.

Creative lawyering may be required when an entity acquires an organization with a valid blanket L approval. Immigration attorneys should carefully examine any existing blanket petitions to determine which entities and corporate structures are listed on the approval notice. In addition, the validity period of any blanket approvals should be reviewed. It is well worth taking measures to ensure a blanket that is valid indefinitely remains so. Rather than pursue a new blanket petition for a newly expanded corporate family, practitioners should consider amending an existing blanket approval that is valid indefinitely but held by what is now a corporate "subsidiary" to include the new corporate parent and all of the corporate parent's existing qualifying organizations.

If both the company being acquired and the company doing the acquiring have L approvals, the blanket approval of either entity could be amended and appended to include all of the entities on the other's blanket approval. However, a company which previously had its own blanket but has been acquired by another entity with its own blanket should use caution if both companies plan to continue to use their own blanket approvals. An amendment to each approval must be filed to reflect changes in the approved relationships that may affect beneficiary eligibility.[11]

When a blanket petition is amended to reflect the name change and to include all of the merged entities, there appears to be no need to amend the individual petitions that were approved under the previous blanket, even if the beneficiaries' individual Approval Notices, Nonimmigrant Petitions based on Blanket L Petition, or Arrival/Departure cards reflect the old name. Most practitioners believe that the required notice of the change to qualifying organizations is satisfied by amending the blanket petition.[12]

In addition, the regulations permit a foreign national admitted to the United States under an approved blanket petition to be reassigned within the organizations listed in the blanket approval without notification to or amendment with USCIS if the employee will be performing virtually the same job duties as he or she was in the initial petition.[13] Therefore, if a foreign national is transferred to "virtually the same" position at a corporate affiliate that has been added to the petitioning company's blanket after a corporate restructure, that blanket-based I-129S petition need not be amended.

While I-129S petition amendments might not be necessary after amending the blanket approval appropriately, in most cases, it is recommended that counsel prepare a document for the company's execution clarifying the nature of the corporate reorganization and any name change and asserting that the visa and the approval notice remain valid. Such a letter can prove useful to the foreign national when questioned upon admission to the United States by a Customs and Border Protection (CBP) officer who may not have sufficient time to review the legality of visa authorization post-corporate reorganization.

INDIVIDUAL L PETITIONS

There is an obligation to notify USCIS when there is a material change to a foreign national's job duties or to the corporate relationship qualifying the petitioner to utilize the L program. Therefore, individual

---

[6] 8 CFR §214.2(*l*)(4)(i)(4).

[7] 8 CFR §214.2(*l*)(4)(i)(4)(A).

[8] 8 CFR §214.2(*l*)(4)(i)(4).

[9] 8 CFR §214.2(*l*)(4)(i)(4)(D).

[10] 8 CFR §214.2(*l*)(4)(i)(4)(B).

[11] 8 CFR §214.2(*l*)(7)(i)(C).

[12] *See id.*

[13] 8 CFR §214.2(*l*)(5)(ii)(G).

petitions that are not under L blanket approval may need an amendment to explain a new corporate relationship to USCIS, unlike I-129S petitions under blanket approval that do not need to be amended. In particular, when a foreign national is transferred from one company to another in the same organization and becomes an employee of the new company, whether necessitated by corporate restructuring or not, an amended individual petition must be filed in order for USCIS to confirm that the new entity is related to the foreign entity in a qualifying capacity.[14]

It also may be appropriate to file an amendment where the corporate relationship between the qualifying entities has changed, even though the relationship still qualifies for the L program and the duties the employee will be providing have not materially changed. If there is a material change in the terms and conditions of employment or the beneficiary's eligibility, an amendment must be filed.[15] For example, while a U.S. parent company may have initially applied for L classification for an employee of its subsidiary abroad, if that parent company and subsidiary are both acquired by a new parent company, it might be necessary to amend the individual employee's petition to explain the new corporate relationship, as this may be considered a material change to the terms and conditions of employment.

Although both USCIS and the Department of State (DOS) have maintained fairly liberal standards for "material change," the prudent practitioner may wish to amend petitions in light of any change that the government may consider "material." If a petitioner has a strong case going in, it is well worth the amendment time and cost to avoid a potential misrepresentation by the foreign national at the port of entry in subsequent trips to the United States. It would be an inopportune time for the government to be notified that, due to corporate restructuring, the foreign national is employed by an employer that has a different name than the one listed on his or her visa or arrival/departure card or I-797 Approval Notice.

While a client may be hesitant to amend an individual L-1 petition for a change that the government may consider immaterial, many practitioners will combine an amendment with an extension of the L validity period in an attempt to maximize the benefit of pursuing an amendment. Although the government has accepted these "amend and extend" petitions, the petitioner runs the risk that USCIS may view this approach as invalid. In reality though, simultaneous "amendment and extension" is a necessity when a client fails to inform the attorney of corporate changes that may have been grounds for an amendment.

A promotion in and of itself may not necessitate an amendment.[16] However, it is important to note that if the job duties of an individual in L-1B classification change, due to corporate restructuring or otherwise, such that the individual's duties are now executive or managerial rather than utilizing specialized knowledge, and an amendment to L-1A status is required, the employee must be performing executive or managerial duties for six months prior to the end of his permitted five years in L-1B status.[17] When an amendment from L-1B to L-1A classification is filed with more than six months remaining in the foreign national's stay in L-1B classification, the individual may remain in the United States for a total of seven years in L status if the amendment is approved by USCIS.[18] Note that the amended petition seeking an "upgrade" to L-1A classification must be *approved* more than six months before the end of L-1B status.

It is also important to note that USCIS and DOS often interpret amendment requirements differently. While most counsel will advise companies to file amendments to petitions to advise regarding a managerial promotion, for example, DOS officers might feel that the notification through consular interview and visa revalidation might be excessive. In these days of zero tolerance, however, the best practice is usually to err on the side of caution and notify the government of any changes in employment which may be viewed as material.

CHANGE OF STATUS

At times, a qualifying corporate relationship no longer exists after corporate restructuring. In this situation, most common in spin-offs and divestitures, it is impossible to salvage L-1 eligibility even by timely notifying the government of the change. In that situation, the foreign national and the company must explore other nonimmigrant visa options, be-

---

[14] *See* legacy INS Memo CO 2141-C, *supra* note 3.

[15] *Id.*

[16] Legacy INS letter from J. Brown, Acting Branch Chief, Business & Trade Services Branch, Benefits Division, INS, HQ 70/6.2.18 (Oct. 14, 1997), *reproduced in* 75 *Interpreter Releases* 130, 155 (Jan. 26, 1998).

[17] 8 CFR §214.2(*l*)(15).

[18] *Id.*

cause the foreign national's L-1 classification technically becomes invalid immediately upon the dissolution of the qualifying corporate relationship.

Just as corporate restructuring may make a foreign national ineligible for continued L classification due to a change in the qualifying corporate relationship, it also may eliminate options for individuals working in the United States in other immigration classifications. In particular, if a U.S. company acquires a foreign company that had a significant investment in the United States and had employees or owners working in the United States in E-1 or E-2 classification, a change in the ownership structure of the company may mean that those employees are no longer eligible for E classification. However, those individuals may be eligible to change status to L-1 classification in certain circumstances.

Some corporate restructuring may have the very positive effect of allowing additional intracompany transfers to the United States. For instance, if a company acquires a new affiliate abroad, it can transfer employees who have served that affiliate abroad in executive, managerial or specialized knowledge positions for one year immediately after the new qualifying corporate relationship has been established. There is no need to wait until the employees have directly worked for the acquiring company for one year before filing an L petition.

THE AFTERMATH

While many clients may be hesitant to spend the time and money to notify their immigration attorney, let alone the government, of changes in corporate structure, the impact on their valued intracompany transfers could be devastating if they do not. A company executive may be denied entry by CBP because she mentions that the company listed as her employer on her visa or approval notice is not her current employer. Or an employee whose specialized knowledge is urgently needed by the U.S. company may have to wait weeks or months while his petition works its way through USCIS processing because the entity that employs him abroad was not added to the blanket approval after a corporate acquisition. Most seriously, valid L-1 classification may be inadvertently dismantled due to inattention by the company and its immigration attorneys to the impact of corporate restructuring. The very real implications of corporate restructuring on intracompany transfers should be affirmatively addressed in order to prevent such ineligibilities from occurring.

SUMMARY OF LAW AND ISSUES REGARDING "ABILITY TO PAY" THE PROFFERED WAGE ON EMPLOYMENT-BASED PETITIONS

*by Roberta Freedman** *

One of the issues that have come to the forefront of our practices in recent years is the issue of whether the petitioning employer on an employment-based visa petition can demonstrate the "ability to pay the proffered wage" stated in the underlying labor certification.

There are a number of likely reasons that practitioners are receiving an increased number of Requests for Evidence (usually called RFEs) on this very thorny issue:

A. Many labor certifications filed under §245(i) of the Immigration and Nationality Act (INA) on or before April 30, 2001, have finally made it through the approval process at the Backlog Elimination Centers. As practitioners will remember, with a limited amount of time to file, counsel and the petitioning employer often had no adequate time to discuss in detail requirements such as the employer's "ability to pay" or a potential request for an increase in the prevailing wage by the Department of Labor (DOL).

B. In recent years, a number of attorneys have been prosecuted for filing labor certifications and immigrant petitions unbeknownst to petitioner.

C. U.S. Citizenship and Immigration Services (USCIS) has added more officers to the Fraud Detection Units and has increased scrutiny of petitions.

The regulation that governs the standard of proof and type of evidence required from the petitioner to evidence the ability to "pay the wage" is located at 8 CFR §204.5(g)(2):

Ability of prospective employer to pay wage. Any petition filed by or for an employment-based im-

migrant which requires an offer of employment must be accompanied by evidence that *the prospective United States employer has the ability to pay the proffered wage*. [emphasis added] The petitioner must demonstrate this ability at the time the priority date is established and continuing until the beneficiary obtains lawful permanent residence. Evidence of this ability shall be either in the form of copies of annual reports, federal tax returns, or audited financial statements. In a case where the prospective United States employer employs 100 or more workers, the director may accept a statement from a financial officer of the organization which establishes the prospective employer's ability to pay the proffered wage. In appropriate cases, additional evidence, such as profit/loss statements, bank account records, or personnel records may be submitted by the petitioner or requested by USCIS.

The regulation provides that:

A. The employer (petitioner) must provide evidence of ability to pay the proffered wage from the time of the filing of the labor certification until permanent residence is obtained.

B. Evidence documenting the ability to pay (also referred to as "initial evidence") must accompany the original filing of the employment-based petition in the form of:

1. Annual reports;

2. Federal tax returns; or

3. Audited financial statements.

C. In cases where the petitioner employs 100 or more workers, USCIS may accept a statement from a financial officer of the organization which confirms this information and the petitioning employer's ability to pay the proffered wage.

D. In certain cases, additional evidence documenting the employer's ability to pay may be submitted by the petitioner or requested by USCIS, including:

1. Profit/loss statements;

2. Bank account records; and/or

* **Roberta Freedman**, a partner of Duane Morris, LLP, in Washington, D.C., has practiced immigration and nationality law exclusively for more than 20 years, and is an active member of AILA. She served as an elected director on the AILA Board of Governors and has served as a member of several AILA committees. She also served as chair for AILA's Washington, D.C. Chapter. Ms. Freedman speaks frequently at AILA and other bar and CLE conferences.

3. Personnel records.

On May 4, 2004, William Yates, USCIS's Associate Director for Operations, issued a memorandum[1] that provided further clarification regarding what evidence would be sufficient to satisfy the regulatory requirements and discussed when an RFE should be issued. The purpose of the memorandum was to issue further clarification of acceptable documentation with the goal of reducing RFEs that were unnecessary. The memorandum indicated that 8 CFR §204.5(g)(2) would be amended.[2] In the interim, guidance was being provided in the form of the memorandum outlining three additional circumstances where a positive determination could be made on the issue of the petitioner's ability to pay if the record, with respect to all of the required initial evidence, and the I-140 Petition, Part 5, were complete. The memo affirmatively states that "USCIS Adjudicators should make a positive ability to pay determination in any one of the following circumstances":

A. Net Income—the initial evidence reflects that the petitioner's net income is equal to or greater than the proffered wage.

B. Net Current Assets—the initial evidence reflects that the petitioner's net current assets are equal to or greater than the proffered wage.

C. Employment of the beneficiary—the record contains credible, verifiable evidence that the petitioner not only is employing the beneficiary but also has paid or currently is paying the proffered wage.[3]

In addition, the memorandum provides some clarification for situations in which the petitioner neither meets the income/assets requirements nor employs the beneficiary, as mentioned above. The petitioner may submit:

A. Profit/Loss Statements, or

B. Bank Account records, and/or

C. Personnel records.[4]

It should be noted, however, that the acceptance of these documents is *discretionary*.

The petitions that practitioners find the most difficult to get approved are those where the petitioner is unable to provide the clearest documentation that falls squarely into what is outlined by the regulations and subsequent memorandum. For example:

A. For some of the years covered from the priority date, the employee did not earn the prevailing wage and the employer's income tax returns did not reflect any net income.

B. The business does not reflect net income for any year, as all profits at the end of the year are distributed to the owners/shareholders of the business.

C. The income tax return of the petitioner does not provide information from which to calculate the petitioner's net current assets for a particular year.

D. The petitioner's business is operated as a sole-proprietorship and all net income is taken as personal income on the individual petitioning employer's income tax return.

The above is a sampling of the difficult situations that petitioners and counsel face when trying to assemble documentation that USCIS will deem sufficient to prove the ability to pay the proffered wage. Examples of alternative evidence that practitioners have submitted, together with the "initial evidence," to obtain a successful outcome on an I-140 petition include:

A. The petitioner has been extended a line of credit by a banking institution. If, for example, a letter from the banking institution can be obtained stating that an unused dollar amount exists on a line of credit that was established from a particular date to the present, that could be helpful to demonstrate funds available to pay the proffered wage during that period of time.

B. Employers frequently have reserve accounts of funds. Evidence of such an account would be helpful to document the ability to pay. On occasion, some business entities, in order to carry on their business or lease office space or property, are required to deposit funds in an

---

[1] U.S. Citizenship and Immigration Services (USCIS) Memorandum, W. Yates, "Determination of Ability to Pay Under 8 CFR §204.5(g)(2)" (May 4, 2004), *published on* AILA InfoNet at Doc. No. 04051262 (*posted* May 12, 2004).

[2] As of this writing, no such amendment to the current regulation has been proposed.

[3] USCIS Memo, *supra* note 1.

[4] *Id.*

account, and this type of evidence should be explored as well.

C. An exhaustive analysis of every single month of the employer's bank statements can also be submitted to document the ability to pay the salary. If, for example, the average monthly ending balance is always equal to or in excess of the monthly gross wage offered to the beneficiary, the argument can be made that such information documents the employer's ability to pay the wage.

D. USCIS may review the petitioner's net current assets to evaluate the ability to pay the proffered wage. Current assets include cash on hand, inventories and receivables expected to be converted to cash within one year. A partnership's year-end current assets are listed on Schedule L, lines 1(d) through 6(d). Its year-end current liabilities are listed on lines 15(d) through 17(d). If a partnership's net current assets are equal to or greater than the proffered wage, then it can be demonstrated that the petitioner would be able to pay the proffered wage out of those net assets. Certain partnerships are not required to file Schedule L, and the income tax return provides no information from which to calculate the petitioner's net current assets.

E. In the case of a sole proprietorship or household employer, a listing of the petitioner's monthly fixed obligations for each year in question may be attached to document that additional funds were available to pay the prevailing wage (see attached chart). Additional evidence of the sole proprietor's current assets may also be submitted.

F. The argument has been made many times without much success that the "depreciation deduction" does not actually represent an actual loss and that such "deduction" should be "added-in" to determine the actual net income of the petitioner. However, if a letter from the certified public accountant (CPA) is attached which outlines specifically the petitioner's position on all of these points, it may bolster the evidence under the "totality of circumstances" test.

G. If the beneficiary will be performing a job that is currently being performed by another individual or contract workers, then documentation should be provided to establish that the

funds available to pay the beneficiary are already being utilized to pay the individual (or individuals) the beneficiary will succeed.

H. The argument has been made many times (not very successfully) that by employing the beneficiary, the petitioner will increase revenues and, therefore, will have the ability to pay the wage. If this can be documented with clear and convincing evidence, this is an additional argument to be made.

I. Some arguments have been accepted which explain and document one particularly negative financial year and request that USCIS review the documentation under a "totality of the circumstances" argument. For example, after 9/11, many businesses in New York City experienced severe financial reversals. If such a downturn occurred over one particular time period, but it can be demonstrated that the business recovered and that the downturn was a result of outside factors, this also could be cited in the arguments submitted to USCIS.

J. If the petitioner can provide documentation that losses sustained by the business can be traced directly to substantial funds being reinvested into the business for expansion and purchase of equipment, then this would be evidence related to documenting the petitioning employer's ability to pay. Such evidence should be well documented and be accompanied by a letter from the accountant.

K. Documentation could be submitted that the petitioner is a subsidiary or owned by a larger entity that has the ability to pay or has pledged the funds necessary to pay the wage.

L. Arguments have been made that officers' compensation will be reduced in order to pay the wage to the beneficiary. The ability of the officer to support himself on a lower salary most certainly should be submitted.

The most challenging aspect of proving the ability to pay is investigating all of the facts and the circumstances of the employer. You will need to review all the documentation and, especially, income tax returns to help the petitioner develop the strongest arguments possible. In those difficult cases, you should seriously consider utilizing the services of a CPA or financial officer of the petitioning entity.

Some practitioners have become concerned, as it was the practice in the past to "refile" a second I-140 petition after the first petition was denied rather than file an appeal of the denial. Under current regulations, the I-140 petition must be filed within six months of the approval of the labor certification. USCIS will reject Form I-140 petitions that require an approved labor certification that are filed with a supporting approved labor certification that has expired.

Exceptions: USCIS will continue to accept amended or duplicate Form I-140 petitions that are filed with a copy of a labor certification that is expired at the time the amended or duplicate Form I-140 petition is filed if the original approved labor certification was filed in support of a previously filed petition during the labor certification validity period.[5]

Thus, clearly, once a Form I-140 is properly filed within the validity dates of an approved labor certification, a second petition may be filed at a later date.

As mentioned, the Administrative Appeals Office (AAO) has somewhat consistently taken a "totality of the circumstances" position in determining whether the employee has the ability to pay the proffered wage. Thus, counsel should work with the employer to collect all documentation which will demonstrate ability to pay the wage which, taken together, would support the I-140 petition.

In summary, it is a "best practice" to review income tax returns and other financial documentation with the employer *prior to filing* the Labor Certification, particularly when the company is small or not currently employing the beneficiary. Otherwise, a review of all possible documentation should be made with the employer and most certainly if it proves challenging, the services of a CPA should be enlisted.

TABLE OF RECURRING HOUSEHOLD MONTHLY EXPENSES OF [EMPLOYER'S NAME]

	2002	2003	2004	2005	2006
Mortgage or Rent Payment					
Auto Payment					
Installment Loan(s)					
Credit Card Payments					
Household Expenses					

The above amounts represent the monthly average of [EMPLOYER'S NAME]'s monthly expenses.

---

[5] USCIS Interoffice Memorandum, D. Neufeld, "Interim Guidance Regarding the Impact of the Department of Labor (DOL) Final Rule . . . on Determining Labor Certification Validity and the Prohibition of Labor Certification Substitution Requests (June 1, 2007), *published on* AILA InfoNet at Doc. No. 07062172 (*posted* June 21, 2007).

USCIS SAYS, 'ALL OR NOTHING':
LATEST DEVELOPMENTS ON SUCCESSOR-IN-INTEREST

by Susan C. Ellison and Paull Hejinian[*]

U.S. Citizenship and Immigration Services (USCIS) has been applying a more stringent standard of "successor-in-interest" in adjudicating I-140 petitions by employers who have taken over labor certifications or petitions filed by companies they have acquired or merged with. This new approach by USCIS changes what was an increasingly open approach by the Department of Labor (DOL), legacy INS, and USCIS until recently. Under this new standard, a new employer can assume a pending case only when it has acquired all the assets and liabilities of the prior employer. This is a standard that does not reflect the realities of most corporate transactions, and recent I-140 denials on this issue have taken some employers (and their attorneys) by surprise.

SHORT HISTORY OF
SUCCESSOR-IN-INTEREST

Responsibility for deciding whether an acquiring company qualifies as a successor-in-interest to a prior employer was assigned to legacy INS in a 1992 agreement with the Department of Labor.[1] Under this agreement, USCIS (and prior to 2003, INS) is responsible during an I-140 adjudication for determining whether an approved labor certification is still valid despite a change in the original sponsoring employer. The burden was placed on the new employer to establish in the I-140 petition that it was a successor-in-interest to the employer named on the labor certification.

The successor-in-interest rule applied by INS required a new employer to demonstrate that it was engaged in the same business as the original employer, that it had the ability to pay the offered wage, that the job opportunity outlined in the labor certification remained the same, and that the new employer had acquired all of the predecessor employer's assets and liabilities.[2] All of these requirements make sense, and are driven by the regulations,[3] except the new standard that the new company assume *all* assets and liabilities.

The legal authority on which legacy INS often relied in requiring assumption of *all* assets and liabilities came from a single Board of Immigration Appeals decision in 1986, *Matter of Dial Auto Repair Shop, Inc.*[4] A close reading of the decision, however, does not reveal any legal analysis of this particular aspect of successor-in-interest, nor is any precedent on the issue cited. In fact, the holding in the case stands for the much broader principle that where "a successorship in interest is recognized, the petitioner bears the burden of proof to establish eligibility in all respects as of the date the application for labor certification is originally accepted for processing by the Department of Labor."[5]

In *Matter of Dial Auto Repair*, the original employer, an auto repair shop, dissolved and ceased doing business. The new employer founded its business at the same location and offered employment to the beneficiary of the original employer's labor certification application. In adjudicating the I-140 petition filed by the new employer, legacy INS denied the petition based on the new employer's failure to establish that the original employer had the ability to pay the wage at the time the petition was filed. Ability to pay was the central issue on appeal, and the Board ultimately based its dismissal of the appeal on the ability-to-pay issue.

The question of whether the new employer qualified as a successor-in-interest was incidental to the

---

[*] **Susan C. Ellison** is a partner in the Boston office of Fragomen, Del Rey, Bernsen & Loewy LLP and a member of the adjunct faculty at Boston College Law School.

Paull Hejinian is a partner in the San Francisco office of Fragomen, Del Rey, Bernsen & Loewy LLP.

[1] Immigration and Naturalization Service (INS) Memorandum, D. Kulick, "Amending Certified Labor Certification Applications" (Apr. 1992), *reprinted in* 69 *Interpreter Releases* 529 (Apr. 27, 1992).

[2] INS Memorandum, J. Puleo, "Amendments to Labor Certifications in I-140 Petitions" (Dec. 10, 1993), *reprinted in* 70 *Interpreter Releases* 1692 (Dec. 20, 1993).

[3] 20 CFR §656.30(c)(2).

[4] *Matter of Dial Auto Repair Shop, Inc.*, 19 I&N Dec. 481 (Comm'r 1986).

[5] *Id.*

legal analysis and final decision. That question was raised at the end of the written decision, and only in the context of being an unresolved issue. Specifically, the Board said, after affirming the original decision, that in order for the new employer to prove its claim of having assumed all of the rights, duties and obligations of the prior employer, the employer would need to provide a copy of the contract or agreement between the two entities, and that if its claim was found to be untrue, there would be grounds for invalidating the labor certification.[6] Rather than creating a rule of law or legal standard to follow, it seems the Board was only restating the assertion made by the employer/petitioner that it was a successor-in-interest because it had assumed all of the assets and liabilities of the original employer.

Over the years, legacy INS gradually relaxed its position on successor-in-interest. In 1995, INS proposed a rule stating that a successor employer must assume "substantially all of the assets and liabilities of the predecessor."[7] The rule was never promulgated but was adopted by USCIS in its *Adjudicator's Field Manual* (AFM):

> Successor in interest occurs when the prospective employer of an alien (and the entity that filed the certified labor certification application form) has undergone a change in ownership, such as an acquisition or merger, or some other form of change such as corporate restructuring or merger with another business entity, and the new or merged, or restructured entity assumes substantially all of the rights, duties, obligations and assets or the original entity.[8]

Further, legacy INS, in private opinion letters addressed to immigration attorneys, explicitly addressed the question of what constitutes a successor-in-interest in the nonimmigrant and immigrant visa petition contexts. In a letter dated March 22, 2001, Efren Hernandez, Director, Business and Trade Services, reiterated INS's position that an amended H-1B petition is not required where "a second entity assumes substantially all of the assets and liabilities of the first entity," and went on to say that INS has "stated both at conferences and in correspondence that the assumption of liabilities refers to immigration-related liabilities, such as LCA obligations and violations . . . . It does not refer to non-immigration-

related obligations and liabilities, such as environmental or tort obligations . . ."[9] In a letter dated October 17, 2001, Hernandez again provided clarification of INS's interpretation of successor-in-interest, this time in a permanent residence scenario.[10] Where the new employer purchased a "significant portion" of the original employer's business assets, acquired a large number of its employees, and assumed the immigration-related rights and obligations for the acquired foreign national employees, Hernandez opined that the new employer was a successor-in-interest, stating that "INS has taken the position that a company is a successor in interest when it has taken on all of the immigration-related liabilities of the company it has acquired, merged, etc."[11] This interpretation, which was widely followed by employers, put the focus of the inquiry on the new company's ability and willingness to take on the foreign worker, rather than on the structure of the corporate change itself.

TEXAS SERVICE CENTER

In a surprising shift from what was generally believed to be current policy, the Texas Service Center recently began issuing Requests for Evidence and even denials of "successor" immigrant visa petitions based on the failure of a new employer to prove assumption of *all* assets and liabilities of the original employer. Even cases where the petitioner has clearly assumed all the immigration-related liability for the prior employer, and the job is otherwise unchanged, USCIS has denied the I-140 petition. When questioned by the American Immigration Lawyers Association in a December 2007 liaison meeting, Texas Service Center officials said that adjudicators "must continue to follow the framework provided in *Matter of Dial Auto Repair Shop, Inc.*"[12] The Texas Service Center went on to dismiss the Efren Hernandez letter of October 2001 as nonbinding, saying that "[l]egacy

---

[6] *Id.*

[7] 60 Fed. Reg. 29711 (June 6, 1995).

[8] AFM ch. 22.2(b)(5).

[9] Letter of Efren Hernandez III, Director, Business and Trade Services, to Steven M. Ladik, HQ 70/6.2.8 (Mar. 22, 2001), *published on* AILA InfoNet at Doc. No. 01032901 (*posted* Mar. 29, 2001).

[10] Letter of Efren Hernandez III, Director, Business and Trade Services, to J. Douglas Donenfeld, HQ 70/6.1.3 (Oct. 17, 2001), *published on* AILA InfoNet at Doc. No. 01101939 (*posted* Oct. 19, 2001).

[11] *Id.*

[12] AILA/TSC Liaison Meeting, Dec. 3, 2007, Questions and Answers No. 11, *published on* AILA InfoNet at Doc. No. 08010365 (*posted* Jan. 3, 2008).

INS and now USCIS endeavor to respond to inquiries from the public in as expeditious a manner as possible. However, our response does not constitute a policy statement regarding the questions posed in such inquiries." The Texas Service Center went on to say that "[i]n the event that USCIS determines it appropriate to issue a formal policy statement, it will certainly take into consideration concerns that have been expressed to USCIS in individual inquiries, as well as those of other members of the public, in doing so." The Texas Service Center also cited the AFM, quoting the manual as saying that successorship occurs when the new entity/employer "assumes the rights, duties, obligations and assets of the original entity," which is demonstrated by submission of a contract or agreement, and evidence of ability to pay.[13] Interestingly, however, as mentioned above, the relevant section of the AFM employs the less stringent "substantially all assets and liabilities" standard.[14]

THE REALITY OF
SUCCESSOR-IN-INTEREST

There is a conflict between USCIS's "all or nothing" method of analyzing corporate acquisitions, and how real-world acquisitions are structured and carried out. A large percentage of acquisition transactions, particularly of closely held companies, are asset sales. In these transactions, the purchasing company acquires a target company's assets, or substantially all of its assets, instead of acquiring its stock. One of the strategic rationales in an asset purchase is avoiding acquisition of the target company's hidden liabilities, such as those stemming from a breach of contract or a defective product. An asset sale also allows the purchasing company to obtain significant tax benefits from the depreciation of the assets. In an asset sale agreement, the purchasing company will typically assume only those liabilities it explicitly designates, such as bank debt, accounts payable, and employment contracts of existing employees. Of course, it can also expressly assume immigration-related responsibilities.

Under the Texas Service Center's restrictive policy, companies involved in asset sales would *never* qualify as successors-in-interest, and a foreign national employee who is "acquired" as a result of the

transaction would not be able to preserve his or her employment-based immigration case status, regardless of whether the job opportunity remained the same, the company/employer had the ability to pay, and the foreign national met the qualifications for the offered position. This seems a harsh and unfair result that does nothing to further the objectives of the permanent residence process.

DEPARTMENT OF LABOR POSITION

The Department of Labor's standards for successor-in-interest are more flexible than these new USCIS standards.[15] Several pre-PERM cases of the Board of Alien Labor Certification Appeals (BALCA) establish that a new employer can substitute for a prior employer as long as the change does not change the nature of the underlying job opportunity.[16] Fortunately, under PERM, some of this flexibility continues. DOL allows a new employer to use the acquired employer's advertising and recruitment, containing the prior employer's company name, as the basis for a PERM case under its own name.[17] In an audit, the DOL will determine whether the new employer is a successor-in-interest based on "the totality of the circumstances, including whether the current employer has assumed the assets and liabilities of the former entity with respect to the job opportunity."[18] Although the rigidity of the electronic filing process makes it very difficult, as a practical matter, to change employers on a pending case, these rules give employers the comfort of allowing a pending case to continue through to approval.

---

[13] *Id.*

[14] *Id.* USCIS in its Answer to Question 11 cites to ch. 22.2(b)(3)(D) of the AFM, which is incorrect. The correct citation is AFM ch. 22(b)(5). *See supra* note 8.

[15] *See* R. Rulon and G. Forney, "Is 'Successor In Interest' Dead and Buried Under PERM?" *Immigration & Nationality Law Handbook* 211 (AILA 2007–08 Ed.).

[16] *Matter of International Contractors, Inc.* 89 INA 278 (BALCA June 13, 1990).

[17] PERM FAQ round 10 (May 9, 2007). If a merger, acquisition, or any other corporate change in ownership occurs between the time of recruitment and the time of submission, resulting in a disparity between the employer's name shown on the advertising used to recruit for a job opportunity and the employer's name on the submitted ETA Form 9089, the employer must be prepared to provide documentation—in the event of an audit—proving that it is a successor in interest, a determination made based on the totality of the circumstances, including whether the current employer has assumed the assets and liabilities of the former entity with respect to the job opportunity. *See www.immigration.com/newsletter1/ dolfaq10perm.pdf.*

[18] *Id.*

CONCLUSION

Corporate transactions are often complex and include all sorts of liability-limiting provisions, but in many cases these transactions do not change the nature of the jobs held by employees. The specific structure of a corporate transaction should not affect the validity of an I-140 as long as the new employer offers the same job opportunity, in the same location, at the same salary. If the purpose of the labor certification is to establish a shortage of U.S. workers for that position, what does the structure of a corporate change matter as long as the labor market test was conducted completely and in good faith?

PROVING AN H-1B OCCUPATION IS A SPECIALIST

by Martin J. Lawler[*]

There are two ways to prove a position is a "specialist occupation" as defined at 8 CFR §214.2(h)(4). One is to show that the "industry standard" for the position is a degree or equivalent work experience.[1] The other is by demonstrating that the job is so complex that it requires a degree or work experience equal to a degree to successfully perform the duties.[2]

PROVING INDUSTRY STANDARD

It can be challenging to prove an industry standard. In the controversial *Louisiana Philharmonic* case,[3] even though the evidence showed 90 percent of philharmonic musicians have degrees in music, the district court upheld the finding of the Administrative Appeals Office (AAO) that musicians are not specialists because they are hired based on auditions not on educational credentials.

For cases involving engineers and other traditionally "professional positions," a statement by the employer that the job is a specialist occupation or requires a degree is usually sufficient. A typical statement is something like this:

> This software engineering job requires a degree in electrical engineering, computer science, mathematics, or a closely related field.

Occupations for which the issue is not so clear, such as a graphic artist, marketing manager, hotel manager and so forth, more evidence is needed. The place to start is the Department of Labor's *Occupational Outlook Handbook* (OOH)[4] on which U.S.

Citizenship and Immigration Services (USCIS) often relies. In *Matter of [Name not Provided]*, (AAO Feb. 23, 2006), it was held that a graphic designer who owned his own firm was a specialist. The service center director had found the petitioner, a start-up company, did not establish that it had "sufficient H-1B caliber work to keep the beneficiary employed on a full time basis for three years." In reversing the director, the AAO stated:

> The AAO routinely consults the *Handbook* for its information about the duties and educational requirements of particular occupations. The proffered position is a graphic designer. On appeal, counsel provides additional documentation regarding the petitioner's clients and work product, and the beneficiary's duties. Despite the fact that the beneficiary may also be engaged in some administrative tasks as a sole proprietor, most of the duties of the position include those of a graphic designer, which the *Handbook* indicates could not be performed without the training and education that are included in a bachelor's degree in graphic design. The petitioner has, thus, established the criteria set forth at 8 CFR §214.2(h)(4)(iii)(A)(1).

The OOH is published yearly, and job requirements change. Thus the latest edition must be referenced.

Some other ways to prove industry standard include expert opinions, newspaper ads showing a degree is required by other employees, and university or major corporate criteria for such a position. These types of proof are often challenged by USCIS, and more evidence may be needed such as the details of the advertised job and testimony from human-resource experts.

PROVING THE COMPLEXITY OF THE JOB

For other specialty occupations, arguing that the job requires a degree because it is complex is more likely to be successful than proving industry standard. The employer is in the best position to give the details of the job duties and explain why the duties require a degreed worker. Employer conclusory statements without detail are insufficient. Also, any independent statements by counsel will be ignored.

---

[*] **Martin J. Lawler** is the author of *Professionals: A Matter of Degree*, a treatise on business visas. Martin has authored many books, book chapters, and articles. He has lectured at Harvard, Stanford, and other universities. At the 2006 AILA annual conference, Lawler organized and chaired a unique three-hour workshop on administrative appeals. He is the 1996 recipient of the AILA Jack Wasserman Memorial Award for excellence in immigration litigation. He also has received a number of AILA presidential awards.

[1] 8 CFR §214.2(h)(4)(iii)(A)(3).

[2] 8 CFR §214.2(h)(4)(iii)(A)(4).

[3] *La. Philharmonic Orchestra v. INS*, 2000 U.S. Dist. LEXIS 3331 (E.D. La. Mar. 15, 2000).

[4] Bureau of Labor Statistics, U.S. Department of Labor, *Occupational Outlook Handbook,* 2008–09 Ed.

A graphic designer is an excellent example of a position that has been found to be a specialty occupation,[5] but not all petitions are granted. Positions at large companies and those involving sophisticated advertising are likely found to be specialty occupations. For a small company, the job of creating local newspaper ads and small company web pages may well be denied a specialist petition and an appeal to the AAO becomes necessary. A firm's letter supporting an H-1B petition for a graphic designer, explaining why the occupation is so complex it requires a graphic arts degree, might include the following:

> We will be placing ads in magazines, such as Wired, trade journals and other press. Quality of graphics, from packaging to user icons and ad campaigns, show our clients that we have quality products. Apple has been very successful with high quality graphics for embedded users (such as icons, layout, etc.) to their advertising. It conveys ease of use to customers. Designing the consumer experience and making it as simple as possible is an integral part of this position. Only a person with a degree in graphic design can have the theoretical, technical, and application expertise to do this job.

The letters from the employer also may explain the projects involved, theories used, interaction with other professionals, responsibilities, independent decisions, and relationships with other degreed specialists.

An employer letter for a color specialist for a post-production film firm where the foreign national had a master's degree in computer science would include something like the following:

> We wish to employ Ms. B, at will, as a color scientist. Color scientists are responsible for maintaining color consistency through all video and film services, which is a very critical aspect of the services we provide our clients. Ms. B's responsibilities will include color space conversion, calibration, sharpening and noise reduction of images, as well as restoration. She will report to the vice president, engineering.

> Ms. B will be responsible for building and programming our look-up tables. A computer science background is required to program this computer-assisted monitoring equipment. We are in the color-correction business for feature films.

> …This requires specific knowledge of differences in color between film and video and the knowledge and ability to look at the film and determine how to make it look different by applying LUTs in the color corrector or video projector so when the image is shot back to film it reflects these differences…. If the programming is not done correctly for the look-up tables, our final output to film is no good and may cause the film to be color-corrected again at great expense ….

> Ms. B will also maintain…digital cinema initiatives specifications for the display device using digital projection devices. Ms. B will also calibrate our film recorders with the labs daily using film output devices.[6]

The AAO held in *Matter of [Name not Provided]* (AAO Jan. 28, 2005)[7] that a chef was a specialty occupation at a restaurant with 140 employees with three outlets, one of which was a venue for the television program, "Sex and The City." The AAO quoted the Department of Labor's OOH and found:

> It is therefore, necessary, to consider the nature of the petitioner's operations and the specific duties of the proffered position when determining whether the job is a specialty occupation. Here, the petitioner is a large specialty restaurant with a complex operational and delivery structure. The duties of the proffered position are more complex than those described in the Handbook for a typical chef's position. Thus, the petitioner's requirement of a bachelor's degree is a reasonable requirement. The petitioner has established that the nature of the specific duties is so specialized and complex that knowledge required to perform the duties is usually associated with the attainment of a baccalaureate or higher degree. 8 CFR §214.2(h)(4)(iii)(A)(4). The proffered position is, therefore, a specialty occupation.

The AAO in *Matter of X* (AAO Nov. 29, 2004)[8] found that an executive housekeeper is a specialist for a leading hotel. The AAO concluded:

> While many duties listed in the job description are routine to any hotel housekeeping position, the level of services and accommodations provided by the petitioner add elements of speciali-

---

[5] *Young China Daily v. Chappell*, 742 F. Supp. 552 (N.D. Cal. 1989).

[6] This case was approved.

[7] 33 *Immig. Rptr.* B2-57 AAO Designation: N/A.

[8] 31 *Immig. Rptr.* B2-27 AAO Designation: D2.

zation and complexity to the nature of the duties. For example, for the past eleven years, the petitioner has been the only hotel in southern California with the American Automobile Association (AAA) five-diamond ranking and the Mobil four-star ranking. The petitioner is one of a group of seven luxury hotels located in the United States and abroad. In addition, the size and variety of the housekeeping staff, as well as the budgetary responsibilities add complexity to the described duties. Viewing these factors, in combination with the expert opinions provided by three individuals very knowledgeable with regard to the lodging industry, the petitioner has established that the position requires a baccalaureate degree in a specific specialty, or its equivalent. Thus, the petitioner has established the fourth criterion of 8 CFR §214.2(h)(4)(iii)(A).

EXPERT TESTIMONY

Excellent evidence about whether the job requires a degree is the testimony from an expert such as a university professor,[9] a professional association manager, or a person who oversees similar professionals elsewhere. An expert opinion must explain the author's credentials and establish his or her ability to give an opinion; show familiarity with the issues in the case, and explain in detail why the duties of the position could not be performed by someone without the required education and other background. The expert should review the case file, interview a manager or executive at the company about the job, and explain what resources he or she used to reach the ultimate conclusion.

An expert's opinion can explain how theories and principles used in certain college courses are applied in different aspects of the job duties. This can be very persuasive. The following is an excerpt from a professor's opinion involving a marketer for a travel business:

The job duties required for the instant position necessitate that an individual be familiar with theoretical and academic concepts in business administration, travel and tourism management, and related areas. These concepts typically are taught in bachelor's-level classes in business administration, travel and tourism management, accounting, hospitality management, operational

management, marketing, financial management, personnel management, budgeting, cost accounting, contract management, quality control, and related subjects, or are learned through substantial professional training and work experience in business administration, travel and tourism management.

PREPONDERANCE OF THE EVIDENCE

Petitions must be proved only by a "preponderance" of the evidence. This standard has been reaffirmed in a USCIS memorandum[10] and in a USCIS Adopted Decision.[11] Preponderance of the evidence means:

The standard of proof should not be confused with the burden of proof. …The standard of proof applied in most administrative immigration proceedings is the "preponderance of the evidence" standard. Thus, even if the director has some doubt as to the truth, if the petitioner submits relevant, probative, and credible evidence that leads the director to believe that the claim is "probably true" or "more likely than not," the applicant or petitioner has satisfied the standard of proof. *See U.S. v. Cardoza-Fonseca*, 480 U.S. 421 (1987) (defining "more likely than not" as a greater than 50 percent probability of something occurring). If the director can articulate a material doubt, it is appropriate for the director to either request additional evidence or, if that doubt leads the director to believe that the claim is probably not true, deny the application or petition.[12]

If a denial says the applicant must present "clear" evidence, an illegal standard of proof has been used.

CLARITY

The employer's supporting letter should be edited to provide concise explanations of the responsibilities of the job. Rewrite "corporate speak," such as "the consultant will provide solutions for clients," to be more plain and descriptive, like "the systems analyst will research and develop software programs customized for each client."

---

[9] *See Hong Kong TV v. Ilchert*, 685 F.2d 712 (N.D. Cal. 1988).

[10] USCIS Memorandum. M. Aytes, "Delegation of Authority for I-751, 'Petition to Remove Conditions on Residence'" (Jan. 11, 2006), *published on* AILA InfoNet at Doc. No. 06021313 (*posted* Jan. 21, 2006).

[11] *Matter of Chawathe* (AAO Jan. 11, 2006).

[12] Aytes Memo, *supra* note 10.

SUMMARY

Often, it is easier to prove that the duties of a job are so complicated its performance requires a degree than to try to use newspaper and Internet ads to prove industry standard. And, yes, even managing a modern dairy can be a highly complex job. So at the right dairy, the dairy manager is a specialist occupation.

BEST PRACTICES IN KEY AREAS OF PERM LABOR CERTIFICATION: THE JOB DESCRIPTION, MINIMUM REQUIREMENTS, AND RECRUITMENT STRATEGIES

by Romy K. Kapoor, Edward Litwin, and Stacy Shore[*]

Success in labor certification practice truly comes from mastering the basics. No matter what the labor certification application form itself may look like—whether it's the old ETA Form 750, the current ETA Form 9089, the proposed ETA Form 9089 pending with the Department of Labor (DOL), or any version they may create in the future—the basic elements of the process always remain the same, as does the goal—proving to DOL that there are no qualified, ready, willing, and able U.S. workers to fill the available job. The key elements to master include crafting the job description, fine-tuning the minimum requirements for the position, drafting the advertisement, and conducting recruitment in a good-faith manner that effectively demonstrates a lack of minimally qualified U.S. workers. An additional key element since the introduction of the Program Electronic Review Management (PERM) process is the audit—preparation for and response to. In this article, we will take these key areas and provide you with some tried and tested best practices.

[*] **Romy K. Kapoor** was the program chair for the AILA 2006 Annual Conference. He is an elected director of AILA's Board of Governors and member of the DOL Liaison Committee. Mr. Kapoor is the founder of Kapoor & Associates, with offices in Atlanta and Orlando. He has spoken extensively on business– and family-based immigration topics for AILA and the State Bars of Georgia and Florida. Mr. Kapoor was named a Georgia Super Lawyer in 2006, 2007, and 2008.

Edward Litwin is the sole shareholder of Litwin & Associates. He is certified as a specialist in immigration law by the California State Bar Board of Legal Specialization. He is included in *The Best Lawyers in America*, *The International Who's Who of Corporate Immigration Lawyers*, *Who's Who in American Law*, *Who's Who in Executives & Professionals*, *National Registry of Who's Who*, and *Strathmore's Who's Who*.

Stacy Shore practices at Trow & Rahal as a senior immigration attorney. She has represented corporations in connection with their business immigration matters for over eight years. Ms. Shore currently serves as chair-elect of the AILA DC Chapter. She is a graduate of Beasley School of Law at Temple University and a member of the District of Columbia and Pennsylvania Bar Associations. Ms. Shore is a frequent speaker on immigration-related topics.

CRAFTING THE FOUNDATION: DRAFTING THE JOB DESCRIPTION

Although the PERM regulations[1] provide specific guidance about the recruitment steps and, to some extent, the level of detail required in job advertisements, they do not provide specific guidance about the content of the job description. On the ETA Form 9089, the job description is listed at Part H, Question 11. Practically speaking, there is great flexibility in the length of the description. If the description does not fit into the designated field on page 3 of the application, there is an option to create an addendum that appears at the end of the application. In light of such wide latitude, the following are some tips for crafting the job description.

The first step in drafting the job description is to talk with an authorized representative of the sponsoring company to determine the job duties. Request a copy of the company's job description for the position. Some companies even maintain job manuals. If the company does not maintain formal job descriptions, ask for a list of the employee's primary job duties.

Although the job description used for a nonimmigrant petition may be helpful as a resource, there are several reasons not to rely on it for the labor certification. One may want to maintain a level of consistency, but sometimes nonimmigrant petitions are drafted in haste with a cursory job description. Also, the job may have changed so that the petition no longer accurately reflects the primary job duties.[2] Furthermore, the labor certification is for a prospective position—the position the employee will hold upon becoming a permanent resident. Usually these positions are the same, but if the employee is on the verge of being promoted, consider using the new position on the labor certification application.

---

[1] 20 CFR §§655.0 to 656.41.

[2] Although the task at hand is the PERM application, if the employer advises that the job has materially changed, one should consider whether an amendment to the nonimmigrant petition is required.

Once a foundation has been provided, evaluate the description to determine which duties should be included and in which order. One must find a balance between being specific enough to describe the primary duties accurately, but general enough so that if the employee receives an inline promotion or changes departments no new labor certification would be required. For example, if the employee is a software consultant working on a long-term project, the description can mention the primary job duties without mentioning the specific project—because in a year or two the employee may be working on a different project. If the job description is too specific, a new labor certification may be required, depending on where the employee is in the permanent residence process.

Another reason to use a more general job description is that the employer may want to sponsor multiple employees in the same or similar occupation. If there are multiple employees, draft the job description so that recruitment can be combined. The particular skills for each position within the occupation may be included in the "specific skills or other requirements" section (H14 on ETA Form 9089). However, some practitioners prefer to list the skills and requirements in the job description itself, particularly if there is a concern that the skills are outside those listed in the O*NET report, thereby requiring business necessity documentation.[3] Also, if the print advertisements will include part or all of the job description, be mindful of the cost for the employer.

Another factor when drafting the job description is anticipating how the state workforce agency (SWA) will categorize the position. The Occupational Employment Statistics (OES) wage survey has a limited number of occupations despite recent efforts to expand the list.[4] If the employee's position could fall under more than one occupation, review the O*NET reports and the *Dictionary of Occupational Titles* (DOT) to determine which occupation is most appropriate for the application.

For example, the OES wage survey does not include the occupation of business analyst. Depending on the crux of the job duties, the SWA may use the occupation of computer systems analyst, business operations specialist, or management analyst, among others. One may suggest a Standard Occupational Classification (SOC) Code to the SWA in the prevailing wage request to aid in its decision-making process. Another option is to provide an alternative survey for business analyst; however, one would need to look to the DOT for the Specific Vocational Preparation (SVP) level since alternative surveys do not include Job Zones.

Also consider whether the job requirements are normal based on the Job Zone assigned, and review the wage levels. If the job duties are beyond those listed in the O*NET report, the SWA may add a point to its worksheet, thereby increasing the prevailing wage level. For example, do not use words such as "manage" or "supervise" unless the person is a true manager; otherwise the SWA may misinterpret the level of responsibility assigned to the employee. To aid the SWA about the level of experience required, begin each job description with guiding language such as "Under close supervision," "Under general supervision," and "Working independently" so that the SWA understands the employee's level of responsibility in this position. Consider these factors when crafting the job description rather than leave the decision to the SWA when the prevailing wage request is submitted.

Furthermore, when drafting the job description, be mindful of whether the employee gained experience with the same employer. To include experience the employee gained with the same employer, one must show that the position in which the employee gained the experience and the position for which certification is being sought are substantially dissimilar.[5] Be sure to chart the two job descriptions carefully so that one may distinguish between the two positions.

FOLLOW THE ZONES: WHEN ARE REQUIREMENTS NORMAL?

Whether job requirements are normal has been under considerable debate over the past three years since the focus on Job Zones emerged with PERM's implementation in 2005. Not only is it difficult to interpret the SVP levels assigned to the Job Zones, the SVP levels for certain positions dropped a point, which is inconsistent with the industry standards. For example, under the new schema, a software en-

---

[3] *See www.foreignlaborcert.doleta.gov/faqsanswers.cfm# jobreq3* (Office of Foreign Labor Certification's frequently asked questions and answers, Job Requirements/Duties, number 3).

[4] *See www.flcdatacenter.com* (Foreign Labor Certification Data Center Online Wage Library).

[5] 20 CFR §656.17(i)(3).

gineer falls under Job Zone 4, which has a listed SVP of 7 to < 8. During past AILA conference presentations, DOL has made clear that 7 to < 8 is really just 7.[6] Since many employers require a master's degree for the position of software engineer, requiring a master's degree plus work experience would elevate the requirements above the designated SVP, thereby creating the need for the employer to provide business necessity documentation. Thus, if an occupation is classified as a Job Zone 4 and the SVP is 7, the normal job requirements may not exceed a master's degree and zero years of experience *or* a bachelor's degree and two years of experience.

The requirements on the labor certification should be the actual minimum hiring requirements.[7] Thus, when the employer states that the minimum requirements are above the SVP limitations, it must be prepared to provide business necessity documentation. With increasing audits, there is more of a chance that the business necessity defense presented may not be deemed satisfactory, so the employer should be prepared to take the risk or lower the requirements to fall within the SVP.

When reviewing whether the requirements are normal, in addition to education and work experience, one must also consider the skills. Practitioners should carefully review O*NET reports to review the skills listed to determine whether the required skills are normal.[8] Some practitioners purposely build several skills into the job description to avoid the risk that they will be deemed not normal. Others list the skills in the current H14 field for special skills and other requirements and compile the required business necessity documentation in preparation for an audit.

As mentioned above, if the position could fall within one or more occupational categories, review the Job Zones to see if they differ. For example, if the position combines the job duties of a financial analyst (Job Zone 4/SVP 7) and an economist (Job Zone 5/SVP 8) and the job requires a master's degree, and if the SWA classifies the position as an economist, the need for business necessity documentation about the education and experience is eliminated. In such cases the SWA's classification makes a significant difference.

In completing the ETA Form 9089, practitioners have learned from experience that it is better to check "not normal" and be ready to provide business necessity than to check "normal" and have the burden to prove the requirements are normal. Prior to PERM, practitioners steered clear of going beyond the SVP; however, with the restrictive Job Zones that are inconsistent with many employers' standard requirements, providing business necessity justification is now normal. Although the documentation is often the same, the burden to show that the job requirements are normal is greater than marking "not normal" on the application and compiling business necessity. With increased audits, the playing field will see more tests, and only time will tell what will work and what will not.

DOCUMENT, DOCUMENT, DOCUMENT: PREPARING FOR BUSINESS NECESSITY

Business necessity documentation most commonly is required when the years of education and/or experience exceed the SVP or if the skills and/or other requirements go beyond those listed on the O*NET report. In addition, an employer also must show business necessity when the job requires a foreign language.[9] In fact, the DOL will automatically audit the application when a foreign language is required, even if the position is for an interpreter or the job is located in Puerto Rico. In such instances, the employer must be prepared to show that the occupation requires knowledge of the foreign language or it is needed to communicate with a large majority of customers, contractors, coworkers, or subordinates.[10]

To establish business necessity, the employer "must demonstrate that the job duties and requirements bear a reasonable relationship to the occupation in the context of the employer's business and are essential to perform the job in a reasonable manner."[11]

[6] Comment made by Elissa M. McGovern, Esq., Regulatory and Policy Manager, Office of Foreign Labor Certification, DOL Panel at AILA National Spring CLE Conference, April 4, 2008. This is also evident to lawyers who have received application denials regarding this issue. AILA continues to challenge this assertion and DOL has confirmed it is looking into the issue further.

[7] 20 CFR §656.17(i).

[8] *See www.foreignlaborcert.doleta.gov/faqsanswers.cfm# jobreq3* (Office of Foreign Labor Certification's frequently asked questions and answers, Job Requirements/Duties, number 3).

[9] 20 CFR §656.17(h)(2).

[10] 20 CFR §656.17(h)(2)(i).

[11] 20 CFR §656.17(h)(1).

When the requirements exceed the SVP, follow these steps to compile business necessity documentation:

- Speak with an informed representative of the company.

- Ask the difficult questions upfront, before recruitment begins.

- Request an explanation *in writing* for any requirements beyond the SVP and/or O*NET report.

- Inquire whether there are any other employees who have less education, experience, or skills than those being required.

- Collect resumes of the employees in the same position to show that all employees have the minimum requirements.

- Review the employer's previous advertisements for the same or similar positions and maintain copies to show that the employer has historically required the education, experience, and/or skills for the position.

- Print advertisements (*i.e.,* newspaper and online ads) from comparable employers to show that the requirements are standard for the industry as well as for the company.

- From company websites, print bios of people who hold the same position to show that they possess the requirements.

- Include the explanations in the recruitment report and attach the corroborating evidence in the audit package.

After a thorough investigation, if there are employees in the same or similar position who do not possess the minimum requirements, ask more questions. Can the position in the labor certification be distinguished from the others? For example, is the proffered position a job that handles a high volume of customers, services the employer's most prestigious clients, or handles more complex projects? Sometimes the employer cannot justify the requirements and it is up to the practitioner to guide the employer to formulate the actual minimum hiring requirements. In this era of increased audits, it is imperative that the employer document business necessity satisfactorily. If DOL finds that the employer willfully misrepresented the requirements, the employer could be required to file all its labor certification applications under supervised recruitment.[12]

---

[12] 20 CFR §656.20(3)(ii)(b).

WALKING THE FINE LINE: POSITION REQUIREMENTS AND THE POTENTIAL MINE FIELD OF DEGREE EQUIVALENCIES / WORK EXPERIENCE / COMBINATION OF DEGREES

One of the trickier tasks in completing the ETA Form 9089, given the constraints inherent in the form, is to determine how best to set forth the minimum requirements for the position, and in particular any alternative requirements. Doing so appropriately has become especially important now as U.S. Citizenship and Immigration Services (USCIS) service centers are closely scrutinizing the listed minimum requirements at the I-140 stage—first, to see if the beneficiary satisfies them; and second, to see if the petition qualifies for the requested EB-2 or EB-3 classification.

One of the first decisions to make is whether or not to use H-7 (alternative field of study). H-4-B (major field of study) allows one to list as many fields of study as desired. For example, "Computer Science, an Engineering discipline, or closely related field" is a typical entry. As such, there would be no need to use H-7. Moreover, one can possibly avoid using the "magic language"[13] with this strategy since the beneficiary qualifies for the position based on the primary educational requirement and not an alternative one.

When it comes to experience requirements, however, there is no way to stuff everything into the primary requirements. So if any experience other than in the type of job offered is acceptable, it should be listed in H-10 (acceptable experience in an alternate occupation). One can list multiple job titles (*e.g.,* "Postdoctoral Fellow or Research Associate"), or even describe the general nature of the acceptable occupation (*e.g.,* "Research involving the design of superstructures in earthquake prone regions"). The magic-language requirement will definitely be triggered if the beneficiary qualifies based on having this alternative experience.

It is important to note that H-8 (acceptable alternate combination of education and experience) can be marked no and H-10 can still be marked yes. H-8 is designed to cover a situation where there is one

---

[13] See R. Kapoor *et al.,* "A Magical Mystery Tour: Selected PERM Issues," *Immigration & Nationality Law Handbook* 180, 187–92 (AILA 2007–08 Ed.) (discussing "magic language" derived from *Matter of Francis Kellogg,* 1994 INA 00465 (BALCA Feb. 2, 1998) (en banc)).

combination of education/experience requirements that is primary (*e.g.,* Master's +2) and another combination that is secondary (Bachelor's + 5).

Overall, section H is one of the least artfully drafted sections of the original ETA Form 9089. The new form that due out in 2008 should significantly revise this section to improve its flow and function.

Nevertheless, no matter the format of the ETA Form 9089, the area of job requirements gets even trickier when the beneficiary does not have a U.S. degree, and even worse when the foreign degree equivalency comes from a combination of education and experience, or from a combination of degrees.[14]

The following are several typical scenarios illustrating how to complete section H of the ETA Form 9089 while anticipating the processing of the I-140 with USCIS.

In the first scenario, the beneficiary has four years of postsecondary education from abroad, from a single source—meaning all four years were taken at one college or university, resulting in the awarding of a Bachelor's degree. Here, no special treatment in the ETA Form 9089 is necessary, other than to check yes to the question in H-9 ("Is a foreign educational equivalent acceptable?"). Nevertheless, one should take care to use a reputable education evaluator who provides a detailed evaluation.

Next is the situation where the Bachelor's equivalency is based on a combination of education and experience. For example, the beneficiary has two years of postsecondary education, but the employer accepts his six years of experience in the field in combination with the two years of education to satisfy the Bachelor's degree requirement for the position. Adapted from the "3-for-1" rule in the H-1B context, this measure of degree equivalency is commonly used. However, this is not a magic ratio. Certainly other ratios—2:1 or even 1:1—can be defined by the employer. But if the beneficiary is already on H-1B with the employer and has qualified

for this status using the 3-for-1 rule, it would certainly be advised to remain consistent in the employment-based permanent residence context.

As for completing Section H, indicate "Bachelor's" in H-4, and then define the equivalency in H-14. For example, a successfully used phrase is "Each three years of progressively responsible work experience in the field will be considered equivalent to one year of college education to satisfy the educational requirement listed in H-4." The beneficiary will not qualify for EB-2 at the I-140 stage, even if the position requires five years of progressively responsible experience in addition to the Bachelor's degree. This is because the EB-2 regulations specifically require a U.S. baccalaureate degree or a foreign equivalent degree, and make no provision for an equivalent degree based on a combination of education and experience.[15]

The next example is where the Bachelor's equivalency is based on a combination of postsecondary degrees or education; for example, a three-year Bachelor's degree followed by a two-year Master's degree or a one-year postgraduate diploma (PGD). Again, "Bachelor's" is indicated in H-4. But the crucial element here is to define the equivalency in H-14 using very specific terms. For example, "A combination of foreign postsecondary education if determined to be equivalent to a U.S. Bachelor's degree in the field is acceptable to satisfy the educational requirement listed in H-4." However, getting EB-2 is unlikely where the combination of degrees include a three-year Bachelor's + one-year PGD, even if five years of progressively responsible experience is required. Here, USCIS has been taking the position that the bachelor's degree is not equivalent to a U.S. bachelor's degree, nor is the PGD; and even the combination of the two is not equivalent to a U.S. bachelor's degree.

Even greater resistance from USCIS can be expected where the position requires a Master's degree, especially if EB-2 classification is requested. Here one must remember the "six-year rule": in general, the beneficiary must have six years of postsecondary education. So any of the following common combination of degrees will be equivalent to a Master's degree and have a high likelihood of being granted EB-2 classification:

- Four-year Bachelor's + two-year Master's

---

[14] An invaluable resource in this area is R. Wada, *AILA's Focus on EB-2 & EB-3 Degree Equivalency* (2007), available from AILA Publications, *www.ailapubs.org*, (800) 982-2839. Also useful are the AILA/NSC liaison meeting minutes from April 12, 2007, *published on* AILA InfoNet at Doc. No. 07060161 (*posted* June 1, 2007), and INS Memorandum, M. Cronin & W. Yates, "Educational and Experience Requirements for Employment-Based Second Preference (EB-2) Immigrants" (Mar. 20, 2000), *published on* AILA InfoNet at Doc. No. 00032703 (*posted* Mar. 27, 2000).

[15] 8 CFR §204.5(k)(2).

- Three-year Bachelor's + one-year PGD + two-year Master's

- Three-year Bachelor's + three-year Master's

- Three-year Bachelor's + three-year PGD

In each of these scenarios, one would indicate "Master's" in H-14. However, there is no need to include any special combination of degree language in H-14, as is critical in the Bachelor's context.

While USCIS will not consider five years of postsecondary education to be equivalent to a Master's degree, EB-2 is possible if the position requires a Bachelor's and five years of progressively responsible experience in the field. For example, a three-year Bachelor's + two-year Master's would be considered equivalent to a U.S. Bachelor's degree, and if the position further requires five years of progressively responsible experience, then EB-2 classification is certainly possible.

TESTING THE JOB MARKET: WHERE TO RECRUIT?

Recruitment must take place within the 30/180-day window.[16] All jobs require two one-day ads[17] and a job order.[18] The regulations are specific about what information needs to be in the ad[19] but not in the job order. The assumption is that the SWAs will direct the employer in crafting a properly worded job order. The ads and job order are fundamental to all labor certifications that require a test of the labor market, both nonprofessional and professional.

Recruitment in a Newspaper of General Circulation

When advertising for professional occupations, the newspapers that must be used are newspapers of "general circulation . . . most appropriate to the occupation . . . and most likely to bring responses from . . . U.S. workers."[20] To be of general circulation, a newspaper must cover the whole area of intended employment.[21] For most locations, there is little question about the newspaper of general circulation. In areas where there are two potential papers, the one with the larger circulation would usually be most appropriate, but that is not always the case.

Recruitment by Choosing the Correct SWA

Choosing a SWA with which the job order is to be placed is normally a matter of selecting the SWA where the employer/employment is located. However, where an employee works off-site or is a "roving" employee, the relevant SWA must be carefully considered. If the alien's employment is stationary, then the SWA over that area of employment is the appropriate one. If the alien's geographic location "roves," then the policy under the old regulations is still applicable; that is, the SWA serving the area of the employer's headquarters will be used.[22]

Recruitment by Using Three Additional Recruitment Steps for Professional Positions

While the regulation lists 10 recruitment steps and how to document them, it has not defined the steps, explained what information needs to be conveyed in each step, or limited their applicability to only certain positions or industries.

Employers normally do not want to spend time and resources on advertisements and other recruitment efforts that are deemed unproductive. Therefore, none of the 10 steps offered by DOL may be accepted easily by some employers. If an employer normally uses any three of the steps listed in its normal, non–labor certification related recruitment, the employer will probably have no problem using these same steps for a labor certification. However, for employers that regularly use fewer than three of these steps, or never use any of them, it could be difficult to persuade them of the need.

---

[16] Recruitment must take place at least 30 days but no more than 180 days before filing the application, whether for a professional or nonprofessional job opportunity. Where the position qualifies as a professional one, with three additional recruitment steps required, one of the additional three steps can be within the 30-day limit. See 20 CFR §656.17.

[17] 20 CFR §§656.17(e)(1)(i)(B), (2)(ii).

[18] 20 CFR §§656.17(e)(1)(i)(A), (2)(i). A posting of notice that the application was filed is also required (20 CFR §656.10(d)(1)), but that is not considered "recruitment." Nonetheless, 20 CFR §656.10(d)(4) requires the posting to include all information listed in the ad, including where the applicants can apply.

[19] 20 CFR §656.17(f).

---

[20] 20 CFR §656.17(e)(1)(i)(B)(1). For nonprofessional occupations, the ad must be placed "in the newspaper of general circulation in the area of intended employment most appropriate to the occupation and the workers likely to apply for the job opportunity." 20 CFR §656.17(e)(2)(ii)(A).

[21] *Matter of MK ENTERPRISE Group, Inc.*, 2007-PER-00019 (BALCA May 16, 2007).

[22] DOL Stakeholders Liaison Minutes (Mar. 15, 2007), *published on* AILA InfoNet at Doc. No. 07041264 (*posted* Apr. 12. 2007).

Recruitment by Using the Right Three Additional Steps

Factors that are important to employers in choosing the three additional steps of recruitment are low price, ease of the process, and quickness of the step. While the following ranking is not a product of any comprehensive, scientific investigation, the 10 steps are listed in the general order of usefulness and attractiveness to many employers:

1. *Employer's website.* Most employers of professionals have a website. Adding a section for job opportunities, if one is not currently on the website, is relatively inexpensive and easy.

2. *Job search websites.* These are quite easy to find. Some of the more well-known include Craigslist, Monster, and CareerBuilder. Often, ads on such websites are available in conjunction with newspaper ads—it is quite possible to obtain newspaper ads and have corresponding website ads included for the same price as the newspaper ad or for only a minimal price increase. Prior to PERM, some certifying officers (COs) did not accept newspaper websites as a separate recruitment source. The PERM regulations specifically allow for this.[23]

3. *Employer referral program with incentives.* This is fairly easy to set up in any company. The program can be publicized by being included in an employee handbook or by being posted. "Incentive" means that employees will receive compensation for every person they refer who is hired.

4. *Campus placement office.* The preamble to the PERM regulations suggested that this step could be used only if the job requires a degree but no experience.[24] However, this limitation was not placed in the regulations, and DOL has rejected it.[25]

5. *Local and ethnic newspaper.* The preamble indicates that local and ethnic newspapers can be used "to the extent they are appropriate for the job opportunity."[26]

6. *Radio and television advertisements.* There is nothing in the regulations that limits the use of radio and television advertisements. Production costs and airtime costs, however, can be expensive. An ad on a community radio or television station may be much more reasonable.

7. *Trade and professional organizations.* These organizations can be used by recruiting through their newsletters or journals. Postings in local offices or reliance on "word of mouth" among the members would not be acceptable.

8. *On-campus recruitment.* Such recruitment normally requires extensive time and resource allocation. On-campus recruitment may not be available year round.

9. *Private employment firms.* Most employers have not used private employment firms for labor certification recruitment purposes. If an applicant is found and hired, their fees tend to be expensive.

10. *Job fairs.* These usually require significant advance planning. They also can require the attendance of one or more of the employers' staff for a whole day. Depending on the occupation and industry, they can be pricey. Some occupations may not be amenable to job fairs. Of course, a job fair that is cheap and can be "staffed" by a mere table with application forms and a box for application submission may be an attractive alternative for employers, as would a previously scheduled job fair that falls within the required time frame.

Good Faith in Recruitment

While the term "good faith" is not used in the regulations themselves, there is an assumption that good faith is an overriding principle in the labor certification process. The preamble to the PERM regulations notes that employers must recruit in good faith,[27] and not doing so could lead to the denial of the PERM application.[28]

"Good faith" is never defined, but it appears that following the PERM recruitment requirements and dealing with the results honestly would reflect good

---

[23] 20 CFR §656.17(e)(ii)(C).

[24] 69 Fed. Reg. 77325656.17(e)(ii)(C).

[24] 69 Fed. Reg. 773, 77345 (Dec. 27, 2004).

[25] PERM FAQ Round 10, *available at www.foreignlaborce rt.doleta.gov/pdf/perm_faqs_5-9-07.pdf.*

[26] 69 Fed. Reg. 77325, 77345 (Dec. 27, 2004).

[27] *Id.* at 77348, *citing Matter of H.C. LaMarche Enterprises, Inc.*, 87 INA 607 (BALCA Oct. 27, 1988) (en banc), *Matter of Wailua Associates*, 88 INA 533 (BALCA June 14, 1989), and *Matter of Quality Rebuilders Corporation*, 93 INA 144 (BALCA June 28, 1994).

[28] 69 Fed. Reg. 77325, 77349 (Dec. 27, 2004).

faith. Failing to promptly contact U.S. applicants, placing undue burdens on applicants, and placing ads out of alphabetical order would not.

Adequate Test of the Labor Market

Another requirement is that there be an adequate test of the labor market. Again, this phrase is not used in the regulations and only slightly referred to in the procedure. One of the jobs of the PERM regulations was to decide how to adequately test the labor market.

Prior to PERM, recruitment could be as little as an ad for three consecutive days. Later, the concept of "pattern of employment" arose, which for a while appeared to require more than a three-day ad. The required recruitment listed by the PERM regulations, discussed below, reflects what an adequate test looks like.

How Much Recruitment Is Necessary?

"Real world" recruitment is usually done by an employer until the position is filled. This may be as little as only one ad (if the job is filled quickly) or weeks of ads (if there are no qualified responses). In some "real world" cases, an employer may not even recruit through newspapers or journals, but merely rely on networking and word-of-mouth. This open-ended concept (recruitment until the position is filled) is unwieldy and potentially time intensive. DOL's task has been to find an acceptable and workable solution between a specific, detailed recruitment protocol on the one hand and an open-ended unstructured recruitment effort on the other. What DOL has come up with is found in the PERM regulations. There are two factors in the test devised by DOL:

1. Adequate recruitment efforts, and

2. Proper evaluation of responses to the recruitment efforts

An adequate test of the labor market is deemed to be two Sunday ads and one 30-day notice with the SWA serving the area of intended employment.[29] That is all that is required. Of course, the responses

must be dealt with appropriately.[30] Basically, for nonprofessional or professional positions, two Sunday ads and a 30-day job order are sufficient for a good-faith test of the labor market.

In addition, for professional positions, employers must choose three additional steps out of 10 suggested by DOL.[31] Choosing any three of the steps will be a good-faith effort, as long as the steps comport with any and all requirements in the regulations.

- *Employer's website*—To document this step, the regulation asks for "dated copies of pages" (plural).[32] This wording easily can be interpreted as requiring more than a one-day post on the website. How many more is currently pure speculation.

- *Job search website*—Dated "pages" (again plural) from one (or more, although more is not required) website[33] would imply more than one day.

- *Employer referral with incentives*—There is no requirement for what the incentives must be. For that reason, a referral program with minimal incentives should be adequate. Since dated copies of the employer's notices or memoranda that include the incentive offered are required,[34] it is safe to infer that the information must be posted more than one day or must be contained in more than one medium.

- *Campus placement offices*—While the heading is listed in the plural, the text is written in the singular: it speaks in terms of documenting "use of a campus placement office" with a copy of the employer's notice of the job opportunity provided to the campus placement office.[35]

- *Local and ethnic newspapers*—Again, this is listed in the plural, but the text requires only a copy of the page that contains the employer's advertisement.[36] A one-day ad appears to be sufficient.

- *Radio and TV*—Documentation required is the text of the ad and written confirmation of when it was aired. The question arises about how many

---

[29] It is interesting to note that the regulations require only two newspaper ads and do not even suggest more than two ads (other than local and ethnic newspapers for professional positions). The model of two Sunday ads had been determined by DOL in its PERM requirements to be adequate to test the labor market. While the wording of the regulations implies that more than 30 days can be used for the SWA notice by suggesting "at least" 30 days for a notice, there is no such implication for newspaper ads.

[30] That is, obviously not throwing away resumes, rejecting U.S. applicants for other than lawful job-related reasons, trying to misinterpret resumes, etc.

[31] 20 CFR §656.17(e)(1)(ii).

[32] 20 CFR §656.17(e)(1)(ii)(B).

[33] 20 CFR §656.17(e)(1)(ii)(C).

[34] 20 CFR §656.17(e)(1)(ii)(G).

[35] 20 CFR §656.17(e)(1)(ii)(H).

[36] 20 CFR §656.17(e)(1)(ii)(I).

times and when the ad must appear or be run. The regulation text appears to allow radio or TV, but does not require both.[37]

- *Trade and professional organizations*—Asking for "pages of newsletters or trade journals containing advertisements"[38] implies printed ads and more than one ad in a newsletter or trade journal. If an organization's electronic journal is used, DOL requires "dated copies of pages,"[39] which apparently means more than one-day placement.

- *On-campus recruitment*—Implies one day, since the regulation states that the documentation necessary to prove this step is "the date [the employer] conducted interviews … ."[40]

- *Private employment firm*—Apparently, only one firm is required, although the requirement of "contracts" (plural) between the employer and "the private employment firm" (not each or every firm) adds ambiguity.[41] In addition, the firm must place "advertisements" (plural), which are part of the documentation that must be assembled.[42]

- *Job fairs*—While the heading is in the plural (implying that more than one fair is necessary) and the text of the regulation initially speaks of "job fairs" (plural), the balance of the information talks about "the fair" and the employer being a "participant in the job fair."[43] The conclusion would be that one job fair may be sufficient to meet this step. However, a conclusion that more than one job fair is required is also supportable.

It appears that minimally complying with the stated requirements complies with the "good faith" and "adequate test" principles.

REJECTING U.S. WORKERS

According to the PERM regulations, employers must prepare and, if audited, submit a recruitment report.[44] Among other things, the report must give the "lawful job-related reasons" for rejecting U.S.

applicants and, in fact, categorize the U.S. applicants by the reason rejected.[45] The regulations also say that a U.S. worker cannot be rejected for lacking skills necessary for the job if the skills can be acquired by the U.S. worker during a "reasonable" period of on-the-job training.[46] The regulations further state that COs may request U.S. applicants' resumes or applications, again sorted by reason for rejection,[47] ostensibly to independently determine whether any applicants were improperly rejected.

A U.S. applicant cannot be rejected if he or she is:[48]

- Able—to perform the job duties.

- Willing—to accept the job as offered. Applicants who want a higher salary than offered, additional benefits, or other accommodations would not be considered "willing."

- Qualified—that is, meets at least the minimum requirements listed on the ETA Form 9089.

- Available—at the time and place of employment. A person who wants to work at some other location or future time is not considered available.

The law is conjunctive, so if a person lacks any of the four qualities listed above, he or she is properly rejected.

With these parameters in mind, what should the employer be aware of when rejecting U.S. applicants?

The U.S. Applicant Is Not Able to Perform the Job Duties

If a person is not physically or mentally able to perform the job duties, he or she can be rejected. An applicant who may meet all the education requirements, but cannot understand enough English to follow directions to do the necessary tasks, may be properly rejected as not able to perform the job duties. An application with poor references may be found as not an able worker.

The U.S. Applicant Is Not Willing to Accept the Position as Stated

A person may be found not *willing* who wants, for example, more pay than is being offered, different hours to accommodate a school schedule, or a different shift because of family reasons. Such persons can be lawfully rejected.

[37] 20 CFR §656.17(e)(1)(ii)(J).

[38] 20 CFR §656.17(e)(1)(ii)(E).

[39] PERM FAQ Round 9, *available at www.foreignlaborcert. doleta.gov/pdf/perm_faqs_11-29-06.pdf.*

[40] 20 CFR §656.17(e)(1)(ii)(D).

[41] 20 CFR §656.17(e)(1)(ii)(F).

[42] *Id.*

[43] 20 CFR §656.17(e)(1)(ii)(A).

[44] 20 CFR §656.17(g)(1).

[45] *Id.*

[46] 20 CFR §656.17(g)(2).

[47] 20 CFR §656.17(g)(1).

[48] *See* 20 CFR §656.24(b)(2).

Documenting this can be tricky. Some Board of Alien Labor Certification Appeals (BALCA) cases appear to require that an actual job offer must be given and rejected. While a written offer turned down by a U.S. applicant is certainly great proof of the applicant's unwillingness to accept the job,[49] most employers may not need to go so far. They can infer that a U.S. applicant who asks for additional accommodation is unwilling to accept the position under the terms and conditions being offered and is withdrawing his or her name from consideration. It should be clear, however, that the applicant is unwilling to accept the job as stated and is not merely suggesting a desired addition or alternative. Documentation such as e-mails or letters from the applicant should be obtained.

The U.S. Applicant Is Not Available

Lack of availability is another lawful reason for rejection. According to the law, U.S. applicants must be *available at the time of the alien's visa application and admission.*[50] This has been interpreted to mean that U.S. applicants must be available at the time of recruitment. The fact that an applicant may be available in the future is not controlling.[51] Therefore, even though it may take the alien years to immigrate due to visa backlogs, the fact that a U.S. applicant will be available in the future is irrelevant. So, where a Bachelor's degree is the minimum education requirement for the job, a student who will graduate in a year or two will not be considered available, even though it may take five years before the alien will be able to immigrate. This approach stands to reason, since the alien as well must meet every requirement at the time the labor certification is filed.[52] Therefore, it is entirely appropriate to reject a U.S. applicant as not being available if that person is not available at the time of the recruitment effort.

The second part of the availability requirement is that U.S. applicants must be *available at the place where the alien is to perform the work.* The employer does not need to accommodate applicants by allowing them to work at some other location. Or, if they are not in the area, the employer is not obligated to relocate them, unless this is the employer's policy.

The availability factor becomes a little more complicated in cases in which the alien is allowed to work at a site different from the employer's. For example, a "roving employee" is one who often travels to customer sites throughout the United States. Due to the nature of the job and the travel it entails, it may be possible for the alien to live in virtually any part of the United States. In many cases, the employer's requirement is that such employees live close to major airports, not in a specific city or geographic location. In such cases, the places where the work will be performed are so diverse that it would be inappropriate for a U.S. applicant to be rejected for not living where the alien may be living. Except for some compelling reason, it would be unlawful to reject a U.S. applicant for choosing to live in some other city.

The U.S. Applicant Is Not Qualified

The U.S. applicant does not meet the education and/or experience requirements

Of the four factors considered when determining whether a U.S. applicant may be properly rejected, the one that may cause the most difficulty for employers is whether U.S. applicants are *qualified.* It is clear, that to be qualified, U.S. applicants must meet the minimum requirements as stated in ETA Form 9089.[53] There are three types of requirements that U.S. applicants (as well as the alien) must meet—education,[54] experience or training (in terms of number of years or months),[55] and other special requirements and specific skills.[56] Assuming that all the employer's requirements have been adequately justified, failure to meet only one of the education, training, or experience requirements is a lawful reason to reject a U.S. applicant.[57]

---

[49] *Matter of Impell Corp.*, 88 INA 298 (BALCA May 31, 1988) (en banc).

[50] INA 212(a)(5)(A)(i)(I).

[51] *Matter of Adry-Mart, Inc.*, 88 INA 243 (BALCA Feb. 1, 1989) (en banc).

[52] Actually, the alien normally must meet all the training and experience requirements at the time of original hire, unless (1) experience was gained in a position not substantially comparable with the position being certified or (2) it is no longer feasible to train a worker to qualify for the position. 20 CFR §656.17(i)(3).

[53] *Matter of Adry-Mart Inc.*, 88 INA 243 (BALCA Feb. 1, 1989) (en banc).

[54] *See* ETA Form 9089, sections H.4, H.7, and H.8.

[55] *See id.*, section H.5, H.6, H.8, and H.10.

[56] *See id.*, section H.14.

[57] 69 Fed. Reg. 77325, 77350 (Dec. 27, 2004). The preamble states: "[A]n applicant's failure to meet the employer's stated minimum requirements is a lawful reason for rejection …."

Although a person who lacks the quantitative requirements of education, training, and experience can be easily and properly rejected, a person missing a specific skill may not be so easily rejected, as discussed below. Such skills are usually identified in H.14 on the Form 9089 and sometimes in H.11, the job description.

The U.S. applicant cannot gain the necessary skill(s) through reasonable on-the-job training

A fundamental change from the old regulations is that a U.S. applicant is able and qualified if he or she can acquire any skills necessary to perform the job duties within a "reasonable period of on-the-job training."[58] This is new territory under the PERM regulations. Of course, the key undefined word in the regulations is "reasonable." When does the amount of time that it would take to train move from "reasonable" to "unreasonable?" And how competent must a U.S. applicant be after a "reasonable" time?

There have been no definitions yet given—by DOL answer to a frequently asked question (FAQ) or BALCA decision—that help to define the term "reasonable." Notwithstanding the lack of definition, the burden still falls on the employer to provide evidence that any skills a U.S. applicant lacks could not be learned in a reasonable period. It appears that two things must be established: (1) the length of time that the training would take, and (2) that the length is unreasonable.

The Length of Time the Training Would Reasonably Take

The first thing that must be established is the correct time that it would reasonably take an applicant to acquire the lacking skill(s) through on-the-job training. This should be determined in months or years. A number of factors should be considered in reaching this determination, including:

1. the complexity of the skills that are lacking

2. the applicant's present skill base from which he or she will be learning

3. the level of competency that is required to reasonably perform the job

4. the industry standard of the normal amount of time that this training takes

Complexity. The more complex the skill, the more training would normally be required. The opposite is also true. For example, the time that it takes for a for-eign specialty chef to become familiar with a restaurant's particular use of ingredients and spices is much less than the time it takes for an engineer to learn a complex software applications program. It is incumbent upon the employer to highlight and emphasize the complexities of the skill(s) to be learned to support the amount of training that would be reasonable.

Skill Base. Each individual's level of education, training, and experience determines what the person brings to the training and how long it would generally take such a person to become proficient. An applicant for a position as a chef in a Thai restaurant who has experience in Thai cuisine would be able to understand the particular restaurant's signature use of Thai spices quicker than an applicant with experience only in Italian cuisine. A software engineer who has experience with C and C+ would be able to pick up C++ much faster than a person with no C or C+ experience. Of course, the less a person has to build on, the longer the on-the-job training will take.

Competency Level. The level of competency would be what would allow the applicant to "perform in the normally accepted manner."[59] Of course, this is open to interpretation as well. The level of competency required for a hospital admitting officer (who does not directly have the patient's life in hand) is far different from a perfusionist, who runs a machine to keep pumping blood through a patient whose heart has been stopped for open heart surgery. Reasonably, the higher the competency required, the more time it would take to train.

Industry Standard. Finally, documentation of the normal time that the industry allots for training can be gathered from industry publications, the Internet, or the employer. The time that similar employers expect it would take for training (or "orientation," as some refer to it) will be helpful in determining a reasonable training period. While there is no science in determining a reasonable period, such a determination requires considerable analysis. "Shooting from the hip" or mere "guesstimation" will not be acceptable. If DOL questions the employer's "reasonable training" conclusion, convincing explanation and documentation will be necessary.

---

[58] 20 CFR §656.17(g)(2).

[59] *See* 20 CFR §656.24(b)(2)(i); 69 Fed. Reg. 77325, 77350 (Dec. 27, 2004).

The Amount of Time for Training is Unreasonable

Once the time it will take to train a U.S. applicant is determined, the employer, to lawfully reject the applicant, must establish that it would be unreasonable to provide such training. The preamble to the PERM regulations states that the reasonableness of a period of training will vary by occupation, industry, and job opportunity.[60] The preamble leaves it up to the COs, who are "experienced in assessing the qualifications of the applicants," to determine the time it would take to acquire a skill.[61]

That being said, to determine that a period will be unreasonable, the factors outlined by DOL—occupation, industry, and job opportunity—should be taken into account. In addition, the inability of the employer to provide resources for training, the wait for the applicant to be proficient, the financial impact on the employer during the wait, and the potential negative impact on clients/customers should be mentioned and analyzed.

THE RECRUITMENT REPORT

The regulations give details about the proper recruitment report.[62] It is not an onerous requirement and need not be a lengthy report. But the supporting documentation to back up the information and assertions contained in the report can always be requested by DOL, which arguably makes the supporting documentation as important as the report itself. Therefore, great care must be taken in ensuring that all information contained in the report is accurately documented.

Signature on the Report

The report must be signed by the employer or the employer's designate. As a matter of practice, the person who signs the recruitment report should be the person who signs the ETA Form 9089. However, that is not required.

Contents of the Report

The report must contain four things, as outlined in the regulations:[63]

1. **A description of the recruitment steps taken.**—This should include information about the two Sunday ads and SWA notice. If the recruitment is for a professional position, the three additional steps should be described.

2. **The results achieved.**—The number of responses received is the minimum information that should be included. Designating the number of responses from each recruitment type, which is not necessary, may be included. Also, the report may include the number of applicants interviewed.

3. **The number of hires.**—If anyone is hired, this needs to be stated. Unless the ad is for multiple positions, hiring a U.S. applicant will fill the position being recruited for and new recruitment efforts must be undertaken.

4. The number of rejected U.S. workers, if any, categorized by reasons for rejection.

Although it is not necessary to submit resumes or applications from U.S. applicants with the recruitment report, they may be requested in an audit.

A sample recruitment report appears at the end of this article.

RESPONDING TO SPECIFIC ISSUES CONTAINED IN AN AUDIT REQUEST

The following specific issues seem to be the focus of current audits:

Normal/Not Normal—Exceeding the SVP

By far the issue raised most frequently in current Audit Notification letters issued by DOL PERM centers is employer requirements that exceed the SVP level of the position that is tied to the Job Zone assigned to it in the O*NET. And it does not seem to matter how H-12 of the ETA Form 9089 is answered—normal or not normal. If the combination of education and experience required exceeds the SVP, the application will be audited and business necessity documentation will be required.

In issuing these audits, DOL adjudicators appear to be looking simply at the job title and the SOC/O*NET assigned by the SWA. From there they look to the Job Zone and the corresponding SVP level, which is expressed in a range (*e.g.,* 7.0 to < 8.0); however, DOL does not seem to recognize this range of SVP values and strictly uses the lower value.[64]

There are no regulations governing the interpretation of the SVP ranges, and DOL's stated position on these ranges is far from clear. As a preliminary

---

[60] 69 Fed. Reg. 77325, 77350–51 (Dec. 27, 2004).

[61] *Id.* at 77350.

[62] 20 CFR §656.17(g).

[63] 20 CFR §656.17(g)(1).

[64] *See* note 6, *supra.*

matter, there have been no conclusive statements from DOL about the rationale behind interpreting what is clearly a range in the O*NET as simply meaning the lower end of that range. This is particularly disturbing since, at the time that the thousands of occupations from the DOT were channeled into 1,100 occupations for the O*NET, SVP levels were initially calculated as an average for the various occupations and then rounded down.[65] In addition, DOL has made contradictory statements about whether the calculation of SVP should include or exclude the value of formal education. For example, the PERM preamble indicates that formal education should be "counted" as part of the value of SVP,[66] but subsequent guidance issued by DOL in May 2005 suggests that formal education is excluded when determining the SVP, at least for wage determination purposes.[67]

Under current DOL interpretations, for example, if a senior software engineer position has minimum requirements of an M.S. degree and two years of experience, an audit is expected, regardless of whether the requirements are marked normal or not normal in H-12. The position will be assigned the SOC/O*NET code of 15-1031.00, with a Job Zone of 4 and an SVP range of 7.0 to < 8.0.

With an SVP of 7 (over two years up to and including four years), the maximum combination education and experience that DOL would consider as not excessive would be a Bachelor's degree with two years of experience, or a Master's degree and no experience. Thus, the example exceeds DOL's expectations of what is "normal" by two years and an audit notification letter is likely.

The audit letter typically comes in two different formats. One is the standard boilerplate version, which contains the usual list of information requested for submission. The fourth bullet point (sometimes highlighted for emphasis by the DOL analyst) requests "[p]roof of business necessity as outlined by §656.17(h) if the answer for question H-12 is no . . .

or the job duties and/or requirements are beyond those defined by the job by the SOC/O*NET code and Occupation Title provided by the State Workforce Agency." In the other version, besides the letter itself, there is also a very helpful attachment giving the audit reasons. On this page the DOL analyst goes into detail about how he or she has calculated that the position's requirements are excessive.

Either way, proof of business necessity must be submitted. While there certainly may be many ways to structure such an audit response, here is one "recipe" for a response that has worked without fail to this point (knocking on wood as this is being typed):

First, it is important to remember, and to put down in writing, the legal definition of "business necessity." Therefore, one should emphasize to the DOL analyst that the employer maintains the job opportunity without unduly restrictive requirements, and that the requirements described are essential to perform the job in a reasonable manner and bear a reasonable relationship to the requirements for the position. For the educational component, this can be done by going through the job duties and responsibilities in a broader sense to make a showing that the position can be performed only by one who has a high level of specific knowledge that could only be acquired through postsecondary education. To the extent possible, try to tie the duties and responsibilities to the specific undergraduate or graduate program of study and curriculum the position requires.

For the experience component, it is crucial to discuss the duties and responsibilities in detail. Argue that one who has not extensively performed similar duties and responsibilities would not have the practical experience needed to fill the position successfully; therefore, the needs of the company and its clients/customers would not be met and the employer's business would suffer. Also, prove that the employer normally requires this combination of education and experience for this specific position. This can be accomplished by documenting the educational and experience background of all current and past employees in this position within the company. Attach a report listing the names, education, and experience of all such employees. Some may choose to attach the resumes of the listed employees. Finally, provide evidence that the requirements are common to the industry in comparable positions among similar organizations. Attach print-outs from Monster, HotJobs, CareerBuilder, and other job search sites for similar positions with organizations in the same industry and similar in size.

---

[65] For an excellent discussion of the history of DOL's statements on SVP, see R. Cohen et al., "Practice Pointers in Resolving PERM Conundrums: Job Requirements, Degree Equivalencies, Experience with the Same Employer, and Timelines," *Immigration & Nationality Law Handbook* 201 (AILA 2007–08 Ed.).

[66] 69 Fed. Reg. 77325, 77332 (Dec. 27, 2004).

[67] DOL Memorandum, E. DeRocco, "Revised Prevailing Wage Determination Guidance" (May 17, 2005), *published on* AILA InfoNet at Doc. No. 05052066 (*posted* May 20, 2005).

Foreign Language Requirement

If there is such as thing as an automatic audit trigger, requiring fluency in a foreign language (other than for something obvious like an interpreter or translator) would be it. Be sure to spend the time up front, prior to filing, to make sure the response documents are in the file.

Audit notification letters tend to have the standard boilerplate language requesting proof of business necessity when H-13 is marked yes. There is also typically a separate attachment with the audit reasons listed, which reiterates that the position requires the capability to speak a foreign language and requests documentation justifying the business necessity for this job requirement. The attachment also quotes 20 CFR §656.17(h)(2), offering guidance on how to document business necessity in this situation. It is advisable to do it exactly that way.

First, one can show that capability in the foreign language is a part of the nature of the occupation.[68] There are obvious examples such as a translator or a Spanish teacher, where the title or the job duties inherently involve usage of a foreign language.

Alternatively, one must demonstrate "[t]he need to communicate with a large majority of the employer's customers, contractors, or employees who cannot communicate effectively in English. . . ."[69] The regulation even provides helpful examples of the kinds of documentation to prove this need. One can furnish "the number and proportion of [the employer's] clients, contractors, or employees who cannot effectively communicate in English, and/or a detailed plan to market products or services in a foreign country."[70] One may also provide "[a] detailed explanation of why the duties of the position for which certification is sought requires [sic] frequent contact and communication with customers, employees or contractors who can not communicate in English and why it is reasonable to believe [these individuals] cannot communicate in English."[71]

If employers do one or both of the above, the audit response experience has generally been very favorable and timely. One recent example involves an art director position for a company in Atlanta that requires the incumbent to speak and write fluently in Spanish. The company has a subsidiary in Bogotá, Colombia, where its production staff is. The audit response documented the existence of this subsidiary. It was shown that the Bogotá office consists of two departments—a design department that provides the creative talent, and a development department that provides the programming talent. The art director works with and communicates stylistic direction to both designers and developers. It was documented that 80 percent of the designers could not communicate in English and that 20 percent of the developers could not. Further it was shown that 50–80 percent of the art director's time was spent working with the production team in Bogotá. These communications were documented in e-mail printouts, instant messenger chat session print-outs, and phone records. The response also detailed the importance of clarity in these communications to the end-design product produced for the company's Fortune 100 clients in the United States. Approval of the labor certification application was received from the Atlanta PERM center five weeks after submission of the audit response.

Again, the type of documents and information needed to successfully respond to a foreign language audit are not quick and easy to obtain. One cannot cut corners here by filing the case and pulling together the business necessity documentation later when (not if) the case is audited.

Experience Gained with the Same Employer

Although DOL had originally proposed eliminating the ability to "count" experience gained with the same employer, the PERM regulations were surprisingly generous about this issue, as was the ETA Form 9089 itself. Significantly, the regulations narrowly define an employer as "an entity with the same Federal Employer Identification Number (FEIN). . . ."[72] Thus, no longer are affiliates or parent/subsidiaries of the employer, either domestically or abroad, considered the "same employer."

Question J-21 of the ETA Form 9089 is written such that it will almost never be answered affirmatively. (If it is, the application will certainly be audited.) It asks, "Did the alien gain any of the qualifying experience with the employer in a position substantially comparable to the job opportunity requested?" The first issue is whether the two employers are the same employer—simply, do they have the same FEIN? Secondly, if they are the same employer, are the positions substantially comparable?

---

[68] *See* 20 CFR §656.17(h)(2)(i).

[69] 20 CFR §656.17(h)(2)(ii)

[70] 20 CFR §656.17(h)(2)(ii)(A).

[71] 20 CFR §656.17(h)(2)(ii)(B).

[72] 20 CFR §656.17(i)(5)(i).

The PERM regulations define "substantially comparable" positions as ones in which the same job duties are performed more than 50 percent of the time.[73] So the only time the employer would answer yes to J-21 would be when it "can demonstrate that it is no longer feasible to train a worker to qualify for the position."[74] This argument is rarely made.

However, answering no to J-21 does not mean the application will not be audited. Especially in cases in which the employer is the same and the job duties as listed on the ETA Form 9089 appear to be somewhat comparable, it is quite possible to receive an audit notification letter. Again the specific attachment to the letter will quote from the PERM regulations, which give fairly clear guidance on what DOL wants to see as proof the positions are not substantially comparable. The regulations suggest providing "position descriptions, the percentage of time spent on the various duties, organizational charts, and payroll records."[75] Again, it is advisable to "take the hint" from DOL and give it exactly what it wants in response. It is also helpful to review the standards set out in the pre-PERM BALCA decision *Matter of Delitizer*.[76] These were referred to in the preamble to the PERM regulations, but were found by DOL to be "unnecessarily complex and in practice difficult to administer."[77] However, it is obvious the documentation listed in the PERM regulations flow from those *Delitizer* standards—"relative job duties and supervisory responsibilities, job requirements, the positions of the jobs in the employer's job hierarchy, whether and by whom the position was filled previously, whether the position is newly created, the prior employment practices of the employer regarding the relative positions, [and] the amount or percentage of time spent performing each job duty in each job and the job salaries."[78]

By mastering these key areas of labor certification, one can be confident of putting clients in the best possible position of completing the first and most important step towards employment-based permanent residence. Knowing the rules and how to best use them is good lawyering to be proud of.

---

[73] 20 CFR §656.17(i)(5)(ii).

[74] *See* 20 CFR §656.17(i)(3)(ii).

[75] 20 CFR §656.17(i)(5)(ii).

[76] *Matter of Delitizer of Newton*, 88 INA 482 (BALCA May 9, 1990) (en banc).

[77] 69 Fed. Reg. 77325, 77353 (Dec. 27, 2004).

[78] *Matter of Delitizer of Newton, supra* note 76, at 9–10.

SAMPLE RECRUITMENT REPORT

[Name of Corporation]

Recruitment Report in Regard to the Labor Certification Application for [name of employee]

1. Description of Recruitment Efforts [The recruitment efforts and dates are already contained on the Form 9089. This part of the report appears to be redundant, but is nevertheless required by the regulation.]

    a. Two Sunday ads placed in the *San Francisco Chronicle*—March 2, 2008 and March 9, 2008.

    b. 30-day job order placed with California EDD, which started February 19, 2008, and ended March 20, 2008.

    c. Employer's website—posted on March 1 through March 10, 2008 [dates posted are optional, as this information is not required by the regulations. As mentioned, the regulations describe "dated pages," connoting more than one day. A 10-day period is used in this sample but there has been no indication that 10 days is required.]

    d. Job Search Website—Posted on *www.sfgate.com*, in conjunction with the *San Francisco Chronicle* ads [Sfgate is the online home of the *San Francisco Chronicle*]. The posting ran from February 9, 2008, to February 29, 2008.

    e. Employee Referral Program with Incentives—This program is in our employee handbook and on line on our website. Employees are eligible for $250 for every referred applicant who is hired.

2. The Results Obtained

    • 10 responses were received from the newspaper ads

    • 1 response was received from the job search website

    • 0 responses were received from all other recruitment efforts

3. The Number of Hires

    • 1 hire—the ad was placed in the plural since we have more than one opening.

    • 4. The Number of U.S. Workers Rejected, Categorized by Reason for Rejection:

    • 5 applicants—did not possess masters degree

- 3 applicants—did not have two years of experience
- 2 applicants—did not have specific skills or other requirements

[name], HR Director

LABOR CERTIFICATION DU JOUR: 2007–08 PERM DEVELOPMENTS

*by Steven A. Clark, Robert H. Cohen, Ester Greenfield, and Deborah J. Notkin**

Our article assists those who want to know: what are some of the issues in labor certification processing that I need to think about now? We discuss four timely topics: the Department of Labor's (DOL) anti-fraud regulation, which became effective on

* **Steven A. Clark**, AILA President 1999–2000, practices business immigration in Cambridge, MA with Flynn & Clark, P.C. A graduate of Yale College and Harvard Law School, he launched the *Ask the Expert* column in *Immigration Law Today*. In addition to chairing AILA's INS and DOL Headquarters Liaison Committees, he served as senior editor of AILA's *Immigration & Nationality Law Handbook*, editor-in-chief of AILA's *Representing Professionals Before the Department of Labor,* and the editor of the chapter on labor certifications in the Matthew Bender treatise *Immigration Law and Practice*. He has served as chair of the Massachusetts Bar Association's Immigration Committee and is Co-Chair of the Boston Bar Association's Immigration Committee.

Robert H. Cohen is a partner with the firm of Porter, Wright, Morris & Arthur LLP, in Columbus, OH. He has practiced immigration law for over 29 years, and his primary areas of practice include business and family immigration representation. Mr. Cohen served as AILA chapter chair in Ohio from 2003 through 2005, and currently serves on AILA's Nebraska Service Center Liaison Committee. He is listed in both *The Best Lawyers in America* and *Super Lawyers* for immigration practice. He is a graduate of Miami University and the University of Cincinnati College of Law.

Ester Greenfield is a director at MacDonald, Hoague & Bayless in Seattle. She is a past chair of the AILA Washington State Chapter and has taught immigration law and an immigration clinic as an adjunct professor at Seattle University. She has served on local and national AILA Department of Labor liaison committees. She was co-editor-in-chief of AILA's *David Stanton Manual on Labor Certification* (3d Ed. 2005), co-editor of AILA's *Department of Labor Directory for Immigration Lawyers* (2002–03 Eds.), and has been an editor of AILA's *Immigration & Nationality Law Handbook* for many years. Ms. Greenfield is listed in *Best Lawyers in America* and *The International Who's Who of Corporate Immigration Lawyers*.

Deborah J. Notkin is a partner in the firm of Barst & Mukamal LLP in New York City, and an AILA past president and member of its executive committee. She served as co-chair of AILA's Labor Liaison Committee, associate editor of AILA's *David Stanton Manual on Labor Certification,* AILA's New York Chapter chair, co-chair of AILA's INS Eastern Liaison Committee, and subcommittee chair for AILA's annual conference. Ms. Notkin appears in *Best Lawyers in America*, *The International Who's Who of Corporate Immigration Lawyers*, and *Chambers USA*.

July 16, 2007; significant decisions from the Board of Alien Labor Certification Appeals (BALCA) in the last year; the impact of layoffs on the ability to file Program Electronic Review Management (PERM) applications; and DOL's efforts to revise and improve the ETA Form 9089.

THE ANTI-FRAUD RULE

The 180-Day Rule

The anti-fraud rule provides that labor certifications approved on or after July 16, 2007, will expire 180 days from issuance unless filed with U.S. Citizenship and Immigration Services (USCIS) in support of an immigrant visa petition (Form I-140).[1] Labor certifications issued prior to July 16, 2007, all expired on Saturday, January 12, 2008.[2] Looking toward the future, the employer must use the labor certification or lose it.

Calculating the Due Date

Will USCIS grant an additional three days for filing since labor certifications are served by mail,[3] or extend the deadline to the next business day when the deadline falls on a weekend or holiday? Evidently not. USCIS Service Center Operations indicated that it would require the I-140 for labor certifications issued prior to July 16, 2007, to be filed by 5:00 PM on Friday, January 11, 2008.

Impact on TNs and E-3s

The anti-fraud rule poses conundrums for employers who wish to sponsor an employee who is currently in the United States in TN or E-3 status for a green card. TN status, unlike H-1B or L-1 status, requires the beneficiary to maintain nonimmigrant intent—a foreign residence that he or she does not

---

[1] 20 CFR §656.30(b)(1).

[2] 20 CFR §656.30(b)(2).

[3] 8 CFR §103.5a(b) provides an additional three days when any notice is served by mail. It is unclear why USCIS did not apply this regulation to the expiration of labor certifications. DOL has no comparable rule of its own. Possibly USCIS was thinking that the rule does not apply to notices by other agencies, or possibly it did not consider the labor certification to be a notice.

intend to abandon.[4] If an immigrant visa petition is filed for an individual in TN status, he or she may face problems when re-entering the United States in TN status, or when seeking a TN extension of stay.[5] The extension application requires the beneficiary to indicate whether an immigrant visa petition has been filed on his or her behalf. A positive response may result in the denial of the extension on the basis the petition evinces intention to remain. However, it is the employer's petition, not the employee's. Moreover, if the petition indicates that the employee will consular process to obtain an immigrant visa, rather than adjust status within the United States, then the border inspector could admit the person on the basis that he or she will depart at a specific time to obtain an appropriate immigrant visa when he or she returns to stay permanently. While this is often the case, there is no guidance compelling such result.

Some employees may choose to change their nonimmigrant status to H-1B before starting the green card process. However, with only 65,000 H-1Bs visas available per year, the chances for success are not that great—50 percent of H-1B petitions filed on April 1, 2007, were rejected, and the acceptance ratio is likely to be even lower in 2008 and beyond unless Congress authorizes additional visa numbers. The 2008 H-1B filing season, starting on April 1, 2008, is likely to include not only this year's demand, but a number of petitions that were rejected last year. Some enterprising nonimmigrants may seek petition filings by more than one employer in order to improve their chance of success.[6] Therefore, changing status from TN to H-1B before starting a labor certification may take more than a year.

Impact of Visa Retrogression

With the EB3 preference category suffering an extensive backlog, an applicant for a green card should establish a priority date by having the labor certification filed as soon as feasible. Canadian citizens who were born in China or India face longer EB backlogs than applicants born in other countries. They are particularly keen to register their priority dates, but also are interested in preserving the ability to travel and to extend their TN visas. Many applicants faced with the dilemma choose to refrain from starting green-card processing until they are able to change nonimmigrant status from TN to H-1B.

Filing Subsequent Petitions

A second I-140 petition can be filed for an employee, based on the labor certification, if more than 180 days have lapsed since the issuance of the labor certification. For example, if the EB2 cut-off date is even earlier than the EB3 cut-off date, employees who have an approved I-140 EB2 petition may ask their employers to file an EB3 petition for them in the event the EB3 classification remains more favorable. USCIS clarified that so long as any I-140 has been filed within 180 days, a second I-140 may be filed after the expiration of the 180-day filing period.[7]

---

[4] More specifically, 8 CFR §214.6(b) requires a temporary entry such that the foreign national's assignment will end at a predictable time and he or she will depart on completion of the assignment. A temporary period has a reasonable, finite end that does not equate to permanent residence. Legacy Immigration and Naturalization Service (INS) specifically declined to provide for "dual intent" because it was felt to be "clearly inconsistent with Article 1608 of the NAFTA. For purpose of Chapter 16 of the NAFTA, Article 1608 of the NAFTA defines 'temporary entry' specifically as 'entry into the territory of a Party by a business person of another Party without the intent to establish permanent residence.'" 63 Fed. Reg. 1331, 1333 (Jan. 9, 1998) (supplementary information to final rule amending 8 CFR §214.6). Dual intent is recognized for those in E status, at least E-1 and E-2. Letter, Bednarz, HQ 214-eC, 245-C (Oct. 1, 1993), *reprinted in* 70 *Interpreter Releases* 1456–58 (Nov. 1, 1993). The Bednarz letter predates the creation of E-3 status in 2005 by Pub. L. No. 109-13, 119 Stat. 231. However, the implementing regulations for E-1, E-2, and E-3 status all provide that the applicant should intend to depart on the termination of the E status. 22 CFR §41.51. The inference may be made that if dual intent applies to E-1 and E-2, it must also apply to E-3, because the regulatory language about intent is the same for all three E statuses. However, there is no specific memorandum or letter confirming this interpretation. Further, the statutory basis for dual intent at INA §214(b) does not include E classifications. By its terms, INA §214(b) does not apply to extensions—only to the application for a visa or for admission to the United States.

[5] *See generally* INS Letter, Y. LaFleur to William Z. Reich (June 18, 1996), *published on* AILA InfoNet at Doc. No. 96061891 (*posted* June 18, 1996), stating that an approved I-140 does not preclude admission as TN absent a specific finding of abandonment of temporary intent. This restated longstanding practice at the border.

[6] USCIS promulgated a final rule prohibiting employers from filing more than one H-1 petition for the same beneficiary. 73 Fed. Reg. 15389 (Mar. 24, 2008).

[7] "USCIS will continue to accept amended or duplicate Form I-140 petitions that are filed with a copy of a labor certification that is expired at the time the amended or duplicate Form I-140 petition is filed, if the original approved labor certification was filed in support of a previously filed petition during the labor certification's validity period. Such

continued

Expired Labor Certifications and AC21 Extensions

One unanswered question is whether an expired labor certification—a labor certification that has not been filed in support of an I-140 petition within 180 days of approval—will be sufficient to confer benefits under AC21[8] and enable an employee in H-1B status to extend his or her H-1B stay in the United States past the six-year limit. This situation could arise if the H-1B employee changed employers before an I-140 petition was filed, and the original employer was not willing to file the I-140 within 180 days of certification.

Employers Must Pay Attorney's Fees and Costs Associated with the Labor Certification

DOL's anti-fraud rule states that all costs of the labor certification, including attorney's fees, must be paid by the employer.[9] DOL promptly published a round of frequently asked questions and answers (FAQs) to explain certain aspects of the new rule.[10] Many employers already bore the costs of labor cer-

tification before the anti-fraud rule went into effect on July 16, 2007. For other employers, however, the rule poses barriers that may be insurmountable. An increasing number of school districts have been filing PERM applications to meet critical needs for bilingual and special needs teachers. Given budget constraints, these efforts will be severely impacted by the requirement that the employer pay the attorney's fees.

Payment Under Pre-existing Fee Arrangements

There are many questions about the impact of the anti-fraud rule on pending fee agreements. DOL asserted that fees could be paid if the obligation accrued before the effective date of the rule,[11] but its position raised more questions than it answered. Unfortunately, it is not clear whether DOL will agree that a fee has accrued if it was billed, but little or no work was done before July 16, 2007. If a fee is collected, then it must be reported in question I-23 on ETA Form 9089 ("Has the employer received payment of any kind for the submission of this application?"), even if the attorney has not yet received payment from the alien. The form should describe the payment, state from whom it was received, and clarify that the payment was for an obligation that accrued prior to July 16, 2007.[12] With the passage of time, the distinctions between fees earned, fees billed, and fees accrued before the effective date, and the problems with denials when they are legitimately reported at item I-23, will fortunately become less relevant. In the meantime, care must be taken not to bill a new invoice to the employee for services under a fee agreement entered into prior to the effective date. DOL FAQs clarify that payment from the employee can only be collected for fees billed prior to the effective date, not new billings.[13] The attorney should be careful to not bill for time entered after the effective date if billing hourly, or for milestones reached after the effective date.

What Fees Are Included in the Rule?

The anti-fraud rule does not bar foreign nationals from paying the attorney's fees in connection with the I-140 petition for immigrant worker, or in connection with the I-485 application for adjustment of status—only in connection with recruitment or legal services to prepare, file, or pursue a labor certifica-

---

filings may occur when a new petition is required due to successor-in-interest, where the petitioning employer wishes to file a new petition subsequent to the denial, revocation or abandonment of the previously filed petition and the labor certification was not invalidated due to material misrepresentation or fraud relating to the labor certification application, in the instances where the amended petition is requesting a different visa classification than the visa classification requested in the previously filed petition, or when the previously filed Form I-140 petition has been determined to have been lost by USCIS or DOS." USCIS Interoffice Memorandum, D. Neufeld, "Interim Guidance Regarding the Impact of the Department of Labor's (DOL) Final Rule, Labor Certification for the Permanent Employment of Aliens in the United States; Reducing the Incentives and Opportunities for Fraud and Abuse and Enhancing Program Integrity, on Determining Labor Certification Validity and the Prohibition of Labor Certification Substitution Requests" (June 1, 2007), *published on* AILA InfoNet at Doc. No. 07062172 (*posted* June 21, 2007).

[8] American Competitiveness in the Twenty-First Century Act of 2000 (AC21), Pub. L. No. 106-313, §§101–16, 114 Stat. 1251, 1251–62.

[9] 20 CFR §656.12(b).

[10] *See* "FAQs on Final Rule to Reduce the Incentives and Opportunities for Fraud and Abuse and Enhancing Program Integrity of May 17, 2007," *available at www.foreignlaborcert.doleta .gov/pdf/fraud_faqs_07-13-07.pdf*, and *published on* AILA InfoNet at Doc. No. 07071675 (*posted* July 16, 2007) (PERM Fraud Rule FAQs Round 1). A second set of anti-fraud FAQs was published by DOL on March 31, 2008, and is available on the DOL website at *www.foreignlaborcert.doleta.gov/pdf/ Fraud_Rule_Round2.pdf* (PERM Fraud Rule FAQs Round 2).

---

[11] PERM Fraud Rule FAQs Round 1, *supra* note 10, at 2–3.

[12] *Id.* at 3.

[13] *Id.*

tion application. One issue is how to allocate attorney's fees among the three stages of the green card process: labor certification (employers must pay), I-140 immigration visa petition (beneficiary may pay), and application for adjustment of status (beneficiary may pay). Some practitioners charge a single flat fee for the entire green card process. How much of the fee can be charged to the immigrant visa petition and application for adjustment of status, the stages of the process for which the beneficiary may pay the fee? If the attorney has a history of allocating the fee in a certain manner among the three processes, use of that allocation may pass muster. If the attorney maintains contemporaneous time records for each part of the process, the amount of time spent on each phase may provide a basis for coming up with a ratio yielding the portion of the overall fee that must be paid by the employer. That ratio may not reflect the realities of the specific case. Hopefully DOL would accept an allocation based on a typical case, since it may be impossible to allocate with mathematical precision for the particular case.

Untangling the Parts the Employee Can Pay For

Prudent practitioners often put in a substantial amount of work in counseling the employee and documenting her or his qualifications before the labor certification is filed. The documentation is typically not submitted until the immigrant visa petition is filed, but it is prepared, analyzed, and reviewed, and credentials evaluations are obtained, in advance of filing the labor certification to ensure that the I-140 petition and I-485 will be successful. If the attorney's time records are sufficiently detailed to document the amount of time spent in counseling, reviewing, and proving up the beneficiary's qualifications for the position, it should be defensible to require the beneficiary to pay for that portion of the analysis and work, even if the work is done before the labor certification has been filed.

Practical Issues Billing Dual Clients

The rule raises some practical issues in setting the fees. Frequently the employee makes the initial contact with counsel, particularly where the employer has not previously filed a labor certification, and will initiate a discussion of fees. The attorney will then have to inform the employee that the employer is an essential part of the equation not only to recruit and file the application, but to pay attorney fees for that phase of the case. Only then does the attorney, or client, have the dubious distinction of informing the employer not only that it is necessary to repeat the recruitment that was just completed,

and file a complex application, but that it is really the employer's application and the employer must pay for it. It is often difficult in this dynamic, or in any case, to assess at the outset whether there will be problems establishing the prevailing wage, or preparing business necessity documentation, or the need to respond to an audit. It may be difficult enough to establish a fee that the employer will be willing to pay if all goes smoothly, but can be a real challenge to convince the employer to agree to undertake the cost of these additional services that the employer clearly must pay for under the rule. Some attorneys may be willing to do all this without an additional fee, but others have staff to pay and children going to college. If the employer is resistant to paying the fee, the employee can not do so. But what if the attorney charges the employee a bit more than usual for the I-140/I-485 and the employer a bit less for the multiple wage challenges, preparing documentation of the language requirement, and the inevitable audit? The DOL FAQs prohibit pro bono representation of the employer,[14] but do not attempt to set standards for an appropriate fee, provided the stated basis for the fee is for services properly payable by the employee. Absent such an inappropriate allocation or egregious charge, one would think that DOL would not want to second guess the charges or get into the business of specifying what is acceptable. After all, it is not unusual for fees to vary, and the client's willingness and ability to pay will be a consideration. That being said, fact is stranger than fiction when it comes to what the government will want to regulate, so caution is advised in grappling with these realities.

Split Fees

Another set of problems arises when the employer and employee share costs on a split percentage basis. If the amount to be paid by the employer covers the usual cost of the labor certification, is it necessary to look further and see who paid for what, and whether it was sufficient? What if the case is terminated before the I-140 and I-485 are prepared? Hopefully, DOL will have the good sense not to raise such issues when the arrangement appears to be a good-faith effort to make an allocation.

Dual Representation and Dual Attorneys

The rule provides that the foreign national may have separate counsel, but if the same attorney represents the employer, as is so often the case given the

---

[14] *Id.* at 4.

impracticality of separate representation, then the costs must be borne by the employer.[15] When employer and employee have separate attorneys, this raises thorny issues as to what roles must be played by the attorneys. Presumably the attorneys could not be from the same firm. But will there be a violation if the employee's attorney drafts an application for the employer's attorney or corporate paralegal to review? The rule does require the employer to pay for the costs incurred in "preparing" the application, but it clearly allows the alien to pay his or her "own costs in connection with a labor certification,"[16] so the rule does not expressly prohibit this. This is commonly done, for instance, in domestic relation cases, in which one attorney drafts, and the other reviews, a prenuptial agreement. In reviewing the documents to determine their validity, the court would not be concerned with which attorney provided the initial draft. However, when the employer's attorney is utterly lacking in familiarity with the labor certification requirements and makes no independent effort to learn them, DOL might be concerned if representation was contrived by the employee's counsel. Would it matter if the employer's attorney was not charging a fee, and was appearing for the employer to accommodate the employee's attorney? If colleagues can make reciprocal arrangements to consult with their clients for a second opinion, or when there is a conflict of interest, then why not here? The FAQs state that the employee's attorney cannot represent the employer *pro bono*, because the attorney would not do it but for the representation of the employee.[17] But if it is a separate person doing so, this logic does not apply. If the attorney can discharge his or her responsibilities to protect the interests of the employer client, then the letter and the spirit of the rule should be satisfied.

Clawback Reimbursement Agreements

A number of employers entered into reimbursement agreements with the employees they sponsored for labor certification. These agreements generally stated that if the employee left the job after a certain milestone in green card processing was reached, the employee would need to reimburse the employer for its costs, fees, and expenses incurred in sponsoring the employee for a green card. After the anti-fraud

rule's effective date, such reimbursement agreements are no longer permitted.[18]

Debarment

Of course, what makes the discussion of fees so interesting is the fact that the attorney, along with the employer, can be penalized for providing false or inaccurate information in the application, participating in or facilitating any action to sell, barter, or purchase a labor certification, or violating any part of the anti-fraud rule, including the attorney fee prohibitions.[19] Penalties include debarment from filing labor certifications for a reasonable period, not to exceed three years.[20] DOL may issue a notice of debarment up to six years after the filing of the application, or the last application filed when there has been a pattern or practice of violations.[21] BALCA can review the notice.[22]

No Modifications

The anti-fraud rule bars requests for modification to an application after July 16, 2007.[23] The supplementary information prefacing the rule indicates that employers will nonetheless be permitted to file motions for reconsideration and to submit evidence subsequent to the application, but such evidence must exist prior to filing the application and be part of the employer's compliance responsibilities under PERM, or be submitted in response to the certifying officer's request.[24]

We Accept No Substitutes!

The rule also bars applications for substitution of the employee filed after July 16, 2007.[25] According to the FAQs, applications filed on or before that date

---

[15] 20 CFR §656.12(b).

[16] *Id.*

[17] PERM Fraud Rule FAQs Round 1, *supra* note 10, at 4.

[18] 20 CFR §656.12(b) simply prohibits recovery of fees and costs from the employee without qualification, but does not expressly refer to these contracts, which may be pre-existing. The FAQs raise the issue of pre-existing contracts to recoup fees and costs, and say that under the rule, such services are to be paid for by the employer. PERM Fraud Rule FAQs Round 1, *supra* note 10. So much for the right to enter into contracts. One wonders if courts would set aside a valid contract on the basis of a rule that does not even expressly mention the contract. Can an FAQ derogate a contract simply because of the sweeping language of the rule?

[19] 20 CFR §656.31(f)(1).

[20] *Id.*

[21] *Id.*

[22] *Id.*; 20 CFR §656.26(a)(3).

[23] 20 CFR §656.11(b).

[24] 72 Fed Reg. 27904, 27916 (May 17, 2007).

[25] 20 CFR §656.11.

will be adjudicated to conclusion.[26] The rule does not address whether DOL will accept a request to substitute an employer under *Matter of International Contractors, Inc.*,[27] but the bar on modifications would preclude such requests made after July 16, 2007. The combined impact of the no-modification and no-substitute rules is to leave the employee in an absolute straightjacket: the employer can not amend the form to correct a simple error, or to reflect a change in circumstances beyond the party's control. The only recourse is to refile, or to request that USCIS acknowledge that the employer is a successor in interest when there has been a change in ownership. The employer is forced to bear the full expense of the process, but if the employee chooses to terminate employment, the employer must start anew if the replacement worker is a foreign national.

BALCA UPDATE

During the first three years of the PERM regulation,[28] from March 2005 to March 2008, BALCA decided 227 PERM appeals. However, many substantive issues still have not been addressed by BALCA. Following the closing of the backlog elimination centers, and the increase in audits on a variety of issues, we expect that the number of appeals on substantive issues will increase over the next couple of years when BALCA is required to address issues such as business necessity and the dichotomy between the requirements suggested by an analysis of the specific vocational preparation (SVP) scale and that suggested by the job zones on O*Net.[29] However, thus far, BALCA has mostly limited itself to determining when to excuse clerical mistakes, finding that it must distinguish between substantive and minor errors on the ETA Form 9089. With some notable exceptions, most errors in completing the 9089 have been determined to be fatal to the application. BALCA has ex-

pressed willingness in some situations to look further and reverse denials based upon technical issues. However, even in the limited circumstances in which a denial is reversed by BALCA, it is not clear that counsel can continue to rely on these decisions for future cases.

In the first decision under the PERM rules, *Matter of HealthAmerica*,[30] BALCA provided hope that minor errors in the completion of the 9089 could be overcome via a motion to reconsider showing that it was a scrivener's error. In *HealthAmerica,* BALCA overruled a PERM denial when the print advertisement actually ran on a Sunday, but the date entered on the 9089 was not a Sunday due to a typographical error. However, it is clear that the same mistake made in an application today (which would require overriding the pop-up screen with advice that the non-Sunday advertisement could result in denial) would be decided differently. It is not safe to assume that *HealthAmerica* will be extended to additional typographical errors.

Leaving Blanks in ETA Form 9089

BALCA has determined in several cases that the failure to complete ETA Form 9089 by leaving portions of section H or J blank is fatal to the application. In *Matter of Alpine Store, Inc.*,[31] BALCA held that the failure to complete the information concerning acceptable alternative experience, item H-8, was a failure to state the minimum requirements. BALCA tied this required to the regulations, which state that the employer must state the actual minimum requirements for the position,[32] and held that this "slight error" was fatal to the application.

Similarly, the failure to complete item H-6 has been found to justify the certifying officer's denial of the application. In *Matter of Best Park*, LLC,[33] BALCA distinguished *HealthAmerica* by noting that in its motion to reconsider, HealthAmerica provided proof of the Sunday advertisements and explained the minor error. In *Best Park*, the employer asserted in the motion to reconsider that the form had been properly completed, and only conceded its error in the appeal following the denial of the motion to reconsider. The employer argued unsuccessfully that the error was still a correctable, minor typographical

---

[26] PERM Fraud Rule FAQs Round 1, *supra* note 10, at 1.

[27] *Matter of International Contractors Inc. and Technical Programming Services,* 89 INA 278 (BALCA June 13, 1990), held that the restriction of the application to the same job opportunity does not preclude allowing a new employer to be substituted if its job is in the same geographic area, and involves the same duties.

[28] 69 Fed. Reg. 77325 (Dec. 27, 2004).

[29] This issue is discussed in R. Cohen, *et al.*, "Practice Pointers in Resolving PERM Conundrums: Job Requirements, Degree Equivalencies, Experience with the Same Employer, and Timelines," *Immigration & Nationality Law Handbook* 201 (AILA 2007–08 Ed.).

[30] 2006 PER 1 (BALCA July 18, 2006).

[31] 2007 PER 00040 (BALCA June 27, 2007).

[32] 20 CFR §656.17(h)(4).

[33] 2007 PER 00065 (BALCA Sept. 18, 2007).

error and that the application should be certified. BALCA disagreed and affirmed the denial. In a similar decision, confusing only because the unrelated employer's name is similar, BALCA again held that the failure to complete item H-6 was fatal to the application.[34] While BALCA took pains to distinguish *HealthAmerica* in the *Best Park* decision, no such effort was made in *Matter of Subhashini Software Solutions*.[35] BALCA held that the failure to complete item H-10 was fatal to the application. It was not a minor error, according to BALCA, but showed that the employer failed to specify the minimum requirements, and therefore could not be corrected after filing.[36]

In *Matter of Phoenix Gear Manufacturing*,[37] the employer failed to note that the position was offered to the alien. This employer argued that the information was contained in other parts of the application, but BALCA rejected this argument without even receiving a brief from the certifying officer justifying his position. However, the decision generated a dissenting opinion from Judge Pamela Lakes Wood, who suggested that the position was clearly being offered to the alien notwithstanding the failure to mark yes in H-16. Judge Wood suggested that the error was analogous to the one in *HealthAmerica*, and she would have remanded the application for further processing.[38]

Lack of Federal Employer Identification Number

BALCA has now clearly stated in numerous cases, every employer, including household employers, must have a Federal Employer Identification Number (FEIN). In *Matter of Maria Gonzales*,[39] BALCA held that the use of a Social Security number is not sufficient to file a PERM application, and the application will be denied without the FEIN.[40] Because many of the household employers are submitting their applications pro se, this mistake continues to mark the BALCA docket, and the *Maria Gonzales* decision may soon be the most cited BALCA opinion.

The Job Order

The decisions on the job order issues appear to fall into two primary categories. First, was the order placed for 30 days, as required by the regulations?[41] Second, did the employer properly observe the 30-day quiet period following the placement of the job order? In a strange variation on this theme, BALCA decided one case that clearly qualifies as the least surprising decision of the season. BALCA held that the employer's assertion that he "was not aware that a job order was needed" was insufficient compliance with the regulations.[42]

The employer in *Matter of Lam Garden Chinese Restaurant*[43] requested the job order for 30 days, and the state workforce agency (SWA) placed it beginning on February 9, 2006, and ending March 9, 2006. Unfortunately, the fact that February only had 28 days in 2006 was overlooked by the SWA, and the job order ran for only 29 days. BALCA held that this was not the employer's error, and while the employer is often bound by SWA errors, the certifying officer has the discretion to take into account that the employer properly processed the application. Thus, in a case clearly limited to these facts, BALCA held that the mistake was SWA's, and it was not likely that the recruiting results would have substantively changed had the job order run one more day. BALCA ordered the application to be certified.

---

[34] *Matter of Best Manufacturing, Inc.*, 2007 PER 00080 (BALCA Dec. 19, 2007).

[35] 2007 PER 00081 (BALCA Dec. 19, 2007).

[36] *Id.*

[37] 2007 PER 00006 (BALCA May 21, 2007).

[38] BALCA has authority to sustain or reverse the denial, but not to remand. 20 CFR §656.27(c). The preamble to the PERM regulation was clear that BALCA did not have the authority to remand a case for further consideration. 69 Fed. Reg. 77325, 77363 (Dec. 27, 2004). While this issue was raised in *HealthAmerica*, BALCA accepted the certifying officer's argument that a remand was not improper because it had not ruled on the application in the first instance. Thus, it was proper to remand for consideration, if not reconsideration. BALCA recognized this "unique gloss on the meaning of the term 'remand,'" and left for further review the question of whether a remand was proper. The only reasonable interpretation of this discussion is that BALCA chose to remand the case because it thought this was the proper result in *HealthAmerica*, but this decision was not to be read as a determination that remands would be proper in future cases.

[39] 2007 PER 00024 (BALCA Apr. 25, 2007).

[40] *See Matter of Maria Gonzales*, 2007 PER 00024 (BALCA Apr. 25, 2007).

[41] 20 CFR §656.17(e)(2)(i).

[42] *Matter of Beck AG Operations, Inc.*, 2008 PER 00005 (BALCA Dec. 18, 2007).

[43] 2008 PER 00014 (BALCA Dec. 17, 2007).

However, there is no such leniency in the quiet-period cases. In several cases, beginning with *Matter of Luyon Corporation*,[44] BALCA has strictly construed the requirement of a 30-day quiet period following the end of the job order. Employers have argued that the 30 days have elapsed, if not before filing, at least before the application was reviewed or decided, and therefore the failure to wait 30 days was harmless. BALCA has rejected this argument in several cases.[45]

One rather troubling decision, however, failed to address a critical question presented by continuous recruiting, or any recruiting that is greater than required by the regulations. In *Matter of Oyassan*,[46] the employer placed the job order for 60 days beginning on June 12, 2006. The application was filed on July 19, 2006, but the job order continued for 60 days and was not removed until August 12, 2006. The employer argued that the quiet period required that the case be filed at least 31 days after the start of the job order. However, BALCA held that it was not the start date addressed by the regulation in question, but the end date. The job order must both start *and end* within the period of 30 to 180 days preceding the filing of the application. The application was denied. While *Oyassan* doesn't squarely present the problem of long-term or continuous recruiting, it would appear that if an employer found it useful to maintain a job order continuously, it would be required to either artificially terminate the date for purposes of the application (one might call this a requirement to misrepresent the termination date) or be permanently ineligible to file a PERM application. It appears to run counter to the theory and intent of the labor certification process to penalize employers for seeking U.S. workers on a continuous basis, but that would appear to be the application of the BALCA decision in *Oyassan*.

Application of the Kellogg Rule

BALCA denied certification in *Matter of Demos Consulting Group, Ltd.*[47] because the employer failed to include the magic *Kellogg* language[48] on the ETA Form 9089. The employer argued that the language was not required because the employee met the primary, and not the alternative requirements. The opinion was not clear on the manner in which the 9089 was prepared, but it appears that H-6 ("Is experience in the job offered required for the job?") was marked yes, with three years' experience noted in item H-6A. Item H-10 ("Is experience in an alternate occupation acceptable?") also appears to have also been marked yes. The decision notes that three years of experience in software development with multi-tiered client server applications would be acceptable, but it does not identify where on the application this requirement was established. It could have been in the text of item H-10B, or possibly item H-14. In any event, it is clear that the individual had this three years of experience. The employer claimed that this experience was the primary requirement, but BALCA determined that it was the alternative requirement, because the primary requirement was three years' experience in the job offered. Thus, the absence of the *Kellogg* language was fatal to the application.

It appears that if item H-6 had been marked no, and H-10 marked yes, experience in the alternative occupation would have been the primary requirement, and the *Kellogg* language would not have been required.[49] However, by requiring experience in the job offered rather than an alternative occupation (even if this alternative occupation is the same as the job offered) with defined experience parameters, the individual was qualified only by virtue of the alternative requirements. While further litigation to find the parameters and meaning of the *Kellogg* language requirements might be expected, we hope that the new form, when it is finalized, will provide further clarity and help to eliminate at least some of the ambiguities of this regulation.

Wrong DOL Address on the Posting

In *Matter of Brooklyn Amity School*,[50] the employer posted the required notice of the filing of an application for permanent employment certifica-

---

[44] 2007 PER 00027 (BALCA June 12, 2007).

[45] *See, e.g., Matter of Syncsort Inc.*, 2007 PER 00067 (BALCA Dec. 18, 2007).

[46] 2007 PER 00069 (BALCA Dec. 18, 2007). *Cf.* DOL PERM FAQ Round #7, *available at www.foreignlaborcert.doleta.gov/pdf/perm_faqs_2-21-06.pdf*, stating that an employer can post a notice of filing indefinitely.

[47] 2007 PER 00020 (BALCA May 16, 2007).

[48] 20 CFR §656.17(h)(4)(ii). *See Matter of Francis Kellogg*, 1994 INA 00465 (BALCA Feb. 2, 1998) (en banc).

[49] See DOL PERM FAQ Round #10, at 2, *available at www.foreignlaborcert.doleta.gov/pdf/perm_faqs_5-9-07.pdf*, which addresses this concern.

[50] 2007 PER 00064 (BALCA Sept. 19, 2007).

tion,[51] but listed the local (New York) address of the regional certifying officer rather than the PERM Processing Center in Atlanta. The regional office was still open in July 2005, as it was wrapping up the pre-PERM cases. BALCA determined that the mistake by the employer was not fatal because the certifying officer still had an office at the posted address and DOL could have received and processed comments in response to the notice. BALCA also noted that because the regional offices are now closed, these facts are not likely to re-occur and employers would be ill-advised to rely upon this case to justify a wrong address. We note, however, that the Chicago office will be transferring all PERM applications to Atlanta in June 2008 and thus, the Atlanta address should be used on all postings for applications filed after the change is announced.[52] While *Brooklyn Amity School* might provide support for continued notices listing Chicago as the contact for comments or complaints, the better practice will be to change the address on all notices posted after DOL provides notice that the PERM cases will all be handled in Atlanta.

Handling Layoffs Under PERM

DOL has had a longstanding concern about employer-specific and industry-wide layoffs in connection with applications for labor certification. These concerns have been codified in the PERM regulations—for the first time, an employer must state affirmatively on the application form whether or not layoffs have taken place within the last six months for the same or similar occupations in the area of intended employment.[53] Employers must also state that laid-off workers have been notified and considered for the position that is the subject of the PERM application.[54]

There has been a lack of guidance since the inception of the PERM regulations, possibly because the unfolding of the PERM program occurred in a period of relatively few layoffs. As 2008 heralded a period of increased layoffs in some industries that are heavy users of the PERM program, further guidance will hopefully be forthcoming.

A layoff is defined as "any involuntary separation of one or more employees without cause or

prejudice."[55] Not every circumstance is clear cut. For example, some employers may cull their workforce of the "poor performers." In many instances, these may be dismissals for cause. But if no replacements are hired to fill the vacancies created and if terminated workers were told they were being dismissed because of a workforce reduction, the actions may be considered layoffs. Whether a termination is a layoff frequently needs to be considered on a case-by-case basis.

The layoffs must have taken place in the "area of intended employment."[56] This terminology reflects a long-established measurable standard under labor certification rules and pertains to all locations in a specific standard metropolitan statistical area or any worksites that are within normal commuting distance of each other.[57] Accordingly, layoffs requiring affirmation on ETA Form 9089 are not limited to those occurring at the worksite indicated on the 9089; they also include layoffs at all the employer's worksite locations in the area of intended employment.

The layoffs must be in the same or similar occupation as the one contained in a PERM application to require an affirmation regarding layoffs on the 9089. A similar occupation is defined as one in which the majority of key duties are the same as the key duties in the position for which labor certification is being sought.[58]

If the employer has laid off similarly employed persons in the same area of intended employment within the past six months, the regulations require that the appropriate laid-off workers be notified and considered. The regulations do not assume that similarly employed workers are deemed to be qualified, but rather require that these laid-off workers be notified and evaluated.[59] The type of notification required is not clear, and it is obviously easier to notify a few laid-off employees than a few hundred. Clear guidance is also lacking on whether all those similarly employed must be considered or if only those who appear to be qualified need to be considered.

Industry-wide layoffs in the area of intended employment are also a concern for DOL, and can have

[51] *See* 20 CFR §656.10(d).

[52] 73 Fed. Reg. 11954 (Mar. 5, 2008).

[53] 20 CFR §656.17(k)(1). *See* ETA Form 9089, p. 5.

[54] 20 CFR §656.17(k)(1). *See* ETA Form 9089, p. 5.

[55] 20 CFR §656.17(k)(1).

[56] For the definition of this term, see 20 CFR §656.3.

[57] *Id.*

[58] 20 CFR §656.17(k)(2).

[59] 69 Fed. Reg. 77325, 77354–55 (Dec. 27, 2004) (supplementary information).

an impact on PERM applications for employers that have not had layoffs but that employ workers in similar occupations in the area of intended employment. While the employer is not required to take affirmative steps in the event of layoffs from other employers in the geographic area, DOL has the authority to require supervised recruitment based on labor market information, including layoffs.[60] DOL typically uncovers layoffs by accessing unemployment claims and Worker Adjustment and Retraining Notification Act[61] (WARN) notices. In addition, the prospect of increased use of supervised recruitment under PERM was affirmed by a representative of the Office of Foreign Labor Certification at the December 2007 New York AILA continuing legal education program.

Under the old labor certification system, similar premises have driven the issue of both employer-applicant layoffs and industry-wide layoffs. While treated similarly, applications under the old system had additional complications as a result of long processing backlogs. Layoffs occurring within six months of filing and layoffs occurring within six months of adjudication were both subject to scrutiny.[62] The recent lengthening of the adjudication time for PERM applications once again raises the specter of how DOL will react to post-filing layoffs of the employer or of other employers in the area of intended employment.

The presence of layoffs in related occupations for which labor certification is being sought clearly places a heavy burden on the employer. Attorneys should inquire at the beginning of a matter about the possible presence of layoffs in the recent past or near future that may impact the PERM application. If layoffs have occurred or are imminent, it may be wise to suggest the option, in cases that don't have timing issues, of postponing PERM filings for a period of time.

THE NEW PERM FORM— CHANGES AND CORRECTIONS

The existing ETA Form 9089 expired in March 2008. In anticipation, DOL published a proposed new form and sought public comment.[63] DOL sent a revised version of the proposed form to the Office of Management and Budget on March 31, 2008.[64] DOL has announced in liaison with its stakeholders that the current form's validity has been extended and that the new form is likely to be effective on January 1, 2009. The comments below are based on the published proposed form as of March 31, 2008; however, the new form may undergo more modifications before it is finalized. DOL's task requires substantial amendments to its processing software and systems as well as finalizing the appearance of the proposed form.

Beneficiary's Name Up Front

The name of the beneficiary will be moved to the first page of the form. This is a modification that will make it much easier to file and track the paper copies of applications manually.

DBA Option

The proposed form provides an option for an employer to indicate that it is doing business as (DBA) a name other than its legal name. This option would help avoid erroneous denials due to the name not being properly recognized. Previously the employers were only prompted to indicate DBA names when registering for a PERM account online.

Alternative Requirements

The proposed revised form modifies how alternative requirements would be stated. The format would allow the employer to provide up to three sets of alternative requirements to the basic set of job requirements. Each alternative would be a complete set of requirements phrased in terms of education, experience, and training. Further, the proposed form allows the employer to require more than one educational degree (such as a technical undergraduate degree and an MBA).

No More Traps for Failure To Include the "Magic Language"

The existing ETA Form 9089 requires the employer to be familiar enough with the regulations to

---

[60] 69 Fed. Reg. 77325, 77354 (Dec. 27, 2004) (supplementary information).

[61] *See* 29 USC §§2101–09.

[62] DOL Memorandum, D. Ziegler, "Clarification of Reduction in Recruitment (RIR) Policy in an Environment of Increased Layoffs" (May 28, 2002), *published on* AILA InfoNet at Doc. No. 02060703 (*posted* June 7, 2002).

---

[63] 72 Fed. Reg. 48689 (Aug. 24, 2007). See AILA InfoNet at Doc. No. 07082466 (*posted* Aug. 24, 2007) for links to a .pdf version of the proposed form and proposed form instructions.

[64] 73 Fed. Reg. 16912 (Mar. 31, 2008).

know that if the beneficiary is currently working for the employer, and qualifies for the job only based on the employer's alternative requirements, the application will be denied unless it states that the employer will accept any suitable combination of education, training, or experience. The existing form has no specific place to insert this language, so most practitioners place it in Box H-14. DOL wisely proposes to include a series of questions indicating whether the "magic language" is required, and then include a checkbox that the employer accepts or does not accept the "magic language."

Roving Employees

DOL's proposed form includes options for roving employees and employees who work out of their homes. Employers need to know where to advertise, where to post notice,[65] and where to seek a prevailing wage determination when the location of the work is not fixed or is based at the employee's home but includes substantial periods of time at other locations. The proposed form provides some checkboxes for the employer to explain whether the worksite is at a business premise, is at the employer's home, is at the employee's home, or is at more than one location. When work is performed at more than one location, the employer may list up to five metropolitan statistical areas where work will be performed. If the location is unknown, the proposed form includes a text box for the employer to explain the location of work.

Employer Must Report Number of Employees in the Job Location

The new form may require employers to specify how many employees they have at the work location where the beneficiary will be employed. Many large employers with multiple worksites do not currently report this information, and some may not have it readily available. DOL representatives have stated that one purpose of requiring this information is to determine whether the employer is filing a greater number of labor certification applications than the current number of workers at the jobsite. This could be a factor that would cause DOL to question whether each of the applications represents a bona fide job opportunity.

Text Boxes Added To Explain Audit Trigger Issues

The proposed form has additional text boxes to provide the opportunity to explain certain issues that could be audit triggers. For example, text boxes are included for the employer to explain the need for a foreign language requirement, and to explain the business necessity for job requirements that exceed the SVP level in the job zone that was assigned by the SWA in the prevailing wage determination. In addition, a text field allows the employer to explain the nature of a layoff and the method by which U.S. workers were notified and considered for the job opportunity. To the extent the form includes more text fields that require interpretation, DOL must be prepared to make its adjudications based on trained human analysts in addition to its automated computer decision matrix. A cogent explanation in the text box may provide enough information to satisfy DOL that a full audit is not required.

Experience and Employment Experience

The proposed form asks if employment experience—not experience—is required. This question assumes that employers would not accept unpaid internships or volunteer experience as qualifying experience. The employer may still require training that is distinct from employment experience.

No Need To Specify Whether Beneficiary Has Experience in the Job Offered or in a Related Occupation

The proposed form would no longer require the employer to decide whether the beneficiary gained experience in the job offered or in a related occupation. Nor would it ask whether experience in the job offered is required. These are welcome modifications. Under the existing 9089, it is confusing to decide how to answer when the beneficiary performed some but not all of the duties in the job description, or when the job description matched the beneficiary's experience closely, but the employee had a very different job title. So long as the beneficiary met all of the job requirements, it doesn't really matter whether the beneficiary gained the experience in a job that was exactly the same as the job offered in the labor certification or in a related occupation.

---

[65] According to minutes from the DOL stakeholders liaison meeting on March 15, 2007, *published on* AILA InfoNet at Doc. No. 07041264 (*posted* Apr. 12, 2007), notice of posting may be at company headquarters when the beneficiary is a roaming employee not assigned to a designated region. However, a DOL FAQ indicates that for Schedule A employees, if the employer does not know where the employee will be placed, the employer must post the notice at the worksite(s) of all of its current clients. DOL PERM FAQ Round #7, *available at www.foreignlaborcert.doleta.gov/pdf/perm_faqs_2-21-06.pdf.* This FAQ by its terms is limited to Schedule A applications.

Fewer/More Employee Details Required

The portion of the new form devoted to the qualifications of the beneficiaries is likely to be different than the existing form. Some details, such as the street address of the educational institution attended, may disappear. The proposed form and its instructions do not require listing the name of the employee's manager at past jobs, nor the telephone number of the prior employer. At the same time, DOL may provide space for beneficiaries to list more than one degree, rather than the highest degree relevant to the occupation. This would be a welcome change and would likely end the occasional incongruous denial on the grounds that the foreign national was not qualified because he or she specified a Ph.D. degree when the job requirement was only a Master's degree.

Substitute Signatures

The proposed form would allow for a substitute to sign the approved labor certification on behalf of the employer or the preparer, in the event there is a change in either after filing. Since beneficiaries may not be substituted, there would be no substitute permitted for the beneficiary's signature.

Form Still in Flux

Extensive analysis of the differences between the existing ETA Form 9089 and the revision proposed by DOL is premature at this time. DOL may make still more revisions before it finalizes the form. One might wonder whether the improvements to the form would justify waiting until the new form is published before filing. Perhaps, for example, an application would not be audited if the employer could provide its explanation of business necessity right on the form. But it would be wiser to not delay a case in anticipation of the new form. The uncertainty in the new form's actual effective date, the reality that DOL will still audit a significant number of applications, and the continued long quota waits in several employment-sponsored categories mean that most employers would be better off filing sooner rather than later.

CONCLUSION

Labor certification practice is no different than most other areas of immigration law, in that the effective practitioner must keep up with practice and policy changes that are formally announced in the *Federal Register* and administrative decisions, and informally gleaned from reported processing trends and liaison reports. Last year's developments in the area of labor certifications are not as dramatic as the 2005 sea change brought about by PERM. Nevertheless, we hope that our discussion of (1) the 2007 anti-fraud rule; (2) recent BALCA decisions; (3) layoffs, and (4) the proposed new ETA Form 9089 serves as a reminder of some of the important PERM trends for practitioners to monitor.

WHAT A DIFFERENCE A FIELD MAKES: FIELD DELINEATION IN THE EB-1 AND EB-2 CLASSIFICATIONS

*by Nathan A. Waxman**

Discernment of both the field and the field's experts, that is true wisdom.[†]

America's early 2008 economic doldrums[1] seem not to have dimmed the enthusiasm of intending immigrants for seeking permanent residence through the four labor certification exempt mechanisms available under the Immigration and Nationality Act involving a qualitative assessment of their professional, scientific, or artistic efforts.[2]

While these four mechanisms under the first and second employment preferences (EB-1, EB-2) vary significantly in substance and procedure, they have in common the qualitative review of the prospective beneficiary's contribution and recognition within his or her field of endeavor.

Considerable attention has been devoted to assessing the nature and type of evidence necessary and sufficient to establish eligibility under these EB-1 and EB-2 labor certification circumvention routes.[3]

This article will not primarily address the evidentiary requirements for these EB-1 and EB-2 mechanisms. On the contrary, the focus will be on a threshold issue that this author believes is critical to the conceptualization and successful preparation of any and all of these petitions: the clear and judicious delineation of the field of endeavor on which the beneficiary's alleged superiority is premised.[4]

WHAT FIELD IS IT AFTER ALL?

The four EB-1 and EB-2 mechanisms addressed in this article share a frame of reference within which the beneficiary's alleged qualitative superiority must be documented with specific reference to a specified field within the arts or sciences (Extraordinary Ability[5] and/or Schedule A, Group II[6]) and academic field (Outstanding Researcher or Professor[7]) or a field within the arts, sciences, business, or the professions (National Interest Waiver [NIW][8]).

Is designating an appropriate field of endeavor really so challenging? Don't our clients typically present themselves with fairly clear, well-defined, and easily discernible fields in which they excel? Transparent congruence between a prospective client's field of endeavor and his or her academic or experiential profile is by no means unusual, but it is no longer necessarily the norm. The postmodern, postindustrial world, with the proliferation and hybridization of technologies and of basic areas of research, has seen the continuous generation of new areas of specialization, from cognitive linguistics to ergonomics to proteomics—fields that stretch the familiar boundaries of academic departments and workplace organization.

This ever-more complex environment provides novel opportunities for employees to apply the skills of one field in the practice of another. The financial industry, for example, employs doctoral-level bio-

---

* Copyright © 2008 by Nathan A. Waxman. All rights reserved. Reprinted with permission.

Nathan A. Waxman practices business and professional employment-based immigration law in New York City with an academic, corporate, and individual client base throughout the United States. He has been a member of AILA since 1985 and writes and lectures extensively on business and immigration topics.

The author wishes to thank Naomi Schorr and Susu Durst for their assistance with this article.

[†] *Bhagavad Gita* 13:2, 13:3 in some editions.

[1] Other considerations might include expanding PERM processing delays, in conjunction with such dire consequences of a declining economy as layoffs and downsizing. Moreover, EB-2 retrogression has increased the appeal of EB-1 for many India- and China-chargeable beneficiaries.

[2] Discussion of EB-1-3 for multinational managers and executives and EB-2 gained through labor certification is excluded, as neither requires documentation of comparative superiority.

[3] *See, e.g.*, A. Cherazi *et al.*, "Employment-Based Petitions Exempt from Labor Certification," *Immigration and Nationality Law Handbook* 291 (2005–06 Ed.).

[4] This article updates and expands the discussion of field of endeavor in N. Waxman, "What's the Angle? Overcoming *NYSDOT*'s Three Legs," 2 *Immigration & Nationality Law Handbook* 203 (2003–04 Ed.).

[5] INA §203(b)(1)(A).

[6] INA §212(a)(5)(A)(ii)(II).

[7] INA §203(b)(1)(A).

[8] INA §203(b)(2)(B).

statisticians and computational astrophysicists to model economic activities and predict trends.

Let's now look at the way field delineation manifests itself in each of the four categories.

EXTRAORDINARY ABILITY[9]

By any reckoning, extraordinary ability is a formidable mechanism for acquiring residence, as it requires documentation that the beneficiary has risen to the very top of his or her field.

First EB-1-1 Precedent Decision: The Price Was Right

The first reported Administrative Appeals Office (AAO) decision in an extraordinary ability case involved Nick Price, a professional golfer who, in the words of the industry journal *Golf Digest*, was "the best player on the planet."[10]

This case, designated a precedent case in 1994, represents the antithesis of the typical scenario confronting most immigration practitioners: that of the consummate practitioner of a canonical field, indisputably at the very top of an easily demarcated field.

Suppose, however, we alter the fact pattern. Had Mr. Price sought extraordinary ability classification years later, beyond his period of sustained recognition as a competitive golfer, but rather while he was initiating a second career as a golf coach, golf historian, or golf commentator, would the outcome be different? Both the service centers and the AAO have expressed skepticism over the EB-1-1 classification of athletes initiating careers in coaching on the cessation of their competitive careers. Absent evidence of a clear nexus between such an applicant's competitive recognition and the as-yet speculative accomplishments of such individuals in post-competition activities, EB-1-1 success is often doubtful.[11] On the con-

trary, should a postcareer athlete, actor, or opera singer successfully mutate into a great mentor or critic, a common denominator might well be denominated, with ensuing favorable result.[12]

Buletini v. INS: Can a Field Be Too Narrowly Defined?

The *Buletini* case[13] has been exhaustively discussed in the EB-1-1 literature. This first reported federal court decision relating to any of our four qualitative assessment mechanisms challenged the legacy Immigration and Naturalization Service (INS) and AAO denials of an EB-1-1 petition of a foreign medical graduate characterized in his petition as a nephrologist. *Buletini* is primarily remembered for its recognition that EB-1-1 could be premised on *either* sustained international or national recognition within a defined field in the arts or sciences. *Buletini* also admonished legacy INS that it was obligated by law to apply its own regulatory criteria to submitted evidence—a mandate sometimes, in the ensuing decade and a half, honored more in the breach than the observance.

However, *Buletini* also is important from the perspective of field delineation. While the petition sought classification of Dr. Buletini as an Albanian nephrologist, the federal court observed that he was better described as

> a physician who practices (that is, attends to patients) in the field of internal medicine, including gynecology, and who holds a specialized degree in general pathology with a concentration in nephrology.

While the court expressed skepticism as to the Albanian physician's qualification "in the narrow field of nephrology," it glowingly commended the eclecticism of his general contribution to the broader field of medicine in Albania, as manifested in such varied accomplishments as his compilation of an unpublished (due to a paper shortage) book, *Alba-*

---

[9] For a recent examination of the EB-1-1, *see* C. Recio, "Recent Adjudications of EB-1 and EB-2 Cases," *Immigration & Nationality Law Handbook* (AILA 2003–04 Ed.), and S. Seltzer, "How to Improve the Impact of Reference Letters Establishing Extraordinary Ability," *Immigration Options for Academics and Researchers* 165 (2005), available from AILA Publications, *www.ailapubs.org*, (800) 982-2839.

[10] *Matter of Price*, 20 I&N Dec. 953 (Assoc. Comm'r AAO 1994). *Price* had been certified on appeal to the appellate unit, and not, like so many meritorious cases in its wake, simply denied by a service center.

[11] Such a scenario may well be appropriate for NIW. *See*, for example, the successful appeal of a sculling coach, *Matter of [name not provided]* NSC 76 863 824 (AAO Sept. 16, 1998), discussed in N. Waxman, "*New York State Department of* continued

---

Transportation: National Interest Waiver One Year Down the Road," 76 *Interpreter Releases* 1141 (Nov. 15, 1999).

[12] *See*, for example, the successful EB-1 case of a martial arts coach turned martial arts movie star (in China) who subsequently segued into an internationally renowned chi-gong teacher, described in N. Waxman, "Mainstreaming the Alternative: An Outline of Immigration Issues and Opportunities in Complimentary and Alternative Health Care," *Immigration Options for Physicians* 237 (2d Ed.), available from AILA Publications, *www.ailapubs.org*, (800) 982-2839.

[13] *Buletini v. INS*, 860 F. Supp 1222 (E.D. Mich. 1994).

nian-German Medical Lexicon, his chronicling the history of public health in Southeastern Albania, and his receipt of impressive (by Albanian standards) compensation and national commendation.

Few of our clients today will demonstrate the breadth of accomplishment of the beleaguered Albanian physician, compelling us to generally narrow rather than expand the characteristics of our clients' fields of endeavor. Two mid-1990s federal court cases regarding National Hockey League (NHL) players illustrate more typical fact patterns.

The Hockey Cases: Position Defines the Field

In *Muni v. INS*[14] and *Grimson v. INS*,[15] the federal court in Chicago rejected the argument that playing on a winning NHL team per se established EB-1-1 eligibility.

Nonetheless, in both cases the Canadian self-petitioners were recognized as being within the small percentage of individuals at the top of their respective fields within the broader realm of professional hockey, *i.e.,* the positions of "defenseman" (Muni) and "enforcer" (Grimson). Unlike Mr. Price, whose consummate achievement as a golf pro placed him at the pinnacle of success in professional golf, these exceptionally capable albeit ferocious players were merely in the upper echelon of their respective subfields within the broader realm of professional hockey.

The Clydesdales: No Run for the Roses, But Head and Shoulders Above Their Field

Our final foray into the variegated world of the arts and sciences concerns the AAO's reversal of the Nebraska Service Center's (NSC) denial of the EB-1-1 self-petition of the indisputably foremost U.S. driver/shower of Clydesdale horses.[16] In addition to winning every conceivable Clydesdale

event, the self-petitioner was commended by the breeder of the celebrated Budweiser Clydesdale as being the "best showman and driver of Clydesdale horses in North America."

The AAO in this entertaining and instructive decision resoundingly rejected NSC's grounding denial on its observation that Clydesdale events constituted only a "small component of the competitive world of horse racing and display." Admittedly, the self petitioner's elephantine equines have been conspicuously absent at Louisville's celebrated "Run for the Roses." Significantly, the AAO recognized that the Clydesdale driver/shower had driven and shown Clydesdale horses at every conceivably appropriate event, TV commercial, or other private or public display of these supersized draft horses. The AAO was so impressed by the concentration of evidence of the petitioner's preeminence within this specialized art that it grounded its favorable decision on the inapplicability of the 10 evidentiary criteria enumerated at 8 CFR §204.5(h)(3) to the showing of Clydesdales. This is the rare instance in which the AAO permitted the substitution of "comparable evidence," as authorized by 8 CFR §204.5(h)(4) when the generally applicable criteria simply do not apply.

The Clydesdale case should serve as a wake-up call to EB-1-1 petitioners and their advocates to forcefully argue the inappropriateness of the *three out of ten* criteria under 8 CFR §204.5(h)(3), and the applicability of the substitution of evidence provision, 8 CFR §204.5(h)(4). Needless to say, the burden of proof on this will reside with the petitioner. In such cases, the paramount importance of appropriate and judicious field delineation is truly highlighted, as petitioners may avail themselves of a rarely recognized opportunity for establishing satisfaction of the EB-1-1 evidentiary criteria.

Outstanding Professor/Researcher

The EB-1-2 mechanism differs in subtle and significant ways from the EB-1-1 in terms of substantive eligibility, requiring that an appropriate academic or research petitioner offer full-time employment to an individual possessing at least three years of teaching and/or research experience in the "academic field."[17]

From the limited perspective of this article, the EB-1-2 category is particularly noteworthy in that it is restricted to *academic* fields, as contrasted with

---

[14] 891 F. Supp. 440 (N.D. Ill. 1995).

[15] 934 F. Supp. 965 (N.D. Ill. 1996). Judge Gettleman admonished the AAO and Nebraska Service Center that Mr. Grimson's "disfavored" conduct (a league record for penalties for fighting) was not a ground for denial, as it was a necessary and accepted element of the game. Indeed, isn't that its main appeal? Legal, albeit disfavored activities should be contrasted with illegal activities, such as importation of elephant tusks. Compare the early 1990 saga of the ivory importer whose unsuccessful appeal was detailed in N. Schorr, "They Don't Shoot Elephants, Do They?: The National Interest Waiver for EB-2," 70 *Interpreter Releases* 773 (June 14, 1993).

[16] *Matter of [name not provided]*, LIN 96 203 50280 (AAO April 27, 1998), 19 Immigr. Rptr. B2-9.

[17] 8 CFR §204.5(i)(3)(ii).

EB-1-1's broad compass within the realm of the arts and sciences.

Perhaps surprisingly, EB-1-2's restriction to academic fields has not constituted a significant challenge to appropriate cases. Casual comparison of the printed college catalogs of the 1960s with their online counterparts today would reveal an astonishing kaleidoscopic proliferation in such fields as "career pilot technology," "air conditioning and refrigeration," and "agribusiness technology."[18] Importantly for our inquiry, EB-1-2 eligibility requires three years of experience in the academic field, not three years of academic institutional experience. While admittedly the experience must be in research or teaching, a broad variety of writers, artists, politicians, or diplomats who have decided to pursue the enviable life of the mind in universities or private think tanks can avail themselves of the EB-1-2 by documenting that their prior activities fell within the loosely denominated realms of research or teaching, should they be offered an appropriate research or professorial position.[19]

In keeping with the seemingly unlimited proliferation of incipient subfields, such as forensic linguistics, or hybridized fields, such as anthropological psycholinguistics or nutritional genomics, it is important to recognize that neither statute nor applicable regulations require that the beneficiary hold a degree in the academic field in which the beneficiary's qualitative superiority is claimed. Indeed, significant apparent divergence in the academic department in which a beneficiary is employed and the beneficiary's academic background should not deter practitioners from handling appropriate cases.

Illustrative of an apparent disconnect resolved through submission of extensive responsive evidence to a request for evidence is the author's recent handling of an EB-1-2 petition for a professor of German holding an undergraduate business degree, and documenting her international recognition in the field of "Orientalism/Neo-Colonial" studies. Eschewing Goethe's The Sorrows of Young Werther and the song cycles of Wagner for the handwritten diaries of 18th century Hessian ministers seeking to convert untouchables in rural South India, this assistant professor of German premised successful review exclusively on testimony outside of Germanic studies, including faculty in fields as diverse as South Asian Studies, Gender Studies, and History of Religions.

Thus, an academic authority on the structuralist Lacan, a post-Freudian psychiatrist, could achieve success despite a career migration from comparative literature through anthropology to semiotics. Indeed, EB-1-2 classification could conceivably be established for a scholar whose international recognition is founded in her deconstructing the ostensibly artificial boundaries between the traditional and emerging academic disciplines. In such an instance, success would entail documentation that the apparent "anti-field" has, in fact, acquired some recognition within the walls of academia as an incipient academic field.

Finally, a note on AAO review of EB-1-2 petitions: Virtually all AAO adjudications of denied EB-1-2 petitions turn on evidentiary considerations or procedural inadequacies.[20] However, it is urged that many otherwise appropriate, albeit unsuccessful, EB-1-2 cases might have achieved success had the petition better articulated the nexus between the beneficiary's prior endeavors and his or her current position. The aforementioned professor of German whose work product was and remains exclusively focused on the investigation of the abortive German and Danish attempt to convert the economically disenfranchised in South India to various Protestant denominations would not have achieved favorable review without the credible documentation of the nexus between her prior work, none of which was published or discussed in the broader field of Germanic studies, and the research and teaching that she was doing at the petitioning institution.

NATIONAL INTEREST WAIVER

Since 1998, intending immigrants seeking EB-2 classification under the national interest waiver (NIW) labor certification exemption mechanism have been subjected to the often dissected[21] three-step analysis imposed by the AAO's New York State Department of Transportation (NYSDOT) precedent

---

[18] See, e.g., the online catalogue of Southwest Texas Junior College, Uvalde, TX, www.swtjc.net.

[19] Cf., e.g., Saul Bellow, who, after an early nonacademic career as a novelist, was appointed as Professor at the Committee on Social Thought at the University of Chicago.

[20] For a recent study of EB-1-2 AAO decisions, see E. Farrell, et al., "Current Trends in EB-1-2 Outstanding Researcher Cases," Immigration Options for Academics and Researchers (2005).

[21] For a recent more detailed dissection of NYSDOT's three-step analysis, and review of prior literature, see N. Waxman, "What's the Angle? Overcoming NYSDOT's Three Legs," Immigration & Nationality Law Handbook (AILA 2003–04 Ed.).

decision.[22] Careful delineation of field of endeavor is indispensable to surmounting each of *NYSDOT*'s three legs. Let us briefly circumnavigate the *NYSDOT* triangle from the limited perspective of appropriate designation of field of endeavor.

Leg 1: Substantial Intrinsic Merit

While *NYSDOT*'s first leg requiring that a field of endeavor fall within an area of "substantial intrinsic merit" rarely has affected nonfrivolous petitions falling within the broader ambit of the sciences, arts, or business, this requirement should not be disregarded. There is little doubt that a dermatologist advancing research or developing clinical care and modalities relating to painful skin conditions or melanoma gets off to a significantly better start with service center adjudicators than an equally qualified clinical dermatologist whose case is premised on a clinical practice specializing in well-established cosmetic procedures.

Leg 2: National in Scope

NYSDOT's second leg mandates that the waiver applicant's prospective service be documented to be national in scope. This restriction was in large part motivated by the legacy agency's stated abhorrence of aliens obtaining residence premised on what the service perceived to be a request for a "blanket waiver," justified primarily by the societal importance of their field of endeavor, whether social work, medicine, or public interest law. *NYSDOT* closes the gap for purely geographically circumscribed practitioners of most professions who cannot convincingly demonstrate the aggregative national impact of their efforts.[23]

Petitioners who anticipate the likelihood of denial under the national impact component of *NYSDOT* always should attempt to argue that their services, however seemingly localized in scope, have a ripple effect on the nation at large, directly analogous to the services performed by the hapless highway engineer as recognized by the AAO in the precedent decision. Accordingly, an art therapist whose services were currently limited by the terms of her H-1 employment to a senior citizen center in the Bronx premised her successful petition handled by the author on her development of nationally disseminated instructional or inspirational materials applying art therapy to overcoming post-traumatic consequences of the conspicuously national problem of child abuse.

Leg 3: Track Record of Success: Influencing the Field as a Whole

By far the greatest challenge confronting NIW beneficiaries is *NYSDOT*'s somewhat inscrutable third leg, which inevitably reduces to whether an alien significantly benefits a circumscribed field of endeavor, as manifested in a record of success convincingly evidencing an influence on that field as a whole.

The *Kaiser* Case: The Difference a Field Can Make

Much has been written about the diversity of NIW scenarios successfully surmounting the *NYSDOT* triangle in the 10 years since its designation as a precedent. However, few cases have manifested the significance of careful field delineation more clearly than that of the engineer whose NIW petition was reversed by the AAO in *Matter of Kaiser Aerospace and Electrics Corporation*.[24]

In *Kaiser*, the AAO recognized the eligibility of a rudder design engineer whose academic credentials were sound but unexceptional and who had neither published internationally nor achieved recognition beyond a narrow range of colleagues and clients. As an employee of a Boeing subcontractor, the *Kaiser* beneficiary's work product was proprietary and his contributions to commercial aircraft safety were not demonstrable through the presentation of objective evidence, such as commentary in trade journals. Nonetheless, he had contributed significantly to the redesign of rudder mechanisms (*i.e.,* actuators) that had been found to be responsible for the Alaska Airlines crash in 2000.[25]

The relevance of *Kaiser* is simply this: the beneficiary was neither a research engineer nor an engineering scholar; his field was "shirt sleeve" rudder engineering. Moreover, the *Kaiser* beneficiary's work product was proprietary and, accordingly, neither nationally acknowledged nor recognized. Nonetheless, the AAO clearly acknowledged the national interest waiver of this relatively obscure figure in rudder engineering, and should be applauded for doing so.

---

[22] *Matter of New York State Department of Transportation,* 22 I&N Dec. 215 (Assoc. Comm'r 1998).

[23] However, by statutory amendment, qualifying physicians working in medically underserved areas qualify through a limited statutory blanket waiver, now incorporated into INA §203(b)(2)(B)(ii).

[24] AAO Mar. 28, 2003, 28 Immig. Rptr. B2-1.

[25] The author is proud to have handled the AAO appeal of the California Service Center's denial of this highly meritorious case.

The ramifications of the aforementioned successful appeal for assessing the comparative appropriateness of the NIW *vis-à-vis* such categories as Extraordinary Ability, Outstanding Researcher, or Schedule A, Group II, are far-reaching. First, a broad class of engineers, financial analysts, chemists, and similar professional workers performing proprietary services, often subject to trade secret limitations on disclosure, may find the NIW the exclusive means for avoiding labor certification. Second, the AAO has admonished the service centers that "[they] must consider the circumstances of the beneficiary's employment." This observation should benefit applicants, in otherwise meritorious cases, whose supporting evidence is concentrated on the declarations of colleagues or customers, and deficient in the ostensibly disinterested testimony of third-party authorities. Advocates should be cautioned, however, to confine petitions alleging the national benefit of proprietary service to cases whose factual contexts are congruent with the *NYSDOT* triangle.

The Importance of Conferring with NIW Clients *Vis a Vis* Fields

Success in the *Kaiser* appeal resulted from AAO's recognition that the beneficiary's field was the narrowly defined area of commercial aircraft rudder engineering, not the broader spectrum of mechanical or aeronautical engineering. Similarly, the Clydesdale decision turned on the demonstrably specialized nature of the field of Clydesdale showing and driving. As suggested above, such easily demarcated client scenarios are by no means universal. The proliferation of new fields and our society's tolerance for—and acceptance of—personal and professional transformation renders conceptualization of many client scenarios far more challenging from the perspective of EB-1 and EB-2 advocacy.

The clear delineation of the field of endeavor allegedly advanced by an EB-1 or EB-2 petitioner should be a *critical* threshold issue unambiguously resolved in the presentation of the petition. The determination of the applicant's field of endeavor should never be left to the desultory curiosity of the overburdened adjudicator. It is incumbent on all applicants, particularly those whose apparent eclecticism renders field definition challenging, or who have recently morphed from nuclear physics postdoctoral fellows to financial analysts, to delineate with clarity what field they allege their services to advance. An applicant's clear presentation of the continuity and coherence within a definable, albeit at

times undeniably incipient, field often distinguishes success from failure in otherwise similar petitions.[26]

Ultimately, many approved petitions have required the delineation of a unitary field through the identification of the *common denominator* linking the applicant's apparently disparate endeavors. Thus, success in the NIW petition of a scientist recently reborn as a financial analyst might be premised on persuasive documentation that the applicant's former research in computational physics relates directly to the applicant's current service as a computational financial analyst. Such a demonstration could establish that the applicant is employing mathematical modeling techniques he or she developed as a computational physicist to the forecasting of futures trends extrapolated from historical econometric data. Similarly, the art therapist developing techniques for retarding memory loss or enhancing socialization in a geriatric population may be able to establish that his or her long-term commitment to applying analogous therapies to other adjustmentally impaired constituencies, such as inmates or recidivist drug addicts, contributes to the national interest in a field broader than his or her immediate occupational endeavor.

Delineation of the applicant's field, although challenging at times, particularly for multitalented clients whose alleged contributions appear to defy ready categorization into a generally recognized area of endeavor, is critical. There is no substitute for extensive consultation between attorney and client in this matter. In many instances, amassing supporting documentation regarding the legitimacy of the field definition will prove to be as challenging as confirming that the applicant's service meaningfully constitutes a substantial benefit to, or in, that field of endeavor. The existence of associations, journals, or topically focused organizations (in some instances virtual) may prove invaluable, particularly in emerg-

---

[26] Actual redacted submissions of cover memoranda, letters to proponents, and testimonial documentation regarding two such cases were published in N. Waxman, "National Interest Waiver: Two Case Studies," *AILA's Immigration Practice Toolbox* 251 (2d Ed.), available from AILA Publications, *www.ailapubs.org*, (800) 982-2839. These real petitions of a doctoral student in "Urban Aesthetics," whose case was predicated on her highly eclectic writings about the city as performance space, and of a Ph.D. in Audiology who had transitioned from hearing-aid designer to business communications consultant, exemplify NIW scenarios in which the common denominator of the self-petitioner's activities had to be carefully delineated.

ing multidisciplinary hybrids such as "postmodernist multimedia conceptual art" or "environmentally friendly meat rendering."

Applicants whose contribution is to an expansive field, such as molecular biology, or even to an established area of endeavor, such as the preservation of a traditional artistic or musical genre, may need to limit the scope of their area of alleged contribution to a definable and defensible subfield. While this practice should be relatively straightforward in scientific disciplines, in which subspecialty journals and committees within professional societies are legion and continually proliferating, the establishment of a legitimate field definition within artistic or cultural areas of endeavor may well be disputed.

Thus, a case premised on preservation of the Rajasthani school (*gharana*) of tabla (traditional drumming) performance would doubtless require extensive academic and artistic documentation to confirm that such a geographical restriction to the generic field of tabla performance corresponds to an actual established genre within classical Indian music of creative endeavor within the genus of tabla performance. Such a demonstration might require proof that the leading exponents of the Rajasthani school are not simply interchangeable with performers in contrasting genre, such as the Delhi or Calcutta performance schools. Similarly, the AAO's approval of a Milwaukee-based *bayan* accordion virtuoso surmounted the third leg on appeal by documenting his national supremacy as a *bayan* accordionist.[27]

SCHEDULE A, GROUP II

Schedule A, Group II's (SAII) recent resurgence largely stems from the now sunset congressional insemination of 50,000 additional visas for both groups I and II of Schedule A in a 2005 appropriations bill.[28] It is conceivable that a future, less deadlocked Congress, less preoccupied with illegal immigration, will revive this generous benefaction. If not, SAII will doubtless revert to an obscure and fairly infrequently utilized alternative to the three previously discussed mechanisms for obtaining resi-

dence while avoiding burdensome and sometimes inappropriate labor certification.

Although SAII appears currently somewhat moribund, a brief review of the ramifications of field of endeavor for obtaining SAII certification is appropriate.[29]

SAII classification is available only to employer-sponsored beneficiaries within the arts and sciences [29].[30] Practitioners should note that beneficiaries must qualify under the Department of Labor's (DOL) regulatory criteria for exceptional ability, which are closely mirrored by the legacy INS EB-1 criteria.[31] More importantly, SAII petitioners must satisfy DOL's regulatory requirement that the alien beneficiary possess "widespread acclaim and international recognition" and that his or her "field of knowledge and/or skill" be one in which colleges and universities offer degrees.[32] DOL's regulations specifically exempt SAII beneficiaries from necessarily having such a degree and, in fact, from the perspective of the DOL regulations, there is no explicit requirement that SAII beneficiaries have gone to college.[33] DOL also requires that the beneficiary have achieved a year of recognition immediately preceding the submission of the petition to U.S. Citizenship and Immigration Services.[34]

Accordingly, SAII eligibility could be appropriate for recently emerged individuals in second or third careers, such as a retired dentist who has become the curator of a Namibian textile collection, or a radiologist who has transitioned into an internationally renowned developer of customized travel packages for high-net-worth clientele. Obviously, such cases will be fairly infrequent, but in such scenarios SAII may be more efficacious than any of the complementary categories, each of which requires, at least implicitly, a longer lead time of international or nationwide recognition.

---

[27] *Matter of [name not provided]*, (no file number available) (AAO Aug.18, 2002) (NSC), discussed in 28 *Bender's Immigr. Bull.* 690 (Apr. 15, 2003).

[28] Emergency Supplemental Appropriations Act for Defense, the Global War on Terror, and Tsunami Relief, 2005, Pub. L. No. 109-13, 119 Stat 231.

[29] For a recent analysis of SAII and its recent revival, *see* R. Kushner Sostrin, "The Revival of Schedule A, Group II: Is 'Exceptional' in Vogue?" *Immigration Options for Academics and Researchers* 443 (2005).

[30] 20 CFR §656.5(b).

[31] 8 CFR §204.5(h)(3).

[32] 20 CFR §656.5(b)(1).

[33] 20 CFR §656.5(b)(1).

[34] 20 CFR §656.5(b)(1).

CONCLUSION

Our study commenced with Lord Krishna's revelation to Arjuna that he, Lord Krishna, the avatar of the god Vishnu, is the one who is knowledgeable in all fields, and that such knowledge constitutes the meaning of true wisdom. Our goal has been to focus the attention of EB-1 and EB-2 advocates on the strategic importance of effective field delineation as a critical initial step in developing an otherwise meritorious EB-1/EB-2 petition.

It is hoped that our modest review of the significance of field definition with regard to the four EB-1 and EB-2 mechanisms for circumventing labor certification through the assessment of the beneficiary's achievements will be of at least some assistance as we guide our most knowledgeable clients to their goal of attaining permanent residence in the United States. As we assist them, let us hope that they, like generations of immigrants preceding them, continue to enable our nation to emerge from the current economic and spiritual malaise.

PERMANENCE AS A FIXTURE IN TIME: PERMANENT RESIDENT CONSIDERATIONS FOR MEDICAL TRAINEES

*by Robert Aronson and Dinesh Shenoy**

This article concerns the various issues when filing a labor certification application for a physician based on a position as a medical trainee—that is, a position engaged in graduate medical education (GME) that carries a professional title of medical resident or clinical trainee. At the core of this discussion is whether such a position in GME can be regarded as "permanent" for purposes of filing a labor certification application. This discussion also examines a wider range of practical, legal, and ethical issues related to structuring an employer-sponsored case for permanent residence on a position as a medical trainee.

GENERAL BACKGROUND ISSUES

GME is defined as "the formal medical education pursued after receipt of an M.D. or other professional degree in the medical sciences. Graduate medical education is usually obtained as an intern, resident, or fellow, or in continuing medical education programs."[1] It is an indispensable credential for practice as a physician, relating to such benefits as state medical licensure,[2] malpractice insurance, medical board accreditation, and scope of professional practice.

At its core, GME exists during a finite period of time in which a physician performs clinical employment services intended to increase the physician's professional competence under the mentorship of attending physicians. Over the course of the program in GME, the scope of the medical trainee's range of independent action and judgment is expected to increase, pursuant to established professional guidelines established both within the individual training institution and in accordance with professional standards set by the Accreditation Council for Graduate Medical Education (ACGME).[3]

GME programs are based in hospitals, clinics, healthcare facilities, or institutions with or without medical school affiliations. Most patient care programs are overseen by the Joint Commission,[4] formerly known as the Joint Commission on the Accreditation of Healthcare Organizations (JCAHO). Accreditation of specific GME programs is issued by the ACGME through its associated residency review committees (RRCs)[5] for medical specialties in conjunction with the relevant member board of the American Board of Medical Specialties (ABMS).[6] The RRCs for accredited programs monitor the quality and training commitment of each program through regular site visits. Although voluntary as a functional matter, accreditation is highly desirable so as to establish that the GME program is being conducted under appropriate professional standards as recognized by the medical community.

* **Robert D. Aronson** is the principal attorney at Aronson & Associates, P.A., practicing in the area of employment-based immigration with a focus on international physicians, biomedical researchers, and healthcare workers. He has written and spoken frequently on immigration topics for physicians to the legal, healthcare, and immigration communities. He was appointed as the legal advisor for the study on international physicians conducted by the Council of Graduate Medical Education (COGME), the advisory body to the secretary of health and human services on healthcare policy in the United States. Mr. Aronson is a graduate of the Indiana University School of Law and was a Fulbright Fellow at the law schools of Harvard University and Moscow State University.

Dinesh Shenoy is an associate attorney with Aronson & Associates PA in Minneapolis, practicing exclusively in the field of immigration law, with an emphasis on employment-based cases. He is a regularly invited speaker at AILA annual conferences and regional events on topics such as advanced employment-based strategies and law practice management. In 2003 he won the AILA Mentor Award for outstanding efforts and excellent counsel to immigration attorneys by providing mentoring assistance.

The authors would like to thank the associate attorneys of Aronson & Associates for their insight into the many issues raised in this article.

[1] *Mosby's Medical Dictionary, Fourth Edition* (1994).

[2] *See* American Medical Association, *State Medical Licensure Requirements and Statistics* (2008).

[3] *See www.acgme.org/acWebsite/home/home.asp.*

[4] *www.jointcommission.org/AboutUs/.*

[5] *www.acgme.org/acWebsite/navPages/nav_comRRC.asp.*

[6] The ABMS, a not-for-profit organization, assists 24 approved medical specialty boards in the development and use of standards in the ongoing evaluation and certification of physicians. *See www.abms.org/.*

GME programs provide graduates with an organized educational program aimed at developing the physician's skill through a course of progressively more independent responsibility for patient care. Programs vary in duration, accreditation, quality, and remuneration. Programs are not to rely on medical trainees to meet service needs, but are to provide structured training and education. However, particularly in inner city and rural communities, medical trainees play an important role in service delivery, particularly to the indigent and medically underserved.

GME can provide much-needed patient care at lower cost to the hospital, because most GME positions are subsidized by the government at approximately $150,000 to the institution per trainee. Roughly 36 percent of patient-service revenue in an average GME program comes from reimbursements from the Medicare Trust Fund, thereby providing the federal government with considerable leverage over many elements of GME, including the size, scope, and duration of a physician's program.[7]

A physician enters a program of training to prepare for practice in a medical specialty, typically culminating in recognition by a specialty board or society. Program durations range from three years for programs like internal medicine to eight years for advanced training like thoracic surgery. Super-sub-specialty training can extend for even longer periods.

The substantial number of international medical graduates (IMGs) who are in H-1B status to pursue their GME has resulted in increased consideration of whether it would be possible to file a labor certification for positions in GME. Particularly given the lengthy time required for many programs of GME—especially in various medical specialties and subspecialties—in combination with the finite period of six years of H-1B eligibility,[8] it is highly desirable, if possible, to initiate a case for permanent residence during the period of medical training. This article deals precisely with the issues related to structuring a labor certification application-based immigration case for a physician in GME.[9]

As a final preliminary background note, we will use the term "intern" to refer to a medical school graduate who is in postgraduate year 1 (PGY-1). We will use the term "resident" to refer to a physician who is doing further advanced training in specified medical disciplines (disproportionately although not exclusively in primary-care medical disciplines) in postgraduate years 2 and above (PGY-2&3 or PGY 2+). We will use the term "fellow" to describe physicians in advanced medical training programs in specialized medical disciplines normally required to fulfill standards set by the relevant ABMS board for eligibility purposes.

IS THE JOB PERMANENT?

For medical trainees, a threshold question is whether or not the position constitutes "permanent" employment that can serve as the subject of a labor certification case (under the general idea that the purpose of the labor certification is to allow the alien to perform the duties at *the time the alien is granted permanent resident status* through either the approval of an I-485 application by U.S. Citizenship and Immigration Services (USCIS) or being admitted to the United States on an immigrant visa issued by a U.S. embassy or consulate overseas).

At first glance, the answer would seem to be a simple "no" for all medical training positions. After all, GME positions are limited to finite periods of training, and one cannot be a physician-in-training forever. Without exception, each state requires a physician to have completed certain stipulated periods of residency training at an accredited program as a term of medical licensure, and there are additional pressures to gain ABMS board eligibility/certification (commonly denoted as BE/BC)[10] in order to practice in a specific medical discipline. Therefore, since training cannot be a permanent, open-ended state of existence, it follows that a labor certification application cannot be filed for a medical trainee. Right?

We believe that the analysis is a little more nuanced. The Department of Labor's (DOL) Board of

---

[7] J. Iglehart, "Medicare and Graduate Medical Education," 338 *New Eng. J. Med.* 402 (1998).

[8] *See* INA §214(g)(4).

[9] Physicians in GME also can be in J-1 status through Educational Commission for Foreign Medical Graduates (ECFMG) sponsorship. This article does not deal with the considerations pertaining to such physicians, who would need to ob-
continued

tain a waiver of the two-year home residence obligation under INA §212(e) as a prerequisite to seriously considering a case for permanent residence.

[10] The purpose of the BC/BE designation is to confirm a physician's fulfillment of certain training and professional standards, indicating a desired level of medical competence in the field of practice. *See www.abms.org.*

Alien Labor Certification Appeals (BALCA) in fact has made quite clear that various positions in GME—*i.e.*, the positions of intern, resident, and fellow—can be the subject of a permanent labor certification.[11] DOL's labor certification regulations do not define the term "permanent." The definition is instead found in BALCA case law, recently restated in *Matter of Crawford & Sons*.[12] According to *Crawford*, permanent employment is employment that can be continuous or carried on throughout the year, whereas employment of the kind exclusively performed at certain seasons or periods of the year cannot be considered permanent.[13] *Crawford* involved the position of landscape gardener, but its central holding (and that of its predecessor case, *Matter of Vito Volpe*[14]) provides the definition of "permanent" that should be applied to all labor certification cases, including to physicians who are working as medical trainees. *Crawford* holds that the duties of landscape gardener cannot be performed year-round and thus are not permanent because there is necessarily a part of each year in the winter during which the duties simply cannot be performed.[15] *Crawford* contrasts landscape gardeners with teachers and professors. Teachers and professors generally teach only during nine to 10 months of each year, roughly the same amount of time landscape gardeners work during each year. However, *Crawford* noted that teaching duties *by their nature* may be performed continuously throughout the year, and therefore the position of teacher or professor is permanent in a way that landscape gardener cannot be.[16]

How does this definition of "permanent" apply to medical trainees? The periods of mandatory and stipulated GME are set by the relevant ABMS board and rigorously enforced by the ACGME. Therefore, any physician desiring to gain a recognized certification reflecting on professional competence in a recognized medical discipline needs to undertake a set, recognized course of medical training. So, how do the various levels of GME satisfy or not satisfy the requirement of permanent employment?

Consider interns first. The typical PGY-1 internship year lasts exactly one year, generally from July 1 to June 30 (although there are certainly instances of off-cycle GME). As contrasted to landscape gardeners, the position of intern lasts fully one year. More importantly, the duties performed by interns (diagnosing and treating patients, albeit under close supervision) may be and are accomplished on a year-round basis. Arguably, then, even the position of intern can be "permanent" enough to support a labor certification.

The case that residents and fellows meet the standards for permanent employment is stronger. The position of resident lasts, in most instances, at least two years. Fellowships invariably last a year, and in most instances for several years. The duties of residents and fellows undoubtedly can be and are performed year-round, with the duties becoming more complex and independent with each passing year. While the jobs of resident and fellow are not indefinite, they satisfy the *Crawford* test despite the fact that residency and fellowship can be characterized as training.

This conclusion bears out in the BALCA case law. The BALCA cases involving intern and resident positions either assume without argument that the positions offered are permanent enough to be the

---

[11] *E.g., Matter of Maimonides Medical Center*, 93 INA 534 (BALCA Nov. 29, 1994) ("position of Resident in Psychiatry PGY-2"); *Matter of Presbyterian Medical Center of Philadelphia*, 96 INA 61 (BALCA July 7, 1997) ("position of Resident PGY II & III"), *Matter of Catholic Medical Center*, 95 INA 547 (BALCA July 24, 1997) (position of "Internal Medicine Physician (Resident)"); *Matters of Albert Einstein Medical Center, et al.*, 96 INA 46, 96 INA 47, 96 INA 59, 96 INA 60, 96 INA 74 (BALCA Feb. 9, 1998) (position of "Resident PGY-II & III"); *Matter of Maricopa Medical Center*, 97 INA 290 (BALCA May 29, 1998) ("position of 'Internist, Resident'"); *Matter of Albert Einstein Medical Center*, 96 INA 0263 (BALCA Jan. 28, 1999), ("position of Medical Resident in Radiology (PGY III and IV years)"). In all these cases, BALCA has either not directly questioned the issue of permanence or ruled in the employer's favor on that issue and has instead ruled on other grounds (in some cases for, others against certification).

[12] 2001 INA 121 (BALCA Jan. 9, 2004).

[13] *Id.* at 4, *reaffirming Matter of Vito Volpe*, 1991 INA 300, at 5 (BALCA Sept. 29, 1994).

[14] *Matter of Vito Volpe*, 1991 INA 300 (BALCA Sept. 29, 1994)

[15] *Matter of Crawford & Sons*, 2001 INA 121 (BALCA Jan. 9, 2004).

[16] *Id. See also Matter of Vito Volpe, supra* note 14, at 9 ("[W]e hold that although these landscaping jobs may be considered 'full time' during ten months of the year, and the need for these jobs occurs year after year, they cannot be considered permanent employment, as they are temporary jobs that are exclusively performed during the warmer growing seasons of the year, *and from their nature, may not be continuous or carried on throughout the year*.") (emphasis added).

subject of a labor certification, or have resolved the permanence issue in favor of the employer and alien and have decided the case on other issues.

IMMIGRANT VISA NUMBER AVAILABILTIY CONSIDERATIONS

Having established that as a threshold matter medical trainee positions may support a permanent labor certification, below we will turn to several practical considerations of actually structuring a labor certification for a medical trainee. Before doing so, however, it is imperative to discuss the timely and major issue of unavailability of immigrant visa numbers. This is because prior to embarking on a labor certification for a medical trainee, both the practitioner and the clients must understand that even if a labor certification and I-140 immigrant petition are ultimately approved for a Medical Trainee, there is a substantial possibility that the alien will not be holding the position by the time that permanent resident status is granted. Indeed, the alien physician likely will not be holding the trainee position described in the labor certification even by the time that an adjustment of status application (I-485) may be filed (or, analogously, certainly not by the time an immigrant visa could be issued overseas).

There are multiple reasons for this reality, including the time required to properly prepare and recruit for a Program Electronic Review Management (PERM) case; delays in the PERM and I-140 processing times at DOL and USCIS; and backlogs in the immigrant visa preference categories. Given that immigrant visa number availability hinges on country of birth, physicians from India[17] and China face very long waits for the availability of an immigrant visa number in the EB-2 category, and there is certainly a plausible expectation that backlogs will also develop in the worldwide EB-2 numbers. Realistically most one-year internships will be completed before an I-485 can be filed, even if the alien is not chargeable to India or China.[18] For labor certifications for the position of resident PGY-2+ and fel-

lows, it may be possible but certainly not guaranteed that the I-485 will be filed while the alien physician beneficiary is working in the underlying GME position.

To file an I-140 petition, an employer's intent to ultimately employ the alien in the offered permanent position must at least exist at the time of I-140 filing.[19] Filing an I-140 petition when it is clear the employer has no intent to ever employ the alien is fraudulent and clearly barred by the INA.[20] However, employment relationships and employers' intent can change over time. With the indefinite suspension of premium processing of I-140s,[21] it may be many months before the I-140 is adjudicated, during which time the employer's future intent might change. The question then becomes whether an I-140 that is still pending (at the end of the internship or residency or fellowship for which labor certification is sought) may and should still be approved after the physician has moved on to the next position or employer.

In the past, USCIS stated that the employer's future intent must still exist at the time the I-140 is *approved*.[22] However, more recently USCIS has re-

---

[17] For a variety of reasons, India is by far the largest single provider of IMGs to the United States, currently accounting for roughly 4.9 percent of physicians now in practice in the United States. F. Mullan: "Doctors for the World: Indian Physician Emigration," 25 *Health Affairs* 380 (2006).

[18] For Indian and Chinese physicians, cross-chargeability to a derivative spouse's different country of birth is possible, 9 *Foreign Affairs Manual* 40.1 N8, though in reality the number of instances of cross-chargeability is small.

[19] INA §204(a)(1)(F) states: "Any employer *desiring and intending* to employ within the United States an alien entitled to classification under [INA §203(b)(1)(B), 203(b)(1)(C), 203(b)(2), or 203(b)(3)] may *file* a petition with the Attorney General for such classification." [Emphasis added.]

[20] INA §212(a)(6)(C)(i). *Cf.* 8 CFR §§292.3(b), 1103.102(c), which make it a ground for being barred from practicing before the Department of Homeland Security immigration agencies if an attorney "knowingly or with reckless disregard makes a false statement of material fact or law, or willfully misleads, misinforms, threatens, or deceives any person (including a party to a case or an officer or employee of the Department of Justice), concerning any material and relevant matter relating to a case."

[21] *See* AILA Liaison/USCIS Question and Answer (Sept. 25, 2007), *published on* AILA InfoNet at Doc. No. 07101962 (*posted* Oct. 22, 2007).

[22] *See* USCIS Memorandum, W. Yates, "Continuing Validity of Form I-140 Petition in Accordance with Section 106(c) of the American Competitiveness in the Twenty-First Century Act of 2000 (AC21) (AD03-16)" (Aug. 4, 2003), *published on* AILA InfoNet at Doc. No. 03081114 (*posted* Aug. 11, 2003) ("In all cases an offer of employment must have been bona fide, and the employer must have had the intent, at the time the Form I-140 was *approved*, to employ the beneficiary upon adjustment.") (emphasis added); *see also* "USCIS Headquarters Response to Issues Raised by AILA at the AILA/USCIS Benefits Liaison Meeting on October 1, 2003,"

continued

versed its position and affirmed that at least in some situations the I-140 should not be denied even if it comes to the attention of USCIS in the course of adjudicating the I-140 that the alien has left the employer. Specifically, in "portability" cases under INA §204(j) (discussed in further detail below), USCIS has instructed adjudicators that an I-140 concurrently filed with an I-485 should be approved even if it has come to their attention that the alien no longer is employed by the I-140 petitioner.[23] These principles are not limited to portability cases—if the alien physician has to cease working in a particular stage of medical training in order to move on to the next position, it makes as much sense that a pending I-140 should still be approved (even if no I-485 has been filed) as in the portability situation.[24] The key fact is that *back at the time of I-140 filing* both employer and employee had the correct intent. If the granting of permanent resident status could occur instantaneously the day after I-140 filing, the intent to employ the alien physician in the medical trainee position would clearly be shown by the alien returning to work the next day in the same trainee position. By the alien physician having actually worked the full year or more in the trainee position described in the labor certification and I-140, it is clear that at the time of I-140 filing, during that year the employer and alien both had the *intent* that the alien fill the position permanently. The fact that the processing time for labor certifications, I-140 petitions, and I-485 applications and waiting times for cut-off

dates to move on the *Visa Bulletin* make it impossible to predict exactly when the alien will get permanent residence does not change the fact that the employer and alien clearly had the necessary intent at the time of I-140 filing, when the alien has in fact worked in the trainee position and completed it successfully.[25] It is the authors' position that as long as the I-140 petition is filed while the petitioner and physician intend to have the employment in a medical trainee position continue for that position's normal duration, the pending I-140 remains valid even if approved after the physician has moved on to the next position. An approved I-140 for a former position need not be withdrawn; legacy Immigration and Naturalization Service guidance confirms that an employer is under no obligation to request withdrawal of an I-140 that it has filed for an alien if its intent changes after filing.[26]

If an I-485 cannot be filed (or immigrant visa obtained[27]) prior to completion of the year(s) of the medical trainee position that formed the subject of the labor certification application, then the alien should be prepared for the prospect that he or she may at most gain an I-140 approval and "lock in" a priority date that can later be retained as the priority date on a new I-140 based on a new labor certifica-

---

published on AILA InfoNet at Doc. No 03112547 (*posted* Nov. 25, 2003) ("The petitioning employer must have the requisite future intent throughout the pendency of the petition/application. Thus, the employer/petitioner on the petition at the time of approval must have had the requisite intent.").

[23] *See* USCIS Memorandum, M. Aytes, "Interim Guidance for Processing I-140 Employment-Based Immigrant Petitions and I-485 and H-1B Petitions Affected by the American Competitiveness in the Twenty-First Century Act of 2000 (AC21) (Public Law 106-313) (Dec. 27, 2005), *published on* AILA InfoNet at Doc. No. 06092763 (*posted* Sep. 27, 2006), *amending* USCIS Interoffice Memorandum, W. Yates, "Interim Guidance for Processing Form I-140 Employment-Based Immigrant Petitions and Form I-485 and H-1B Petitions Affected by the American Competitiveness in the Twenty-First Century Act of 2000 (AC21) (Public Law 106-313)" (May 12, 2005), *published on* AILA InfoNet at Doc. No. 05051810 (*posted* May 18, 2005) Q&A 1, 2.

[24] As one well-known immigration attorney often would say to the authors, "What is sauce for the goose is sauce for the gander."

[25] Indeed, USCIS has repeatedly confirmed that the alien has no obligation to work for the sponsoring employer while the I-140 petition is pending. *See* USCIS Memorandum, *supra* note 23, Q&A 10. *See also* USCIS Memorandum, *supra* note 22, at 3 ("It should be noted that there is no requirement in statute or regulations that the beneficiary of a Form I-140 actually be in the underlying employment until permanent residence is authorized.").

[26] INS Letter, Thomas Simmons to Richard Steele, Oct. 20, 1999, *published on* AILA InfoNet at Doc. No. 00042507 (*posted* Apr. 25, 2000) ("While Service regulations at [8 CFR] section 205.1(a)(iii) outline the reasons for an automatic revocation of an employment-based immigrant petition, there is no specific requirement that the employer notify the Service."). The termination of the employment relationship does not automatically revoke a pending or approved I-140 petition. *Cf.* 8 CFR § 205.1(a)(iii).

[27] As of the time of writing this article, premium processing has not been restored for I-140s, and USCIS reports that it is not likely to bring it back in the near future. *See* AILA Liaison/USCIS Q&A, *supra* note 21. This reduces the potential benefit of immigrant visa processing as a faster alternative to adjustment of status. While an I-485 may be concurrently filed with an I-140 if an immigrant visa number is currently available, *see* 8 CFR §245.2(a)(2)(i)(B), an immigrant visa cannot be issued by a U.S. consulate abroad before USCIS first approves the I-140 petition and forwards it to the Department of State (DOS).

tion filed by a future employer.[28] In the case of Indian and Chinese EB-2 aliens at the present time (and possibly all EB-2 aliens in the future, if a retrogression occurs in the worldwide EB-2 category), there is a realistic possibility that they will need to wait several years beyond I-140 filing or approval for their priority dates to be reached. Priority date cut-offs on the *Visa Bulletin* do not advance in steady fashion but instead tend to stay frozen and then make random jumps backward or forward at different times through a given fiscal year, as occurred from June to August 2007, and most recently with the severe backward movement of the India EB-2 cutoff in the January 2008 *Visa Bulletin*.[29]

It is quite possible that several years after locking in a priority date for an I-140 filed for the position of medical trainee an alien will see his or her priority date reached, long after the alien has moved on to a new position with a different employer. In this situation, which has been common for the past two years and will remain common for years to come (absent an increase in the employment-based immigrant visa quotas), there is debate among practitioners as to whether an alien can file an I-485 in the future when the priority date is reached.

The "aggressive" position: In favor of filing the I-485 long after the trainee position ended is the argument that *back when the I-140 was filed*, both the employer and alien had the required intent that the alien would fill the position if permanent residence were immediately granted on that date. It is only the accident of the alien's birth and the per-country limits imposed by INA §202 that prevented the alien from concurrently filing an I-485 at the time of I-140 filing. Therefore, the alien may file an I-485 without any new I-140 by the alien's current employer.

The "conservative" position: Against the filing of the I-485 long after the position ended is the argument that the filing of an I-485 based on a pending or approved I-140 is a statement of the alien's *present* intent (intent on the date of *I-485 filing*) to

work for the I-140 petitioner in the future at the time the I-485 is approved. Since the alien clearly will not be going back to being an intern or resident or fellow and the alien is already working full-time as a physician, to file an I-485 now based only on the approved I-140 from back in the physician's internship/residency/fellowship days would be fraudulent conduct, and the alien risks becoming deportable.

The aggressive position is questionable and concerning, and the debate can be mooted if the physician can be sponsored for a new labor certification at his or her postresidency or postfellowship employment. To avoid putting too many eggs in one basket, the physician who completes the several years of training and emerges with an approved I-140 but no pending I-485 should seek to be sponsored on a new labor certification at a post-GME job. The physician can then invoke the priority date retention provision 8 CFR §204.5(e) when the new employer files the new I-140 petition. It goes without saying that if a physician filed an I-485 taking the "aggressive" position argued above, he or she should maintain H-1B status while the I-485 is pending and not switch to using an EAD, in the event of I-485 denial on grounds that the I-485 could not be filed because the alien no longer intended to work for the I-140 petitioner on the date of I-485 filing.

APPLICABILITY OF ADJUSTMENT PORTABILTY

If the timing works out such that the physician is able to file the I-485 while still in the GME position, but then moves on to a post-GME position of practicing physician before the I-485 is approved, it becomes necessary to analyze whether the I-485 will be approved under the "portability" rule.[30] In its essence, this rule states that as long as more than 180 days have passed since I-485 filing, the adjustment application remains approvable even though the applicant no longer intends to work for the I-140 petitioner but instead has moved to new employment in a "same or similar" occupation. USCIS guidance directs adjudicators to compare the job duties of the two positions, as well as the applicable Standard Occupational Classification (SOC) codes and the difference in salary.[31] It is generally true that physicians experience a considerable increase in salary upon completion of GME;

---

[28] The priority date accorded by an *approved* I-140 in the EB-1, EB-2, or EB-3 categories can be retained by the alien on any subsequently approved I-140 that is also in the EB-1, EB-2, or EB-3 categories. 8 CFR §204.5(e).

[29] Current and archived *Visa Bulletins* are available on the DOS consular affairs website at *http://travel.state.gov/visa/frvi/bulletin/bulletin_1360.html,* or through AILA InfoNet, *www.aila.org* (Agencies Liaison—Department of State—Visa Bulletins).

[30] INA §204(j).

[31] *See* USCIS Memorandum, *supra* note 23, Q&A 3.

however, this is only one factor, and practitioners should emphasize to USCIS that the similarity of the job duties is more important than any salary discrepancy. The SOC code category 29-1060 for physicians and surgeons includes all categories of physicians, with no distinction placed between physicians engaged in GME and those that have completed their GME.[32] That is a strong factor in favor of finding that post-GME positions and GME positions are sufficiently the "same or similar." In the end, the physician's core duties both during GME and afterwards will consist of diagnosing and treating illness, and thus arguably should support I-485 approval under the portability rule. Nonetheless, caution mandates that any physician in H-1B status who has filed an I-485 application and who will rely on the portability rule be advised to maintain H-1B status at all times independent of the I-485 application, because determinations on the applicability of the portability rule are made only at the very end of the I-485 case. As noted above, it is equally the case here that a good backup plan is to have the new employer file a new labor certification case as well. If a new labor certification is approved and the previous priority date retained on the new employer's I-140, there is long-standing USCIS guidance pre-dating the portability rule that allows the pending I-485 to be transferred to the new I-140 petition.[33]

ACTUAL MINIMUM REQUIREMENTS

Any enthusiasm for sponsoring a medical trainee for a permanent labor certification must be tempered with the realization that it is not a simple business to define the actual minimum requirements for the position accurately while still ensuring success at the I-140 stage if the labor certification is approved. The actual minimum requirements might not be ones the alien physician can satisfy while still keeping consistent with Department of State and USCIS regulations and case law.

The educational requirement of an M.D. degree (plus the requirement of the authorization to hold the position, whether through a full state medical license or other state-issued licensure documents) generally should not present a problem, since these are not

credentials obtained through employment at the sponsoring employer. The difficulty arises when considering the required work experience, captured in Sections H6 and H10 of the Form ETA 9089 application. DOL regulations require that the position requirements stated in Section H of the ETA 9089 "must be those normally required for the occupation[.]"[34] In the GME context, this rule can lead to a direct clash with the rule that:[35]

If the alien beneficiary already is employed by the employer, in considering whether the job requirements represent the employer's actual minimums, DOL will review the training and experience *possessed by the alien beneficiary at the time of hiring by the employer*, including as a contract employee. The employer cannot require domestic worker applicants to possess training and/or experience *beyond what the alien possessed at the time of hire* unless:

(i) The alien gained the experience while working for the employer, including as a contract employee, in *a position not substantially comparable to the position for which certification is being sought*, or

(ii) The employer can demonstrate that it is no longer feasible to train a worker to qualify for the position.

We will consider the impact of these two competing rules in the cases of interns, residents, and fellows in order.

For the position of intern, it is not customary to require work experience, since the position of intern is the first post-M.D. work experience the physician gains. Therefore, a labor certification for an intern that contains no experience requirement in Sections H6 or H10 should not run afoul of the prohibition against counting experience gained at the same employer.

The position of resident presents considerably more difficulty by comparison. A GME program cannot admit a physician to the position of resident (PGY-2 and beyond) if the physician does not have at least one year of experience as an intern. Therefore, it is expected that Section H of the ETA 9089 will reflect a requirement of at least one year of same or related work experience as an intern. But nearly all residents have completed their internship year at the same employer, thus prohibiting them from counting their

---

[32] *www.bls.gov/soc/soc_j1g0.htm.*

[33] *See* INS Memorandum, M. Pearson, "Transferring Section 245 Adjustment Applications to New or Subsequent Family or Employment-Based Immigrant Visa Petitions" (May 9, 2000), *published on* AILA InfoNet at Doc. No. 00062110 (posted June 21, 2000).

[34] 20 CFR §656.17(h)(1).

[35] 20 CFR §656.17(i)(3) (emphasis added).

internship year toward satisfying the experience requirement of a labor certification for the position of resident with that same employer.

The prohibition against requiring domestic applicants to possess training and/or experience beyond what the alien possessed at the time of hire does contain two exceptions that an employer may claim in an audit if a resident's qualifying year of work experience as an intern was gained at the same employer. Considering these exceptions in reverse order from how they appear in the regulation, if the employer continues to train interns who are one year behind the current class of residents of which a sponsored foreign national is a part, arguably it is feasible for the employer to train a worker for the position of resident (thus undercutting the second exemption from the prohibition against counting internship experience at the same employer.)

This leaves the first exemption, which allows the sponsored foreign national employee to count the internship year as qualifying work experience toward the position of resident if the position of intern is "not substantially comparable to the position [of resident] for which certification is being sought." This first exemption is the one more likely to succeed. DOL regulations define a "substantially comparable job or position . . . [as] a job or position requiring performance of the same job duties more than 50 percent of the time. This requirement can be documented by furnishing position descriptions, the percentage of time spent on the various duties, organization charts, and payroll records."[36]

To count the alien physician's internship year as qualifying experience that may satisfy sections H6 and H10 on the ETA 9089 therefore requires distinguishing the job duties of intern and resident by more than 50 percent. Prior to the PERM regulations, the *Delitizer* test was applied to this situation to determine whether experience gained at the same employer could be counted towards the labor certification (whether or not the prior positions were "sufficiently dissimilar," as compared to the current standard of "not substantially comparable.")[37] The implementation of PERM re-

placed *Delitizer*'s multifactor test with the 50 percent rule.[38] Though the BALCA case law[39] on this issue pre-dates the implementation of the PERM regulations, it is still highly informative due to the similarity of the *Delitizer* test to the 50 percent rule. In two precedent cases, BALCA found that the positions of intern and resident were not sufficiently dissimilar and that the positions lie on a continuum with no significant change in the duties (other than augmented responsibilities). Certification was denied because the sponsored physicians gained their PGY-1 experience at the same employer.[40]

However, at least one later precedent BALCA case did distinguish these two earlier decisions successfully and found that the position of Resident PGY-2&3 was sufficiently dissimilar from the position of PGY-1, such that requiring PGY-1 experience was in fact an actual minimum requirement, even though all the sponsored alien physicians gained their PGY-1 experience at the same employer.[41] Characterizing the two previous cases' holdings as stemming from a failure of the employers to document the differences between the PGY-1 and later postgraduate years sufficiently, the deci-

---

[36] 20 CFR §656.17(i)(5)(ii).

[37] *See Matters of Albert Einstein Medical Center, et al., supra* note 11 at 3, *citing Brent-Wood Products Inc.*, 88 INA 259 (BALCA Feb. 28, 1989) (en banc) and *The Cinnamon Buns Inc.*, 93-INA-99 (BALCA July 6, 1994), and enumerating the various factors to be considered when comparing the two positions, as provided in *Delitizer Corp. of Newton*, 88 INA 482 (BALCA May 10, 1990) (en banc).

[38] In the supplementary information to the PERM regulation, DOL agreed with the majority of commenters that there are legitimate situations in which experience gained with the same employer in a different position should be allowed to count towards the experience requirement for the position for which certification is sought, but found that "the specific *Delitizer* criteria are unnecessarily complex and in practice difficult to administer." 69 Fed. Reg. 77326, 77354 (Dec. 27, 2004).

[39] *See* note 11, *supra.*

[40] *See Matter of Maimonides Medical Center, supra* note 11, at 4 (position of resident in psychiatry PGY-2 required one year of PGY-1 level experience; "[I]n reality a residency is in fact one job, and was acknowledged by Employer, as such the progression of a psychiatric residency through the various levels of a residency to the staff psychiatrist position is essentially on a continuum with augmented responsibilities throughout but with no significant change in the essential duties[.]"); *Matter of Presbyterian Medical Center, supra* note 11 at 5, (position of resident PGY-2&3 required one year of experience in the job offered or related occupation of PGY-1; held, following *Maimonides*, that the positions of PGY-2&3 are on a continuum with PGY-1 and not sufficiently dissimilar; thus it did not reflect the employer's actual minimum requirements to require PGY-1 experience when the alien gained the PGY-1 experience with the same employer.).

[41] *See Matters of Albert Einstein Medical Center, et al., supra* note 11, at 5.

sion in *Albert Einstein Medical Center*[42] emphasized that the employer had indeed documented the different supervisory, teaching, and staff interaction responsibilities of residents and interns in satisfaction of the regulations. The *Albert Einstein Medical Center* decision provides guideposts for the evidence that practitioners should gather to address this issue in the planning stages of the case, since an audit is more likely to be triggered.

As for the position of fellows, the same issue arises as with residents if the PGY-2-and-beyond experience required for the fellowship is gained at the same employer. If a foreign physician does a fellowship at a different employer than his or her residency training, then this issue does not arise.

CONSIDERATIONS FOR FILING LABOR CERTIFICATION APPLICATION FOR MEDICAL TRAINEE

The next question we consider is what factors would lead an academic institution to file a labor certification application for a medical trainee. After all, when all is said and done, a labor certification requires the active commitment and involvement of the employer, and the physician will not remain employed for a lengthy period of time by the academic institution (unless the intention is to hire the physician on completion of the period of GME). The temporariness of a foreign physician's period of GME employment may temper an academic institution's willingness to undertake the complex and expensive labor certification process. This is particularly true given the recent DOL rule requiring all attorney's fees and recruitment costs for the labor certification stage of a permanent residence case be paid by the employer without reimbursement by the employee.[43]

As noted above, the average medical trainee accounts for roughly $150,000 in billed revenues from Medicare per year, but draws a salary well below the compensation level of an attending physician. Particularly as Medicare reimbursement rates drop, there are increased pressures within many teaching hospitals to look to medical trainees as highly lucrative providers of clinical care to the indigent and medically underserved—mandates that potentially call into question the proper balance between clinical service and medical training. Regardless of how that question is resolved, however, the fact is that medical trainees are a key part of hospitals' ability to treat patients. This is a factor in favor of persuading employers to make the commitment of effort and money to sponsor a medical trainee for a labor certification if for no other reason than to attract qualified IMGs to commit to GME training in the sponsoring institution.

Given the growing shortages of physicians[44] and the role of many community-based teaching hospitals as primary providers of clinical services to medically vulnerable populations qualifying for lower reimbursement schedules, it has been our observation that various hospitals—largely those in the inner city—become much more receptive to provide permanent resident sponsorship (as well as H-1B status) precisely as a recruitment effort intended to attract IMGs to their programs.

CONCLUSION

This article is not intended to present a monolithic conclusion on permanent resident options for medical trainees. Rather, we have sought to present to the practitioner some of the more nettlesome issues that affect labor certification practice for physicians. We again want to stress that the basic themes of the "normal" labor certification application process apply fully in the physician context. But there are, unquestionably, nuances and special considerations of which the practitioner needs to be aware when formulating a labor certification case based on a position in GME.

If we can share one overarching final thought, it would be the following: The practitioner's basic challenge in representing physicians in labor certification (or other) cases is not simply to understand immigration law, but equally importantly to understand the environment in which physicians work— the culture, professional pressures, lexicon, aspirations, economics, credentialing requirements, and overall complexities of practicing medicine in the United States. In our opinion, both the challenge and the ultimate satisfaction of representing physicians—and an indispensable requirement for quality professional representation—requires an understanding of certain factors unique to the medical profession. This article is one attempt to orient the immi-

[42] *Id.*

[43] *See* 72 Fed. Reg. 27904 (May 17, 2007).

[44] *See generally* R. Aronson & D. Shenoy, "Zeno's Revenge: The Paradoxes of Interested Government Agency J-1 Waivers for Physicians," 04-4 and 04-5 *Immigration Briefings* (Apr. & May 2004).

gration practitioner to considerations peculiar to physicians engaged in programs of GME.

HABEAS CORPUS AFTER THE REAL ID ACT OF 2005: CREATIVE USES

*by Lisa S. Brodyaga**

INTRODUCTION

We all know that, particularly in the past 12 years, Congress has chipped away at the availability of habeas corpus under 28 USC §2241. With the Antiterrorism and Effective Death Penalty Act of 1996 (AEDPA)[1] and the Illegal Immigration Reform and Immigrant Responsibility Act of 1996 (IIRAIRA),[2] Congress made an initial attempt in 1996 to scale back, if not fully eliminate, the availability of habeas corpus to review deportation/removal orders.[3] This effort was largely nullified by the courts, culminating in *INS v. St. Cyr*,[4] which held that these provisions did not speak "with sufficient clarity to bar jurisdiction pursuant to the general habeas statute."[5] Congress revisited the issue, in light of *St. Cyr*, in the REAL ID Act of 2005.[6] With REAL ID we lost, for the most part, the ability to challenge deportation and removal orders through ha-

beas,[7] although we retain the ability to challenge detention issues in habeas corpus.[8] This includes, for example, cases arising under *Zadvydas v. Davis*,[9] such as those involving whether the Department of Homeland Security (DHS) can hold a person beyond the 90-day removal period as a "danger to the community" based on mental illness;[10] challenges to mandatory detention based on an inordinate delay in completing removal proceedings;[11] and cases involving such incidental is-

---

* **Lisa S. Brodyaga** is the cofounder of Refugio Del Rio Grande, Inc., a nonprofit refugee camp and law office, where she has been a staff attorney since 1985. She has a B.A. from George Washington University (1968) and a J.D. from Catholic University (1974). Ms. Brodyaga has been certified by the Texas Board of Legal Specialization since 1981 in immigration and nationality law. She is the recipient of several national awards for advocacy, including awards from the National Lawyers Guild and AILA. Ms. Brodyaga has been a member of the National Lawyers Guild's National Immigration Project since approximately 1974.

[1] Pub. L. No. 104-132, 110 Stat. 1214.

[2] Pub. L. No. 104-208, div. C, 110 Stat. 3009, 3009-546 to 3009-724.

[3] In §306 of IIRAIRA, Congress enacted what is now INA §242 [8 USC §1252]. It included a series of provisions which legacy Immigration and Naturalization Service (INS) argued were intended to repeal habeas review of deportation orders. Specifically, former INA §242(a)(2)(C) [8 USC §1252(a)(2)(C)], captioned "matters not subject to judicial review," stated: "Notwithstanding any other provision of law, no court shall have jurisdiction to review any final order of removal against an alien who is removable by reason of having committed" certain enumerated criminal offenses.

[4] 533 U.S. 289 (2001).

[5] *Id.* at 312–13. The Court also held that IIRAIRA's repeal of INA §212(c) relief was not retroactive, at least for those lawful permanent residents (LPRs) who pled guilty prior to its enactment.

[6] Pub. L. No. 109-13, div. B, 119 Stat. 231, 302–23.

[7] The REAL ID Act added language specifically referencing habeas corpus to the phrases in INA §242 [8 USC §1252] restricting jurisdiction "notwithstanding any other provision of law." *See* INA §242(a)(5) [8 USC §1252(a)(5)]; *see also* INA §242(b)(9) [8 USC §1252(b)(9)]. However, it also included a new section, INA §242(a)(2)(D) [8 USC §1252(a)(2)(D)], which excludes "constitutional claims and questions of law" from the jurisdictional bars. This was obviously an attempt to avoid constitutional issues, by incorporating the holding of *Swain v. Pressley*, 430 U.S. 372 (1977) (substitution of collateral remedy for habeas corpus is not an unconstitutional suspension of the writ of habeas corpus if the substituted remedy "is neither inadequate nor ineffective" to test the legality of the custody at issue).

[8] *See Ochieng v. Mukasey*, 2008 WL 324219 (10th Cir. 2008), *quoting Singh v. Gonzales*, 499 F.3d 969, 978 (9th Cir. 2007), which concluded that "both §§1252(a)(5) and 1252(b)(9) apply only to those claims seeking judicial review of orders of removal" and noted that the legislative history stated that the REAL ID Act "would not preclude habeas review over challenges to detention that are independent of challenges to removal orders."

[9] 533 U.S. 678 (2001) (holding, *inter alia*, that the post–removal-period detention statute, INA §241(a)(6) [8 USC §1231(a)(6)], read in light of the Constitution's demands, implicitly limits an alien's detention to a period reasonably necessary to bring about that alien's removal from the United States, and does not permit indefinite detention).

[10] *See Tran v. Mukasey*, 515 F.3d 478 (5th Cir 2008) (statute authorizing detention beyond the 90-day removal period does not authorize the continued and potentially indefinite detention where removal is not reasonably foreseeable based on a determination that the alien's mental illness makes him a risk to the community).

[11] *See Demore v. Kim*, 538 U.S. 510 (2003) (upholding mandatory detention under INA §237(c) [8 USC §1227(c)], but with the safeguard of a *Joseph* hearing to determine whether that section applies); *Ly v. Hansen*, 351 F.3d 263, 271 (6th Cir. 2003) (finding unreasonable incarceration for one and a half years when there was no chance of actual, final removal); *Hussain v. Mukasey*, 510 F.3d 739, 743 (7th Cir.

continued

sues as the regulation governing the release of detained alien juveniles.[12]

Less well-known, however, is the fact that habeas corpus can be an effective tool for challenging agency action, or inaction, in countless other circumstances. The effectiveness of a habeas action is often magnified when it is coupled with a traditional action, where available, such as review under the Administrative Procedure Act,[13] mandamus, or actions invoking general federal jurisdiction under 28 USC §1331 seeking declaratory or injunctive relief (or both). In such cases, one might ask: if there is jurisdiction in mandamus, or under 28 USC §1331, why bother with habeas?

Often the reason is procedure.[14] Habeas cases move more rapidly than regular civil actions.[15] And from the client's perspective, most immigration litigation involves real urgency. Whether one is challenging the denial of an application for advance parole in the context of an adjustment application, a refusal to issue proof of lawful permanent resident (LPR) status, or the failure to take action on a long-stalled I-130, the client is often desperate. Complaints such as "I haven't been able to go home for years, and my mother is very ill," or, "I can't support my family without employment authorization," or, "My children are growing up thousands of miles away, and I can't bring them to the United States until they adjudicate my I-130s," sound in violation of recognized liberty interests: the rights to travel, to

seek employment in the common occupations of the community, and to participate in family life and in the rearing of one's children.

To invoke the Great Writ, two elements must coincide: some form of "custody," *i.e.,* a significant impingement on a liberty interest,[16] and the violation of a right protected by the laws, treaties, or Constitution of the United States. One must also navigate the jurisdictional restrictions of INA §242 [8 USC §1252], but this is usually possible where the two conditions mentioned above exist.

Part I of this article provides a general historical perspective, while Part II focuses on lesser-known situations in which habeas can help resolve clients' dilemmas created by unlawful, unconstitutional, of just plain arbitrary action (or inaction) on the part of government officials. Arguments and authorities are provided, as well as citations to other cases.[17] The intent is not only to provide tools for analogous situations, but to aid in the development of the process of "creative" lawyering, so that you can invoke the Great Writ in novel situations not addressed in this article.

PART I: GENERAL PRINCIPLES OF HABEAS CORPUS

Constitutional Bases

Habeas corpus is a statutory procedure with constitutional underpinnings.[18] The degree to which the Constitution protects the right of noncitizens to invoke the Great Writ has been examined by the U.S. Supreme Court in a number of cases.[19]

Historical Development

A survey of habeas decisions from 20th century shows that constitutionally mandated review encompasses claims alleging a wide variety of errors. First, the U.S. Supreme Court consistently reviewed habeas petitions and overturned deportation or ex-

---

2007) (noting, in *dicta,* that inordinate delay before a removal order was entered "might well justify relief").

[12] *See Reno v. Flores*, 507 U.S. 292 (1993).

[13] 5 USC §§551–59.

[14] The fact that it only costs $5 to file a habeas does not hurt, but cannot be a controlling factor.

[15] 28 USC §2243 Issuance of writ; return; hearing; decision

A court, justice or judge entertaining an application for a writ of habeas corpus shall forthwith award the writ or issue an order directing the respondent to show cause why the writ should not be granted, unless it appears from the application that the applicant or person detained is not entitled thereto. The writ, or order to show cause shall be directed to the person having custody of the person detained. It shall be returned within three days unless for good cause additional time, not exceeding twenty days, is allowed. The person to whom the writ or order is directed shall make a return certifying the true cause of the detention. When the writ or order is returned a day shall be set for hearing, not more than five days after the return unless for good cause additional time is allowed.

[16] *See, e.g., Jones v. Cunningham,* 371 U.S. 236, 240 (1963).

[17] Pleadings can be accessed through PACER (Public Access to Court Electronic Records). *See http://pacer.psc.uscourts.gov/.* In the district courts where it is fully implemented, PACER allows attorneys to access virtually all pleadings, other than those filed under seal.

[18] *See INS v. St. Cyr,* 533 U.S. 289 (2001).

[19] *See, e.g., Heikkila v. Barber,* 345 U.S. 229 (1953); *INS v. St. Cyr,* 533 U.S. 289 (2001).

clusion orders for errors of statutory construction.[20] Also during this period, two cases involving the denial of discretionary relief reached the Supreme Court.[21] Notably, both were decided shortly after the Court had specifically confirmed that Congress intended the courts to engage in only that review "required by the Constitution."[22] These cases illustrate that the Suspension Clause[23] requires the review of the denial of discretionary relief for both constitutional and nonconstitutional error.

In *U.S. ex rel. Accardi v. Shaughnessy*,[24] the Court vacated a decision denying discretionary relief because the agency had allegedly exercised its discretion in a manner inconsistent with "existing valid regulations."[25] *Accardi* is particularly significant because the majority ruled in favor of the immigrant over the objection of the dissent that habeas review did not encompass the denial of discretionary relief, and was available only to challenge the finding of deportability. The *Accardi* dissenters argued that:

> Petitioner ... does not question his deportability or the validity of the order to deport him. The hearings in question relate only to whether carrying out an entirely legal deportation order is to be suspended. ... Congress vested in the Attorney General ... discretion as to whether to suspend deportation. ... *We think a refusal to exercise that discretion is not reviewable on habeas corpus.* ...[26]

In granting habeas relief, and ordering a hearing to determine whether the attorney general had lawfully exercised his discretion, the *Accardi* majority necessarily rejected this claim.

In *U.S. ex rel. Hintopoulos v. Shaughnessy*,[27] the Court rejected the petitioner's contention that he was improperly denied discretionary relief, but did so on the merits, after concluding that the agency had "applied the correct legal standards in deciding whether ... the statutory prerequisites for [discretionary] suspension of deportation [had been met]."[28]

Clearly, there were limitations on habeas review. Permissible review looked for errors that could fairly be characterized as involving the "Constitution or laws" of the United States, such as the use of improper criteria in the exercise of discretion,[29] failure to abide by binding regulations, for example, by relying on nonrecord factors,[30] or, more generally, anything that resulted in the lack of a "fair hearing."[31] For example, in *Kwock Jan Fat v. White*,[32] the Supreme Court remanded for a hearing on a habeas petition, and set out the following parameters of review:

> It is fully settled that the decision by the Secretary of Labor, of such a question as we have here, is final, and conclusive upon the courts, unless it be shown that the proceedings were "manifestly unfair," were "such as to prevent a fair investigation," or show "manifest abuse" of the discretion committed to the executive officers by the statute, ... or that "their authority was not fairly exercised, that is, consistently with the fundamental principles of justice embraced within the conception of due process of law" ... . The decision must be after a hearing in good faith, however sum-

---

[20] *See Fong Haw Tan v. Phelan*, 333 U.S. 6, 9–10 (1948) (rejecting executive's interpretation of multiple criminal sentence deportation provision); *Delgadillo v. Carmichael*, 332 U.S. 388, 390–91 (1947) (rejecting the executive's interpretation of "entry"); *Kessler v. Strecker*, 307 U.S. 22, 29–30 (1939) (rejecting executive's interpretation of ideological deportation provision); *Mahler v. Eby*, 264 U.S. 32, 44–45 (1924) (rejecting executive's interpretation of findings necessary for deportation after conviction under Espionage and Selective Service Acts); *Gegiow v. Uhl*, 239 U.S. 3, 8–10 (1915) (rejecting executive's broad interpretation of public charge exclusion provision).

[21] *U.S. ex rel. Accardi v. Shaughnessy*, 347 U.S. 260 (1954); *U.S. ex rel. Hintopoulos v. Shaughnessy*, 353 U.S. 72 (1957).

[22] *Heikkila v. Barber*, 345 U.S. 229 (1953).

[23] U.S. Const., art. 1, §9, cl. 2 ("The Privilege of the Writ of Habeas Corpus shall not be suspended, unless when in Cases of Rebellion or Invasion the public Safety may require it.").

[24] 347 U.S. 260 (1954).

[25] *Id.* at 268.

[26] *Id.* at 269 (Jackson, J. dissenting) (emphasis added).

[27] 353 U.S. 72 (1957).

[28] *Id.* at 77. *Hintopoulos* was cited in *INS v. St. Cyr*, 533 U.S. 289, 307 (2001), for the proposition that the denial of discretionary relief was reviewable for errors of law.

[29] *U.S. ex rel. Hintopoulos v. Shaughnessy*, 353 U.S. 72 (1957). *See also Carlson v. Landon*, 342 U.S. 524, 541 (1952), in which the Court sustained a decision to detain certain aliens, finding no abuse of discretion in the conclusion that "evidence of membership [in the Communist Party] plus personal activity in supporting and extending the Party's philosophy concerning violence" made the aliens "a menace to the public interest."

[30] *U.S. ex rel. Accardi v. Shaughnessy*, 347 U.S. 260 (1954).

[31] *U.S. ex rel. Tisi v. Tod*, 264 U.S. 131 (1924).

[32] 253 U.S. 454 (1920).

mary ... and it must find adequate support in the evidence ... .[33]

A few years later, the Court discussed the requirement of a "fair hearing" in terms that underscored the difference between habeas and direct review, but that still encompassed certain abuses of discretion, and lack of evidence to support the factual findings.[34]

U.S. ex rel. Tisi v. Tod[35] shows that a complaint that the Board of Immigration Appeals (BIA) simply reached an incorrect determination was not reviewable in habeas, unless the result derives from an error of law, or is so "flagrant" as to constitute a denial of a "fair hearing," to wit, a violation of the Constitution of the United States.[36] That a "manifest abuse of discretion" constitutes a denial of a "fair hearing" was apparently first acknowledged in *Low Wah Suey v. Backus*:[37]

A series of decisions in this court has settled that such hearings before executive officers may be made conclusive when fairly conducted. In order to successfully attack by judicial proceedings the conclusions and orders made upon such hearings it must be shown that the proceedings were manifestly unfair, that the action of the executive officers was such as to prevent a fair investigation or that there was a manifest abuse of the discretion committed to them by the statute. In other cases the order of the executive officers within the authority of the statute is final.[38]

Swain v. Pressley

Another important case is *Swain v. Pressley*,[39] which held that the substitution of collateral remedy for habeas corpus is not an unconstitutional suspension of the writ of habeas corpus if the substituted remedy "is neither inadequate nor ineffective" to test the legality of the custody at issue.[40]

Until recently, *Swain* was an under-appreciated and little utilized tool, and there was very little judicial precedent examining its scope in the immigration context. In *INS v. St. Cyr*, the Supreme Court cited *Swain* for the proposition that "Congress could, without raising any constitutional questions, provide an adequate substitute through the courts of appeals,"[41] which is precisely what Congress purported to do in the REAL ID Act. Litigation is ongoing as to whether that attempt was adequate. Under some circumstances, petitions for review under INA §242 [8 USC §1252] are (arguably) "inadequate and ineffective" to test the legality of a deportation order. Areas of ongoing litigation relate to the time limits for filing such a petition and the potential need for factual development to demonstrate the unconstitutionality of the order at issue. As discussed below, litigation has not been successful in either area, but neither has yet gone to the Supreme Court.

Timeliness

When deportation orders were challenged in habeas corpus, there was no time limit to file the petition.[42] By contrast, under INA §242(a) [8 USC §1252(a)], a petition for review must be filed within 30 days of the issuance of the order being challenged. What happens, then, if no petition is filed within 30 days? Does that mean that the order cannot be challenged at all? Or can you argue that, under the circumstances, a petition for review is an ""ineffective or inadequate" substitute for habeas corpus?

Although there is still no definitive answer to that question, all known attempts to date have failed.[43]

---

[33] *Id.* at 457–58.

[34] *Tisi v. Tod, supra* note 31, at 133–34.

[35] 264 U.S. 131 (1924).

[36] This is the same conclusion reached by the Fifth Circuit in *Toscano-Gil v. Trominski*, 210 F.3d 470 (5th Cir. 2000).

[37] 225 U.S. 460 (1912).

[38] *Id.* at 468 (emphasis added)

[39] 430 U.S. 372 (1977).

[40] In *Swain*, a prisoner in custody pursuant to a sentence imposed by the Superior Court of the District of Columbia filed for a writ of habeas corpus to review of the constitutionality of the proceedings that led to his conviction and sentence. The U.S. District Court for the District of Columbia dis-

continued

missed the action, but the U.S. Court of Appeals for the District of Columbia Circuit reversed. Certiorari was granted. The Supreme Court reversed, holding that the statute prohibiting the district court from entertaining an application for a writ of habeas corpus, unless the statutory remedy by motion was inadequate or ineffective to test legality of the detention, did not unconstitutionally suspend the privilege of writ of habeas corpus.

[41] 533 U.S. 289, 314 n.38 (2001).

[42] *U.S. ex rel Marcello v. District Director*, 634 F.2d 964, 971 (5th Cir.1981) (habeas review remained available even where the alien did not avail himself of direct review, so long as there was no finding of a "deliberate bypass" of such review).

[43] *Ruiz-Martinez v. Mukasey*, 516 F.3d 102, 114 (2d Cir. 2008):

Although this Court has not yet addressed the question, other Circuits, with which we now join, have determined that the provision of the REAL ID Act at issue here is not unconstitutional because "it provides, through review by a federal court of appeals, an adequate and effective remedy

continued

Notwithstanding cases such as *Ruiz-Martinez v. Mukasey*,[44] resolution may still depend in part on the circumstances, such as whether there was a compelling reason for the delay. But even without a clear answer, the invocation of *Swain* may be effective in other ways, at least in those circuits that have not yet definitively addressed the issue.

For example, in one case, a petition for review timely mailed, a few months after Katrina, to the U.S. court of Appeals for the Fifth Circuit (in New Orleans) either never arrived, or was misplaced by the clerk's office. The fact that it was not docketed did not come to light until after the passage of the 30 days. At the suggestion of the clerk's office, a second (tardy) petition was filed, with affidavits, and other evidence, to show timely mailing. There was virtually indisputable evidence that the petition had been sent, through the U.S. Postal Service, well before the deadline, which evidence was unchallenged by the Office of Immigration Litigation (OIL). This evidence, coupled with the presumption of receipt,[45] should have established that the petition for review

had been timely filed. The Fifth Circuit disagreed, and dismissed the petition as untimely.[46]

A petition for habeas corpus was filed, invoking *Swain*.[47] ICE filed a motion to dismiss the petition for lack of jurisdiction. But before the judge ruled on the motion, local ICE counsel agreed to a joint motion to reopen before the BIA. This allowed the petitioner to seek (and win) cancellation of removal under *Lopez v. Gonzales*,[48] which was issued while his habeas petition was pending, since his offense was no longer considered to be an aggravated felony. While solving the immediate problem, this left the underlying issue unresolved in this circuit.[49]

Factual Development

The second area in which arguably there may exist a *Swain*-type problem, particularly in cases in which the record was closed prior to the REAL ID Act, relates to the development of facts required to assert a constitutional claim that directly attacks the INA in some manner, *i.e.*, one over which the Executive Office for Immigration Review would lack jurisdiction.[50] Under INA §242(a)(1) [8 USC §1252(a)(1)], the circuit court is precluded from remanding for purposes of taking new evidence under 28 U.S.C. §2347(c).[51] This means that one must at least make an offer of proof to preserve whatever constitutional issues are present that may require factual development.

---

to test the legality of an alien's detention." *Alexandre v. U.S. Att'y Gen.*, 452 F.3d 1204, 1206 (11th Cir.2006); *see also Mohammed v. Gonzales*, 477 F.3d 522, 526 (8th Cir.2007) (holding that, because the REAL ID Act "created [a] remedy as broad in scope as a habeas petition," the Act is "an adequate substitute" for habeas corpus); *Puri v. Gonzales*, 464 F.3d 1038, 1041 (9th Cir.2006) (determining that the REAL ID Act "provided an adequate substitute for habeas proceedings"); *see also Iasu v. Smith*, 511 F.3d 881, 888–90 (9th Cir.2007) (same). In *De Ping Wang v. Dep't of Homeland Sec.*, 484 F.3d 615 (2d Cir.2006), we wrote that "[i]t is possible that in some future case, the particular circumstances that prevented a petitioner from seeking review within the 30-day time limit of § 1252(b)(1) would require us to reexamine whether that limit ought to be treated as jurisdictional now that the petition for review is the exclusive means of obtaining judicial intervention in deportation cases." 484 F.3d at 618–19 (internal quotation marks omitted). We now consider the "future case[s]" we presaged in *De Ping Wang*.

[44] *Id.*

[45] There is a well-established presumption that a piece of U.S. mail deposited in a proper receptacle was delivered in a timely fashion. *See Warfield v. Byron*, 436 F.3d 551, 556 (5th Cir. 2006), *quoting Beck v. Somerset Technologies, Inc.*, 882 F.2d 993, 996 (5th Cir. 1989) ("Proof that a letter properly directed was placed in a U.S. post office mail receptacle creates a presumption that it reached its destination in the usual time and was actually received by the person to whom it was addressed."). *See also Hagner v. U.S.*, 285 U.S. 427, 430 (1932).

[46] *Briseno-Zapata v. Gonzales*, No 06-60693 (5th Cir. 2006).

[47] *Briseno-Zapata v. Gonzales*, No. 06-156 (S.D. Tex., Brownsville Division).

[48] 127 S. Ct. 625 (2006) (holding that whether simple possession of a controlled substance is an aggravated felony is determined with reference to federal standards).

[49] The more compelling the facts, the more likely it is that the government will look for a way to avoid litigation, given that bad facts (from their perspective) tend to make bad law.

[50] *See Matter of Cenatice*, 16 I&N Dec. 162 (BIA 1977).

[51] *See U.S. ex rel. Accardi v. Shaughnessy*, 347 U.S. 260 (1954) (remanding habeas petition to allow immigrant to present evidence in support of his claim that the attorney general had improperly influenced the BIA's decision to deny relief); *Garcia v. Boldin*, 691 F.2d 1172 (5th Cir. 1982) (where alleged unfairness is extrinsic to administrative record on which deportation order is based, court of appeals may remand case to agency for further inquiry and findings).

The Interaction Between The Requirements of "Custody" and of the Violation of a Right Protected by Law, Treaty, or the U.S. Constitution

Custody is not synonymous with detention. Rather, a person is in "custody" whenever there is a significant abridgment of a liberty interest.[52] This includes the simple fact of being under a final order of removal.[53] Although under the REAL ID Act, that order can no longer be reviewed in habeas, its existence still creates "custody." Further, in the context of noncitizens, violation of any right protected by law, treaty, or the Constitution will often, if not always, result in the abridgment of a significant liberty interest, and thus custody, for habeas purposes.[54]

Since regulations have the force and effect of law,[55] a regulatory violation can be considered a violation of "law" under 28 USC §2241. Given that many circuits consider that noncitizens have no due process rights in discretionary relief,[56] and that a due process violation is generally cognizable only to the extent there is prejudice,[57] a regulatory violation should be cast as a violation of law whenever possible.

Liberty Interests That Will Support a Finding of "Custody"

There are numerous liberty interests the deprivation of which may support a finding of "custody." These include rights to family relationships, travel, and work at the common occupations of the community.

Family Relationships

One very significant liberty interest, the deprivation of which may constitute "custody" for habeas purposes, is the right to participate in family life.[58] These are protected interests, even for resident aliens.[59] In *Landon v. Plasencia*,[60] the U.S. Supreme Court stated:

> Plasencia's interest here is, without question, a weighty one. She stands to lose the right "to stay and live and work in this land of freedom." ... *Further, she may lose the right to rejoin her immediate family, a right that ranks high among the interests of the individual.*

The Right to Travel

Interstate travel is also a fundamental right, and therefore subject to few restrictions. That right has three components. As explained by the U.S. Supreme Court in *Saenz v. Roe*:[61]

---

[52] *See Jones v. Cunningham*, 371 U.S. 236, 243 (1963).

[53] *See Rosales v. BICE*, 426 F.3d 733, 735 (5th Cir. 2005); *Simmonds v. INS*, 326 F.3d 351, 354 (2d Cir. 2003); *Aguilera v. Kirkpatrick*, 241 F.3d 1286, 1291 (10th Cir. 2001); *Mustata v. DOJ*, 179 F.3d 1017, 1021 n.4 (6th Cir. 1999); *Nakaranurack v. U.S.,* 68 F.3d 290, 293 (9th Cir. 1995).

[54] *See, e.g., Koetting v. Thompson*, 995 F.2d 37 (5th Cir. 1993) (although a "detainer" issued in connection with a parole violation does not constitute custody for habeas purposes where no liberty interest in impinged, custody does exist where the detainer implicates such an interest by interfering with the petitioner's ability to defend against the parole revocation proceedings).

[55] *U.S. ex rel. Accardi v. Shaughnessy*, 347 U.S. 260, 265 (1954) (regulations issued by the attorney general in supplementation of immigration acts have the force and effect of law).

[56] *See Assaad v. Ashcroft,* 378 F.3d 471, 475 (5th Cir. 2004):

> Assaad's motion to reopen does not allege a violation of his Fifth Amendment right to due process because "the failure to receive relief that is purely discretionary in nature does not amount to a deprivation of a liberty interest." *Mejia Rodriguez v. Reno*, 178 F.3d 1139, 1146 (11th Cir. 1999) (*citing Conn. Bd. of Pardons v. Dumschat*, 452 U.S. 458, 465, 69 L. Ed. 2d 158, 101 S. Ct. 2460 (1981)); *accord Nativi-Gomez v. Ashcroft*, 344 F.3d 805, 808 (8th Cir. 2003); see also *Munoz v. Ashcroft*, 339 F.3d 950, 954 (9th Cir. 2003) ("Since discretionary relief is a privilege ... , denial of such relief cannot violate a substantive interest protected by the Due Process clause."); *cf. Hallmark v. Johnson*, 118 F.3d 1073, 1080 (5th Cir. 1997) ("[A] statute which 'provides no more than a mere hope that the benefit will be obtained ... is not protected by due process.'" (alteration in original) (*quoting Greenholtz v. Inmates of Neb. Penal & Corr. Complex*, 442 U.S. 1, 11 ... (1979)).

[57] *See Ali v. Gonzales,* 435 F.3d 544, 547 (5th Cir. 2006) (proof of due process denial requires showing of substantial prejudice).

[58] *See, e.g.,* M.L.B. v. S.L.J., 519 U.S. 102 (1996) ("The interest of parents in their relationship with their children is sufficiently fundamental to come within the finite class of liberty interests protected by the Fourteenth Amendment."); *Santosky v. Kramer*, 455 U.S. 745, 760 (1982) ("[T]he child and his parents share a vital interest in preventing erroneous termination of their natural relationship."); *Moore v. City of East Cleveland*, 431 U.S. 494 (1977) (freedom of personal choice in matters of family life is one of the liberties protected by due process).

[59] *See Landon v. Plasencia*, 459 U.S. 21 (1982). *But see Aguilar v. ICE,* 510 F.3d 1 (1st Cir. 2007), holding, in the context of the New Bedford workplace raids, that the undocumented aliens had not alleged facts that sufficiently "shocked the conscience" to survive dismissal of their claim that the manner in which they were detained, and transferred, interfered with their substantive due process family rights.

[60] *Landon v. Plasencia, supra* note 59, at 34 (emphasis added).

[61] 526 U.S. 489, 500 (1999).

The "right to travel" discussed in our cases embraces at least three different components. It protects the right of a citizen of one State to enter and to leave another State, the right to be treated as a welcome visitor rather than an unfriendly alien when temporarily present in the second State, and, for those travelers who elect to become permanent residents, the right to be treated like other citizens of that State.

The right to travel abroad is less absolute, as it derives from the due process clause of the Fifth Amendment. It is therefore subject to more restrictions, such as foreign policy considerations.[62] The Supreme Court has stated:[63]

In Kent, the Court held that Congress had not authorized the Secretary of State to inquire of passport applicants as to affiliation with the Communist Party. The Court noted that the right to travel "is a part of the 'liberty' of which the citizen cannot be deprived without due process of law," id. at 125, and stated that it would "construe narrowly all delegated powers that curtail or dilute" that right. *Id.*, at 129. Fn25 Subsequently, in *Aptheker v. Secretary of State,* 378 U.S. 500, 514 (1964), the Court held that a provision of the Subversive Activities Control Act of 1950, 64 Stat. 993, forbidding the issuance of a passport to a member of the Communist Party, "sweeps too widely and too indiscriminately across the liberty guaranteed in the Fifth Amendment."

> FN25. In Kent, 357 U.S., at 126-127, the constitutional right to travel within the United States and the right to travel abroad were treated indiscriminately. That position has been rejected in subsequent cases. *See Haig v. Agee,* 453 U.S. 280, 306 (1981) ("the freedom to travel outside the United States must be distinguished from the right to travel within the United States"); *Califano v. Aznavorian,* 439 U.S. 170, 176-177 (1978).

Both Kent and Aptheker, however, were qualified the following Term in *Zemel v. Rusk,* 381 U.S. 1 (1965). In that case, the Court sustained against constitutional attack a refusal by the Secretary of State to validate the passports of United States citizens for travel to Cuba. The Secretary of State in Zemel, as here, made no effort selectively to deny passports on the basis of political belief or affiliation, but simply imposed a general ban on travel to Cuba following the break in diplomatic and consular relations with that country in 1961. The Court in Zemel distinguished Kent on grounds equally applicable to Aptheker.

There are still some useful "teeth" to this right,[64] under cases such as *Hernandez v. Cremer,*[65] in which the court held that an applicant for admission with facially valid documents showing birth in the United States is entitled to "fair procedures" in determining whether he or she will be admitted or placed in exclusion proceedings.

For example, U.S. Customs and Border Protection (CBP) tends to believe that it has the same right to turn back claimants to U.S. citizenship at the Mexican border that it has with respect to noncitizens. One such case involves a man of Mexican descent who was born in a hospital in McAllen, TX, but raised largely in Mexico and who did not speak much English. He had a U.S. passport, as well as identification cards from two states where he had been recently working. But on return from a visit to his grandmother in Mexico, a CBP officer apparently decided that he could not be a native-born U.S. citizen if he did not speak English, and stripped the man naked, threatening that if he did not sign a "confession" admitting foreign birth, he would go to prison for eight months. Denied even the ability to use the phone to call his parents, the applicant signed the confession. All his documents were confiscated, and he was returned to Mexico, without even a receipt to show that he had ever possessed them. After he had spent almost two years in Mexico, his parents finally located legal help, and he was returned to the United States. A *Bivens* action is pending against the CBP officer involved.[66]

The Right to Employment

Numerous types of immigration applications implicate the right to be employed. The restraints on liberty caused by the denial of such applications therefore also may constitute a deprivation of the

---

[62] *See Regan v. Wald,* 468 U.S. 222 (1984).

[63] *Id.* at 240–42.

[64] Although not yet tested, this may also be useful in the context of the new travel restrictions on U.S. citizens—requiring that they have U.S. passports to return from even a brief visit to Mexico—which are subject to take effect in June 2009.

[65] 913 F.2d 230 (5th Cir. 1990).

[66] *Martinez v. Cantu et al.,* Civ. No. M-08-087 (S.D. Tex. McAllen Div.).

right to be employed, a recognized liberty interest. For example, as held by the Fifth Circuit:[67]

> Stidham has properly demonstrated the violation of a clearly established right by showing that the defendants deprived him of his liberty interest without due process of law. The Supreme Court has said that "the right to work for a living in the common occupations of the community is of the very essence of the personal freedom and opportunity that it was the purpose of the [Fourteenth] Amendment to secure." *Truax v. Raich,* 239 U.S. 33, 41, 36 S.Ct. 7, 60 L.Ed. 131 (1915). We have confirmed the principle that one has a constitutionally protected liberty interest in pursuing a chosen occupation. *See Ferrell v. Dallas Independent School Dist.,* 392 F.2d 697, 703 (5th Cir.1968) (noting that the right of professional musicians to follow their chosen occupation free from unreasonable governmental interference comes within the liberty concept of the Fifth Amendment); *Shaw v. Hospital Authority,* 507 F.2d 625, 628 (5th Cir.1975) (holding that a podiatrist's application for staff privileges at a public hospital for purposes of engaging in his occupation as a podiatrist involved a liberty interest protected by the Fourteenth Amendment); *San Jacinto Savings & Loan v. Kacal,* 928 F.2d 697, 704 (5th Cir.1991) (finding that the owner of an arcade had a protectable liberty interest in operating her business).

Due Process and Discretionary Relief

The right to review of discretionary decisions has been severely limited by INA §242(a)(2)(B) [8 USC §1252(a)(2)(B)], as enacted by IIRAIRA and amended by the REAL ID Act. Although INA §242(a)(2)(D) [8 USC §1252(a)(2)(D)] exempts "constitutional claims and questions of law" from the jurisdictional bar, the statute now provides as follows:

> Notwithstanding any other provision of law (statutory or nonstatutory), including section 2241 of Title 28, or any other habeas corpus provision, and sections 1361 and 1651 of such title, and except as provided in [INA §242(a)(2)(D)], and regardless of whether the judgment, decision, or action is made in removal proceedings, no court shall have jurisdiction to review—

> (i) any judgment regarding the granting of relief under [INA §§212(h), 212(i), 240A, 240B, or 245], or

> (ii) any other decision or action of the Attorney General or the Secretary of Homeland Security the authority for which is specified under this subchapter to be in the discretion of the Attorney General or the Secretary of Homeland Security, other than the granting of relief under [INA §208(a)].

However, whether one can complain of a due process violation in the denial of discretionary relief is still an open question. *INS v. St. Cyr*[68] established that noncitizens can assert violations of law relating to discretionary relief. And notwithstanding circuit court decisions to the contrary,[69] there are strong arguments that immigrants also have due process rights in such relief, where there are standards guiding the exercise of discretion, regardless of whether those standards are established by statute, regulation, or settled course of adjudication.

In *Board of Regents v. Roth*,[70] the U.S. Supreme Court found a constitutionally protected interest in discretionary benefits, because the existence of governing rules and standards mandated that discretion be exercised in conformity with those rules and standards. The Court stated:[71]

> *Goldsmith* v. *Board of Tax Appeals,* 270 U.S. 117, is a related case. There, the petitioner was a lawyer who had been refused admission to practice before the Board of Tax Appeals. The Board had "published rules for admission of persons entitled to practice before it, by which attorneys at law admitted to courts of the United States and the States, and the District of Columbia, as well as certified public accountants duly qualified under the law of any State or the District, are made eligible. . . . The rules further provide that the Board may in its discretion deny admission to any applicant, or suspend or disbar any person after admission." *Id.,* at 119. The Board denied admission to the petitioner under its discretionary power, without a prior hearing and a statement of the reasons for the denial. Although this Court disposed of the case on other grounds, it stated, in an opinion by Mr. Chief Justice Taft, *that the*

---

[67] *Stidham v. Texas Com'n on Private Sec.,* 418 F.3d 486, 491 (5th Cir. 2005).

[68] 533 U.S. 289 (2001).

[69] *See, e.g., Assaad v. Ashcroft,* 378 F.3d 471 (5th Cir. 2004).

[70] 408 U.S. 564 (1972).

[71] *Id.* at 577 n.15 (emphasis added).

existence of the Board's eligibility rules gave the petitioner an interest and claim to practice before the Board to which procedural due process requirements applied. It said that the Board's discretionary power "must be construed to mean the exercise of a discretion to be exercised after fair investigation, with such a notice, hearing and opportunity to answer for the applicant as would constitute due process." Id., at 123.

In *Olim v. Wakinekona*,[72] the Supreme Court defined the test for the existence of a constitutionally protected interest in discretionary relief as follows:[73]

[A] State creates a protected liberty interest by placing substantive limitations on official discretion. An inmate must show "that particularized standards or criteria guide the State's decisionmakers." Connecticut Board of Pardons v. Dumschat, 452 U.S. 458, 467 (1981) (BRENNAN, J., concurring). If the decisionmaker is not "required to base its decisions on objective and defined criteria," but instead "can deny the requested relief for any constitutionally permissible reason or for no reason at all," ibid., the State has not created a constitutionally protected liberty interest.

No court has yet addressed this argument, and the cases in which the doctrine has been applied are generally those in which the type of relief involved would not support an argument under *Roth*. For example, *Assaad v. Ashcroft*[74] involved a "hardship" waiver, where conditional residency was obtained by a marriage to a U.S. citizen that fell apart in less than two years. There are no substantive restraints on the exercise of discretion in such applications, either by regulation or administrative decision. Such relief is thus truly in the "unfettered" discretion of the attorney general. By contrast, cancellation of removal under INA §240A(a) [8 USC §1229b(a)], and its predecessor, INA §212(c) relief, are subject to a long line of decisions defining the conditions for, and specifying the manner in which, discretion is exercised. The BIA stated in *Matter of C–V–T–*:[75]

[T]he Board ruled in Matter of Marin, 16 I&N Dec. 581, 584–85 (BIA 1978), that in exercising discretion under section 212(c) of the Act, an Immigration Judge, upon review of the record as a whole,

"must balance the adverse factors evidencing the alien's undesirability as a permanent resident with the social and humane considerations presented in his [or her] behalf to determine whether the granting of . . . relief appears in the best interest of this country." We find this general standard equally appropriate in considering requests for cancellation of removal under section 240A(a) of the Act.

We also find that the factors we have enunciated as pertinent to the exercise of discretion under section 212(c) are equally relevant to the exercise of discretion under section 240A(a) of the Act.

In *INS v. St. Cyr*, the Supreme Court described the result of this process as follows:[76]

[T]he *Board developed criteria, comparable to common-law rules, for deciding when deportation is appropriate*. Those criteria, which have been set forth in several Board opinions, see, *e.g., In re Marin*, 16 I. & N. Dec. 581 (1978), include the seriousness of the offense, evidence of either rehabilitation or recidivism, the duration of the alien's residence, the impact of deportation on the family, the number of citizens in the family, and the character of any service in the Armed Forces.

Once such a list—albeit nonexclusive—of factors to be considered, and more importantly, *the procedure by which they are to be evaluated*, are established, it can no longer be said that the attorney general has "unfettered" discretion in adjudicating such an application. As the Supreme Court has stated:[77]

Though the agency's discretion is unfettered at the outset, if it announces and follows—by rule or by settled course of adjudication—a general policy by which its exercise of discretion will be governed, an irrational departure from that policy (as opposed to an avowed alteration of it) could constitute action that must be overturned as "arbitrary, capricious, [or] an abuse of discretion" within the meaning of the Administrative Procedure Act.

Under this ruling, when the attorney general has established criteria for the exercise of such discretion, such as "by settled course of adjudication," he or she is no longer free to "deny the requested relief for any constitutionally permissible reason or for no reason at all."[78] Thus, in contrast to the immigrant in

---

[72] 461 U.S. 238 (1983).

[73] *Id.* at 249 (emphasis added)

[74] 378 F.3d 471 (5th Cir. 2004).

[75] 22 I&N Dec. 7, 11 (BIA 1998).

[76] 533 U.S. 289, 296 (2001) (emphasis added).

[77] *INS v. Yang*, 519 U.S. 26, 32 (1996).

[78] *See Diaz-Resendez v. INS,* 960 F.2d 493 (5th Cir. 1992) ("Concluding that the Board's decision is arbitrary and *be-*
continued

Assaad v. Ashcroft, LPRs have constitutionally protected interests in applications for cancellation of removal under INA §240A(a) [8 USC §1229b(a)], and other forms of discretionary relief where similar showings of settled standards can be made.

Habeas Corpus and the Administrative Procedure Act

General Principles

The judicial review provisions of the Administrative Procedure Act[79] do not, in and of themselves, confer jurisdiction. Therefore, a specific grant of jurisdiction is necessary, usually under 28 USC §1331 and/or habeas corpus under 28 USC §2241. Significantly, however, 5 USC §703 specifically mentions habeas as an appropriate vehicle, where no specific statutory remedy exists:

> The form of proceeding for judicial review is the special statutory review proceeding relevant to the subject matter in a court specified by statute or, in the absence or inadequacy thereof, any applicable form of legal action, including actions for declaratory judgments or writs of prohibitory or mandatory injunction or habeas corpus, in a court of competent jurisdiction. If no special statutory review proceeding is applicable, the action for judicial review may be brought against the United States, the agency by its official title, or the appropriate officer. Except to the extent that prior, adequate, and exclusive opportunity for judicial review is provided by law, agency action is subject to judicial review in civil or criminal proceedings for judicial enforcement.

The INA is notably stingy in its specific grants of jurisdiction. Such grants exist for: (1) judicial review of removal orders;[80] (2) naturalization cases;[81] and (3) denial of rights or privileges as a U.S. citizen.[82] There are no specific grants, for example, for challenging an "arriving alien" determination, a threat to reinstate a deportation order against an "arriving alien," or a claim that an "arriving alien" falls under the visa waiver program.

PART II—SPECIFIC EXAMPLES

Issues Involving "Arriving Aliens"

Challenging an "arriving alien" designation for bond purposes

Habeas corpus is also the appropriate remedy where an immigration judge refuses to entertain a challenge to a designation of "arriving alien" in bond proceedings. Under 8 CFR §1003.19(h)(2)(i), an immigration judge may not redetermine custody of various classes of aliens:

> (A) Aliens in exclusion proceedings;
>
> (B) Arriving aliens in removal proceedings, including aliens paroled after arrival pursuant to [INA §212(d)(5)];
>
> (C) Aliens described in [INA §237(a)(4)];
>
> (D) Aliens in removal proceedings subject to [INA §236(c)(1)] (as in effect after expiration of the Transition Period Custody Rules); and
>
> (E) Aliens in deportation proceedings subject to [INA §242(a)(2)] (as in effect prior to April 1, 1997, and as amended by [AEDPA §440(c)].

A partial exception to this bar is found in §1003.19(h)(2)(ii):

> Nothing in this paragraph shall be construed as prohibiting an alien from seeking a redetermination of custody conditions by the Service in accordance with [8 CFR] part 1235 or 1236 . . . . In addition, with respect to [8 CFR §§1003.19(h)(2)(i)(C), (D), and (E)], nothing in this paragraph shall be construed as prohibiting an alien from seeking a determination by an immigration judge that the alien is not properly included within any of those paragraphs.

Some immigration judges interpret the absence of any mention of subsection (h)(2)(i)(B) (the bar for "arriving aliens") as implying an alien may not challenge the designation as an "arriving alien" in bond proceedings. There is no statute clearly mandating this result. What is involved is checking a box on a notice to appear, alleging that someone is an "arriving alien." However, this designation is not a fact per se, but a mixed finding of law and fact. In *Demore v. Kim*,[83] the U.S. Supreme Court held that Congress could constitutionally mandate that certain criminal aliens be detained for the "brief period" necessary for removal proceedings. In so holding,

---

yond the pale of its discretion we grant review, vacate and remand.") (emphasis added).

[79] 5 USC §§701–06.

[80] INA §242; 8 USC §1252.

[81] INA §336; 8 USC §1447.

[82] INA §360; 8 USC §1503.

---

[83] 538 U.S. 510 (2003).

the Court relied heavily on the existence of a safety valve, a so-called "*Joseph* hearing,"[84] by which the alien could challenge whether he was properly included within the statutory category of those subject to mandatory detention.[85] There is no such safety valve when the reason for the mandatory detention is an administrative designation of the alien as an "arriving alien."

In *Garza-Garcia v. Moore*,[86] this interpretation was found to be inconsistent with the statute:

> The Court holds that 8 C.F.R. § 1003.19(h)(2)(ii) is an invalid exercise of executive power because it is arbitrary and inconsistent with 8 U.S.C. § 1226(c). Accordingly, to the extent that the government is still pursuing administrative remedies and the IJ's order terminating proceedings is still not final, we ORDER the immigration judge to conduct a *Joseph* hearing to determine whether or not Garza is properly designated an arriving alien subject to mandatory detention during the pendency of his removal proceedings. If the Immigration Judge finds Garza is improperly designated, he will then be eligible for release in accordance with the general bond provisions and based on the Immigration Judge's discretion.

ICE released him, without waiting for the immigration judge to conduct a *Joseph*-type hearing.

An "Arriving Alien" Is Not Inadmissible Under the Visa Waiver Program

In *Hebel v. Cabrera et al.*,[87] the issue was whether ICE had properly detained a person returning to the United States with an advance parole, on the theory that he was still under the Visa Waiver Program (VWP). The government argued that because he had been "admitted" under the VWP, he was still subject to that program, notwithstanding his subsequent departures and returns with advance parole, issued on the basis of an adjustment application filed through his U.S. citizen wife.[88] ICE also argued that it had made a determination under the VWP that he was inadmissible, and that such a determination

was the equivalent of a removal order, which could be challenged only at the circuit court of appeals. The district court disagreed, denying the government's motion to dismiss, and ordering the alien's release. ICE released him on the advance parole, but immediately took him back into custody, as an "arriving alien," where he remained until the immigration judge granted both the I-601 and I-485.

Appropriate Evidence of LPR Status
Refusal to Provide Proof of LPR Status

The question of providing adequate proof of LPR status arises in various contexts. Under INA §264(d) [8 USC §1304(d)], DHS has a nondiscretionary duty to provide noncitizens with "a certificate of alien registration or an alien registration receipt card in such form and manner and at such time as shall be prescribed under regulations issued by the Attorney General."[89] The refusal to provide such documentation, therefore, violates the laws of the United States.

Ongoing I-90 Litigation

Recent litigation challenging demands by DHS that LPRs produce extensive documentation with respect to any arrests or convictions as a precondition of renewing their green cards appears headed for successful resolution.[90] The plaintiffs in *Pantoja-Castillo et al. v. Sanchez et al.*[91] had to confront OIL's argument that habeas corpus was an improper vehicle for such a challenge, and that the slow train of litigation under 28 USC §1331 was the only available vehicle.[92] On August 2, 2007, when the action was filed, the lead plaintiff had no valid proof of LPR status. His old I-551 had expired in 2006, and the initial extension thereof had expired at the end of May 2007. When he requested a further ex-

---

[84] *See Matter of Joseph*, 22 I&N Dec. 799 (BIA 1999).

[85] *Demore v. Kim*, 538 U.S. 510, 514 (2003).

[86] Civ. No. B-07-067 (S.D. Tex. 2007).

[87] Civ. No. M-06-174 (S.D. Tex. 2006).

[88] His second advance parole document was issued after his I-485 had been denied, on the basis that he had appealed the denial of his I-601, and filed a motion to reopen the adjustment application, should the appeal be granted.

[89] *See* 8 CFR §264.1 ("Prescribed Registration Forms") and 8 CFR §299.1 (showing I-551 as the "Prescribed Form" for a "Permanent Resident Card" and I-688 as the prescribed form for a "Temporary Resident Card"); *Loa-Herrera v. Trominski*, 231 F.3d 984,988 n.8 (5th Cir. 2000), quoting *Etuk v. Slattery*, 936 F.2d 1433, 1444 (2d Cir. 1991) ("The INA mandates that the Attorney General provide LPRs who register with proof of their legal status.").

[90] *Pantoja-Castillo et al. v. Sanchez et al.*, Civ. No. M-07-204 (S.D. Tex.). The plaintiffs survived a motion to dismiss, and, at the time of this writing, were in the final stages of negotiating a settlement agreement, acceding to virtually all of their demands.

[91] *Id.*

[92] The action was styled as a Petition for Writ of Habeas Corpus and Complaint for Injunctive and Declaratory Relief.

tension, or an I-94 temporary proof of LPR status, U.S. Citizenship and Immigration Services (USCIS) refused. He had therefore had been without valid proof of LPR status for over two months when the action was filed.

The plaintiffs argued that leaving LPRs without documents for months on end, making it difficult if not impossible for them to obtain employment, obtain or renew drivers' licenses, travel outside—or even within—the United States, and leaving them vulnerable to detention by DHS (or others) imposed significant restrictions on their liberty that are not shared by other LPRs, which constituted custody for habeas purposes. As explained in *Jones v. Cunningham*:[93]

Of course, that writ always could and still can reach behind prison walls and iron bars. But it can do more. It is not now and never has been a static, narrow, formalistic remedy; its scope has grown to achieve its grand purpose—the protection of individuals against erosion of their right to be free from wrongful restraints upon their liberty.

In particular, the restraints on the LPRs' liberty caused by the lack of valid immigration documents showing their entitlement to be employed were both significant and wrongful.[94]

Therefore, when *Pantoja-Castillo et al.* was instituted, the lead plaintiff was clearly being deprived of a protected liberty interest, to wit, "the right to work for a living in the common occupations of the community," and was "in custody" for habeas purposes. For purposes of habeas jurisdiction, custody is determined at the moment the petition is filed, and jurisdiction is not defeated by the later release from the unlawful custody.[95] The issue may be mooted, but that is a separate question, determined independently.[96]

Issues Involving the Adequacy of Documents Showing Status

Some cases just never seem to go away. In *Loa-Herrera et al. v. Trominski et al.*,[97] the plaintiffs challenged, *inter alia,* the fact that legacy Immigration and Naturalization Service did not always give appropriate proof of status to LPRs in deportation proceedings.[98] If it gave anything, it was an I-94, on which it usually put all kinds of extraneous notations about how the person was in proceedings because of a drug conviction, etc. The plaintiffs argued that such notations were improper under the statute, and tended to make it difficult for the LPR to obtain employment; *i.e.,* it deprived them of a liberty interest. Initially, the district court certified the class, and granted all relief. Legacy INS appealed, and the Fifth Circuit vacated the decision, allegedly because INS had been deprived of an opportunity to be heard at the district level.[99] On remand, the district court reversed itself and denied all relief, on the theory that this was what the Fifth Circuit had intended. This time, the plaintiffs prevailed on appeal. The Fifth Circuit remanded for the district court to consider the plaintiffs' arguments. The plaintiffs are now back before the district court, still asserting that ICE has no right to divulge sensitive personal information on the temporary I-551.

Wrongful Expulsion or Attempt

"Involuntary" Voluntary Departure

A recurring problem in the Houston district court (and perhaps others) is what could be called involuntary prehearing voluntary departure. Ironically, the practice is reminiscent of the situation that led to *Nunez v. Boldin*,[100] in which the court ruled that legacy INS was obligated to notify detained Guatemalans and Salvadorans of their right to seek asylum. The primary difference is that the current victims are now mostly Mexican, and it is hard to get a class action established, given the rapidity with which ICE can physically remove them. In one recent case, counsel was able to get a temporary restraining order before ICE got the person out of the country.[101] He

---

[93] 371 U.S. 236, 243 (1963).

[94] *See Stidham v. Texas Com'n on Private Sec.*, 418 F.3d 486 (5th Cir. 2005).

[95] *Zalawadia v. Ashcroft,* 371 F.3d 292, 297 (5th Cir. 2004) ("The Supreme Court has made it clear that the 'in custody' determination is made at the time the habeas petition is filed. Spencer v. Kemna, 523 U.S. 1, 7, 140 L. Ed. 2d 43, 118 S. Ct. 978 (1998); Carafas v. La Vallee, 391 U.S. 234, 237–38, 20 L. Ed. 2d 554, 88 S. Ct. 1556 (1968).").

[96] For example, in *Lopez v. Gonzales,* 127 S. Ct. 625 (2006), the resident had been deported before the case was decided by the Supreme Court, but the Court noted that it was not moot.

---

[97] Civ. No. B-94-215 (S.D. Tex.).

[98] The plaintiffs also challenged ICE's practice of confiscating documents such as Social Security cards, driver's licenses, etc.

[99] *Loa-Herrera v. Trominski,* 231 F.3d 984 (5th Cir. 2000).

[100] 537 F. Supp. 578 (S.D. Tex. 1982).

[101] Temporary Restraining Order, *Adame-Gutierrez v. Freeman,* Civ. No. B-08-065 (S.D. Tex. Feb. 13, 2008). The original-
continued

was taken off the bus, and put into proceedings. Since this occurred very rapidly, mooting the case, counsel has been unable to mount a class action, and the problem continues.

Unlawful Expulsion

Another issue that has surfaced repeatedly involves noncitizens whom ICE takes it upon themselves to remove from the United States, with little or not opportunity to challenge the lawfulness of the expulsion. Often, this involves a claim that there is an outstanding order of removal/deportation, notwithstanding that the person has previously departed and returned, sometimes lawfully and sometimes not.

For example, in *Arellano v. Adame*,[102] the alien had been under a final order of deportation, but had erroneously adjusted his status, through his U.S. citizen wife. Thereafter, he came and went frequently from Mexico, using his I-551. Eventually, USCIS discovered the fact that he had an old deportation order, and issued a notice of intent to rescind his LPR status. While this was ongoing, ICE picked him up, with the stated intent of executing the old deportation order. It literally became a race to the courthouse, which plaintiff's counsel won by three minutes.[103]

The same thing occurs with applicants for adjustment of status who were previously granted voluntary departure by an immigration judge, and left in a timely fashion, but did not, for whatever reason, fully (or successfully) document their departure at the time. In some cases, this may have been the result of ignorance on the part of the noncitizen. In others, it may be caused by DHS sloppiness. In such cases, USCIS sometimes denies the adjustment application, and calls in ICE, which may attempt to immediately "execute" the alleged prior deportation order, on the theory that the noncitizen has not adequately proven that ho or she departed the United States, much less that the departure occurred while the immigration judge's

grant of voluntary departure was still in effect. In *Ramirez-Rodriguez v. Cantu et al.*,[104] the plaintiff litigated such a case to the point where DHS capitulated, and allowed him to return in the *status quo ante*, to continue his adjustment application.

If the client is Mexican, and the adjustment interview occurs near the border, a race to the courthouse may sometimes occur. Notwithstanding precedent to the effect that a deportation order cannot be challenged in habeas corpus once it has been executed, because there is no longer any "custody" for habeas purposes,[105] counsel have successfully used habeas corpus as a vehicle to bring the client back. This success derives from a combination of factors.

First, you should arrange for the noncitizen to be physically on U.S. soil at the moment the petition is filed. Usually, this entails meeting the client at the port of entry,[106] obtaining his or her signature on the petition, and then rushing to file it while the client is still waiting at the bridge.[107] The legal theory is that he or she is in "custody" for habeas purposes because he or she is being deprived of various "rights" discussed above; *e.g.*, the rights to travel, to work at the common occupations of the community, to rejoin

---

[102] Civ. No. B-06-130 (S.D. Tex. 2006).

[103] Because there was electronic filing, counsel could document the exact minute in which the petition was filed. And because ICE knew it was a race, they noted the time when they physically expelled Mr. Arellano—three minutes later. This case illustrates the importance of the fact that once habeas jurisdiction attaches, it remains, regardless of whether the alien is deported or custody ceases. *Zalawadia v. Ashcroft*, 371 F.3d 292 (5th Cir. 2004).

nal petition was sketchy, given the time pressure, but accomplished the objective. This illustrates the fact that, since habeas is often an emergency procedure, the courts are generally understanding and tolerant of bare-bones pleadings.

[104] Civ. No. M-06-233 (S.D. Tex. 2006).

[105] *Macias v. Greene*, 28 F. Supp. 2d 635, 638–39 (D. Colo. 1998) (alien who had been deported to Mexico was not physically in the United States, and was not in "custody" for purposes of challenging the denial of suspension of deportation through a habeas action).

[106] An applicant for admission at a port of entry who has not made an "entry" is under "official restraint" by DHS. *See, e.g., Matter of Patel*, 20 I&N Dec. 368, 373–74 (BIA 1991) (internal citations and original footnotes omitted):

Reading *Matter of V–Q–* to hold that freedom from official restraint is not an essential element to effecting an entry into the United States would be inconsistent with decades of caselaw on the "entry" issue, including the very cases relied upon in *Matter of V–Q–*. ... *The critical point is such cases is that freedom from official restraint exists, not that such freedom has been exercised.*

In *Patel*, the BIA also quoted *Correa v. Thornburgh*, 901 F.2d 1166, 1172 (2d Cir. 1990), defining "freedom from official restraint" as meaning that the individual "is no longer under constraint emanating from the government that would otherwise prevent her from physically passing on." *Id.* at 374. One who is in the waiting room of the International Bridge, but lacks appropriate documents to enter or be paroled into the United States, is under such constraint.

[107] In one case, CBP chased the client back to Mexico before counsel completed the process, so counsel had him come part-way back and wait on the U.S. side of the bridge while counsel filed the petition.

family in the United States, and participate in the rearing of children, which rights could be enjoyed by otherwise similarly situated noncitizens who were not expelled from the United States in violation of the laws and Constitution of the United States.[108] As in most such cases, the government threw in the towel, and allowed the petitioner to return to the United States in the *status quo ante* once it was established to its satisfaction that the person had actually departed during the period of voluntary departure given by the immigration judge.

Return After Successful Petition for Review

Another issue that may or may not be limited to the Great State of Texas involves individuals, usually those who had been under mandatory detention while they challenged their removal orders, who were physically removed following an adverse BIA decision, but then prevailed at the circuit court. There are a number of such cases that followed *Lopez v. Gonzales*.[109]

In a recent nonprecedent case, the local ICE attorney took the position on remand to the BIA that the BIA lacked jurisdiction, because the person had been deported. Notwithstanding language in *Lopez* to the effect that the case was not moot, because the noncitizen would be eligible for cancellation on remand, the BIA agreed. The BIA reasoned that while the U.S. Supreme Court could determine *its* jurisdiction, the BIA had the same prerogative, and that 8 CFR §1003.4 had divested it of jurisdiction. The BIA therefore purported to return the file to the Fifth Circuit "without action."

Since this was not an order of removal, there would have been no review at the Fifth Circuit. Therefore, counsel filed a motion to reconsider, and a habeas action,[110] using the sitting-at-the-port-of-entry procedure. Once the habeas was filed, and it became clear that ICE's position, and that of the BIA, were ridiculous, ICE filed a pleading with the BIA to the effect that it had changed its mind, and urged the BIA to grant the plaintiff's motion to re-

consider. The BIA complied, so the APA review was moot.[111]

EADs for N-600 Applicants

Another case that simply will not go away involves a class action, filed in 1996, asserting that applicants for certificates of citizenship (N-600s) should be entitled to employment authorization documents (EADs) while their applications are pending.[112] The lead plaintiff and her husband, a Mexican national, filed simultaneous applications with legacy INS. She filed an N-600, and he filed an I-485, based on an I-130 from his wife, asserting her claim to U.S. citizenship. His I-485 was held in abeyance, pending resolution of her citizenship claim, but he was issued an EAD. Counsel asserted that this violated Equal Protection: the husband could get employment authorization, based on his wife's claim to citizenship, but she could not. The district court agreed, certified the class, and issued judgment in plaintiffs' favor. After several more years of litigation, an agreed amended final order was issued. Shortly thereafter, USCIS stopped issuing EADs to class members,[113] and counsel filed an enforcement action. The case is now at the Fifth Circuit.[114]

Denial of Advance Parole

In *Mendoza-Hernandez v. Sanchez*,[115] plaintiff challenged the denial of an application for an advance parole, in the context of a long-delayed adjustment application. The action was combined with a mandamus, demanding that DHS adjudicate the

---

[108] *See, e.g., Ramirez-Rodriguez v. Cantu et al.*, Civ. No. M-06-233 (S.D. Tex. 2006).

[109] *See, e.g., Torres-Ramos v. Gonzales*, No. 05-60906 (5th Cir.); *Cavazos v. Gonzales*, No. 05-60798 (5th Cir.); *Garza-Arizpe v. Gonzales*, No. 06-60630 (5th Cir.); *Vasquez-Montoya v. Gonzales*, No. 06-60765 (5th Cir.).

[110] *Torres-Ramos v. Gonzales*, No. 05-60906 (5th Cir.).

[111] One can ask whether the BIA determined its jurisdiction in the first instance, or ICE. Initially, the BIA found ICE's argument more persuasive than the holding of the Supreme Court in *Lopez*. Notably, the BIA did not purport to change its mind, but only accepted ICE's suggestion that they grant the motion to reconsider. Conceptually, this could not be done without reconsidering jurisdiction, but the BIA did not bother with this detail.

[112] *Dominguez-Perez et al. v. Chertoff et al.*, Civ. No. B-96-116 (S.D. Tex.).

[113] USCIS routinely issues requests for evidence (RFEs) of physical presence in support of N-600s. It now asserts that this stops the clock for issuance of an EAD. It cites 8 CFR §103.2(b)(10)(ii), which stops time for interim benefits on a given application where an RFE is issued with respect thereto. It can be argued, however, that the regulation would only apply if there were an RFE for more evidence on the I-765, *e.g.,* proof that the N-600 was still pending.

[114] No. 07-40934 (5th Cir).

[115] Civ. No. B-06-178 (S.D. Tex.).

underlying I-485. DHS quickly granted the adjustment application.

Orders of Supervision

In another class action, counsel successfully used habeas corpus as a vehicle for obtaining orders of supervision for aliens under final orders of removal, where DHS has allowed them to remain for discretionary reasons, such as extremely ill U.S. citizen children.[116] Again, the liberty interests asserted are the right to be employed, and to engage in interstate travel.[117]

Challenging Mandatory Detention

As discussed above, there are a number of ways in which one can challenge mandatory detention in habeas corpus. If a detained client is arguably not subject to mandatory detention, but after a *Joseph* hearing both the immigration judge and the BIA found that INA §237(c) [8 USC §1227(c)] applies, this determination can be challenged in habeas corpus.[118] One can also challenge mandatory detention when the removal proceedings are inordinately delayed,[119] or when there are other reasons to believe that the provisions of INA §237(c) [8 USC §1227(c)] are being applied in a manner that violates either the laws or Constitution of the United States.

For example, also by joining a habeas petition with a class action complaint, the author's law office obtained a declaratory judgment that a conviction for a nondeportable offense occurring after the end of the transitional period (October 8, 1998) does not trigger mandatory detention.[120] As in our I-90 litigation, DHS kept mooting out our named plaintiffs, and we had to keep adding people. When we were down to one person, the court certified the class, and granted relief. At the time, we believed that this was only a local problem, so our class was defined locally. Apparently, the problem has since arisen in other jurisdictions.

---

[116] *Zamora-Garcia et al. v. Moore et al.*, Civ. No. M-05-331 (S.D. Tex.).

[117] *See, e.g., Saenz v. Roe,* 526 U.S. 489 (1999).

[118] *Demore v. Kim*, 538 U.S. 510 (2003).

[119] *Ly v. Hansen* 351 F.3d 263 (6th Cir. 2003); *Hussain v. Mukasey*, 510 F.3d 739 (7th Cir. 2007).

[120] *Cavazos et al v. Moore et al*, Civ. No. M-03-347 (S.D. Tex. 2005).

U.S. Supreme Court–Savvy Immigration Practice

by Nancy Morawetz[*]

INTRODUCTION

Today's legal terrain in immigration law increases the need for sophisticated immigration practitioners to think about the role of the Supreme Court. With the Illegal Immigration Reform and Immigrant Responsibility Act of 1996[1] and the REAL ID Act of 2005[2] placing cases directly into the courts of appeals, and cases frequently turning on legal questions, rather than issues of substantial evidence and discretion, there are more and more legal questions on which the circuits are divided. These splits in the circuits create issues that may be deemed worthy of U.S. Supreme Court review. In many cases, circuit splits will attract the interest of a new bar made up of law firms and law school clinics that specialize in Supreme Court practice but that may have little or no immigration law experience. In some cases, these attorneys or law clinics may contact immigration lawyers to discuss the possibility of handling a case on a petition for writ of certiorari to the Supreme Court or of handling a case in which the Supreme Court has recently granted certiorari.

This article presents a checklist of issues for immigration attorneys to consider if they are considering seeking Supreme Court intervention in their cases. The checklist is meant to help attorneys ensure that they have given consideration to the many interests that their clients may have in connection with a possible petition for certiorari. It is also de-signed to help attorneys with their choices as to who should handle a case in the Supreme Court, should they decide to pursue that route. The American Immigration Law Foundation (AILF) also has helped to establish a Supreme Court Immigration Law Working Group to assist attorneys in thinking through these decisions. The function of this group is not to engage in Supreme Court practice, but rather to assist lawyers as they navigate the choices they face when a case is a potential candidate for Supreme Court review.

This checklist is a work in progress and will continue to be revised as we develop greater experience with the dilemmas faced by attorneys and their clients, as well as experience with the Supreme Court's treatment of these cases. If you have comments for the Supreme Court Immigration Law Working Group, please forward them to *clearing-house@ailf.org*.

BACKGROUND

In recent years, there have been several important victories for immigrants in the Supreme Court. These cases typically have involved a nationally based immigration office that played a lead role either in handling the cases at the Supreme Court or in coordinating amicus briefing and advising on the cases when they reached the Supreme Court. For example, in the litigation leading up to the decision in *INS v. St. Cyr*,[3] the Immigrant Rights Project of the American Civil Liberties Union tracked and coordinated litigation in the district and circuit courts, and then served as lead counsel in the case at the Supreme Court.[4] Its highly developed legal arguments and sophisticated strategy paid off in the Court's decision. Similarly, two years ago the Immigrant Defense Project of the New York State Defenders' Association (IDP) identified the drug aggravated felony issue as one that would be taken by the Supreme Court and developed a strategy to influence which cases might be taken and what

---

[*] **Nancy Morawetz** is a professor of clinical law at New York University School of Law, where she has taught since 1987. She currently teaches in the Immigrant Rights Clinic (IRC). Through her work with students in the IRC and her pro bono work, Professor Morawetz has engaged in litigation and legislative and media advocacy to curb the harshness of current detention and deportation policies. Professor Morawetz is also the author of numerous articles on deportation and judicial review.

This article, © Nancy Morawetz, was prepared in consultation with the Supreme Court Immigration Law Working Group. It may be copied in whole without permission so long as the publication indicates that it was first published in the *Immigration & Nationality Law Handbook* (AILA 2008–09 Ed.).

[1] Pub. L. No. 104-208, div. C, 110 Stat. 3009, 3009-546 to 3009-724.

[2] Pub. L. No. 109-13, div. B, 119 Stat. 231, 302–23.

---

[3] 533 U.S. 29 (2001).

[4] For a description of the litigation campaign that culminated in the *St. Cyr* decision, *see* N. Morawetz, "INS v. St. Cyr: The Campaign to Preserve Court Review and Stop Retroactive Application of Deportation Laws," in D. Martin & P. Schuck, eds., *Immigration Stories* (2005).

amicus filings would be submitted. This effort also paid off when the Supreme Court issued an 8-1 ruling rejecting the government's overbroad reading of the drug aggravated felony category in *Lopez v. Gonzales*.[5]

The Supreme Court, however, is often not friendly to immigrants, and there is reason to expect a tough fight in any case that goes to the Court.[6] The fight is tough for several reasons: (1) many Justices are rarely, if ever, favorably disposed to the arguments of immigrants; (2) the government has available tactics that allow it to change the rules of the game following a grant of certiorari by issuing new regulations or new precedent decisions, or persuading Congress to change the governing statute; and (3) the Supreme Court may allow the government to present new arguments that it did not raise below. The government also enjoys a special status at the Supreme Court, and the Court gives it deference when deciding which cases to hear. As a result, the government can act strategically so as to put its legal position in the best light. Given how tough the fight is likely to be, immigrant advocates have to be as prepared as possible and to work as collaboratively as possible.

The checklist that follows is designed to assist lawyers in evaluating how to approach issues that might be prospects for Supreme Court resolution. In some cases, for example, there is little chance of success, and a significant chance of making the law worse in ways that will affect the client and his or her family and community. In other cases, there may be another case that would serve as a better vehicle for seeking Supreme Court review. In all cases, better information will help develop the issues so that there is the best chance of a good outcome.

The checklist also addresses the question of how individual counsel should approach offers from pro bono counsel and others to handle Supreme Court advocacy in a case. In some cases, one or more pro bono attorneys from a law clinic or a law firm in Supreme Court practice will contact an attorney whose client lost a case in the court of appeals. In such a situation, there may be an opportunity to negotiate or otherwise talk through with the prospective counsel aspects of the possible representation at the Supreme Court. This kind of negotiation can help to assure that the case is handled in a way that is best for the client and for the development of the legal issues.

The checklist begins with steps to take at the agency and circuit court level. These steps are included because they are of vital importance in any case that might later be considered for Supreme Court review or that might be affected by developments in Supreme Court caselaw.

THE CHECKLIST

At the Agency

❑ Preserve claims

Even if you have no plan to take a case to the Supreme Court, it is wise to prepare for the possibility of Supreme Court resolution of an issue at the earliest possible time. Just as it makes sense to preserve claims for circuit review that are doomed at the Board of Immigration Appeals (BIA), it makes sense to preserve issues related to splits in the circuits even if your circuit has an adverse ruling. If you fail to make an application for relief, or argue a claim, your client may not get the benefit of a later favorable Supreme Court precedent. It is always better to practice defensively and avoid a contention that you have waived a claim.

❑ Build a factual record

If a case ultimately goes to any appellate court, you will be stuck largely with the record that you developed below. It is therefore important to build in facts related to the equities of the case or anything else that may seem obvious to practitioners but will be unknown and beyond the record for an appellate court. For example, it can be helpful to make clear that a client's family members are U.S. citizens, both as an equity and as establishing eligibility for forms of relief if, for example, the BIA's subsequent aggravated felony determination is reversed.

In the Circuit Courts

❑ Seek Supreme-Court-proof victories

It is almost always better to win a case on grounds that will not be affected by later adverse Supreme Court precedent. So, no matter how interesting or creative a claim may be, look for ways to win for your client that are less flashy but hold out the promise of a secure victory.

---

[5] 127 S.Ct. 625 (2006). For a description of IDP's litigation work leading up to and following the *Lopez* decision, *see* www.nysda.org/idp/webPages/drugLitigationInit.htm.

[6] *See, e.g., Fernandez-Vargas v. Gonzales*, 548 U.S. 30 (2006); *INS v. Aguirre-Aguirre*, 526 U.S. 415 (1999).

❑ **Preserve issues**

Just as it is important to preserve issues at the agency for later circuit review, it is essential to preserve issues at the circuit for later Supreme Court review. This is true even if the circuit precedent is unfavorable. Issues that have not been preserved are likely to be barred.

❑ **Seek circuit solutions to bad circuit precedent**

Even if the circuit law is bad, it may be possible to seek a change in circuit law through a petition for rehearing or for rehearing en banc. On occasion, circuits will change their precedent, such as when they wish to comport with agency rulings or the rulings of other circuits.

A petition for rehearing or rehearing en banc also may serve to delay a decision on whether to file a petition for writ of certiorari.

❑ **Pay attention to requests from the government for extensions of time**

If the government seeks an extension of time to petition for rehearing or to file a petition for certiorari, it is a sign that the Office of the Solicitor General is seriously considering taking the case to the Supreme Court. This is an important early warning sign that you should communicate to AILF's Supreme Court Advisory Committee.

Considering Certiorari

❑ **Make a realistic assessment of the likelihood of success in the Supreme Court on the legal issue**

It is natural to believe in the strength of your arguments. But in thinking about taking the case to the Supreme Court, you must consider the strength of the arguments as they will appear to that Court. The Supreme Court is a very different institution from the circuit courts. It is unlikely to be seriously influenced by the decisions of the lower courts, or to feel as strictly bound by its own precedents as the lower courts. Assessment your likelihood of success will benefit from close consultation with people who are familiar with Supreme Court litigation in the immigration field.

❑ **Consider the ways in which the government can alter the legal landscape while the case is on appeal**

In assessing the likelihood of success, it is important to consider the many ways in which the government can alter the legal landscape between the time a petition for writ of certiorari is filed and

the time the case is resolved. The government can strengthen its case by issuing decisions or regulations to which it will later claim deference is due. Although there will be arguments against deference to these new decisions, they will complicate the legal context of the case.

- Certification of a BIA decision to the Attorney General

  In *INS v. Elramly*,[7] for example, the solicitor general's position was weakened by the BIA's decision in *Matter of Soriano*,[8] interpreting the scope of the Antiterrorism and Effective Death Penalty Act of 1996 (AEDPA).[9] While the case was pending before the Supreme Court, the attorney general certified the legal issue to herself and vacated the *Soriano* decision.[10] The solicitor general then informed the Supreme Court of the vacatur of *Soriano*. The Supreme Court proceeded to vacate and remand the case for reconsideration in light of AEDPA.

- Issuance of a precedent decision by the BIA

  After the Supreme Court granted certiorari in *Ali v. Achim*,[11] for example, the BIA issued a precedent decision supporting the government's position.[12] This new decision provided the government with an opportunity to argue for deference to its reading of the law.

- Issuance of new regulations

  In *Dada v. Mukasey*,[13] for example, the Department of Homeland Security issued proposed regulations while the case was pending that read the INA as allowing for termination of voluntary departure upon a motion to reopen.[14] These proposed regulations offered a new agency interpretation of the governing statute.

---

[7] 518 U.S. 1051 (1996).

[8] 21 I&N Dec. 516 (BIA 1996).

[9] Pub. L. No. 104-132, 110 Stat. 1214.

[10] 21 I&N Dec. 516 (A.G. 1997).

[11] 128 S. Ct. 828 (2007) (granting certiorari to review the decision in *Ali v. Achim*, 468 F.3d 462 (7th Cir. 2006)).

[12] *Matter of N–A–M–*, 24 I&N Dec. 336 (BIA 2007) (issued 29 days after the grant of certiorari in *Ali*).

[13] No. 06-1181 (argued Jan. 8, 2008).

[14] 72 Fed. Reg. 67674 (Nov. 30, 2007).

❑ **Assess whether your client's case would make a good "lead case" on the issue or whether it would be better if another case took the lead**

Due to the volume of immigration cases being heard by the circuit courts, it is highly likely that any given legal issue will arise in many different cases. As a result, there is often a possibility of identifying other cases that raise the same legal issue and assessing which case would be the most favorable vehicle for Supreme Court review. Although counsel cannot control what case the Court will take, there are various mechanisms that can make a case more or less likely to serve as a lead case, such as extensions of time to seek certiorari or a brief that signals that another case is a better lead case.

A good lead case presents the Court with a sense of the real consequences of the adverse ruling below. In general, it is good for a lead case to be one in which the issues and the factual record were well developed before the agency and the courts below. It is also helpful for the record to contain sympathetic facts that are tied to the legal issue in the case and demonstrate the importance of construing the law in the way that would benefit the client.

❑ **Assess whether there are other approaches to resolution of the issue short of Supreme Court review**

In many situations, it will be possible to resolve a legal question in some way without Supreme Court intervention. For example, the government may be persuaded to issues new regulations, or the BIA or attorney general may be persuaded to alter their precedent. For example, following litigation on the right of "arriving aliens" to seek adjustment,[15] the agency altered its regulations to address a split in the circuit courts,[16] and the legal issue that divided the circuits never reached the Supreme Court.

❑ **Determine whether the issue on which the Supreme Court might take certiorari will really help the client; what further obstacles does the client face in receiving relief?**

Sometimes there is a solid legal argument to challenge the decision of the circuit court, but success on that claim actually will not help the

client. For example, with relief from removal, there may be another eligibility problem. Or with removal, there may be an alternate ground of removal the client cannot contest.

❑ **If it would be better to allow another case to take the lead, or for the issues to be resolved in another way, examine alternative options for your client**

There are often alternative steps that can be taken to assist a client, either by preserving the chance for relief under an alternative case or through alternative immigration remedies. For example, it may be possible to postpone briefing or argument of the circuit case or disposition of a rehearing request pending resolution of another case. There may be alternative immigration remedies for the client also.

❑ **Consult with national immigration experts by contacting the AILF Supreme Court Working Group at *clearinghouse@ailf.org***

Supreme Court litigation is tricky and requires consideration of a wide range of potential consequences. It is helpful to have national experts with whom to consult about these choices and to assist in coordination of related litigation.

❑ **Counsel your client about the implications of seeking certiorari**

The decision whether to seek certiorari belongs to your client. Your client deserves to know in plenty of time the deadline for seeking certiorari, and whether you are prepared to undertake representation at that stage. You have no obligation to take a case to the Supreme Court, but you do have an obligation to provide your client with a timely assessment of his or her options.

Client counseling ideally should include the full range of considerations that might bear on the client's choice. These include a realistic assessment of the chances of prevailing at the end of the case, including prevailing on the legal issues that the Court might consider and the many things that could interfere with such a ruling (such as a change in regulations or precedent decisions). In addition, clients may be concerned about the implications of pursuing their case for others in a similar situation, including family and community members. Finally, further litigation may have implications for the client's detention.

Clients who take their cases to the Supreme Court also should be advised about the scrutiny their

---

[15] *See, e.g., Succar v. Ashcroft,* 394 F.3d 8 (1st Cir. 2005).

[16] 71 Fed. Reg. 27585 (May 12, 2006).

cases will receive, as well as the scrutiny that they will face with respect to their conduct during, and possibly after, the course of the litigation.

❑ **With assistance from a national team, evaluate possible Supreme Court representatives and arrangements**

In the last several years, there has been an increase in law school clinic and law firm interest in Supreme Court practice in the immigration area. The Supreme Court Immigration Law Working Group has had some experience with different firms and law clinics and will continue to develop this experience. If you receive an offer from a law firm or law clinic to handle a Supreme Court case pro bono, you can draw on the expertise of the Working Group to make decisions that are best for your client and for the development of caselaw that will affect others. The Working Group will help you think through some of the factors that bear on who is best suited to assist in Supreme Court representation, such as:

– the experience of the firm and the lead lawyer in immigration law

– the firm's track record of working with immigration experts

– the firm's willingness to share authority with individual counsel

– the firm's willingness to pursue strategies that benefit the client but may affect the prominence of the case, such as allowing another case to take the lead

– the firm's willingness not to appear on an opposition to certiorari if that would improve the chances of certiorari being denied

– the firm's overall experience in Supreme Court litigation

– the firm's familiarity with Supreme Court practice in immigration cases

– the firm's recognition of the dangers in this area of practice, *e.g.*, summary reversal of the Ninth Circuit

– the firm's thoughtfulness about an amicus plan—in advance of seeking certiorari—and willingness to devote resources to developing an amicus plan or to work with others on such a plan

– the firm's willingness to allow timely review of briefs by immigration experts so as to avoid unnecessary bad dicta in the case

– the firm's willingness to engage in or support relevant media work

– the firm's willingness to pursue related cases

– the firm's willingness to allow experts to decide who is best suited to argue the case

Steps to Take Once the Supreme Court has Granted a Writ of Certiorari in a Parallel Case

❑ **Preserve issues administratively**

It is dangerous to count on being able to reopen a case following a favorable Supreme Court decision. Reopening has a discretionary element, and there is the danger that reopening will be denied on alternative grounds that prevent you from being able to pursue relief that your client should be entitled to under the later precedent. A far better course is to preserve the issues in the first place, so that any favorable precedent must be applied in your client's case.

❑ **Seek postponement of briefing or argument if your client is not in detention**

For clients who are not in detention, it may be possible to delay briefing or a disposition either administratively or in the circuit courts due to a pending case.

❑ **Coordinate with national advocates**

To the extent possible, identify and be in touch with national advocates about cases that raise the same issues as a case in the Supreme Court. In some situations, your client's situation may be useful to present in an amicus brief to illustrate the effect of the rule sought by the government. In other situations, there may be value in seeking certiorari in a parallel case.

CONCLUSION

Increased Supreme Court activity is a likely reality, given the number of legal issues being resolved at the courts of appeals and the increased resources being devoted to Supreme Court litigation by law firms and law clinics. Being savvy about these issues will benefit both your clients and the client community at large.

JUDICIAL REVIEW OF MOTIONS TO REOPEN

*by Robert Pauw**

INTRODUCTION

A motion to reopen or reconsider does not have to be filed in order to exhaust administrative remedies. Motions to reopen and motions to reconsider "are not 'remedies available … as of right' within the meaning of 8 USC §1252(d)(1)," and, therefore, a petitioner is not required to file a motion to reopen or reconsider in order to exhaust administrative remedies.[1]

Although a motion to reopen is not required in order to exhaust administrative remedies, in some cases, it may be advisable to file a motion to reopen in order to avoid exhaustion problems.[2] Filing a mo-

tion to reopen may be the only way to make certain that an issue has been presented to the Board of Administrative Appeals (BIA or Board) for its consideration. For example, where a person has filed an appeal to the BIA pro se or has been represented by prior counsel who did not present all of the relevant issues on appeal to the BIA, filing a motion to reopen may be necessary in order to clearly present the issue to the BIA. The motion to reopen should not be seen as a substitute for filing a petition for review with the court of appeals. If a petition for review is not filed, then judicial review of the Board's initial decision may be foreclosed. The only issues reviewable would be those that arise in connection with the motion to reopen. Thus, in order to ensure judicial review of all relevant issues, it may be necessary to file two petitions for review: first, an appeal from the BIA's initial decision; and second, if the BIA denies the motion to reopen, an appeal from the denial of this motion. The two petitions for review will be consolidated before the court of appeals.[3]

IJ/BIA DECISION

A petitioner seeking to reopen removal proceedings must file a motion to reopen either with the IJ or with the BIA, depending on who made the decision that is being reopened. If the motion to reopen is filed with the IJ and the IJ denies the motion, then an appeal must generally be filed to the BIA in order to exhaust administrative remedies before seeking judicial review. Judicial review of the denial of the motion to reopen occurs by filing a petition for review to the appropriate court of appeals.[4]

Judicial Review of the Motion to Reopen

As explained by the U.S. Supreme Court, there are at least three reasons why the Board may deny a motion to reopen:

First, it may hold that the movant has not established a prima facie case for the underlying substantive relief sought …. Second, the BIA may hold that the movant has not introduced previ-

* **Robert Pauw** specializes in immigration-related litigation and has been counsel for plaintiffs in several significant immigration cases, including *Reno v. Catholic Social Services*, 509 U.S. 43 (1993); *Quezada-Bucio v. Ridge*, 317 F. Supp. 2d 1221 (W.D. Wash. 2004); *Immigrant Assistance Project v. INS*, 306 F.3d 842 (9th Cir. 2002), 976 F.2d 1198 (9th Cir. 1992), 717 F. Supp. 1444, 709 F. Supp. 998 (W.D. Wash. 1989); *Walters v. Reno*, 145 F.3d 1032 (9th Cir. 1998); and *Gete v. INS*, 121 F.3d 1285 (9th Cir. 1997). Mr. Pauw is a partner in the Seattle law firm of Gibbs Houston Pauw and teaches immigration law at Seattle University School of Law. Mr. Pauw is a 1983 graduate of Harvard Law School and one of the founding members of the Northwest Immigrant Rights Project in Seattle. In June 1999, he received the American Immigration Lawyers Association's Jack Wasserman Award for Excellence in Litigation. His published articles include "Plenary Power: An Outmoded Doctrine," 51 *Emory L.J.* 1095 (2002); and "A New Look at Deportation as Punishment: Why at Least Some of the Constitution's Criminal Procedure Protections Must Apply," 52 *Admin. L. Rev.* 1202 (2000).

[1] *Noriega-Lopez v. Ashcroft*, 335 F.3d 874, 881 (9th Cir. 2003); *Rhoa-Zamora v. INS*, 971 F.2d 26, 31 (7th Cir. 1992), *cert. denied*, 508 U.S. 906 (1993). There is an exception where a new form of relief becomes available after the Board's decision is issued and where regulations allow reopening in order to apply for that form of relief. *See, e.g., Huang v. Ashcroft*, 390 F.3d 1118, 1123 (9th Cir. 2004) (where administrative record with respect to the petitioner's CAT claim was undeveloped, motion to reopen was required as a matter of prudential exhaustion).

[2] The fact that a motion to reopen or reconsider has been filed does not render the original order of removal non-final; the court of appeals still has jurisdiction to hear the original petition. *See, e.g., Stone v. INS*, 514 U.S. 386 (1995); *Jaggernauth v. Att'y Gen.*, 432 F.3d 1346, 1351 (11th Cir. 2005).

[3] INA §242(b)(6).

[4] *Id.*

ously unavailable, material evidence .... Third, in cases in which the ultimate grant of relief is discretionary ... the BIA may ... simply determine that even if [the other requirements] were met, the movant would not be entitled to the discretionary grant of relief.[5]

The jurisdictional question is whether INA §242(a)(2)(B) precludes judicial review of the denial of the motion to reopen. Whether the court has jurisdiction, and if so the scope of review, depends on the reasons given by the BIA for denying the motion.

Cases Not Involving Discretionary Decisions Under INA §242(a)(2)(B)

In cases where the motion to reopen does not involve a request for discretionary relief covered by INA §242)(a)(2)(B), the BIA's decision will be reviewed for abuse of discretion. For example, the respondent may move to reopen an in absentia order on the basis of a failure of notice; or to file an application for CAT relief or some other non-discretionary form of relief; or to reconsider an application for asylum or withholding of removal based on changed circumstances. Generally, where the motion to reopen does not involve an application for discretionary relief, §242(a)(2)(B) does not deprive the court of jurisdiction and the court reviews for abuse of discretion.[6] Under the "abuse of discretion" standard, the court will reverse the Board's denial of a motion to reopen "if its discretion (1) provides no rational explanation, (2) inexplicably departs from established policies, (3) is devoid of any reasoning, or (4) contains only summary or conclusory statements."[7]

In some cases, the Board will deny the motion to reopen because the respondent failed to comply with certain procedural requirements. For example, the Board may deny the motion to reopen because the respondent did not establish that the new evidence

was unavailable at the prior hearing. In these cases, the court has jurisdiction and reviews for abuse of discretion.[8]

If there is a constitutional claim or a question of law presented, then the court reviews the decision de novo.[9]

Cases Involving Discretionary Relief Under INA §242(a)(2)(b)

Discretionary Relief Not Previously Applied for

Where a motion to reopen is filed in order to file apply for a discretionary form of relief that has not been previously applied for, the court has jurisdiction to review the Board's decision and reviews for abuse of discretion. For example, in *Medina-Morales v. Ashcroft*,[10] the respondent withdrew his application for adjustment of status before the IJ because his stepfather (who filed the I-130 petition) failed to appear at the removal hearing. The respondent subsequently filed a motion to reopen accompanied by an affidavit explaining why the stepfather had not been able to attend the hearing. The IJ and the BIA denied the motion to reopen. On appeal, the U.S. Ninth Circuit Court of Appeals held that because the IJ had never ruled on the application for adjustment of status, Medina-Morales was not seeking review of a judgment regarding adjustment of status, which would be barred under §242(a)(2)(B). Instead, the denial of the motion to reopen was held to be a decision under INA §212(a)(6)(A) (the ground of deportation relied on by the IJ in finding deportability), which is not barred from judicial review under §242(a)(2)(B).

Similarly, in *Arrozal v. INS*,[11] where the petitioner filed a motion to reopen in order to apply for suspension of deportation, the court held that the Board's denial of the motion to reopen must be considered to be an order under §241(a)(2) (the ground of deportability) because Arrozal had not previously applied for suspension of deportation and neither the IJ nor the Board had ruled on suspension of deportation. Thus, IIRAIRA §309(c)(4)(E) (the precursor of §242(a)(2)(B)) did not bar judicial review and the

---

[5] *INS v. Abudu*, 485 U.S. 94, 104–05 (1988).

[6] *See INS v. Doherty*, 502 U.S. 314, 324, 112 S.Ct. 719, 116 L.Ed.2d 823 (1992) (prior to IIRAIRA) ("the abuse-of-discretion standard applies to motions to reopen regardless of the underlying basis of the alien's request [for relief]").

[7] *Melnitsenko v. Mukasey*, 517 F.3d 42 (2d Cir. 2008). *See, e.g., Singh v. INS*, 213 F.3d 1050 (9th Cir. 2000) (applying abuse of discretion standard to denial of motion to reopen *in absentia* proceedings); *Toufighi v. Mukasey*, 510 F.3d 1059 (9th Cir. Dec. 13, 2007) (where BIA finds that there are no "changed circumstances" for an asylum applicant, the court reviews the BIA's decision for abuse of discretion); *Montano-Cisneros*, 514 F.3d 1224 (11th Cir. 2008).

[8] *Bhasin v. Gonzales*, 423 F.3d 977 (9th Cir. 2005).

[9] *See, e.g., Mohammed v. Gonzales*, 400 F.3d 785, 791–92 (9th Cir. 2005); *Cerezo v. Mukasey*, 512 F.3d 1163 (9th Cir. 2008).

[10] *Medina-Morales v. Ashcroft*, 371 F.3d 520 (9th Cir. 2004).

[11] *Arrozal v. INS*, 159 F.3d 429 (9th Cir.1998).

court reviewed the denial of the motion to reopen for abuse of discretion.[12]

Discretionary Relief Previously Applied for

If the Board denies a motion to reopen for failure to establish a prima facie case for discretionary relief, where there has already been an unreviewable discretionary determination concerning the application, then §242(a)(2)(B) bars the court from taking jurisdiction to review the denial of the motion to reopen For example, in *Fernandez v. Gonzales.*[13] The Board denied the respondent's application for cancellation of removal for failure to show adequate hardship. Under §242(a)(2)(B), that decision is not subject to judicial review. The respondent then submitted a motion to reopen with additional evidence of hardships. The Board denied the motion to reopen for failure to establish a prima facie case. Under these circumstances, §242(a)(2)(B) bars judicial review. As the court explained: "Otherwise, petitioners could make an end-run around the bar to review of their direct appeals simply by filing a motion to reopen."[14]

Exceptions. In *Fernandez*, the court recognized an exception to this general rule. If there is a new basis for the discretionary relief, and the evidence offered is not just cumulative, then the court does have jurisdiction:

> Where the relief sought is formally the same as was previously denied but the evidence submitted with a motion to reopen is directed at a different basis for providing the same relief, the circumstances can take the matter out of the realm of §1252(a)(2)(B)(i). This category covers cases in which the newly-submitted evidence is not cumulative, and thus directed at collaterally attacking the agency's initial decision on the same basis as it was originally made, but does seek the same type of discretionary relief as was originally sought. . . . An example would be the submission of evidence, subsequent to a denial of cancellation of removal, concerning a newly-

discovered, life-threatening medical condition afflicting a qualifying relative.[15]

Fernandez also recognizes a second exception for cases in which the respondent presents an independent claim such as ineffective assistance of counsel. In order to establish ineffective assistance of counsel, the petitioner must establish that (1) prior counsel rendered assistance that was inadequate;[16] and (2) the petitioner was prejudiced by the inadequate assistance.[17] The court has jurisdiction to review both the Board's decision regarding the adequacy of prior representation and the Board's decision regarding prejudice. Where the ineffectiveness claim regards discretionary relief, the court's decision regarding prejudice may involve an assessment of discretionary factors. For example, in a cancellation of removal case the prejudice analysis may involve an examination of the discretionary hardship decision. Nonetheless, if the Board denies the motion to reopen based on a failure to show prejudice, §242(a)(2)(B) does not bar the court from reviewing that determination.[18]

Delay in Filing the Motion to Reopen

A petitioner has 90 days to file a motion to reopen after the decision of the IJ or the BIA. 8 CFR §1003.2(c)(2); §1003.23(b)(1). This 90 day deadline is subject to equitable tolling. For example, if the 90 day deadline is missed because of ineffective assistance of counsel or because of misinformation from the government, then the motion may be allowed even if it is filed more than 90 days after the Board's decision.[19] However, the motion to reopen

---

[12] *See also Pilica v. Ashcroft*, 388 F.3d 941 (6th Cir. 2004) (where the petitioner appeals the Board's denial of the motion to reopen in which he sought to apply for adjustment of status for the first time, s/he does not appeal from a discretionary determination denying adjustment of status and the court reviews for abuse of discretion); *Subhan v. Ashcroft*, 383 F.3d 591 (7th Cir. 2004) (exercising jurisdiction where no judgment regarding adjustment of status had ever been made).

[13] *Fernandez v. Gonzales*, 439 F.3d 592, 601 (9th Cir. 2006).

[14] *Id.*

[15] *Id.* at 601–02.

[16] *See Strickland v. Washington*, 466 U.S. 668, 688 (1984) ("The proper measure of attorney performance remains simply reasonableness under prevailing professional norms.").

[17] *Maravilla Maravilla v. Ashcroft*, 381 F.3d 855, 859 (9th Cir.2004) (BIA "should have asked only whether [prior counsel's] deficient performance may have affected the proceedings").

[18] *See Ontiveros-Lopez v. INS*, 213 F.3d 1121 (9th Cir. 2000) (reviewing Board's decision for abuse of discretion); *Lara-Torres v. Ashcroft*, 383 F.3d 968 (9th Cir. 2004), *amended by* 404 F.3d 1105 (9th Cir. 2005) (applying abuse of discretion standard).

[19] *See, e.g., Socop-Gonzalez v. INS*, 272 F.3d 1176 (9th Cir. 2001); *Gaberov v. Mukasey*, 516 F.3d 590 (7th Cir. 2008); *Iavorski v. INS*, 232 F.3d 124 (2d Cir.2000).

must be filed promptly after the petitioner discovers that prior counsel rendered ineffective assistance.[20]

Motion to Reopen to Apply for Benefits Outside Removal Proceedings

In some cases, a person in removal proceedings may become eligible for immigration benefits that are not granted by the immigration judge or the BIA. Recently, for example, the Department of Homeland Security (DHS) issued regulations according to which "arriving aliens" are eligible to apply for adjustment of status. According to these regulations, the immigration judge and the Board do not have jurisdiction to consider an application for adjustment of status filed by an "arriving alien". Thus, an "arriving alien" who is in removal proceedings cannot file a motion to reopen to apply for the benefit before the immigration judge. But if a final order of removal is issued, then the person may be removed from the United States before he is given an opportunity to apply for the benefit that he is eligible for. In such a situation, the person may file a motion to reopen and ask for a continuance pending the decision on the application for adjustment of status. Two courts—the Second Circuit and the Ninth Circuit—have held that the Board abuses its discretion if it denies the motion to reopen solely on the grounds that it has no jurisdiction to grant the benefit. In *Kalilu v. Mukasey*,[21] the Ninth Circuit explained:

> The opportunity that the Interim Rule affords for an arriving alien in removal proceedings to establish his eligibility for adjustment based on a bona fide marriage is rendered worthless where the BIA, as it purports to do in the present case, denies a motion to reopen (or continue) that is sought in order to provide time for USCIS to adjudicate a pending application. Without a reopening or a continuance, an alien is subject to a final order of removal, despite the fact that he may have a prima facie valid I-130 and adjustment application pending before USCIS.[22]

Similarly, in *Sheng Gao Ni v. BIA*,[23] the Second Circuit held that the Board abused its discretion in denying a motion to reopen filed by an "arriving alien":

> The BIA erred, nevertheless, because a rote recital of a jurisdictional statement - even if technically accurate - does not adequately discharge the BIA's duty to "consider the facts of record relevant to the motion" and provide a "rational explanation" for its ruling. . . . The BIA did not consider . . . whether petitioners' newfound ability to file adjustment applications with the USCIS warranted a favorable exercise of its discretion to reopen and continue the proceedings and thereby lift the removal orders. Accordingly, the reason set forth by the BIA for its denial of the motions—a lack of jurisdiction over adjustment applications—was unresponsive to the relief petitioners sought and therefore did not provide a "rational explanation" for the denial.[24]

The Second Circuit left open the possibility that the Board could properly deny the motion to reopen if, for example, it appears unlikely that the petitioner would be granted adjustment of status.[25]

Motion to Reopen After Departure from the United States

According to DHS regulations:

> A motion to reopen or a motion to reconsider [filed with the BIA] shall not be made by or on behalf of a person who is the subject of exclusion, deportation, or removal proceedings subsequent to his or her departure from the Untied States. Any departure from the United States, including the deportation or removal of a person who is the subject of exclusion, deportation, or removal proceedings, occurring after the filing of a motion to reopen or a motion to reconsider, shall constitute a withdrawal of such motion.[26]

This "post-departure bar" has been challenged on the basis of INA §240(c)(7), which gives individuals an unqualified right to file one motion to reopen within 90 days of the final order of removal. Several courts have overturned Board decisions denying a

---

[20] *See, e.g., Valeriano v. Gonzales,* 474 F.3d 669 (9th Cir. Jan. 23, 2007) (equitable tolling is not available where petitioner waited more than 90 days after discovering prior attorney's IAC; even if petitioner was waiting for DHS's response to a request for a joint motion to reopen, DHS's response was "non vital" and so petitioner's delay in filing the motion to reopen was not reasonable); *Jin Bo Zhao v. INS,* 452 F.3d 154, 159 (2d Cir.2006) ("We conclude that the five-month period ... is not too long for Zhao to merit equitable tolling.").

[21] *Kalilu v. Mukasey,* 516 F.3d 777 (9th Cir. 2008).

[22] *Id.* at 780.

[23] *Sheng Gao Ni v. BIA,* 520 F.3d 125 (2d Cir. 2008).

[24] *Id.* at *4.

[25] *Cf. Matter of Velarde-Pacheco,* 23 I&N Dec. 253, 255 (BIA 2002) (motion to reopen can be denied if there is not a "strong likelihood that the respondent's marriage is bona fide").

[26] 8 CFR §1003.2(d). *See also* 8 CFR §1003.23(b)(1) (similar rule for motions to reopen filed with the IJ).

motion to reopen based on the "post-departure bar," including the following:

William v. Gonzales[27]—INA §240(c)(7)(A) provides the petitioner with the right to file one motion to reopen, regardless of whether he is in the U.S. or outside the U.S., and therefore 8 CFR §1003.2(d) (barring a motion to reopen after the petitioner departs from the U.S.) is invalid.

Reynoso-Cisneros v. Gonzales[28]—motion to reopen is not barred after petitioner has been lawfully removed after conclusion of removal proceedings and reenters unlawfully; 8 CFR §1003.2(d) and §1003.23(b)(1) bar motions to reopen only if the petitioner departs from the U.S. while s/he is subject of removal proceedings.

Zi-Xing Lin v. Gonzales[29]—8 CFR §1003.23(b)(1) "is phrased in the present tense and so by its terms applies only to a person who departs the United States while he or she 'is the subject of removal ... proceedings.'"

Avila-Sanchez v. Mukasey[30]—the petitioner was told (incorrectly) in 1998 that he was not eligible for 212(c) relief and was deported, and he then illegally reentered; the Board denied the "*Soriano* motion to reopen" because it was filed after the petitioner had been deported; the court held that the fact that the BIA makes an "interpretive error" does not make the prior deportation unlawful and the petitioner is not eligible for reopening.

Cardoso-Tlaseca v. Gonzales[31]—where a conviction that constitutes a "key part of [the] removal proceeding" has been vacated, the petitioner is entitled to reopen the proceedings even after departure from the United States.

Contreras-Rodriguez v. Attorney General[32]—the post-departure bar does not apply to a motion to reopen an *in absentia* order based on lack of proper notice.

See also Pena-Muriel v. Gonzales[33]—and Order dated October 24, 2007, Case No. 05-1937 (rejecting the argument that by rescinding INA §106 when it enacted IIRIRA, Congress intended to eliminate the post-departure bar to motions to reopen, noting, however that the Court was not deciding whether 8 CFR §1003.23(b)(1) conflicts with INA §240(c)(7)).

Preserving Voluntary Departure

Judicial review of a denial of a motion to reopen often involves review of the underlying order of removal.[34] There are not many circumstances in which the petitioner will seek review of the denial of a motion to reopen, but not seek review of the underlying order of removal. In filing the initial petition for review, the petitioner should seek a stay of the voluntary departure period if voluntary departure was granted by the Board.[35]

An important issue in the context of motions to reopen is whether the voluntary departure period is tolled pending the Board's consideration of a motion to reopen. Suppose that a person is granted voluntary departure for 60 days, and that he or she becomes eligible for adjustment of status and has to file a motion to reopen in order to apply for this benefit. The person has 90 days after the Board's decision to file a motion to reopen. However, if the voluntary departure period is not tolled, then the right to file a motion to reopen becomes meaningless. Even if the motion to reopen is filed before the voluntary departure period expires, the Board will not issue a decision on the motion to reopen before the voluntary departure period expires. And once the voluntary departure period expires, the person is no longer eligible for adjustment of status.[36] Thus, if the voluntary departure period is not tolled, the right to file a motion to reopen will, in many cases, be illusory.

---

[27] *William v. Gonzales*, 499 F.3d 329 (4th Cir. 2007).

[28] *Reynoso-Cisneros v. Gonzales*, 491 F.3d 1001 (9th Cir. 2007).

[29] *Zi-Xing Lin v. Gonzales*, 473 F.3d 979 (9th Cir. 2007).

[30] *Avila-Sanchez v. Mukasey*, 509 F.3d 1037 (9th Cir. 2007).

[31] *Cardoso-Tlaseca v. Gonzales*, 460 F.3d 1102 (9th Cir. 2006).

[32] *Contreras-Rodriguez v. Att'y Gen.*, 462 F.3d 1314 (11th Cir. 2006).

[33] *See also Pena-Muriel v. Gonzales*, 489 F.3d 438 (1st Cir. 2007).

[34] *See* INA §242(b)(6) (requiring that the consolidation of the appeal from the order of removal and the appeal from the denial of the motion to reopen).

[35] *See* AILF Practice Advisory, "Protecting the Voluntary Departure Period During Court of Appeals Review" (Oct. 25, 2005), *available at www.ailf.org/lac/lac_pa_102505.pdf.*

[36] *See* INA §240B(d)(1)(B) (a person who overstays voluntary departure is not eligible for a variety of benefits, including adjustment of status).

Different courts have taken different positions on whether voluntary departure is tolled upon the filing of a motion to reopen. The U.S. Third, Eighth, Ninth and Eleventh Circuit Courts of Appeals hold that the filing of a motion to reopen automatically tolls the voluntary departure period.[37] At the time of this writing, the Supreme Court has held oral argument in the case but has not issued a decision.

In addition, DHS has promulgated proposed regulations according to which the filing of a motion to reopen would automatically terminate any period of voluntary departure that was previously granted.[38] Under these proposed regulations, a person who has been granted voluntary departure and who becomes eligible for some form of relief from removal faces a difficult dilemma: either s/he departs from the United States (thereby abandoning the benefit that s/he is eligible for) or files a motion to reopen knowing that if the motion is denied then s/he will lose voluntary departure and be deported from the United States. In other words, if the motion to reopen is denied then the person will be penalized by being banished from the United States for a period of ten years.[39]

DENIAL OF MOTION TO REOPEN BY OTHER AGENCIES

If the petitioner seeks judicial review of a decision made outside removal proceedings—for example a decision by DHS or CIS—a motion to reopen is not required in order to exhaust administrative remedies. APA §704 ("agency action otherwise final is final . . . whether or not there has been presented or determined an application . . . for any form of reconsideration"). In many cases the petitioner will seek review of the underlying agency decision rather than filing a motion to reopen. If a motion to reopen is filed and denied, then judicial review of the denial is possible in a complaint for declaratory and injunctive relief pursuant to the Administrative Procedures Act.

Jurisdiction

Generally, the district court will have jurisdiction under 28 USC §1331:

> The district courts shall have original jurisdiction of all civil actions arising under the Constitution, laws, or treaties of the United States.

According to the Administrative Procedures Act, the district court's jurisdiction may be limited in two circumstances: (1) judicial review is precluded by statute, or (2) the agency action is committed to agency discretion by law.[40] These limitations on judicial review are to be narrowly interpreted.[41]

Exhaustion Issues

There are two APA provisions that are relevant to the issue of exhaustion of administrative remedies.

APA §702: A person suffering legal wrong because of agency action, or adversely affected or aggrieved by agency action within the meaning of a relevant statute, is entitled to judicial review thereof.

APA §704: Agency action made reviewable by statute and final agency action for which there is no other adequate remedy in a court are subject to judicial review. A preliminary, procedural, or intermediate agency action or ruling not directly reviewable is subject to review on the review of the final agency action. Except as otherwise expressly required by statute, agency action otherwise final is final for the purposes of this section whether or not there has been presented or determined an application for a declaratory order, for any form of reconsideration, or, unless the agency otherwise requires by rule and provides

---

[37] *See Kanivets v. Gonzales*, 424 F.3d 330 (34d Cir. 2005); *Sidikhouya v. Gonzales*, 407 F.3d 950 (8th Cir. 2005); *Azarte v. Ashcroft*, 394 F.3d 1278 (9th Cir. 2005); *Ugokwe v. Attorney General*, 453 F.3d 1325 (11th Cir. 2006). The First, Fourth, and Fifth Circuits have held otherwise. *See Chedad v. Gonzales*, 497 F.3d 57 (1st Cir. 2007); *Dekoladenu v. Gonzales*, 459 F.3d 500 (4th Cir. 2006); *Banda-Ortiz v. Gonzales*, 445 F.3d 387 (5th Cir. 2006). This issue is currently under consideration by the Supreme Court in *Dada v. Mukasey*, Case No. 06-1181, *cert granted sub nom. Dada v. Keisler*, 2007 U.S. LEXIS 9061 (September 25, 2007).

[38] 72 Fed Reg. 67674 (Nov. 30, 2007), *published on* AILA InfoNet at Doc. No. 07112965 (*posted* Nov. 30, 2007).

[39] *See* INA §212(a)(9)(A).

[40] 5 USC §701(a).

[41] *See, e.g., Abbott Laboratories v. Gardner*, 387 U.S. 136, 140 (1967) (courts must presume that judicial review is available unless there is a "showing of clear and convincing evidence of a . . . legislative intent" to restrict access); *Hernandez v. Ashcroft*, 345 F.3d 824, 846 (9th Cir. 2003) (there is a "strong presumption in favor of judicial review of administrative action"); *Heckler v. Chaney*, 470 U.S. 821, 830 (agency action is "committed to agency discretion by law" only "in those rare instances where statutes are drawn in such broad terms that in a given case there is no law to apply" and where there is "no meaningful standard against which to judge the agency's exercise of discretion" and thus "it is impossible to evaluate agency action for abuse of discretion").

that the action meanwhile is inoperative, for an appeal to superior agency authority.

If an agency action has become "final" for the purposes of §704, courts cannot impose additional exhaustion requirements as a prerequisite to judicial review.[42] Under §704, an administrative decision is "final"—and no further exhaustion of administrative remedies can be required—if the following conditions are met: (1) the lawsuit challenging the decision is brought pursuant to the Administrative Procedures Act; (2) there is no statute that mandates an administrative appeal; and (3) if an agency rule requires an administrative appeal, then the administrative decision is made inoperative during such appeal.[43]

In most non-removal cases, the statute does not require exhaustion of administrative remedies.[44] Thus, an appeal can be filed directly to the district court without exhausting administrative appeals unless (a) the governing regulations require an administrative appeal to be taken, and (b) a provision stays the administrative decision pending the administrative appeal.[45]

Review of Discretionary Decisions

Prior to the REAL ID Act, it was an open issue whether §242(a)(2)(B) applies to limit judicial review of discretionary decisions made outside the context of removal proceedings. Several district courts held that §242(a)(2)(B) applies only to decisions made during removal proceedings before an immigration judge.[46] On the other hand, two circuit

courts held that §242(a)(2)(B) applies to decisions made outside the context of removal proceedings.[47]

The REAL ID Act resolved this issue. After the REAL ID Act, the limitation on judicial review of discretionary decisions applies whether the decision is made within or outside the context of removal proceedings.[48] This does not mean that agency decisions that involve discretionary aspects are not subject to judicial review. Although the discretionary aspects of such decisions may not be subject to judicial review, the decisions are reviewable for legal and constitutional error.[49]

---

[42] *See Darby v. Cisneros*, 509 U.S. 137, 146 (1993).

[43] 509 U.S. at 154.

[44] The INA requires exhaustion of administrative remedies under the following circumstances: INA §242(d) (removal cases), INA §245A(f)(4) (legalization cases), INA §201(e)(3) (SAW legalization cases), INA §310 (naturalization cases), and INA §336(b) (naturalization delay cases). Other than these cases, the INA does not require exhaustion of administrative remedies.

[45] Several courts have required exhaustion of the administrative appeal where an individual has filed an optional administrative appeal and then also filed an APA action while the administrative appeal was still pending. *See, e.g., Ma v. Reno*, 114 F.3d 128 (9th Cir. 1997); *Acura v. Reich*, 90 F.3d 1403 (9th Cir. 1996). Under *Darby*, these courts should not have required exhaustion of administrative remedies. However, because the administrative appeal had been filed and was pending, the court reasoned that there was not a "final" agency decision and refused to consider the plaintiff's claims.

[46] *See, e.g., Mart v. Beebe*, 94 F.Supp.2d 1120, 1123–24 (D. Or. 2000) (§242(a)(2)(B) does not bar review of district director's denial of application for adjustment of status based on DV lottery program); *Shanti v. Reno*, 36 F.Supp.2d 1151, *continued*

1157–60 (D. Minn. 1999) (district court has jurisdiction to review INS's denial of H-1B petition).

[47] *See CDI Information Services, Inc. v. Reno*, 278 F.3d 616, 618-620 (6th Cir. 2002) (no jurisdiction to review denial of request for extension of H-1B visa); *Samirah v. O'Connell*, 335 F.3d 545 (7th Cir. 2003) (no jurisdiction to review of revocation of advance parole).

[48] *See* INA §242(a)(2)(B) (the limitation on review of discretionary decisions applies "regardless of whether the judgment, decision, or action is made in removal proceedings").

[49] *See, e.g., Ramadan v. Gonzales*, 479 F.3d 646 (9th Cir. 2007) (judicial review of questions of law includes "mixed questions of law and fact").

The Government Burden of Proof in Asserting That a Conviction Bars Eligibility for Relief: Ninth Circuit Law

by Katherine Brady and Angie Junck[*]

This article discusses beneficial new case law in the Ninth Circuit holding that the government bears the burden of document production and proof when it alleges that a conviction under a divisible statute bars immigration relief such as cancellation of removal. The article focuses on the aggravated-felony bar, but its discussion of the categorical and modified categorical analyses applies to any offense with immigration consequences, including such crimes as domestic violence, controlled substance offenses, and crimes involving moral turpitude.[1]

To determine whether a past conviction is an aggravated felony or has adverse immigration consequences for other reasons, immigration authorities will identify the elements of the offense by applying the categorical and modified categorical analyses.[2] It is accepted that the government bears the burden of proving that a conviction under a divisible statute[3] is a basis for *deportability*, but the government sometimes asserts that the *noncitizen* bears the burden of document production to prove that a conviction under a divisible statute is not a *bar to relief*.

Example: Mikhail is a permanent resident who was convicted under a statute that prohibits sale (an aggravated felony) or transportation (a deportable offense, but not an aggravated felony) of heroin. Because the record of conviction is vague between the two offenses, the government cannot prove that Mikhail is deportable for having committed an aggravated felony. However, because Mikhail is deportable for conviction of a controlled substance offense, he needs to apply for cancellation of removal as a defense in removal proceedings. Conviction of an aggravated

[*] **Katherine Brady** is a senior staff attorney at the ILRC. She has served with the ILRC since 1987 and has contributed to numerous ILRC projects. Her expertise includes the immigration consequences of criminal convictions; issues affecting immigrant children and mixed families; immigration consultant and consumer fraud; naturalization; family immigration; legal status for immigrant victims of domestic violence through the Violence Against Women Act (VAWA); and trial skills. She is the primary author of ILRC's *Defending Immigrants in the Ninth Circuit: The Impact of Crimes Under California and Other State Laws*, and for many years was co-author of the section on defending noncitizens in *California Criminal Law: Procedure and Practice*, published by Continuing Education of the Bar. She also is a co-author of the ILRC's *Special Immigrant Juvenile Status* and *Immigration Benchbook for Juvenile and Family Courts*. She has helped found coalitions and projects to address these issues, including serving as a co-founder of the Defending Immigrants Partnership and the Immigrant Justice Network. She authored briefs in key Ninth Circuit cases on immigration and crimes. In 2007, she received the Carol King award for advocacy from the National Immigration Project of the National Lawyers Guild. Prior to working at the ILRC, Ms. Brady was in private practice with the immigration firm of Park and Associates. She is conversant in Spanish.

Angie Junck is a staff attorney with the Immigrant Legal Resource Center (ILRC) in San Francisco. Her work focuses on the intersection between criminal and immigration law. She is a co-author of ILRC's *Defending Immigrants in the Ninth Circuit: The Impact of Crimes Under California and Other State Laws* and has also co-written other ILRC manuals, including *A Guide for Immigration Advocates* and *Naturalization and U.S. Citizenship*. Her efforts to mitigate the difficult immigration consequences for criminal convictions of immigrants is at the core of the ILRC's Defending Immigrants Project to assist public defenders and the Immigrant Justice Network, a project to build a movement to shift public perception of immigrants in the criminal justice system. Ms. Junck is a co-chair of the Detention Watch Network's Public Awareness Committee and is on the advisory board of the California Coalition for Women Prisoners. Prior to joining the ILRC, she worked on postconviction relief for immigrants at the Law Offices of Norton Tooby and advocated on behalf of incarcerated survivors of domestic violence as a coordinator of the statewide coalition Free Battered Women and a member of the Habeas Project.

---

[1] For a review of law in all circuits, see National Immigration Project of the National Lawyers Guild Practice Advisory, J. Dahlstrom & D. Kesselbrenner, "The Burden of Proof to Overcome the Aggravated Felony Bar to Cancellation of Removal" (Mar. 22, 2007), *available at www.nationalimmigrationproject.org/CrimPage/Practice_Adv._Burden_Proof_Ag_Fel_3.07.pdf.*

[2] For an explanation of the categorical and modified categorical analyses, see M. Kramer, *Immigration Consequences of Criminal Activity* 157–59 (3d Ed.), available from AILA Publications, *www.ailapubs.org*, (800) 982-2839.

[3] A divisible statute is one that describes acts that do constitute an immigration-related offense and acts that may not. *See* M. Kramer, *supra* note 2, at 158.

felony is a bar to cancellation. The government asserts that now it is *Mikhail* who has the burden of producing documents to prove that the conviction was *not* for sale of heroin, since he must establish eligibility for relief.

To support its contention, the government cites 8 CFR §1240.8(d), which provides that an applicant for relief bears the "burden of establishing that he or she is eligible for any requested benefit or privilege and that it should be granted in the exercise of discretion. If the evidence indicates one or more of the grounds for mandatory denial of the application for relief may apply, the alien shall have the burden of proving by a *preponderance of the evidence* that such grounds do not apply." (Emphasis added.)

The Ninth Circuit has ruled that, *in the context of a conviction analyzed under the modified categorical analysis*, the applicant for relief has met his or her burden where the record of conviction in a divisible statute is *inconclusive* about whether the conviction is a bar. In *Cisneros-Perez v. Gonzales*,[4] the Ninth Circuit held that the government had the burden of producing documents to prove that a conviction under a divisible statute was a crime of domestic violence, and hence a bar to nonpermanent resident cancellation under INA §240A(b). Because the government did not produce sufficient documents to prove a domestic relationship, the court ordered the case remanded to permit the applicant to apply for cancellation.[5] In *Sandoval-Lua v. Gonzales*,[6] the issue was whether the deportable permanent resident was barred from applying for cancellation of removal because of a conviction for an aggravated felony, when the documents in the record (which apparently had been produced by the government) were not sufficient to establish under the modified categorical analysis that the offense was an aggravated felony. The court held that the applicant has met the requirements of 8 CFR §1240.8(d) where the record of conviction in the case is inconclusive about whether the offense of conviction con-

stitutes an aggravated felony. The respondent must show by a preponderance of the evidence that the offense is not *necessarily* an aggravated felony; an inconclusive record establishes this.[7] Note that it appears that the inconclusive documents in *Sandoval-Lua* were provided by the government, and the court imposed no duty on the applicant to attempt to obtain more documents.

In *Kepilino v. Gonzales*,[8] the court considered an application for admission to the United States. Acknowledging the applicable rules concerning burden of proof, the court held that because the government failed to produce sufficient documents to show that the conviction at issue involved prostitution, the applicant met her burden and showed she was admissible.[9] Advocates have reported success in using

---

[4] 451 F.3d 1053 (9th Cir. 2006).

[5] "Because Cisneros-Perez's conviction does not categorically qualify as a crime of domestic violence, we consider whether to examine his conviction under the 'modified' categorical approach and, if so, whether the government has established under that approach that Cisneros-Perez committed a crime of domestic violence." *Id.* at 1058 (reversing and remanding to apply for cancellation). Thanks to Holly Cooper and Michael K. Mehr for their valuable insights on this case.

[6] 499 F.3d 1121 (9th Cir. 2007).

[7] The court stated:

> We are thus left to consider this question: Does an alien seeking to prove his eligibility for cancellation of removal under 8 U.S.C. § 1229b(a) carry his burden of establishing by a preponderance of the evidence that he has not been convicted of an aggravated felony when the alien produces an *inconclusive* record of conviction? We conclude that he does. By submitting an inconclusive record of conviction, Lua has affirmatively proven under the modified categorical analysis that he was not necessarily "convicted of any aggravated felony." 8 U.S.C. § 1229b(a)(3).
>
> Under the modified categorical analysis, our concern is with the nature of Lua's [California Health & Safety Code] § 11379(a) conviction, not with the conduct underlying the conviction; consequently, we must determine whether the judicially noticeable documents establish that Lua's conviction necessarily was for all of the elements constituting an aggravated felony under 8 U.S.C. § 1101(a)(43)(B). If the record of conviction does not so establish, Lua's § 11379(a) conviction cannot amount to the generic offense, and Lua has carried his burden.

Id. at 1130–31 (9th Cir. 2007) (footnote omitted).

[8] 454 F.3d 1057 (9th Cir. 2006).

[9] *Id.*, holding that the government failed to meet its burden of proving that a conviction under a divisible statute established that the applicant for admission was inadmissible under the prostitution ground, reversing the immigration judge.

III. Burden of Production

Kepilino's possession of a valid Korean passport and immigrant visa issued by South Korea is prima facie evidence that Kepilino is admissible to the United States. See Pazcoguin v. Radcliffe, 292 F.3d 1209, 1212 (9th Cir. 2002). In light of this evidence, the burden shifted to the Government to produce "some evidence" to show that she was not admissible. *Id.* at 1213. The IJ found that the Government met this burden by offering proof of Kepilino's conviction under H.R.S. section 712-1200. Accordingly, the burden of production shifted back
continued

Cisneros-Perez and *Kepilino* to persuade immigration judges to adhere to this standard.

The government is not, however, required to charge in the notice to appear all convictions that will serve as a bar to relief, either as aggravated felonies or as convictions that will "stop the clock" for cancellation.[10]

---

to Kepilino for her to prove "clearly and beyond doubt" that she is entitled to be admitted and is not inadmissible under section 212(a)(2)(D)(i). Toro-Romero v. Ashcroft, 382 F.3d 930, 936 (9th Cir. 2004). For the reasons set forth below, we find that the evidence shows "clearly and beyond doubt" that Kepilino is not inadmissible under section 212(a)(2)(D)(i).

Id. at 1059–60. The court's "reasons set forth below" were the government's failure to provide documents sufficient to characterize the offense as "prostitution," and the lack of any other evidence that the person had engaged in prostitution.

[10] *Salviejo-Fernandez v. Gonzales*, 455 F.3d 1063 (9th Cir. 2006) (due process does not require that the notice to appear sent to the alien include a conviction that is not charged as a ground of removability but is asserted as a bar to relief from removal); *Matter of Jurado*, 24 I&N Dec. 29 (BIA 2006) (notice to appear is not required to charge offense that will stop the clock on seven years residence required for cancellation).

GETTING OUT: STRATEGIES FOR CHALLENGING UNLAWFUL DETENTION IN FEDERAL COURT

by Jeff Joseph and Aaron Hall[*]

Despite its innumerable other problems, the REAL ID Act of 2005[1] did not affect the federal court's powers to review unconstitutional detention. The federal courts have consistently held that habeas corpus review of detention decisions survives the jurisdictional-stripping provisions of §106(a) of the REAL ID Act.[2] Practitioners can, and should, continue to rely on writs of habeas corpus to challenge unconstitutional detention by the Department of Homeland Security (DHS).

The purpose of this article is to discuss recent developments in federal litigation of detention claims and provide arguments and strategies for federal challenges to unconstitutional detention.

I'M EXHAUSTED!

Setting Yourself Up for Federal Court Review

The first step in a federal court challenge to unconstitutional detention does not occur in federal court. The first step in obtaining federal court review is before DHS and the immigration judge (IJ). Gen-erally, federal courts require that an individual exhaust all administrative remedies mandated by law before seeking federal court redress for constitutional violations.[3]

Be aware, however, that in the detention context, there is no statutory exhaustion requirement for judicial challenges to DHS custody.[4] The U.S. Supreme Court in *McCarthy v. Madigan* specifically provided that where Congress has not clearly required exhaustion, "sound judicial discretion governs."[5]

In determining whether judicial discretion is warranted, the court will consider: (1) whether available remedies provide a genuine opportunity for adequate relief; (2) whether irreparable injury may occur without immediate judicial relief; (3) whether administrative appeal would be futile; and (4) in certain instances, whether a plaintiff has raised a substantial constitutional question.[6] Before going into federal court, you will want to be able to demonstrate that at least one (if not all) of the factors is present in your case. Exhaustion may also be excused if "the interest of the individual in retaining prompt access to a federal judicial forum [outweighs] countervailing institutional interests favoring exhaustion."[7]

Despite the lack of a statutory requirement to exhaust, it is prudent to try to do so. File a written request for release with the field director for detention and removal and file a motion for bond determination with the IJ—even if you know that the field director will deny your request, or that the IJ will not entertain a bond motion. By getting a written order to that ef-

[*] **Jeff Joseph** is senior partner in the Joseph Law Firm, a full-service immigration law firm. Mr. Joseph is a past chair of the Colorado Chapter of AILA and former member of the national board of governors of AILA. He is on the AILA EOIR Liaison Committee. In 2004, Mr. Joseph received the Joseph Minsky Young Lawyer of the Year Award from AILA. He has been named a Colorado Super Lawyer for the past three years and is an adjunct professor of immigration law at the University of Denver College of Law.

Aaron Hall is a law clerk and future associate attorney with Joseph Law Firm, PC. Prior to joining Joseph Law Firm, P.C. as a law clerk, Mr. Hall had experience working with detained noncitizens at the Rocky Mountain Immigrant Advocacy Center (RMIAN). He is currently in his final year of law school at the University of Colorado.

This article updates J. Joseph *et al.*, "Getting Out: Strategies For Challenging Unlawful Detention In Federal Court," *Immigration & Nationality Law Handbook* 213 (AILA 2006–07 Ed.).

[1] Pub. L. No. 109-13, div. B, 119 Stat. 231, 302–23.

[2] *See, e.g.*, H.R. Rep. No. 109-72, at 300 (2005); *Hernandez v. Gonzales*, 424 F.3d 42, 42 (1st Cir. 2005); *Forbes v. Att'y Gen.*, No. 05-3659, 2006 WL 615984 (3d Cir. 2006); *Gul v. Rozos*, No. 05-30327, 2006 WL 140540 (5th Cir. 2006); *Armentero v. INS*, 412 F.3d 1088, 1099 (9th Cir. 2005).

[3] *McCarthy v. Madigan,* 503 U.S. 140, 144 (1992), superseded by statutory amendment as noted in *Booth v. Churner,* 532 U.S. 731, 738 (2001), but still good law as there is no statutory exhaustion requirement in the immigration detention context.

[4] *Tam v. INS*, 14 F. Supp. 2d 1184, 1189 (E.D. Cal. 1998) ("Congress has not specifically mandated exhaustion before judicial review of [INS] custody determination.").

[5] *McCarthy v. Madigan*, 503 U.S. at 144.

[6] *Howell v. INS*, 72 F.3d 288, 291 (2d Cir. 1995).

[7] *McCarty v. Madigan*, 503 U.S. at 146.

fect, you can demonstrate that you have exhausted your administrative remedies. When you file the habeas, attach as exhibits copies of your requests for release and bond motion and any written decisions.

If the issue is jurisdictional, *i.e.*, whether your client is subject to mandatory detention, and therefore whether the judge has jurisdiction to redetermine bond, file a motion for a *Matter of Joseph* hearing.[8] In *Matter of Joseph*, the Board of Immigration Appeals (BIA) held that the judge has jurisdiction to determine, in the first instance, whether someone is properly classified as subject to INA §236(c) and held under mandatory detention.[9] In other words, the IJ has jurisdiction to determine whether he or she has jurisdiction over an individual whom U.S. Immigration and Customs Enforcement (ICE) alleges is subject to mandatory detention. Although *Matter of Joseph* deals specifically with §236(c), argue that *Matter of Joseph* stands for the general proposition that IJs have jurisdiction to determine their jurisdiction over other bond decisions, such as whether someone is properly classified as an arriving alien.

Argue, too, that appeal of the bond issue to the BIA is not required because appeal would take a minimum of six months and since a final order of removal is likely to be issued before you receive a decision on the bond and the petitioner would remain in custody during that time, exhaustion is futile. Also, argue that appeal to the BIA would be futile because the habeas petition raises substantial constitutional questions that the BIA cannot address.

Finally, in your petition, lay out the irreparable harm that is caused by your client's continued detention. Argue that your client suffers irreparable injury every day in the form of loss of liberty. Argue that mandatory detention separates the family and penalizes your client for pursuing claims against deportation. It also causes your client to face the indefinite loss of income that may be necessary to support your client's family and deprives U.S. citizen family members of financial, physical, and emotional support.

SOMEBODY'S GONNA' GET SUED HERE!

Where Do You File the Habeas Petition?

One of the issues that will certainly be on the forefront of detention-related litigation in the next few years is where to file the habeas. Who is the custodian of your client? What is the proper venue? These are confusing questions today.

- Your client may have been arrested in Miami (Eleventh Circuit), detained and processed at Krome (Eleventh Circuit), transferred to Oakdale, LA (Fifth Circuit), after a natural disaster such as a hurricane, but appear by video conference before a judge in Arlington (Fourth Circuit).

- A client may be convicted of first-time drug possession in Idaho (Ninth Circuit), where *Lujan-Armendariz* says that a first-time drug possession offense that is expunged pursuant to a state rehabilitative statute is not a conviction for immigration purposes. In the Ninth Circuit your client is not removable. However, the Denver detention district has jurisdiction over Idaho, so your client may be detained in Denver (Tenth Circuit). In the Tenth Circuit, your client is removable.

Where do you file the habeas? DHS has consistently argued that the "immediate custodian" rule should apply and that the only proper respondent to a habeas action is the field director with immediate physical control over your client. This is a very narrow and inflexible approach to habeas venue considerations, but it has been adopted by the majority of circuit courts which have considered the issue.[10]

Under the rule adopted by these circuit courts, the detained alien challenging removal must name the warden of the detention facility in a petition for habeas corpus and must file the habeas in the place where he or she is detained.

The Supreme Court in *Rumsfeld v. Padilla*,[11] applying the immediate custodian rule, held that Padilla's challenge to his detention as an enemy combatant at a naval brig in South Carolina under military custody was a "core challenge" to "present physical confinement" and that the proper respon-

---

[8] *Matter of Joseph*, 22 I&N Dec. 799, 1999 WL 339053 (BIA 1999). *See* further discussion, *infra*.

[9] *Id.*

[10] *Kholyaviskiy v. Achim*, 443 F. 3d 946, 953 (7th Cir. 2006); *Roman v. Ashcroft*, 340 F.3d 314, 322 (6th Cir. 2003); *Vasquez v. Reno*, 233 F.3d 688, 693 (1st Cir. 2000); *Yi v. Maugans*, 24 F.3d 500, 507 (3d Cir. 1994); *Henderson v. INS*, 157 F.3d 106, 126 (2d Cir. 1998).

[11] 542 U.S. 426 (2004).

dent is the warden of the facility where the detainee is being held.[12] The Court also held that the habeas challenge may only be brought in the district court that has territorial jurisdiction over the detainee's immediate custodian.[13] Nevertheless, the Court specifically reserved applying the decision to immigration habeas petitions and left open the question of whether the immediate custodian rule applies in the immigration habeas context.[14]

On the other side of the equation, the Ninth Circuit adopted the "functional custodian" approach in *Armentero v. INS*.[15] Under this approach, the proper custodian is the attorney general or secretary of DHS, and the habeas can be filed in any jurisdiction because the attorney general has the ultimate power to cause the petitioner to be present.

After analyzing five Supreme Court cases, culminating in *Braden v. 30th Judicial Circuit Court of Kentucky*,[16] the Ninth Circuit in *Armentero* concluded that, "read as a whole, the Supreme Court's pertinent case law indicates that the concept of custodian is a broad one that includes any person empowered to end restraint of a habeas petitioner's liberty, not just the petitioner's immediate on-site, immediate physical custodian."[17]

The court acknowledged the First Circuit decision in *Vazquez* and agreed that "while a petitioner's immediate physical custodian is typically a proper respondent in traditional habeas petitions, the statutory custodian requirement of 28 U.S.C. §2241 is sufficiently flexible to permit the naming of respondents who are not immediate physical custodians if practicality, efficiency, and the interests of justice so demand."[18] The court went on to state that the circumstances surrounding immigration-related detention of aliens demand such flexibility.[19] "Although held at the behest of federal authorities, immigration detainees are physically detained in a host of institutions, ranging from specialized immigration detention centers to federal prisons to state and local pris-

ons and jails."[20] It also noted that "[i]mmigration detainees are frequently transferred among federal, state, and local institutions across the country."[21] The court then recognized many problems encountered by aliens who have been transferred and whose habeas petitions are constrained by the "immediate custodian" approach[22]: access to counsel, dismissal or frequent transfer of petitions for lack of personal jurisdiction over the respondent, pro hac vice rules of the transferee district, and overload of court dockets in those areas with large immigration detention facilities.[23]

The issue of who is the proper custodian for detention-based challenges is likely to reach critical mass in the near future as ICE conducts more and more worksite enforcement raids and arrests individuals in large numbers. As we saw after the Swift raids, these individuals were arrested in one location, held for some time at that location, and then, often, transported around the country to various other locations. It was often days or weeks before these individuals were even able to contact family members and notify them as to their whereabouts. In circumstances such as this, it makes sense that an individual should be able to file a habeas corpus in any appropriate court and that the courts should be flexible in applying custodian rules.

Although DHS will raise the issue of forum shopping, the same argument can be raised against application of the immediate custodian rule. Because ICE routinely transfers immigration detainees to remote detention centers, permitting suit only in the district court of confinement gives the government complete control over where the action can be filed and thus, the circuit court law that will govern.

NO MORE *DEMORE*

Challenging the Application of §236(c) in Federal Court

In 1996, Congress considerably expanded the breadth of the mandatory detention provisions.[24] Currently under INA §236(c), most noncitizens with inadmissible or removable criminal offenses are confined in mandatory administrative detention be-

---

[12] *Id.* at 438.

[13] *Id.* at 444.

[14] *Id.* at 436 n.8.

[15] 340 F.3d 1058 (9th Cir. 2003).

[16] 410 U.S. 484 (1973).

[17] *Armentero v. INS*, 340 F.3d at 1064.

[18] *Id.* at 1068.

[19] *Id.*

---

[20] *Id.*

[21] *Id.* at 1069.

[22] *Id.*

[23] *Id.*

[24] INA §236(c).

fore a final removal order. In *Kim v. Ziglar*, the Ninth Circuit found the mandatory detention provisions to be unconstitutional as applied to lawful permanent residents.[25] It held that a permanent resident in removal proceedings is entitled to an individualized bond hearing and cannot be automatically detained without bond under INA §236(c). In *Demore v. Kim*, the Supreme Court reversed *Kim v. Ziglar*. The Supreme Court held that certain classes of lawful permanent residents may be detained without individualized bond hearings used to determine whether they posed a flight risk or danger to the community.[26]

This section will present arguments that you can raise to challenge the applicability and breadth of *Demore v. Kim*.

How Can I Challenge Mandatory Detention Under §236(c)?

The starting point for any analysis is determining whether the mandatory detention provisions apply to you or your client.

Was Your Client Released Before the Transitional Period Custody Rules Expired?[27]

First, the mandatory detention provisions should only apply to individuals who were released from physical criminal custody on or after October 9, 1998.[28] The logical extension should be that only release for a removable/inadmissible offense listed in INA §236(c) should subject a person to mandatory detention. Thus, if your client was released from physical custody before October 9, 1998, your client could be eligible for a bond hearing. Moreover, if your client was released from physical criminal custody on or after October 9, 1998, for a criminal offense that is not enumerated in INA §236(c), your client may also be eligible for a bond hearing.

Did Your Client Plead Guilty to a Criminal Offense Enumerated in INA §236(c) Before April 1, 1997?

INA §236(c) should not apply retroactively to individuals who pleaded guilty to a criminal offense before April 1, 1997, IIRAIRA's general effective date, but

were released after October 8, 1998. At least one district court has found that §236(c) should not apply retroactively. In *Boonkue v. Ridge*,[29] the petitioner was convicted in 1994 for felony issuing checks with insufficient funds; probation was revoked in 1998, and he was released after serving his sentence in 1999, but was not detained by ICE until 2004.

Was Your Client Given Only Probation for the Criminal Offense?

Mandatory detention should not apply to persons sentenced to probation only after October 8, 1998, because "release" in that statute means release from physical confinement.[30]

Was Your Client Released from Criminal Custody Only to Later Be Taken into ICE Custody?

Mandatory detention provisions should only apply to persons taken into DHS custody immediately upon release from criminal incarceration for an offense enumerated in §236(c).[31]

Does the American Baptist Church v. Thornburgh *Settlement Protect Your Salvadoran or Guatemalan Client from Mandatory Detention?*

Most lawyers are unaware that the *American Baptist Church v. Thornburgh*[32] settlement may exempt a client from mandatory detention. Paragraph 17 of the settlement states,

> The INS may only detain class members, eligible for relief under paragraph 2, who are otherwise subject to detention under current law and who: (1) have been convicted of a crime involving moral turpitude for which the sentence actually

---

[25] 276 F.3d 523 (9th Cir. 2001).

[26] 538 U.S. 510 (2003).

[27] On October 9, 1998, the legislative authority expired for the exercise of discretion to release noncitizens under the Transition Period Custody Rules (TPCR) of IIRAIRA §303(b)(2).

[28] *Garcia-Garcia v. Chertoff*, 2007 WL 4258836 (E.D. Cal. 2007); *Matter of Adeniji*, 22 I&N Dec. 1102 (BIA 1999); *Matter of West*, 22 I&N Dec. 1405 (BIA 2000).

[29] 2004 WL 1146525 (D. Or. 2004); *See also Cox v. Monica*, 2007 WL 1804335 (M.D. Pa. 2007).

[30] *Matter of Nguyen*, A25 404 392 (BIA 2000); *In re West*, 22 I&N Dec. 1405(BIA 2000); *In re Adeniji*, 22 I&N Dec. 1102 (BIA 1999); *see also Tenrreiro v. Ashcroft*, 2004 WL 1354277 (D. Or. 2004), *order vacated on reconsideration on other grounds*, 2004 WL 1588217 (D. Or. 2004) (convicted of theft in 2003 and received probation with no incarceration).

[31] *Quezada-Bucio v. Ridge*, 03-CV-03668-ORD (Apr. 7, 2004 W.D. Wa.); *Tenrreio v. Ashcroft*, 2004 WL 1354277 (D. Or. 2004), *order vacated on reconsideration on other grounds*, 2004 WL 1588217 (D. Or. 2004); *Zabadi v. Chertoff*, 2005 WL 3157377 (N.D. Cal. 2005). *But see Matter of Rojas*, 23 I&N Dec. 117 (BIA 2001) (finding §236(c) could apply to individuals not immediately taken into custody after release but leaving open the issue of whether the offense had to be one enumerated in INA §236(c)).

[32] *American Baptist Church v. Thornburgh*, 760 F. Supp. 796 (N.D. Cal. 1991).

imposed exceeded a term of imprisonment in excess of six months; or (2) pose a national security risk; or (3) pose a threat to public safety.[33]

The distinction of *ABC* members under paragraph 17 is important because it appears to exempt members from mandatory detention. The paragraph categorically prohibits ICE from detaining class members unless they meet the criteria.[34]

Do the Mandatory Detention Provisions Apply to Your Client if You Are Challenging That Your Client Is Not Even Removable or Inadmissible?

Often detainees are challenging the premise that they are even removable. For example, a detainee may be claiming U.S. citizenship through acquisition or be challenging that the offense is removable as an aggravated felony. Persons in this situation should argue that they are entitled to a hearing pursuant to *Matter of Joseph*,[35] where they can show through a special hearing that they are not properly included in the mandatory detention category. A person who is denied a *Joseph* hearing should appeal to the BIA to exhaust his or her administrative remedies (unless exhaustion is not required) to then pursue a federal challenge to the *Joseph* finding.[36]

Although the BIA found in *Joseph* that the noncitizen had to show that DHS was "substantially unlikely" to establish the charges, advocates and pro se detainees should argue that the proper standard is "likelihood of success on the merits of the charge."

Also, *Demore v. Kim* left open the possibility that a lawful permanent resident who has not yet conceded removability could still challenge detention. The majority appeared to give considerable weight to Kim's alleged concession of deportability.

In *Tijani v. Willis*,[37] the Ninth Circuit avoided deciding the constitutional issue and interpreted the authority conferred by INA §236(c) as applying only to expeditious removal of criminal aliens. "Two

years and four months of process is not expeditious; and the foreseeable process in this court, where the government's brief in the appeal has not yet been filed, is a year or more."[38]

The concurring opinion by Judge Tashima strongly criticized *Joseph* and held that the *Joseph* standard was egregiously unconstitutional because it placed the burden on the defendant to prove that he should not be physically detained, making the burden all but insurmountable.[39] The court found that INA §236(c) should apply to mandatory detention more narrowly, holding that only immigrants who could not raise a "substantial argument" against their removability should be subject to mandatory detention.[40] The opinion criticized *Joseph* for establishing a system of detention by default.[41]

If your client is contesting removability yet is still held in detention for an extended period under §236(c), you should argue that he or she is entitled to a bail hearing. General immigration detention statutes do not authorize attorney general to incarcerate detainees for indefinite period; rather, statutes at issue permit detention only while removal remains reasonably foreseeable.[42]

Finally, if your client is claiming U.S. citizenship by birth, derivation, or acquisition, you should challenge the applicability of §236(c) through a *Joseph* hearing or a writ of habeas corpus.

What if My Client Is Detained for an Unreasonable Period Under §236(c) and There Is No Final Order or the Order Is Stayed?

In the seminal case of *Ly v. Hansen*,[43] the Sixth Circuit granted a petition for a writ of habeas corpus and construed the pre–removal detention statute §236(c) to include an implicit requirement that removal proceedings be concluded in a reasonable time. The court held that the reasonableness of the length of detention was to be analyzed on a case by

---

[33] *Id.* at 804.

[34] *But see ABC* Settlement Wire 15 (Apr. 24, 1991) (*see* 68 *Interpreter Releases* 910 (July 22, 1991) (stating that *ABC* members convicted of aggravated felonies are subject to the mandatory detention provisions of the Immigration Act).

[35] 22 I&N Dec. 799 (BIA 1999).

[36] *See* discussion, *supra*.

[37] 430 F.3d 1241 (9th Cir. 2005); *see also Hussain v. Gonzales*, 492 F. Supp. 2d 1024, 1035 (E.D. Wis. 2007) (distinguishing from *Tijani* in part because alien in *Tijani* was contesting removability).

[38] 430 F.3d at 1242 (9th Cir. 2005).

[39] *Id.* at 1246.

[40] *Id.*

[41] *Id.* at 1244.

[42] *Nadarajah v. Gonzales*, 443 F.3d 1069 (9th Cir. 2006); *Judulang v. Chertoff*, 535 F. Supp 2d 1129 (S.D. Cal. 2008) (where alien's appeal raised a substantial issue and was likely to take at least another year, he was entitled to habeas relief in form of a bail hearing based on finding that his detention for two and a half years was not reasonable).

[43] 351 F.3d 263 (6th Cir. 2003).

case basis in habeas review.[44] The court deemed the 18-month detainment of Ly while his removal proceedings were pending to be unreasonable. Courts seem to be realizing that the vast majority of detained cases are not completed in the 90 days that *Demore* said was usual. Courts are now distinguishing *Demore* by considering the length of detention and releasing individuals on bond if the detention period has exceeded what the Supreme Court was considering to be a "reasonable" period.[45]

Does a Stay of Removal in the District Court or Circuit Court of Appeals Affect Ability to Be Released?

In *Lawson v. Gerlinski*,[46] the petitioner secured a stay of removal while challenging his removal order in circuit court. The petitioner simultaneously pursued a writ of habeas corpus in district court. The court found that the price for securing a stay of removal should not be prolonged incarceration. Where detention becomes prolonged, special care must be exercised so that confinement does not continue beyond the time when the original justifications for custody are no longer tenable.

In *Oyedeji v. Ashcroft*,[47] the court found that a noncitizen with removable convictions who filed a stay of removal and a petition for review challenging his removal could be released. The court found petitioner's convictions did not conclusively establish that he was a danger to the community or a flight risk. Further, the court found the alien's incarceration for more than four years after he petitioned for the stay of removal was unreasonable.

In *Haynes v. DHS*,[48] the court ordered DHS to provide petitioner with a meaningful review pursuant to 8 CFR §241.4(i). The petitioner had filed a petition for review and stay of removal. Petitioner challenged his prolonged confinement by filing a writ of habeas corpus. DHS argued that his stay of removal tolled the 90-day removal period. The court, however, found the DHS position inconsistent with the constitutional command that liberty be taken away only for appropriate reasons and only after the individual was afforded meaningful opportunity to be heard.[49]

In *Parlak v. Baker*,[50] the court granted the habeas petition where the detained noncitizen, who had not been convicted of a crime inside the United States, claimed that his eight-month detention violated due process. The court stated that, given the legal intricacies surrounding petitioner's removal, it would very likely take years for a final determination of his status, and it could not ignore the fact that petitioner was facing a significant period of detention for an indeterminate time. The prospect of prolonged detention, the court found, amounted to a violation of due process.

In *Diomande v. Wrona*,[51] the court granted the petition for writ of habeas corpus, finding that detention where removal proceedings had been pending for 21 months violated due process.

In *Uritsky v. Ridge*,[52] the court found that detention of a 19-year-old lawful permanent resident for almost one year while removal proceedings and Service appeal was pending was not justified by "sufficiently compelling government need."[53]

---

[44] *Id.* at 273.

[45] *Id. Cf. Yang v. Chertoff*, 2005 WL 2177097 (E.D. Mich. Sep 08, 2005) (holding three-month detainment during removal proceedings to be reasonable); *Leonardo v. Crawford*, 2008 WL 853604 (D. Ariz. Mar 27, 2008) (alien's own contributions in contributing to the delay through continuances taken into account when considering reasonableness); *Araiza-Morales v. Stine*, 2006 WL 3021495 (E.D. Ky. Oct 23, 2006) (holding two month delay not unreasonable); *Gjoliku v. Chertoff*, 2007 WL 518809 (W.D. Mich. Feb 14, 2007) (fact that petitioner contributed to much of the delay negates his argument that the delay was unreasonable); *Madrane v. Hogan*, 520 F. Supp. 2d 654 (M.D. Pa. 2007) (detainment of almost 3 years during proceedings unreasonable even though petitioner had contributed to the delay); *Diomande v. Wrona*, 2005 WL 3369498 (E.D. Mich. 2005. Dec. 12, 2005) (detainment of nearly two years unreasonable); *Fuller v. Gonzales*, 2005 WL 818614 (D.Conn. April 08, 2005) (more than two years unreasonable); *Parlak v. Baker*, 374 F.Supp.2d 551 (E.D. Mich. 2005) (judge ordered release of alien following eight months of detainment, noting that the legal complexity of the case meant that it would likely take years to before final resolution).

[46] 332 F. Supp. 2d 735 (M.D. Penn 2004).

[47] 332 F. Supp. 747 (M.D. Penn. 2004).

[48] 2005 U.S. Dist. LEXIS 13662 (M.D. Penn. 2005).

[49] *But see Bah v. Cangemi*, 489 F. Supp. 2d 905 (D. Minn. 2007) (holding that stay of removal effectively tolls the removal period).

[50] 374 F. Supp. 2d 551 (E.D. Mich. 2005).

[51] 2005 U.S. Dist. LEXIS 33795 (E.D. Mich. 2005).

[52] 286 F. Supp. 842 (E.D. Mich. 2003).

[53] *But see Sanusi v. INS*, 100 Fed. App. 49 (2d Cir. 2004); *Suarez v. Acting Director*, 2004 WL 1811494 (W.D.N.Y. 2004) (finding 90-day period does not start until after the final decision on appeal).

REMOVE ME OR RELEASE ME

Challenging Post-Removal Detention Under *Zadvydas*

When Does the 90-Day Removal Period Start Counting?

Typically, the issuance of a final administrative order by the IJ or the BIA triggers the removal period during which the alien is subject to mandatory detention pending removal within 90 days.[54] Since mandatory detention of aliens post-removal is statutorily limited to the 90-day period, it is important to analyze whether the period has been triggered, because if it has not, your client is arguably entitled to apply for reasonable bond.[55]

INA §241(a)(1)(B) offers clear guidance. It provides that the removal period begins on the *latest* of the following: (1) the date the order of removal becomes administratively final; (2) if a court orders a stay of removal, the date of the court's final order; or (3) if the alien is detained or confined (except under an immigration process), the date the alien is released from detention or confinement.[56] The statute also provides that the removal period is stayed if the alien fails to apply for a travel document or obstructs the deportation process.[57]

If the alien is subject to a final administrative order, the removal period is deemed to have commenced on the date that the BIA issued its decision. But, as most practitioners know, it is common DHS practice in nondetained cases to begin counting the 90-day period only after the alien is taken into custody for execution of the removal order. For example, if a noncitizen is subject to an old order of deportation or removal and detained at an adjustment interview, ICE will begin counting the 90 days as of the date of the alien's arrest.

A challenge to this practice will usually be of little use since ICE is likely to obtain a travel document within the 90-day period, and release through an independent arbiter is remote at best. However, you may want to consider challenging ICE's practice of commencing the counting of the 90-day period where removal is unlikely or impossible.

The argument in such cases is that the statute clearly states that the removal period commenced upon issuance of the final administrative order, not arrest of the alien. Therefore, so you should argue, the 90-day period has run and the noncitizen is eligible for release. This might lead to the alien's earlier release.

There do not appear to be any administrative or judicial decisions analyzing this question, but the Supreme Court decision in *Zadvaydas v. Davis*,[58] which holds that a six-month period of post–removal-order detention is presumptively reasonable, may cause a federal district court to take pause before considering release.

If a noncitizen is not removed from the United States within the 90-day removal period, the statute provides that the noncitizen be released subject to an order of supervision.[59] The removal period, however, may be extended for many reasons, including flight risk or failure to cooperate with the removal order. This does not mean that if your client is denied release at 90 days, he or she must remain in indefinite detention. The Supreme Court in *Zadvydas* read an implicit limitation into the statute's post–removal-period detention provision, which it defined as "the period reasonably necessary to bring about [the individual's] removal."[60] The Court allowed provided for six months for the government to effectuate removal unless the noncitizen's removal was reasonably foreseeable.

What About Those Who Are from Countries That Won't Take Them Back or Accept Them?

Many individuals with a final order of removal may be awaiting travel documents from their embassies that may not be forthcoming. The majority of individuals in this situation are from Vietnam, Laos, Iran, Iraq, or native stateless Palestinians. Any of these individuals could be physically deported to their countries, but often the embassies refuse travel document requests or the country may have no diplomatic relationship with the United States. Practitioners should be cautioned, however, that lengthy delays in issuance of a travel document do not necessarily mean that your client will not eventually be physically removed.

---

[54] INA §241(a).

[55] *Id.*

[56] INA §241(a)(1)(B).

[57] INA §241(a)(1)(C).

[58] *Zadvydas v. Davis*, 533 U.S. 678 (2001).

[59] INA §241(a)(3).

[60] *Zadvydas*, 533 U.S. 678.

In 2005, the Supreme Court extended the *Zadvydas* decision to inadmissible aliens in *Clark v. Martinez*,[61] which involved two Mariel Cubans found inadmissible due to prior convictions in the United States. In *Jama v. Immigration and Customs Enforcement*, the Supreme Court also held that noncitizens may be removed to a country without advance consent from that country's government.[62] The Court refused to read an acceptance requirement into the removal statute when Congress had not indicated such in the plain language. The country at issue in *Jama* was Somalia.

In *Ali v. Ashcroft*,[63] the Ninth Circuit ruled that where there is no functioning government to receive a national, immigration authorities cannot carry out a valid removal order. The Ninth Circuit upheld the district court's certification of a nationwide habeas and declaratory class composed of all persons in the United States who were subject to orders of removal to Somalia. It further upheld the district court order that the named petitioners be released from detention because there was no significant likelihood of removal in the reasonably foreseeable future. After the Supreme Court's decision in *Jama,* the Ninth Circuit abrogated the decision in *Ali,* and found that, based on the Supreme Court decision in *Jama,* Somalia did have a functioning government, and, therefore, ICE could remove the respondent to Somalia.[64]

What if ICE Is Refusing to Release the Client After the Removal Period Because It Says the Client Is Mentally Ill or Specially Dangerous Under 8 CFR §§241.14, 1241.14?

In *Thai v. Ashcroft*,[65] the Ninth Circuit held that the Supreme Court's construction of §241(a)(6) did not authorize the continued and potentially indefinite detention of an alien based on a determination that the alien's mental illness made him specially dangerous to the community. The court also held that the danger of criminal conduct by an alien was not automatically a matter of national security as that term was used in *Zadvydas*.

What If the Client is in the Post-Removal Period, Has a Petition for Review Pending, and Has Received a Stay of Removal?

The applicability of the removal period is also at issue when a noncitizen has filed a petition for review and the circuit court has issued a stay of removal. The statute clearly provides that if the final administrative order is judicially reviewed *and* if a court issues a stay, the removal period does not begin until the court issues a final order.[66] Therefore, the removal period has not yet begun and the alien's detention is governed by INA §236, which governs custody decisions prior to the removal period.[67] Only after judicial review is complete does the removal period begin and INA §241(a)(2), the mandatory detention period governing the removal period, come into play.

Nevertheless, ICE's practice is to continue to detain petitioners even where the court of appeals has issued a stay of removal, presumably on the theory that the stay is an action which "interferes" with removal under §241(a)(1)(C).[68] However, most federal courts have generally rejected this analysis and held that if the case is being judicially reviewed and the court enters a stay, the mandatory detention provision of the 90-day removal period does not apply.[69] Therefore, practitioners whose clients have sought judicial review *and* obtained a stay from the court should strenuously argue that their client is not subject to detention. Since the client is under a final administra-

[61] 543 U.S. 371 (2005).

[62] *Jama v. Immigration Customs and Enforcement*, 543 U.S. 335 (2005).

[63] 346 F.3d 873 (9th Cir. 2003).

[64] *Ali v. Gonzales,* 421 F.3d 795 (9th Cir. 2005).

[65] *Thai v. Ashcroft*, 389 F.3d 967 (9th Cir. 2004); *see also Tran v. Mukasey*, 515 F.3d 478 (5th Cir. 2008).

[66] INA §241(a)(1)(B)(ii).

[67] *See generally Demore v. Kim*, 538 U.S. 510 (2003).

[68] At least one circuit court has accepted this analysis. *See Akinwale v. Ashcroft*, 287 F.3d 1050, n.4 (11th Cir. 2002). *But see Arevalo v. Ashcroft,* 260 F.Supp.2d 347 (D. Mass. 2003); *Rodriguez-Carabantes v. Chertoff,* 2007 WL 1268500 (W.D. Wash. May 1, 2007); *Al Bassrei v. Clark,* 2006 WL 3691394 (W.D. Wash. Aug. 6, 2006); *Cesar v. Achim,* ___ F. Supp. ___, 2008 WL 829486 (E.D. Wis. Mar. 27, 2008).

[69] *See Bejjani v. Ashcroft*, 271 F.3d 670 (6th Cir 2001) (because of a court-ordered stay, removal period did not begin until the date of the court's final order. Thus, INS did not have authority to detain) (abrogated in part on other grounds by *Fernandez-Vargas v. Gonzalez,* 548 U.S. 30 (2006)); *Clavis v. Ashcroft*, 281 F. Supp. 2d 490, 493 (E.D.N.Y. 2003) ("Because the court entered a temporary stay of deportation, up to this point petitioner has remained in INS custody pursuant to Section 236."); *Milbin v. Ashcroft*, 293 F. Supp. 2d 158, 161 (D. Conn. 2003) ("Until this decision is filed, Milbin continues to be subject to mandatory detention under 236(c), as the Court's stay order…remains in effect."); *Rodriguez-Carabantes v. Chertoff,* 2007 WL 1268500 (W.D. Wash. May 1, 2007) (citing *Beijani*). *But cf. De La Teja v. U.S.*, 321 F.3d 1357, 1362–63 (11th Cir. 2003).

tive order, INA §236—which governs pre-order detention—arguably does not apply. Since a stay has been issued, the detention provisions of the 90-day removal period do not apply. While not precisely applicable because it covers supervision of noncitizens "after the 90-day period," INA §241(a)(3) may provide guidance for the release of noncitizens who have been granted stays of removal or deportation while their cases are being judicially reviewed.

Alternatively, practitioners might argue that detention is governed by INA §236, which provides that "the Attorney General...may release the alien on bond of at least $1,500."[70]

The proper court in which to test the detention issue raised by a noncitizen under a final order of removal is in habeas proceedings in the federal district court. While the REAL ID Act divested the district courts of jurisdiction to entertain challenges to removal orders, its provisions did not disturb district court jurisdiction over challenges to unlawful detention.[71]

But once the habeas is granted, who hears the bond motion? Since the noncitizen is under a final administrative order, there is no clear jurisdiction in the immigration courts. While there is nothing to prevent the court from remanding the matter to the agency for a bond hearing, the order may be met with confusion by an IJ who does not clearly understand his or her jurisdiction to consider bond where the noncitizen is under a final order of removal.

Unfortunately, the state of the law is of little help. It could be argued that INA §236 controls the detention because the removal period has not yet been triggered. The applicable standard for release,

therefore, is set forth in the statute and case law.[72] Practitioners might alternatively argue that there is a gap in the law; INA §236(c) controls pre–final order cases, and INA §241 applies to cases post–final order. Since the noncitizen has been granted a stay of removal, INA §241(a)(1)(B) places him or her in a statutory gap between the two provisions. Therefore, since neither detention provision directly applies, and since the client is under a final administrative order, the court might look for guidance to INA §241(a)(3), which governs release after the removal period, for guidance. Under these circumstances, 8 CFR §241.4(e), which sets forth factors for release, could be applied by analogy.

For practical purposes, it might make sense to move the district court to hear the merits of bond itself. Practitioners should argue to the court that it has the inherent power to release a habeas applicant on bond.[73] The government will likely assert, at least about in the context of noncitizens convicted of criminal offenses, that its authority to detain an alien under a final administrative order, which is set forth in INA §241(a)(6), is entitled to de minimis review;[74] that the scope of review of its discretionary decisions in the immigration context is extremely limited;[75] that detention of a noncitizen for up to six months is presumptively reasonable;[76] and that detention thereafter is appropriate so long as removal is reasonably foreseeable.[77] Further, the government will likely attack the district court's inherent authority to release as a limited power "to be exercised in special cases only."[78]

---

[70] The government will likely respond, in part, by asserting that the final administrative order divested the noncitizens of his or her lawful permanent resident status, citing INA §101(a)(20), which defines "lawfully admitted for permanent residence" as "the status of having been lawfully accorded the privilege of residing permanently in the United States as an immigrant in accordance with the immigration laws, such status not having changed." The entry of a final administrative order, so the government will likely assert, changes a legal permanent resident's status. 8 CFR §1.1 provides that lawful permanent residency status terminates upon entry of a final administrative order. However, the BIA has held that if a person appeals the BIA's decision and it is overturned, that person never lost legal permanent resident status. See Matter of Farinas, 12 I&N Dec. 467 (BIA 1967) (holding that a person not properly found deportable remains a lawful permanent resident).

[71] Supra note 2.

[72] INA §236(a) provides that "an alien may be arrested and detained pending a decision on whether the alien is to be removed from the United States ... pending such decision, the Attorney General ... may release the alien on ... bond of at least $1,500." BIA precedent also strongly favors release of a noncitizen in removal proceedings. Matter of Patel, 15 I&N Dec. 666 (BIA 1976) (an alien should not be detained or required to post bond unless he is a national security threat or flight risk).

[73] Ewing v. U.S., 240 F. 241 (6th Cir. 1917).

[74] See Carlson v. Landon, 342 U.S. 524 (1952); Reno v. Flores, 507 U.S. 292 (1993) (upholding the attorney general's custody scheme for juvenile aliens because these rules met "the (unexacting) standard of rationality advancing some legitimate governmental purpose").

[75] See Jean v. Nelson, 727 F.2d 957 (11th Cir. 1984), aff'd, 472 U.S. 846 (1984)

[76] Zadvydas v. Davis, 533 U.S. 678, 678 (2001).

[77] Id. at 701.

[78] Mapp v. Ashcroft, 241 F.3d 221 (2d Cir. 2001) ("[A] habeas petitioner should be granted bail only in unusual cases,
continued

Yet, neither the statute nor the case law suggests that DHS can hold a noncitizen pending judicial review unless the person proves his or her case is "special." The "special circumstances," so the practitioner should argue, apply where an individual files a habeas application and collaterally attacks a criminal conviction. In that context, the applicant will usually not be released from detention unless there are "special circumstances or a high probability of success." The Supreme Court has made it clear, however, that a different standard applies to civil detention.[79]

WELCOME TO THE UNITED STATES, HERE ARE THE HANDCUFFS

Challenging the Detention of Arriving Aliens

Generally, an IJ is divested of jurisdiction for an arriving alien in a bond hearing.[80] Challenge the denial of a bond hearing for returning lawful permanent resident aliens who are being treated as arriving aliens because of IIRAIRA's new definition of admission. The categorical denial to lawful permanent resident aliens of the right to a bond hearing may raise serious constitutional issues.

One also could challenge the lack of proper notice for a person seeking admission on an advance parole. In *Shahwan v. Chertoff*,[81] the district court found that where an alien was granted advance parole and the immigration authorities failed to warn him of the prospect of detention without the possibility of bond, such notice would be insufficient. As a result, the court remanded the case to the IJ for a bond hearing. The petitioner in this case was apprehended and categorized as an arriving alien because he had falsely represented himself as a U.S. citizen on a passport application.

Finally, in *Nadarajah v. Gonzalez*,[82] the Ninth Circuit found that detention for five years despite

having prevailed at every administrative level of review and never having been charged with any crime would be counter to the *Zadvydas* and *Clark* holdings. In *Nadarajah*, DHS claimed the authority to indefinitely detain a person seeking admission and pursuing asylum under INA §§235(b)(1)(B)(ii) and (b)(2)(A). The court disagreed and concluded that the statutes at issue permit detention only while removal remains reasonably foreseeable. Further, after a presumptively reasonable six-month detention, "once the alien provides good reason to believe that there is no significant likelihood of removal in the reasonably foreseeable future, the Government must respond with evidence sufficient to rebut that showing."

PRISON OF A DIFFERENT KIND

Challenging the Detention of Refugees

In a disturbing nationwide trend, ICE appears to be apprehending refugees with criminal convictions (often nonremovable criminal convictions) and detaining them from 18 months to two years without filing a notice to appear. ICE detains the refugees for such lengthy periods because it compels them to submit adjustment of status applications to the local U.S. Citizenship and Immigration Services (USCIS) office and the processing times for such applications are well over a year for refugees. ICE claims authority for the detention because refugees are considered arriving aliens or INA §209 permits "custody" of a refugee seeking admission. Most IJs will conduct a bond hearing finding that refugees are not arriving aliens but are subject to the limits of INA §236(c) even though no removal proceedings are pending.[83] The BIA has found in many unpublished decisions that they have no jurisdiction over such custody because it falls under §209(a). Further, the BIA found in an unpublished case that they have no authority to review the legality of an arrest.

Advocates should distinguish between the terms "custody" and "detention." As §209 only permits "custody," argue that custody is a temporary arrest and does not authorize long-term detention.[84] Fur-

---

or when extraordinary or exceptional circumstances exist, which make the grant of bail necessary to make the habeas remedy effective.").

[79] *Aronson v. May*, 85 S. Ct. 3 (1964); *Yanish v. Barber*, 73 S. Ct. 1105 (1953).

[80] 8 CFR §1003.19(h)(2)(i)(B).

[81] 2005 WL 3369991 (N.D. Cal. 2005).

[82] 443 F.3d 1069 (9th Cir. 2006); *see also Martinez v. Gonzales*, 504 F. Supp. 2d 887 (C.D. Cal. 2007) ("The Ninth Circuit did not limit its holding in *Nadarajah* to the facts of that case or otherwise indicate that it was crafting a rule of limited application because of the relatively unusual posture of the petitioner's application for relief from removal.").

[83] 8 CFR §1003.19(h)(2)(i)(B) (only divests IJs of jurisdiction over an arriving alien where removal proceedings are pending).

[84] *See* Legal Opinion No. 97-2, 1997 WL 33169234, Office of General Counsel, Legal Opinion on Whether a Personal Interview Is Required for All Refugee and Asylee Adjustment of Status Applications under INA §209 ("The crucial question here is whether the use of the term 'custody' requires the Service to take actual physical control over refugees adjusting status when their admissibility is determined.
continued

thermore, even if §209 is accepted as a detention-authorizing statute, courts should be authorized to conduct individualized bond hearings. Additionally, it could be argued that holding refugees for indefinite periods without charges violates due process. Finally, the arriving alien categorization of unadjusted refugees should have no bearing on custody because 8 CFR §1003.19(h)(2)(i)(B) only divests IJs of jurisdiction over an arriving alien where removal proceedings are pending.

ICE'S TRUMP CARD

Challenging the Automatic Stay Provisions of 8 CFR §1003.19

Even if the IJ redetermines bond and gives your client a bond, the fight may not be over. The regulations provide that ICE may file an automatic stay of the IJ's decision in any case where the bond is initially set above $10,000 and the judge lowers the bond below $10,000.[85] ICE must file Form EOIR-43 with the Executive Office for Immigration Review seeking an automatic stay of the IJ's custody decision. Although the Supreme Court determined in *Demore v. Kim*[86] that mandatory detention during removal proceedings is constitutionally permissible, the Court was interpreting §236(c). However, the automatic stay comes into play in cases where the judge already has determined that the respondent is not subject to mandatory detention under INA §236(c) and should be released on bond.

Many district courts that have considered the constitutionality of the automatic stay provisions have found them to be unconstitutional.[87] The first

challenge that can be raised is that the automatic stay is ultra vires, since there is no statutory authority for the stay regulation and the statute allows the attorney general, by way of the IJ, to redetermine bond. ICE's exercise of the automatic stay provisions at 8 CFR §1003.19(i)(2) effectively allows it to bypass §236(a), which authorizes release, and to secure the mandatory detention of anyone regardless of whether they are subject to §236(c).[88]

After an individualized hearing before an IJ on whether or not your client is a flight risk or a danger to the community, as required by longstanding BIA precedent,[89] and after assessing the positive and negative equities in the case, the IJ is in the best position to redetermine bond because as the trier of fact, he or she is in the best position to determine the flight risk and danger potential of the applicant, and such determination should not be unilaterally thwarted by ICE through an ultra vires regulation without statutory authority. "Due process is not satisfied where the individualized custody determination afforded to Petitioner was effectively a charade."[90] "In effect, the automatic stay provision renders the Immigration Judge's bail determination an empty gesture."[91]

The government's principal justifications for the automatic stay are to ensure the presence of criminal aliens at their removal proceedings and to protect the public from dangerous criminal aliens. Yet in some cases ICE invokes the automatic stay for cases in which the respondent has been living freely and crime-free in the community for decades.

Furthermore, 8 CFR §1003.19(i)(2) contains definite time requirements for the filing of the stay and appeal but *no* time limits for when the BIA or attorney general must render a decision on the stay or appeal. This distinguishes the case from the Supreme Court decision in *Demore v. Kim*. The Court stated, "Congress . . . may require that persons . . .

Current practice does not include the taking of this type of custody over a refugee, and it seems doubtful that Congress intended the Service to detain refugees applying for adjustment of status. Both in common usage and as a technical legal term, custody denotes many different types of control over a person short of physical restraint. Webster's Dictionary defines custody as 'judicial or penal safekeeping: control of a thing or individual with such actual or constructive possession as fulfills the purpose of the law or duty requiring it...'.Therefore, it is reasonable to interpret 'custody' in Section 209(a) to mean something other than physical restraint. It should be understood to mean sufficient control over an alien to carry out the purpose of Section 209(a).").

[85] 8 CFR §1003.19(i).

[86] 538 U.S. 510 (2003).

[87] *Zavala v. Ridge*, 310 F. Supp. 2d 1071 (N.D. Cal. 2004) (citing other cases); *see also Zabadi v. Chertoff*, 2005 WL 1514122 (N.D. Cal. 2005).

[88] *Almonte-Vargas v. Elwood*, Civ. Act. No. 02-CV-2666, 2002 U.S. Dist. LEXIS 12387 (E.D. Pa. June 28, 2002) ("It is the operation of the appeal and automatic stay, and not §1226(c) that is technically responsible for her continued detention"); *contra Galarza-Solis v. Ashcroft*, 2004 WL 728199 (N.D. Ill. 2004) (questioning validity of holdings in *Almonte-Vargas* in wake of *Demore*).

[89] *Carlson v. Landon*, 243 U.S. 524 (1952); *Matter of Patel*, 15 I&N Dec. 666 (BIA 1976); *Matter of Moise*, 12 I&N Dec. 102 (BIA 1967).

[90] *Almonte-Vargas v. Elwood*, 2002 U.S. Dist. LEXIS 123897, at 5.

[91] *Ashley v. Ridge*, 2003 U.S. Dist. LEXIS 19335, at 16.

be detained for the brief period necessary for their removal proceedings."[92] The time limitation has been a consistent concern of the Court in addressing detention without bond.[93] The cases addressing the automatic stay confirm that the period can be more than six months.[94]

CONCLUSION

"Freedom from bodily restraint has always been at the core of the liberty protected by the Due Process Clause from arbitrary governmental action."[95] The authors hope that this article has given you some tools, arguments, and strategies for protecting your clients' liberty.

[92] *Demore v. Kim*, 538 U.S. 510 (2003).

[93] *Zadvydas v. Davis*, 533 U.S. at 690 ("a statute permitting indefinite detention would raise a serious constitutional problem"); *Reno v. Flores*, 507 U.S. 292, 314 (1993) (noting that juveniles would remain in custody only an average of 30 days, and that individual abuses would be remedied through habeas).

[94] *Ashley v. Ridge*, 2003 U.S. Dist. LEXIS 19335 (Aug. 19, 2003, to Oct. 29, 2003, when the Court vacated the stay); *Bezman v. Ashcroft*, 245 F. Supp. 2d 446 (July 31, 2002, to Feb. 21, 2003, when the Court vacated the stay); *Uritsky v. Ridge*, 2003 U.S. Dist. LEXIS 17698 (Apr. 3, 2003, to Sept. 29, 2003, when the Court vacated the stay); *Almonte-Vargas v. Elwood*, 2002 U.S. Dist. LEXIS 12387 (Feb. 27, 2002, to June 28, 2002, when the Court vacated the stay); *Grant v. Zemski*, 54 F. Supp. 2d 437, 439 (E.D. Pa. 1999) (noting that BIA appeals of detention decisions can take three to six months).

[95] *Foucha v. Louisiana*, 504 U.S. 71, 80 (1992).

LEGAL STRATEGIES INVOLVING MOTIONS TO REOPEN, RECONSIDER, AND RESCIND BEFORE THE BOARD OF IMMIGRATION APPEALS

by Zachary Nightingale and Avantika Shastri[*]

INTRODUCTION

This updated article[1] is intended to provide a broad overview of motions to reconsider, reopen, and rescind before the Board of Immigration Appeals (BIA). The regulations governing such motions appear at 8 CFR §1003.2.[2] Filing such motions can be a powerful tool to have facts or arguments of your client's case considered (or reconsidered) prior

to the execution of a deportation or removal order. It may also be the only way to have certain facts considered if your client has already been issued a final order of deportation or removal.

There are different regimes for each kind of motion, some of which have been created by regulation and others by case law. Recognizing the different sources of law is important because many relevant rules are not found in the regulations themselves, but are instead based on legal interpretation contained in precedent decisions or in statutory language[3] not yet embodied in regulations.

When determining which type of motion to file, and what the relevant rules are, there are several preliminary questions: the kind of proceeding, the function of the motion, the timing of the motion, the evidentiary requirements of each motion, and the practical effect of the motion on delaying or preventing removal. Notably, the filing of each kind of motion is not restricted to one motion at a time, to one judge at a time, or to one adjudicator at a time. Thus, thoughtful and creative filing of the motions based on the procedural posture of the case may maximize your client's chances of receiving a rehearing.

This article will focus primarily on the different regimes for motions to reconsider and reopen, with updates of recent case law, with general updates related to motions to rescind. The article concludes with general or strategic considerations when filing these motions.

---

[*] **Zachary Nightingale**, a partner at Van Der Hout, Brigagliano & Nightingale, LLP, in San Francisco, received his J.D. and M.S. (mathematics) from Stanford and A.B. from U.C. Berkeley. His practice focuses on deportation defense and litigation in immigration and federal court. Mr. Nightingale was honored with AILA's 2003 Jack Wasserman Memorial Award for excellence in litigation. He has litigated *Quintero-Salazar v. Keisler*, 506 F.3d 688 (9th Cir. 2007), and *Li v. Ashcroft*, 389 F.3d 892 (9th Cir. 2004).

Avantika Shastri is an associate attorney at Van Der Hout, Brigagliano & Nightingale, LLP. Her practice focuses on deportation defense and litigation before the federal courts and administrative agencies. This article also includes arguments developed by other members of the firm.

[1] This article updates and supplements the authors' article "Here We Go Again: Motions to Reopen, Reconsider, and Rescind Before the Board of Immigration Appeals," *Immigration & Nationality Law Handbook* 169 (AILA 2006–07 Ed.).

[2] Motions to reopen and reconsider may also be filed before the immigration judge, *see* 8 CFR §1003.23, and the Administrative Appeals Office, *see* 8 CFR §§103.3, 1103.3. Although this article will primarily address motions to the BIA, the suggestions made here will almost always apply to motions made to the immigration court as well.

There are two additional kinds of motions that are related but will not be discussed in depth in this article. First, if an appeal of an order is pending or a motion to reopen has been granted by the BIA, you may file a motion to remand before the BIA to return jurisdiction of a case pending before the BIA to the immigration judge. *See* 8 CFR §1003.2(c)(4); *Matter of Coelho*, 20 I&N Dec. 464 (BIA 1992); *Matter of L–V–K–*, 22 I&N Dec. 976, 980 (BIA 1999); *see also Board of Immigration Appeals Practice Manual* (BIA Practice Manual), ch. 5.8. Motions to remand are subject to the same substantive requirements as motions to reopen, but are not limited in time or number. *See* discussion *infra*. Second, when proceedings have been administratively closed or continued indefinitely and you wish to "reopen" those proceedings, the proper motion is a motion to recalendar, not a motion to remand. *See* BIA Practice Manual, ch. 5.9(h).

[3] Both language in the Immigration and Nationality Act of 1952 (INA), Pub. L. No. 82-414, 66 Stat. 163, as well as in uncodified provisions of other statutes such as the Violence Against Women Reauthorization Act of 2005 (VAWA 2005), Pub. L. No. 109-162, §§3(a), 801–34, 119 Stat. 2960, 2964–71, 3053–77 (2006); the Nicaraguan Adjustment and Central American Relief Act, Pub. L. No. 105-100, tit. II, 111 Stat. 2160, 2193–201 (1997); the Haitian Refugee Immigration Fairness Act of 1998, Pub. L. No. 105-277, div. A, §101(h), tit. IX (secs. 901–04), 112 Stat. 2681, 2681-538 to 2681-542; and other statutes not explicitly incorporated into the INA.

193

MOTIONS FOR RECONSIDERATION

A motion to reconsider is a vehicle for requesting reconsideration of a previously issue legal decision, when there are no new facts that also need to be considered.[4] A motion to reconsider is a "request that the Board reexamine its decision in light of additional legal arguments, a change of law, or perhaps an argument or aspect of the case which was overlooked."[5]

A motion to reconsider must be filed with the BIA within 30 days of its decision.[6] A party may file only one motion to reconsider any given decision and may not seek reconsideration of a previous decision denying a motion to reconsider.[7] Motions to reconsider filed before July 31, 1996, do not count towards the one-motion limit.[8] In contrast to motions to reopen, there are no regulatory exceptions to these numerical and time limitations, except that the BIA may reconsider on its own motion at any time.[9] There may be equity-based exceptions to those limitations, however.[10]

A motion to reconsider may be made even if the case was dismissed for lack of jurisdiction if the dismissal was due to an untimely appeal.[11] In *Matter of Lopez*,[12] the BIA held that it retained jurisdiction

---

[4] *See* INA §240(c)(5); 8 CFR §1003.2(b).

[5] *Matter of Ramos*, 23 I&N Dec. 336, 338 (BIA 2002), *aff'd*, 979 F.2d 212 (11th Cir. 1992) (unpublished table decision); *Asemota v. Gonzales*, 420 F.3d 32, 34 (1st Cir. 2005); *Kui Rong Ma v. Ashcroft*, 361 F.3d 553, 558 (9th Cir. 2004); *see also* BIA Practice Manual, ch. 5.7.

[6] INA §240(c)(5)(B); 8 CFR §1003.2(b)(2).

[7] INA §240(c)(5)(A); 8 CFR §1003.2(b)(2).

[8] *See* 8 CFR §1003.2(b)(2).

[9] *See* 8 CFR §1003.2(a). *Cf.* 8 CFR §1003.2(c)(3).

[10] *See* discussion *infra*. In addition, there are other cases in which untimely motions to reconsider may be filed. For example, following a BIA decision, your client's prior representative may have missed the 30-day jurisdictional deadline to file a petition for review in the court of appeals and the 30-day motion to reconsider deadline. Even if the failure to file were the result of deficient representation, the circuit courts have not found ineffective assistance of counsel to be a sufficient basis for accepting a late petition for review. However, the ineffective assistance of counsel may be a valid basis to file a late motion to reconsider with the BIA. Even if such motion were denied, a petition for review of that denial could be timely filed to ultimately obtain review in the circuit court. *See Ray v. Gonzales*, 439 F.3d 582, 590 (9th Cir. 2006).

[11] *Matter of Lopez*, 22 I&N Dec. 16, 17 (BIA 1998), *modifying Matter of Mladineo*, 14 I&N Dec. 591 (BIA 1974).

[12] *Id.*

over a motion to reconsider its dismissal of an untimely appeal to the extent that the motion challenges the finding of untimeliness or requests consideration of the reasons for untimeliness.

The only supporting materials required for a motion to reconsider are a statement of the party's arguments regarding the BIA's alleged errors and "pertinent authority."[13] It is implicit in 8 CFR §1003.2(b)(1) that the BIA will reconsider the party's case using the same record evidence used in making its prior decision.[14]

In *Matter of Cerna*,[15] the BIA held that motions to reopen and motions to reconsider are separate and distinct motions with different requirements.[16] In *Cerna*, the BIA stated:

A motion to reconsider asserts that at the time of the Board's previous decision an error was made. It questions the Board's decision for alleged errors in appraising the facts and the law. When we reconsider a decision, we are in effect placing ourselves back in time and considering the case as though a decision in the case on the record before us had never been entered. If the respondent was eligible for relief at the time the original decision was entered, then in reconsidering the decision we would treat his status as that which it had been at the time of the initial decision. The very nature of a motion to reconsider is that the original decision was defective in some regard.

In contrast, in regard to motions to reopen, the BIA stated:

A motion to reopen proceedings, however, is a fundamentally different motion. It does not contest the correctness of (or simply request a re-evaluation of) the prior decision on the previous factual record. Rather, a motion to reopen proceedings seeks to reopen proceedings so that new evidence can be presented and so that a new decision can be entered, normally after a further evidentiary hearing.

---

[13] *See Matter of Ramos*, 23 I&N Dec. 336, 338 (BIA 2002). *See also Matter of O–S–G–*, 24 I&N Dec. 56, 58–59 (BIA 2006) (enumerating requirements for motion to reconsider a summary affirmance order).

[14] *Matter of Ramos*, *supra* note 13, at 338.

[15] 20 I&N Dec. 399, 402–03 (BIA 1991).

[16] The BIA has made this same distinction between motions to reopen and to rescind. *See Matter of M–S–*, 22 I&N Dec. 349 (BIA 1998).

Despite this allegedly clear distinction, in practice, the difference is not always so readily apparent, especially when a change in law after the final order affects your client's legal rights. Furthermore, there may be a strategic reason to characterize a motion as either reopening or reconsideration, given that each has separate evidentiary and jurisdictional requirements.

In confusing circumstances, always refer to relevant precedent in the particular jurisdiction. It may be best to file a motion within the jurisdictional time for a reconsideration motion to best preserve your client's legal options. The motion can always be supplemented, and if necessary be characterized as either or even both types of motions. If you face numerical or time bars to jurisdiction, then it still may be possible to file based on equitable reasons for untimely filing.[17]

MOTIONS TO REOPEN

A motion to reopen is a vehicle for presenting new facts, unavailable at the time of the original proceedings, to the BIA or to the immigration judge.[18] A motion to reopen must demonstrate a prima facie case for relief and will not be granted unless it appears to the BIA that the evidence sought to be offered is material and was not available and could not have been discovered or presented at the former hearing.[19] The applicant must submit any applications for relief at the time that he or she submits the motion.[20] A motion to reopen does *not* lead to an automatic stay of removal; the applicant must still request a stay from the BIA.[21] There are strict jurisdictional requirements for motions to reopen. Unless subject to one of the specific exceptions in the regulations, a party may file only one motion to reopen, and that motion must be filed no later than 90 days after the administrative decision was rendered.[22] Motions to reopen filed before September 30, 1996, do not count towards the one-motion limit.[23] A statutory exception not reflected in the regulations is that a motion to reopen to apply for relief as a battered spouse, parent, or child does *not* count towards the one-motion limitation.[24]

There are several regulatory exceptions to these time and numerical limitations.[25]

Notably, in a motion to reopen, the applicant has the burden of making a prima facie case for relief.[26] The BIA has found that "a respondent demonstrates prima facie eligibility for relief where the evidence reveals a reasonable likelihood that the statutory requirements for relief have been satisfied."[27] It has "not required a conclusive showing that eligibility for relief has been established. Rather, [it has] reopened proceedings where the new facts alleged, when coupled with the facts already of record, satisfy us that it would be worthwhile to develop the issues further at a plenary hearing on reopening."[28]

Thus, applicants will want to submit documentation that not only relates to why the evidence or issues were not raised in the prior hearing, and what the new evidence is, but also relates to the underlying merits of the claim, including any discretionary issues in addition to the basic requirements for relief. If the applicant is filing for a new form of relief, the application must be attached to the motion to reopen.[29] A filing fee may also be required.[30]

Statutory and Regulatory Bases for Motions to Reopen

Asylum Applications

Pursuant to 8 CFR §1003.2(c)(3), a motion to reopen may be filed to apply or reapply for asylum or withholding of deportation/removal based on

---

[17] *See* discussion *infra*.

[18] *See* INA §240(c)(6); 8 CFR §1003.2(c).

[19] *See* 8 CFR §1003.2(c)(1).

[20] *Id.*

[21] *See* 8 CFR §1003.2(f); *see also* discussion *infra*.

[22] *See* INA §240(c)(6)(C)(i); 8 CFR §1003.2(c)(2).

[23] *See* 8 CFR §1003.2(c)(2).

[24] INA §240(c)(7)(A).

[25] *See* 8 CFR §1003.2(c)(3); *see also* 8 CFR §§208.24(e), (f), 1208.24(e), (f) (providing for Department of Homeland Security (DHS) motion to reopen a grant of asylum or withholding of deportation). *Cf.* 8 CFR §§208.17(d)–(f), 1208.17(d)–(f) (motion for new hearing, rather than motion to reopen, required to terminate prior grants of deferral of removal under CAT).

[26] *See* INS v. Abudu, 485 U.S. 94 (1988) (also enumerating other reasons why the BIA may deny a motion to reopen).

[27] *Matter of S–V–*, 22 I&N Dec. 1306, 1308 (BIA 2000), citing *Matter of L–O–G–*, 21 I&N Dec. 413, 419 (BIA 1996).

[28] *Id.* (citations omitted). *See e.g., Ordonez v. INS*, 345 F.3d 777, 784–87 (9th Cir. 2003); *Kay v. Ashcroft*, 387 F.3d 664, 675 (7th Cir. 2004); *Shardar v. Ashcroft*, 382 F.3d 318, 325 (3d Cir. 2004).

[29] 8 CFR §1003.2(c)(1).

[30] *See* 8 CFR §1003.2(g)(2)(i), *citing* 8 CFR §1003.8.

changed circumstances arising in the country of nationality or in the country to which deportation has been ordered.[31] In such cases, the numeric and time limitations on motions to reopen *do not* apply.[32] The applicant must show that the evidence is material and could not have been presented earlier.[33]

However, it appears to be an open question whether a successive asylum application based on changed *personal* circumstances or some other kind of change in circumstances, aside from changed circumstances in the country of nationality, may be filed after a final order of removal (either with or without a motion to reopen). In *Matter of C–W–L–*, the BIA held that changed personal circumstances could not be the basis for an asylum application after a final order of removal had been issued.[34] It compared the asylum provisions at INA §208(a)(2)(D), which allow for successive asylum applications on certain grounds, with the motion to reopen provisions at INA §240(c)(7)(C)(ii), which allow motions to reopen for asylum outside of the time and numeric limitations. The statutory and regulatory language at INA §208 appears to permit *successive* asylum claims on broader bases than those permitted for motions to reopen based on asylum, which are limited to claims of changed circumstances in the country of nationality.[35] The BIA held that, based on its review of the INA, regulations, and legislative history, successive asylum applications filed on bases other than changed circumstances in the country of origin were permitted only prior to a final order of

removal. After a final order of removal, such applications were impermissible, and the only applications that could be considered required a motion to reopen and showing changed circumstances in the country of nationality.

The BIA acknowledged that other cases had appeared to suggest that a noncitizen could file a successive asylum application based on personal circumstances without a motion to reopen, but the BIA dismissed the language from these cases as dicta.[36] The BIA's reasoning has been followed in four circuits.[37]

However, given the broad statutory language of INA §208, it appears arguable whether the motion to reopen provisions at INA §240 apply to limit the asylum statute, and that congressional intent may have been to allow successive asylum applications without a motion to reopen. Notably, in *He v. Gonzales*,[38] the U.S. Court of Appeals for the Ninth Circuit suggested that, although the petitioner was barred from filing an untimely motion to reopen based on changed personal circumstances, a second asylum application might be possible.

It also appears to be an open question whether a noncitizen would have to meet the time or numerical requirements for a motion to reopen for a claim to protection under the Convention Against Torture (CAT),[39] or a second application based on a claim separate from the first application under CAT. The requirement under CAT that the United States not repatriate an applicant to a country where he or she faces torture would appear to require a mechanism for making a CAT claim even after the 90-day reopening period has expired if the basis of the CAT case arises after that deadline. Therefore, again, such

---

[31] 8 CFR §1003.2(c)(3)(ii); *Matter of C–W–L–*, 24 I&N Dec. 346, 348–54 (BIA 2007) (holding that a successive asylum application based on changed country conditions *must* be accompanied by a motion to reopen).

[32] 8 CFR §1003.2(c)(3).

[33] *Id. See, e.g., Kebe v. Gonzales*, 473 F.3d 855, 858 (7th Cir. 2007) (remanding for consideration of changed circumstances); *Shardar v. Att'y Gen.*, 503 F.3d 308, 316 (3d Cir. 2007) (finding changed circumstances); *Li v. Att'y Gen.*, 488 F.3d 1371 (11th Cir. 2007) (changed circumstances); *Alemu v. Mukasey* 509 F.3d 907, 910 (8th Cir. 2007) (no changed circumstances); *Norani v. Gonzales*, 451 F.3d 292, 295 (2d Cir. 2006) (changed circumstances); *Malty v. Ashcroft*, 381 F.3d 942 (9th Cir. 2004) (changed circumstances); *see also Matter of S–Y–G–*, 24 I&N Dec. 247 (BIA 2007) (no changed circumstances); *Matter of J–J–*, 21 I&N Dec. 976 (BIA 1997) (same).

[34] *Matter of C–W–L–, supra* note 31, at 352–53.

[35] *Compare* INA §208(a)(2)(D) and 8 CFR §§208.4(a)(4),(5), 1208.4(a)(4), (5) *with* INA §240(c)(7)(C)(ii) and 8 CFR §1003.2(c)(3)(ii).

[36] *See Haddad v. Gonzales*, 437 F.3d 515, 518–19 (6th Cir. 2006); *Guan v. BIA*, 345 F.3d 47, 49 (2d Cir. 2003).

[37] *See Zheng v. Mukasey*, 509 F.3d 869, 871 (8th Cir. 2007); *Chen v. Gonzales*, 498 F.3d 758 (7th Cir. 2007); *Wang v. BIA*, 437 F.3d 270, 273–74 (2d Cir.2006); *see also He v. Gonzales*, 501 F.3d 1128, 1133 n.9 (9th Cir. 2007) (agreeing that petitioner was barred from untimely motion to reopen, but not agreeing that successive application was barred); *Ni v. Gonzales*, 494 F.3d 260, 273–74 (2d Cir.2007) (Calabresi, J., concurring) (suggesting that petitioner could file a second asylum application based on changed personal circumstances).

[38] 501 F.3d 1128 (9th Cir. 2007).

[39] Convention Against Torture and Other Cruel, Inhuman or Degrading Treatment or Punishment, Dec. 10, 1984, 1465 U.N.T.S. 85 (entered into force June 26, 1987).

a situation would appear to be one in which a late motion to reopen would have be accepted based on changed circumstances within the United States in order to uphold the CAT treaty obligations.

Relief Under Former INA §212(c)

A motion to reopen proceeding for consideration of an application for relief under former INA §212(c) may be granted if the applicant demonstrates that he or she was statutorily eligible for such relief prior to the entry of the administratively final order of deportation.[40] Such motions had to be filed by April 26, 2005.[41] Since the expiration of that regulatory deadline, the numerical and time limitations applicable to motions to reopen presumably apply in such cases as well.

Battered Spouses, Parents, and Children

Applicants in removal, exclusion, and deportation proceedings may file one motion to reopen at any time based on domestic violence, *in addition to* one motion to reopen based on other causes.[42] The motion to reopen must be filed within one year of the entry of the final order of removal unless this time limitation is waived by the Attorney General.[43]

The motion may be applied on behalf of battered spouses, children, and parents.[44] The case may be reopened for applying for adjustment as a self-petitioner under INA §204(a), special rule cancellation under INA §240A(b)(2), and Violence Against Women Act (VAWA) suspension of deportation under INA §244(a)(3) (as in effect on March 31, 1997).[45]

An applicant must be physically present in the United States at the time of filing of the motion. Notably, there is a mandatory stay for qualified aliens (as defined in 8 USC §1641(c)(1)(B)) pending the final disposition of the motion, including exhaustion of all appeals if the motion establishes that the alien is a qualified alien.[46]

Bases to Reopen Established by Case Law

Ineffective Assistance of Counsel

An applicant effectively may have been prevented from presenting evidence in a prior hearing because of deficient legal advice (or advice from someone purporting to be a lawyer). A claim of ineffective assistance may be used to explain the error below that resulted in the delay in presenting "new evidence" (which may have, in fact, existed and/or been known earlier in the case), and/or the error that may have prevented the new information from being timely presented in a motion to reopen. While we will not claim to recount all of the ways in which ineffective assistance could take place, it is worth noting that the courts have found ineffective assistance and sometimes equity-based remedies in numerous situations.[47]

A claim of ineffective assistance of counsel almost always requires complying with the basic procedural requirements laid out by the BIA, or an explanation as to why they have not been followed. In *Matter of Lozada*,[48] the BIA first held that ineffective assistance of counsel could constitute a ground for reopening if certain procedural hurdles were met.[49]

Procedural Requirements of *Lozada*

Lozada explicitly sets forth three requirements for supporting a claim of ineffective assistance of counsel:

1. an affidavit by the alien setting forth the agreement with counsel regarding the alien's representation

2. evidence that counsel was informed of the allegations and allowed to respond

3. an indication that a complaint has been lodged with the relevant state bar, or reasons explaining why not

The BIA and the circuit courts generally have been fairly strict about requiring these procedural hurdles to be met before reopening any case. How-

---

[40] 8 CFR §1003.2(c)(1). *See also* 8 CFR §§212.3, 1212.3.

[41] *See* 8 CFR §1003.44(h).

[42] *See* INA §§240(c)(7)(A), (C)(iv). *See also Sanchez v. Keisler*, 505 F.3d 641, 648 (7th Cir. 2007). Certain provisions of VAWA relating to reopening deportation proceedings were contained only in the statute and never promulgated into the regulations.

[43] *See* INA §240(c)(7)(C)(iv)(III) (the requirement may be waived if the applicant demonstrates extraordinary circumstances or extreme hardship to his or her child). Notably, the "extraordinary circumstances" requirement is distinct from the "exceptional circumstances" required to rescind *in absentia* orders. *See* INA §240(e)(1).

[44] *See* INA §240(c)(7)(C)(iv).

[45] INA §240(c)(7)(C)(iv)(I).

[46] INA §240(c)(7)(C)(iv).

[47] *See also* discussion *infra*.

[48] 19 I&N Dec. 637, 639 (BIA), *aff'd*, 857 F.2d 10 (1st Cir. 1988).

[49] *See also Matter of Assaad*, 23 I&N Dec. 553 (BIA 2003); *Matter of Rivera*, 21 I&N Dec. 599 (BIA 1988).

ever, there are cases in which the circuit courts have found that an applicant effectively met the requirements for demonstrating ineffective assistance even when he or she did not meet one or more of the strict *Lozada* requirements.[50] In most of these cases, the courts found that ineffective assistance was clear by the fact that the prior counsel acknowledged his or her mistake or because the record clearly demonstrated clear legal errors by prior counsel.

Substantive Requirements of *Lozada*

The substantive requirements of a Lozada claim generally involve showing (1) fundamental unfairness, and (2) prejudice.

The standard for fundamental unfairness is fairly easy to meet, given that ineffective assistance of counsel constitutes a due process violation under the Fifth Amendment, a principle that has been accepted in most circuits. The courts have found ineffective assistance in a variety of cases, aside from simply failing to file timely briefs and applications.[51]

Similarly, the standard for prejudice used by many courts is also fairly low, and requires showing only that the outcome of the case *may* have been affected by the ineffective assistance of counsel.[52] Notably, the Ninth Circuit has held that prejudice

may be *presumed* in cases in which the petitioner was deprived of appellate review because of the ineffective assistance of prior counsel.[53]

A motion to reopen based on ineffective assistance of counsel not only should provide evidence showing your client's prior counsel's ineffective assistance (such as that required by *Lozada*), but should provide clear and strong evidence of your client's eligibility for relief. Evidence in support of your client's eligibility for relief is important to show the *prejudice* your client has suffered from his or her prior counsel's ineffective assistance. In addition to any necessary applications for relief, this evidence should address all the elements required for relief, such as evidence of qualifying relatives, hardship, and good moral character. It also should provide any evidence necessary to support a positive exercise of discretion.

Vacature of Convictions

Numerous courts have observed that the overturning of a conviction on which deportability was premised is an appropriate basis for reopening administrative proceedings.[54]

The BIA itself has found that a conviction that was overturned for reasons of having been illegally entered in the first place will be recognized as no longer having immigration consequences.[55] How-

---

[50] *See e.g., Fadiga v. Att'y Gen.*, 488 F.3d 142, 157 (3d Cir. 2007); *Lo v. Ashcroft*, 341 F.3d 934, 938 (9th Cir. 2003); *Escobar-Grijalva v. INS*, 206 F.3d 1331, 1335, *as amended by* 213 F.3d 1221 (9th Cir.2000); *Castillo-Perez v. INS*, 212 F.3d 518, 526 (9th Cir. 2000); *Esposito v. INS*, 987 F.2d 108, 111 (2d Cir. 1993); *Figeroa v. INS*, 886 F.2d 76, 79 (4th Cir. 1989).

[51] *See, e.g., Grigoryan v. Gonzales*, No. 05-77020 (9th Cir. Feb. 5, 2008) (prior counsel filed boilerplate brief); *Sanchez v. Keisler*, 505 F.3d 641, 648 (7th Cir. 2007) (prior counsel inexplicably abandoned claim for relief); *Fadiga v. Att'y Gen.*, 488 F.3d 142, 163 (3d Cir. 2007) (prior counsel failed to ensure evidentiary consistency and witnesses); *Mai v. Gonzales*, 473 F.3d 162, 167 (5th Cir. 2006) (prior counsel admitted, despite petitioner's denials, false claim to citizenship charge).

It is important to note that, when reviewing evidence in a motion to reopen, the BIA may not make independent credibility determinations. *See Bhasin v. Gonzales*, 423 F.3d 977, 986–87 (9th Cir.2005) ("We have long held that credibility determinations on motions to reopen are inappropriate.").

[52] *See, e.g., Fadiga v. Att'y Gen.*, *supra* note 51, at 159 (3d Cir. 2007) (prejudice requires showing "reasonable likelihood that the result would have been different if the error[s] ... had not occurred"); *Maravilla Maravilla v. Ashcroft*, 381 F.3d 855, 858 (9th Cir. 2004) ("Petitioners must demonstrate that counsel's performance was so inadequate that it 'may have affected the outcome of the proceedings.'").

[53] *See Grigoryan v. Gonzales*, *supra* note 51 (and Ninth Circuit case law cited therein).

[54] *See e.g., De Faria v. INS*, 13 F.3d 422, 423 (1st Cir. 1994); *Johnson v. Ashcroft*, 378 F.3d 164, 171 (2d Cir. 2004); *Escobar v. INS*, 935 F.2d 650, 652 (4th Cir. 1991) (noting that legacy INS had requested BIA to "reopen and terminate" deportation proceedings following expungement of conviction); *Cardoso-Tlaseca v. Gonzales*, 460 F.3d 1102, 1107 (9th Cir. 2006) (requiring reopening where vacate of conviction changed eligibility for relief, even if underlying removability not fully eliminated); *Wiedersperg v. INS*, 896 F.2d 1179, 1182–83 (9th Cir. 1990) (abuse of discretion to deny reopening where conviction establishing deportability was vacated on its merits); *Becerra-Jimenez v. INS*, 829 F.2d 996, 1000–02 (10th Cir. 1987) (due to expungement of convictions, court remands for agency consideration of motion to reopen); *Haghi v. Russell*, 744 F. Supp. 249, 251–52 (D. Col. 1990) (vacation of conviction is "new and material evidence" within 8 CFR §1003.2).

[55] *See, e.g., Matter of Adamiak*, 23 I&N Dec. 878, 879 (BIA 2006); *Matter of Rodriguez-Ruiz*, 22 I&N Dec. 1378 (BIA 2000). Cf. *Matter of Song*, 23 I&N Dec. 173 (BIA 2001) (finding that the modification of a sentence for theft to less than one year meant that the conviction no longer constituted an aggravated felony); *Matter of Cota-Vargas*, 23 I&N Dec. 849 (BIA 2005) (holding that a trial court's decision to mod-
continued

ever, a conviction vacated for other reasons (such as rehabilitation or other equity, or to avoid immigration consequences) will continue to have the same immigration consequences. In *Matter of Pickering,*[56] the BIA held that a criminal conviction that was vacated for reasons *solely* related to rehabilitation or immigration hardships would continue to operate as a "conviction" within the meaning of INA §101(a)(48)(A). The BIA concluded in *Pickering* that "there is a significant distinction between convictions vacated on the basis of a procedural or substantive defect in the underlying proceedings and those vacated because of post-conviction events, such as rehabilitation or immigration hardships."[57]

The circuit courts have applied this same analysis in looking at the specific nature of the vacatur when considering whether a conviction continues to have immigration consequences.[58]

It is very likely that the BIA and the circuit courts would apply this same rule to motions to reopen based on vacated convictions. The Ninth Circuit, for example, has found that a "technical" expungement does not carry the same significance as a legal vacate when a respondent tries to reopen a deportation order based on that conviction. In *Hernandez-Almanza v. DOJ,*[59] the Ninth Circuit affirmed a BIA decision refusing to reopen deportation proceedings for an alien who had his state court conviction vacated because he had returned to the

United States illegally and successfully attacked his state court conviction only after new deportation proceedings had begun against him. The Ninth Circuit distinguished *Hernandez-Almanza* in two subsequent cases, *Estrada-Rosales v. INS*[60] and *Wiedersperg v. INS.*[61] Among other things, the court emphasized in each of those subsequent cases that the vacature of the conviction went to the merits and the conviction was the sole ground for the petitioner's deportation. It therefore found that the motion to reopen should have been granted.

There is a conflict between the BIA and circuit courts regarding which party bears the burden of proving *why* a conviction has been vacated in the context of a motion to reopen. In *Matter of Chavez-Martinez,*[62] the BIA held that burden of proof is on the respondent to show that his conviction has been vacated on procedural or substantive grounds.[63] In contrast, the Ninth Circuit has held that once a noncitizen provides evidence of a vacature, the Department of Homeland Security (DHS) bears the burden of showing that the noncitizen's conviction remains valid for immigration purposes.[64]

Although we are not aware of any case law explicitly to have held so in this context, motions to reopen based on elimination of the factual predicate for the deportation order should be granted without regard to the time and numerical limitations of the statute and regulations. The reason is grounded in due process: it is basically unfair to uphold a deportation or removal order that is based on a criminal conviction that has been rendered invalid. If the conviction on which the removal order was based was invalid, then due process requires that the removal order be invalid as well. Because such a situation invokes constitutional (*i.e.,* due process) concerns, neither statutory nor regulatory requirements could override the underlying constitutional issue.

ify or reduce an alien's criminal sentence nunc pro tunc is entitled to full faith and credit by the immigration judge and the BIA, and such a modified or reduced sentence is recognized as valid for purposes of the immigration law without regard to the trial court's reasons for effecting the modification or reduction).

[56] 23 I&N Dec. 621 (BIA 2003), *rev'd on other grounds by Pickering v. Gonzales*, 465 F.3d 263 (6th Cir. 2006).

[57] *Id.* at 624. *See also Matter of Roldan*, 22 I&N Dec. 512 (BIA 1999) (finding that vacature of a conviction pursuant to a state rehabilitative statute did not eliminate the immigration consequences); *Pickering v. Gonzales*, 465 F.3d 263, 269 (6th Cir. 2006) (finding the BIA had failed to require the government to show that the conviction remains valid for immigration purposes).

[58] *See, e.g., Herrera-Inirio v. INS*, 208 F.3d 299, 306 (1st Cir. 2000); *U.S. v. Campbell*, 167 F.3d 94, 98 (2d Cir. 1999); *Zaitona v. INS*, 9 F.3d 432, 436–37 (6th Cir. 1993); *Beltran-Leon v. INS*, 134 F.3d 1379, 1380–81 (9th Cir. 1998). *But cf. Renteria-Gonzales v. INS*, 310 F.3d 825 (5th Cir. 2002) (finding no reason to distinguish between reasons for vacature and upholding original conviction).

[59] 547 F.2d 100 (9th Cir. 1976).

[60] 645 F.2d 819 (9th Cir. 1981).

[61] 896 F.2d 1179 (9th Cir. 1990).

[62] 24 I&N Dec. 272, 273 (BIA 2007).

[63] *See also Rumierz v. Gonzales*, 456 F.3d 31, 40–41 (1st Cir. 2006) (holding that the alien bears the burden of proving that a conviction was not vacated solely for immigration reasons).

[64] *See Nath v. Gonzales*, 467 F.3d 1185, 1188–89 (9th Cir. 2006); *Cardoso-Tlaseca v. Gonzales*, 460 F.3d 1102, 1107 (9th Cir. 2006); *Pickering v. Gonzales*, 465 F.3d 263, 269 (6th Cir. 2006).

Marriage During Proceedings

Until recent BIA precedent changed the law, if an individual in deportation or removal proceedings were to enter into a marriage and the marriage could be the basis for an application for adjustment of status, a motion to reopen could not be filed until the relevant immediate relative visa petition was *approved*.[65]

However, in *Matter of Velarde*,[66] the BIA modified this position to allow for motions to reopen when (1) the application for adjustment of status and the visa petition are timely filed within 90 days of the final order, (2) the motion is not numerically barred or barred by *Matter of Shaar*,[67] or on any other procedural grounds, and (3) the motion presents clear and convincing evidence that the marriage is bona fide.[68]

The BIA suggested that a *Velarde* motion would generally be granted if DHS does not oppose the motion or bases its opposition solely on the prior case law.[69]

---

[65] *See Matter of Arthur*, 20 I&N Dec. 475 (BIA 2002).

[66] 23 I&N Dec. 253 (BIA 2002).

[67] 21 I&N Dec. 541 (BIA 1996). In *Matter of Shaar*, the BIA held that INA §240B(d) (1994) barred reopening of deportation orders for certain forms of relief, including adjustment of status, if the applicant had failed to timely depart the United States pursuant to a grant of voluntary departure. *See infra* for a more detailed discussion of *Shaar*.

[68] *See also Ilic-Lee v. Mukasey*, 507 F.3d 1044, 1051 (6th Cir. 2007) (upholding BIA's denial of motion to reopen based on pending adjustment application because, "[w]hile at best, the evidence might demonstrate a legal marriage, it does not suggest a bona fide marriage …"); *Palma-Mazariegos v. Keisler*, 504 F.3d 144, 147 (1st Cir. 2007) (upholding denial because adjustment application was not attached to the motion to reopen).

[69] *See, e.g., Matter of Garcia*, 16 I&N Dec. at 653 (stating that the BIA "shall hereafter generally reopen the deportation proceedings in such cases unless clear ineligibility is apparent in the record"); *Melnitsenko v. Mukasey*, No. 06-3189-ag (L), 07-0110-ag (Con). (2d Cir. 2008) (finding that the BIA abused its discretion by denying a motion based solely on DHS opposition); *Kalilu v. Mukasey*, No. 06-75425 (9th Cir. Feb. 14, 2008) (finding that the BIA abused its discretion in denying a motion to reopen based on a pending I-130); *Sarr v. Gonzales*, 485 F.3d 354, 363 (6th Cir. 2007) (holding that DHS opposition alone was not a sufficient basis to deny a motion to reopen); *Bull v. INS*, 790 F.2d 869 (11th Cir. 1986) (finding abuse of discretion to deny continuance based on pending visa petition).

For more about the eligibility of arriving aliens to adjust status based on marriage, *see* American Immigration Law Foundation
continued

MOTIONS TO RESCIND

Motions to rescind are a special kind of motion to reopen. They call for the reopening of a removal order on the ground that the order was unlawfully executed. They have their own specific filing deadlines and provide a mandatory stay of removal. The BIA has stated that whereas a motion to reopen permits you to raise new facts for consideration or for relief in regard to a prior order, motions to rescind eliminate the prior order of removal completely and return the respondent to the status he or she held prior to the removal proceedings.[70] The regulations for motions to rescind for the BIA, at 8 CFR §1003.2(c), refer to the regulations for motions to rescind before the immigration judge, at 8 CFR §1003.23(b)(4)(ii).

The jurisdictional rules for motions to rescind are different depending on whether the proceedings are for deportation, exclusion, or removal. Motions to rescind in removal proceedings are not subject to the 90-day time limitations for filing a motion to reopen.[71] Motions to rescind in deportation or exclusion proceedings are not subject to the 90-day time limitations *or* the numerical limitations for motions to reopen.[72]

A motion to rescind requires showing one of the following: (1) the failure to appear was caused by "exceptional circumstances" as defined by INA §240(e)(1); (2) a failure to receive notice in accordance with INA §§239(a)(1) or (2); or (3) that the alien was in federal or state custody and the failure to appear was through no fault of the alien.[73]

Exceptional circumstances warranting a motion to reopen are defined at INA §240(e). For cases initiated before June 13, 1992, the standard for reopening is "reasonable cause," rather than "exceptional circumstances."[74] The BIA has interpreted what does and does not constitute exceptional circumstances in

---

(AILF) Practice Advisory, M. Kenney, "Adjustment of Status of 'Arriving Aliens' Under the Interim Regulations: Challenging the BIA's Denial of a Motion to Reopen, Remand, or Continue a Case" (Apr. 16, 2007), *available at www.ailf.org/lac/pa/lac_pa_070416_biaarraliens.pdf*.

[70] *See Matter of M–S–*, 22 I&N Dec. 349 (BIA 1998).

[71] *See* 8 CFR §1003.2(c)(3).

[72] *Id.*

[73] *See* INA §240(b)(5); 8 CFR §§1003.23(b)(4)(ii), (iii).

[74] *See* INA §242(b) (1982); *Matter of Ruiz*, 20 I&N Dec. 91 (BIA 1989).

several cases.[75] Notably, domestic violence is now recognized as an "exceptional circumstance" warranting reopening of an *in absentia* order.[76] In the U.S. Court of Appeals for the Third Circuit, the timely filing of a motion to reopen also may constitute an exceptional circumstance.[77]

Proper notice is defined at INA §239(a).[78] The case law distinguishes between the service of the charging documents, to which a presumption of proper delivery may not be applied, and the service of hearing notices, for which a presumption of proper delivery may apply.[79] In addition, although there was a presumption of effective delivery for hearing notices, which were required to be sent by certified mail prior to 1997, circuit courts have not upheld that presumption after the changes made by the Illegal Immigration Reform and Immigrant Responsibility Act of 1996,[80] which allow service by regular mail.[81]

Thus, in such cases, the applicant must provide detailed statements and evidence in support of reasonable cause, and show attempts to notify the court in advance or immediately afterwards. It is also helps to show prior diligence in attending hearings,

eligibility for relief, and that the noncitizen had no reason to miss the hearing.[82]

There may be circumstances in which you have a choice between filing a motion to rescind (because your client was issued an *in absentia* removal order) and a motion to reopen (because there was a due process violation or your client recently has become eligible for a form of relief). In such cases, the question of which type of motion is preferable to file may arise. Notably, in *Matter of M–S–*,[83] the BIA held that a respondent could file a motion to reopen an *in absentia* removal order without filing a motion to rescind. In *M–S–*, the BIA held that a motion to reopen and a motion to rescind were distinct motions and that an *in absentia* order could be reopened pursuant to a motion to reopen, without requiring the applicant to rescind the prior removal order first, if the alien was not contesting the finding of deportability but was instead applying for a form of relief that had not been previously considered. It also held that the respondent, because she had not been given proper notice of failing to appear, was not subject to the limitations on discretionary relief under INA §242B(c)(3) [1994]. The BIA stated that the immigration judge could consider why she failed to appear at her prior hearing in the exercise of discretion.

Thus, if circumstances would allow a client to choose between these two motions, clients and their counsel should be aware of the following differences in the motions, some of which are noted in *Matter of M–S–*:

(1) a motion to reopen an *in absentia* order cannot be used to challenge the finding of deportability or removability, but only to present an application for relief

(2) an automatic stay will follow from filing a motion to rescind but not a motion to reopen

(3) the standards for showing exceptional circumstances or lack of notice for a motion to rescind may or may not be more difficult than showing lack of notice of consequences for failing to appear, depending on the particular facts

(4) eligibility for a given form of relief may depend on whether the individual had been properly notified of the consequences of failing to appear at the hearing, including the loss of eligibility for

---

[75] *See e.g.*, AILF Practice Advisory, B. Werlin, "Rescinding an In Absentia Order of Removal," (amended Sept. 21, 2004), *available at* www.ailf.org/lac/pa/lac_pa_092 104.pdf; B. Jobe, "Strategies for Reopening In Absentia Deportation Proceedings and Mitigating the Effects of the Time and Numerical Limitations on Motions to Reopen," *11th Annual AILA California Chapters Conference Handbook* 121 (1998).

[76] *See* INA §240(e)(1) (stating that these circumstances must be "beyond the control of the alien").

[77] *See Barrios v. Att'y Gen.*, 399 F.3d 272 (3d Cir. 2005).

[78] *See also Matter of G–Y–R–*, 23 I&N Dec. 181 (BIA 2001) (en banc) (holding that the notice to appear must be properly served before the address obligations of INA §239(a)(1)(F) and the possible penalty of an in absentia order attach).

[79] *See e.g.*, *Matter of Grivalja*, 21 I&N Dec. 27, 37 (BIA 1995); *Chaidez v. Gonzales*, 486 F.3d 1079, 1085 (9th Cir. 2007), *Adeyemo v. Ashcroft*, 383 F.3d 558 (7th Cir. 2004); *Fuentes-Argueta v. INS*, 101 F.3d 867 (2d Cir. 1996).

[80] Pub. L. No. 104-208, div. C, 110 Stat. 3009, 3009-546 to 3009-724.

[81] *See, e.g.*, *Kozak v. Gonzales*, 502 F.3d 34, 36 (1st Cir. 2007); *Gonzalez v. Att'y Gen.*, 506 F.3d 274, 279 (3d Cir. 2007); *Lopes v. Gonzales*, 468 F.3d 81, 84 (2d Cir. 2006); *Nibagwire v. Gonzales*, 450 F.3d 153, 157 (4th Cir. 2006); *Ghounem v. Ashcroft*, 378 F.3d 740, 744–45 (8th Cir. 2004); *Salta v. INS*, 314 F.3d 1076, 1079 (9th Cir. 2002). *But see Gurung v. Ashcroft*, 371 F.3d 718, 722 (10th Cir. 2004) (finding that the prior presumptions continued to apply).

[82] *See, e.g.*, *Terezov v. Gonzales*, 480 F.3d 558, 563 (7th Cir. 2007); *Sembiring v. Gonzales*, 499 F.3d 981, 991 (9th Cir. 2007); *Joshi v. Ashcroft*, 389 F.3d 732, 735 (7th Cir. 2004).

[83] 22 I&N Dec. 349 (BIA 1998) (en banc).

certain forms of relief (as specified under INA §240(b)(7) or the applicable statute in force at that time)

GENERAL STRATEGY AND CONSIDERATIONS

Exceptions to the Strict Jurisdictional Bars

Equitable Tolling of Time or Numerical Limitations

Each motion has specific numerical and time bars. However, there are several situations in which exceptions to these bars will apply.

Some circuit courts have recognized equity-based exceptions to the strict regulatory and statutory time and numerical restrictions on motions to reopen.[84]

Where equitable tolling has been permitted, a noncitizen has to provide evidence demonstrating the reasons for the untimely filing, and show due diligence in filing once he or she has become aware of the reasons preventing him or her from filing. These inquiries are very fact-intensive, and thus should be investigated and demonstrated carefully by counsel.

Motions to Supplement a Pending Motion

The numerical limit to motions to reopen often can be as problematic as the time limit. For example, if one motion to reopen is pending, and another issue that also would be the proper subject of a motion to reopen arises, it is not clear how to style the second filing in order to properly raise the new issue.

If a motion to reopen is already pending, then it may be preferable to file a motion to supplement the earlier motion. In *Wang v. Ashcroft*,[85] the U.S. Court of Appeals for the Fifth Circuit found it "plausible" that a second motion to reopen was in fact a supplement to a prior motion to reopen, and that therefore the second motion might not be barred numerically.[86]

Joint Motions with DHS

If your client is barred on other grounds, it may be possible to file a joint motion before the BIA with the cooperation of DHS, which bypasses the need to meet any filing requirements.[87] However, do not wait for DHS to agree to a joint motion to reopen if it means passing the 90-day deadline.[88]

Requesting Sua Sponte Reopening

In extraordinary cases the BIA may exercise its sua sponte powers to reopen a case.[89]

The BIA has specified that the sua sponte authority is not intended to provide an exception allowing reopening in cases otherwise jurisdictionally barred.[90] For this reason, counsel will want to explain in the motion why sua sponte reopening is particularly warranted in that case.

---

motion to remand as something other than a barred second motion to reopen, such as a motion to supplement).

[87] *See* 8 CFR §1003.2(c)(3)(iii); *see also* INS Memorandum , D. Martin, HQ COU 90/16.11-P (Dec. 23, 1997), *reprinted in* 75 *Interpreter Releases* 259, 275 (Feb. 23, 1998) (laying out factors that would lead the government to consent to reopening the case); INS Memorandum, B. Cooper, HQCOU 90/16.22.1 (May 17, 2001), *reprinted in* 78 *Interpreter Releases* 1166, 1181–84 (July 16, 2001) (same).

[88] *See Valeriano v. Gonzales*, 474 F.3d 669, 673–74 (9th Cir. 2007) (finding that equitable tolling was not merited when prior counsel waited for response to request for joint motion and thereby missed the 90-day deadline).

[89] *See* 8 CFR §1003.2(a); *see also, e.g., Matter of X–G–W–*, 22 I&N Dec. 71, 72 (BIA 1998) (finding that a significant change in the immigration law made relief available to the applicant on the basis of the same asylum application he filed initially, and he had filed his motion promptly following the new developments). *Cf. Matter of G–C–L–*, 23 I&N Dec. 359 (BIA 2002); *Matter of G–D–* 22 I&N Dec. 1132, 1136 (BIA 1999) (en banc) (finding that the BIA's decision in *Matter of O–Z– & I–Z–*, 22 I&N Dec. 23 (BIA 1998), constituted an "incremental" change in the law, which did not warrant reconsideration of the case); *Matter of J–J–*, 21 I&N Dec. 976, 984 (BIA 1997).

For example, currently, given that over 90 days have passed since the Supreme Court's decision in *Lopez v. Gonzales*, 127 S.Ct. 625 (2006), a motion for sua sponte reopening on that basis would presumably be the only means to reopen your client's case. *See* New York State Defender's Association, Immigration Defense Project, Practice Advisory: Removal Defense of Immigrants in Drug Possession Cases—The Impact of *Lopez v. Gonzales* (Apr. 12, 2007), *available at* www.nysda.org/idp/docs/07_PostLopez AdvisoryforRemovalDefense41207.pdf.

[90] *Matter of J–J–, supra* note 89.

---

[84] *See, e.g., Jobe v. INS*, 238 F.3d 96, 100–01 (1st Cir. 2001); *Iavorski v. INS*, 232 F.3d 124, 129–35 (2d Cir. 2000); *Borges v. Gonzales*, 402 F.3d 398, 406 (3d Cir. 2005); *Scorteanu v. INS*, 339 F.3d 407, 413 (6th Cir. 2003); *Iturribaria v. INS*, 321 F.3d 889, 897 (9th Cir. 2003). *But cf. Mejia-Rodriguez v. Reno*, 178 F.3d 1139 (11th Cir. 1999) (upholding 90-day limitation as not raising a constitutional concern). *See* the discussion *supra* regarding ineffective assistance of counsel.

[85] 260 F.3d 448, 452 (5th Cir. 2001).

[86] *See also Guzman v. INS*, 318 F.3d 911, 913 (9th Cir. 2003) (holding that it was within the discretion of the BIA to treat a
continued

Of course, counsel will have to bring a case warranting reopening to the BIA's attention by filing a request to the BIA to exercise its sua sponte authority to reopen a case. We recommend that such a request be made as an additional basis to reopen in any case in which an exception to the jurisdictional requirements is being requested.

Obtaining Review After Your Client Has Been Removed from the United States

The need to file a motion to reopen *after* your client has departed the United States can present a particularly difficult problem. Generally, such motions are barred under 8 CFR §1003.2(d). If your client has re-entered the United States illegally, the problem can be compounded. However, there may be grounds for arguing that the prior deportation order was unlawful and therefore the case must be reopened, and there may even be case law to support such an argument.

Recently, the U.S. Courts of Appeal for the Fourth, Ninth, and Eleventh Circuits have found that the regulations at 8 CFR §003.2(d) do not apply to a noncitizen who files a motion to reopen after he or she has left the United States, or before proceedings have begun against him or her, and therefore is not the subject of proceedings at the time of departure. In *William v. Gonzales*,[91] the Fourth Circuit held that the postdeparture bar contained in 8 CFR §1003.2(d) is invalid on the grounds that it conflicts with the statutory language of INA §240(c)(7)(A) [8 USC §1229a(c)(7)(A)]. It therefore allowed for a motion to reopen to be filed from outside of the United States after a final order had been executed. In *Lin v. Gonzales*,[92] the Ninth Circuit found that a noncitizen could file a motion to reopen before the immigration judge after he left the United States and executed his removal order.[93] Finally, in *Contreras-Rodriguez v. Att'y Gen.*,[94] the Eleventh Circuit held that the postdeparture bar does not apply to a motion to reopen

and rescind an *in absentia* removal order based on lack of proper notice.[95]

In addition, under Ninth Circuit and BIA case law, a motion to reopen prior deportation proceedings may be filed after a noncitizen has re-entered the United States after being deported if the applicant was deported pursuant to an unlawful order. Either a due process violation or gross miscarriage of justice has been found to render the prior deportation order unlawful.[96]

Notably, in *Cardoso-Tlaseca v. Gonzales*,[97] the Ninth Circuit granted reopening based on a vacated conviction, even though the petitioner remained removable for another conviction. Specifically, in that case, the conviction that was vacated rendered the petitioner both deportable and ineligible for a waiver. Once the conviction was vacated, the petitioner remained deportable but was now eligible for relief. The court rejected the argument that the vacated state court conviction must be the "the sole

---

[91] 499 F.3d 329 (4th Cir. 2007).

[92] 473 F.3d 979 (9th Cir. 2007).

[93] *See also Reynoso-Cisneros v. Gonzales*, 491 F.3d 1001, 1002 (9th Cir. 2007) (extending the holding of *Lin* to motions to reopen filed with the BIA under 8 CFR §1003.2(d)); *Singh v. Gonzales*, 412 F.3d 1117, 1121 (9th Cir. 2005) (holding that the petitioner was not barred from filing a motion to reopen because he had departed the United States before proceedings had been commenced against him).

[94] 462 F.3d 1314, 1317 (11th Cir. 2006).

[95] *But see Navarro-Miranda v. Ashcroft*, 330 F.3d 672 (5th Cir. 2003) (upholding the BIA's finding that it did not have jurisdiction to reopen, even sua sponte, the case when it was filed after the petitioner left the United States).

[96] *See, e.g., Cardoso-Tlaseca v. Gonzales*, 460 F.3d 1102, 1107 (9th Cir. 2006) (due process violation); *Matter of Farinas*, 12 I&N Dec. 467 (BIA 1967) (gross miscarriage of justice); *Matter of Malone*, 11 I&N Dec. 730 (BIA 1966) (gross miscarriage of justice); *Hernandez-Almanza v. DOJ*, 547 F.2d 100 (9th Cir. 1976) (gross miscarriage of justice); *Mendez v. INS*, 563 F.2d 956 (9th Cir. 1977) (due process violation); *Estrada-Rosales v. INS*, 645 F.2d 819 (9th Cir. 1981) (due process violation); *Wiedersperg v. INS*, 896 F.2d 1179 (9th Cir. 1990) (due process violation).

However, although this may provide a jurisdictional argument as to why the case should be reopened, difficult issues may remain about how to address any subsequent unlawful entries into the United States. *See, e.g., Hernandez-Almanza, supra.*

If your client was a lawful permanent resident prior to his or her removal, then reopening or reconsidering his or her case may allow you to argue that your client should be restored to the status your client held before his or her unlawful order, and that the subsequent entry would have been authorized. However, your client's presence in the United States could subject him or her to reinstatement of removal under INA §241(a)(5), expedited removal under INA §235, or administrative removal under INA §238(b), or a new removal proceeding under INA §240. Each of these presents its own complications, but would also potentially present a venue in which to challenge the prior removal (or in which to appeal based on the invalidity of the prior removal). These concerns are beyond the scope of this article, but should be seriously considered when planning a legal strategy.

[97] 460 F.3d 1102, 1107 (9th Cir. 2006).

ground of deportability," and instead held that reopening was warranted where the conviction was a "key part" of the deportation proceeding. The decision does not indicate whether or not the petitioner had returned illegally to the United States after his removal, although it appears he did not.

Effect on Your Client's Eligibility for a Stay of Removal

Each motion may have different practical effects on your client's eligibility to have his or her removal stayed while the motion is pending. A motion to rescind or a motion to reopen based on domestic violence may automatically stay your client's deportation and permit your client to litigate the merits of his or her hearing.[98] A motion to rescind an *in absentia* deportation order will invoke an automatic stay of deportation while the case is pending before the immigration court and the BIA. A similar motion to rescind an *in absentia removal* order, however, will invoke an automatic stay only until the immigration judge adjudicates the motion, but not while any appeal is pending before the BIA.[99]

General motions to reopen or reconsider will *not* mandate an automatic stay of removal.[100] Instead, in such cases, a separate motion for a stay, with supporting documentation, should be filed before the BIA. In some cases, deportation officers will respect these motions, and on proof of filing, informally delay your client's removal. However, if your client's removal is imminent, then you may ask the BIA to expedite the adjudication of your motion for a stay.[101]

Tolling the Voluntary Departure Period

An additional issue arises if your client has been granted voluntary departure but also would like to file a motion to reopen or reconsider. The U.S. Supreme Court is currently considering whether the filing of a motion to reopen removal proceedings automatically tolls the period within which an alien must depart the United States under an order granting voluntary departure.[102] The Supreme Court also appears to be considering whether a noncitizen who has been granted voluntary departure and has filed a

timely motion to reopen should be permitted to withdraw the request for voluntary departure prior to the expiration of the departure period. In addition, DHS has submitted proposed regulations that would terminate a grant of voluntary departure if the respondent files a motion to reopen prior to the expiration of the voluntary departure.[103] Thus, the law on this topic may change in the very near future.

In *Matter of Shaar*, the BIA held that filing a motion to reopen *deportation* proceedings does not stop the voluntary departure period from running.[104] Under INA §240B(d) (1994), any person who was granted voluntary departure but fails to timely depart faces certain civil penalties. These penalties include being barred for 10 years from being granted cancellation of removal, adjustment of status, change of status, registry, and voluntary departure.

However, in some circumstances, facts or legal arguments that may warrant filing a motion to reopen or reconsider arise after voluntary departure has been granted. Often in these cases, the new facts rendered the noncitizen eligible for a form of relief from which the noncitizen would be barred if he or she overstayed the voluntary departure period. However, because the BIA rarely adjudicates the motions within the brief voluntary departure period, those persons would be faced with a difficult decision under *Shaar*: whether to voluntarily depart in a timely manner (and not be subject to the bar, but thereby abandon the motion to reopen) or to litigate the motion to reopen only to be barred from the very relief for which they otherwise would be eligible.[105]

Four courts have found that the filing of a motion automatically tolls the voluntary departure period.[106] In these circuits, it then becomes crucial to file the motion to reopen (with the stay request, if needed) as soon as possible so as to preserve as much of the

---

[98] *See* 8 CFR §1003.3(f); INA §240(c)(7)(C)(iv).

[99] *Compare* 8 CFR §1003.23(b)(4)(ii) *with* 8 CFR §1003.23(b)(4)(iii)(C).

[100] *See* 8 CFR §1003.3(f).

[101] *See* BIA Practice Manual, ch. 6.

[102] *See Dada v. Keisler*, cert. granted, 2007 U.S. LEXIS 9061 (No. 06-1181, U.S. Sept. 25, 2007).

[103] *See* 72 Fed. Reg. 67674 (Nov. 30, 2007).

[104] 21 I&N Dec. 541 (BIA 1996), *aff'd*, 141 F.3d 953 (9th Cir. 1998) (upholding *Shaar* for pre-IIRAIRA cases).

[105] In such cases, persons with final orders of deportation would be in a better position than those granted voluntary departure, since overstaying their removal order did not subject them to the same bars to relief under INA §240B(d) (1994). Counsel should therefore strongly consider not requesting voluntary departure before the immigration court under some circumstances.

[106] *See Ugokwe v. Att'y Gen.*, 453 F.3d 1325, 1331 (11th Cir. 2006); *Kanivets v. Gonzales*, 424 F.3d 330, 335 (3d Cir. 2005); *Sidikhouya v. Gonzales*, 407 F.3d 950, 952 (8th Cir. 2005); *Azarte v. Ashcroft*, 394 F.3d 1278, 1289 (9th Cir. 2005).

voluntary departure period as possible.[107] Three courts have concluded otherwise.[108]

New Criminal Issues

A requirement for filing motions is that the party state whether any new criminal proceedings have commenced against the client since the last action by the BIA.[109] Thus, in some cases, it may be in your client's interest to postpone the filing of the motion until new criminal charges have been dismissed or otherwise concluded. The government can file a motion to reopen based on new charges for removal.[110]

Use of Motions to Reopen by the Government

The regulations make clear that the government may also file motions to reopen. Importantly, the government may move to reopen, without any limitations, deportation or exclusion cases in which it has discovered fraud in the underlying proceedings, or if it believes that your client has committed a crime that would support termination of asylum.[111] Notably, the government does *not* have to file a motion to reopen to terminate a deferral of removal that has been granted under CAT.[112]

The government has also used motions to reopen to lodge new charges of deportability. Pursuant to 8 CFR §1240.10(e), DHS "may at any time during a hearing lodge additional charges of deportability, including factual allegations, against the respondent." This regulation has been held to be applicable to reopened proceedings.[113]

However, the government is subject to the same substantive requirements for motions to reopen. For example, in *Ivanov v. Gonzales*,[114] the U.S. Court of Appeals for the Eighth Circuit held that "no part of the regulation exempts DHS from the requirement that a party seeking to reopen proceedings must show that the evidence it offers 'was not available and could not have been discovered or presented at the former hearing.'"[115]

Scope of Review on Remand/Reopening

If the BIA grants reopening and remand, another issue that may arise is whether new evidence or new applications, which were unavailable at the time that the motion to reopen was submitted to the BIA, may be submitted before the immigration judge.

The regulations and case law suggest that new issues may be raised at this time.

The regulations do not expressly limit the scope of the judge's jurisdiction in the case of a case remanded from the BIA.[116] Nor is this authority limited by the regulations regarding the BIA's power to remand for further factfinding.[117] Thus, at a minimum, the regulations show that the judge has jurisdiction to determine removability in "any" removal hearing, including removal hearings on remand when the BIA has not specifically retained jurisdiction.[118]

More importantly, the BIA has upheld this authority explicitly, finding that an immigration court's jurisdiction on remand is not limited unless the BIA's decision specifically limits the scope of what the immigration judge may hear. If the BIA does not do so, the court may hear a wide range of

---

[107] For more information, *see* AILF Practice Advisory, "Staying the Voluntary Departure Period When Filing a Motion to Reopen" (updated Dec. 16, 2005), *available at* www.ailf.org/lac/pa/lac_pa_121605.pdf.

[108] *See Chedad v. Gonzales*, 497 F.3d 57, 64 (1st Cir. 2007); *Dekoladenu v. Gonzales*, 459 F.3d 500, 507 (4th Cir. 2006), petition for cert. pending, No. 06-1252 (filed Mar. 22, 2007); *Banda-Ortiz v. Gonzales*, 445 F.3d 387, 391 (5th Cir. 2006).

[109] *See* 8 CFR §1003.2(e).

[110] *See infra.*

[111] *See* 8 CFR §1003.3(c)(3)(iv); *see also* 8 CFR §§208(e), (f), 1208.24(e), (f) (applying this rule to removal proceedings and to prior grants of withholding of deportation).

[112] *See* 8 CFR §§208.17(d), 1208.17(d) (requiring only that the government file a motion before the immigration court to schedule a hearing to consider whether the deferral of removal should be reconsidered).

[113] *See, e.g., De Faria v. INS*, 13 F.3d 422, 423 (1st Cir. 1994), *citing Rosenberg v. Fleuti*, 374 U.S. 449, 450 (1963).

[114] 487 F.3d 635, 639 (8th Cir. 2007).

[115] *See also Matter of Guevara*, 20 I&N Dec. 238 (BIA 1991) ("[I]n the instant case, the Service does not seek to advance additional charges of deportability, nor does it seek to advance additional factual allegations. The Service does not wish to modify its case against the respondent at all, but rather requests the opportunity to make a second effort at proving the same allegations and charge which have already been advanced unsuccessfully."); *Bravo-Pedroza v. Gonzales*, 475 F.3d 1358, 1359 (9th Cir. 2007) (finding res judicata barred initiation of a second deportation case against noncitizen on basis of the same charges, where new charges could have been brought during prior proceeding); *Ramon-Sepulveda v. INS*, 743 F.2d 1307, 1310 (9th Cir. 1984) (finding BIA abused its discretion when it granted reopening on the basis of newly discovered evidence in the form of a birth certificate, because there was no indication that the birth certificate could not have been discovered before the hearing).

[116] 8 CFR §1240.1(a)(1)(i).

[117] *See* 8 CFR §1003.2(d)(3)(iv).

[118] 8 CFR §1240.1(a)(1)(i).

matters and/or accept new evidence for any cognizable form of relief. Specifically, in *Matter of Patel*, the BIA explained that: [119]

> [W]hen the Board remands a case to an immigration judge for further proceedings, it divests itself of jurisdiction of that case unless jurisdiction is expressly retained. Further, when this is done, unless the Board qualifies or limits the remand for a specific purpose, the remand is effective for the stated purpose and for consideration of any and all matters which the Service officer deems appropriate in the exercise of his administrative discretion or which are brought to his attention in compliance with appropriate regulations.

Thus, an IJ's jurisdiction on remand is not limited unless the BIA sets forth specific limitations.

Since its decision in *Patel* in 1978, the BIA has continued to issue decisions consistent with its holding in that case. [120]

The BIA's decision in *Patel* was later interpreted by the Third Circuit in *Johnson v. Ashcroft* [121] as permitting an immigration court to assume jurisdiction over matters other than those for which the remand was initially granted, even where the BIA states the purpose for the remand. The *Johnson* court found that "if the Board did not include … qualifications or limitations, then the immigration judge could appropriately consider the stated purpose and

'any and all matters' deemed appropriate or brought under relevant regulations." [122]

CONCLUSION

Many times, a motion after the final order will be the only way to preserve your client's right to relief from removal. As is evident, the regulatory framework and case law for motions to reopen, reconsider, and rescind are constantly evolving at the BIA and in the circuit courts. Thus, when strategizing in this complicated area, it is important to review not only the current regulations but also the administrative and judicial case law (as well as other statutes when applicable) carefully.

---

[119] 16 I&N Dec. 600, 601 (BIA 1978) (emphasis added).

[120] *See, e.g., Matter of M–D–*, 24 I&N Dec. 138, 141–42 (BIA 2007) (clarifying that, when a case is remanded for background checks, "since no final order exists and a remand has traditionally been treated as effective for all purposes, the immigration judge has authority to consider additional evidence if it is material, was not previously available, and could not have been discovered or presented at the former hearing. …); *Matter of Deanda-Romo*, 23 I&N Dec. 597 (BIA 2003) (remanding for cancellation of removal, but noting in footnote that respondent might be eligible for adjustment as well); *Matter of Alcantara-Perez*, 23 I&N Dec. 882, 884 (BIA 2006) (stating that if no new issues arise when a case is remanded for background checks, the immigration judge simply should issue the order but may hold a new hearing if new issues have arisen). The BIA knows how and clearly does limit the scope of a remand if it wants to do so, which is distinct from merely stating the purpose of the remand. *Cf. Matter of Yewondwosen*, 21 I&N Dec. 1025, 1027 (BIA 1997) ("We underscore the limited scope of this decision. In view of the foregoing, the respondent's motion to remand to apply for adjustment of status will be granted.").

[121] 286 F.3d 696 (3d Cir. 2002).

[122] *Id.* at 702. *See also Verano-Velasco v. Att'y Gen.*, 456 F.3d 1372, 1373 n.1 (11th Cir. 2006) (remanding with note that, "This ruling is based upon appellant's motion to reopen, therefore, we do not reach the remaining issues on appeal. However, the effect of this reversal is that the entire case is remanded for further proceedings and reconsideration."). *But see Potdar v. Keisler*, 505 F.3d 680, 684 (7th Cir. 2007) (holding that the BIA's order reopening the case did not resurrect jurisdiction over the issues underlying the initial exclusion order).

IMMIGRATION LAWSUITS AND THE APA:
THE BASICS OF A DISTRICT COURT ACTION

by Mary A. Kenney[*]

INTRODUCTION

Suits under the Administrative Procedure Act (APA)[1] can be an effective means of challenging unlawful agency decisions or action in immigration cases outside of the removal context. This article will discuss the primary issues involved in an APA suit and provide examples of how these issues have been decided in immigration cases. It also will outline arguments that can be made in showing compliance with the various procedural requirements for an APA action.

The cases cited in this article are examples only and do not constitute the results of an exhaustive search of relevant case law in all jurisdictions. Moreover, the information in this article does not substitute for individual legal advice supplied by a lawyer familiar with a client's case.

OVERVIEW OF THE APA

The APA is a federal statute that regulates federal agency action in a number of ways. This article focuses on the provisions of the APA that allow an individual to sue the United States in federal district court for unlawful action (including the unlawful failure to act) by federal agencies or agency officials or employees. The suit must be for nonmonetary relief, such as an injunction. The relevant portions of the APA are found at 5 USC §701 *et seq.*

As discussed in this article, the APA states that a person who is suffering a legal wrong because of agency action, or who is adversely affected by agency action within the meaning of a relevant statute, is entitled to judicial review.[2] The APA creates a "cause of action." It provides an individual with a basis to sue a federal agency when Congress has not specifically provided such a basis anywhere else in the law. The APA also provides a waiver of sovereign immunity that allows a person to sue the federal government over unlawful agency action for nonmonetary damages.

The APA is *not* a jurisdictional statute—it does not give a court the initial authority to hear the case. In APA cases, jurisdiction will be based on the "federal question" statute.[3]

What Types of Immigration-Related Claims Can Be Brought Under the APA?

The APA has been used to remedy unlawful agency action in various types of immigration cases that fall outside the removal context.[4] The following are just a few examples of successful APA challenges:

- U.S. Citizenship and Immigration Services (USCIS) denial of an adjustment of status reversed where the agency erred in finding the plaintiff ineligible[5]

- Legacy Immigration and Naturalization Service (INS) denial of a religious worker visa petition reversed where it was based on the improper application of a regulation[6]

- Preliminary injunction granted where there was a reasonable question whether the Executive Office for Immigration Review's (EOIR) directives to immigration judges violated the APA[7]

---

[*] **Mary A. Kenney** is a senior attorney with the Legal Action Center of the American Immigration Law Foundation (AILF). Mary has litigated cases at the Board of Immigration Appeals and in federal courts around the country, including class actions. Prior to joining AILF, she was the executive director for the Texas Lawyers' Committee, a statewide immigrant and refugee rights project.

This article is adapted from an AILF practice advisory originally published May 9, 2007. Copyright © 2008 American Immigration Law Foundation. See *www.ailf.org/copyright* for information on reprinting this practice advisory.

[1] 5 USC §701 *et seq.*

[2] 5 USC §702.

[3] 28 USC §1331.

[4] The Immigration and Nationality Act (INA) specifies that a petition for review in a federal court of appeals is the "sole and exclusive means for judicial review" of an order of removal. INA §242(a)(5); *see also* INA §242(b)(9). Consequently, an APA action is not possible in the removal context.

[5] *Pinho v. Gonzales*, 432 F.3d 193 (3d Cir. 2005).

[6] *Camphill Soltane v. DOJ*, 381 F.3d 143 (3d Cir. 2004).

[7] *Baharona-Gomez v. Reno*, 167 F.3d 1228 (9th Cir. 1999).

- USCIS denial of specific consent to pursue special immigrant juvenile (SIJ) status in state court reversed[8]

- USCIS denial of an H-1B visa reversed where the Administrative Appeals Office (AAO) made findings that were not based on evidence in the record and ignored contrary evidence that was in the record[9]

Forum/Venue

Where Is an APA Suit Filed?

An APA suit is filed in a federal district court. Venue in suits against the federal government or a federal official acting in his or her official capacity, including APA suits, can be brought in any judicial district where (1) a defendant resides; (2) a substantial part of the events or omissions giving rise to the claim occurred; or (3) the plaintiff resides, if no real property is involved in the action.[10]

An APA suit is a civil action, and therefore the Federal Rules of Civil Procedure and the district court's local rules apply. The local rules are available on the courts' websites.

Statute of Limitations

When Can an APA Suit Be Filed?

The APA does not contain a statute of limitations. However, there is a general six-year statute of limitations for civil actions brought against the United States.[11] All courts that have considered the question of what statute of limitations applies to APA actions agree that the six-year limitations period is applicable.[12] Note, however, that there are no cases

specifically addressing this issue in the immigration context.

Jurisdiction

What Is the Jurisdictional Basis for an APA Suit?

Practice Tip: The "federal question" statute[13] is the basis for jurisdiction in an APA suit for review of agency action. The APA itself can also be listed in the jurisdictional section of a complaint. While the APA does not provide an independent grant of jurisdiction to the court, it does waive sovereign immunity in suits against the government for injunctive relief. Such a waiver is necessary for the court to exercise its jurisdiction.[14]

The APA is not an independent grant of subject matter jurisdiction to the federal courts.[15] In contrast, 28 USC §1331 provides a general grant of subject matter jurisdiction to federal district courts in civil actions over "federal questions" arising under the Constitution, laws, or treaties of the United States.

The U.S. Supreme Court has found that 28 USC §1331 serves as the jurisdictional basis for federal courts "to review agency action."[16] Courts of appeals uniformly agree that 28 USC §1331 is the jurisdictional basis for a suit to review agency action under the APA.[17] A plaintiff's erroneous reliance on the APA as the sole ground of jurisdiction, without al-

---

[8] *Young Zheng v. Pogash*, 416 F. Supp. 2d 550 (S.D. Tex. 2006).

[9] *Fred 26 Imps., Inc. v. DHS*, 445 F. Supp. 2d 1174 (C.D. Cal. 2006).

[10] 28 USC §1391(e).

[11] 28 USC §2401(a). The one exception to the six-year statute of limitations is for suits that accrue under a statute that was adopted after December 1, 1990, in which case a four-year statute of limitations is applicable. 28 USC §1658. The APA itself was enacted prior to 1990, so §1658 would not apply to it. However, it is unclear whether §1658 would apply if the APA suit challenged conduct as violating a statute that was enacted after December 1, 1990. In such cases, the safer practice would be to file within four years if possible.

[12] *See, e.g., Trafalgar Capital Assocs. v. Cuomo*, 159 F.3d 21, 34 (1st Cir. 1998); *Polanco v. DEA*, 158 F.3d 647, 656 (2d Cir. 1998); *Pennsylvania Dept. of Public Welfare v. DHHS*, 101 F.3d 939, 944–45 (3d Cir. 1996); *Jersey Heights Neighborhood Assoc. v. Glendening*, 174 F.3d 180, 186
continued

(4th Cir. 1999); *Dunn McCampbell Royalty Interest Inc. v. National Park Service*, 112 F.3d 1283, 1286 (5th Cir. 1997); *Sierra Club v. Slater*, 120 F.3d 623, 631 (6th Cir. 1997); *Sierra Club v. U.S. Army Corps of Engineers*, 446 F.3d 808, 815 (8th Cir. 2006); *Turtle Island Restoration Network v. U.S. Dept. of Commerce*, 438 F.3d 937, 942–43 (9th Cir. 2006); *Daingerfield Island Protective Society v. Babbitt*, 40 F.3d 442, 445 (D.C. Cir. 1994).

[13] 28 USC §1331.

[14] *See FDIC v. Meyer*, 510 U.S. 471 (1994) (sovereign immunity is jurisdictional in nature).

[15] *See Califano v. Sanders*, 430 U.S. 99 (1977).

[16] *Id.* at 105; *see also Bowen v. Massachusetts*, 487 U.S. 879, 891 n.16 (1988) ("[I]t is common ground that if review is proper under the APA, the District Court has jurisdiction under 28 USC §1331.").

[17] *See, e.g., Ana International Inc. v. Way*, 393 F.3d 886, 890 (9th Cir. 2004) (finding that this rule applies in the immigration context); *Yeboah v. DOJ*, 345 F.3d 216, 220 (3d Cir. 2003) (SIJ visa case); *Sabhari v. Reno*, 197 F.3d 938, 943 (8th Cir. 1999) (immigrant visa case); *Sigman Coal Co. v. Apfel*, 226 F.3d 291, 301 (4th Cir. 2000), aff'd sub. nom, *Barnhart v. Sigmon Coal Co.*, 534 U.S. 438 (2002); *Trudeau v. FTC*, 456 F.3d 178, 185 (D.C. Cir. 2006).

leging jurisdiction under 28 USC §1331, can result in dismissal of the case.[18]

Because an APA Action Is Against the Federal Government, Does the APA Include a Waiver of Sovereign Immunity?

Yes. The United States is immune from suit and can only be sued if there is a specific waiver of this immunity. The APA includes a statutory waiver of sovereign immunity for suits that seek nonmonetary relief.

The APA's waiver of sovereign immunity states:

An action in a court of the United States seeking relief other than money damages and stating a claim that an agency . . . acted or failed to act . . . shall not be dismissed nor relief therein be denied on the ground that it is against the United States or that the United States is an indispensable party. The United States may be named as a defendant in any such action, and a judgment or decree may be entered against the United States.[19]

The waiver of sovereign immunity found in the APA applies to suits that seek relief other than money damages. Generally, this would include suits for injunctive and declaratory relief.[20]

Are There Other Jurisdictional Grounds That Can or Must Be Included in an APA Complaint?

Whether there are other jurisdictional grounds to include in the complaint will depend on the nature of the lawsuit and the claims that are raised. It is best to include all potential grounds of jurisdiction.

Practice Tip: If you are raising a claim directly under the Constitution, include the Constitution as a basis for jurisdiction. Similarly, if you are raising a claim directly under an immigration statute, include that statute as a basis for jurisdiction.[21] If you have a claim for mandamus, include the federal mandamus statute as a basis for jurisdiction in the complaint.[22] In contrast, the Declaratory Judgment Act[23] is a procedural statute that does not confer jurisdiction.[24] As such, the Declaratory Judgment Act provides for relief rather than for jurisdiction. The jurisdictional basis for relief under the Declaratory Judgment Act to be pled in the complaint is 28 USC §1331.

Cause of Action

What Does It Mean for the APA To Provide a Cause of Action?

The courts have made clear that, while the APA is not a basis for federal jurisdiction, 5 USC §704 provides a "cause of action" for parties who have been adversely affected by agency action.[25] Section

[18] *See, e.g., Figgens v. USCIS,* No. 1:05-CV-107 TS, 2006 U.S. Dist. LEXIS 28734 (N.D. Ut. May 8, 2006) (case dismissed where viable ground of jurisdiction was not pled along with the APA). In *Figgens*, the plaintiffs erroneously relied on INA §279 for jurisdiction. That statute was amended in 1996 such that it now provides a district court with jurisdiction only over actions *brought by the United States*. It does *not* provide jurisdiction for cases *against the United States*. At the same time, however, it also does not bar jurisdiction based on some other ground in suits *against* the United States. *See Sabhari v. Reno,* 197 F.3d 938, 942 (8th Cir. 1999).

[19] 5 USC §702.

[20] *See, e.g., Trudeau v. FTC,* 456 F.3d 178, 186 (D.C. Cir. 2006); *Sabhari v. Reno,* 197 F.3d 938, 943 (8th Cir. 1999) (challenge to the denial of an immigrant visa petition); *Shah v. Chertoff,* No. 3:05-CV-1608-BH (K) ECF, 2006 U.S. Dist. LEXIS 73754, at *5–6 (N.D. Tex. 2006) (government motion to dismiss denied in challenge to denial of an L-1A visa extension). The APA's waiver of sovereign immunity applies to agency action or inaction, including action or inaction by an agency officer or employee. Several courts have held that this waiver can apply in suits against unlawful agency action even if the suit is not brought under the APA. *Trudeau, supra,* at 186; *Presbyterian Church v. U.S.,* 870 F.2d 518, 524–25 (9th Cir. 1989) (waiver found in a challenge to legacy INS investigation brought directly under the Constitution).

[21] *See e.g., Ngwanyia v. Ashcroft,* 302 F. Supp. 2d 1076, 1084 n. 14 (D. Minn. 2004) (complaint alleged that USCIS's failure to provide employment authorization to asylees violated the APA, the due process clause of the Constitution, and INA §208(c)(1)(B), although court ultimately held only that USCIS practice violated the APA).

[22] 28 USC §1361. For more on mandamus actions, see AILF Practice Advisory, "Mandamus Actions: Avoiding Dismissal and Proving the Case" (Aug. 15, 2005), *available at www.ailf.org/lac/lac_pa_index.shtml.*

[23] 28 USC §2201.

[24] *Skelly Oil Co. v. Phillips Petroleum Co.,* 339 U.S. 667, 671 (1950); *see also Fleet Bank Nat'l Assoc. v. Burke,* 160 F.3d 883, 886 (2d Cir. 1998); *State ex rel. Missouri Highway and Transportation Com'n v. Cuffley,* 112 F.3d 1332, 1334 (8th Cir. 1997).

[25] *See Bennett v. Spear,* 520 U.S. 154, 175 (1997) (stating that §704 provides a cause of action for all "final agency action for which there is no other adequate remedy in a court"); *Japan Whaling Ass'n v. Am. Cetacean Soc'y,* 478 U.S. 221, 230 n.4 (1986) (holding that §704 expressly creates a "right of action" absent clear and convincing evidence of legislative intention to preclude review); *Md. Dep't of Human Res. v. DHHS,* 763 F.2d 1441, 1445 n.5 (D.C. Cir. 1985) (describing the APA as a "generic" cause of action for persons aggrieved by agency action).

704 states in relevant part: "Actions Reviewable. Agency action made reviewable by statute and final agency action for which there is no other adequate remedy in a court are subject to judicial review."

As a "cause of action," the APA provides an individual with a basis to sue a federal agency for unlawful agency action when Congress has not specifically provided such a basis anywhere else in the law. It also "permits the courts to provide redress for a particular kind of 'claim.'"[26] Because the APA creates this specific cause of action, the Supreme Court has held that a separate indication of congressional intent of the right to sue is not necessary.[27]

What "Agency Action" Is Reviewable Under the APA?

The APA states that a person who is suffering a legal wrong because of agency action, or who is adversely affected by agency action within the meaning of a relevant statute, is entitled to judicial review.[28] "Agency action" is defined to include "the whole or a part of an agency rule, order, license, sanction, relief, or the equivalent or denial thereof, or failure to act."[29] Thus, for example, an agency action may include the denial of a visa petition or an application for adjustment. It can also include the agency's failure to adjudicate a visa petition or adjustment application.

Limitations on Judicial Review Under the APA

There are a number of limitations on when a suit can be brought under the APA. The following sections will briefly discuss some of the most frequently encountered of these various limitations.

No Judicial Review Where Another Statute Specifically Precludes Review

The APA does not apply to the extent that another statute precludes judicial review over the issues challenged in the suit.[30] There are a number of bars to judicial review found in the INA.[31] However, the existence of these bars will not necessarily limit APA review. For example, one court specifically found that INA §242(a)(2)(B) does not bar an APA action challenging a denial of an adjustment application on nondiscretionary grounds, even though such action would be barred if the adjustment application had been denied on a discretionary basis.[32]

Practice Tip: Determine if there is a statutory bar to judicial review in the INA that could impact the APA claim, and if so, exactly what the scope and impact of that bar is.

No Review of Agency Action Committed to Agency Discretion by Law

5 USC §701(a)(2) states that agency action is reviewable under the APA except "where it is committed to agency discretion by law." The government takes an expansive view of what constitutes agency action committed to agency discretion by law, and will move to dismiss a case on this basis. Fortunately, courts have taken a more limited view. The Supreme Court has set forth several important guiding principles.

First, the Court has held that the APA embodies "a basic presumption of judicial review," explaining further that "only upon a showing of 'clear and convincing evidence' of a contrary legislative intent should the courts restrict access to judicial review."[33]

Under 5 USC §701(a)(2), the presumption of judicial review over agency action can be overcome where such action is committed to agency discretion

---

[26] *Trudeau v. FTC,* 456 F.3d 178, 189 (D.C. Cir. 2006).

[27] *Japan Whaling Assoc., supra* note 25, at 230 n.4; *see also Chrysler Corp. v. Brown*, 441 U.S. 281, 317 (1979) (finding that a private right of action is not necessary because review is available under the APA); *Central S.D. Cooperative Grazing District v. Sec'y of the U.S. Dep't of Agriculture*, 266 F.3d 889, 894 (8th Cir. 2001) ("Although [the statute at issue] does not authorize a private right of action, the [APA] provides for judicial review of agency action."); *Hernandez-Avalos v. INS*, 50 F.3d 842, 846 (10th Cir. 1995) (a plaintiff who has alleged a cause of action under the APA need not rely on an implied right of action under any other statute).

[28] 5 USC §702.

[29] 5 USC §551(13).

[30] 5 USC §701(a)(1).

[31] *See, e.g.,* INA §§212(h), (i)(2) (precluding judicial review of certain discretionary waivers); 242(a)(2)(B) (precluding review of certain discretionary decisions in the nonremoval context); 242(a)(5) (designating a petition for review in court of appeals as the "sole and exclusive means" of review of a final order of removal).

[32] *Pinho v. Gonzales,* 432 F.3d 193, 204 (3d Cir. 2005) ("Determination of eligibility for adjustment—unlike the granting of adjustment itself—is a purely legal question and does not implicate agency discretion."). For more on INA §242(a)(2)(B), the bar to review of discretionary decisions, see AILF Practice Advisory, M. Kenney, "Federal Court Jurisdiction over Discretionary Decisions After Real ID: Mandamus, Other Affirmative Suits and Petitions for Review" (Apr. 5, 2006), *available at www.ailf.org/lac/lac_pa_topics.shtml*.

[33] *Abbott Laboratories v. Gardner,* 387 U.S. 136, 140, 141 (1967).

by law. However, the Supreme Court has held that such circumstances are "rare," and only occur "where the relevant statute 'is drawn so that a court would have no meaningful standard against which to judge the agency's exercise of discretion.'"[34] In such rare circumstances, the courts may find that there is no law for the court to apply to judge the agency's exercise of discretion. Furthermore, in these cases, the court will find that the grant of discretion to the agency is unfettered and not subject to review under the APA.

Therefore, the first step in any analysis under §701(a)(2) is to look at the statute to see if it sets forth a standard against which to measure the agency action. For example, in *Spencer Enterprises, Inc. v. U.S.*,[35] the court determined that the statute setting forth eligibility requirements for employment-based investor visas provided a standard to measure USCIS's decision whether to approve a preference petition for such a visa. As such, the court found that there was law to apply and that there could be judicial review under the APA.

Similarly, the court in *Pinho v. Gonzales*[36] found that under the APA, it could review the denial of an adjustment of status application by USCIS where the denial was based on a statutory eligibility issue. The court found that the adjustment provision in the INA set forth standards for eligibility to guide its review. It distinguished such statutory eligibility issues from denials of adjustment applications in the exercise of discretion.[37] Still another court found statutory guidelines under which it could review eligibility for an extension of an L-1A visa in an APA case, as distinct from a denial of such an extension on discretionary grounds.[38]

In contrast, courts have found that agency action is wholly committed to agency discretion in limited circumstances in which neither the statute nor the regulations provide any guidelines for the exercise of discretion. For example, courts have held that the BIA's refusal to reopen a case sua sponte is unreviewable.[39] Similarly, the U.S. Court of Appeals for the Fifth Circuit held that under prior law, the APA did not apply to review of a grant of prehearing voluntary departure because there were no guidelines for the exercise of this discretionary authority set forth in the law.[40] A number of courts have held that the APA does not apply to the discretionary waiver of a foreign residency requirement under INA §212(e) for the same reason.[41]

Practice Tip: Even when a statute provides unfettered discretion to an agency, if the agency adopts regulations or practices to guide its exercise of discretion, these can provide the necessary standard for judicial review of the agency action under the APA. Thus, look at regulations and agency guidelines to see if they contain factors that an agency must consider in reaching its decision. If so, judicial review arguably can be exercised under the APA.

For example, in *M.B. v. Quarantillo*, the court found that the regulations that governed SIJ visa petitions set forth "the material matters to be included in a petition."[42] The court found that these regulations, coupled with agency field guidance, provided sufficient standards by which to review the agency action. As such, judicial review could be exercised under the APA. Similarly, a number of courts have found that the regulations limit when the BIA can affirm the decision of an immigration judge without issuing an opinion, and that these regulations therefore supply the "law to apply" for judicial review.[43]

---

[34] *Lincoln v. Vigil*, 508 U.S. 182, 190–91 (1993) (*quoting Heckler v. Chaney*, 470 U.S. 821, 830 (1985)).

[35] 345 F.3d 683, 688 (9th Cir. 2003).

[36] 432 F.3d 193, 204 (3d Cir. 2005).

[37] The court considered the question of discretion under both the APA standard and INA §242(a)(2)(B), the statutory bar to review of discretionary immigration decisions, finding that the two standards were "partly duplicative." *Id.* at 200 n.9; *see also Spencer Enterprises, Inc. v. U.S.*, 345 F.3d 683 (9th Cir. 2003) (discussing both APA and INA restrictions on review of discretionary decisions); *Shah v. Chertoff*, No. 3:05-CV-1608-BH (K) ECF, 2006 U.S. Dist. LEXIS 73754 (N.D. Tex. 2006) (same). Note, however, that the scope of the two limits on judicial review differs due to different statutory language and context.

[38] *Shah v. Chertoff, supra* note 37, at *28.

---

[39] *See, e.g., Luis v. INS,* 196 F.3d 36, 40 (1st Cir. 1999) (*citing Heckler v. Chaney,* 470 U.S. 821, 831 (1985)); *Harchenko v. INS,* 379 F.3d 405, 410–11 (6th Cir. 2004). While *Luis* and *Harchenko* are removal cases, and thus were not brought under the APA, the same reasoning would apply to an APA case.

[40] *Perales v. Casillas,* 903 F.2d 1043, 1050 (5th Cir. 1990).

[41] *See, e.g., Singh v. Moyer,* 867 F.2d 1035, 1039 (7th Cir. 1989); *Abdelhamid v. Ilchert,* 774 F.2d 1447, 1450 (9th Cir. 1985); *Dina v. Att'y Gen.,* 793 F.2d 473, 476–77 (2d Cir. 1986) (per curiam).

[42] 301 F.3d 109, 113 (3d Cir. 2002).

[43] *See, e.g., Haoud v. Ashcroft,* 350 F.3d 201, 206 (1st Cir. 2003); *Smirko v. Ashcroft,* 387 F.3d 279, 291–92 (3d Cir. 2004). *But see Ngure v. Ashcroft,* 367 F.3d 975, 987 (8th Cir.
continued

Exhaustion of Administrative Remedies

Generally, before seeking federal court review of a decision of an administrative agency, an individual must exhaust all administrative remedies. If the individual fails to do this, the court may refuse to review the case. In *Darby v. Cisneros*,[44] the Supreme Court held, however, that in federal court cases brought under the APA, a plaintiff can only be required to exhaust administrative remedies that are *mandated* by either a statute or regulation.

For a case to be exempt from the exhaustion requirement under *Darby*, the following criteria must be met:

- the federal suit is brought pursuant to the APA;

- there is no statute that mandates an administrative appeal;

- either: (1) there is no regulation that mandates an administrative appeal; or (2) if there is a regulation that mandates an administrative appeal, it does not also stay the administrative decision pending the administrative appeal; and

- the adverse agency decision being challenged is final for purposes of the APA.[45]

The *Darby* rule has been applied in immigration cases brought under the APA, with the courts concluding in each that no exhaustion of administrative remedies was required.[46]

Final Agency Action

5 USC §704 states that "final agency action" for which there is no other adequate remedy in a court is subject to review under the APA.[47] This "finality" requirement is somewhat intertwined with exhaustion; if there are administrative remedies that must be exhausted in accord with *Darby v. Cisneros*, agency action generally will not be "final" until such exhaustion has taken place.[48]

The "finality" requirement is also distinct from the exhaustion requirement, however. Even when exhaustion of administrative remedies is not required under the *Darby* analysis, the APA still requires that the agency decision be "final" in order for it to be challenged in federal district court. The Supreme Court indicated that generally two conditions must be satisfied for agency action to be "final": (1) the action must mark the "'consummation' of the agency's decision-making process" and cannot be "of a mere tentative or interlocutory nature;" and (2) the action must be one by which "rights or obligations have been determined," or from which "legal consequences will flow."[49]

Under this standard, USCIS's denial of "specific consent" for a state court dependency hearing for an SIJ visa was held to be final agency action.[50] Similarly, an AAO denial of an adjustment application has been found to be a final agency decision when there are no removal proceedings pending in which the issue could be raised.[51]

Other immigration agency actions, however, are not final under the APA. For example, one court held

2004) (finding no review because decision committed to agency discretion by law).

[44] 509 U.S. 137 (1993).

[45] For a full discussion of each of these requirements, see AILF Practice Advisory, "Failure to Appeal to the AAO: Does it Bar All Federal Court Review of the Case?" (July 22, 2004), *available at www.ailf.org/lac/lac_pa_topics.shtml.*

[46] *See, e.g., Bangura v. Hansen*, 434 F.3d 487, 498 (6th Cir. 2006) (APA challenge to denial of a spousal immigration petition); *Pinho v. Gonzales*, 432 F.3d 193, 202 (3d Cir. 2005) (applying *Darby* and finding that possibility that removal proceedings could be instituted in future in which adjustment application could be renewed did not establish a mandatory exhaustion requirement); *Duran Gonzales v. DHS*, No. C06-1411P, 2006 U.S. Dist. LEXIS 82502, *8–9 (W.D. Wash. Nov. 13, 2006) (APA challenge to DHS's willful refusal to follow Ninth Circuit law), *vacated on other grounds*, 508 F.3d 1227 (9th Cir. 2007); *Hillcrest Baptist Church v. U.S.*, No. C06-1042Z, 2007 U.S. Dist. LEXIS 12782, *6 (W.D. Wash. Feb. 23, 2007) (adjustment of status in a religious worker case).

[47] 5 USC §704.

[48] *See Pinho v. Gonzales*, 432 F.3d 193, 200 (3d Cir. 2005) ("Finality requires exhaustion of administrative remedies."); *see also Air Espana v. Brien*, 165 F.3d 148 (2d Cir. 1999) (legacy INS fine against airline carriers was not final when airlines' voluntary appeal to the Board of immigration Appeals was still pending); *Beverly Enterprise, Inc. v. Herman*, 50 F. Supp. 2d 7, 12 (D.D.C. 1999) (Department of Labor determination that plaintiff employer violated the Immigration Nursing Relief Act not final when plaintiff's administrative appeal was still pending).

[49] *Bennett v. Spear*, 520 U.S. 154, 177–78 (1997).

[50] *Young Zheng v. Pogash*, 416 F. Supp. 2d 550, 556 n.9 (S.D. Tex. 2006).

[51] *Pinho v. Gonzales*, 432 F.3d 193, 202 (3d Cir. 2005). *But see Barut v. USCIS*, No. 06-3246-CV-S-RED, 2006 U.S. Dist. LEXIS 61424 (W.D. Mo. 2006) (adjustment denial is not a final agency action because application can be renewed in removal proceedings).

that USCIS's finding of marriage fraud was not final agency action; rather, it would only become final action when the visa petition was denied.[52] Similarly, a court found that USCIS's denial of temporary protected status was not final agency action where the plaintiff was placed in removal proceedings and could renew the claim in these proceedings.[53]

Parties to an APA Suit

Who Has Standing To Bring an APA Suit?

In all federal litigation, Article III of the Constitution imposes a requirement that a plaintiff have "standing" to sue, which generally requires that the plaintiff have suffered a sufficient injury-in-fact.[54] However, the APA imposes an *additional* standing requirement. The APA states that:

A person suffering legal wrong because of agency action, or adversely affected or aggrieved by agency action within the meaning of a relevant statute, is entitled to judicial review thereof.[55]

The Supreme Court has interpreted this provision as requiring a plaintiff not only to have an injury but also to demonstrate standing under the APA by showing that "the interests sought to be protected by the [plaintiff are] arguably within the zone of interests to be protected or regulated by the statute ... in question."[56]

The "zone of interest" test does not require a plaintiff to establish that Congress specifically intended to benefit the plaintiff. Rather, there is a two-step inquiry. "First, the court must determine what interests the statute *arguably* was intended to protect, and second, the court must determine whether

the 'plaintiff's interests affected by the agency action in question are among them.'"[57] One court has described this test as "a fairly weak prudential restraint, requiring some non-trivial relation between the interests protected by the statute and the interest the plaintiff seeks to vindicate."[58] Even so, the "zone of interest" test "denies a right of review if the plaintiff's interests are ... marginally related or inconsistent with the purposes implicit in the statute."[59]

Applying this test in the immigration context, numerous courts have held that a noncitizen beneficiary of a family– or employment-based visa petition is within the "zone of interest" of the statute and thus has standing to sue over the denial or revocation of a visa petition.[60] An applicant for an SIJ visa also has been found to fall within the zone of interest of that provision.[61] In contrast, several courts held that noncitizens who were serving criminal sentences for deportable offenses were not within the "zone of interest" of former INA §242(i) and thus had no standing to challenge legacy INS's failure to initiate deportation proceedings prior to completion of their criminal sentences.[62]

Who Can Be Named as a Defendant?

The APA provides that the United States can be named as a defendant in an APA action.[63] It also specifies, however, that an action seeking mandatory or injunctive relief "shall specify the Federal officer or officers (by name or by title), and their successors in office, personally responsible for compliance."[64]

Practice Tip: In light of the above, consider naming as defendants in the complaint the specific individual within the agency who can carry out any in-

---

[52] *Bangura v. Hansen,* 434 F.3d 487, 501 (6th Cir. 2006).

[53] *Hernandez v. DHS,* No. 06-CV-12457-DT, 2006 U.S. Dist. LEXIS 71786 (E.D. Mich. 2006); *see also E.J.'s Luncheonette v. De Haan,* 01 CIV 5603 (LMM), 2002 U.S. Dist. LEXIS 105 (S.D.N.Y. 2002) (denial of a request for reduction in recruitment as part of a labor certification was not final agency action; instead, only a notice of findings that denied the labor certification would be final action); *Transport Robert (1973) Ltee v. INS,* 940 F. Supp. 338 (D.D.C. 1996) (letter from legacy INS associate commissioner refusing to certify truck drivers as B-1 business visitors was not final agency action).

[54] *See, e.g., Valley Forge Christian College v. Americans United for Separation of Church and State, Inc.,* 454 U.S. 464, 472 (1982).

[55] 5 USC §702.

[56] *Association of Data Processing Service Organizations, Inc. v. Camp,* 397 U.S. 150, 153 (1970).

[57] *Bangura v. Hansen,* 434 F.3d 487, 499 (6th Cir. 2006) (*quoting NCUA v. First National Bank & Trust Co.,* 522 U.S. 479, 492 (1998)).

[58] *Hernandez-Avalos v. INS,* 50 F.3d 842, 846 (10th Cir. 1995).

[59] *NCUA v. First National Bank & Trust Co.,* 522 U.S. 479, 491 (1998) (quotations omitted).

[60] *See, e.g., Bangura, supra* note 57, at 499–500; *Abboud v. INS,* 140 F.3d 843, 847 (9th Cir. 1998); *Ghaley v. INS,* 48 F.3d 1426, 1434 n.6 (7th Cir. 1995); *Taneja v. Smith,* 795 F.2d 355, 358 n.7 (4th Cir. 1986).

[61] *Yu v. Brown,* 36 F. Supp. 2d 922 (D.N.M. 1999).

[62] *See Campos v. INS,* 62 F.3d 311, 314 (9th Cir. 1995); *Hernandez-Avalos v. INS,* 50 F.3d 842, 847–48 (10th Cir. 1995); *Giddings v. Chandler,* 979 F.2d 1104, 1109–10 (5th Cir. 1992).

[63] 5 USC §702.

[64] *Id.*

junction or other mandatory order of the court that you seek in the lawsuit. Note, however, that this does not mean this individual is being sued in his or her individual capacity. Instead, the individual is named as a defendant in his or her official capacity within the agency.[65]

Standard of Review

What Is the Scope and Standard of Review in an APA Suit?

The APA provides for two general types of relief, and generally sets forth the scope of review for each.

First, the court can "compel agency action unlawfully withheld or unreasonably delayed."[66] This provision is similar to a mandamus action to compel delayed agency decision-making or action. A "central point" is that the "only agency action that can be compelled under the APA is action legally required."[67] Moreover, a court may only compel an agency "to take action upon a matter, without directing how it shall act."[68] Congress need not have set a definitive deadline for an agency to act, however, in order for a court to find a delay unreasonable; 5 USC §706(1) mandates that all action be done within a reasonable amount of time.[69]

Second, the APA states that a court can "hold unlawful and set aside agency actions, findings and conclusions" that meet one or more of six standards.[70] Four of these standards apply to all cases without limitation, and thus most often would apply to the type of suit discussed in this article. These four standards are:

- Arbitrary, capricious, an abuse of discretion, or otherwise not in accordance with the law;

- Contrary to constitutional right, power, privilege or immunity;

- In excess of statutory jurisdiction, authority, or limitations, or short of statutory right; or

- Without observance of procedures required by law.[71]

Discovery

Can Discovery Be Carried Out Against the Government Agency in an APA Suit?

Yes, in certain cases. As a general rule, judicial review under the APA is limited to the administrative record that was before the agency when it made its decision.[72] As a result, discovery often is not allowed in APA cases. This is particularly true in challenges to a decision or agency action in an individual case. In such cases, the government frequently will object to any discovery, arguing that the administrative record is sufficient.

However, there are exceptions to the general rule. The primary exception applies when there is no administrative record for the court to review, or the record may be insufficient with respect to the claims in the suit. Such an incomplete record "may frustrate judicial review,"[73] and discovery may be necessary to supplement the agency record.[74] This often will be the case when the suit challenges a pattern or practice of agency decisions or action, rather than the decision in one individual case. In such pattern-and-practice cases, there is not a single agency record to be reviewed, and the court may permit discovery.

Even in individual cases, however, discovery may be necessary to supplement the agency record. To remedy an incomplete or inadequate record, the district court may allow discovery, although the court may narrowly tailor the scope of discovery to

---

[65] For more on this topic, see AILF Practice Advisory, "Whom To Sue And Whom To Serve In Immigration-Related District Court Litigation" (updated Apr. 7, 2006), available at www.ailf.org/lac/lac_pa_topics.shtml.

[66] 5 USC §706(1).

[67] Norton v. S. Utah Wilderness Alliance, 542 U.S. 55, 63 (2004).

[68] Id.

[69] Kaplan v. Chertoff, 481 F. Supp. 2d 370, 399 (E.D. Pa. 2007) (finding that an APA claim was adequately stated against both USCIS and the Federal Bureau of Investigation with respect to delays in adjustment of status and naturalization applications).

[70] 5 USC §706(2).

---

[71] Id. at (A)–(D); see also Citizens to Preserve Overton Park, Inc. v. Volpe, 401 U.S. 402, 414 (1971) ("In all cases agency action must be set aside if the action was 'arbitrary, capricious, an abuse of discretion or otherwise no in accordance with law' or if the action failed to meet statutory, procedural, or constitutional requirements.").

[72] Citizens to Preserve Overton Park, Inc., supra note 71, at 420; see also Camp v. Pitts, 411 U.S. 138, 142 (1973) ("[T]he focal point for judicial review [in an APA suit] should be the administrative record already in existence, not some new record made initially in the reviewing court.").

[73] Voyageurs National Park Assoc. v. Norton, 381 F.3d 759, 766 (8th Cir. 2004).

[74] See also Animal Defense Council v. Hodel, 840 F.2d 1432, 1436 (9th Cir. 1988) (court may inquire outside the record when necessary to explain the agency's action or when the agency has relied on documents not in the record).

respond to whatever is missing in the agency record.[75] In particular, the Supreme Court has said that inquiry into the mental processes of the agency decision-maker is to be avoided unless it is "the only way there can be effective judicial review."[76]

For example, in an APA challenge to the denial of a marriage-based visa petition for alleged fraud, the plaintiffs sought to depose two agency employees engaged in the investigation of the visa petition.[77] The plaintiffs argued that these depositions were necessary because the record was incomplete, in that there was no contemporaneous administrative record to explain why USCIS deviated from its normal practices and procedures when investigating the marriage petition.[78] The district court agreed with this, but more narrowly tailored the discovery, ordering that the defendant USCIS was to submit the information that plaintiffs sought in affidavits rather than by deposition.[79]

Attorney's Fees

Is It Possible To Get Attorney's Fees in These Cases?

Yes. The Equal Access to Justice Act (EAJA)[80] authorizes payment of attorney's fees and costs for successful litigation against the government in the federal courts so long as certain requirements of the Act are met.[81]

Practice Tip: In anticipation of a favorable court order in the case, consider requesting attorney's fees under EAJA as part of the relief identified in the complaint.

---

[75] *Voyageurs National Park Assoc., supra* note 73, at 766.

[76] *Citizens to Preserve Overton Park, Inc., supra* note 71, at 420.

[77] *Sabhari v. Cangemi*, No. 04-1104 ADM/JSM, 2005 U.S. Dist. LEXIS 3550 (D. Minn. Mar. 9, 2005).

[78] *Id* at *6.

[79] *Id.*

[80] 28 USC §2412(d); 5 USC §504 *et seq.*

[81] For more on EAJA fees, see AILF Practice Advisory, "Requesting Attorney's Fees Under the Equal Access to Justice Act" (updated Apr. 7, 2006), *available at* www.ailf.org/lac/lac_pa_index.shtml.

WAIVERS OF HIV-BASED INADMISSIBILITY FOR IMMIGRANTS

by Paul O'Dwyer[*]

INTRODUCTION[1]

In 1993, Congress amended the Immigration and Nationality Act (INA) to specify infection with the human immunodeficiency virus (HIV) virus as a communicable disease of public health significance which renders an alien inadmissible to the United States. The statute provides that "any alien who is determined to have a communicable disease of public health significance, which shall include infection with the etiolic agent for acquired immune deficiency, is inadmissible."[2] Waivers of this ground of inadmissibility can be found at INA §§212(g)(1), 209(c) (adjustment of status for asylees and refugees), and 210(c)(2)(B)(ii) (adjustment of status for special agricultural workers), and in the regulations at 8 CFR §§212.7(b), 209.1 and 209.2.

HIV is unique as being the only such disease to be specified in the Act; all other excludable communicable diseases of public health significance are so designated by the Secretary of the Department of Health and Human Services (HHS).[3]

APPLICABILITY

All applicants for adjustment of status in the United States (and for immigrant visas overseas) are required to undergo a medical exam, conducted by a designated civil surgeon, to determine eligibility for adjustment of status and/or an immigrant visa.[4] All such applicants over the age of 15 are required to undergo an HIV test, a chest X-ray and a syphilis test.[5] Applicants under the age of 15 are excused from the tests for HIV and syphilis unless there is reason to suspect that such applicant is HIV-positive or has syphilis.[6]

If the results of a medical exam indicate an HIV-positive test result, the alien is inadmissible. Depending on the section of the law under which the person is seeking adjustment, he or she may be eligible for a waiver of inadmissibility. The availability of waivers, and the procedural and substantive requirements for getting a waiver, vary according to the section of the law under which the person is seeking admission or adjustment. There is no need for a medical examination for aliens seeking admission under §249 of the INA (registry cases), §289 (Indian cases), or §240 (lawful admission cases).

SECTION 245 ADJUSTMENTS

Aliens seeking to adjust status based on an approved immediate relative petition or petition for alien worker seek admission to the U.S. pursuant to INA §245. For such aliens who are HIV-positive, INA §212(g) authorizes a waiver, *provided* the applicant is either:

- The spouse or unmarried son or daughter or minor unmarried adopted child, of either a U.S. citizen or lawful permanent resident (LPR) or alien who has been issued an immigrant visa;[7]

- The parent of a U.S. citizen, LPR or alien who has been issued an immigrant visa;[8]

- A VAWA self-petitioner.[9]

A waiver can be issued in accordance with such terms, conditions and controls, if any, as the Attorney General, after consultation with the HHS Secretary, may prescribe.[10] Those "terms, conditions and controls" are set forth in a 2002 memorandum known as the Williams memorandum.[11] The Wil-

---

[*] **Paul O'Dwyer** is a graduate of the National University of Ireland and the Kings' Inns, Dublin. Mr. O'Dwyer practices immigration law and family and matrimonial law in New York City.

[1] A very useful resource on this topic is an article by Lynn Neugebauer, supervising attorney at Safe Horizon Immigration Law Project in Queens, New York, "HIV as a Ground of Inadmissibility," *Immigration & Nationality Law Handbook* 400 (AILA 2007–08 Ed.).

[2] INA §212(a)(1)(A)(i).

[3] 42 CFR §54.2(b).

[4] INA §§221(d), 245(a)(2); 8 CFR §245.5.

[5] 42 CFR §34.3(b)(1).

[6] 42 CFR §34.3(b)(1)(V).

[7] INA §212(g)(1)(A).

[8] INA §212(g)(1)(B).

[9] INA §212(g)(1)(C).

[10] INA §212(g).

[11] Legacy Immigration and Naturalization Service (INS) Memorandum J. Williams, "Medical Examinations, Vaccination Requirements, Waivers of Medical Ground of Inadmissibility, and Designation of Civil Surgeon and Revocation of
continued

liams memo provides that an application for an HIV waiver pursuant to INA §212(g) is made on Form I-601, and the required fee must be paid.[12] The applicant must submit documentary evidence establishing eligibility for the waiver: *i.e.,* evidence of the qualifying familial relationship, along with evidence establishing:

- That the danger to the public health of the United States created by the alien's admission is minimal;

- The possibility of infection created by his or her admission is minimal;

- That there would be no costs incurred by any level of government agency without the prior consent of that agency.[13]

The Williams memo states that evidence sufficient to meet the first two requirements may "include but [is] not limited to: (a) evidence that the applicant has arranged for medical treatment in the United States; (b) the applicant's awareness of the nature and severity of his or her medical condition; (c) evidence of counseling; (d) the applicant's willingness to attend educational seminars and counseling sessions; and (e) the applicant's knowledge of the modes of transmission of the disease."[14]

Note that the memo does *not* require proof of private health insurance; instead, it requires the showing that no U.S. government agency will incur any costs without that agency's prior consent. However, even if the government agency consents to provide treatment (thus "incurring cost"), in accordance with the Williams memo requirement, such consent will probably trigger a non-waiveable public charge bar to admissibility.[15] Therefore, if possible, the applicant should endeavor to obtain private health insurance prior to the adjustment interview. The Williams memo suggests that in order to satisfy the third requirement, adjustment applicants (including those seeking adjustment under the Nicaraguan Adjustment and Central American Relief Act (NACARA) and the Haitian Refugee Immigration Fairness Act of 1998 (HRIFA)) may submit evidence of private insurance, personal financial re-

sources, or proof that a hospital research organization or other type of facility will provide care at no cost to the government, or any other evidence establishing the ability to cover the cost of medical treatment for HIV/AIDS.[16]

Violence Against Women Act (VAWA) applicants for adjustment of status are also eligible for a waiver on the same grounds as §245 adjustment applicants, except that the applicant does not need a qualifying family relationship to establish eligibility.[17]

The I-601 (the waiver application form) can be filed at the interview, if the alien is unaware that he or she is inadmissible because of HIV, or unaware until the interview of the need to file the I-601, or it can be submitted after the interview has concluded but before there has been a final determination, or it can be filed with the medical exam and the adjustment package. There is no need to wait for a determination of inadmissibility to be made in order to file the I-601, and so filing it initially with the medical exam and the adjustment package can save time later. At a minimum, it should contain the following:

- The completed Form I-601;

- An HIV supplement requiring the signature of the applicant, his or her doctor, and a local designated health official (except in New York where there is no need for a signature from a designated health official), along with the address where the applicant intends to live in the United States (see attached, Appendix A);

- A letter from the treating physician, HIV clinic, or an AIDS organization confirming that the applicant has received counseling, including instruction on HIV prevention, and attended educational seminars and/or support groups;

- A letter from a doctor or a clinic that has treated the applicant, including a statement of the current status of the applicant's health, whether or not the applicant is taking HIV medication, and confirming that the applicant is compliant with any treatment;

- A copy of the applicant's medical insurance card and/or medical insurance policy;

- An affidavit from the applicant (and/or his or her spouse or partner, if appropriate) indicating that he or she is aware of the implications of his or

---

Such Designation (AD 01-03)" (Oct. 17, 2002), *published on* AILA InfoNet at Document No. 03031763 (*posted* Mar. 17, 2003).

[12] *Id.* at 19.

[13] *Id.* at 20.

[14] *Id.*

[15] INA §212(a)(4).

---

[16] Williams Memo, *supra* note 11, at 20.

[17] INA §212(g)(1)(C).

her health condition, that he or she has been counseled with regard to modes of transmission, how to prevent it, and that he or she takes adequate steps to ensure that HIV is not transmitted to anybody else.

Once the waiver application has been reviewed it is then sent to the Centers for Disease Control and Prevention (CDC) in Atlanta, Georgia, which then creates a file for the applicant and returns the I-601 to U.S. Citizenship and Immigration Services (US-CIS) to be adjudicated. Once the individual's application for adjustment of status is granted, he or she will receive a letter from the CDC requesting that the doctor who executed the 1-601 verify that the applicant is following up on his or her HIV-related care. Once this verification is provided to the CDC, the applicant's file at that agency is closed.

APPLICATIONS FOR ADJUSTMENTS BASED ON ASYLEE STATUS

Pursuant to INA §209(b) and the relevant regulations,[18] an alien who is physically present in the United States can seek adjustment of status within one year of being granted asylum. Asylee adjustment applications are also subject to the HIV ground of inadmissibility, but the waiver application requirements are governed by INA §209(c) and are different from those for adjustment applications under §245. To qualify for a waiver under §209(c), there is no requirement for a qualifying relative, and such a waiver is to be granted "for humanitarian purposes, to assure family unity, or when it is otherwise in the public interest."[19]

Most asylee adjustment applicants are not interviewed, and therefore the medical exam is normally submitted along with the application for adjustment. The medical exam is usually opened by USCIS at the Service Center, and if the person seems ineligible because of HIV, a request for evidence would be issued, requesting that a waiver be filed. Waivers of medical inadmissibility in asylee adjustments are filed on Form I-602 (not I-601). As with §245 adjustment waivers, however, the waiver application package should include, at a minimum: a letter from either a treating physician or a support group or counseling center, confirming that the applicant has been counseled regarding modes of transmission; a letter from the treating physician, confirming that

the alien is receiving HIV care and detailing the type of treatment being received; a copy of either private insurance or a Medicaid card, or the equivalent; and an affidavit from the applicant setting forth the humanitarian, public interest and/or family factors which merit granting the waiver. Note that merely asserting that the applicant has been granted asylum in the United States will generally not be considered a sufficient humanitarian or public interest reason, because even if adjustment is not granted, the applicant will still retain his or her asylee status and will not be returned to the country of origin.

Refugees present in the United States for more than one year can also adjust status under INA §209; however, refugees are typically given medical exams prior to entering the United States. HIV waivers are available pursuant to INA §209(c) and are processed overseas.

Special immigrant juveniles are also eligible for a waiver of the HIV ground of inadmissibility on the same grounds as asylees—for humanitarian purposes, for reasons of family unity, or when otherwise in the public interest—and need not have a qualifying family member.

APPEALS

A denial of an HIV waiver may be appealed from the district director to the Administrative Appeals Office in Washington, D.C., or via a motion to reopen or reconsider at the district office if the reason for the denial can be cured. The applicants who are filing a waiver under INA §245 should be mindful that there is no requirement to show hardship to the qualifying relative. Many SAOs and DAOs will deny HIV waivers based on a mistaken understanding that the qualifying family member also must demonstrate hardship. Thus, it is important to remind them that there is no requirement to show hardship to the family member, in contrast to a §212(h) waiver.

CONCLUSION

The HIV ground of inadmissibility may soon be repealed. As of the time of writing this article, Section 305 of Senate Bill 2731, the "United States Global Leadership Against HIV/AIDS, Tuberculosis, and Malaria Reauthorization Act of 2008," would remove HIV as a ground of inadmissibility, by deleting from INA §212(a)(1)(A)(i) the words "which shall include infection with the etiolic agent for acquired immune deficiency." This bill passed the Senate Foreign Relations Committee on March

---

[18] 8 CFR §209.2.

[19] INA §209(c).

13, 2008, and is expected to go to the full Senate floor after the Easter recess. A similar bill was approved by the House of Representatives Foreign Relations Committee on March 11, 2008, but without the Senate's Section 305 amendment. Rep. Barbara Lee (D-CA) has sponsored a House version of the amendment. If this legislation passes, full responsibility for determining which medical conditions are bases for inadmissibility would return to the HHS Secretary.[20] Thus, HIV could conceivably be designated by HHS as a ground of inadmissibility, but that is generally believed to be unlikely.

If this legislation does not pass and the HIV ground of inadmissibility remains in force, it is important for practitioners to be aware that it can, in certain circumstances, be waived, and to understand fully the requirements for such a waiver to be granted.

---

[20] INA §212(a)(1)(A)(i).

COMMUNICABLE DISEASE, INADMISSIBILITY, WAIVERS, AND RELATED ISSUES

*by Sana Loue**

INADMISSIBILITY AND COMMUNICABLE DISEASE

The Immigration and Nationality Act (INA) provides for the inadmissibility of any alien

i. who is determined (in accordance with regulations prescribed by the Secretary of Health and Human Services) to have a communicable disease of public health significance ...

ii. except as provided in [INA §212(a)(1)(C)], who seeks admission as an immigrant, or who seeks adjustment of status to the status of an alien lawfully admitted for permanent residence, and who has failed to present documentation of having received vaccination against vaccine-preventable diseases, which shall include at least the following diseases: mumps, measles, rubella, polio, tetanus and diphtheria toxoids, pertussis, influenza type B and hepatitis B, and any other vaccinations against vaccine-preventable diseases recom-

mended by the Advisory Committee for Immunization Practices.[1]

The vaccination requirement does not apply, however, to adopted children within the meaning of the INA[2] who are 10 years of age or younger and are applying as an immediate relative, and the

> adoptive parent or prospective adoptive parent of the child, who has sponsored the child for admission as an immediate relative, has executed an affidavit stating that the parent is aware of the provisions [relating to vaccinations] and will ensure that, within 30 days of the child's admission, or at the earliest time that is medically appropriate, the child will receive the [required] vaccinations.[3]

It is important to note that paragraph (i) applies to *all* aliens, while the vaccination requirement contained in paragraph (ii) is relevant only to individuals applying for permanent residence or adjustment of status.

Current regulations provide that "communicable diseases of public health significance" include[4]

- Chancroid
- Gonorrhea
- Granuloma inguinale
- Human immunodeficiency virus (HIV) infection
- Infectious leprosy
- Lymphogranuloma venereum
- Syphilis, infectious stage
- Active tuberculosis

The determination of whether an alien has one of these enumerated conditions is made in the context of a medical examination undertaken by a civil surgeon in connection with an application for adjustment of status, a panel physician in connection with an application for an immigrant visa, or through in-

* **Sana Loue**, J.D., Ph.D., MP.H., is a professor in the Department of Epidemiology and Biostatistics of the School of Medicine of Case Western Reserve University in Cleveland. She holds secondary appointments in the Department of Bioethics, the Department of Psychiatry, and the Center for Global Health. Prior to joining the university, she practiced immigration law and AIDS-related law for 14 years, following a career in social work and secondary education. She is the author or senior editor of more than 20 books and of over 60 articles, some of which have been cited in court decisions, as well as multiple chapters in books and government monographs. Professor Loue teaches cross-disciplinary courses focusing on ethics, law, and epidemiology; mental health epidemiology; and sexuality, public health, and the law. She has taught in Romania, Uganda, Chile, and Vietnam. Professor Loue's empirical research focuses on HIV prevention among vulnerable and marginalized populations, including immigrants, non-English speakers, injection drug users, and severely mentally ill persons. Professor Loue has served on numerous advisory boards of nonprofit organizations and governmental task forces. She received the Fulbright award to teach and conduct research in Romania during 1999 and 2000. Professor Loue is a member of the American Immigration Lawyers Association (AILA) and is a past chair of AILA's San Diego Chapter.

[1] INA §§212(a)(1)(A)(i), (ii); 8 USC §§1182(a)(1)(A)(i), (ii).

[2] INA §101(b)(1)(F); 8 USC §1101(b)(1)(F).

[3] INA §212(a)(1)(C); 8 USC §1182(a)(1)(C).

[4] 42 CFR §34.2(b).

spection at the port of entry upon arrival to the United States.[5] Those applying for a nonimmigrant visa as a student, a fiancé(e), or an exchange visitor, or for refugee status, are also required to undergo a medical examination.[6]

MEDICAL EXAMINATION AND TREATMENT

Statute and regulation provide for the medical examination of those aliens who are applying for a visa at an embassy or consulate of the United States, arriving in the United States, applying for adjustment of status, or required to have a medical examination to determine their admissibility to the United States.[7] That medical examination includes relevant x-ray examinations and serologic testing to determine if the individual may be infected with any of the enumerated communicable diseases.[8] The procedures for the detection of each listed condition are quite lengthy; for this reason, this article provides an overview that focuses specifically on tuberculosis and sexually transmitted diseases, which are of more frequent concern than are the other communicable diseases.[9]

Tuberculosis

Tuberculosis has been of particular concern worldwide, due to the increase in prevalence of multidrug resistant tuberculosis and the relative ease of its transmission. Pulmonary tuberculosis results from exposure to the bacilli Mycobacterium tuberculosis in airborne droplet nuclei. Individuals are exposed to the bacilli through the coughing, sneezing, or singing of persons who have laryngeal or pulmonary tuberculosis.

Although individuals may be exposed to tuberculosis, they may not become infected. Among those who do become infected, the infection may not manifest for some time. It is important here to distinguish between tuberculosis exposure, infection, and disease.

Not everyone who is exposed will develop tuberculosis infection. Individuals who are infected, but who do not have tuberculosis disease, will not transmit tuberculosis to others. Only a portion of those who are infected will go on to develop disease. Approximately 5 percent of individuals with intact immune systems develop active disease, compared to approximately half of those with compromised immune systems. The risk of contracting tuberculosis increases with increasing frequency and duration of exposure to an individual with active disease.

Approximately 90 to 95 percent of individuals who become infected develop latent tuberculosis after the initial lesions heal. Individuals with latent infection do not feel sick, do not have any symptoms of tuberculosis, and cannot transmit the disease to others. However, they may remain at risk of reactivation of the disease. Exogenous reinfection (infection due to an exposure that originates outside of that individual) or endogenous reactivation of a latent focus (reactivation of the individual's initial infection due to factors relating to that specific individual, such as a weakened immune system) may lead to progressive pulmonary tuberculosis, which, if untreated, can result in death. Individuals with advanced disease may experience fatigue, fever, night sweats, cough, chest pain, and hoarseness, and may spit up blood that is actually derived from the lungs or bronchial tubes (hemoptysis).[10]

Extrapulmonary tuberculosis, which is less common than pulmonary tuberculosis, may occur in any organ or tissue, including the kidneys, bone, eyes, intestines, and lymph nodes. The infection results from exposure to tuberculous cattle through the ingestion of unpasteurized dairy products. Unlike pulmonary tuberculosis, extrapulmonary tuberculosis is not usually communicable.

1991 Instructions for Tuberculosis Screening

The original instructions for the examination of aliens for tuberculosis were issued in 1991. In general, they require the following:

- A review of the individual's medical history, including a history of tuberculosis, if any
- Treatment records for any past tuberculosis
- A tuberculin skin test for individuals under the age of 15 who are suspected of having tuberculo-

---

[5] 42 CFR §§34.2(c), (o).

[6] 42 CFR §§34.3(b)(1)(ii), (iii).

[7] INA §232; 8 USC §1222; 42 USC §252; 42 CFR §34.1.

[8] Centers for Disease Control and Prevention (CDC), *Technical Instructions for Medical Examination of Aliens in the United States* (for civil surgeons), *available at www.cdc.gov/ncidod/dq/pdf/ti-civil.pdf*; CDC, *Technical Instructions for Medical Examination of Aliens* (for panel physicians), *available at www.cdc.gov/ncidod/dq/pdf/ti-alien.pdf*.

[9] Issues relating to HIV infection are addressed in a separate article in this handbook. *See* A. Stevenson, "Substance Use, Health-Related Inadmissibility, and Waivers."

[10] C.W. Fox & R.B. George, "Current Concepts in the Management and Prevention of Tuberculosis in Adults," 144 *J. La. Med. Ass'n* 363 (1992).

sis or contact with an individual known to have tuberculosis

- A chest x-ray for individuals 15 years of age or older and those under the age of 15 who had a positive tuberculin skin test
- A sputum smear examination of individuals with a chest x-ray that suggested active pulmonary tuberculosis.[11]

It should be noted, however, that a 2007 update to the 1991 instructions asserts that the 1991 instructions require a tuberculin skin test of all applicants age 2 and older, regardless of whether they are suspected of having tuberculosis or were in contact with an individual known to have tuberculosis.[12]

The 1991 instructions for tuberculosis were found to be inadequate because they did not require the examination of individuals 15 years or younger, failed to detect infection in persons with negative sputum smears but positive cultures, and did not provide guidance for the treatment of infected individuals prior to travel. Scientific research has underscored the inadequacy of those procedures and their implementation. As an example, from 1992 to 1994, it was found that 51 percent of the chest radiographs of Tibetan immigrants to Minneapolis were abnormal, despite initial tuberculosis screening by U.S.-authorized physicians in India prior to immigration to the United States. A comparison with the results from the chest radiograph evaluations conducted in India indicated that 79 percent of the Tibetans had unchanged readings and 21 percent showed evidence of potentially progressive disease.[13]

2007 Instructions for Tuberculosis Screening

In 2007, the Centers for Disease Control and Prevention (CDC) issued revised requirements for tuberculosis screening and treatment.[14] Immigrants and nonimmigrants in the above-specified categories who are age 15 and older from countries where the incidence of tuberculosis is less than 20 cases per 100,000 persons will be required to have a medical examination taken, a physical examination, and a chest x-ray. If any of these suggest that the individual may have tuberculosis infection, he or she will be required to undergo, in addition, three sputum smears and cultures for *Mycobacterium tuberculosis* and drug susceptibility testing on the finding of a positive culture.[15]

New requirements have been established for applicants from countries with an incidence rate of 20 or more cases of tuberculosis infection per 100,000.[16] These are enumerated in Table 1 below. Individuals subject to tuberculosis screening from all other countries remain subject to the screening procedures established in 1991.

Table 1. Revised TB Screening Requirements for Immigrants and Applicants for Student, Fiancé(e) Exchange Visitor, and Refugee Status from Countries with Incidence Rate of ≥20 Per 100,000

Applicants 2–14 years old	Applicants 15 years old and older
Medical history	Medical history
Physical examination	Physical examination
Tuberculin skin test	Chest x-ray
Chest x-ray if tuberculin skin test is ≥ 5mm	Three sputum smears and cultures for *Mycobacterium tuberculosis* if medical history, physical examination, or chest x-ray found to suggest tuberculosis or HIV infection
	Drug susceptibility testing if culture found to be positive

This represents the following changes from the previous procedures:

- a tuberculin skin test for all applicants under the age of 15 in countries for which the World Health Organization has estimated an incidence of more than 20 cases of tuberculosis per 100,000 population;

---

[11] Civil surgeon instructions, *supra* note 8; Panel physician instructions, *supra* note 8.

[12] *www.cdc.gov/ncidod/dq/updates.htm.*

[13] D. Truong, *et al.*, "Tuberculosis Among Tibetan Immigrants from India and Nepal in Minnesota, 1992-1995," 277 *JAMA* 735 (1997).

[14] CDC, "CDC Immigration Requirements: Technical Instructions for Tuberculosis Screening and Treatment" (2007), *available at www.cdc.gov/ncidod/dq/pdf/ti_tb_8_9_2007.pdf.*

[15] *Id.* at 3.

[16] *Id.* at 4. Incidence refers to new cases of the disease, whereas prevalence refers to existing cases, which includes new cases plus cases that have already been diagnosed.

- a chest x-ray for all applicants under the age of 15 whose tuberculin skin test is greater than or equal to 5mm;

- a mycobacterial culture for all applicants whose chest x-ray suggests that they may have tuberculosis disease; and

- the completion of treatment consistent with the guidelines of the American Thoracic Society/CDC/Infectious Diseases of America prior to immigration to the United States.[17]

Table 2 enumerates the countries and populations that have been designated as being subject to the new screening requirements as countries having an incidence of ≥20 cases per 100,000 and the dates on which this is to commence.[18]

Table 2. Populations Subject to Screening Pursuant to 2007 Technical Instructions for Tuberculosis Screening and Treatment

Country	Population	Commencement
Botswana	All applicants	3/3/2008
Kenya	Refugees (including Ethiopians, Somalis, and Sudanese)	1/1/2008
Lesotho	All applicants	3/3/2008
Mexico	All applicants	10/1/2007
Mozambique	All applicants	3/3/2008
Namibia	All applicants	3/3/2008
Nepal	Refugees (Bhutanese)	12/13/2007
Philippines	All applicants	10/1/2007
South Africa	All applicants	3/3/2008
Swaziland	All applicants	3/3/2008
Tanzania	Refugees (Burundian)	1/1/2008
Thailand	Refugees (including Burmese and Hmong refugees)	4/9/2007
Turkey	All applicants	2/4/2008
Vietnam	All applicants	2/1/2008

The revised Technical Instructions also provide for new tuberculosis classifications for all applicants suspected of having tuberculosis infection and for contacts of cases with tuberculosis disease.

---

[17] Background on the 2007 Technical Instructions for Tuberculosis Screening and Treatment, *www.cdc.gov/ncidod/dq/ titb_background_2007.htm.*

[18] *www.cdc.gov/ncidod/dq/panel_2007.htm.*

Sexually Transmitted Disease (Other than HIV)

The instructions relating to screening for sexually transmitted infections, other than HIV, were issued in 1991.[19] All applicants for adjustment of status or an immigrant visa who are 15 years of age or older are required to be evaluated for syphilis, gonorrhea, chancroid, granuloma inguinale, and lymphogranuloma venereum on the basis of a medical history and physical examination. In addition, all applicants 15 years of age and older must be tested for syphilis; those under the age of 15 must be tested if there is reason to suspect that they might be infected. Individuals found to be positive for any of these diseases are to be treated with the standard recommended treatment.

Vaccination Requirements

In 2007, the CDC issued new technical instructions for vaccination that are specifically for panel physicians.[20] These instructions supersede all previous instructions, memoranda, and letters to panel physicians.[21] These revised instructions reflect significant changes relating to the timing of administration of vaccines for rotavirus, hepatitis A, meningococcal meningitis, zoster, hepatitis B, influenza, tetanus, pertussis, and diphtheria.

Although vaccination for human papillomavirus is controversial even within the United States, it is now required for female immigrant visa applicants ages 11 through 26.[22] It, like all vaccinations, is not required for V and K visa applicants or refugees at the time of their initial admission to the United States.[23] However, it will be required at the time of their application for adjustment of status or permanent resident status.[24]

A determination whether a vaccination is to be administered for a specific disease will be made by the panel physician through consideration of the applicant's age, his or her medical history and records, vaccinations that may be lacking, possible contrain-

---

[19] Civil surgeon instructions, *supra* note 8, at III-6 to III-7; Panel physician instructions, *supra* note 8, at III-6 to III-8.

[20] CDC, *CDC Immigration Requirements: Technical Instructions for Vaccination* (2007), *available at www.cdc.gov/ ncidod/dq/pdf/ti_vacc.pdf.*

[21] *Id.* at iii (Preface).

[22] *Id.* at 1.

[23] *Id.* at 3.

[24] *Id.*

dications and precautions, and laboratory records.[25] The panel physician is not required to administer the vaccinations but may refer the applicant to another physician for these.[26]

CLASS A AND CLASS B CERTIFICATES

If the panel physician finds that the individual has a communicable disease that would render him or her inadmissible, he or she will issue a Class A certificate, which establishes the individual's inadmissibility on the basis of the communicable disease.[27] In the case of tuberculosis, a Class A certificate will be issued, travel clearance denied, and treatment initiated if the individual is found to have:

- a positive sputum smear;
- a positive culture;
- a component of the medical history, physical examination, or chest x-ray that is suggestive of tuberculosis and has either a positive sputum smear or culture;
- completed therapy for tuberculosis and has either a positive sputum smear or culture.[28]

Individuals will be classified as "Class B1 TB pulmonary" and issued a Class B certificate if they have completed tuberculosis therapy and have both a negative culture and negative sputum smears.[29] In such cases, they will receive travel clearance that is valid for three months from the time the evaluation was completed.[30] The culture results must be known within eight weeks of collection.[31]

Individuals will not have a TB classification if there is no evidence of tuberculosis in their medical history, physical examination, or chest x-ray and their sputum smears and culture are negative. Such individuals who do not have HIV infection will be given a six-month travel clearance, while those who are HIV-positive will receive a three-month travel clearance.[32] Individuals with equivocal results may be required to undergo additional screening procedures prior to being granted travel clearance.[33]

Individuals who are found to be positive for syphilis must undergo standard treatment. Once the recommended treatment has been completed, it is no longer a Class A condition. It may be a Class B condition, however, if the individual suffers from residual disability as a result of the infection, such as a neurologic abnormality resulting from previously untreated neurosyphilis.[34]

As indicated above, the technical instructions for both panel physicians and civil surgeons mandate the provision of treatment if an individual is found to have gonorrhea, chancroid, granuloma inguinale, or lymphogranuloma venereum. Once the recommended treatment has been completed, these are no longer Class A or Class B conditions and no certificate will be issued.[35]

WAIVERS OF INADMISSIBILITY
Waiver of Inadmissibility for Communicable Disease

A waiver of inadmissibility for tuberculosis or a sexually transmitted disease other than HIV is potentially available for an individual who[36]

(A) is the spouse or the unmarried son or daughter, or the minor unmarried lawfully adopted child, of a United States citizen, or of an alien lawfully admitted for permanent residence, or of an alien who had been issued an immigrant visa,

(B) has a son or daughter who is a United States citizen, or an alien lawfully admitted for permanent residence, or an alien who has been issued an immigrant visa; or

(C) is a VAWA self-petitioner.

Individuals undergoing pulmonary or laryngeal tuberculosis treatment may petition for a Class A waiver. Instructions to panel physicians indicate that

[25] *Id.* at 2.
[26] *Id.*
[27] 42 CFR §34.4(b).
[28] Tuberculosis screening and treatment instructions, *supra* note 12, at 10, Table 1.
[29] *Id.*
[30] *Id.*
[31] *Id.*
[32] *Id.*
[33] *Id.*
[34] Civil surgeon instructions, *supra* note 8, at III-6; Panel physician instructions, *supra* note 8, at III-6. Aliens excludable under the former INA §212(a)(6) [8 USC §1182(a)(6)] relating to "dangerous contagious diseases" who were cured by treatment received after arriving in the United States were admissible. *Klapholz v. Esperdy*, 201 F. Supp. 294 (S.D.N.Y. 1961), *aff'd on other grounds*, 302 F.2d 928 (2d Cir. 1962).
[35] Civil surgeon instructions, *supra* note 8, at III-7; Panel physician instructions, *supra* note 8, at III-7.
[36] INA §212(g)(1); 8 USC §1182(g)(1).

"[w]aivers should be pursued for any immigrant or refugee who has a complicated clinical course and would benefit from receiving treatment of [his or her] tuberculosis in the United States."[37]

Application for a waiver is made on Form I-601[38] and is submitted in conjunction with the application for adjustment of status or for the immigrant visa in conjunction with consular processing. The form is filed with the U.S. Citizenship and Immigration Services office having jurisdiction over the individual's place of residence if applying for adjustment of status or with the U.S. embassy or consulate if applying from outside of the United States.[39] The Division of Global Migration and Quarantine (DGMQ) within the CDC is responsible for the review of the waiver form and any supporting medical documentation.[40]

No fee is required if the waiver is needed because of tuberculosis.[41] Individuals with active or suspected tuberculosis must certify that on their admission to the United States they will:[42]

- Go directly to the physician that is predesignated on Form I-601

- Present all x-rays used in the examination to substantiate the diagnosis

- Submit to whatever examination, x-rays, treatment, or isolation that may be deemed necessary, and

- Continue with the prescribed inpatient or outpatient treatment until discharged.

The waiver application must also be endorsed by a state or local health department having jurisdiction over the alien's intended place of residence.[43]

The client's sponsoring family member will be required to arrange for the alien's medical care and have a private physician or local health department officer complete Section B of the form. Section B requires that the physician or health department officer certify that he or she will submit a completed "Report on Alien with Tuberculosis Waiver" to the CDC within 30 days of the alien's presentation or notify the CDC within a specified time period if the alien does not present for follow-up. The statement must verify:[44]

(1) that within 30 days after the client's reporting for care the DGMQ will be provided with a report detailing the client's presumptive diagnosis, test results, and plans for the client's future care or the failure of the client to present to the facility for such an evaluation, and

(2) that the client or his or her sponsoring family member has made arrangements to pay for any charges that might be incurred after the client's arrival in the United States for his or her care that is associated with the tuberculosis.

The application must be endorsed by a medical facility or department, such as a hospital or clinic, that is approved by the U.S. Public Health Service. The endorsement indicates recognition of the physician or facility that will be providing care for the tuberculosis. Additionally, the client or his or her sponsoring family member may be required to post a bond to ensure that he or she will not become a public charge.[45]

Form I-602 is used by refugee applicants for a waiver. Applicants must specify the ground on which they are seeking waiver: humanitarian reasons, to assure family unity, and/or because such waiver would be in the public interest. Applicants subject to inadmissibility because of tuberculosis must make a similar certification to that noted above and must also obtain the certification of a local or state health department official.

Waiver of Inadmissibility for Vaccination Requirement

The INA provides for the possibility of a waiver of the vaccination requirement for an alien[46]

(A) who receives vaccination against the vaccine-preventable disease or diseases for which the alien has failed to present documentation of previous vaccination,

---

[37] Tuberculosis screening and treatment instructions, *supra* note 12, at 15.

[38] 8 CFR §212.7(b)(1).

[39] *See* 8 CFR §212.7(b)(2).

[40] *See* www.cdc.gov/ncidod/dq/waiver.htm.

[41] Instructions for I-601, Application for Waiver of Grounds of Inadmissibility.

[42] Form I-601, p. 3.

[43] *See id.*

[44] *Id.*

[45] 8 CFR §212.7(b)(5).

[46] INA §212(g)(2); 8 USC §1182(g)(2).

(B) for whom a civil surgeon, medical officer, or panel physician ... certifies ... that such vaccination would not be medically appropriate, or

(C) [when] the requirement of such a vaccination would be contrary to the alien's religious belief or moral convictions ....

In cases in which the administration of the vaccine would be medically inappropriate, the civil surgeon must indicate this on the supplement to Form I-693 for vaccinations and the panel physician must note this on Form 3025, the Vaccination Documentation Worksheet, to be used in conjunction with Form DS-2053, Medical Examination for Immigrant or Refugee Applicant.[47] The physician must indicate which of the following reasons provides the basis for the waiver:[48]

- The vaccine is not age appropriate
- Administration of the vaccine is medically contraindicated
- There is an insufficient time interval between doses
- The vaccine is seasonal
- The vaccine is unavailable

An individual seeking a waiver of the vaccination requirement on the basis of religious objections must demonstrate that he or she (1) is opposed to vaccinations in any form; (2) those objections are premised on religious belief or moral convictions, regardless of whether or not the individual is a member of a recognized religion; and (3) the religious or moral belief is sincere, regardless of whether it is part of a recognized religion. If the waiver is for a child, the parents must satisfy these requirements.[49]

QUARANTINE AND ISOLATION PROVISIONS

Unlike the provisions relating to inadmissibility, which apply to all aliens, and the vaccination requirements that apply to only those individuals seeking permanent residence or adjustment of status,

provisions relating to quarantine and isolation apply to *all* individuals, including nonimmigrants and U.S. citizens. It is important that immigration attorneys be aware of the controlling provisions, because situations may arise in which their immigration clients are detained by health authorities despite admissibility. Knowledge of these provisions may help attorneys to better prepare their clients who are coming from areas of the world that have a high prevalence of the diseases for which quarantine and isolation are authorized. As an example, the prevalence of tuberculosis is significantly higher in parts of Africa and Southeast Asia than in countries of Western Europe and the United States. Consequently, individuals from these areas are at increased risk of exposure to the disease.[50]

The CDC bears the responsibility and authorization for the implementation of measures designed to prevent the entry and spread of communicable disease from foreign countries into the United States and between states. This authority has been delegated to the CDC from the U.S. Department of Health and Human Services, pursuant to section 361 of the Public Health Service Act.[51] Accordingly, the CDC is permitted to apprehend, examine, and, if necessary, detain individuals who are "coming into a State or possession from a foreign country or possession"[52] and those who are

reasonably believed to be infected with a communicable disease in a qualifying stage and (a) to be moving or about to move from a State to another State; or (B) to be a probable source of infection to individuals who, while infected with such disease in a qualifying stage, will be moving from a State to another State.[53]

A "qualifying stage" refers to a disease that is in a communicable stage or one that is in a precommunicable stage but could cause a public health emergency if it were to be transmitted to other individu-

[47] CDC, *Technical Instructions to Civil Surgeons for Vaccination Requirements (2003)*, available at www.cdc.gov/ncidod/dq/pdf/ti-03/ti-iz-cs-clrd.pdf; Technical instructions for vaccination, *supra* note 20; 9 *Foreign Affairs Manual* (FAM) 40.11 PN4.2.

[48] *Technical Instructions to Civil Surgeons for Vaccination Requirements*, *supra* note 47.

[49] 9 FAM 40.11 PN4.3.

[50] E. Corbett, *et al.*, "The Growing Burden of Tuberculosis: Global Trends and Interactions with the HIV Epidemic," 163 *Arch. Internal Med.* 1009 (2003); C. Dye, *et al.*, "Global Burden of Tuberculosis: Estimated Incidence, Prevalence, and Mortality by Country," 282 *JAMA* 677 (1999).

[51] 42 USC §264.

[52] 42 USC §264(c).

[53] 42 USC §264(d)(1). *See also* 42 CFR Parts 70, 71. The regulations regulating foreign quarantine are made applicable to aliens arriving at ports of the United States by 42 CFR §34.6.

als.[54] In some circumstances, the CDC may detain the entire crew and all passengers of a plane or vessel to investigate.

In order to carry out its designated responsibility, the CDC may impose quarantine or isolation measures to prevent the transmission of communicable diseases. Although the terms "quarantine" and "isolation" are often used interchangeably, they actually refer to different concepts. "Quarantine" is a mechanism utilized "to separate and restrict the movement of well persons who may have been exposed to a communicable disease to see if they become ill."[55] Individuals may have been unknowingly exposed to a disease, or they may actually be infected with the disease but are not yet displaying any symptoms of the infection. In such circumstances, quarantine may help to prevent the spread of the disease.[56] In the United States, underlying racism and xenophobia have sometimes provided the underlying motivation and impetus to utilize such measures. As an example, the San Francisco Board of Health attempted in the early 20th century to quarantine only Chinese residents for bubonic plague,[57] and, in more recent years, the United States became known as the only country in the world to establish an internment camp for the quarantine of HIV-seropositive asylum seekers—all of whom were black and Haitian.[58]

In contrast, isolation is used "to separate ill persons who have a communicable disease from those who are healthy."[59] This also helps to prevent the transmission of infectious disease. Hospitals often isolate individuals with infectious tuberculosis in order to prevent transmission to others.[60]

Several public health events in recent years have prompted the issuance of quarantine or isolation orders by the CDC. In 1963, a passenger arriving in the United States was quarantined due to suspected smallpox. In 2007, a U.S. citizen traveler suspected of having multidrug resistant tuberculosis was placed in isolation.[61] During the Severe Acute Respiratory Syndrome (SARS) outbreak of 2003, the CDC did not issue a quarantine or isolation order but, instead, conducted active surveillance, visual screening of passengers, and distributed travel health alert notices.[62]

By executive order of the president, diseases for which individuals may be quarantined or isolated currently include:[63]

- cholera
- diphtheria
- infectious tuberculosis
- plague, smallpox
- yellow fever
- viral hemorrhagic fevers (Lassa, Marburg, Ebola, Crimean-Congo, South American, and others)
- Severe Acute Respiratory Syndrome (SARS)
- influenza caused by novel or reemergent influenza that are causing, or have the potential to cause, a pandemic.

U.S. Customs and Border Protection and the U.S. Coast Guard are authorized to act to enforce federal quarantine orders.[64] State, local, and tribal health authorities may enforce isolation and quarantine within their borders. In cases of conflict, federal law prevails.

The Surgeon General can also order that the entry of persons from one or more countries be suspended entirely if there exists there a communicable disease for which

> there is serious danger of the introduction of such disease into the United States, and that this danger is so increased by the introduction of persons or property from such country that a suspension

---

[54] 42 USC §264(d)(2).

[55] *www.cdc.gov/ncidod/dq/facts2.htm.*

[56] *Id.*

[57] *See Wong Wai v. Williamson,* 103 F. 1 (N.D. Cal. 1900).

[58] *See Haitian Centers Council Inc. v. Sale,* 825 F. Supp. 1028, 1045 (E.D.N.Y. 1993). For a brief review of the use of quarantine measures, *see* F. Batisan, "Law in the Time of Cholera: Disease, State Power, and Quarantines Past and Future," 80 *Temple L. Rev.* 53 (2007). For an analysis of the constitutional limits of the power to isolate and quarantine, *see* M. Daubert, Comment, "Pandemic Fears and Contemporary Quarantine: Protecting Liberty Through a Continuum of Due Process Rights," 54 *Buff. L. Rev.* 1299 (2007).

[59] *www.cdc.gov/ncidod/dq/facts2.htm.*

[60] *Id.*

[61] A. Young, "Atlantan Quarantined with Deadly TB Strain," *Atlanta-Journal Constitution,* May 30, 2007; L. Altman, "Agency Warns of Surge in Drug-Resistant TB," *N.Y. Times,* June 6, 2007.

[62] *www.cdc.gov/ncidod/dq/facts2.htm.*

[63] Exec. Order No. 13295, 68 Fed. Reg. 17255 (Apr. 4, 2003), as amended by Exec. Order No. 13375, 70 Fed. Reg. 17299 (Apr. 1, 2005).

[64] 42 USC §268(b).

of the right to introduce such persons and property is required in the interest of the public health [65] ....

As an example, if there were a SARS epidemic in a particular country, the Surgeon General has the authority to suspend the entry of all individuals seeking entry from that country, even if they held a valid visa and were admissible.

KEY PRACTICE POINTS

- The provisions relating to inadmissibility due to communicable disease of public health significance are applicable to all individuals seeking entry into the United States, other than U.S. citizens, although it is highly unlikely that they would be applied to individuals already holding permanent residence.

- In general, other than HIV, inadmissibility due to a sexually transmitted disease is unlikely if the individual receives treatment for the infection.

- Screening procedures for tuberculosis vary depending on the region of the world from which the client is seeking entry.

- Clients found to have tuberculosis disease may be required to follow up with a public health official after arrival in the United States. It is critical that they do this, particularly because scientific research suggests that the screening and treatment provided in conjunction with the immigration-related medical examination may not be adequate. A failure to follow up may place their own health and the health of others at serious risk.

- The vaccination requirements do not apply to refugees and V and K visa applicants at the time of their initial admission to the United States.

- All individuals are subject to quarantine and isolation provisions, including U.S. citizens and permanent residents.

- History suggests that racism and xenophobia have provided the impetus for the use of quarantine procedures with specific groups of persons. This may be an issue to consider should litigation be required to contest quarantine orders that appear to be directed against specific groups.

---

[65] 42 USC §265.

SUBSTANCE USE, HEALTH-RELATED INADMISSIBILITY, AND WAIVERS

by Andrew J. Stevenson[*]

The apprehension in the silence on your client's end of the phone is palpable. His case initially seemed straightforward, even predictable, to you. But then something unexpected happened at the medical examination.

He explains: "Well … um … the doctor really focused in on some questions when I went in. A couple of months back, I was at my neighbor's, and there were some drugs there. When the doctor asked if I had ever done illegal drugs, I said, 'well, not me, but I was at my neighbor's, you know, this party, and I didn't do any but they were there around me. Since I didn't do any, they shouldn't show up on any test, but I was right there, so …' The doctor asked me again if *I* had ever done any drugs, and I said, 'well, yeah, not that time, but I did just *try* marijuana a couple of times. That was about a year ago, though; since then, never again, and I never got charged or convicted of anything.' *Is this going to be a problem for my case?*"

The short answer for this client is: yes, it could be a problem and it may even result in denial of his case. In fact, any applicant for U.S. immigration benefits who has even a minor history of substance use may be subjected to scrutiny upon consular processing of their visa or adjustment of status. This is not only limited to applicants who have a history of drug use, but may also include applicants who have struggled with alcoholism. The Department of State (DOS) and U.S. Citizenship and Immigration Services (USCIS) also have recently increased scrutiny on applicants with a history of arrests or convictions for alcohol-related offenses, including Driving Under the Influence (DUI).

This article will focus on how U.S. immigration authorities define and identify substance use as a health-related ground of inadmissibility, and how they determine whether an applicant's substance use actually triggers inadmissibility. It also discusses what appeals of these determinations may be made and what waivers of inadmissibility are available. Understanding this topic is important for practitioners, especially because substance use issues are frequently undisclosed or underreported by clients, and they may arise unexpectedly at critical stages of a case.

HEALTH-RELATED INADMISSIBILITY BASED ON SUBSTANCE USE

An applicant's history of substance use can trigger health-related inadmissibility under two distinct sections of the INA.

First, INA §212(a)(1)(A)(iv) declares inadmissible any alien "who is determined … to be a drug abuser or addict." This section is applied against applicants who have engaged in non-medical use of psychoactive substances. It is not necessarily limited to illegal drug use.

Second, INA §212(a)(1)(A)(iii) declares inadmissible any alien:

> who is determined … (I) to have a physical or mental disorder and behavior associated with the disorder that may pose, or has posed, a threat to the property, safety, or welfare of the alien or others, or (II) to have had a physical or mental disorder and a history of behavior associated with the disorder, which behavior has posed a threat to the property, safety, or welfare of the alien or others and which behavior is likely to recur or to lead to other harmful behavior ….

Drug or alcohol use may be deemed a "mental disorder" under this section. This ground of inadmissibility may be applied against applicants who have a history of drug- or alcohol-related incidents, arrests or convictions[1] that have involved personal injury or property damage.

---

[*] **Andrew J. Stevenson** is an associate in the law firm Wolfsdorf Immigration Law Group, LLP, in Santa Monica, CA. He practices exclusively in the area of immigration and nationality law, focusing primarily on inadmissibility issues and waivers, immigration analysis of U.S. and foreign criminal convictions, and family-based immigration. He has published a number of articles and received the American Immigration Law Foundation's Edward L. Dubroff Award for excellence in scholarly writing on immigration. He is a member of the California State Bar and AILA, and is a liaison to U.S. Customs and Border Protection for AILA's Southern California Chapter.

---

[1] In addition to health-related inadmissibility, it is important to keep in mind that applicants with any criminal convictions related to drugs or alcohol may also be subject to criminal inadmissibility at INA §212(a)(2).

In order to be declared inadmissible pursuant to either of these sections, a civil surgeon or panel physician must examine the applicant and classify him or her as having a "Class A" condition. The civil surgeon or panel physician's Class A diagnosis would confirm that the applicant is a "drug abuser or addict" or has a "physical or mental disorder" with associated harmful behavior,[2] and would automatically trigger inadmissibility.[3]

Alternatively, the civil surgeon or panel physician could classify the applicant as having a "Class B" condition, either as a drug abuser or addict in remission, or as a person with a mental disorder which is controlled by medication or in remission with no associated harmful behavior. A Class B diagnosis does not render the applicant inadmissible on health-related grounds,[4] although it does suggest to immigration authorities that follow-up medical care may be necessary in the United States.[5]

U.S. GOVERNMENT DEFINITIONS AND CLASSIFICATIONS OF INADMISSIBILITY

"Drug Abusers or Addicts"

Federal regulations and policy define which applicants may be classified as "drug abusers" and "drug addicts," and provide substantial guidance as to how applicants can be found inadmissible.

---

[2] *See* 42 CFR §34.2(d).

[3] See 9 *Foreign Affairs Manual* (FAM) 40.11 N3.3(1); U.S. Citizenship and Immigration Services (USCIS) *Adjudicator's Field Manual* (AFM) ch. 23.3(a), available at: *www.uscis.gov* (search for "adjudicator's field manual"). AILA Publications offers the 2007 edition of the USCIS *Adjudicator's Field Manual*. Visit *www.ailapubs.org* for more information and to see a table of contents.

[4] *See* 9 FAM 40.11 N3.3(2); AFM ch. 23.3(a).

[5] If the reviewing physician deems the applicant will necessarily or likely undergo medical treatment in the United States related to the diagnosis, this could lead to public charge inadmissibility issues. *See* Centers for Disease Control and Prevention (CDC), Division of Global Migration and Quarantine, *Instructions to Panel Physicians for Completing New U.S. Department of State MEDICAL EXAMINATION FOR IMMIGRANT OR REFUGEE APPLICANT (DS-2053) and Associated WORKSHEETS (DS-3024, DS-3025, and DS-3026)*, at 1, *available at: www.cdc.gov/Ncidod/dq/pdf/ds-forms-instructions.pdf*, [hereinafter Panel Physicians Forms Instructions] (noting that one purpose of the migration health assessment is to "determine if medical conditions or mental disorders exist that would … [r]equire the applicant to receive long-term institutionalization or maintenance income provided by the U.S. government after resettlement that is to become a *public charge*").

42 CFR §34.2(g) defines "drug abuse" as the "non-medical use of a controlled substance listed in section 202 of the Controlled Substances Act,[6] as amended (21 USC §802), which *has not necessarily resulted in physical or psychological dependence.*"[7] Similarly, 42 CFR §34.2(h) defines "drug addiction" as the "non-medical use of a controlled substance listed in section 202 of the Controlled Substances Act … which *has resulted in physical or psychological dependence.*"[8] The Technical Instructions written by the Centers for Disease Control and Prevention (CDC's) Division of Global Migration and Quarantine for Civil Surgeons and Panel Physicians clarify that "non-medical use" of "psychoactive substances" not listed in the Controlled Substances Act can also be grounds for a finding of drug abuse or addiction, but only if such use has resulted in "harmful or dysfunctional behavior patterns … or physical disorders."[9]

The phrase "non-medical use"—a central part of the regulatory definition for "drug addiction" or "drug abuse"—is defined as "more than experimentation with the substance."[10] Although "experimentation" is not explicitly defined, the Technical Instructions provide the example of "a single use of marijuana or other non-prescribed psychoactive substances such as amphetamines or barbiturates."[11] According to this strict definition, any applicant who has used marijuana, cocaine, amphetamines, barbiturates or any other controlled substance more than once may be declared inadmissible as a "drug abuser."[12]

---

[6] Section 202 of the Controlled Substances Act lists a wide range of substances, from "commonly abused" illicit drugs to prescription drugs with widely accepted medical uses.

[7] (Emphasis added).

[8] (Emphasis added). Note that a criminal conviction classifying the defendant as an "addict" is not necessarily determinative for immigration purposes. *See Matter of K–C–B–*, 6 I&N Dec. 274 (BIA 1954).

[9] *See* CDC, Division of Global Migration and Quarantine, *Technical Instructions for Medical Examination of Aliens* [for panel physicians]; CDC, Division of Global Migration and Quarantine, *Technical Instructions for Medical Examination of Aliens in the United States* [for civil surgeons], §III(C)(2)(a)(2), *available at www.cdc.gov/NCIDOD/dq/technica.htm* [collectively hereinafter CDC-DGMQ Technical Instructions].

[10] *Id.* at §III(C)(2)(c). *See also* 9 FAM 40.11 N9.1(c).

[11] CDC-DGMQ Technical Instructions, §III(C)(2)(c). *See also* 9 FAM §40.11 N9.1(c).

[12] The American Immigration Lawyers Association (AILA), through its Department of State (DOS) liaison committee, has vigorously contested the Technical Instructions' defini-
continued

Notwithstanding the number of times an applicant may have engaged in substance use, the *recency* of substance use is also a critical element in determining inadmissibility. The Technical Instructions state that an applicant who is currently using or has used a controlled substance in the past three years will be classified with a Class A condition[13] and will be declared inadmissible. The Instructions clarify that use of any controlled substance in the past three years is "illegal and qualifies as a Class A condition, whether or not harmful behavior is documented."[14] Any applicant who has used an unlisted (*i.e.,* non-controlled) psychoactive substance in the past two years will also be classified with a Class A condition and declared inadmissible.[15]

In contrast, any applicant who has a history of substance use, but has not used a controlled substance in the past three years and has not used an unlisted psychoactive substance in the past two years will be considered in "remission." The Technical Instructions direct that applicants in "remission" should be classified with a Class B condition,

---

tion of "drug abuse" as overly broad, alleging that it is inconsistent with CDC's *Instructions to Panel Physicians for Completing Medical History and Physical Examination Worksheet (DS-3026). See* AILA, "Practice Alert on 'Drug Abuser or Addict' Grounds of Inadmissibility," *published on* AILA InfoNet at Doc. No. 06020110 (*posted* Feb. 1, 2006), at 2. The CDC's instructions to panel physicians completing Medical History Form DS-3026 appear to imply that the phrase "drug abuse" should be defined as a "maladaptive pattern of substance use" leading to "recurrent" or "continued use," as directed by the *Diagnostic and Statistical Manual of Mental Disorders. See* Panel Physicians Forms Instructions, *supra* note 5, at 11. Accordingly, AILA-DOS liaison attorneys argued that a panel physician's analysis of whether an applicant is a "drug abuser" use should be made not just in light of the number of times of use, but also with regard to whether the applicant's use represents a "maladaptive pattern." However, AILA's appeals to DOS have not resulted in any policy changes, as DOS subsequently directed consular officers to defer to the "professional judgments" of CDC's panel physicians. *See* AILA, "Visa Office Clarification on Drug Abuse/Addict Ineligibility Standard," *published on* AILA InfoNet at Doc. No. 06052460 (*posted* May 24, 2006), at 1–2. In the aftermath of these liaison inquiries, consular practitioners consistently report that panel physicians make Class A findings of "drug abuse" according to the strict definition of the Technical Instructions—when an applicant has used a controlled substance more than once, and the last use occurred within the past three years.

[13] *See* CDC-DGMQ Technical Instructions, §III, Table 6.

[14] *Id.* at §III(C)(2)(a)(1).

[15] *See id.* at §III, Table 6.

and thus should not automatically be declared inadmissible as "drug abusers or addicts."[16]

To aid panel physicians and civil surgeons in distinguishing between circumstances warranting Class A and Class B determinations, the Technical Instructions include a Table entitled "Reporting Results of Evaluation for Psychoactive Substance Abuse."[17] A copy of this table is attached to this article as Appendix 1.

Drug- and Alcohol-Related Offenses as "Mental Disorders" with Associated Harmful Behavior

Federal policy and practice manuals also define when incidents of substance use may be classified as mental disorders with associated harmful behavior sufficient to trigger health-related inadmissibility.

The Technical Instructions indicate that alcoholism, alcohol abuse and drug abuse can all be classified as "mental disorders."[18] However, "the mere presence of a physical or mental disorder does not by itself render [an] applicant ineligible" for a visa."[19] In order for an applicant to be inadmissible, one or more incidents of substance use "must be associated with a ... display of harmful behavior."[20]

"Harmful behavior" is defined as "a dangerous action or series of actions by the alien that has resulted in injury (psychological or physical) to the alien or another person, or that has threatened the health or safety of the alien or another person, or that has resulted in property damage."[21] A criminal conviction "is not determinative" as to whether the applicant has a history of harmful behavior.[22] Therefore, the nature of the behavior must be qualitatively examined by the medical examiner.[23]

Generally, the Technical Instructions direct that Class A certifications should only be made under this

---

[16] *See id.*

[17] *Id.*

[18] *See id.* at §III, Table 4 (items 7–8).

[19] 9 FAM 40.11 N8.

[20] *See id.*

[21] CDC-DGMQ Technical Instructions, §III(B)(2)(c); 9 FAM 40.11 N8.1(a).

[22] *See* 9 FAM 40.11 N8.1(b).

[23] Alcohol or drug use is not, by itself, considered a mental disorder with associated harmful behavior. *See* CDC-DGMQ Technical Instructions, §III, Table 4, "Mental Disorders for which Harmful Behavior Is an Element of the Diagnostic Criteria" (noting that "behavior [is] necessary to establish the diagnosis" of inadmissibility on this ground based on alcohol and drug use).

section if an applicant currently engages in substance use associated with harmful behavior, or has a history of substance use with harmful behavior which is likely to recur.[24] Conversely, if an applicant's pattern of substance use and associated harmful behavior is controlled by medication[25] or is in remission,[26] and thus the harmful behavior is unlikely to recur, a Class B diagnosis may be made.[27]

Similar to the table regarding drug abuser or addict determinations, the Technical Instructions also include a Table entitled "Reporting Results of Evaluation for Mental and Physical Disorders with Associated Harmful Behavior."[28] A copy of this table is attached to this article as Appendix 2.

U.S. GOVERNMENT IDENTIFICATION AND INVESTIGATION OF AN APPLICANT'S SUBSTANCE USE

There are various ways in which an applicant's substance use may be disclosed by the applicant or affirmatively identified by U.S. immigration authorities. In all applications for immigrant visas or adjustment of status, substance use questions arise as part of the required medical examination by a civil surgeon or panel physician.[29] Additionally, applicants must disclose on many forms whether they are a "drug abuser or addict," have ever used illicit drugs, or have a substance-related "mental disorder" with associated harmful behavior.[30] Likewise, if an applicant has ever been arrested or convicted for a drug- or alcohol-related offense, this must also be disclosed on many forms. In some instances, regardless of whether the applicant has already completed a medical examination, USCIS or DOS officials may order the applicant to be re-examined by a civil surgeon or panel physician regarding substance use issues.

Medical Examination and Screening by Civil Surgeons and Panel Physicians

As part of the required medical examination for immigrant visa applicants, a civil surgeon or panel physician interviews all applicants regarding their medical history and conditions. The Technical Instructions direct the medical examiner to ask "specific questions about psychoactive drug and alcohol use [and] history of harmful behavior."[31] Initial substance use screening questions are normally general (*e.g.,* "have you ever used illegal drugs"), but if an applicant reveals a history of use, questions become much more detailed regarding the substance(s) used, frequency of use, and date of last use. While not necessarily commonplace, some panel physicians have been reported to ask non-affirmative and confusing questions regarding substance use (*e.g.,* "have you used drugs less than 10 times"). Medical examiners also frequently take blood or urine samples, which may be tested to detect substance use.

Additionally, the examining physician will inquire about records and likely ask to review all available documents pertaining to hospitalizations and institutionalizations,[32] including the applicant's participation in rehabilitation programs. Examiners may also ask to review police, military, school, employment or other records for evidence of "harmful behavior … nonmedical use of psychoactive substances or evidence of alcohol abuse or dependence."[33] An examiner might even go so far as to interview the applicant's family regarding substance use "when practical and clinically relevant … as this information may not be included in medical records."[34] The examining physician might ask questions, for example, to an applicant's spouse if he or she is undergoing a medical examination for immigration purposes on the same day as the applicant.

Finally, if the civil surgeon or panel physician cannot make a "definitive diagnosis" of whether the applicant has a Class A or Class B condition, he or she may refer the applicant to a specific medical or mental health specialist to evaluate their condition.[35] After receiving a report from the specialist, the

---

[24] *See id.* at Table 5.

[25] Applicants whose condition is controlled by medication may be required to certify in writing that they "will continue medication or other treatment to control the disorder and prevent harmful behavior." *See id.* at p. III-13, n. ****.

[26] "Remission" is defined as "no pattern of the behavioral element of the disorder for the past 2 years." *See id.*

[27] *See id.* at Table 5.

[28] *Id.*

[29] *See* CDC-DGMQ Technical Instructions, §III(C)(1).

[30] *See, e.g.,* Form DS-156, Question 38; Form DS-230 Part II, Question 30a; Form I-485, Part 3, Question 1a. U.S. Customs and Border Protection (CBP) Form I-94W Question A, also screens these issues for applicants for admission under the Visa Waiver Program.

---

[31] CDC-DGMQ Technical Instructions, §H(A)(1)(a)(4).

[32] *See id.* at §§II(A)(1)(a)(1)–(2).

[33] *Id.* at §III(B)(3)(b).

[34] *Id.* at §III(B)(3)(c).

[35] *See id.* at §II(C).

medical examiner will complete his or her report and diagnosis to DOS or USCIS.[36]

Referrals for Medical Examination or Re-Examination of Certain Applicants

DOS and USCIS officials also may ask screening questions regarding an applicant's substance use at in-person interviews, often as part of reviewing immigration forms. If information disclosed on an immigration form or an answer to a verbal question highlights that an applicant has engaged in substance use, the DOS or USCIS officer may refer the applicant to a panel physician or civil surgeon for examination or re-examination. As a practical matter, these referrals commonly occur when an applicant discloses substance use or convictions for the first time in an interview with immigration officials.

Applicants with DUI Arrests or Convictions

Over the past several years, DOS and the Department of Homeland Security (DHS) have issued specific guidance regarding alcohol use and applicants with DUI arrests or convictions. Agency memoranda and policy clearly reflect that U.S. immigration authorities consider drunk driving a serious mental disorder with great potential for harmful behavior. However, DOS and USCIS officials will not make any health-related inadmissibility determinations without first receiving a report and Class A diagnosis of the applicant by a medical professional. Thus, immigration and consular officers may refer applicants with a record of alcohol-related arrests or convictions to be examined or re-examined by a panel physician or civil surgeon with regard to these incidents.

These referrals commonly occur at the consular level with nonimmigrant visa (NIV) applicants who have a record of DUI arrests or convictions, but have not previously visited a panel physician. They may also occur for consular immigrant visa (IV) applicants who did not discuss their record of DUI arrests or conviction with the panel physician during their medical examination. Likewise, USCIS will refer adjustment of status (AOS) applicants to civil surgeons for further review if the applicant has a record of arrests or convictions, and no discussion of the applicant's record appears in the medical examination report.

In June 2007, DOS released a cable mandating referrals to panel physicians for *all* visa applicants with "a single drunk driving arrest or conviction within the last three calendar years or two or more drunk driving arrests or convictions in any time period" or where "there is any other evidence to suggest an alcohol problem."[37] In the cases of IV applicants who already have undergone examination by a panel physician, medical examiners are directed to "evaluat[e] for the presence of a mental disorder previously unnoticed before ... [becoming] aware of [an] alcohol-related arrest."[38] The cable clarifies that incidents of alcohol abuse or drunk driving alone are not a sufficient basis for health-related inadmissibility, and must be accompanied by harmful behavior to make an applicant ineligible to receive a visa.[39] However, this policy of mandatory referrals to panel physicians for further examination will add an extra step which complicates and delays consular processing for many applicants.

Similarly, USCIS officers are required to refer AOS applicants for re-examination by a civil surgeon "when the criminal record of [the] applicant ... reveals a significant history of alcohol-related driving arrests and/or convictions, and the Form I-693 medical report does not reflect that the alcohol-related driving incidents were considered by the civil surgeon."[40] However, not all applicants with a record of DUI arrests or convictions will be re-examined. Referral for re-examination is only mandatory for applicants with a "significant criminal record of alcohol-related driving incidents," namely:

- One or more arrest/conviction for DUI/DWI while the applicant's driver's license was suspended, revoked or restricted at the time of the arrest due to a previous DUI/DWI incident;

- One or more arrest/conviction for DUI/DWI where personal injury or death resulted from the incident(s);

- One or more conviction for DUI/DWI where the conviction was a felony in the jurisdiction in

---

[36] *Id.* at §III(B)(4)(c).

[37] DOS Cable, "Guidance on Processing Visa Applicants with Drunk Driving Hits" (June 7, 2007), *published on* AILA InfoNet at Doc. No. 07071760 (*posted* July 16, 2007), at 1.

[38] *Id.*

[39] *Id.*; *see also* 9 FAM 40.11 N8.3 (revised pursuant to the 6/7/07 DOS cable).

[40] Department of Homeland Security (DHS) Memorandum, W. Yates, "Requesting Medical Re-examination: Aliens Involved in Significant Alcohol-Related Driving Incidents and Similar Scenarios" (Jan. 16, 2004), *published on* AILA InfoNet at Doc. No. 04022362 (*posted* Jan. 23, 2004), at 2–3.

which it occurred or where a sentence of incarceration was actually imposed;

- Two or more arrests/convictions for DUI/DWI within the preceding two years; or

- Three or more arrests/convictions for DUI/DWI where one arrest/conviction was within the preceding two years.[41]

In the re-examination, the civil surgeon will investigate the applicant's "mental status … specifically addressing the incidents revealed in the criminal record"[42] and must make a Class A diagnosis to trigger health-related inadmissibility.

PRACTICE POINTERS: PREPARING YOUR CLIENT FOR A MEDICAL EXAMINATION OR A REFERRAL TO A MEDICAL EXAMINER

If a client has disclosed a record of substance use or related arrests or convictions to you, you should prepare your client to affirmatively disclose these facts to the panel physician, civil surgeon or immigration officer. Any applicant who gives incomplete or inconsistent answers to a medical examiner regarding substance use may be subjected to further investigation of his or her medical history. If evidence of substance use is ultimately discovered through documents or interviews that contradict the applicant's attestations to the medical examiner, these inconsistencies may be documented in the medical examination report. According to such a report or other inconsistent statements made at the time of interview, a DOS or USCIS officer could declare an applicant inadmissible not only on health-related grounds, but also on the basis of fraud or willful misrepresentation.[43]

Immigration practitioners may also affirmatively address substance use and drug- and alcohol-related arrests and convictions in a short brief to support their client's admissibility. This may be submitted to DOS, attached to the requisite DS forms, or to USCIS, attached to Form I-485. A declaration from the applicant should be submitted with the legal brief, detailing which substances were used, frequency of use, date of last use, whether the applicant's use ever involved harmful behavior, and whether the applicant was ever arrested or convicted for substance-related offenses. Letters of support from friends, family, religious leaders or others also may be submitted to support an applicant's claims of being an infrequent user, in remission or having a history of no harmful behavior associated with use. The brief also should include copies of all applicable medical or criminal documentation for agency review, including:

- Medical records regarding hospitalization or treatment for substance use, including participation in rehabilitation programs;

- Documentation of any prescribed medication related to the above treatment;

- Certified court disposition(s) of any criminal case(s) relating to DUI/substance use; and/or

- Police report(s) relating to arrest(s) for DUI/substance use.

Copies of these documents should also be prepared to provide to the medical examiner upon request. Failure to provide these documents may result in delays in adjudication or issuance of a request for evidence (RFE).

As a practical matter, DOS and USCIS referrals to panel physicians and civil surgeons for examination or re-examination of substance use will, at minimum, delay the adjudication of an applicant's case. It may take as long as several months from the time of referral until the time of adjudication. This is especially true if the case is pending abroad, and it depends on the country, the appointment availability of panel physicians, and whether or not an applicant is referred to a psychiatrist or other specialist for further evaluation. At the same time, in some countries, referral to adjudication may take as little as one to two weeks. Other country-specific complications may also arise. For example, in Mexico, the only panel physicians certified to review applicants for health-related inadmissibility in the entire country are located in Ciudad Juarez. NIV applicants from all over Mexico who are referred for medical examination due to a DUI arrest in the past three years have no choice but to travel to Ciudad Juarez, and then back again to the post where they applied to await final adjudication and visa issuance. Different countries or consular posts, depending on local culture and other factors, may also define "other evidence suggesting an alcohol problem" in very different ways and therefore will have varying referral

---

[41] *Id.* at 3.

[42] *Id.*

[43] *See* INA §212(a)(6)(C)(i). This is an especially important consideration because health-related inadmissibility based on substance use may be merely temporary (until an applicant has been in remission for several years), whereas fraud-based inadmissibility is permanent.

processes. In the United States, obtaining a referral-based appointment with a civil surgeon may present fewer challenges, but USCIS adjudication time may vary greatly depending on the Field Office with jurisdiction over the case.

APPEALS AND WAIVERS OF HEALTH-RELATED INADMISSIBILITY DETERMINATIONS BASED ON SUBSTANCE USE

If an applicant is declared inadmissible on health-related grounds because of substance use, he or she still may have several options to be admitted to the United States. First, although on a practical level this strategy may have a very low chance of success, the applicant may request an advisory opinion or a medical re-examination by the CDC to contest a Class A diagnosis triggering inadmissibility. Second, the applicant may be eligible for a waiver of inadmissibility.

Seeking an Advisory Opinion or Medical Re-examination by the CDC after an Erroneous Class A Determination by a Medical Examiner

If a visa applicant disagrees with a determination made by a panel physician characterizing the applicant as inadmissible on health-related grounds, he or she may request that the consular officer seek an advisory opinion from the CDC.[44] A CDC consultant physician will then review the panel physician's report and Class A diagnosis of the applicant, and will provide the consular officer with an opinion as to whether the diagnosis was correctly made.[45]

42 CFR §34.8 also authorizes the CDC to re-examine the medical condition of an applicant classified by a civil surgeon or a panel physician as having a Class A condition triggering inadmissibility. However, there is no regulatory authority for applicants or attorneys to initiate this re-examination process directly with CDC. It appears that appealing parties must communicate with DHS to request a re-examination, although the process for doing so is unclear.[46] As part

of the re-examination process, "a board of medical officers" convened by CDC will review all records submitted by the applicant and other witnesses, medical history documents and reports submitted by other physicians who have examined the applicant's mental condition.[47] The board will notify the applicant of a time and place for an official medical re-examination, and may discretionarily allow oral or written medical expert testimony on the applicant's behalf.[48] The board's decision is final and cannot be appealed or reconsidered except upon express authorization of the Director of the CDC.[49]

As a practical matter, either of these options may be a futile exercise for an applicant deemed inadmissible pursuant to findings in the medical examiner's report. According to practitioners' reports, CDC advisory opinions very rarely result in reversal of a panel physician's Class A diagnosis of an applicant. Additionally, CDC re-examinations of applicants rarely occur at all,[50] although their uncommonness may be attributable to logistical difficulties in initiating the re-examination process through DHS.

Waivers of Health-Related Inadmissibility Based on Substance Use

Nonimmigrant Visa Waivers

INA §212(d)(3) allows for discretionary waivers of all grounds of health-related inadmissibility for NIV applicants.[51] In considering whether to grant an NIV waiver, a consular officer will consider and balance three factors: (1) the recency and seriousness of the condition causing inadmissibility, (2) the reasons for the applicant's travel to the United States, and (3) the positive or negative effect, if any, of the applicant's travel on U.S. public interests.[52] It is important

---

[44] AILA Liaison Update, "Visa Office Clarification on Drug Abuse/Addict Ineligibility Standard," *published on* AILA InfoNet at Doc. No. 06052460 (*posted* May 24, 2006).

[45] *Id.*

[46] *See* 42 CFR §34.8(a)(2) (stating that re-examination may occur "[u]pon an appeal *to the INS* by an alien who … has been certified for a Class A condition") (emphasis added). A CDC representative acknowledged to the author that there is no clear interagency procedure set in place for applicants to communicate with DHS to request a medical re-examination by CDC. Telephone interview with Joe Foster, Legal Coun-
continued

sel, CDC (Feb. 29, 2008). However, the CDC representative also maintained that, according to federal regulations, it is not appropriate for applicants or attorneys to request such an examination directly from the CDC. *Id.* Clarifying how an applicant should request a medical re-examination from CDC appears to be an issue ripe for AILA liaison clarification with USCIS.

[47] *See* 42 CFR §34.8(c).

[48] *See id.* at §§34.8(d)–(f).

[49] *Id.* at §34.8(k).

[50] Telephone interview Joe Foster, Legal Counsel, CDC (Feb. 29, 2008).

[51] *See also* 9 FAM 40.11 N11.

[52] 9 FAM 40.301 N3(b); *see also Matter of Hranka*, 16 I&N Dec. 491 (BIA 1978) (the seminal case in the area of INA §212(d)(3) waivers).

238

IMMIGRATION & NATIONALITY LAW HANDBOOK, 2008–09

to note that waivers are not "limited to humanitarian or other exceptional cases" and that a consular officer can recommend a waiver "for any legitimate purpose."[53] Consular officers may recommend multiple-entry waivers for applicants deemed inadmissible as drug abusers, but waivers for applicants classified as drug addicts or having mental disorders are only eligible for single-entry waivers.[54]

To support an NIV waiver application, there is no required form,[55] but practitioners may submit supporting evidence to the consular officer. Such evidence should include a declaration from the applicant and letters of support from friends, family, religious leaders or others with a personal or professional relationship with the applicant. These statements should directly address the applicant's substance use, but should highlight that he or she is an infrequent user, in remission or has no history of harmful behavior associated with use. The statements should also emphasize that the applicant poses no threat or risk to U.S. national security or public health based on his or her history of substance use. Depending on the type of visa the applicant is seeking, you also may be able to present compelling evidence regarding the importance of the applicant's travel to the United States. For example, if the applicant has been invited to engage in business activities in the United States, you may wish to include letters of support from U.S. business partners describing the importance of the applicant's contributions and the positive ways his or her travel stands to affect the U.S. economy. If the applicant will only be a temporary visitor for personal or family reasons, it is still recommendable to submit evidence to clarify the personal importance of the trip to the United States. Finally, if the applicant may need medical treatment in the United States related to a past history of substance use or seeks entry to attend a rehabilitation facility, it is critically important to submit evidence of financial resources proving the applicant's ability to pay for treatment.[56]

As a matter of procedure, a consular officer must determine that an applicant is inadmissible to the United States before the post may consider a §212(d)(3) waiver application. The applicant may be found inadmissible pursuant to a panel physician's Class A diagnosis made during the preceding three years, or the consular officer may directly refer the applicant for a new medical examination if substance use problems arise during the visa interview. In cases where the applicant is referred to a panel physician, the applicant should be prepared to disclose his or her substance use history, as well as provide related records to the panel physician. If drug use during the past three years will be at issue, it is recommended that the applicant also obtain independent drug test results showing that he or she has not used for a significant period of time. Clean drug tests can be significant proof that an applicant's use is neither recent nor serious, and can strongly support issuance of a waiver even if use has occurred within the past three years.

Once an applicant is declared inadmissible, evidence supporting the waiver application may be submitted, and the reviewing consular officer or his or her supervisor will make a recommendation either to grant or deny the waiver.[57] If the recommendation is favorable, DOS forwards the application to the Admissibility Review Office (ARO) in Washington, D.C. for final adjudication. NIV waivers routinely take 30-60 days to reach a final adjudication, and if approved, the consular post will issue the visa with a "§212(d)(3)" annotation.

Although all §212(d)(3) waivers are adjudicated on a case-by-case basis, the factors in the DOS's *Foreign Affairs Manual* (FAM) and controlling case law are a good common-sense guide for which waiver cases may be viable. Applicants who can present documentation proving remission or rehabilitation over a significant period of time, or can otherwise reasonably distance themselves from their last use by a year or more, may have better chances of being granted a waiver. Likewise, applicants with a very compelling reason to travel to the United States or whose presence would measurably benefit the United States may also present viable waiver cases. Conversely, applicants who are found to have recently engaged in substance use (especially if linked to harm

[53] 9 FAM 40.301 N3(a). The FAM provides several examples of a "legitimate purpose," including "family visits, medical treatment (whether or not available abroad), business conferences, tourism, etc." *Id.*

[54] *Id.* at N.6.3(1) & (2).

[55] The one exception is for visa-exempt Canadian applicants, who must submit NIV waivers on Form I-192 to CBP officials at a port of entry.

[56] *See* 9 FAM 40.11 N11.

[57] If the consular post's recommendation is to deny the waiver, the post will forward the waiver application request to a central DOS authority for review and recommendation. *See* 9 FAM 40.301 N6.2-1.

to self or others), have a long pattern of use with no demonstrable rehabilitation and have no compelling reason to visit the United States may encounter difficulties in obtaining a waiver.

Immigrant Visa Waivers

IV waivers are categorically unavailable for applicants declared inadmissible as drug abusers or addicts.[58]

However, INA §212(g)(3) does authorize IV waivers for applicants diagnosed with a mental disorder with associated harmful behavior.[59] The waiver application must be submitted on Form I-601 to DOS or USCIS, and is forwarded to CDC's Division of Global Migration and Quarantine (DGMQ) for review. Form I-601 must be accompanied by a medical report or a statement that arrangements have been made for submission of a medical report, including "a complete medical history of the alien ... [and] [f]indings as to the current physical ... [and] mental condition of the alien, with information as to prognosis ... and with a report of a psychiatric examination."[60]

With regard to substance use and associated harmful behavior, this waiver may apply most commonly to applicants with criminal convictions implicating that alcohol abuse has resulted in harm to self, others or property. This may include, but is not limited to: DUI incidents resulting in damage to a person or property, and domestic violence, battery or assault incidents in which alcohol use was involved and well-documented in court and law enforcement documents reviewed by immigration officials. In some rare cases, applicants with multiple DUI convictions, even without any associated harm to persons or property, may be classified by panel physicians as "threaten[ing] the health or safety of the alien or others," and thus require a waiver to overcome inadmissibility.

In response to these scenarios, the medical reports and waiver application should be prepared very carefully, preferably by medical professionals who have a previous history with and knowledge of the applicant, and always with the guidance of an immigration attorney. Generally, the physician's report should detail

any treatment the applicant has received, medication he or she has been prescribed, rehabilitation and the applicant's ability to function productively and self-sufficiently. Similarly, the psychiatric examination should highlight the applicant's progress toward rehabilitation and, if appropriate, the unlikely nature of recurring harmful behavior related to substance use. All reports should describe the applicant's habits or pattern of consuming alcohol. Medical professionals should comment as to how, if at all, this pattern of alcohol use inhibits the applicant's ability to function professionally or care for others in family and social relationships. The reports should specifically mention whether the applicant's alcohol use has habitually or on any specific occasion posed danger to any other person or property or caused any harm. It should also mention whether the applicant's drinking has caused any harm or is particularly dangerous to his or her health. The reports should certify, to the extent that it is accurate, that the applicant is a fully functioning member of society whose use of alcohol is not detrimental or dangerous to his or anyone else's health or safety. If the applicant has an established record of harming or endangering self, others or property while under the influence, the report should address each incident and how the applicant has rehabilitated: physically, through remission, and psychologically, through therapy or self-examination. If medication or a specific treatment plan was prescribed or suggested by a medical professional, this should be reviewed in detail, and the applicant's positive performance and rehabilitation should be emphasized. Additionally, the reports should recognize completion of classes (regarding substance use or rehabilitation from particular criminal behavior) or participation in groups such as Alcoholics Anonymous.

As a matter of law, the medical reports are the most important pieces of the IV waiver application package. However, as a practical matter, other documents can also be helpful to establish an overall tone of rehabilitation and reform from prior incidents of alcohol use or abuse. A conciliatory affidavit from the applicant describing his or her personal strides to rehabilitate and achieve change to better the lives their family may be appropriate or meaningful. Likewise, affidavits or letters of support from family and close friends regarding the applicant's rehabilitation and positive character may help round out the waiver application.

If the IV waiver is approved, the applicant must provide a post-entry evaluation report conducted by a medical facility approved by the U.S. Public

---

[58] See INA §212(g) (setting forth immigrant visa waiver options for all health-related inadmissibility categories except §212(a)(1)(A)(iv)); see also 9 FAM 40.11 N10.4.

[59] See also 9 FAM 40.11 N10.3.

[60] See DHS, USCIS, "Instructions for I-601, Application for Waiver of Grounds of Inadmissibility."

Health Service to CDC within 30 days after entering the United States.[61] DHS may also restrict the waiver to certain terms, conditions or controls it deems appropriate on a case-by-case basis, which may include posting of a bond.[62]

CONCLUSION

Health-related inadmissibility due to drug or alcohol use is an important issue to understand because it can result in unexpected denials at the critical end-stages of visa applications. The CDC's technical instructions are somewhat difficult to wade through and the definitions of inadmissibility are harsh. If an applicant's substance use is not disclosed or discovered until the time of his or her visa interview, the case may be complicated and delayed by a referral to a panel physician or civil surgeon. However, a basic understanding of all these issues can be a great asset in analyzing your client's record, anticipating adverse consequences, setting client expectations and making sure the case doesn't "go to pot."

---

[61] *See* 8 CFR §212.7(b)(4)(ii).

[62] INA §212(g)(3); 8 CFR §212.7(b)(5).

APPENDIX 1

Table 6

Reporting Results of Evaluation for Psychoactive Substance Abuse

Findings	Record on Medical Report Form
Current nonmedical use or use within the last 3 years of a substance listed in section 202 of the Controlled Substances Act	Class A condition List substance(s) used.
History of nonmedical use of a substance listed in section 202 of the Controlled Substances Act No use in last 3 years	Class B condition Note whether dysfunctional behavior or associated physical disorder is present.
Current abuse or abuse within the last 2 years of a psychoactive substance other than those listed in section 202 of the Controlled Substances Act	Class A condition List substance(s) used.
History of abuse of a psychoactive substance other than those listed in section 202 of the Controlled Substances act No use in the last 2 years	Class B condition Note whether dysfunctional behavior or associated physical disorder is present.

from CDC's Technical Instructions to Panel Physicians / Civil Surgeons

APPENDIX 2

Table 5

Reporting Results of the Evaluation for Mental and Physical
Disorders with Associated Harmful Behavior*

Findings	Record on Medical Report Form
No current evidence of physical or mental disorder No history of physical or mental disorder and no history of harmful behavior	No Class A or Class B condition
Mental shortcomings due solely to lack of education and no harmful behavior	No Class A or Class B condition
Mental condition, with or without harmful behavior, attributable to remediable physical causes; or temporary--caused by a toxin, medically prescribed drug, or disease	(Treat underlying condition or refer for treatment; complete medical report form after reevaluation.)
History of physical or mental disorder and history of associated harmful behavior Physical or mental disorder not currently present and harmful behavior not likely to recur **	No Class A or Class B condition (Report diagnosis and reason(s) for judging that harmful behavior will not recur.)
Current evidence of a physical or mental disorder and associated harmful behavior or history of associated harmful behavior	Class A condition (Report diagnosis and description of harmful behavior.)
History of physical or mental disorder and history of associated harmful behavior, and harmful behavior likely to recur	Class A condition (Report diagnosis, description of harmful behavior, and reason(s) for judging that harmful behavior is likely to recur.)
Current evidence of a physical or mental disorder but no history of associated harmful behavior	Class B condition (Report diagnosis.)
History of physical or mental disorder and history of associated harmful behavior Physical or mental condition controlled by medication or in remission.*** No currently associated harmful behavior, and behavior judged not likely to recur.****	Class B condition (Report diagnosis, description of harmful behavior and reason(s) for judging that behavior is not likely to recur.)

*Includes alcohol abuse/dependence, which, under the new law, is to be considered as any other
mental or physical disorder with associated harmful behavior.

**E.g., an otherwise normal person with a history of a physical or mental disorder and associated
harmful behavior that is unlikely to recur (e.g., suicide attempt during reactive depression over
the death of a spouse, and the person is no longer considered a suicidal risk).

***E.g., an alien with a history of harmful behavior due to a disorder or condition that continues
but that has been managed with medication (e.g., person who has a manic-depressive illness that is
treated with lithium) or that is in remission.

****The behavior can be judged not likely to recur if the alien is able to demonstrate that the
disorder is in remission, remission being defined as no pattern of the behavioral element of the
disorder for the past 2 years (5 years in the case of antisocial personality disorder, impulse
control disorders not otherwise classified, paraphilias that involve behaviors that threaten others,
and conduct disorders); or the alien's condition is controlled by medication and the alien certifies
in writing that he or she will continue medication or other treatment to control the disorder and
prevent harmful behavior.

III-13

from CDC's Technical Instructions to Panel Physicians / Civil Surgeons

Waivers of the Joint-Filing Requirement to Remove Conditions on Resident Status: I-751 Waivers

by Karen R. Seiden[*]

INTRODUCTION

The Immigration Marriage Fraud Amendments of 1986[1] (IMFA) contained, among other elements, a requirement to file a Petition for Removal of Condition during the 90-day period preceding the second anniversary of the noncitizen's acquisition of resident status. This petition was to be filed jointly by the U.S. citizen or lawful permanent resident (LPR) spouse and the conditional resident (CR). IMFA also allowed for a waiver of the joint-filing requirement based on specified grounds if the joint petition could not be filed. IMFA was modified by the Immigration Act of 1990[2] (IMMACT90), which broadened the grounds for filing for a waiver of the joint-filing requirement.[3] Currently, INA §216(c)(4) allows a CR to obtain a waiver of the joint-filing requirement and remove the condition on resident status if the CR can show that he or she qualifies on one of three distinct bases: (1) extreme hardship to the CR if removed, (2) a good-faith marriage that has been terminated, or (3) a good-faith marriage during which the CR or child suffered battery or extreme cruelty at the hands of the spouse.[4] The CR files the waiver on Form I-751.

On the surface, the law appears straightforward. However, as immigration practitioners are aware, seemingly simple statements of law are often rife with controversy, contradiction, and varying interpretation. Such is the case with the joint-filing waivers. Each basis for a waiver of the joint-filing requirement will be looked at separately and some common facets and issues will be addressed.

THE WAIVER BASES

Hardship Waiver

Under Immigration and Nationality Act (INA) §216(c)(4)(A), a CR who can show that "extreme hardship would result if such alien is removed" is eligible to have the joint-filing requirement waived and the conditional basis of resident status removed.[5] The extreme hardship can be to the CR, a dependent child, or a subsequent spouse.[6] The marriage that gave rise to the conditional resident status may have been terminated or not; termination of the marriage is not required, and subsequent remarriage is not a bar to the hardship waiver.[7] Currently, areas of concern and controversy regarding this provision include the definition of "extreme hardship," the period of time in which the hardship must have arisen, and whether the applicant must evidence a good-faith marriage.

Extreme Hardship

As with all areas of immigration law in which extreme hardship is required, neither the INA nor the regulations define the term. The regulations state only, "The director shall bear in mind that any removal from the United States is likely to result in a certain degree of hardship, and that only in those

---

[*] **Karen R. Seiden** is a solo practitioner in Sunnyvale, CA, focusing exclusively on issues of immigration and nationality law for over 13 years. She has been an AILA member since 1995 and is an active member of the Santa Clara Valley chapter.

[1] Pub. L. No. 99-639, 100 Stat. 3537.

[2] Pub. L. No. 101-649, 104 Stat. 4978.

[3] IMMACT90 §701; INA §216(c)(4).

[4] INA §216(c)(4), which states:

> The Attorney General, in the Attorney General's discretion, may remove the conditional basis of the permanent resident status for an alien who fails to meet the requirements of [joint filing under INA §216(c)(1)] if the alien demonstrates - (A) extreme hardship would result if such alien is removed, (B) the qualifying marriage was entered into in good faith by the alien spouse, but the qualifying marriage has been terminated (other than through the death of the spouse) and the alien was not at fault in failing to meet the requirements of [joint filing under INA §216(c)(1)], or (C) the qualifying marriage was entered into in good faith by the alien spouse and during the mar-

continued

> riage the alien spouse or child was battered by or was the subject of extreme cruelty perpetrated by his or her spouse or citizen or permanent resident parent and the alien was not at fault for failing to meet the requirements of [joint filing under INA §216(c)(1)].

[5] *See also* 8 CFR §§216.5(a)(1)(i), (e)(1), 1216.5(a)(1)(i), (e)(1).

[6] INS Memorandum, CO-216-C, "IMF in General", #57 (Mar. 5, 1990).

[7] *Id.* at #3.

cases where the hardship is extreme should the application for a waiver be granted."[8] Therefore, removal alone will not support a determination of extreme hardship. Remarriage to another U.S. citizen, alone, also does not support a determination of extreme hardship.[9] Although extreme hardship waivers have been available for many years, there is not much guidance from the Board of Immigration Appeals (BIA) as to what *does* rise to the level of extreme hardship. The principal case on this topic is *Matter of Anderson.*[10] In *Anderson*, the BIA set out 10 criteria relevant to determining whether a deportation would cause extreme hardship. These include (1) the alien's age; (2) family ties in the United States and abroad; (3) length of residence in the United States; (4) health conditions; (5) economic and political conditions in the alien's home country; (6) occupation and work skills; (7) immigration history; (8) position in the community; (9) whether the alien is of special assistance to the United States or to the community; and (10) whether there are alternate means to adjust status.[11] Practitioners are well advised to use and evidence *all* factors that will give rise to hardship, including seemingly minor ones, as these can be viewed in the aggregate.[12]

The Period in Which the Extreme Hardship Must Arise

The INA provides, "In determining extreme hardship, the Attorney General shall consider circumstances occurring *only during the period that the alien was admitted for permanent residence on a conditional basis.*"[13] However, the regulations state, "In considering an application for a waiver based upon an alien's claim that extreme hardship would result from the alien's removal from the Unites Sates, the director shall take into account only those factors that arose *subsequent to the alien's entry as a conditional permanent resident.*"[14] A reading of the two provisions "exposes a clear conflict between the relevant statute and the agency's corresponding

regulation, which, to date… has not been acknowledged let alone reconciled."[15]

In *Singh v. DOJ*,[16] the U.S. Court of Appeals for the Second Circuit reviewed a denial of a motion to remand for the purpose of application for an extreme hardship waiver. The immigration judge (IJ) and the BIA had denied the motion, in relevant part, because the petitioner had asserted hardship that arose *after* his conditional resident status had ended. The BIA predicated its decision and the government defended on the basis of the wording of INA §216(c)(4). The Second Circuit noted that "while the BIA decision concords with the *statutory* language, the regulation that the BIA panel ignored better comports with the legislative history of [IMFA]."[17] Additionally, "[a]t least since *United States ex rel. Accardi v. Shaughnessy*, 347 U.S. 260, 74 S. Ct. 499, 98 L. Ed. 681 (1954), the Supreme Court has held that an administrative agency must adhere to its own regulations."[18] Since the relevant regulation clearly states that factors arising subsequent to the grant of conditional resident status, without reference to the period closing if conditional resident status is terminated, the Second Circuit found that the BIA had contravened agency regulations, so it remanded the case.[19]

On remand, the BIA acknowledged that it had not previously addressed the regulation specifically.[20] However, the BIA found that there is no conflict between the regulation and INA §216(c)(4)(A).[21] The BIA supported this conclusion by pointing out, "[T]he statute provides both a start date and an end date for the period during which the relevant circumstances must occur. In contrast, the regulation provides only the start date for the relevant circumstances …. The regulation does not contain any language that specifically contradicts the language of the statute."[22] The BIA continued,

[W]e are mindful of the fundamental canons of statutory construction that a statute and its implementing regulations should be read as a whole, and, where possible, afforded a harmoni-

---

[8] 8 CFR §§216.5(e)(1), 1216.5(e)(1).

[9] INS Memorandum, *supra* note 6, at #9 and #50.

[10] 16 I&N Dec. 596 (BIA 1978).

[11] *Id.* at 597.

[12] *See id.*

[13] INA §216(c)(4) (emphasis added).

[14] 8 CFR §§216.5(e)(1), 1216.5(e)(1) (emphasis added).

---

[15] *Singh v. DOJ*, 461 F.3d 290, 295 (2d Cir. 2006).

[16] *Id.*

[17] *Id.* at 296 (emphasis added).

[18] *Id.* (citations omitted).

[19] *Id.* (referring to 8 CFR §§216.5(e)(1), 1216.5(e)(1)).

[20] *Matter of Singh,* 24 I&N Dec. 331, 333 (BIA 2007).

[21] *Id.*

[22] *Id.*

ous interpretation, and that the words of a statute must be read in their context and with a view to their place in the overall regulatory scheme to see whether the regulation harmonizes with the plain language of the statute.

In the matter before us we find no conflict between the statute and the implementing regulation. Both provide the same start date for the evidence we may consider. The regulation is silent about a termination point for the evidence, so we look to the statute and find that a termination point is clearly set out there.[23]

While it does not appear that debate about the period during which the extreme hardship must arise has yet concluded, based on the BIA's decision above, practitioners should carefully consider when the issues that form the basis of the claimed hardship arose.

Is a Showing of Good-Faith Marriage Required?

Another evolving area of controversy relating to the hardship waiver is whether a showing of a good-faith marriage is required. Generally, U.S. Citizenship and Immigration Services (USCIS) looks at the bona fides of the marriage in assessing whether to grant a hardship waiver. In *Velazquez v. INS*,[24] the district court held that legacy Immigration and Naturalization Service's (INS) interpretation was permissible and consistent with the statutory scheme and was "not contrary to the plain and unambiguous language of the statue."[25]

However, the U.S. Court of Appeals for the Fifth Circuit reached a different conclusion in assessing the same statute. In *Waggoner v. Gonzales*,[26] the court looked to *Chevron*[27] principles to determine whether an extreme hardship waiver under INA §216(c)(4)(A) requires that the qualifying marriage be entered into in good faith. The court first queried whether Congress had spoken directly with respect to this question. The court noted that the statute lists three grounds for excusing the failure to meet the joint-petition requirement, with the hardship basis being the first listed. The court continued, "Unlike the second and third grounds, the extreme hardship exception does not list the requirement of a good-

faith marriage."[28] Applying the canon of statutory construction *expressio unius est exclusio alterius* (the expression of one thing is the exclusion of another), the court found that extreme hardship is the *only* requirement.[29] The court bolstered its finding by pointing out, "[T]o read the extreme hardship exception as implicitly requiring a good faith marriage would render superfluous the words setting forth that requirement in the second and third exceptions."[30] The court further noted that "the three grounds are set forth disjunctively as separate and independent bases to excuse the joint petition and interview requirement,"[31] pointing to the BIA's decision in *Matter of Balsillie*.[32] The court concluded that, applying the canons of statutory construction, "the statutory language unambiguously does not require a good faith marriage to qualify for an extreme hardship waiver."[33] It is also of note that the court not only acknowledged the *Velazquez* decision, but criticized it as well.[34]

Good-Faith Marriage That Has Been Terminated

Under INA §216(c)(4)(B), a CR who can show that "the qualifying marriage was entered into in good faith by the alien spouse, but the qualifying marriage has been terminated (other than through the death of the spouse) and the alien was not at fault in failing to meet the requirements of [joint filing under INA §216(c)(1)]"[35] is eligible to have the joint-filing requirement waived and the conditional basis of resident status removed.[36]

Basic Requirements

Good-Faith Marriage

There is no controversy that the good-faith waiver requires a showing that the CR entered into the marriage in good faith. The job for the practitioner is to determine what documents will evidence this requirement and how to present certain docu-

---

[23] *Id.* at 333, 334.

[24] 876 F. Supp. 1071 (D. Minn. 1995).

[25] *Id.* at 1077.

[26] *Waggoner v. Gonzales*, 488 F.3d 632 (5th Cir. 2007).

[27] *Chevron U.S.A., Inc. v. Natural Res. Def. Council, Inc.*, 467 U.S. 837 (1984).

[28] *Waggoner v. Gonzales, supra* note 26, at 636.

[29] *Id., citing U.S. v. Shah*, 44 F.3d 285, 293 (5th Cir. 1995).

[30] *Id., citing Bustamante-Barrera v. Gonzales*, 447 F.3d 388, 397 (5th Cir. 2006).

[31] *Id.*

[32] 20 I&N Dec. 486, 491 (BIA 1992).

[33] *Waggoner v. Gonzales, supra* note 26, at 636.

[34] *Id.* (reviewing the *Velazquez* court's analysis of the issue and finding that analysis to be in error).

[35] INA §213(c)(4)(B).

[36] *See also* 8 CFR §§216.5(a)(1)(ii), (e)(2), 1216.5(a)(1)(ii), (e)(2).

mentation. The burden of proof of evidencing the good faith lies squarely with the applicant.[37]

The INA makes clear that *any credible evidence* relevant to the application must be considered.[38] However, the INA also gives sole discretion to the attorney general to determine what evidence is credible and the weight the evidence will be afforded.[39] Therefore, practitioners need be ready to support an applicant's credibility, in general, and the credibility of evidence presented, specifically. Additionally, practitioners need be ready to argue the relevancy of the evidence presented.

There is ample legal material on evidencing a good-faith marriage. For this waiver, one may begin with the regulation at 8 CFR §§216.5(e)(2), 1216.5(e)(2), which states:

> In considering whether an alien entered into a qualifying marriage in good faith, the director shall consider evidence relating to the amount of commitment by both parties to the martial relationship. Such evidence may include - (i) Documentation relating to the degree to which the financial assets and liabilities of the parties were combined; (ii) Documentation concerning the length of time during which the parties cohabited after the marriage and after the alien obtained permanent residence; (iii) Birth certificates of children born to the marriage; and (iv) Other evidence as deemed pertinent by the director.

As this particular waiver basis requires the marriage to have been terminated, it is common that practitioners find themselves with clients who have relatively little postmarriage documentation. However, it must be remembered that the governing question in determining whether a marriage was entered into in good faith is whether the couple intended "to establish a life together *at the time they were married.*"[40] Although the regulations set out some criteria for determining whether a marriage

was bona fide, it is important to note that, on their face, the regulations do not set out an all-inclusive list. The regulations state, "Such evidence *may* include... ," not that the evidence *must* include.[41] Furthermore, there is "no set formula to be applied in determining whether a marriage was entered into in good faith. 'The concept of establishing a life as marital partners contains no federal dictate about the kind of life that the partners may choose to lead.'"[42]

Successful case preparation often includes documenting not only the couple's relationship after marriage but before marriage. This may include an affidavit by the CR, affidavits by others who knew of the nature of the relationship, and, in the best-case scenario, an affidavit from the spouse attesting to the bona fides of the relationship. Also, if the couple commingled assets before marriage, cohabitated before marriage, or have any documentation of the type that the government commonly seeks from postmarriage life, such documents should also be included, as they certainly help establish the CR's intent at the time of the marriage.

Marriage Terminated

The good-faith marriage waiver basis requires that the qualifying marriage be terminated.[43] Although it has always been clear that this requirement must be fulfilled before the good-faith waiver could be granted, for many years legacy INS accepted filing of the waiver petition with proof that marriage termination proceedings were *pending*. Under this routine, the CR could file the waiver before the end of the two-year period to avoid the possibility of having conditional resident status terminated and immigration court proceedings initiated. However, in April 2003, Acting Associate Director of Operations William Yates issued a memorandum ending this practice.[44]

The Yates memo bases it determination on the relevant statute,[45] *Matter of Anderson,*[46] and the in-

---

[37] *See* 8 CFR §§216.5(a)(1), 1216.5(a)(1) ("and the conditional resident alien is able to establish that ...").

[38] INA §213(c)(4) (final paragraph) ("In acting on applications under [INA §216(c)(4)], the Attorney General *shall* consider any credible evidence relevant to the application.") (emphasis added).

[39] *Id.* ("The determination of what evidence is credible and the weight to be given that evidence shall be within the sole discretion of the Attorney General.").

[40] *Bark v. INS,* 511 F.2d 1200, 1201 (9th Cir. 1975), *emphasis added.*

[41] 8 CFR §[1]216.5(e)(2).

[42] *Damon v. Ashcroft,* 360 F.3d 1084, 1089 (9th Cir. 2004), *quoting Bark, 511 F.2d at 1201).*

[43] 8 CFR §[1]216(e)(2).

[44] Bureau of Citizenship and Immigration Services Memorandum, W. Yates, "Filing a Waiver of the Joint Filing Requirement Prior to Final Termination of the Marriage" (Apr. 10, 2003), *published on* AILA InfoNet at Doc. No. 03050643 (*posted* May 6, 2003).

[45] INA §216(c)(4)(B).

[46] 16 I&N Dec. 596 (BIA 1978).

structions to Form I-751. The Yates memo states, "The statute clearly requires that the marriage already be terminated and, thus, the mere commencement of divorce proceedings is not sufficient.[47] The Yates memo continues, citing *Matter of Anderson*:

> Further, in *Matter of Anderson*, [citation omitted], it was determined that an alien spouse:

> [W]as ineligible to apply for a waiver under section 216(c)(4)(B) [of the Act] because she remained married to her husband ... if the respondent had become statutorily eligible to apply for the section 216(c)(4)(B) waiver by virtue of changed circumstances, *i.e.*, through the termination of her marriage ... she could have sought a continuance from the immigration judge to pursue her alternative application with the Service.

The Yates memo also points out that the instructions to Form I-751 state, "If you are filing to waive the joint filing requirement because your marriage has been terminated, also submit a copy of the divorce decree or other document terminating or annulling the marriage with your petition."

Although it is hard to argue against USCIS's conclusion that filing for the good-faith waiver requires an already terminated marriage, it places many CRs in a precarious situation, especially in light of USCIS's recent push to issue notices to appear (NTAs). Marriage termination is a creature of state law and the time needed to complete the termination, as well as the circumstances, varies widely. While some CRs may be fortunate enough to have the termination well before the conditional residence period will expire, thereby allowing them to submit the waiver application without fear of conditional resident status termination, other CRs may find themselves well into removal proceedings before the marriage is terminated, leaving them to the vagaries of immigration court judge and BIA rulings. Planning a strategy for all contingencies as early as possible is a key to ultimate success for the CR.

Good-Faith Marriage—Battery/ Extreme Cruelty (Abuse)

The abuse waiver basis was not part of IMFA, which allowed only the two previously discussed waiver bases.[48] It was not until IMMACT90 that the abuse waiver became part of the law.[49]

Under INA §216(c)(4)(C), a CR who can show that "the qualifying marriage was entered into in good faith by the alien spouse and during the marriage the alien spouse or child was battered by or was the subject of extreme cruelty perpetrated by his or her spouse or citizen or permanent resident parent and the alien was not at fault in failing to meet the [joint filing requirements of INA §216(c)(1)]" is eligible to have the joint-filing requirement waived and the conditional basis of resident status removed.[50] The CR may apply for the waiver regardless of his or her current marital status and regardless of whether he or she is still living with the spouse.[51] The CR parent of a battered or abused child may apply for the waiver regardless of the child's citizenship or immigration status.[52] Information in the application and supporting documents must be kept strictly confidential.[53]

The Requirements

Good-Faith Marriage

As with the waiver based on a good-faith marriage that has been terminated, the battery waiver clearly requires that the CR evidence a good-faith marriage to qualify for the waiver. The discussion regarding what constitutes a good-faith marriage issues appears above, and should be referenced for use for the battery waiver as well.

Battery/Extreme Cruelty

Any Credible Evidence

The implementing regulations that followed the 1990 enactment of this waiver required that extreme cruelty be documented with evidence from a licensed clinical social worker, psychologist, or professional.[54] This greatly restricted the use of the abuse waiver, because the abused CR's circumstances often did not allow for access to the required professionals. In response to this reality, Congress

---

[47] USCIS Memorandum, W. Yates, "Filing a Waiver of the Joint Filing Requirement Prior to Final Termination of the Marriage" (April 10, 2003).

[48] Note that the *good faith waiver* had different requirements in its original form. *See* Pub. L. No. 99-639, 100 Stat. 3537.

[49] Pub. L. No. 101-649, 104 Stat. 4978.

[50] *See also* 8 CFR §216.5(a)(1)(iii), (e)(3), 1216.5(a)(1)(iii), (e)(3).

[51] 8 CFR §§216.5(e)(3)(ii), 1216.5(e)(3)(ii).

[52] 8 CFR §§216.5(e)(3), 1216.5(e)(3).

[53] INA §216(c)(4).

[54] 8 CFR §§216.5(e)(3)(iv), 1216.5(e)(3)(iv).

amended INA §216(c)(4) in 1994. The amendment provided for use of *any credible evidence* in support of the waiver.[55] To date, the regulations have not been changed to incorporate the modification to the INA.[56] However, anecdotal evidence demonstrates that USCIS has approved cases under the "any credible evidence" standard.

Battery/Extreme Cruelty Standards

The INA does not provide any guidance as to what constitutes battery or extreme cruelty. The regulations, however, do state that "'was battered by or was the subject of extreme cruelty' includes, but is not limited to, being the victim of any act or threatened act of violence."[57] The acts of violence given as examples are, to say the least, some of the most egregious.[58] Practitioners should note that less egregious acts also suffice to meet the required showing for battery and extreme cruelty.

As battery and mental cruelty are not defined in the INA or regulations, one must look to other sources for guidance. The circuit courts, the BIA, and the Administrative Appeals Office have each considered battery and mental cruelty in some context—suspension of deportation/cancellation of removal provisions of the Violence Against Women Act (VAWA),[59] I-360 battered spouse petitions, etc. Although there remains a paucity of precedent decisions by the BIA, a number of unpublished decisions can prove instructive for practitioners.[60] Addition-

ally, the regulations relating to VAWA self-petitions may prove helpful. For example, the VAWA self-petitioning regulations state that certain acts that initially may not appear violent may be considered acts of violence if they are part of an overall pattern of violence. The U.S. Court of Appeals for the Ninth Circuit used such a concept in *Hernandez v. Ashcroft*.[61] The applicant had applied for VAWA suspension of deportation. Although the applicant had not been *battered* in the United States, the Ninth Circuit found that she had been the victim of extreme cruelty during the contrite phase of the domestic violence cycle.[62] The court reasoned, "The interaction that took place in the United States presents a well-recognized stage within the cycle of violence, one which is both psychologically and practically crucial to maintaining the batterer's control."[63]

Although what constitutes battery or extreme cruelty is not well defined by the INA or regulations, the regulations do address the *forms of evidence*.[64] The regulations state that evidence of physical abuse may include, but is not limited to, expert testimony in the form of reports and affidavits from:

- police
- judges
- medical personnel
- school officials
- social service agency personnel[65]

It must be remembered that this section of the regulations was added at the same time as the section on the need for a licensed professional evaluation for extreme cruelty.[66] Both came about before Congress added the *any credible evidence* statement to the INA.[67] Therefore, practitioners should remember that documentation of the battery/extreme

---

[55] INA §216(c)(4). Note, however, that the determination of what is credible is at the sole discretion of the attorney general.

[56] *See* 8 CFR §§216.5(e)(3), 1216.5(e)(3), which continue to require that licensed professionals evaluate mental cruelty.

[57] 8 CFR §§216.5(e)(3)(i), 1216.5(e)(3)(i).

[58] 8 CFR §§216.5(e)(3)(i), 1216.5(e)(3)(i) include: being the victim of any act or threatened act of violence, including any forceful detention, which results or threatens to result in physical or mental injury; and psychological or sexual abuse or exploitation, including rape, molestation, incest (if the victim is a minor) or forced prostitution.

[59] First enacted as Pub. L. No. 103-322, 108 Stat. 1796 (1994).

[60] *See, e.g., Matter of —,* EAC03-208-50844, 33 Immig. Rptr. B2-35 (AAO May 25, 2005) (dismissal of appeal of petitioner seeking classification as battered spouse on finding that petitioner failed to submit sufficient evidence of alleged forced sexual contact or conduct otherwise rising to level of abuse or extreme cruelty); *Matter of Pattree Huynh,* A78 887 859, 2004 WL 2952112 (BIA Nov. 16, 2004) (applicant testified regarding her husband's threats to kill her and incidents of choking during their short marriage); *Matter of Christina Ekeman,* A74 896 291, 2004 WL 3187294 (BIA *continued*

Dec. 9, 2004) (extreme cruelty established by medical records, court documents, and affidavits attesting to abuse); *In re —,* EAC01-195-51136, WL 2897922 (AAO 2004) (denial of I-360 upheld where evidence included petitioner statement, statements from friends and relatives, letter from social worker attesting to depression of petitioner, and evidence of spouse's adultery.)

[61] 345 F.3d 824 (9th Cir. 2003).

[62] *Id.* at 828 (9th Cir. 2003).

[63] *Id.*

[64] 8 CFR §§216.5(e)(3)(iii), 1216.5(e)(3)(iii).

[65] *Id.*

[66] *See* 8 CFR§216.5(e)(3)(iv), 1216.5(e)(3)(iv).

[67] INA §216(c)(4).

cruelty should include any evidence that can meet the *any credible evidence* standard.

The "Fourth" Waiver—Death of Citizen or LPR Spouse

There is one other circumstance under which a CR may file the I-751 waiver petition. Although not explicit in the INA, a CR may file for a waiver of the joint-filing requirement if the CR entered into the marriage in good faith but the petitioning spouse died during the first two years of the marriage.[68] The CR will need to prove the bona fides of the marriage and provide the spouse's death certificate.[69]

GENERAL CONSIDERATIONS

When to File

Neither the statute nor the regulations require the waiver application to be filed within the 90-day period before the second anniversary of the grant of conditional residence. Therefore, the waiver petition may be filed at any time.[70] For example, a CR whose spouse dies or who suffers battery or extreme cruelty before the 90-day period may file a waiver application immediately. The CR also may file the waiver application after the 90-day period. This would be appropriate, for example, if filing is based on the good-faith marriage/termination basis and the marriage terminates after the 90-day period has passed. The CR also may submit a waiver application after a joint petition has been denied or the conditional status has been terminated.[71] It is generally advisable to file the waiver application at the earliest possible

moment, especially when NTA issuance may be avoided by doing so. A CR who is in immigration court proceedings may file a waiver application only until a final order of removal has been entered.[72]

Jurisdiction to Adjudicate the Waiver

Original jurisdiction for a waiver of the joint-filing requirement lies with USCIS.[73] No direct administrative appeal is available; however, the CR may seek review of the denial before an IJ in proceedings.[74] Although the IJ reviews the waiver application de novo, the IJ may review only the basis on which USCIS denied the petition.[75] Therefore, if the CR had applied for a waiver based on extreme hardship and the waiver was denied by USCIS, for example, and then the marriage was terminated, the IJ may *not* review the waiver application on the good-faith marriage basis. The CR would need to submit a new waiver application on the good-faith marriage basis to USCIS.[76] The IJ should grant a continuance, if necessary, so that USCIS can adjudicate the waiver.[77] The CR bears the burden of proof to establish eligibility for the waiver requested.[78]

Judicial Review

The Circuit Courts have split over the question of whether a decision of the BIA denying a waiver is reviewable. Judicial review of any decision or action of the attorney general the authority for which is specified to be in the discretion of the attorney general is precluded.[79] Below is a brief overview of where some of the circuits stand on this matter:

First Circuit

Cho v. Gonzales, 404 F.3d 96 (1st Cir. 2005) (court may review BIA decision that an eligibility condition was not demonstrated. No review of discretion to grant or deny once eligibility established.).

---

[68] 8 CFR §§216.4(a)(1), 1216.4(a)(1); Instructions, Form I-751.

[69] Instructions, Form I-751.

[70] *See Matter of Stowers*, 22 I&N Dec. 605 (BIA 1999) ("[I]n certain situations it is appropriate to file a waiver application before or after the 90-day petitioning period, even where the Service affirmatively has terminated an alien's conditional resident status.").

[71] *See* Letter from Edward H. Skerrett, Chief, Nonimmigrant Branch, INS Office of Adjudications, to lawyer Paul Parsons (Nov. 6, 1992), *reproduced in* 70 *Interpreter Releases* 254 (Mar. 1, 1993) ("Neither the submission of the new Form I-751 [waiver application] nor of a motion to reopen or reconsider a previously adjudicated Form I-751 [joint petition] should be formally rejected solely because the alien's conditional resident status has been terminated and the alien placed in deportation proceedings."); Opinion of William P. Cook, INS Acting Gen. Counsel, File No. CO 216-P (Jan. 9, 1990), *reproduced in* 67 *Interpreter Releases* 168 (Feb. 5, 1990) (a noncitizen may file a waiver after the 90-day petitioning period following denial of a timely filed joint petition).

[72] 8 CFR §§216.5(a)(2), 1216.5(a)(2).

[73] 8 CFR §§216.5(c), 1216.5(c) ("Form I-751 shall be filed with the regional service center director having jurisdiction over the alien's place of residence.").

[74] 8 CFR §§216.5(f), 1216.5(f).

[75] *Matter of Lemhammad*, 20 I&N Dec. 316 (BIA 1991).

[76] *Matter of Stowers*, 22 I&N Dec. 605 (BIA 1999), *citing Matter of Lemhammad*, 20 I&N Dec. 316 (BIA 1991).

[77] *Id.*

[78] 8 CFR §§216.5(a)(1), 1216.5(a)(1).

[79] INA §242(a)(2)(B)(ii).

Second Circuit

Atsilov v. Gonzales, 468 F.3d 112 (2d Cir. 2006) (whether to grant the relief prescribed in INA §216(c)(4) to an alien who is admittedly eligible for such relief is ultimately a decision of the attorney general specified to be in the attorney general's discretion. IJ expressly found eligibility for waiver but denied review of denial of waiver. No jurisdiction to review discretionary decision.).

Third Circuit

Ventura v. Att'y Gen., 2008 U.S. App. LEXIS 3796 (3d Cir. 2008), *citing Sukwanputra v. Gonzales,* 434 F.3d 627, 634 (3d Cir. 2006)*, and referencing Jarbough v. Att'y Gen.,* 483 F.3d 184, 188 (3d Cir. 2007) (extreme hardship waiver denial by the BIA not reviewable. Although the REAL ID Act of 2005[80] restored judicial review of constitutional claims or questions of law, "factual or discretionary determinations continue to fall outside the jurisdiction of the court of appeals entertaining a petition for review.").

Urena-Tavarez v. Ashcroft, 367 F.3d 154 (3d Cir. 2004) (All determinations under INA §216(c)(4) are left to the attorney general's pure discretion. Court may not review such determination.).

Fifth Circuit

Assaad v. Ashcroft, 378 F.3d 471 (5th Cir. 2004) (INA §242(a)(2)(B)(ii) bars jurisdiction of threshold eligibility determinations under INA §216(c)(4).).

Eighth Circuit

Nguyen v. Mukasey, No. 07-3889, 2008 U.S. App. LEXIS 8353 (3d Cir. 2008) ("Although respondent is correct that we lack jurisdiction to review either the BIA's discretionary decision to deny a hardship waiver ... or the BIA's determinations, in relation to a hardship-waiver decision, as to what evidence is credible and how much weight to five that evidence ... we have jurisdiction to review constitutional claims or questions of law raised in a petition for review ... and we may also review the nondiscretionary determination underlying the denial of relief, such as the predicate legal question of whether the IJ properly applied the law to the facts determining the alien's eligibility for discretionary relief."). (Citations omitted). (Referencing *Pinos-Gonzalez v. Mukasey,* No. 07-1299, 2008 WL 58677 (8th Cir. 2008) and *Reyes-Vasquez v. Ashcroft,* 395 F.3d 903, 906 (8th Cir. 2005)).

Suvorov v. Gonzales, 441 F.3d 618 (8th Cir. 2006) (REAL ID Act prohibits court from reviewing discretionary determinations of the attorney general, such as a denial of a waiver under INA §216(c)(4). Whether the qualifying marriage was entered into in good faith by the alien spouse is a discretionary factual determination of the IJ.).

Ebrahim v. Gonzales, 471 F.3d 880 (8th Cir. 2008) (no jurisdiction to review, following *Suvorov, supra.*)

Ninth Circuit

Medina-Morales v. Ashcroft, 371 F.3d 520 (9th Cir. 2004) (INA §242(a)(2)(B)(ii) applies only to acts over which a statute gives the attorney general pure discretion unguided by legal standards or statutory guidelines.).

Oropeza-Wong v. Gonzales, 406 F.3d 1135 (9th Cir. 2005) (court held that determinations made with respect to statutory waivers under INA §216(c)(4) are not purely discretionary and are therefore generally subject to review. Court is generally free to review BIA decisions that marriages were not entered into in good faith. Although not at question in the matter, the court noted that all three waiver bases will usually require factual and legal determinations, thus making review possible in certain situation.).

FINAL WORDS

In all, although the law provides for waivers of the joint-filing requirement for CRs, each waiver basis presents legal and standard-of-proof requirements that may be difficult to evidence. These potential obstacles, though, should not be seen as insurmountable. Early planning, if possible, is the surest way to success. However, even cases that come to practitioners later in the game can have successful outcomes. Knowledge of the differing requirements for each waiver basis, including circuit court decisions that may cause requirements to differ in different locations, is critical to strategic planning and action. Which waiver basis or bases are selected for filing and the timing of the filings are keys in the successful prosecution of I-751 joint-filing waivers. Practitioners who arm themselves with these competencies will truly be able to be an advocate for the client in need.

---

[80] Pub. L. No. 109-13, div. B, 119 Stat. 231, 302–23.

SUCCESSFUL I-601 WAIVERS: THE FORM AND A LETTER ARE NOT ENOUGH

by David N. Simmons and Laurel Scott[*]

INTRODUCTION

An I-601 waiver of inadmissibility is required whenever an alien is inadmissible under INA §212(a), and there is a provision for the inadmissibility to be waived. Many government officials, most notarios, and even some attorneys (who should know better), will suggest that Form I-601 and a letter from a U.S. citizen or permanent resident relative is enough to have a waiver granted. This is not the case. Filing a waiver case requires knowledge of the standard, knowledge of the case, and the ability to make a clear, concise presentation of the facts.

This article is designed to provide attorneys with "how to" guidelines for preparing and winning I-601 cases. The authors have both been highly successful in preparing and I-601 cases. However, this article also will discuss when not to file an I-601, thus "winning" the case by not losing.

Please read this article with the understanding that it provides suggestions and guidance, not a checklist. You must analyze each case you encounter. In so doing, you may find that information provided in this article will differ from what is best for your client. Finally, reading this article is no substitute for your own understanding of the Immigration and Nationality Act, the Code of Federal Regulations, and the controlling legal authority.

---

[*] **David N. Simmons** practices immigration law in Denver, graduate of University of Denver Law. He is an adjunct professor at the University of Denver Sturm College of Law, teaching Immigration Law in Spanish as part of the Spanish in the Law program. He served as AILA Colorado Chapter chair and served as an NSC liaison. He is the current pro-bono chair of the Colorado Chapter. He has spoken and written on several immigration-related subjects.

Laurel Scott is the founding attorney of Scott and Associates, Attorneys at Law, PLLC, formerly known as The Law Office of Laurel Scott. She has previously co-authored an article on I-601 waivers that appeared on *ILW.com*. She has been the featured speaker, discussing this subject, at AILA events in Houston, Philadelphia, and Boston. She is a member of AILA's Refugee, Asylum, and International Programs Liaison Committee, as well as Houston's Unauthorized Practice of Law Committee under the Supreme Court of Texas.

EXTREME HARDSHIP DEFINED

The Legal Standard

Extreme hardship is a two-part test. You must prove that the qualifying relative would suffer extreme hardship if he or she moved to the applicant's country. You must also prove that the qualifying relative can't simply remain in the United States without the applicant. The term "extreme hardship" is very vaguely defined as "greater than the normal hardship" you would expect a qualifying relative to experience if a visa applicant is denied a visa.

The Standard Applied

Envision a married couple. Jane, a U.S. citizen is married to José, a Mexican national. José cannot adjust in the United States. Because José has been unlawfully present in the United States, he needs a waiver in order to get an immigrant visa. Jane may say she does not want to move to Mexico because it has a high unemployment rate, wages are low, crime rates are high, public health standards are not as good, she won't have medical insurance, she won't be able to pay her student loans and credit card bills, education for their future children won't be as good, and Jane doesn't speak Spanish. She will say that she can't remain in the United States without her husband as she would be depressed and would experience separation anxiety and she would miss his added income. All of this is "normal hardship."

When the adjudicator has seen the same arguments thousands of times, he or she becomes wary of reading what is essentially the same letter over and over. If an attorney has a difficult time creating a case that shows *greater* than the usual hardship, the attorney should instead try to make a case that shows *different* than the usual hardship. What is "greater" is highly subjective, while what is "different" may be obvious.

EXPLAINING EXTREME HARDSHIP TO THE CLIENT

When the attorney consults with the client, it is important that the attorney explain to the clients what standard needs to be met. The clients need to be able to understand the case so they can make an informed decision on whether to attempt the waiver process, and they need to be able to understand the case so they can provide essential participation in the representation.

MITIGATING AND AGGRAVATING FACTORS

The decision to grant a waiver will be affected by aggravating and mitigating factors unrelated to extreme hardship. The adjudicator may consider the entire record, not just the extreme hardship factors, and may deny a waiver as a matter of discretion even if he or she finds extreme hardship. Mitigating factors include the length of the marriage or relationship, whether there are small children involved, whether the applicant has voluntarily entered into the waiver process, and the applicant's limited culpability for the violation. For example, if the applicant is inadmissible for prior unlawful presence only and entered the United States without inspection at age 2, that is a huge mitigating factor. If the applicant is inadmissible for misrepresentation, but only because someone practicing law without a license committed misrepresentation on his behalf without his knowledge *and the attorney can prove it*, that's a big mitigating factor. Mitigating factors will *decrease* the extreme hardship threshold that you will have to meet. Conversely, aggravating factors will *increase* that hardship threshold. Aggravating factors include prior criminal record, even if the applicant is not inadmissible on criminal grounds, multiple violations of immigration law, multiple prior marriages (in a marriage-based case), and whether the applicant is a deportation absconder. Additionally, while it is not exactly an aggravating factor, if the qualifying relative is originally from the same country as the applicant, having immigrated to the United States as an adult, there will automatically be a presumption that it is not an extreme hardship for the qualifying relative to move back to his or her country of origin; overcoming this presumption can be difficult if not impossible.

Aggravating factors must be addressed in the waiver packet. Failure to do so may cause a denial, or a delay in processing. For example, failure to address an aggravating factor when filing a waiver packet in Mexico will almost always result in the case being referred out of the Pilot Program and into the lengthy normal process for adjudication.

FACTORS TO SUPPORT AN ARGUMENT OF EXTREME HARDSHIP

There are many possible arguments to make to support a waiver case. Most can be divided into a few categories. Here are some of those categories with comments on what needs to be shown.

Qualifying Relative's Medical Problem

If the qualifying relative has a very serious medical problem, such as active cancer or recommended back surgery, the attorney might prove that the alien's presence is needed for direct nursing-type care. If the qualifying relative has a chronic, manageable medical problem, the attorney might prove that the problem cannot be adequately managed abroad either due to climate conditions, public health, or medical facilities. If possible, prove that people living in that country with that medical condition have trouble managing it, whereas people living in the United States have less difficulty or no difficulty.

Caring for the Sick, Elderly, or Disabled

The authors cannot overstress this: it is not enough to prove that the alien has a sick or old relative. The attorney must prove how the burden of caring for that person is alleviated by the alien's presence or worsened by the alien's absence. If there is another person, such as an adult sibling, potentially available to take care of the sick, elderly, or disabled person, the attorney must prove why that other person is unable to handle the care or unable to do it alone without great difficulty.

Financial Hardship

A good financial argument usually involves either the qualifying relative's financial dependence on the alien and/or another relative's financial dependence on either one of them. Beware of the difference between "financial dependence" (where the affected relative cannot meet his or her basic needs without the support provided) and "financial convenience" (where the affected relative's lifestyle might change without the support provided, but the relative's basic needs will still be met). Another good financial argument would include the qualifying relative's inability to maintain employment in the United States if he or she is too depressed or distracted by the alien's absence. Evidence for such an argument must be convincing. Note that lower standard of living and inability to pay U.S. debts if you move abroad are NOT good financial hardship arguments.

Minor Child from a Prior Relationship

If the qualifying relative has a child from a prior relationship and the noncustodial parent's rights have not been terminated, the child cannot legally be taken abroad without the noncustodial parent's permission. This can be an argument for not moving abroad, but under *Matter of Ige*, I&N Dec. 3230 (BIA 1994), the attorney must show why the child cannot simply be left in the custody of the noncustodial parent. The argument can be made either for the qualifying relative's child or for the alien's child if the alien's child currently resides with the qualifying relative and would have to go back to the noncustodial parent in the alien's absence.

Domestic Violence Concerns

Former abusive spouses or boyfriends often do not leave the abused alone until another man comes into the picture. For many women the potential long-term absence of the alien brings concerns over the return of the prior abusive spouse or boyfriend. These concerns unfortunately are not without merit. This argument is especially strong when there is a child of the prior abusive relationship and the qualifying relative would be afraid to contact the child's father to ask for cooperation in getting the child a passport.

Racism Abroad

If the qualifying relative has a minority race or ethnicity in the US that is the target of racism in the alien's home country, the qualifying relative may have more trouble adjusting to life abroad than the typical American. But beware that prejudice and discrimination experienced by any American in that country would probably be considered normal hardship.

Heightened Concerns over Moving Abroad

Country conditions regarding civil strife and/or crime are normally not very strong as they are such common arguments to make. However, if the qualifying relative was previously the victim of a violent crime or experienced political violence or oppression (*e.g.*, naturalized citizen from that country having originally come as a refugee or asylee), the qualifying relative will have a heightened fear of those factors, greater than most Americans would experience.

Unavailable Career, Community or Religion Abroad

It may be that the qualifying relative's identity is intertwined with his/her career, community or religion more than the usual American. If the qualifying relative would no longer be able to continue with that career or be a part of a comparable community or religion in the alien's home country, then this may be greater hardships than normally experienced. Understand the difference between the financial impact of job loss, which is normal hardship, and the identity crisis precipitated by loss of certain careers. When making this argument, the focus is not so much on the qualifying relative's success in that career as it is on the importance of that career to the qualifying relative's identity. Beware that the loss of "community of family" will almost always be considered normal hardship.

Depression

Very rarely will depression and separation anxiety be a strong argument, simply because it is such an ***overwhelmingly common*** argument to make. Occasionally you will have someone who has been hospitalized for the depression or who has developed a drug problem because of it or has lost a job because of it, etc. and you do, in fact, have a strong hardship argument to make based on depression. But this is the exception, not the rule, and there is no reason to be sending the majority of clients to the psychologist for evaluation. In most cases the client is spending $600 to $800 on a psychological evaluation to support a very weak argument.

ANALYSIS OF THE JURISDICTION

When a potential waiver applicant is considering whether to voluntarily come forward and enter into the waiver process—either for an in-country waiver accompanying adjustment of status or a foreign-filed waiver—one must also consider the location where the waiver will be adjudicated. Some CIS offices have a reputation for lenience on waivers, while others do not. Bear in mind that common grounds of inadmissibility may be different at different CIS offices and it may not be so much that one office is more lenient as it is that they are simply getting more cases with lots of mitigating factors and fewer cases with aggravating factors. For example, it is very common with Mexican cases for the applicant to have unlawful presence only and no other grounds of inadmissibility, whereas for Albanian cases it is more common for the applicant to have a prior denied asylum case that led to a final order for deportation that the applicant ignored. The expected result would be to see more approvals on Mexican cases than on Albanian cases due to these different grounds of inadmissibility, as opposed to greater lenience on the part of the adjudicating officers. Also, processing times and administrative issues cannot be ignored. Families may find themselves in a Catch-22: the stronger their extreme hardship case; the less likely they are to voluntarily enter into the foreign-filed waiver process if it means an unavoidable lengthy separation.

One problem with the great latitude given the adjudicator in defining extreme hardship is that for borderline cases, it may all come down to which adjudicator is assigned the case and even how he/she is feeling that day. Certainly adjudicators attempt to avoid inconsistency, but adjudicators are human and with such a variable and vague guideline for the standard of extreme hardship, some inconsistency may be unavoidable. The wild card of inconsistency is a risk to be taken into consideration. An attorney may have gotten a nearly identical case approved at the same office last month, but that doesn't guarantee that you'll get this next case approved.

THE CLIENT DECIDES
WHETHER TO PROCEED

There are plenty of times when the attorney is not hired until after a finding of inadmissibility has been made and the client has no choice but to apply for a waiver. But there are also plenty of times when the attorney is contacted while the alien is residing unlawfully in the US 'undetected'. In such a situation, the attorney is responsible for informing and educating the client on the risks of voluntarily entering into the waiver process. No voluntary waiver application is risk-free. For some attorneys, exposing the client to any risk is unacceptable. However, attorneys adopting this stance should consider that residing unlawfully in the US is not without its consequences. There is the inability to get a driver's license, the constant fear, the apprehension about calling the police when victimized, the exposure to exploitation from employers, inability to get federal student aid, etc. For many, the consequences of unlawful presence outweigh the risks of the voluntarily filed waiver. For others it will not. This is why the attorney needs to maximize his or her ability to assess the risks for a given case and clearly explain them to the client. Ultimately, the client is an adult, capable of making important decisions for his/her own life. The attorney is responsible for making all of the decisions throughout the course of the waiver process, but whether or not to attempt it at all is the client's decision.

ASSIGNING TASKS TO
ATTORNEY AND CLIENT

A waiver case, like all immigration cases, is a joint effort between attorney and client. The client is responsible for communicating the facts of the case to the attorney. The attorney is responsible for determining which arguments will be the strongest and what supporting documents will prove those arguments. The client is responsible for obtaining all 'personal supporting documents' according to the attorney's instructions. 'Personal supporting documents' include things such as medical records, doctor or psychiatrist letters, letters from friends or neighbors attesting to various facts, and any other document that pertains entirely to the client. The attorney is responsible for obtaining 'non-personal supporting documents' such as country condition reports, medical articles, newspaper articles, and any other supporting document not pertaining entirely to the client. The attorney is responsible for reviewing all supporting documents to make sure they support the arguments presented. The qualifying relative is responsible for writing his/her one to three page letter *affidavit* describing the hardship. Once all the supporting documents are collected, the attorney prepares the brief, if desired, and puts the packet together.

Preparation of the Application

A successful I-601 waiver case requires more than good arguments. The arguments must be supported by credible evidence, well organized, and clearly presented. The adjudicator may only have minutes to make a decision in each case. The attorney must make the most of those minutes. In preparing the application, it is helpful to think of the final product as more than just a legal submission. Ideally, it is well packaged, well organized, and easy to read and understand. The proper approach to the application recognizes that packaging and marketing the case is as important as any legal arguments.

The I-601 Form

In most cases, the I-601 is not a difficult form to complete. The information requested is largely biographical, and can be provided by the client. There are two important points to remember in completing the form. First, leaving blank spaces is not a good idea. If a particular question does not apply to the client, this should be indicated by answering "not applicable," or "none." Second, a client may be reluctant to answer all the questions completely, out of fear of providing adverse information (or what the client perceives to be adverse information) to the Government. The attorney should not allow a client to do this. There are obvious ethical and legal reasons (loss of license to practice, or going to prison) for this. There is also a good tactical reason. A form that provides all of the requested information, even the adverse facts, is more credible.

Question 10 asks for the basis of the client's inadmissibility. This is not the place for a long narrative, spilling over onto a continuation page. Instead, the attorney should provide a brief statement, and cite the appropriate section of INA §212. The ideal response will look like these examples:

"INA 212(a)(9)(B)(i)(II): Unlawful presence between December 2002 and June 2008."

"INA 212(a)(2)(A)(i)(I): Crime Involving Moral Turpitude; Conviction of Theft by Receiving, Colorado Revised Statutes 18-4-410(3.5), July 9, 1998; Sentenced to two years probation."

This type of response will serve to inform the adjudicator of the need for the waiver, and set the stage for the presentation of the evidence.

Tuberculosis and HIV Medical Waivers

If a client is seeking a waiver under INA §212(g) because of a diagnosis of Tuberculosis or HIV, the client must complete an additional page of the I-601 form. These pages both require four signatures: the alien; the alien's sponsor; a physician or health facility representative; and a state or local health agency representative. While completing these pages of the form is relatively straightforward, the attorney should allow additional time to obtain the signatures. The facility and agency representatives may have their own prerequisites to signing, and may not be able to accommodate a last-minute request. Remember that HIV and TB waivers are all about public health and health insurance, rather than extreme hardship.

The Qualifying Relative's Affidavit

The key document in a successful I-601 waiver application is the affidavit from the qualifying relative. The affidavit should serve several purposes. First, it should tell the relative's story. Second, it should introduce the supporting evidence. Finally, it should serve as the basis for organizing that evidence into a coherent package. An example of a successful affidavit is attached to this article for illustration.

Writing the Affidavit

The most important thing to remember is that the relative writes the affidavit. The attorney only edits the relative's work. Preparing a good affidavit takes time and energy. It takes close cooperation between the relative and the attorney, similar to the cooperation required to prepare a witness to testify at trial. This is reasonable, because an affidavit is testimony—although presented in written form.

Preparation of the affidavit began at the initial interview. While the attorney discussed the various aspects of the client's case, and began to assign tasks to the alien and relative, they all were agreeing on the principal points that the relative needs to make. The preparation continued while the attorney, client, and relative begin to gather evidence. When it is time to draft the affidavit, both the attorney and the relative should have a clear idea of what needs to be said. While an attorney should discuss extreme hardship at the initial interview and evaluate the case, drafting the waiver should not begin until a few months before filing the I-601. At the time of filing the I-130, the case may be nine months or more away from filing the I-601 waiver packet. If drafting starts too early, the facts of the case may change over time, and the affidavit may be out of date when it is time to file.

Drafting the affidavit begins with a conversation between the attorney and the relative. The attorney should take notes. They should discuss the points that need to be made. This does not mean that the attorney should tell the relative what to say. Rather, the attorney should advise the relative what topics need to be covered. At the end of the conversation, the attorney should have an outline that the relative can use to begin the affidavit.

The relative should then draft the affidavit entirely on his or her own. The format of the draft is not important, nor does it matter whether the draft is handwritten, typed, written using a computer, or block-lettered on a Big Chief tablet with crayon. What matters is that this is the relative's work. When the draft is finished, the relative should bring it to the attorney to begin the editing process.

Editing the Affidavit

In editing, the attorney must constantly remember that the relative is the author of the affidavit. The purpose of editing the affidavit is to ensure that the author's story is as compelling as possible, and that the affidavit effectively introduces and presents the supporting evidence. The attorney may be tempted to clean up the relative's grammar and syntax. This temptation should be indulged as infrequently as possible.

Unless the relative has written the affidavit using a computer, the attorney should first transcribe the affidavit. If the document was written in a foreign language, it should be translated into English so that the attorney can edit the English translation.

The attorney should then perform the first edit. Usually, this will involve removing repetition, making sure that the affidavit follows a recognizable organizational pattern, and taking out unnecessary conclusory or argumentative statements. In order to do this without destroying the author's style, the attorney should focus on the deletion or relocation of sentences, phrases, or paragraphs. Rewriting of individual sentences should be avoided whenever possible.

Once the first edit is complete, the relative should review and approve the attorney's changes. If the relative has any concerns, the attorney should make sure that the concerns are resolved. The result should be a document the relative agrees clearly and completely describes his or her hardships and concerns.

Supporting Evidence

Once the affidavit is complete, the attorney should begin organizing the supporting evidence. Much of the evidence already will be available; a result of the assignment of tasks at the original interview. Organize the evidence by topic, following the order in which each topic is presented in the affidavit.

Ideally, the attorney will have more evidence than required. The attorney should not automatically use everything available. It is not enough to be convincing, the packet also must be *concise.* The attorney should eliminate anything that is unnecessarily duplicative, and anything that does not add support to the affidavit. The goal is quality, not quantity. The adjudicator will be more easily persuaded by (and more inclined to read) 20 strong documents than 200 weak ones. This is especially important for the Pilot Program in Mexico where adjudicators have only about 15 minutes per case in which to make a decision. If a packet is too large, it may be referred to the normal process simply because it cannot be reviewed quickly enough.

On the other hand, the attorney should not hesitate to ask for more evidence if it appears to be necessary. Clients generally do not like being asked to provide more evidence; it generally means more work for them. It also can frustrate a client who feels that he or she already has "given everything." However, if the attorney has prepared the client and the relative by explaining at the initial interview that additional documents may be requested; the reluctance probably will be minimized.

Evidence will fall into two categories. Primary evidence will directly support the relative's assertions in the affidavit. An example would be a letter from a medical expert providing a diagnosis of the relative's medical condition. Secondary evidence adds depth and credibility to the primary evidence. Examples

would include a downloaded copy of the medical expert's biography and résumé, billing statements from a medical provider showing that the relative has been treated for the described condition, or copies of the relative's medical history. Ideally, every assertion in the affidavit will be supported by both primary and secondary evidence. However, don't overdo it.

Other Affidavits

In some cases, the attorney may need to obtain more than one affidavit. The most common example is when there is more than one qualifying relative. In that case, each relative should provide his or her own affidavit, supported with the appropriate evidence. Another example is when the alien has a criminal record. Even when the convictions do not trigger a basis of inadmissibility, an adjudicator may consider the convictions to be an adverse factor justifying a denial of the waiver application in the exercise of discretion.

In these cases, each affidavit should be dealt with separately and presented with its own supporting evidence. In the case of an applicant with a criminal record, evidence should be provided to show the nature of the underlying offense, the disposition of the case, and the applicant's having reformed and being unlikely to commit another crime.

The Supporting Brief

If the case involves a complex legal matter, or if the attorney feels that a brief will assist the examining officer in making a decision, the attorney may wish to submit a brief. The brief should be separate from the cover letter, and should be clearly marked. A brightly-colored cover page, with the words "legal brief, please read first" printed in large font would be an appropriate way of getting the adjudicator's attention.

The Attorney Letter

Dozens of decisions from various immigration-related administrative appeals have declared that statements of counsel are not evidence. Regardless, an attorney cover letter is still an important part of any application. The attorney cover letter should serve as a table of contents for the entire application, and as a record of what was submitted.

Final Organization

The application should be assembled with the attorney letter, followed by the fee check and Form I-601. Any brief is next, then each affidavit with its supporting documents. The documents should be numbered and tabbed, to make each document easier for the examining officer to locate while reading the related affidavit.

When assembling the application package, the entire package can be fastened together, or each component (attorney letter, application and fee, brief, each affidavit and documents) kept separate, and the entire package joined with a rubber band or a large fastener. If the entire package is joined, it is a good idea to separate each component with a piece of brightly-colored paper. The key is to make the application easy to read and each part of the application easy to locate.

Submitting the Application

Copy the entire application for the client file. Make a second copy for the client, if appropriate. The application should include the originals of all affidavits and any supporting letters, as well as original certified copies of criminal records. This adds credibility to the application. However, keep any other original documents and file copies. Original documents are often difficult to replace, and are not usually required.

Finally, if the alien is not filing the application personally, send the application via a delivery method that will provide proof of delivery. This is invaluable for preserving the application if the government loses it.

CONCLUSION

When preparing a waiver, if affidavits and supporting evidence sound like hard work, it's because it is. However, the rewards are great. The successful attorney will find his or her name being referred by satisfied clients, with the opportunity for more business. However, the greatest reward will be that with each successful case, the alien and his or her family will have an opportunity to live legally in the United States and begin building their own version of the American dream.

[SAMPLE AFFIDAVIT]

UNITED STATES DEPARTMENT OF HOMELAND SECURITY
UNITED STATES CITIZENSHIP AND IMMIGRATION SERVICES
City and County of Denver
State of Colorado
Affidavit of Qualifying Relative
In Support of I-601 Waiver of Ground of Excludability
On behalf of: Alien Applicant

I, Qualifying Relative hereby declare under the penalty of perjury that the following information is true and correct. My date of birth is November 31, 1972. I was born in Smalltown, Colorado.

I am presently residing at my address, Denver, CO. I have been living at this address for three months.

I am writing this letter in support of the I-601 petition that I have filed on behalf my husband Alien Applicant. Relocation to Mexico would cause me and my family extreme and severe hardship due to the lack of educational and employment opportunities as well as a lack of health care and treatment of preexisting conditions, economic issues and future child bearing plans.

EDUCATION

I am the first and only person in my immediate family who has graduated from college. I began attending State College in spring 1998, part-time, while working as an administrative assistant for Residential Properties, full – time. In Fall 2000, as my school responsibilities became more demanding, I was forced to make a choice between my employment endeavors and my educational goals. I chose to pursue my educational goals and began attending the University of Colorado at Denver as a full time student. At this time, I was living alone and surviving off of money borrowed from federal student loans, which provided only enough financial support to pay for my tuition, books, rent, food, household expenses, and any other additional living expenses.

I graduated from the University of Colorado at Denver in May 2005 with a bachelor's degree in Political Science and Sociology. **EXHIBIT 1: University of Colorado Bachelor's Degree**

In January 2005, one semester prior to my graduation, I began a Masters and Teacher Licensure program, the IPTE program, through the University of Colorado at Denver's, School of Education and Human Development. **EXHIBIT 2**

   a. **PLACE examination results**

   b. **Secondary Social Studies License**

   c. **Teacher welcome letter from the State of Colorado**

   d. **University of Colorado at Denver official school transcripts (includes Bachelor's & Masters classes & credits)**

   e. **Letter from UCD's School of Education and Human Development advisor, Lori Sisneros.**

Upon finishing the IPTE program and passing a Colorado state examination, the *PLACE*, in May 2006 I was granted my Secondary Social Studies Teaching License through the Colorado Department of Education. I am currently working on finishing my Masters degree of Arts in Education; I have four more classes left to complete my Masters.

I currently hold a substitute teachers license through the State of Colorado as well. **EXHIBIT 3: Colorado Three—Year Substitute Teacher License**

Relocating to Mexico would not allow me to use my education that I worked so hard on to finish. I am specifically licensed to teach an explicit profession in the state of Colorado and not in any other state or country, *Secondary Social Studies*.

As a newly licensed teacher, I am required by the state of Colorado to successfully complete a State Board approved Induction Program. Induction is a program of training, support, and supervision that is provided by the district I work for. This type of induction program is not offered and/or available in Mexico. **EXHIBIT 4: Colorado State Induction Requirements & Information for Teachers**

To be a teacher in Mexico, one does not need to have a teaching license nor does one need to have a bachelor's degree, however one does need to be able to speak Spanish. I do not speak Spanish therefore my only options as a teacher in Mexico would be to teach English, though, I did not study and earn my license in English – I studied and earned my license in secondary social studies, which only enables me to teach History, Geography, Economics, Psychology and Civics (Government). It would be very difficult for me to be a teacher in Mexico.

Moreover, the skills and educational pedagogy I have studied and have experience with are very specific to the United States. I am extensively familiar with the secondary education system, including the state and federal laws, rules and regulations that govern the education profession. My pedagogy and skills are not the same as the pedagogy and skills practiced by teachers in Mexico; I would feel isolated and inadequate. My license and my education would mean nothing; they would be complete wastes in Mexico.

If I had to relocate to Mexico, I would lose the opportunity to finish my Masters degree because the program I have started and am almost finished with is not available at any university in Mexico. On top of that, since I do not speak Spanish I wouldn't be able to study and attend any university, regardless of the Masters programs offered. Relocating to Mexico would mean that all the classes I have completed towards my Masters degree thus far would be squandered.

Completing my educational goals has been life changing for my future and me. My family is very proud of me given that I am the only one in my family with a higher education; they feel a sense of pride and accomplishment. My education has opened doors for me that would have not been opened otherwise. Because of my education I have been able to pursue my dream of teaching, work closely with my community and be a productive member of my society.

EMPLOYMENT OPPORTUNITIES

I have recently accepted a contracted social studies teaching position, with the Learning Academy, a Denver Public School, beginning in the Fall 2007. My yearly income will begin at $35,000, and will significantly increase when I finish my Masters degree and any education beyond that. **EXHIBIT 5**

   a. **Denver Public School Teaching Contract for 2007/08**

   b. **Salary verification**

   c. **Pro-comp salary increases information**

I would not have the same employment opportunity if I had to relocate to Mexico because Mexico has a very bad economy, consequently affecting employment opportunities. A teacher's income in Mexico is very low and on top of that, most teachers' salary does not increase with seniority and further education (contract attached).

When I resided in Guerrero, Mexico, from October 2006 to May 2007, I was fortunate enough to find work teaching English for a small English/Computer school, **EXHIBIT 6: Teaching Contract** My hourly wage was $2.30 taxed, with no benefits, no salary increases, no paid time off, no professional development and no room for advancement. I worked Wednesday, Thursday and Friday nights beginning at 4pm and ending at 9pm. I also worked on Saturday and Sunday from 8am to 4pm, straight with no breaks, which was to say the least, exhausting.

Teaching eight classes a day, back to back, without a break for eight hours straight, not only jeopardized my health and well being but it also affected the quality of my teaching and my interaction with the students. I was never paid on time and when I did get paid, the wages I was given did not reflect my time spent teaching, in other words, I did not get paid accurately (contract attached).

FINANCIAL CONSIDERATIONS

I am a person who genuinely helps stimulate the economy. I have many debts and financial responsibilities in the United States. Without my job in the U.S. I would be unable to repay these loans. Due to my wage in the U.S I am also accustomed to a certain standard of living.

Since, I will be unemployed if living in Mexico this standard of living would be impossible to maintain. This would be a hardship for me because I have worked very hard to be where I am at financially. Changing my lifestyle that I have enjoyed for 34 years would cause a lot of unrest in my life. I owe College Invest five student loans in the amounts of:

   1. $39,245.13

   2. $44,571.24

   3. $3,895.62

   4. $5,726.30

5. $3,100.66   **TOTAL: $96,538.95**

The above total does not include my Sallie Mae Student Loan which is $34,594.59.

My father is a co-signor on the Sallie Mae Student Loan. If I had to relocate to Mexico, I would be unable to repay this loan because I would not be able to find a job that would pay me sufficiently so that I could pay off my student loans. Consequentially my father would be burdened with the repayment of this loan. My father is not able to repay this loan due to his financial situation. His credit would be ruined. This burden would deeply affect my father's already deteriorating physical and mental health.

Payment on all of these student loans would begin when I stop attending graduate school or when I finish graduate school. **EXHIBIT 7: College Invest Student Loan Amounts** Since Mexico has a high unemployment rate I would not be able to find a job that would pay me sufficiently so that I could pay off my student loans.

If I had to relocate to Mexico my future employability in the United States would be jeopardized because as a licensed teacher, my license is only good and valid for five years, from the date of issue. If I did not work as a teacher within the first five years from the date my license was issued, my license could possibly be terminated and/or I would have to take additional education classes as well as another state examination. This would severely affect my chances for future employment with any school district in the state of Colorado.

HEALTH ISSUES/CONCERNS

A move to Mexico would cause severe hardship. My health care or lack thereof and health conditions are also something to consider. Five years ago, in 2002 I was diagnosed with depression and severe generalized anxiety disorder. Before I met Alien, in 2004, I was facing relentless financial and economic hardships that were making life unbearable. I was close to quitting school altogether to move in with my parents in Smallcity, CO. **EXHIBIT 8: Letter from Dr. Physician and Medical Records from visits with Dr. Physician at the Health Center**

My physical, mental and overall well-being was in danger as I was diagnosed by the school psychiatrist, Dr. Physician, with depression and generalized anxiety disorder. Dr. Physician prescribed Zoloft and Clonazepam for me to help cope with the depression and anxiety, though the medications were effective, they did not help much; as a matter of fact I gained 40 pounds from taking them.

When I met Alien in 2004, I was still taking the Zoloft and the Clonazepam, however being and living with him helped my physical and mental condition tremendously. He not only helped me with my personal, financial and educational hardships I was facing at that time, but with his support and guidance I was able to finish my Bachelor's degree *as well as*, began and finish the Teacher Licensure and Masters of Arts in Education program I enrolled in afterwards. I have also lost 40 pounds. I could not have progressed both physically and mentally without him.

At this time, I am experiencing extreme anxiety and insomnia from being separated from my husband. My doctor, Dr. Medical has been prescribing a mild tranquilizer, Lorezapam to help me cope with the anxiety and insomnia. This has been a long-term condition that I fear will to turn into something more extreme if my husband and I are not reunited. **EXHIBIT 9: Letter from Dr. Medical**

I have been seeing the same physician for three years. Finding a doctor in Mexico that I could communicate my health concerns with would be impossible since I don't speak Spanish. Concern for my health and the lack of treatment available would cause me much more anxiety and distress than needed.

PERSONAL CONSIDERATIONS/FAMILY TIES

I was born in Smalltown, CO in 1972 where my parents grew up and where their parents grew up. My father and mother met in Smalltown, CO, where my mother was living after a marriage and divorce in 1970. My mother had five children from her prior marriage that she was taking care of and raising in Smalltown, CO. when she met my father. My father, who was drafted as a soldier into the armed forces and enlisted into the Army at the age of 18, had just finished serving his time in the Vietnam War when he met my mother.

All of my mother's children from her prior marriage are United States Citizens. Their names are:

• First Child – currently resides in Denver, CO.

• Second Child – currently resides in Salt Lake City, Utah

• Third Child - deceased

• Fourth Child – currently resides in Denver, CO.

• Fifth Child – currently resides in Aurora, CO.

Two years after my father and mother met, in 1972, I was born and two years later in 1974, my sister was born. That same year my family moved to Smallcity, CO, where The Industry employed my father. I grew up in Smallcity, CO, where I attended and graduated from High School in 1991.

In 1994 in Smallcity, CO, my sister Third Child passed away from *Fulminant Hepatic Failure* – acute liver failure. **EXHIBIT 10: Third Child's Death Certificate**

My sister was 30 years old and had four children whom she was raising alone. After her death, my parents gained custody of her children, who were at the time, 6, 8, 9 and 11 years old.

Their names are:

- Oldest Niece
- Oldest Nephew
- Younger Niece
- Younger Nephew

At the time of my sister's death, my sister I and I were the only children of my parents left living in Smallcity as all of our other siblings were living in other cities, raising their own families. Because of this, we helped our parents with the raising and supporting of my sisters children. My sister now lives in California with her husband and two daughters.

I am incredibly close to my nephews and nieces; I am like a mother to them. Presently, they all live in and around Denver, with children of their own that we, Alien and I help them with. My nephews and nieces have formed an emotional attachment to my husband. They love him greatly and would be devastated if he could not be here in the United States with them. It would be traumatic and devastating for us all if I had to be move away from them, as they have never had a mother and for most of their lives, I have been the closest thing to a mother they have ever had. On top of that, my parents cannot imagine the thought of losing another child. They are still suffering from the loss of my sister.

My mother has been diagnosed by her doctor with ASCVD (arteriosclerotic cardiovascular disease), diabetes mellitus type 2, depression, anxiety, reflux esophagus, chronic abdominal pain and somatoform disorder (see attached information sheet) She is required to take numerous and various medications for her physical and mental condition. She depends on my father for everything, including her medication administration, her food and transportation. He also bathes and dresses her. My father also takes care of the household needs. Since I am the oldest daughter, with no family responsibilities of my own, I feel it is my obligation to help my father take care of my mother. For example, I drive to Smallcity and clean, cook and take care of my mother. I administer her medications, talk with her doctors, drive her to any of her doctor appointments, fill out any paperwork needed for her medical insurance (Medicare and Champ VA) and I take care of any other paper work needed.

In 2002, In Smallcity, my mother had a quadruple bypass surgery. Her recovery was exceptionally slow and complicated; she was in and out of the hospital numerous times after her surgery. **EXHIBIT 11: Medical Records of Mother.**

My father suffers from diabetes mellitus type 2, hypertension, eczematous dermatitis, peripheral neuropathy and PTSD. He is also required to take numerous medications for his mental and physical conditions. Since my mother is not physically or mentally healthy to assist with the care of my father, it is my responsibility to do so. I help my father in various ways ranging from going with him to his visits a the Veterans Hospital because he has a hard time concentrating and talking with his doctors, with the filling out of various and numerous health insurance forms, medical forms and any other forms needed by the Veterans Administration. I help him with managing the household bills and expenses, including the care and maintenance of the house.

EXHIBIT 12: Medical Records of Father.

My father is 60 years old and my mother is 69 years old. They both suffer from an array of physical and mental health problems stemming from my sister's death, my mother's heart surgery, and my father's past experiences as a soldier in the Army and his time spent in the Vietnam War.

Since I am the oldest daughter of my mother and father, with no family responsibilities of my own, I feel it is my responsibility to take care of my parents. Whenever my father has to travel to Denver for his doctor's appointments at the Veterans Hospital (there is not a veterans hospital in Smallcity), I have to either stay with my mother here in Denver or travel to Smallcity to stay with her because she cannot be left alone.

They both depend on me as their health has been declining, and I expect that they will need more of my help in the near future.

I am the oldest child. I do not have children of my own, and I do not own a home. My job gives me enough flexibility to travel back and forth to Smallcity to help with the care and management of my parents in their times of need. Normally, they can take care of themselves, however with their failing health and age, there are episodes in which they need a lot of help from me and during those times I, in turn, need help from my spouse.

FUTURE CHILDREN

My husband and I are anxiously waiting the day that we will be blessed with children. This would be extremely difficult for me if living in Mexico, not to mention an extreme hardship. If I was to deliver our children in Mexico I would face many problems causing me much more worrisome nights than necessary.

I do not speak Spanish so I would be unable to communicate my concerns accurately with nurses and doctors. I would be extremely uncomfortable with someone I had no prior relationship with. And most importantly I would not have the same health benefits in Mexico that I have in the U.S., my health insurance in the U.S, will cover a very large part of maternity costs including a significant time off for maternity leave. I would be unable to afford the same kind of care if living in Mexico. **EXHIBIT 13: Medical/Health Insurance Plan – Kaiser Permanente and Kaiser Permanente Enrollment Form**

When we do have children, I know my family will play a major role in their upbringing. My mom cannot wait for grandchildren from my husband and I. The thought of raising them in Mexico with less educational opportunities than the United States and keeping them away from the grandparents make my stomach turn. I do not want our children to grow up without the same educational and economic opportunities that I had. It would be impossible for me to travel back and forth between the U.S and Mexico to see my parents; our finances if living in Mexico would not allow it.

LIVING IN MEXICO

I moved to Guerrero, Mexico, where Alien's family is from, with Alien in October 2006. At that time, I gave up my lifestyle, all of my responsibilities and family ties here in the United States to be with my husband. **EXHIBIT 14: a. Letter from Bank of America regarding taking the Volkswagen to Mexico and Rental Contract** In Mexico we lived in a house that was owned by his parents and we were responsible for paying rent including all of the utilities for the home.

My husband is a licensed architect in Mexico and took responsibility for one project when we lived there. He was supposed to get paid by his clients when he completed architectural drawings, models and blueprints, which sometimes took up to four weeks. Once completed, Raul rarely got paid on time and many times he didn't get paid at all.

Since I worked as a teacher and made $2.30 an hour, I did not make enough money to cover all of our household expenses. Our combined income only allowed us enough to pay our rent and buy food. At times we had no electricity, gas or water.

Life in Mexico was extremely hard for me to adjust to for various reasons. The lack of income was difficult to deal with because it changed my lifestyle completely. In the United States I was accustomed to a certain lifestyle, not a glamorous one by all means, but one that allowed me to find a job and pay my monthly household living expenses. Indeed, while attending college in the United States I faced financial hardships, I still had and have the opportunity to improve my circumstances through my education, experience and skills, which is why I worked so hard on my education. In Mexico, I did and do not have the opportunity to improve my circumstances through my education, experience and skills, because Mexico just did and does not have the demand or the need for my skills. When I lived in Mexico I felt stressed out and anxiety ridden all of the time, because of the lack of money, we could not pay our bills, and I could not find a decent paying job – I felt hopeless and helpless.

While I was living in Mexico I felt very alone and isolated, I became introverted and depressed again. There were several things I could not do in Mexico that I was able to do in the United States, and having to depend on my husband to help me with everything, including communicating with others, was especially difficult for me to adapt to. I could not drive because the traffic in town is horrendous and I felt scared. While I was living there, I witnessed several car crashes, including one head on collision on the highway – the vision of that crash and the people involved will be forever embedded in my memory. I could not call home to talk with my family because the long distance telephone charges to the United States were and still are enormously expensive. This was tough for me to deal with because of my parent's declining age and health problems. I could not communicate with my husband's family because I do not speak the language, Spanish. I could not go to the market and buy groceries because of the language barrier. I had no friends or family to talk with and communicate my concerns and fears to. My husband did help me at times but because of his work schedule, he could not be with me all of the time.

I did go to the clinic with my husband to speak with a physician about my depression and anxiety. The doctor gave me a prescription for Lorezapam to help cope with my condition.

I moved back to the United States in April 2007, leaving my husband behind in Mexico. My readjustment back to the United States has been difficult as well, especially without having my husband here.

CONCLUSION

One could say life would be over if my husband was not allowed to return to the U.S and I had to relocate to Mexico. I would be emotionally, physically and mentally traumatized since I do not speak Spanish and therefore, would not be able to communicate. I would be unemployable and helpless.

Separating myself from the educational opportunities, the health care, my career, the standard of living, and my family relationships would be devastating and could lead to further more serious hardships and/or health issues. I have high hopes for my career and my future as an educator. Living in Mexico would make this impossible. I have good health care and health issues that need to be treated and taken care of in the U.S. I have debts that must be paid and a standard of living to continue. My relationship with my family would be torn apart and they too would suffer a significant loss. It is imperative for my husband to be allowed to return to the United States so that we can continue our love and our life together.

My husband is a good man who possesses great integrity, wisdom and love for our family. Taking both of us away from our lives in the United States of America would be devastating.

I declare under the penalty of perjury that the preceding statement is true and correct to the best of my knowledge.

By:_____
Qualifying Relative

Signed and sworn to before me on this _____ day of July 2007.

Witness my hand and Official Seal.

Notary Name :_____

WHAT TO DO WHEN UNLAWFUL PRESENCE BEWITCHES YOUR IMMIGRANT VISA CASE

by Robert D. Ahlgren and Michael E. Piston[*]

Consular processing of immigrant visas has always been with us. However, as the remaining dim hopes for the reinstatement of Immigration and Nationality Act (INA) §245(i) continue to fade and disappear, and U.S. Citizenship and Immigration Services (USCIS) adjudicators become increasingly more vigorous in leaping on the smallest violations to deny adjustment of status to even the most law-abiding noncitizens, attorneys are increasingly forced to deal with consular processing in order to obtain permanent residence for their clients. However, before sending a client off to "pick up a visa" at a U.S. consulate abroad, it is, of course, of critical importance to ensure that the client will be coming back in relatively short order, rather than languishing outside the United States for three years or more (maybe much more) as a result of being found inadmissible for one reason or other. Perhaps most prominent among the grounds of inadmissibility one must be aware of are those contained in INA §212(a)(9), particularly those imposing excruciating long sentences of exile on persons who have been "unlawfully present" in the United States.

THE IMPACT OF UNLAWFUL PRESENCE

Unlawful presence plays a key role in assessing the feasibility of consular processing for your clients. Unlawful presence can trigger bars to future admissibility. Depending on the length of time your client has been "unlawfully present" in the United States in current or prior entries, and the manner in which your client has entered the country, either recently or in the past, on leaving your client may be barred from re-entering the United States for three years, 10 years, or life, with a waiver difficult or even impossible to obtain.[1]

CALCULATING UNLAWFUL PRESENCE

The INA provides: "For purposes of this paragraph [INA §212(a)(9)] an alien is deemed to be unlawfully present in the United States after the expiration of the period of stay authorized by the Attorney General or is present in the United States without being admitted or paroled."[2] Therefore, the primary key to understanding what constitutes unlawful presence is to determine what constitutes a period of stay authorized by the attorney general.

Periods of Stay Authorized by the Attorney General

We now enter difficult terrain. The statute expands on the above definition of unlawful presence only by indicating some exceptions to the rule. There are no regulations interpreting the concept of unlawful presence. We have only a variety of policy statements from legacy Immigration and Naturalization Service (INS), USCIS, and the Department of State (DOS), mostly in the form of memoranda.

Generally speaking, a noncitizen who is admitted to the United States on a nonimmigrant visa or in parole status until a certain date—typically as indicated on his or her Form I-94 (or, in the case of a citizen of a visa waiver country, Form I-94W)—who remains in the United States past the expiration date, or enters the United States without being admitted or paroled (that is, without inspection), is unlawfully present.

When status is extended, unlawful presence does not begin until the expiration of the date on the new

---

[*] **Robert D. Ahlgren** is a principal in the law office of Robert D. Ahlgren & Associates, P.C. in Chicago. He is a former chair of the Chicago Chapter of AILA and was a member of the Board of Governors of AILA for several years. Mr. Ahlgren is a frequent writer and lecturer on immigration and nationality law.

Michael E. Piston is the senior partner in Piston & Carpenter P.C. in Troy, MI. He has been practicing immigration law exclusively for over 20 years, and has spoken at numerous AILA and ILW conferences and workshops.

[1] Of course, due to previous periods of unlawful presence, a person also may be subject to these bars even if he or she remains in the United States and adjusts status.

[2] INA §212(a)(9)(B)(ii). This authority was actually transferred to the secretary of homeland security as a result of the Homeland Security Act of 2002, Pub. L. No. 107-296, 116 Stat. 2135. However, we will continue to refer to use the term "authorized by the Attorney General" to refer to periods in which a noncitizen is allowed to lawfully remain in the United States.

I-94. Unlawful presence does not accrue during the gap between the expiration of the original I-94 and the approval of an application for extension of stay, even if the application was filed after the original I-94 expired. The approval of an application for extension of stay is retroactive to the date of the expiration of the previous status.[3]

Unlawful presence does not accrue while a non-frivolous application for extension of stay is pending even if it is ultimately denied, provided that the application was filed before the previous status expired, and as long as the applicant did not work without authorization before the application was filed or while it was pending.[4] However, lawful presence may not be extended by filing a second application for extension of stay while the first is pending, unless the I-94 has yet to expire, or the first application is eventually approved.[5]

Unlawful presence can begin prior to the expiration of an I-94 if an immigration judge makes a determination of a status violation in exclusion, deportation, or removal proceedings, or, if legacy INS or the Department of Homeland Security (DHS)[6] made such a determination when adjudicating a benefit application.[7] If the immigration judge finds there was a status

violation, unlawful presence begins to accrue as of the date of the order, whether or not the decision is appealed. A DHS determination of status violation may arise, for example, during the adjudication of an application for extension or change of nonimmigrant status, reinstatement of nonimmigrant status (such as F-1 or J-1), employment authorization, or adjustment of status. In the case of a DHS determination of a nonimmigrant status violation, unlawful presence begins on the date of the decision denying the immigration benefit, whether or not it is appealed.[8]

Since F and J nonimmigrants normally are not admitted to the United States for a fixed term, but rather for "duration of status" (reflected by the notation "D/S" on the I-94), a DHS or Executive Office for Immigration Review (EOIR) determination of status violation is the only way that such a nonimmigrant may become unlawfully present.[9] The same rule also applies to Canadian citizens who are admitted to the United States as visitors without an I-94.[10]

Query, however, whether this same rule applies to a non-Canadian citizen who is not issued an I-94 when entering the United States, perhaps because the inspecting officer mistakenly believed that the person was Canadian.[11] While no agency guidance appears to address this situation, the definition of unlawful presence suggests application of the same

---

[3] INS Memorandum, M. Pearson, "Period of Stay Authorized by the Attorney General After 120 Day Tolling Period for Purposes of section 212(a)(9)(B) of the Immigration and Nationality Act (the Act)" (Mar. 3, 2000), *published on* AILA InfoNet at Doc. No. 00030774 (*posted* Mar. 7, 2000); INA §212(A)(9)(B)(iv).

[4] INA §212(A)(9)(B)(iv); Applications to Change NIV Status or Extend NIV Stay, 00 State 102274 (May 30, 2000), *published* on AILA InfoNet at Doc. No. 00060202 (*posted* June 2, 2000); 9 *Foreign Affairs Manual* (FAM) 40.92 N1.

[5] INS Memorandum, T. Cook, "Guidance on Interpretation of 'Period of Stay Authorized by the Attorney General' in Determining 'Unlawful Presence' Under Section 212(a)(9)(B)(ii) of the Immigration and Nationality Act" (Apr. 2, 2003), *published on* AILA InfoNet at Doc. No. 03042140 (*posted* Apr. 21, 2003).

[6] The DHS assumed the functions and responsibilities of legacy INS on March 1, 2003. *See* Homeland Security Act of 2002, Pub. L. No. 107-296, 116 Stat. 2135. Therefore, for simplicity, any reference to DHS or its components (USCIS, U.S. Immigration and Customs Enforcement (ICE), or U.S. Customs and Border Protection (CBP)) should also be understood to refer to legacy INS during periods prior to that date.

[7] Thus, unlawful presence does not begin to run from the date of a status violation (including unauthorized employment). One is not unlawfully present as long as one possesses an unexpired I-94, at least absent an express government finding of
continued

violation of status. INS Memorandum, P. Virtue, "Section 212(a)(9)(B) Relating to Unlawful Presence" (Sept. 19, 1997), *published* on AILA InfoNet at Doc. No. 97092240 (*posted* Sept. 22, 1997); 9 FAM 40.92 N1. *But see* K3 Visa Implementation, 01 State 167548 (Sept. 2001), *published* on AILA InfoNet at Doc. No. 01092702 (*posted* Sept. 27, 2001). The DOS cable indicates that the grant of permanent residence to a K-3 renders any dependent K-4 nonimmigrants who didn't adjust with the K-3 unlawfully present. Presumably, the FAM note overrules this unorthodox comment.

[8] *See* Virtue Memo, supra note 7; 9 FAM 40.92 N1.

[9] 9 FAM 40.92 N1; P.L. 104-208 Update No. 36: 212(a)(9)(A)–(C), 212(a)(6)(A) and (B), 98 State 060539 (Apr. 4, 1998), *published* on AILA InfoNet at Doc. No. 98040490 (*posted* Apr. 4, 1998).

[10] DOS Advisory Opinion, "INA 212(a)(9)(B) and Canadians," *published on* AILA InfoNet at Doc. No. 99102090 (*posted* Oct. 20, 1999). While there is no equivalent legacy INS or DHS memorandum, it seems reasonable to assume that DHS follows the same rule, given that DOS indicated that this rule was based on information from legacy INS's general counsel.

[11] Or because the person was a Mexican national using a border crossing card; I-94s are not typically issued for travel within 25 miles of the border.

rule applies to Canadians without I-94s. Thus, it can be argued that since the noncitizen was never granted a period of stay by the DHS, but was nevertheless admitted, in the absence of a formal finding by DHS or EOIR that the person has violated nonimmigrant status, there is never a time when the person is present in the United States after a period of stay authorized by the attorney general, and so the person never would become unlawfully present.

Periods of stay authorized by the attorney general also include periods when the following applications are pending:

- Adjustment of status or registry, if the application is properly filed[12] and not filed for the first time with an immigration judge during removal proceedings. The period of authorized stay continues during administrative and judicial review, provided that the applicant is eligible to renew the denied application in proceedings and has a legal basis for renewing that application;[13]

- Temporary residence (legalization) INA §§245(a) and/or 210 through administrative appeal;[14]

- Temporary and permanent residence by Cuban or Haitian entrants under Pub. L. No. 99-603 §202(b), through administrative appeal.[15]

A period of stay authorized by the attorney general also exists if one of the following statuses has been granted:

- Voluntary departure[16]

- Temporary protected status[17]

- Refugee and asylee status[18]

- Withholding or deferral of removal under the United Nations Convention Against Torture[19]

- Suspension of deportation, or cancellation of removal[20]

- Deferred enforced departure[21]

- Deferred action[22]

- Parolees (until the status expires)[23]

Conditional permanent resident (CPR) status, of course, is a period of stay authorized by the attorney general, at least during the initial two-year validity period on the CPR's Form I-551 (except when that status is terminated pursuant to INA §216(b)).[24] Further, that stay is extended when a timely petition (one filed before the CPR's I-551 expires) to remove conditions of residence (Form I-751 or I-829) is pending, including its renewal in removal proceedings. If, however, the petition is not timely filed, the alien is unlawfully present while the petition is pending unless USCIS agrees that there was good cause for the late filing.[25]

However, it may be argued plausibly that even a CPR who files a conventional I-751 or I-829 petition after his or her I-551 expires is in a period of stay authorized by the attorney general, even if USCIS does not find that the CPR had good cause for late filing. First, USCIS regulations provide that once an I-751 or I-829 has been "properly filed,"[26] CPR status will be extended automatically until such time

---

[12] "An application or petition received in a USCIS office shall be stamped to show the time and date of actual receipt and, unless otherwise specified in part 204 or part 245 or part 245a of this chapter, shall be regarded as properly filed when so stamped, if it is signed and executed and the required filing fee is attached or a waiver of the filing fee is granted." 8 CFR §103.2(a)(7)(i).

[13] *See* Pearson Memo, *supra* note 3; INS Memorandum, P. Virtue, "Additional Guidance for Implementing Sections 212(a)(6) and 212(a)(9) of the Immigration and Nationality Act" (June 17, 1997), *published on* AILA InfoNet at Doc. No. 97061790 (*posted* June 17, 1997); INS Memorandum, J. Williams, "Unlawful Presence" (June 12, 2002), *published on* AILA InfoNet at Doc. No. 02062040 (*posted* June 20, 2002).

[14] *See* Pearson Memo, *supra* note 3.

[15] *See id.*

[16] *See* Virtue Memo, *supra* note 7.

[17] *See* Pearson Memo, *supra* note 3.

[18] *See* Williams Memo, *supra* note 13.

[19] *See id.*

[20] *See* Pearson Memo, *supra* note 3.

[21] *See id.*

[22] *See* Williams Memo, *supra* note 13; *See also* 9 FAM 40.92 N1 (apparently deferring to legacy INS's definition of "period of stay authorized by the Attorney General," but only specifically mentioning some of the periods of stay that legacy INS so designated).

[23] *See* Virtue Memo, *supra* note 7. Presumably the failure to repeat this period in the Williams Memo, *supra* note 13, was an oversight.

[24] Virtue Memo, *supra* note 7.

[25] *See id.*; Letter of B. Cooper, INS General Counsel, to H. Klasko & D. Buffenstein (Dec. 10, 1999), *published on* AILA InfoNet at Doc. No. 99122271 (*posted* Dec. 22, 1999).

[26] An I-751 petition need not be "timely" filed to be "properly" filed. *See* 8 CFR §103.2(a)(7)(i). Neither must a Form I-829, although it must have the documentation required by 8 CFR §216.6(a)(4). *See* 8 CFR §216.6(a)(1).

as a director has adjudicated the petition.[27] The regulations do not make any exception for untimely filed I-751s or I-829s.

Second, even a CPR whose I-751 has been denied by USCIS is entitled to temporary evidence of permanent residence while in removal proceedings.[28] It is difficult to see how it can be maintained plausibly that a person in actual possession of temporary evidence of permanent residence is not in a period of stay authorized by the attorney general.

Also, since an I-751 filed by a CPR seeking a waiver of the joint petition requirement[29] may be filed at any time before the CPR is subject to a final order of removal,[30] presumably the filing of an I-751 for waiver purposes always will be timely as long as there is no such final order entered, regardless of when the CPR's initial I-551 expired.[31]

Exceptions

No one, regardless of immigration status, was unlawfully present in the United States prior to April 1, 1997, the effective date of INA §§212(a)(9)(B) and (C).[32] There are also certain situations in which one may not be in a period of stay authorized by the attorney general, but still not be unlawfully present for the purposes of INA §212(a)(9)(B) (only). These are described in INA §212(a)(9)(B)(iii), which provides that:

Minors.—No period of time in which an alien is under 18 years of age shall be taken into account

in determining the period of unlawful presence in the United States under clause (i).[33]

Asylees.—No period of time in which an alien has a bona fide application for asylum[34] pending under section 208 shall be taken into account in determining the period of unlawful presence in the United States under clause (i) unless the alien during such period was employed without authorization in the United States. The tolling of any unlawful presence continues during administrative and judicial review.[35]

Family unity.—No period of time in which the alien is a beneficiary of family unity protection pursuant to section 301 of the Immigration Act of 1990 shall be taken into account in determining the period of unlawful presence in the United States under clause (i).

Battered women and children.—Clause (i) shall not apply to an alien who would be described in paragraph (6)(A)(ii) if "violation of the terms of the alien's nonimmigrant visa" were substituted for "unlawful entry into the United States" in subclause (III) of that paragraph.

Victims of a severe form of trafficking in persons—Clause (i) shall not apply to an alien who demonstrates that the severe form of trafficking (as that term is defined in section 103 of the Trafficking Victims Protection Act of 2000 (22 USC 7102)) was at least one central reason for the alien's unlawful presence in the United States.

INA §212(a)(9)(B)(iv) also provides for "tolling" of unlawful presence for 120 days following the filing of nonfrivolous, timely applications for change or extension of status, for the purposes of the three-year bar (INA §212(a)(9)(B)(i)(I)) only, provided that the applicant has not engaged in unauthorized employment before or during that application. How-

---

[27] 8 CFR §§216.4(a), 216.6(a)(1).

[28] *See* INS Memorandum, K. Redman, "Status of Conditional Residents in Proceedings" (Oct. 9, 1997); *published in* 74 *Interpreter Releases* 1731 (Nov. 7, 1997); INS General Counsel Opinion, D. Martin, "Status of a Conditional Permanent Resident After Denial of I-751 During Pendency of Review by EOIR," 96 Op. Gen. Counsel 12 (Aug. 6, 1996). Inexplicably, no similar accommodation appears to have been ordered for alien entrepreneurs seeking to renew a denied I-829 in removal proceedings.

[29] *See* INA §216(c)(4).

[30] *See* 8 CFR §216.5(a)(2); *Matter of Stowers*, 22 I&N Dec. 605 (BIA 1999).

[31] Thus it may be prudent for a CPR filing an untimely joint petition for the lifting of conditions to apply also for a hardship waiver of that requirement, where applicable, thereby presumably cutting off the further accrual of unlawful presence.

[32] *See Matter of Rodarte-Roman*, 23 I&N Dec. 905 (BIA 2006).

---

[33] "Clause (i)" apparently refers to INA §212(a)(9)(B)(i), which begins the definitions and exceptions.

[34] Defined as having any arguable basis in law or fact. INS Memorandum, B. Cooper, "INA 212(a)(9)(B)(iii)(II): Asylee Exception to Unlawful Presence" (June 8, 1999), *published on* AILA InfoNet at Doc. No. 99082590 (*posted* Aug. 25, 1999).

[35] *Id.* This rule applies even if the asylum application was denied (not referred) by legacy INS, regardless of when removal proceedings eventually were commenced. INS Memorandum, M. Pearson "Asylum-Related Issues/AILA Meeting" (Aug. 2, 1999), *published* on AILA InfoNet at Doc. No. 99082591 (*posted* Aug. 25, 1999).

ever, this section has been rendered largely superfluous by legacy INS[36] and DOS[37] policy statements making all time such applications are pending periods of stay authorized by the attorney general. Nevertheless, this statutory provision still may prove applicable to persons in removal proceedings, in that the Board of Immigration Appeals (BIA) has held that legacy INS policy memoranda are not binding on it.[38]

Finally, a little-known exception is contained in a legacy INS memorandum providing that "[a]n alien lawfully present in the United States in a nonimmigrant status on September 10, 2001, who was prevented from departing the United States after the alien's period of lawful admission expired as a direct result of a specified terrorist activity shall not be considered to have accrued unlawful presence during the period between September 11, 2001 and November 11, 2001."[39]

WHEN UNLAWFUL PRESENCE CAUSES INADMISSIBILITY

Of course, not all persons who have been unlawfully present in the United States are necessarily inadmissible. Rather, the precise consequences of periods of unlawful presence turn on the specific provisions of three sections of the INA: §§212(a)(9)(B)(i)(I), (II), and (C)(i)(II).

The Three-Year Bar

INA §212(a)(9)(B)(i)(I) provides that a noncitizen is inadmissible if he or she:

was unlawfully present in the United States for a period of more than 180 days but less than 1 year, voluntarily departed the United States (whether or not pursuant to section 244(e) [sic][40]) prior to the commencement of proceedings under section 235(b)(1) or section 240, and again seeks admission within 3 years of the date of [his or her] departure or removal . . .

This can be broken down into four elements, all of which must be satisfied before the noncitizen will be deemed inadmissible. The noncitizen must:

1. Be unlawfully present in the United States for more than 180 days but less than one year.

Comment: Legacy INS has confirmed that the 180 days of unlawful presence must be during one continuous period of presence.[41] Thus, if one was unlawfully present in the United States for 100 days, then left, reentered, and was unlawfully present for another 100 days, one still would not have satisfied the first part of this test, even though one's cumulative period of unlawful presence would be more than 180 days. Also, please note that 180 days is *not* six months. Rather, given that there are 365 or 366 days in a year, and 12 months, it follows that six months will be approximately 182 or 183 days, and a client who thinks he or she needs to leave the United States within six months of becoming unlawfully present may end up barred.[42] Needless to say, in advising clients it is extremely important to be precise as to the last day that they may remain in the United States without becoming inadmissible.[43]

2. Have voluntarily departed the United States.

Comment: The statute says, "whether or not pursuant to section 244(e)." The requirement that one have voluntarily departed the United States, therefore, includes any exiting of the country not under a final order of removal, even if it is not pursuant to a

---

[36] *See* Pearson Memo, *supra* note 3.

[37] *See* DOS Cable, *supra* note 4.

[38] *Matter of L–K–*, 23 I&N Dec. 677 (BIA 2004); *Ortega-Cervantes v. Gonzales,* 501 F.3d 1111 (9th Cir. 2007). *But see Matter of Cano*, A78 131 147, 2006 WL 3088790 (BIA Aug. 8, 2006). In *Cano* the BIA vacated an immigration judge's (IJ) decision denying the respondent adjustment of status on the grounds that he was inadmissible under INA §212(a)(9)(B)(i)(I) due to a period of unlawful presence while he was an applicant for adjustment of status, and remanded the proceedings to the IJ for a determination as to whether DHS continued to adhere to the INS policy that the period during which a Form I-485 is pending is a period of stay authorized by the attorney general.

[39] *See* INS Memorandum, S. Anderson, "Procedures for Preservation of Immigration Benefits for Victims of Terrorism (Title IV, Subtitle C (Sections 421-428), of the USA PATRIOT Act) P.L. 107-56 (October 26, 2001)" (Jan. 31, 2002), *published* on AILA InfoNet at Doc. No. 02032533 (*posted* Mar. 25, 2002).

[40] Probably should be §240B.

[41] *See* INS Memorandum, P. Virtue, "Implementation of Section 212(a)(6)(A) and 212(a)(9) Grounds of Inadmissibility" (Mar. 31, 1997), *published on* AILA InfoNet at Doc. No. 97033190 (*posted* Mar. 31, 1997).

[42] In addition, lingering in the United States without a legal status will count heavily against the client in any future applications that require a favorable exercise of consular or agency discretion, even if it does not result in a 212(a)(9)(B) or (C) bar.

[43] See *www.timeanddate.com/date/dateadd.html* for a date calculator that will assist in making precise calculations.

formal grant of voluntary departure under section 240B of the INA (formerly INA §244(e)).[44]

3. Have departed prior to the commencement of proceedings under INA §235(b)(1) or INA §240.

Comment: This language creates the paradoxical situation in which a noncitizen can actually benefit from being placed in removal proceedings. If a noncitizen has been unlawfully present in the United States for over 180 days but less than a year and leaves the United States prior to the commencement of removal proceedings, he or she will be subject to the three-year bar. But, if the noncitizen leaves the United States after the commencement of removal proceedings, he or she won't be subject to a bar if the period of unlawful presence in the United States is not one year or more.[45]

However, one must be very careful in relying on this loophole in the rules pertaining to unlawful presence. One must be aware of what constitutes the commencement of removal proceedings. It is not merely the issuance of a notice to appear. Rather, removal proceedings are commenced only by the filing of the notice to appear with the immigration court or by the issuance and service of Form I-860, Notice and Order of Expedited Removal.[46] Further, it can be quite difficult to get DHS to issue a notice to appear against one's client, and more difficult still to cause it to file the notice with the immigration court in a timely manner. Therefore, this is by no means a reliable technique for avoiding the three-year bar for clients who have been unlawfully present for over 180 days.[47]

Often discussions of this provision seem to suggest that once placed in removal proceedings, one should not leave the United States without an order of voluntary departure. Actually this is not always strictly necessary. Per legacy INS, INA §212(a)(9)(A) (bar after removal) applies only if the alien has departed or been removed from the United States after the issuance of a removal order.[48] Therefore, leaving the United States after the commencement of removal proceedings, but prior to the issuance of a removal order, should not result in one being subject to the bar at INA §212(a)(9)(A) even if a removal order is issued after one's departure.[49]

The *Foreign Affairs Manual* (FAM) also warns that a person who leaves the United States after the commencement of removal proceedings may be inadmissible for five years under INA §212(a)(6)(B) for failure to attend a hearing.[50] However, here again it is apparent that this ground of inadmissibility only applies to a person who leaves the United States following a failure to appear at a hearing, not before. INA §212(a)(6)(B) provides that "[a]ny alien who without reasonable cause fails or refuses to attend or remain in attendance at a proceeding to determine the alien's inadmissibility or deportability and who seeks admission to the United States within 5 years of such alien's subsequent departure or removal is

---

[44] *See Matter of Lemus-Losa*, 24 I&N Dec. 373 (BIA 2007).

[45] Letter of P. Chang, INS Branch Chief, Residence and Status Services Branch, to E. Lichtman (Mar. 23, 1998), *published* on AILA InfoNet at Doc. No. 98032391 (*posted* Mar. 23, 1998); Cooper Letter, *supra* note 25. A denied applicant for adjustment of status or registry also benefits from the commencement of removal proceedings, since his or her renewal of the denied application apparently has the effect of negating unlawful presence from the time of the denial of the application to the time of its renewal, and forward until a final order of removal is entered. Pearson Memo, *supra* note 3; *Matter of Reyes*, A73 616 942, 2007 WL 4711458 (BIA Dec. 27, 2007).

[46] *See* 8 CFR §245.1(c)(8)(i).

[47] Decisions about whether (and when) to initiate removal proceedings are committed to the unreviewable discretion of DHS. *Matter of Bahta*, 22 I&N Dec. 1381, 1391 (BIA 2000); *Matter of U–M–*, 20 I&N Dec. 327, 333 (BIA 1991); *Matter of Geronimo*, 13 I&N Dec. 680, 681 (BIA 1971).

[48] *See* INS Memorandum, L. Crocetti, "Processing of Section 245(i) Adjustment Applications on or After the October 1, 1997 Sunset Date; Clarification Regarding the Applicability of Certain New Grounds of Inadmissibility to 245(i) Applications" (May 1, 1997), *published* on AILA InfoNet at Doc. No. 97050191 (*posted* May. 1, 1997) ("It should be noted that new section 212(a)(9)(A) of the Act applies only if the alien has departed or been removed from the United States subsequent to issuance of an order.").

[49] *Accord* 20 CFR §40.91(b) ("An alien who has otherwise been removed from the United States under any provision of law, or who departed while an order of removal was in effect, is ineligible for a visa under INA §212(a)(9)(A)(ii) for 10 years following such removal or departure from the United States."). One supposes it is theoretically possible that the government might argue that a person who leaves the United States prior to the issuance of a removal order, is outside the United States when it is issued, and then returns to the United States and departs again may then be subject to the INA §212(a)(9)(A) bar. Such a strained reading of the law, however, seems inconsistent with the general rule that a removal order is not applicable to subsequent entries (otherwise there would be no need for INA §241(a)(5)). Nevertheless, clients should be counseled regarding this presumably remote possibility.

[50] *See* 9 FAM 40.92 N2.1.

inadmissible." Needless to say, a "subsequent departure" is one which occurs after, not before, the failure to appear.

However, if one left the United States, was ordered removed in absentia, returned to the country, and then departed again, one might well become subject to this bar. Nevertheless, this bar seems unlikely to be enforced in such a situation, if for no other reason than one would be hard pressed to think of better "reasonable cause" for not attending a removal hearing than the fact that one has already left the country.[51]

4. Be again seeking admission to the United States within three years of the date of his or her departure or removal.

Comment: Note that this phrase refers to the noncitizen's "departure or removal" as a precondition to the imposition of the three-year bar. Thus, merely having been unlawfully present in the United States for over 180 days is not a bar to adjustment of status if one has not left the country since that unlawful presence occurred.[52]

Further, there appears to be no requirement that one remain outside the United States during the three-year period before seeking adjustment of status. Thus, the Administrative Appeals Office (AAO) has found in at least three unpublished decisions that an applicant for adjustment of status who departed the United States with advance parole while his application for adjustment of status was pending (and then returned as a parolee to continue to pursue his adjustment application) was no longer inadmissible at the time of its decision because by then more than three years had passed since his last departure.[53]

The 10-Year Bar

INA §212(a)(9)(B)(i)(II), containing the 10-year bar, is a simpler section that breaks down into only two elements. A noncitizen is inadmissible if he or she:

1. Has been unlawfully present in the United States for one year or more, and

2. Again seeks admission within 10 years of the date of his or her departure or removal from the United States.

Comment: The commencement of removal proceedings will not exempt one from the 10-year bar, and although it still requires a departure from the United States, that departure need not be voluntary and can be under an order of removal. Like INA §212(a)(9)(B)(i)(I), the unlawful presence must have occurred during a single continuous stay in the United States.

It is probably of little current significance that INA §212(a)(9)(B) does not apply to applicants for a "V" nonimmigrant visa.[54]

The "Permanent" 10-Year Bar

INA §212(a)(9)(C)(i)(I) provides that any alien who has been unlawfully present in the United States for an aggregate period of more than one year, and who enters or attempts to re-enter the United States without being admitted, is inadmissible.

Here the period of unlawful presence referred to by the statute is the aggregate of all periods of unlawful presence prior to an entry (or attempted entry) without inspection.[55] So, for example, if one is unlawfully present in the United States for four months, leaves, re-enters, is unlawfully present for another four months, leaves, is unlawfully present a third time, for five months, then leaves the United States and returns without inspection, one is subject to the permanent bar of INA §212(a)(9)(C)(i)(I).

---

[51] The legacy INS general counsel was reported to have agreed with this statement in an AILA liaison meeting. "Highlights of AILA–INS General Counsel Liaison Meeting" (July 10, 1998), *published on* AILA InfoNet at Doc. No. 98081090 (*posted* Aug. 10, 1998).

[52] *See* Virtue Memo, *supra* note 41; *Matter of Rodarte-Roman,* 23 I&N Dec. 905 (BIA 2006) (to be rendered inadmissible for 10 years pursuant to INA §212(a)(9)(B)(i)(II), a noncitizen must depart the United States after having been unlawfully present in the United States for one year or longer).

[53] *See Matter of [name not provided]* [file number not provided] (AAO June 2, 2004) (accessed at *www.uscis.gov/err/Administrative%20Decisions%20after %20August%201%202000/h2/2004/jun0204_01h2212.pdf*) ; *Matter of [name not provided]* [file number not provided] 2006 WL 4739219 (AAO Aug. 29, 2006); *Matter of [name not provided]* [file number not provided] 2004 WL 3480617
continued

(AAO Oct. 21, 2004). However, note that if a person subject to the bar entered the United States as a nonimmigrant without a waiver, he or she might be barred from adjustment under INA §§245(a) or (k) on the grounds that his or her admission was not "lawful." *Cf. Matter of Koloamatangi,* 23 I&N Dec. 548 (BIA 2003) (an alien who acquired permanent resident status through fraud or misrepresentation has never been "lawfully admitted for permanent residence" and is therefore ineligible for cancellation of removal under INA §240A(a)).

[54] INA §214(q)(2).

[55] *See* Virtue Memo, *supra* note 41.

Note also that it is only an entry, or attempted entry, without inspection that triggers the bar.[56]

Waiver of Inadmissibility Due to Unlawful Presence

INA §212(a)(9)(B)(v) provides the standard for a waiver of the three– or ten-year bars to admissibility due to unlawful presence in the United States. The attorney general may waive the bars in the case of an immigrant who is the spouse or son or daughter of a U.S. citizen or of an alien lawfully admitted for permanent residence, if it is established to the satisfaction of the attorney general that the refusal of admission to such immigrant alien would result in extreme hardship to the citizen or lawfully resident spouse or parent of such alien.

Comment: Note that there is no waiver of the unlawful presence bar for a noncitizen through an immediate relative who is a U.S. citizen or permanent resident child, regardless of how much hardship the child would suffer as a result of the removal.

Waiver of the "Permanent" 10-Year Bar

The "permanent" bar imposed by INA §212(a)(9)(C)(i)(I) "shall not apply to an alien seeking admission more than 10 years after the date of the alien's last departure from the United States if, prior to the alien's reembarkation at a place outside the United States or attempt to be readmitted from a foreign contiguous territory, the Secretary of Homeland Security has consented to the alien's reapplying for admission."

Comment: The earliest it is possible to apply for this waiver is 10 years after the last departure from the United States. Therefore, if the bar applies in a given case, the applicant must be outside the country to apply, and the prior 10 years must be spent outside the United States. American consulates, on a finding that a permanent 10-year bar applies, note on the denial form that the earliest a request for a waiver of inadmissibility (Form I-601) will be entertained is a specific date that is 10 years from the last day the applicant was in the United States, as determined from discussions with the client.

As of this year, 2008, we will begin to see the first of the applicants requesting a waiver of the "permanent" 10-year bar. Although clients have been cautioned to maintain evidence of having lived outside the United States, doing so is sometimes very difficult. We do not know what adjudications officials will require to prove presence outside the United States. Obviously, hardship issues may be greatly affected by the requirement to live abroad.

Violence Against Women Act (VAWA) Waiver

The secretary of homeland security may waive the permanent 10-year bar in the case of a VAWA self-petitioner if there is a connection between the petitioner's battering or subjection to extreme cruelty and his or her removal, departure from the United States, re-entry or re-entries into the United States, or attempted re-entry into the United States.[57]

NEW GUIDANCE

Unfortunately, what little new information has emerged regarding the INA §212(a)(9) bars to admissibility since the 2007–08 AILA annual conference is uniformly negative.

New Federal Decisions

The biggest and worst new development is the U.S. Court of Appeals for the Ninth Circuit's disappointing decision in *Duran Gonzales v. DHS*,[58] overruling *Perez-Gonzalez v. Ashcroft*,[59] and holding instead that INA §212(a)(9)(C)(i)(II) inadmissibility is in fact a bar to adjustment of status under INA §245(i).[60] Although the decision actually construed INA §212(a)(9)(C)(i)(II) (the permanent bar to admission for persons who entered, or tried to enter, without inspection [EWIs] following removal), its reasoning casts into considerable doubt the Ninth Circuit's *Acosta v. Gonzales*[61] decision, which holds that INA §212(a)(9)(C)(i)(I) (the permanent bar to admission of EWIs who previously had been unlawfully present for over a year in the United States) was not a bar to adjustment under §245(i).

---

[56] *See id.* The Visa Office endorsed this interpretation in a visa advisory opinion addressed to one of the authors, stating that "the mere fact that an alien knows he/she is inadmissible (when seeking admission to the U.S.) does not render him/her an attempted illegal entrant under INA 212(a)(9)(C)."

[57] INA §212(a)(9)(C)(iii).

[58] 508 F.3d 1227 (9th Cir 2007). However, on February 27, 2008, the plaintiffs filed a petition for rehearing en banc, asking the entire Ninth Circuit to rehear the decision. The decision is not final as long as a motion for rehearing en banc is pending.

[59] 379 F.3d 783 (9th Cir. 2004).

[60] As to INA §245(i), see *infra*.

[61] 439 F.3d 550, 554 (9th Cir. 2006).

The common question in all these cases is whether Congress intended that a person who was rendered inadmissible to the United States as a result of entering (or attempting to enter) the country without inspection should be barred from adjusting his or her status to permanent resident under INA §245(i). Immigrant advocates argued that it did not, relying primarily on the express statement in INA §245(i)(1)(A)(i) that noncitizens who entered without inspection could adjust status in the United States if they otherwise met the requirements of §245(i). Government attorneys, however, countered that this language didn't apply to persons barred under §212(a)(9)(C), since it contained bars to admission, rather than adjustment, and §245(i)(2)(A) expressly requires immigrants to be admissible to the United States for permanent residence as a condition of adjustment of status. In *Perez-Gonzalez v. Ashcroft, Padilla-Caldera v. Gonzalez,*[62] and *Acosta v. Gonzales,* the courts decided that while the statute was ambiguous, Congress's intent in adopting §245(i) would be best served by permitting persons inadmissible under §212(a)(9)(C) to apply to adjust status under §245(i).

However, when DHS appealed a district court preliminary injunction ordering it to comply with *Perez-Gonzalez* within the Ninth Circuit, the court in *Duran Gonzales* overruled *Perez-Gonzalez,* holding that it had been superseded in effect by the BIA's decision in *Matter of Torres-Garcia.*[63] In *Torres-Garcia,* the BIA ruled that §212(a)(9)(C)(i)(II) did bar immigrants from adjusting status under §245(i). The Ninth Circuit found the U.S. Supreme Court's decisions in *Chevron USA, Inc. v. Natural Resources Defense Council*[64] and *National Cable & Telecommunications Ass'n v. Brand X Internet Services*[65] required it to defer to the BIA construction of the INA, since its construction was a "permissible" (reasonable) interpretation of a statutory ambiguity.

While, as discussed, *Perez-Gonzalez* involved the permanent bar on EWIs with prior removal orders contained in §212(a)(9)(C)(i)(II), its reasoning seems likely to be used to deny §245(i) adjustment to EWIs re-entering after being unlawfully present for over a year who are inadmissible under §212(a)(9)(C)(i)(I), despite the Ninth Circuit's con-

trary decision in *Acosta.* As in *Perez-Gonzalez,* there was a published decision of the BIA after *Acosta* holding that immigrants inadmissible under §212(a)(9)(C)(i)(I) are barred from adjustment under §245(i).[66] The BIA's reasoning in that case, *Matter of Briones,* appears fundamentally the same as it used in *Torres-Garcia:* §245(i)(2)(A) requires that applicants for adjustment be admissible, and an adjustment applicant subject to §212(a)(9)(C)(i)(I) is not. Therefore, it is not unlikely that the Ninth Circuit may soon conclude that it must defer to the BIA's decision in *Briones* and overrule *Acosta* as well.

Also vulnerable is the U.S. Court of Appeals for the Tenth Circuit's decision in *Padilla-Caldera v Gonzales.*[67] There, like the Ninth Circuit in *Acosta,* the Tenth Circuit held that INA §212(a)(9)(C)(i)(I) is not a bar to adjustment of status under §245(i). If the traditionally pro-immigrant Ninth Circuit abandons its *Acosta* decision, there will be tremendous pressure on the relatively pro-government Tenth Circuit to follow suit, particularly since two other circuit courts of appeals have agreed with the BIA that §245(i) does not trump §212(a)(9)(C).[68]

New BIA Decisions

Were that not bad enough, the BIA has been busy steadily extending the reach of INA §212(a)(9) inadmissibility while making it more difficult for immigrants to waive its restrictions. As previously noted, the BIA held in *Matter of Briones* that §212(a)(9)(C)(i)(I) is a bar to adjustment under INA §245(i). Unsurprisingly, it has also concluded that INA §212(a)(9)(B)(i)(II)'s 10-year bar on those who departed the United States after a year or more of unlawful presence is a bar to adjustment of status despite the fact that the heading for §212(a)(9) refers to "Aliens Previously Removed."[69] More distressing still is footnote 5 of the *Matter of Briones* opinion, suggesting that Congress stripped immigration judges of jurisdiction to grant a waiver of the §212(a)(9)(C)(i) bar, even in those rare instances when such a waiver might be available, by technical corrections to the waiver provision that transferred

---

[62] 453 F.3d 1237 (10th Cir 2005).

[63] 23 I&N Dec. 866 (BIA 2006).

[64] 467 U.S. 837 (1984).

[65] 545 U.S. 967 (2005).

[66] *Matter of Briones,* 24 I&N Dec. 355 (BIA 2007).

[67] 453 F.3d 1237 (10th Cir 2005).

[68] *Tenesaca Delgado v. Mukasey,* 2008 WL 323234 (2d Cir. 2008); *Mortera-Cruz v. Gonzales,* 409 F.3d 246 (5th Cir. 2005).

[69] *Matter of Lemus-Losa,* 24 I&N Dec. 373 (BIA 2007).

authority to adjudicate such waivers to USCIS from the attorney general.[70]

A PRACTICAL GUIDE TO APPLYING FOR A WAIVER OF INADMISSIBILITY DUE TO UNLAWFUL PRESENCE

Despite the daunting prospect of leaving the United States to apply for an immigrant visa abroad when a waiver of inadmissibility for unlawful presence will be needed, many clients are motivated to do so due to their lack of other options for obtaining permanent residence in the United States. When representing someone in such a case, practitioners must make sure that the client understands the risks. Additionally, before taking on the case, the practitioner must make sure that the client is eligible for a waiver, and that he or she is not subject to a "permanent" bar, *i.e.,* ineligibility for a waiver for 10 years or more. The correct legal advice is frequently that no visa can be applied for by a prospective immigrant until 10 years have passed. After these considerations have been made, the task of preparing a waiver application will require great time and care on the part of the client as well as the attorney.

Documenting Hardship to the Qualifying Relative

Pursuant to INA §212(a)(9)(B)(v), a waiver of unlawful presence depends on a showing of extreme hardship to a qualifying relative. Section 212(a)(9)(B)(v) provides in pertinent part:

> The Attorney General has sole discretion to waive clause (i) in the case of an immigrant who is the *spouse, son, or daughter of a United States citizen or of an alien lawfully admitted for permanent residence*, if it is established to the satisfaction of the Attorney General that the refusal of admission to such immigrant alien would result in *extreme hardship to the citizen or lawfully resident spouse or parent of such an alien . . . .* (Emphasis added.)

Step One: Who is the Qualifying Relative?

Before beginning to document extreme hardship, one must analyze who the qualifying relative is in the case. Under INA §212(a)(9)(B)(v), the waiver applicant's qualifying relative(s) would be his or her citizen or lawfully resident spouse and/or citizen or lawfully resident parent(s). As mentioned, children,

regardless of how they might suffer, are not qualifying relatives under the statute.[71] If the applicant has more than one qualifying relative, then the attorney would be wise to document extreme hardship as to each of those qualifying relatives, although the hardship of the different qualifying relatives may overlap significantly. Proving hardship to more than one qualifying relative may increase the applicant's chance of success greatly. Hardship is always to be considered cumulatively.[72]

Step Two: The In-Depth Client Interview

The next step is to uncover all of the ways in which the applicant's qualifying relative will suffer if the waiver of unlawful presence is denied.[73] An in-depth interview with the applicant and his or her qualifying relative(s) is essential because most applicants need substantial guidance in identifying all of the ways in which their qualifying relatives will suffer. It is not as easy as simply asking the qualifying relatives how they will suffer. It is easier to ask simple questions and build on them. It is important to examine and document how the qualifying relatives would suffer if they move abroad with the applicant *and* how they would suffer if they remain in the United States without the applicant.

Start with the basics

Where the spouse is the qualifying relative, ask about the history of the couple's relationship: how and when did the couple meet, when did they begin dating, and when were they married. It is important to get a sense of how the couple supports each other and what their daily routine is like. Also ask other basic questions about where they live, with whom they live, whether they own or rent their home, and what they do for a living. Where the parent is the qualifying relative, ask about the qualifying relative's daily routine and all of the ways the applicant is involved in that routine. Do not overlook the need to factor in the presence or absence of other sons or daughters who are lawfully in the United States. The adjudicating officer will not.

The next topic to discuss is emotional hardship. The above questions about the relationship between

---

[70] *See* Pub. L. No. 109-271, §6(b)(1)(C), 120 Stat. 750, 762 (2006).

[71] But see discussion under the heading **Children**, *infra.*

[72] *See Salameda v. INS* 78 F.3d 447 (7th Cir. 1995); *Hernandez-Cordero v. INS,* 783 F 2d 1266 (5th Cir. 1986).

[73] Please note that there are many published cases discussing "extreme hardship." One of the principal cases often discussed in matters involving "extreme hardship" is *Matter of Cervantes-Gonzalez,* 22 I&N Dec. 560 (BIA 1999).

the applicant and the qualifying relative will lay a foundation for arguing that the destruction of this relationship will cause extreme emotional hardship. It is also, however, important to search for special factors in the qualifying relative's life and past that would play a role in how he or she would suffer emotionally. For example, if the spouse is the qualifying relative, it is helpful to respectfully—and perhaps indirectly—elicit information about whether the qualifying relative's prior spouse had been physically and mentally abusive. This would strengthen the argument that the destruction of this new marriage would be especially hurtful. Similarly, evidence that the couple has supported each other through particularly traumatic events can strengthen the argument.

The separation of the qualifying relative from other family members besides the applicant may also produce significant emotional hardship. Ask the qualifying relative about his family in the United States and whether he has any family in the home country. Try to get a sense of what his family means to him and how he would feel if he had to abandon his family in the United States to be with the applicant in the home country. It is also beneficial to ask how far away he lives from his relatives, how often they get together, and what they enjoy doing together. Another special factor to consider is whether the qualifying relative grew up without his parents around and thus knows firsthand how difficult a separation like that can be. All of these factors contribute to the extreme emotional hardship the qualifying relative will suffer.

Medical and Physical Hardship

This area of hardship should be thoroughly examined, as it may be given significantly more weight by officers than other types of hardship. For example, Mr. Warren Janssen of the USCIS office in Ciudad Juarez, Mexico, has noted that the strongest waiver applications include evidence of health-related factors, which he considers to have a more extreme impact than emotional hardship, family separation, or financial inconvenience.[74] Many times when clients are asked whether they have any health or medical concerns, they will quickly respond that everyone is healthy. If the client responds in this way, it is worth the effort to try other ways of asking

this same question. It is often helpful to ask whether anyone in the family takes any medications, or when was the last time anyone needed to visit the doctor. If the qualifying relative—or any of the qualifying relative's dependent relatives—has medical concerns, asking about the type of ongoing or specialized treatment, the availability and quality of such treatment in the home country, the anticipated duration of the treatment, and whether the condition is chronic or acute is especially helpful. Examine whether the stress of relocation or separation will have a deleterious impact on the qualifying relative's health.

Financial Hardship

Ask both the qualifying relative and the applicant about future employability in the applicant's home country and the current conditions. Asking whether they have any work history in the applicant's home country is also important, as that factors into whether they could easily find employment there. Also investigate whether the qualifying relative will lose his home, business, or professional practice if the applicant's waiver is not granted and the qualifying relative is left to support himself in the United States. Further, consider what additional expenses the qualifying relative might incur if he remains in the United States without the applicant. For example, would he have to hire a childcare provider or home healthcare worker in the applicant's absence? Also, would he have to send part of his income to the applicant? Would he lose his health insurance and be forced to pay significant medical bills out of pocket? Finally, discuss the family's current financial situation, including salaries, household and personal expenses, and debt to understand how, specifically, the family will suffer financially if the applicant is not able to return to the United States.

Children

In all cases, but especially when the spouse is the qualifying relative, a thorough discussion about the applicant's children is critical. There is a strong argument that any suffering of one's child directly and significantly impacts the parent. Therefore, discuss the children's education, extracurricular activities, health, and special education needs, if any. Focus particularly on the impact that a separation from one or more parent would have on the child. Also discuss how the child would suffer if taken to live in the applicant's home country.

Although some of these topics and questions are uncomfortable and may feel invasive, they are all

---

[74] *See* C. Wheeler, "Update from the U.S. Consulate in Ciudad Juarez," *available at www.ilw.com/articles/2005,1215-wheeler.shtm.*

crucial to a thorough analysis of a qualifying relative's extreme hardship.

Step Three: Documenting Hardship to the Qualifying Relative

The waiver application must be very well-documented to have a good chance of success. *All* claims of hardship must be supported by documentary evidence. Thus, the waiver package will likely include the waiver application on Form I-601, a brief, exhibits, and a list of the supporting exhibits.

Each USCIS office around the globe (as well as in the United States in adjustment of status cases) adjudicates waivers of unlawful presence differently, some requiring significantly more evidence of extreme hardship than others. It is critically important to research waiver approval rates and the level of hardship required in the country in which the waiver will be adjudicated before deciding whether to send your client back to that country. Talk to other practitioners who have filed waivers in that same country. Different countries may have different preferences regarding how a waiver is documented. For example, Mr. Janssen has specified particular requirements for waiver application packages filed in Ciudad Juarez, indicating that his office prefers, among other things, a cover letter in bulleted format.[75]

The rest of this section will focus on the documents that may be included as supporting exhibits. The most important piece of evidence that will be submitted is most likely the affidavit of the qualifying relative. This affidavit should include a very specific discussion as to how the qualifying relative will suffer if the applicant's waiver is denied. It is important to be as detailed and specific as possible. Narrative-style affidavits can be especially persuasive. One or more in-depth interviews should uncover the information for a well-written affidavit.

Other very helpful pieces of evidence are affidavits from family members and friends of the qualifying relative. These affidavits serve two important purposes. The first is to show the family and community ties that the qualifying relative has in the United States. The second is to document the qualifying relative's suffering if the applicant's waiver is denied.

It is also beneficial to include an affidavit of the applicant. This affidavit offers the applicant an opportunity to tell his or her story. For example, the applicant for the unlawful presence waiver can explain why he or she came to the United States and what life was like in the home country. The applicant also should mention significant ways in which his or her qualifying relative will suffer. Additionally, the applicant should apologize for entering the country unlawfully or for overstaying his or her period of lawful presence. For an applicant who has committed a crime (any crime, whether or not a separate waiver is needed), it is also helpful to explain what happened (if mitigating factors exist) and what lessons the applicant learned.

If the applicant has committed a crime, even if it is not a ground of inadmissibility itself, special consideration should be given to uncovering documents to show rehabilitation. Proof that the applicant has participated in community organizations, church, volunteer groups, or a local school is helpful.

Also, it is helpful to include documents evidencing the qualifying relative's educational and professional ties in the United States. Include, for example, copies of high school and college diplomas, certificates of achievement, and employment letters.

If the qualifying relative has any medical condition, there are a number of different documents to gather: a letter from the treating doctor or professional, prescriptions, and medical records, if legible. Doctor's letters should describe the medical condition, the prognosis, the current treatment, the patient's physical limitations, the need for assistance, and the need for continued medical care. If the extreme hardship argument includes the fact that the qualifying relative has a sick relative who depends on his or her care or assistance, these medical documents should also be gathered for that relative. The key to this type of argument is that there must be a connection between the sick relative's medical condition and the qualifying relative. It may not be enough simply to point out that a relative of the qualifying relative is sick and needs care in the United States.

It is important to note that mental health conditions, like depression or anxiety issues, also may constitute very persuasive evidence. If the mental condition is undiagnosed, the qualifying relative may seek a psychological evaluation. Psychological evaluations should describe the mental health condition of the qualifying relative, and may go so far as to describe the relationship between the waiver process and the condition, the likely psychological effects of a waiver denial, and the need for future treatment.

---

[75] *Id.*

To document the financial hardship, copies of all bills and other evidence of the qualifying relative's expenses and debt are important. Suggest to clients expenses and debts they may not think of right away. The goal is to obtain a list of all of the qualifying relative's anticipated expenses, which can then be compared against the qualifying relative's income.

If the qualifying relative has dependent children, include school records, proof of extracurricular activities, and evidence of any special education or health care need. It is also important to include evidence showing the child has firmly established his or her life in the United States.

To show the hardship the qualifying relative would suffer in the applicant's home country, submit newspaper articles and government reports, such as the DOS *Country Report on Human Rights Practices* or newspaper articles. Also consider other ways to show country conditions, such as photographs of the applicant's home town or letters from family or friends who live there. Although the USCIS Ciudad Juarez office in particular has suggested that such evidence need not be submitted,[76] it may be very important in other countries.

WHAT TO DO ABOUT A WRONG DETERMINATION

Preventative Medicine

Sometimes a denial of an unlawful presence waiver occurs because the client was not eligible due to previous problems with immigration or criminal authorities. It is unfortunate when the consular officer knows more about the client's life than the attorney. The importance of sitting down with your client and going over the facts of the case, perhaps several times, cannot be overstressed. Simply put, you must get the story. It almost always takes more than one interview to extract the client's history.

Clients often fail to differentiate between legal technicalities such as voluntary departure, voluntary return, removal, arrest, conviction, and dismissal. Again, it is the attorney's responsibility to know about each and every time the client has interacted with the authorities, the result of the incident, and how it might affect the client's case. Additionally, it is important to prepare your client to discuss all of these incidents with the interviewing DOS officer. The responses a client makes during a consular in-

terview or interrogation can be very influential on the outcome of the case.

Typical Reasons for Denial

Misrepresentations, fraud, criminal activity, lack of evidence establishing extreme hardship to the qualifying relative(s), or finding an applicant is subject to a ground of inadmissibility for which a waiver is not available are all common reasons that result in the denial of an immigrant visa. In certain circumstances, a phone call or fax to the consular post issuing the adverse finding can give the attorney a clear understanding of the reason for the denial. If the consular post has the option, send a fax with specific questions or concerns directed toward the immigrant visa team. However, practitioners should be wary of the consular call center operators, who are often poorly trained and unable to relay the information their database shows. Always attempt to speak to an actual officer.

Unless there is a clear misunderstanding between the consular officer and the applicant, or a clear misapplication of the law which a practitioner could easily clarify, the only alternative available, when the ultimate result of the immigrant visa interview and waiver application process is a denial of the waiver, and thus the application for an immigrant visa, is to file an appeal on Form I-290B.[77]

Filing an Appeal or Motion to Reopen and Reconsider

The affected[78] party must file a notice of appeal of a waiver denial with the AAO on Form I-290B.[79] This process is extremely important, because it is an attorney's last opportunity to convince USCIS that the client's waiver application should have been granted.

The notice of appeal on Form I-290B must be filed at the field office where the decision was made within 30 days of the date of decision, or 33 days if the decision was mailed.[80] The Form I-290B should be filed along with a brief. However, additional time to file a brief may be requested.[81] When additional time has been allowed to submit a supporting brief, and it is not sent along with the notice of appeal, that

---

[76] *Id.*

[77] *See* 8 CFR §103.3(a)(2)(vi).

[78] *See* 8 CFR §103.3(a)(1)(iii)(B).

[79] *See* 8 CFR §103.3(a)(2)(i).

[80] *See* 8 CFR §§103.3(a)(2)(i), 103.5a(b).

[81] *See* 8 CFR §103.3(a)(2)(vii).

brief must be filed with the AAO, not the office that made the decision to deny the waiver application.[82] An appeal filed on Form I-290B also may be treated as a motion to reopen or reconsider.[83] As a result, it is an opportunity to supplement the record, when perhaps the original waiver application was not sufficiently supported by documents showing extreme hardship to a qualifying relative. In fact, it is the last chance to do so.

As with any other application for a visa or admission, the burden of proving eligibility remains entirely with the applicant.[84] A typical waiver denial will include a clear reminder of this fact, and often cite an abundance of cases discussing the ever elusive concept of "extreme hardship."

When preparing an appeal, the notice of decision (denial) must be carefully scrutinized. Many of the cases mentioned in the denial may be distinguished easily because of radical differences in the facts of the case cited and your client's situation. Read each cited case carefully. One case commonly used to determine whether "extreme hardship" exists is *Matter of Cervantes-Gonzalez*.[85] Even if the denial your client received does not cite *Cervantes*, it may be helpful to the attorney preparing the appeal to consider the factors discussed in *Cervantes* in explaining how the qualifying relatives will be and likely are suffering extreme hardship, and how the adjudicating officer erred in deciding that the client failed to demonstrate extreme hardship.

Because the adjudicating officer may treat the appeal as a motion to reopen or reconsider, that officer may decide to take a favorable action.[86] In the event the officer decides not to approve the application, the officer will forward the appeal and the record of proceeding to the AAO.[87] As of the writing of this article, processing time stated by USCIS for an I-290B is 18 months.[88]

If the AAO dismisses the appeal, all hope should not be lost. Clients can start over again by scheduling a new immigrant visa appointment. Depending on consulate-specific guidelines, scheduling a new appointment can be as simple as calling the consulate's call center and explaining to the operator that the case was previously denied. As long as the underlying petition remains valid, applicants have the opportunity to attend a subsequent immigrant visa interview and submit a second, third, or fourth waiver application. In some instances, it may be necessary to file a new visa petition, making the process quite lengthy.

SECTION 245(i)

How Does INA §245(i) Interact with Unlawful Presence, Bars, and Waivers?

Given the risk of proceeding abroad to apply for a visa when (hopefully) the attorney and client are aware a waiver will be necessary to return to the United States, the best option, nearly always, is to remain in the United States and adjust status.

INA §245(i) is a special adjustment of status provision that allows certain noncitizens who would otherwise be ineligible to adjust status and obtain lawful permanent residence from within the United States to do so.[89]

Those who qualify for adjustment under §245(i) need not leave the United States to process their immigrant visas abroad in U.S. consulates. As a result, §245(i) helps individuals who have been unlawfully present in the United States because they entered without inspection, overstayed the time allotted on their I-94 cards, or violated the status of their nonimmigrant visas. It is especially relevant here because it allows clients who have accrued at least 180 days of unlawful presence but who have not departed since accruing such unlawful presence to adjust their status and become lawful permanent residents without incurring a three– or ten-year bar.

If such individuals were to process their immigrant visas abroad, they would have to depart the United States and then seek admission within less than three or ten years of their departure, thereby incurring inadmissibility under INA §§212(a)(9)(B)(i)(I) or (II). They would have to apply for a waiver under INA §212(a)(B)(9)(v) for unlawful presence. If it is at all possible for a client to remain in the United States to adjust status and avoid consular processing, it is nearly always a good idea.

---

[82] *See* 8 CFR §103.3(a)(2)(viii).

[83] *See* 8 CFR §103.3(a)(2)(iii).

[84] *See* INA §291.

[85] 22 I&N Dec. 560 (BIA 1999).

[86] *See* 8 CFR§103.3(a)(2)(iii).

[87] *See id.*

[88] *www.uscis.gov* (search for "AAO processing times").

---

[89] Section 245(i)'s implementing regulations are located at 8 CFR §§245.10, 1245.10.

INA §245(i) is available to individuals who:

(1) are the beneficiaries of a family-based petition (under INA §204) or labor certification filed on or before April 30, 2001,[90]

(2) pay a $1,000 penalty,[91] and

(3) are otherwise admissible for permanent residence.[92]

Those who are beneficiaries of petitions filed after January 14, 1998 (but on or before April 30, 2001) must additionally show that they were physically present in the United States as of December 21, 2000.[93]

It is the third element above, admissibility for permanent residence, that tends to cause the most complications. Exactly when and how §245(i) "cures" inadmissibility due to unlawful entries and/or presence must be examined carefully in each case.

Section 245(i) is available to overstays and to those who have worked without authorization.

By its express terms, §245(i) is available to those classes of individuals named in INA §245(c) who are ineligible to adjust status under INA §245(a), including those who have overstayed their visas or who have worked without authorization prior to applying for adjustment.[94]

Section 245(i) is available those who have entered without inspection.

Section 245(i) states that it is available to individuals who entered the United States without inspection.[95] Thus, §245(i) trumps inadmissibility arising from an uninspected entry.[96] This is incredibly important for those who entered without inspection and have remained more than 180 days or a year,

because they can adjust their status without having to leave the United States and incur a three– or ten-year bar from re-entry, requiring a waiver.

However, attorneys must be very careful in finding out exactly how many uninspected entries a client has attempted or accomplished, and in calculating how much unlawful presence that client accrued after an entry, when the client departed the United States, and when he or she returned or attempted to return. Section 245(i) will allow an individual to adjust status despite an entry without inspection, but, in most jurisdictions, it will not waive bars accrued due to unlawful presence under INA §§212(a)(9)(B)(i)(I) or (II).[97]

As discussed in the section on unlawful presence above, individuals who have been unlawfully present in the United States for an aggregate period of one year or more and who subsequently depart and reenter EWI are inadmissible under INA §212(a)(9)(C)(i)(I). Such individuals are only eligible to apply for a waiver of inadmissibility after they have departed the United States and remained outside for at least 10 years.[98]

The BIA's current position is that an individual who is inadmissible under this section is ineligible to adjust status under §245(i).[99] The BIA further holds that such an individual cannot "cure" his or her inadmissibility under §212(a)(9)(C)(i)(I) by seeking a waiver under §212(a)(9)(C)(ii), because such an application can only be made 10 years after the applicant's last departure from the United States.[100]

The Fifth Circuit has deferred to the BIA's interpretation of this issue.[101]

---

[90] INA §245(i)(1)(B).

[91] INA §245(i)(1)(C).

[92] INA §245(i)(2)(a). *See also* 8 CFR §§245.1(b)(3), 1245.1(b)(3).

[93] INA §245(i)(1)(C). *See also* INS Memorandum, J. Cronin, HQ 70/23.1-P (Jan. 26, 2001), *reprinted in* 78 *Interpreter Releases* 325, 346–52 (Feb. 5, 2001). December 21, 2000, is the date of enactment of the Legal Immigration and Family Equity Act (LIFE Act), Pub. L. No. 106-553, §1(a)(2) (appx. B, H.R. 5548, §§1101–04), 114 Stat. 2762, 2762A-142 to 2762A-149 (2000), which extended the sunset of §245(i).

[94] INA §245(i)(1)(A)(ii).

[95] INA §245(i)(1)(A)(i).

[96] *See* INS Memorandum, D. Martin, "Request for Legal Opinion: The Impact of the 1996 Act on Section 245(i) of the Act" (Feb. 19, 1997), *published on* AILA InfoNet at Doc. No. 97021991 (*posted* Feb. 19, 1997).

---

[97] *See Matter of Briones*, 24 I&N Dec. 355 (BIA 2007), and the discussion *supra*.

[98] INA §212(a)(9)(C)(ii). For more details, see section on unlawful presence *supra*.

[99] *Matter of Briones*, 24 I&N Dec. 355 (BIA 2007).

[100] *Id.* at 358–59.

[101] *Mortera-Cruz v. Gonzales*, 409 F.3d 246, 255 n.9 (5th Cir. 2005) ("In the instant case, the basis for Mortera's inadmissibility is [INA §212(a)(9)(C)(i)(I)], which involves an illegal reentry after accumulating more than one year of illegal presence, whereas [the appellant in *Berrum-Garcia v. Comfort*, 390 F.3d 1158, 1166–68 (10th Cir. 2004)] was inadmissible under [INA §212(a)(9)(C)(i)(II)]. For the purposes of our analysis, this is a distinction without a difference because both provisions are subject to the same default penalty of lifetime inadmissibility.").

In some jurisdictions, §245(i) may overcome the bar under§212(a)(9)(C)(i)(I), which attaches when a person accrues over one year of unlawful presence, departs the United States, and then re-enters or attempts to re-enter without inspection.

The Ninth and Tenth Circuits have differed with the BIA about the effect of §245(i) on the "permanent" 10-year bar under §212(a)(9)(C)(i)(I).[102] The Tenth Circuit in *Padilla-Caldera v. Gonzales* found that despite section 245(i)'s requirement that individuals must be admissible to permanent residence, §245(i) nevertheless should be interpreted to overcome inadmissibility under §212(a)(9)(C)(i)(I) arising from an EWI re-entry after accruing more than one year of unlawful presence.[103]

In *Acosta v. Gonzales*,[104] the Ninth Circuit cited *Padilla-Caldera* and largely followed its reasoning. However, it must be noted that the court in *Acosta* explicitly found itself to be bound by *Perez-Gonzalez v. Ashcroft*. As discussed above in the section on new guidance, there is significant doubt about *Acosta*'s continued viability after the Ninth Circuit's recent decision in *Duran-Gonzales v. DHS*[105] overruling *Perez-Gonzalez*. Specifically, in *Duran-Gonzales*, the Ninth Circuit found that pursuant to the U.S. Supreme Court's decision in *National Cable and Telecommunications Association v. Brand X Internet Services*,[106] the Ninth Circuit was required to give effect to the BIA's contrary interpretation of an ambiguity in the INA, allowing the BIA interpretation to trump the Ninth Circuit's interpretation. Thus, the Ninth Circuit in *Duran-Gonzales* applied BIA precedent and found the applicant ineligible for §245(i).

Following this reasoning, it seems likely that the Ninth Circuit will also find that *Brand X* requires deference to the BIA's position that §245(i) is unavailable to individuals who have entered without inspection after having accrued one year or more of unlawful presence. Whether other courts will apply *Brand X* in the area of immigration law in the same manner as the Ninth Circuit remains to be seen.

Section 245(i) will not overcome the permanent bar that arises under §212(a)(9)(C)(i)(II) when an individual who has previously been ordered deported or removed departs the country and then enters or attempts to enter without inspection.

One who enters or attempts to re-enter illegally after having been ordered deported or removed is ineligible for §245(i) adjustment, as discussed previously. According to the BIA and the several circuit courts that have addressed the issue, §245(i) does not cure the permanent bar to admissibility that attaches pursuant to §212(a)(9)(C)(i)(II).[107]

Despite the somewhat unhappy news about the limits of protection that §245(i) may provide, helping your clients avoid the consequences of the three– or ten-year bars due to unlawful presence by adjusting under §245(i) is an incredibly powerful tool. Whether an employer submitted an application for labor certification for your client, a family member submitted a petition, or your client was a derivative of a parent or spouse, your client may be eligible to adjust under INA §245(i) and avoid having to apply for a waiver at a U.S. consulate.

Again, talk to your clients in detail about their personal history, their parents, siblings, aunts, uncles, and children. If the client is eligible to obtain a green card but for an issue that §245(i) may cure, you must carefully consider all possibilities about whether that client could have been a beneficiary or derivative beneficiary of a visa petition, or application for labor certification that was "approvable when filed" on or before April 30, 2001.[108] If so, that client may be able to adjust status in the United States.

---

[102] *Padilla-Caldera v. Gonzales*, 453 F.3d 1237 (10th Cir. 2005); *Acosta v. Gonzales*, 439 F.3d 550 (9th Cir. 2006).

[103] *Padilla-Caldera, supra* note 102, at 1241–44.

[104] 439 F.3d 550 (9th Cir. 2006).

[105] 508 F.3d 1227 (9th Cir 2007).

[106] 545 U.S. 967 (2005).

[107] *Matter of Torres-Garcia*, 23 I&N Dec. 866, 867, 877 (BIA 2006). *See also Lattab v. Ashcroft*, 384 F.3d 8, 21 (1st Cir. 2004); *Tenesaca Delgado v. Mukasey*, No. 06-5035, 2008 WL 323234 (2d Cir. Feb. 7, 2008); *Berrum-Garcia*, 390 F.3d 1158, 1163 (10th Cir. 2004) (finding it irrelevant whether the applicant's application for adjustment was filed before or after the reinstatement decision was made); *Warner v. Ashcroft*, 381 F.3d 534, 540 (6th Cir. 2004); *Lino v. Gonzales*, 467 F.3d 1077, 1079 (7th Cir. 2006); *Flores v. Ashcroft*, 354 F.3d 727, 731 (8th Cir. 2003); *Gonzales v. DHS*, 508 F.3d 1227 (9th Cir. 2007), *overruling Perez-Gonzalez v. Ashcroft*, 379 F.3d 783, 793–95 (9th Cir. 2004); *De Sandoval v. Att'y Gen.*, 440 F.3d 1276, 1284–85 (11th Cir. 2006).

[108] *See* 8 CFR §245.10.

Retained Western Hemisphere Priority Dates

From time to time the question has come up whether or not a Western Hemisphere Priority Date (WHPD) can be the basis for INA §245(i) eligibility. Although many assume that such an old priority date must confer §245(i) eligibility, a closer examination reveals that it only sometimes does. This is due to the manner in which these priority dates were established. Therefore, an explanation of the WHPD is in order. Additionally, since there are still many cases in which a WHPD is available, it is worthwhile to briefly review the WHPD system. In other places, more detailed explanations have been offered.[109]

Before January 1, 1977

Prior to 1977, the system for immigrating to the United States for persons born in independent countries of the Western Hemisphere was different from the system for the rest of the world. For Western Hemisphere natives, there were two immigrant classifications: immediate relatives and special immigrants. The latter were specifically exempted from the labor certification requirements of then INA §212(a)(14).[110] Persons from the rest of the world

had the immediate relative classification and a preference system similar to what we have today.

The only petitions filed in Western Hemisphere processing were immediate relative I-130s, which were filed with legacy INS. On approval, these petitions were forwarded to appropriate American consulates for visa processing. As today, these cases were not subject to any quota system and were processed without delay.

Within the special immigrant category there were several subdivisions encompassing family– and employment-based groups. For all these groups, a priority date was obtained from the appropriate consulate and all special immigrants were processed uniformly in chronological order according to the priority date.

Priority dates for special immigrants were obtained in one of three ways. In labor certification cases, the Department of Labor forwarded the approved labor certification to the consulate for priority date issuance. In other employment-based cases, evidence of eligibility was sent by the prospective immigrant directly to the consulate to obtain the priority date. These cases included situations in which the individual could establish that he or she would not be a public charge based on independent means of financial support without having to work and certain cases in which a person was a member of the professions, a qualified investor, or on the equivalent of Schedule A.

Lawful permanent residents seeking to immigrate their parents (yes, parents), spouses, or children (no adult sons or daughters) would file an I-550 application (not petition) with legacy INS. This was a carbonized form that requested legacy INS to send verification to a designated consulate of the lawful permanent residence status of the applicant. The carbon copy was kept in the applicant's INS file and can be obtained today by Freedom of Information Act procedures. On receipt of the verification, the consulate would issue a priority date.

Parents of a U.S. citizen child under age 21 could immigrate together with their minor children by filing an FS-497 form with the consulate. These are the famous "baby cases."

Why Everything at the Consulate?

There was no adjustment of status for natives of the Western Hemisphere (other than Cubans under

---

[109] One of your co-authors, Robert Ahlgren, has done work in the past on this topic, and the father/daughter team of Bob and Kathrin Mautino have also provided extensive coverage. *See* R. Ahlgren, "Western Hemisphere Immigration and the *Silva* Case," 8 *AILA Immigration Journal*, (July–Sept. 1985); R. Ahlgren, "Pre-1977 Western Hemisphere Priority Dates: The Never-Ending Story," 1 *Immigration & Nationality Law Handbook* 352 (AILA 2002–03 Ed.); R. Mautino, "Save the Western Hemisphere Priority Date Program," 71 *Interpreter Releases* 513 (Apr. 18, 1994); "Western Hemisphere Derivative Priority Dates: Don't Forget to Use Them," 2 *Immigration & Nationality Law Handbook* 141 (AILA 1992–93 Ed.); K. Mautino, "Pulling the Rabbit Out of the Hat: Using Western Hemisphere Priority Dates to Move Business and Family Based Immigration," *Immigration & Nationality Law Handbook* 409 (AILA 2006–07 Ed.). *See also* C. Gordon, S. Mailman, & S. Yale-Loehr, *Immigration Law and Procedure* §3:35.01(4).

[110] INA §101(a)(27) (pre-1977) ("The term *special immigrant* means (A) an immigrant who was born in any independent foreign country of the Western Hemisphere or in the Canal zone and the spouse and children of any such immigrant, if accompanying, or following to join him: Provided that no immigrant visa shall be issued pursuant to this clause until the consular officer is in receipt of a determination made by the Secretary of Labor pursuant to the provision of §212(a)(14).").

On the other hand, pre-1977 INA §212(a)(14) contained the following all important exemptions: "The exclusion of aliens under this paragraph shall apply to special immigrants defined in §101(a)(27)(A) (other than parents, spouses, chil-
continued

dren of United States citizens or of aliens lawfully admitted to the United States for permanent residence.").

the Cuban Adjustment Act of 1966[111]). Consequently, all cases that were accorded a priority date were placed on registration lists of the American consulates. Normally, cases were assigned to the American consulate that had jurisdiction over the place of the alien's last foreign residence. However, "stateside criteria processing" was available for many years for people in some of these categories who were living in the United States. This meant that visa processing was available at American consulates in Canada for nationals of third countries processing under the Western Hemisphere system.[112]

Principals and Derivatives

Significantly, once a priority date was established for the principal applicant, normal derivative eligibility applied: the priority date was also available to a spouse and any minor, unmarried children.[113] The derivative relationship had to exist only by the time of visa immigrant application, not necessarily before.[114] Thus, siblings of minor U.S. citizen children were said to have obtained permanent residency through the sibling relationship, and spouses and children acquired after the issuance of the priority date, but before the issuance of the visa, immigrated on the earlier priority date. Derivative eligibility was the explanation for these realities and explains the confusion that exists even today among Western Hemisphere immigrants who believe that lawful permanent residents can file immigrant petitions for their siblings or their parents. The priority was also cross-chargeable between hemispheres and between countries.

After-Acquired Spouse and Children

In addition to according priority dates to normal derivative visa applicants, a special procedure was established for the after-acquired spouse of a perma-

nent resident. If a marriage between a lawful permanent resident and a native of the Western Hemisphere occurred in the home country, the American consulate would recognize the date of the marriage as the priority date in a subsequent application for a spouse or child, not, as usual, the date of the filing of the I-550. This was possible because the I-550 was an application for recognition of a relationship, not a petition to accord preference or immediate relative classifications. The FAM provided that in such a case the date of the marriage would be recognized as the priority date if it took place prior to any admission.[115]

Immediate Relatives

Then (as now) immediate relatives were outside the regular system for family immigration. As mentioned above, the I-130 petition was used in Western Hemisphere immigration only for immediate relatives. The filing date was recognized as the priority date. Significantly, this date eventually was assigned to dependants of immediate relatives for whom separate petitions were never filed. This departure from the norm was the result of litigation.[116]

Continuing Validity of Priority Dates

Once a person had immigrated to the United States, the spouse and children were eligible for the original priority date, provided that those relationships existed at the time of the original issuance of the priority date. Therefore, it was possible for a lawful permanent resident to be in the United States many years and still petition for the spouse and minor children using the original priority date.[117]

Additionally, any child born to a principal applicant after the priority date for that applicant had been established was entitled to the priority date as long as the marriage predated the priority date. Thus people immi-

---

[111] Pub. L. No. 89-732, 80 Stat. 1161.

[112] Stateside criteria processing continued after January 1, 1977 for Western Hemisphere natives (and derivatives from wherever) who were not eligible to adjust status. It ended on December 31, 1987, except for cases in the pipeline. Some of us were still doing stateside criteria processing as late as 1989. Compare the policy behind the generous stateside criteria processing with the motive behind the 10-year bars! Have the 10-year bars achieved a more human and reasonable result than the more enlightened stateside criteria processing system, particularly in view of the fact that family members denied for the 10-year bar are becoming an ever-larger group of people living within the United States as well as abroad who see themselves as unjustly disenfranchised?

[113] *See* INA §203(a)(8); 8 CFR §204.1(a).

[114] *See* 9 FAM 4.2.32, N2 (1971).

[115] 9 FAM 42.62 N23 (1971).

[116] *Barajas v. Shultz,* No. 87-0870 (S.D. Cal., June 15, 1987). *See* 65 *Interpreter Releases* 617 (June 13, 1988).

[117] The term of art for this is "following to join." To initiate the case, of course, it was necessary to file an I-550 to establish that the derivative beneficiaries were indeed following to join a lawful permanent resident. After-acquired children could immigrate on the original priority date as derivatives of an accompanying parent. 9 FAM 40.1 N7.2-2 (1971).

Also, since a copy of the I-550 is retained in the file of the petitioner, an I-864 can be filed and directed to the American consulate (or a copy of the I-550), and the consul will recognize the filing date of the I-550 as the priority date of the beneficiary named in the I-550.

grated with priority dates established before their birth. For this reason, American consulates in the Western Hemisphere became accustomed to maintaining indices of families so that they could quickly recognize earlier priority dates when appropriate.

The Waiting List

As noted, by whatever route a native of an independent country of the Western Hemisphere established a priority date, except as an immediate relative, that person became equal to all others in the Western Hemisphere with the same priority date. In other words, an applicant had to wait on the waiting list until the priority date was reached. No category moved ahead of another, and all independent countries in the Western Hemisphere were covered by the same pool of visas. In the early years of this system, 1968 to 1973, the waiting period was relatively short, sometimes only a few months. However, by 1974, the waiting period was over a year, and by early 1976 it had become three years. Being "special (Western Hemisphere) immigrants" seemed less special all the time.

The 1976 Act and Its Aftermath

Despite the various problems that developed under the old system, there was at least some certainty that an applicant eventually would be called for a final visa appointment. The 1976 amendments to the INA[118] changed that certainty. The new law provided that after January 1, 1977, Western Hemisphere special immigrant applicants with priority dates would be reclassified as nonpreference applicants, and they would have to file under the preference system that was already in effect for the Eastern Hemisphere. This meant that regardless of what might eventually happen to nonpreference waiting lists, Western Hemisphere natives who were eligible to apply for a visa as the parents of lawful permanent residents or minor citizen children had to register their cases before the new amendments took effect on January 1, 1977, because the preference system has no category for these cases.

In any event, it was desirable to escape nonpreference, because the waiting period was long and getting longer. Nonpreference actually became permanently unavailable in 1981.

The Savings Clause

The 1976 amendments, however, did include an extremely important savings clause in section 9. That clause allowed any Western Hemisphere priority date obtained prior to January 1, 1977, to remain available to the applicant and his or her derivative family for use in any preference status for which the principal or the family could become eligible.[119] This savings clause was the humane response to the thousands of visa applicants who had been waiting with full expectation of eventual immigration. It remains part of the immigration law, although it is not codified. It is usually found in the appendix to printed versions of the INA. From time to time, attempts have been made to abolish it, but it has survived to keep on giving.

Discovering a WHPD

In looking for a WHPD, careful review of the situation of any client whose family may have such a date is necessary. Begin looking for a pre-1977 priority date if your client or anyone in his or her family is a Western Hemisphere native (or has a parent or spouse who was), and either the person obtained lawful permanent resident status before 1977 or someone petitioned for him or her (or for a parent or spouse) before 1977. You can also ask if anyone in the family ever had a "Silva letter."

For example, when presented with a Mexican second-preference spousal case, there will be immediate visa availability if the beneficiary has a pre-1977 priority date. It is possible that such a beneficiary would still have the right to an early priority date derivatively obtained as a sibling in a "baby case." Likewise, do not fail to inquire if a pre-1977 priority date was obtained for the family by a lawful permanent resident sibling filing for the parents. In both situations, the priority date would be available to this beneficiary if he or she was under the age of 21

---

[118] Immigration and Nationality Act Amendments of 1976, Pub. L. No. 94-571, 90 Stat. 2703.

[119] Section 9(b) provides that "an alien chargeable to the numerical limitation contained in section 21(e) of the Act of October 3, 1965 (79 Stat. 921), who established a priority date at a consular office on the basis of entitlement to immigrant status under statutory or regulatory provisions in existence on the day before the effective date of this Act shall be deemed to be entitled to immigrant status under section 203(a)(8) of the Immigration and Nationality Act and shall be accorded the priority date previously established by him. Any petition filed by, or in behalf of, such an alien to accord him a preference status under section 203(a) shall, upon approval, be deemed to have been filed as of the priority date previously established by such alien . . . ."

at the time the parents obtained the priority date or, as we have seen, not even born yet.

These cases are showing up somewhat more frequently now when many middle– and upper-middle-class Mexicans who had established a priority date before January 1, 1977, but decided to return to or stay in Mexico, now are interested in leaving because of security issues such as kidnapping for ransom.

How to Prove a WHPD

Evidence of the pre-1977 priority date is no longer available from the consulates. The applicant, however, may have original documents from the consulate showing the priority date. If an I-550 application was part of the case, a copy will be in the applicant's INS file, as mentioned above. This shows the priority date, because the consulates gave the date of filing the I-550 as the priority date.

Also, many people have in their INS files a document called a "Silva letter." This letter was an early form of temporary protected status and was only issued to persons who submitted proof of a WHPD. This proof and a copy of the Silva letter will be in the INS files of anyone who received a Silva letter. People readily remember if they received a Silva letter.[120]

However, if an applicant has original documents showing the priority date, the National Visa Center (NVC) has a Problem Resolution Unit that has become aware of the savings clause and will issue new priority dates upon being given evidence of the early priority date. The NVC has also understood the after-acquired child cases referred to above and has recognized priority dates that actually were earlier than the birth of the applicant. In adjustment of status cases it is usually necessary to provide all the information about retained WHPD in a package, including the statute, regulations, FAM cites, and so forth. Frequently, in USCIS offices, there are few if any officers who are familiar with retained WHPDs.

It should be noted that once a priority date has been used, it cannot be used again for the same person to obtain permanent residency a second time. However, the fact that a principal beneficiary has immigrated on the priority date does not preclude a derivative beneficiary from using that same priority date even many years later. Most current WHPD cases involve derivatives.

A Retained WHPD and §245(i)

Although a WHPD can obviously be a great help in immigrating someone, it only confers eligibility for the benefits of INA §245(i) if it was established by the filing of an I-130 or the filing of a labor certification, either with a state department of labor in the case of regular labor certification cases, or directly with the consulate in the Schedule A situations. This is because §245(i) itself clearly specifies that only labor certifications filed pursuant to regulations of the secretary of labor and petitions filed for classification under INA §204 can establish the requisite §245(i) priority date.[121]

CONCLUSION

Given the increasingly unforgiving decisions of the BIA towards immigrants subject to the INA §212(a)(9) bars and the increasingly limited discretion the courts have to review those decisions, the role of immigration attorneys in assisting their clients in avoiding or seeking waivers of these bars to inadmissibility has become more critical than ever. Clients should be counseled to avoid unlawful presence at every juncture, and their complete immigration histories need to be carefully scrutinized to detect possible periods of unlawful presence and analyze their consequences. Clients who are potentially subject to §212(a)(9) bars need to understand exactly what their risk is, and what their options are, before leaving the United States to seek immigrant visas abroad.

---

[120] The Silva letter was part of a remedy in a successful class action case, *Silva v. Bell*, 605 F.2d 978 (7th Cir. 1979), which is revisited in some of the articles in note 109, *supra*.

[121] INA §245(i)(1)(B)(i).

EFFECTIVE ADVISING ON STUDENT ISSUES – SEVIS, WORK, TRAVEL, AND THE CAP GAP

by Elizabeth Goss and Connie L. Burk[*]

BACKGROUND AND KEY QUESTIONS

What Is the Student and Exchange Visitor Information System (SEVIS)?

The Department of Homeland Security (DHS) created this internet-based system in order to maintain current information on nonimmigrant students (F and M visas) and J Exchange Visitors (EVs) and their dependents. SEVIS tracks F, M, and J visa holders from the time they receive their visa program documents (Form I-20 or Form DS-2019) until they complete their programs including Practical and Academic training periods post-completion of degree. Under SEVIS, universities are required to provide regular electronic reports to DHS on each student or EV. SEVIS houses the information provided by these institutions and U.S. Citizenship and Immigration Services (USCIS), U.S. embassies, consulates, and ports of entry all have certain access to information through this system.

Is SEVIS New?

The requirement that schools provide the federal government with information about each student's or research scholar's status is not new. Most of the information that is reported to SEVIS has been required by the DHS for many years. But the prior paper-based system precluded widespread coordination among schools and governmental agencies. In 1996, Congress passed legislation directing the DHS (then the Immigration and Naturalization Service (INS)) to move to a new electronic data collection system, which came to be known as SEVIS. Technical challenges and lack of funding delayed the program for several years. However, in October 2001, Congress passed the Uniting and Strengthening America by Providing Appropriate Tools Required to Intercept and Obstruct Terrorism (USA PATRIOT) Act of 2001,[1] which authorized additional SEVIS funding and required nationwide compliance by January 30, 2003.

SEVIS is a networked management system and has introduced comprehensive technological elements and challenges to foreign student and scholar administration and advising. The institution or organization is responsible for transmitting electronic information for any reportable events during the participant's stay in the United States while in F, M, or J status. Ultimately, SEVIS is intended to entirely replace the old manual, paper-driven procedures.

Historical Background

The 1993 World Trade Center bombing served as the initial catalyst for today's SEVIS. Shortly after the first attack on the World Trade Center, government officials concluded that some of the suspected bombers had entered the United States on student visas. In 1996, as a result of these findings, Congress passed the Illegal Immigration Reform and Immigrant Responsibility Act of 1996 (IIRAIRA),[2] mandating tighter controls for foreign student and scholar programs in the form of an Internet-based tracking system called the Coordinated Interagency Partnership Regulating International Students (CIPRIS). Although IIRAIRA mandated that all

[*] **Elizabeth Goss,** a partner in Tocci, Goss & Lee, PC, in Boston, specializes in the representation of physicians, researchers, trainees, and students in the higher education, healthcare and the biopharma/biotech fields securing their temporary and permanent visas. In addition, she has extensive experience representing multinational corporations and entrepreneurial ventures in a wide array of immigration matters. Ms. Goss previously served as Tufts University's Foreign Student & Scholar Advisor/Director of the International Affairs Office for the Health Sciences campus and affiliated hospitals.

Connie L. Burk is the director of international affairs at the University of Tennessee Health Science Center in Memphis. She came to Memphis as an F-1 student from Denmark and obtained bachelor's and master's degrees in English from the University of Memphis. She has worked with international students since 1993 and also with international scholars and staff since 1997, when she accepted her present position. She has been involved with workshop curriculum development for NAFSA: Association of International Educators, where she currently serves on the Policy and Practice Committee.

The authors thank **Lynda Hagerty**, an associate at Tocci, Goss & Lee, PC, in Boston, for her assistance with this article.

[1] Pub. L. No. 107-56, 115 Stat. 272.

[2] Pub. L. No. 104-208, div. C, 110 Stat. 3009, 3009-546 to 3009-724.

programs be on board with this system within a reasonable time frame, enthusiasm for the project eventually waned. Inadequate funding, programming complications, and fierce opposition to CIPRIS by various entities combined to stall nationwide implementation. Despite the lack of enthusiasm for the program, in 1999, CIPRIS was still being tested in 20 schools in the southern United States. At this time, legacy INS officials began referring to the program by a new acronym, SEVIS.[3]

The tragedy of September 11 and the perception that several of the hijackers held student visas renewed incentives for implementation of the SEVIS system. The USA PATRIOT Act amended §641 of IIRAIRA to require full implementation of SEVIS by January 1, 2003. The Enhanced Border Security and Visa Entry Reform Act of 2002, Pub. L. No. 107-173, 116 Stat. 543, added and clarified requirements for collection of information. Section 641 of IIRAIRA required Immigration and Customs Enforcement (ICE) to collect current information on an ongoing basis from schools and exchange programs related to visitors during the course of their stay. It also mandated that institutions report any failure of participants to enroll within 30 days of the registration deadline. The initial January 30, 2003, deadline was extended to February 15, 2003, to accommodate government implementation issues. From February 15, 2003, forward, all institutions issuing sponsoring visas for F and J status immigrants were required to use the SEVIS system. As of August 1, 2003, all institutions were required to have completed the enrollment of all of their active students and EVs in SEVIS. Since that time, the challenging questions and implementation issues continue to arise on a regular basis. Of particular importance is the increased institutional responsibility in reporting student activities, both during and after attendance in a particular program.

WHAT YOU NEED TO KNOW ABOUT SEVIS AND SEVP TODAY

SEVIS and SEVP Administration

ICE is the DHS agency that administers the Student and Exchange Visitor (SEVP) program. SEVIS

(Student and Exchange Visitor Information System) is the document issuance system and database developed for schools and exchange visitor programs to issue Forms I-20 and DS-2019, respectively.

Notably, only schools and exchange programs approved by SEVP to use SEVIS may issue I-20s or DS-2019s. SEVP maintains a list of approved schools as well as statistics on the number of students and exchange visitors on its website, www.ice.gov/sevis.

Data entered in SEVIS by users or Designated School Officials (DSOs) and Responsible Officers (ROs) can be seen by various government agencies as the student or exchange visitor moves through the process of applying for a visa and admission to the U.S. However, it is not entirely clear at this time exactly what information can be viewed by which agency. As SEVIS has aged, more information has become available to more agencies, so past problems with comments and fields in the SEVIS record not being visible to the consulate, for example, seem to have been resolved. However, many issues still remain with interagency communications and ability to share important information.

Systematic SEVIS Problems: Lookout Flags

Currently, one of the most problematic areas is the systematic "flagging" of individual student records. A "flag" on a SEVIS record occurs as the result of a termination of a past SEVIS record regardless of the reason for the termination. Some records may be terminated simply due to improper updates or technical problems with the SEVIS system itself. SEVIS terminations generate a lookout or a flag placed in the SEVIS record through ICE's Compliance Enforcement Unit's TEC database system. This system feeds information to both the Department of State (DOS) and the Customs and Border Protection (CPB) systems. Although both agencies have been instructed that the presence of such a flag is not grounds for denial, flags must be resolved before a visa can be issued by DOS or entry can be granted by CPB. These unresolved flags can cause students delays when applying for a visa or admission to the United States. A consular officer, CPB officer, DSO or RO may request removal of this flag from the SEVIS Help Desk. Flag removal takes one week, and there is no way to expedite this process. If the student needs to travel during this one-week period and must apply for a visa, it is possible for consular officers to place a note in the record for the port of entry that flag removal has been requested.[4]

Another flag removal option is to use DHS TRIP, from which the issue will be referred to ICE/SEVP.[5] The advantage of using DHS TRIP is that students may use this system themselves to seek resolution without going through the school (this may be useful if the student has already graduated, the school is closed for the holidays, etc.).

SEVIS Conflict of Benefits vs. Reporting Requirements

The April 2008 29-month Optional Practical Training (OPT) Rule is a prime example of the conflict that is inherent in the SEVIS system today. This new rule will be discussed in more detail herein. The creation of this OPT Rule highlights an area where an additional benefit to certain students is coupled with substantial additional reporting and administrative burdens for schools during a period after an F-1 student has completed his/her studies. This conundrum is typical of the tension between the usefulness of the system and the perceived "policing" actions required. It is important to review the types of work authorization available to F-1 students and how the benefits are granted under the SEVIS system to provide a comprehensive understanding of the additional benefits and burdens schools, students and potential employers now face.

WHEN CAN AN F-1 WORK?

Background

The primary purpose of an individual present in F-1 student status in the United States is to study. As a benefit of F-1 status, students have several good options for work experience during and after studies. Although not directly involved in the process, attorneys should be aware of the options available for students, particularly in light of the current H-1B quota issues facing would-be temporary workers each year.

Practice Note: Updated Social Security Administration (SSA) policies on the issuance of Social Security Numbers (SSN). Pursuant to the SSA's Program Operations Manual System (POMS), effective November 1, 2007, SSA will no longer process applications for SSNs more than 30 days

in advance of the scheduled employment start date for students in possession of DSO-authorized employment categories where no employment authorization document (EAD) is required. SSA will only process application for SSNs for EAD-authorized categories of employment on or after the effective date of the EAD. POMS RM 00203.407 Section K.8.

On-Campus Work Options

On-Campus Work Authorization

Once an F-1 student arrives and registers at a college or university, he or she may engage in on-campus employment based solely on maintenance of status and which does not displace a U.S. worker.[6] Work is authorized part-time (20 hours a week inclusive of any scholarship, fellowship or assistantship) during school and full-time employment on campus during summer and semester breaks. USCIS has also confirmed that a student who enters the country within the 30 days prior to the I-20 report date is also eligible for on-campus work. Further, graduate students who are transferring from one program to another are allowed to work on-campus during the transition period; however, the student is limited to working for the institution that "holds" the SEVIS record.[7] If a student wishes to work at the transfer-in school, that school must have completed the transfer event prior to the student working on campus. Authorization to work is "incident" to status; thus no formal authorization is necessary for this type of employment. However, as a matter of practice, many schools may provide a letter to the student to confirm on-campus work eligibility. In addition, in order to obtain an SSN, a student will likely need a letter to provide to the SSA.

Who Qualifies as an On-Campus Employer?

An on-campus employer includes school-sponsored positions, such as work study programs, graduate research, or assistantships. Certain private companies on school campuses may also hire F-1 students if the nature of services they provide are directly beneficial to students; some classic examples of such employers are food service companies and campus book stores.[8] Certain off-site employers are also eligible to hire F-1 students. An on-campus,

---

[4] SEVIS Conference Call. NAFSA Questions. September 26, 2007.

[5] SEVIS Conference Call. NAFSA Questions. July 18, 2007.

[6] 8 CFR §214.2(f)(9)(i).

[7] Students are not allowed to work on-campus upon completion of studies.

[8] 8 CFR §214.2(f)(9)(i).

off-site location is defined as a "location which is educationally affiliated with the school …[,] associated with the school's established curriculum or related to contractually funded research projects at the post-graduate level … [and] the employment must be an integral part of student's educational program."[9] Often, this type of employer has at a minimum a direct contract or a formal affiliation agreement with the sponsoring institution.[10]

> **Practice Note:** The regulations are ambiguous as to whether companies that lease space on campus—such as bank branch offices or restaurant chains operating in student centers—qualify as on-campus companies for the purpose of F-1 student employment. Institutions will likely have specific policies for on-campus employment based on the facts and circumstances at their individual campuses.

Off-Campus Work During Studies—Requires Application and Employment Authorization Document (EAD)

Unforeseen Economic Hardship

If a student, after one full academic year of student status with an institution, suffers an unforeseeable economic hardship, he or she may be eligible to apply for employment authorization through the USCIS regional service center. Examples of this type of circumstance range from the very personal, such as the death of a parent who was the primary financial sponsor, to a very public government decision to devaluate a currency due to the individual economic circumstances facing an individual country.[11]

USCIS will issue EADs valid for one year. Work is authorized part-time, 20 hours per week, during school for on– or off-campus employment, and full-time authorization during school breaks. Work authorization can be obtained in one-year intervals and the issuance of this work authorization does not limit subsequent or concurrent applications for on-campus employment or OPT. The authorization ends if a student transfers from one institution to another. A student must have maintained valid F-1 status for at least one year and must prove that the economic hardship occurred *after* accrual of F-1 status. No

appeal or motion to reconsider or reopen will be allowed if denied.[12]

Internship with an International Organization

This type of work authorization is extremely rare and must be well documented by both the international organization and the sponsoring institution.[13] However, it is a good option for those who qualify. Work authorization can be obtained in one-year intervals (full– or part-time) and, similar to economic hardship cases, the issuance of this work authorization does not limit subsequent or concurrent applications for on-campus employment or OPT.

Special Student Relief Program

This program was instituted in June of 1998 to assist students affected by the Asian economic crisis at that time. USCIS has not since rescinded the provisions of this program, and it is technically still an option for those students who qualify. However, this provision only applies to those students from specific countries here on or before June 1998. At this stage, very few students, if any, would qualify.

Practical Training

Curricular Practical Training (CPT)

An F-1 student may have an option to seek authorization from the DSO for up to one year of employment in CPT. To qualify, a student must be enrolled in a program for one full academic year, except if the employment being sought is a requirement of a graduate program. Employment must be "an integral part of an established curriculum" at an institution. Each institution will have varying policies on how established curriculum" is defined; however, as a baseline, the educational work opportunities at the very least must either be required for all students or be available for credit.[14] If the employment meets the institutional policies of the sponsor, the DSO can recommend either full– or part-time CPT on the student's I-20 form for up to a maximum of 12 months at one time. Students may seek additional periods if available, based on the designations of the specific programs. Employment is authorized for a specific employer by the DSO directly on the I-20. No separate EAD is required to begin work.

---

[9] *Id.*

[10] 8 CFR §214.2(f)(9)(i); 56 Fed. Reg. 55608, 55609–10 (Oct. 29, 1991).

[11] 8 CFR §214.2(f)(9)(ii)(C).

[12] 8 CFR §214.2(f)(9)(ii)(F)(2).

[13] 8 CFR §214.2(f)(9)(iii). (Note that definitions are within the International Organization Immunities Act, 59 Stat. 669 (Dec. 29, 1945).

[14] 8 CFR §214.2(f)(10)(i).

Practice Note: If a student engages in one year or more of full-time CPT per academic level prior to graduation, the student is no longer eligible for any OPT after graduation.[15] Strategically, requesting 11 months of CPT would still permit the student to later complete 12 months of OPT. In addition, no amount of part-time CPT triggers a bar to OPT.[16]

Optional Practical Training (OPT)—Generally

All eligible college, university, seminary, and conservatory students are eligible for one year of OPT as long as the F-1 student can show at least one year of continuous enrollment and maintenance of status.[17] This type of work authorization is typically granted post-graduation and it is required to be used in the student's field of study. The OPT can be authorized for a maximum of 12 months, either pre-completion or post-program completion. A combination of pre– and post-authorization is also allowed. In addition, a student may specifically request pre-completion part-time authorization that will be deducted according to the amount of time requested.[18] Under normal circumstances, a student can use time spent outside the United States in an approved study abroad program to qualify for the one-year continuous enrollment period if the student spent at least one full academic semester in the United States prior to study abroad. In addition, a student granted reinstatement to F-1 student status is also allowed to count the time prior to and through the reinstatement period for the purposes of qualifying for OPT.[19] A student must apply to the USCIS regional service center for an EAD prior to completion of studies to qualify for this benefit.[20]

Practice Note: A 12-month period of OPT is currently available at each educational level. Pre-

viously, the regulations had allowed only for a total of 12 months of practical training for each student, regardless of the number of degrees by a student.[21]

Practice Note: Note that F-2 visa holders and English language students are not, under any circumstances, allowed to work in the United States.[22] Also, F-1 and F-3 border students are only allowed to work pursuant to CPT and OPT regulations.[23]

Practice Note: A student is only authorized to work under the specific circumstances outlined above. Students who engage in unauthorized employment are deemed to have violated their status and are not eligible for reinstatement.[24]

INTERIM FINAL RULE MODIFICATIONS TO THE OPT PROGRAM—APRIL 8, 2008[25]

Summary

The USCIS interim rule was issued in response to several critical and outstanding areas of concern including: the current H-1B quota crisis causing key U.S. industries to be unable to retain talented individuals in the key areas of Science, Technology, Engineering and Mathematics ("STEM" fields); defining additional reporting requirements in F-1 student programs; and the H-1B Cap Gap. The rule also changes the period within which a student may apply for the general 12-month period of post-completion OPT, returning to the pre-SEVIS rule that a student may apply for OPT within the time frame of 90 days before completion of his or her course of study, or within 60 days after completion of studies.

17-Month Extensions of OPT Time Available for STEM Students

The rule allows for certain students with degrees in STEM fields to apply for extension of OPT for an additional 17-month period.[26] The new rule is de-

---

[15] 8 CFR §214.2(f)(10)(i).

[16] Department of Homeland Security (DHS)/p. 35 of NAFSA's 10/29/2003 SEVIS Liaison Call Summary Compilation. §2.4.5.5.3.3 of DHS's SEVIS RTI user Manual (Vol. II).

[17] 8 CFR §214.2(f)(10)(ii).

[18] In this instance, the DSO should enter in SEVIS OPT remarks field that OPT request is for pre-completion—there is no other specific application procedure for this.

[19] Legacy Immigration and Naturalization Service (INS) letter from Jacquelyn Bednarz to Lisa Enfield, Esq. HQ21f-C (updated 1973), *reprinted in* 70 *Interpreter Releases* 1120–21 (Aug. 23, 1993).

[20] 8 CFR §214.2(f)(10)(ii)(A)(3).

[21] 8 CFR §214.2(f)(10).

[22] 8 CFR §§214.2(f)(15)(i), 214.2(f)(10)(ii).

[23] 8 CFR §214.2(f)(18)(iv).

[24] 8 CFR §214.2(f)(16).

[25] 73 Fed. Reg. 18944 (Apr. 8, 2008) (modifying 8 CFR Parts 214 and 274(a)). *See also* USCIS News Release, *www.dhs.gov/xnews/releases/pr_1207334008610.shtm*; USCIS Regulation, *www.dhs.gov/xlibrary/assets/press_opt_ifr .pdf*.

[26] 8 CFR §214.2(f)(10)(ii)(C).

signed to provide students who qualify at least two chances to be selected in the H-1B cap "lottery" during their OPT period. STEM extension eligibility is limited to students who have completed a Baccalaureate, Masters or Ph.D. degree that is designated in SEVIS under a specific Classification of Instructional Program (CIP) code including Actual Science, Computer Science, Engineering, Engineering Technologies, Biology and Biological Sciences, Mathematics, Statistics, Military Technologies, Physical Sciences, Science Technologies or Medical Scientists.[27] Students also must be participating in their initial 12-month period of post-completion OPT and otherwise be maintaining status at the time of application for the additional 17-month period.

Under the special extension provisions, the employer also must meet specific requirements, including enrollment in USCIS's electronic I-9 reporting system, "E-Verify." Employers also must agree to report termination or departure of the student within a 48-hour period to the DSO holding the student record. Procedurally, the students will be required to request an updated I-20 and file a new I-765 application, noting the proper code, to extend their employment authorization with the applicable documents and fees.[28]

> **Practice Pointer**: The rule provides for a significant departure from the normal practice of EAD extension filings by extending the student's employment authorization by regulation during the time that the request for a STEM extension of OPT is pending.[29]

E-Verify Participation—Problematic?

USCIS's condition of the use of its voluntary "E-Verify" program for the 17-month extension is problematic for several reasons. First, it is currently used by very few employers. Second, the government admits that significant data integrity issues have yet to be resolved. For example, system errors can arise due to an individual's inconsistent use of his or her middle name versus middle initial on his or her social security card and other official documents used for I-9 verification. If an employer submits to the E-Verify process, the employer is committing to using an electronic database to check whether the name and SSN presented by all new hires match the records in the SSA database, and whether any immigration documents presented by the employee match information contained in the DHS's database. Use of this system for employers with large numbers of employees is complicated. To implement the E-Verify system, companies would have to make significant investment in training human resources staff and may cause an additional workload responding to various flags in the system as well as potential increased exposure to risks of government audits or discrimination charges. For some employers, the benefit of additional OPT time for employees will outweigh the burden of participating in the E-Verify program.

New School Reporting Requirements on Maintenance of Employment for all Periods of Post-Completion OPT

Prior to the new regulation, employment during post-completion OPT periods was not specifically tracked by colleges and universities. The regulations now require that a DSO track and confirm a student is maintaining F-1 status during the period of post-completion OPT. Now, a student may not aggregate more than 90 days of unemployment during the initial 12-month period of OPT. In addition, students with an approved 17-month OPT extension may not aggregate more than 120 days of unemployment during the entire 29-month period of OPT.[30]

Additional reporting requirements for all F-1 students in OPT status include any name or address changes along with any interruption of employment to the DSO. Students granted a 17-month extension also must report any change of legal name, residential or mailing address, employer name address and/or loss of employment, and must make a "validation report" every six months to their DSO regarding their current employment status. Clearly, the DSO is assuming a significant administrative burden with the implementation of this new rule.

---

[27] 8 CFR §214.2(f)(10)(ii)(C)(2) STEM Designated Degree Program List, published on the SEVP website at *www.ice.gov/sevis* and *http://nced.ed.gov/pubs2002/cip2000/.*

[28] New form I-765 changes the eligibility codes for an F-1 student seeking OPT—the eligibility code (c)(3)(i) will no longer be used and has been replaced with the following codes: (c)(3)(A) for pre-completion OPT; (B) for post-completion OPT; and (C) for the 17-month STEM OPT extension.

[29] 8 CFR §274a.12(b)(6)(iv).

---

[30] USCIS has stated this reporting requirement will only be applied to post-completion OPT Employment Authorization Documents issued on or after April 8, 2008. *www.nafsa.org/regulatory_infomration.sec/29_month_opt_r ule_updates.*

SPECIAL CONSIDERATIONS DURING AND AFTER OPT

Travel and Re-Entry on OPT

One of the major challenges facing students each year is if and when they are able to travel during their OPT period. The regulations allow travel and under certain circumstances students have even been able to secure a new visa stamp at a U.S. consulate or Embassy during this time to re-enter after completion of their degree. However, it is prudent to note that OPT is a benefit of the F-1 visa status, and the purpose of the F-1 student visa has already been met in the award of the student's degree. If students are traveling post-graduation, circumstances for a smooth re-entry vary widely depending on a number of factors such as nonimmigrant intent, job offer in hand, and time left on OPT. Prior to traveling, it is always wise to advise that the student contact his or her DSO to learn the most up-to-date information. USCIS often changes its stance on this issue and CBP officials across the United States are not uniform in their document requirements USCIS's current policy states that an F-1 student is able to re-enter the United States with an EAD receipt notice, endorsed I-20 within six months for OPT and a valid visa stamp.[31] However, students should be cautioned that, as a matter of best practice, it is advisable to travel only when they have their approved EAD in hand.

Transferring and Starting New Full-Time Course of Study During F-1 OPT

If a student is issued an EAD for OPT and subsequently enrolls in a new degree program for the next semester and the card is not expired, enrollment in a full-time course of study will invalidate the OPT.[32] OPT automatically terminates when the student transfers to another school or begins study at another education level. In the SEVIS system, the OPT canceled when the SEVIS record is transferred to the new school.

Cap-Gap Relief for OPT Students

The April 8, 2008, interim rule also instituted a permanent "Cap-Gap" rule allowing F-1 OPT students with an expiring OPT period within a federal fiscal calendar year (e.g., federal year (FY) 2008 is defined as 10/1/07 to 9/30/08) to be automatically extended in both F-1 OPT status and work authorization incident to status while an H-1B application is filed and pending and, if approved, until the start date of the next fiscal year. For example, if a student's OPT expires on 6/15/08 (and his or her EAD card expires accordingly), and if the student has a valid H-1B application that has been accepted and is pending with USCS, his or her status and work authorization is automatically extended until the matter is adjudicated. If the H-1B application is rejected or denied on the merits in August, for example, the status and work authorization would end on the date of rejection and/or denial. If approved however, the student's OPT status and work authorization is valid until the beginning of the next FY, which always begins on October 1 of each year. In the example, the student's OPT status and work authorization would be automatically extended until 10/1/2008, when both the new FY 09 begins as well as the change of status to H-1B.

CONCLUSION

The panic that most students have today concerning the increasing difficulties students are encountering changing status and remaining in the United States after OPT due to the H-1B quota crisis increases daily. The OPT extension rule for those students qualifying in the STEM discipline provides some relief in this area. However, the disciplines are limited, and the employer requirement of participating in E-Verify may not be workable for every organization. Thus, other options are still to be explored with your clients if they are not selected for the H-1B lottery, including approaches such as returning to school for further studies, preferably in a program that allows curricular practical training work options as a benefit of that program. Also consider other categories that an individual may qualify for during that period. For example, is the student married, or is he or she under 21 with parents present in the United States, and does he or she qualify for a change of status to a dependent visa status (F-2, H-4, J-2 with no 212(e) requirement, etc.)?

---

[31] 8 CFR §214.2(f)(13)(ii), DOS Field Cable (Jan. 13, 2004); ICE-CPB training—May 2004 SEVIS Liaison Call SEVP Resources Qu.2.N in FAQ for F-Non-immigrants Entry and Exit.

[32] 8 CFR §214.2(f)(10)(ii)(B).

J-1 TRAINING AND INTERNSHIP PROGRAMS: UPDATES AND WHAT'S NEW

by Laura A. Edgerton, Amy M. Nice, and Lois Magee[*]

On June 19, 2007, the Department of State (DOS) issued an interim final rule concerning the processing of J-1 visas for trainees and a new subset of trainees—interns.[1] The interim final rule took effect on July 19, 2007. DOS's Bureau of Educational and Cultural Affairs (ECA) manages the J-1 program through its Office of Exchange Coordination and Designation. This article summarizes what we believe to be the key changes in the J-1 training and internship category and in ECA's oversight of the category.

PURPOSE OF REGULATORY CHANGES

The stated purpose of the interim final rule is to, among other things, "eliminate the distinction between 'non-specialty occupations' and 'specialty occupations,' establish a new internship program, and modify the selection criteria for participation in a training program."[2] The new regulations also increase the ability of DOS to monitor quality and compliance among participants more closely.

One of the major changes in the new rules addressed new training program eligibility requirements. The purpose behind this change was to deal with perceived abuses by host organizations that were enabling the J-1 to be used in situations in which a work visa (such as an H-1B) was more appropriate, but unavailable.[3] Although recognizing that "work is an essential component of on-the-job training, and that in many respects there are no conceptual or legal distinctions between an employee and a trainee," the changes aim to ensure that the visa is used appropriately for training, learning and cultural exchange, rather than work, purposes.[4]

Another major conceptual change underlying the interim final rule is that all qualifying credentials of participants are now limited to education and experience obtained abroad. ECA felt this change was necessary to ensure that the intern or trainee had established ties abroad and would be more likely to return home after completing his or her J-1 training program.[5]

NEW PARTICIPANT ELIGIBILITY REQUIREMENTS

Education/Work Experience Requirements for Trainees vs. Interns

In addition to the interim final rule's imposition of a new educational and work experience requirement for trainees, the rule establishes the new intern subset of the trainee category, which is subject to different requirements and is aimed at current students and recent graduates.

Trainee Requirements

The interim rule now focuses on the *amount* of prior experience that the trainee has acquired, rather

[*] **Laura A. Edgerton** is a partner with Bashyam Spiro & Edgerton, LLP, based in Raleigh. She is the current Carolinas Chapter chair and the former chair of AILA's Young Lawyers Division. She has been practicing immigration law for more than a decade and focuses her practice on business immigration issues. She is a frequent lecturer on immigration topics at local and national conferences and has also served as an AILA mentor for many years.

Amy M. Nice manages the immigration practice of Dickstein Shapiro LLP, in Washington, DC. Ms. Nice has served as chair, co-chair and member of AILA's USIA Liaison, VSC Liaison, State Department Liaison, and SSA Liaison committees. She has twice been the recipient of the AILA Presidential Award. She is a frequent speaker and is included in *The Best Lawyers in America*, the Lawdragon 3000, and *Chambers USA: America's Leading Lawyers for Business*. Ms. Nice is a graduate of George Washington University (J.D.).

Lois Magee, director of the American Immigration Law Foundation's Exchange Visitor Program, has been affiliated with a number of citizen exchange organizations, including the International Christian Youth Exchange, AFS Intercultural Programs, and the YMCA International Branch. She has worked with and written on J-1 visa programs for over 20 years. Ms. Magee holds a master's degree in international administration from the School for International Training in Brattleboro, VT.

[1] 72 Fed. Reg. 33669 (June 19, 2007).

[2] *Id.* at 33669 (summary).

[3] *Id.* at 33670.

[4] *Id.*

[5] *See id.*

than the type of training.[6] It still remains a requirement that the individual be training for a skilled occupation, and that training for the purpose of pursuing an unskilled occupation is not permitted. The new rules also limit the amount of time that can be spent on clerical tasks—which is considered unskilled work—to 20 percent.[7] Accordingly, the new regulations require that to be eligible to participate in a training program, trainees must have either (1) a degree or professional certificate from a postsecondary academic institution outside the United States and at least one year of prior related work experience in their occupational field acquired outside the United States, or (2) five years of work experience outside the United States in their occupational field.[8]

Intern Requirements

To qualify as a bona fide intern, the candidate must (1) be currently enrolled and pursuing studies at a degree– or certificate-granting postsecondary academic institution, or (2) have graduated from such institution no more than 12 months prior to the exchange visitor program begin date and be entering the United States to participate in an internship program related to his or her specific academic field.[9]

English-Language Fluency

Under the new regulations, J-1 trainees and interns must have sufficient English fluency to be able to fully participate and understand the training that they are receiving. To meet this standard, applicants' fluency must be verified by a recognized English language test (*e.g.*, TOEFL), by signed documentation from an academic institution or English language school, or through a documented interview conducted by program sponsors or a third party in person, by videoconferencing or by web camera.[10]

Training in a Designated Occupational Category

To be eligible for a J-1 training or internship program under the new regulations, the applicant must be receiving training in one of the following occupational categories: agriculture, forestry, and fishing; arts and culture; certain types of aviation; construction and building trades; education, social sciences, library science, counseling and social services;

health-related occupations; hospitality and tourism; information media and communications; management, business, commerce and finance; public administration and law; the sciences, engineering, architecture, mathematics, and industrial occupations; or "such other occupational categories that the Department may from time to time include in training and internship programs."[11]

TRAINING PLAN ELIGIBILITY REQUIREMENTS

New Form for Placement Plan

The interim final rule mandates the use of the new DS-7002 form[12] to describe the training/intern placement plan (T/IPP).[13] This new form can be requested by a consular officer as a prerequisite to issuing a J-1 visa to a trainee or intern.[14] In order for the T/IPP to be sufficient under the new regulations, it must identify goals and objectives, detail the knowledge, skills, or techniques to be imparted, and describe the methods of evaluation and supervision.[15] If the training or internship has rotations, then a description of these elements must be provided for each rotation.[16]

The DS-7002 T/IPP contains two primary pages. The signature page must be completed for each training supervisor. That is, if the intern or trainee will rotate through three different departments, three different signature pages must be submitted. Page 2 of the T/IPP must be completed for each separate phase of the training.

The new rules also impose special T/IPP requirements depending on whether the applicant is a trainee or an intern. For *trainees*, the regulations state that the T/IPP must be divided into specific and various phases and components, and for each phase or component must describe the methodology of training and provide a chronology or syllabus.[17] For *interns*, the T/IPP must describe the role of the intern in the organization and, if applicable, identify various departments or functional areas in which the

---

[6] *Id.*

[7] 22 CFR §62.22(j)(4).

[8] 22 CFR §62.2 (definition of "trainee").

[9] 22 CFR §62.22(a); *see also* 22 CFR §62.2 (definition of "intern").

[10] 22 CFR §62.22(d).

[11] 22 CFR §62.22(c)(2).

[12] The form is reproduced at the end of this article.

[13] 22 CFR §62.22(i)(1).

[14] *Id.*

[15] 22 CFR §62.22(i)(2).

[16] *Id.*

[17] 22 CFR §62.22(i)(3).

intern will work. It also must identify the specific tasks and activities the intern will complete.[18]

Conflicting guidance has been given to various J program sponsors as to when a section of training rises to the level that a separate T/IPP is needed. It appears that ECA and individual consular posts may have different views. By way of general guidelines, no training program of longer than six months should be summarized in a single phase. Progressive phases should instead be described on separate "page 2" submissions. While early guidance from ECA had indicated that phases should not exceed five months, consular posts have expressed concern about having to scan excessive documents when numerous, separate "page 2" submissions are part of the T/IPP. As a result, some training program sponsors require a separate DS-7002 for each rotation, phase, or component of the training, while others have revised their instructions. The best advice is to check with the specific program sponsors for their expectations before translating the training plan into a T/IPP on the DS-7002.

Individualized Plans

The interim final regulations for intern and trainee programs make it clear that ECA requires *individualized* T/IPPs.[19] There is a clear expectation that the training program reflect the needs of the specific trainee or intern. While this expectation is not "new," because ECA has been advising sponsors of this concern for some time, there has never been a regulatory imperative to ensure compliance or any regulatory text underlying ECA's position. For many years, J program sponsors were encouraged by ECA to provide sample training plans to model what was expected from host companies. Over time, that led to the "cloning" of plans, and an inability for host companies to document they were delivering training that helped the career development of a particular J-1 participant. To address this concern, the next section focuses on how to write an effective training plan under the new regulations.

How to Write a Training Plan

The development of an effective training program is central to a successful J trainee or intern application. Yet, many employers struggle to understand how to put together a program that is bona fide training. Typically, the employer can pull up a job

description with no difficulty, but, unless there is a professional trainer on staff, writing a training program can be a real challenge. A training plan is a 180-degree departure from a job description. A job description describes what an employee will do for a company; a training plan details what the company will do for the trainee or intern. While a job description puts the employee's skills to work, a training plan works on the development of the skills. Although this seems obvious, thinking in this way allows the employer to begin to understand what constitutes bona fide training.

Effective training recognizes that different people have distinct learning styles. The best training plans combine a variety of training activities. Classroom instruction provides a theoretical base helpful in understanding the reason for acquiring a certain skill. Guided research projects provide a more universal view of how competency is developed. Learning journals provide the opportunity for reflection, and a tangible record of skills acquisition for future reference. Special projects provide active engagement in the skill being developed.

Questions to Answer in Developing a Training Plan

A training plan is just that—a plan. Starting with the needs of the trainee or intern and the resources of the training site, defining the desired outcomes of the training, scheduling training activities that progressively develop the necessary skills to achieve planned outcomes, providing on-going periods of reflection and feedback, and identifying the criteria to determine that skills and competencies have been acquired are the bare bones of an effective training plan. The steps can be summarized as following:

- Step one: What does the trainee or intern need to learn?

- Step two: What human and physical resources does the training site have in order to teach these skills?

- Step three: By the end of the training, or training phase, what will the trainee or intern have learned to do?

- Step four: How and when will the trainee or intern learn these skills?

- Step five: When and how will the trainee reflect on and receive feedback on his or her performance during the training activity?

---

[18] 22 CFR §62.22(i)(4).

[19] 72 Fed. Reg. 33669, 33670 (June 19, 2007).

- Step six: How will we know the trainee or intern has mastered the skill? When and how will this be measured?

Components of a Training Plan

Effective training includes four key components: defined outcomes, experiential learning, reflection and feedback, and formal evaluation. A training program has clearly defined outcomes.

Training Outcomes

The outcomes are based on the learning needs of the potential intern or trainee and the human and physical resources at the potential training site. Consider the example of the new driver. It is not enough to simply hand the trainee the keys and say, "Here. Take the car and go learn how to drive." A good training program instead identifies the final objectives of the training: for example, "the new driver will be able to identify and avoid potential hazards while driving"; "the new driver will be able to fill the gas tank at a self serve station"; "the new driver will be able to control the vehicle on icy roads." Without clearly defined outcomes, no training program exists. The outcomes define and guide what training will occur.

Experiential Learning as Training

Experiential learning is the key difference between the classroom and training experience. Training takes the individual beyond theoretical knowledge into the practical application of skills. Thus, classroom experience forms part of a training program, but it alone does not represent the whole. Experiential learning is the justification for on-the-job training. However, just as the classroom learning does not qualify as an entire training program, neither does on-the-job training. Again, the J regulations are very clear on this point.[20] What moves on-the-job training, or any other training activity, away from a mere means of gaining experience and positions it as a legitimate training activity is reflection and feedback.

Reflection and Feedback

Reflection and feedback provide the opportunity for the trainee and the trainer to acknowledge what has been learned, and to refine and expand on skills learned through the training activities. Let's again use the example of the new driver. Merely having the experience of driving by itself is not a training experience. Until the new driver has the opportunity to reflect on the experience and to receive feedback, an active awareness of the skills learned does not occur. Feedback, however, is more than an admonition to "watch out for the curb." It is an active dialog about what has been learned, as well as how and why. A common rule of thumb for reflection and feedback is that this element of training takes at least as long as the preceding training activity.

Evaluation

The fourth component of training is formal evaluation. Formal evaluation tracks and measures the progress of acquiring the skills and competencies to reach the defined outcomes. It is separate from reflection and feedback in that it occurs at planned intervals in order to measure change. In the new driver example, formal evaluation is the licensing test. Evaluation differs from reflection and feedback, which are subjective, in that it is an objective measure against predetermined criteria.

Program Exclusions

In formulating training programs, bear in mind that programs having any of the following characteristics are *not* eligible for J-1 classification:

- Trainees or interns are placed in unskilled or casual labor positions, in positions that require child/elder care, or clinical or other work involving patient care (*e.g.*, physical therapy, nursing, early childhood education).[21]

- Trainees or interns are placed into positions, occupations, or businesses that could bring the J-1 program or DOS into notoriety or disrepute. (Although undefined, "notoriety or disrepute" is generally thought by the exchange community to mean that anything that might be the subject of negative newspaper or television reporting needs to be avoided.)[22]

- Staffing or employment agencies are engaged or involved in any way to recruit, screen, orient, place, evaluate, or train candidates for participation in a trainee or internship program.[23]

---

[20] 22 CFR §62.22(b)(1)(ii): The requirements in these regulations for trainees are designed to distinguish between bona fide training, which is permitted, and merely gaining additional work experience, which is not permitted.

[21] 22 CFR §62.22(j).

[22] *Id.*

[23] *Id.*

- The T/IPP involves more than 20 percent clerical work or involves tasks that are not necessary for completion of the training or internship program.[24]
- "Hospitality and tourism" training and internship programs of six months or longer that do not have at least three departmental or functional rotations.[25]
- Interns are placed in the field of aviation. (Trainees may be placed in certain aviation training programs.)[26]

PROGRAM SPONSOR OBLIGATIONS TO SCREEN HOST COMPANIES

In addition to the above changes, the new regulations mandate that each host company providing training have a Dun & Bradstreet identification number (DUNS), which is provided to the program sponsor.[27] ECA felt that the DUNS number provided a benchmark for assessing a company's reliability. Academic institutions, government entities, and family farms who are acting as the training provider are exempt from the DUNS requirement.[28] Furthermore, each training-program sponsor is required to have a written agreement with any third party that provides training or acts in any manner on behalf of the program sponsor.[29] Written agreements are also required with any partner organizations the program sponsor may use outside the United States.[30] One of the new program sponsor requirements that is most vexing to the exchange community is the requirement that every host organization providing training be visited by the program sponsor.[31] Program sponsors must conduct site visits for any host company providing training that has not successfully trained J-1 participants through that sponsor previously, if the training provider either has less than $3 million in annual revenues or less than 25 employees.[32] These new program-sponsor obligations are probably best thought of as part of ECA's implementation

of the "know your customer" constraint established in the Patriot Act.[33]

DURATION OF TRAINEE AND INTERN PARTICIPATION

Interns may have J-1 internships lasting only 12 months, while trainees may have J-1 trainee status for up to 18 months.[34] However, "hospitality and tourism" training programs can be of no more than 12 months duration.[35] Agriculture training programs also are limited to 12 months, unless the additional six months of the program consists of classroom participation and studies.[36] Note as a practical matter that any 18-month training program that is classified as "management, business, commerce and finance" for an assignment in a hospitality or tourism industry employer will be carefully reviewed by ECA to confirm that it is really management or business training.

An intern may participate in multiple internships while enrolled as a student abroad, or within one year of graduating, as long as each successive J-1 intern period addresses the development of new skills.[37] A trainee may participate in more than one period of J-1 trainee status if he or she spends at least two years outside the United States after his or her initial training period.[38] Likewise, if an individual comes to the United States as a J-1 intern but no longer qualifies for intern designation because he or she is not enrolled in school abroad or it has been more than 12 months since his or her graduation, the individual can come to the United States as a trainee if he or she spends at least two years outside the United States after his or her last J-1 internship period.[39]

CONCLUSION

The interim final rule of June 19, 2007, attempts to strike a balance between addressing the perceived abuses[40] of the training category of the J-1 visa with

[24] *Id.*
[25] *Id.*
[26] *Id.*
[27] 22 CFR §62.22(g)(3).
[28] *Id.*
[29] 22 CFR §62.22(g)(1).
[30] 22 CFR §62.22(g)(2).
[31] 22 CFR §62.22(g)(4).
[32] *Id.*

[33] Uniting and Strengthening America by Providing Appropriate Tools Required to Intercept and Obstruct Terrorism Act of 2001, Pub. L. No. 107-56, 115 Stat. 272.
[34] 22 CFR §62.22(k).
[35] *Id.*
[36] *Id.*
[37] 22 CFR §62.22(n).
[38] *Id.*
[39] *Id.*
[40] DOS, "Stronger Action Needed to Improve Oversight and Assess Risks of the Summer Work Travel and Trainee Cate-
continued

regard to the intent of the Fulbright-Hays Act,[41] and
the need to expand citizen exchange to promote the
public policy objectives of the United States. As the
need grows to build the United States's national
"soft power"[42] to improve our image and position
overseas, the exchange of international trainees and
interns is more than merely developing the skills and
competencies of young professionals. Each J-1 program is part of a larger picture of promoting stability, goodwill, and U.S. interests around the world.
The changes brought by the interim final rule seek to
strengthen the likelihood of the J-1 visa successfully
achieving this idealistic intent. It is an intent we can
all support.

---

gories of the Exchange Visitor Program" (GAO-06-106, Oct.
2005), *available at www.gao.gov/new.items/d06106.pdf.*

[41] 22 USC §2451 *et seq.*

[42] Remarks delivered by Secretary of Defense Robert M.
Gates, Landon Lecture, Manhattan, KS, Nov. 26, 2007.

U.S. Department of State

*OMB APPROVAL NO. 1405-0170
EXPIRATION DATE: 07-31-2009
ESTIMATED BURDEN: 60 minutes

TRAINING/INTERNSHIP PLACEMENT PLAN

Check one:	Occupational Field		Number of Years of Experience
[X] Trainee			
[ ] Intern	Level of Degree BSci	Date Awarded (mm-dd-yyyy)	Field of Study

PARTICIPANT INFORMATION

Trainee/Intern Name (Last, First, MI)	U.S. Residence Address
U.S. Telephone Number	FAX Number	Email Address

SITE OF ACTIVITY INFORMATION

Host Organization	Address
Supervisor's Name (Last, First, MI)	Email Address
Phone Number	FAX Number	Supervisor's Title
Dates of Program (mm-dd-yyyy) From _____ To _____	Hours Per Week	Will Trainee/Intern receive a stipend? [ ] Yes [ ] No	If so, how much? $ _____ per

CONTRACT AGREEMENT

NOTE- Sponsors will not approve any contracts, and Trainees/Interns may not begin their programs until both a Training/Internship Placement Plan *(page 2)* and proof of required insurance that meets 22 CFR 62.14 is on file with the sponsor.

Trainee/Intern- I hereby acknowledge, understand and agree to the attached Training/Internship Placement Plan.

Trainee/Intern Signature	Date (mm-dd-yyyy)

Supervisor- I certify that I will provide on-site supervision and that this training/internship is known and approved by this company/business or organization *(site of activity)*. I will ensure that the required insurance is in place that meets 22 CFR 62.14 and provide the sponsor with written evaluations of the trainee/intern's performance, including the number of hours performed, the type of training, and the quality of the performance. At minimum, I will submit the evaluation at the mid-point and end of the program.

Supervisor's Signature	Date (mm-dd-yyyy)

Sponsor- I approve the attached Training/Internship Placement Plan. I certify the following:

1. Sufficient planning, equipment, and trained personnel will be dedicated to provide the training/internship specified;
2. The training/internship program is not designed to recruit and train aliens for employment in the United States;
3. Trainees/Interns will not displace full-time or part-time U.S. employees; and
4. That training and internship programs in the field of agriculture meet all requirements of the Employment Relationship under the Fair Labor Standards Act and the Migrant and Seasonal Agricultural Worker Protection Act *(29 CFR Part 500)*.

I understand that false certification may subject me to criminal prosecution under 18 U.S.C. 1001, which reads: "Except as otherwise provided in this section, whoever, in any matter within the jurisdiction of the executive, legislative, or judicial branch of the Government of the United States, knowingly and willfully falsifies, conceals, or covers up by any trick, scheme, or device a material fact; makes any materially false, fictitious, or fraudulent statement or representation; or makes or uses any false writing or document knowing the same to contain any materially false, fictitious, or fraudulent statement or entry; shall be fined under this title or imprisoned not more than 5 years, or both."

Sponsor's Signature (RO/ARO)	Date (mm-dd-yyyy)
Program Sponsor Name	Program Number

DS-7002
04-2007
*Public reporting burden for this collection of information is estimated to average 60 minutes per response, including time required for searching existing data sources, gathering the necessary data, providing the information required, and reviewing the final collection. Persons are not required to provide this information in the absence of a valid OMB approval number. Send comments on the accuracy of this estimate of the burden and recommendations for reducing it to: U.S. Department of State (A/ISS/DIR) 1800 G St. NW, Washington, DC 20520.

Page 1 of 2

Program Sponsor Name	Program Number

TRAINING/INTERNSHIP PLACEMENT PLAN

An acceptable Training/Internship Placement Plan should cover a definite period of time and should consist of definite phases of training or tasks performed with a specific objective for each phase. The plan must also contain information on how the trainees/interns will accomplish those objectives (i.e. classes, individual instruction, shadowing, etc.). Each phase must build upon the previous phase to show a progression in the training/internship. A separate copy of page 2 must be completed for each phase if applicable (i.e.; if the trainee/intern is rotating through different departments).

Name of Trainee/Intern (Last, First, MI)	Field of Training/Internship

Name of Phase	Start Date for this Phase _____ (mm-dd-yyyy)	End Date for this Phase _____ (mm-dd-yyyy)	Phase _____ of _____

Specific Objective for This Phase

Skills to be Imparted for This Phase

Justification for On-The-Job Training

Chronology or Syllabus of Training or Tasks Performed During This Phase

Method of Evaluation and the Frequency of Supervision During This Phase

DS-7002   Page 2 of 2

WHAT ARE YOUR INTENTIONS ANYWAY? IMMIGRANT INTENT, "DUAL INTENT," AND PRECONCEIVED INTENT IN IMMIGRATION PRACTICE

by Dagmar Butte, Rómulo E. Guevara, and Marketa Lindt[*]

INTRODUCTION

There can be no question that the doctrine of immigrant intent has always been at the core of immigration law. It is a complex concept, which has not always been understood or properly applied. The rules of intent in nonimmigrant visa eligibility vary from visa to visa. Adjustment of status also presents its own set of challenges, especially because much of the relevant case law is old and not at the forefront of the minds of examiners. Whether immigrant intent exists in a wish or desire, or something more definite or preconceived, courts have generally been more liberal in the interpretation of the doctrine, while immigration authorities have tried to narrow it—the U.S. Department of State (DOS) through the *Foreign Affairs Manual* (FAM) and the unfettered discretion of its consular officers, and the Department of Homeland Security (DHS) through the wide discretionary power in adjustment of status adjudications.

This article will explore the different facets of immigrant intent from the perspective of nonimmigrant and immigrant visa classifications and the way courts and immigration authorities have treated the subject. The discussion will also analyze the "dual intent" doctrine and whether it is limited to Hs and Ls. It will further address whether dual intent has always existed in the nonimmigrant classifications that are commonly thought not to have it. Finally, practical and timing considerations will be offered for handling the intent doctrine in nonimmigrant and immigrant visa processing. This article is not intended to be an exhaustive study of the topic but is designed to sensitize practitioners to the existence of these rules of engagement and encourage them to consider the issue before filing for a benefit on behalf of a client.

THE DOCTRINE OF IMMIGRANT INTENT

The General Presumption Framework

Under Section 214(b) of the Immigration and Nationality Act (INA), a legal presumption exists that every foreign national is an intending immigrant until he or she establishes to the satisfaction of the relevant immigration authority that he or she is eligibile for a nonimmigrant status under INA

§101(a)(15). Once the presumption is overcome, the foreign national will be able to obtain a nonimmigrant visa and subsequent admission to the United States.[1] But how does a foreign national overcome the presumption?

[*] **Dagmar Butte**, a shareholder of Parker, Bush & Lane in Portland, OR, has practiced immigration law since 1992 and is currently an elected member of the board of governors of the American Immigration Lawyers Association (AILA) and an ambassador for the American Immigration Law Foundation (AILF). She writes and speaks annually for AILA national, regional, and local seminars as well as privately sponsored seminars and Lewis & Clark Law School sponsored immigration events. She has served as associate editor of *Immigration Options for Artists and Entertainers* (AILA 2007), and has chaired and been a member of several national AILA committees, including Strategic Planning, USCIS Headquarters & General Counsel, Due Process, Detention and Removal, Publications, and various seminar planning committees. In her spare time, she is an adjunct professor of law at Lewis & Clark Law School.

Rómulo E. Guevara, an attorney with Fragomen, Del Rey, Bernsen & Loewy, LLP, in Phoenix, has practiced immigration law since 1997 and is currently chairman of AILA Distance Learning Committee, and a member of the AILA Board of Publications. Mr. Guevara frequently writes, edits, and speaks for AILA national, regional, and local seminars, in addition to private organizations. He served as associate editor of *Immigration Practice Toolbox* (AILA 2d Ed.) and *Business Immigration from a New Perspective: 2007 Alaskan Cruise Conference Handbook* (AILA 2007), and co-edited *Understanding Immigration Policy, Practicing It Effectively: 2006 AILA Fall CLE Conference Handbook*. He also served as a committee member for the AILA 2007 Annual Conference. Mr. Guevara is a graduate of Hofstra University School of Law in New York.

Marketa Lindt practices business immigration law at Sidley Austin LLP in Chicago, where she focuses her practice on employer-side workforce planning, visa processing, and employer sanctions counseling. She currently serves on the national AILA-ICE Liaison Committee and the Interior Enforcement Committee. During 2005–06, she was chair of AILA's Chicago Chapter and served on AILA's Board of Governors. She has previously served on a number of national AILA government liaison committees, including those with the Department of Labor, USCIS Nebraska Service Center, and the Social Security Administration. Ms. Lindt is named as a leading business immigration lawyer and Illinois lawyer by Who's Who Legal, and is a previous recipient of AILA's Joseph Minsky Young Lawyer Award. Ms. Lindt is

continued

Among the elements that many of the nonimmigrant visa classifications require in order to overcome the presumption is that the foreign national maintain a "residence" abroad that he or she does not intend to abandon.[2] The INA defines "residence" as "a place of general abode," which means "his principal, actual dwelling place in fact, *without regard to intent*."[3] The latter phrase thus suggests an objective, rather than subjective, test. An exemption from the intent to abandon a foreign residence exists specifically for two nonimmigrant classifications, as will be discussed below.

For the immigrant visa classifications, the applicant for the visa or holder of the status must establish the eligibility for the classification with respect to the corresponding immigrant intent requirement, but must also seek the immigration authority's favorable exercise of discretion. A detailed discussion of adjustment of status appears after the nonimmigrant visa discussion below.

Nonimmigrant Intent vs. Preconceived Intent

The issue of immigrant intent raises the challenge of how to identify it. Is it a whim or desire? Or must it be something more definite or fixed? Courts have been consistently more liberal in recognizing that the U.S. government cannot legislate a prohibition against a person's wish to live in the United States.

In *Matter of H–R–*,[4] the Board of Immigration Appeals (BIA) said, "[T]he fact that the applicant previously expressed a desire to enter the United States as an immigrant—and may still have such desire—does not of itself preclude the issuance of a nonimmigrant visa to him or preclude his being a *bona fide* nonimmigrant."[5] Similarly, in *Matter of Hosseinpour*,[6] the BIA continued this line of thinking

and stated, "[A] desire to remain in this country permanently in accordance to the law, should the opportunity to do so present itself, is not necessarily inconsistent with lawful nonimmigrant status."[7] Thus, there is a long line of cases that makes a clear distinction between a person's general desire to remain in the United States—which is *not* prohibited—and a person's preconceived (fixed) intent to remain permanently in the United States when entering in a temporary visa classification—which *is* prohibited.[8] Therefore, while a foreign national entering the United States in a temporary category, such as an F-1 student, may harbor a generalized wish to live in the United States, he or she may not seek to enter in F-1 status with the specific intention of remaining in the United States after the completion of the F-1 program of study. The specific intention of remaining in the United States objectively would mean the foreign national also intends to abandon his foreign residence.

The Exemption from the Presumption of Immigrant Intent

As an analysis of nonimmigrant visa classifications will reveal below, the vast majority of nonimmigrant visa classifications require, as part of the intent doctrine, that the holder maintain a residence abroad that he or she does not intend to abandon.[9] However, the INA contains an exemption, which in practice has evolved into a distinct legal concept to address the situation in which a nonimmigrant in the United States may hold a temporary visa classification while simultaneously pursuing permanent status in the United States.

Under INA §214(h), "[T]he fact that an alien is the beneficiary of an application for a preference status ... or has otherwise sought permanent residence in the United States shall not constitute evidence of an intention to abandon a foreign residence for purposes of obtaining a visa as a nonimmigrant"

---

also past chair of the Chicago Bar Association Immigration & Nationality Law Committee. Ms. Lindt is a frequent speaker and writer for AILA national and regional conferences.

[1] INA §214(b). The three visa classifications exempted by the INA provision are H-1B (but *not* the Singaporean and Chilean H-1B1), L, and V.

[2] INA §101(a)(15).

[3] INA §101(a)(33) (emphasis added).

[4] 7 I&N Dec. 651 (RC 1958).

[5] *Id.*, citing *U.S. v. Reimer*, 10 F. Supp. 992 (S.D.N.Y. 1935); *Chryssikos v. Commissioner of Immigration*, 3 F.2d 372 (C.C.A. 2, 1924); *U.S. ex rel. Rizzo v. Curran*, 13 F.2d 233 (S.D.N.Y. 1925).

[6] 15 I&N Dec. 191 (BIA 1975).

[7] *Id.* at 192. *See also Choy v. Barber*, 279 F.2d 642 (9th Cir. 1960); *Brownell v. Carija*, 254 F.2d 78 (D.C. Cir. 1957); *Ameeriar v. INS*, 438 F.2d 1028 (3d Cir. 1971) (Gibbons, J. dissenting); *Jain v. INS*, 612 F.2d 683 (2d Cir. 1979).

[8] *Lauvik v. INS*, 910 F.2d 658, 660 (9th Cir. 1990) ("At most, Luvik may have *wanted* to remain permanently, but there was no evidence that he *intended* to remain if that was not legally possible."). *See also Ameeriar v. INS*, 438 F.2d 1028, 1033 (3d Cir. 1971) ("[A]bsent an administrative error, any alien who arrives in the United States with a fixed intention to remain permanently has misrepresented his intention to the immigration authorities.").

[9] INA §101(a)(15).

in H-1B or L-1 status. The language of this section is consistent with the definition of "residence" and the objective test that arises from it.[10]

Although commonly (and perhaps incorrectly) known as "dual intent," the notion that the individual will intend to depart the United States but simultaneously have a permissible long-term intent to remain permanently is an exemption from the prohibition of abandonment of foreign residence rather than a separate doctrine.[11] H-1Bs and L-1s are expressly exempted from §214(b) immigrant presumption, as are V visa holders. Other classifications for which statute or regulations permit the holder to pursue permanent residence with more limited degrees of the exemption are E, O-1, and P (except essential support personnel). On the other hand, a number of visa classifications, including B, F-1, J, Q, and TN, bear specific statutory and regulatory requirements regarding an applicant's temporary intent, in some cases requiring return to a residence abroad after completing the allotted temporary period of stay in the United States.[12]

Many people are caught unaware of the application of the intent doctrine in two contexts: (1) when applying for, renewing, or seeking admission as nonimmigrants, and (2) when applying for adjustment of status to permanent residence status. An analysis and discussion of these different contexts follows.

THE INTENT DOCTRINE IN NONIMMIGRANT VISA CLASSIFICATIONS

Classifications Containing Explicit Presumption of Immigrant Intent

B-1/B-2 Visitors

Legal standard: Under the B visa category, the alien must intend to visit the United States for business or pleasure and maintain "a residence in a foreign country which he has no intention of abandoning."[13] As stated earlier, the INA defines "residence"

as "the place of general abode or the principal, actual dwelling place in fact."[14] This does not mean that the foreign national must maintain an independent household to qualify as a person who has a residence in a foreign country that he or she has no intention of abandoning. If the alien customarily resides in the household of another, that household is the residence in fact.[15] Again, it is an objective test.

In the context of a visa application, the applicant must establish to the consular officer his or her ties to the home country, such as family, employment, and social.[16] Therefore, the inquiry regarding the intent issue is two-fold. First, does the applicant for the B visa or status intend to carry out the activities permitted under the B-1 or B-2 visa classification? Second, does the applicant have sufficient ties to the home country that will not be abandoned during the nonimmigrant stay in the United States? If the answer is no, the visa will be denied under INA §214(b).[17]

There are a number of interesting variations on the required temporary intent requirement for B visa holders. While a B-1 nonimmigrant may not intend to remain in the United States permanently, the classification is the appropriate one to use for preliminary visits to the United States before applying for a longer-term classification such as an E-2 investor.[18] In limited circumstances, the U.S. consulate may relax the nonimmigrant intent requirement to grant B-2 classification to individuals who have relatives who are U.S. citizens or who reside in the United States. For example, DOS permits B-2 status for certain applicants who seek to enter the United States temporarily to meet family or prospective spouses.[19] DOS also

---

[10] INA §101(a)(33).

[11] *Matter of H–R–*, 7 I&N Dec 651 (RC 1958), *citing U.S. v. Reimer*, 10 F. Supp. 992 (S.D.N.Y. 1935); *Chryssikos v. Commissioner of Immigration*, 3 F.2d 372 (C.C.A. 2, 1924); *U.S. ex rel. Rizzo v. Curran*, 13 F.2d 233 (S.D.N.Y. 1925).

[12] *See also* INA §214(b), Basis of Refusal Not Equivalent to Inadmissibility or Immigrant Intent, 04 State 274068 (Dec. 28, 2004), *published on* AILA InfoNet at Doc. No. 05032279 (*posted* Mar. 22, 2005).

[13] INA §101(a)(15)(B); *see also* 22 CFR §41.31; 9 FAM 41.31.

[14] INA §101(a)(33).

[15] 9 FAM 41.31 N2.

[16] 9 FAM 41.31 N3.4.

[17] When there are intended changes to the activity and underlying status subsequent to U.S. entry, the 30/60 day rule may come into play. A separate discussion that will address these issues and consequences appears later in this article.

[18] For example, the FAM permits a B-1 for a person seeking investment in the United States, including investment that would subsequently qualify him or her for status as an E-2 investor. 9 FAM 41.31 N9.7.

[19] The FAM includes the following permissible B-2 classifications: (1) the fiancé(e) of a U.S. citizen or lawful permanent resident who intends to return to a residence abroad soon after the marriage; (2) a fiancé(e) who wishes to travel to the United States to marry a nonimmigrant alien in the United States in a valid nonimmigrant F, H, J, L, M, O, P, or Q status; (3) a spouse married by proxy to an alien in the United States in a nonimmigrant status to join the spouse

continued

permits use of the B-2 to permit cohabiting partners of nonimmigrants in longer-term categories to accompany their partners to the United States.[20] This is consistent with case law discussed above.

Practical considerations:

- For citizens of countries in the Visa Waiver Program, the B-1/B-2 determination is made at the port of entry rather than at the consulate. Due to the nonimmigrant intent requirement, the inspector is unlikely to grant entry in B-1/B-2 status under the Visa Waiver Program if he or she is aware that the applicant is the beneficiary of an immigrant petition or otherwise intends to immigrate to the United States, unless the argument and evidence follows the analysis or framework of the established case law.

- The application for a standard B-1/B-2 visa is made at the U.S. consulate abroad. Again, due to the nonimmigrant intent requirement, at the time of application the consular officer is unlikely to grant an application for a B-1/B-2 if the applicant is the beneficiary of an immigrant petition and the evidence does not follow the analysis discussed in the case law.

- If the applicant is from a Visa Waiver Program country but falls into one of the special classifications in the FAM, it is typically advisable to apply for a specially annotated B-1/B-2 visa at the U.S. consulate abroad rather than to apply for entry under the Visa Waiver Program. Obtaining a B visa at the consulate before traveling minimizes the risk of an adverse decision at the port of entry. Applicants should present sufficient documentation and a legal analysis to demonstrate that the applicant qualifies for the special FAM classification.

- As the 90-day nonimmigrant admission under the Visa Waiver Program cannot be extended, the nonimmigrant intent issue does not arise in the context of an extension. An entrant under the Visa Waiver Program can only file for adjustment of status in limited circumstances, such as the spouse of a U.S. citizen petitioner. But a Visa Waiver Program entrant who files for adjustment of status after entry may face accusations of preconceived intent (as discussed below).

- In practice, a request for an extension of B-1 or B-2 status pursuant to admission under a B-1/B-2 visa is typically granted, but it is advisable to submit evidence of the residence abroad to establish eligibility.

- From a practical standpoint, it is typically not advisable to file for employment-based permanent residence for an individual in B-1 status if the B-1 I-94 validity period is expected to remain valid. The processing times for the permanent residence filing typically exceed the B-1 holder's ability to remain in the United States under the original B-1 admission, and it would be extremely difficult to obtain an extension from U.S. Citizenship and Immigration Services (USCIS) for the B-1 status if the individual had indicated the intention to remain in the United States as the beneficiary of an immigrant petition. However, keep in mind the 30/60 day rule,[21] which may permit permanent residence filing if the intent rule is properly documented.

F-1 Students

Legal standard: An F-1 academic student must maintain "a residence in a foreign country which he has no intention of abandoning."[22] Fortunately, DOS has recognized that F-1 students, by nature of their stage in life, typically do not have the same material evidence of ties to the home country as B visitors. In the FAM, DOS states:

The context of the residence abroad requirement for student visas inherently differs from the context for B visitor visas or other short-term visas. The statute clearly pre-supposes that the natural circumstances and conditions of being a student do not disqualify that applicant from obtaining a student visa. It is natural that the student does not possess ties of property, employment, family obli-

---

already in the United States; (4) an alien spouse or child, including an adopted alien child, of a U.S. citizen or resident alien who seeks to travel to accompany or follow to join the spouse or parent for a temporary visit to the United States. 9 FAM 41.31 N14.

[20] The B-2 classification is appropriate for aliens who are members of the household of another alien in long-term nonimmigrant status, but who are not eligible for derivative status under that alien's visa classification. Such aliens may include cohabiting partners or elderly parents of temporary workers, students, diplomats posted to the United States, etc. B-2 classification may also be accorded to a spouse or child who qualifies for derivative status (other than derivative A or G status) but for whom it may be inconvenient or impossible to apply for the proper H-4, L-2, F-2, or other derivative visa. *Id.*

[21] 9 FAM 40.63 N4.7.

[22] INA §101(a)(15)(F).

gation, and continuity of life typical of B visa applicants. These ties are typically weakly held by student applicants, as the student is often single, unemployed, without property, and is at the stage in life of deciding and developing his or her future plans. This general condition is further accentuated in light of the student's proposed extended absence from his or her homeland. ... Nonetheless, the Consular Officer must be satisfied at the time of application for a visa that an alien possesses the present intent to depart the U.S. at the conclusion of his or her studies. That this intention is subject to change or even likely to change is NOT a sufficient reason to deny a visa.[23]

Similarly, in a 2005 memorandum, DOS instructs consular officers to narrow the scope of inquiry for F-1 students to their immediate intent rather than ties to the home country,[24] which is consistent with the long line of case law on the intent doctrine.

Practical considerations:

- As F-1 status does not permit the exemption, it is advisable for the employee to convert the employee to an exempt category such as H-1B before filing an immigrant petition. An F-1 worker who files an adjustment of status application may face a charge of preconceived intent during the adjustment of status process (as discussed below).

- If there is no alternative option, the employer will need to strategically plan a permanent residence filing for an F-1 student. After the employer has filed an immigrant petition on behalf of the F-1 worker, it is unlikely that a subsequent F-1 extension or visa issuance will be granted, unless the argument and evidence follows the case law discussed above. There are also risks in traveling abroad and seeking readmission after an employer has filed an immigrant petition on behalf of the F-1 worker.

- F-1 workers will abandon a pending adjustment of status application if they travel internationally before the advance parole is approved.

J-1 Exchange Visitors

Legal standard: In the J-1 visa category, the applicant must have no intention to abandon the for-

eign residence.[25] In the FAM, DOS states that while it is natural for an exchange visitor to expect to reside outside of the homeland for extended periods of time, the consular officer should also refrain from automatically presuming an intent to return due to the presence of a mandated two-year foreign residence requirement:

> The context of the residence abroad requirement for exchange visitor visas inherently differs from the context for B visitor visas or other short-term visas. The statute clearly presupposes that the natural circumstances and conditions of being an exchange visitor do not disqualify that applicant from obtaining a J visa. It is natural that the exchange visitor proposes an extended absence from his homeland (see 9 FAM 41.11 N2). Nonetheless, the consular officer must be satisfied at the time of the application for a visa that an alien possesses the present intent to depart the U.S. at the conclusion of his or her program. However, consular officers should not automatically assume that an exchange visitor visa applicant will return to a residence abroad merely because the applicant is subject to the two-year foreign residence requirement of INA §212(e) and the special restrictions of that section relating to changing nonimmigrant classification and adjusting to lawful permanent residence (LPR) status. A factor to consider is whether the skills that the alien expects to acquire in the United States can be readily and effectively utilized in the country to which he or she is returning.[26]

The converse situation occurs when the J-1 exchange visitor seeks to apply for a waiver of the foreign residence requirement and thereby arguably expresses an intention to remain in the United States after the expiration of the J-1 visa. In general, J-1 visa holders are required to return to the home country for two years before becoming eligible to apply for an H or L visa or for adjustment of status.[27] In some cases, the J-1 holder can request a waiver of the two-year home residence requirement.[28] Given

---

[23] 9 FAM 41.61 N5.

[24] Students and Immigrant Intent, 05 State 180015 (Sept. 28, 2005), *published on* AILA InfoNet at Doc. No. 05110115 (*posted* Nov. 1, 2005). *See also* 9 FAM 41.61 N5.1–5.4.

[25] INA §101(a)(15)(J); 22 CFR Part 62; 9 FAM 41.62 N1.

[26] 9 FAM 41.62 N5.

[27] This applies to a J-1 holder whose program was financed, in whole or in part, by the U.S. government, its agents, or by the alien's foreign government, whose program involved a field subject to the DOS skills list, or who received medical graduate education or training. INA §212(e).

[28] INA §212(e).

that the J-1 holder is already in the United States and that the completion date of his or her exchange program is in sight, does the act of requesting a waiver of the two-year residence requirement represent an intent to remain in the United States and thereby violate the nonimmigrant intent requirement of the J-1? DOS has stated that the act of filing a request for a waiver of the two-year home residency will not, in and of itself, bar an extension of the J-1, but that the individual cannot obtain an extension after the waiver is granted.[29]

Practical considerations:

- As J-1 status does not permit the exemption, it is advisable for the employer to convert the employee to a category that permits the exemption, such as H-1B, before filing an immigrant petition. A J-1 worker who files an adjustment of status application may face a charge of preconceived intent during the adjustment of status process (as discussed below).

- If there is no alternative option, the employer will need to strategically plan a permanent residence filing for a J-1 student. After the employer has filed an immigrant petition on behalf of the J-1 worker, it is unlikely that a subsequent J-1 extension or visa issuance will be granted, unless the argument and evidence are consistent with the case law discussed above. There are also risks in traveling abroad and seeking readmission after an employer has filed an immigrant petition on behalf of the J-1 worker.

- J-1 workers will abandon a pending adjustment of status application if they travel internationally before the advance parole is approved.

Q Cultural Exchange Visitors

Legal standard: A foreign national who is coming to participate in an approved international cultural exchange program must meet the same basic standard as the B, F, and J visa holders—he or she must have "a residence in a foreign country which he has no intention of abandoning."[30] There is not much additional guidance devoted to the Q visa, other than a restatement in the FAM that a "Q nonimmigrant must establish to the satisfaction of the consular officer that he or she has a residence out-

side the United States which he or she has no intention of abandoning."[31]

Practical considerations:

- As Q status does not permit the exemption, it is advisable for the employer to convert the employee to a category that permits an exemption, such as H-1B, before filing an immigrant petition. A Q worker who files an adjustment of status application may face a charge of preconceived intent during the adjustment of status process (as discussed below).

- If there is no alternative option, the employer will need to strategically plan a permanent residence filing for a Q worker. After the employer has filed an immigrant petition on behalf of the Q worker, it is unlikely that a subsequent Q extension or visa issuance will be granted, unless the argument and supporting evidence follows the established case law. There are also risks in traveling abroad and seeking readmission after an employer has filed an immigrant petition on behalf of the Q worker.

- Q workers will abandon a pending adjustment of status application if they travel internationally before the advance parole is approved.

TN NAFTA Professionals

Legal standard: While a Canadian or Mexican professional who seeks to apply for classification under the North American Free Trade Agreement (NAFTA) is not exempted from INA §214(b), the temporary intent requirement is more generous than for the B-1, F-1, J-1, and Q classifications. While the preceding classifications require the applicant to maintain a foreign residence that he or she does not intend to abandon, the TN classification has a lesser nonimmigrant intent requirement. The TN holder must enter only "without the intent to establish permanent residence."[32] The regulations further require that the TN holder's proposed stay must have a:

> reasonable, finite end that does not equate to permanent residence. In order to establish that the alien's entry will be temporary, the alien must demonstrate to the satisfaction of the inspecting immigration officer that his or her work assignment in the United States will end at a predict-

---

[29] Letter, Jin, USIA G.C. (Dec. 18, 1995), *reprinted in* 69 *Interpreter Releases* 47, 51 (Jan. 9, 1998).

[30] INA §101(a)(15)(Q).

[31] 9 FAM 41.57 N5.3.

[32] 8 CFR §214.6(b).

able time and that he or she will depart upon completion of the assignment.[33]

The FAM provides the following additional clarification:

NAFTA Chapter 16 provides the following definition: "Temporary Entry means an entry into the United States without the intent to establish permanent residence." ... The circumstances surrounding an application should reasonably and convincingly indicate that the alien's temporary work assignment in the United States will end predictably and that the alien will depart upon completion of the assignment. An intent to immigrate in the future which is in no way connected to the proposed immediate trip need not in itself result in a finding that the immediate trip is not temporary. An extended stay, even in terms of years, may be temporary, as long as there is no immediate intent to immigrate.[34]

There is no limitation in the statute or regulations regarding the number of times that a TN visa holder can request renewal of the status. This provides the TN holder with a fair amount of flexibility, including the ability to apply for and even hold H-1B status and subsequently revert back to TN status, as long as he or she can demonstrate that the TN assignment is temporary.

However, the situation is more complicated if the TN holder's employer begins permanent residence processing on his or her behalf. In a 1996 legacy Immigration and Naturalization Service (INS) letter, the agency stated that the fact that an applicant for TN admission is the beneficiary of an approved I-140 petition should not be, in and of itself, the reason to deny an application for admission if the applicant's intent is to remain in the United States temporarily.[35] Nevertheless, the filing of the I-140 petition on behalf of the individual should be taken into account with all other factors in determining eligibility for TN classification.[36]

Practical considerations:

- As TN status does not permit the exemption, it is advisable for the employer to convert the employee to a category that permits the exemption,

such as H-1B, before filing an immigrant petition. A TN worker who files an adjustment of status application may face a charge of preconceived intent during the adjustment of status process (as discussed below).

- If there is no alternative option, the employer will need to strategically plan a permanent residence filing for a TN worker. After the employer has filed an immigrant petition on behalf of the TN worker, the employer may experience problems obtaining subsequent TN extensions or visa issuance, unless the argument and evidence are consistent with the case law. There are also risks in traveling abroad and seeking readmission after an employer has filed an immigrant petition on behalf of the TN worker.

- TN workers will abandon a pending adjustment of status application if they travel internationally before the advance parole is approved.

Classifications Exempt from the Presumption of Immigrant Intent

Currently, the nonimmigrant visa classifications that are exempted from the presumption of immigrant intent are H-1B, L-1, and V, and—with certain limitations—E, O-1, and P (except essential support personnel).

H-1B Specialty Workers

Legal standard: In addition to being statutorily exempted from INA §214(b), the foreign national may "legitimately come to the United States for a temporary period as an ... H-1B nonimmigrant and depart voluntarily at the end of his or her authorized stay and, at the same time, lawfully seek to become a permanent resident of the United States."[37] The regulatory provisions also explicitly state that a labor certification or immigrant petition will not be a basis for the denial of a petition or request for extension of H-1B status.[38] DOS further instructs consular officers that "intent of the H-1 applicant in regard to NIV or IV status is totally irrelevant. Thus, not only shall the consular officers not refuse an H-1 visa on this basis, facts relating for foreign residence and

---

[33] *Id. See also* 22 CFR §49.59(c).

[34] 9 FAM 41.59 N5.

[35] LaFleur letter, INS HQ 1815-C (June 18, 1996), *reprinted in* 73 *Interpreter Releases* 970, 979–80 (July 22, 1996).

[36] *Id.*

[37] 8 CFR §214.2(h)(16)(i). *See also* 9 FAM 41.53 N3.1.

[38] 8 CFR §214.2(h)(16)(i). In contrast, the approval of a labor certification or filing of an immigrant petition can be the basis of denying an extension of stay for holders of H-2A, H-2B, and H-3 classification. 8 CFR §214.2(h)(16)(ii).

NIV intent shall not be considered by the officer when adjudicating the H-1 visa application."[39]

In 1999, legacy INS issued a regulation permitting H-1B holders expanded privileges of travel while an adjustment of status application is pending, which the agency discussed in the context of INA §214(b) and the special intent exemption for H-1B and L-1 workers.[40] In the preamble to the interim rule, legacy INS stated:

> Under Section 214(b) of the Immigration and Nationality Act, (Act), most nonimmigrants who apply for adjustment of status to that of permanent residents of the United States are presumed to be intending immigrants and, therefore, are no longer eligible to maintain nonimmigrant status. Section 214(h) of the Act, however, permits aliens described in section 101(a)(15)(H)(i) and (L) of the Act, *i.e.,* temporary workers in specialty occupations, intracompany managerial or executive transferees, and their dependent spouses and children, to maintain their nonimmi-

grant status during the pendency of their applications for adjustment of status.[41]

Practical considerations:

- Due to the full exemption for H-1B beneficiaries, the employer may begin processing for permanent residence at any time without jeopardizing H-1B status.

- Within the allotted time periods, H-1B holders may apply for extensions of stay, visa renewals, and re-entry into the United States in H-1B status regardless of the stage of the permanent residence process.

- Due to the special travel provision for H-1B visa holders, it is not necessary to apply for or wait for advance parole issuance before traveling internationally after an adjustment of status application has been filed.

A Notable Exception—The H-1B1 Under the Chile/Singapore Free Trade Agreement: In 2003, the U.S. trade agreements with Chile and Singapore created the new H-1B1 classifications for nationals of those countries.[42] Although the H-1B1 regulations

---

[39] DOS Cable, 91 State 171115 (May 24, 1991), *reprinted in* 68 *Interpreter Releases* 681–84 (June 3, 1991).

[40] 64 Fed. Reg. 29208 (June 1, 1999), promulgating revised 8 CFR §245.2(a)(4)(ii):

> Under section 245 of the Act. (A) … Except as provided in paragraph (a)(4)(ii)(B) and (C) of this section, the departure of an applicant who is not under exclusion, deportation, or removal proceedings shall be deemed an abandonment of the application constituting grounds for termination of any pending application for adjustment of status, unless the applicant was previously granted advance parole by the Service for such absences, and was inspected upon returning to the United States. … (B) The travel outside of the United States by an applicant for adjustment who is not under exclusion, deportation, or removal proceedings shall not be deemed an abandonment of the application if he or she was previously granted advance parole by the Service for such absences, and was inspected and paroled upon returning to the United States. … (C) The travel outside of the United States by an applicant for adjustment of status who is not under exclusion, deportation, or removal proceeding and who is in lawful H-1 or L-1 status shall not be deemed an abandonment of the application if, upon returning to this country, the alien remains eligible for H or L status, is coming to resume employment with the same employer for whom he or she had previously been authorized to work as an H-1 or L-1 nonimmigrant, and, is in possession of a valid H or L visa (if required) and the original I-797 receipt notice for the application for adjustment of status.

[41] *Id.* at 29209. Interestingly, the rule's preamble went on to discuss the exemption in terms of dual intent by stating:

> In addition, the Service is considering expanding the dual intent concept to cover other long term nonimmigrants who are visiting this country as traders (E-1), investors (E-2), students (F-1, J-1 or M-1), or scholars (J-1), etc. These nonimmigrants, who are typically authorized to stay in this country for considerable lengths of time, often need to make short overseas travels during their authorized stay. Under the exemption (often referred to as dual intent) doctrine, these nonimmigrants would be able to maintain valid nonimmigrant status and travel overseas without advance parole while applying for adjustment of status.

Id. However, the agency has not taken the necessary steps to expand this concept of full intent exemption beyond H-1B and L-1 classifications. In fact, when AILA recently asked the agency whether it would consider permitting E-1, E-2, E-3, and O-1 holders to travel without advance parole while an adjustment of status application is pending, USCIS replied that the agency "appreciates the impact on the business community and has taken the request under advisement. We hope to promulgate regulations in the future, but are now focusing our limited resources on other DHS priorities." AILA/USCIS Questions and Answers (Apr. 2, 2008), *published on* AILA InfoNet at Doc. No. 08040235 (*posted* Apr. 2, 2008).

[42] United States-Chile Free Trade Agreement Implementation Act, Pub. L. No. 108-77, 117 Stat. 909 (2003); United States-Singapore Free Trade Agreement Implementation Act, Pub. L. No. 108-78, 117 Stat. 947 (2003).

in many ways track the H-1B regulations, there are several significant differences. For example, the H-1B1 classification is granted in one-year increments only, is subject to INA §214(b), and requires that the applicant not intend to establish permanent residence in the United States.[43] The FAM provision contains an intent requirement for the H-1B1 that is virtually identical to that of the TN, another classification arising from a U.S. free trade agreement:

Both agreements provide for the temporary entry of professionals into the United States. Temporary entry is defined in both agreements as "an entry into the United States without the intent to establish permanent residence." The alien must satisfy the consular officer that the proposed stay is temporary. A temporary period has a reasonable, finite end that does not equate to permanent residence. The circumstances surrounding an application should reasonably and convincingly indicate that the alien's temporary work assignment in the United States will end predictably and that the alien will depart upon completion of the assignment. An intent to immigrate in the future, which is in no way connected to the proposed immediate trip, need not in itself result in a finding that the immediate trip is not temporary. An extended stay, even in terms of years, may be temporary, as long as there is no immediate intent to immigrate.[44]

Practical considerations:

- As the H-1B1 does not permit the full exemption, employers who wish to sponsor H-1B1 holders for permanent residence should either convert such employees to H-1B status, which permits full exemption, or should follow a strategy similar to that for TN holders (as discussed above).

- If permanent residence is sought, an extension or new visa stamp may be difficult to obtain unless the argument and evidence are consistent with the case law discussed above.

- The H-1B1 is not subject to the 240-day automatic extension of work authorization upon a timely filed extension.[45] Thus, these limitations pose another layer of concern that may make this

specialty occupation carve-out more of a short-term value.

L-1 Intracompany Transferees

Legal standard: Like H-1B visa holders, L-1 visa holders are statutorily exempted from INA §214(b) and, by regulation, may "legitimately come to the United States for a temporary period as an L-1 nonimmigrant and, at the same time, depart voluntarily at the end of his or her authorized stay and, at the same time, lawfully seek to become a permanent resident of the United States provided he or she intends to depart voluntarily at the end of his or her authorized stay."[46] The regulatory provisions also explicitly state that a labor certification or immigrant petition is not a basis for the denial of a petition or request for extension for L-1 status.[47] In 1999, legacy INS issued a regulation permitting L-1 holders expanded privileges of travel while an adjustment of status application is pending, which the agency discussed in the context of INA §214(b) and the special intent exemption for H-1B and L-1 workers.[48]

Practical considerations:

- Due to the full exemption for L-1 beneficiaries, the employer may begin processing for permanent residence at any time without jeopardizing L-1 status.

- Within the allotted time periods, L-1 holders may apply for extensions of stay, visa renewals, and re-entry into the United States in H-1B status, regardless of the stage of the permanent residence process.

- Due to the special travel provision for L-1 holders, it is not necessary to apply for or wait for advance parole issuance before traveling internationally after an adjustment of status application has been filed.

V Visa (LIFE Act)

The V classification is the third category of visas explicitly exempted from INA §214(b) by statute. It stands to reason that a visa classification specifically enacted to permit certain spouses and children of lawful permanent residents to obtain expedited entry into the United States permits the exemption. A further discussion of the exemption for V visa holders

---

[43] *See* U.S. Customs and Border Protection Memorandum, J. Ahern, "Free Trade Agreements with Chile and Singapore" (Apr.19, 2004), *published on* AILA InfoNet at Doc. 05040166 (*posted* Apr. 1, 2005).

[44] 9 FAM 41.53 N28.5.

[45] 8 CFR §274a.12(b)(20).

[46] 8 CFR §214.2(*l*)(16). *See also* FAM 41.53 N3.1.

[47] 8 CFR §214.2(*l*)(16).

[48] *See* note 40, *supra*.

can be found in the comments accompanying the V visa regulation.[49]

E-1/E-2/E-3 Nonimmigrant Treaty Classifications

Legal standard: The classic E treaty classifications—E-1 treaty trader and E-2 treaty investor—*do not* enjoy the same level of full exemption as the H-1B or L classifications, but E-1 and E-2 holders may pursue permanent residence in the United States in most circumstances.[50] By regulation, foreign nationals under INA 101(a)(15)(E)

> shall maintain an intention to depart the United States upon the expiration or termination of E-1 or E-2 status. However, an application for initial admission, change of status, or extension of stay in E classification may not be denied solely on the basis of an approved request for permanent labor certification or a filed or approved immigrant visa preference petition.[51]

The FAM further states:

> An applicant for an E visa need not establish intent to proceed to the United States for a specific temporary period of time. Nor does an applicant for an E visa need to have a residence in a foreign country which the applicant does not intend to abandon. The alien may sell his or her residence and move all household effects to the U.S. The alien's expression of an unequivocal intent to return when the E status ends is normally sufficient, in the absence of specific indications of evidence that the alien's intent is to the contrary. If there are such objective indications, inquiry is justified to assess the applicant's true intent.[52]

On May 11, 2005, Congress enacted the E-3 classification for Australian professionals, codified at INA §101(a)(15)(E). DOS subsequently amended its regulations to include the new E-3 category. In its regulations, DOS imposes the identical intent requirement for all of the E classifications, requiring only that the foreign national "intends to depart upon the termination" of the status.[53] The FAM further clarifies:

a. Temporary entry for treaty aliens in specialty occupations is the same standard used for treaty traders/investors.

b. The alien's expression of an unequivocal intent to return when the E-3 status ends is normally sufficient, in the absence of specific evidence that the alien's intent is to the contrary.

c. The applicant must satisfy you that he or she plans to depart the United States upon termination of status; however, he or she does not need to establish intent to proceed to the United States for a specific temporary period of time. Nor does an applicant for an E-3 visa need to have a residence in a foreign country that the applicant does not intend to abandon.

d. The alien may sell his or her residence and move all household effects to the United States.

e. An E-3 applicant may be a beneficiary of an immigrant visa (IV) petition filed on his or her behalf.[54]

Practical considerations:

- Although the E classifications have a more limited exemption standard than the H-1B and L-1 classifications, in practical terms employers can begin processing for permanent residence at any time without jeopardizing E status. However, some practitioners may find it advisable to time the permanent residence process in a way to avoid the need for E extensions midstream.

- E visa holders are not protected by the special exemption travel provision for H-1B and L-1 holders, and therefore will abandon a pending adjustment of status application if they travel internationally before the advance parole is approved.

- E-3s are not allowed the 240-day automatic extension of work authorization upon a timely filed extension,[55] which may create timing issues.

O-1 Extraordinary Ability

Legal standard: Similar to those governing E classifications, the regulatory provisions describing the O-1 extraordinary ability classification permit the intent exemption. The regulations state, "The ap-

---

[49] 66 Fed. Reg. 46697 (Sept. 7, 2001).

[50] Letter, Bednarz, HQ 214e-C, 245-C (Oct. 1, 1993), *reprinted in* 70 *Interpreter Releases* 1444, 1456–58 (Nov. 1, 1993). *See also Lauvik v. INS*, 910 F.2d 658, 660–61 (9th Cir. 1990).

[51] 8 CFR §214.2(e)(5).

[52] FAM 41.51 N15.

[53] 22 CFR §§41.51(a)–(c).

[54] 9 FAM 41.51 N16.6.

[55] *See* 8 CFR §274a.12(b)(20).

proval of a permanent labor certification or the filing of a preference petition for an alien shall not be the basis for denying an O-1 petition, a request for admission, change of status, or extension of stay."[56] The regulation goes on to say that an alien may have a legitimate temporary need to be in the United States in O-1 status, complete the assignment, and return to his or her home country, but at the same time seek permanent residence in the United States.[57] However, despite the intent exemption for the O-1, the statute explicitly imposes a nonimmigrant intent requirement on O-2 support personnel.[58]

The INA does not require an applicant for an O-1 visa to have a residence abroad that he or she does not intend to abandon, nor does it address the issue of temporariness of stay for O-1 nonimmigrants. As a consequence, the FAM directs consular officers to not apply any standard of temporariness or immigrant intent unless there are specific indications or evidence that the alien does not intend to comply with the terms of the petition approved on his or her behalf.[59]

Unlike the O-1 nonimmigrant, the O-2 visa applicant must satisfy the consular officer that he or she has a residence abroad and no intent to abandon that residence.[60]

Practical considerations:

- Although the O-1 classification has a more limited intent exemption standard than the H-1B and L-1 classifications, in practical terms employers can begin processing for permanent residence at any time without jeopardizing O-1 status. However, some practitioners may find it advisable to time the permanent residence process to avoid the need for O-1 extensions midstream.

- O-1 visa holders are not protected by the special intent exemption travel provision for H-1B and L-1 holders, and therefore will abandon a pending adjustment of status application if they travel internationally before the advance parole is approved.

- As the O-2 support personnel category requires nonimmigrant intent and an unrelinquished for-

eign residence, filing for permanent residence requires a strategic approach. After the employer has filed an immigrant petition on behalf of the O-2 worker, it is unlikely that a subsequent O-2 visa will be granted or an existing one extended. There are also risks in traveling abroad and seeking readmission after an employer has filed an immigrant petition on behalf of the O-2 support personnel worker.

P Performers, Artists, and Athletes

Legal standard: The P visa provision contains an interesting contradiction in that it requires maintenance of a foreign residence, but at the same time states that pursuing permanent residence does not in and of itself disqualify an individual from P status. The statutory definition of the P classification begins with the clause "an alien having a foreign residence which the alien has no intention of abandoning."[61] The FAM emphasizes, "[E]very P visa applicant must satisfy the consular officer that he or she has a residence abroad which he or she has no intention of abandoning."[62]

However, the regulations also provide, "The approval of a permanent labor certification or the filing of a preference petition for an alien shall not be the basis for denying a P petition, a request to extend such a petition, or the alien's admission, change of status, or extension of stay."[63] The regulations state further, "The alien may legitimately come to the United States for a temporary period as a P nonimmigrant and depart voluntarily at the end of his or her authorized stay and, at the same time, lawfully seek to become a permanent resident of the United States."[64]

Like with the limitation on the intent exemption for O-2 support personnel, the regulations state that the provision permitting the intent exemption for

---

[56] 8 CFR §214.2(o)(13).

[57] *Id.*

[58] INA §101(a)(15)(O)(ii) requires that the O-2 holder have "a foreign residence which the alien has no intention of abandoning." Also, 8 CFR §214.2(o)(13) refers only to O-1 petitions, not to O-2 support personnel.

[59] 9 FAM 41.55 N5.1.

[60] *Id.*

[61] INA §101(a)(15)(P).

[62] 9 FAM 41.56 N9.1.

[63] 8 CFR §214.2(p)(15).

[64] *Id.* The FAM states, "DHS has determined that the approval of a permanent labor certification or the filing of a preference petition for an alien shall not be a basis for denying a P petition, a request to extend such a petition, or the alien's application for admission, change of status, or extension of stay. The alien may legitimately come to the United States for a temporary period as a P nonimmigrant and depart voluntarily at the end of his or her authorized stay and, at the same time, lawfully seek to become a permanent resident of the United States." 9 FAM 41.56 N9.2.

aliens holding P status does not extend to "essential support personnel" accompanying a P-1 alien.[65]

Practical considerations:

- Although the P classifications have a more limited intent exemption standard than the H-1B and L-1 classifications, in practical terms employers can begin processing for permanent residence at any time without jeopardizing P status. However, due to the foreign-residence requirement, some practitioners may find it advisable to time the permanent residence process in a way to avoid the need for P extensions midstream.

- P visa holders are not protected by the special intent exemption travel provision for H-1B and L-1 holders, and therefore will abandon a pending adjustment of status application if they travel internationally before the advance parole is approved.

- As the P essential support personnel category requires nonimmigrant intent and an unrelinquished foreign residence, filing for permanent residence requires a strategic approach. After the employer has filed an immigrant petition on behalf of the P-2 worker, it is unlikely that a subsequent P-2 visa will be issued or an existing one extended. There are also risks in traveling abroad and seeking readmission after an employer has filed an immigrant petition on behalf of the P essential support personnel worker.

Classifications for Which the Intent Doctrine is Silent

R-1 Religious Workers

Legal standard: Neither the statutory nor regulatory provisions for R classification make specific reference to a nonimmigrant intent requirement. The FAM confirms that there is no requirement for an unrelinquished foreign residence:

> There is no requirement in the INA that applicants for R status establish that they have a residence in a foreign country which they have no intention of abandoning. The INA limits R nonimmigrants to a total period of stay not to exceed five years. The alien's stated intention to depart the United States when his or her status ends is normally sufficient to satisfy INA §101(a)(15)(R)(ii), absent specific indications or evidence that the alien's intent is to the contrary.[66]

Practical considerations:

- Although the R classifications have a more limited intent exemption standard than the H-1B and L-1 classifications, in practical terms employers can begin processing for permanent residence at any time without jeopardizing R status. However, some practitioners may find it advisable to time the permanent residence process in a way to avoid the need for R extensions or re-entries midstream.

- R visa holders are not protected by the special intent exemption travel provision for H-1B and L-1 holders, and therefore will abandon a pending adjustment of status application if they travel internationally before the advance parole is approved.

I International Media Personnel

- Similarly, neither the statute nor regulations for I classification make reference to a nonimmigrant intent requirement. The FAM confirms the lack of nonimmigrant intent requirement for this category.[67]

THE INTENT DOCTRINE IN ADJUSTMENT OF STATUS

Prevalence of the Adjustment of Status Option

Ordinarily, when an individual seeks permanent resident status in the United States, there are two primary methods for reaching the end goal: adjustment of status in the United States or consular processing at a U.S. consular post abroad. These days, most applicants prefer adjustment of status because the process for both family-based and employment-based applicants is typically faster and less expensive. In most family– and employment-based applications for which the priority date is current, the immigrant petition (Forms I-130 or I-140) can be filed concurrently with the adjustment of status application. As a result, typically a family-based adjustment of status application with a current priority date—most commonly encountered in the immediate relative category—takes between four and eight months to process. The same application would take a year or more if the applicant chose to process through a consulate. An employment-based application—again assuming the beneficiary's priority date is current—also often is adjudicated within one year.

Another advantage to filing for adjustment of status in the United States is the applicant's ability to file Form I-765 to obtain work authorization while the adjustment case is in process. Work authorization in this context is available even if the beneficiary falls out of status before the work permit is adjudicated, for example if there are only six weeks remaining on a TN when a Canadian nurse marries his U.S. sweetheart and wants to keep working. In some cases, an applicant who files for adjustment based on an immediate relative petition can obtain work authorization and avoid unlawful presence bars even when he or she was not in lawful status when the immigrant petition and Form I-485 were filed.[68] In employment-based filings, the statute even provides for green card portability, permitting adjustment applicants to switch to a same or similar position with a different employer before the adjustment is adjudicated as long as the change in position occurs at least 180 days after the filing of the adjustment of status application.[69]

Adjustment of status has not always been the preferred route. Not long ago, when USCIS processing times were 18 to 24 months for a straightforward I-485 and green card portability was not an option, applicants often would opt for consular processing. As circumstances evolve, beneficiaries again may elect to consular process despite the increased costs associated with foreign travel and the inconvenience of interrupting a life in the United States to spend a period of time overseas. However, currently adjustment is viewed by most applicants as the preferred route.

Preconceived Intent Issues

The current preference for adjustment of status processing has consequences for the continued viability of the person's underlying nonimmigrant visa and the ultimate approvability of the adjustment application. Unless the individual is in the United States in a nonimmigrant category that permits the exemption, the person seeking adjustment of status must be able to show that he or she did not have immigrant intent at the time he or she entered in the nonimmigrant status.[70] While this is less frequently a problem for employment-based applicants, who are usually in the United States in H or L status and therefore may have immigrant intent, it can be a problematic issue for employment-based applicants who are in a status such as B, F, J, Q, R, or TN, or some other status that does not explicitly allow the

exemption. It is also a significant issue for family-based adjustment applicants who are not in a status that permits either immigrant intent or the exemption. A finding of preconceived intent to immigrate or being deemed inadmissible as a nonimmigrant based on present immigrant intent is a potential basis for discretionary denial of adjustment of status.[71]

Changed Circumstances and the 30/60 Day Rule

What if there are changes to the activities contemplated under a particular nonimmigrant visa status? What effect does engaging in such activities have on the representations made to the consulate at the time of application?

DOS created a narrowing framework to the intent doctrine based on timeframes within entry, known as the "30/60 day rule." DOS analysis creates three sets of presumptions, depending on whether activities take place within 30 days of U.S. entry, between 30 and 60 days after entry, or more than 60 days after entry.[72] The types of actions that raise red flags under this framework include B-2 changing to F-1, B-2 applying for adjustment of status, and TN applying for adjustment of status. If a foreign national applies for a B-2 visa, enters the United States, and then files an adjustment of status within 30 days of entry, the consulate is likely to presume that the alien had preconceived intent when applying for a U.S. nonimmigrant visa. If the action falls between 30 and 60 days, the DOS framework creates a rebuttable presumption of misrepresentation, against which the foreign national can provide documentation to show nonimmigrant intent. If the consulate is not persuaded with the rebuttal evidence, the foreign national can seek an advisory opinion from DOS. Finally, if the action occurs after the 60th day, it does not trigger a presumption of misrepresentation or preconceived intent.[73]

The 30/60 day rule is technically a DOS rule. USCIS does not contain a similar rule, but it often relies on the rule in its adjudication process. Practitioners are urged to keep the 30/60 day rule in mind even in adjustment of status cases.

---

[68] INA §245.

[69] INA §204(j).

[70] INA §214(b).

[71] *See Jain v. INS*, 612 F.2d 683, 688–89 (2d Cir. 1979); *Von Pervieux v. INS*, 572 F.2d 114, 118 (3d Cir. 1978).

[72] 9 FAM 40.63 N4.

[73] *Id.*

Practical Considerations: Ways to Avoid the Intent Trap

▪ First, remember that the question of intent arises in relation to the foreign national's subjective intention at the time he or she entered or applied for his or her underlying nonimmigrant status, not at the time he or she applies for adjustment. If the foreign national had no intention to stay at the time he or she applied, but circumstances changed thereafter, then there is not necessarily an intent problem.[74] Documentation of these cases is limited only by the attorney's creativity.[75]

▪ Second, question the foreign national to determine whether the distinction in *Lauvik v. INS*[76] applies—did the foreign national have a long-term desire to remain in the United States at the time of nonimmigrant entry or application for the nonimmigrant status, but no short-term or immediate intent to immigrate?[77]

▪ Third, foreign nationals should be counseled not to take any actions that communicate a present intent to immigrate prior to application for or entry in nonimmigrant status. People who abandon their foreign residences, leave their jobs, close their bank accounts, and liquidate their assets have a difficult time proving they did not have a present intent to immigrate. This is true even if their present intent was to move to a new place when they returned, use the asset sale proceeds to finance their trip, or change jobs or banks when they returned. In a world in which people are increasingly transitory, these factors are important, because often foreign nationals are unaware of the potential consequences of their actions.

▪ Fourth and finally, foreign nationals should not engage in a rapid sequence of events leading up to the application for permanent residence that make the conclusion of preconceived intent to immigrate all but inescapable. The BIA has repeatedly applied this "rapid sequence of events" test in denying adjustment or analyzing whether adjustment should be denied based on preconceived intent.[78] In essence, this is a "smell" test—if it seems as though the foreign national client changed his or her mind very quickly without any sort of reasonable explanation, it is very likely that USCIS, in its discretion, will deny adjustment of status based on preconceived intent by looking at the totality of the circumstances that suggests the existence of preconceived intent.

Practical Considerations: When the Intent Trap Cannot Be Avoided

In immediate-relative family cases, despite the presumption of immigrant intent, there is a line of cases that protects at a minimum immediate relatives—and possibly others—from denial of their

---

[74] For example, your client who entered in R status may be dating an American but have no intention of marrying that person. She renews her R status in the United States and then four or five months later decides to marry. As long as you and you client can document this change in the relationship, the case should be approved for adjustment of status.

[75] For example, in the R marriage case in the preceding footnote, if the proposal was made in a public place, the adjustment applicant could present the sales receipt for the ring, the credit card bill for the restaurant, affidavits from family or friends to whom she communicated the proposal, etc. Do not rely on the assumption that religious workers are inherently truthful, since it is clear from the changes to the R and religious worker immigrant categories that USCIS does not agree with that proposition.

[76] 910 F.2d 658 (9th Cir. 1990).

[77] For example, a foreign national enters as a student and thinks it would be wonderful to get a job and eventually stay in the United States. However, at the time of entry in F-1 status the student has no idea where he or she might work, no job offer, and no firm and specific opportunity to immigrate despite his or her ardent desire to do so. Under *Lauvik*, this person has no intent problem. In another example, some practitioners believe that even the promise of a nursing job by a specific hospital on graduation from nursing school—necessarily a permanent residence application if the nurse does not qualify for H-1 or TN—is not sufficient to create a problem under *Lauvik* until such time as an application is actually filed, because things could change.

[78] *See, e.g., Matter of Patel*, 19 I&N Dec. 774 (BIA 1988), citing *Matter of Lasike*, 17 I&N Dec. 445, 446–48 (1980) (deportation upheld where alien refused to depart after denial of adjustment of status to special immigrant minister because none of his documentary evidence established that he had been carrying on vocation of minister of a religious denomination for two years prior to denial of application; discretionary denial of adjustment based on preconceived intent upheld where alien applied for "ministerial recognition" only 11 days after entry with tourist visa and five months later obtained "Christian Worker's Certificate" entitling him to conduct religious services, letter of recommendation for ministry overseas predated his entry, and he started employment immediately upon entry but falsely stated in his request for extension of tourist visa that his intent was only to continue in his visitor status); *Matter of Ro*, 16 I&N Dec. 93 (1977) (denial of application for adjustment on preconceived intent where petitioner applied for adjustment of status within 16 days of his entry into the United States).

adjustment applications if the only basis for the denial is alleged preconceived intent.

In *Matter of Cavazos*,[79] the BIA reversed an immigration judge who denied adjustment to the spouse of a U.S. citizen solely on the basis of preconceived immigrant intent. The BIA held that in the case of immediate relatives seeking a grant of adjustment of status, the INS Operating Instructions in effect in 1977 and then 8 CFR §§242.5(a)(2) and (3) essentially negated "preconceived intent as an adverse factor in meritorious case."[80] In other words, if the only adverse factor is preconceived intent, immediate relative adjustment applications should be granted.

Practitioners should be aware, however, that there are some issues relating to the decisions in *Matter of Cavazos* and the case following it, *Matter of Ibrahim*.[81] First, because these cases are quite old, often USCIS examiners are not aware of their existence. Second, there have been a number of recent cases—involving Visa Waiver entrants and other nonimmigrants—in which preconceived intent was one of several factors considered in denying adjustment, and the consequences were quite severe.[82]

Therefore, sometimes there are intent-related fact patterns in both the family-based and employment-based context making it simply unadvisable for the applicant to proceed with adjustment of status. In those situations, the foreign national may need to file the permanent residence case through consular processing. And in some cases, the foreign national may be able to gain admittance to the United States while the consular case is pending.

- For example, if a foreign national is from a visa waiver country and is married a U.S. citizen, he or she may be able to enter the United States as a visitor while the I-130 and the consular applications are pending. While entry under these circumstances is discretionary with the admitting U.S. Customs and Border Protection (CBP) officer, entry is often granted. The key is to be truthful and to carefully document both the intent to depart on completion of the temporary stay and the intent to consular process.

- In another case, an applicant from Germany was permitted to enter on visa waiver three times during the 13 months it took to process the immigrant visa.

- In a third case, a Canadian applicant who was the beneficiary of a pending I-130 was permitted to enter as a visitor to help her husband, who was immobilized from a broken leg. In seeking entry, the foreign national assured the CBP officer of her intent to process at the U.S. consulate in Montreal, and provided a copy of the I-130 indicating consular processing, the filing receipt, and a physician's letter documenting her husband's medical condition.

CONCLUSION

As is evident from the foregoing discussion, there are abundant complexities within the doctrine of intent. Most of it is subject to interpretation and all of it is extremely fact-specific. The case law supports a more reasonable and traditional approach to the intent doctrine than the agencies have employed in practice. There is also much that the practitioner can affect positively by addressing the issue earlier and developing strategies to deal with the problem at the outset of the matter. While most practitioners clearly would prefer to not come face to face with the issue at all, the authors hope that this article at least shifts the moment of facing the issue from the visa or adjustment interview to the first contact that counsel has with the client.

---

[79] 17 I&N Dec. 215 (BIA 1980).

[80] *Id.* The BIA followed the same reasoning in *Matter of Ibrahim*, 18 I&N Dec. 55 (BIA 1981). Interestingly, these decisions were actually later incorporated into the same Operating Instruction that they had cited.

[81] 18 I&N Dec. 55 (BIA 1981).

[82] For example, a visa waiver entrant whose adjustment is denied based on preconceived intent in conjunction with other facts is unable to appeal or challenge that denial as a result of entering under the Visa Waiver Program, and if that person is subject to the re-entry bars contained in INA §212(a)(9)(B) as a result of a visa overstay, the person would not be eligible to consular process without a waiver. In regard to the denials it should be noted that the authors found no cases in which preconceived intent was the sole basis for the denial of the adjustment application—the denial always found other culpable conduct. In one case for example, the denial was based on a combination of preconceived intent and alien smuggling, and thus the BIA's departure from its usual policy and case law was justified. *Mamoka v. INS*, 43 F.3d 184 (5th Cir. 1995); *Matter of Patel*, 19 I&N Dec. 774 (BIA 1988), citing *Matter of Lasike*, 17 I&N Dec. 445, 446–48 (1980).

WHERE THE PROPOSED REGULATIONS FOR THE RELIGIOUS WORKER VISA PROGRAM ARE TAKING US—A COMPARATIVE ANALYSIS

by David Grunblatt, Daniel Retter, and Michael C. Runde[*]

INTRODUCTION

As this article goes to press, the proposed regulations relating to "special immigrant and non-immigrant religious workers" remain just that—proposed—after opportunities for comment were made available from April to June 2007[1] and once again from November 1 to November 16, 2007.[2]

The objective of U.S. Citizenship and Immigration Services (USCIS) in promulgating these proposed regulations was announced in the preamble to

---

[*] **David Grunblatt** is a partner at Proskauer Rose LLP, heading its immigration practice group. He served as chair of AILA's New York Chapter, was formerly chair of the Committee on Ethics and Professional Responsibility, and is currently chair of the Vermont Service Center Liaison Committee. He was formerly chair of the New York State Bar Association's Committee on Immigration and Nationality Law and was chair of the Committee on Immigration and Nationality Law at the New York County Lawyers Association.

Daniel Retter practices in New York City as of counsel to the law firm of Herrick Feinstein LLP, with offices in New York and New Jersey. He was the secretary of the AILA South Florida Chapter and former co-chair of the Unauthorized Practice of Law Committee of the AILA New York Chapter. Mr. Retter also maintains a fully staffed office in Moscow, where he spends one week each month. He has been an adjunct professor at Fordham Law School and Queens College teaching immigration law. He has contributed to AILA's *Immigration & Nationality Law Handbook*, and has lectured at previous AILA conferences.

Michael C. Runde practices immigration law as a shareholder of Hochstatter, McCarthy & Rivas, S.C. Mr. Runde served as chair of AILA's Wisconsin Chapter. His practice is concentrated in business and employment immigration, including religious worker matters. He speaks regularly on employment-based immigration issues, and is currently on several AILA national committees. Mr. Runde is a graduate of the University of Notre Dame Law School. He is listed in *The Best Lawyers in America* and *The International Who's Who of Corporate Immigration Lawyers*.

The authors thank John Huleatt and the legal team at Church Communities International for allowing them to use and modify their schematic analysis of 8 CFR §§204.5 and 214.2 as proposed.

[1] *See* 72 Fed. Reg. 20442 (Apr. 25, 2007) (proposed regulations).

[2] *See* 72 Fed. Reg. 61821 (Nov. 1, 2007) (reopening comment period).

the proposed regulation and in a communication to the public on April 19, 2007: "The proposed rule focuses on how the agency can best ensure the integrity of the religious worker program by eliminating opportunities for fraud in the program, while, at the same time, streamlining the process for legitimate petitioners."[3]

Whether or not this proposed regulation or a version very similar has become final by the time you are reading this article, what we can conclude confidently is that USCIS has not been successful in fulfilling either of these objectives.

In its comments and summary preceding the proposed regulation, USCIS blithely concludes that this rule does not raise any concerns under the Religious Freedom Restoration Act of 1993.[4] However, it is clear that many of the documentary requirements and obligations imposed on a religious entity are burdensome, intrusive, and totally unnecessary as tools to fulfill the USCIS mandate to reduce fraud.

USCIS relies heavily on a 1999 Government Accountability Office report[5] that purported to find a high incident of false statements by petitioners with regard to applicant members of religious organizations, and on a USCIS Office of Fraud Detection and National Security assessment, which purported to find a 33 percent rate of fraud in the program.[6]

With these concerns in mind, USCIS proposed a number of changes, summarized in its April 19, 2007, announcement.

---

[3] *See* USCIS Fact Sheet, "USCIS Proposes Revisions for Religious Worker Visa Classifications" (Apr. 19, 2007), *published on* AILA InfoNet at Doc. No. 07041912 (*posted* Apr. 19, 2007).

[4] 72 Fed. Reg. 20442, 20445 (Apr. 25, 2007). The Religious Freedom Restoration Act, Pub. L. No. 103-141, 107 Stat. 1488, is codified as amended at 42 USC 2000bb *et seq.*

[5] Government Accountability Office, "Visa Issuance: Issues Concerning the Religious Worker Visa Program" (GAO/NCIAD-99-67, Mar. 26, 1999), *available at* www.gao.gov/archive/1999/ns99067.pdf.

[6] A summary of the assessment is available at www.uscis.gov/files/nativedocuments/Relig_Worker_Fraud_Jul06.pdf.

PETITIONING REQUIREMENTS

▪ USCIS proposes to require the filing of a petition in every instance. (The requirement already exists for special immigrants and for organizations seeking to extend the stay or adjust status for nonimmigrant religious workers already in the United States.)[7]

Comment: This requirement imposes a significant additional burden on sponsoring religious entities, but many would concede that there is a very rational relationship between this requirement and USCIS's fraud prevention objective. A strict time limit should be imposed on USCIS for adjudication of such petitions.

▪ The Petition for a Nonimmigrant Worker (Form I-129) or Petition for Special Immigrant (Form I-360) must be completed and submitted by the employing U.S. organization.[8]

Comment: It is unclear as to what "fraud prevention" objective is fulfilled by this additional restriction on the filing of I-360 petitions. It also is inaccurate to characterize in all instances the relationship between the entity and the individual (who may be engaging in a religious vocation) as employer–employee.

▪ Petitioning employers are required to submit an attestation (included in the Forms I-129 and I-360) verifying the worker's qualifications, the nature of the job offered, and the legitimacy of the organization.[9]

Comment: The notion of including an attestation is not in and of itself burdensome and inappropriate. What is problematic, as you see when reviewing the regulatory language described below, is the content of these attestations.

ON-SITE INSPECTIONS

▪ The regulation notifies petitioner that USCIS may conduct on-site inspections of the organization, a practice that was already implemented prior to promulgation of this proposed regulation.

Comment: It is reasonable for USCIS to assume that inspections would increase deterrence and detection of fraudulent petitions, and the intru-

siveness of the process may have to be tolerated. The regulation, however, fails to provide the opportunity for a religious entity to respond to a negative report and provide appropriate explanation. USCIS should be obligated to produce a written report articulating the basis for any negative finding and describing the circumstances of the visit to assure that the inspector understood the nature of the entity. This is particularly important given the "all or none" context created by a site visit. The wrong person coming to the wrong place at the wrong time can come to the wrong conclusion. In addition, undue delay has been associated with the implementation of the site-visits program.

EVIDENTIARY REQUIREMENTS FOR PETITIONING ORGANIZATIONS

▪ The proposed regulations require that a petitioning organization submit a currently valid determination letter from the Internal Revenue Service showing that it is exempt from income taxation as a religious organization.[10]

Comment: No enforcement objective is fulfilled by restricting eligibility to those organizations that actually have Internal Revenue Code §501(c)(3) designation. As a practical matter, such a designation always would be supplemented in any petition (usually at the request of USCIS) with factual substantiation of the qualifications of the organization as a religious entity. As a practical matter, the 501(c)(3) designation is almost meaningless and an unnecessary burden. This is compounded by the fact that no one fully understands what is meant by a "currently valid" determination.

NONIMMIGRANT RELIGIOUS WORKER CLASSIFICATION

▪ USCIS is proposing to reduce the standard initial period of stay for nonimmigrant religious workers from three years to one. The revision gives the agency the opportunity to review whether the terms of the R-1 visa have been met. (Requests for two potential extensions of two years each will be considered.)[11]

Comment: Limiting the initial petition approval period to one year is clearly onerous and burden-

---

[7] *See* USCIS Fact Sheet, *supra* note 3.

[8] *Id.*

[9] *Id.*

[10] *Id.*

[11] *Id.*

some and has no similar parallel in the nonimmigrant category, with the exception of L-1 "new businesses."[12] While USCIS may have an interest in a "second look" or "look back" subsequent to approval of the petition, requiring the refiling of a petition almost as soon as it has been granted (given the considerable backlogs in processing) is on its face unreasonable.

SPECIAL IMMIGRANT RELIGIOUS WORKERS

- USCIS is expanding its interpretation of prior work experience to include work that is not in the exact same position as the job offered.[13]

Comment: This is a reasonable and welcome change.

- The proposed regulations allow for a short break in the continuity of the required two-year prior experience when the beneficiary was engaged in further religious training or on a sabbatical.[14]

Comment: This is a reasonable and welcome change.

NEW DEFINITIONS AND PROPOSED CHANGES TO EXISTING DEFINITIONS

- To streamline the regulations, the proposal focuses on the distinctions between workers in a "religious vocation" and workers in a "religious occupation," whether in a professional capacity or not.[15]

Comment: This is a simplification of the definitions, but does not eliminate the confusion generated by the language of the definitions.

- A definition of "denominational membership" is added to clarify how a petitioner can establish that the beneficiary is a member in the same religious denomination as the U.S. employer seeking to employ him or her.[16]

Comment: A broader and expansive definition of denominational membership should have been considered. Given that in many religious groupings there are a myriad of very closely related entities with similar systems of belief and practice,

they should not be classified as separate denominations, even if they are conventionally viewed as separate.

- Expands the definition of "religious occupation" to focus on the duties that "primarily, directly, and substantially relate[] to the religious beliefs or creed of the denomination." Such a change distinguishes between committed religious work and nonqualifying work that, while it may be incident to religious duties, cannot by itself warrant classification in the religious worker category.[17]

Comment: It is hard to know whether in real world situations (*e.g.,* with respect to hospital workers) this distinction can be made easily.

- A clear distinction is made between "bona fide nonprofit religious organizations" and "bona fide organizations which are affiliated with the religious denomination" to account for the two types of petitioners who may seek to employ religious workers.[18]

Comment: The technical requirements for unaffiliated religious denomination appear to be restrictive.

- "Ministers" are defined as individuals duly authorized by religious denominations to conduct religious worship and other duties performed by clergy. The proposal adds that the minister must be "fully trained according to the denomination's standards."[19]

Comment: The implicit assumption that there would be a minimum requirement of formal training within a seminary may not be applicable to many denominations.

- The term "religious denomination" applies to a religious group or community of believers governed or administered under some form of ecclesiastical government.[20]

Comment: Many very well-established religions do not have an "ecclesiastical government" associated with them.

- The proposed regulations redefine "religious vocation" to mean a formal lifetime commitment to a religious way of life.[21]

---

[12] *See* 8 CFR §214.2(*l*)(7)(i)(A)(3).

[13] *See* USCIS Fact Sheet, *supra* note 3.

[14] *Id.*

[15] *Id.*

[16] *Id.*

[17] *Id.*

[18] *Id.*

[19] *Id.*

[20] *Id.*

[21] *Id.*

Comment: The inclusion of "lifetime commitment" is unnecessarily restrictive and precludes those truly in a vocation on an interim basis as prescribed in many religious denominations.

As reflected in our comments, it is disappointing that USCIS was not more sensitive to the burden that it is imposing on religious entities. The analysis of the regulation that you will find in the schematic below, which places the language of the current (prior) regulation side by side with the proposed (new) regulation with comments, illustrates this further.

CONCLUSION

While this proposed regulation has introduced a few improvements, over all it clearly will have the effect of making it much more difficult for the religious community to make use of the religious worker visa program.

Advocates have requested that at the very least, USCIS should take additional remedial steps to alleviate the burden, recognizing the current policy and implementation of this regulation will generate very significant delays in processing. Specifically, it has been suggested that the "240-day rule" which allows for ongoing employment or participation in the vocation while an extension is pending,[22] is insufficient, and USCIS should administratively toll the number of days during which the I-129 petition is pending due to security reviews and site visits.

In addition, concurrent filing of the I-360 petition and an application for adjustment of status should be permitted, and premium processing should be reinstituted.

The religious community shares with the Department of Homeland Security the desire that the religious worker visa program be implemented in a fair manner, free of fraud. A much more effective fraud reduction program could be implemented, if the Department were to reach out to the religious community and work together with the religious entities to learn how they operate and what their concerns are. Knowing them better and working with them is the best way to learn how to identify what is legitimate and what is not legitimate when reviewing petitions and applications associated with religious workers.

---

[22] 8 CFR §274a.12(b)(20).

8 CFR 204.5(m)
Petitions for employment-based immigrants

Current 8 CFR §204.5	Proposed 8 CFR §204.5	Comments
(m) Religious workers—	(m) Religious workers –	
(1) An alien, or any person in behalf of the alien, may file an I-360 visa petition for classification under section 203(b)(4) of the Act as a section 101(a)(27)(C) special immigrant religious worker. Such a petition may be filed by or for an alien, who (either abroad or in the United States) for at least the two years immediately preceding the filing of the petition has been a member of a religious denomination which has a bona fide nonprofit religious organization in the United States. The alien must be coming to the United States solely for the purpose of	(1) Any prospective employer may file a Form I-360, Petition for Amerasian, Widow(er), or Special Immigrant visa petition, on behalf of an alien for classification under section 203(b)(4) of the Act as a section 101(a)(27)(C) of the Act special immigrant religious worker. Such a petition may be filed for an alien who (either abroad or in the United States) for at least the two years immediately preceding the filing of the petition has been a member of a religious denomination that has a bona fide nonprofit religious organization in the United States. The alien must be coming to the United States solely for the purpose of working, on a compensated, full-time basis, in one of the following capacities:	"Compensated, full-time basis" in last sentence does not contemplate vocation/vow of poverty. The requirement of full-time compensated employment with proof based on minimum hours per week and income tax requirements is stricter than what Congress intended with the creation of the religious worker program, which was supposed to lift the burdens of employment visa categories from persons engaged in religious work. The statute does not include a compensation requirement. This is a stricter version of what legacy INS proposed in 1995 and never enacted. Fraudulent filings should be challenged and pursued aggressively. There is no argument against that. But the strictness of these regulations in many cases has nothing to do with fraud per se, but rather appears poised to simplify adjudications by creating "prove it or lose it" bright lines. The case has not been made that the proposals are the least restrictive means of furthering a compelling governmental interest in dealing with fraudulent filings. The result is the creation of burdensome new requirements for legitimate bona fide religious organizations. Where a bona fide religious organization has a need for a religious worker to further its religious goals, and can obtain that worker only by changing its operations to comply with standards that appear to be strict for strictness stake, is that not unnecessary interference with a religious organization's practices?
carrying on the vocation of a minister of that religious denomination,	(i) The vocation of a minister of that religious denomination; or	
working for the organization at the organization's request in a professional capacity in a religious vocation	(ii) A religious vocation; or	This is a good change. This schematic—(i), (ii), or (iii)—is more practical and focused.
or occupation	(iii) A religious occupation.	
	(3) A break in the continuity of the required religious work during the two years immediately preceding the filing of the petition will not affect eligibility so long as:	
	(i) The alien was still employed as a religious worker on a compensated, full-time basis,	While the concept is a good one, the word "compensated" should be stricken. How realistic is it to expect that one who is on break from religious work will continue to receive compensation during the break?
	(ii) The break did not exceed two years, and	
	(iii) The nature of the break was for further religious training or for sabbatical that did	

Current 8 CFR §204.5	Proposed 8 CFR §204.5	Comments
	not involve unauthorized work in the United States. However, the alien must have been a member of the petitioner's denomination throughout the two years of qualifying employment.	
(2) Definitions. As used in this section:	(4) Definitions. As used in this paragraph the term:	
Bona fide nonprofit religious organization in the United States means an organization exempt from taxation as described in section 501(c)(3) of the Internal Revenue Code of 1986 as it relates to religious organizations, or one that has never sought such exemption but establishes to the satisfaction of the Service that it would be eligible therefore if it had applied for tax exempt status.	Bona fide nonprofit religious organization in the United States means a religious organization exempt from taxation as described in section 501(c)(3) of the Internal Revenue Code of 1986 or subsequent amendment, as a religious organization and possessing a currently valid determination letter from the IRS confirming such exemption. A church must petition as a bona fide nonprofit religious organization and may not petition as a bona fide organization that is affiliated with an organization as a means to avoid the evidentiary requirements applicable to churches.	Churches are religious organizations, but not all bona fide religious organizations are churches. It is not clear what is meant by the term "church." There is no definition of a "currently valid" determination letter. Other government agencies make determinations as to "religious" organizations, including the states.
Bona fide organization which is affiliated with the religious denomination means an organization which is closely associated with the religious denomination and which is exempt from taxation as described in section 501(c)(3) of the Internal Revenue Code of 1986 as it relates to religious organizations.	Bona fide organization which is affiliated with the religious denomination means an organization which is closely associated with and routinely and substantially acts to further the religious goals of the religious denomination, as attested to by a bona fide nonprofit religious organization in the United States within the denomination. The bona fide nonprofit religious organization attesting to the petitioning organization's affiliation must be exempt from taxation as described in section 501(c)(3) of the Internal Revenue Code of 1986 or subsequent amendment, and as evidenced by a currently valid determination letter from the IRS confirming the bona fide nonprofit religious organization's exemption. "Affiliation" for this particular purpose does not require legal relationship in the form of ownership or control by the denomination or by religious organizations within the denomination, but it does require a solid and public commitment by the affiliated organization to the tenets of the religious denomination.	Need to define "currently valid." If this means updating valid but old documentation, this is overly burdensome.
	Denominational membership means membership during at least the two-year period immediately preceding the filing date of the petition, in the same type of religious denomination as the United States religious organization where the alien will be employed. Membership in religious denominations, including interdenominational organizations, sharing forms of government and worship, creeds, and disciplinary practices may be sufficient to show denominational membership. The denominational membership requirement shall be interpreted in a manner to allow qualification of persons who have demonstrated a sincere commitment to the religious faith of the United States organization of employment,	Is this really a major "fraud" concern? "Denomination" should be broadly construed to accommodate religious constituencies, which many have very similar, but multiple, "denominations."

Current 8 CFR §204.5	Proposed 8 CFR §204.5	Comments
	and to prevent qualification by persons who may have taken on the faith of the United States organization for purposes of facilitating eligibility for United States immigrant or nonimmigrant status.	
Minister means an individual duly authorized by a recognized religious denomination to conduct religious worship and to perform other duties usually performed by authorized members of the clergy of that religion. In all cases, there must be a reasonable connection between the activities performed and the religious calling of the minister. The term does not include a lay preacher not authorized to perform such duties.	Minister means an individual duly authorized by a religious denomination, and fully trained according to the denomination's standards, to conduct religious worship and to perform other duties usually performed by authorized members of the clergy of that denomination. The term does not include a lay preacher or a person not authorized to perform such duties. In all cases, there must be a rational relationship between the activities performed and the religious calling of the minister. The minister must also intend to work solely as a minister in the United States, but the performance of administrative duties incident to the predominant, essentially religious duties does not exclude one from the definition of minister.	
Professional capacity means an activity in a religious vocation or occupation for which the minimum of a United States baccalaureate degree or a foreign equivalent degree is required.		
Religious denomination means a religious group or community of believers having some form of ecclesiastical government, a creed or statement of faith, some form of worship, a formal or informal code of doctrine and discipline, religious services and ceremonies, established places of religious worship, religious congregations, or comparable indicia of a bona fide religious denomination. For the purposes of this definition, an inter-denominational religious organization which is exempt from taxation pursuant to section 501(c)(3) of the Internal Revenue Code of 1986 will be treated as a religious denomination.	Religious denomination means a religious group or community of believers governed or administered under a common type of ecclesiastical government. Members of a denomination must share a recognized common creed or statement of faith, a common form of worship, a common formal code of doctrine and discipline, religious services and ceremonies, common established places of religious worship, religious congregations, or comparable indicia of a bona fide religious denomination. For the purposes of this definition, religious organizations that are recognized as tax exempt under a group tax exemption issued pursuant to section 501(c)(3) of the Internal Revenue Code of 1986 or subsequent amendment, as a religious organization will be presumed to belong to the same religious denomination, but such official affiliation is not necessary for denominational membership.	(1) Some denominations do not have "ecclesiastical government" as contemplated by the proposed rule. This includes religions with a long history of acceptance as religious denominations, such as Judaism.
Religious occupation means an activity which relates to a traditional religious function. Examples of individuals in religious occupations include, but are not limited to, liturgical workers, religious instructors, religious counselors, cantors, catechists, workers in religious hospitals or religious health care facilities, missionaries, religious translators, or religious broadcasters. This group does not include janitors, maintenance workers, clerks, fund raisers, or persons solely involved in the solicitation	Religious occupation means habitual employment in an occupation the duties of which primarily relate to a traditional religious function and which is recognized as a compensated religious occupation within the denomination. The duties of the position must be primarily, directly and substantively related to, and must clearly involve inculcating or carrying out the religious creed and/or beliefs of the denomination. The position must be traditionally recognized by the religious organization or similar organizations as a compensated	Definition of "religious occupation" recognizes (by distinction) a vocation as not requiring compensation: "A religious occupation, in contrast to a vocation, must be salaried, or otherwise compensated by stipend, room and board, or other support … ." The "religious vocation" definition is less clear.

Some find the listing of specific occupations troubling, if it will lead adjudications to preclude others, such as "Mohel" (circumciser). |

Current 8 CFR §204.5	Proposed 8 CFR §204.5	Comments
of donations.	occupation within the denomination. A religious occupation, in contrast to a vocation, must be salaried, or otherwise compensated by stipend, room and board, or other support that is reflected in an alien's W-2, wage transmittal statements, or income tax returns. Examples of occupations that can qualify as a religious occupation include liturgical workers, religious instructors, religious counselors, cantors, catechists, missionaries, religious translators, religious broadcasters, youth ministers, religious choir directors or music ministers, or ritual slaughter supervisors. "Religious occupation" does not include positions whose duties are primarily administrative or supportive in nature, and any administrative duties must be incident to the substantive, traditionally religious functions. Examples of non-qualifying administrative and support positions include, but are not limited to: janitors; maintenance workers; clerks; secretaries; fund raisers; secular musicians; secular translators; those who sell literature, volunteer as ushers during worship services, serve in the choir, volunteer part-time to assist the clergy or teach religion classes; or similar persons engaged in primarily secular, administrative or support duties. It is expected that members of religious organizations volunteer their time even in traditionally religious functions, and immigration status will not be conferred to lay persons who have arranged to be paid for traditionally volunteer work in order to obtain immigration status. Religious study or training for religious work does not constitute religious work, but a religious worker may pursue study or training incident to status. For nonimmigrant purposes, prior experience or training is not required, the petition must demonstrate that the alien truly intends to take up the described religious occupation, and the position must require at least 20 hours per week of compensated service. For immigrant petitions only, the position offered must be permanent and full-time, and the alien's experience in the preceding years must have been full-time. Full-time is considered to be 35 hours per week.	
Religious vocation means a calling to religious life evidenced by the demonstration of commitment practiced in the religious denomination, such as the taking of vows. Examples of individuals with a religious vocation include, but are not limited to, nuns, monks, and religious brothers and sisters.	Religious vocation means a formal lifetime commitment to a religious way of life. There must be evidence that the religious denomination has a traditional established class of individuals whose lives are dedicated to religious practices and functions, as distinguished from the secular members of the religion. It requires that the individual make a formal lifetime commitment through vows, or other investitures or ceremonies, to this class of individuals and	This definition should make clear on its face that compensation is not required for a religious vocation. Suggest: "In contrast to a religious occupation, a religious vocation requires no salary or compensation." The term "religious practices and functions" is troublesome. In current law, a religious vocation relates to a person's status in life and within the religion. A religious vocation is not defined by the person's daily activities for a minimum

Current 8 CFR §204.5	Proposed 8 CFR §204.5	Comments
	religious way of life. Examples of individuals with a religious vocation include, but are not limited to nuns, monks, and religious brothers and sisters.	number of hours per week. Vocation activities are assigned by the religious superior and further the religious mission of the organization. If a bona fide religious organization establishes that a person has a religious vocation and is serving the organization's religious mission, it is unduly restrictive to make a judgment of the vocation based on the type of daily activity and duties the person performs. Moreover, insertion of the word "lifetime" has the potential for denying vocation status based on the type of vows one in a vocation may profess. In some legitimate traditions, periodic renewal of vows is common. The fact that they are renewed periodically does not mean they are not legitimate evidence of commitment practiced in that religion.
	Religious worker means an individual engaged in and, according to the denomination's standards, qualified for a religious occupation or vocation, whether or not in a professional capacity. Such individuals may work in a religious vocation if they have made a formal lifetime commitment to a religious way of life and in a religious occupation if the duties predominantly involve traditional religious functions.	
	(5) Form and filing requirements. The Form I-360, Petition for Amerasian, Widow(er), or Special Immigrant, along with the fee specified in 8 CFR 103.7(b)(1), and supporting evidence must be filed at the appropriate USCIS service center. Such a petition must be filed by the prospective United States employer on behalf of an alien who is either abroad or in the United States. After the date stated in section 101(a)(27)(C) of the Act (as amended), immigration or adjustment of status on the basis of this section is limited solely to ministers of religion.	This simply avoids the need to amend the regulations every time Congress extends the sunset date provision; it does not make the special immigrant workers in a religious vocation or occupation permanent.
(3) Initial evidence. Unless otherwise specified, each petition for a religious worker must be accompanied by:	(6) Attestation. The Form I-360 contains an attestation section which an authorized official of the prospective employer must complete, sign and date. The term "prospective employer" refers to the organization or institution where the alien will be performing the proffered duties. The attestation includes a statement which certifies under penalty of perjury that the contents of the attestation are true and correct to the best of his or her knowledge. This attestation must be submitted by the prospective employer along with the petition. In the Form I-360, the prospective employer must specifically attest to the following:	Consider replacing "employer" with "petitioner."
(i) Evidence that the organization qualifies as a nonprofit organization in the form of	(i) That the prospective employer is a bona fide non-profit religious organization or a bona fide organization which is affiliated	Should not be obligatory. Original regulation more reasonable. Qualification under Internal Revenue Code (IRC) §501(c)(3) is

Current 8 CFR §204.5	Proposed 8 CFR §204.5	Comments
either: (A) Documentation showing that it is exempt from taxation in accordance with section 501(c)(3) of the Internal Revenue Code of 1986 as it relates to religious organizations (in appropriate cases, evidence of the organization's assets and methods of operation and the organization's papers of incorporation under applicable state law may be requested); or (B) Such documentation as is required by the Internal Revenue Service to establish eligibility for exemption under section 501(c)(3) of the Internal Revenue Code of 1986 as it relates to religious organizations; and	with the religious denomination and is exempt from taxation in accordance with section 501(c)(3) of the Internal Revenue Code of 1986 or subsequent amendment;	not the only evidence that an organization fulfills the requirements of being a religious entity. *See* IRC §501(d), which provides tax exemption to certain religious organizations that conduct their finances through a "common Treasury."
	(ii) The number of members of the prospective employer's organization, the number and positions (with brief descriptions) of employees in the prospective employer's organization, the number of aliens holding R visa status currently employed or employed within the past five years by the prospective employer's organization, and the number of special immigrant religious worker and R visa petitions and applications filed by or on behalf of any aliens to be employed as ministers or religious workers for the prospective employer in the past five years;	Consider alternative to "employer" and "employee." Note inconsistency between "members of" and "employees in." The terms are not defined. Context seems to indicate the drafter considers worshipers and congregants to be members and religious workers to be employees. This terminology is not uniform in many religious organizations.
	(iii) The title of the position offered to the alien, the complete package of compensation being offered and a detailed description of the alien's proposed daily duties;	Reference to compensation with no exception for vocation/vow of poverty.
	(iv) That the alien will be employed at least 35 hours per week and such services are needed on a full-time basis;	
	(v) The specific location(s) of the proposed employment;	
	(vi) That the alien has worked as a compensated, full-time religious worker for the two years immediately preceding the filing of the application and is otherwise qualified for the position offered;	Should strike "compensated." Those in a vocation—are they "compensated"?
(ii) A letter from an authorized official of the religious organization in the United States which (as applicable to the particular alien) establishes:		
(A) That, immediately prior to the filing of the petition, the alien has the required two years of membership in the denomination and the required two years of experience in the religious vocation, professional religious work, or other religious work; and	(vii) That the alien has been a member of the denomination for at least two years immediately preceding the filing of the application;	
	(viii) That the alien will not be engaged in secular employment, and any compensation for religious work will be paid to the alien by the attesting employer;	Add the phrase "if the position is not a religious vocation" after "that" and before "the" for consistency with 8 CFR §214.2(r)(6)(vii).

Current 8 CFR §204.5	Proposed 8 CFR §204.5	Comments
		What is meant by secular employment? Would a worker in a religious vocation who has professed the religious vow of poverty for a religious organization whose mission is health care be performing "secular" employment when he or she cares for the sick in a hospital? In 8 CFR §214.2(r)(6)(vii) dealing with the attestation, there seems to be language allowing secular employment when the worker is in a vocation.
	(ix) That the prospective employer has the ability and intention to compensate the alien at a level at which the alien and accompanying family members will not become a public charge, and that funds to pay the alien's compensation do not include any monies obtained from the alien, excluding reasonable donations or tithing to the religious organization, and that the petitioner will notify USCIS of any changes to the alien's employment; and	"Compensated" in first sentence does not contemplate vocation/vow of poverty. Could fix this by adding "or otherwise supported." Analogous section 8 CFR §214.2(r)(6)(vii) in nonimmigrant regulations has "ability to compensate and otherwise support" (and preferable to that would be "compensate *or* otherwise support"). It is important to note that many religious organizations have uneven and unpredictable cash flow, relying on donations and contributions that are episodic or in response to a particular financial need of the entity. Using "I-140-like" criteria in addressing the issue of compensation and support is inappropriate.
	(7) Evidence relating to the petitioning organization. A petition shall include the following initial evidence relating to the petitioning organization:	
	(i) A currently valid determination letter from the Internal Revenue Service (IRS) showing that the organization is exempt from taxation in accordance with section 501(c)(3) of the Internal Revenue Code of 1986 or subsequent amendment, as a religious organization; or	Need to define "currently valid."
	(ii) For religious organizations that are recognized as tax exempt under a group tax exemption, a currently valid determination letter from the IRS establishing that the group is an organization as described in sections 509(a)(1) of the Internal Revenue Code of 1986 or subsequent amendment, and that the group's tax exemption is in accordance with section 501(c)(3) of the Internal Revenue Code of 1986 or subsequent amendment, as a religious organization; or	Need to define "currently valid." Tying bona fide religious organization status solely to IRC standards is restrictive. Although a central organization holding a group tax-exemption ruling may be a church, not all of the subordinate organizations covered by a group ruling are necessarily churches, but they may be legitimate religious organizations. It would be better to continue to allow the organization to submit an IRC determination of tax exemption or other qualifying evidence showing good-faith religious organization status. What about IRC §501(d) religious organizations with a common treasury—also tax exempt?
	(iii) For a bona fide organization which is affiliated with the religious denomination, if the organization was granted a section 501(c)(3) exemption as something other than a religious organization:	Should not be exclusive.

Current 8 CFR §204.5	Proposed 8 CFR §204.5	Comments
	(A) A currently valid determination letter from the IRS showing that the organization is exempt from taxation in accordance with section 501(c)(3) of the Internal Revenue Code of 1986 or subsequent amendment, not necessarily as a religious organization;	Should not be exclusive.
	(B) Documentation that establishes the religious nature and purpose of the organization, such as a copy of the organizing instrument of the organization that specifies the purposes of the organization;	
	(C) Organizational literature, such as brochures, calendars, flyers and other literature describing the religious purpose and nature of the activities of the organization;	
	(D) A Religious Denomination Certification. The Form I-360 contains a "Religious Denomination Certification" section which the petitioner must have the attesting religious organization complete, sign and date. The "Religious Denomination Certification" includes a statement certifying under penalty of perjury that the petitioning organization is affiliated with the religious denomination. The certification must be submitted by the petitioner along with the petition and attestation; and	
	(E) A currently valid determination letter from the IRS evidencing that the attesting organization is exempt from taxation in accordance with section 501(c)(3) of the Internal Revenue Code of 1986 or subsequent amendment, as a religious organization.	Need to define "currently valid."
(B) That, if the alien is a minister, he or she has authorization to conduct religious worship and to perform other duties usually performed by authorized members of the clergy, including a detailed description of such authorized duties. In appropriate cases, the certificate of ordination or authorization may be requested; or	(8) Evidence relating to the qualifications of a minister. If the alien is a minister, the petitioner must submit as initial evidence a copy of the alien's certificate of ordination or similar documents reflecting acceptance of the alien's qualifications as a minister in the religious denomination, as well as evidence that the alien has completed any course of prescribed theological education at an accredited theological institution normally required or recognized by that religious denomination, including transcripts, curriculum, and documentation that establishes that the theological institution is accredited by the denomination. For denominations that do not require a prescribed theological education, the petitioner must submit evidence of the denomination's requirements for ordination to minister, evidence of the duties allowed to be performed by virtue of ordination, evidence of the denomination's gradations of ordination, if any, and evidence of the alien's completion of the denomination's requirements for ordination.	"Accredited" should be deleted. In the normally understood meaning of the term, it implies an outside quality review process. This is a difficult requirement for denominations that have a requirement of traditional, formal education for ministers of religion. Seminaries abroad are not likely to be accredited. Ministers fair poorly under these regulations. Under the proposal, a minister's qualifications cannot include foreign non-accredited education, and the minister is precluded from using religious worker status to study at an accredited seminary in the United States to acquire minister status.
(C) That, if the alien is a religious professional, he or she has at least a United States baccalaureate or its foreign equivalent		

Current 8 CFR §204.5	Proposed 8 CFR §204.5	Comments
required for entry into the religious profession. In all professional cases, an official academic record showing that the alien has the required degree must be submitted; or		
(D) That, if the alien is to work in another religious vocation or occupation, he or she is qualified in the religious vocation or occupation. Evidence of such qualifications may include, but need not be limited to, evidence establishing that the alien is a nun, monk, or religious brother, or that the type of work to be done relates to a traditional religious function.	(9) Evidence relating to the alien's prior employment. Initial evidence must include evidence of the alien's prior religious employment. If the alien was employed in the United States during the two years immediately preceding the filing of the application, the petitioner must submit the alien's W-2 wage statements, the employer's wage transmittal statements, and the transcripts of the alien's processed income tax returns for the preceding two years reflecting such work. If more than six months of such employment is not yet reflected in the documents such as W-2s, wage transmittal statements or income tax returns required to be completed or filed at the time of filing the petition, then pay stubs relating to payment for such employment shall also be presented for work not yet reflected in such documents. If the alien was employed outside the United States during such two years, the petitioner must submit comparable evidence of compensation and religious work. Aliens who have taken a vow of poverty or similar formal lifetime commitment to a religious way of life may submit evidence of such commitment in lieu of the above documentary requirements, but must also submit evidence of all financial support (including stipends, room and board, or other support) received in the preceding two years. Qualifying prior experience (that is, during the two years immediately preceding the petition or preceding any acceptable break in the continuity of the religious work) must have occurred after the age of 14, and, if acquired in the United States, must have been authorized under United States immigration law.	Consider how to present evidence of financial support (subsistence maintenance) when no employment-related documentation is available.
(iii) If the alien is to work in a non-ministerial and non-professional capacity for a bona fide religious organization which is affiliated with the religious denomination, the letter from the authorized official must explain how the affiliation exists. A tax-exempt certificate indicating that the affiliated organization is exempt from taxation in accordance with section 501(c)(3) of the Internal Revenue Code of 1986 as it relates to religious organizations is required in this instance.		
	(10) Audits, inspections, assessment, verification, spot checks, and site visits. The supporting evidence submitted may be verified by USCIS through any means determined appropriate by USCIS, up to and including an on-site inspection of the peti-	A written report available to the petitioner, if there is a negative finding, should be mandated. An opportunity to rebut such findings should be mandated.

Current 8 CFR §204.5	Proposed 8 CFR §204.5	Comments
	tioning organization. The inspection may include a tour of the organization's facilities, an interview with the organization's officials, a review of selected organization records relating to compliance with immigration laws and regulations, and an interview with any other individuals or review of any other records that the USCIS considers pertinent to the integrity of the organization. An inspection may include the organization headquarters, or satellite locations, or the work locations planned for the applicable employee. If USCIS decides to conduct a pre-approval inspection, satisfactory completion of such inspection will be a condition for approval of any petition.	

8 CFR 214.2(r)
Special requirements for admission, extension, and maintenance of status

Current 8 CFR §204.5	Proposed 8 CFR §204.5	Comments
(r) Religious workers—	(r) Religious workers—	
(1) General. Under section 101(a)(15)(R) of the Act, an alien who, for at least the two (2) years immediately preceding the time of application for admission, has been a member of a religious denomination having a bona fide nonprofit religious organization in the United States, may be admitted temporarily to the United States to carry on the activities of a religious worker for a period not to exceed five (5) years. The alien must be coming to the United States for one of the following purposes:	(1) General. Under section 101(a)(15)(R) of the Act, an alien who, for at least the two years immediately preceding the time of application for admission, has been a member of a religious denomination having a bona fide nonprofit religious organization in the United States, may be admitted temporarily to the United States to carry on the activities of a religious worker for a period not to exceed five years. The alien must be coming to or remaining in the United States solely for one of the following purposes:	
	(i) As an employee of a religious organization within the denomination, or of a bona fide organization which is affiliated with the religious denomination, at the request of the organization;	Categories are different than for immigrant class. Suggest consistency with 8 CFR §204.5(m)(1). Either include "employees of ..." for both immigrant and nonimmigrant, or not at all.

Also, suggest separating "religious vocation" and "religious occupation" as in 8 CFR §§204.5(m)(1)(ii) and (iii). |
solely to carry on the vocation of a minister of the religious denomination;	(ii) To carry on the vocation of a minister of the religious denomination; or	
to work for the religious organization at the request of the organization in a professional capacity;		
or to work for the organization, or a bona fide organization which is affiliated with the religious denomination, at the request of the organization in a religious vocation or occupation.	(iii) To work in a religious vocation or occupation.	Consider adding "in a religious organization within the denomination, or of a bona fide organization that is affiliated with the religious denomination" to clarify that working within a bona fide affiliate applies to (i)–(iii). Alternatively, rephrase so that the qualifying phrase is in (1) so as to apply to subparagraphs (i)–(iii).
	(2) An alien may work for more than one qualifying employer as long as each qualifying employer submits the Form I-129 and R Classification Supplement, and, where applicable, accompanying documentation, submitted either in a single petition or through an additional petition.	
(2) Definitions. As used in this section:	(3) Definitions. As used in this paragraph, as applicable to the proposed employment and to the membership in the two years preceding the filing of the petition, the definitions of terms set forth at 8 CFR 204.5(m)(1), concerning immigrant religious workers, shall apply to nonimmigrant religious workers.	This creates ambiguity about whether the definitions of 8 CFR §204.5(m)(1) apply throughout or only as enumerated to proposed employment and membership in preceding years. They should apply throughout as in 8 CFR §204.5(m)(1).
Bona fide nonprofit religious organization in the United States means an organization exempt from taxation as described in section 501(c)(3) of the Internal Revenue Code of 1986 as it relates to religious organizations, or one that has never sought		

Current 8 CFR §204.5	Proposed 8 CFR §204.5	Comments
such exemption but establishes to the satisfaction of the Service that it would be eligible therefore if it had applied for tax exempt status. Bona fide organization which is affiliated with the religious denomination means an organization which is both closely associated with the religious denomination and exempt from taxation as described in <u>section 501(c)(3) of the Internal Revenue Code</u> of 1986 as it relates to religious organizations. Minister means an individual duly authorized by a recognized religious denomination to conduct religious worship and to perform other duties usually performed by authorized members of the clergy of that religion. In all cases, there must be a reasonable connection between the activities performed and the religious calling of the minister. The term does not include a lay preacher not authorized to perform such duties. Professional capacity means an activity in a religious vocation or occupation for which the minimum of a United States baccalaureate degree or a foreign equivalent degree is required. Religious denomination means a religious group or community of believers having some form of ecclesiastical government, a creed or statement of faith, some form of worship, a formal or informal code of doctrine and discipline, religious services and ceremonies, established places of religious worship, and religious congregations, or comparable indicia of a bona fide religious denomination. For the purposes of this definition, an interdenominational religious organization which is exempt from taxation pursuant to <u>section 501(c)(3) of the Internal Revenue Code</u> of 1986 will be treated as a religious denomination. Religious occupation means an activity which relates to a traditional religious function. Examples of persons in religious occupations include, but are not limited to, liturgical workers, religious instructors, religious counselors, cantors, catechists, workers in religious hospitals or religious health care facilities, missionaries, religious translators, or religious broadcasters. This group does not include janitors, maintenance workers, clerks, fund raisers, or persons involved solely in the solicitation of donations. Religious vocation means a calling to religious life evidenced by the demonstration of commitment practiced in the religious denomination, such as the taking of vows. Examples of persons with a religious voca-		

Current 8 CFR §204.5	Proposed 8 CFR §204.5	Comments
tion include, but are not limited to, nuns, monks, and religious brothers and sisters.		
	(4) Requirements for admission/change of status; time limits.	
[Out of order] (4) Initial admission. The initial admission of a religious worker, spouse, and unmarried children under twenty-one years of age shall not exceed three (3) years. A Form I-94, Arrival-Departure Record, shall be provided to every alien who qualifies for admission as an R nonimmigrant. The Form I-94 for the religious worker shall be endorsed with the name and location of the specific organizational unit of the religious organization for which the alien will be providing services within the United States. The admission symbol for the religious worker shall be R-1; the admission symbol for the worker's spouse and children shall be R-2.	(i) Principal applicant. If otherwise admissible, an alien who meets the requirements of section 101(a)(15)(R) of the Act may be admitted as an R-1 alien or changed to R-1 status for an initial period of up to one year from date of initial admission. If visa-exempt, the alien must present the original Notice of Action, Form I-797 approval notice (not a copy), at the port of entry.	Under current regulations, the standard period of stay is three years, with one potential extension of two years. This proposal to change the standard stay period to one year (with two potential extensions of two years each) is not as flexible. See also 8 CFR §214.5(r)(4)(iii). A better proposal would be for an initial period of two years, with a possible three-year extension. With USCIS's current processing delays, its proposal is totally unrealistic. Short periods also increase the expense to the organization.
[Out of order] (8) Spouse and children. The religious worker's spouse and unmarried children under twenty-one years of age are entitled to the same nonimmigrant classification and length of stay as the religious worker, if the religious worker will be employed and residing primarily in the United States, and if the spouse and unmarried minor children are accompanying or following to join the religious worker in the United States. Neither the spouse nor any child may accept employment while in the United States in R-2 nonimmigrant status.	(ii) Spouse and children. The spouse and children of an R-1 alien who are accompanying or following to join the principal may be accorded R-2 status and admitted or have their R-2 status extended for the same period of time and subject to the same limits as the principal, regardless of the time such spouse and children may have spent in the United States in R-2 status. Neither the spouse nor children may accept employment while in the United States in R-2 status.	
[Out of order] (5) Extension of stay. The organizational unit of the religious organization employing the nonimmigrant religious worker admitted under this section shall use Form I-129, Petition for a Nonimmigrant Worker, along with the appropriate fee, to extend the stay of the worker. The petition shall be filed at the Service Center having jurisdiction over the place of employment. An extension may be authorized for a period of up to two (2) years.	(iii) Extension of stay or readmission. An R-1 alien who is maintaining status or is seeking readmission and who satisfies the eligibility requirements of this section may be granted an extension of R-1 stay or readmission in R-1 status for the validity period of the petition, up to 2 years, provided the total period of time spent in R-1 status does not exceed a maximum of five years. A petition for an extension of R-1 status must be filed by the United States employer on Form I-129, Petition for a Nonimmigrant Worker, along with the R Classification Supplement containing the attestation, the fee specified in 8 CFR 103.7(b)(1), and the supporting evidence, at the appropriate USCIS service center.	See above at (i). Under current regulations, the standard period of stay is three years, with one potential extension of two years. This proposal to change the standard stay period to one year (with two potential extensions of two years each) is not as flexible.
The worker's total period of stay may not exceed five (5) years. The petition must be accompanied by a letter from an authorized official of the organizational unit confirming the worker's continuing eligibility for classification as an R-1 nonimmigrant.	(iv) Limitation on total stay. An alien who has spent five years in the United States under section 101(a)(15)(R) of the Act may not be readmitted to, or receive extension of stay in, the United States under the R visa classification unless the alien has resided abroad and been physically present outside the United States for the immediate prior year. The limitations in this paragraph shall not apply to R-1 aliens who did not	The five years applies to time "in the United States" rather than to the time of the approved petition. This should eliminate the current inconsistency in approvals of extensions, for which USCIS often includes time outside the United States as part of the five-year limit. This is a physical presence test. USCIS is adding another exception to the five-year limit for seasonal or intermittent R-1 service. This is a wel-

Current 8 CFR §204.5	Proposed 8 CFR §204.5	Comments
	reside continually in the United States and whose employment in the United States was seasonal or intermittent or was for an aggregate of six months or less per year. In addition, the limitations shall not apply to aliens who reside abroad and regularly commute to the United States to engage in part-time employment. To qualify for this exception, the petitioner and the alien must provide clear and convincing proof that the alien qualifies for such an exception. Such proof shall consist of evidence such as arrival and departure records, transcripts of processed income tax returns, and records of employment abroad. The primary purpose of the spouse or child must be to join or accompany the principal R-1 alien in the United States. USCIS may limit, deny or revoke on notice any stay for an R-2 that is not primarily intended for this purpose or is intended to evade the normal requirements of the nonimmigrant classification that otherwise would apply when the principal alien is absent from the United States.	come proposal, consistent with policy in other nonimmigration classifications.
	(5) Jurisdiction and procedures for obtaining R-1 status. A petitioner seeking to classify an alien as a religious worker, by initial petition or by change of status, shall file a petition on Form I-129, Petition for a Nonimmigrant Worker, along with the R Classification Supplement containing the attestation, the fee specified in 8 CFR 103.7(b)(1), and supporting evidence, at the appropriate USCIS service center. The Form I-129, Petition for a Nonimmigrant Worker, must be submitted by the employer in the United States seeking to employ the religious worker.	Requiring the I-129 for obtaining R-1 status and renewal is cumbersome, but probably not negotiable. The reference to "employment" in the last sentence should be changed to "petitioner" for consistency with the rest of the paragraph and to include religious orders or other petitioners if the religious worker is not an employee. Time limits for adjudication should be imposed.
(3) Initial evidence. An alien seeking classification as a nonimmigrant religious worker shall present to a United States consular officer, or, if visa exempt, to an immigration officer at a United States port of entry, documentation which establishes to the satisfaction of the consular or immigration officer that the alien will be providing services to a bona fide nonprofit religious organization in the United States or to an affiliated religious organization as defined in paragraph (r)(2) of this section, and that the alien meets the criteria to perform such services. If the alien is in the United States in another valid nonimmigrant classification and desires to change nonimmigrant status to classification as a nonimmigrant religious worker, this documentation should be presented with an application for change of status (Form I-129, Petition for a Nonimmigrant Worker). The documentation shall consist of:	(6) Attestation. The Form I-129, Petition for a Nonimmigrant Worker, contains an attestation section in the R Classification Supplement, which the authorized official of the prospective employer must complete, sign and date. The term "prospective employer" refers to the organization or institution where the alien will be performing the proffered duties. The attestation includes a statement which certifies under penalty of perjury that the contents of the attestation are true and correct to the best of his or her knowledge. This attestation must be submitted by the prospective employer along with the petition. In the Form I-129 R Classification Supplement, the prospective employer must specifically attest to the following:	Again, the use of "employer" narrowly interpreted does not contemplate a religious worker working in a religious vocation pursuant to a vow of poverty when no employment relationship is present. It runs counter to USCIS's stated goal in the summary to the proposed regulations to use employment records and compensation as objective proof to weed out fraudulent applicants, but consider using "petitioner" wherever possible instead of "employer." Also, consider alternatives such as adding "or religious organization within which the alien works in a religious vocation pursuant to a vow of poverty." Needless to say the latter alternative is protracted and would be difficult to build in throughout. *General Comment: This applies throughout where "employer" is used*
(i) Evidence that the organization qualifies as a non-profit organization, in the form of	(i) That the prospective employer is a bona fide non-profit religious organization or a	The attempt in the proposed regulations to tie bona fide religious organization status

Current 8 CFR §204.5	Proposed 8 CFR §204.5	Comments
either: (A) Documentation showing that it is exempt from taxation in accordance with <u>section 501(c)(3) of the Internal Revenue Code</u> of 1986 as it relates to religious organizations (in appropriate cases, evidence of the organization's assets and methods of operation and the organization's papers of incorporation under applicable state law may be requested); or (B) Such documentation as is required by the Internal Revenue Service to establish eligibility for exemption under <u>section 501(c)(3) of the Internal Revenue Code</u> of 1986 as it relates to religious organizations; and	bona fide organization which is affiliated with the religious denomination and is exempt from taxation in accordance with section 501(c)(3) of the Internal Revenue Code of 1986 or subsequent amendment;	to particular sections of the IRC is misplaced. There are numerous problems with this approach, such as that of a "currently valid" letter; an exemption under the 1986 IRC (many exemption letters pre-date the 1986 code); confusion over the term "church"; the expense of a private ruling for an organization that does not have one; and the requirement that organizations in a group ruling must be "churches." There is a recurrence here of the problem from several years ago that resulted in a USCIS memorandum that clarified that status as a "church" is only one method of qualifying as a religious organization. *See* USCIS Memorandum, W. Yates, "Extension of the Special Immigrant Religious Worker Program and Clarification of Tax Exempt Status Requirements for Religious Organizations" (Dec. 17, 2003), *published on* AILA InfoNet at Doc. No. 04011211 (*posted* Jan. 12, 2004).
	(ii) The number of members of the prospective employer's organization, the number and positions (with brief descriptions) of employees in the prospective employer's organization, the number of aliens holding R visa status currently employed or employed within the past five years by the prospective employer's organization, and the number of special immigrant religious worker and R visa petitions and applications filed by or on behalf of any aliens to be employed as ministers or religious workers for the prospective employer in the past five years;	Consider use of "petitioner" and "beneficiary."
	(iii) The title of the position offered to the alien, the complete package of compensation being offered and a detailed description of the alien's proposed daily duties;	Compensation? Should include alternative means of support.
	(iv) That the position that the alien is being offered requires at least 20 hours per week of compensated service;	
[Out of order] (E) The name and location of the specific organizational unit of the religious organization for which the alien will be providing services within the United States; and	(v) The specific location(s) of the proposed employment and that the alien is otherwise qualified for the position offered;	Employment?
(ii) A letter from an authorized official of the specific organizational unit of the religious organization which will be employing the alien or engaging the alien's services in the United States. If the alien is to be employed, this letter should come from the organizational unit that will maintain the alien's Form I-9, Employment Eligibility Verification, that is, the organizational unit that is either paying the alien a salary or otherwise remunerating the alien in exchange for services rendered. This letter must establish:		

Current 8 CFR §204.5	Proposed 8 CFR §204.5	Comments
(A) That, if the alien's religious membership was maintained, in whole or in part, outside the United States, the foreign and United States religious organizations belong to the same religious denomination; (B) That, immediately prior to the application for the nonimmigrant visa or application for admission to the United States, the alien has the required two (2) years of membership in the religious denomination;	(vi) That the alien has been a member of the denomination for at least 2 years;	
(C) As appropriate: (1) That, if the alien is a minister, he or she is authorized to conduct religious worship for that denomination and to perform other duties usually performed by authorized members of the clergy of that denomination, including a detailed description of those duties; (2) That, if the alien is a religious professional, he or she has at least a United States baccalaureate degree or its foreign equivalent and that at least such a degree is required for entry into the religious profession; or (3) That, if the alien is to work in another religious vocation or occupation, he or she is qualified in the religious vocation or occupation. Evidence of such qualifications may include, but need not be limited to, evidence establishing that the alien is a monk, nun, or religious brother or that the type of work to be done relates to a traditional religious function;		
	(vii) That, if the position is not a religious vocation, the alien will not be engaged in secular employment, and any compensation for religious work will be paid to the alien by the attesting employer,	
(D) The arrangements made, if any, for remuneration for services to be rendered by the alien, including the amount and source of any salary, a description of any other types of remuneration to be received (including housing, food, clothing, and any other benefits to which a monetary value may be affixed), and a statement whether such remuneration shall be in exchange for services rendered; [(E) is out of order above.]	(viii) That the prospective employer has the ability and intention to compensate and otherwise support (through housing, for example) the alien at a level at which the alien and accompanying family members will not become public charges, and that funds to pay the alien's compensation do not include any monies obtained from the alien, excluding reasonable donations or tithing to the religious organization; and	*Cf.* 8 CFR §204.5(m)(6)(ix), which does not include "and otherwise support qualification"; this version is preferable, but "compensate or otherwise support" (rather than "compensate and otherwise support") would be a further improvement. Consider replacing "employer" with "petitioner" here.
(F) If the alien is to work in a non-ministerial and nonprofessional capacity for a bona fide organization which is affiliated with a religious denomination, the existence of the affiliation; and		
	(ix) That the petitioner will notify USCIS of any changes to the alien's employment and reapply by filing a new Form I-129 on behalf of the alien within 60 days of the	Note use of the word "any" here. This is problematic, because of the important requirement of maintaining nonimmigrant status. If a religious instructor changes

Current 8 CFR §204.5	Proposed 8 CFR §204.5	Comments
	occurrence of any change.	class periods from Tuesday to Wednesday, should that require an amended petition? This is stricter than the requirement for H's and L's.
(iii) Any appropriate additional evidence which the examining officer may request relating to the religious organization, the alien, or the affiliated organization. Such additional documentation may include, but need not be limited to, diplomas, degrees, financial statements, or certificates of ordination. No prior petition, labor certification, or prior approval shall be required.		
	(7) Evidence relating to the petitioning organization. The petitioner must submit the following initial evidence relating to the petitioning organization:	Note use of "petitioning organization" here rather than "prospective employer." In general, "petitioner" or "petitioning organization" would be preferable throughout, as it would include religious workers in vocations pursuant to vows of poverty.
	(i) A currently valid determination letter from the Internal Revenue Service (IRS) showing that the organization is exempt from taxation in accordance with section 501(c)(3) of the Internal Revenue Code of 1986 or subsequent amendment, as a religious organization; or	Need to define what "currently valid" is. Many religious organizations will have received a determination letter decades ago.
	(ii) For religious organizations that are recognized as tax exempt under a group tax exemption, a currently valid determination letter from the IRS establishing that the group is an organization as described in sections 509(a)(1) of the Internal Revenue Code of 1986 or subsequent amendment, and that the group's tax exemption is in accordance with section 501(c)(3) of the Internal Revenue Code of 1986 or subsequent amendment, as a religious organization; or	Need to define what "currently valid" is.
	(iii) For a bona fide organization which is affiliated with the religious denomination, if the organization was granted a section 501(c)(3) exemption as something other than a religious organization:	
	(A) A currently valid determination letter from the IRS showing that the organization is exempt from taxation in accordance with section 501(c)(3) of the Internal Revenue Code of 1986 or subsequent amendment, (not necessarily as a religious organization),	Need to define what "currently valid" is. See comment to proposed (6)(i) re: IRC §501(c)(3).
	(B) Documentation that establishes the religious nature and purpose of the organization, such as a copy of the organizing instrument of the organization that specifies the purposes of the organization,	
	(C) Organizational literature, such as brochures, calendars, flyers and other literature describing the religious purpose and nature	

Current 8 CFR §204.5	Proposed 8 CFR §204.5	Comments
	of the activities of the organization, and	
	(D) A Religious Denomination Certification. The Form I-129 contains a "Religious Denomination Certification" section which the petitioner must have the attesting religious organization complete, sign and date. The "Religious Denomination Certification" includes a statement certifying under penalty of perjury that the petitioning organization is affiliated with the religious denomination. The certification must be submitted by the petitioner along with the petition and attestation.	
	(E) A currently valid determination IRS letter evidencing that the attesting organization is exempt from taxation in accordance with section 501(c)(3) of the Internal Revenue Code of 1986 or subsequent amendment, as a religious organization.	Need to define what "currently valid" is.
	(8) Evidence relating to the qualifications of a minister. If the alien is a minister, the petitioner must submit as initial evidence a copy of the alien's certificate of ordination or similar documents reflecting acceptance of the alien's qualifications as a minister in the religious denomination, as well as evidence that the alien has completed any course of prescribed theological education at an accredited theological institution normally required or recognized by that religious denomination, including transcripts, curriculum, and documentation which establishes that the theological education is accredited by the denomination. For denominations that do not require a prescribed theological education, the petitioner must submit evidence of the denomination's requirements for ordination to minister, evidence of the duties allowed to be performed by virtue of ordination, evidence of the denomination's gradations of ordination, if any, and evidence of the alien's completion of the denomination's requirements for ordination.	
(6) Change of employers. A different or additional organizational unit of the religious denomination seeking to employ or engage the services of a religious worker admitted under this section shall file Form I-129 with the appropriate fee. The petition shall be filed with the Service Center having jurisdiction over the place of employment. The petition must be accompanied by evidence establishing that the alien will continue to qualify as a religious worker under this section. Any unauthorized change to a new religious organizational unit will constitute a failure to maintain status within the meaning of section 241(a)(1)(C)(i) of the Act.	(9) Change or addition of employers; employer obligations. An alien admitted in the R-1 classification shall engage only in employment that is consistent with the approved petition, the attestation contained in the supplement and supporting documents submitted to USCIS. A different or additional employer seeking to employ the alien must obtain prior approval of such employment through the filing of an additional Form I-129, Petition for a Nonimmigrant Worker, with the R Classification Supplement, supporting documents and the appropriate fee. Any compensated work for an unauthorized religious organization will constitute a failure to maintain status within the meaning of section 237(a)(1)(C)(i) of the Act. When an alien who has obtained R-1 classification is working less than the	Consider antifraud implications of listing one site and having individual move to a different location and not present when site visit occurs. When must petitioner notify USCIS of moves? Under proposed (6)(ix) above, *any* change requires notification to USCIS for approval.

Notification to USCIS when a religious worker has left the position is reasonable and should serve to lessen the extent to which these regulations seek to micromanage the employment of a religious worker. The time for giving notice should be extended so that it is also reasonable. For H's and L's there is no time period at all. |

Current 8 CFR §204.5	Proposed 8 CFR §204.5	Comments
	required number of hours or has been released from or has otherwise terminated employment before the expiration of a period of authorized R-1 stay, the employer through whom R-1 classification has been obtained must notify DHS within 7 days of such release or termination, using reporting procedures set forth in the instructions to Form I-129, Petition for a Nonimmigrant Worker, which can be found on the USCIS internet website at *www.uscis.gov.*	
	(10) Evidence of previous R-1 employment. Any request for R-1 status, admission beyond the first year of R-1 status, or any period of extension of stay, must include initial evidence of the previous R-1 employment in the form of the alien's W-2 wage statements, the employer's wage transmittal statements, and transcripts of the alien's processed income tax returns for any preceding period spent in the United States in R-1 status. For any period of such employment not yet reflected in the documents such as W-2s, wage transmittal statements or income tax returns required to be completed or filed at the time of filing the petition, then pay stubs relating to payment for such employment shall be presented for work not yet reflected in such documents. Aliens who have taken a vow of poverty or similar formal lifetime commitment to a religious way of life may submit evidence of such commitment in lieu of the above documentary requirements, but must also submit evidence of all financial support (including stipends, room and board, or other support) received while in R-1 status.	The carve-out for vow of poverty is helpful.
	(11) Nonimmigrant intent. The filing or approval of a permanent labor certification or the filing of a preference petition for an alien shall not be a basis for denying an R petition, a request to extend such a petition, or the alien's application for admission, change of status, or extension of stay. The alien may legitimately come to the United States for a temporary period as an R nonimmigrant and depart voluntarily at the end of his or her authorized stay and, at the same time, lawfully seek to become a permanent resident of the United States.	
	(12) Audits, inspections, assessment, verification, spot checks, and site visits. The supporting evidence submitted may be verified by USCIS through any means determined appropriate by USCIS, up to and including an on-site inspection of the petitioning organization. The inspection may include a tour of the organization's facilities, an interview with the organization's officials, a review of selected organization records relating to compliance with immigration laws and regulations, and an interview with any other individuals or	There is no process outlined for challenging the findings of a site visit, as erroneous as they could possibly be, based on the inspector's lack of understanding of a situation.

If an organization establishes itself as a bona fide religious organization—based, for example, on an initial site inspection, other evidence that is publicly available, or proper filing and approval—that organization should be considered for treatment like that accorded to blanket L employers. The organization's |

Current 8 CFR §204.5	Proposed 8 CFR §204.5	Comments
	review of any other records that the USCIS considers pertinent to the integrity of the organization. An inspection may include the organization headquarters, or satellite locations, or the work locations planned for the applicable employee. If USCIS decides to conduct a pre-approval inspection, satisfactory completion of such inspection will be a condition for approval of any petition.	established status should carry weight in deferring to the organization's determination of when one is properly trained or educated for a religious worker position, and what the normal incidents of the position are, such as whether it is compensated or not. There is no justification shown for the meddling in a bona fide religious organization's internal affairs as seen in these regulations.

"DOs" AND "DON'TS" FOR ATTORNEYS REPRESENTING VISA APPLICANTS (AND FOR CONSULAR OFFICERS, TOO!)

by Liam Schwartz, Anastasia Tonello, and Avi Friedman[*]

As lawyers, we are often frustrated by an inability to gain real-time responses from consular posts to questions that are not addressed on consular websites. U.S. consular officers (conoffs) sometimes appear to insulate themselves from attorney communications. Admittedly, conoffs may justifiably wish to cut off communications with an attorney who is perceived as under-prepared or over-zealous. But refusing to communicate with attorneys will not necessarily make them go away.

The working relationship between conoffs and attorneys can and should be a "win-win" situation.

---

[*] **Liam Schwartz** is a principal in Liam Schwartz & Associates, practicing in Israel. Mr. Schwartz is the immediate past chair of AILA's DOS Liaison Committee. His other recent AILA activities include: Moderator, *Current Issues in Nonimmigrant Visa Processing: A Roundtable with Visa Consuls*; Panelist, *3rd Biennial Global Immigration Conference*; Organizer, AILA Tours of U.S. Consulate General, Vancouver and of U.S. Embassy, London; Discussion Leader, *DOS Open Forum*; Discussion Leader, *DOS—Standards in Visa Processing*; Organizing Committee Member, 2007 Spring CLE Conference; Author, Tel-Aviv and Jerusalem chapters for *The Visa Processing Guide;* Consular Affairs Mentor.

Anastasia Tonello, a dual U.S./U.K. citizen and resident, is a partner at Laura Devine Solicitors in London and Laura Devine Attorneys LLC in New York. She has practiced immigration law in London and New York since 1998. Ms. Tonello received a B.A. from Indiana University and a J.D. from the University of Notre Dame. She was admitted to the Bar of the State of New York in 1999 and is a solicitor of the Supreme Court of England U.K. Edition and *Chambers Guide* to the U.K. Legal Profession. Ms. Tonello is active in both the Rome District and New York AILA chapters, serving as interim secretary for the Rome District and social co-chair in New York. Ms. Tonello is a frequent speaker at AILA conferences and has published several articles.

Avi Friedman is a senior associate with Wolfsdorf Immigration Law Group. Mr. Friedman is currently serving on the 2007–08 AILA Department of State Liaison Committee and is also serving his fifth term as the consular affairs liaison for AILA's Southern California Chapter. He has extensive experience with assisting applicants with visa interviews at U.S. consular posts worldwide, with a focus on in-person attorney/client representation at U.S. border posts in Canada and Mexico. He is listed in The California edition of the *2007 Who's Who of Corporate Immigration Lawyers* and *Southern California Super Lawyers,* Rising Stars Edition.

Conoffs can benefit from letting the attorney "work" for them on behalf of their clients, for example, through proper case preparation and legal citations. Attorneys, in turn, can benefit from obtaining the background information necessary to best serve the client/applicant.

We believe that the ultimate success of this process lies with holding attorneys and consular officers accountable for maintaining a constructive working relationship. It is with this in mind that we offer the following list of "DOs" and "DON'Ts." In addition to general suggestions for attorneys, the list relates to special processing issues: E visa applications in London; Third Party National (TCN) visa processing in Canada and Mexico; and Special Advisory Opinions (SAOs).

The list ends with a number of proposed "DOs" and "DON'Ts" for consular officers involved in the visa application process. These proposals are offered with respect, and in recognition of the many pressures placed on visa officers in the course of their work. We hope these proposals will underline the belief expressed by William D. Morgan—who did more than anyone to promote the consular function within the State Department—that in reality, lawyers are "our friends and supporters."

ATTORNEY ACCOUNTABILITY

General

- To ensure that clients receive the most efficient service, the best place to start to learn about a consular post's visa operations, and any special application procedures, is the post's website. In recent years, the Department of State (DOS) has achieved significant progress in making individual consular post websites more uniform and helpful to the public. Consular post websites may be accessed through the State Department's own website: *www.usembassy.gov.* Other valuable sources of information are the AILA *Visa Processing Guide and Consular Posts Handbook* and the AILA mentor program.

- Be sensitive to overseas posts' limited resources—use the post's e-mail and public telephone information services for routine questions and information. In this regard, don't insist on talking to a consular officer simply to obtain general information that is available through automated or other easily available sources; the local Foreign Service National (FSN) staff can often provide this information as well (if not better) than anyone else.

- When inquiring about a pending case, observe post procedures for such inquiries and respect any special rules concerning hours for or preferred means of inquiry.

- Utilize the interview scheduling procedure detailed on the post's website. In most cases, scheduling an appointment is possible only through a post's Internet-based appointment system.

- Recognize that consular officers cannot pre-adjudicate visa applications. Decisions on visa issuance (and on related matters, such as the need for "additional administrative processing") will only be made at the time of the visa interview.

- If you have questions about a pending case or visa refusal, don't telephone cold and expect the consular officer to recall your client's case. Instead, contact the post in writing first before calling. Explain in a detailed e-mail or fax message the nature of the inquiry and include any relevant documents. If necessary, you can then follow up with a phone call (always best to call in the afternoon after visa interviews have been completed for the day). *TIP*: Make sure the post has a G-28 on file before seeking to discuss a case.

- Explain to the client that expeditious consular processing of the visa application is not covered by the $1,000 that may have been spent to obtain USCIS premium processing.

- On November 17, 2007, DOS instructed consular posts (Cable No. 155679) to verify the details of approved nonimmigrant visa petitions via a report called "PIMS" (Petition Information Management Service). The electronic PIMS record created by the Kentucky Consular Center (KCC) now serves as the primary source of evidence used in determining petition approval. This applies to all nonimmigrant petition-based visa categories (H, L, O, P, and Q). The PIMS Petition Report contains a record of all petitioners recorded by the KCC as having approved petitions since 2004. In addition, many of the records contain information from KCC's Fraud Prevention Unit. Reportedly, this change has resulted in delays at many posts from interview to visa issuance for these categories. Parenthetically, some

of the Canadian posts permit attorneys to submit applicant's information in advance and will then attempt to undertake the PIMS clearance procedure prior to the visa interview, thereby limiting the time applicants have to wait until the passport is returned.

Preparing the Application

- Prepare well in advance, as there may be heavy delays at the post—especially during summer and holiday seasons.

- Unless the case involves a unique factual or legal situation, refrain from giving a "heads-up" to the consulate to "pave the way" for the application.

- Learn as much as you can about the facts of the case and the relevant immigration history of the applicant and any employing company. The more an attorney knows about a client, the greater the potential for the attorney to assist her client in a concrete way. This is particularly true of more complicated applications, such as work visa requests.

- Help the client prepare for the interview, and fully brief him or her on the visa interview process so that the interview can be as effective as possible for both the client and the interviewing officer.

- Advise the client on the eligibility requirements of the visa for which he or she intends to apply, and alert him or her to the possibility of delay (for example, due to the need for a Special Advisory Opinion) or of visa refusal.

- Ensure that clients read and understand their application forms before coming to the interview. This is particularly critical if the applicant does not have a good command of the language used in the form.

- Make sure the client fills out the visa application form carefully and accurately, answers all questions completely, and signs the DS-156 form before submission.

- Stress to the applicant the importance of answering all questions truthfully, both on the application form and during the interview, and warn of the possibility of permanent exclusion if he or she makes any material false statements.

- If applicable, inform the client of the importance of being upfront about any previous arrest or conviction or past problems with U.S. immigration or consular officials, and make sure the applicant is prepared to present relevant court or immigration records as well as police certificates at the time of interview. If you suspect the visa application will be denied because of a specific ground of ineligibility (such as a past criminal conviction), brief the client about the waiver process and prepare the waiver application for the client to submit, if possible, to the interviewing officer immediately after the denial.

- Make sure the applicant is prepared to explain and, if necessary, document previous stays in the United States.

- Send supporting documents directly to the client, not to the post. The best way to ensure that the documentation you wish to submit in support of the application is immediately available at the time of the interview is to have the applicant hand-carry it to the interview.

- Contact the post first (particularly in time-sensitive cases), if you plan to submit nonimmigrant visa applications for a large group of aliens, such as sports teams, performance groups, delegations, groups of workers, etc. This allows the post to advise the attorney in advance on application procedures and the types of materials the applicants will need to bring with them. Advance notice helps ensure that both the post and the applicants are prepared for the group application and thereby facilitates prompt and efficient processing.

- In group-visa application cases, assist the applicants to arrange their supporting documentation in an orderly fashion. This facilitates more efficient review of the cases and helps speed up the interview process.

- Recognize that a neat and well-organized document package in itself does not lead to visa issuance. Applicants are all individuals, and, while documents for one may have assisted in showing eligibility, the same documents may not be enough for another alien with differing circumstances.

Application and Interview

- Have the applicant apply at the appropriate post, *i.e.,* where he or she resides or last resided abroad, or at a post designated to process "homeless" applications.

- Consider Third Country National Processing (TCN) in Canada or Mexico so the applicant can possibly avoid the added cost and time delays of processing in his or her home country post.

- Respect whatever rules the consulate has established for attorney presence at interviews.

- Alert the client that visa interviews can be an unpleasant and even intimidating experience. The client will often wait for several hours to be called for an interview that lasts only three minutes. During these critical 180 seconds, the applicant stands and the consul sits on opposite sides of heavy bullet-proof glass.

- Stress to the client that the consular officer interviews people, not documents. While it is important to submit a well-documented case, the consul's decision to issue or deny the visa will be made primarily on how well the client presents his or her case at the interview window. Accordingly, your role as attorney in preparing the client for the visa interview cannot be overstated.

- Impress upon the client that the visa process has become subject to an increased level of unforeseeable delay, also known as "administrative review." Reasons for administrative review include: the applicant has a criminal conviction; the applicant has a name and date of birth that closely parallel those of a known criminal; the applicant is a national of a country listed as a state sponsor of terrorism; the applicant will be exposed to sensitive technology during his or her visit to the United States.

- Have the client review the application documents as if preparing for a school exam. The night before the interview, encourage the client to write a statement of his or her eligibility for the visa. Ensure that he or she understands the basic requirements for the visa. For example, practitioners need to make sure the client understands that when he or she applies for a B-2 visa, the applicant has the burden of convincing the consular officer that he or she is only coming to the United States to visit and that he or she has strong ties to his or her home country. Or the H-1B applicant should understand that he or she may need to show that the job requires a degree and that he or she must have a degree or degree equivalent that is relevant to the job.

- Tip for the client: don't give up jobs, take kids out of school, commit to lease payments on a U.S. home, or put the family dog up for adoption in anticipation of receiving a visa. The reality of nonimmigrant visa processing in 2008 is that "it ain't over 'til it's over"—in this case, until you actually see the visa stamp in your passport.

In the Event of a Visa Denial

- If you are present at the interview and the client is refused, accept that it may be necessary to submit any countervailing arguments or requests for review in writing, given the time and crowd pressures in many nonimmigrant visa units. Don't argue the case at length at the window.

- If you are not present and the visa application is denied, debrief the client ASAP about what was said at the interview. Bearing in mind that clients may add their own "spin" to their recollection of the interview Q&A, it is always best to also contact the consulate to ask for the official version of the grounds for the visa denial.

- When presenting arguments following a denial, cite the specific section of the *Foreign Affairs Manual* (FAM) or other relevant law or regulation that supports your client's position, and be sure to include specific facts about your client's case that show that the cited law/regulation applies.

- Don't settle for a bad decision if you have a good case and you believe an error was made. Reapply or seek review within the consulate, and, if unsuccessful and the issue is a legal one, seek an advisory opinion from the Visa Office. Consult with an AILA mentor or seek the advice of other members through the InfoNet Message Center.

- If the reviewing consular officer upholds the refusal and you remain convinced that an error has been committed, you may seek an advisory opinion from the Visa Office—if the issue is legal in nature. Bear in mind that factual determinations by the consular officer are nonreviewable—period!

- When asking for review of a case, present your case succinctly, addressing all relevant facts and citing legal authority for your arguments. Don't overwhelm the consular officer with large volumes of unnecessary documents, either in the application process or when seeking review.

- If your client has been refused and you already have exhausted all opportunities for review and been unable to overcome the refusal, do not seek repeated further reviews unless you have new arguments to raise or new information to provide. Accept that some cases cannot be saved, and preserve your efforts (and built-up goodwill) for cases that merit it.

- Whatever the outcome, maintain a courteous and professional tone throughout. A confrontational manner or abusive tone is usually counterproductive, and does not serve your client's interests.

Miscellaneous Tips

- Recognize the time pressures that most consulates are under, and don't call with unnecessary frequency or drop by without an appointment in the hope of being able to meet with a consular officer.

- Inform the post if you have ceased representing an applicant or have taken over a case from another attorney.

- Don't rely on FOIA requests to obtain information on the reasons for a visa refusal or other visa-related information, as this procedure is not an effective means to obtain such information. Visa records are confidential under §222(f) of the Immigration and Nationality Act and, through that provision, are generally exempt from release under FOIA. The only visa records that can be obtained under a FOIA request are documents either submitted by or sent to the applicant. Thus, the applicant will not learn anything new about the case from any documents that might be obtained through a FOIA request. If you do not believe you have received sufficient information about the grounds of refusal or other issues, you should write to the post or the Visa Office.

Special Considerations for E Visa Applications in London

- Check the embassy's website repeatedly throughout your case preparation process as procedures, required documentation and formats change regularly with little notice.

- Do follow the instructions regarding required format, documentation, and presentation of the case.

- If a business plan is included with the application, do read it and ensure it makes good business sense.

- Do provide an e-mail address on the DS-156E so that the E visa unit can contact you with any issues.

- Do not push the E visa unit to expedite cases unless there are extraordinary circumstances. Most likely, they will not expedite; and dealing with expedite requests takes time away from adjudications.

- Do make sure your initial applicant is able to demonstrate strong ties to the United Kingdom and an intent to return.

- For British applicants, do make sure they are able to demonstrate a U.K. domicile (which may be different than the U.K. tax domicile).

- Do make sure your initial applicant is well-versed on the finances, investment, and operations of the business. If the initial applicant is not a senior member of the business, ensure the applicant has the contact information for a senior employee in the company who can answer these types of questions about the company.

- Closely review 9 FAM 41.51 on E visa requirements and make sure your case deals with all relevant sections.

- Deal with shortcomings in your application and explain them. The treaty officer will not ignore them and neither should you.

Special Considerations for TCN Processing in Mexico and Canada

- Don't send TCN visa applicants to a border post if they initially entered the United States on a B-1/B-2 visa and subsequently were approved for a student or work category (regardless of whether they have a change of status approval issued by U.S. Citizenship and Immigration Services (USCIS). Generally, only "clearly approvable" TCN cases should be processed in Canada or Mexico. Cases with complex admissibility issues are usually not suitable for TCN processing at a border post.

- Attorneys can represent clients at posts in Canada but not at posts in Mexico (where counsel is no longer even allowed in the door). The scope of attorney representation varies in Canada, depending on the post, from complete representation at the visa interview to limited representation requiring the attorney to remain in the waiting area. Attorneys need to be conscious that interfering or disruptive actions while representing clients at a consular post may adversely impact the outcome of a case.

- Do advise your client to obtain the applicable visa for entering Canada or Mexico. Counsel may also require a work visa if representing or accompanying the client at the visa interview. Contact the Mexican or Canadian consulate and review their respective websites for information on visa/entry requirements. U.S. attorneys representing clients at U.S. posts in Mexico are advised to obtain an FM-3 work visa from a Mexican consulate/embassy having jurisdiction over their place of residence.

- Do make sure that your client is not subject to INA §222(g). Section 222(g) generally prohibits a visa applicant who is out of status from applying for an NIV at a border post. Applicants in J or F status with D/S (Duration of Status) are not subject to §222(g) *unless* USCIS or an immigration judge has made a formal finding that the alien has violated his or her visa status. However, while not subject to §222(g), many border posts will not approve NIV applicants outside the grace period (60-day grace period for F; 30-day grace period for J).

- Applicants from the "List of 26" countries (a classified list of predominantly Muslim countries) may not apply at posts in Mexico (unless they are resident in the consular district); such applicants can generally apply in Canada. If applying in Canada, they should be prepared to wait either in Canada or outside of Canada (if they have a multiple entry Canadian visa) while routine security checks are pending. Also, remind these applicants that they must have complied with special registration and departure registration requirements.

- Don't submit TCN E visa applications in Canada (the E program in Canada is limited to Canadian citizens and permanent residents only). Options in Mexico also are limited but some Mexican posts may allow TCN E visa renewal applications where the company is on the "Business List" at their home post (*i.e.*, list of E Registered Companies in Japan) or if the company is listed in the Fortune 500.

- Make sure to pay the visa application fee in advance. Posts in Mexico require the visa application fee to be paid in advance at a branch of Banamex. Posts in Canada require the visa application fee to be paid in advance at a branch of Scotiabank. Reciprocity fees in Mexico and Canada usually are paid in U.S. cash at the post after the visa has been approved (some posts also accept credit card payment for reciprocity fees).

- Don't plan on your client re-entering the United States under Automatic Revalidation if they are denied their visa or are subjected to a security check. On April 1, 2002, DOS changed the automatic revalidation provision of 22 CFR §42.112(d). Automatic revalidation applies for trips to Canada or Mexico of 30 days or less provided that the applicant is not rejected for a visa application and not from the DOS designated State Sponsors of Terrorism (T-5) (which includes Iran, Cuba, Sudan, Syria, and North Korea). If an applicant is denied a visa at a border post or is a national of a T-5 country, it is necessary to have a valid U.S. visa (or advance parole) to re-enter the United States. Rejected visa applicants must now travel back to their home country directly from Mexico or Canada. Prior to this change, applicants who were denied a visa were able to return to the United States using an expired visa and a valid Form I-94 (which automatically revalidated their visa).

- Some posts in Canada accept Australian E-3 visa applicants and Singapore and Chilean H-1B1 visa applicants under the Singapore and Chilean Free Trade Agreements; but this is done on a case-by-case basis.

Special Considerations for Security Advisory Opinions (SAOs)

- Do anticipate a possible Visas Condor security clearance if your client was subject to special registration. While the exact criteria of the Visas Condor are classified, it appears to be based on several factors including:

  1. Information disclosed on Form DS-157 (such as travel to predominantly Muslim countries in the last 10 years, prior employment, military service, specialized skills or training)

  2. Country of Birth, Citizenship, or Residence—persons born in the T-5 State Sponsors of Terrorism and/or "List of 26" countries will likely be subject to a Condor security check.

  3. Most Condor SAOs clear within seven to 15 days.

- Don't anticipate a quick resolution for a Visas Donkey SAO. A Donkey clearance is a name "hit" based on noncriminal issues and is not nationality-specific. For instance, a U.K. citizen with the name "Mohammad Khan" or "Muhammad Ali" will very likely be subject to a Donkey clearance. These clearances can take 10 to 14 weeks to process, while a few take substantially longer.

- Don't expect to still find the Technology Alert List (TAL) on the DOS website. The last unclassified version is published on AILA InfoNet at Doc. No. 03030449 (*posted* Mar. 4, 2003). Fortunately, most Visas Mantis SAOs are processed within 15 days. Applicants potentially involved in "dual use" activities should anticipate a Mantis SAO and should bring to their interview a de-

tailed and complete résumé, a complete publications list, abstracts of papers or other published materials, and a detailed letter from their employer and/or U.S. sponsor explaining the nature of the proposed work or meeting/presentation, or project descriptions (in lay terms). The employer/sponsor should explain why the work has no possible military application and, if applicable, that the information is in the public domain or found in academic courses.

- Millions of records from the FBI's National Crime Information Center (NCIC) have been incorporated into the Consular Lookout and Support System (CLASS) name-check database. As DOS is not a "law enforcement agency," consuls do not have access to the specifics of an arrest or a conviction and cannot tell whether the person before them is a murderer or jaywalker. Accordingly, if there is a hit in the system for a prior arrest and/or conviction or a false "hit," the consul is required to submit the applicant's full set of fingerprints along with the prevailing processing fee to the FBI to request the record and/or to confirm that there is no record. Applicants may present certified final court dispositions, arrest records, and legal briefs at the time of the interview, but the consul cannot issue the visa until it has received the record from the FBI.

- Do expect false hits to occur for visa applicants with common names (*e.g.,* John Smith or Juan Gonzalez). As many as half of the names recently entered into the CLASS system are Latino. This has resulted in an alarming number of false hits and delays for persons with common Latino names. Fortunately, posts have now implemented an electronic fingerprinting program, which allows the post to process clearances on false hits in the same day, while clearances for positive hits are often cleared by the next day.

- Do ask your client if they ever have had any alcohol-related incidents. DOS issued guidance in 2007 requiring consular officers to refer nonimmigrant visa applicants with prior drunk driving issues to panel physicians for medical examination in the following circumstances[1]:

---

[1] DOS Cable, "Guidance on Processing Visa Applicants with Drunk Driving Hits," *published on* AILA InfoNet at Doc. No. 07071670 (*posted* July 16, 2007).

1. if an applicant has a single drunk driving arrest or conviction within the last three calendar years, or

2. two or more drunk driving arrests or drunk driving convictions in any time period.

- Do request a consular officer to expedite an SAO for exigent circumstances. It is advisable to submit an expedite request letter from the petitioner detailing the emergent reasons for the applicant's urgent return to the United States. Clearly, physicians in medically underserved areas and medical researchers are strong candidates for such a request.

- If a security check has been pending for over 45 days, attorneys can inquire via e-mail to *legalnet@state.gov*. The subject-line caption should state "Overdue SAO". Also, attorneys may call the Visa Office Public Inquiries line at (202) 663-1225 or fax (202) 663-3899.

CONSULAR OFFICER ACCOUNTABILITY

We respectfully propose that the State Department's Visa Office reaffirm guidance on working with attorneys sent to consular officers in 1999 (99 State 21138)[2] by sending an updated version to all U.S. consular posts. This renewed guidance would set forth standards for conoff accountability in the visa process. Such standards might include the following:

- Consulates shall post their preferred method and manner of communications on their website, and shall use their best efforts to respond initially to an attorney's inquiry within a specified time frame of no more than two full business days.

- Posts will create attorney inquiry e-mail addresses for legal and procedural issues not referenced on the post's website, similar to that provided by the National Visa Center. After receipt of a legitimate inquiry from the attorney, a post shall use its best efforts to reply to such an inquiry within two business days of receipt.

- Consular officers shall always provide a denial letter to the applicant for a nonimmigrant or immigrant visa, which clearly advises of the precise obstacle to visa issuance, in recognition of the provisions of 9 FAM 41.121 N2 ("Refused Applicants Have Reasonable Opportunity to Establish Eligibility"). Denial letters shall not consist merely of a pre-printed form with a box checked indicating the section of law.

- A uniform mechanism shall be adopted by posts for redress by attorneys of both procedural and legal errors concerning a visa denial. For example, if a post requires the original of an L blanket approval, there should be a way to address such a procedural error on a same day or next day basis. Thus, consulates shall devote resources to allow for phone calls or e-mails to try to address such issues post-interview in a required format.

- If the attorney believes that the consular officer is not applying the applicable law or regulation, the attorney will submit the required form, and such issue shall be noted in bold on the attorney's refusal reply as "LEGAL APPLICATION ISSUE." Posts shall use best efforts to reply to such refusal inquiries within two business days or less, so that if an advisory opinion must be sought, it can be commenced as soon as possible.

- It is a waste of resources, however, to have to request an advisory opinion on a legal or procedural matter clearly established in FAM or regulations. For such matters, we would request some type of inquiry methodology to quickly address such simple matters as for example, the application of dual intent to an H-1B case. We would suggest an e-mail or phone inquiry option on a same-day basis for applicants in these situations.

- Consular officers and staff shall not inquire as to attorneys' fees paid by an applicant or to demean the value of attorney representation to an applicant. In addition, consular officers and staff shall not slander or denigrate the attorney's work on a case. If the consular officer believes the attorney has committed malpractice, the officer should advise the attorney's state bar via a complaint.

CONCLUSION

An effective—and efficient—visa application process is the goal of consular officers and attorneys alike. Achieving this goal relies in large part on ensuring the accountability of conoff and counsel to the process. The authors hope that this within "DOs" and "DON'Ts" makes at least a small contribution toward facilitating a "win-win" relationship between consular officers and attorneys, in which visa applicants are the true victors.

---

[2] *Published on* AILA InfoNet at Doc. No. 03010241 (*posted* Jan. 2, 2003).

CHALLENGES TO THE USE OF DIPLOMATIC ASSURANCES IN THE APPLICATION FOR PROTECTION UNDER THE CONVENTION AGAINST TORTURE

by Ivan Yacub [*]

INTRODUCTION

This paper discusses the U.S. commitment to protecting victims of torture and the regulations known as diplomatic assurances. In this paper, it is argued that the implementing regulation violates the plain language of the Convention Against Torture and Other Cruel, Inhuman or Degrading Treatment or Punishment (CAT).[1] There are two compelling reasons why the regulatory language of diplomatic assurances is an unreasonable interpretation of CAT. First, it lacks common sense to interpret the U.S. treaty obligation not to repatriate a foreign national to a country where he or she has a clear probability of persecution and at the same time grant the torturing nation the authority to provide diplomatic assurances that the alien will not be tortured.[2] Second, the plain language of the regulation violates procedural due process as that concept is interpreted in *Matthews v. Eldridge*.[3]

SOURCE OF LAW

The United States has a longstanding history of protecting victims of torture. Prior to signing and ratifying CAT, the United States protected victims of torture under two principles of international law: customary international law and *jus cogens*. Customary international law is "the consistent practice of states followed by them from a sense of legal obligation."[4] Customary international law is binding on nations if those nations consent to the custom.[5]

In contrast to the principle of customary international law, *jus cogens* "embraces customary laws considered binding on all parties."[6] "Whereas customary international law derives solely from the consent of states, the fundamental and universal norms constituting *jus cogens* transcend such consent, as exemplified by the theories underlying the judgments of the Nuremberg tribunals following World War II. The legitimacy of the Nuremberg prosecutions rested not on the consent of the Axis Powers and individual defendants, but on the nature of the acts they committed; acts that the laws of all civilized nations define as criminals."[7]

The right to be free from torture is a fundamental right and possesses *jus cogens* recognition.[8]

President Ronald Reagan signed CAT in 1988 against the backdrop of almost universal condemnation of torture.[9] The U.S. Senate gave its advice and

---

[*] **Ivan Yacub** practices immigration law and is the owner of Yacub Law Office in Falls Church, VA. Mr. Yacub is a graduate of University of Maryland School of Law. He is an AILA liaison with the Arlington, VA immigration court and is the recipient of the AILA Washington, D.C. Chapter's Outstanding Service Award (2007).

[1] Dec. 10, 1984, 1465 U.N.T.S. 85 (entered into force June 26, 1987).

[2] *See U.S. v. Howell*, 78 U.S. 432, 436 (1870) (holding that statutes must not be construed to be "[a]t war with common sense"); *see also Macheod v. U. S.*, 229 U.S. 416, 434 (1913) (holding that statutes should be construed consistently with American obligations under international law).

[3] 424 U.S. 319 (1976).

[4] *Siderman de Blake v. Republic of Argentina*, 965 F.2d 699, 714 (9th Cir. 1992), *citing* Restatement (Third) of the Foreign Relations of Law of the United States §102(2).

[5] *Id.* at 715. *See also The Paquete Habana*, 175 U.S. 677, 700 (1900), incorporating customary international law into U.S. domestic law.

[6] *Siderman de Blake, supra* note 4, quoting Klein, "A Theory for the Application of the Customary International Law of Human Rights by Domestic Courts," 13 *Yale J. Int'l L.* 332, 351 (1988).

[7] *Id.* at 715.

[8] *Id.* at 716. *See also Committee of U.S. Citizens Living in Nicaragua v. Reagan*, 859 F.2d 929, 941 (D.C. Cir. 1988) (holding that "genocide, slavery, murder, torture, prolonged arbitrary detention, and racial discrimination" are the "few norms that arguably do meet the stringent criteria for jus cogens").

[9] The courts were not in agreement as to whether torture was universally recognized as a violation of international law. *See Sosa v. Alvarez-Machain*, 542 U.S. 692, 732 n.20 (2004). *Compare Tel-Oren v. Libyan Arab Republic*, 726 F.2d 774, 791–95 (D.C. Cir. 1984) (Edwards, J., concurring) (insufficient consensus in 1984 that torture by private actors violates international law) *with Kadic v. Kardzic*, 70 F.3d

continued

consent in October 1990.[10] Congress enacted the Foreign Affairs Reform and Restructuring Act of 1998 (FARRA)[11] to implement the United States' treaty commitment under CAT. Section 2244(b) of FARRA mandates the "heads of the appropriate agencies" to "prescribe regulations to implement the obligations of the United States under Article 3 of [CAT] . . . ." To this end, legacy Immigration and Naturalization Service (INS) promulgated regulations "[t]o grant protection under CAT whenever it determines that an 'alien is more likely than not to be tortured in the country of removal.'"[12]

THE SCOPE OF CAT

CAT radically modified the forms of relief an alien could seek in immigration court. Prior to CAT, an alien fearing harm in his or her country of origin could seek relief in the form of asylum[13] or withholding of removal.[14] Although asylum and withholding of removal provided refuge to countless individuals fleeing persecution, the statutes limited the relief to those aliens who fear persecution on account of race, religion, nationality, membership in a particular social group, or political opinion. In addition, under both asylum and withholding of removal, criminal aliens had limited forms of relief. For example, aggravated felons are statutorily ineligible to obtain asylum.[15] Aggravated felons who received an aggregate sentence of five years or more are ineligible to receive withholding of removal.[16] Unlike asylum and withholding of removal, CAT does not contain restrictions based on criminal grounds. Only CAT provides protection to any alien who possesses a clear probability of torture. Also unlike asylum and withholding, CAT is a blanket provision against torture; there is no requirement that the torture inflicted against the alien be on account of an enumerated ground.

With these precepts in mind, legacy INS promulgated regulations pursuant to FARRA.[17] Under the regulations, an alien must show a clear probability of torture.[18] Torture is defined as "[a]ny act by severe pain or suffering, whether physical or mental, is inflicted on a person for such purposes as obtaining from him or her or a third person information or a confession, punishing him or her for an act he or she or a third person has committed or is suspect of committing, or intimidating or coercing him or her or a third person, or for any reason based on discrimination of any kind, when such pain or suffering is inflicted by or at the instigation or with the consent or acquiescence of a public official or other person acting in an official capacity."[19]

The tribunal will examine if there is evidence of past torture, evidence of "gross flagrant or mass violations of human rights," and other evidence indicative of the likelihood that the alien will be subject to torture.[20] Based on the totality of the evidence, the immigration judge will decide whether the alien must receive protection under CAT.[21]

Aliens in removal proceedings possess a statutory and regulatory right to seek protection under CAT. Once the notice to appear is filed with the immigration court, removal proceedings are "the

---

232, 239–41 (2d Cir. 1995) (sufficient consensus in 1995 that genocide by private actors violates international law).

[10] Sen. Exec. Rpt. 101-30 (1990).

[11] Pub. L. No. 105-277, div. G, 112 Stat. 2681, 2681-761 to 2681-854.

[12] *Wang v. Ashcroft*, 320 F.3d 130, 133 (2d Cir. 2003), *citing* 8 CFR §§208.16–208.18 (2002).

[13] *See* INA §208. To obtain protection in the form of asylum, the alien either must have suffered persecution or possess a well-founded fear of persecution on account of an enumerated ground. An alien who suffered persecution on account of an enumerated ground will be presumed to possess a well-founded fear of persecution. *Matter of D–I–M–*, 24 I&N Dec. 448, 450 (BIA 2008). Even in the absence of past persecution, an asylum applicant may show that he or she possesses a well-founded fear of persecution. Meeting this burden, the applicant must show by a preponderance of the evidence that he or she possesses a reasonable fear of harm on account of the enumerated grounds. *INS v. Cardoza-Fonseca*, 480 U.S. 421, 424 (1987).

[14] *See* INA §241(b)(3). To be granted withholding of removal, the applicant must show a clear probability of persecution. The clear probability of persecution requires the applicant to show that it is more likely than not that he or she will face persecution on account of the enumerated grounds. The more-likely-than-not standard is interpreted as being more than a 50 percent likelihood of future persecution. *Cardoza-Fonseca*, *supra* note 13, at 431. However, as with asylum, an alien who suffered past persecution is presumed to possess a clear probability of persecution. 8 CFR §208.16(b)(1)(i).

[15] INA §208(b)(2)(B).

[16] INA §241(b)(3)(B).

[17] 8 CFR §§208.16–208.18.

[18] 8 CFR §208.16(c)(2).

[19] 8 CFR §208.18(a)(1).

[20] 8 CFR §208.16(c)(3).

[21] 8 CFR §208.16(c)(4).

sole and exclusive procedure for determining whether an alien may be admitted to the United States or, if the alien has been so admitted, removed from the United States."[22]

In addition to possessing a statutory and regulatory right to an adversarial hearing, an alien fearing torture possesses a right to a hearing under the due process clause of the Fifth Amendment.[23]

Constitutionally, statutorily, and under the regulations, an alien who faces torture possesses a right to an adversarial hearing before an immigration judge. However, if the government obtains diplomatic assurances from the nation accused of committing torture that the alien will not be tortured, the alien is deprived of an adversarial or any other type of hearing to contest the diplomatic assurances. As the regulations plainly state: "Once assurances are provided ... the alien's claim for protection under the Convention Against Torture shall not be considered further by an immigration judge, the Board of Immigration Appeals, or an asylum officer."[24]

INTERPRETATION OF CAT

It is absurd and lacks common sense to interpret article 3 of CAT to permit a torturing nation to provide diplomatic assurances that an alien will not be tortured and not permit the alien to challenge such "assurances" in court. After all, the United States is obligated by its treaty commitment not to return an alien to a country where he or she faces a significant risk of torture. Therefore, common sense dictates that if the torturing nation provides diplomatic assurances that the alien will not be tortured, the alien must be permitted to challenge such assurances.

Congress Has Directly Spoken on the Issue, and the Regulation Divesting the Immigration Court of Jurisdiction to Adjudicate a CAT Claim Is Invalid

The regulation governing diplomatic assurances is troubling in two respects. First, it purports to divest the immigration court of jurisdiction to adjudicate CAT claims. Second, under the regulation, the alien is not permitted to challenge the validity of the diplomatic assurances. Under *Chevron USA, Inc. v. Natural Resources Defense Council, Inc.*,[25] in determining the validity of administrative regulations, courts must first decide whether Congress has addressed the issue. As the *Chevron* Court held, the "[j]udiciary is the final authority on issues of statutory construction, and must reject administrative constructions which are contrary to the clear congressional intent. ... If a court, employing traditional tools of statutory construction, ascertains that Congress had an intention on the precise question at issue, that intention is the law, and must be given effect."[26]

In plain terms, Congress has addressed the issue. There are two relevant statutory authorities that contradict the regulation governing diplomatic assurances. First, under INA §240(a)(3), Congress conferred sole and exclusive jurisdiction to the immigration court to determine whether an alien "may be admitted to the United States, or, if the alien has been so admitted, removed from the United States." Second, under INA §240(b)(4)(B), Congress set forth the rights of aliens in removal proceedings. As that section of the INA plainly states: "[T]he alien shall have a reasonable opportunity to examine the evidence against the alien, to present evidence on the alien's own behalf, and to cross-examine witnesses presented by the Government . . . ."

---

[22] INA §240(a)(3).

[23] *Khouzam v. Hogan*, 2008 WL 98545, *17 (M.D. Pa. 2008) (*Khouzam II*). The diplomatic assurances regulations do not state at what part of the proceedings they are applicable. In *Khouzam II*, the Department of Homeland Security obtained diplomatic assurances after the immigration judge granted relief. This could create a res judicata problem. *See Astoria Federal Savings and Loan Association v. Solimino*, 501 U.S. 104 (1991) (applying the doctrine of res judicata to administrative proceedings); *Medina v. INS*, 993 F.2d 499 (5th Cir. 1993), and *Hamdan v. Gonzales*, 425 F.3d 1051 (7th Cir. 2005) (applying the doctrine of res judicata to immigration proceedings).

[24] 8 CFR §208.18(c)(3).

[25] 467 U.S. 837 (1984).

[26] *Chevron USA, Inc. v. Natural Resources Defense Council, Inc.*, 467 U.S. 837, 843 n.9 (1984). A reviewing court must defer to the agency's interpretation of a statute if (1) Congress has not spoken to the precise issue, or (2) the agency interpretation is reasonable. If Congress has spoken on the issue, courts must give effect to the plain language of the statute. *Id.* at 843. However, if the statute is silent or ambiguous, courts must defer to the agency's reasonable interpretation of the statute. *Id.* at 844. "In determining whether Congress has specifically addressed the question at issue, a reviewing court should not confine itself to examining a particular statutory provision in isolation. The meaning—or ambiguity—of certain words or phrases may only become evident when placed in context." *Food and Drug Admin. v. Brown & Williamson Tobacco Corp.*, 529 U.S. 120, 133 (2000).

What is clear from the Congressional enactment is that an alien in removal proceedings may only have his or her case heard before an immigration judge, and in immigration court, the alien possesses a plethora of rights, including the right to inspect evidence, present evidence, and cross-examine adverse witnesses.[27]

Although congressional enactment is plain, the CAT diplomatic assurances regulations contradict the plain language of the Immigration and Nationality Act (INA). Under the CAT diplomatic assurances regulation, the torturing nation provides diplomatic assurances to the U.S. secretary of state. The regulations do not provide a forum for the alien to examine the evidence regarding the "assurances," to present evidence regarding the reliability of the "assurances," or to cross-examine adverse witnesses. Thus, the regulation is in clear conflict with INA §240(b)(4)(B).

The diplomatic assurances regulations also conflict with INA §240(a)(3). Although in removal proceedings the immigration court is the "sole and exclusive" tribunal to determine the admissibility or the removal of an alien, under 8 CFR §208.18(c)(3), once assurances are provided, the application for protection under CAT "shall not be considered further by an immigration judge, the Board of Immigration Appeals, or an asylum officer." Thus, without an opportunity to challenge the assurances provided by the torturing nation, the fate of the alien is essentially decided under a shroud of secrecy. Courts have traditionally held that secrecy in immigration proceedings is highly disfavored.[28] It is so disfavored to rely on secret evidence that on bond and removal hearings, such process has been compared to Joseph K.'s predicament in Kafka's *The Trial*.[29]

It is impossible to reconcile the congressional mandate that aliens in removal proceedings must have their cases heard by an immigration judge with the regulation that divests the immigration court of jurisdiction to hear the case. A regulation that is inconsistent with the statute must be invalidated.[30]

The Diplomatic Assurances Regulation Is an Unreasonable Interpretation of the Treaty

Assuming that the regulation is not in clear conflict with the INA, the regulation is an unreasonable interpretation of the United States' commitment to protect victims who face torture in their countries. Thus, even under the *Chevron* deferential standard—courts must defer to reasonable agency interpretations—the diplomatic assurances regulation must be struck down.

Although the INA confers jurisdiction on immigration courts to hear CAT claims, CAT is silent on the issue of diplomatic assurances. In *Khouzam v. Hogan* (*Khouzam II*),[31] the district court found that Congress has not directly spoken on the issue of how CAT application must be adjudicated. Thus, the court found the use of diplomatic assurances in the context of adjudicating a CAT claim to be reasonable. A reviewing court must defer to the agency's interpretation of CAT unless such interpretation is unreasonable.[32]

However, the level of deference of an agency's interpretation of a statute is not absolute. "It has been called a golden rule of statutory interpretation that unreasonableness of the result produced by one among alternative possible interpretations of a statute is reason for rejecting that interpretation in favor of another which would produce a reasonable result."[33]

Reading CAT in the context of the United States' treaty obligation not to return aliens who face a certainty of being tortured, it lacks common sense to rely on diplomatic assurances from the torturing nation that the removed alien will be able to reside safely and without being tortured. For more than a century the U.S. Supreme Court has held that statutes must be interpreted consistent with notions of common sense.[34] In *U.S. v. Brown*,[35] a criminal defendant argued that a penal statute must be construed narrowly. Refusing to give such construction, the Supreme Court held: "We are mindful of the maxim that penal statutes are to be strictly construed. And we would not hesitate, present any compelling reason, to apply it and accept the restricted interpreta-

---

[27] INA §§240(a)(3), (b)(4)(B).

[28] *Kiareldeen v. Reno*, 71 F. Supp. 2d 402, 412 (D.N.J. 1999).

[29] *Id.*; *Rafeedie v. INS*, 800 F.2d 506, 524 (D.C. Cir. 1989).

[30] *C.I.R. v. Standard Life & Acc. Ins. Co.*, 433 U.S. 148, 163 (1977).

---

[31] 2008 WL 98545 (M.D. Pa. 2008).

[32] *Chevron*, *supra* note 26, at 843.

[33] *Kelly v. U.S.*, 924 F.2d 335, 361 (1st Cir. 1991), *citing* 2A Sands, *Sutherland Stat. Const.* §45.12 (4th Ed. 1984–85).

[34] *States v. Howell*, 78 U.S. 432, 436 (1870). *See also Brown & Williamson*, *supra* note 26, at 133 ("We must be guided by a degree of common sense . . . .").

[35] 333 U.S. 18 (1948).

tion. But no such reason is to be found here. The canon in favor of strict construction is not an inexorable command to override common sense and evident statutory purpose."[36]

There are two compelling reasons why it is unreasonable to interpret CAT as permitting diplomatic assurances. First, by simply informing the torturing nation that an alien is seeking relief under CAT, the U.S. government will be placing an alien at even greater risk of harm than before. Second, the torturing nation does not possess any incentive to be truthful about whether the alien will be tortured.

CAT, in a similar vein with asylum and withholding of removal, is grounded on the United States' humanitarian obligation not to return aliens fearing torture. Simply informing a nation that engages in human rights abuses that an asylum applicant filed an application for protection in the United States may be sufficient to trigger a "new risk" of persecution. For example, in *Lin v. U.S. Dep't of Justice*,[37] the Department of Homeland Security (DHS) trial attorney submitted documents of Lin's detention to the U.S. consulate in China for authentication. The documents were given to the Chinese government to determine whether the documents were forgery. By submitting the documents to the Chinese government, the DHS placed the alien in further fear of harm. As the U.S. Court of Appeals for the Second Circuit held: "The government through its own negligence has potentially exposed Lin and his family to risks beyond those he claims caused him to flee China."[38]

Diplomatic assurances fall within the "new risk" of harm identified in *Lin*. In order to obtain diplomatic assurances, the U.S. government must inform the torturing nation that the alien (1) has requested CAT relief in the United States, and (2) alleges that the nation is more likely than not to torture the alien. Thus, by informing the torturing nation that the alien is seeking protection, the alien faces new fears of torture if returned. Relying on and accepting as credible a torturing nation's Diplomatic assurances that the alien will not be tortured lacks common sense.

At the core of diplomatic assurances is the issue of whether such assurances are "reliable."[39] If the "assurances" are valid and the trier of fact believes that the alien does not face a clear probability of persecution, the CAT claim may be denied.[40]

There is a stigma attached to a nation known as a "torturer." In fact, torture is such a heinous crime that for "[p]urposes of civil liability, the torturer has become—like the pirate and slave trader before him—*hostis humani generis,* an enemy of all mankind."[41] That is why nations may be willing to provide "reasonable assurances" that they will not engage in torture regardless of their true intentions. This makes the concept of diplomatic assurances meaningless. There is no reason a nation would not provide them, so they should be read with much scrutiny and skepticism. This skepticism is heightened by the fact that once an alien is removed to the nation where he or she faces torture, there is no mechanism for the United States to follow up the fate of the individual. The harm, if any, would be irreparable.

Further reason for skepticism is the fact that numerous nations that systematically use torture as a means to punish or obtain confessions outlaw torture in their constitutions. In Sudan, for example, the State Department reports: "Although the Interim National Constitution, adopted in July 2005 and hereafter referred to as the "interim constitution," prohibits such practices, government security forces continued to torture, beat, and harass suspected political opponents and others."[42] The lack of credibility and the strong incentives torturing nations have to deceive the United States regarding their policies was recognized by the *Lin* court: "We agree with the IJ that the Consular Report is entirely based on the opinions of Chinese government officials who appear to have powerful incentives to be less than candid on the subject of their government's persecution of political dissidents."[43]

If the torturing nation—a nation that has strong incentives both to punish the alien for making an

---

[36] *Id.* at 25.

[37] 459 F.3d 255 (2d Cir. 2006).

[38] *Id.* at 268. *But see Abdel-Rahman v. Gonzalez,* 493 F.3d 444, 454 (4th Cir. 2007); *Averianova v. Mukasey,* 509 F.3d 890, 898 (8th Cir. 2007) (holding that disclosure of identity does not necessarily create a "new risk" for asylum purposes).

[39] *See* 8 CFR §208.18(c)(2).

[40] 8 CFR §208.16(c)(2).

[41] *Sosa v. Alvarez-Machain,* 542 U.S. 692, 733 (2004), *citing Filartiga v. Pena-Irala,* 630 F.2d 876, 890 (2d Cir. 1980).

[42] Department of State, 2006 Country Reports on Human Practices (Sudan), *available at www.state.gov/g/drl/rls/hrrpt/2006/78759.htm.*

[43] *Lin v. U.S. Dep't of Justice,* 459 F.3d 255, 269–70 (2d Cir. 2006).

accusation that that country engages in torture and to deceive the United States about the fact that it engages in torture—is permitted to provide diplomatic assurances, those assurances must be provided in the context of an adversarial hearing in front of an immigration judge. Then, the immigration judge, after reviewing the diplomatic assurances and other evidence presented by the alien to rebut such assurances, will be able to decide whether the alien must be protected under CAT.

Under a Traditional Procedural Due Process Analysis the Regulation Must Be Understood To Be Invalid

The diplomatic assurances regulation violates basic principles of due process. Under the regulations, an alien who believes he or she will be tortured does not possess a right to a meaningful hearing as to whether the diplomatic assurances are valid. The only "hearing" that the alien receives under the diplomatic assurances regulation is a determination by the secretary of state and the attorney general as to whether the assurances are "sufficiently reliable."[44] The alien cannot participate or opine regarding the validity of the assurances; in fact, the alien may not even be placed on notice that the secretary of state and the attorney general received diplomatic assurances from the torturing nation. Without being subject to review in any forum and under a cloak of secrecy, the attorney general is permitted to divest the immigration court of jurisdiction to further adjudicate the nature of the alien's fear of torture. The ultimate decision of whether the torturing nation provided adequate assurances is decided behind closed doors. This lack of process offends fundamental notions of fairness under *Mathews v. Eldridge*.[45] As the U.S. Court of Appeals for the Third Circuit held in *Dia v. Ashcroft*, "an alien: (1) is entitled to 'factfinding based on a record produced before a decision maker and disclosed to' him or her; (2) must be allowed to make arguments on his or her own behalf; and (3) has the right to 'an individualized determination of his [or her] interests.'"[46]

The right of an alien to challenge the validity of the diplomatic assurances is governed by the Fifth Amendment's Due Process Clause. It is without dispute that an alien has a "liberty" interest cognizable under the Due Process Clause. As was stated in *Khouzam II*: "Freedom from torture falls squarely within the concept of 'liberty' protected by the Fifth Amendment."[47] An alien cannot be deprived of his or her "liberty" interest without due process.[48] Of course not every interest protected under the Due Process Clause merits the same type of hearing. The amount of process and by extension the type of hearing an individual will receive rests on balancing the individual's stake in a hearing and the risk of an erroneous adjudication against the administrative cost in providing the alien with the requested hearing.[49]

In CAT claims, the right to be free from torture is weighty. The *Khouzam II* court held that the right to be free from torture constitutes a "fundamental and universal right, a right deserving of the highest status under international law, a norm of *jus cogens*."[50]

The problem with the diplomatic assurances regulation is the second prong of the *Mathews* test, the possibility of an erroneous adjudication. Because the regulation divests the Board of Immigration Appeals and the immigration court of the right to test the validity of the diplomatic assurances, an alien seeking protection under article 3 of CAT does not have a meaningful forum to challenge the diplomatic assurances. Moreover, in light of the fact that the assurances are provided by representatives of governments that engage in torture, and that such governments have a strong incentive in hiding their human rights abuses practices, at a very minimum, and consistent with procedural due process, the alien must be allowed to challenge the evidence contained in the diplomatic assurances.

In the asylum context, courts are in agreement that asylum applicants possess a due process right to an adversarial hearing. In *Yiu Sing Chun v. Sava*,[51] the Second Circuit held that because "the severity of harm to the erroneously excluded asylee outweighs the administrative burden of providing an asylum hearing, if the regulations did not do so already the INS arguably would be required to provide a hearing before an immigration judge to determine whether

---

[44] 8 CFR §208.18(c)(2).

[45] 424 U.S. 319 (1976).

[46] *Dia v. Ashcroft*, 353 F.3d 228, 240 (3d Cir. 2003), *citing Abdulai v. Ashcroft*, 239 F.3d 542, 549 (3d Cir. 2001).

[47] *Khouzam II*, *supra* note 23, at *17.

[48] *Mathews v. Eldridge*, 424 U.S. 319, 331 (1976).

[49] *Id.* at 335.

[50] *Khouzam II*, *supra* note 23, at *6, *citing Siderman de Blake*, *supra* note 4, at 717.

[51] 708 F.2d 869, 877 (2d Cir. 1983).

applicants for asylum are, in fact, refugees within the meaning of the Act."[52]

The nature of harm sought to be prevented under CAT is similar to that faced by an asylum applicant—in both cases the applicant fears for his or her life. Therefore, it stands to reason that if in the case of asylum applicants the government must provide the alien with an adversarial hearing and an opportunity to rebut the evidence presented against him or her, the same must be true for an alien seeking protection under CAT. As such, if DHS believes that the diplomatic assurances are valid, the diplomatic assurances must be adjudicated in an adversarial hearing with the right of the CAT applicant to challenge the evidence. The right to an adversarial hearing when a person fears torture is consistent with notions of procedural fairness.

Further, the cost to the government is minimal. In a CAT claim the alien is not seeking to create a new tribunal to adjudicate his or her CAT claim in conjunction with the diplomatic assurances. Rather, the alien requests that the immigration court, a forum that has experience hearing CAT claims, adjudicate the alien's claim under CAT and permit the alien to challenge the validity of diplomatic assurances in the adversarial hearing.

This process of hearing the CAT claim in an adversarial setting and permitting the alien to challenge the assurances provided by the torturing nation is consistent with how other countries adjudicate CAT claims. In *Zicherman v. Korean Air Lines Co., Ltd.*,[53] the U.S. Supreme Court held that post-ratification conduct of parties to treaties is persuasive as to how the treaty must be interpreted. The Supreme Court recently reiterated this principle in *Sanchez-Llamas v. Oregon*.[54] Post-ratification conduct permits nations to provide diplomatic assurances, but at the same time, the alien claiming protection under CAT can be permitted to challenge such assurances. As the *Khouzam II* court points out: "Austria, Canada, Germany, Netherlands, Russia, Sweden, Switzerland, Turkey and the United Kingdom, all parties to CAT, provide for judicial review of the reliability and sufficiency of diplomatic assurances. For example, in Suresh v. Canada (Minister of Citizenship & Immigration) (2002) 1 S.C.R. 3, the Supreme Court of Canada held that '[w]here the

Minister is relying on written assurances from a foreign government that a person would not be tortured, the refugee must be given an opportunity to present evidence and make submissions as to the value of the assurances.'"[55] A UK court has stated: "[t]he state's obligation is not only not to deport persons to a state where they face a real risk of torture, but also to ensure that the proceedings in which that issue was considered were fair. Proceedings are not fair if evidence is used that is not seen by the [claimant] and his . . . advocates."[56] In fact, as the *Khouzam II* court observed, "the United States is the only government that purports to deny a person subject to transfer the right to challenge the reliability and sufficiency of diplomatic assurances against torture before an independent, impartial body."[57]

The due process violation goes beyond the fact that the alien's fate is essentially tried in secrecy. Although statutorily and under the regulations, an alien has an absolute right to appeal the denial of CAT in the court of appeals,[58] by "trying" the case between the attorney general, the secretary of state, and the torturing nation, without any meaningful record created of the proceedings, the alien is deprived of his or her right to seek judicial review of the diplomatic assurances.

By allowing the CAT applicant to be "tried" under secrecy and denying the applicant participation in his or her own hearing, without the right to challenge the reliability of the assurances, the process is constitutionally deficient.[59] Under FARRA and the implementing regulations, an alien possesses a right to judicial review. However, under the diplomatic assurances regulations there is no adequate record for the court of appeals to review. As the *Dia* court held: "We have always required that the review process be a meaningful one, aided by a reasoned opinion from the agency."[60]

To comply with *Mathews* and *Dia*, the regulations as written must be struck down. If in the process of removing an alien, the government obtains

---

[52] *Accord Marincas v. Lewis*, 92 F.3d 195 (3d Cir. 1996).

[53] 516 U.S. 217, 227 (1996).

[54] 126 S.Ct. 2669 (2006).

[55] *Khouzam II, supra* note 23, at *17.

[56] *MT, RB, and U v. Secretary of State for the Home Department,* cited in *Khouzam II, supra* note 23, at *17.

[57] *Khouzam II, supra* note 23, at *17.

[58] An alien may seek judicial review of a denied CAT application "as part of the review of a final order of removal pursuant to section 242 of the [INA]. . . ." 8 CFR §208.18(e)(1).

[59] *Dia v. Ashcroft, supra* note 46, at 240.

[60] *Id.* at 244.

diplomatic assurances that the alien will not be tortured in his or her country, those assurances must be made part of the administrative record. The immigration judge should be able to consider the validity of the assurances provided and the nature of the fear that the alien possesses of being tortured. After carefully weighing the evidence, the immigration judge can do what immigration judges routinely do—decide cases on the basis of a complete record. Justice requires nothing less.

CONCLUSION

Because of the futility doctrine, it is not necessary to raise the issues presented in this article in immigration court. The immigration judge will not have authority to rule on the validity of the regulation. After all, "[a]n agency has the duty to follow its own federal regulations, even when those regulations provide greater protection than is constitutionally required."[61] In fact, if the immigration court does not follow its own regulations, it "can lead to reversal of an agency order and a new hearing."[62] Further, the immigration court is without authority to decide the constitutionality of a regulation.[63] Although typically an alien must exhaust his or her administrative remedies prior to filing a petition in federal court, if exhaustion itself is futile, the alien may file the petition immediately.[64]

Remember, in federal court is it of utmost importance to plead at least the issues discussed above when challenging the diplomatic assurances regulations. The *Khouzam II* court took an important step in holding the regulations unconstitutional, and it is likely that other courts will either invalidate the regulations as being unreasonable under the *Chevron* analysis, or as a violation of the Fifth Amendment Due Process Clause.

---

[61] *Nelson v. INS*, 232 F.3d 258, 262 (1st Cir. 2000).

[62] *Id.*

[63] *Ashley v. Ridge*, 288 F. Supp. 2d 662, 667 (D.N.J. 2003).

[64] *Id.*

ANY REAL CHANGE?
CREDIBILITY AND CORROBORATION AFTER THE REAL ID ACT

by Deborah Anker, Emily Gumper, Jean C. Han, and Matthew Muller[*]

INTRODUCTION

Congress passed the REAL ID Act on May 11, 2005.[1] Its provisions included several amendments addressing evidentiary standards in asylum, withholding of removal, and Convention Against Torture claims.[2] Citing a need for uniform standards,[3] the bill's authors largely encoded existing case law relating to credibility and corroboration.

Since its enactment, practitioners have generally assumed that the REAL ID Act would lead to more restrictive interpretations by adjudicators and appellate bodies.[4] The purported aim of the REAL ID Act—preventing abuse of the U.S. asylum system by terrorists—as well as the tenor of debate surrounding its enactment contribute to this sense. However, as this article will explain, there is no basis in the REAL ID Act for the notion that Congress issued judges and other adjudicators a blank check

to make and uphold evidentiary decisions as they see fit. To the contrary, the REAL ID Act sets forth detailed standards and procedures for making evidentiary determinations, as well as admonitions to extend refugees the benefit of the doubt and uphold international standards.[5] Nonetheless, advocates' and commentators' negative impressions are in danger of becoming a self-fulfilling prophecy, as adjudicators base their decisions on the general sense that REAL ID gives them free reign, overlooking the actual dictates of Congress.

This article concerns the proper interpretation of the REAL ID Act according to widely accepted principles of statutory construction. Those principles direct us primarily toward the text of the statute,[6] revisions in the text from prior iterations of the bill,[7] and the conference report accompanying the final bill as the key indicators of congressional intent.[8] As detailed in this article, these indicators show that Congress intended to enact objective, uniform credibility and corroboration standards based on pre-existing administrative standards. Advocates should welcome this goal, considering that much of the criticism surrounding credibility and corroboration determination can be traced to inconsistency in adjudication and the unwillingness or inability of the

[*] **Deborah Anker** is a clinical professor of law at Harvard Law School and director of the Harvard Immigration and Refugee Clinical Program. **Emily Gumper** is a 2007 graduate of Harvard Law School. **Jean C. Han** and **Matthew Muller** are clinical teaching and advocacy fellows with the Harvard Immigration and Refugee Clinical Program. The authors would like to thank all of the attorneys and advocates who took the time to share their observations, including in particular (but not limited to) Christine Brigagliano, Ira Kurzban, Mario Russell, Debi Sanders, Debbie Smith, Virgil Wiebe, and John Willshire-Carrera.

[1] Pub. L. No. 109-13, div. B, 119 Stat. 231, 302–23.

[2] Except where otherwise noted, references to evidentiary standards for asylum in this article also encompass those applicable to withholding of removal and Convention Against Torture relief. REAL ID Act §101(a) encoded credibility and burden of proof standards for asylum claims. REAL ID Act §101(c) incorporated these standards by reference for withholding of removal determinations. Using nearly the same language as §101(a), REAL ID Act §101(d) extended materially identical evidentiary standards to "Other Requests for Relief From Removal," which would include Convention Against Torture claims.

[3] See H. Rep. No. 109-72 at 165 (2005) [Hereinafter "Conference Report"].

[4] See, e.g., M. Silenzi Cianciarulo, "Terrorism and Asylum Seekers: Why the Real ID Act is a False Promise," 43 *Harv. J. on Legis.* 101, 103 (2006).

[5] As discussed below, the committee report accompanying the REAL ID Act emphasized that unreasonable demands must not be placed on protection seekers, and reaffirmed the principle that applicants may carry their burden of proof through detailed and credible testimony alone. Conference Report, *supra* note 3, at 165–69 (discussed further below).

[6] See, e.g., Reiter v. Sonotone Corp., 442 U.S. 330, 337 (1979) ("[O]ur starting point must be the language employed by Congress.").

[7] See, e.g., INS v. Cardoza-Fonseca, 480 U.S. 421, 443–44 (1987).

[8] See, e.g., Garcia v. U.S., 469 U.S. 70, 76 (1984) ("In surveying legislative history we have repeatedly stated that the authoritative source for finding the Legislature's intent lies in the Committee Reports on the bill, which represen[t] the considered and collective understanding of those Congressmen involved in drafting and studying proposed legislation.") (internal quotations omitted). See also Zuber v. Allen, 396 U.S. 168, 186 (1969) ("Floor debates reflect at best the understanding of individual Congressmen.").

Board of Immigration Appeals (BIA) to effectively enforce (and in some cases apply) its own credibility and corroboration standards.[9]

Congress's goal may be fulfilled through minimizing arbitrariness in administrative decision-making and requiring transparent justification of decisions in terms of uniform rules. Adjudicators who assume that REAL ID extended them *carte blanche* in credibility and corroboration determinations are acting directly contrary to Congressional intent. This article aims to equip advocates with a robust understanding of the REAL ID Act that will allow them to confront adjudicators and judges who are failing to apply the correct standards and procedures specified by Congress.

As part of their research for this article, the authors spoke with practitioners in a variety of locations and practice settings about what they saw on the ground in terms of changes arising from the REAL ID Act's credibility and corroboration requirements. Reports have run the range from no change to a perceivable difference in standards employed by the asylum office and immigration courts. To the extent that changes have been noted, they are most often in the form of increased expectations and demands for corroboration of applicants' claims (although many practitioners considered this a trend that predates the REAL ID Act). Where practitioners have seen changes in agency practice purportedly pursuant to REAL ID—especially spiraling demands for corroboration—these changes may well be in

defiance of the Act's standards and purpose rather than in keeping with them.

This article begins with an overview of the applicant's burden of proof in refugee determination or asylum cases, followed by an overview of the relevant REAL ID provisions. The article then discusses the statute's credibility and corroboration provisions in more detail, and their implications for some specific issues of testimony and evidence.[10] In particular, this article draws on the BIA's decision in *Matter of S–M–J–*,[11] which was repeatedly cited by Congress as embodying the correct corroboration framework under the REAL ID Act.[12]

THE REFUGEE'S BURDEN

Applicants for asylum, withholding of removal, and Convention Against Torture protection[13] face unique evidentiary challenges in establishing their claims. Not only are they far from the place where the events underlying their claims took place, but, in addition, they will often have fled under conditions incompatible with the gathering of evidence to support their cases. Accordingly, the special situation of the refugee shapes the standards that govern asylum applications under the U.S. statute and the international law it implements and by which it is bound. While asylum applicants bear the burden of proof with regard to their claims, the BIA, federal courts, and now Congress have developed corroboration and credibility standards that recognize the difficulties refugees face in establishing their claims.

Although significant domestic authority exists on credibility and corroboration in asylum claims, international law and standards have been incorporated into that authority and remain a critical touch-

[9] This institutional breakdown—concentrated in the immigration courts and the BIA—has been well-documented elsewhere. *See generally* S. Legomsky, "Deportation and the War on Independence," 91 *Cornell L. Rev.* 369 (2006); G. Seipp & S. Feal, "Overwhelmed Circuit Courts Lashing Out at the BIA and Selected Immigration Judges: Is Streamlining to Blame?," 82 *Interpreter Releases* (Dec. 19, 2005) (detailing various cases in which immigration judges or the BIA have been chastised by the circuit courts). Former Attorney General John Ashcroft's 2002 implementation of major changes in the BIA has seriously undermined the BIA's independent reviewing role and produced arbitrariness and lack of uniformity in administrative decisions. In the wake of these changes, the federal courts have been forced to step in to provide meaningful review of immigration judge decisions that have often been summarily affirmed by the BIA. *See* J. Palmer, S. Yale-Loehr, & E. Cronin, "Why Are So Many People Challenging Board of Immigration Appeals Decisions in Federal Court? An Empirical Analysis of the Recent Surge in Petitions for Review," 20 *Geo. Immigr. L.J.* 1, 29–32 (2005) (BIA streamlining changes have effectively shifted the backlog of immigration appeals from the BIA to the circuit courts).

[10] For the most thorough and complete treatment of asylum-related credibility and corroboration—elaborating, for example, on the appropriate factors in credibility evaluations and categories of corroborative documentation generally required by adjudicators and courts—practitioners and researchers should consult comprehensive texts in the field.

[11] 21 I&N Dec. 722 (BIA 1997).

[12] Conference Report, *supra* note 3, at 166 ("Congress anticipates that the standards in *Matter of S–M–J–*, including the Board's conclusions on situations where corroborating evidence is or is not required, will guide" interpretations of the REAL ID Act's burden of proof provisions.).

[13] As used in the remainder of this article, the term "asylum" refers collectively to U.S. asylum, withholding of removal, and Convention Against Torture relief, except where otherwise noted.

stone. As recognized by the BIA in *Matter of S–M–J–*[14] (a case Congress sought to encode by passing the REAL ID Act),[15] the fundamental purpose of U.S. asylum law is to implement U.S. obligations under the United Nations Convention Relating to the Status of Refugees.[16] In addition to being binding on the United States,[17] the Convention and associated standards have proven to be an important persuasive force in domestic adjudications. U.S. advocates have argued successfully for interpretations of domestic law that comport with international standards.[18] In *Matter of S–M–J–*, the BIA cited to and quoted repeatedly from United Nations High Commissioner for Refugees (UNHCR) guidelines on the adjudication of asylum claims.[19] It noted that even government attorneys prosecuting removal cases have a duty to "uphold international refugee law" and "extend refuge where such refuge is warranted."[20] As such, practitioners, adjudicators, and Department of Homeland Security [DHS] counsel alike should be familiar with both domestic and international author-ity pertaining to evidentiary standards in asylum and related relief.

Consistent with the REAL ID Act,[21] international standards emphasize the special weight that must be given to an applicant's credible testimony, since it is often the only evidence a refugee can produce. According to the UNHCR, an applicant's claim must be evaluated within an evidentiary framework that recognizes the difficulties of proof in asylum cases and extends applicants the "benefit of the doubt" when their testimony is credible but corroborating evidence is not reasonably available.[22]

Although not always hewing to this standard in practice, the BIA has endorsed the international "benefit of the doubt" principle in case law that has now been encoded by the REAL ID Act. This case law notes that asylum applicants are expected to provide detailed and credible testimony addressing the legal elements of their claims, but stresses that this testimony alone may satisfy the applicant's burden when outside corroboration is not reasonably available.[23] Quoting from the UNHCR *Handbook on Procedures and Criteria for Determining Refugee Status Under the 1951 Convention and the 1967 Protocol Relating to the Status of Refugees*, the BIA in *Matter of S–M–J–* acknowledged that:

> [a]fter the applicant has made a genuine effort to substantiate his story there may still be a lack of evidence for some of his statements . . . . [I]t is hardly possible for a refugee to "prove" every part of his case . . . . It is therefore frequently necessary to give the applicant the benefit of the doubt.[24]

The BIA also directed adjudicators to ensure that "[u]nreasonable demands are not placed on an asylum applicant to present evidence to corroborate par-

---

[14] *Matter of S–M–J–*, 21 I&N Dec. 722, 723 (BIA 1997).

[15] *See* Conference Report, *supra* note 2.

[16] United Nations Convention Relating to the Status of Refugees, July 28, 1951, 189 U.N.T.S. 150 (entered into force Apr. 22, 1954); United Nations Protocol Relating to the Status of Refugees, 606 U.N.T.S. 267 (entered into force Oct. 4, 1967) [hereinafter Refugee Convention].

[17] *See, e.g., INS v. Stevic*, 467 U.S. 407, 416, 426 n.20 (1984) (stating that the United States obligated itself to follow the terms of the Refugee Convention by acceding to the Refugee Protocol, and noting the clear intent of Congress to conform U.S. law to the Refugee Convention. In addition, the BIA and federal courts have looked to materials published by the Office of the United Nations High Commissioner for Refugees (UNHCR) for guidance in interpreting the Convention. *See, e.g., INS v. Cardoza-Fonseca*, 480 U.S. 421, 437–39, 439 n.2 (1987) (the UNHCR *Handbook, infra* note 22, "provides significant guidance" in interpreting the Convention); *Matter of Acosta*, 19 I&N Dec. 211, 221 (BIA 1985).

[18] *See, e.g., INS v. Cardoza-Fonseca*, *supra* note 17 (discussing conformance of U.S. law to international standards regarding the refugee definition). For a recent example, *see Yusupov v. Att'y Gen.*, Nos. 05-4232, 05-5411, & 06-3160 (3d Cir. Mar. 14, 2008) (recognizing the intent of Congress to conform U.S. law to its treaty obligations and citing international law, other countries' interpretations of the Refugee Convention, and the understandings of international scholars as interpretative guidance).

[19] *Matter of S–M–J–*, *supra* note 14, at 724–25, 729 (quoting the UNHCR *Handbook, infra* note 22); *see also id.* at 735, 738, 740 (Rosenberg, Bd. Mem., concurring) (quoting the same).

[20] *Id.* at 727.

[21] *See* Conference Report, *supra* note 3, at 165 (discussed further below).

[22] *See* UNHCR, Handbook on Procedures and Criteria for Determining Refugee Status Under the 1951 Convention and the 1967 Protocol Relating to the Status of Refugees, ¶¶196, 203–05 (1992) (also quoted in Matter of S–M–J–, *supra* note 14, at 725).

[23] *Matter of S–M–J–*, *supra* note 14, at 722; *Matter of Dass*, 20 I&N Dec. 120 (BIA 1989); *Matter of Mogharrabi*, 19 I&N Dec. 439, 445 (BIA 1987); 8 CFR §208.13(a) ("The testimony of the applicant, if credible, may be sufficient to sustain the burden of proof without corroboration.").

[24] *Matter of S–M–J–*, *supra* note 14, at 725 (quoting UNHCR *Handbook, supra* note 22, at ¶203).

ticular experiences"[25] and quoted UNHCR guidance stating that "while the burden of proof in principle rests on the applicant, the duty to ascertain and evaluate all the relevant facts is shared between the applicant and the examiner."[26]

THE REAL ID ACT

The REAL ID Act codifies evidentiary standards in asylum and related claims, requiring a uniform, objective approach based on existing case law. It also specifies the standard of review that federal courts must apply to agency decisions regarding the availability of corroborating evidence.[27] The REAL ID provisions addressing credibility and corroboration standards apply only to applications initiated after the May 11, 2005, effective date of the Act.[28] The standard of review provision became effective on the same date, and applies regardless of when the final administrative removal order was issued.[29]

Evidentiary Standards Essentially Unchanged

Given that credibility and corroboration cases subject to REAL ID took some time to reach the BIA and circuit courts, a large body of post-REAL ID appellate case law has not yet developed. However, the picture emerging is that administrative and judicial bodies seem to agree in principle that there has been little or no shift in standards from pre-REAL ID case law. To the extent that the REAL ID Act does supersede case law in some circuits, it is best seen as mandating a uniform approach rather than signaling any significant shift in evidentiary standards.[30]

The text and legislative history of REAL ID confirm the view that the new provisions aimed to pro-mote consistency and encode current case law rather than announce new standards.[31] In particular, the conference report[32] emphasized that with certain explicit exceptions, Congress intended existing case law standards to remain valid.[33] The conference report quotes at length from *Matter of S–M–J–* and sets forth Congress's intent that this decision guide adjudicators in interpreting the REAL ID Act's burden of proof provisions.[34] The credibility provisions likewise were enacted to bring about "a uniform standard for credibility" based on standards already articulated in case law.[35]

CREDIBILITY AND THE REAL ID ACT

An applicant's credible testimony is the lynchpin of a successful asylum claim. Extensive evidence corroborating a claim will frequently be unavailable; therefore, it is critical that the applicant's testimony is found credible. Credibility assessments are typically the most important determinations in asylum adjudications. They may also be the most complex. Beyond the usual criteria animating adjudicatory credibility determinations, special factors inherent in

---

[25] *Id.*

[26] UNHCR *Handbook*, *supra* note 22, at ¶196.

[27] INA §242(b)(4)(D).

[28] REAL ID Act §101(h)(2), 119 Stat. at 305; *see also Matter of S–B–*, 24 I&N Dec. 42, 45 (BIA 2006) (where an application was filed with the Asylum Office before May 11, 2005, and then renewed in immigration court on or after May 11, 2005, the REAL ID Act provisions were not applicable to credibility determinations made in adjudicating the application).

[29] REAL ID Act §101(h)(3), 119 Stat. at 305–06.

[30] *See* Conference Report, *supra* note 3, at 163, 165, 167 (stating that the REAL ID Act was intended to "bring clarity and consistency to evidentiary determinations by codifying standards for determining the credibility of applicant testimony, and determining when corroborating evidence may be required").

[31] One BIA decision has indirectly addressed the REAL ID credibility provisions in reversing an immigration judge (IJ) who improperly applied the provisions in a case filed prior to their effective date. *See Matter of S–B–*, *supra* note 28 (where IJ improperly relied on REAL ID credibility provisions rather than pre-REAL ID Sixth Circuit precedent in a case filed prior to REAL ID's effective date, the BIA reversed and remanded the IJ's decision on the grounds that "the standards articulated by the Sixth Circuit differ in significant respects from the REAL ID Act credibility provisions when applied to the credibility determination in this case"). In addition, various federal court decisions have noted possible variations between law applicable to credibility and corroboration determinations in claims filed before and after REAL ID's effective date. *See, e.g., Diallo v. Gonzales*, 439 F.3d 764, 766 n.1 (7th Cir. 2006).

[32] Committee reports are the most authoritative sources on the meaning of legislation. *Thornburg v. Gingles*, 478 U.S. 30, 43 n.7 (1986) ("We have repeatedly recognized that the authoritative source for legislative intent lies in the Committee Reports on the bill."); *U.S. v. Awadallah*, 349 F.3d 42, 54 (2d Cir. 2003) ("[T]he authoritative source for finding the Legislature's intent lies in the Committee Reports on the bill, which represen[t] the considered and collective understanding of those Congressmen involved in drafting and studying proposed legislation.") (internal quotation marks omitted) (alteration in original).

[33] *See* Conference Report, *supra* note 3, at 166.

[34] *Id.*

[35] *Id.* at 166–67.

asylum claims—including cultural and language differences, psychological trauma, and the circumstances of flight from persecution—present particular challenges.[36]

Although it can be determinative of a claim, credibility is not a legal element of asylum protection. Agency guidance stresses that there is no moral component to credibility determinations, stating that "the purpose of evaluating an asylum applicant's credibility is solely to determine eligibility, not to punish the applicant if he or she is untruthful."[37] Relief cannot be denied simply because an applicant made misrepresentations in the applicant's claim. However, the BIA or an immigration judge (IJ) may impose penalties for filing a "frivolous" asylum application if respondents knowingly fabricate material elements of their claims.[38]

Prior to the enactment of REAL ID, general criteria for assessing the credibility of an applicant's testimony arose from BIA and federal court case law. The criteria most often cited as being determinative include specificity of testimony, internal consistency, plausibility, and consistency with known facts about the country of origin.[39] Demeanor has also been a factor considered by adjudicators, generally in conjunction with other criteria, discussed below.[40] Both federal court and agency pronouncements on credibility have recognized the special circumstances present in asylum adjudications and have aimed to take account of these circumstances.[41]

The REAL ID Act's Credibility Provision

Considering the totality of the circumstances, and all relevant factors, a trier of fact may base a credibility determination on the demeanor, candor, or responsiveness of the applicant or witness, the inherent plausibility of the applicant's or witness's account, the consistency between the applicant's or witness's written and oral statements (whenever made and whether or not under oath, *and considering the circumstances under which the statements were made*), the internal consistency of each such statement, the consistency of such statements with other evidence of record (including the reports of the Department of State on country conditions), and any inaccuracies or falsehoods in such statements, without regard to whether an inconsistency, inaccuracy, or falsehood goes to the heart of the applicant's claim, *or any other relevant factor*. There is no presumption of credibility, however, if no adverse credibility determination is explicitly made, the applicant or witness shall have a rebuttable presumption of credibility on appeal.[42]

Several courts interpreting the phrase "[c]onsidering the totality of the circumstances, and all relevant factors" have found it to be central to interpretation of the statutory language. These courts have found that the phrase is compulsory, *i.e.*, triers of facts *must* consider "the totality of the circumstances" and "all relevant factors" in evaluating credibility.[43] This follows in part from the placement of the phrase at the beginning of the statutory provision, and the nonpermissive language.

The trier of fact also should articulate the factors he or she has relied on in assessing credibility, so as to assure compliance with the statutory mandate that he or she considered all relevant factors and the totality of the circumstances. The conference report states that "[w]hile the trier of fact is not required to state expressly that the trier has considered each factor in assessing credibility, Congress expects that the trier of fact will describe those factors that form the basis of the trier's opinion," including "where the trier of fact bases a credibility determination in part or in whole on the demeanor of the applicant."[44]

---

[36] For detailed treatment of these issues, *see*, for example, M. Kagan, "Is Truth in the Eye of the Beholder? Objective Credibility Assessment in Refugee Status Determination," 17 *Geo. Immigr. L.J.* 367 (2003).

[37] *See* Asylum Officer Basic Training Course (AOBTC) Lesson Plan: Credibility II.B. (Mar. 1999), *available at* www.asylumlaw.org/docs/united_states/asylum_officer_training_credibility_031999.pdf.

[38] INA §208(d)(6); 8 CFR §§208.20, 1208.20 (discussed further below). As at least one court has noted, the "frivolous application" provision is somewhat inaptly named and might be better thought of and explained to clients as pertaining to "fraudulent" applications. *Barreto-Clara v. Att'y Gen.*, 275 F.3d 1334, 1339 n.11 (11th Cir. 2001).

[39] *See, e.g., Matter of Mogharrabi*, 19 I&N Dec. 439, 445 (BIA 1987) (incorporating these criteria into those for evaluation of the applicant's testimony generally).

[40] *See, e.g., Matter of A–S–*, 21 I&N Dec. 1106, 1109 (BIA 1998).

[41] *See, e.g., Matter of S–M–J–, supra* note 14, at 725; *Fiadjoe v. Att'y Gen.*, 411 F.3d 135, 153–60 (3d Cir. 2005).

[42] INA §208(b)(1)(B)(iii) (emphasis added).

[43] *See, e.g., Sarr v. Gonzales*, 474 F.3d 783 (10th Cir. 2007); *Uanreroro v. Gonzales*, 443 F.3d 1197, 1210 (10th Cir. 2006); *Kadia v. Gonzales*, 2007 U.S. App. LEXIS 21456, at 9–11 (7th Cir. 2007).

[44] Conference Report, *supra* note 3, at 167.

When a factor has not been discussed by the adjudicator, it is properly assumed not to have been a basis for the adjudicator's decision.[45]

Administrative agencies, appellate tribunals, and courts have increasingly insisted that adjudicators explain the specific reasoning behind negative credibility findings. The BIA has held that a refugee status decision-maker may not reject an applicant on credibility grounds without "specific and cogent reasons," such as inconsistencies, vagueness, or material omissions in testimony or evidence.[46]

The REAL ID Act's "totality of the circumstances" standard provides adjudicators with the flexibility to synthesize and weigh a constellation of factors relating to the credibility of an applicant's testimony on any given issue. As the BIA has explained, a credibility determination "apprehends the overall evaluation of testimony in light of its rationality or internal consistency and the manner in which it hangs together with other evidence."[47] At the same time, the legislative history makes it clear that credibility findings are not discretionary[48] and must be adequately explained by the adjudicator. Although an asylum decision-maker need not recite and discuss every conceivable factor that could potentially be relevant to an adjudication, at a minimum "Congress expects that the trier of fact will describe those factors that form the basis of the trier's opinion."[49] In other words, a conclusory credibility determination or one that omits a discussion of factors actually relied on by the adjudicator is unacceptable under the REAL ID Act. Furthermore, as discussed below, adjudicators may not rely on one factor in isolation in determining whether the applicant's testimony is credible. The adjudicator's credibility determination must include two basic elements: a factual analysis of truthfulness and a legal analysis of materiality to the claim.[50]

The Asylum Officer Basic Training Course (AOBTC) lesson plan on credibility provides that a credibility finding must be based on objective facts only.[51] As one prominent practitioner and commentator has noted in underscoring the importance of objectivity and transparency in credibility determinations:

Credibility assessments can embody a struggle between norms of subjective and objective decision-making. Subjective assessments are highly personal to the decision-maker, dependent on personal judgment, perceptions, and disposition, and often lacking an articulated logic. They are very difficult to review and are likely be inconsistent from one decision-maker to another. Objective credibility assessments apply standard criteria and require adjudicators to conduct a more structured inquiry. Because objective assessments tend to involve more specific and concrete explanations for decisions, they also are easier for appellate tribunals to review. . . .

Unstructured and unreviewable credibility assessments lead to inconsistent decision-making and great risks of mistaken refusals to protect people in danger. Allowing a central part of refugee status determination to be essentially subjective generates serious doubts about the fairness and effectiveness of the adjudication system. Applying a common approach to credibility assessment, which so often determines the outcome of refugee cases, would bolster confidence in a [refugee status determination] system.[52]

---

[45] "Inconsistencies due to an unscrupulous preparer without other evidence of dishonesty (such as evasiveness in answering questions ...) do not provide a specific and cogent basis for an adverse credibility finding." *Alvarez-Santos v. INS*, 332 F.3d 1245, 1254 (9th Cir. 2003) (recognizing that asylum applications are frequently filled out by "poor, illiterate people who do not speak English" or by "preparers, whether lawyers or non-lawyers [who] are not always scrupulous" but finding on the facts independent reasons to discredit testimony).

[46] *Matter of A–S–*, supra note 40, at 1109 (BIA 1998); see also *Matter of J–B–N–*, 24 I&N Dec. 260 (BIA 2007) (noting that the BIA generally defers to an IJ's factual findings on credibility, and upholding findings in instant case where IJ articulated reasons and considered relevant factors and totality of circumstances, as required by REAL ID).

[47] *Matter of A–S–*, supra note 40, at 1112 (citation omitted).

[48] See infra under the heading The REAL ID Act's Corroboration Provision.

[49] Conference Report, supra note 3, at 167.

[50] "[J]udges are expected—unlike juries—to give reasons for their conclusions, even on credibility. The reasons must be 'cogent' and 'specific,' *Gailius v. INS*, 147 F.3d 34, 46–47 (1st Cir.1998), and must be 'reasonably grounded in the record, viewed as a whole, *Cordero-Trejo* [v. INS, 40 F.3d 482, 487 (1st Cir. 1994)]. It is not our task to 'invent explanations that may justify' the agency's conclusion. *Dia v. Ashcroft*, 353 F.3d 228, 260 (3d Cir.2003) (en banc)." *Castaneda-Castillo v. Gonzales*, 488 F.3d 17, 22 (1st Cir. 2007).

[51] AOBTC Lesson Plan: Credibility, supra note 37, at II.C.

[52] M. Kagan, supra note 36, at 374, 377.

Prominent in Congress's formulation of the credibility standard is the requirement that asylum adjudicators consider "all relevant factors."[53] This requirement is consistent with pre-REAL ID domestic and international standards recognizing that, in addition to the factors animating a typical adjudicative credibility determination, asylum adjudicators must consider, for example, how language and cultural barriers, psychological trauma, and circumstances of flight affect an applicant's testimony and the adjudicator's perceptions. Along these lines, the conference report emphasizes that any credibility determination "must be reasonable and take into consideration the individual circumstances of the specific witness and/or applicant."[54] Both the statute and the accompanying conference report send a clear message that, in reaching credibility determinations, adjudicators must consider mitigating factors surrounding such circumstances as incomplete or inconsistent statements. The AOBTC lesson plan on credibility exemplifies this objective, holistic, and individualized approach to assessing credibility. Even before setting forth the general credibility criteria, the lesson plan discusses a list of factors that could affect assessment under the general criteria, and directs asylum officers always to bear these in mind when making credibility determinations.[55] Various types of such factors are considered below in the context of each individual credibility criterion.

Some Key Factors in Credibility Determinations

Consistency

Several criteria specifically mentioned by REAL ID as relevant to credibility fall under the general heading of consistency. REAL ID provides that credibility rulings can be based on the internal consistency of an applicant's claim, including both consistency within the applicant's testimony and consistency between the oral and written statements of an applicant.[56] A credibility determination may also weigh external consistency—the consistency of the statement with any evidence in the record other than such testimony or statements of the applicant.

Internal Consistency

Adverse credibility determinations grounded in inconsistencies or omissions must be based on evidence in the record. The BIA in *Matter of A–S–*[57] set forward the criteria for determining whether such support exists in the record. First, the discrepancies and omissions must actually be present in the record. Second, the discrepancies and omissions must provide specific and cogent reasons to conclude that the applicant provided testimony that was not credible. Finally, the applicant must have had an opportunity to explain the discrepancies and omissions and must have failed to do so.[58]

Available background evidence on country conditions is relevant to credibility. In addition to corroborating an applicant's claim, such background evidence can aid adjudicators by providing context for the applicant's testimony regarding specific events, harm that he or she suffered, and the reasons for his or her particular fear of return. There is no one-size-fits-all assessment available for these situations, however. Instead, an adjudicator must engage in a close and individualized credibility determination.

Minor Inconsistencies

Since an asylum applicant's testimony is the lynchpin of his or her claim, discounting that testimony based entirely on only minor inconsistencies or falsities in the claim would have particularly harsh results wholly inconsistent with domestic case law and international standards. Although the language of REAL ID allows adjudicators to consider any inconsistencies, such statements must be properly weighed in the overall context, and in light of all the circumstances.

Specifically, in *Matter of A–S–*, the BIA established a three-part test whereby the BIA will defer to an adverse credibility determination based on inconsistencies and omissions in an applicant's asylum claim. In such a case a review of the record must reveal that: (1) the discrepancies and omissions described by the IJ are actually present in the record; (2) such discrepancies and omissions provide specific and cogent reasons to conclude that the applicant provided incredible testimony; and (3) the applicant has failed to provide a convincing explanation for the discrepancies and omissions.[59] This test

---

[53] INA §208(b)(1)(B)(iii).

[54] Conference Report, *supra* note 3, at 167.

[55] AOBTC Lesson Plan: Credibility, *supra* note 37, at II, III.

[56] INA §208(b)(1)(B)(iii). *See also Matter of A–S–*, *supra* note 40 (discussing generally both types of inconsistencies as well as omissions).

[57] *Matter of A–S–*, *supra* note 40, at 1109.

[58] *Id.* at 1109–11.

[59] *Id.* at 1109.

is still valid and applicable, even when the credibility finding was predicated on nonmaterial events, as per the REAL ID Act.[60]

External Consistency and the Role of Corroboration in Credibility Determinations

The AOBTC lesson plan on credibility states that "the facts alleged by the applicant should be plausible, in light of country conditions and logic."[61] Both U.S. and international standards stress the importance of background evidence on human rights conditions and relevant persecutory practices in an applicant's country of origin. Such country-condition evidence serves as both an objective basis for assessing a claim and a background against which to evaluate the applicant's credibility.[62] Comparison of an applicant's testimony to country conditions reports is an evaluation of its external consistency. As such, the holistic and individualized approach outlined above applies as well when examining the credibility of testimony in light of corroborating evidence (or its absence).

To the extent that an applicant's detailed testimony comports with patterns and practices documented in human rights and country condition reports, it may be considered more credible. Conversely, where an applicant's testimony deviates significantly from what country documentation suggests is to be expected, the testimony is less believable. When making inferences about credibility in either situation, adjudicators must cleave to REAL ID's requirement of considering all relevant factors.[63] Just as testimony conforming to country reports may not per se establish that the applicant has met the criteria of

the refugee definition and asylum eligibility, testimony inconsistent with external documentation does not preclude eligibility, but might be explained by a number of factors. For this reason, it is particularly important that applicants be provided a clear opportunity to address inconsistent evidence and explain why their testimony and experience do not conform to that evidence. This clarification process will also help uncover any misunderstandings of the applicant's testimony resulting from language and cultural and psychological dynamics.

Asylum adjudicators also may find that an applicant's failure to produce corroboration affects his or her credibility. However, adjudicators should be cautious about making adverse credibility inferences simply because an applicant's testimony is uncorroborated by widely available human rights documentation. As the AOBTC lesson plan on credibility observes:

In some instances, the asylum officer may be the first to learn about human rights abuses or other developments in another country. In some refugee producing countries, freedom of expression and association is non-existent, and human rights monitors are prevented from visiting. This makes it difficult for organizations that document human rights abuses to obtain up-to-date information. Even where human rights monitors have access to a country, they are not able to document every human rights abuse that occurs.[64]

In most cases in which reasonably expected corroboration is absent, the approach most consistent with the REAL ID Act will be to find that the applicant failed to carry his or her burden of proof under the corroboration standards discussed *infra*. Where adjudicators determine that the absence of reasonably available corroboration both prevents an applicant from carrying his or her burden of proof and undermines the applicant's credibility, each finding should be addressed independently and explained in the record. As with conflicting background evidence (and in conformity with REAL ID's corroboration standards), the applicant should be advised of the expected corroboration and have the opportunity to explain why it is not reasonably available. As emphasized above, adjudicators should always bear in mind the evidentiary difficulties and circumstances surrounding a refugee's flight from persecution be-

---

[60] *Id. See also Matter of J–Y–C–*, 24 I&N Dec. 260 (analyzing the applicant's testimony to *see* whether the discrepancies did in fact exist and reviewing the IJ's decision to ensure that he had examined the totality of the circumstances).

[61] AOBTC Lesson Plan: Credibility, *supra* note 37, at IV.A.3.a.

[62] James Hathaway describes the relationship between background evidence and the individual's testimony:

[T]he purpose of eliciting evidence from the claimant herself . . . is to establish how circumstances in the homeland impact on her own security, and why she feels compelled to seek protection abroad. Against the backdrop of human rights reports from the country of origin, the determination authority must decide whether the individual applicant faces a reasonable chance of serious harm if returned to her home.

J. Hathaway, *Law of Refugee Status* (1991) at 86–87.

[63] *See* INA §208(b)(1)(B)(iii).

[64] AOBTC Lesson Plan: Credibility, *supra* note 37, at IV.B.10.

fore making negative credibility inferences based on lack of corroboration.

When upholding adverse credibility determinations, the BIA and circuit courts have often found it relevant that no attempt was made to explain inconsistencies in the record.[65]

Specificity and Detail

BIA case law provides that an applicant's testimony generally may be considered credible when it is detailed and coherent.[66] Similarly, the AOBTC lesson plan on credibility includes "detail" in its list of key credibility factors and states that "the applicant's ability or inability to provide detailed descriptions of the main points of the claim is often critical to the credibility evaluation."[67] The language of the REAL ID Act echoes and reinforces the importance of this criterion by providing that an applicant may establish his or her claim by offering credible, persuasive testimony that "refers to specific facts sufficient to demonstrate that the applicant is a refugee."[68]

Since "a genuine refugee should be able to provide sufficient detail to indicate first-hand knowledge of the events that form the basis of the claim,"[69] a lack of specificity or detail in testimony may reflect adversely on the testimony's credibility.[70] However, other factors that may explain the lack of specificity must be considered.[71] The AOBTC lesson plan on credibility includes in its considerations for assessing credibility based on the specificity of testimony (1) factors that impair memory, (2) types of recall varying from person to person, and (3) the adjudicator's duty to elicit detail.[72] As noted also below, post-traumatic stress and related difficulties cause applicants to block the memory of certain events from their own consciousness.

Where an IJ harbors doubts about an applicant's testimony because of meagerness or lack of detail, the IJ should probe for the additional details.[73]

Demeanor

The REAL ID Act provides that demeanor is one of the factors on which adjudicators may rely in making credibility determinations.[74] Legacy Immigration and Naturalization Service defined demeanor as "all those subtle aspects of a person's self-presentation that affect one's judgement [sic] of that person's statements."[75] According to one commentator, demeanor comprises "an assessment of a person's general physical appearance, composure or lack of composure, maintenance of eye contact, and manner of speech, including intonation, speed, and fluency."[76]

More than any other credibility criteria, assessments of demeanor are subjective and highly dependent on the cultural backgrounds and personal dispositions of the adjudicator and applicant. The nonverbal cues that people tend to rely on to decide if another person is telling the truth vary widely

---

[65] See, e.g., Bojoques-Villanueva, 194 F.3d 14, 18 (1st Cir. 1999) ("There was no attempt, although there was ample time, to elaborate upon or explain the mother's varying interpretation.").

[66] Matter of Mogharrabi, supra note 39, at 445; see also Estrada v. INS, 775 F.2d 1018, 1021 (9th Cir. 1985) (stating that specific, credible evidence must be presented); Cardoza-Fonseca v. INS, 767 F.2d 1448, 1453 (9th Cir. 1985), aff'd, 480 U.S. 421 (1987) (holding that applicant must point to "specific facts" to support his or her claim for asylum); Ghasemimehr v. INS, 7 F.3d 1389, 1390 (8th Cir. 1993) (noting that applicant must present credible, direct, and specific evidence). In many of the decisions, it is difficult to separate the question of specificity or detail, as they relate to the assessment of credibility, from those same issues as they relate to the determination of whether the applicant has met his or her burden of proof in establishing a well-founded fear.

[67] AOBTC Lesson Plan: Credibility, supra note 37, at IV.A.2.a.

[68] INA §208(b)(1)(B)(ii).

[69] AOBTC Lesson Plan: Credibility, supra note 37, at IV.A.2.a.

[70] See, e.g., Estrada v. INS, supra note 66, at 1021 (noting that applicant did not provide sufficient detail about the number of threats made against him, their nature, and their source). But see Argueta v. INS, 759 F.2d 1395, 1397

(9th Cir. 1985) (deciding that applicant's testimony was sufficiently specific where he clearly identified the persons threatening him as members of a death squad, detailed the substance of those threats, and observed a close friend being kidnapped the next day by men believed to be the same as those who had threatened him).

[71] See INA §208(b)(1)(B)(iii) (requiring that "all relevant factors" be considered).

[72] AOBTC Lesson Plan: Credibility, supra note 37, at IV.A.2.b.

[73] You Hao Yang v. BIA, 440 F.3d 72, 74 (2d Cir. 2006) (per curiam).

[74] See Matter of J–B–N–, supra note 46 (upholding IJ's credibility determination where IJ considered demeanor, along with other factors).

[75] Immigration and Naturalization Service, Basic Law Manual: U.S. Law and INS Refugee Asylum Adjudications 109 (1994).

[76] J. Ruppel, "The Need for a Benefit of the Doubt Standard in Credibility Evaluations of Asylum Applicants," 23 Colum. Hum Rts. L. Rev. 1, 7 (1991–92).

continued

from culture to culture. In addition, trauma can have an enormous impact on a person's memory; it can result in repression of memory and detachment in affect when recounting events.[77]

For all these reasons, the AOBTC lesson plan on credibility emphasizes that "[d]emeanor is generally an unreliable indicator of credibility, particularly in the asylum context where cultural differences and effects of trauma make it difficult to read accurately non-verbal signals."[78] The conference report also states this rule in the context of credibility determinations based on demeanor. It specifies that adjudicators must explain the basis for a credibility assessment "even where the trier of fact bases a credibility determination in part or in whole on the demeanor of the applicant."[79] The established rule that the trier of fact must offer a specific cogent reason for his or her disbelief of the applicant's testimony[80]

should apply with particular force to demeanor-based rulings in asylum cases.[81]

CORROBORATION AND THE REAL ID ACT

The Benefit-of-the-Doubt Principle

While applicants bear the burden of proof, the situation of asylum seekers requires that their testimony be given special evidentiary weight. The UNHCR *Handbook* provides that when outside corroboration is not reasonably available and "the applicant's account appears credible, he should, unless there are good reasons to the contrary, be given the benefit of the doubt."[82] This principle was articulated in U.S. case law soon after enactment of the 1980 Refugee Act.[83] The BIA in *Matter of S–M–J–* reaffirmed the principle and stressed that "[u]nreasonable demands are not placed on an asylum applicant to present evidence to corroborate particular experiences."[84] In keeping with prior case law and international guidance, Congress encoded the benefit of the doubt principle in U.S. law with the REAL ID Act.

The REAL ID Act's Corroboration Provision

Sustaining burden.—The testimony of the applicant may be sufficient to sustain the applicant's burden without corroboration, but only if the applicant satisfies the trier of fact that the applicant's testimony is credible, is persuasive, and refers to specific facts sufficient to demonstrate that the applicant is a

---

[77] A significant barrier to understanding the demeanor of applicants who have experienced trauma is the likely repression of traumatic memories. Such repression only adds to the difficulty of answering questions. Their "detachment when recounting tragic events, sometimes perceived as an indication of fabrication, may reflect psychological mechanisms employed to cope with past traumatic experiences, rather than duplicity." *Id.* at 20; *see also Zubeda v. Ashcroft*, 333 F.3d 463, 477 (3d Cir. 2003). One such mechanism is post-traumatic stress disorder, a disorder catalogued by the American Psychiatric Association in its *Diagnostic and Statistical Manual of Mental Disorders* (DSM) as having symptoms including "impaired memory, difficulty in concentrating and a numbing of responsiveness to the external world." *Id.* at 470 (citing to the third edition of the DSM published in 1980). Various psychological responses to torture have been noted and catalogued in the *Manual on the Effective Investigation and Documentation of Torture and Other Cruel, Inhuman or Degrading Treatment or Punishment* submitted to the United Nations Office of the High Commissioner for Human Rights. *Id.* at 477 n.16. The Asylum Office has developed a lesson plan elaborating the effects of torture. *See* Asylum Officer Basic Training Course (AOBTC) Lesson Plan: Interviewing Part V: Interviewing Survivors (Sept. 2001), *available at www.asylumlaw.org/docs/united_sta tes/asylum_officer_training_interview5_092001.pdf.*

[78] AOBTC Lesson Plan: Credibility, *supra* note 37, at IV.A.5.b.

[79] Conference Report, *supra* note 3, at 167.

[80] *See Damaize-Job v. INS*, 787 F.2d 1332, 1338 (9th Cir. 1986); *Garcia-Ramos v. INS*, 775 F.2d 1370, 1374, 1375 & n.9 (9th Cir. 1985) (remanding to the BIA in case of ambiguous ruling on IJ's clearly erroneous credibility findings based on out-of-wedlock child and inconsequential inconsistency where applicant would be eligible if credibility determination were positive).

[81] *See* J. Ruppel, *supra* note 76, at 12–14.

[82] UNHCR *Handbook, supra* note 22, at ¶196 ("It is a general legal principle that the burden of proof lies on the person submitting a claim. Often, however, an applicant may not be able to support his statement by documentary or other proof, and cases in which an applicant can provide evidence of all his statements will be the exception rather than the rule. In most cases a person fleeing from persecution will have arrived with the barest necessities and very frequently even without personal documents. Thus, while the burden of proof in principle rests on the applicant, the duty to ascertain and evaluate all the relevant facts is shared between the applicant and the examiner. Indeed, in some cases, it may be for the examiner to use all the means at his disposal to produce the necessary evidence in support of the application. Even such independent research may not, however, always be successful and there may also be statements that are not susceptible of proof. In such cases, if the applicant's account appears credible, he should, unless there are good reasons to the contrary, be given the benefit of the doubt.").

[83] *See, e.g., Matter of Mogharrabhi, supra* note 39, at 445; *Canjura-Flores v. INS*, 784 F.2d 885, 888 (9th Cir. 1985).

[84] *Matter of S–M–J–, supra* note 14, at 725.

refugee. In determining whether the applicant has met the applicant's burden, the trier of fact may weigh the credible testimony along with other evidence of record. Where the trier of fact determines that the applicant should provide evidence that corroborates otherwise credible testimony, such evidence must be provided unless the applicant does not have the evidence and cannot reasonably obtain the evidence.[85]

As noted, the first sentence of this section upholds the benefit-of-the-doubt principle. The remaining sentences in the section codify the dominant rule that applicants may be required to provide reasonably available corroborating evidence of their testimony or, in the alternative, to provide a reasonable explanation for the lack of such corroborating evidence.

The conference report accompanying the REAL ID Act also emphasized that testimony alone can be sufficient to sustain a claim, and recognized the evidentiary challenges refugees face:

> As a preliminary matter, new clause 208(b)(1)(B)(ii) of the INA codifies the BIA case law standard that the testimony of an asylum applicant can be sufficient to sustain the asylum applicant's burden of proof without corroboration, where the adjudicator determines that such testimony is credible, persuasive, and refers to specific facts demonstrating refugee status. Many aliens validly seeking asylum arrive in the United States with little or no evidence to corroborate their claims. This clause recognizes that a lack of extrinsic or corroborating evidence will not necessarily defeat an asylum claim where such evidence is not reasonably available to the applicant.

Quoting extensively from *Matter of S–M–J–*, the conference report states explicitly that the REAL ID Act provision is "based upon the standard set forth" in that case, and that "Congress anticipates that the standards in *Matter of S–M–J–*, including the BIA's conclusions on situations where corroborating evidence is or is not required, will guide the BIA and the courts in interpreting this clause."[86]

Also noteworthy—as with the credibility provision discussed above—is language the final REAL ID Act burden of proof provision *did not* contain. The version of the Act passed by the House specified that "[w]here the trier of fact determines, *in the trier of fact's discretion*, that the applicant should provide evidence which corroborates otherwise credible testimony, such evidence must be provided unless the applicant does not have the evidence and cannot reasonably obtain the evidence without departing the United States."[87] However, the final Act rejected the phrase "in the trier of fact's discretion," ensuring that adjudicators' determinations as to when corroboration is required would be subject to review according to existing standards set forth in *Matter of S–M–J–* and related case law.

It is important to note that the question of whether corroboration of particular testimony or events should be required in a given case is distinct from the question of whether that corroboration is reasonably available or whether an applicant has offered a sufficient explanation for not producing reasonably available evidence. The REAL ID Act specifies that determinations concerning the availability of corroboration are questions of fact and are reviewed for substantial evidence.[88] However, a determination of whether the evidence submitted is sufficient to bear the burden of proof is a legal question that the BIA and circuit courts may address under a less deferential standard of review.[89]

Corroboration and *Matter of S–M–J–*

Matter of S–M–J– (the ruling of which was codified in REAL ID) did not overturn the general rule that credible applicant testimony may suffice to sustain the applicant's burden of proof. BIA member Lory Rosenberg's concurring opinion underscored this point: "Our opinion should not be read to impose upon the individual asylum applicant the necessity of providing more than her credible testimony to satisfy her burden, if that is all that is available."[90] Rosenberg further stated that "perhaps what is most important about this decision is what we are not holding . . . . [W]e do not presume that certain forms of supporting evidence of material facts 'easily subject to verification' . . . are readily available in the case of every applicant or necessarily required for the alien to satisfy her burden of proof. In other words, there is no presumption that the 'absence of

---

[85] INA §208(b)(1)(B)(ii).

[86] Conference Report, *supra* note 3, at 166.

[87] H.R. 1268 §101(a)(3)(iii), 109th Cong. (2005) (emphasis added).

[88] *See* INA §242(b)(4).

[89] *See, e.g., Secaida-Rosales v. INS*, 331 F.3d 297, 306–07 (2d Cir. 2003).

[90] *Matter of S–M–J–, supra* note 14, at 736 (Rosenberg, Bd. Mem., concurring).

such corroborating evidence' alone supports a finding that an applicant has failed to meet her burden of proof."[91]

S–M–J– placed two critical qualifications on its corroboration requirement.[92] First, the BIA emphasized that "unreasonable demands should not be placed on the applicant" to corroborate particular experiences," specifying "corroboration from the persecutor" as a clear example of such an unreasonable demand.[93] Second, the BIA stipulated that, when documentation may be required but the applicant cannot provide it, the applicant must be given an opportunity to explain why that documentation has not been presented.[94] These limitations are central to the S–M–J– holding and merit close consideration.

Reasonable Availability of Corroboration

The circuit courts have frequently overturned the BIA for not following the standards set forth in S–M–J– governing when it is "reasonable to expect" corroboration. In particular, S–M–J– contains the following guidance about the reasonableness inquiry:

- *It is per se unreasonable to expect the persecutor to provide corroboration of particular experiences.* As S–M–J– specifies, "[u]nreasonable demands are not placed on an asylum applicant to present evidence to corroborate particular experiences (*e.g.,* evidence from the persecutor)."[95]

- Expected corroboration must be of "material facts which are central to the applicant's claim and easily subject to verification."[96] S–M–J– provides as examples "evidence of [the applicant's] place of birth, media accounts of large demonstrations, evidence of a publicly held office, or documentation of medical treatment."[97] Of course, even this kind of documentation is not always reasonably available.[98]

- It is unreasonable to expect "specific documentary corroboration of an applicant's particular experiences . . . . unless the supporting documentation is of the type that would normally be created or available in the particular country and is accessible to the alien, such as through friends, relatives, or co-workers."[99] This rule places a crucial limitation on the preceding rule. As the concurrence notes, "we do not presume that certain forms of supporting evidence of material facts 'easily subject to verification' . . . are readily available in the case of every applicant or necessarily required for the alien to satisfy her burden of proof."[100]

These limitations are required, if the principle that applicants should provide reasonable corroboration of credible testimony is not to eviscerate the principle that the applicant's testimony alone may be sufficient to meet her burden of proof. The circuit courts have been vigilant in this regard. Thus, the U.S. Court of Appeals for the Seventh Circuit in *Dawoud v. Gonzales* overturned a BIA decision (ef-

---

[91] *Id.* at 733.

[92] *See id.* at 742 ("In our decision today we have set forth two 'reasonableness' determinations that need to be made in assessing the adequacy of the asylum applicant's evidence. One is whether it is reasonable to expect that the applicant's personal experiences are easily subject to verification. The other is whether in such a case, the explanation given by an applicant for failing to provide such documentation is a reasonable one.") (Rosenberg, Bd. Mem., concurring).

[93] *Id.* at 725 ("Where the record contains general country condition information, and an applicant's claim relies primarily on personal experiences not reasonably subject to verification, corroborating documentary evidence of the asylum applicant's particular experience is not required. Unreasonable demands are not placed on an asylum applicant to present evidence to corroborate particular experiences (*e.g.,* corroboration from the persecutor). However, *where it is reasonable to expect corroborating evidence for certain alleged facts pertaining to the specifics of an applicant's claim, such evidence should be provided.*" (Emphasis added.)

[94] *Id.* at 723–24 ("If such evidence is unavailable, the applicant must explain its unavailability, and the Immigration Judge must insure that the applicant's explanation is included in the record.").

[95] *Id.* at 725 (also quoted in Conference Report, *supra* note 3, at 166).

[96] *Id.*

[97] *Id.* at 725; *see also* Asylum Officer Basic Training Course (AOBTC) Lesson Plan: Asylum Eligibility Part IV: Burden of Proof, Standards of Proof, and Evidence" IV.D.1.b. (Nov. 2001), *available at* www.asylumlaw.org/docs/united_states/asylum_officer_training_eligibility4_112001.pdf (listing examples of possible documentation, including death certificates; baptismal certificates; prison records; arrest warrants; affidavits of or letters from government officials, friends, or family members; union membership cards; and political party cards).

[98] *Matter of S–M–J–, supra* note 14, at 725.

[99] *Id.* at 726.

[100] *Id.* at 734 (Rosenberg, Bd. Mem., concurring).

fectively an IJ decision) for failing to apply the BIA's own *S–M–J–* rule:

> We have repeatedly rejected IJs' decisions that a credible asylum applicant's claim can be rejected solely because she did not supply corroborating evidence. . . . The regulation, in our view, cannot bear an interpretation that would exclude all possibility of an applicant's relying exclusively on credible but uncorroborated testimony, so long as that testimony is specific, detailed, and convincing. . . . The policy behind a rule permitting reliance solely on credible testimony is simple. Many asylum applicants flee their home countries under circumstances of great urgency. Some are literally running for their lives and have to abandon their families, friends, jobs, and material possessions without a word of explanation. They often have nothing but the shirts on their backs when they arrive in this country. To expect these individuals to stop and collect dossiers of paperwork before fleeing is both unrealistic and strikingly insensitive to the harrowing conditions they face.[101]

Notice and Opportunity to Explain

Matter of S–M–J– requires adjudicators to provide applicants with notice of specific deficiencies, *i.e.,* corroborating evidence the adjudicator has determined it is reasonable to expect applicants to provide.[102] Unless the applicant is on notice that such corroborating evidence is expected, he or she will be deprived of the opportunity to meet his or her burden of proof by producing the evidence or explaining its absence.[103]

Requirements Imposed on Adjudicators as Prerequisite of Judicial Review of Corroboration Determination

In addition to overturning BIA decisions for failure to apply *S–M–J–*'s reasonableness requirements, the circuit courts frequently have overturned the BIA for failing to explain its reasoning in applying the rule as a prerequisite to judicial review. These courts have held that an adjudicator making an adverse determination under the *S–M–J–* rule must include in the record the following:

- A clear finding as to the credibility of the applicant

- The specific corroborating evidence that the adjudicator found it was reasonable to expect,[104] and the adjudicator's reasons for this determination

- The explanations provided by the applicant for the failure to produce this evidence, and the adjudicator's reasons for not crediting the applicant's explanation[105]

Requiring the adjudicator to provide these explanations, as the courts have noted, is a basic prerequisite for the court to fulfill its reviewing role. The U.S. Court of Appeals for the Third Circuit made

---

[101] *Dawoud v. Gonzales*, 424 F.3d 608, 612–13 (7th Cir. 2005) (internal citations omitted).

[102] *Matter of S–M–J–* provides the example of an applicant who claimed persecution based on her activities as a union vice-president for two years, and notes that she "should provide some corroborating evidence indicating that she held the office of vice-president or an explanation of why she did not provide corroborating evidence." *Matter of S–M–J–*, *supra* note 14, at 725–26.

[103] *See Toure v. Att'y Gen.*, 443 F.3d 310 (3d Cir. 2006) ("Indeed, it is impossible for us to determine 'whether a reasonable trier of fact would be compelled to conclude that the corroborating evidence is unavailable,' unless a petitioner is given the opportunity to testify as to its availability.").

[104] *See Qiu v. Ashcroft*, 329 F.3d 140, 153 (2d Cir. 2003) (IJ erred by requiring unspecified evidence to corroborate "forcedness" of wife's sterilization).

[105] *See Diallo v. INS*, 232 F.3d 279, 287 (2d Cir. 2000) ("First, the BIA should decide explictly whether or not Diallo's testimony was credible. . . . Second, if the BIA finds that Diallo's testimony was credible, it should decide whether additional corroboration is nonetheless required to meet his burden of proof. If the BIA insists on further corroboration, it should explain specifically, either in its decision or otherwise in the record: (1) why it is reasonable under the BIA's standards to expect such corroboration; and (2) why Diallo's proffered explanations for the lack of such corroboration are insufficient."); *see also Abdulai v. Ashcroft*, 239 F.3d 532, 554 (3d Cir. 2001) ("The BIA's rule contemplates a three-part inquiry: (1) an identification of the facts for which 'it is reasonable to expect corroboration;' (2) an inquiry as to whether the applicant has provided information corroborating the relevant facts; and, if he or she has not, (3) an analysis of whether the applicant has adequately explained his or her failure to do so."); *Gontcharova v. Ashcroft*, 384 F.3d 873, 877 (7th Cir. 2004) (accepting BIA corroboration rule but imposing *Diallo* requirements on IJ); *El-Sheikh v. Ashcroft*, 388 F.3d 643 (8th Cir. 2004); *Niang v. Gonzales*, 195 Fed. Appx 371, 377 (6th Cir. 2006) ("In summary, if the BIA insists on further corroboration, it must explain in its decision (1) why it is reasonable under its standards to expect such corroboration in this case; and (2) why Niang's explanations for lack of corroboration are insufficient.") (citing *Diallo*).

this point forcefully in its 2001 decision in *Abdulai v. Ashcroft*:

> [T]he availability of judicial review (which is specifically provided in the INA) necessarily contemplates *something* for us to review. . . . Because the BIA's failure of explanation makes it impossible for us to review its rationale, we grant Abdulai's petition for review, vacate the Board's order, and remand the matter to it for further proceedings consistent with this opinion.[106]

REAL ID and the Legacy of S–M–J–

REAL ID codifies the *S–M–J–* rule that an adjudicator may require an applicant to provide reasonably available documentary evidence to corroborate his or her credible testimony or to provide an explanation for not providing such corroboration.[107] The statute restates the *S–M–J–* rule that the requirement to corroborate credible testimony must be reasonable.[108] The conference report accompanying the

final version of REAL ID expressly states that the provision as amended is intended to codify *S–M–J–*:

> Codifying the BIA's corroboration standards, new clause 208(b)(1)(B)(ii) in the INA states that if an adjudicator determines that an asylum applicant should provide corroborating evidence for otherwise credible testimony, such corroborating evidence must be provided unless the applicant does not have it and cannot reasonably obtain it. Although this provision makes it possible for an alien to prove eligibility for asylum without corroborating evidence, the inability to obtain corroborating evidence does not relieve the applicant from sustaining the burden of proof, that is, the alien must satisfy his burden through other evidence. *This provision is based upon the standard set forth in the BIA's decision in Matter of S–M–J–.*...[109]

The report then cited those portions of the *S–M–J–* decision that place reasonableness limitations on the corroboration determination, stating that these standards were to govern application of REAL ID:

> With respect to evidence to support the applicant's specific claim, the BIA explained: "*Unreasonable demands are not placed on an asylum applicant to present evidence to corroborate particular experiences* (*e.g.,* corroboration from the persecutor). However, where it is *reasonable to expect* corroborating evidence for certain alleged facts pertaining to the specifics of an applicant's claim, such evidence should be provided. That is, an asylum applicant should provide documentary support for material facts which are central to his or her claim and easily subject to verification, such as evidence of his or her place of birth, media accounts of large demonstrations, evidence of a publicly held office, or documentation of medical treatment. If the applicant does not provide such information, an explanation should be given as to why such information was not presented. . . . The absence of such corroborating evidence can lead to a finding that the applicant has failed to meet her burden of proof." Id. at 725-26. *Congress anticipates that the standards in Matter of S–M–J–, including the BIA's conclusions on situations where corroborating evidence is or is*

---

[106] *Abdulai v. Ashcroft, supra* note 105, at 555 (emphasis in original); *see also Gontcharova v. Ashcroft, supra* note 105, at 877 ("[W]e do not reject the BIA's corroboration rule out of hand. In order that we may review its application, however, an IJ must explain his use of it."); *Poradisova v. Gonzales,* 420 F.3d 70 (2d Cir. 2005) ("Despite our generally deferential review of IJ and BIA opinions, we require a certain minimum level of analysis from the IJ and BIA opinions denying asylum, and indeed must require such if judicial review is to be meaningful.").

[107] *See* "Asylum Documentation Under the REAL ID Act," 9 *Immigr. Lit. Bull.* 15 (June 30, 2005), *available at www.justice.gov/civil/oil/9news6.pdf* (noting that in REAL ID corroboration provision Congress had adopted *S–M–J–* rule); V. Wiebe, "Maybe You Should, Yes You Must, No You Can't: Shifting Standards and Practices for Assuring Document Reliability in Asylum and Withholding of Removal Cases," *Imm. Briefings* (Nov. 2006) (in passing REAL ID, Congress "essentially enshrined" rule arrived at by Second, Third, Sixth, and Eight Circuits, where "these circuits based their standard largely on the line of cases culminating in *Matter of S–M–J–* . . . .").

[108] Some commentators have misinterpreted REAL ID to require corroboration whenever the judge determines it is needed, as opposed to when it is reasonable to expect corroboration. *See* M. Silenzi Cianciarulo, *supra* note 4, at 127 (REAL ID Act's corroboration provision differs from *S–M–J–* approach because it "does not hold specifically adjudicators to a standard of reasonableness when determining whether corroboration is necessary or whether the corroboration provided is sufficient."); Congressional Research Service Report, M. John Garcia, M. Mikyung Lee, & T. Tatelman, "Immigration: Analysis of the Major Provisions of the REAL ID Act of 2005" at 6–7 (May 25, 2005), *available at http://fpc.state.gov/documents/organization/47141.pdf*

continued

(claiming decision to require corroboration is in trier of fact's discretion).

[109] Conference Report, *supra* note 3, at 291 (emphasis added).

not required, will guide the BIA and the courts in interpreting this clause.[110]

Finally, the legislative history of REAL ID demonstrates that under its provisions only reasonably available corroborating evidence may be required. As noted, the original version of the bill, introduced in the House of Representatives as House Bill 418, stated that the corroboration determination was to be "in the trier of fact's discretion."[111] When the bill was amended in conference, this clause was omitted.

Because REAL ID codifies *S–M–J–* and because Congress expressed its clear intent that adjudicators look to the standards set forth in *S–M–J–* in deciding when a credible applicant should produce corroborating evidence, adjudicators must make corroboration determinations in light of these standards.

Does REAL ID Change the Scope of Judicial Review of Determinations About Corroboration?

In addition to codifying substantive standards for when corroboration would be required, REAL ID added the following provision with regard to the standard of review applicable to corroboration determinations:

No court shall reverse a determination made by a trier of fact with respect to the availability of corroborating evidence, as described in [INA] section 208(b)(1)(b), 240(c)(4)(B), or 241(b)(3)(C), unless the court finds, pursuant to section 242(b)(4)(B), that a reasonable trier of fact is compelled to conclude that such corroborating evidence is unavailable.[112]

The conference report contains the following statement with regard to this provision:

Judicial Review of Corroboration Determinations: Subsection 101(e) of Division B would amend paragraph 242(b)(4) of the INA by establishing a specific standard of review for reversal of determinations concerning the availability of corroborating evidence by an adjudicator considering an application for asylum, withholding of removal, or other applications for relief or protection. This subsection would apply the prevailing standard of review for factual determinations in subparagraph 242(b)(4)(B) of the INA to determinations about the availability of corroborat-

ing evidence, itself a factual determination. This provision underscores that the appropriate standard of review for such determinations is the deferential factual review standard.[113]

Thus, the aim of the provision was to clarify that the standard of review generally applicable to factual findings is applicable to the factual determination that corroborating evidence is reasonably available.

First, the question what level of review applies to administrative determinations is distinct from the question of what form administrative determinations must take if review is to be possible at all. Thus, a number of decisions issued after the REAL ID standard of review provision was enacted have emphasized that this provision does not upset the requirement that judges explain why it was reasonable to expect corroboration and why the applicant's explanations of its absence were not accepted. Thus, in a 2006 case, the Third Circuit reasoned as follows:

We do not believe that the REAL ID Act changes our disposition of this case. We do not interpret 8 USC §1252(b)(4)(D) to alter our rules that (1) an IJ has a duty to develop the applicant's testimony, especially regarding an issue that she may find dispositive, and (2) as a logical predicate to appellate review, the BIA must adequately explain the reasons for its decisions. Indeed, it is impossible for us to determine "whether a reasonable trier of fact would be compelled to conclude that such corroborating evidence is unavailable," 8 USC §1252(b)(4)(D), unless a petitioner is given the opportunity to testify as it its availability.[114]

---

[110] *Id.* at 291–92 (emphasis added).

[111] *See* H.R. 418, §101(a)(3), 109th Cong. (2005).

[112] INA §242(b)(4).

---

[113] *See* Conference Report, *supra* note 3, at 294.

[114] *Toure v. Att'y Gen.*, *supra* note 103, at 325 (citations omitted); *see also Hor v. Gonzales,* 421 F.3d 497, 500–01 (7th Cir. 2005) ("The government points to the recently enacted REAL ID Act of 2005, which provides that 'no court shall reverse a determination made by a trier of fact [in a removal case] with respect to the availability of corroborating evidence . . . unless the court finds . . . that a reasonable trier of fact is compelled to conclude the evidence is available.' All that means is that an immigration judge's determination that if there were evidence to corroborate the alien's testimony the alien could and should have presented it is entitled to reasonable deference. The precondition to deference is that the immigration judge explain (unless it is obvious) why he thinks corroborating evidence, if it existed, would be available to the alien.") (citations omitted); *Ikama-Obambi v. Gonzales,* 470 F.3d 720, 725 (2006) (requiring IJ explanations of reasons while applying REAL ID standard of review).

CONCLUSION

This article has discussed generally the implications of REAL ID on assessments of credibility and corroboration requirements in asylum and related protection cases. As to credibility, the statute provides that all inconsistencies may be considered and that the trier of fact also may evaluate the applicant's "demeanor." However, the statute also states that the trier of fact must evaluate credibility *considering the totality of circumstances* and in light of *all relevant factors*. The adjudicator, therefore, must take into account, for example, when and where the statement was made and various other factors, including the applicant's familiarity with U.S. legal culture and processes, whether or not the applicant was or is represented or detained at the time of any statement, etc. Most critically, the trier of fact must make his or her assessment and the factors on which it is based explicit in the decision.

With respect to corroboration, REAL ID restates the international legal rule, elaborated in its seminal *S–M–J–* ruling, that the applicant's credible testimony may be sufficient to meet her burden of proof without corroboration, that reasonably available corroboration should generally be provided, that the applicant should be given an opportunity to explain why she could not present such evidence, that adjudicators should make their rulings and reasoning explicit, and that all parties involved in the adjudication –applicant, adjudicator and district counsel—are to reasonably assist in providing corroborative evidence, including background materials related to the country of origin. Although not discussed at length in this article, the last point—the joint nature of the enterprise, reasonably shared among applicant, adjudicator and district counsel—is especially important in cases where applicants are detained and/or unrepresented.

Before the enactment of REAL ID's credibility and corroboration provisions, the BIA and immigration judges were not in many cases complying with the BIA's own *S–M–J–* ruling that required applicants only to present reasonably available corroborative evidence, consistent with international legal standards. Practitioners report increased corroboration demands that violate the *S–M–J–* and REAL ID rule. It is to be hoped that administrative authorities will comply better in the future, that courts will monitor and ensure that they do, and that eligible refugees and torture survivors will receive the protection and welcoming that U.S. law and tradition, and the international regime on which it is based, require.

CORROBORATION: SOME MAJOR PRACTICE POINTERS

Below are a few general practice pointers. We know that many times it is difficult to follow these, such as when your client is in detention or when (which is often the case) you have limited resources.

Spend as much time as possible with your client, preparing his or her testimony, and trying to understand your client's story from his or her point of view. Use the client's own thought process to refer to the timing of events. Several asylum books and manuals discuss interviewing and establishing credibility; these are important resources.[115]

Professor Virgil Wiebe (who runs an asylum clinic), Serena Parker, Erin Corcoran, and Anna Marie Gallagher make the following suggestions regarding corroboration,[116] which we have amplified:

- Corroborate the claim with contemporaneous original documents relating specifically to your client's claim, such as arrest warrants, medical records, death certificates, photos, school records, political party identification cards, newspaper articles, etc.

- Corroborate the claim with documentary evidence produced specifically for the asylum claim, such as medical and psychiatric reports confirming physical and psychological injury, affidavits, letters, faxes, or e-mails from family, friends, and colleagues confirming central facts of your claim;

- Corroborate country conditions that support your claim through State Department reports, human rights groups, UN documents, expert affidavits, etc.;

---

[115] *See, e.g.*, R. Germain, *AILA's Asylum Primer: A Practical Guide to U.S. Asylum Law and Procedure* (5th ed. 2007), available from AILA Publications, *www.ailapubs.org*, (800) 982-2839; Immigrant Legal Resource Center, *Winning Asylum Cases* (2004); Midwest Immigrant & Human Rights Center, *Basic Procedural Manual for Asylum Representation Affirmatively and in Removal Proceedings* (2006). For a general book on U.S. asylum law, *see* D. Anker, *Law of Asylum in the United States* (1999 and 2002 Supp.) The AOBTC lesson plans are another excellent resource. *See www.asylumlaw.org/legal_tools/index.cfm?category=119& countryID=194.*

[116] V. Wiebe, *et al.*, "Asking for a Note from Your Torturer: Corroboration and Authentication Requirements in Asylum, Withholding and Torture Convention Claims," 1 *Immigration & Nationality Law Handbook* 414 (AILA 2001-02 Ed.).

- Corroborate (and in any case establish on the record) all efforts you have made to obtain evidence, explaining unsuccessful efforts to obtain evidence, or why it was imprudent to even try to obtain evidence in the home country. (A country condition expert may be able to verify that phones and faxes are routinely tapped, mail opened, family members of suspects are followed, the postal system is nonfunctioning, phones don't work, etc.). Be sure to explain and put on the record reasonable time and resource constraints that limited your ability to obtain documentation.

Practitioners should keep in mind the following:

- Remember these principles from the discussion in this article and the *S–M–J–* case (a decision encoded in REAL ID):

- It is per se unreasonable to expect corroboration of particular experiences from the persecutor

- Expected corroboration must be of material facts which are central to the applicant's claim and easily subject to verification

- It is unreasonable to expect specific documentary corroboration of an applicant's particular experiences unless the supporting documentation is of the type that would normally be created or available in the particular country and is accessible to the alien, such as through friends, relatives, or coworkers.

- Consider asking the adjudicator where he or she sees gaps in evidence and corroboration. Emphasize to the adjudicator that he or she has the obligation to give your client the opportunity to correct/rebut/supply such evidence before the proceedings are complete and a decision is made;

- Again, remember that unreasonable demands for corroborative evidence cannot be made, and point this out to adjudicators (for example, diligent efforts to obtain an arrest warrant may either be futile or place your client's friends and family who seek such documentation in greater danger, particularly if such efforts would alert the very persecutors from whom asylum applicants flee);

- If unreasonable demands for corroborative evidence have been made and your case is on appeal, be sure to make the argument that requiring excessive and unreasonable corroboration is impermissible under the BIA's *S–M–J–* ruling and REAL ID;

- Local practices and adjudicative cultures vary. Know what the Asylum Office or IJ in your area generally expects. Summary indexes of corroborative materials are very helpful. This is generally a list of documents under various descriptive headings (*e.g.,* "Corroboration of Identity" or "Corroboration of Persecution of HIV/AIDS Patients in X") and may also include excerpts of the most relevant material from the full documents. Note that some asylum offices and immigration judges prefer focused documentation material, rather than volume.

- Be sure to preserve the record in case of appeal, including lodging appropriate objections and making all available arguments when credibility and corroboration issues arise.

REINSTATEMENT OF REMOVAL

by Trina Realmuto*

A person who has been removed and who subsequently unlawfully re-enters the United States may be subject to reinstatement of removal under Immigration and Nationality Act (INA) §241(a)(5) [8 USC §1231(a)(5)]. This practice advisory provides an overview of the reinstatement statute and implementing regulations, including how the reinstatement process is currently being carried out by the Department of Homeland Security (DHS). The advisory addresses who is subject to reinstatement, where to obtain federal court review of reinstatement orders, and what arguments are available to challenge the legality of reinstatement orders in federal court, including challenges to the underlying removal order. It also addresses the U.S. Supreme Court's decision in *Fernandez-Vargas v. Gonzales*,[1] regarding the retroactive application of the reinstatement provision. Finally, the advisory includes a list of federal circuit court of appeals cases that have addressed the reinstatement provision.

The first inquiry, before a client's reinstatement case is litigated in federal court, is whether the client would be eligible for relief from removal but for the reinstatement order. If the client is not or not likely to be eligible for ultimate relief, the client may be better advised not to pursue litigation.

Court decisions addressing INA §241(a)(5) may change the existing law or create new law. Counsel are advised to independently confirm whether the law in their circuit has changed since the date of this advisory.

BACKGROUND

What is reinstatement of removal?

Reinstatement of removal is the term for removal pursuant to INA §241(a)(5), as added by IIRAIRA[2] §305(a). The regulations implementing the statute are located at 8 CFR §241.8. Section 241(a)(5) took effect on April 1, 1997.[3] The provision states:

> (5) Reinstatement of removal orders against aliens illegally reentering.
>
> If the Attorney General finds that an alien has reentered the United States illegally after having been removed or having departed voluntarily, under an order of removal, the prior order of removal is reinstated from its original date and is not subject to being reopened or reviewed, the alien is not eligible and may not apply for any relief under this Act,[4] and the alien shall be removed under the prior order at any time after the reentry.

Who is subject to reinstatement of removal?

Noncitizens who return to the United States illegally after having been removed under a prior order of deportation, exclusion, or removal are subject to removal under INA §241(a)(5) unless they meet a statutory or judicial exemption.

Who is statutorily exempt from reinstatement of removal under INA §241(a)(5)?

Congress has enacted legislation that specifically exempts the following individuals from being subject to reinstatement of removal:

- Individuals applying for adjustment of status under INA §245A (the legalization program) who are covered by certain class action lawsuits.[5]

---

[1] 548 U.S. 30 (2006).

---

[2] Illegal Immigration Reform and Immigrant Responsibility Act of 1996 (IIRAIRA), Pub. L. No. 104-208, div. C, 110 Stat. 3009, 3009-546 to 3009-724.

[3] IIRAIRA §309(a).

[4] Some online versions incorrectly use the word "chapter" rather than "Act."

[5] *See* Legal Immigration and Family Equity Act (LIFE Act), Pub. L. No. 106-553, §1(a)(2) (appx. B, H.R. 5548, §§1101–04), 114 Stat. 2762, 2762A-142 to 2762A-149 (2000). The relevant class action lawsuits include *Catholic Social Services, Inc. v. Meese, vacated sub nom. Reno v. Catholic So-*
continued

- Nicaraguan and Cuban applicants for adjustment under §202 of the Nicaraguan Adjustment and Central American Relief Act of 1997 (NACARA).[6]

- Salvadoran, Guatemalan, and Eastern European applicants under NACARA §203.[7]

- Haitian applicants for adjustment under the Haitian Refugee Immigration Fairness Act of 1998 (HRIFA).[8]

Who is judicially exempt from reinstatement of removal under INA §241(a)(5)?

Litigation has resulted in some court-created exemptions to INA §241(a)(5). That is, some courts have said that certain people are not subject to having their prior orders reinstated. As of the date of this advisory, these should include individuals in the:

- First, Seventh, and Eleventh Circuits, who applied for discretionary relief before April 1, 1997;[9]

- Tenth Circuit, who took affirmative steps to legalize their immigration status prior to April 1, 1997.[10]

- Ninth Circuit, who filed an application for adjustment of status and application for permission to reapply for admission to the United States af-

ter deportation or removal prior to the reinstatement determination.[11]

After issuance of a reinstatement order, can a person apply for any "relief" from removal?

A final reinstatement order triggers INA §241(a)(5)'s bar to relief. However, DHS previously has taken the position that withholding of removal is not a form of relief because it is mandatory, not discretionary. Thus, if a person expresses a fear of return during the reinstatement process, the regulations provide for an interview with an asylum officer.[12] If an asylum officer determines that the person has a "reasonable fear of persecution or torture," the person may apply for withholding before an immigration judge.[13] The person arguably also might be eligible to apply for asylum.[14]

What is the process for assessing whether a client is subject to INA §241(a)(5)?

First, determine whether the client has a prior deportation, exclusion, or removal order. To verify whether a prior order exists, attorneys may (1) call the Executive Office for Immigration Review (EOIR) ((800) 898-7180); (2) file a Freedom of Information Act request with DHS/EOIR; and/or (3) file a fingerprint records request with the Federal Bureau of Investigation.

Second, determine whether the client departed under the prior order. If the client has not departed since the prior order was issued, he or she cannot be subject to reinstatement, because INA §241(a)(5) requires an illegal reentry "after having been removed or having departed voluntarily, under an order of removal." However, in this situation, DHS could attempt to execute the outstanding order.

---

cial Services, Inc., 509 U.S. 43 (1993); *League of United Latin American Citizens v. INS, vacated sub nom. Reno v. Catholic Social Services, Inc.*, 509 U.S. 43 (1993); and *Zambrano v. INS, vacated sub nom. INS v. Zambrano*, 509 U.S. 918 (1993). LIFE Act, H.R. 5548 §1104(b), as amended by LIFE Act Amendments of 2000 (Life Act Amendments), Pub. L. No. 106-554, appx. D, div. B, §1503(a), 114 Stat. 2763, 2763A-324.

[6] Pub. L. No. 105-100, §202(a)(2), as added by LIFE Act Amendments §1505(a)(1), 114 Stat. at 2763A-326; 8 CFR §241.8(d).

[7] IIRAIRA §309, as amended by LIFE Act Amendments §1505(c), 114 Stat. at 2763A-327.

[8] Pub. L. No. 105-277, div. A, §101(h), sec. 902(a), as added by LIFE Act Amendments §1505(b)(1), 114 Stat. at 2763A-326 to 2763-327; 8 CFR §241.8(d).

[9] *Arevalo v. Ashcroft*, 344 F.3d 1 (1st Cir. 2003); *Faiz-Mohammed v. Ashcroft*, 395 F.3d 799 (7th Cir. 2005); *Sarmiento-Cisneros v. Ashcroft*, 381 F.3d 1277 (11th Cir. 2004). Although these decisions pre-dated the Supreme Court's decision in *Fernandez-Vargas*, AILF believes that *Fernandez-Vargas* should not impact the continuing validity of these decisions. *See* discussion in retroactivity section below.

[10] *Valdez-Sanchez v. Gonzales*, 485 F.3d 1084, 1089–90 (10th Cir. 2007) (finding that it would be fundamentally unfair to apply the reinstatement provision to an individual who had applied for lawful residence status prior to April 1, 1997).

---

[11] These people are entitled to *adjudication* of the I-212 waiver application. If the waiver application is approved, they are not subject to reinstatement. If the waiver application is denied, they *are* subject to the reinstatement provision. *See Duran Gonzales v. DHS*, 508 F.3d 1227, 1242 n.14 (2007) (effectively overruling *Perez-Gonzalez v. Ashcroft*, 379 F.3d 783 (9th Cir. 2004), but not as to its holding that a successful I-212 waiver application would "avoid" the reinstatement provision). For more detailed and current information on the *Duran Gonzales* class action lawsuit, please *see* AILF's website at *www.ailf.org/lac/lac_lit.shtml*.

[12] 8 CFR §241.8(e).

[13] *See* 8 CFR §208.31(e).

[14] *See* the discussion of *Fernandez-Vargas* in the retroactivity section below.

Third, determine whether the client returned to the United States illegally. In general, a person enters legally when he or she is admitted following inspection and authorization by an immigration officer. However, whether an entry is legal or not can involve complex entry and admission issues.

Individuals who meet all three statutory conditions and who do not fall under a statutory or judicial exemption are subject to reinstatement under §241(a)(5).

What happens when a person's removal order is reinstated?

Once a person is identified as subject to INA §241(a)(5), a DHS officer completes the top portion of the Form I-871, Notice of Intent to Reinstate. This notice contains the factual allegations against the individual, including alienage, the date of the prior order, and the date of illegally re-entry. The notice states that there is no right to a hearing before an immigration judge, but the individual can make an oral or written statement to an immigration officer. The notice contains a space for the individual to sign to acknowledge receipt of the notice and to indicate whether he or she wishes to make a statement to contest the determination. The regulations provide, "If the alien wishes to make a statement, the officer shall allow the alien to do so and shall consider whether the alien's statement warrants reconsideration of the determination."[15]

When there is an identity dispute over whether the individual was in fact previously subject to a prior order, DHS is supposed to compare the individual's fingerprints with those in its file before it issues the order. In the absence of such fingerprints, the regulations provide that DHS cannot remove the individual.[16]

A DHS officer issues a reinstatement order by completing the bottom portion of Form I-871, labeled "Decision, Order and Officer's Certification." The Decision, Order and Officer's Certification box on Form I-871 is the actual reinstatement order. Often the DHS officer will sign the top and bottom portions of the form on the same day. Thus, reinstatement orders may be issued and even executed within a period of hours.

FEDERAL COURT JURISDICTION OVER REINSTATEMENT ORDERS AND TRANSFER UNDER 28 USC §1631

Can reinstatement orders be appealed and, if so, to which court?

Yes. Every circuit court to address jurisdiction over reinstatement orders has concluded that judicial review is available in the court of appeals having jurisdiction over the place the reinstatement order was issued.[17] Notably, a person can file a petition for review challenging a reinstatement order even after it has been executed and the person has been physically removed.

A petition for review must be filed within 30 days of the date of the reinstatement order.[18] If the petitioner has not yet been removed, a motion for a stay of removal may be filed simultaneously with a petition for review.

The 30-day deadline for filing a petition for review is jurisdictional, meaning that the court of appeals will *not* be able to exercise jurisdiction over an *untimely* petition for review. The Decision, Order and Officer's Certification box on the I-871, when signed by the DHS officer, is the final order. The date it is completed is the date the reinstatement order is administratively final and the judicial review clock begins to run.[19]

---

[15] 8 CFR §241.8(a)(3).

[16] 8 CFR §241.8(a)(2).

---

[17] *Arevalo v. Ashcroft*, 344 F.3d 1, 9 (1st Cir. 2003); *Delgado v. Mukasey*, 2008 U.S. App. LEXIS 2655, *3 (2d Cir. 2008), *Avila-Macias v. Ashcroft*, 328 F.3d 108, 110 (3d Cir. 2003); *Velasquez-Gabriel v. Crocetti*, 263 F.3d. 102, 105 (4th Cir. 2001); *Ojeda-Terrazas v. Ashcroft*, 290 F.3d 292, 295 (5th Cir. 2002); *Bejjani v. INS*, 271 F.3d 670, 674 (6th Cir. 2001), *abrogated on other grounds by Fernandez-Vargas*, 126 S.Ct. at 2427 & n.5; *Gomez-Chavez v. INS*, 308 F.3d 796, 800 (7th Cir. 2002); *Alvarez-Portillo v. Ashcroft*, 280 F.3d 858 (8th Cir. 2002), *overruled on other grounds by Gonzalez v. Chertoff*, 454 F.3d 813, 818 n.4 (8th Cir. 2006); *Castro-Cortez et al. v. INS*, 239 F.3d 1037, 1043–44 (9th Cir. 2001), *abrogated on other grounds by Fernandez-Vargas*, 126 S.Ct. at 2427 & n.5; *Duran-Hernandez v. Ashcroft*, 348 F.3d 1158, 1162 n.3 (10th Cir. 2003); *Sarmiento-Cisneros v. Ashcroft*, 381 F.3d 1277, 1278 (11th Cir. 2004).

[18] INA §242(b)(1).

[19] *See generally Ponta-Garca v. Ashcroft*, 386 F.3d 341, 343 (1st Cir. 2004). Courts have not addressed the question of when the appeal period begins if the date of the reinstatement order is different from the date of service. In addition, courts have not yet addressed if or how the finality of the reinstatement order is affected by referral to an asylum officer for a reasonable fear interview or by referral to an immigration judge for a withholding application. Therefore, out of

continued

If a person would otherwise be statutorily barred from filing a petition for review of a removal order, does the statutory bar also apply to reinstatement orders?

Courts that are statutorily barred under INA §242(a)(2)(C) from considering petitions for review filed by persons with certain criminal convictions may nonetheless review a reinstatement order if the petition for review raises a question of law or constitutional issue.[20]

What if federal court review of the reinstatement order was sought in the wrong court?

Under 28 USC §1631, a court may transfer an action filed in the wrong court to cure a lack of jurisdiction. The transfer statute may be invoked to obtain a court of appeals' review of claims raised in an improperly filed district court action or claims raised in a petition for review filed with the wrong court of appeals. A court of appeals can transfer an improperly filed district court action to itself. In addition, one court of appeals can transfer a petition for review to another court of appeals. Transfer can be requested by a party or invoked *sua sponte* by a court.

In general, transfer is appropriate under §1631 if three conditions are met: (1) the transferring court lacks jurisdiction; (2) the transferee court could have exercised jurisdiction at the time the action or appeal was filed; and (3) the transfer is in the interest of justice. Importantly, the statute provides that the court "shall" transfer the case to the appropriate court if these conditions are met.

In the reinstatement context, several courts have invoked the transfer statute.[21] Courts have invoked

the statute based on justifiable reliance on a statute or court decision,[22] to preserve review that would otherwise be time barred for failure to file a timely petition for review,[23] or to prevent undue delay.[24]

FEDERAL COURT CHALLENGES TO THE PRIOR REMOVAL ORDER (UNDERLYING THE REINSTATEMENT ORDER)

Do the federal courts have jurisdiction to consider a challenge to a prior order even though INA §241(a)(5) says the prior order "is not subject to being . . . reviewed"?

AILF believes there must be some opportunity to challenge the legality of a prior order before DHS can use the order as the basis for a reinstatement order. To date, the Fifth, Third, and Tenth Circuits have found jurisdiction to review the prior order in certain circumstances.[25] The Ninth Circuit has held that it cannot review the prior order.[26]

What is the statutory basis for the federal courts to review the prior order?

INA §242(a)(2)(D) provides for review of legal and constitutional questions notwithstanding INA §§242(a)(2)(B) and (C) "or any other provision [of the INA (other than INA §242)] which limits or eliminates judicial review." The reinstatement provision, INA §241(a)(5), provides that "the prior order

---

an abundance of caution, one might presume that the judicial review clock begins ticking on the date the reinstatement order is issued, notwithstanding referral to an asylum officer or immigration judge. Arguably, filing a petition for review of the reinstatement order in this situation should not impact the agency's jurisdiction or willingness to consider and decide the withholding application.

[20] *See* INA §242(a)(2)(D); *see also, e.g., Debeato v. AG*, 505 F.3d 231, 234 (3d Cir. 2007); *Ramirez-Molina v. Ziglar*, 436 F.3d 508, 513 (5th Cir. 2006).

[21] Although the REAL ID Act of 2005, Pub. L. No. 109-13, div. B, 119 Stat. 231, 302–23, eliminated district court jurisdiction to review removal orders through habeas corpus actions as of the date of enactment, May 11, 2005, the elimination of this habeas review does not impact the district court's authority to transfer improperly filed habeas actions to the court of appeals when the requirements of §1631 are met.
continued

Indeed, §1631 provides that such transfer is appropriate to cure a court's "want of jurisdiction."

[22] *See Castro-Cortez v. INS*, 239 F.3d 1037, 1046–47 (9th Cir. 2001), *abrogated on other grounds by Fernandez-Vargas*, 126 S.Ct. at 2427 & n.5 (decided prior to the REAL ID Act's elimination of habeas jurisdiction over final removal orders; transferring habeas petition when "petitioners had good reason to believe that direct review [of reinstatement order] was not available and that a habeas corpus petition was their only avenue to secure judicial review").

[23] *See, e.g., Lopez v. Heinauer*, 332 F.3d 507, 510–11 (8th Cir. 2003) (transferring habeas action because without transfer "the petitioner will have lost his opportunity to present the merits of the claim due to a statute of limitations bar").

[24] *See, e.g., Arevalo v. Ashcroft*, 344 F.3d 1, 6 (noting district court transfer of habeas action seeking review of a reinstatement order), 16 (retransferring case to the district court for further proceedings) (1st Cir. 2003); *Cruz v. Ridge*, 383 F.3d 62, 65 (2d Cir. 2004) (discussing jurisdiction to review transfer order in reinstatement case).

[25] *Ramirez-Molina v. Ziglar*, 436 F.3d 508 (5th Cir. 2006); *Debeato v. AG*, 505 F.3d 231, 234–35 (3d Cir. 2007); *Lorenzo v. Mukasey*, 508 F.3d 1278, 1281 (10th Cir. 2007).

[26] *Martinez-Merino v. Keisler*, 504 F.3d 1068, 1071 (9th Cir. 2007).

of removal … is not subject to being … reviewed …." Because §241(a)(5) is a provision "which limits or eliminates judicial review" within the meaning of INA §242(a)(2)(D), it follows that courts may review legal and constitutional challenges to prior removal orders.

Post-REAL ID, what have the circuit courts held regarding review of prior orders?

The Fifth, Third, and Tenth Circuits have adopted the construction of INA §242(a)(2)(D) set forth above. The Fifth Circuit ultimately dismissed the petition for review, however, because the petitioner had a meaningful opportunity to seek judicial review of the underlying order in the prior removal proceeding but did not do so.[27] The Third Circuit reviewed the prior order but upheld its validity under a "gross miscarriage of justice" standard.[28] The Tenth Circuit held that, while §242(a)(2)(D) provides a basis for reviewing underlying orders, it does not trump INA §242(e)'s limitations on review of expedited removal orders.[29] Thus, the court held that it could not review the underlying expedited order at issue in that case.

Although the Eighth Circuit also has addressed the issue of collateral review, the decision pre-dated the REAL ID Act's enactment of INA §242(a)(2)(D) and thus did not address it. In *Ochoa-Carrillo v. Gonzales*,[30] the petitioner claimed she was not the person named in the prior expedited removal order being reinstated. She argued that the district court had habeas corpus jurisdiction to review her claim pursuant to INA §242(e)(2) (authorizing limited habeas corpus review of expedited removal orders). The court disagreed, finding that habeas corpus review under INA §242(e)(2) is not available in a reinstatement proceeding because review of the underlying order is barred.

The Ninth Circuit has held that it lacks jurisdiction to review any challenge to a prior order.[31] In so holding, the court said it was bound by the en banc decision in *Morales-Izquierdo v. Ashcroft*.[32] However, the *Morales-Izquierdo* court did not address §242(a)(2)(D). Petitioner, supported by AILF and other amici curiae working on this issue, sought rehearing on this basis. The court ordered the government to respond and a decision as to whether the case will be reheard is pending as of the date of this advisory.

Prior to the enactment of the REAL ID Act, would the federal courts review prior orders in reinstatement cases?

Although pre-REAL ID case law is helpful to understanding the historical development of collateral review, practitioners should *not* rely on these cases in formulating jurisdictional arguments. The REAL ID Act's enactment of INA §242(a)(2)(D) radically altered the relevant legal arguments in this area.

Prior to the REAL ID Act, and with little or no analysis, several courts stated that they could not review prior removal orders.[33] Only the Fourth and Ninth Circuits addressed whether the bar also precluded habeas review when an individual alleged a colorable constitutional claim that he or she was denied judicial review in the first proceeding.[34] Both courts held that such individuals may obtain habeas review of the prior order.[35] Applying the rationale of *INS v. St. Cyr*,[36] these courts reasoned that it would raise a serious constitutional question if *all* review of the prior order were barred. Thus, these circuits interpreted INA §241(a)(5)'s bar to review to preclude only direct review in the courts of appeals, not habeas corpus review.[37]

---

[27] *Ramirez-Molina, supra* note 25, at 515.

[28] *Debeato, supra* note 25, at 237.

[29] *Lorenzo, supra* note 25, at 1282–84.

[30] 446 F.3d 781 (8th Cir. 2006).

[31] *Martinez-Merino, supra* note 26, at 1071.

[32] 486 F.3d 484 (9th Cir. 2007).

---

[33] *Arevalo v. Ashcroft*, 344 F.3d 1, 9 (1st Cir. 2003); *Avila-Macias v. Ashcroft*, 328 F.3d 108, 115 (3d Cir. 2003); *Smith v. Ashcroft*, 295 F.3d 425, 428–29 (4th Cir. 2002); *Ojeda-Terrazas v. Ashcroft*, 290 F.3d 292, 295 (5th Cir. 2002); *Gomez-Chavez v. INS*, 308 F.3d 796, 801 (7th Cir. 2002); *Briseno-Sanchez v. Heinauer*, 319 F.3d 324, 327–28 (8th Cir. 2003); *Alvarenga-Villalobos v. Ashcroft*, 271 F.3d 1169, 1173 (9th Cir. 2001); *Garcia-Marrufo v. Ashcroft*, 376 F.3d 1061 (10th Cir. 2004).

[34] *Smith v. Ashcroft*, 295 F.3d 425, 428–29 (4th Cir. 2002); *Arreola-Arreola v. Ashcroft*, 383 F.3d 956, 963–64 (9th Cir. 2004).

[35] *But cf. Alvarenga-Villalobos v. Ashcroft*, 271 F.3d 1169 (9th Cir. 2001) (finding review of prior order precluded where petitioner voluntarily waived appeal in the first proceeding).

[36] 533 U.S. 289 (2001).

[37] *See also Sifuentes-Barraza v. Garcia*, 252 F. Supp. 2d 354, 360 (W.D. Tex. 2003) (also applying the rationale of *St. Cyr* to permit habeas review of prior order); *Chacon-Corral v. Weber*, 259 F. Supp. 2d 1151 (D. Col. 2003) (applying the rationale of *U.S. v. Mendoza-Lopez*, 481 U.S. 828 (1987), to permit habeas review of prior order). *Accord Avila-Macias v. Ashcroft*, 328 F.3d 108, 115 (3d Cir. 2003) (whether the dis-

continued

ADMINISTRATIVE CHALLENGES
TO PRIOR ORDERS

Can the agency reopen or reconsider a prior order if my client is potentially or presently subject to a reinstatement order?

If a person is potentially or presently subject to reinstatement, practitioners should not automatically rule out the possibility of an administrative challenge to the prior order even though the statute says the prior order "is not subject to being reopened or reviewed …."

Why should I bother asking the agency to reconsider or reopen the prior order when the reinstatement statute bars review or reopening of the prior order?

The law on collateral review is still developing. The courts may hold that a prior order cannot be reopened or collaterally reviewed *in a reinstatement case*. However, such a holding would not necessarily bar reopening or review in a *direct challenge* to the prior order.

Indeed, the First Circuit has suggested that an administrative motion is an appropriate avenue to remedy errors in the reinstatement process. In *Ponta-Garca v. Ashcroft*,[38] the court dismissed an untimely petition for review of a reinstatement order. Notably, however, the petitioner had filed a motion to reconsider or reopen the reinstatement decision with the local DHS field office director. Although the court rejected the petitioner's contention that the motion tolled the petition for review deadline, the court stated, "Should the eventual disposition of that motion not be in the petitioner's favor, he may, of course, file a separate petition for review with respect thereto."[39] The court encouraged the government "to reexamine the case with care."[40]

In addition, the Ninth Circuit has suggested that a motion to reopen might be available when the prior order was issued in absentia.[41]

Where can I find the regulations governing motions to reopen or reconsider if ICE issued the underlying order?

The regulations at 8 CFR §103.5 govern motions to reopen or reconsider decisions made by DHS officers. The applicable regulations include the following:

> A motion to reopen must state the new facts to be provided in the reopened proceeding and be supported by affidavits or other documentary evidence.[42]

> A motion to reconsider must state the reasons for reconsideration and be supported by any pertinent precedent decisions to establish that the decision was based on an incorrect application of law or Service policy.[43]

Motions to reopen or reconsider must be filed within 30 days of the decision or proceeding.[44] The deadline for reopening "may be excused in the discretion of the Service where it is demonstrated that the delay was reasonable and was beyond the control of the applicant or petitioner."[45]

The INA contains some restrictions on direct *federal* court review of expedited removal orders.[46] Arguably, these restrictions do not apply to requests for administrative review.

How do I ask for reopening or reconsideration if the BIA issued the underlying order?

If the Board of Immigration Appeals (BIA) issued the underlying order, the respondent may file a motion to reopen or motion to reconsider, as appropriate, in accordance with the governing regulations. It is advisable to inform the BIA that DHS has reinstated the order as DHS will likely point this out in its response. If the challenge to the underlying order is based in whole or in part on an ineffective assistance of counsel claim, the respondent must comply with the procedural requirements of the BIA's decision in *Matter of Lozada*.[47]

---

trict court has jurisdiction over collateral challenge can be "can be raised and decided" in district court via habeas).

[38] 386 F.3d 341 (1st Cir. 2004).

[39] *Id.* at 343 n.1.

[40] *Id.* at 343.

[41] *Morales-Izquierdo v. Ashcroft*, 486 F.3d 484, 496 n.13 (9th Cir. 2007) (en banc).

[42] 8 CFR §103.5(a)(2).

[43] 8 CFR §103.5(a)(3).

[44] 8 CFR §103.5(a)(1)(i).

[45] *Id.*

[46] *See* INA §242(e).

[47] 19 I&N Dec. 637 (BIA 1988).

What if the client already has been deported based on the reinstatement order?

The regulations governing motions to reopen and reconsider before DHS do not contain a jurisdictional bar to review of motions filed by people outside the United States. Accordingly, the motions should not be denied for this reason. If DHS nevertheless were to take this position, a circuit court could reverse it on petition for review.

The regulations governing motions to reopen and reconsider before immigration judges and the BIA purport to bar review if the person has departed the United States.[48] To date, at least one court has struck down this postdeparture regulatory bar because it conflicts with the motion to reopen statute.[49] Some courts also have held that these regulations do not apply in certain cases, such as when the motion to reopen is filed after departure,[50] when the motion seeks reopening of an in absentia order,[51] when the basis of the order has been nullified,[52] and when the order was unlawfully executed.[53] The BIA also has conducted collateral review of a prior order notwithstanding a person's departure.[54]

What if the BIA or DHS denies the motion to reopen or motion to reconsider?

The courts of appeals should have jurisdiction to consider a petition for review of a BIA or DHS denial of a motion to reopen or motion to reconsider.[55]

Is there a way to "challenge" the prior order through consular processing?

Maybe. Individuals who are applying for visas from abroad and who have viable claims that their prior order or reinstatement order is unlawful can try to convince a consular officer that they are not subject to INA §§212(a)(9)(A) or (C), and, thus do not need a waiver of their previous removal order(s). One could argue that a person is not inadmissible based on an unlawful order, and/or that an I-212 waiver should not be required for unlawful orders.

"RETROACTIVE" APPLICATION OF INA §241(A)(5)

Did "reinstatement" exist prior to INA §241(a)(5)'s April 1, 1997, effective date?

Yes, but the *only* individuals subject to reinstatement under the former INA §242(f) were those who had been previously deported (not excluded) on grounds relating to certain criminal convictions, failing to register, or falsification of documents, or security or terrorist-related grounds and subsequently re-entered the country illegally.

How does reinstatement under former INA §242(f) compare with reinstatement under current INA §241(a)(5)?

Under pre-IIRAIRA reinstatement procedures, legacy Immigration and Naturalization Service was required to issue an order to show cause charging the individual with deportability under former INA §242(f).[56] At a deportation hearing, an immigration judge would determine deportability and adjudicate any application for relief. The regulations further provided that reinstatement proceedings were to be conducted in general accordance with the rules governing deportation hearings before immigration judges.[57]

The current reinstatement provision substantively differs from its predecessor provision. The new provision expands the scope of individuals subject to reinstatement proceedings and broadens the consequences of issuance of a reinstatement order by providing that the prior order is not subject to "being reopened or reviewed" and that the individual is "not eligible and many not apply for any relief under the INA."[58]

---

[48] *See* 8 CFR §§1003.23(b)(1) (immigration court), 1003.2(d) (BIA).

[49] *See William v. Gonzales,* 499 F.3d 329 (4th Cir. 2007).

[50] *Zi-Xing Lin v. Gonzales,* 473 F.3d 979 (9th Cir. 2007); *Reynoso-Cisneros v. Gonzales,* 491 F.3d 1001 (9th Cir. 2007).

[51] *Contreras-Rodriguez v. Att'y Gen.,* 462 F.3d 1314 (11th Cir. 2006). *See also Morales-Izquierdo v. Ashcroft,* 486 F.3d 484, 496 n.13 (9th Cir. 2007) (en banc) (suggesting possibility).

[52] *Cardoso-Tlaseca v. Gonzales,* 460 F.3d 1102 (9th Cir. 2006); *Wiedersperg v. INS,* 896 F.2d 1179, 1181 (9th Cir. 1990); *Estrada-Rosales v. INS,* 645 F.2d 819 (9th Cir. 1981).

[53] *Mendez v. INS,* 563 F.2d 956 (9th Cir. 1977).

[54] *Matter of Malone,* 11 I&N Dec. 780 (BIA 1966); *Matter of Farinas,* 12 I&N Dec. 467 (BIA 1967); *Matter of Roman,* 19 I&N Dec. 855, 856–57 (BIA 1988).

[55] *Ponta-Garca v. Ashcroft,* 386 F.3d 341, 343 n.1 (1st Cir. 2004) (suggesting availability of such review).

---

[56] 8 CFR §242.23 (1995).

[57] *Id.*

[58] INA §241(a)(5).

What did the Supreme Court hold in *Fernandez-Vargas*?

In *Fernandez-Vargas v. Gonzales*,[59] the U.S. Supreme Court held that INA §241(a)(5) may be applied to an individual who (1) re-entered the United States before April 1, 1997, and (2) did not take any affirmative steps to legalize his or her unlawful status in the United States before that date. The petitioner in *Fernandez-Vargas* was last deported in 1981 and re-entered illegally shortly thereafter. Although he fathered a U.S. citizen son in 1989 (before April 1, 1997), he did not marry the boy's U.S. citizen mother or file an application for adjustment of status and request to waive his prior deportation order until March 2001 (after April 1, 1997).

What was the Supreme Court's rationale in *Fernandez-Vargas*?

The Court's decision rested on the retroactivity analysis from *Landgraf v. USI Film Products*.[60] First, the Court noted that Congress did not expressly prescribe whether the statute could be applied retroactively. The Court then concluded that application of traditional statutory construction rules failed to indicate whether Congress intended the provision to apply retroactively or prospectively. Next, the Court moved on to consider whether application of INA §241(a)(5) would produce a retroactive effect. A statute has a retroactive effect only when it applies to conduct completed prior to the change in law.

The Court concluded that "Fernandez-Vargas has no retroactivity claim based on a new disability consequent to a completed act ...." The Court reasoned that, in reinstatement cases, "it is the conduct of remaining in the country after entry that is the predicate action" triggering §241(a)(5)'s application, not the person's illegal reentry. The Court stated that §241(a)(5) does not penalize illegal re-entry but, rather, establishes a process to "stop an indefinitely continuing [immigration] violation." Therefore, because the petitioner continued his illegal presence after §241(a)(5) took effect, his conduct was not completed prior to the change in law.

The Court also noted that the petitioner had six months following §241(a)(5)'s enactment in which he could have left the United States before the statute took effect.

Can persons who took affirmative steps to legalize their status prior to April 1, 1997, claim that INA §241(a)(5) should not apply retroactively to them?

Yes. Importantly, the Court in *Fernandez-Vargas* expressly declined to decide whether the provision can be applied retroactively to someone who took affirmative steps to legalize his or her status, such as by filing an adjustment of status application, an immigrant visa petition, labor certification application, or asylum application, or by seeking temporary protected status. Indeed, there are several places in the decision where the Court expressly noted that the petitioner's situation was different from a petitioner who took some action to legalize his or her status before the change in law.[61]

Before the *Fernandez-Vargas* decision, the First, Seventh, and Eleventh Circuits held that INA §241(a)(5) does not apply retroactively to a person who applied for adjustment of status prior to April 1, 1997.[62] AILF believes these decisions are still good law.[63]

Two circuits have addressed retroactivity claims after *Fernandez-Vargas*. The Tenth Circuit has held that §241(a)(5) cannot be applied retroactively to an individuals who had applied for lawful residency

---

[59] 548 U.S. 30 (2006).

[60] 511 U.S. 244 (1994).

[61] 548 U.S. 30, 126 S.Ct. 2422, 2425 (2006) (limiting holding to the "continuing violator of the INA *now before us*"); 2427 n.5 (noting that whether a noncitizen's marriage or application for adjustment of status before April 1, 1997, renders §241(a)(5) impermissibly retroactive as applied are "facts not in play here"); 2432 n.10 (noting that petitioner's retroactivity claim was not based on a claim that §241(a)(5) cancelled vested rights, because he "never availed himself" of cancellation, adjustment, or voluntary departure and did not take an "action that enhanced their significance to him in particular"); 2433 & n.12 (declining to express an opinion on whether §241(a)(5) would have retroactive effect had the petitioner married a U.S. citizen and applied for adjustment of status before the change in law); 2434 (concluding "that §241(a)(5) has no retroactive effect when applied to aliens *like Fernandez-Vargas* ...."). (Emphasis added.)

[62] *Arevalo v. Ashcroft*, 344 F.3d 1 (1st Cir. 2003); *Faiz-Mohammed v. Ashcroft*, 395 F.3d 799 (7th Cir. 2005); *Sarmiento-Cisneros v. Ashcroft*, 381 F.3d 1277 (11th Cir. 2004). *Cf. Velasquez-Gabriel v. Crocetti*, 263 F.3d 102, 110 (4th Cir. 2001) (reasoning that §241(a)(5) did not have an impermissible effect because the petitioner did not file an adjustment application before April 1, 1997).

[63] *See also Valdez-Sanchez v. Gonzales*, 485 F.3d 1084, 1089–90 (10th Cir. 2007) (discussing ongoing validity of these cases).

prior to April 1, 1997.[64] The Fifth Circuit has held that §241(a)(5) can apply retroactively to someone who married a U.S. citizen and filed an I-130 visa petition but did *not* file an adjustment application before April 1, 1997.[65]

How does *Fernandez-Vargas* impact potential asylum applicants?

Footnote 4 of the *Fernandez-Vargas* decision states: "Notwithstanding the absolute terms in which the bar on relief is stated, even an alien subject to §241(a)(5) may seek withholding of removal" under INA §41(b)(3)(A) or 8 CFR §§241.8(e) and 208.31. Interestingly, the parenthetical following the Court's citation of 8 CFR §208.31, the regulation regarding the "reasonable fear" process, describes it as "raising the possibility of asylum to aliens whose removal order has been reinstated under INA §241(a)(5)." Since the Supreme Court has indicated that asylum remains available, individuals subject to reinstatement who have potential asylum claims may pursue these claims and cite to footnote 4 for the authority to do so.

Does *Fernandez-Vargas* overturn any circuit court case law?

Yes, the decision overturns the Sixth Circuit's opinion in *Bejjani v. INS*,[66] and the Ninth Circuit's decision in *Castro-Cortez v. INS*.[67] These courts had held that INA §241(a)(5) cannot apply retroactively to pre-April 1, 1997, re-entrants.

The *Fernandez-Vargas* decision also may have overturned the Third Circuit's decision in *Dinnall v. Gonzales*[68] (holding that §241(a)(5) cannot apply retroactively if the person was eligible for voluntary departure before April 1, 1997). The Supreme Court

suggests a petitioner must take "some action" towards legalizing status to prevail on a retroactivity claim.[69]

Are there any defenses available to people in removal proceedings who are subject to reinstatement pursuant to *Fernandez-Vargas* when DHS moves to terminate proceedings in order to reinstate?

Possibly. Once removal proceedings have commenced in immigration court, only the immigration judge has the authority to terminate proceedings.[70] A motion to terminate "must be adjudicated on the record and pursuant to the regulations as would any other motion;" it is "not just an automatic grant ... but an informed adjudication by the Immigration Judge ... based on an evaluation of the factors underlying the Service's motion."[71] Thus, an immigration judge can refuse to terminate proceedings to permit DHS to issue a reinstatement order if the judge believes that reinstatement is not lawful or if reinstatement would have an impermissible retroactive effect.

In addition, an immigration judge could refuse to terminate proceedings if he or she concludes that DHS waived its opportunity to pursue reinstatement against the person. Arguably, when DHS issues a notice to appear and is aware the petitioner is subject to reinstatement—but nonetheless chooses to initiate removal proceedings, rather than reinstatement proceedings—it waives its opportunity to subject the person to reinstatement under INA §241(a)(5).

This waiver argument applies equally to immigration cases within the jurisdiction of the Sixth and Ninth Circuits, in which the *Bejjani* and *Castro-Cortez* courts, respectively, had held that §241(a)(5) did not apply retroactively to a pre-IIRAIRA re-entrant. By deciding not to petition the Supreme Court for certiorari in those cases, arguably, the government acquiesced to the holdings in those decisions.

DUE PROCESS CONSIDERATIONS

What are the due process concerns in the reinstatement process?

The due process concerns in the reinstatement process include, but are not limited to:

- Lack of a full and fair hearing;

---

[64] *Valdez-Sanchez v. Gonzales,* 485 F.3d 1084 (10th Cir. 2007).

[65] *Silva Rosa v. Gonzales*, 490 F.3d 403 (5th Cir. 2007). Prior to *Fernandez-Vargas*, the courts were divided on whether the filing of immigrant visa petition prior to April 1, 1997, was sufficient to invoke retroactivity concerns. *Compare Lopez-Flores v. DHS*, 376 F.3d 793 (8th Cir. 2004) (holding that §241(a)(5) cannot be applied retroactively when a person filed an I-140 petition before April 1, 1997) *with Labojewski v. Gonzales*, 407 F.3d 814, 822 (7th Cir. 2005) (holding that the filing of an I-130 petition before April 1, 1997, is not sufficient to render §241(a)(5) impermissibly retroactive).

[66] 271 F.3d 670 (6th Cir. 2001).

[67] 239 F.3d 1037 (9th Cir. 2001).

[68] 421 F.3d 247 (3d Cir. 2005).

[69] *Fernandez-Vargas v. Gonzales,* 548 U.S. 30, 126 S.Ct. 2422, 2433 n.10 (2006).

[70] *Matter of G–N–C–,* 22 I&N Dec. 281, 284 (BIA 1998); 8 CFR §1239.2(c).

[71] *Matter of G–N–C–, supra* note 70, at 284.

- Lack of an impartial adjudicator;
- Lack of a meaningful opportunity to present evidence;
- Lack of a meaningful opportunity to cross-examine evidence;
- Inability to develop an adequate administrative record;
- Right-to-counsel issues, including lack of access to counsel during the reinstatement process and lack of notice to existing counsel in violation of 8 CFR §292.5; and
- Lack of notice of the right to seek federal court review.

How have the circuit courts ruled on due process claims?

To date, no court has found that the current reinstatement process violates due process.

Some courts, however, have expressed concern regarding the due process issues surrounding the reinstatement process.[72] Nonetheless, courts have upheld the reinstatement procedures.[73] In many cases, however, the petitioner was unable to show actual and specific prejudice from the alleged due process violation. Petitioners who challenge the existence (or, possibly, the legality) of the prior order, departure, or re-entry might be able to establish prejudice.

One court held that the reinstatement procedures, including fingerprinting procedures, did not violate petitioner's due process rights where the petitioner argued that she was not the person named in the prior removal order.[74]

Notably, consistent with the canon of constitutional avoidance, if a petitioner raises a nonconstitutional claim along with a due process challenge to a reinstatement order, presumptively courts will rule on the nonconstitutional claim before reaching the due process issue.

OTHER POTENTIAL ARGUMENTS AND ISSUES

Can someone who is eligible for adjustment of status under INA §245(i) argue that INA §245(i) trumps the bar to relief in INA §241(a)(5)?

Unless it already has been rejected by the relevant circuit court, this argument may be available. Unfortunately, however, many circuits have rejected this argument.[75]

Can someone challenge the existence of the factual elements of reinstatement?

Yes, a person can challenge a reinstatement order by arguing that he or she was not previously ordered removed, did not depart under a removal order, or re-entered the country pursuant to a legal admission. A few courts have addressed such claims.[76]

What is the implication of the *Morales-Izquierdo* case?

Although the Ninth Circuit previously held that only immigration judges can issue reinstatement orders, an en banc panel of the court reversed this conclusion in *Morales-Izquierdo v. Ashcroft*.[77] Thus, DHS officers within the Ninth Circuit can issue reinstatement orders. The en banc panel further rejected

---

[72] *See, e.g., Castro-Cortez v. INS,* 239 F.3d 1037, 1047–50 (9th Cir. 2001), *abrogated on other grounds by Fernandez-Vargas v. Gonzales,* 548 U.S. 30, 126 S.Ct. 2422, 2427 & n.5 (2006); *U.S. v. Charleswell,* 456 F.3d 347 (3d Cir. 2006); *Lattab v. Ashcroft,* 384 F.3d 8, 21 n.6 (1st Cir. 2004); *Bejjani v. INS,* 271 F.3d 670, 675–76 (6th Cir. 2001); *Alvarez-Portillo v. Ashcroft,* 280 F.3d 858, 867 (8th Cir. 2002), *overruled on other grounds by Gonzalez v. Chertoff,* 454 F.3d 813, 818 n.4 (8th Cir. 2006).

[73] *See, e.g., Morales-Izquierdo v. Ashcroft,* 486 F.3d 484 (9th Cir. 2007) (en banc); *Warner v. Ashcroft,* 381 F.3d 534, 539 (6th Cir. 2004); *Lattab v. Ashcroft,* 384 F.3d 8, 20–21 (1st Cir. 2004); *Ojeda-Terrazas v. Ashcroft,* 290 F.3d 292, 302 (5th Cir. 2002); *Gomez-Chavez v. INS,* 308 F.3d 796, 802 (7th Cir. 2002); *Briseno-Sanchez v. Heinauer,* 319 F.3d 324, 327–28 (8th Cir. 2003); *Duran-Hernandez v. Ashcroft,* 348 F.3d 1158, 1162–63 (10th Cir. 2003); *Ochoa-Carrillo v. Gonzales,* 437 F.3d 842 (8th Cir. 2006).

[74] *Ochoa-Carrillo, supra* note 73, at 845–48. *But see Rafaelano v. Wilson,* 471 F.3d 1091 (9th Cir. 2006) (transferring *continued*

case to BIA to resolve factual dispute regarding the existence of the prior order).

[75] *See Delgado v. Mukasey,* 2008 U.S. App. LEXIS 2655 (2d Cir. Feb. 7, 2008) (rejecting argument and discussing similar decisions of the First, Sixth, Seventh, Tenth, and Eleventh Circuits).

[76] *See, e.g., Ochoa-Carrillo supra* note 73, at 845–48 (rejecting challenge to the existence of a prior order against petitioner); *Rafaelano v. Wilson, supra* note 74 (transferring case to BIA to resolve factual dispute regarding whether person was previously departed under a removal order or pursuant to a grant of voluntary departure). *Accord Batista v. Ashcroft,* 270 F.3d 8 (1st Cir. 2001) (transferring case to district court to resolve genuine issue of fact regarding citizenship claim made by person subject to reinstatement order).

[77] 486 F.3d 484 (9th Cir. 2007).

petitioner's due process arguments and refused to consider his collateral attack on the prior order.[78]

Can a person with an approved I-212 waiver application avoid reinstatement?

In all circuits that have decided this issue, with the exception of the Ninth Circuit, an approved I-212 waiver application generally will not protect a person from issuance of a reinstatement order.

In the Ninth Circuit, pursuant to *Perez-Gonzalez v. Ashcroft*,[79] persons who file an I-212 waiver application prior to a reinstatement determination are entitled to adjudication of the I-212 waiver application. If the waiver application is approved, they are not subject to reinstatement. If the waiver application is denied, they *are* subject to the reinstatement provision.[80]

What avenues are available to individuals who are otherwise eligible for an immigrant or nonimmigrant visa but for having previously been subject to a reinstatement order?

People applying for a visa abroad must establish that they are admissible. A person who was deported based on a reinstatement order may be inadmissible under INA §212(a)(9)(C)(i)(II).

Importantly, the Department of State has interpreted INA §212(a)(9)(C)(i)(II) as *only* applying to re-entries after April 1, 1997.[81] Therefore, if the person's reinstatement order was based on a pre-April 1, 1997 re-entry, he or she is not inadmissible under INA §212(a)(9)(C)(i)(II). However, the person may still be inadmissible under INA §212(a)(9)(A) for having been previously removed, but could apply for a waiver under INA §212(a)(9)(A)(ii).[82]

If the person's reinstatement order was based on a post-1997 re-entry, he or she is inadmissible under INA §212(a)(9)(C)(i)(II) and generally cannot apply for a waiver of inadmissibility unless 10 years have elapsed since the date of last departure from the United States.[83] Whether a person must wait the 10 years to apply for such waiver is the subject of litigation in *Duran Gonzales*, the Ninth Circuit class action referenced in the question above.

Individuals who are applying for visas abroad and who have viable claims that their prior order or reinstatement order is unlawful also can try to convince a consular officer that they are not subject to INA §§212(a)(9)(A) or (C) and thus they do not need a waiver of their previous removal order(s). The argument is that the person should not be subjected to inadmissibility based on an unlawful order, and/or that an I-212 waiver should not be required where the order was unlawful.

ADDENDUM OF PUBLISHED APPELLATE COURT REINSTATEMENT DECISIONS

Supreme Court

- *Fernandez-Vargas v. Gonzales*, 547 U.S. 30, 126 S. Ct. 2422 (2006)

First Circuit

- *Batista v. Ashcroft*, 270 F.3d 8 (1st Cir. 2001)
- *Arevalo v. Ashcroft*, 344 F.3d 1 (1st Cir. 2003)
- *Ponta-Garca v. Ashcroft*, 386 F.3d 341 (1st Cir. 2004)
- *Lattab v. Ashcroft*, 384 F.3d 8 (1st Cir. 2004)

Second Circuit

- *Cruz v. Ridge*, 383 F.3d 62 (2d Cir. 2004)
- *Delgado v. Mukasey*, 2008 U.S. App. LEXIS 2655 (2d Cir. Feb. 7, 2008)

---

[78] *But see* the discussion of *Martinez-Merino v. Keisler*, 504 F.3d 1068 (9th Cir. 2007), in the collateral review section above.

[79] 379 F.3d 783 (9th Cir. 2004).

[80] *See Duran Gonzales v. DHS*, 508 F.3d 1227, 1242 n.14 (2007) (effectively overruling *Perez-Gonzalez*, but not as to its holding that a successful I-212 waiver application would "avoid" the reinstatement provision). For more detailed and current information on the *Duran Gonzales* litigation, please *see* AILF's website at *www.ailf.org/lac/lac_lit.shtml*.

[81] *See* P.L. 104-208 Update No. 36: 212(a)(9)(A)–(C), 212(a)(6)(A) and (B), 98 State 060539 (Apr. 4, 1998), *published on* AILA InfoNet at Doc. No. 98040490 (posted Apr. 4, 1998). *See also* INS Memorandum, P. Virtue, "Additional Guidance for Implementing Sections 212(a)(6) and 212(a)(9) of the Immigration and Nationality Act (Act)" (June 17, 1997), *published on* AILA InfoNet at Doc. No. 97061790 (*posted* June 17, 1997) (adopting same interpretation).

[82] *See also* 8 CFR §§212.2(b) (nonimmigrant visas), 212.2(d) (immigrant visas).

[83] *See Matter of Torres-Garcia*, 23 I&N Dec. 866 (BIA 2006) (holding that a person who enters the United States without inspection after removal is not eligible for a waiver of inadmissibility unless 10 years have elapsed since the date of last departure from the United States).

Third Circuit

- *Avila-Macias v. Ashcroft*, 328 F.3d 108 (3d Cir. 2003)

- *Dinnall v. Gonzales*, 421 F.3d 247 (3d Cir. 2005)

- *U.S. v. Charleswell*, 456 F.3d 347 (3d Cir. 2006)

- *Debeato v. AG*, 505 F.3d 231 (3d Cir. 2007)

Fourth Circuit

- *Velasquez-Gabriel v. Crocetti*, 263 F.3d. 102 (4th Cir. 2001)

- *Smith v. Ashcroft*, 295 F.3d 425 (4th Cir. 2002)

Fifth Circuit

- *Ojeda-Terrazas v. Ashcroft*, 290 F.3d 292, 295 (5th Cir. 2002)

- *Ramirez-Molina v. Ziglar*, 436 F.3d 508 (5th Cir. 2006)

- *Silva Rosa v. Gonzales*, 490 F.3d 403 (5th Cir. 2007)

Sixth Circuit

- *Bejjani v. INS*, 271 F.3d 670 (6th Cir. 2001), *abrogated by Fernandez-Vargas Gonzales,* 547 U.S. 30, 126 S. Ct. 2422, 2427 & n.5 (2006)

- *Warner v. Ashcroft*, 381 F.3d 534 (6th Cir. 2004)

Seventh Circuit

- *Gomez-Chavez v. INS*, 308 F.3d 796 (7th Cir. 2002)

- Faiz-Mohammed v. Ashcroft, 395 F.3d 799 (7th Cir. 2005)

- *Labojewski v. Gonzales*, 407 F.3d 814 (7th Cir. 2005)

- *Lino v. Gonzales*, 467 F.3d 1077 (7th Cir. 2006)

Eighth Circuit

- *Alvarez-Portillo v. Ashcroft,* 280 F.3d 858 (8th Cir. 2002), *overruled by Gonzalez v. Chertoff,* 454 F.3d 813, 818 n.4 (8th Cir. 2006).

- *Briseno-Sanchez v. Heinauer,* 319 F.3d 324 (8th Cir. 2003)

- *Lopez v. Heinauer*, 332 F.3d 507 (8th Cir. 2003)

- *Flores v. Ashcroft*, 354 F.3d 727 (8th Cir. 2003)

- *Lopez-Flores v. DHS,* 376 F.3d 793 (8th Cir. 2004)

- *Ochoa-Carrillo v. Gonzales,* 437 F.3d 842 (8th Cir. 2006)

- *Ochoa-Carrillo v. Gonzales,* 446 F.3d 781 (8th Cir. 2006)

Ninth Circuit

- *Castro-Cortez et al. v. INS*, 239 F.3d 1037 (9th Cir. 2001), *abrogated by Fernandez-Vargas Gonzales,* 547 U.S. 30, 126 S. Ct. 2422, 2427 & n.5 (2006)

- *Gallo-Alvarez v. Ashcroft*, 266 F.3d 1123 (9th Cir. 2001)

- *Alvarenga-Villalobos v. Ashcroft*, 271 F.3d 1169 (9th Cir. 2001)

- *Padilla v. Ashcroft*, 334 F.3d 921 (9th Cir. 2003)

- Perez-Gonzalez v. Ashcroft, 379 F.3d 783 (9th Cir. 2004), effectively overruled in part by Duran Gonzales v. DHS, 508 F.3d 1227 (2007)

- *Arreola-Arreola v. Ashcroft*, 383 F.3d 956 (9th Cir. 2004), *overruled by Morales-Izquierdo v. Ashcroft*, 486 F.3d 484 (9th Cir. 2007) (en banc)

- *Rafaelano v. Wilson*, 471 F.3d 1091 (9th Cir. 2006)

- *Morales-Izquierdo v. Ashcroft*, 486 F.3d 484 (9th Cir. 2007) (en banc)

- *Martinez-Merino v. Keisler*, 504 F.3d 1068 (9th Cir. 2007)

Tenth Circuit

- *Duran-Hernandez v. Ashcroft,* 348 F.3d 1158 (10th Cir. 2003)

- *Garcia-Marrufo v. Ashcroft*, 376 F.3d 1061 (10th Cir. 2004)

- *Fernandez-Vargas v. Ashcroft*, 394 F.3d 881 (10th Cir. 2005), *affirmed* 547 U.S. 30 (2006)

- *Berum-Garcia v. Comfort*, 390 F.3d 1158 (10th Cir. 2004)

- *Valdez-Sanchez v. Gonzales*, 485 F.3d 1084 (10th Cir. 2007)

- *Lorenzo v. Mukasey*, 508 F.3d 1278 (10th Cir. 2007)

Eleventh Circuit

- *Sarmiento-Cisneros v. Ashcroft*, 381 F.3d 1277 (11th Cir. 2004)

- *Guijosa De Sandoval v. AG*, 440 F.3d 1276 (11th Cir. 2006)

THE INS AND OUTS OF EXPEDITED REMOVAL: PRACTICAL STRATEGIES TO SERVE YOUR CLIENT

*by David Koelsch and Michael B. Berger**

Hanan, a young woman from Lebanon, married a U.S. citizen in Lebanon and embarked on a honeymoon cruise to the United States When she arrived in Boston, she presented a tourist visa and her Lebanese passport. U.S. Customs and Border Protection (CBP) officers questioned her regarding why she was attempting to enter the United States on a tourist visa if she was married to a U.S. citizen. Unable to answer the CBP officers' questions or to speak with her husband while she was questioned, she was detained and transported by CBP to Logan International Airport and placed on an outbound flight. While Hanan's intent was to enter the United States to begin a new life with her husband, her possession of a tourist visa was problematic and, at first glance, the decision to summarily deport her appears to be a correct application of expedited removal.

However, the situation was not as simple as it appeared. Hanan feared returning to Lebanon because, shortly before her marriage, Hezbollah militants had threatened her life on the basis of her marriage to a U.S. citizen and their assumption that she must be a spy for the Central Intelligence Agency. When Hanan returned to Lebanon, she went into hiding, while her family and her husband completed the process for her to obtain an immigrant visa to the United States. Although she and her family lived in fear for months, she ultimately received the immigrant visa and attempted to re-enter the United States at Detroit Metropolitan Airport. Because

Hanan was in the CBP database as being subjected to expedited removal once before, she endured a five-hour interview.

Through the quick intervention of her immigration attorney and evidence that Hanan should be admitted to the United States, Hanan was released to her husband and allowed to enter the United States as a lawful permanent resident. Hanan was lucky—she managed to avoid harm in her home country and she was finally admitted to the United States. Others are not as fortunate due to the vagaries of the expedited removal process. But do not abandon all hope: there are ways in which you, as an immigration attorney, can prepare your clients to avoid and, if necessary, survive expedited removal. Read on.

EXPEDITED REMOVAL: THE BASICS

A solid, working knowledge of the scope, exceptions and challenges to expedited removal is essential for every immigration attorney. Even if an attorney does not practice in the sub-area of removal defense, expedited removal affects a variety of clients, including visitors for business and pleasure, students, skilled workers, and even returning lawful permanent residents. In fact, in just the past 10 years, more than 500,000 people have been removed from the United States under the expedited removal process. Decisions by the Department of Homeland Security (DHS) to remove persons under expedited removal are not reviewable and raise serious due process and humanitarian concerns.

Expedited removal was enacted as part of the Illegal Immigration Reform and Immigrant Responsibility Act of 1996 (IIRAIRA)[1] and is codified at §235 of the Immigration and Nationality Act (INA). Expedited removal allows CBP inspectors at ports of entry to order the summary removal of an "arriving alien," without any right to a hearing or a review of the order, upon a determination that the arriving alien is inadmissible under INA §§212(a)(6)(C) or 212(a)(7) based, respectively, on material misrepre-

* **David Koelsch** is a professor and director of the immigration law clinic at the University of Detroit Mercy School of Law. He practices in the areas of asylum law and also handles VAWA, special immigrant juvenile, cancellation, and family-based adjustment cases. He has served two terms as secretary of the Michigan AILA chapter and has organized the largest contingent of student members of AILA. Professor Koelsch received his law degree from the Catholic University of America.

Michael B. Berger is a senior partner in the firm of Berger and Berger in Buffalo, with offices in Rochester and Atlanta. Mr. Berger is a graduate of SUNY Buffalo School of Law. His practice includes all aspects of immigration and nationality law. Mr. Berger was one of the founders of AILA's Upstate New York Chapter. Mr. Berger was voted among the top lawyers in New York in the field of immigration law.

[1] Pub. L. No. 104-208, div. C, 110 Stat. 3009, 3009-546 to 3009-724.

sentations or failure to produce documents showing a valid immigrant or nonimmigrant visa.

Who is and who is not an arriving alien is a critical threshold determination in the expedited removal process. The concept of an arriving alien is set forth in INA §101(a)(13) and the term is defined at 8 CFR §§1.1(q), 1001.1(q). The shorthand method of determining whether a person is an arriving alien is to examine whether that person had permission to enter the United States. In most cases, the inquiry ends if the person lacks a valid visa. Likewise, the place of attempted entry is irrelevant because CBP will declare persons attempting to enter the United States by land, sea (except Cubans), or air to be arriving aliens. Expedited removal proceedings also are not limited to persons attempting to enter the United States; expedited removal may also be applied to persons who entered the country without a visa or parole if they cannot prove that they have been in the United States for two or more years.[2] This last extension of expedited removal means that even attorneys in the heartland, far from the coasts and land borders, need to understand how expedited removal operates.

Despite the broad definition of arriving alien, the term and its application are limited in a few respects. For example, aliens paroled into the United States for "urgent humanitarian reasons" or due to a "significant public benefit" under INA §212(d)(5)(A) are not deemed to be arriving aliens. Cubans seeking entry at an airport or by sea also are not subject to expedited removal.[3] In addition, a lawful permanent resident is not normally deemed to be an arriving alien unless he or she falls into the exceptions listed at INA §101(a)(13).[4] Likewise, unaccompanied minors are not normally subject to expedited removal.[5]

The consequences of expedited removal are dramatic in both the short- and long-term. The immediate impact is that an alien is denied entry into the United States.[6] The more long-term problem is that an alien who is found to be inadmissible as a result of expedited removal is barred from entry into the

United States for a period of five years.[7] Even more draconian consequences occur when a CBP officer renders a finding of inadmissibility pursuant to INA §212(a)(6)(C)'s fraud prohibitions, which may create a permanent bar on entry to the United States.[8]

EXPEDITED REMOVAL PROCESS

At an Airport, Border Crossing or Seaport

Upon arrival at a port of entry, each person is screened by CBP officers in primary inspection. Officers question a person regarding their expected length of stay and the purpose for their visit and the officer examines each person's passport or other travel documents. If the CBP officer has any concerns regarding the issuance or authenticity of any identity or travel documents or any reason to suspect that the person may lack the proper intent or authority to enter the United States, the officer will direct the person to secondary inspection. Of the more than 300 million people per year screened for entry into the United States in recent years, only approximately 8 million are forwarded to secondary inspection.

In secondary inspection, CBP officers again question the person and perform additional security and document verification. CBP officers question the person regarding the reasons for their travel to the United States, the route that they traveled, how they obtained their travel documents, who paid for their travel, and whether they have any relatives in the United States. Ninety percent of persons placed in secondary inspection are allowed to enter the United States after a delay of up to one hour. Attorneys are not allowed to represent persons in secondary inspection and persons must be able to articulate to CBP's satisfaction the answers to any question posed by a CBP officer.[9] The remaining 10 percent of persons in secondary inspection without correct documentation to enter the United States, unable to clear security checks, or who lack the requisite nonimmigrant or immigrant intent, may then be subject to the expedited removal process.

---

[2] INA §§235(b)(1)(A)(iii)(I)–(II).

[3] 67 Fed. Reg. 68924–26 (Nov. 13, 2002).

[4] 8 CFR §235.3(b).

[5] Legacy Immigration and Naturalization Service (INS) Memorandum, P. Virtue, "Unaccompanied Minors Subject to Expedited Removal" (Aug. 21, 1997), *published on* AILA InfoNet at Doc. No. 97082191 (*posted* Aug. 21, 1997).

[6] 8 CFR §235.3(b).

---

[7] INA §235.

[8] *Id.*

[9] Customs and Border Protection (CBP) *Inspector's Field Manual* (IFM) ch. 2.9. AILA Publications offers the 2007 edition of the *CBP Inspector's Field Manual*. Visit *www.ailapubs.org* for more information and to see a table of contents.

Upon Encounter with Immigration Agents

A lesser-known practice that is being employed more and more frequently is to subject persons whom U.S. Immigration and Customs Enforcement (ICE) or CBP encounters within the United States to expedited removal if they are unable to prove that they were admitted or paroled and that they have been in the United States continuously for two or more years.[10] Given the difficulty of proving entry if persons entered without inspection, and due to stepped-up ICE worksite enforcement actions, expedited removal may become much more common in the interior of the United States. Whether conducted at a port of entry or elsewhere, the expedited removal process is the same and the same risks and opportunities apply for immigration attorneys and their clients.

Secondary Inspection

If CBP determines that the person lacks correct documentation, poses unresolved security issues, or lacks nonimmigrant or immigrant intent, CBP then conducts a more extensive interview which is documented on the Form I-867B. There are several mandatory questions that CBP officers must ask and record on the I-867B but CBP officers may also stray from the mandatory questions and there is no upward limit on the number of questions CBP officers may ask. As an intended safeguard to the veracity of the information gathered on the I-867B, CBP officers must have the individuals read or have read to them their statements on the I-867B. Persons may make any corrections before initialing each correction and each page of the I-867B and signing the I-867B.

If, after the completion of the I-867B interview, CBP officers determine that the person is inadmissible to the United States, the person is held by CBP at the port of entry and summarily deported from the United States, without an opportunity for a hearing or other review of his or her application for admission or the procedures used by CBP. At the airport, the deportation process consists of waiting for the next outbound flight that retraces the person's travel to the United States. At a border crossing, the person is accompanied by CBP to the Canadian or Mexican side of the border and released. At a seaport, depending on the availability of an outbound ship, persons may be transported to a nearby airport and placed on an outbound flight.

Credible Fear of Persecution

A very important determination that can be made at the time of entry is whether a person possesses a "credible fear" of returning to their home country. Based on the questions recorded on the I-867B, the CBP officers conducting secondary inspection may determine that the person has articulated a fear of returning to his or her home country. At that point, the person is interviewed by an asylum officer. The credible fear interviews are generally conducted telephonically by asylum officers from one of the regional asylum offices. A person may consult with an immigration attorney prior to the interview with the asylum officer. However, while attorneys may be present with the person during the interview, attorneys are not allowed to question their client, answer any questions from the asylum officer or raise objections to the asylum officer's questions. The asylum officer then makes a finding as to whether an alien has made a credible claim of fear of persecution or torture.[11]

If the asylum officer makes a positive credible fear finding, the person will be eligible to have a hearing before an immigration judge.[12] If the asylum officer makes a negative finding, the person may still request a review of his or her claim before an immigration judge.[13] A credible fear of persecution is established if there is a significant possibility, taking into account the credibility of the statements made by the person in support of his or her claim and such other facts as are known to the asylum officer, that the person could establish eligibility for asylum under INA §208.[14] In making such a determination, the asylum officer will consider whether the person's case presents novel or unique issues that merit consideration in a full hearing before an immigration judge.[15]

Detention During Process

A person subject to expedited removal is detained without bond pending his or her removal although, in many cases, women and minors will not be detained due to humanitarian concerns. Men are generally only released if they need complicated and

---

[10] INA §§235(b)(1)(A)(iii)(I)–(II).

[11] 8 CFR §235.3(b)(4).

[12] INA §235(b)(1)(B).

[13] *Id.*

[14] INA §235(b)(1)(B)(v).

[15] *See* 8 CFR §208.30(e)(2).

pressing medical treatment.[16] The detention may be relatively short and last only as long as it takes CBP to render a decision that the person is not eligible for admission to the United States and place them on an out-bound flight or to escort them back across a land border. However, detention may continue if out-bound flights are not regularly scheduled or if the person requests protection in the United States, in which case the person would remain in detention while an immigration judge considers their asylum, withholding, or Convention Against Torture claim.

CLIENT-REPRESENTATION STRATEGIES

As harsh as expedited removal undoubtedly is, there are opportunities for immigration attorneys to engage in proactive and defensive client representation. Immigration attorneys are also encouraged to work within AILA to shed light on the abuses of the expedited removal process and advocate for reform. For example, immigration attorneys should advise all clients regarding the inspection process prior to their entry to the United States and explain the significance of secondary inspection and the expedited removal process. By explaining the process, immigration attorneys can minimize clients' fears and the unease their clients may experience during the expedited removal interview. If an immigration attorney is aware that a client or potential client has a fear of returning to their home country and is advised of that fact before the person arrives in the United States, the attorney may also advise the client of the types of questions that are asked during an expedited removal interview and the importance of providing detailed and accurate responses to questions.

The statements made by your client and recorded on the I-867B will be very important to the immigration judge's deliberations. There are several means to either amplify or diminish the significance of such statements. For example, if your client's statement that he or she was persecuted and how is recorded on the I-867B and that statement is consistent with their later-filed asylum application, highlight the fact that the I-867B was made contemporaneously with their arrival in the United States and reflects their very real fear of returning to their home country. A more likely scenario is when ICE Chief Counsel uses the I-867B to impeach the credibility of your client and alleges that the statements on the I-867B do not comport with the substance of their asylum application or that the I-

867B statements do not provide as many details as contained in the asylum application or certain material inconsistencies exist.

Defensive tactics include always anticipating that ICE chief counsel will use the I-867B statements to impeach your client's credibility. To that end, you would do well to obtain from your client information regarding any details of the interview that they can remember, including the questions they were asked and their responses. In certain instances, you may wish to prepare an affidavit for your client to swear to and sign regarding the I-867B interview and then file that affidavit with the asylum application to signal to ICE chief counsel that any effort to use the I-867B against your client will bring a vigorous challenge.

You may also distance your clients from their statements on the I-867B by asking them—of course, not for the first time in open court—whether the interview with the CBP office was interpreted and, if so, whether the interpreter was competent, whether they read or had read to them and truly understood the contents of the I-867B, how long they had been traveling before the I-867B interview, their physical, mental and emotional state at the time, and any other factors that may reduce the accuracy of the I-867B in the eyes of the immigration judge. In general, immigration judges recognize the inherent one-sided nature of the I-867B interview and allow asylum applicants to alter somewhat their claim for protection and provide many more details to substantiate their fear of return on the asylum application and through in-court testimony.

CONCLUDING THOUGHTS

Expedited removal is the black hole of immigration law. Persons subjected to expedited removal have, in many cases, just arrived in the United States after a long and exhausting journey, are separated from their traveling companions or their loved ones who were to meet them on their arrival, are placed in a segregated and locked area of airport screening, are unrepresented by an attorney, are peppered with questions the answers to which may determine their ultimate fate, and then are forced to sign a form which they may or may not fully understand. Then, if they are fortunate enough to demonstrate a credible fear of persecution in their home country, their statements at the expedited removal interview are used against them months and even years after they were recorded. To many ordinary U.S. citizens, expedited removal is an affront to due process but, as immigration attorneys know, due process concerns

---

[16] 8 CFR §235.3(b)(2)(iii).

often take a back seat during the treatment of non-citizens by the DHS.

Forewarned is forearmed. Immigration attorneys would do well to discuss the entry screening process and expedited removal with all arriving clients, and should also advise any clients or potential clients who may be subject to expedited removal in the interior of the United States. Once clients are in the expedited removal black hole, contact with them is very limited. Yet once clients emerge from expedited removal, attorneys can take certain steps to mitigate negative effects of expedited removal. Expedited removal is now one decade old and it continues to be applied in new and different contexts. A thorough understanding of expedited removal is critical for all immigration attorneys and their clients.

ADVANCED ISSUES IN RELIEF FROM REMOVAL

by Ron Russell, Mary Holper, Mark Silverman, and Joseph A. Vail*

This article will discuss numerous issues facing individuals in removal proceedings. While a number of issues will be presented, this article does not encompass the many types of relief that may be available or the many legal issues that may arise in removal proceedings.

CANCELLATION FOR NONPERMANENT RESIDENTS

Nonpermanent residents placed in removal proceedings may be eligible to apply for cancellation of removal under section 240A(b) of the Immigration and Nationality Act (INA).[1] Eligibility for relief under this section requires establishing the following:[2]

1. Physical presence in the United States for a continuous period of not less than 10 years immediately preceding the date of such application;

2. Good moral character for the 10-year period;

3. The applicant has not been convicted of an offense under INA §§212(a)(2) (criminal and related grounds), 237(a)(2) (criminal offenses), or 237(a)(3) (failure to register or falsification of documents); and

4. Removal would result in exceptional and extremely unusual hardship to the applicant's spouse, parent, or child, who is a citizen or a lawful permanent resident (LPR) of the United States.[3]

This article will discuss two common hurdles that nonpermanent residents must overcome to establish eligibility for cancellation.

Stop-Time Issues

As noted above, applicants must establish continuous physical presence for the 10 years prior to

* **Ron Russell** (B.A. University of Louisville, J.D. University of Louisville Brandeis School of Law, 1989) practices exclusively in immigration law in Louisville at Russell Immigration Law Firm. He served as chair of AILA's Mid-South Chapter and also served on the AILA Board of Governors. He served on the 2002 and 2003 AILA Annual Conference Program Committee, as well as the Essential Workers Committee. Mr. Russell has spoken at numerous AILA regional and national conferences on various aspects of immigration law.

Mary Holper is the supervising attorney for the Boston College Immigration and Asylum Project and a Human Rights Fellow at the Boston College Center for Human Rights and International Justice. With the help of students in the immigration clinic at Boston College Law School, she conducts "Know Your Rights" presentations to ICE detainees and provides them with legal representation in removal proceedings. She previously was a detention attorney for CLINIC and an Equal Justice Works Fellow at the CAIR Coalition in Washington, D.C. She is an author and recipient of several distinguished awards.

Mark Silverman is the Director of Immigration Policy at the Immigrant Legal Resource Center (ILRC), where he has worked as an attorney since 1983. Mr. Silverman has done over 400 presentations and trainings for immigrant communities throughout California. He also has made a large number of presentations on various aspects of the law to lawyers and other legal workers, and is the author or co-author of more than 10 manuals on various aspects of immigration law.

Joseph A. Vail is a former immigration judge with the U.S. Department of Justice. While serving as a judge, Mr. Vail adjudicated almost 3,200 cases over a four-year period. Previously, while in private practice for 11 years, he represented noncitizens in deportation proceedings, averaging 125 cases a year. In July 1999, Mr. Vail started the immigration clinic at the University of Houston Law Center, where he also teaches several courses on immigration law. He entered the field of immigration law in 1980 as a volunteer through Volunteers in Service to America (VISTA). He then worked for three years as a legal aid attorney with Gulf Coast Legal Foundation in Houston and later with AYUDA, Inc., in Washington, D.C. Mr. Vail is the recipient of the Texas state bar's Pro Bono Attorney Award for 1994 and AILA's Elmer Fried Excellence in Teaching Award for 2005. He is a 1980 graduate of Widener Law School and is board-certified by the state bar of Texas in immigration and nationality law.

---

[1] *See* 8 CFR §§1240.11(a), 1240.20. Certain individuals are statutorily ineligible for relief. INA §240A(c) (crewmen admitted after June 30, 1964; J-1 exchange visitors, either admitted in such status or obtained such status after admission, even if not subject to two-year return requirement under INA §212(e); exchange visitors defined in INA §101(a)(15)(J); certain persecutors under the INA; and individuals previously granted cancellation, suspension, or relief under former INA §212(c)).

[2] INA §240A(b)(1).

[3] Special rules of eligibility exist for persons battered or subject to extreme cruelty by someone who was or is a citizen or a permanent resident of the United States. INA §240A(b)(2)(A).

submitting the application for cancellation of re-moval. A period of continuous physical presence is deemed to end whenever the applicant is served with a notice to appear (NTA) or when the applicant has committed an offense listed at INA §212(a)(2) that makes him or her inadmissible under §212(a)(2) or removable under INA §237(a)(4), whichever occurs first.[4] If an applicant has departed the United States for any period in excess of 90 days, or for any period in the aggregate exceeding 180 days, the continuous physical presence requirement cannot be met.[5] How-ever, if the applicant left the United States pursuant to a grant of voluntary departure, continuous physi-cal presence ceases, even if the departure is for less than 90 days.[6] Although a person's acceptance of withdrawal of an application for admission is com-parable to a voluntary departure under the threat of removal, the Board of Immigration Appeals (BIA) has ruled that when a person departs and attempts to re-enter, continuous physical presence is not broken unless, during that attempted re-entry, the person was formally excluded or made subject to an order of expedited removal, was offered and accepted the opportunity to withdraw an application for admis-sion, or was subjected to some other formal, docu-mented process pursuant to which he or she was de-termined to be inadmissible to the United States.[7]

Exceptions to the physical presence requirement exist if an applicant has served at least 24 months in active duty status in the U.S. armed forces and, if separated, has received an honorable discharge and was in the United States at the time of enlistment or induction.[8]

This provision of the law cutting off the accrual of continuous physical presence is referred to as the "stop-time rule." The rule has also been interpreted to cut off the accrual of the required 10 years of con-tinuous physical presence by the commission of the crime, not the conviction.[9] In other words, if the date of the commission of the offense for which the ap-plicant has been convicted occurs before the appli-cant acquired 10 years in the United States, eligibil-ity cannot be established. In such case, postconvic-

tion relief may be the only recourse to establishing 10 years of continuous physical presence. Postcon-viction relief must meet the requirements found in *Matter of Pickering*.[10]

Some courts have ruled that the stop-time rule cannot apply retroactively to guilty pleas entered prior to the enactment of the Illegal Immigrant Re-form and Immigrant Responsibility Act (IIRAIRA) and the proceedings were initiated under IIRAIRA.[11] Another court has rejected the retroactive applica-tion of the stop-time rule to commission of certain crimes.[12] Check the federal law in your circuit to see if any court has ruled on the issue.

The BIA has carved out certain limits on applica-tion of the stop-time rule. In *Matter of Campos-Torres*,[13] the BIA held that convictions that create a ground of removal, but not a ground of inadmissibility under INA §212(a)(2) (such as crimes involving do-mestic violence, aggravated felonies that do not lead to inadmissibility under another category, violation of law relating to firearms, and high-speed flight), do not stop the accrual of time to meet the physical presence re-quirement for cancellation of removal.

Further limiting the application of the stop-time rule in *Matter of Deanda-Romo*,[14] the BIA held, in a case involving LPR cancellation,[15] that when a crime of moral turpitude meets the petty-offense exception to inadmissibility[16] and occurs within seven years of admission, commission of a second crime of moral turpitude after the accrual of seven years of continu-ous presence does not invoke the stop-time rule. The BIA reasoned the first offense did not create a ground of inadmissibility and therefore could not trigger the stop-time rule.

The stop-time rule does not apply to other eligi-bility requirements for cancellation of removal, in-cluding issues of qualifying relatives, hardship, or good moral character.[17] In *Matter of Bautista Go-*

---

[4] INA §240A(d)(1).

[5] INA §240A(d)(2).

[6] *Matter of Romalez-Alcaide*, 23 I&N Dec. 423 (BIA 2002).

[7] *Matter of Avilez-Nava*, 23 I&N Dec. 799 (BIA 2005).

[8] INA §240A(d)(3).

[9] *Matter of Perez*, 22 I&N Dec. 689 (BIA 1999).

[10] 23 I&N Dec. 621 (BIA 2003).

[11] *Mulholland v. Ashcroft*, 2004 U.S. Dist. LEXIS 21426 (E.D.N.Y. 2004); *Generi v. Ashcroft*, 2004 U.S. Dist. LEXIS 6396 (W.D. Mich. 2004).

[12] *Henry v. Ashcroft*, 175 F. Supp.2d 688 (S.D.N.Y. 2001).

[13] 22 I&N Dec. 1289 (BIA 2000).

[14] 23 I&N Dec. 597 (BIA 2003).

[15] INA §240A(a) (requiring continuous residence for seven years).

[16] *See* INA §212(a)(2)(A)(ii)(II).

[17] *Matter of Bautista Gomez*, 23 I&N Dec. 893 (BIA 2006).

mez,[18] the BIA held that the stop-time rule and regulatory limitations on motions to reopen for cancellation[19] did not apply to an applicant who did not have a qualifying relative when the NTA was served.

The 10 years of continuous physical presence is cut off when the person is served with an NTA.[20] One court has ruled the applicant met the 10-year physical presence requirement under the stop-time rule even though the NTA was served on the 365th day of the 10th year.[21] However, one court has held if the applicant with a conviction left the United States and re-entered lawfully, the clock could restart, allowing accrual of a new 10-year period of continuous presence for cancellation of removal.[22]

Exceptional and Extremely Unusual Hardship

One of the most difficult issues in proving eligibility for cancellation of removal for nonpermanent residents is establishing the hardship standard under INA §240A(b)(1)(D).[23] Three precedent decisions by the BIA provide a starting point in analyzing whether an applicant can establish the required level of hardship.

The hardship requirement in its current form was first addressed by the BIA in *Matter of Monreal*.[24] The applicant in *Monreal* had two citizen children in the United States, ages 12 and 8. A 14-year-old U.S. citizen child resided in Mexico with the applicant's wife, who returned with their child to Mexico prior to his hearing. While rejecting the idea that an applicant must show that his or her removal would be "unconscionable,"[25] the BIA ruled that Congress intended that cancellation of removal should be available "only in compelling cases."[26] Further, the hardship to the qualifying relative must be "substantially beyond the ordinary hardship suffered when a close family member leaves this country."[27]

The BIA referenced factors presented in *Matter of Anderson*,[28] such as the age, health, and circumstances of the qualifying relative, as well the effects of a lower standard of living or adverse country conditions.[29] The decision also provided examples of "strong cases": an applicant whose parents "are solely dependent upon him for support," a child with "very serious health issues," or "compelling special needs in school" and remarked that all hardship issues should be "considered in the aggregate."[30]

However, the BIA noted the respondent could support his family in Mexico and that the children (one of whom could speak, read, and write in Spanish), while they would suffer some hardship, would not encounter the level of hardship required by Congress. Nor did the applicant show that his permanent resident parents, who were employed and had other children living in the United States, would suffer the necessary hardship under the statute.

The BIA again addressed the hardship standard in *Matter of Andazola-Rivas*.[31] The qualifying relatives included two children, ages 11 and 6, neither of whom were fluent in Spanish. The BIA considered the lower educational possibilities in Mexico, and general emotional and financial hardship if the respondent were to return to Mexico with her children. But the BIA found that the applicant had not shown "that her children would be deprived of all schooling or of an opportunity to obtain any education."[32] The respondent had assets (a bank account of $7,000, two cars, a retirement plan, and a house with mortgage), indicating that the respondent and her children would not be penniless if returned to Mexico. As such, the BIA ruled that the respondent's hardship was not distinguishable from that found in *Monreal* and concluded that the respondent had not proven her children would suffer sufficient hardship if required to live in Mexico.

However, in *Matter of Recinas*,[33] the BIA ruled that a single mother who was the sole supporter of her six children, four of whom were U.S. citizens, and who did not have close relatives in Mexico but had considerable family ties in the United States, met the

---

[18] *Id.*

[19] *See* 8 CFR §1003.23(b)(3).

[20] INA §240A(d)(1)(A).

[21] *Lagandaon v. Ashcroft*, 383 F.3d 983 (9th Cir. 2004).

[22] *Okeke v. Gonzales*, 407 F.3d 585 (3d Cir. 2005).

[23] Under the prior suspension statute, an applicant only had to show extreme hardship to the qualifying relative to establish eligibility for relief.

[24] 23 I&N Dec. 56 (BIA 2001).

[25] *Id.* at 61.

[26] *Id.* at 59.

[27] *Id.* at 62.

---

[28] 16 I&N Dec. 596 (BIA 1978).

[29] *Matter of Monreal*, 23 I&N Dec. 56, 63 (BIA 2001).

[30] *Id.*

[31] 23 I&N Dec. 319 (BIA 2002).

[32] *Id.* at 323.

[33] 23 I&N Dec. 467 (BIA 2002).

hardship standard. The BIA opined that "the hardship standard is not so restrictive that only a handful of applicants, such as those with serious medical condition, will qualify for relief."[34] The BIA used a cumulative analysis to conclude that "the heavy financial and familial burden on the adult respondent, the lack of support from the children's father, the United States citizen children's unfamiliarity with the Spanish language, the lawful residence in this country of all of respondent's immediate family and the concomitant lack of family in Mexico combine to render the hardship in this case well beyond that which is normally experienced in most cases of removal."[35]

Since a number of these same hardship factors existed in the BIA's previous decisions on the issue, the BIA explained: "We emphasize that the respondent is a single parent who is solely responsible for the care of six children and who has no family to return to in Mexico. These are critical factors that distinguish her case from many other cancellation of removal claims."[36] Additionally, while hardship factors to respondent are generally not considered in assessing the level of hardship to qualifying relatives, "to the extent that they affect the potential level of hardship to the qualifying relative, they can be considered."[37] These additional factors sufficiently raised the level of hardship to grant relief.

The BIA reiterated that *Monreal* and *Andazola-Rivas* remain the "seminal cases" interpreting exceptional and extremely unusual hardship, and that the decision in *Recinas* cannot be read in isolation. The BIA noted that *Recinas* involved "unusual factors" not found in most cases.[38] Whether the factors presented in *Recinas* are truly unusual, the arguably more generous analysis of certain factors provides a framework that practitioners can use in presenting as strong a hardship case as possible.

Most notably, practitioners should emphasize factors such as qualifying relatives' dependence on the financial support of the applicant; lack of meaningful financial support in the country to which removal is proposed; inability of qualifying relatives to speak, read, or write the language of the country of removal; lack of close family in the country of

removal; and the existence of close family in the United States. Of course other hardship may be even more important in obtaining relief, but in cases in which medical and serious educational issues are not present, the above factors may prove crucial in obtaining relief or in laying the groundwork for a successful appeal to the BIA.

Interestingly, in *Recinas*, the BIA also remanded the cases of two of the respondent's children, to be held in abeyance until they had a qualifying relative (their mother) through whom they could establish eligibility for cancellation of removal. So under *Recinas*, a child or spouse who is not eligible for cancellation of removal can assert "potential" eligibility based on a grant of cancellation to a parent or spouse that is likely to make such person a qualifying relative.

CANCELLATION OF REMOVAL FOR PERMANENT RESIDENTS

Eligibility

Cancellation of removal is available to certain long-term permanent residents who can make the case for mercy before the immigration court. The LPR can seek such relief if he or she is placed in removal proceedings and charged with deportability under INA §237 or if he or she is charged as an "arriving alien" on returning to the United States from a trip abroad.[39] In order to be eligible for cancellation of removal, the LPR must meet three statutory requirements: (1) five years of permanent residence, (2) seven years of continuous residence after admission in any status, and (3) no aggravated felony conviction.[40] Once a permanent resident has met these requirements, he or she must fill out a form EOIR-42A,[41] pay the $100 fee[42] (or ask the immigration court for a fee waiver)[43], complete biometrics, submit any supporting documentation, and attend an individual hearing on the merits of his or her application. The immigration judge will allow testimony from the LPR and any family members, friends, doctors, expert witnesses, or others. The judge will determine whether the good in

[34] *Id.* at 470.

[35] *Id.* at 472.

[36] *Id.* at 471.

[37] *Id.*

[38] *Id.* at 472.

[39] Under INA §101(a)(13)(C), an LPR is not deemed to be seeking admission to the United States unless, for example, he or she has committed an offense identified in INA §212(a)(2).

[40] INA §240A(a).

[41] 8 CFR §1240.20(a).

[42] 8 CFR §1103.7(b)(4)(i).

[43] *See* 8 CFR §1003.24(d).

the LPR's life outweighs the bad and make a discretionary decision on the application.

Relief under LPR cancellation is a "one-time only" type of relief that cannot be granted twice to the same person. An LPR is not eligible for cancellation of removal if he or she has previously been granted cancellation, suspension of deportation, or a waiver of exclusion under former INA §212(c).[44] Thus, it is important to question the noncitizen carefully regarding previous encounters with immigration and what happened during those proceedings.

Example: Jack is in removal proceedings, and he appears to be eligible for LPR cancellation. You ask him about any previous contacts with immigration, and he says that he was in deportation proceedings before, but, after his family came to testify for him and the judge listened to him talk about how sorry he was for his crimes, he won the right to stay. You will want to do a Freedom of Information Act (FOIA) request to the Executive Office for Immigration Review, or ask to review the tapes of his hearing at the immigration court, because it sounds like Jack already got LPR cancellation of removal or a §212(c) waiver and cannot now apply for LPR cancellation.

Others who are not eligible for LPR cancellation are LPRs who entered as a crewman after June 30, 1964, certain individuals who had J nonimmigrant status, certain persecutors of others, and LPRs who are covered in the security-related grounds of inadmissibility or deportability.[45]

Lawful Admission, Continuous Presence, and the "Stop-Time" Rule

As noted above, to be eligible for cancellation of removal, an LPR must show that he or she has been lawfully admitted for permanent residence for at least five years.[46] Therefore, if permanent residence was acquired through fraud or misrepresentation, the noncitizen has not been "lawfully admitted for permanent residence," and therefore is not eligible for LPR cancellation.[47] If the noncitizen failed to reveal a prior criminal conviction or arrest in the original application for permanent residence, the Department of Homeland Security (DHS) will argue that LPR status

was based on a misrepresentation.[48] Therefore, it is important to question the noncitizen carefully about the dates of criminal activity and obtain the original application if the criminal activity preceded the grant of permanent residence. The noncitizen may also have the option of applying for a *nunc pro tunc* INA §212(h) waiver and concurrent INA §212(i) waiver in this situation,[49] especially if the noncitizen is a returning LPR charged as an arriving alien.[50]

As mentioned above, an LPR must show seven years of continuous presence after admission in any status.[51] Even if the LPR was admitted as a nonimmigrant and later adjusted status, the first admission as a nonimmigrant will be the starting point for counting seven years of continuous presence.[52] This seven years is "stopped" either when the LPR is served with a notice to appear or when the LPR commits an offense referred to in INA §212(a)(2) that renders the LPR inadmissible under INA §212(a)(2) or removable under INA §237(a)(2) or 237(a)(4), whichever is earliest.[53] It is important to

---

[48] It is possible that the noncitizen did not commit a fraud if, for example, the noncitizen failed to report an event that he or she did not perceive as an arrest, or stated that he or she suffered no conviction because a state court told him or her it was not a conviction. All of these arguments are relevant to whether the noncitizen made a willful misrepresentation of a material fact. *See, e.g., Forbes v. INS*, 48 F.3d 439 (9th Cir. 1995) (failure of immigrant visa applicant to disclose an arrest that ultimately resulted in dismissal was willful but not material misrepresentation); *but see Solis-Muela v. INS*, 13 F.3d 372 (10th Cir. 1993) (material misrepresentation where applicant for immigrant visa admitted arrest but failed to disclose a conviction).

[49] *See Matter of Millard*, 11 I&N Dec. 175 (BIA 1965) (INA §212(h) waiver can be granted *nunc pro tunc* in deportation proceedings to cure a ground of inadmissibility existing at the time of entry).

[50] *See Matter of Abosi*, 24 I&N Dec. 204 (BIA 2007) (returning LPR charged as an arriving alien can apply for a "stand-alone" INA §212(h) waiver). Courts are split on whether persons in removal proceedings who are charged with deportability can apply for a "stand-alone" §212(h) waiver. *See, e.g., Klementanovsky v. Gonzales*, 501 F.3d 788 (7th Cir. 2007) (no equal protection violation where "stand-alone" §212(h) waiver is only available to noncitizens in exclusion proceedings, not those in deportation proceedings); *Yeung v. INS*, 76 F.3d 337 (11th Cir. 1995) (equal protection violation if BIA only allows noncitizens in exclusion proceedings and not those in deportation proceedings to apply for "stand-alone" §212(h) waiver).

[51] INA §240A(a)(2).

[52] *Matter of Blancas-Lara*, 23 I&N Dec. 458 (BIA 2002).

[53] INA §240A(d)(1).

---

[44] INA §240A(c)(6).

[45] INA §240A(c)(1)–(5).

[46] INA §240A(a)(1).

[47] *Matter of Koloamatangi*, 23 I&N Dec. 548 (BIA 2003); *Mejia-Orellana v. Gonzales*, 502 F.3d 13 (1st Cir. 2007).

note that the relevant date for determining if the stop-time provision applies is the date of *commission* of the offense, not the date of conviction for the offense. Also, the BIA has held that the offense need not be charged on the notice to appear, so long as it is a ground of removal, to stop the seven years of continuous presence for LPR cancellation purposes.[54] Once the LPR's time is stopped, it can be difficult to argue that the continuous presence should start anew.[55]

Example: Jane was admitted as a visitor in 1990. She adjusted status in 1995. In 1993, she had some law enforcement encounter that she says resulted in a dismissal. In 2000, she was convicted for possession of cocaine. She is now in removal proceedings charged as deportable under INA §237(a)(2)(B). You can make an expedited FOIA request in Jane's case, because she is in removal proceedings. You should check to see if she admitted to the 1993 arrest in her application to adjust status, and if not, analyze whether she made a willful misrepresentation of a material fact, or else DHS can say that she was not "lawfully admitted" due to the misrepresentation. If she passes this hurdle, she is eligible for LPR cancellation because she accrued seven years of continuous presence, which began in 1990 at her lawful admission as a visitor, before her 2000 conviction.

The wording of the stop-time provision at INA §240A(d)(1) has given practitioners a few arguments to avoid the harsh consequences of the rule. In *Matter of Deanda-Romo*,[56] the BIA held that the seven years of continuous presence was not stopped by the commission of a first crime involving moral turpitude because it fit within the petty-offense exception at INA §212(a)(2)(A)(ii)(II). In *Matter of Campos-Torres*,[57] the BIA held that a firearms conviction did not stop the LPR's seven years of continuous presence because the offense is not described in INA §212(a)(2), since the firearms ground of deportability does not have a corresponding ground of inadmissibility. The firearms offense *will* stop the LPR's seven years or continuous presence, however, if it is also an offense that is described in INA §212(a)(2), such as a crime involving moral turpitude that does not fit within the petty-offense exception.[58]

Aggravated Felonies

The most common bar to LPR cancellation is a conviction for an aggravated felony.[59] Look carefully through the aggravated felony definition at INA §101(a)(43), as there are many categories of aggravated felonies. Also, look carefully at the records of conviction and statutes under which the noncitizen was convicted, as there may be ways to argue that a particular conviction does not amount to an aggravated felony. For example, a common-law assault and battery conviction with a one-year sentence is not necessarily a crime of violence aggravated felony;[60] even an assault statute requiring the causation of injury with a dangerous weapon or deadly instrument has been held not to be a crime of violence aggravated felony.[61] Many practitioners make a wrong assumption that assault offenses are automatically crimes of violence and therefore aggravated felonies if the sentence is one year. Just because DHS says your client has been convicted of an aggravated felony does not make it true.

In *Lopez v. Gonzales*,[62] the U.S. Supreme Court decided that a felony simple possession of a controlled substance was not an aggravated felony under INA §101(a)(43)(B). Although the Supreme Court's only reference to whether two simple possession convictions would amount to an aggravated felony was in a

---

[54] *Matter of Jurado-Delgado*, 24 I&N Dec. 29 (BIA 2006).

[55] Practitioners can argue that for LPR cancellation, the continuous presence need not immediately precede the application. This is different from non-LPR cancellation of removal, which requires that the noncitizen prove continuous presence *immediately preceding* the application. *See* INA §240A(b)(1)(A). Also, the U.S. Court of Appeals for the Seventh Circuit held in the context of a non-LPR cancellation of removal case that if the applicant is lawfully admitted to the United States after a clock-stopping event, the stop-time rule does not prevent a new clock from running. *See Okeke v. Gonzales*, 407 F.3d 585 (3d Cir. 2005).

[56] 23 I&N Dec. 597 (BIA 2003).

[57] 22 I&N Dec. 1289 (BIA 2000).

[58] *Compare Matter of S*, 8 I&N Dec. 344 (BIA 1959) (possession of a firearm with intent to use it is a crime involving moral turpitude) *with Matter of Granados*, 16 I&N Dec. 726 (BIA 1979) (possession of a firearm is not a crime involving moral turpitude).

[59] INA §240A(a)(3).

[60] *See, e.g., Flores v. Ashcroft*, 350 F.3d 666 (7th Cir. 2003) (simple battery is not a crime of violence under 18 USC §16); *Matter of Sanudo*, 23 I&N Dec. 968 (BIA 2006) (holding, in a case arising under the jurisdiction of the U.S. Court of Appeals for the Ninth Circuit, that an assault offense was not a crime of violence; following *Ortega-Mendez v. Gonzales*, 450 F.3d 1010 (9th Cir. 2006)).

[61] *Garcia v. Gonzales*, 455 F.3d 465 (4th Cir. 2006).

[62] 127 S.Ct. 625 (2006).

footnote,[63] other courts and the BIA have decided this issue. Following *Lopez*, the BIA chimed in on the issue with two decisions issued on the same day, *Matter of Thomas*[64] and *Matter of Carachuri-Rosendo*.[65] In *Matter of Thomas*, the BIA held that a second conviction for simple possession that was not prosecuted under a state recidivist statute was not an aggravated felony. In *Matter of Carachuri-Rosendo*, the BIA held that a second offense that was not prosecuted under the state recidivist statute was not an aggravated felony, except in the circuit courts of appeals that had already decided that two simple possession offenses alone amount to an aggravated felony conviction. Those circuits are the Fifth,[66] Second,[67] and Seventh.[68] The Fifth and Second Circuits did not have the benefit of the Supreme Court's opinion in *Lopez* when the cases were decided. Nonetheless, the BIA reasoned that, until these circuits reversed themselves in light of *Lopez*, their holdings would stand in cases arising in those circuits. In *Matter of Aruna*,[69] the BIA held that a state court marijuana conviction need not exclude the possibility of distribution of a small amount of marijuana for no remuneration as provided at 21 USC §841(b)(4) to constitute a drug trafficking aggravated felony. The Third Circuit reached a contrary conclusion in *Jeune v. Attorney General*,[70] holding that the record of conviction must exclude that possibility under a categorical analysis of the conviction.

In *Matter of Babaisakov*,[71] the BIA lightened the burden on the government to prove that a conviction was a fraud aggravated felony under INA §101(a)(43)(M)(i). The BIA held that evidence outside the traditional record of conviction (such as a presentence report) could be used to prove that the monetary loss to the victim exceeded $10,000; it was not necessary to rely on documents within the record of conviction to prove such loss. The BIA made this decision despite many circuits deciding

otherwise when interpreting INA §101(a)(43)(M).[72] The holding also departs greatly from the categorical approach that immigration judges and the BIA have traditionally used in order to avoid a retrial of the underlying criminal case.[73] This arguably opens the door to "mini-trials" on the issue of loss amount, since there is a burden of proof differential— preponderance of the evidence at sentencing as opposed to clear and convincing evidence required to establish a ground of removal in immigration court.

Finally, in the theft offense category of aggravated felonies, the BIA decided that a welfare fraud offense, which punished obtaining public assistance by fraud, was not a theft offense under INA §101(a)(43)(G). In *Matter of Garcia-Madrugada*,[74] the BIA followed the reasoning of the Fourth Circuit in *Soliman v. Gonzales*,[75] which distinguished between fraud and theft within the aggravated felony definition. According to this reasoning, fraud offenses involve unlawfully obtained consent of the owner, whereas theft offenses involve takings without the consent of the owner. However, the Third Circuit in *Nugent v. Ashcroft*[76] held in a case involving a hybrid offense—theft by deception—that in order to establish an aggravated felony, DHS had to meet the definition for aggravated felony for theft (sentence of a year or more) as well as for fraud and deceit (loss of more than $10,000).

LPR Cancellation Discretion

In *Matter of C–V–T–*,[77] the BIA described the factors that an immigration judge weighs when deciding an application for LPR cancellation. The BIA adopted the same factors that judges weighed to decide waivers of deportability under former INA §212(c), which were described by the BIA in *Matter of Marin*.[78] The positive factors are: (1) family ties in the United States, particularly ties to lawful permanent residents or U.S. citizens; (2) residence of long duration in the United States (particularly when the inception of residence occurred at a young age);

[63] *Id.* at 630 n.6.

[64] 24 I&N Dec. 416 (BIA 2007).

[65] 24 I&N Dec. 382 (BIA 2007).

[66] *U.S. v. Sanchez-Villalobos*, 412 F.3d 572 (5th Cir. 2005).

[67] *U.S. v. Simpson*, 319 F.3d 81 (2d Cir. 2002).

[68] *U.S. v. Pacheco-Diaz*, 506 F.3d 545 (7th Cir. 2007).

[69] 24 I&N Dec. 452 (BIA 2008).

[70] 476 F.3d 199 (3d Cir. 2007).

[71] 24 I&N Dec. 306 (BIA 2007).

[72] *See, e.g., Dulal-Whiteway v. DHS*, 501 F.3d 116 (2d Cir. 2007); *Kawashima v. Gonzales*, 503 F.3d 997 (9th Cir. 2007); *Conteh v. Gonzales*, 461 F.3d 45 (1st Cir. 2006).

[73] *See Matter of Pichard-Sufren*, 21 I&N Dec. 330 (BIA 1996).

[74] 24 I&N Dec. 436 (BIA 2008).

[75] 419 F.3d 276 (4th Cir. 2005).

[76] 367 F.3d 162 (3d Cir. 2004).

[77] 22 I&N Dec. 7 (BIA 1998).

[78] 16 I&N Dec. 581 (BIA 1978).

(3) evidence of hardship to the respondent and his or her family if deportation occurs; (4) service in the U.S. armed forces; (5) a history of employment; (6) the existence of property or business ties; (7) evidence of value and service to the community; (8) proof of genuine rehabilitation if a criminal record exists; and (9) other evidence attesting to the person's good character. Adverse factors include: (1) nature and underlying circumstances of the grounds of removal; (2) the presence of additional significant violations of the immigration laws; (3) the nature, recency, and seriousness of a criminal record; and (4) the presence of other evidence indicative of a respondent's bad character or undesirability as a permanent resident of the United States.

Unlike persons seeking discretionary waivers under former INA §212(c), however, LPRs applying for cancellation of removal need not show "unusual or outstanding equities," which was necessary for §212(c) waiver applicants to offset serious criminal behavior. In *Matter of Sotelo*,[79] the BIA decided that because the aggravated felony bar to LPR cancellation weeded out the applicants with the most serious criminal behavior, it was not necessary for any LPR cancellation applicant to meet such a heightened standard. Cases deciding waivers under former INA §212(c) are still instructive when arguing LPR cancellation cases. For example, the BIA determined that rehabilitation, while important, is not a prerequisite to obtaining a waiver[80] and that a person who is in custody can still show rehabilitation.[81]

There are many effective ways to win a discretionary case for LPR cancellation:

(1) *Pack the courtroom.* In order to show community support and family ties, nothing beats packing the courtroom. Even if the immigration judge does not wish to hear repetitive testimony from each family member, friend, and other supporting witness, the impact of seeing a "standing-room only" courtroom will help win the case. On direct exam, ask your client who appeared in court that day and what your client's relationship is to each person.

(2) *Know your client's criminal record.* The EOIR-42A asks about every *arrest* and every conviction. It is important to order your client's state rap sheets in addition to his or her FBI report, because there may be criminal convictions or arrests outside of the jurisdiction where your client lives. Also obtain police reports from all arrests, because your client may be asked to explain the circumstances behind every arrest, especially if his or her version of events differs from the events described in the police report.

(3) *Prepare your client to explain questionable behavior.* Your client may be asked about his or her income and the amount of money spent on a drug or alcohol addiction. Questions such as this will try to demonstrate that your client had some illicit means of income, such as drug dealing or prostitution. Prepare your client to answer questions about exact income and exact expenditures on drugs or alcohol.

(4) *Show the hardship to your client and your client's family.* Include country conditions reports, especially if your client would be deported to a country that is especially poor or where human rights abuses are rampant. Do not assume that these reports are only relevant to an application for asylum, withholding of removal, or relief under the Convention Against Torture. You also want to include any medical issues that your client has and the availability of treatment in his or her home country. In cases in which your client has a serious medical issue, have the client's doctor testify to what would happen if the client could not continue his or her medications.

(5) *Show rehabilitation through psychological tests or psychiatric evaluations.* For clients with a particularly violent criminal conviction or addiction-related convictions, you may wish to ask a psychologist to perform a psychological test, such as the violence risk assessment test or the Maryland Addictions Questionnaire. If psychological tests are not useful in your case, have your client evaluated by a psychiatrist to show that he or she is capable of rehabilitation.

(6) *Prepare a prehearing memo to describe how your client meets the Matter of C–V–T– factors.* A prehearing memorandum can be a very effective way to convince the immigration judge that your client merits discretionary relief. This also can convince the DHS trial attorney to not appeal the case if the judge grants LPR cancellation.

INA §212(c) WAIVERS

Although a waiver of deportability under former INA §212(c) is not possible under the current INA, the waivers are still available to persons who were convicted of certain aggravated felonies prior to

---

[79] 23 I&N Dec. 201 (BIA 2001).

[80] *Matter of Edwards*, 20 I&N Dec. 191 (BIA 1990).

[81] *Matter of Arreguin*, 21 I&N Dec. 38 (BIA 1995).

April 24, 1996. The U.S. Supreme Court decided in *INS v. St. Cyr*[82] that an LPR who pleaded guilty to an aggravated felony prior to April 24, 1996, was eligible for a §212(c) waiver. Many old convictions can be waived using former §212(c) relief, provided that the LPR did not serve more than five years in prison for an aggravated felony.[83] For convictions before November 29, 1990, the LPR could serve more than five years in prison for an aggravated felony and still be eligible for a §212(c) waiver.[84] The regulations pertaining to such waivers are at 8 CFR §§1003.44 and 1212.3.

Comparable Ground of Inadmissibility

Currently, the most significant bar to §212(c) relief is for LPRs whose ground of deportability have no corresponding ground of inadmissibility. The BIA and several circuit courts of appeals have decided that the waiver is not available to an LPR who is deportable unless there is a corresponding ground of inadmissibility.[85] Only the Second Circuit has decided that §212(c) relief should be available to persons whose conviction has no corresponding ground of inadmissibility.[86] Thus, LPRs outside of the Second Circuit who were convicted of pre- April 24, 1996, crimes of violence, theft offenses, and sexual abuse of a minor convictions, among others, are not eligible for waivers under former INA §212(c).

Trial v. Plea

Another significant bar to §212(c) relief is conviction after a trial. Only persons who were convicted on a guilty or nolo contendere plea are eligible for a §212(c) waiver.[87] However, circuit courts have disagreed with the regulations and have allowed LPRs to apply for §212(c) relief even if the deportable offense resulted from a jury trial.[88] In all of these decisions, the courts discussed how much a person had to rely on the availability of a §212(c) waiver in making decisions during the criminal process; this discussion was necessary to determine whether the repeal of the 212(c) waiver had an impermissible retroactive effect. Some courts have allowed the LPR to apply for 212(c) relief if he or she can show reliance on its availability when deciding to wait and accrue evidence to make a stronger §212(c) waiver application.[89] Other courts have limited the Supreme Court's decision in *St. Cyr* to its facts, stating that only LPRs who gave up their right to trial and took a guilty plea can show they relied on the availability of §212(c) relief.[90] One court dismissed the importance of showing reliance on the availability of the waiver, and instead determined that any conviction preceding the change in law would be enough to show an impermissible retroactive effect.[91]

SUSPENSION OF DEPORTATION AND CANCELLATION OF REMOVAL BENEFITS UNDER NACARA[92]

The Nicaraguan Adjustment and Central American Relief Act (NACARA),[93] which was signed into law on November 19, 1997, provides significant benefits to Salvadorans, Guatemalans, and nationals of former Soviet bloc and Eastern European nations. The legislation gives them the opportunity to apply for suspension of deportation under rules that preceded IIRAIRA.

The interim rule[94] implementing section 203 of NACARA establishes a streamlined procedure for processing cases of applicants who are class mem-

---

[82] 533 U.S. 289 (2001).

[83] 8 CFR §1212.3(f)(4)(i).

[84] 8 CFR §1212.3(f)(4)(ii).

[85] 8 CFR §1212.3(f)(5); *Matter of Blake*, 23 I&N Dec. 722 (BIA 2005); *see also Vue v. Gonzales*, 496 F.3d 858 (8th Cir. 2007); *Vo v. AG*, 482 F.3d 363 (5th Cir. 2007); *Caroleo v. Gonzales*, 476 F.3d 158 (3d Cir. 2007); *Valere v. Gonzales*, 473 F.3d 757 (7th Cir. 2007); *Kim v. Gonzales*, 468 F.3d 58 (1st Cir. 2006).

[86] *Blake v. Carbone*, 489 F.3d 88 (2d Cir. 2007). As of the time of this writing, the Ninth Circuit has withdrawn its opinion in *Abebe v. Gonzales*, 493 F.3d 1092 (9th Cir. 2007) and is rehearing the issue en banc.

[87] 8 CFR §1212.3(h).

[88] *See, e.g., Hem v. Maurer*, 458 F.3d 1185 (10th Cir. 2006); *Ponnapula v. Ashcroft*, 373 F.3d 480 (3d Cir. 2004).

[89] *See, e.g., Carranza de Salinas v. Gonzales*, 47 F.3d 200 (5th Cir. 2007); *Restrepo v. McElroy*, 369 F.3d 627 (2d Cir. 2004).

[90] *See, e.g., Dias v. INS*, 311 F.3d 456 (1st Cir. 2002); *Chambers v. Reno*, 307 F.3d 284 (4th Cir. 2002); *Armendariz-Montoya v. Sonchik*, 291 F.3d 1116 (9th Cir. 2002); *Brooks v. Ashcroft*, 283 F.3d 1268 (11th Cir. 2002).

[91] *Atkinson v. AG*, 479 F.3d 222 (3d Cir. 2007).

[92] This section of the article, which is excerpted from Chapter 1 of the Immigrant Legal Resource Center's *Winning NACARA Suspension Cases*, analyzes §203 of NACARA. This article provides an update on implementation of NACARA, drawing on the interim regulations and on policy statements that legacy INS/DHS and EOIR have issued to date.

[93] Pub. L. No. 105-100, tit. II, 111 Stat. 2160, 2193–201 (1997).

[94] 64 Fed. Reg. 27855 (May 21, 1999).

bers in *American Baptist Churches v. Thornburgh*[95] (*ABC*), affording them a rebuttable presumption that they meet the "extreme hardship" requirement for suspension or special rule cancellation. The interim rule took effect on June 21, 1999.

Framework for Analyzing NACARA Cases

The NACARA statute is complicated, and the regulations add a further level of complexity. To assist practitioners in analyzing NACARA cases, the following four-step process, which can be divided into two parts, may be useful:

First, the practitioner analyzes his or her client's NACARA and then suspension/cancellation eligibility.

- *NACARA eligibility*: Is the person eligible to apply for suspension of deportation or special cancellation of removal under NACARA's more generous requirements? Is the person eligible for the rebuttable presumption of extreme hardship?

- *Remedy*: Is the person eligible for NACARA suspension or special rule cancellation? Are there any suspension/cancellation eligibility issues?

After that eligibility determination, there are additional considerations of where, when, and how to bring the case, including:

- *Application Procedures*: Is the person eligible for an asylum office adjudication?

- *Evaluation of the Case*: How strong is the case based on a hardship claim, as well as other suspension or cancellation requirements and information from the prior three steps? Should the person be preparing to file for NACARA now, or should he or she wait?

Each of these aspects of analyzing NACARA cases is discussed in detail below.

Analysis of NACARA Cases

Eligibility Requirements and the Rebuttable Presumption of Hardship

Under NACARA, certain individuals are potentially eligible to apply for suspension of deportation/cancellation of removal based on the more generous suspension of deportation standards that were in place before IIRAIRA took effect on April 1, 1997. The following groups of persons are eligible for suspension/cancellation benefits as NACARA

principals and dependents, provided that they have not been convicted of an aggravated felony:

- *Salvadoran nationals*: (1) who first entered the United States on or before September 19, 1990, and registered for benefits under the *ABC* settlement agreement on or before October 31, 1991 (either by applying for temporary protected status (TPS) or by submitting an *ABC* registration),[96] unless apprehended at the time of entry after December 19, 1990,[97] or (2) who filed an application for asylum with legacy INS on or before April 1, 1990.[98]

- *Guatemalan nationals*: (1) who first entered the United States on or before October 1, 1990, and registered for *ABC* benefits on or before December 31, 1991,[99] unless apprehended at the time of entry after December 19, 1990, or (2) who filed an application for asylum with legacy INS on or before April 1, 1990.[100]

In *Chaly-Garcia v. U.S.*,[101] the court expanded what may constitute *ABC* registration, holding that in addition to sending in the *ABC* registration form, a Guatemalan has met the registration requirement when he or she has provided written notice of either (1) intent to apply for a de novo asylum adjudication or (2) an intent to receive the benefits of the *ABC* agreement. Chaly-Garcia met the registration requirement by indicating in writing on his asylum application (I-589) that he wanted to take advantage of the "new asylum program for Guatemalans."[102]

---

[95] 760 F.2d 796 (N.D. Cal. 1991).

[96] IIRAIRA §309(c)(5)(C)(i)(I)(aa), *amended by* NACARA §203(a)(1); *see* 8 CFR §§240.61(a)(1), 1240.61(a)(1).

[97] IIRAIRA §309(c)(5)(C)(i)(I), *amended by* NACARA §203(a)(1); *see* 8 CFR §§240.60, 240.61(a)(1), 1240.60, 1240.61(a)(1).

[98] IIRAIRA §309(c)(5)(C)(i)(II), *amended by* NACARA §203(a)(1); *see* 8 CFR §§240.60, 240.61(a)(2), 1240.60, 1240.61(a)(2).

[99] IIRAIRA §309(c)(5)(C)(i)(I)(bb), *amended by* NACARA §203(a)(1); *see* 8 CFR §§240.60, 240.61(a)(1), 1240.60, 1240.61(a)(1).

[100] IIRAIRA §309(c)(5)(C)(i)(II), *amended by* NACARA §203(a)(1); *see* 8 CFR §§240.61(a)(2), 1240.61(a)(2).

[101] 508 F. 3d 1201 (9th Cir. 2007) (successfully litigated by AILA member Stephen Manning).

[102] *See* Immigrant Law Group LLP, "Federal Court Decision Assists Central Americans Seeking Asylum: *Chaly-Garcia* Background & Frequently Asked Questions" (Jan. 14, 2008), *available at http://ilgrp.com/docs/ChalyGarciaFAQ.pdf*. For more information, *see http://ilgrp.com*, or contact Stephen

continued

Filed with Legacy INS

The regulations wisely clarify that a person satisfies the eligibility prong of filing an asylum application with legacy INS on or before April 1, 1990, "either by filing an application with the Service or filing an application with the Immigration Court and serving a copy of that application on the Service."[103]

Filed an application for asylum is defined as the proper filing by a principal or "filing a derivative asylum application by being properly included as a dependent spouse or child in any asylum application *pursuant to the regulations and procedures in effect at the time of filing* of the principal or derivative asylum application."[104] For example, if a child was properly included as a dependent (or derivative) applicant in her father's application in 1988, she would be eligible to apply for NACARA, because she filed an asylum application prior to April 1, 1990.

Is the Person Eligible for the Rebuttable Presumption of Extreme Hardship?

If person is in one of the categories described above, he or she is eligible for the rebuttable presumption of extreme hardship.[105] All Salvadorans and Guatemalans who are eligible for NACARA as principals are presumed to have established the requisite extreme hardship requirement, because the regulations specifically provide the presumption to both groups of NACARA principals from those countries—those who registered for *ABC* either directly or via TPS, and those who applied for asylum on or before April 1, 1990.[106] Therefore, for purposes of the presumption, all NACARA-eligible principals from El Salvador and Guatemala are *ABC* class members whether or not they ever registered or applied for asylum pursuant to the *ABC* settlement. The supplementary information section of the NACARA interim rule states that a result of the unusual immigration history of the *ABC* class "is the creation of a large class of individuals who share certain strong predictors of extreme hardship."[107] These characteristics include the fact that *ABC* class members came to the United States on or before

1990 during a period of civil strife in El Salvador and Guatemala. They were entitled to special asylum adjudication procedures as a result of a settlement of litigation that alleged discriminatory treatment of Guatemalan and Salvadoran asylum applicants.

Grounds of Inadmissibility or Deportation That Bar Eligibility for "Regular" Seven-Year NACARA Suspension or Cancellation

USCIS has taken the correct and good position that grounds of deportation apply only to persons who were admitted, and grounds of inadmissibility apply only to those persons who are in the United States without having been admitted. For example, a person who was not admitted would not be subject to the deportation ground for a firearms offense (INA §237(a)(2)).[108] Appendix A to this article summarizes the ineligibility bars for suspension and special rule cancellation.

ADJUSTMENT OF STATUS

Introduction

Adjustment of status is a term of art in the immigration world. It generally refers to the procedure for seeking LPR status while in the United States. For those individuals placed into removal proceedings, it is sometimes an available form of relief. Generally, adjustment of status requires first an approved visa petition through a U.S. citizen family member, an employer, or a diversity (a/k/a "lottery") visa. There are other possible means of adjustment (*e.g.,* cancellation of removal) that do not require an approved visa petition.

Adjustment of Status—Requirements Under INA §245(a)

The INA sets out requirements for eligibility to adjust status in the United States.[109] These include:

- inspection and admission or parole into the United States

- eligible to receive an immigrant visa

- admissible to the United States under INA §212(a)

- immediate availability of a visa

Manning, whose contact information may be found in the AILA membership directory.

[103] 8 CFR §§240.61(a)(2), 1240.61(a)(2).

[104] 8 CFR §§240.60, 1240.60 (emphasis added).

[105] 8 CFR §§240.64(d), 1240.64(d).

[106] 8 CFR §§240.61(a)(1), (2), 1240.61(a)(1), (2).

[107] 64 Fed. Reg. 27855, 27866 (May 21, 1999).

---

[108] USCIS Memorandum, J. Langlois, "Revision to the NACARA Lesson Plan and Change to NACARA Quality Assurance Review Categories" (Sept. 6, 2007), *published on* AILA InfoNet at Doc. No. 07092562 (*posted* Sept. 25, 2007).

[109] INA §245(a); 8 CFR §§245.1(a), 1245.1(a).

Inspection and Admission

Admission means the lawful entry of the alien into the United States after inspection and admission by an immigration officer.[110] An inspection occurs when the alien physically presents him- or herself for questioning and makes no false claims to citizenship even if he or she is asked no questions by the immigration officer and volunteers no information.[111] The BIA has stated that "admission" occurs when the inspecting officer indicates to the individual that he or she is not inadmissible.[112] That communication occurs when the inspector permits the alien to enter. DHS has argued since the passage of INA §101(a)(13) in 1996 that the BIA's holding on this matter is no longer the law and that more than just appearing before an officer at the border and refraining from making a false claim to citizenship is required to prove an inspection and admission. This claim is based on the language in INA §101(a)(13), which indicates that admission now means lawful "inspection and authorization by an immigration officer." However, the BIA has not pulled back from its position.

The U.S. Court of Appeals for the Sixth Circuit has held that when an individual has been inspected and admitted on a temporary visa and later adjusts to lawful permanent resident status; the date of admission is the entry date on the temporary visa, not the later adjustment date.[113] The court held that the alien's adjustment did not constitute an admission to the United States for calculating whether a conviction for a crime involving moral turpitude occurred within five years of admission. The court distinguished this case from the BIA's prior decision in *Matter of Rosas-Ramirez*,[114] in which the BIA held that the date of admission was the date of adjustment. In *Rosas-Ramirez*, the alien entered the United States illegally, so his adjustment date became his admission date, while in *Zhang* the alien entered lawfully with a visa, so the BIA ruled that his admission date was his adjustment date.

Parolees/Arriving Aliens

For parolees in removal proceedings there have been changes in the law. Attorney General John Ashcroft had promulgated a regulation making arriving aliens in removal proceedings ineligible for adjustment.[115] However, the regulations classify parolees as arriving aliens,[116] and the INA states that those paroled into the United States are eligible to adjust.[117] The government took the position that parolees were no longer eligible to adjust before the court unless they were paroled into the United States specifically for the purpose of adjustment of status, or given advance parole so that they could resume an adjustment of status application. Several courts found that the regulation contravened the statutory provision permitting paroled aliens to adjust status, even in removal proceedings, and that therefore the regulation was invalid.[118] In 2006, the regulations were amended to remove the adjustment of status prohibition against arriving aliens in removal proceedings.[119] USCIS now has the sole authority to grant or deny adjustment of status petitions for paroled aliens who have been placed into removal proceedings, except that the immigration court will have jurisdiction if: (1) the alien departed from and returned to the United States pursuant to a grant of advance parole to pursue the previously filed application for adjustment; (2) the application was denied by USCIS; and (3) the alien was placed into removal proceedings upon return to the United States or after denial of the adjustment application.[120]

Maintaining Lawful Status

The regulations require in addition to inspection and admission, or parole, that an applicant for adjustment maintain lawful status in the United States.[121] There are exceptions to this requirement.

---

[110] INA §101(a)(13).

[111] *Matter of Areguillin*, 17 I&N Dec. 308 (BIA 1980); *Morelos-Ontiveros v. INS*, 927 F.2d 610 (9th Cir. 1991).

[112] *Matter of Areguillin, supra* note 111.

[113] *Zhang v. Mukasey*, 509 F.3d 313 (6th Cir. 2007).

[114] 22 I&N Dec. 616 (BIA 1999).

[115] Former 8 CFR §245.1(c)(8).

[116] 8 CFR §§1.1(q), 1001.1(q).

[117] INA §245(a).

[118] *Succar v. Ashcroft*, 394 F.3d 8 (1st Cir. 2005); *Rivera v. Ashcroft*, 394 F.3d 37 (1st Cir. 2005); *Bona v. Gonzales*, 425 F.3d 663 (9th Cir. 2005).

[119] 71 Fed. Reg. 27585 (May 12, 2006). *See* USCIS Memorandum, M. Aytes, "Eligibility of Arriving Aliens in Removal Proceedings to Apply for Adjustment of Status and Jurisdiction to Adjudicate Applications for Adjustment of Status" (Jan. 12, 2007), *published on* AILA InfoNet at Doc. No. 07030661 (*posted* Mar. 6, 2007).

[120] 8 CFR §§245.2(a)(1), 1245.2(a)(1)(ii).

[121] 8 CFR §§245.1(b)(6); 1245.1(b)(6).

The following groups need not have maintained continuous lawful status in the U.S. in order to adjust status here:

- applicants under INA §245(i)[122]

- immediate relatives of U.S. citizens as defined in INA §201(b)[123]

- special immigrants under INA §101(a)(27)(H) (foreign medical graduates)[124]

- INA §101(a)(27)(I) (former employees of international organizations and family members)[125]

- special immigrants under INA §101(a)(27)(J) (special immigrant children)[126]

- INA §101(a)(27)(K) (immigrants who have served honorably in the U.S. military)[127]

In addition, applicants for adjustment under certain special programs such as the Haitian Refugee Immigration Fairness Act,[128] NACARA,[129] and the Immigration Reform and Control Act of 1986 (IRCA) programs[130] have not had to maintain lawful status to qualify for adjustment to permanent status. Asylees adjusting under INA §209 need not have maintained lawful status, nor are registry applicants under INA §249 required to do so.

Adjustment of Status Under INA §245(i)

Unlike applicants for adjustment under INA §245(a), applicants for adjustment under INA §245(i) may adjust regardless of manner of entry or maintenance of lawful status. The following are the requirements for adjustment under §245(i):

- Physical presence in the United States

- An approved visa petition (employment, family)

- The family visa petition or the labor certification were filed before April 30, 2001, and were prima facie approvable when filed

- If the qualifying visa petition or labor certification was filed after January 14, 1998, the alien must have been physically present in the United States since December 21, 2000

- Eligibility to receive an immigrant visa and an immigrant visa is immediately available

- Admissible as an immigrant

- Payment of a $1,000 fee (in addition to the filing fee), although this is not required for children under the age of 17, or spouses and children of aliens granted Special Agricultural Worker or legalization status under IRCA who were present in the United States since May 5, 1988, who were in that relationship with the legalized alien (as a spouse or child) since that date, and who have applied for Family Unity benefits.

An alien who has previously filed for adjustment of status under INA §245(a) and has been denied may file a new application for adjustment pursuant to INA §245(i) if eligible and if he or she pays the $1,000 fee.[131] The denial, withdrawal, or revocation of the visa petition filed before April 30, 2001, does not preclude eligibility under the grandfather clause as long as it was approvable when filed.[132] An alien seeking to establish eligibility for adjustment of status under INA §245(i) on the basis of a marriage-based visa petition must prove that the marriage was meritorious at its inception.[133] For purposes of the grandfather clause, the immigration judge does not need to conduct a new hearing to determine if the petition was approvable when filed if an original review was made on the merits.[134]

There are numerous grounds of inadmissibility that cannot be waived for adjustment under INA §245(i), including drug trafficking offenses, most drug possession offenses, fraud involving false claims to citizenship, murder, crimes relating to torture, and human trafficking.[135] Individuals who are deportable under INA §237(a)(4)(B) (terrorism ground) cannot adjust.[136]

---

[122] 8 CFR §§245.1(b), 1245.1(b).

[123] 8 CFR §§245.1(b)(6), 1245.1(b)(6).

[124] *Id.*

[125] *Id.*

[126] *Id.*

[127] 8 CFR §§245.1(b)(10), 1245.1(b)(10).

[128] *See* 8 CFR §§245.15, 1245.15.

[129] *See* 8 CFR §§245.13, 1245.13.

[130] *See* 8 CFR §245a.2(b).

[131] 8 CFR §§245.10(f)(2), 1245.10(f)(2).

[132] 8 CFR §§245.10(a)(3), 1245.10(a)(3).

[133] *Matter of Jara Riero*, 24 I&N Dec. 267 (BIA 2007).

[134] *Eccheveria v. Keisler*, 505 F.3d 16 (1st Cir. 2007).

[135] 8 CFR §§245.10(b)(3), 1245.10(b)(3), require that the applicant not be inadmissible or that all grounds of inadmissibility be waived. However, INA provides no waiver for the grounds stated.

[136] 8 CFR §§245.10(g), 1245.10(g).

Inadmissibility for INA §245(i) Adjustment Under INA §§212(a)(9)(B) & (C)

The most contested areas of inadmissibility involve INA §212(a)(9)(B) (unlawful presence) and INA §212(a)(9)(C) (returning to the United States after a removal order or unlawful presence in the aggregate of more than one year).

The BIA has ruled that an alien who is unlawfully present in the United States for an aggregate period of more than one year, then departs the country and seeks admission within 10 years of the date of his or her departure, is inadmissible under INA §212(a)(9)(B)(i)(II), and ineligible for adjustment under INA §245(i), even when the alien's departure was not made pursuant to an order of removal or was not a voluntary departure at the conclusion of removal proceedings.[137]

An alien inadmissible under INA §212(a)(9)(C)(i)(I) who has departed the United States after a removal order, or accrual of one year or more of unlawful presence, who then re-enters or attempts to re-enter, is ineligible for adjustment under INA §245(i). It is the entry or attempted entry after a removal order, or one year or more of illegal presence, which triggers INA §212(a)(9)(C).[138] The BIA has found that adjustment of status under INA §245(i) is not available to individuals inadmissible under INA §212(a)(9)(C) even when permission to re-apply under 8 CFR §212.2 is granted during the 10-year waiting period after the removal or departure.[139] According to the BIA, 8 CFR §212.2, permitting an alien in the United States to seek adjustment under INA §245(i) in conjunction with an I-212 waiver, contradicts INA §212(a)(9)(C).[140] A grant of permission to re-apply under 8 CFR 212.2 is not an authorization to be admitted.[141]

The Ninth Circuit Court of Appeals had initially held in *Perez-Gonzalez v. Ashcroft*[142] that an alien who was inadmissible under INA §212(a)(9)(C)(i) could apply for adjustment of status in conjunction with an I-212 application for retroactive waiver of inadmissibility filed before the prior deportation order was reinstated. However, in a later decision the Ninth Circuit rejected *Perez-Gonzalez* and held that an alien who is inadmissible under INA §212(a)(9)(C) is not eligible to adjust status, thereby adopting the position of the BIA discussed above.[143] However, at least one circuit court of appeals has disagreed.[144]

Aliens Restricted Under INA §245(a) Who May Adjust Under INA §245(i)

The regulations highlight several groups of aliens ineligible for adjustment under INA §245(a) who may adjust only through INA §245(i).[145] These include:

- aliens who entered in transit without a visa

- aliens serving aboard a vessel or aircraft on arrival, destined to serve on a U.S. vessel

- aliens not admitted or paroled into the United States following inspection by an immigration officer

- aliens employed without authorization in the United States after January 1, 1977 (unless the alien qualifies as an immediate relative or special immigrant juvenile, or under one of the other exceptions at 8 CFR §245.1(b)(4))

- aliens who have failed (other than through no fault of their own or for technical reasons) to maintain continuously a lawful status since entry into the United States on or after November 6, 1986 (unless immediate relatives or in special immigrant status as defined in INA §§101(a)(27)(H), (I), or (J))

- aliens admitted on the visa waiver program, or, other than immediate relatives, those on the visa waiver pilot program

- aliens seeking adjustment based on employment-based visa petitions who have not maintained lawful status

- aliens who have engaged in unauthorized employment in the United States (unless immediate relatives or in special immigrant status as defined in INA §§101(a)(27)(H), (I), (J), or (K))

---

[137] *Matter of Lemus-Losa,* 24 I&N Dec. 373 (BIA 2007).

[138] *Matter of Briones,* 24 I&N Dec. 355 (BIA 2007).

[139] *Matter of Torres-Garcia,* 23 I&N Dec. 866 (BIA 2006).

[140] *Id.*

[141] *Id.; see also* USCIS Memorandum, M. Aytes & D. Carpenter, "Effect of *Perez-Gonzalez v. Ashcroft* on Adjudication of Form I-212 Applications Filed by Aliens Who Are Subject to Reinstated Removal Orders Under INA §241(a)(5)" (Mar. 31, 2006), *published on* AILA InfoNet at Doc. No. 06080967 (*posted* Aug. 9, 2006).

[142] 379 F.3d 783 (9th Cir. 2004).

[143] *Gonzales v. DHS,* 508 F.3d 1227 (9th Cir. 2007).

[144] *Padilla-Caldera v. Gonzales,* 426 F.3d 1294 (10th Cir. 2005).

[145] 8 CFR §§245.1(b), 1245.1(b).

Recent Cases on Adjustment of Status

The courts have rendered in recent years several precedent decisions touching on adjustment of status. They are too numerous to list here, but some of them are highlighted below.

Adjustment of Status and the Child Status Protection Act

The Child Status Protection Act[146] provides protection to individuals who were children, and whose petitions were approved prior to August 6, 2002, the effective date of the Act, even where the adjustment of status is filed after August 6, 2002.[147]

Returning Lawful Permanent Residents

A returning lawful permanent resident seeking to overcome a ground of inadmissibility is not required to apply for adjustment of status in conjunction with a waiver of inadmissibility under INA §212(h). He need only seek the waiver.[148]

Authority of Immigration Judges in Employment-Based Adjustment of Status

The U.S. Court of Appeals for the Fifth Circuit joined other circuit courts in recently holding that immigration judges have jurisdiction to determine whether an employment-based visa petition qualifies for portability under INA §204(j) when the adjustment of status application has been filed and remains unadjudicated for 180 days or more.[149]

Adjustment of Status and the Visa Waiver Program

An alien who overstays his or her authorized time under the Visa Waiver Program and files for adjustment of status after the overstay, but before the issuance of a removal order, has waived his or her right to contest a subsequent removal order through a renewed application for adjustment of status, or to seek review of the adjustment.[150] However, an alien who applies for adjustment of status while in lawful status under the Visa Waiver Program is not bound by the Visa Waiver Program no-contest rule waiving the right to contest a removal action by the government.[151]

Reinstatement of Removal Orders

The elimination of the availability of adjustment of status under INA §241(a)(5) without providing the alien a hearing before the immigration court does not violate due process. Those re-entering the United States without prior consent are barred from seeking adjustment of status under INA §241(a)(5).[152]

Waiver of Inadmissibility for Criminal Activity

The U.S. attorney general does not exceed discretionary authority by requiring a heightened showing of hardship by aliens convicted of dangerous or violent crimes before granting a waiver of criminal grounds of inadmissibility.[153]

The court of appeals lacks jurisdiction to review an immigration judge's discretionary denial of adjustment of status or waiver of inadmissibility.[154]

Continuances to Seek Adjustment

An immigration judge does not abuse discretion in denying a continuance to pursue a labor certification or a family-based visa where no evidence is submitted to the court to show that the respondent would be eligible to adjust on the employment-based petition under INA §245(i), or that a family visa petition was filed.[155] Nor did a judge abuse discretion to grant a continuance for adjustment of status where multiple continuances had been granted and no evidence was submitted to show that the labor certification was submitted prior to April 30, 2001.[156] However other courts have found an abuse of discretion where an immigration judge denied a motion for continuance while an employment-based petition was pending.[157] One court found that the immigration judge abused his discretion in denying a continuance on a family-based adjustment case where the respondent sought the continuance to have a document translated, the government was not opposed to the continuance, and the biometrics had not yet been completed.[158]

---

[146] Pub. L. No. 107-208, 116 Stat. 927 (2002).

[147] *Matter of Avila-Perez*, 24 I&N Dec. 78 (BIA 2007).

[148] *Matter of Abosi*, 24 I&N Dec. 204 (BIA 2007).

[149] *Sung v. Keisler*, 505 F.3d 372_(5th Cir. 2007); *see also Matovski v. Gonzales*, 492 F.3d 722 (6th Cir. 2007); *Perez-Vargas v. Gonzales*, 478 F.3d 191 (4th Cir. 2007).

[150] *Lacey v. Gonzales*, 499 F.3d 514 (6th Cir. 2006).

[151] *Freeman v. Gonzales*, 444 F.3d 1031 (9th Cir. 2005).

[152] *De Sandoval v. Att'y Gen.*, 440 F.3d 1276 (11th Cir. 2006).

[153] *Jean v. Gonzales*, 452 F.3d 392 (5th Cir. 2006).

[154] *Onikoyi v. Gonzales*, 454 F.3d 1 (1st Cir. 2006).

[155] *Ramchandani v. Gonzales*, 434 F.3d 337 (5th Cir. 2005).

[156] *Ali v. Gonzales*, 440 F. 3d 678 (5th Cir. 2006); *see also Zafar v. Att'y Gen.*, 461 F.3d 1357 (11th Cir. 2006); *Lendo v. INS*, 493 F.3d 439 (4th Cir. 2007).

[157] *Haswanee v. Att'y Gen.*, 471 F.3d. 1212 (11th Cir. 2006).

[158] *Badwan v. Gonzales*, 494 F.3d 566 (6th Cir. 2007).

Overstaying a Period of Voluntary Departure

An application for adjustment of status was properly pretermitted by the immigration judge, even where a motion to reopen had been granted, in a case where the respondent had overstayed a prior grant of voluntary departure.[159] A decision by an immigration judge to refuse to reopen proceedings for adjustment was upheld where the respondent had filed his application for adjustment after the expiration of the voluntary departure period.[160] The voluntary departure period was not tolled by the filing of the motion to reopen.[161]

Adjustment of Status After Withholding of Removal

Individuals who have won asylum and those who were admitted to the United States as refugees may apply for adjustment of status under INA §209. However, there is no provision for the adjustment of persons who have won relief from removal in the form of withholding of removal under INA §241(b)(3), withholding of removal under the Convention Against Torture,[162] and deferral of removal under the Convention Against Torture.[163] The regulations state that an immigration judge who grants deferral of removal under the Convention Against Torture must first enter an order of removal.[164] In *Matter of I–S– and C–S–*,[165] the BIA held that when an immigration judge issues a decision granting an application for withholding of removal under INA §241(b)(3), the judge must first enter a removal order. The BIA reasoned that although no regulation clearly requires this entry of removal order, the regulations "contemplate that the Immigration Judge will enter an order that leads to a final conclusion of the removal proceedings."[166]

Therefore, if a noncitizen becomes eligible to adjust status following a grant of withholding of removal, the removal proceedings must be reopened in order to apply for adjustment of status. Because the availability of adjustment of status often will arise long after the 90-day deadline for such motion,[167] the noncitizen must rely on a joint motion to reopen[168] or a *sua sponte* motion to reopen.[169] Battered spouses may also be eligible for a special motion to reopen under the Violence Against Women Act (VAWA).[170]

Adjustment Bars Under INA §212(a)(9)(C)

INA §212(a)(9)(C) creates a 10-year bar, with no waivers available to shorten that period, for aliens who have an aggregate of more than 180 days' unlawful presence or who have been ordered removed and who enter or attempt to enter without inspection. Neither an application for permission to seek readmission after removal or deportation, nor an application for adjustment of status pursuant to INA §245(i) will take precedence over this bar of inadmissibility.[171]

VOLUNTARY DEPARTURE

Introduction

Voluntary departure is a limited form of relief. It provides no permanent status. It does not allow the individual to remain in the country for any extended period of time. It provides a short period of time for an individual to wrap up his or her affairs in the country and depart at his or her own expense in lieu of removal. There are no provisions for work authorization during this period. The main benefit is that recipients of a grant of voluntary departure are free to leave under their own power on a day of their choosing, and their record is kept clean of a removal order. The maximum period for which a grant of voluntary departure can be given is 120 days. In certain cases, discussed below, the maximum period is 60 days. Failure to depart within the time granted by the judge carries severe consequences; *i.e.*, the voluntary departure order converts into a removal order and the person cannot return for a period of 10 years, and the person is not eligible for most forms of relief for that same period.

There are two types of voluntary departure. They are:

---

[159] *Chedad v. Gonzales*, 497 F.3d 57 (1st Cir. 2007).

[160] *Naeem v. Gonzales*, 469 F.3d 33 (1st Cir 2006).

[161] *Id.*

[162] *See* 8 CFR §§208.16, 1208.16 (eligibility and procedures for withholding of removal).

[163] *See* 8 CFR §§208.17, 1208.17 (eligibility and procedures for deferral of removal).

[164] 8 CFR §§208.17(b)(1), 1208.17(b)(1).

[165] 24 I&N Dec. 432 (BIA 2008).

[166] *Id.* at 433.

[167] INA §240(c)(7)(C)(i).

[168] 8 CFR §§1003.2(c)(3)(iii), 1003.23(b)(4)(iv).

[169] 8 CFR §§1003.2(a), 1003.23(b)(1).

[170] INA §240(c)(7)(C)(iv).

[171] *Matter of Torres-Garcia*, 23 I&N Dec. 866 (BIA 2006); *Matter of Briones*, 24 I&N Dec. 355 (BIA 2007).

- Voluntary departure prior to completion of proceedings; and

- Voluntary departure at the conclusion of proceedings.

The two types of voluntary departure have different requirements. They will be discussed individually below.

Voluntary Departure Prior to Completion of Proceedings: INA §240B(a)

This form of voluntary departure is usually sought by itself when there will be no other relief sought, or no other contested issue.

Eligibility Requirements

- Not removable as an aggravated felon;[172]

- Not removable as a terrorist under INA §237(a)(4)(B);[173]

- Concedes removability;[174]

- Waives all appeal issues;[175] and

- Makes no additional request for relief.[176]

Arriving Aliens

If an alien is an arriving alien for whom removal proceedings under INA §240 are started at the time of arrival, he or she is not eligible for voluntary departure.[177]

Period of Time Granted

The maximum period allowed for this type of voluntary departure is 120 days.[178]

Documentary Requirements

The alien must present a travel document to prove he or she will be permitted entry into the country of departure, unless the country does not require it or DHS already has it.[179]

Bond

The attorney general (*i.e.,* immigration judge) may require the posting of a voluntary departure bond, to be surrendered upon proof that the person timely departed the United States.[180]

When Sought

The request must be made prior to, or at, the master calendar hearing at which the case is initially calendared for a hearing on the merits.[181] If a request for other relief has been made and a case is set for a merits hearing, the individual may still be able to obtain voluntary departure prior to the completion of proceedings if the request for relief is withdrawn before the grant of any voluntary departure.[182]

Appeal

To obtain this type of voluntary departure, the applicant must abandon all challenges and appeals of any issue, accepting the voluntary departure decision of the judge.[183] The immigration judge has the duty to inform an eligible immigrant of the availability and requirements of voluntary departure and to provide the alien the opportunity to apply for this relief.[184] However, one court has ruled that the failure by the immigration judge to advise the respondent of the types and availability of voluntary departure is not a denial of due process.[185] An alien does not forfeit the right to apply for voluntary departure prior to completion of proceedings by appealing an erroneous denial of this relief.[186]

Voluntary Departure at the Conclusion of Proceedings: INA §240B(b)

This type of voluntary departure is generally sought as an alternative to other forms of relief (*e.g.,* asylum, adjustment of status). It is requested at the master calendar hearing from the judge, along with whatever primary forms of relief are sought. Seeking this form of voluntary departure does not mean that one must abandon any contested issues or appeals.

---

[172] INA §240B(a)(i).

[173] *Id.*

[174] 8 CFR §1240.26(b)(1)(i)(C).

[175] 8 CFR §1240.26(b)(1)(i)(D).

[176] 8 CFR §1240.26(b)(1)(i)(B).

[177] INA §240B(a)(4).

[178] INA §240B(a)(2); 8 CFR §240.25(c).

[179] 8 CFR §1240.26(b)(3)(i).

[180] INA §240B(a)(3).

[181] 8 CFR §1240.26(b)(1)(i)(A).

[182] 8 CFR §1240.26(b)(1)(i)(B).

[183] *Matter of Ocampo-Ugalde,* 22 I&N Dec. 1301 (BIA 2000).

[184] *Matter of Cordova,* 21 I&N Dec. 966 (BIA 1999). In addition, voluntary departure prior to completion of proceedings may not be granted by the immigration judge without an express waiver from the alien or the alien's representative of the right to appeal. *Matter of Ocampo-Ugalde, supra* note 183, at 1305.

[185] *Garcia-Mateo v. Keisler,* 503 F.3d 698 (8th Cir. 2007).

[186] *Matter of Cordova, supra* note 184.

_____

_____

_____

_____

_____

_____

_____

_____

_____

_____

_____

_____

_____

_____

_____

_____

_____

_____

_____

_____

_____

_____

_____

_____

_____

_____

_____

_____

_____

_____

_____

_____

_____

_____

_____

_____

_____

_____

_____

_____

conclusion of proceedings, but not if sought from ICE or prior to the completion of proceedings with the immigration judge.

- *Willingness to Depart and Ability to Pay Costs*—required for voluntary departure at the conclusion of proceedings.[203]

- *Date of applying*—voluntary departure not available at the conclusion of proceedings if the alien has not been present for one year prior to the service of the NTA.[204]

- Aggravated Felons and Terrorists—not eligible.

Should Voluntary Departure Be Sought?

Finally, there is an issue as to whether voluntary departure should be sought at all. If the alien has no intention of departing, he or she is only creating an additional bar to future admission should he or she seek voluntary departure, receive it, then refuse to depart. In that situation, the 10-year bar to future benefits under INA §240B(d) arises. When the voluntary departure period expires, it converts into an order of removal and the individual also faces the bar to admissibility under INA §212(a)(9)(A) for the removal, as well as the bar to future benefits mentioned above. Many experienced practitioners often will forego seeking voluntary departure if there is a significant possibility that the person will not depart. The decision to seek or forego voluntary departure is one that must be analyzed in light of the effect that the failure to depart will have on future possible forms of relief.[205] In addition, a grant of voluntary departure and compliance with the order does not cure bars of inadmissibility relating to unlawful presence pursuant to INA §212(a)(9)(B).

Failure to Depart During Voluntary Departure Period

An individual granted voluntary departure who voluntarily fails to depart the United States within the time specified is subject to a civil penalty between $1,000 and $5,000, and is ineligible for a period of 10 years for cancellation of removal, adjustment of status, change of nonimmigrant status, and registry.[206] These restrictions do not apply to VAWA applicants if the extreme cruelty or battery was "at least one central reason" for the failure to depart during the voluntary departure period.[207]

The BIA has ruled that an alien did not "voluntarily" fail to depart when the accredited representative representing her did not advise her of the departure requirement until after the expiration of the voluntary departure period.[208] The BIA is without power to create an "exceptional circumstances" standard for failure to depart.[209] An individual who is ordered deported "in absentia" has not remained beyond a granted period of voluntary departure, and the 10-year bar is not applicable, since no voluntary departure is granted in an "in absentia" proceeding.[210]

Motions to Reopen; Tolling of Voluntary Departure

In 1996 the BIA ruled in a precedent decision that a motion to reopen proceedings for adjustment of status was properly dismissed where the voluntary departure period previously granted to the alien had run out while the motion to reopen was pending.[211] Since then the circuit courts have been split in their decisions on whether a motion to reopen tolls the voluntary departure period. Several courts have held that the filing of a motion to reopen does not toll a period of voluntary departure.[212] For example, the First Circuit has held that when the alien files a motion to reopen during the permitted 90-day period for moving to reopen, he or she is ineligible for relief if the voluntary departure period has expired at the time of filing the motion.[213] That same court has also held that an order by the BIA to reopen removal proceedings to permit an individual to adjust status does not retroactively nullify the violation of the terms of a prior voluntary departure order.[214] Likewise, the Second Circuit found that an alien's failure to depart during the voluntary departure period ren-

[203] INA §240B(b)(1)(D).

[204] INA §240B(b)(1)(A).

[205] *See* American Immigration Law Foundation Practice Advisory, "Failure to Depart After a Grant of Voluntary Departure: The Consequences and Arguments to Avoid Them" (updated Feb. 21, 2006), *available at www.ailf.org/lac/pa/lac_pa_022106.pdf.*

[206] INA §240B(d)(1).

[207] INA §240B(d)(2).

[208] *Matter of Zmijewska,* 24 I&N Dec. 87 (BIA 2007).

[209] *Id.*

[210] *Matter of Singh,* 21 I&N Dec. 998 (BIA 1997).

[211] *Matter of Shaar,* 21 I&N Dec. 541 (BIA 1996), *aff'd, Shaar v. INS,* 141 F.3d 953 (9th Cir. 1998).

[212] *Dekoladenu v. Gonzales,* 459 F.3d 500 (4th Cir. 2006); *Banda-Ortiz v. Gonzales,* 445 F.3d 387 (5th Cir. 2006).

[213] *Naeem v. Gonzales,* 469 F.3d 33 (1st Cir. 2006).

[214] *Dacosta v. Gonzales,* 449 F.3d 45 (1st Cir. 2006) (motion to reopen for adjustment was filed after the expiration of the voluntary departure period).

dered him statutorily ineligible for adjustment of status even though a motion to reopen proceedings for adjustment had been granted.[215] The Fifth Circuit has held that an alien who files a timely motion to reopen before the expiration of voluntary departure without actually requesting that voluntary departure be tolled or reinstated does not stay the period of voluntary departure and the respondent is therefore subject to the 10-year bar on relief under INA §240B(d).[216] The Second Circuit has also ruled that an individual granted voluntary departure who wishes to stay the period of voluntary departure must expressly request a stay of the voluntary departure period.[217] The court in that case also ruled that the alien, failing to request a stay of voluntary departure, was not entitled to *nunc pro tunc* relief on the request for stay of voluntary departure.[218]

However, several circuits have held that a timely filed motion to reopen (filed prior to the expiration of voluntary departure period) serves to toll the time allotted for voluntary departure.[219] Because of the conflict between courts on the issue of tolling the period of voluntary departure, the Supreme Court has granted certiorari on this issue.[220]

---

[215] *Singh v. Gonzales,* 468 F.3d 135 (2d Cir. 2006).

[216] *Banda-Ortiz v. Gonzales,* 445 F.3d 387 (5th Cir. 2006).

[217] *Iouri v. Ashcroft,* 464 F.3d 172 (2d Cir. 2006).

[218] *Id.*

[219] *Kanivets v. Gonzales,* 424 F.3d 330 (3d Cir. 2005); *Ugokwe v. Att'y Gen.,* 453 F.3d 1325 (11th Cir. 2006); *Barroso v. Gonzales,* 429 F.3d 1195 (9th Cir. 2005); *Sidikhouya v. Gonzales,* 407 F. 3d 950 (8th Cir. 2005).

[220] *Dada v. Keisler,* 128 S.Ct. 36 (2007).

Appendix A (Part I)

Bars to NACARA Seven-Year
Special Cancellation of Removal

	Grounds of deportation that don't bar NACARA eligibility	Grounds of deportation barring NACARA eligibility	Grounds of inadmissibility barring NACARA
Immigration Violations			
Inadmissible/excludable at entry	INA §237(a)(1)(A)		
Present in violation of the law	§237(a)(1)(B)		
Violated status	§237(a)(1)(C)		
Termination of conditional residency	§237(a)(1)(D)		
Alien smuggling	§237(a)(1)(E)		
Marriage fraud	§237(a)(1)(G)		
Criminal Offenses			
Crimes involving moral turpitude		§237(a)(2)(A)*	§212(a)(2)(A)(i)(I)* [g]
Aggravated Felony		§237(a)(2)(A)(iii)	
Multiple criminal convictions			212(a)(2)(B)* [g]
High speed flight		§237(a)(2)(A)(iv)*	
Drug trafficker			§212(a)(2)C* [g]
Drug conviction		§237(a)(2)(B)(I)*	§212(a)(2)(A)(i)(II)* [g]
Drug abuser or addict		§237(a)(2)(B)(ii)*	§212(a)(2)(A)(i)(II)*
Firearm convictions		§237(a)(2)(C)*	
Miscellaneous crimes (espionage, Selective Service, sabotage)		§237(a)(2)(D)*	
Domestic violence and violations of protection orders		§237(a)(2)(E)*	
Prostitution or commercialized vice			§212(a)(2)D* [g]
Asserted immunity from prosecution			§212(a)(2)E*
Failure to register as an alien and conviction for falsification of documents		§237(a)(3)*	
Security and related grounds		§237(a)(4)	§212(a)(3)
Within five years of entry has become a public charge	§237(a)(5)		
Unlawful voting	§237(a)(6)		

*These grounds do not bar applicants from applying under the 10-year cancellation provision of NACARA.

Also: [g] = ground of inadmissibility is also a statutory preclusion to establishing **good moral character** (GMC) if within last seven years. The applicant may be statutorily barred or determined not to have the requisite GMC based on other reasons not enumerated in this chart. The GMC bar for drug convictions does not apply to simple possession of 30 grams or less of marijuana.

Notes: Present without being admitted or paroled (previously "entry without inspection") is a ground of inadmissibility—INA §212(a)(6)(A). It is *not* a bar to NACARA eligibility. Persecution of others, a bar to restriction on removal for persons who have—INA §241(b)(3)(B)(i)—is also a bar to NACARA.

Created by Cristina Fabie and Mark Silverman, ILRC

Appendix A (Part II)

Bars to NACARA Seven-Year Suspension

	Grounds of deportation which don't bar NACARA eligibility**	Grounds of deportation barring NACARA eligibility**
Immigration Violations		
Inadmissible/excludable at entry	INA §241(a)(1)(A)	
Present in violation of the law	§241(a)(1)(B)	
Violated status	§241(a)(1)(C)	
Termination of conditional residency	§241(a)(1)(D)	
Alien smuggling	§241(a)(1)(E)	
Marriage fraud	§241(a)(1)(G)	
Criminal Offenses		
Crimes involving moral turpitude		§241(a)(2)(A)(i)*
Aggravated felony		§241(a)(2)(A)(iii)
Multiple criminal convictions		§241(a)(2)(A)(ii)*
High-speed flight	***	
Drug conviction		§241(a)(2)(B)(i)*
Drug abuser or addict		§241(a)(2)(B)(ii)*
Firearm convictions		§241(a)(2)(C)*
Miscellaneous crimes (espionage, Selective Service, sabotage)		§241(a)(2)(D)
Domestic violence, and violations of protection orders	***	
Failure to register as an alien and conviction for falsification of documents		§241(a)(3)(B)*
Document fraud		§241(a)(3)(C)*
Security and related grounds		§241(a)(4)* [not for (4)(D)]
Within five years of entry has become a public charge	§241(a)(5)	

* These grounds do not bar applicants from applying under the 10-year suspension provision of NACARA.

** These section numbers are given as they were prior to the enactment of IIRAIRA; however, they still apply to NACARA suspension of deportation cases.

*** These grounds were added by IIRAIRA and therefore should not apply to NACARA suspension of deportation cases.

Note: The applicant may fail to meet the Good Moral Character requirement for other reasons not listed on this chart.

Notes: Persecution of others, a bar to restriction on removal for persons who have—INA §241(b)(3)(B)(i)— is also a bar to NACARA special rule cancellation, but it does not appear to be a bar to suspension of deportation.

Created by Mark Silverman and Lisa Klapal, ILRC

MOTIONS TO SUPPRESS: BREATHING NEW LIFE INTO THE EXCLUSIONARY RULE IN REMOVAL PROCEEDINGS

by Maria T. Baldini-Potermin, Rex Chen, and Erich C. Straub[*]

INTRODUCTION

While there are a myriad of possible suppression issues in immigration court, this article focuses on suppression motions based on the Fourth and Fifth Amendment and the immigration statutes and regulations that relate to these constitutional rights. It is not meant to be an exhaustive review of the theories or strategies involved in motions to suppress.

The first section will focus on the basics of these two amendments as they relate to law enforcement encounters generally, and immigration officers specifically. The second section will focus on theories for pursuing suppression in immigration court, particularly given the absence of a strong exclusionary rule in immigration proceedings. The third section will address some of the issues to consider when litigating motions to suppress in immigration court.

FOURTH AMENDMENT AND THE EXCLUSIONARY RULE

The Fourth Amendment to the U.S. Constitution protects individuals against unreasonable searches and seizures by the government. It regulates two of the most common law-enforcement encounters: (1) an investigative or *Terry*[1] stop, which must be sup-

ported by reasonable suspicion of criminal activity, and (2) an arrest, which must be supported by probable cause that a crime has been or is being committed.[2] When the government violates the Fourth Amendment, the exclusionary rule provides that any evidence obtained is generally not admissible in criminal proceedings against an individual.[3] Under the "fruit of the poisonous tree" doctrine, any additional evidence that is obtained as a result of the original, illegally obtained evidence is likewise inadmissible.[4]

In *INS v. Lopez-Mendoza*,[5] the U.S. Supreme Court held that the exclusionary rule is generally not applicable to immigration proceedings. Specifically, the Court held: "At issue here is the exclusion of credible evidence gathered in connection with peaceful arrests by INS officers. We hold that evidence derived from such arrests need not be suppressed in an INS civil deportation hearing."[6] The Court did allow for the possibility of suppression for "egregious" Fourth Amendment violations that rise to the level of due process violations under the Fifth Amendment. Further, the Court stated that "conclusions concerning the exclusionary rule's value might change, if there developed good reason to believe that Fourth Amendment violations by [immigration] officers were widespread."[7] While *Lopez-Mendoza* makes it clear that suppression standards under im-

* **Maria T. Baldini-Potermin** is an attorney with Gostynska Frakt, Ltd., Chicago, Illinois. She focuses on deportation defense, family-based immigration, federal litigation, naturalization, waivers, and immigration consequences of convictions. She regularly speaks at immigration law conferences, has served on several local and national committees, and received the Chicago Chapter's 2004 Joseph Minsky Mentor Award. She was an accredited representative at Pro-BAR and on the southern border from 1990 to 1994. J.D. *cum laude*, University of Minnesota, Law School, and adjunct clinical professor, Immigration Law Clinic, 1997–99.

Rex Chen is the supervising attorney at Catholic Charities of the Archdiocese of Newark. He has given several trainings on suppression motions and manages a wiki that allows immigration attorneys to collaborate on suppression strategies. Rex also maintains a blog on Third Circuit immigration decisions.

Erich C. Straub is an attorney practicing in Milwaukee, Wisconsin in the areas of deportation defense, family-based immigration and the immigration consequences of criminal convictions. He is currently chair of the AILA Wisconsin

Chapter. He is also a faculty member for AILF's Litigation Institute and serves on AILF's Litigation Advisory Committee. Since 2005, he has been listed in *Best Lawyers in America* in the area of immigration law. Prior to focusing his practice on immigration, he was a criminal defense attorney and has litigated suppression motions in both criminal and immigration court.

[1] *Terry v. Ohio*, 392 U.S. 1 (1968).

[2] *Beck v. Ohio*, 379 U.S. 89 (1964).

[3] *Weeks v. U.S.*, 232 U.S. 383 (1914); *Mapp v. Ohio*, 367 U.S. 643 (1961).

[4] *Silverthorne Lumber Co. v. U.S.*, 251 U.S. 385 (1920).

[5] 468 U.S. 1032 (1984).

[6] *Id.* at 1051.

[7] *Id.* at 1050; *see also Almeida-Amaral v. Gonzales*, 461 F.3d 231, 234 (2d Cir. 2006).

continued

migration and criminal law are distinct, a solid understanding of both is critical for the immigration practitioner. This is particularly true in the present enforcement environment, in which state and local law enforcement officers are playing a greater role in the initiation of removal proceedings, and clients increasingly find themselves facing criminal charges such as identity theft.

Before embarking on a summary of the constitutional parameters of police encounters, it is important to have a basic understanding of situations in which the Fourth Amendment is generally not applicable. A voluntary or consensual police encounter does not implicate the Fourth Amendment, and an officer is generally free to approach and question an individual as long as a seizure does not occur.[8] An officer may request "voluntary" production of identification and travel information or ask for consent to search luggage without any specific evidence of wrongdoing.[9] Similarly, an immigration officer is authorized by regulation to ask a person any question, irrespective of evidence of unlawful status or criminal conduct, as long as the officer does not restrain the freedom of the person to walk away.[10]

Immigration officers also are permitted more expansive power to detain, search, and interrogate at the border[11] and international airports.[12] The "border exception" to the Fourth Amendment also applies at fixed immigration checkpoints on roads leading away from the border[13] and mobile immigration checkpoints.[14] Within a reasonable distance of the border, an immigration officer is authorized to board and search any vessels within the territorial waters of the United States, as well as railway cars, aircraft, conveyances or vehicles. Except for unusual circumstances, a reasonable distance from the border has been defined as 100 miles.[15] An immigration officer also is permitted to patrol private lands, not including dwellings, within 25 miles of the border.[16]

Investigative or *Terry* Stop

An investigative or *Terry* stop is considered a seizure of a person, but not an arrest.[17] A seizure occurs when an officer uses physical force or a show of authority to restrain the liberty of a person, and a "reasonable" person under the circumstances would not feel free to leave.[18] A seizure justified under *Terry* must be temporary and limited in scope to the purpose of the stop.[19] An officer is also required to use the least intrusive means available to verify or dispel the officer's suspicion.[20] For Fourth Amendment purposes, a stop can only be justified if an officer has reasonable suspicion of criminal activity.[21] Reasonable suspicion must be based on specific and articulable facts and cannot be based on "an inchoate and unparticularized suspicion or hunch."[22] The amount of evidence required for reasonable suspicion is less than probable cause.[23]

The most common type of investigative or *Terry* stop is a traffic stop. Many traffic stops do not involve criminal activity, so an officer is only required to have probable cause of a traffic violation rather that reasonable suspicion of criminal activity.[24] In all other respects, traffic stops are analyzed under *Terry* principles.[25]

Once the initial stop is valid under *Terry*, an officer may order the driver[26] and passengers[27] out of the vehicle and perform a "pat-down" or frisk of any person that the officer has reasonable suspicion may be armed and dangerous. A search of the passenger area of a car is also permissible when there is reasonable suspicion that any person is dangerous and may gain

---

[8] *Florida v. Bostick*, 501 U.S. 429 (1991).

[9] *Florida v. Royer*, 460 U.S. 491 (1983).

[10] 8 CFR §287.8(b)(2).

[11] *U.S. v. Flores-Montano*, 541 U.S. 149 (2004).

[12] *U.S. v. Montoya de Hernandez*, 473 U.S. 531 (1985); 8 USC §1357(c).

[13] *U.S. v. Martinez-Fuerte*, 428 U.S. 543 (1976).

[14] *Melnitsenko v. Mukasey*, 2008 U.S. App. LEXIS 2549, 2008 WL 339344, at *4 (2d Cir. 2008) (holding that stop and search of a noncitizen for three hours at a mobile checkpoint without being given *Miranda* or other warnings did not rise to the level of egregiousness required for suppression under the Fourth Amendment).

---

[15] 8 CFR §287.1(a)(2).

[16] 8 USC §1357(a)(3).

[17] *Terry v. Ohio*, *supra* note 1.

[18] *U.S. v. Mendenhall*, 446 U.S. 544 (1980).

[19] *Florida v. Royer*, *supra* note 9.

[20] *Id.*

[21] *Terry v. Ohio*, *supra* note 1.

[22] *Id.* at 27.

[23] *U.S. v. Arvizu*, 534 U.S. 266 (2002).

[24] *Whren v. U.S.*, 517 U.S. 806 (1996).

[25] *Berkemer v. McCarty*, 468 U.S. 420 (1984).

[26] *Pennsylvania v. Mimms*, 434 U.S. 106 (1977).

[27] *Maryland v. Wilson*, 519 U.S. 408 (1997).

immediate access to a weapon.[28] In practice, courts will usually find that any reasonable suspicion of criminal activity justifies a person being ordered out of a vehicle and frisked and the passenger area of the vehicle being searched. In addition to questions related to the suspected criminal activity or traffic violation, an officer is also permitted to ask basic questions to determine identity.[29] In practice, an officer will usually request some form of photo identification verifying name, date of birth and address.

In addition to requesting a form of identification, it is quite common for an officer to ask additional questions that are unrelated to the original justification for the stop. The U.S. Supreme Court has held that, as long as the initial seizure is justified, questions regarding immigration status are permissible even if an officer does not have reasonable suspicion of a violation of immigration law.[30] The person being detained is not required to answer the questioning,[31] and if the original suspicion justifying the stop has been dispelled, continued detention by the officer to investigate immigration status is no longer justified under the Fourth Amendment.[32] Under such circumstances, it is critical that a person stand firm in his or her right to refuse to answer immigration questioning. Unfortunately, law enforcement officers understand and make full use of their power to intimidate, and frequently the person being detained will answer such questions under the belief that full cooperation will make things go smoother.

Under immigration regulations, an immigration officer must also justify investigative stops under *Terry*. To temporarily detain an individual, an immigration officer must have reasonable suspicion based upon articulable facts that the person is unlawfully present in the United States.[33] As the basis for a stop is reasonable suspicion of an immigration violation, questions regarding immigration status are permissible and an individual's refusal to answer will normally be used as justification for an arrest.

Practice Pointer—Analysis of an Investigative or Terry Stop

1. Which law enforcement agencies were involved in the encounter with the noncitizen?

   a. If an officer from the Department of Homeland Security was involved, when did the officer come upon the scene of the seizure?

   b. What was the role of the Department of Homeland Security (DHS) officer?

2. Was there a seizure?

   a. Did the officer use physical force or did the officer demonstrate a show of authority to restrain the liberty of the noncitizen?

   b. Did the noncitizen feel that he or she was free to leave? Why or why not?

3. Was the seizure a stop rather than an arrest?

   a. Was the detention temporary?

   b. Did the officer use the least intrusive means to dispel the reasonable suspicion?

   c. Did the officer also have reasonable suspicion that a noncitizen might be armed or dangerous?

4. Did the officer have reasonable suspicion of criminal activity or probable cause of a traffic violation?

   a. What may have been the specific and articulable facts known to the officer?

   b. What did the officer say when he or she questioned the noncitizen as to the reason for the stop?

      i. In what language did the noncitizen initially respond to the officer?

      ii. What did the noncitizen say in response to the officer?

      iii. Did the noncitizen give the officer any papers or other items? If yes, what did he or she give the officer?

5. Was the detention limited to the initial justification for the stop?

   If not, was the evidence obtained beyond this scope of the stop?

6. Is there circumstantial evidence that the officer conducted a race-based stop?

7. What are the legal arguments for suppression in immigration proceedings?

---

[28] *Michigan v. Long*, 463 U.S. 1032 (1983).

[29] *Berkemer v. McCarty, supra* note 25.

[30] *Muehler v. Mena*, 544 U.S. 93 (2005).

[31] *Florida v. Royer, supra* note 9.

[32] The Supreme Court has held that Mexican appearance alone does not create reasonable suspicion of an immigration violation. In a border area, the following factors may support reasonable suspicion: smuggling or unusual traffic patterns; vehicles typically used for smuggling; erratic driving or other evasive behavior; and a manner of dress or haircut indicative of nationality. *U.S. v. Brignoni-Ponce*, 422 U.S. 873 (1975).

[33] 8 CFR §287.8(b)(2).

Arrest

A *Terry* stop becomes an arrest when an individual's detention is no longer temporary and/or the officer's actions are no longer limited to the least intrusive means necessary to verify or dispel the suspicion justifying the stop.[34] In determining whether a seizure is a *Terry* stop or an arrest, it is also important to remember that reasonable suspicion that a person may be armed or dangerous will expand what is considered temporary or the least intrusive means. An arrest requires that an officer have probable cause, which has been defined as trustworthy knowledge of facts and circumstances that would lead a reasonable person to conclude that the suspect had committed or was committing a crime.[35]

A lawful arrest under the Fourth Amendment expands the ability of any law enforcement officer to search beyond the scope of a *Terry* frisk. Under the "search incident to arrest" doctrine, an officer is justified in searching a person for weapons or evidence,[36] including the contents of a wallet or purse.[37] It is also permissible to search the area within a person's "immediate control" and from which the person might grab a weapon or piece of evidence.[38] If a person is arrested in a home or dwelling, a "protective sweep" or search is authorized if an officer has reasonable suspicion that an area may conceal someone or who poses a danger.[39] If a person is arrested while in control of an automobile, an officer may search the passenger area of vehicle[40] or impound the vehicle and perform an "inventory search" of all compartments and items therein.[41] In most instances, a detailed law-enforcement inventory policy will provide Fourth Amendment justification for an officer to make an exhaustive search of the person and all items or containers within the person's immediate control or anywhere in his or her vehicle.

As a practical matter, most arrests are conducted without a warrant and are justified based on an objective analysis of whether the arresting officer had probable cause. In most instances, "exigent circum-

stances" will be used to excuse the Fourth Amendment warrant requirement. Exigent circumstances occur when there is a compelling need for official action and no time to obtain a warrant.[42] However, the U.S. Supreme Court has firmly held that, absent exigent circumstances, a warrantless entry into a residence to make an arrest is presumptively unreasonable.[43] Immigration regulations also require an immigration officer to have a warrant before entering a residence or the "curtilage"[44] of a residence.[45]

Under statutory and regulatory authority, an immigration officer is allowed to arrest a person if there is probable cause of the following: (1) a noncitizen is entering, attempting to enter, or present in U.S. in violation of immigration law;[46] (2) a person has committed a felony immigration violation;[47] or (3) a person has committed any felony offense under U.S. law that comes to the immigration officers attention during the performance of immigration enforcement related duties.[48] An immigration officer is also authorized to arrest a person for any crime (felony or misdemeanor) that is committed in the officer's presence.[49] A warrant is required for the immigration officer to arrest in each of these scenarios unless the officer reasonably believes that the person is likely to escape before a warrant can be obtained.[50] During the actual arrest, an immigration officer must reveal his or her identity as an officer and state the reason for the arrest as soon as it is practical or safe to do so.[51]

Practice Pointer—Analysis of an Arrest

1. Which law enforcement agencies were involved in the encounter with the noncitizen?

    a. If an officer from the Department of Homeland Security was involved, when did the officer come upon the scene of the seizure?

---

[34] *Florida v. Royer, supra* note 9.

[35] *Beck v. Ohio, supra* note 2.

[36] *U.S. v. Robinson*, 414 U.S. 218 (1973).

[37] *U.S. v. Molinaro*, 877 F.2d 1341 (7th Cir. 1989).

[38] *Chimel v. California*, 395 U.S. 752 (1969).

[39] *Maryland v. Buie*, 494 U.S. 325 (1990)

[40] *New York v. Belton*, 453 U.S. 454 (1981).

[41] *Colorado v. Bertine*, 479 U.S. 367 (1987).

[42] *Michigan v. Tyler*, 436 U.S. 499.

[43] *Payton v. New York*, 445 U.S. 573 (1985).

[44] Curtilage has been defined as the land immediately surrounding and associated with the home that an individual may reasonably expect to remain private. *Oliver v. U.S.*, 466 U.S. 210 (1984).

[45] 8 CFR §287.8(f)(2).

[46] 8 USC §1357(a)(2); 8 CFR §287.8(c)(2)(i).

[47] 8 USC §1357(a)(5).

[48] 8 USC §1357(a)(5)(B); 8 CFR §287.5(c)(4)(i).

[49] 8 USC §1357(a)(5)(A).

[50] 8 USC §§1357(a)(2), (4), and (5); 8 CFR §287.8(c)(2)(ii).

[51] 8 CFR §287.8(c)(2)(iii).

    b. What was the role of the DHS officer?

2. Was there a seizure?

    a. Did the officer use physical force or did the officer demonstrate a show of authority to restrain the liberty of the noncitizen?

    b. Did the noncitizen feel that he or she was free to leave? Why or why not?

3. Was the seizure a stop rather than an arrest?

    a. Was the detention temporary?

    b. Did the officer use the least intrusive means to dispel the reasonable suspicion?

    c. Did the officer also have reasonable suspicion that a noncitizen might be armed or dangerous?

4. What evidence was obtained?

    a. Who obtained the evidence?

    b. Was the evidence obtained pursuant to the more expansive powers to search incident to an arrest?

5. What are the legal arguments for suppression in immigration proceedings?

Custodial Interrogation

The U.S. Supreme Court has held that police coercion can render a statement involuntary, and thus, inadmissible under the Fifth and Fourteenth Amendment due process clauses.[52] This principle is reflected in the immigration regulations, which prohibit an immigration officer from using threats, coercion, or physical abuse to obtain a statement or induce a waiver of rights.[53] The Board of Immigration Appeals (BIA) has found that suppression is appropriate if a statement is involuntary and thus "fundamentally unfair" under the Fifth Amendment.[54] Use of a coerced statement in removal proceedings has been considered a violation of due process in at least one circuit court decision.[55]

Miranda[56] warnings are perhaps the best-known constitutional protection in the context of custodial

interrogation. Because *Miranda* is based on the Fifth Amendment right against self-incrimination, an officer's failure to give the warnings can only justify suppression in criminal proceedings.[57] However, there is a hint of *Miranda* in 8 CFR §287.3(c), which applies to removal proceedings and requires an immigration officer to do the following when arresting a noncitizen without a warrant:

1) advise the noncitizen that any statement made may be used against the noncitizen in subsequent proceedings;

2) advise the noncitizen of the right to be represented by counsel at no expense to the government; and

3) provide the noncitizen with a list of free legal service organizations and attorneys.

Unlike *Miranda*, the regulation does not contain an explicit requirement that the warnings be given before an immigration officer takes a statement, and in practice, they are routinely given after a statement is taken. While not as powerful a tool as *Miranda*, an officer's compliance with these regulations is relevant to any inquiry into the voluntariness of a statement,[58] and as discussed later, the regulatory violation itself may provide a basis for suppression.

Practice Pointer—Analysis of a Custodial Interrogation

1. Was there a seizure?

2. What did the officer(s) say to the noncitizen or what questions did the officer(s) ask the noncitizen to answer?

    a. What did the noncitizen say in response to the officer?

    b. In what language did the conversation take place?

    c. Was the noncitizen advised of his or her rights under *Miranda* at any point? If yes, when? By which officer?

    d. At any point, did the officer(s) threaten the noncitizen or a member of his or her family with jail, physical harm, deportation, etc. if he or she did not provide information as requested?

    e. At any point, did the officer(s) use physical force against the noncitizen? What kind of force?

---

[52] *Jackson v. Denno*, 378 U.S. 368 (1964).

[53] 8 CFR §287.8(c)(2)(vii).

[54] *Matter of Toro*, 17 I&N Dec. 340 (BIA 1980); *Matter of Garcia*, 17 I&N 319 (BIA 1980) (where a noncitizen makes a prima facie showing that admissions were involuntary, only those admissions support a finding of deportability, and immigration authorities present no contrary evidence, deportation proceedings will be terminated).

[55] *Navia-Duran v. INS*, 568 F.2d 803 (1st Cir. 1977).

[56] *Miranda v. Arizona*, 384 U.S. 436 (1966).

[57] *Navia-Duran v. INS*, 568 F.2d 803 (1st Cir. 1977).

[58] *Id.*

f. At any point, did the officer(s) use other forms of physical abuse, such as refusing to provide food, water, warm clothing, restroom facilities, or medical care to the noncitizen?

3. Were there personal characteristics that made a noncitizen particularly susceptible to threats, coercion, or physical abuse?

4. What are the legal arguments for suppression in immigration proceedings?

Worksite Enforcement Actions

An immigration officer must have a warrant or the consent of the owner (or person in control) to enter nonpublic areas of a business, a farm, or an outdoor agricultural operation.[59] The warrant requirement does not extend to the area of a business or activity that is open to the general public.[60] An immigration officer is also authorized to make a warrantless entry to "open fields" that are not farms or agricultural operations.[61] The "open fields" doctrine is a recognized exception to the Fourth Amendment warrant requirement.[62]

The U.S. Supreme Court has concluded that workers are not seized under the Fourth Amendment during a factory sweep, even when immigration officers station themselves at all exits and individually approach workers to ask questions about their immigration status.[63] Given the Supreme Court's ruling, practitioners seeking to suppress evidence obtained from an individual in a workplace investigation need to focus on the particular actions taken by the officers. An analysis of whether a seizure has occurred focuses upon whether a reasonable person under the same circumstances would have concluded that he or she was not free to leave, so the extent to which officers may have controlled the movement of workers and degree of force employed are particularly relevant factors.

LEGAL THEORIES FOR SUPPRESSION IN IMMIGRATION COURT

Egregious Fourth Amendment Violations

At least one court has identified two different categories of egregious Fourth Amendment viola-

tions: (1) a seizure for a grossly improper consideration such as race and (2) a seizure that was sufficiently severe—for example, if the initial stop is particularly lengthy or there is a show or use of force.[64] In addition to race, a seizure based on a foreign-sounding name has also been found to be egregious.[65] A common strategy is to prove that the innocent reasons offered by U.S. Immigration and Customs Enforcement (ICE) counsel for the illegal seizure or search are not plausible, leaving the improper motive as the only justification. Immigration case law on particularly lengthy seizures or the unreasonable use of force is not yet well developed, but practitioners should continue to push such theories by emphasizing the severity of illegal searches and seizures in suppression motions.

In announcing the egregious violation standard in *INS v. Lopez-Mendoza*, the U.S. Supreme Court was concerned that a broad exclusionary rule could have a severe impact on chaotic mass arrests in the field because they "occur in crowded and confused circumstances."[66] Although ICE has conducted ongoing worksite enforcement actions and arrested 4,940 noncitizens in fiscal year 2007,[67] ICE also has focused its efforts on other operations[68] as well as on collabora-

---

[59] 8 CFR §287.8(f)(2).

[60] 8 CFR §287.8(f)(4).

[61] *Id.*

[62] *Oliver v. U.S.*, 466 U.S. 170 (1984).

[63] *INS v. Delgado*, 466 U.S. 210 (1984).

[64] *Almeida-Amaral v. Gonzales*, 461 F.3d 231 (2d Cir. 2006).

[65] *Orhorhaghe v. INS*, 38 F.3d 488 (9th Cir. 1994).

[66] *INS v. Lopez-Mendoza*, 468 U.S. 1032, 1049 (1984).

[67] *See* DHS Fact Sheet, "Border Security and Enforcement" (Feb. 29, 2008), *available at www.dhs.gov/xnews/ releases/pr_1204311226540.shtm*.

[68] *See, e.g.,* ICE News Release, "Area ICE Fugitive Operations Teams Record Nearly 150 Arrests in January" (Feb. 11, 2008), *available at www.ice.gov/pi/news/newsreleases/ articles/080211sandiego.htm* (discussing the existence of 75 fugitive operations teams and the nearly 72,000 arrests of noncitizens with outstanding deportation/removal orders since 2003); *www.ice.gov/pi/investigations/comshield/ newsreleases.htm* (linking to news releases discussing the operations to arrest noncitizens suspected of being gang members); *www.ice.gov/pi/predator/newsreleases.htm* (linking to news releases regarding the arrest of noncitizens convicted of sex offenses); *www.ice.gov/partners/dro/ cap.htm* (discussing the Criminal Alien Program: collaborative efforts of local, state, and federal law enforcement authorities and ICE to identify noncitizens who may be subject to being removed from the United States); E. Londoño, "U.S. Steps Up Deportation of Immigrant Criminals," *Wash. Post*, Feb. 27, 2008, p. A1, *available at www.washingtonpost.com/ wp-dyn/content/article/2008/02/26/AR2008022603705.html* (stating that ICE identified and placed 164,000 noncitizen criminals in removal proceedings in fiscal year 2007).

tive efforts with local law enforcement[69] to arrest and remove noncitizens. Thus, one of the key justifications for the egregious violation standard may not be factually applicable in many cases, and practitioners should make this distinction whenever possible.

It is also important to remember that before *Lopez-Mendoza*, the traditional view was that suppression was appropriate in immigration court for Fourth Amendment violations.[70] In *Lopez-Mendoza*, the Supreme Court made its decision based on legacy Immigration and Naturalization Service (INS) conduct in the 1980s. Legacy INS was able to convince the Court that it had effective training, supervision, regulations, and punishment for its officers who violated constitutional rights of noncitizens.[71]

ICE officers today may not receive the same level of training about noncitizens' rights or governmental oversight of ICE's current operations as INS officers received in the 1980s. Thus, it may become possible to demonstrate that the Supreme Court's view of the conduct of agents who enforce immigration laws is no longer valid. Since ICE raided the Swift & Co. meatpacking plants in December 2006, many questions have arisen about ICE's techniques, and hearings are being conducted about the alleged constitutional violations of individuals' rights by ICE and local law enforcement.[72] Lawsuits remain pending in federal district courts regarding worksite raids, and the formal discovery process may yield documents and information that will be helpful to counsel filing motions to suppress in removal proceedings.[73] The information and sworn testimony obtained may be useful in motions to suppress before the immigration court to demonstrate a pattern and practice of ICE actions that violate the immigration statute, federal regulations, federal guidelines, and the Fourth and Fifth Amendments.

With the advent of mandatory detention, the prison-like features of today's detention centers, and the techniques being used by ICE officers (such as early morning team arrests of noncitizens at their homes),[74] there are strong arguments that removal proceedings are now (after the Illegal Immigration Reform and Immigrant Responsibility Act[75]) very similar to criminal proceedings. The government also has repeatedly stated that it will use immigration law as an extension of criminal law in order to exhaust every opportunity to detain individuals suspected of involvement in terrorism.[76] Given these quasi-criminal features of present immigration removal proceedings, the finding in *Lopez-Mendoza* of sufficient constitutional safeguards may be ripe for challenge.

Fifth Amendment Violations

Fifth Amendment violations also form the basis of a standard evidentiary objection to the admission of evidence in removal proceedings. The BIA has ruled that for evidence to be admissible in removal proceedings, the use of the evidence must be fundamentally fair, such that it would not deprive the respondent of due process under the Fifth Amendment.[77] Also, in *INS v. Lopez-Mendoza*,[78] the U.S. Supreme Court explicitly left open the potential to suppress evidence if the government violated liberties that might transgress notions of fundamental fairness. In footnote 5 of the decision, the Court noted that the BIA had suppressed evidence for violations such as repeatedly refusing the respondent's request for counsel[79] and a nighttime warrantless entry into a person's residence.[80]

When there is evidence that government officials conducted interrogations in such a manner that the noncitizen's statement and/or other evidence was obtained through coercion, grounds exist to argue for suppression of the statements and other evidence obtained in violation of a noncitizen's Fifth Amendment rights. For example, suppression was

---

[69] *See www.ice.gov/partners/287g/Section287_g.htm* (discussing the efforts to train local law enforcement officers to enforce the provisions of the Immigration and Nationality Act).

[70] *Matter of Sandoval*, 17 I&N Dec. 70 (BIA 1979).

[71] *INS v. Lopez-Mendoza, supra* note 66, at 1044–45.

[72] *See* O. Garcia, "New Panel to Report on Possible ICE Misconduct to Congress," *Associated Press*, Feb. 23, 2008.

[73] *See id.* The American Immigration Law Foundation (AILF) maintains on its website updated information on lawsuits regarding ICE raids. *See www.ailf.org/lac/clearinghouse_122106_ICE.shtml*.

[74] *See, e.g.,* M. Martinez, "Advocates Organize to Thwart US Immigration Agents," *Chi. Trib.*, Mar. 1, 2008.

[75] Pub. L. No. 104-208, div. C, 110 Stat. 3009, 3009-546 to 3009-724 (1996).

[76] Speech by Attorney General John Ashcroft, Oct. 25, 2001, at the U.S. Conference of Mayors; Press conference by DHS Secretary Michael Chertoff, Apr. 20, 2006.

[77] *Matter of Grijalva*, 19 I&N Dec. 713, 722 (BIA 1988); *Matter of Toro*, 17 I&N Dec. 340 (BIA 1980).

[78] 468 U.S. 1032 (1984).

[79] *Matter of Garcia*, 17 I&N Dec.319, 321 (BIA 1980).

[80] *Matter of Ramira-Cordova*, No. A21 095 659 (BIA Feb. 21, 1980).

deemed appropriate after legacy INS agents misinformed the respondent that she had to leave the United States within two weeks, and then conducted an illegal interrogation for over two hours late at night in an INS station.[81]

Other Fifth Amendment violations are also worth pursuing, even if there are few cases directly on point. For example, the BIA has held that illegal electronic surveillance could form the basis for suppression under the Fifth Amendment.[82] It may also be appropriate to argue that numerous regulatory and statutory violations, when considered cumulatively, violated a noncitizen's Fifth Amendment rights.[83]

Regulatory Violations

In *Matter of Garcia-Flores*,[84] the BIA ruled that suppression is appropriate when: (1) a regulation is violated; (2) the regulation is intended to benefit the noncitizen; (3) there is proof that the violation prejudiced the noncitizen. The U.S. Court of Appeals for the Second Circuit has expanded *Garcia-Flores* and does not require proof of prejudice if the regulation implicates a fundamental constitutional or statutory right.[85] As previously stated, immigration regulations actually codify the *Terry* standard of reasonable suspicion and at least mimic *Miranda* warnings. The constitutional principles contained in these regulations provide fertile ground for suppression, even when prejudice may be difficult to demonstrate.

Federal Policy or Guidelines Violations

With the creation of DHS on March 1, 2003,[86] DHS and the Federal Bureau of Investigation (FBI) are no longer in the same executive branch depart-

ment. Many of the memoranda that bound legacy INS are applicable to DHS, such as the Attorney General Guidelines for INS Undercover Operations.[87] These memoranda are also binding on the Department of Justice agencies, such as the FBI, that work in conjunction with the DHS on joint operations. Thus, where DHS or another agency working with DHS violates applicable guidelines, a motion to suppress may be brought and be ultimately successful in removal proceedings.

DISCOVERY ISSUES AND STRATEGIES IN REMOVAL PROCEEDINGS

There are many resources available to counsel for motions to suppress.[88] Many AILA chapters have begun forming committees to address the ongoing raids. Counsel should reach out to other attorneys working on motions to suppress locally and nationally to coordinate efforts to create the record before the Immigration Court and adequately raise and preserve all legal and constitutional challenges for review by the federal circuit courts of appeals and eventually the U.S. Supreme Court.

As motions to suppress evidence are litigated around the United States, case law will develop. For favorable precedent to be issued by the BIA and the federal courts of appeals, the record before the immigration court must be fully developed. Issues that are not raised and developed before the immigration court and later the BIA may be deemed to be waived for failure to exhaust administrative remedies.[89]

[81] *Navia-Duran v. INS*, 568 F.2d 803 (1st Cir. 1977).

[82] *Matter of Hemblen*, 14 I&N Dec. 739 (BIA 1974).

[83] *See INS v. Lopez-Mendoza, supra* note 66, at 1051 (leaving open the question whether to suppress evidence in deportation proceedings for egregious violations of "other liberties" that might transgress fundamental fairness).

[84] 17 I&N Dec. 325 (BIA 1980).

[85] *Montero v. INS*, 124 F.3d 381 (2d Cir. 1997).

[86] The Homeland Security Act of 2002, Pub. L. No. 107-296, 116 Stat. 2135, abolished legacy INS and transferred its responsibilities to three bureaus within DHS, which is headed by the Secretary of Homeland Security. Unlike the INS, DHS has its own secretary and is not under the authority of the attorney general in the Department of Justice. The Executive Office for Immigration Review (EOIR), which includes the BIA and the immigration courts, remains under the direction of the attorney general. *See* 8 USC §1103; 8 CFR §§1001.1, 1003, 1003.1, and 1003.9.

[87] *Pieniazek v. Ashcroft*, 449 F.3d 792, 794 (7th Cir. 2006) (holding that the 1984 Attorney General Guidelines for INS Undercover Operations continue to govern the actions of DHS, and remanding the case for additional consideration of the motion to suppress).

[88] *See, e.g.,* the "Community Resource Kit" developed by the National Immigration Project of the National Lawyers Guild, *available at www.nationalimmigrationproject.org/commresourcekit.html*. The executive director of that organization, Dan Kesselbrenner, is a good resource regarding challenges to ICE enforcement actions and lawsuits pending throughout the United States. The National Immigration Project also maintains a brief bank with sample motions to suppress and supporting briefs. For more on motions to suppress, see A. Gallagher & T. Hutchins, *Immigration Pleading and Practice Manual*, ch. VII. (Motion to Suppress Evidence); National Immigration Project of the National Lawyers Guild, *National Immigration Law and Defense* §7:6.

[89] INA §242(d)(1); 8 USC §1252(d)(1) (stating that a federal circuit court of appeals may review a final order of removal only if the noncitizen has exhausted all administrative remedies available as of right). Case law continues to develop

continued

The courts of appeals repeatedly have emphasized that statutory and regulatory claims should be made before constitutional claims. Statutory and regulatory claims can be and are routinely decided by the immigration court and the BIA. Constitutional claims should be fully briefed and raised before the immigration judge and the BIA as well to preserve them for judicial review.

Litigating a motion to suppress can be an emotionally charged experience, particularly when counsel strongly believes that a noncitizen's rights were violated. Allegations of fact must be supported by evidence that is admissible and relevant. The BIA has looked closely at attorney conduct in the past few years and has sanctioned attorneys for misrepresentations before the immigration court and other tribunals.[90] Counsel should know the evidence to avoid getting into a situation in which statements by counsel regarding the case are seen as less than forthright.

Finally, counsel should have a frank discussion with the noncitizen client about his or her prior immigration history, eligibility for immigration relief if a motion to suppress is not granted, and any immediate immigration relief before preparing to litigate a motion to suppress before the immigration court. For example, a noncitizen may have prior negative immigration history, such as a prior voluntary departure or deportation order, which the ICE assistant chief counsel can use as evidence of alienage, thereby mooting out the legal basis of a motion to suppress in the current removal proceeding. Another noncitizen may have a current visa petition and be eligible to apply for an immigrant visa abroad at a U.S. embassy or consulate; in this case, the noncitizen may prefer to work out an agreement with ICE assistant chief counsel to have the immigration judge grant the noncitizen voluntary departure instead of ordering removal. Leaving the United States under a grant of voluntary departure eliminates the need to apply for a waiver of inadmissibility after a removal order and can expedite the visa processing,

particularly when a noncitizen may not require a waiver other than one for unlawful presence. Ultimately, the noncitizen needs to decide whether he or she wants to pursue the motion to suppress, particularly when he or she is detained in DHS custody.

Discovery Issues

Under the Immigration and Nationality Act, a noncitizen has the right to examine evidence offered by DHS against him or her, to present evidence on his or her own behalf, and to cross-examine witnesses presented by DHS.[91] Requests under the Freedom of Information Act (FOIA)[92] should be made as soon as possible for a noncitizen with USCIS, U.S. Customs and Border Protection, and ICE. For noncitizens in removal proceedings, USCIS has established a "fast-track" or "Notice to Appear" FOIA process.[93] A continuance may be granted by the immigration judge for "good cause," which has been found to include the processing of a FOIA request made to obtain exculpatory evidence.[94]

FOIA requests may also be made under state and local laws. Such requests may result in the release of information relevant to joint ICE and local law enforcement policies (or the nonexistence of such policies). The information may also be helpful in the analysis of a motion to suppress and likelihood of success. A noncitizen can obtain the names of state or local law enforcement officers involved in the enforcement of immigration law and, where relevant, request subpoenas from the immigration judge to require the appearance of such officers before the immigration court.[95]

Warnings:

- Counsel should take care in pleadings before the immigration court. A motion to suppress will be of no avail if the noncitizen or counsel admits to

---

regarding what constitutes exhaustion of administrative remedies, with splits among the circuit courts of appeals. Counsel should review the federal circuit court of appeals precedent applicable to the jurisdiction in which the removal proceedings are venued.

[90] 8 CFR §§1003.1(d)(2)(5), 1003.101–106, and 1292.3; *see also Matter of Shah*, 24 I&N Dec. 282 (BIA 2007); *Matter of Krivonos*, 24 I&N Dec. 292 (BIA 2007); *Matter of Jean-Joseph*, 24 I&N Dec. 294 (BIA 2007); *Matter of Ramos*, 23 I&N Dec. 843 (BIA 2005).

[91] INA §240(b)(4); 8 USC §1229a(b)(4); *see also Ibarra-Flores v. Gonzales*, 439 F.3d 614, 620–21 (9th Cir. 2006) (directing the immigration judge on remand to order DHS to produce evidence related to the noncitizen's eligibility for relief from removal); *Immigration Court Practice Manual* ch. 4.15(e).

[92] 5 USC §552.

[93] *See* 72 Fed. Reg. 9017 (Feb. 28, 2007).

[94] *Pieniazek v. Ashcroft*, 449 F.3d 792, 794 (7th Cir. 2006).

[95] INA §240(b)(1); 8 USC §1229a(b)(1).

the factual allegations in the notice to appear that support the charge of removability.[96]

- Requests for bifurcated hearings on the issues of removability and relief are not always granted. One of the contested areas of removal practice continues to be the requirement of some immigration judges that a noncitizen completely fill out and file all applications for relief and supporting documentation before a contested hearing to determine removability has been held or removability has been determined.

- The new *Immigration Court Practice Manual*[97] does not resolve the issues involved. Chapter 3.3(c)(i) states that all application forms should be filled out completely. Application forms typically require information regarding place of birth, country of nationality and citizenship, and date of entry/admission to the United States, which can be used to establish alienage.[98]

- Counsel must take care in preparation of the applications and supporting documentation to protect the record if a motion to suppress is pending and to raise due process arguments for appellate review when an immigration judge deems an application abandoned for failure to completely fill out the form prior to a contested hearing on removability. Similarly, care must be taken regarding motions to change venue.[99]

ICE Tactics During a Suppression Hearing

At a suppression hearing, one of the most common tactics by ICE counsel is to call the noncitizen to testify. ICE must first present other evidence of alienage before calling a noncitizen to testify about alienage.[100] ICE counsel will then seek to essentially bypass the motion to suppress and prove alienage by questioning the noncitizen about his or her immigration status. To counter this tactic, counsel must carefully prepare the

noncitizen to assert his or her Fifth Amendment right against self-incrimination. Immigration judges frequently permit ICE counsel to continue asking questions regarding immigration status, so the noncitizen should be prepared to assert the right repeatedly. Similarly, immigration judges may ask questions regarding immigration status or place of birth.

Although unlawful presence of a noncitizen is only a civil violation under federal law, unlawful reentry and other criminal immigration crimes provide a sufficient justification for invoking the Fifth Amendment.[101] Federal and state criminal statutes regarding the possession or use of false identification documents or identity theft may also provide a basis for a noncitizen to invoke her right against self-incrimination. While an immigration judge may draw a negative inference from a noncitizen's refusal to testify in court, his or her silence alone will be insufficient for ICE to meet its burden to prove alienage and removability.[102]

Others tactics used by ICE counsel include calling a noncitizen's family members to testify against the noncitizen regarding his or her place of birth or to introduce Form I-213 with statements taken from other family members who were present before, during, or after the noncitizen's arrest. ICE may also use information obtained from other sources, such as a school application obtained by a subpoena.[103] Counsel should consider opposing motions for subpoenas to the immigration court if it appears that ICE is on a fishing expedition to obtain information about the noncitizen's place of birth, nationality, and citizenship. Counsel can counter by asking the immigration judge to issue subpoenas for the release of law enforcement documents (*i.e.*, written policies, internal guidelines, etc.) and the appearance of federal and local law enforcement officers before the immigration court.

Finally, ICE may question a noncitizen on the stand to obtain information about his or her parents' nationality, citizenship, and immigration status in the United States. Counsel should be prepared to

---

[96] *See, e.g., Miguel v. INS*, 359 F.3d 408 (6th Cir. 2004) (holding that even when a noncitizen had a basis for a motion to suppress before the immigration court, the motion to suppress was moot because the noncitizen admitted the factual allegations that constituted the elements of the charge of removability before the immigration court).

[97] *Available at www.usdoj.gov/eoir/vll/OCIJPracManual/ocij_page1.htm.*

[98] 8 CFR §§208.3(c), 1208.3(c) (DHS can use information on an asylum application filed affirmatively to establish alienage in removal proceedings).

[99] *See Immigration Court Practice Manual*, ch. 5.10(c).

[100] *Matter of Tang*, 13 I&N Dec. 691 (BIA 1971).

[101] *See Kastigar v. U.S.*, 406 U.S. 441, 444 (1972); *Bigby v. INS*, 21 F.3d 1059 (11th Cir. 1994); *Tashnizi v. INS*, 585 F.2d 781 (5th Cir. 1978); *Matter of King & Yang*, 16 I&N Dec. 502 (BIA 1978).

[102] *U.S. ex rel. Bilokumsky v. Tod*, 263 U.S. 149, 154 (1928); *Matter of Guevara*, 20 I&N Dec. 238 (BIA 1991).

[103] 8 CFR §§1003.35, 1287.4(a)(2)(ii); *Immigration Court Practice Manual* ch. 4.20 and appxs. F and N.

object on the basis of relevancy and any other applicable grounds.

Negotiations and Pretrial Conferences with ICE Assistant Chief Counsel and the Immigration Court

Release from custody is the initial and often foremost concern of noncitizens detained by ICE. Counsel should interview a noncitizen client and anyone who witnessed the arrest to obtain as much credible information as possible before speaking with ICE assistant chief counsel about the noncitizen and her situation. In negotiations with ICE assistant chief counsel, counsel should be cautious and not stretch the "facts" about a noncitizen client and what happened during his or her arrest and detention. Likewise, counsel should not threaten to go to the media with a noncitizen client's story unless the noncitizen is prepared to do so and understands the impact that his or her family may face once the story is out.

Counsel should be on guard in discussions with ICE assistant chief counsel not to give information that could be used against the noncitizen in the removal proceedings part of the case. For example, ICE assistant chief counsel may insist on seeing foreign identity documents to verify a noncitizen's identity before agreeing to a bond or release on his or her own recognizance. Providing such a document to ICE may undermine a motion to suppress evidence in the removal proceedings, as this is evidence of citizenship and nationality that—ICE could argue—it obtained independently from the alleged violations that form the basis of a motion to suppress.

Often counsel tend to try to be agreeable in pretrial discussions or at an initial master calendar with the immigration court and ICE assistant chief counsel, in order to appear cooperative and noncombative. A motion to suppress, however, is almost never perceived as a routine matter and is likely to be viewed with hostility by ICE assistant chief counsel and possibly even the immigration judge. Counsel should be prepared mentally to encounter such a response. If counsel does not feel comfortable litigating a motion to suppress, counsel should refer the matter to another attorney or a legal services provider that is willing to take on the matter and zealously represent the noncitizen before the immigration court.

CONCLUSION

With the predicted increase in ICE enforcement actions, motions to suppress will continue to be a major tool for immigration counsel in the upcoming years. Additional theories not covered in this article are being litigated in motions to suppress around the United States, and new theories will be developed over time. Working together will be critical to raising the issues and developing circuit court of appeals precedent favorable to noncitizens whose rights have been violated by ICE and other law enforcement agencies. Through coordinated action, counsel can breathe new life into suppression motions in removal proceedings.

UPDATE 2008: CRIMES INVOLVING MORAL TURPITUDE, AGGRAVATED FELONIES, AND GOOD SOLUTIONS TO COMMON PROBLEMS

by Mary E. Kramer[*]

INTRODUCTION

In 2007 and early 2008, the federal courts and Board of Immigration Appeals (BIA) continued to issue significant decisions defining "crime involving moral turpitude" and "aggravated felony." Both the BIA and the courts claim to apply a categorical and modified categorical approach to defining these

[*] **Mary E. Kramer** has been in private practice for 17 years and is a sole practitioner in Miami. Her practice is limited to immigration law with a concentration on cases involving individuals with criminal records. She handles more than 150 cases per year involving adjustment of status, visa applications before consulates, naturalization and affirmative INA §212(c) waivers before U.S. Citizenship and Immigration Services, and representation of clients before the immigration courts and the Board of Immigration Appeals. Additionally, Ms. Kramer works with criminal lawyers on their pending criminal cases and cooperating witness work.

Ms. Kramer is a past-president of the AILA South Florida Chapter. She currently serves as liaison between the chapter and U.S. Immigration and Customs Enforcement's Detention and Removal Office, working on policies and standards involving the South Florida region's detention centers and deportation offices. She also serves on the board of directors of Catholic Charities Legal Services, Inc., a nonprofit organization assisting low-income people with immigration matters in South Florida.

Ms. Kramer was a founding co-supervising attorney of the AILA South Florida Legal Assistance Project, a pro bono project serving the Miami immigration court. In November 2002 she received the U.S. attorney general's Meritorious Public Service Award based on her work with this project, which was also featured in the March/April 2003 issue of AILA's *Immigration Law Today*. Ms. Kramer also volunteers for the Florida Bar, having recently finished a term as chair of a local grievance committee, and presently serving on a committee on unauthorized practice of law.

Ms. Kramer has authored numerous articles about, and has frequently lectured on, immigration consequences of criminal activity. She enjoys guest lecturing for law schools and colleges that teach aspects of immigration law.

Ms. Kramer graduated cum laude from the College of Saint Benedict, in St. Joseph, MN, and earned her J.D. from the University of Wisconsin at Madison. While in school, she interned for the Harlingen immigration court, and after graduation worked as a judicial law clerk to the Miami immigration court before entering private practice. Ms. Kramer is a member of the Wisconsin and Florida state bars.

terms. As case law reveals, however, the two entities are not always in agreement as to what these approaches mean or, more importantly, where they lead.

This chapter first summarizes a few recent decisions and highlights the importance of research, writing—and most of all—*appealing*, in criminal-alien cases. It then presents a series of scenarios highlighting client concerns in this new age of security checks, outdated resident cards, driver's license concerns, and the generally heightened level of enforcement.

CRIMES OF ASSAULT AND BATTERY

Moral Turpitude

In *Matter of Sejas,* the BIA held that simple assault and battery against a family or household member under Virginia law is not a crime involving moral turpitude.[1] The Board reiterated that neither the seriousness of a criminal offense nor the severity of the sentence imposed is determinative of whether a crime involves moral turpitude.[2] The Board further noted that it is the statutory elements or definition of the crime, as opposed to the specific conduct in the case, that determines whether a crime involves moral turpitude.[3] Applying these basic tenets, the Board observed that a conviction for assault and battery in Virginia does not require the actual infliction of physical injury and may include any touching, however slight. Without the intent to cause bodily harm, it could not be said that Virginia's statute necessarily described a crime involving moral turpitude. In reaching this conclusion, the Board relied upon its 2006 decision in *Matter of Sanudo,*[4] wherein it found that California's simple battery statute did not involve moral turpitude (nor was it a crime of violence[5]) because the statute

---

[1] *Matter of Sejas,* 24 I&N Dec. 236 (BIA 2007).

[2] *Matter of Serna,* 20 I&N Dec. 579, 581 (BIA 1992).

[3] *Matter of Torres-Varela,* 23 I&N Dec. 78 (BIA 2001).

[4] *Matter of Sanudo,* 23 I&N Dec. 968 (BIA 2006).

[5] Reference is made to the federal definition of crime of violence at 18 USC §16, which is the key definitional phrase for the domestic violence ground of removability at INA §237(a)(2)(E).

did not involve a specific intent to inflict bodily harm, and encompassed such innocuous conduct as touching.

A similar analysis was used by the Seventh Circuit in *Garcia-Meza v. Mukasey*,[6] wherein the court overturned the BIA and instead found that aggravated battery on a police officer under Illinois law was not a crime involving moral turpitude because the state statute did not include as an element that the officer sustain bodily injury. The court noted that the title, or caption, of an offense is not determinative to the inquiry of moral turpitude: "states are free to give whatever names they like to crimes. . . ."[7] Moreover, much of the behavior envisioned by the statute could be minor, such as spitting.[8] The court further found that the defendant's knowledge that the victim was a police officer did not determine moral turpitude. In the end, the court found that the BIA's analysis (that aggravated battery on a police officer did involve moral turpitude) represented a misapprehension of Illinois law and was accordingly vacated.

Aggravated Felony

Assault and battery offenses may also be relevant to the aggravated felony definition at §101(a)(43)(F) of the Immigration and Nationality Act (INA), which includes crimes of violence under 18 USC §16 where a sentence of imprisonment of one year or longer is imposed. Certainly these two classifications, aggravated felony crime of violence and crime involving moral turpitude, are not synonyms. Sometimes, an offense might qualify as an aggravated felony crime of violence, but not necessarily a crime involving moral turpitude—which requires that the act be "base, vile or depraved. . . ."[9] But there is overlap, and the two analyses can be hard to distinguish.

In *Hernandez v. U.S. Attorney General*,[10] the Eleventh Circuit reviewed Georgia's simple battery statute to determine whether a defendant/respondent who had been sentenced to 12 months imprisonment (suspended for probation, subsequently violated) for simple battery was removable as an aggravated felony. The statute in question contains two subsections:

> [A] person commits the offense of simple battery when he or she either: (1) Intentionally makes physical contact of an insulting or provoking nature with the person of another; or (2) Intentionally causes physical harm to another.[11]

Thus subsection (1) refers to any contact—which could include simple touching. Subsection (2) refers to intentional causation of physical harm. The Eleventh Circuit found that *both* subsections qualify as a "crime of violence" under 18 USC §16(a), concluding that even simple physical contact satisfied the "use of physical force" definition.[12] In so doing, the Eleventh Circuit specifically disagreed with the Seventh Circuit's decision in *Flores v. Ashcroft*,[13] and the Ninth Circuit's decision in *Ortega-Mendez v. Gonzales*,[14] regarding simple battery (touching, slight contact, etc.) not meeting the definition of "crime of violence." Note that although the Eleventh Circuit does not mention *Matter of Sanudo* or any other BIA precedent, *Sanudo* and *Sejas* (discussed above) rely heavily on *Ortega-Mendez v. Gonzales*. Accordingly, the Eleventh Circuit appears to take a more strict approach to the definition of "crime of violence" under 18 USC §16, which in turn affects its application in both the aggravated felony definition as well as crimes of domestic violence.[15] The Eleventh Circuit cites to a string of its own precedent wherein various battery-type crimes (aggravated battery, battery on an officer) were all found to be crimes of violence; this circuit's position is in strong contrast to both the BIA and its sister circuits.[16] Arguably, the Eleventh Circuit's position is too strict. Four years ago, the Supreme Court analyzed the term "crime of violence" in *Leocal v. Ashcroft*.[17] In *Leocal* the Court focused on the different criminal intent levels (specific intent, recklessness, and negligence) and found that acts of

---

[6] *Garcia-Meza v. Mukasey*, No. 07-2215, 2008 U.S. App. LEXIS 2487 (7th Cir. Feb. 5, 2008).

[7] *Id.*

[8] *Id.*

[9] *Matter of L–V–C*, 22 I&N Dec. 594 (BIA 1990); *Matter of Short*, 20 I&N Dec. 136 (BIA 1989).

[10] 513 F.3d 1336 (11th Cir. 2008).

[11] Ga. Code Ann. §§16-5-23(a)(1)–(2).

[12] 513 F.3d 1336, at 1341.

[13] 350 F.3d 666 (7th Cir. 2003).

[14] 450 F.3d 1010 (9th Cir. 2006).

[15] Crimes of domestic violence are a ground of removability at INA §237(a)(2)(E).

[16] *Compare Popal v. Gonzales*, 416 F.3d 249 (3d Cir. 2005) (finding that simple assault under 18 Pa. Cons. Stat. §2701(a) is not a crime of violence.)

[17] 543 U.S. 1 (2004).

negligence[18] do not meet the definition of "crime of violence." However, the Court's decision also includes helpful language regarding the phrase "crime of violence" in holding that the term requires the intentional employment of physical force that is "violent" in nature. Consider the following:

> In construing both parts of §16, we cannot forget that we ultimately are determining the meaning of the term "crime of violence." The ordinary meaning of this term, combined with §16's emphasis on the use of physical force against another person (or the risk of having to use such force in committing a crime), suggests a category of violent, active crimes that cannot be said naturally to include DUI offenses. [19]

It remains to be seen whether the Eleventh Circuit will ameliorate its strict interpretation of "crime of violence," or be instructed to do so (again, as *Leocal* originated in the Eleventh Circuit) by the Supreme Court. In any event, it is important that the various state statutes be reviewed on a case-by-case basis to determine the elements of the assault or battery-type crime in light of applicable case law, including both federal and BIA precedent.

FALSE VERSUS FRAUD

Crimes involving fraud or an intent to deceive are understood to be crimes involving moral turpitude.[20] Further, a conviction for a crime involving fraud or deceit where there is a loss to a victim exceeding $10,000 is an aggravated felony under INA §101(a)(43)(M). However, a false statement is not the equivalent of a fraudulent statement, and in certain cases—depending on the elements of the stat-ute—a false statement will not qualify as a crime involving moral turpitude.

In *Blanco v. Mukasey*,[21] the Ninth Circuit overturned the BIA and held that the misdemeanor crime of false identification to a peace officer under California Penal Code §148.9(a) was not a crime involving moral turpitude. This penal section states as follows:

> Any person who falsely represents or identifies himself or herself as another person or as a fictitious person to any peace officer . . . upon a lawful detention or arrest of the person, either to evade the process of the court, or to evade the proper identification of the person by the investigating officer is guilty of a misdemeanor.

The court noted that in order to obtain a conviction under this provision, the prosecutor does not need to show that the defendant had a specific intent to obtain a benefit or otherwise cause another to be liable on his behalf; in other words, the statute does not require a showing that the offender knowingly attempted to obtain anything of value.[22]

The court's general analysis on false versus fraud is more important than the actual offense at issue. The court wrote that a false statement translates into a fraudulent statement—hence a crime involving moral turpitude—only where the falsity is made with the intent to procure something of value; the false statement must be employed to obtain something tangible.[23] Where the only benefit is to evade or impede law enforcement, the crime does not involve moral turpitude.[24]

FAILURE TO REGISTER AS A SEX OFFENDER

Regulatory violations are generally found *not* to involve moral turpitude. In *Plasencia-Ayala v. Mukasey*,[25] the Ninth Circuit found that a conviction for

---

[18] Acts involving reckless behavior are dealt with on a case-by-case basis, and may or may not meet the definition of "crime of violence." The Supreme Court stated in *Leocal* that an act of recklessness may qualify as a crime of violence under 18 USC §16(b) if the act carries a significant risk that the use of physical force against another might be required in committing the crime; the classic example, provided by the Court, is burglary. *Leocal*, at 10. An act of recklessness will generally not qualify as a crime of violence under 18 USC subsection (a). *See, e.g.*, *Popal v. Gonzales*, 416 F.3d 249 (3d Cir. 2005). For further discussion on the levels of intent, including reckless behavior, *see* M. Kramer, *Immigration Consequences of Criminal Activity* (3rd Ed.), available from AILA Publications, *www.ailapubs.org*, (800) 982-2839.

[19] *Leocal* at 8.

[20] *Jordan v. DeGeorge*, 341 U.S. 223 (1951); *Matter of Bart*, 20 I&N Dec. 436 (BIA 1992).

[21] No. 06-71385, 2008 US. App. LEXIS 4497 (9th Cir. Mar. 3, 2008).

[22] *Id.* at 8.

[23] The federal courts and BIA have generally found that an offense involving a false statement as to a material fact is a crime involving moral turpitude. *See, e.g., Zaitona v. INS*, 9 F.3d 432, 437 (6th Cir. 1993). However, a false statement linked to deceit or trickery may also be a crime involving moral turpitude, without the element of materiality. Matter of Jurado, 24 I&N Dec. 29 (BIA 2006).

[24] *Blanco v. Mukasey, supra* note 21.

[25] No. 06-73728, 2008 U.S. App. LEXIS 2696 (9th Cir. Feb. 7, 2008).

failure to register as a sex offender in violation of Nevada law did not qualify as a crime involving moral turpitude because it caused no direct or particularized injury. The court distinguished between the preceding sexual offense—which the court termed "reprehensible"—from the act of registering, which was basically a law enforcement tool designed to prevent future sex crimes.[26] In this decision, the Ninth Circuit specifically criticizes the Board of Immigration Appeals' decision in *Matter of Tobar-Lobo,*[27] wherein the BIA found that a conviction for failure to register as a sex offender is a crime involving moral turpitude.

FIREARMS OFFENSES

Firearms offenses "described by" INA §101(a)(43)(E), which references certain federal firearm offenses under the United States Criminal Code, are aggravated felonies. Subsection (ii) references specific code sections under 18 USC §§922 and 924. In *Negrete-Rodriguez v. Mukasey,*[28] the Seventh Circuit Court of Appeals found that unlawful possession of a firearm by a felon in violation of an Illinois state statute could qualify as an aggravated felony offense under INA §101(a)(43)(E)(ii) even though it was not a federal conviction, and even though the state statute did not include a jurisdictional element of affecting commerce or other interstate nexus. In so doing, the court followed the BIA's analysis in an earlier case, *Matter of Vasquez-Muniz,*[29] and the Ninth Circuit in *United States v. Castillo-Rivera.*[30] Thus although the INA references specific federal statutes at INA §101(a)(43)(E), the courts are content to include state offenses that describe similar conduct within the definition of aggravated felony, even though the state statute lacks the essential federal jurisdictional element. The BIA and most recently the Ninth Circuit have found that the element of federal jurisdiction that renders the offense a federal crime need not be present in the state statute in order to comply with the "described by" language of §101(a)(43)(E). This appears at odds with those offenses that constitute aggravated

felonies only by way of reference to specific federal statutes, thus morphing a state statute, which lacks a critical element of the offense (jurisdiction), into an aggravated felony. This is also an apparent conflict with other sections of §101(a)(43)—where Congress wanted a broad description of offense conduct to qualify as an aggravated felony offense (for example, crimes of fraud or deceit, perjury, counterfeiting), it did not reference specific code sections.

CONTROLLED SUBSTANCE OFFENSES

In December 2007, the Board issued two side-by-side decisions that illustrate its understanding and application of the Supreme Court's decision in *Lopez v. Gonzales.*[31] The overall state of the law regarding state convictions for straight possession of a controlled substance is best described as fluid: the outcome in a particular case will vary depending upon the jurisdiction.

In *Lopez v. Gonzales,* the Supreme Court held that a state offense constitutes a "felony punishable under the Controlled Substance Act" only if it proscribes conduct *punishable* as a felony under federal law. For a state-controlled substance offense to qualify as an aggravated felony drug trafficking crime,[32] it must correspond to an offense under federal law that carries a maximum term of imprisonment exceeding one year. Under *Lopez,* the state's designation of a controlled substance violation as a felony or misdemeanor is not controlling; it is the federal law's hypothetical treatment of the offense that controls.

This holding in turn raised the question of whether a multiple (second or subsequent) offense for possession of a controlled substance—which can be punished as a felony under federal law—would automatically be considered an "aggravated felony" for immigration purposes, even though the state jurisdiction may consider a minor subsequent offense as a misdemeanor. The issue arises because federal law does indeed employ a recidivist procedure, which calls for specific charging requirements that must be followed in order to charge a subsequent offense as a felony.[33] A subsequent possession offense cannot be a felony unless these procedures are followed and a prior, final conviction is established. The "recidivist" argument defense attorneys now raise is that in the absence of a

---

[26] *Id.* at 23.

[27] 24 I&N Dec. 143 (BIA 2007).

[28] *Pablo Negrete-Rodriguez v. Michael B. Mukasey,* Nos. 06-1931 & 06-2938, 2008 U.S. App. LEXIS 4491 (7th Cir. March 3, 2008) (As of this writing, this decision has not been designated a federal reporter citation.)

[29] 23 I&N Dec. 207 (BIA 2002).

[30] 244 F.3d 1020 (9th Cir. 2001).

---

[31] 127 S.Ct. 625 (2006).

[32] INA §101(a)(43)(B).

[33] 21 USC §851, entitled "Proceedings to establish previous convictions."

recidivist statute existing and being followed in the particular state jurisdiction, it is not fair and cannot legally be argued that the controlled substance offense qualifies as a hypothetical federal felony— hence an aggravated felony.

Thus in *Matter of Carachuri-Rosendo*,[34] the Board found that absent controlling authority in the particular jurisdiction, an alien's subsequent (*e.g.,* second or multiple) state conviction for simple possession of a controlled substance will not qualify as an aggravated felony unless the defendant/respondent's status as a recidivist drug offender was either admitted by him or determined by the judge or jury, in the context of a recidivist prosecution. In *Carachuri,* which arose in the Fifth Circuit, the Board found that the respondent's second offense for possession of a controlled substance did qualify as an aggravated felony because of controlling precedent case law. The BIA referred to *United States v. Sanchez-Villalobos*,[35] wherein the court of appeals—in a sentencing guidelines case—held that the defendant's second offense was conduct punishable as a felony under the Controlled Substances Act. The Fifth Circuit did not require that the state conviction have been entered in a proceeding that complied with the procedural requirements for federal recidivist treatment in order to be considered a "felony under federal law." [36] The Board found that this analysis is "reconcilable" with the Supreme Court's holding in *Lopez*.[37]

A different result was reached based on a lack of controlling precedent in *Matter of Thomas*,[38] which involved a subsequent conviction for simple possession of a controlled substance in Florida—within the Eleventh Circuit. The Board found that the respondent's second offense for possession of a controlled substance did not qualify as an aggravated felony because the conviction did not arise from a state proceeding in which his status as a recidivist drug offender was either admitted or determined by a judge or jury. It would appear the Board's default position is that unless a circuit has specifically ruled otherwise, a second or subsequent (state) simple possession conviction will not be deemed an aggra-

vated felony unless the state has a criminal law procedure for charging as a recidivist and the prior offense(s) was specifically charged, pled to, and found by the judge or jury in arriving at a felony conviction. *Matter of Thomas* arose in the state of Florida, which does not have a specific recidivist procedure; apparently the conviction record contained no reference to a prior offense, nor an admission thereto.

The Element of Trafficking

It is important to recall that the above line of cases, starting with *Lopez*, address the issue of simple—or straight—possession offenses. A controlled substance offense that involves the element of illicit trafficking (sale, distribution, importation) will be considered a drug trafficking crime, even if classified as a misdemeanor by the state.[39] This point was reiterated in *Matter of Aruna*,[40] wherein the respondent was convicted of conspiracy to distribute marijuana, a misdemeanor under Maryland law. The respondent argued that federal law contains an exception for distribution of a small amount of marijuana for no remuneration,[41] and that there was no evidence in his case that remuneration was involved, or that the amount of drug involved was more than a "small amount." The respondent therefore argued that the misdemeanor conviction did not qualify as a hypothetical federal felony. The Board found that the classification "misdemeanor" was irrelevant to the analysis of whether this offense was an aggravated felony drug trafficking crime. The Board further found that in a federal prosecution the defendant has the burden of establishing no remuneration and a small amount; these are not elements of the crime that the prosecution must establish. Noting that the respondent did not attempt to establish either of these facts in his hearing before the immigration judge, the Board found that that the Maryland statute's elements correspond to the elements of the federal felony crime of conspiracy to distribute an indeterminate quantity of marijuana. Interestingly, the Board seems to leave open the window of possibility for respondents to establish as an evidentiary matter in immigration court the theory that their of-

---

[34] 24 I&N Dec. 382 (BIA 2007).

[35] 412 F.3d 572, 576–77 (5th Cir. 2005), cert. denied, 546 U.S. 1137 (2006).

[36] *Id.* at 576.

[37] *Matter of Carachuri*, 24 I&N Dec. 382, 386 (BIA 2007).

[38] 24 I&N Dec. 416 (BIA 2007).

---

[39] *Matter of Davis,* 20 I&N Dec. 536 (BIA 1992), *overruled in part on other grounds by Matter of Yanez-Garcia,* 23 I&N Dec. 390 (BIA 1992).

[40] 24 I&N Dec. 452 (BIA 2008).

[41] Reference is made to 21 USC §841(b)(4).

fense involved a small amount of marijuana, not for remuneration.[42]

CLIENT SCENARIOS: POSSIBLE SOLUTIONS TO TYPICAL (OR ATYPICAL) CASES

An attorney faces different situations when representing a lawful permanent resident (LPR). Some common situations are discussed below.

LPR with Aggravated Felony Firearm Conviction

Juan has been a lawful permanent resident for twenty years. In 1992, he was convicted in federal court of conspiracy to transfer machine guns in violation of 18 USC §371, the underlying conspiracy being 18 USC 922(o). This is his only conviction. It is now 2008. Without speaking to an attorney first, Juan applied for naturalization. He now comes to your law office, notice to appear (NTA) in hand; he is charged with removability under INA §§237(a)(2)(A)(iii) and 237(a)(2)(C). Incidentally, he is married to an American citizen and has three U.S. citizen children.

Is Juan removable? He is removable for an aggravated felony offense pursuant to the definition at INA §101(a)(43)(U) (attempts and conspiracies) as it relates to INA §101(a)(43)(E)(ii). Arguably, he is also removable for a firearms offense, even though the underlying conviction is actually conspiracy under 18 USC §371 (not a per se firearms offense). Whether he is removable for this second charge does not impact the finding of removability nor possible relief, as discussed below.

Juan is not eligible for cancellation of removal under INA §240A(a) because the conviction is an aggravated felony. He is not eligible for a pre-AEDPA (Antiterrorism and Effective Death Penalty Act of 1996) §212(c) waiver, even though the offense precedes 1996, because this waiver does not waive firearm offense or aggravated felony offenses with no corresponding ground of inadmissibility at INA §212(a).[43] However, for the same reason that §212(c) cannot waive an aggravated felony or firearms offense (because these are not grounds of inadmissibil-

ity), adjustment of status does act as a form of relief for Juan's aggravated felony/firearm conviction.[44] Juan is eligible to seek adjustment of status and readjust, but his spouse or an adult child will have to file immediately an I-130 visa petition. He is not in mandatory detention, and the immigration judge, it is hoped, will grant a continuance pending adjudication of the I-130.[45] No additional waiver is required.

Juan may be granted readjustment, hence avoiding removal. However, with a post–November 1990 conviction for an aggravated felony offense, he is not eligible for naturalization.[46] The only exception would be if Juan can obtain a full and unconditional executive pardon.[47] The regulations do allow a person with an aggravated felony conviction to go on to receive naturalization if they receive a full and unconditional pardon from either the governor (for a state offense) or the president (for a federal offense). (Note that receiving a pardon prior to removal proceedings would waive removability for the aggravated felony, but not the firearms offense; arguably the conviction would remain in effect for purposes of cancellation eligibility under §240A(a). Thus the client would still have to proceed on adjustment of status to waive the remaining firearm offense.)

LPR with Conviction; Needs to Renew Resident Card

Marcela comes to your office and shows you her expired resident card. She does not have a driver's license because it has also expired. She is afraid to apply for a new card because she has a 1995 conviction for controlled substance trafficking. For this offense, she served three months in jail and three years' probation. The Department of Homeland Security does not know about this conviction. She became a lawful permanent resident in 1992. She is

---

[42] *Matter of Aruna*, 24 I&N Dec. 452, 457–58, note 5 (BIA 2008). The Third Circuit has charted a different course. *Jeune v. Att'y Gen.*, 476 F.3d 199 (3d Cir. 2007) (DHS must prove it is not a small amount of marijuana distributed for no remuneration).

[43] *Matter of Blake*, 23 I&N Dec. 722 (BIA 2005).

[44] *Matter of Rainford*, 20 I&N Dec. 598 (BIA 1992); *Matter of Kanga,* 22 I&N Dec. 1206 (BIA 2000). However, *see Ali v. Mukasey*, No. 07-1970 (7th Cir. Apr. 4, 2008) (review of presentence report found elements of fraud in a conspiracy to traffic in firearms case, sustaining a finding of crime of moral turpitude, thus requiring a §212(h) waiver for which the alien was not eligible).

[45] Another twist would be if Juan had some other basis for adjustment of status; for example, a Cuban national could readjust under the Cuban Adjustment Act without an underlying petition.

[46] An aggravated felony conviction entered after November 29, 1990 (IMMACT90), is a bar to establishing good moral character for purposes of naturalization. INA §101(f)(8).

[47] 8 CFR §316.10(c)(2).

single, but cares for her elderly parents, who are U.S. citizens. They are in their 80s, have various health problems, including the fact that her mother is blind. She has no other siblings. She is from a country in West Africa. Marcela has no other convictions.

Marcela is subject to removal for the controlled substance offense.[48] She is not subject to mandatory detention because the offense predates October 8, 1998. If she applies for a new resident card, she will provide biometrics, and DHS will ask her to provide certified copies of her conviction record. At that point, one of two things may happen: DHS might send her a new resident card and take no enforcement action against her, or, they may issue an NTA. If placed in removal proceedings, Marcela is eligible for a waiver under the pre-AEDPA INA §212(c). Again, she is not mandatory detention. Thus taking an action to trigger removal proceedings may not be a bad idea, as it could potentially resolve the problem; however, the risk is that she will not receive a waiver and instead be ordered removed.

This is not counsel's decision. It is Marcela's. Counsel's role is to explain the possible scenarios and explain the balancing criteria of §212(c); obviously, her parents' age, illness, and dependence upon her will be the key to this case, along with other relevant criteria as set forth in case law.[49]

One strategy—depending on everything else being in order (such as taxes and employment history)—would be to file affirmatively for §212(c) with USCIS and also file form I-90 to replace the expired card. Three facts—that Marcela's offense occurred twelve years ago, her parents' are dependent on her, and her native country is in Africa—work together for a strong waiver case, and an affirmative application in a relaxed, informal interview setting is the best solution. The alternative is to spend the rest of her life afraid of DHS, holding on to an expired card, and worse yet, confront DHS when her parents have passed away and her strongest equities no longer exist. Again, assuming other relevant factors in Marcela's life are in good order, an affirmative waiver is the best alternative.

Another viable strategy, depending upon the law of the state, would be to seek post-conviction relief (a vacatur of the conviction) so that Marcela would no longer be removable for the conviction.[50] Bearing in mind that once she receives the waiver, Marcela is no longer prejudiced by the conviction, post-conviction relief must be sought prior to a waiver being granted. Post-conviction relief criteria varies by state; if a motion to vacate is a meritorious and viable option, it is preferable to simply seeking §212(c) because, even with a grant of §212(c), Marcela is barred from receiving naturalization unless she can one day receive a pardon.[51]

Legal Permanent Residence and §212(h)

Boris is a native and citizen of a former country of the USSR, and is Jewish. He and his family members were admitted as refugees in July 1, 1997, when he was still a teenager. They applied for adjustment of status on July 1, 1998. In January 1999, they were approved for residency, but received a rollback date of July 1, 1997. Boris' resident cards states he is a resident since July 1, 1997.

On or about August 1, 2002, Boris was involved in bank fraud involving three transactions. His activities were not detected for over a year, and would have gone undetected, except that a co-conspirator was arrested on unrelated charges one day and turned Boris in. On August 1, 2005, while returning from a trip abroad, he was admitted by U.S. Customs and Border Protection (CBP) but arrested by federal authorities. He was eventually convicted, sentenced to three months in prison, a period of probation, and $9,000 restitution. Upon release from prison, Boris was transferred to an Immigration and Customs Enforcement (ICE) detention facility. The notice to appear was served on July 1, 2007.

Boris was charged with commission of one crime involving moral turpitude within five years of the date of entry under INA §237(a)(2)(A)(i)(I).

Boris is eligible for bond, and counsel asks for a bond hearing. He is not mandatory detention because he is charged with only one crime and he served less than one year.[52] Boris is released on bond. At the master hearing, counsel moves to dis-

---

[48] INA §§237(a)(2)(A)(i), (a)(2)(A)(iii), and (a)(2)(B).

[49] See, e.g., Matter of Marin, 16 I&N Dec. 581 (BIA 1978).

[50] Prior to filing a motion to vacate a conviction, counsel should review Matter of Pickering, 23 I&N Dec. 621 (BIA 2003), rev'd, Pickering v. Gonzales, 465 F. 3d 263 (6th Cir. 2006). A motion to vacate must meet certain standards set by the BIA (and affirmed by most federal courts) in order to be viable for immigration law purposes—i.e., effectively eliminating the conviction.

[51] See notes 41 and 42, supra.

[52] INA §236(c).

miss the charge and terminate removal proceedings because the commission of the crime occurred more than five years after the date of admission, the operative date being the rollback date. The immigration judge denies the motion to terminate, finding that the date Boris was actually adjusted (as a clerical matter) is the operative date for purposes of §237(a)(2)(A)(i)(I). Counsel could file an interlocutory appeal on this issue alone, but the BIA rarely reviews interlocutory appeals, so counsel reserves appeal on removability and moves on.[53]

Boris is not eligible for cancellation of removal under INA §240A(a) because he did not accumulate an ongoing lawful residence before commission of the crime. He was admitted on July 1, 1997; the offense was in August of 2002, which tolled the continuous residence period.[54] Boris does not have the required seven years.

However, counsel applies for a waiver under INA §212(h). Boris is eligible for this waiver because he has not been convicted of an aggravated felony (loss under $10,000) and the seven-year required residence period for 212(h) purposes tolls upon filing of the NTA with the court (or service upon the respondent, depending upon the jurisdiction)—Boris accumulated 12 years of an ongoing lawful residence prior to initiation of proceedings.

Counsel successfully argues that Boris does not need a concurrent adjustment of status application, even though these are "deportation track" proceedings under INA §237, because Boris was inadmissible at the time of admission; accordingly, he seeks nunc pro tunc approval of his §212(h) waiver.[55] The application for a waiver is retroactive to the date of his last admission. However, if the IJ did insist on an application for adjustment, Boris' wife is a U.S. citizen and may file an I-130 petition for him. In the exercise of caution, this petition should be filed early on in the course of representation, so that the petition is approved, or at least pending, when and if the issue of a concurrent adjustment arises.

Based on extreme hardship to his parents, spouse, and two U.S. citizen children, Boris receives a waiver under INA §212(h).[56]

Cooperating Witness and Family Members

Felix is from a country in South America known for its problems with drug trafficking, cartels, and armed guerilla and paramilitary groups. There is a heavy U.S. law enforcement presence in this country. He and his family members have been brought to the United States on special public benefit paroles (SPBP) by the FBI. Felix is under federal indictment for money laundering and racketeering; however, he is also cooperating with the FBI against his former "colleagues"—members of the cartel that he did business with. His wife, two children, and parents were paroled in for their safety along with Felix. The FBI is worried for their safety. The FBI is also responsible for their presence in the United States and must monitor their status. The FBI and Felix relate to counsel that the cartel members against whom he is now cooperating are associated with a paramilitary organization in the country (designated as a terrorist group by the U.S. State Department) that finances their political mission in large part with funds derived from drug trafficking. Felix has information about the paramilitary organization's operations. Felix and his family members have been promised protection and "S" status from the FBI. What can counsel do to help? What are counsel's recommendations?

Counsel recommends asylum applications for Felix's family members. (Note with these serious charges, whether convicted or not, Felix is unlikely to qualify for asylum; however, this scenario is about taking care of family members.) Years ago, the recommendation may have been nonimmigrant visas such as E or L. However, with increased scrutiny (background checks) at American consulates, it is quite possible that the spouse and parents of Felix will not be issued visas on account of the family connection. Certainly the source of wealth or funds for an E or L will be closely scrutinized.

The key to a successful asylum application is establishing and explaining the link between the cartel and the paramilitary group, explaining that the ille-

---

[53] Counsel is aware that Boris could have been charged with multiple offenses based on multiple transactions; this would make Boris mandatory detention. Thus counsel preserves the issue for appeal but does not file an interlocutory appeal.

[54] INA §240A(d). *Matter of Perez*, 22 I&N Dec. 689 (BIA 1999) (stop time rule applies at time of commission of crime, not conviction).

[55] *Matter of Abosi*, 24 I&N Dec. 204 (BIA 2007), which must be read in conjunction with *Matter of Sanchez*, 17 I&N Dec. 218 (BIA 1980).

[56] Note there is an argument to be made that Boris is also eligible for a waiver under INA §209(c), but ICE would likely contest an LPR filing for a §209(c) waiver, as the BIA has ruled that an LPR cannot apply for a refugee waiver. *Matter of S–I–K–*, 24 I&N Dec. 324 (BIA 2007); *Matter of Smriko*, 23 I&N Dec. 836 (BIA 2005).

gal activity is a means of perpetuating the essentially political mission. Admittedly, in cases like this (which can be seen, actually, in troubled countries across the globe) is that the lines between illegal activity and political goals becomes blurred; it is counsel's job through research and writing to articulate the complicated situation and establish a nexus.[57] Asylum in this case is based on imputed political opinion and social group (family/cooperating witnesses).

The arrival with "SPBP" (witness) paroles is a strong, key start: the U.S. government believed these persons were in danger and whisked them away from the home country. And clearly, the law enforcement agency's willingness to assist with an affidavit or testimony, confirming the facts and developing the link with the paramilitary organization, is a key component of the case. With the law enforcement agency's assistance, an asylum case is very strong. Moreover, the agency is generally pleased to assist because a grant of asylum means they are no longer responsible for the family and corresponding paperwork.

The elusive S status is often thrown around in initial plea negotiations. The truth is, S status is very hard to obtain and takes a long time. Even with outstanding cooperation and a dedicated, loyal agent, the application must go through a high bureaucratic ladder and there is no guarantee of success. Felix is not eligible for asylum because of his criminal activity, but at least counsel can ensure the family members are safe and taken care of. It would be a major mistake to forego asylum and let the family members wait years for S status. Asylum should be filed within one year of admission.[58] If it is not approved, there is no law or regulation that says the agency cannot file for S status for family members later.

---

[57] *See* the enumerated grounds for asylum at INA §101(a)(42) and INA §208(b). For more background information on the law of asylum, *see* R. Germain, *AILA's Asylum Primer* (5th Ed.), available from AILA Publications, *www.ailapubs.org*, (800) 982-2839.

[58] INA §208(a)(2)(B).

UNDERSTANDING ACCESS TO FEDERAL AND STATE PUBLIC BENEFITS FOR IMMIGRANT VICTIMS OF DOMESTIC VIOLENCE

by Julie E. Dinnerstein and Barbara Weiner*

INTRODUCTION

The year 1996 is remembered by most immigration lawyers as the year that gave us the Antiterrorism and Effective Death Penalty Act[1] and the Illegal Immigration Reform and Immigrant Responsibility Act (IIRAIRA).[2] But for those of us working with poor clients on a regular basis, 1996 also is remembered as the year that brought us the Personal Responsibility and Work Opportunity Reconciliation Act (PRWORA).[3] With the stroke of a pen, President Bill Clinton fulfilled his campaign promise to fundamentally "change welfare as we know it."[4] As one reporter noted at the time, "[i]n a sweeping reversal of Federal policy, President Clinton today ended six decades of guaranteed help to the nation's poorest children by signing into law a vast welfare overhaul requiring the 50 states to deal more directly with the social burdens and the budget expense of poverty."[5] Practically speaking, this historic change has meant that advocates assisting clients in accessing public benefits must navigate a complicated 50-state hodgepodge of a system in which rules for eligibility may vary state by state. By changing federally funded assistance from an entitlement program to a block grant program with a combination of options for and restrictions on states' use of federal funds, each state must, to a certain extent, chart its own course in administering welfare programs. Into this complicated patchwork, the federal government implemented a wave of restrictions on immigrant access to benefits.

In this article, we map out some of the key concepts in immigrant access to public benefits in the post-1996 regime[6] and focus on how the law plays out for some particularly vulnerable groups of immigrants—those who have been victimized by domestic violence and other, gender-related forms of harm. As New Yorkers, we tend to reference the laws of New York by way of example, but the ap-

* **Julie E. Dinnerstein** is the co-director of Sanctuary for Families' Immigration Intervention and Brooklyn Family Justice Center Legal Projects. She also teaches immigration law at the School of Professional Studies at the City University of New York and serves as a part-time counselor at the Center for Public Interest Law, Columbia Law School. Previous positions include deputy director for immigration policy and training at the New York Immigration Coalition, associate at Cleary, Gottlieb, Steen & Hamilton, and law clerk to the Honorable Jack B. Weinstein of the U.S. District Court for the Eastern District of New York. Ms. Dinnerstein is a recipient of the Columbia Law School Public Interest Law Foundation's 2005 Public Interest Achievement Award and an honoree at the 8th Annual AILA New York Chapter Immigration Law Symposium. Ms. Dinnerstein is a graduate of Columbia College and Columbia Law School, where she served as an editor on the *Columbia Journal of Gender and Law* and the *Columbia Law Review*.

Since 1990, **Barbara Weiner** has been a staff attorney with the Empire Justice Center, a statewide legal services support center that provides advice and training to both lawyers and community advocates who serve the low-income community across New York. The Empire Justice Center is also a public interest law firm that has undertaken major impact litigation in poverty law areas, including public benefits, housing, and health. Ms. Weiner has been co-counsel in several of these cases. Ms. Weiner's practice focuses on public-benefits law, in particular the Food Stamp Program. She also provides representation to low-income immigrants, particularly to victims of domestic violence and to immigrants in need of public benefits. She is an expert on the impact of immigration status on the access of noncitizens to federal, state, and local public-benefit programs. Ms. Weiner has provided substantial training and technical assistance to local legal services programs and community advocates in these areas. In addition, she regularly meets with the public benefits policy staff at the New York Office of Temporary and Disability Assistance to further the interests of the low-income community in the state's administration of its public benefit programs.

[1] Pub. L. No. 104-132, 110 Stat. 1214.

[2] Pub. L. No. 104-208, div. C, 110 Stat. 3009, 3009-546 to 3009-724.

[3] Pub. L. No. 104-93, 110 Stat. 2105.

[4] F. Clines, "Clinton Signs Bill Cutting Welfare; States in New Role," *N.Y. Times* (Aug. 23, 1996), *available via search at www.nytimes.com*.

[5] *Id.*

[6] This article offers a brief introduction to immigrant access to public benefits. For a more in-depth treatment of this topic along with a state-by-state review, see National Immigration Law Center (NILC), *Guide to Immigrant Eligibility for Federal Programs* 39 (4th Ed. 2002), and the ongoing updates to this book posted at *www.nilc.org/pubs/Guide_update.htm*.

proach we use illustrates how attorneys in every state of the union can walk through federal law and the provisions in their own states.

Key Concepts

The Federal/State Divide

In most states, basic benefit programs for the assistance of low-income individuals and families, such as cash assistance and health insurance programs, have both a federal and state dimension. For example, New York has both a cash assistance program that is funded through federal, state, and local funds (the Family Assistance program) and a program funded solely with state and local dollars (the Safety Net program).[7] Generally the state or local benefit agency administering these programs first will determine whether the applicant is eligible for the federally funded program. It is only if the applicant is ineligible for the federally funded program that a determination will be made whether the applicant may be eligible for comparable benefits under a state-funded program.

With PRWORA, the federal government explicitly authorized state governments to pick and choose among public benefits eligibility options for some lawful immigrants for federally funded cash (Temporary Aid to Needy Families (TANF)) and health insurance (Medicaid) programs,[8] and to restrict immigrants' access to state programs (as long as immigrants in the state are subject to the same restrictions to state-administered federally funded programs).[9] For example, federal funds may be—but are not required to be—used to provide cash assistance to certain lawful permanent residents (LPRs). A state could choose *not* to grant cash assistance to LPRs, imposing even more restrictive prohibitions on immigrant access than the federal government, as long as the same rules applied to state-funded cash assistance programs. While as far as the authors are aware, no state has taken up the federal government

on this opportunity to reject federal dollars for lawful immigrants, the intent was to allow states to impose even harsher restrictions on immigrant access to public benefits than those authorized by Congress.

Finally, PRWORA purported to prohibit states from providing benefits to any noncitizen unless he or she is in a federally qualified status, has a nonimmigrant visa, or has been paroled into the United States on a humanitarian basis, except "through the enactment of a State law after August 22, 1996, which affirmatively provides for such eligibility."[10] The authority of Congress to impose such a requirement on the states with respect to the states' own programs has not been tested in the courts.

The Creation of the "Qualified Alien"

In 1996, for the first time, Congress embedded immigrant eligibility rules for public benefits directly into Title 8 of the U.S. Code, which contains the Immigration and Nationality Act (INA)[11] and other provisions governing noncitizens in the United States. This centralized approach, attempting to corral all the immigrant restrictions into one location within Title 8, signaled a new drive to incorporate public-benefit rules into national immigration policy.[12] Previously, immigrant access provisions were scattered throughout the U.S. Code and placed within the statutory provisions relating to the programs in question.

The mechanism for implementing these centralized restrictions came through the congressional creation of a new benefits-related eligibility category, "qualified alien,"[13] a classification that includes, in its current amended form:

- LPRs;[14]
- asylees, refugees, and those granted withholding of removal under the INA[15]

---

[7] *See* N.Y. Soc. Serv. Law §§122(a), (b) (describing noncitizen eligibility for Family Assistance, New York's cash assistance program that includes federal Temporary Aid to Needy Families (TANF) funds), and (c) (describing noncitizen eligibility for Safety Net Assistance, New York's non-federally funded cash assistance program, for noncitizens who are qualified immigrants not yet eligible for federally funded assistance and noncitizen permanently residing under color of law (PRUCOL)).

[8] 8 USC §1612(b)(1).

[9] 8 USC §1624.

[10] 8 USC §1621(d). One imagines that the expectation was that it would be difficult for a state to affirmatively and publicly enact legislation that provided benefits to people not lawfully in the country. In reality, some states did just that. *See, e.g.,* 1997 N.Y. Laws 436 (Aug. 20, 1997).

[11] Pub. L. No. 82-414, 66 Stat. 163.

[12] *See, e.g.,* 8 USC §1601(2)(a) (stating that noncitizens "within the Nation's borders [should] not depend on public resources to meet their needs").

[13] 8 USC §1641. Note that in this article, except where statutory text is explicitly quoted, a "qualified alien" is referred to as "qualified immigrant."

[14] 8 USC §1641(b)(1).

- parolees for one year or more;[16]

- Cuban/Haitian entrants;[17] and

- some, but by no means all, battered immigrants.[18]

In addition, under this new regime, some groups within the qualified immigrant classification—for example, the humanitarian-related categories, Cuban/Haitian entrants, and Amerasians—are given enhanced access to benefit programs as compared to the qualified immigrant group as a whole.[19] Victims of trafficking who have been granted continued presence or T nonimmigrant status, categories not in existence when PRWORA was enacted, are added to the group receiving special treatment.[20]

Others, including some LPRs currently or formerly in the military, as well as those who can be credited with a substantial work history, also are singled out for special treatment.[21] Not only do all of these groups have enhanced access to federal benefit programs, they cannot be excluded by the states from participation in state-funded programs.[22]

Still other groups, such as Canadian-born Native Americans residing in the United States, members of certain Indian tribes, and lawfully residing Hmong

and Highland Laotians, though not included in the qualified immigrant category, are explicitly provided access to certain federal programs.[23]

In true Orwellian fashion, however, noncitizens who are "qualified aliens" under federal law may find that they are not actually qualified to receive any of the public benefits they seek. As one provision of Title 8 helpfully explains, "[i]n general[, n]otwithstanding any other provision of law and except as provided . . . an alien who is a qualified alien . . . is *not* eligible for any specified Federal Program. . . ."[24] For a number of programs, eligibility lies not in the fact of being a qualified immigrant alone but rather in finding one's way into one of the myriad of exceptions to the general bar to eligibility imposed on qualified immigrants. In other words, eligibility often involves being a qualified alien plus meeting some additional eligibility criteria, which vary across the covered programs. Determining that a noncitizen is a qualified immigrant is just the first step in the intricate analysis of eligibility review, which must include a program-by-program analysis and a review of the federal *and* state legislative regime in place in your state.

It is worth noting that this effort to consolidate benefit eligibility criteria for noncitizens in Title 8, begun in 1996, remains incomplete to this day, leaving some contradictory passages in federal statute,[25] as well as seemingly unintentional inconsistencies in immigrant eligibility across programs.[26] In other words, the conundrum that is the "qualified alien" of 8 USC §1641 in all its incoherent glory does not even directly relate back to all immigrant restrictions across the federal program spectrum.

The End of "PRUCOL" as We Knew It

In the decade preceding 1996, an eligibility concept known as PRUCOL developed in public benefits law. PRUCOL is an acronym for "permanently residing under color of law." Noncitizens who were not LPRs but were residing indefinitely in the United

---

[15] 8 USC §§1641(b)(2) (asylees), (3) (refugees), (5) (withholding under the INA), and (6) (relating to "conditional entrants," the term used prior to 1980 for refugees admitted to the United States).

[16] 8 USC §1641(b)(4).

[17] 8 USC §1641(b)(7).

[18] 8 USC §1641(c).

[19] 8 USC §1612(a)(2).

[20] *See* 22 USC §7105(b)(1)(A) ("[A]n alien who is a victim of a severe form of trafficking in persons shall be eligible for benefits and services under any Federal or State program or activity funded or administered by any official or agency described in subparagraph (B) to the same extent as an alien who is admitted to the United States as a refugee under section 207 of the Immigration and Nationality Act."). Under the terms outlined in 22 USC §§7105(b)(1)(C) and (E), a trafficked noncitizen who has not yet been granted or even applied for T nonimmigrant status may be certified by the secretary of health and human services as "a person whose continued presence in the United States the Attorney General and the Secretary of Homeland Security is ensuring in order to effectuate prosecution of traffickers in persons." 22 USC §7105(b)(1)(E)(i)(II)(bb). A noncitizen who has received such certification is generally referred to as someone who is in "continued presence" for public benefits purposes.

[21] 8 USC §§1612(a)(2)(B), (C).

[22] 8 USC §1622(b).

[23] 8 USC §§1612(a)(2)(G), (K)

[24] 8 USC §1612(a)(1) (emphasis added).

[25] *See, e.g.,* 7 USC §2015(f); 8 USC §§1612(a)(2)(D)(ii), (G), (I), (J), (K), and (L) (providing contradictory criteria for immigrant eligibility for food stamps, with the provisions in Title 8 generally followed over those in Title 7).

[26] *See, e.g.,* 42 USC §1436a(a) (housing) and 20 USC §1091(a)(5) (financial aid for education), which contain immigrant eligibility criteria never directly linked to the immigrant eligibility criteria in Title 8.

States and in circumstances in which they were not likely to be deported were called PRUCOL. As such, within each benefit program, they were considered eligible for benefits.

This concept of PRUCOL is entirely related to benefit eligibility and has no function in immigration law. Through promulgation of program-specific regulations and litigation, each federal program came to define the PRUCOL classification somewhat differently. In the Supplemental Security Income (SSI) context, the PRUCOL category came to have one of its most expansive definitions, when a federal court held, in the year before the PRUCOL category was eliminated from federal law, that:

> PRUCOL includes "any . . . alien residing in the United States 'with the knowledge and permission' of the [Immigration and Naturalization Service (INS)], whose departure the INS 'does not contemplate enforcing.'" . . . . The term "does not contemplate enforcing" includes aliens whose residence in the United States is "continued by virtue of official permission or acquiescence." . . . The expansive definition of PRUCOL . . . must . . . include scenarios in which INS does not respond to requests by the Commissioner, yet in which official acquiescence to an individual's presence is nevertheless present. . . . Such a situation would be present when INS is made aware on numerous occasions of the presence of an illegal alien yet does not take action to enforce the departure.[27]

Until the 1996 welfare reform legislation, this concept of PRUCOL eligibility was used in determining eligibility in both federal and state benefits. With the 1996 legislation, PRUCOL as a benefit eligibility classification for federal programs was entirely eliminated. A few of the categories that were previously included in the concept of PRUCOL, such as asylum and humanitarian parole, were taken into the qualified immigrant classification, but most other categories were simply eliminated as grounds for federal benefits eligibility.

However, in the years since 1996, some states have continued to provide state benefits to immigrants considered PRUCOL.[28] As with the prior federal use of the term, even within a state the contours of the definition of PRUCOL vary between benefit programs.[29]

Federal Means-Tested Public Benefits

In determining whether a noncitizen is affected by many of the strict immigration restrictions of PRWORA, one must frequently determine whether a benefit in question is a "federal means-tested public benefit." While PRWORA, as amended, defined a number of programs that are *not* federal means-tested public benefits,[30] identifying which programs are federal means-tested benefits was left to individual administrative agencies. Ultimately, by *Federal Register* notice and other announcements, the following federal programs have been identified as federal means-tested benefits:

- Supplemental Security Income (SSI);[31]
- Medicaid;[32]
- TANF;[33]
- Food Stamps;[34] and

---

for unemployment benefits for any noncitizen who "was permanently residing in the United States under color of law at the time the [employment] services [for which unemployment benefits are sought] were performed"); N.Y. Soc. Serv. Law §122(c) (eligibility for state-funded cash and medical assistance programs for noncitizens who are PRUCOL).

[29] In New York, for example, those in PRUCOL are eligible for both state-funded cash and medical assistance programs. *See* N.Y. Soc. Serv. Law §122(c), as modified by *Aliessa v. Novello*, 96 N.Y.2d 418 (2001). However, the definition of PRUCOL for the cash assistance program is much narrower than the definition of PRUCOL for the medical assistance program. Compare General Information System (GIS) Message, R. Sykes, "Permanently Residing Under the Color of Law (PRUCOL)" (Feb. 20, 2007), *available at http://otda .state.ny.us/main/gis/2007/07dc001.rtf* (describing those in PRUCOL eligible for New York's cash assistance program) with the much more expansive definition of PRUCOL used for the state's medical assistance program described in New York Department of Health Informational Letter, D. Bachrach, "Clarification of PRUCOL Status for Purposes of Medicaid Eligibility" (Mar. 15, 2007), *available at www.health.state .ny.us/health_care/medicaid/publications/docs/inf/07inf-2.pdf* (describing those in PRUCOL who are eligible for New York's medical assistance program).

[30] 8 USC §1613(c)(2) (a list which, as amended, includes supplemental nutrition program for Women, Infant and Children (WIC), school breakfast and lunch programs, Head Start, and food stamps for children under 18).

[31] 62 Fed. Reg. 45284 (Aug. 26, 1997).

[32] 62 Fed. Reg. 45256 (Aug. 26, 1997).

[33] *Id.*

---

[27] *Farjam v. Comm'r of the Social Security Administration,* No. CV-94-4486, 1995 U.S. Dist. LEXIS 21418, at *11–*13 (2d Cir. Aug. 18, 1995) (internal citations omitted).

[28] *See, e.g.,* Cal. Code Regs. tit. 22, §50301(a)(4) (listing noncitizens who are PRUCOL as "eligible for full Medi-Cal benefits"); Me. Rev. Stat. Ann. tit. 26, §1192.11 (eligibility

continued

- State Children's Health Insurance Program (SCHIP)[35]

It is noteworthy that the Department of Housing and Urban Development failed to identify any housing program as a federal-means tested public benefit, so no housing programs are covered by this term.[36]

The Five-Year Bar

Subject to a host of exceptions, a noncitizen entering the United States after August 22, 1996, "is not eligible for any Federal means-tested public benefit for a period of 5 years beginning on the date of the alien's entry into the United States with a status within the meaning of the term 'qualified alien.'"[37] As there are a number of qualified immigrant statuses that a noncitizen may pass through on his or her way to becoming an LPR, counting the number of years a noncitizen has been in qualified immigrant status can be a daunting task. Furthermore, as the nature of the five-year bar varies depending on a variety of factors—including, but not limited to, the program for which eligibility is sought, the particular immigration status of the qualified immigrant, and certain demographic characteristics (such as age and disability)[38]—identifying which noncitizen is subject to the five year bar is never as easy as the kind of counting to five you learned in kindergarten.

40 Quarters

PRWORA provides that LPRs who can be credited with 40 qualifying quarters are eligible for most state and federal benefit programs without restriction. It is only LPRs, not all qualified immigrants, who get all of the advantages of the special 40-quarter rules. Thus, in the post-1996 regime, knowing the number of Social Security "qualifying quarters"[39] with which an LPR can be credited has be-

came critical. Unfortunately, many people in the benefits-eligibility world (government administrators, advocates or immigrants themselves) find it challenging to figure out just how to count to 40 quarters (which is not surprising when you consider the just mentioned challenges of counting to five).[40]

The first issue, of course, is what constitutes a "qualifying quarter." The National Immigration Law Center (NILC) has described the term in plain English:

> Qualifying quarters are determined based on the total amount of a worker's earnings each year, without regard to the months in which the work was performed (i.e., with sufficient earnings, all four quarters could be credited based on income earned in a single quarter).[41]

As NILC goes on to explain, "[t]he amount of earnings needed to earn a qualifying quarter changes each year."[42] In 2001, for example, a person needed to earn and pay taxes in the United States on $3,320 in order to be credited with all four qualifying quarters for the calendar year.[43]

The second issue is whose quarters an individual gets to count. In addition to his or her own quarters, an LPR can count any quarters credited to (1) his or her parents before the noncitizen's 18th birthday;[44] and (2) his or her spouse during the course of the marriage, as long as the couple is (a) still legally married, or (b) the noncitizen is a surviving widow.[45] Note, however, that that the noncitizen cannot get any credit for any quarter after 1996 dur-

---

[34] 63 Fed. Reg. 36653 (July 7, 1998). Note, however, that by statutory amendment, food stamps to children under 18 are not considered a "federal means-tested benefit" for purposes of the five-year bar. 8 USC §1613(c)(2)(L).

[35] Letter from Sally K. Richardson, Director, Center for Medicaid and State Operations, Health Care Financing Administration and Claude Earl Fox, M.D., M.P.H., Acting Administrator, Health Resources and Service Administration, to State Health Officials (Jan. 14, 1998), available at www.cms.hhs.gov/smdl/downloads/sho011498.pdf.

[36] 65 Fed. Reg. 49994 (Aug. 16, 2000).

[37] 8 USC §1613(a).

[38] 8 USC §1613(b).

[39] See 42 USC §401 et seq.

[40] Fortunately, actual counting is not required. A person may request his or her own Social Security Statement by phone call or in writing. For information, see www.ssa.gov/mystatement/. With respecting to finding out about family members' quarters which may be credited to a noncitizen, while there is no direct way for a noncitizen to find out about his or her family members' qualifying quarters, the benefits granting agency from which the noncitizen seeks a benefit is authorized to obtain the information directly from the Department of Social Security. 8 USC §1645 ("[T]he Commissioner of Social Security is authorized to disclose quarters of coverage information concerning an alien and an alien's spouse or parents to a government agency for the purposes of this title.").

[41] NILC Guide, supra note 6, at 39 (describing the post-1978 method for determining quarters).

[42] Id.

[43] Id. at 40.

[44] 8 USC §1645.

[45] Id.; see also INA §213A(a)(3)(B); 8 USC §1183a(a)(3)(B).

ing which the noncitizen or the relevant family member received a "Federal means-tested public benefit."[46]

The third issue is why you should care. As we shall see, the concept of 40 quarters matters in determining eligibility for SSI and, for some, food stamps.

Affidavits of Support

As most immigration practitioners are well aware, family-sponsored immigrants and those sponsored by family businesses must generally submit an enforceable affidavit of support in connection with their applications for LPR status.[47] In the affidavit of support, the sponsor agrees to provide financial support to the intending immigrant when he or she becomes an LPR.[48]

Affidavits of support remain in effect until either the sponsor dies or the sponsored immigrant (1) becomes a citizen; (2) may be credited with 40 quarters; (3) abandons his or her LPR status; (4) has his or her LPR status terminated and then readjusts to LPR status on a new basis; or (5) dies.[49] Termination of the familial relationship, for example, through divorce, does not end the affidavit of support obligation.[50]

The affidavits of support lead to three specific issues discussed in turn below: sponsor deeming, sponsor liability, and reporting.

Sponsor Deeming

During the period in which an affidavit of support is in effect, an LPR applying for any federal means-tested benefit is treated as having access to the money of the financial sponsor who signed an affidavit of support on that LPR's behalf.[51] This is often a legal fiction, because if the LPR did indeed have access to support from his or her financial sponsor, he or she would likely not be seeking a public benefit.

From a practical perspective, if the LPR "would, in the absence of the assistance provided by the agency, be unable to obtain food and shelter,"[52] the sponsor-deeming provisions of the law will not prevent an LPR from accessing public benefits. This is known as the "indigence exception" to sponsor deeming.

In addition, a sponsored immigrant who is a victim of domestic violence at the hands of her sponsor or the sponsor's family living in the same household will also be exempted from having the income and resources of the sponsor deemed to her.[53]

Sponsor Liability

Any government or nongovernmental entity can seek reimbursement for any means-tested public benefits provided to an LPR from that LPR's financial sponsor who signed an affidavit of support under INA §213A.[54] Much to the chagrin of anti-immigrant zealots, few government entities have taken advantage of this option.[55]

Reporting

There are two distinct issues with respect to reporting.

---

[46] INA §213A(a)(3)(A)(ii); 8 USC §1183a(a)(3)(A)(ii) (with respect to the noncitizen's own work and taxpaying history); INA §213A(a)(3)(B); 8 USC §1183a(a)(3)(B); 8 USC §1645 (with respect to the relevant family member's work and taxpaying history).

[47] INA §§212(a)(4)(C), (D); 8 USC §§1182(a)(4)(C), (D); INA §213A; 8 USC §1183a. An extended discussion of current affidavit of support rules is beyond the scope of this article. A good discussion of the current requirements can be found in C. Wheeler, "New Affidavit of Support Rules and How They Affect Your Practice," 11-15 *Bender's Immigr. Bull.* 1 (Aug. 1, 2006).

[48] INA §213A(a)(1); 8 USC §1183a(a)(1).

[49] 8 USC §1631(b); INA §§213A(a)(2), (3); 8 USC §§1183a(a)(2), (3); 8 CFR §213a.2(e)(2).

[50] *See Stump v. Stump,* No. 1:04-CV-253-TS 2005, 2005 U.S. Dist LEXIS 45729 (N.D. Ind. May 27, 2005), 2005 U.S. Dist LEXIS 26022 (N.D. Ind. Oct. 25, 2005) (allowing a sponsored immigrant to seek support from a divorcing spouse based on an affidavit of support). For criticism of the *Stump* court's position with respect to whether a private right of action lies in connection with an affidavit of support, see C. Wheeler, "Alien vs. Sponsor: Legal Enforceability of the Affidavit of Support," 10-23 *Bender's Immigr. Bull.* 3 (Dec. 1, 2005).

[51] 8 USC §1631(a).

[52] 8 USC §1631(e).

[53] 8 USC §1631(f).

[54] INA §§213A(b), (c); 8 USC §§1183a(b), (c).

[55] K. Beaucar Vlahos, "Lawmaker: Immigration Sponsors Should Repay Welfare Saturday," *FoxNews.com* (Mar. 22, 2003), *available at www.foxnews.com/story/0,2933,81894, 00.html* (describing concerns of Representative Tom Tancredo and Dan Stein, executive director of the Federation for American Immigration Reform, that states have not pursued financial sponsors for reimbursement).

First, if a sponsored immigrant avails him- or herself of the indigence exception to sponsor deeming and successfully obtains public benefits despite the existence of a current, enforceable affidavit of support, the government entity distributing the public benefit is supposed to send the name of both sponsor and sponsored immigrant to federal immigration authorities.[56] There is little evidence of any agency sending this information to federal immigration authorities and, to the extent that any agency has done so, it does not appear that federal immigration authorities have done much, if anything, with such information.

Second (and unrelated to the existence of an affidavit of support), state and federal agencies administering certain programs are required to report "the name and address of, and other identifying information on, any individual who the [state, or federal agency, as the case may be] knows is not lawfully present in the United States"[57] to federal immigration authorities. Federal agencies have taken a narrow view of what it means to "know" that someone is not lawfully present, finding only that knowledge of a final, unreviewable order of deportation, exclusion, or removal rises to the level of knowledge of a noncitizen's unlawful presence.[58]

These reporting requirements, while not always clearly understood either by immigrants or employees of benefit-granting agencies, have had a chilling effect on the willingness of households with immigrant family members to apply for benefits on behalf of *any* household member, including U.S. citizen children who face no immigration status bars to access.[59]

Public Charge

Finally, there is the issue of public charge. Noncitizens who are found "likely at any time to become a public charge"[60] are inadmissible. This means that noncitizens seeking nonimmigrant visas, as well as those seeking to become LPRs, may be denied status on the basis of being likely to become a public charge.[61] For family-sponsored immigrants as well as those sponsored by family-owned businesses to overcome this bar, as noted above, they must have affidavits of support filed in connection with their applications to become LPRs.[62] In addition, regardless of whether the intending immigrant falls into a category that requires an affidavit of support, a government officer adjudicating the application of a would-be LPR must engage in a general analysis of factors relating to the noncitizen's likelihood of needing public benefits in the future,[63] which analysis includes a review of past receipt of some public benefits.[64]

Concern with respect to public charge is widespread, and keeps immigrants away from receiving public benefits, even those benefits that have no effect on their immigration status.[65] Furthermore, "[t]he misapplication [by some government agencies] of the public charge ground of inadmissibility has contributed significantly to the chilling effect on immigrants' access to services."[66]

Despite the fear and the confusion, the field guidance issued by the Department of Justice provides clear guidelines as to which benefits may be considered with respect to a "totality of the circumstances" review.[67] Under the field guidance, only "[c]ash assistance for income maintenance and institutionalization for long-term care at government expense may be considered for public charge purposes."[68] The receipt of past or current income maintenance benefits does not necessarily require a finding of inadmissibility on public charge grounds.

---

[56] 8 USC §1631(e)(2); 8 CFR 213a.4(c).

[57] 42 USC §608(g) (TANF); 42 USC §1383(e) (SSI); 42 USC §1437y (low-income housing).

[58] 65 Fed. Reg. 58301 (Aug. 28, 2000).

[59] *See generally* T. Broder, "Overview of Immigrant Eligibility for Federal Programs" (Oct. 2007), *available at* www.nilc.org/immspbs/special/pb_issues_overview_2007-10 .pdf; N. Bernstein, "Recourse Grows Slim for Immigrants Who Fall Ill," *N.Y. Times* (Mar. 3, 2006), *available via* search at www.nytimes.com.

[60] INA §212(a)(4)(A); 8 USC §1182(a)(4)(A).

[61] INA §212(a)(4); 8 USC §1182(a)(4). As most immigration lawyers know, but many others do not realize, accessing public benefits does not affect an LPR's eligibility to become a U.S. citizen.

[62] INA §§212(a)(4)(C), (D); 8 USC §§1182(a)(4)(C), (D).

[63] INA §212(a)(4)B); 8 USC §1182(a)(4)(B).

[64] 64 Fed. Reg. 28689 (May 26, 1999). Note that this field guidance, issued nine years ago, remains, at the time of this writing, the most recent federal pronouncement on what immigration adjudicators should consider in making public charge determinations.

[65] *See, e.g.,* N. Bernstein, *supra* note 59 (describing immigrant fears of seeking health care).

[66] T. Broder, *supra* note 59, at 5.

[67] 64 Fed. Reg. 28689, 28690 (May 26, 1999).

[68] *Id.* at 28692.

As the field guidance further explains, "[p]ast or current receipt of such cash benefits does not lead to a *per se* determination that an alien is . . . inadmissible . . . as a public charge. Rather, such benefits should be taken into account under the totality of the circumstances test. . . ."[69]

Perhaps most significant, and most commonly forgotten, are a list of "supplemental non-cash benefits or special-purpose cash benefits that [a noncitizen] may receive that should *not* be considered for public charge purposes."[70] These benefits include:[71]

1. Medicaid and other health insurance and health services (including public assistance for immunizations and for testing and treatment of symptoms of communicable diseases; use of health clinics, short-term rehabilitation services, and emergency medical services) other than support for long-term institutional care;

2. State Children's Health Insurance Program (SCHIP);

3. Nutrition programs, including Food Stamps, the Special Supplemental Nutrition Program for Women, Infants and Children (WIC), the National School Lunch and School Breakfast Program, and other supplementary and emergency food assistance programs;

4. Housing benefits;

5. Child care services;

6. Energy assistance, such as the Low Income Home Energy Assistance Program (LIHEAP);

7. Emergency disaster relief;

8. Foster care and adoption assistance;

9. Educational assistance, including benefits under the Head Start Act[72] and aid for elementary, secondary, or higher education;

10. Job training programs; and

11. In-kind, community-based programs, services, or assistance (such as soup kitchens, crisis counseling and intervention, and short-term shelter).

From this review of key concepts, we turn next to how these concepts affect immigrants seeking bene-

fits, with a focus on immigrant victims of domestic violence.

Vulnerable Immigrants

Immigrant victims of domestic violence and other forms of violence, such as sexual assault and trafficking, are often those in most desperate need of public benefits, to escape violence and secure safety and stability for themselves and their children. Unfortunately, due to complicated rules for accessing public benefits, many do not receive the benefits for which they are eligible.

Some immigrant victims either have (or are eligible for) immigration status relating to the violence that they have suffered. The rules relating to public benefits eligibility often track the specific, abuse-related basis on which the victims have sought to obtain, or already have obtained, immigration status.

These victims include those who are eligible for immigration status based on their relationship to abusive U.S. citizens or LPRs,[73] including those eligible to file:

▪ Violence Against Women Act (VAWA) self-petitions on Form I-360;[74]

▪ Battered spouse and child waivers petitions on Form I-751;[75]

▪ VAWA suspension of deportation on Form EOIR-40;[76] and

---

[69] *Id.*

[70] *Id.* at 28693.

[71] *Id.* (internal citations omitted).

[72] 42 USC §9801 *et seq.*

[73] For a summary of these forms of relief, see J. Dinnerstein, "Options for Immigrant Victims of Domestic Violence," *Immigration & Nationality Law Handbook* 482 (AILA 2007–08 Ed.).

[74] VAWA self-petitions on Form I-360 are filed pursuant to INA §§204(a)(1)(A)(iii) (abused spouse of U.S. citizen (USC)); (iv) (abused child of USC); (vii) (abused parent of USC); (B)(ii) (abused spouse of LPR); and (iii) (abused child of LPR). Approved VAWA self-petitioners are granted deferred action status, which can be renewed every year until they become LPRs. Those VAWA self-petitioners related to abusive USCs are usually eligible to apply for adjustment of status and become LPRs and become LPRs relatively quickly, whereas those VAWA self-petitioners related to abusive LPRs generally must wait several years until they become eligible to apply for adjustment of status and become LPRs.

[75] Battered spouse and child waiver petitions are filed on Form I-751. *See* INA §216(c)(4)(C). On approval, battered spouse or child waiver petitioners are LPRs without condition.

[76] VAWA suspension applications on Form EOIR-40 are filed pursuant to INA §244(a)(3) (as in effect before the title III-A effective date in IIRAIRA §309). On approval, VAWA suspension applicants become LPRs.

- VAWA cancellation on Form EOIR-42B.[77]

Other immigrants are eligible for immigration status based on having been trafficked[78] or been victims of criminal activity who have cooperated with the investigation or prosecution of criminal activity committed against them.[79]

Finally, despite the fact that neither the statute nor the regulations relating to asylum have been revised to include gender-related violence,[80] those fleeing gender violence are increasingly successful in obtaining asylum.[81]

Other immigrant victims of domestic violence may have no connection between the violence that they experience and their current immigration status (such as immigrants sponsored for LPR status by employers or nonabusive family members or those in temporary, nonimmigrant statuses) or lack of immigration status (such as those with no current prospects for obtaining immigration status and those who are the beneficiaries of approved or pending immigrant relative petitions filed by nonabusive family members). In these cases, there is often little to no correlation between the public benefits sought, the violence suffered, and the noncitizen's immigration status.

We now review how a noncitizen's experience as a victim of domestic violence or a gender-related harm may or may not affect the applicability of some of the key concepts reviewed above.

The Federal/State Divide

While the federal/state divide generally will not affect access to public benefits for victims, it is worth exploring whether your state has any special rules regarding access to benefits or special programs providing services to immigrant victims.[82] The state programs may require only that the noncitizen be a victim[83] or, alternatively, may be tied to an application for or grant of a specific immigration benefit for victims.[84]

The "Qualified Alien" Designation

Some noncitizens are qualified immigrants because they are (1) domestic violence victims; (2) seeking certain forms of immigration relief; and (3) need the benefits that they seek to escape the domestic violence.[85] In order to be a qualified immigrant in this manner, a noncitizen must be the spouse or child (but not parent) of an abusive U.S. citizen or LPR, and must have filed and made out a prima facie case for, or had approved, one of the following forms of relief:

- a VAWA self-petition on Form I-360[86]

- a VAWA cancellation application on Form EOIR-42B[87]

- a VAWA suspension on Form EOIR-40[88]

In addition, abused spouses and children of U.S. citizens and LPRs who are the beneficiaries of ap-

---

[77] VAWA cancellation applications on Form EOIR-42B are filed pursuant to INA §240A(b)(2). On approval, VAWA cancellation applicants become LPRs.

[78] INA §101(a)(15)(T); 8 USC §1101(a)(15)(T); INA §214(o); 8 USC §1184(o); 8 CFR §214.11 (relating to T nonimmigrant status); INA §245(l); 8 USC §1255(l) (adjustment of status for those in T nonimmigrant status); see also 22 USC §§7105(b)(1)(C), (E) (relating to certification of continued presence in connection with public benefits access for victims of trafficking).

[79] INA §101(a)(15)(U); 8 USC §1101(a)(15)(U); INA §214(p); 8 USC §1184(p); 8 CFR §214.14 (relating to U nonimmigrant status); INA §245(m); 8 USC §1255(m) (adjustment of status for those in U nonimmigrant status).

[80] Cf. 65 Fed. Reg. 76588 (Dec. 7, 2000) (proposed rule meant to "aid in the assessment of claims made by applicants who have suffered or fear domestic violence," which has never been promulgated in interim or final form).

[81] While a discussion of gender-based violence is beyond the scope of this article, those interested in learning about the latest developments in case law, statutes, and regulations, as well as a history of asylum for victims of gender-based violence, are advised to consult the comprehensive information and resources available at the website of the Center for Gender and Refugee Studies, http://cgrs.uchastings.edu/.

[82] See, e.g., Or. Rev. Stat. §411.117(1)(f) (providing access to state TANF program for noncitizen victims of domestic violence who might not otherwise be eligible); Fla. Stat. §409.9531(1) (mandating the Department of Children and Family Services to "[p]rovide services to immigrant survivors of human trafficking, domestic violence, and other serious crimes, during the interim period between the time the survivor applies for a visa and receives such visa from the United States Department of Homeland Security or receives certification from the United States Department of Health and Human Services").

[83] See, e.g., Or. Rev. Stat. §411.117(1)(f).

[84] See, e.g., Fla. Stat. §409.9531(1).

[85] 8 USC §1641(c).

[86] 8 USC §1641(c)(1)(B)(i) (family of abusive U.S. citizens), (ii) (family of abusive LPRs).

[87] 8 USC §1641(c)(1)(B)(iii).

[88] 8 USC §1641(c)(1)(B)(v).

proved or pending immigrant relative petitions on Form I-130 petitions filed by their abusive spouse or parent are also designated as qualified immigrants, without any specific requirement that they file for an immigration benefit relating to the abuse.[89]

As noted, some victims of gender violence obtain asylum, refugee, or withholding of removal status. As asylees, refugees, or persons granted withholding under the INA, these noncitizens are also qualified immigrants.[90]

Finally, those granted continued presence or T nonimmigrant status, while not technically qualified immigrants, are eligible for benefits on the same basis as refugees in qualified immigrant status.[91]

The End of PRUCOL as We Knew It

For those who live in states in which PRUCOL remains a meaningful category for public benefits eligibility, an application for or the granting of any victim-related form of immigration status may bring a noncitizen into the PRUCOL category. In New York, for example, a noncitizen granted interim relief under the U visa statute is considered PRUCOL and eligible for cash assistance.[92]

Federal Means-Tested Public Benefits

The fact that a noncitizen is a victim or is seeking or has been granted a victim-related immigration benefit generally will not enhance the access of that noncitizen to programs defined as "federal means-tested benefits," unless the victim has obtained asylum, refugee, continued presence, or T status based on the violence.[93]

The Five-Year Bar

Victims in asylum, refugee, continued presence, and T status are not subject to the five-year bar in ac-

cessing federal means-tested benefits.[94] With the exception of federal food-stamp eligibility for qualified immigrants under 18,[95] all other immigrant victims are subject to the five-year bar, whether or not they have been granted a victim-related immigration status.

40 Quarters

To the extent that eligibility for a benefit program is made easier for LPRs who can be credited with 40 qualifying work quarters, an immigrant victim may be able to take advantage of the abusive spouse's or parent's work history. Even after a domestic violence victim has fled an abusive spouse or parent, as long at the abuser remains the legal spouse—or in the case of a noncitizen under 18, the parent—of that noncitizen, he or she can continue to count the quarters of the abuser.[96] In practical terms, for example, if you represent a domestic violence victim who is an LPR and who has been married to her spouse for five years, during which time both spouses worked full-time and paid taxes (thereby being credited with 20 quarters each), it may be in the victim's best interest to stay legally married in order to ensure that she can access the public benefits she needs.

Affidavits of Support

For an immigrant victim of domestic violence who has obtained conditional or permanent resident status based on the Form I-130 filed by an abusive family member, the affidavit of support in no way will be affected by the fact that the immigrant has suffered domestic violence. (Conversely, if a victim of domestic violence has sponsored a family member who has obtained conditional or permanent resident status, the fact of victimization does nothing to relieve the victim from the obligations of the affidavit of support.)

If a noncitizen is seeking to become an LPR based on any of the forms of relief that are specific to victims of violence, no affidavit of support is required.[97]

---

[89] 8 USC §1641(c)(1)(B)(iv). Advocates should be on the lookout not only for I-130 approval notices, but other documents, such as a V visa or an expired conditional green card, that provide evidence of a filed or approved I-130.

[90] 8 USC §1641(b).

[91] See 22 USC §7105(b)(1)(A) ("[A]n alien who is a victim of a severe form of trafficking in persons shall be eligible for benefits and services under any Federal or State program or activity funded or administered by any official or agency described in subparagraph (B) to the same extent as an alien who is admitted to the United States as a refugee under section 207 of the Immigration and Nationality Act").

[92] GIS Message, supra note 29.

[93] 8 USC §1613(b)(1); 22 USC §7105(b)(1)(A).

[94] 8 USC §1613(b)(1); 22 USC §7105(b)(1)(A).

[95] 8 USC §1613(c)(2)(L).

[96] 8 USC §1645.

[97] The affidavit of support requirement is described in the public charge ground of inadmissibility under INA §§212(a)(4)(C)(ii), (D). If a noncitizen is not subject to the public charge ground of inadmissibility or is explicitly exempt from the affidavit of support requirement, no affidavit of support is required. See INA §207(c); 8 USC §1159(c) (explicitly exempting refugees and asylees seeking to adjust

continued

Sponsor Deeming

For immigrants who have obtained conditional or permanent immigration status based on an abusive spouse's or parent's sponsorship, in addition to the exception for the indigent,[98] there is a specific exception for domestic violence victims.[99] A noncitizen must be out of the household of the abusive family member and establish a connection between the abuse and the need for a benefit in order to qualify for this exception to sponsor deeming.[100] In addition, after the first 12 months in which a noncitizen avails him- or herself of this sponsor deeming exception, there must be some form of recognition of the abuse either by a judge (who may be an administrative judge) in the form of an order, or by federal immigration authorities.[101]

Sponsor Liability

When an affidavit of support is in effect, the victimization of the sponsored immigrant (or the sponsor) will in no way affect sponsor liability.

Reporting

Reporting requirements are not affected by the victimization of a noncitizen.

Public Charge

As noted above, most noncitizens seeking to become LPRs in connection with a form of immigration relief specific for victims of domestic and other forms of violence are not required to establish that they are not likely to become a public charge as part of their applications for LPR status. In addition, it is worth noting that there is an explicit provision barring consideration of any public benefits that a noncitizen has received under the special rules for do-

mestic violence victims who are qualified immigrants under 8 USC §1641(c) in making a public charge determination.[102]

Benefits Eligibility

At long last, after having reviewed a number of the public benefits concepts that pervade the post-1996 world, and having reviewed how immigrant victims of domestic and other forms of violence are impacted by those concepts, we finally arrive at a review of eligibility for public benefits for these vulnerable immigrants.

Income Maintenance Programs (Cash)

Temporary Aid to Need Families

Victims in asylum, refugee, continued presence, and T status are immediately eligible for federal TANF benefits.[103] Other victims, whether or not they have been granted a victim-related immigration status, have no special access to federally funded TANF, but rather do not become eligible until they have been qualified immigrants for five years.[104]

Many states, however, have TANF-replacement programs.[105] As noted above, some of these replacement programs are linked specifically to a nonimmigrant's status as a domestic violence victim or as a current or potential beneficiary of a special form of immigrant relief for victims.[106]

---

status from the public charge ground of inadmissibility); INA §212(a)(4)(C)(i)(III); 8 USC §1182(a)(4)(C)(i)(III) (exempting VAWA self-petitioners and derivatives from the affidavit of support requirement); INA §240A(b)(2)(iv); 8 USC §1229b(b)(2)(iv) (no requirement that those seeking VAWA cancellation overcome the public charge ground of inadmissibility); INA §245(*l*); 8 USC §1255(*l*) (allowing for a waiver of the public charge ground of inadmissibility for those in T nonimmigrant status seeking to adjust status); INA §245(m); 8 USC §1255(m) (no requirement that those in U nonimmigrant status seeking to adjust status overcome the public charge ground of inadmissibility).

[98] 8 USC §1631(e).

[99] 8 USC §1631(f).

[100] *Id.*

[101] *Id.*

[102] INA §212(s); 8 USC §1182(s).

[103] 8 USC §1613(b)(1) (exempting, among others, asylees and refugees, from the bar to federal means-tested benefits until noncitizens have been qualified immigrants for five years); 22 USC §7105(b)(1)(A) (granting those in continued presence and T nonimmigrant status access to the same benefits as refugees); 62 Fed. Reg. 45256 (Aug. 26, 1997) (designating TANF as a federal means-tested public benefit).

[104] 8 USC §1613(a) (describing bar to federal means-tested benefits until noncitizens have been qualified immigrants for five years); 62 Fed. Reg. 45256 (Aug. 26, 1997) (designating TANF as a federal means-tested public benefit).

[105] T. Broder, *supra* note 59, at 4.4. For a list of state-funded replacement programs, see NILC *Guide, supra* note 6, at table 8.

[106] *See, e.g.,* Or. Rev. Stat. §411.117(1)(f) (relating to domestic violence victims); Fla. Stat. §409.9531(1) (relating to victims applying for certain forms of immigration relief); New York State Office of Temporary and Disability Assistance Informational Letter, R. Sykes, "Battered Aliens Eligibility for Benefits" (06-INF-14, rev. May 5, 2006), *available at* www.otda.state.ny.us/main/directives/2006/INF/06-INF-14.pdf (describing cash assistance eligibility of VAWA self-petitioners).

It is also critical to remember that "[i]n nearly all states, eligible children may receive TANF even if their parents are ineligible based on their immigration status."[107]

Supplemental Security Income

Victims in asylum, refugee, continued presence, and T status are eligible for SSI only during their first seven years in such status.[108] Otherwise, all victims are subject to the same rules that make SSI inaccessible to the majority of immigrants who are not yet naturalized citizens.[109]

A handful of states have SSI-replacement programs,[110] one of which, in California, takes into consideration whether the noncitizen may have been trafficked or may be eligible for U nonimmigrant status as a crime victim.[111]

Health Insurance

Medicaid and State Children's Health Insurance Program

Victims in asylum, refugee, continued presence, and T status are eligible for Medicaid.[112] Other victims, whether or not they have been granted a victim-related immigration status, have no special access to federally-funded Medicaid and SCHIP, but

rather do not become eligible until they have been qualified immigrants for five years.[113]

Many states, however, have health insurance replacement programs,[114] one of which, in California, takes into consideration whether the noncitizen may have been trafficked or may be eligible for U nonimmigrant status as a crime victim.[115]

Emergency Medicaid

There are no immigrant access restrictions on emergency Medicaid.[116]

Food

Food Stamps

Victims in asylum, refugee, continued presence, and T status are eligible for food stamps.[117] Other victims, whether or not they have been granted a victim-related immigration status, generally have no special access to federally-funded food stamps, but rather do not become eligible until they have been qualified immigrants for five years.[118]

Note, however, that there is an important exception to this more general rule denying access to food stamps during the first five years in qualified immigrant status. All noncitizens *under 18* who are in qualified immigrant status are immediately eligible for food stamps, regardless of time in qualified immigrant status.[119] This means, for example, that

---

[107] NILC *Guide*, *supra* note 6, at 100.

[108] 8 USC §1612(a)(2)(A) (describing time-limited exception to general rule limiting access to SSI to noncitizens for those in asylee and refugee status during their first seven years in such status); 22 USC §7105(b)(1)(A) (granting those in continued presence and T nonimmigrant status access to the same benefits as refugees).

[109] *See* 8 USC §1612(a)(3)(A) (identifying SSI as a program for which qualified immigrants are generally *not* eligible); 8 USC §1612(a)(2) (listing categories of exceptions to the general rule that qualified immigrants are not eligible for SSI).

[110] For a list of state-funded replacement programs, see NILC *Guide*, *supra* note 6, at table 9.

[111] *Id.*

[112] 8 USC §1612(b)(2)(a)(i) (exempting refugees and asylees, among others, from bar on accessing Medicaid during first seven years in status); 22 USC §7105(b)(1)(A) (granting those in continued presence and T nonimmigrant status access to the same benefits as refugees); 8 USC §1613(b)(1) (exempting refugees and asylees, among others, from five-year bar on accessing federal means-tested benefits); 62 Fed. Reg. 45256 (Aug. 26, 1997) (designating Medicaid as a federal means-tested public benefit).

[113] 8 USC §1613(a) (describing bar to federal means-tested benefits until noncitizens have been qualified immigrants for five years); 62 Fed. Reg. 45256 (Aug. 26, 1997) (designating Medicaid as a federal means-tested public benefit); Letter from Sally K. Richardson, *supra* note 35 (designating SCHIP as a federal means-tested benefit).

[114] For a list of state-funded replacement programs, see NILC *Guide*, *supra* note 6, at tables 10 and 11.

[115] *Id.*

[116] 8 USC §§1611(b)(1)(A), 1613(c)(2)(A).

[117] 8 USC §1613(b)(1) (exempting, among others, asylees and refugees, from the bar to federal means-tested benefits until noncitizens have been qualified immigrants); 22 USC §7105(b)(1)(A) (granting those in continued presence and T nonimmigrant status access to the same benefits as refugees); 63 Fed. Reg. 36653 (July 7, 1998) (designating food stamps as a federal means-tested benefit).

[118] 8 USC §1613(a) (describing bar to federal means-tested benefits until noncitizens have been qualified immigrants for five years); 63 Fed. Reg. 36653 (July 7, 1998) (designating food stamps as a federal means-tested benefit).

[119] 8 USC §1613(c)(2)(L) (food stamps to children under 18 defined by statute not to be a "federal means-tested benefit," and thus qualified immigrants under 18 are not subject to the

continued

children of adult VAWA self-petitioners, as well as VAWA self-petitioning children, as qualified immigrants,[120] are eligible for food stamps as soon as they receive prima facie determinations on their self-petitions.

Women, Infant, and Children

There are no immigration restrictions on access to supplemental nutrition programs for pregnant women, nursing mothers during their infants' first year of life, and children through their fifth birthdays.[121]

School Breakfast and School Lunch Programs

There are no immigration restrictions on access to school breakfast and school lunch programs.[122]

Housing

Long-Term Housing

Victims in asylum, refugee, continued presence, and T status are eligible for federally funded housing subsidies.[123] Other victims, whether or not they have been granted a victim-related immigration status, generally have no special access to federally funded housing.[124]

Crisis Shelter

There are no immigrant restrictions on federal funds for crisis shelters.[125] Practitioners are advised, however, to learn the actual practices of local shelters for domestic violence victims and others in need of short-term shelter, to determine how noncitizens are treated and what limitations on access there are, if any, based on immigration status.

Child Care

In determining eligibility for child care assistance, with respect to programs in which there is an immigration status requirement, it is status of the child, not the parent or guardian, that is taken into consideration.[126] With respect to child care programs funded through Head Start, there are no immigration restrictions.[127]

Education

Head Start Through 12th Grade

Free public school education, from Head Start through 12th grade, cannot be denied to children based on immigration status, or lack thereof.[128]

University Education

Tuition. IIRAIRA explicitly sought to prevent states from offering in-state tuition rates to all students living within a state without regard to immigration status.[129] The relevant IIRAIRA provision, however, only relates to noncitizens who are "not

---

five-year bar to federal-means tested benefits when it comes to food stamps).

[120] 8 USC §1641(c)(1)(B).

[121] 8 USC §1613(c)(2)(D) (exemption of WIC from immigration restrictions); 42 USC §1786 (describing eligibility for WIC).

[122] 8 USC §1613(c)(2)(c) (exemption of school breakfast and lunch programs from immigration restrictions); 42 USC §1751 *et seq.* (describing the school breakfast and lunch programs).

[123] 42 USC §1436a(a)(3) (describing access of asylees and refugees to housing); 22 USC §7105(b)(1)(A) (granting those in continued presence and T nonimmigrant status access to the same benefits as refugees).

[124] Note that immigrant eligibility rules for federally funded long-term housing assistance do not track eligibility rules in 8 USC §1641 (defining qualified immigrants).

[125] 8 USC §§1611(b)(1)(D), (c)(2)(G).

[126] U.S. Department of Health and Human Services (DHHS), Administration on Children, Youth and Families (ACYF), Program Instruction, J. Harrell, "Clarification of Interpretation of 'Federal Public Benefit' Regarding Child Care and Development Fund (CCDF) Services" (ACYF-PI-CC-98-08, Nov. 25, 1998), *available at www.acf.hhs.gov/programs/ccb/law/guidance/current/pi9808/pi9808.htm.*

[127] *Id.* ("Head Start and Early Head Start have been determined not to provide 'Federal public benefits' because non-post secondary education benefits were expressly omitted from the statutory definition in title IV of PRWORA. Therefore, Head Start providers are not required to implement PRWORA's verification requirements."); 8 USC §1613(c)(2)(J) (indicating that Head Start is not a federal means-tested public benefit program).

[128] *Plyler v. Doe*, 457 U.S. 202 (1982) (holding based on the Equal Protection Clause of the 14ht Amendment to the U.S. Constitution); *see also* 8 USC §1611(c)(1)(B) (defining a "Federal Public Benefit" to include postsecondary education, but not primary or secondary education); 8 USC §1613(c)(2)(J) (indicating that Head Start is not a federal means-tested public benefit; 8 USC §§1613(c)(2)(H), (I) (indicating that certain programs relating to primary and secondary education are not federal means-tested public benefits); DHS ACYF Program Instruction, *supra* note 126.

[129] *See* 8 USC §1623 ("Notwithstanding any other provision of law, an alien who is not lawfully present in the United States shall not be eligible on the basis of residence within a State (or a political subdivision) for any postsecondary education benefit unless a citizen or national of the United States is eligible for such a benefit (in no less an amount, duration, and scope) without regard to whether the citizen or national is such a resident.").

lawfully present."[130] As victims granted any of the victim-related immigration statuses discussed in this article are all "lawfully present," none should be excluded from in-state tuition on the basis of this provision; the reality of who is excluded from in-state tuition, however, is likely to vary state to state.

Furthermore, a number of states have found ways around the immigration prohibitions altogether. They find routes for providing in-state tuition rates to those who attend and graduate from in-state high schools, or, in at least one state, from in-state General Education Diploma (GED) programs.[131]

Financial Aid. Although there are no restrictions on private loans, grants, and scholarships, federal law and regulation limit federal financial aid to those who are U.S. citizens, nationals, LPRs, and those who are "in the United States for other than a temporary purpose with the intention of becoming a citizen or permanent resident."[132] The statutory and regulatory language is quite expansive, and it would seem, on the language alone, to include a broad group of noncitizens, including all of those who have been granted victim-related immigration status. For reasons that are unclear—although perhaps based on inattention on the part of both government administrators and immigrant advocates—by policy letter (rather than statute or regulation) financial aid is available to some, but not all, of those defined as qualified immigrants.[133] In practical terms, under current interpretation (whose narrowness is supported neither by regulation nor statute), victims in asylum, refugee, continued presence, and T status are eligible for financial aid, and others are not.[134]

Because of this chasm between the words of the statute and regulations on the one hand, and the implementation of federal financial aid programs on the other, this is an area ripe for litigation.

CONCLUSION

Learning one's way around the labyrinth of state and federal statutes, regulations, and policies governing immigrant access to benefits can be daunting. Nonetheless, those of us engaged in helping vulnerable immigrant victims secure safety must rise to the challenge. By understanding the possibilities and limitations of the current regime, we can help our clients access benefits and services to the maximum extent possible on a daily basis, and we can fight to change both law and policy so that, in the long term, persons on our shores are not held back in their efforts to escape violence by lack of access to federal and state benefits.

---

[130] *Id.*

[131] *See, e.g.,* N.Y. Educ. L. §6301 (including within the definition of those eligible for in-state tuition anyone who has "attended an approved New York high school for two or more years, graduated from an approved New York high school and applied for attendance at an institution or educational unit of the state university within five years of receiving a New York state high school diploma; or . . . attended an approved New York state program for general equivalency diploma exam preparation, received a general equivalency diploma issued within New York state and applied for attendance at an institution or educational unit of the state university within five years of receiving a general equivalency diploma issued within New York state"); *see generally* NILC, "Basic Facts About In-State Tuition for Undocumented Immigrant Students" (April 2006), *available at www.nilc.org/immlawpolicy/DREAM/in-state_tuition_basic facts_041706.pdf.*

[132] 20 USC §1091(a)(5); 34 CFR §668.33(a)(2)(ii).

[133] U.S. Department of Education Dear Colleague Letter, E. Hicks, "Student Eligibility Issues" (GEN-98-2, Jan. 1998), *available at www.nasfaa.org/publications/1998/gen-98-*
continued

2.html (listing indigenous Canadians, LPRs, asylees, refugees, parolees, those granted withholding under the INA, and conditional entrants as eligible for financial aid).

[134] *Id.* (with respect to asylees and refugees); U.S. Department of Education Dear Colleague Letter, J. Manning and T. Shaw, "Eligibility for Title IV Program Assistance for Victims of Human Trafficking" (GEN-06-09, May 2006), *available at www.nasfaa.org/publications/2006/gen0609.html* (with respect to those in continued presence and T status).

THE "NEW" AND EXCITING
U: NO LONGER JUST MY IMAGINARY FRIEND

*by Julie E. Dinnerstein**

For several years now, I have been giving talks and trainings on the "U" visa, my imaginary friend. I called the U[1] my imaginary friend because, although created by law on October 28, 2000,[2] and amended by statute on January 5, 2006,[3] no actual U visas had ever been issued and no one had ever been granted U nonimmigrant status. Without implementing regulations, there were simply no forms to fill out and no visas to be had. Nonetheless, like an imaginary friend, there was something to the U, even without its being in existence.

Pursuant to a series of memoranda,[4] noncitizens in the United States who believed themselves eligible for U nonimmigrant status could contact federal immigration authorities to seek some form of temporary status. Starting in October 2003, such noncitizens were specifically directed to submit their requests for interim relief under the U statute to the Violence Against Women Act (VAWA) Unit of the Vermont Service Center of U.S. Citizenship and Immigration Services (USCIS).[5] By the end of May 2007, close to 9,000 requests for interim relief had been submitted and close to 7,500 of these requests had been granted.[6]

---

* **Julie E. Dinnerstein** is the co-director of Sanctuary for Families' Immigration Intervention and Brooklyn Family Justice Center Legal Projects. She also teaches immigration law at the School of Professional Studies at the City University of New York and serves as a part-time counselor at the Center for Public Interest Law, Columbia Law School. Previous positions include deputy director for immigration policy and training at the New York Immigration Coalition, associate at Cleary, Gottlieb, Steen & Hamilton, and law clerk to the Honorable Jack B. Weinstein of the U.S. District Court for the Eastern District of New York. Ms. Dinnerstein is a recipient of the Columbia Law School Public Interest Law Foundation's 2005 Public Interest Achievement Award and an honoree at the 8th Annual AILA New York Chapter Immigration Law Symposium. Ms. Dinnerstein is a graduate of Columbia College and Columbia Law School, where she served as an editor on the *Columbia Journal of Gender and Law* and the *Columbia Law Review*. Her understanding of the "U" statute and the many immigrants who may benefit from this statutory provision has been developed in working on applications for U interim relief for over 400 immigrant victims of criminal activity, in collaboration with her insightful and hard-working colleagues, past and present, at the Immigration Intervention Project at Sanctuary for Families over the years: Genia Blaser, Molly Bowen, Lori Cohen, Mailyssa Guercy-Adodo, Sarah Gunther, Colleen Hodgetts, Carolien Hardenbol, Abja Midha, Avideh Moussavian, Laura Polstein, Archana Pyati, Carmen Rey, Hilary Sunghee Seo, and Kathleen Slocum. To them, she owes an enormous debt of gratitude.

[1] For purposes of this article, "U," unless otherwise indicated, refers to U nonimmigrant status and the U visa.

[2] Battered Immigrant Women Protection Act of 2000, Pub. L. No. 106-386, §1513, 114 Stat. 1464, 1533–37, part of the Violence Against Women Act of 2000 (VAWA 2000), improving access to self-petitioning under the Violence Against Women Act of 1994 (VAWA 1994), Pub. L. No. 103-322, 108 Stat. 1796.

[3] Violence Against Women Reauthorization Act of 2005 (VAWA 2005), Pub. L. No. 109-162, §§3(a), 801–34, 119 Stat. 2960, 2964–71, 3053–77 (2006), as amended by Pub. L. No. 109-271, 120 Stat. 750 (2006).

[4] Immigration and Naturalization Service (INS) Memorandum, M. Cronin, "Victims of Trafficking and Violence Protection Act of 2000 (VTVPA) Policy Memorandum #2—"T" and "U" Nonimmigrant Visas (Aug. 30, 2001), *available at www.asistaonline.org/Uvisa/Policy_Memo_-_Cronin_-_8-30-01.pdf*; INS Memorandum, L. Blackman, "Automatic Administrative Relief for Aliens Eligible for Nonimmigrant Status Under Sections 101(a)(15)(T) and (U) of the Immigration and Nationality Act" (May 23, 2002), *available at www.asistaonline.org/Blackman__Anderson__May_8__20 02.pdf*; U.S. Citizenship and Immigration Services (USCIS) Memorandum, W. Yates, "Centralization of Interim Relief for U Nonimmigrant Status Applicants" (Oct. 8, 2003), *published on* AILA InfoNet at Doc. No. 03101420 (*posted* Oct. 14, 2003); USCIS Memorandum, W. Yates, "Assessment of Deferred Action in Requests for Interim Relief from U Nonimmigrant Status Eligible Aliens in Removal Proceedings" (May 6, 2004), *available at www.asistaonline.org/Uvisa /deferred%20action.pdf*; USCIS Memorandum, M. Aytes, "Application for U Nonimmigrant Status: Revisions to *Adjudicator's Field Manual (AFM)* Chapter 39 (*AFM* Update AD06-11)" (Jan. 6, 2006), *published on* AILA InfoNet at Doc. No. 06011763 (*posted* Jan. 17, 2006), and *available at www.asistaonline.org/Uvisa/apps.4%20U%20status.pdf*.

[5] *See* Yates Memorandum, Oct. 8, 2003, *supra* note 4.

[6] *See* Declaration of M. Young, Supervisory Adjudications Officer for USCIS, ¶¶3, 7, Exhibit D to Defendants' Motion to Dismiss Plaintiffs' Complaint, *Catholic Charities CYO v. Chertoff*, C 07-1307 PJH (N.D. Cal. May 29, 2007).

These noncitizen would-be U applicants generally were granted deferred action, which allowed them to apply to the Vermont Service Center[7] for employment authorization documents (EADs, popularly known as work permits),[8] and, in some states, like New York, to apply for certain forms of public assistance.[9] With work permits, Social Security numbers, and public assistance, many noncitizen recipients of interim relief under the U statute began to feel like they really had something substantial. Nonetheless, as with an imaginary friend, something was missing—the U itself.

In the Fall of 2007, however, this imaginary world changed. Implementing interim regulations were issued on September 17, 2007,[10] and amended, with respect to fees, on September 27, 2007.[11] The regulations became effective on October 17, 2007, 11 days shy of the seven year anniversary of the creation of the U under federal law, when the VAWA Unit of the Vermont Service Center of USCIS began accepting petitions for U nonimmigrant status on Form I-918. At the time of this writing, we have yet to see the issuance of a single U. Nonetheless, at this early stage of a new era—when the imaginary friend becomes a real nonimmigrant status that will ultimately allow its holders to apply for lawful permanent resident (LPR) status—this article sets out to describe the U itself and what we know of the evolving landscape, providing an initial

how-to guide for preparing U petitions. Readers are cautioned that the suggestions provided in this article are preliminary and must be read in conjunction with ongoing discussions among U practitioners, as we all develop experience with the U petitioning process.

WHAT IS THE U?

The U nonimmigrant classification was created to "facilitate the reporting of crimes to law enforcement officials by trafficked, exploited, victimized, and abused [noncitizens] who are not in lawful immigration status," and, in accordance with "the humanitarian interests of the United States," to create "a means to regularize the status of cooperating individuals."[12] The U is classified as a nonimmigrant status. Like the "K," "T" and "V,"[13] however, the U is nonimmigrant in name only. It is intended for noncitizens who will eventually become eligible to apply for permanent immigrant status.

Unlike the vast majority of nonimmigrant classifications, the U may be granted to a noncitizen in the United States who is out of immigration status. Furthermore, those petitioning for U nonimmigrant status are eligible for a broad waiver of grounds of inadmissibility, including entry without inspection and false claims to U.S. citizenship, to name just two grounds of inadmissibility that generally spell the death knell to a nonimmigrant classification petition.[14]

The granting of a U visa or status confers "lawful temporary resident status"[15] on a noncitizen. While the exact meaning of this phrase remains unclear as it applies to those in U nonimmigrant status, at a minimum, such status will result in employment authorization and lawful status for up to four years, which may, under certain circumstances, be extended.[16] After three years in U status, a noncitizen who has been continuously present in the United States may apply for lawful permanent residence,[17] which status may be granted "on humanitarian

---

[7] 69 Fed. Reg. 77768 (Dec. 28, 2004) ("The adjudications for Forms I-765 filed by aliens who have been granted deferred action based upon (1) an approved Form I-360 (as a battered spouse or child of a U.S. citizen or lawful permanent resident); (2) a pending bona fide application for T nonimmigrant status (Form I-914); or (3) U nonimmigrant status interim relief [a]re centralized at the Vermont Service Center.").

[8] 8 CFR §274a.12(c)(14).

[9] N.Y. Soc. Serv. Law §122(c)(ii) (relating to "persons residing under color of law"), as modified by *Aliessa v. Novello*, 96 N.Y.2d 418 (2001), allowing noncitizens granted deferred action to receive Medical Assistance (public health insurance) and Safety Net Assistance (cash assistance); *see also* New York State Department of Health, Informational Letter, "Clarification of PRUCOL Status for Purposes of Medicaid Eligibility," 07 OHIP/INF-2 (Mar. 15, 2007), *available at www.health.state.ny.us/health_care/medicaid/publications/docs/inf/07inf-2.pdf*; New York State Office of Temporary and Disability Assistance, General Information System Memorandum, R. Sykes, "Permanently Residing Under of the Color of Law (PRUCOL)" (Feb. 20, 2007), *available at www.otda.state.ny.us/main/gis/2007/07dc001.rtf*.

[10] 72 Fed. Reg. 53014 (Sept. 17, 2007).

[11] 72 Fed. Reg. 54813 (Sept. 27, 2007).

---

[12] VAWA 2000 §1513(a)(2)(B), 114 Stat. at 1534.

[13] INA §§101(a)(15)(K), (T), and (V).

[14] INA §212(d)(14) (allowing all grounds other than Nazi persecution, genocide, torture, or extrajudicial killing to be waived).

[15] INA §214(p)(3)(B).

[16] INA §214(p)(6); *see also* 8 CFR §214.14(g)(2).

[17] INA §245(m).

grounds, to ensure family unity, or [when it] is otherwise in the public interest."[18]

WHO IS ELIGIBLE FOR THE U?

The U is for victims of criminal activity in areas over which U.S. law enforcement (or any of law enforcement within the United States, including state, local, territorial, and tribal authorities) has jurisdiction.

Victims of a certain statutory list of criminal activities, as well as victims of any "attempt, conspiracy, or solicitation to commit any of the [listed] crimes"[19] may be eligible for U status. The criteria for U status are as follows:

- the noncitizen has suffered substantial abuse as a result of having been a victim of qualifying criminal activity

- the noncitizen (or, in the case of a noncitizen under 16,[20] the parent, guardian, or next friend) has information about the qualifying criminal activity

- the noncitizen (or, in the case of a noncitizen under 16,[21] the parent, guardian, or next friend) "has been helpful, is being helpful, or is likely to be helpful"[22] to the investigation *or* prosecution of the qualifying crime or criminal activity

- the noncitizen has received certification from the relevant U.S. government authority (which may be a state or local authority) of such past, current, or future helpfulness

- the criminal activity violated the laws of the United States (or any state, local, territorial, and tribal authorities within the United States);

- the crime, the criminal activity, or the attempt, conspiracy, or solicitation to commit the criminal activity involved one or more of the following 26 acts:

  - rape

  - torture

  - trafficking

  - incest

  - domestic violence

  - sexual assault

  - abusive sexual contact

  - prostitution

  - sexual exploitation

  - female genital mutilation

  - being held hostage

  - peonage

  - involuntary servitude

  - slave trade

  - kidnapping

  - abduction

  - unlawful criminal restraint

  - false imprisonment

  - blackmail

  - extortion

  - manslaughter

  - murder

  - felonious assault

  - witness tampering

  - obstruction of justice;

  - perjury

Such bad acts are defined as the "qualifying crime or qualifying criminal activity" in the regulations.[23]

Each aspect of these basic eligibility requirements is explored in detail below.

The Crime or Criminal Activity

The statutory list of qualifying criminal activities[24] is echoed in the regulations.[25] While many terms are self-explanatory, a few require further examination.

A careful eye should be turned to each listed statutory criminal activity to see if an argument can be made that the victim of a differently named crime or criminal activity may, in essence, be a victim of a listed criminal activity. For example, New York does not have any crimes called "domestic violence" in its penal code. However, under the general catch-

---

[18] INA §245(m)(1)(B).

[19] INA §101(a)(15)(U)(iii).

[20] The reference to being "under 16" is the age on the date of the crime, not the application for a U visa or nonimmigrant status. 8 CFR §214.14(b)(2).

[21] *Id.*

[22] INA §101(a)(15)(U)(i)(III).

[23] 8 CFR §214.14(a)(9).

[24] INA §101(a)(15)(U)(iii).

[25] 8 CFR §214.14(a)(9).

all of "any similar activity,"[26] criminal acts between family members (such as assault, menacing, and harassment) may fall within the definition of "domestic violence" for purposes of the U statute. With respect to this example, practitioners assisting victims of domestic violence are advised to submit documents (birth certificates of children in common, marriage certificates, etc.) to establish the familial relationship between the U petitioner and the criminal perpetrator in order to demonstrate that the criminal activity with another name is actually domestic violence.

The U practitioner must keep in mind that the U statute predominantly uses the term "criminal activity" rather than "crime,"[27] and that the regulations define the qualifying bad acts as "crime[s] *or* criminal activit[ies]."[28] The repeated and predominant use of the phrase "criminal activity" over "crime" suggests that the U statute covers a wider scope of bad acts than simply those prosecuted as crimes. The expansive understanding of bad acts that qualify as the basis for a U petition is further supported by the regulations' references to "child protective services, the Equal Employment Opportunity Commission, and the Department of Labor"[29] as potential certifiers of criminal activity. When you are working with a noncitizen who has been the victim of bad acts that come within the scope of the U statute, it may be worth contacting the relevant federal, state, local, territorial, or tribal authority "that has responsibility for the detection, investigation, prosecution, conviction, or sentencing of [the] qualifying criminal activity"[30] to see if you might be able to enlist such authority's involvement in your client's case (if no such involvement exists already) and obtain that authority's support for your client's U petition.

Finally, practitioners must keep in mind that it is not only the commission of a crime or criminal activity that gives rise to a U petition, but also an "attempt, conspiracy, or solicitation to commit any of the [qualifying] crimes."[31]

The Victim of the Criminal Activity

As with everything else in immigration law, the meaning of the term "victim" for purposes of the U statute is not straightforward. The regulations define the term "victim" as the person "who is directly and proximately harmed by ... criminal activity."[32] This definition is broader than one might think.

On first reading the statute, one might wonder what kind of immigration benefit a victim of a murder or manslaughter might seek from the U.S. government. After all, once a person is dead, the U.S. government's jurisdiction over such a person's future travels would seem severely curtailed, to say the least. It turns out, however, that for U purposes the definition of a victim of murder or manslaughter includes, in addition to a living survivor of an attempted murder, certain immediate family members of the deceased victim.[33]

In a similar vein, certain immediate family members of victims of crimes who are incompetent or incapacitated are also deemed victims under the U regulations.[34]

Some criminal activities on the list do not, per se, convey how a person might be victimized. The regulations provide guidance as to how some victims may come within the purview of the U statute. A victim of a witness tampering, obstruction of justice, or perjury offense may be eligible for U nonimmigrant status, the regulations explain, if:

> the perpetrator committed [one of these criminal activities], at least in principal part, as a means:
>
> (1) To avoid or frustrate efforts to investigate, arrest, prosecute, or otherwise bring to justice the perpetrator for other criminal activity; or
>
> (2) To further the perpetrator's abuse or exploitation of or undue control over the petitioner through manipulation of the legal system.[35]

Information About the Criminal Activity

The noncitizen—or, in the case of a victim who is deceased, incompetent, incapacitated, or 15 years old or younger, certain family members—must have

---

[26] INA §101(a)(15)(U)(iii).

[27] *See generally* INA §101(a)(15)(U).

[28] 8 CFR §214.14(a)(9) (emphasis added).

[29] 8 CFR §214.14(a)(2).

[30] 8 CFR §214.14(c)(2)(i).

[31] INA §101(a)(15)(U)(iii).

---

[32] 72 Fed. Reg. 53014, 53016 (Sept. 17, 2007).

[33] 8 CFR §214.14(a)(14)(i).

[34] *Id.*

[35] 8 CFR §214.14(a)(14)(ii)(B).

"credible and reliable information establishing that he or she has knowledge of the details concerning the qualifying criminal activity on which his or her petition is based. The alien must possess specific facts regarding the criminal activity . . . ."[36] The regulatory provision requiring "knowledge of the details" and "specific facts" seems intentionally narrower than the statutory requirement of "information concerning the criminal activity."[37] To the extent that a victim has little or no knowledge of the criminal assailant or the immediate facts surrounding the criminal activity (for example, an assault victim who was attacked from behind and left unconscious) but cooperates fully with any law enforcement investigation or prosecution, that victim should be eligible for a U visa or nonimmigrant status. Any attempt to exclude such a victim through the "knowledge of the details" and "specific facts" requirements imposed by the regulations but not by the statute is likely *ultra vires* and should be challenged.

Cooperation

A victim must not only cooperate with the investigation or prosecution of the crime or criminal activity, but also must receive certification to that effect in order to be eligible for a U.[38]

The question of ongoing cooperation, however, is a tricky one. While it is true that an affirmative finding that a noncitizen "unreasonably refused to provide assistance in a criminal investigation or prosecution" is a basis for denying a green card to a noncitizen in U nonimmigrant status,[39] there is no ongoing statutory requirement that the victim continue to assist in the investigation or prosecution of criminal activity in order to be eligible for a U. The statute explicitly authorizes the granting of U nonimmigrant status to a noncitizen who "has been helpful, is being helpful or is likely to be helpful to ... authorities investigating or prosecuting"[40] qualifying criminal activity. The language of the Form I-918, Supplement B, U Nonimmigrant Status Certification[41] and

the regulatory language indicates that a certification may be withdrawn and that such withdrawal would result in the revocation of U nonimmigrant status.[42] Although this language tends to suggest some kind of ongoing cooperation requirement, it is important to remember (and remind federal immigration authorities, as necessary) that cooperation in the investigation *or* prosecution, which cooperation is certified, is all that is required by statute to be eligible for a U visa or U nonimmigrant status.

Substantial Physical or Mental Harm

As with other areas of immigration law relating to victims of domestic violence and related harms, USCIS takes an expansive view of what constitutes harm. According to the regulations, "[p]hysical or mental abuse means injury or harm to the victim's physical person, or harm to or impairment of the emotional or psychological soundness of the victim."[43] The regulations further go on to explain that the harm suffered may be understood either as a result of (1) the single criminal event that gives rise to the U petition or (2) "[a] series of acts taken together [that] may be considered to constitute substantial physical or mental abuse even where no single act alone rises to that level."[44] This regulatory description of harm will be of particular importance working with victims of domestic violence when the criminal activity investigated or prosecuted giving rise to the U petition may not, in and of itself, have been the cause of substantial physical or mental harm, but the victim, over time, has suffered substantially.

HOW DOES A NONCITIZEN APPLY FOR A U VISA OR NONIMMIGRANT STATUS?

An overview on the petitioning process, followed by a more detailed discussion of each element of the petitioning process, is provided below.[45]

Overview

A noncitizen U petitioner submits the following to:

VAWA Unit/Vermont Service Center/USCIS
75 Lower Welden Street
St. Albans, VT 05479

---

[36] 8 CFR §214.14(b)(2).

[37] INA §101(a)(15)(U)(i)(II).

[38] *See* INA §§101(a)(15)(U)(i); 214(p)(1); 8 CFR §214.14(c)(2)(i).

[39] INA §245(m).

[40] INA §101(a)(15)(U)(i)(III).

[41] *See* Form I-918, Supplement B, U Nonimmigrant Status Certification, pt. 4, question 4 ("Has unreasonably refused to provide assistance in a criminal investigation and/or prosecution of the crime detailed above").

[42] 8 CFR §214.14(h)(2).

[43] 8 CFR §214.14(a)(8).

[44] 8 CFR §214.14(b)(1).

[45] Please also review appendices to this article, which include checklists and charts to guide the practitioner through the U petitioning process.

All petitioners

- Form I-918;

- Form I-918, Supplement B, completed by a certifying official, except that, in the case of "petitioners who requested and received U interim relief prior to the filing of the I-918, no new Supplement B will be required";[46]

- A "signed statement by the petitioner describing the facts of the victimization," except that "[w]hen the petitioner is under the age of 16, incapacitated, or incompetent, a parent, guardian, or next friend may submit a statement on behalf of the petitioner";[47]

- Evidence of substantial physical or mental harm suffered as a result of the victimization; and

- A biometric fee ($80 at the time of this writing)[48] for every petitioner between the ages of 14 and 79, or a fee waiver request for the biometric fee.[49]

Some petitioners

- Form I-192, including payment for the form (at the time of this writing, a $545 fee, which fee is nonwaivable),[50] if subject to any waivable ground of inadmissibility;

- Form I-193, including payment for the form (at the time of this writing, a $545 fee, which fee is

nonwaivable),[51] if unable to present a valid, unexpired passport; and

- Form I-918, Supplement A,[52] signed by the petitioner and, if the derivative beneficiary is present in the United States, by the derivative beneficiary, for each derivative family member accompanying or following to join the U visa principal petitioner, including a biometric fee ($80 at the time of this writing)[53] for every petitioner between the ages of 14 and 79 or a fee waiver request for the biometric fee.[54]

Derivative beneficiaries

A family member of the U visa petitioner who is eligible for U nonimmigrant status as a derivative, in addition to being the beneficiary of a Form I-918, Supplement A signed by the U petitioner (and derivative, if he or she is in the United States), as noted above, will also file:

- Form I-192, including payment for the form (at the time of this writing, a $545 fee, which fee is nonwaivable),[55] if subject to any waivable ground of inadmissibility;

- Form I-193, including payment for the form (at the time of this writing, a $545 fee, which fee is nonwaivable),[56] if unable to present a valid, unexpired passport;

- Form I-765, along with the fee ($340 at the time of this writing)[57] or a fee waiver request,[58] if he or she is present in the United States and wants an employment authorization document.

Form I-918

The noncitizen begins the petitioning process by filling out Form I-918,[59] a form that over 18 pages manages to ask for some basic biographic informa-

---

[46] Per 8 CFR §214.14(c)(1), "A petitioner who received interim relief is not required to submit initial evidence with Form I-918 if he or she wishes to rely on the law enforcement certification and other evidence that was submitted with the request for interim relief." Per Instructions for Form I-918, p. 5, "[P]etitioners who requested and received U interim relief ... are not required to file Supplement B".

[47] 8 CFR §214.14(c)(2)(iii).

[48] 8 CFR §103.7(b)(1) (listing biometric fee).

[49] 8 CFR §103.7(c)(5) (listing the biometric fee as a fee for which a fee waiver may be sought).

[50] See 8 CFR §103.7(b)(1) (fee); 8 CFR §103(c)(5) (not listing Form I-192 as a form for which a fee waiver is available). Note, however, that USCIS has announced that while there is no fee waiver currently available for I-192, it intends to publish a regulation in the future that will allow waivers of the I-192 fee for applicants filing for both U nonimmigrant status as well as T nonimmigrant status (victims of human trafficking). USCIS Update, "USCIS Announces Update for Processing Petitions for Nonimmigrant Victims of Criminal Activity: U-Visas Provide Temporary Immigration Benefits to Victims Who Help Law Enforcement" (Apr. 10, 2008), *available at www.uscis.gov/files/article/U-Visa_10Apr08.pdf.*

[51] See 8 CFR §103.7(b)(1) (fee); 8 CFR §103(c)(5) (not listing Form I-193 as a form for which a fee waiver is available).

[52] Note that the Form I-918, Supplement A may be filed either with the I-918 or at a later date.

[53] 8 CFR §103.7(b)(1) (listing biometric fee).

[54] 8 CFR §103.7(c)(5) (listing the biometric fee as a fee for which a fee waiver may be sought).

[55] See note 50, supra.

[56] See note 51, supra.

[57] 8 CFR §103.7(b)(1) (listing fee for Form I-765).

[58] 8 CFR §103.7(c)(5) (listing Form I-765 as a form for which a fee waiver may be sought).

[59] Available at www.uscis.gov/files/form/I-918.pdf.

tion, as well as some truly bizarre questions (my favorite of which, at part 3, question 4.3, queries whether the petitioner has ever used a nuclear weapon against anyone).

While most of the questions on the form are relatively straightforward (albeit, with respect to a few, a bit far-fetched), question 11 at part 3 presents some problems. The question asks, "Have you EVER been present or nearby when any person was: a. Intentionally killed, tortured, beaten, or injured; b. Displaced or moved from his or her residence by force, compulsion or duress; c. In any way compelled or forced to engage in any kind of sexual contact or relations." While the question seems designed to ascertain whether the U petitioner may be implicated by association in any inadmissible activity, on the plain language of the question, I imagine the answer to at least one of those questions will be "yes" for almost all U petitioners who themselves have been present at the time that they were beaten or sexually abused. For now, our office is answering "yes" when filling out I-918s on behalf of those who have been beaten, thrown out of their residences, or sexually abused. This will be a question to watch as practitioners develop an approach to it over the next several months.

Form I-918, Supplement A

A U petitioner may ask USCIS to grant a U nonimmigrant visa or status to certain families members pursuant to the terms outlined in 8 CFR §214.14(f). The following "qualifying family members"[60] are eligible for derivative U status:

- Spouses of U petitioners (U-2);

- Children of U petitioners (U-3);

- Parents of U petitioners who are under 21 (U-4); and

- Unmarried siblings under 18 of U petitioners who are under 21 (U-5).

With respect to U petitioners who are under 21 and their siblings under 18, the statute makes clear that these age cut-offs are on the date of application;[61] but the statute is silent with respect to the date that a child of an adult (21 or over) U petitioner must be under 21. For now, our office is working under the assumption that the child of an adult petitioner similarly must be under 21 on the date of application.

With respect to derivatives previously granted interim relief under the U statute, the derivative's age is frozen as of the date of filing for U interim relief.[62]

As noted above, a Form I-918, Supplement A, must be filed for each and every family member who is accompanying or following to join the principal petitioner. The Supplement A may be filed at the same time that the Form I-918 is filed, or it may be filed later.[63]

As with principal U petitioners, Form I-192 must be filed for those seeking waivers of inadmissibility and Form I-193 must be filed by those seeking waivers of the general requirement of a valid, unexpired passport.

While no separate application for an EAD is required for the I-918 petitioner him- or herself, derivative beneficiaries on whose behalf I-918, Supplement A's are filed must file separate applications for EADs on Form I-765 and either pay the required fee ($340 at the time of this writing)[64] or apply for a fee waiver.[65]

Form I-918, Supplement B

A law enforcement certification is required by regulation[66] and by statute.[67] Except for those granted interim relief,[68] who are exempt from the requirement of filing any new certification,[69] the

---

[60] For the definition of the term "qualifying family members," see 8 CFR §214.14(a)(10); see also INA §101(a)(15)(u)(ii).

[61] See INA §101(a)(15)(U)(ii)(I).

[62] USCIS Memorandum, M. Aytes, "New Classification for Victims of Criminal Activity—Eligibility for "U" Nonimmigrant Status" (Mar. 27, 2008), published on AILA InfoNet at Doc. No. 08040256 (posted Apr. 2, 2008).

[63] 8 CFR §214.14(f)(2).

[64] 8 CFR §103.7(b)(1) (listing fee for Form I-765).

[65] 8 CFR §103.7(c)(5) (listing Form I-765 as a form for which a fee waiver may be sought).

[66] 8 CFR §214.14(c)(2)(i).

[67] INA §§101(a)(15)(U)(i); 214(p)(1).

[68] The term "U interim relief" is defined by regulation at 8 CFR §214.14(a)(13).

[69] See 8 CFR §214.14(c)(1) ("A petitioner who received interim relief is not required to submit initial evidence with Form I-918 if he or she wishes to rely on the law enforcement certification and other evidence that was submitted with the request for interim relief."); see also Instructions for Form I-918, p. 5, available at www.uscis.gov/files/form/ I-918instr.pdf ("[P]etitioners who requested and received U interim relief ... are not required to file Supplement B.").

Form I-918, Supplement B, U Nonimmigrant Status Certification[70] must have been signed:

- "within the six months preceding the submission of the Form I-918;"[71]

- by a certifying official,[72] which means:

  - the head of a certifying agency;[73]

  - a person with supervisory responsibilities who has been specifically designated to sign U certifications by the head of a certifying agency; or

  - a judge.

If the certifying official is neither a judge nor the head of the certifying agency, the petitioner should include "evidence of the agency head's written designation of the certifying official for this specific purpose."[74] A sample letter that may satisfy this requirement is provided at the end of this article.

Signed Statement

Generally, the signed statement will be provided by the victim him- or herself. However, if the victim is incapacitated, incompetent, or under 16 years of age, a "parent, guardian or next friend"[75] may provide the signed statement.

The regulations[76] require that the signed statement include a description of the following:

- the substantial physical or mental suffering that has resulted from either:

  - the qualifying criminal activity alone; or

  - a series of events over time that include the qualifying criminal activity;

- specific information and facts about the qualifying criminal activity;

- the cooperation of the victim, or, in the alternative, of the "parent, guardian or next friend;"[77] and

- the location of the crime.[78]

Evidence of Substantial Harm

The U petitioner may submit "any credible evidence"[79] in establishing eligibility for the U. This evidentiary standard is of particular importance when the U petitioner may be relying on his or her statement, or his or her statement combined with the statements of others to establish substantial harm. If medical records, court documents, newspaper articles, or other documents exist to substantiate the substantial harm suffered, they of course should be obtained and submitted. Nonetheless, if no such external documents exist, a U petitioner may establish the substantial harm suffered through his or her statement alone.

Form I-192

Under INA §212(d)(14), USCIS may waive the vast majority of grounds of inadmissibility for U petitioners.[80] While the statutory language is broad, the regulations (in a way that may be *ultra vires*) indicate that "[i]n cases involving violent or dangerous crimes or inadmissibility based on the security and related grounds in section 212(a)(3) of the [INA], USCIS will only exercise favorable discretion in extraordinary circumstances."[81] Despite this language, the waiver available to noncitizens seeking U visas or nonimmigrant status (either as principal petitioners or as derivatives)—which waiver will be granted if USCIS "determines that it is in the public or national interest to exercise discretion to waive the applicable ground(s) of inadmissibility"[82]—is a much more generous waiver of grounds of inadmissibility than is available to noncitizens in most other contexts.

A noncitizen may apply for this waiver through the filing of a Form I-192 with the Vermont Service

---

[70] The requirements for the certification are described at 8 CFR §214.14(c)(2)(i).

[71] 8 CFR §214.14(c)(2).

[72] The term "certifying official" is defined at 8 CFR §214.14(a)(3).

[73] The term "certifying agency" is defined at 8 CFR §214.14(a)(2).

[74] Instructions for I-918, Supplement B, U Nonimmigrant Status Certification.

[75] 8 CFR §214.14(c)(2)(iii).

[76] 8 CFR §214.14(c)(2)(iii) (requiring that the signed statement cover all of the eligibility elements identified in 8 CFR §214.14(b)).

[77] 8 CFR §214.14(b)(3).

[78] The statement must affirm that "[t]he qualifying criminal activity occurred in the United States (including Indian country and U.S. military installations) or in the territories or possession of the United Sates, or violated a U.S. federal law that provides for extraterritorial jurisdiction to prosecute the offense in a U.S. federal court." 8 CFR §214.14(b)(4).

[79] INA §214(p)(4); 8 CFR §214.14(c)(4).

[80] Only "[p]articipants in Nazi persecution, genocide, or the commission of any act of torture or extrajudicial killing" may not apply for a waiver of inadmissibility under INA §214(d).

[81] 8 CFR §212.17(b)(2).

[82] 8 CFR §212.17(b)(1).

Center,[83] a form which, at the time of this writing, costs $545[84] to file and for which no fee waiver is available.[85] The form is a single page and relatively easy to fill out. As the form is predominantly designed for people outside the United States seeking to enter, some of the questions may seem inapplicable to U petitioners filing inside the United States. To that end, I provide some suggested responses to the questions in Form I-192 for those filing the form from within the United States:

- In response to Questions 7, 8, and 9, I suggest writing "not applicable."

- In response to Question 10, I suggest writing "permanent."

- In response to Question 11, I suggest writing "obtaining U nonimmigrant status."

At the time of this writing, it remains unclear what kinds of documentation will be required to support a request for the favorable exercise of discretion. At a minimum, it would seem appropriate to provide a statement from the petitioner describing the sympathetic circumstances of the act that gave rise to the inadmissibility (if such sympathetic circumstances exist) and the reasons why the U petitioner or derivative seeks to stay in (or enter) the United States.

Form I-193

In general, "[a]ny nonimmigrant who ... is not in possession of a passport valid for a minimum of six months from the date of the expiration of the initial period of the alien's admission or contemplated initial period of stay ... is inadmissible."[86] Noncitizens who are filing Form I-918 or who are beneficiaries of Form I-918, Supplement A, may file a Form I-193 with the Vermont Service Center to seek a waiver of the passport requirement.[87] This waiver may be granted by the director of the Vermont Service Center "in the exercise of his or her discretion, on a case-by-case basis ... if satisfied that the nonimmigrant cannot present the required documents because of an unforeseen emergency."[88] As with the

Form I-192, at the time of this writing, the Form I-193 costs $545[89] to file and no fee waiver is available.[90]

Form I-765

Principal U petitioners filing Form I-918 are *not* required to file any additional applications or petitions to obtain employment authorization. Instead, "USCIS automatically will issue an initial EAD to [those granted U-1 nonimmigrant status] who are in the United States."[91] The noncitizen U petitioner in the United States should simply check the yes box next to the statement "I want an Employment Authorization Document" on the second page of Form I-918. A noncitizen who enters the United States on a U-1 visa may contact the Vermont Service Center after admission to obtain an EAD.[92]

In contrast, derivative beneficiaries submitting Form I-918, Supplement A, must apply for EADs on Form I-765 from within the United States.[93] At the time of this writing, the Form I-765 costs $340.[94] In contrast to Forms I-192 and I-193, a fee waiver is available.[95]

Although the instructions to Form I-765 have not yet been updated to reflect the regulatory basis for the I-765 filings of U derivatives, note that the answer to Question 16 on the form is "(a)(20)," reflecting the fact that U derivatives are eligible for employment under 8 CFR §274.12(a)(20).

SPECIAL CONSIDERATIONS

Noncitizens Currently or Previously in Exclusion, Deportation, or Removal Proceedings

Regardless of whether a noncitizen is currently in immigration proceedings or has previously been ordered removed, deported, or excluded, "USCIS has sole jurisdiction over all petitions for U nonimmi-

---

[83] 8 CFR §212.17(a).

[84] 8 CFR §103.7(b)(1).

[85] 8 CFR §103.7(c)(5). However, USCIS has announced its intention to introduce a fee waiver for the I-192 filed in connection with Forms I-914 and I-918. *See supra* note 50.

[86] INA §212(a)(7)(B).

[87] 8 CFR §212.1(p).

[88] 8 CFR §212.1(g); *see also* 8 CFR §212.1(p).

[89] 8 CFR §103.7(b)(1).

[90] 8 CFR §103.7(c)(5).

[91] 8 CFR §214.14(c)(7); *see also* 8 CFR §274a.12(a)(19).

[92] *See* 8 CFR §214.14(c)(7).

[93] 8 CFR §212.14(f)(7) ("For qualifying family members within the United States, the Form I-765 may be filed concurrently with Form I-918, Supplement A, or at any time thereafter. For qualifying family members who are outside the United States, Form I-765 only may be filed after admission to the United States in U nonimmigrant status."); *see also* 8 CFR §274a.12(a)(20).

[94] 8 CFR §103.7(b)(1).

[95] 8 CFR §103.7(c)(5).

grant status."[96] When a noncitizen is in removal proceedings, "U.S. Immigration and Customs Enforcement (ICE) counsel may agree, as a matter of discretion, to file, at the request of the alien petitioner, a joint motion to terminate proceedings without prejudice ... while a petition for U nonimmigrant status is being adjudicated by USCIS."[97] Once USCIS grants U nonimmigrant status, any prior exclusion, deportation, or removal order *issued by the secretary of homeland security* "will be deemed canceled by operation of law as of the date of USCIS' approval."[98] In contrast, any prior exclusion, deportation, or removal ordered *issued by an immigration judge or the Board of Immigration Appeals* remains in effect. A petitioner "may seek cancellation of such order by filing, with the immigration judge or the Board, a motion to reopen and terminate removal proceedings. ICE counsel may agree, as a matter of discretion, to join such a motion to overcome any applicable time and numerical limitations of 8 CFR 1003.2 and 1003.23."[99]

Note, furthermore, that "[t]he filing of a petition for U ... nonimmigrant status has no effect on ICE's authority to execute a final order, although the alien may file a request for a stay of removal pursuant to 8 CFR 241.6(a) and 8 CFR 1241.6(a)."[100]

U Petitioners Previously Granted Interim Relief

Noncitizens previously granted U interim relief[101] enjoy certain benefits. First, noncitizens previously granted U interim relief, on the filing and approval of Form I-918, will be granted U nonimmigrant status dating back to the initial date that the applica-

tion for interim relief was approved.[102] This means that some U petitioners will be deemed to have been in U nonimmigrant status for more than four years on the date that such status is granted. As U nonimmigrant status is meant to be extended beyond four years only after law enforcement certification of a need for such extension,[103] it is unclear how USCIS will handle the grants of U status for those who first received interim relief more than four years ago.

Second, noncitizens previously granted U interim relief are exempt from the requirement that they provide a newly executed Form I-918, Supplement B certification with the filing of the Form I-918;[104] instead, U petitioners may rely on whatever form of law enforcement certification they have previously provided in their requests for interim relief. Similarly, other than filing the required forms and fees (or fee waivers, as the case may be), no additional evidence is required to be filed, although supplementary evidence may be submitted should the petitioner so choose.[105]

There is no explicit deadline for perfecting the request for a U visa or nonimmigrant status through the filing of a Form I-918.[106] Although USCIS initially indicated it would reconsider previous grants of deferred action for those who did not file within 180 days of the interim regulations going into effect, USCIS has retreated from this position.[107]

Effect of Statutory Cap

The U statute limits the granting of principal U (*i.e.*, U-1) status to 10,000 per year.[108] Luckily, how-

---

[96] 8 CFR §214.14(c)(1).

[97] 8 CFR §214.14(c)(1)(i).

[98] 8 CFR §214.14(c)(5)(i) (with respect to U-1 status and I-918 petitioners); 8 CFR §214.14(f)(6) (with respect to U-2, U-3, U-4, and U-5 status and beneficiaries of I-918, Supplement A's).

[99] 8 CFR §214.14(c)(5)(i) (with respect to U-1 status and I-918 petitioners); 8 CFR §214.14(f)(6) (with respect to U-2, U-3, U-4, and U-5 status and beneficiaries of I-918, Supplement A's).

[100] 8 CFR §214.14(c)(1)(ii) (with respect to U-1 status and I-918 petitioners); 8 CFR §214.14(f)(2)(ii) (with respect to U-2, U-3, U-4, and U-5 status and beneficiaries of I-918, Supplement A's).

[101] The term "U interim relief" is defined at 8 CFR §214.14(a)(13).

[102] 8 CFR §212.14(c)(6) (with respect to U-1 status); 8 CFR §212.14(f)(6)(i) (with respect to U-2, U-3, U-4, and U-5 status).

[103] INA §214(p)(6). Note, however, that the regulations are inexplicably more generous with respect to extensions, allowing them not only for law enforcement purposes but to ensure family unity. *See* 8 CFR §214.14(g).

[104] *See* 8 CFR §214.14(c)(1) ("A petitioner who received interim relief is not required to submit initial evidence with Form I-918 if he or she wishes to rely on the law enforcement certification and other evidence that was submitted with the request for interim relief."); *see also* Instructions for Form I-918 ("[P]etitioners who requested and received U interim relief ... are not required to file Supplement B.").

[105] *See* 8 CFR §214.14(c)(1).

[106] 72 Fed. Reg. 53014 (Sept. 17, 2007).

[107] *See* USCIS Update, *supra* note 50.

[108] INA §214(p)(2)(A); 8 CFR §214.14(d)(1). Note, however, that the statutory cap does not apply to derivatives. INA §212(p)(2)(B).

ever, when a noncitizen is eligible for a U-1 visa or nonimmigrant status but does not receive it because the statutory cap has been reached for that fiscal year, USCIS will place the U-1 petitioner on a waiting list and "will grant deferred action or parole to U-1 petitioners and qualifying family members while the U-1 petitioners are on the waiting list."[109]

HOW DOES A NONCITIZEN APPLY FOR LAWFUL PERMANENT RESIDENT STATUS?

The statutory basis for granting LPR status, like the U visa statute itself, is quite generous.[110] Other than not being inadmissible under INA §212(a)(3)(E) (relating to Nazis, extrajudicial murder, genocide, and torture) and not being subject to an affirmative finding of having "unreasonably refused to provide assistance in a criminal investigation or prosecution,"[111] the noncitizen in U nonimmigrant status must meet the following criteria to adjust to LPR status:

- Presence in the United States for at least three years since the grant of U nonimmigrant status; and

- His or her "continued presence in the United States is justified on humanitarian grounds, to ensure family unity, or is otherwise in the public interest."[112]

Unfortunately, although regulations were promulgated with respect to U visas and nonimmigrant status, no similar regulations have been promulgated for the adjustment of status of those in U nonimmigrant status. The issue is sure to jump to the forefront early on, as hundreds of Form I-918 petitioners will be deemed to have been in U nonimmigrant status for over three years as of the date of approval of the Form I-918.

WHERE DO WE GO FROM HERE?

This article was written and updated in the months following the promulgation of interim U regulations, prior to the adjudication of a single petition for U nonimmigrant status on Form I-918. The ideas and suggestions in this article are based on a careful reading of the statute and regulations, combined with years of experience with both the U interim relief process and with the adjudication of other petition types (notably the I-360 and I-751) for domestic violence victims. Nonetheless, the reader once again is reminded that the U petitioning process is in its infancy and, as diligent immigration practitioners, we must pay close attention to the benefits and pitfalls of the U petitioning process as it develops over time.

---

[109] 8 CFR §214.14(d)(2).

[110] *See generally* INA §245(m).

[111] INA §245(m)(1).

[112] INA §245(m)(1)(B).

Preparing a U visa or nonimmigrant status petition: Which forms will you need?
(prepared by Sanctuary for Families)

Question	Answer	Form	Cost[*]
Does U.S. Citizenship and Immigration Services (USCIS) have a current, safe address on file?	If your answer is no, then you will need to file a Change of Address on Form AR-11 which you may send to the following address: USCIS/ Change of Address/ PO Box 7134/ London, KY 40742-7134. If USCIS has a current, safe address for you, then you do not need to file this form. Should you move, be sure to remember to file an AR-11 within 10 days of moving.	AR-11	Free
Are you represented by an attorney or an accredited representative?	If your answer is yes, then the attorney or accredited representative must file a Notice of Appearance on Form G-28 (to be printed on blue paper). If you are representing yourself (not recommended), then no G-28 is required.	G-28	Free
Are you inadmissible to the United States? Examples include (but are not limited to): ➤ Being HIV+; ➤ Being convicted (including receiving a "Conditional Discharge" (CD)) of any of a long list of crimes (including some misdemeanors and violations); ➤ Previously lying to federal immigration authorities (such as by submitting applications with false information or presenting false documents); ➤ Previously lying to a government official about being a U.S. citizen; ➤ Entering the U.S. without inspection by coming across the border when no one was looking; ➤ Receiving an order of exclusion, deportation or removal, but not leaving the U.S. or staying outside the U.S. for less than the required amount of time; ➤ Living in the U.S. without immigration authorization, then leaving and either returning or seeking return to the U.S.; ➤ Helping other people to enter into the U.S. unlawfully; and ➤ Unlawfully voting	If the answer is yes, then you will need to ask for a waiver under INA §212(d)(14), 8 CFR §212.17 for one or more grounds of inadmissibility by filing an Application for Advance Permission to Enter as Nonimmigrant on Form I-192. If you are not subject to any ground of inadmissibility, then you do not need to file an I-192.	I-192	$545

[*] As of May 4, 2008, there are fee waivers available for biometric fees and Form I-765 but no fee waivers available for Forms I-192 and 193. Fees and fee waivers change frequently. (For example, USCIS has announced its intention to create a fee waiver for Form I-192, but has not done so as of the time of this writing. USCIS Update, "USCIS Announces Update for Processing Petitions for Nonimmigrant Victims of Criminal Activity: U-Visas Provide Temporary Immigration Benefits to Victims Who Help Law Enforcement" (Apr. 10, 2008), *available at www.uscis.gov/files/article/U-Visa_10Apr08.pdf.* Check the USCIS web site at *www.uscis.gov* for current fees and fee waiver rules.

Question	Answer	Form	Cost*
Do you have a passport that is valid for at least 6 months, or can you obtain one?	If the answer is no, then you will need to ask for a waiver of the requirement that you hold a passport by filing Form I-193 Application for Waiver of Passport and/or Visa. If you have or can obtain a valid passport, you do not need to file an I-193.	I-193	$545
Are you a principal U petitioner (U-1) or a derivative U petitioner (U-2, U-3, U-4, or U-5)?	If you are a derivative on the U nonimmigrant status petition of a family member who has been a victim of criminal activity and you are in the U.S. and you would like to be authorized to work, you must file an Application for an Employment Authorization Document (EAD) on Form I-765. If in the U.S., you may file Form I-765 concurrently with Form I-918, Supplement A or at any time thereafter. If outside the U.S., you must wait until you enter the U.S. before filing Form I-765. If you are a principal U petitioner filing for A U visa or nonimmigrant status because you have been the primary victim of a crime, then you do not need to file a separate application for a work permit. You may request a work permit by checking a box on the Form I-918 (if inside the US) or by requesting a work permit with the Vermont Service Center upon entering the US (if the Form I-918 is filed outside the US).	I-765	$340
Are you a principal U petitioner (U-1) who is applying for A U visa or nonimmigrant status because you have been a crime victim (or are the surviving spouse or child of a murder victim)?	If the answer is yes, then you will file a Petition for U Nonimmigrant Status on Form I-918. If you are seeking a U visa or nonimmigrant status as a derivative, there is a different form for you to file.	I-918	$80 biometric fee
Are you a derivative U petitioner (U-2, U-3, U-4, or U-5), seeking a U visa or nonimmigrant status where your familial relationship to the primary crime victim is: ➢ Spouse (U-2); ➢ Unmarried child under 21 (U-3); ➢ Parent (if the primary crime victim is under 21) (U-4); or ➢ Sibling (if the primary crime victim is under 21 and you are under 18) (U-5).	If the answer is yes, then your family member who is the principal U petitioner and primary crime victim, will file a Petition for Qualifying Family Member of U-1 Recipient on Form I-918, Supplement A. If you, the derivative family member, are in the U.S., you will also sign this form. Remember that an I-918, Supp. A must be filed for each and every derivative family member and can be filed simultaneously with the principal's U nonimmigrant status petition or later on. Remember also that each derivative family member who would like work authorization must file an I-765, which form can only be filed from within the U.S.	I-918, Supp. A	$80 biometric fee
Have you previously received deferred action based on a pre-10/17/07 U visa or nonimmigrant status application?	If the answer is yes, you have previously received deferred action on a pre-10/17/07 request for a U visa, then you do not need to file U Nonimmigrant Status Certification, Supplement B. If the answer is no, and you the principal U petitioner, then you must obtain an I-918, Supp. B, signed by (a) a judge; (b) the head of a certifying agency; or (c) a specific designee of the head of a certifying agency.	I-918, Supp. B	Free

U visa or nonimmigrant status check list
Preparing a Petition for U Nonimmigrant Status on Form I-918
(prepared by Sanctuary for Families)

Actions for initial client meeting:

☐ Review client checklist.[1]

☐ Be sure to record:
  ➢ Safe home, cell, work and alternative telephone numbers;
  ➢ Safe mailing address;
  ➢ Safe e-mail (if any);
  ➢ Alien numbers for all family members who have them; and
  ➢ Social security numbers for all family members of who have them.

☐ Check whether there are any pending or final immigration proceedings against U petitioner or derivative family members by dialing 1 800 898 7180.[2]

☐ Have client sign releases (both general[3] and Health Insurance Portability and Accountability Act (HIPPA)[4]) to facilitate obtaining records.

☐ If a Freedom of Information Act (FOIA) request has not previously been filed with U.S. Citizenship and Immigration Services (USCIS), one should be filed on Form G-639 with the National Records Center/ PO Box 648010/ Lee's Summit, MO 64064.[5]

☐ If USCIS does not have a current, safe address on file, a Change of Address on Form AR-11 with a safe address (which may be legal or social service agency office) should be filed with USCIS/ Change of Address/ PO Box 7134/ London, KY 40742-7134.

☐ For men who are between the ages of 18 and 26, if Selective Service (the "draft") registration form has not previously been filed, one should be filed on-line at www.sss.gov. If the would-be registrant does not have a social security number, the web site should redirect the would-be registrant to a paper form that can be printed out. If no such form appears, then the would-be registrant should be directed to a local post office to obtain a registration card to be mailed in.

☐ Any U petitioner (primary or derivative) who entered without inspection (EWI), believes he or she may have previously been in immigration proceedings or ordered removed or has a criminal record[6] should obtain fingerprints to send to the FBI, using the legal office as the mailing address.

---

1   A model client checklist is included below and is available on the *probono.net/ny/family* website (registration is free) in the library under immigration.
2   If a noncitizen has a final exclusion, deportation, or removal proceedings and has not been granted deferred action or another form or postorder protection from execution of the order, you may wish to file for a stay of removal.
3   A model release is available on the *probono.net/ny/family* website (registration is free) in the library under immigration.
4   An example of a generic HIPAA release that also complies with New York state laws is available as a fillable form at *www.nycourts.gov/forms/Hipaa_fillable.pdf*.
5   In most circumstances, it will not be necessary to wait for the results of a FOIA before filing the U nonimmigrant status petition. This is particularly true if an application for interim U relief has already been filed.
6   If your client has a criminal record and has previously filed for an application for interim relief under the U statute and received deferred action, you may have no good options other than to file Petition for U Nonimmigrant Status on Form I-918 and a waiver of inadmissibility on Form I-192, as federal immigration authorities are already aware of your client and his or her current lack of immigration status outside of the current grant of deferred action. If, however, your client has a criminal record and no previous petitions or applications for U nonimmigrant status relief have been filed, it will be critical to

> ➤ Persons wishing to be fingerprinted can be fingerprinted and obtain a standard 10 fingerprint form, FD258, from any private or law enforcement source.

> ➤ Residents of New York City can obtain a standard fingerprint form, FD258 (which is __different__ from a good conduct certificate) from the Public Inquiry Department of the New York Police Department located at 1 Police Plaza in Room 152A. Requests can be made from 9 a.m. to 3 p.m., Monday through Friday. The client can take the 4, 5 or 6 to the Brooklyn Bridge/City Hall Stop, the J, M or Z to Chambers Street or the N or R to City Hall. Clients should bring a valid identity document and a $15 money order.

> ➤ Per the FBI web site: "The subject of a record in the system may obtain a copy thereof by making a request in writing with the envelope and the letter clearly marked "Privacy Act Request." The request must include the requester's full name, date of birth and place of birth, a certified check or money order in the amount of $18 made payable to the Treasurer of the United States, and a set of rolled-inked fingerprint impressions placed upon fingerprint cards or forms commonly utilized for applicant or law enforcement purposes by law enforcement agencies. The requester must also provide a return address for transmitting the information. Such requests for access to information must be addressed to the Federal Bureau of Investigation, CJIS Division, Attn: SCU, Mod. D-2, 1000 Custer Hollow Road, Clarksburg, WV 26306." See http://foia.fbi.gov/firs552.htm.

☐ Grounds of inadmissibility under INA §212(a) should be reviewed. Common grounds of inadmissibility include:

> ➤ Being HIV+;

> ➤ Being convicted (including receiving a "Conditional Discharge" (CD) or any other form of post-plea disposition) of any of a long list of crimes (including some misdemeanors and violations);

> ➤ Previously lying to federal immigration authorities (such as by submitting applications with false information or presenting false documents);

> ➤ Previously lying to government officials about being a U.S. citizen;

> ➤ Entering the U.S. without inspection by coming across the border when no one was looking;

> ➤ Receiving an order of exclusion, deportation or removal, but not leaving the U.S. or staying outside the U.S. for less than the required amount of time;

> ➤ Living in the U.S. without immigration authorization, then leaving and either returning or seeking return to the U.S.

> ➤ Helping other people to enter the U.S. unlawfully; and

> ➤ Unlawful voting.

Note that most, but not all, grounds of inadmissibility may be waived under INA §212(d)(14). If a U petitioner or derivative family member may be subject to a ground of inadmissibility, the likelihood of success of a waiver of the ground(s) of inadmissibility filed on Form I-192 should be considered in light of the regulations at 8 CFR §212.17.

---

understand the nature of your client's criminal record before continuing with any immigration filing. Resources available include www.criminalandimmigrationlaw.com; www.nlada.org/Defender/Defender_Immigrants/Defender_Immigrants/ Defender_Immigrants_Consequence; www.nationalimmigrationproject.org/ImmRightsRes/IRR.html#imm_consq_crim _convctns; www.immigrantdefenseproject.org (New York, Connecticut, New Jersey and Vermont); and www.ilrc.org/online resource.php (California and Arizona).

☐ Interview the client to learn client's story, including relevant immigration history, qualifying criminal activities of which he or she has been a victim, nature of cooperation with investigating or prosecuting authorities and substantial harm suffered.

☐ Review Form I-918 and any answers that might require an explanatory affidavit.

☐ Review Form I-192, if it will be filed, and review sympathetic nature of the circumstances surrounding the events which have made the client inadmissible and aspects on the client's life which tend to suggest that USCIS should favorably exercise discretion; such information will be required for an affidavit in support of the I-192.

☐ Review Form I-193, if it will be filed, and the reasons why the noncitizen is unable to obtain a passport.

☐ Review with client the universe of documents to be gathered, including all of those on the pre-meeting check-list and come up with a plan of action, including determining a time-frame, identifying which documents will be gathered and prepared, and who will do the gathering and preparing (i.e., the client, the lawyer, the paralegal or someone else).

Follow-up actions after first and second meetings:

☐ Draft affidavit from U petitioner describing (1) substantial physical or mental abuse suffered as a result of the U crime itself or a series of actions over time, of which the U crime was just one of many actions; (2) knowledge of U criminal activity; (3) helpfulness to the investigation or prosecution;[7] and (4) nature (i.e., domestic violence) and place (i.e. in the United States) of U criminal activity.

☐ Draft additional affidavits that may be required to provide (1) additional information on responses to questions on Form I-918; (2) support for the request for a waiver of inadmissibility on Form I-192, if such waiver will be filed; and (3) support for the request for a waiver of the passport requirement, if such waiver will be filed.

☐ Gather supporting documents, per discussion at first meeting.

☐ For a client who has not previously been granted deferred action through interim relief under the U statute, obtain a signed Supplement B to Form I-918[8] that certifies the primary U petitioner's helpfulness in the investigation or prosecution; the signature must be obtained from the head of a certifying agency (as defined by 8 CFR §214.14(a)(2)), a specific designee of the head of a certifying agency,[9] or a judge.

☐ Identify which forms are to be filed by reviewing the directions to Form I-918[10] and Sanctuary for Families' question and answer chart on forms.[11]

---

7   Descriptions should be limited to helpfulness rather than any noncooperation after such time as a law enforcement agency provides a certification of helpfulness. Post-helpful noncooperation may be the basis for revoking a U status or not granting lawful permanent resident status to a noncitizen in U nonimmigrant status. *See* 8 CFR §214.14(h)(2)(i)(A) (revocation) and INA §245(m)(1) (statutory provisions regarding the granting of lawful permanent resident status to those in U nonimmigrant status).

8   Supplement B to Form I-918 is found at the last three pages of Form I-918, *available at www.uscis.gov/files/form/I-918.pdf.*

9   If the certifying official is neither a judge nor the head of the certifying agency, the petitioner should include "evidence of the agency head's written designation of the certifying official for this specific purpose." Instructions for I-918, Supplement B, U Nonimmigrant Status Certification.

10 *www.uscis.gov/files/form/I-918instr.pdf.*

11 The chart "Preparing a U nonimmigrant status petition: Which forms will you need?" is included above and is available on the *probono.net/ny/family* website (registration is free) in the library under immigration.

☐ Ensure that you understand the immigration consequences of any interactions between your client and any criminal justice systems in the U.S. or abroad.

Actions for second meeting:

☐ If client has obtained fingerprints, submit to the FBI for background check, per instructions above.

☐ Review and have all relevant forms signed.

☐ Review and have the client sign his or her affidavit(s).

☐ Review supporting documents that have been gathered.

Actions for final client meeting (which can be either the second or the third meeting):

☐ Confirm that all required forms have been completely filled out and signed.

☐ Obtain checks or money orders for all required fees or, for indigent clients, draft fee waiver requests following the instructions at 8 CFR §103.7(c) for fees that are waivable which, at the time of this writing, include the biometric fee and the fee for Form I-765 required for derivative beneficiaries (but not principal U petitioners) in the U.S. who seek work permits.

Final submission checklist

☐ Brief (one to two page) cover letter;[12]

☐ Index of documents;[13]

☐ Signed Form I-918;

☐ Biometric fee ($80) in check or money order made out the **U.S. Department of Homeland Security** or fee waiver request for Form I-918;

☐ Signed Form I-918, Supplement A for each derivative family member;

☐ Proof of previous grant of deferred action under interim U relief procedures or original Form I-918, Supplement B,

> ➤ Signed in the six months proceeding the filing the I-918;
> ➤ Signed by:
> > o a judge; or
> > o the head of the certifying agency; or
> > o a specified designee of the certifying agency where the designee has supervisory responsibilities and the agency head the head has explicitly designated said certifier.[14]

---

12 See "Cover letter accompany U petition submission" available on the probono.net/ny/family web site (registration is free) in the library under immigration.

13 See Model index accompanying Petition for U Nonimmibrant Status on Form I-918 on the probono.net/ny/family web site (registration is free) in the library under immigration.

14 If the certifying official is neither a judge nor the head of the certifying agency, the petitioner should include "evidence of the agency head's written designation of the certifying official for this specific purpose." Instructions for I-918, Supplement B,

☐ Copies of identity and status documents (passports, birth certificates, marriage certificates, divorce decrees and death certificates) for petitioner and each derivative family member.

☐ Signed statement from U petitioner (or from parent, guardian or next friend where U petitioner is 15 or younger at time of the crime, incapacitated or incompetent).

☐ Supporting documentation of facts surrounding crime and substantial harm suffered (police, court and hospital records, supporting statements, etc.).

☐ Copies of immigration documents indicating lawful entry, such as I-94 card, if available.

☐ Signed Notice of Appearance on Form G-28 (printed out on blue paper) for principal and for each family member represented.

☐ 2 passport photos for I-918 principal petitioner, if he or she wants a work permit.

☐ Signed Form I-192 for petitioner and each derivative family member who is inadmissible under INA §212(a), along with:
  ➢ Supporting statement an other evidence, if any, supporting request for favorable exercise of discretion;
  ➢ A check or money order for $545 made out the **U.S. Department of Homeland Security** for each Form I-192 (as no fee waiver available).

☐ Signed Form I-193 for petitioner and each derivative family member who does not have a passport and cannot obtain one, along with:
  ➢ Supporting statement an other evidence, if any, supporting request for favorable exercise of discretion and explaining why passport cannot be obtained;
  ➢ A check or money order for $545 made out the **U.S. Department of Homeland Security** for each Form I-193 (as no fee waiver available).

☐ Signed Form I-765 for each derivative beneficiary present in the U.S. on whose behalf a Form I-918, Supplement A has been filed, along with:
  ➢ 2 passport photos;
  ➢ A check or money order for $175 made out the **U.S. Department of Homeland Security** or a fee waiver request for each Form I-765.

The Petition for U Nonimmigrant Status on Form I-918 and all additional forms and supporting materials are submitted to:
VAWA Unit
USCIS – Vermont Service Center
75 Lower Welden Street
St. Albans, VT 05479-0001
Should a legal representative with a G-28 on file need to contact the VAWA Unit post-filing, he or she may leave a voicemail at **1 802 527 4888** or send a fax to **1 802 527 4859**.

U Visa and Nonimmigrant Status Checklist
For clients to review prior to meeting with an attorney or paralegal
(prepared by Sanctuary for Families)

<u>Documents to be gathered before meeting with lawyer or paralegal:</u>

☐ Birth certificates and any marriage certificates, divorce/annulment decrees or death certificates[*] relating to:

> ➢ the primary U petitioner;
> ➢ the children of the U petitioner, whether in the U.S. or abroad;
> ➢ the parents of the U petitioner (where the primary crime victim is under 21), whether in the U.S. or abroad; and
> ➢ the siblings under 18 of the U petitioner (where the primary crime victim is under 21), whether in the U.S. or abroad.

All documents that are not in English must be accompanied by certified translations.

☐ Valid passports, for each U petitioner and derivative.[†]

☐ I-94 cards, if any, of U petitioner and any family members in the U.S.

☐ Copies of any documents previously submitted to or received from federal immigration authorities.

☐ Work permits of each U petitioner and derivative (for those who have work permits).

☐ 2 passport pictures for each family member in the US who would like a work permit (both principal U petitioner and derivative family members).

☐ Social security cards (or numbers, if the card is unavailable) of each U petitioner and derivative (for those who have social security numbers).

☐ All police reports concerning incidents of violence against U petitioner by abuser who perpetrated the U crime.

☐ All orders of protection between the U petitioner, the U petitioner's family and abuser who perpetrated U crime.

☐ All documents relating to any court (i.e., divorce, civil suit) cases involving the U petitioner, the petitioner's family and the person who committed the criminal activity.

☐ All hospital and other medical records concerning incidents of violence or trauma resulting from such incidents suffered by U petitioner and family members.

☐ Letters from counselors, case managers and shelter workers who interacted with U petitioner and family members in connection with incidents of violence against U petitioner by perpetrator of the U criminal activity.

☐ Statement from U petitioner (or parent if the U petitioner was 16 or under at the time of the crime) describing criminal activities and the harm suffered.

---

[*] For deceased family members.

[†] Noncitizens who are unable to obtain passports must file Form I-193 to waive the passport requirement. As of May 4, 2008, the fee for this form is $545.

U VISAS AND NONIMMIGRANT STATUS
ACCESS FOR NON-CITIZENS AND THEIR FAMILIES, DEPENDING ON AGE, COMPETENCE AND CAPACITY

Issue	Age/Capacity	U visa and nonimmigrant status requirement or benefit
Cooperation	16 years of age or older (on date of crime)	• Must possess information on the crime. • Must have been helpful or be likely to be helpful in the future to a law enforcement agency.
	15 years of age or younger	Parent, guardian or next friend: • Must possess information on the crime. • Must have been helpful or be likely to be helpful in the future.
	Incapacitated or incompetent	Parent, guardian or next friend: • Must possess information on the crime. • Must have been helpful or be likely to be helpful in the future.
Submission of a statement with the U visa or nonimmigrant status petition	16 years of age or older (on date of crime)	Must prepare and submit a "signed statement . . . describing the facts of the victimization."
	15 years of age or younger	Either the petitioner <u>or</u> a parent, guardian or next friend must prepare and a submit a "signed statement . . . describing the facts of the victimization."
	Incapacitated or incompetent	Either the petitioner <u>or</u> a parent, guardian or next friend must prepare and a submit a "signed statement . . . describing the facts of the victimization."
Derivative family members eligible for U visas and nonimmigrant status[1]	21 years or older (on the date of application)	The following family members may receive visas at the same time as (or following to join) the principal applicant: • Spouse (U-2); • Unmarried children under 21 (U-3).
	20 years old or younger (on the date of application)	The following family members may receive visas at the same time as (or following to join) the principal applicant: • Spouse (U-2); • Unmarried children under 21 (U-3); • Parent (U-4); and • Unmarried siblings under 18 (U-5).

---

[1] Please be aware that the issues with respect to the date on which a noncitizen must be a certain age to either be a derivative or include derivative family members is unclear in both statute and regulations at the time of this writing. The age approach suggested in this chart should be taken only as a guideline.

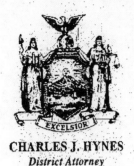

CHARLES J. HYNES
District Attorney

OFFICE OF THE DISTRICT ATTORNEY, KINGS COUNTY

RENAISSANCE PLAZA at 350 JAY STREET
BROOKLYN, N.Y. 11201-2908
(718) 250-2000

October 18, 2007

Violence Against Women Act (VAWA) Unit
Vermont Service Center
U.S. Citizenship and Immigration Services
75 Lower Welden Street
St. Albans, VT 05479

Dear Sir or Madam:

I am the elected District Attorney of Kings County, New York. In this capacity, I am the Chief Law Enforcement Officer for Kings County and I am responsible for prosecuting New York State crimes committed in Kings County, New York and my office is a certifying agency, as such term is defined at 8 C.F.R. §214.14(a)(2).

Pursuant to 8 C.F.R.§ 214.14(a)(3) and 8 C.F.R.§ 214.14(c)(2)(i), I hereby specifically designate Deirdre Bialo-Padin, Domestic Violence Bureau Chief to sign I-918 Supplement B, U Nonimmigrant Status Certification forms. Ms. Bialo-Padin has supervisory responsibilities. In addition, I specifically designate Amy P. Feinstein, Chief Assistant District Attorney to sign I-918 Supplement B, U Nonimmigrant Status Certification forms. Ms. Feinstein also has supervisory responsibilities. This specific designation shall remain in force until revoked in writing.

Very truly yours,

Charles J. Hynes

ADVANCED ISSUES IN WORKING WITH NONCITIZEN CRIME VICTIMS: WINNING U AND T VISAS, WORKING WITH LAW ENFORCEMENT, AND ETHICAL CONSIDERATIONS FOR ALL IMMIGRATION PRACTITIONERS ENCOUNTERING VICTIMS OF TRAFFICKING AND CRIMES

by Lea M. Webb, Gail Pendleton, and B. Kent Felty*

INTRODUCTION

This article covers ethical considerations in working with crime victims; practice pointers on U visas and working with law enforcement; and practice pointers on T visas, including ethical issues for business immigration practitioners who may unwittingly help human traffickers. The section on ethical considerations is a necessary introduction for anyone who plans to represent a crime victim seeking immigration status.

ETHICAL CONSIDERATIONS: WORKING WITH IMMIGRANT CRIME VICTIMS

Ethics color every day in the life of an attorney. The codes of ethics and professional conduct to which we are bound are a sort of Constitution—a guiding principle by which to judge the work that we do and how we do it. The "U" and "T" visas present some of the same challenges as any other work, and some previously not contemplated. It is "new" and not often encountered, but that may be because we are still not looking. When we begin to do the work, we face situations that are unlike the usual family– and employment-based application, and we are presented with the need to work alongside traditional foes. There is a great deal to consider, but basic ethical standards can prevent most common pitfalls. This article references the American Bar Association (ABA) *Model Rules of Professional Conduct*, but you should consult your state code before you begin your work.[1]

Competence

Every practitioner of immigration law does not offer every service, but we are responsible under most state codes for identifying the issues at hand pursuant to the rules requiring competence.[2] "Perhaps the most fundamental legal skill consists of determining what kind of legal problems a situation may involve ...."[3] Taking the issues as they present

* **Lea M. Webb** is a founding partner of Webb & Pillich, LLC, in Cincinnati. Her practice is limited to immigration law. Ms. Webb received her B.A. from Centre College in Danville, KY in 1992 and her J.D./M.A. in Women's Studies and Law from the University of Cincinnati College of Law in 2001. On graduation, she was awarded a National Association for Public Interest Law (now Equal Justice Works) fellowship to begin a program serving immigrant victims of crime at Legal Aid of the Bluegrass in north, central, and east Kentucky, and continued the project until 2005. Ms. Webb is an active volunteer and consultant with several nonprofit agencies that provide services and training to benefit immigrants, especially immigrant victims of crime. She authored the section of this article on ethical considerations in working with crime victims.

Gail Pendleton is the co-founder and co-chair of the National Network to End Violence Against Immigrant Women, and co-director of ASISTA, a national immigration law technical assistance project funded by the federal Office on Violence Against Women. Formerly associate director of the National Immigration Project of the National Lawyers Guild, where she worked for 20 years, she is now an independent consultant, providing innovative multidisciplinary training on immigration options for immigrant survivors of domestic violence, sexual assault, and trafficking. She received AILA's Human Rights Award in 2001. Ms. Pendleton received her J.D. in 1985 from N.Y.U. School of Law and her A.B. from Harvard/Radcliffe College in 1981. She authored the section of this article on U visas.

B. Kent Felty is special counsel at The Mastin Law Firm in Greenwood Village, CO. Mr. Felty has appeared on NBC Nightly News with Tom Brokaw and on National Public Radio's This American Life, as well as in print in various national and international publications in connection with his groundbreaking litigation for victims of human trafficking. He was plaintiffs' counsel for 52 Indian citizens in *Chellen v. John Pickle Co.*, 344 F. Supp. 2d 1278, 446 F. Supp. 2d 1247 (N.D. Okla. 2004, N.D. Okla. 2006), in which a judgment in excess of $1.3 million was awarded. Mr. Felty also successfully argued for the implementation of civil RICO statutes in a human trafficking scheme involving 215 Indian citizens in Louisiana. *Abraham v. Singh*, 480 F.3d 351 (5th Cir. 2007). He received his B.A. from Louisiana State University and his J.D. from the University of Tulsa. Mr. Felty currently has a general immigration practice. He authored the section of this article on T visas.

---

[1] *See www.abanet.org/cpr/links.html#States* for links to state ethics codes and opinions.

[2] Model Rules of Prof'l Conduct, R. 1.1.

[3] *Id.* at cmt. 2.

in practice, we must begin with consultations or screening for benefits and relief. "General practice" immigration attorneys usually use a screening tool to assess the complete immigration possibilities and liabilities of a client. We look for the traditionally taught three bases of immigration relief: family, employment, and humanitarian. Since 2000, there has existed a fourth basis: crime victim. It is critical to screen in a way that will allow you to identify victims of crime. Similar to screening for a basis for an asylum claim, simple and direct questions can be asked, such as:

- Have you ever been intentionally injured by anyone?

- Have you ever called the police, or wanted to call the police, because someone did something to you?

- Has anyone ever threatened to hurt you or your family?

- Has anyone ever done anything bad to you?

Any immigration practitioner may encounter a crime victim who is eligible for crime victim benefits. Victims of rape, domestic violence, extortion, forced labor, and many other crimes undoubtedly walk into an attorney's offices frequently without realizing that they may apply for an immigration benefit.[4] In the author's experience, approximately 10 percent of persons screened could be identified as a victim of crime.

If an attorney is consulting with a couple who intend to have a marriage-based case, or a family that hopes to resettle in the United States due to a business venture, the attorney may identify problems that cause him or her to advise against filing for a benefit (*e.g.*, inadmissibility issues). In that case, the attorney may be inclined to say, "There is simply nothing you can file now." If the attorney has failed to screen for a

crime-victim basis, he or she may be foreclosing possibilities of investigation in many cases.

This brings to light an important practice pointer, which is not contemplated by codes of professional responsibility. Victims of domestic violence or rape will likely not self-identify, and cannot be questioned about victimization in front of friends or family. For this reason it is always preferable to make sure that each person answers his or her own questionnaire, and that cases are only assessed in person and in private. When the author's firm receives calls regarding family members that have been detained, we advise the calling family member that we cannot assess the case without speaking to the detainee. There are many details about presence and entries that are hard for family members to answer, but whether a person has been or is being abused is most certainly not an appropriate question for a friend or family member, who may have no reason to know, or every reason not to answer properly.

On the flip side of the your-client-may-be-a-victim chip is … you guessed it—your-client-may-be-a-perpetrator.[5] You need to be prepared to advise your client how to stay out of the victim/perpetrator game. When your client wants you to make a phone call, or write a letter, or take action in court to intimidate or retaliate against an immigrant employee or family member, you must take a deep breath and speak candidly. If an employee wants to quit, neither you nor the client should do anything to threaten or harm that employee. Yes, you can notify U.S. Citizenship and Immigration Services (USCIS), and may even have a responsibility to do so, but USCIS is not U.S. Immigration and Customs Enforcement (ICE). You may need to file civil suit over damages or file a criminal complaint if there was criminal action, but calling the police or threatening legal action that is inappropriate is simply designed to retaliate for hurt feelings—and may be seen as a part of a pattern of abuse. Advising your clients not to be abusively controlling will help them and may keep you from becoming part of a criminal investigation.

---

[4] The Bureau of Justice Statistics reports that there were 23 million crimes committed in 2005 in the United States alone against persons 12 years old or older. *See www.ojp.usdoj.gov/bjs/cvictgen.htm* (criminal victimization statistics from the Department of Justice, Office of Justice Programs, Bureau of Justice Statistics); Family Violence Prevention Fund, "The Facts on Immigrant Women and Domestic Violence," *available at www.endabuse.org/resources/facts/Immigrant.pdf*. If we add the number of crimes committed against children and the disproportionately high number of crimes committed against immigrants, we can *see* why I have found that in 10 percent of the screenings I conduct, the person has been the victim of crime.

---

[5] *See generally www.usdoj.gov/whatwedo/whatwedo_ctip.html;* M. Herbst, "Are H-1B Workers Getting Bilked? Business Week (Jan. 31, 2008), *available at www.businessweek.com/magazine/content/08_06/b4070057782750.htm;* Southern Poverty Law Center, "Holding the Deportation Card," *www.splcenter.org/legal/guestreport/guest4.jsp*.

Scope of Representation

Because the crime-victim bases are multifaceted, any contract with the client should specify exactly what you will try to achieve, and possible limitations. Immigrant crime victims must be certified by law enforcement, abuse-investigating officials, or judges as cooperating (past, present, or possibly in the future) in either the investigation or prosecution of the crime(s) of which they have been a victim.[6] If you are hired by someone who previously cooperated, but has not yet been certified, you should limit the scope of your representation clearly. If you cannot achieve certification, you will not (except, possibly, in the case of some victims under age 16) be able to apply for the benefit.

Clients "Under a Disability or with Diminished Capacity"

ABA Model Rule 1.14 is called "Client with Diminished Capacity." Victims of crime generally do not have "diminished capacity," but some crime victims are suffering in the throes of trauma. Often, this is a result of the crime. It can make serving the client very challenging. I have found that the *Model Rules* admonishment works very well:

> When a client's capacity to make adequately considered decisions in connection with a representation is diminished, whether because of minority, mental impairment or for some other reason, the lawyer shall, *as far as reasonably possible, maintain a normal client-lawyer relationship with the client.*

Over the past eight years, I have had the great honor to work with many victims of abuse and crime, and I have seen many of them in mental states that are temporary but terribly severe and hopeless. Maintaining a professional (yet kind and understanding) relationship is essential. Resisting urges to help too much in order to maintain a lawyer/client relationship allows the client to maintain dignity throughout. Advising the client honestly when depression or despair are driving her or his decisions is essential. Reminding the client that you are only an attorney helps to keep you from overextending yourself. Representing a client in these situations is mentally and emotionally draining. You are only an attorney. Do the best you can. Be understanding and kind, but know where your boundaries are and communicate that to the client as you advise

and refer the client for additional mental health or medical services.

Integrity Is Everything

The recognition that crime victims are normal, traumatized people is important also in your consideration of "candor toward the tribunal." When representing a person who is cooperating with law enforcement, the law enforcement agency is, practically speaking, part of the tribunal—it will decide whether or not the cooperation was reasonable. We are guiding our clients through cooperating. Under the *Model Rules*, attorneys are to give adverse information to the tribunal if it is material.[7] Maintaining an open and honest relationship with law enforcement is crucial to cooperating successfully. Law enforcement will benefit from knowing the shortcomings of the case, or of your client as a witness, and providing these are crucial as investigations are underway. Good investigators and prosecutors have no problem working with real humans, and will appreciate your help working with your client.

Of course, no attorney may make any false or misleading statement in representing a client.[8] Therefore, you must have earnest discussions with your client before beginning any work with a law enforcement agency. Revealing shortcomings, prior crimes/convictions, issues of false document use, prior entries/exits/removals, etc., is better up front than after some action has been taken by law enforcement dependent on your client as a witness.

WINNING U VISAS

This section provides practice pointers on how to prepare winning U visa applications. It is not intended as a comprehensive background piece on U procedures and options,[9] but instead is designed for practitioners who have read such information and seek practice pointers based on the experience of those who helped shape the law and now work with USCIS to implement it as Congress intended.

Congress created the U visa in 2000.[10] In 2007, the Department of Homeland Security (DHS) issued

---

[6] INA §214(p)(1); 8 USC §1184(p)(1).

[7] Model Rules of Prof'l Conduct R. 3.3(d).

[8] *Id.* R. 4.1 (Truthfulness in Statements to Others).

[9] For more information on the U visa, *see* J. Dinnerstein, "The 'New' And Exciting U: No Longer Just My Imaginary Friend," in this volume.

[10] Battered Immigrant Women Protection Act of 2000, Pub. L. No. 106-386, §1513, 114 Stat. 1464, 1533–37, part of the

continued

the implementing regulations.[11] Before then, USCIS had created an "interim relief" process that allowed eligible crime victims to obtain deferred action status and gain work authorization.[12]

History and Purpose

Since 1993, the National Network to End Violence Against Immigrant Women has worked with Congress to enhance access to safety and justice for victims of crimes, especially gender-based crimes committed inside the United States. This began with the Violence Against Women Act (VAWA) of 1994.[13] To ensure the law was implemented uniformly and to handle these cases, legacy Immigration and Naturalization Service created a special unit, which resides at the Vermont Service Center.[14] That unit now also handles all U applications.[15] At the same time that Congress was negotiating the U visa with the Network, it was creating the T visa.[16] As a result of this confluence, the structure of the U resembles that of the T, but its eligibility requirements derive from experience working with noncitizen survivors of domestic violence, sexual assault, and stalking.

The U has a dual purpose. Congress intended it both to provide humanitarian relief to immigrant victims of crime *and* to give law enforcement a tool for "community" policing among immigrants. By certifying victims of crime who have been or are likely to be helpful in investigations or prosecutions, law enforcement is able to build relationships of trust with victims and communities that have his-

torically lacked trust in law enforcement.[17] Unlike the T visa, there is no alternative to showing helpfulness for a U visa applicant.[18] So learning to work with your local law enforcement agencies is required for making the U work.

YOU MUST READ THESE BEFORE YOU BEGIN

Read the supplementary information to the regulations.[19] These reflect the agency's experience with, and commitment to, helping victims of crime. Use this language to bolster arguments for your client's eligibility. Also read the notes from the question-and-answer with DHS officials on the U visa interim regulations, available on the ASISTA website.[20] This is information formally provided by USCIS to the Network at a November 2007 conference, and later confirmed and supplemented via e-mail with ASISTA.

Summary of Requirements

To win a U visa, an applicant must show that he or she:

- is a victim of an enumerated crime or "similar criminal activity;"

- possesses useful information about the qualifying crime;

- has been, is being, or is likely to be helpful in investigation or prosecution of an enumerated crime;

- has suffered substantial mental or physical injury from that crime or abuse of which the crime was a part; and (if applicable)

- merits a waiver of inadmissibility.[21]

The special "any credible evidence" standard applies to all elements of the U requirements.[22] The

---

Victims of Trafficking and Violence Protection Act of 2000 (VTVPA).

[11] 72 Fed. Reg. 53014 (Sept. 17, 2007).

[12] Immigration and Naturalization Service (INS) Memorandum, M. Cronin, "Victims of Trafficking and Violence Protection Act of 2000 (VTVPA) Policy Memorandum #2—"T" and "U" Nonimmigrant Visas (Aug. 30, 2001), *available at* www.asistaonline.org/Uvisa/Policy_Memo_-_Cronin_-_8-30-01.pdf.

[13] Pub. L. No. 103-322, §§40701–03, 108 Stat. 1796, 1953–55 (VAWA 1994).

[14] INS Memorandum, P. Virtue, "Supplemental Guidance on Battered Alien Self-Petitioning Process and Related Issues; IIRAIRA Section 384" (May 5, 1997), *published on* AILA InfoNet at Doc. No. 97050590 (*posted* May 5, 1997).

[15] USCIS Memorandum, W. Yates, "Centralization of Interim Relief for U Nonimmigrant Status Applicants" (Oct. 8, 2003), *published on* AILA InfoNet at Doc. No. 03101420 (*posted* Oct. 14, 2003); *see* USCIS Form I-918.

[16] *See* section on trafficking, *infra*.

---

[17] VTVPA §1513(a), 114 Stat. at 1533–34.

[18] *Compare* lack of "shall" requirement at INA §101(a)(15)(T) [8 USC 1101(a)(15)(T)], *with* INA §214(p) [8 USC §1184(p)].

[19] 72 Fed. Reg. 53014 (Sept. 17, 2007).

[20]   www.asistaonline.org/Questions%20for%20CIS%20re%20U%20Visas.doc.

[21] INA §101(a)(15)(U); 8 USC §1101(a)(15)(U). An applicant under 16 may satisfy the information-possession and helpfulness requirements if his or her "parent, guardian, or next friend" provides the required assistance. INA §101(a)(15)(U)(i)(III); 8 USC §1101(a)(15)(U)(i)(III); 8 CFR §§214.14(b)(2) (information possession), (3) (helpfulness).

[22] 8 CFR §214.14(c)(4).

law enforcement certification[23] supplies evidence of the first three eligibility requirements.[24] Everyone should explore and submit additional evidence of victimization, possession of useful evidence, and helpfulness, as well as substantial physical or mental harm.[25] This could include "primary evidence, such as court documents and copies of evidence your client provided to law enforcement, and "any credible evidence," such as declarations from others (besides law enforcers) who can corroborate and elaborate on the information supplied in the original certification.

What Crimes?

The list of crimes in the statute includes:[26]

- Rape
- Torture
- Trafficking
- Incest
- Domestic violence
- Sexual assault
- Prostitution
- Female genital mutilation
- Being held hostage
- Peonage
- Involuntary servitude
- Slave trade
- Kidnapping
- Abduction
- False Imprisonment
- Blackmail
- Extortion
- Manslaughter
- Murder
- Felonious assault
- Witness tampering
- Obstruction of justice
- Perjury
- Attempt, conspiracy, or solicitation to commit any of these crimes.

It is essential to recognize that the list is not exclusive, but descriptive. The supplementary information in the regulations points out that the statutory list of qualifying crimes

> is not a list of specific statutory violations, but instead a list of general categories of criminal activity. It is also a non-exclusive list. . . . [T]he criminal activity listed is stated in broad terms. . . . In addition, qualifying criminal activity may occur during the commission of non-qualifying criminal activity. For varying reasons, the perpetrator may not be charged or prosecuted for the qualifying criminal activity, but instead, for the non-qualifying criminal activity.[27]

The statute requires helpfulness in an investigation *or* prosecution. As noted below in the section on work-

ing with law enforcement, many crimes may be investigated initially but only one charged or prosecuted, or no prosecution may occur at all. This is one reason you need to work closely with law enforcement to help explain what they can certify for your client.

Partnering with Advocates

If you are working with a victim of domestic violence or sexual assault,[28] you should partner with an advocate with experience working with this population.[29] Advocates from these arenas can help you and your client to:

- do the safety planning necessary for each individual case;

- ensure your client is accessing any civil and criminal remedies he or she needs;

- monitor what is happening in the civil and criminal systems that may affect your client's immigration options;

- provide a "trusted" connection to law enforcement to pursue U visas;[30]

- help your client navigate the various systems she or he encounters, which otherwise may revictimize the client or send her/him to ICE; and

- work with your client to collect and prepare the documentation you need, including your client's declaration and supporting evidence on substantial physical or mental abuse.

Safety Planning

Abusers (and perpetrators) may respond violently to attempts by their victims to escape their control or bring them to justice. This includes when the victim contacts law enforcement or files for immigration status. Unless you are trained in working with survi-

---

[23] Form I-918, Supplement B.

[24] 8 CFR §214.14(c)(2)(i).

[25] 8 CFR §§214.14(c)(2)(ii), (iii).

[26] INA §101(a)(15)(U)(iii); 8 USC §1101(a)(15)(U)(iii).

[27] 72 Fed. Reg. 53014, 53018 (Sept. 17, 2007) (supplementary information).

[28] An extremely helpful guide for attorneys working with domestic violence victims generally is the new Standards of Practice for Lawyers Representing Victims of Domestic Violence, Sexual Assault and Stalking in Civil Protection Order Cases (2007), a project of the ABA Commission on Domestic Violence, *available at www.abanet.org/domviol/docs/ StandardsCommentary.pdf*. Make sure you get the version with commentary. Though designed for those in civil courts, the rules and guidelines apply with equal force or by analogy to those representing noncitizen victims of domestic violence.

[29] Contact the National Network to End Violence Against Immigrant Women to find advocates in your area who work with immigrant victims of crimes by sending an e-mail to Ana Manigat, *ana@nationalimmigrationproject.org*.

[30] The advocates often have existing relationships with allies in the system.

vors of violence, advocates must help you and your client identify risks and dangers and develop a "safety plan." As noted in the section on ethics, these cases are not like most other immigration cases. Your client may end up dead if you take actions that trigger violence from the perpetrator. An additional benefit to working with advocates is that they often already have contacts and resources for helping to keep your client safe and feeling as secure as possible.

Documenting Your Case

In addition to the forms, you should supply:

- a declaration from the applicant;[31]

- a certification that he or she "has been, is being or is likely to be helpful" in investigating or prosecuting an enumerated crime;[32]

- any additional documentation available supporting the claims in his or her declaration;[33]

- identification of inadmissibility grounds and why he or she meets the waiver standard;[34] and

- applications for any derivatives he or she wishes to include.[35]

Write a "road map" cover letter that bullet points how your client meets the eligibility requirements and highlights any special issues, such as inadmissibility waivers and derivatives. Explain here, if necessary, why this documentation meets the "any credible evidence" standard.

Although the VAWA/crime victim unit understands the "any credible evidence" standard, the adjudicators will want to see any primary documents they think should exist based on your client's story. If your client doesn't have them, explain why, and then explain why the other evidence you supplied is credible and all you can find to document that particular eligibility requirement.

Create an index for your documents that organizes them by eligibility element (repeating documents is fine), with a brief summary of how each document demonstrates that eligibility requirement. Highlight within each document the portion that shows eligibility. (This process should sound famil-

iar to those of you who have done asylum cases; victims-of-crime cases are very similar to asylum cases in this and many other respects.)

Preparing and Presenting the Applicant's Declaration

Every U applicant must supply a declaration describing his or her case.[36]

Such declarations should explain how the applicant:

- is a victim of an enumerated crime,

- possesses information about that crime,[37]

- suffered substantial mental or physical abuse as a result of the crime,[38] and

- is helping, was helping, or may help law enforcement in the crime's investigation, or prosecution.[39]

Your client's declaration will be scrutinized closely for credibility. Experience with the self-petitioning process teaches that it is extremely difficult to rehabilitate your client's credibility once it is called into question by discrepancies in his or her application.

As with asylum applicants and victims of domestic violence, getting your client's story will take time. The declaration also should be in your client's own words; declarations that sound like they were written by you will be disregarded by the VAWA unit and may even raise credibility concerns. *Use trained advocates* to help your clients tell their full story, in their own words.

Showing Substantial Physical or Mental Abuse (Harm)

The regulations provide a broad definition of "substantial abuse."[40] While your client's declaration will be the first document the unit reviews, other documentation of your client's suffering should be included if at all possible. Advocates who work with victims of crimes may be extremely helpful, because they are considered "experts" by law.[41] Sometimes, asking the advocate to explain your client's declaration, putting it into a victim-of-crime context, can be

---

[31] *See infra* for details on the declaration.

[32] 8 CFR §214.14(c)(2)(ii).

[33] Id.

[34] 8 CFR §214.14(c)(2)(iv).

[35] 8 CFR §214.14(f).

[36] 8 CFR §214.14(c)(2)(iii).

[37] 8 CFR §214.14(b)(2).

[38] 8 CFR §214.14(b)(1).

[39] 8 CFR §214.14(c)(2)(ii).

[40] 8 CFR §214.14(b)(1).

[41] This advice is based on the author's discussions with VAWA unit adjudicators and supervisors during trainings at the Vermont Service Center and for the field.

very helpful. Most crime victims will not self-describe as suffering from trauma, for instance, or as having grave difficulties coping with basic life functions. Advocates can explain harms, objectively, based on work with your client or review of the client's declaration. This is especially important if the client has no physical impairment. To help an advocate or your client with beginning to write a statement, you might ask him or her to address the list of factors cited in the regulations, which include:[42]

- the nature of the injury;
- the severity of the perpetrator's conduct;
- the severity of the harm suffered;
- the duration of the infliction of harm;
- any permanent or serious harm to appearance;
- health and physical or mental soundness; and
- any aggravation of a victim's pre-existing conditions.

The Subjective Perspective

USCIS will evaluate the kind and degree of harm suffered by the applicant "based upon that applicant's individual experience."[43] This last factor demonstrates that USCIS is looking at U visas based on its experience with domestic violence survivors and trafficking victims. USCIS has seen that victims of such abuse are often severely traumatized by acts that would have little or no effect on a nonvictim. It understands that perceptions of actions or threats can differ greatly according to an individual's history of violence. Perpetrators and abusers use this history/developed perception to threaten victims with acts that may seem innocuous to others.

Both your client and any corroborating declarations should explain this subjective context, as well as highlight how your client's experience objectively meets the eligibility requirements.

Overcoming Inadmissibility

The attorney's most important job is identifying inadmissibility.[44] As noted already, much of the other work in preparing the claim can be done by advocates working with your client while addressing his or her other issues as a victim.

A U visa applicant can apply for a waiver of all grounds of inadmissibility except those concerning Nazis or perpetrators of genocide, torture, or extrajudicial killing.[45] The standard for granting the waiver is that it be "in the national or public interest to do so."[46] The standard is novel, and the regulations provide no guidance on its contours, but the self-petitioning and trafficking experience provide some clues. If you meet the standard you can overcome false claims to citizenship, aggravated felonies, and other inadmissibility grounds that generally bar status. The VAWA unit has final discretion, of course, to determine whether your client merits "forgiveness." We have been advised that unlike most other immigration cases, you are in a much better position to obtain the waiver if you are straightforward about your client's inadmissibility from the outset.[47] If the agency later discovers inadmissibility that you did not flag, your client likely will be found to lack credibility generally, and may end up deported.

Some Possible Strategies

The following suggestions are based on experience, but you should check the ASISTA website[48] for updates, since at the time of writing we have no official guidance on how USCIS will interpret the waiver standard. You should provide both general arguments and individualized arguments.

General Argument

Many U applicants will trigger inadmissibility for being "present without admission or parole"[49] or for unlawful presence[50] and other inadmissibility issues arising from being undocumented.[51] Congress targeted the most vulnerable victims of crimes, especially the undocumented, because they are the most afraid to access justice for fear of removal.[52] It is therefore generally in the national and public interest to grant waivers to those whose inadmissibility is directly connected to being undocumented. Individualize this by showing how being undocu-

---

[42] 8 CFR §214.14(b)(1).

[43] 72 Fed. Reg. 53013, 53018 (Sept. 17, 2007).

[44] INA §212(a); 8 USC §1182(a).

[45] INA §212(d)(14); 8 USC §1182(d)(14).

[46] Id.

[47] See also U Visa Q & A, supra note 20.

[48] www.asistaonline.org.

[49] INA §212(a)(6)(A); 8 USC §1182(a)(6)(A).

[50] INA §§212(a)(9)(B), (C); 8 USC §§1182(a)(9)(B), (C).

[51] E.g., fraud and false claims to citizenship on entry, triggering INA §212(a)(6)(C) [8 USC §1182(a)(6)(C)].

[52] See VTVPA §1513(a), 114 Stat. at 1533–34.

mented made your client more vulnerable to crime or more fearful of accessing justice.

Individualize

Do not rely solely on general arguments. Although we hope USCIS eventually will agree that inadmissibility for being undocumented, for instance, merits a blanket waiver, do not expect that to happen soon. In the meantime, you must show how your client personally merits the waiver. Using the factors for showing good moral character, extreme hardship to VAWA applicants, and extreme hardship to trafficking victims may help you frame your argument. How does empowering one victim help to change social acceptance of violence or oppression of victims?

How would you show your client's good moral character? How has your client or your client's children contributed to the community? How can you document this? (Think clergy, children's teachers, or others who can talk about how your client is helping others and her children.)

Review the VAWA extreme hardship factors. These are no longer a requirement for self-petitioners, but they are still in the law for VAWA cancellation applications[53] and are familiar to the unit adjudicating U visas.[54] Like these factors, the extreme hardship factors for trafficking[55] generally look at the connection between the crime and the victim's experience, or juxtapose what the victim and his or her children need here against what would happen if they returned to their home country. Tie these, if possible, to the applicant doing something that enriches the community or our society generally, and you should have a persuasive argument that it is in the national or public interest for your client not to be removed.

Getting the Law Enforcement Certification: Working with Law Enforcement

You are ineligible for a U visa without a certification from law enforcement that your client "has been, is being or is likely to be helpful" in investigating or prosecuting an enumerated crime.[56] You

will probably be working mostly with police departments or district attorneys, or both. Note, however, that the regulations recognize that other agencies, such as Child Protective Services, the Department of Labor (DOL), and the Equal Employment Opportunity Commission (EEOC), may sign certifications.[57] Judges can also certify the cooperation of your client.[58] Form I-918, Supplement B is the form the certifier must use.

At the time of this writing, the interim regulations impose a requirement, not found in statute, that only supervisors or heads of certifying agencies may sign certifications.[59] You should monitor the regulations to see if USCIS rectifies this unnecessary requirement. Fortunately, the Form I-918B (as of this writing) also states that "if the certification is not signed by the head of the certifying agency, please attach evidence of the agency head's written designation of the certifying official for this specific purpose."[60] This provides an opening for law enforcement to provide certifications from those to whom a head of an agency has delegated authority, regardless of that person's title. Work with your local law enforcement agencies to set up a system for obtaining certifications that provides the agencies with maximum flexibility in designating who may certify, while clearly showing that the head of the agency has thoughtfully delegated authority to the officers he or she believed most qualified to certify.[61]

Approaching Law Enforcement: A Few Practice Pointers

These practice pointers are derived from several years' experience training law enforcement on how to work with noncitizen crime victims.[62] They may seem like basic social psychology, but you should determine whether you possess the skill set neces-

---

[53] 8 CFR §§1240.20(c) (VAWA cancellation), 1240.58(c) (VAWA suspension).

[54] See INS Memorandum, P. Virtue, "Extreme Hardship" and Documentary Requirements Involving Battered Spouses and Children" (Oct. 16,1998).

[55] 8 CFR §214.11(i)(1).

[56] 8 CFR §214.14(c)(2)(ii).

[57] 8 CFR §214.14(a)(2).

[58] Note that civil protection orders against domestic violence or stalking often become criminal in nature when violated.

[59] 8 CFR §214.14(a)(3)(i).

[60] Form I-918, Supplement B, Instructions, at 2.

[61] Please contact Gail Pendleton, glpendleton@earthlink.net, if the regulatory limitations are inhibiting your ability to obtain certifications. This information will help inform USCIS and Congress about why and how USCIS must alter the regulations and the form.

[62] Some of these practice pointers are excerpted from Collaborating to Help Trafficking Survivors: Emerging Issues and Practice Pointers, 2006, a manual written by the author for the Family Violence Prevention Fund.

sary to pursue them effectively. You will serve your clients better if you acknowledge that others are better skilled and positioned to approach and work with law enforcement on certifications, especially given the mutually unflattering stereotypes and assumptions law enforcement and attorneys often have of each other.

Think about what law enforcement's experience with attorneys is likely to have been. Whom do they already trust? What can you offer them that would help them (*e.g.,* your client, explanations of immigration law)? Try to understand their priorities (prosecuting perpetrators and keeping communities safe, not just helping your client). Realize that they see the worst sides of our society and the violence humans commit on each other every day. When deciding whether to accept the representation, consider whether you already have a relationship with law enforcement that will not serve a cooperating victim-witness.

Partner with Domestic Violence, Sexual Assault, and Crime Victim Advocates

If there's one message you take from this article, this is it: You *must* partner with advocates to do these cases correctly. Advocates who work with victims of crimes are likely to have existing connections with law enforcement and know which allies to approach.[63] Law enforcement people are much more likely to respond favorably to a request from an advocate they know than to a request from an unknown attorney.

Don't Wait for a Real Case

You do not want to be explaining all of the information and possibilities below in the context of a real case, when an individual's life is at risk. The mere act of discussing the issues below with law enforcement will help forge the personal relationships you will need when you need help with individual cases. Work with your advocate partners to set up meetings, discussions, and trainings, and use hypothetical situations to explore how law enforcement will handle different kinds of cases.

Use the Form

The certification form[64] is a useful tool for your first meetings with law enforcement, because it answers some of the concerns they often raise when initially approached to sign certifications for undocumented victims of crime. For instance, the form explains that while the certification is necessary for obtaining status, it is not sufficient. This answers any law enforcement concerns that they will be giving status to noncitizens by signing a certification or that they will be liable if, for some reason, the victim is unqualified for U status. The form explains that USCIS considers the "totality of the circumstances" in determining whether someone is eligible for a U visa.[65]

Both the regulations and the form fail to mention that the crimes listed are just general categories, not the specific names of the crimes as they appear in state statutes. For instance, the statute lists "domestic violence" as a crime; many states do not have crimes specifically called domestic violence, but use a variety of crimes to investigate and prosecute domestic violence. Share the useful parts of the regulations' supplementary information[66] to explain this to law enforcement and ask them for examples they encounter that demonstrate the point.

Use Domestic Violence as an Example

A good example to explore is domestic violence, because police and prosecutors often have had significant experience and training on this issue. As noted above, law enforcement may use many crimes to investigate and prosecute domestic violence, such as misdemeanor assaults, choking, strangulation, and stalking. None of these are listed in the statute, but they all qualify if the certifier notes that the investigation/prosecution of these crimes was in the domestic violence context.

This is also a good example for exploring the flexibility of the "investigation or prosecution" language. Police may arrive at a scene of domestic violence, but end up charging the abuser with drug possession, because it's easier to prove and will put the abuser away for a longer period of time. This should still qualify your victim client, because the police investigated domestic violence, even though they ended up charging another crime.

---

[63] For referrals to advocates in your area already working with noncitizen crime victims, contact the National Network to End Violence Against Immigrant Women by sending an e-mail to Ana Manigat, *ana@nationalimmigrationproject.org.*

[64] Form I-918B.

[65] 72 Fed. Reg. 53014, 53024 (Sept. 17, 2007) (supplementary information).

[66] *Id.*

Do Not Lecture; Ask Law Enforcement for Help

This is a good time to discuss how to present your information. Lecturing law enforcement about what they "should" or "must" certify will backfire. Congress wants this to be a tool to help them. Emphasize this and ask for their help in figuring out how it will help noncitizen crime victims. They are the experts on what crimes are investigated, not you.

Use the history of how the U visa came into being and the express statutory findings and purpose to show law enforcement that Congress was thoughtful and incremental in deciding that undocumented crime victims needed the U visa, and that it particularly wanted to help law enforcement reach this vulnerable population. The statute provides:[67]

FINDINGS AND PURPOSE-

(1) FINDINGS- Congress makes the following findings:

(A) Immigrant women and children are often targeted to be victims of crimes committed against them in the United States, including rape, torture, kidnapping, trafficking, incest, domestic violence, sexual assault, female genital mutilation, forced prostitution, involuntary servitude, being held hostage or being criminally restrained.

(B) All women and children who are victims of these crimes committed against them in the United States must be able to report these crimes to law enforcement and fully participate in the investigation of the crimes committed against them and the prosecution of the perpetrators of such crimes.

(2) PURPOSE-

(A) The purpose of this section is to create a new nonimmigrant visa classification that will strengthen the ability of law enforcement agencies to detect, investigate, and prosecute cases of domestic violence, sexual assault, trafficking of aliens, and other crimes described in section 101(a)(15)(U)(iii) of the Immigration and Nationality Act committed against aliens, while offering protection to victims of such offenses in keeping with the humanitarian interests of the United States. This visa will encourage law enforcement officials to better serve immigrant crime victims and to prosecute crimes committed against aliens.

_____

[67] VTVPA §1513(a), 114 Stat. at 1533–34 (emphasis added).

(B) Creating a new nonimmigrant visa classification *will facilitate the reporting of crimes to law enforcement officials* by trafficked, exploited, victimized, and abused *aliens who are not in lawful immigration status*. It also gives law enforcement officials a means to regularize the status of cooperating individuals during investigations or prosecutions. Providing temporary legal status to aliens who have been severely victimized by criminal activity also comports with the humanitarian interests of the United States.

Negotiating "Helpfulness"

Domestic violence and sexual assault advocates have experience negotiating victim access and helpfulness with law enforcement. They are better positioned to explain why victims, especially your client, may be unwilling to do exactly what law enforcement wants. The more comfortable a victim feels working with law enforcement, the more likely the victim will be willing to provide help. Some law enforcement officials report that they have found that signing certifications early on in the process encourages victims to be more forthcoming. It also may undermine attempts by defense attorneys to use the certification against victims, impugning their motivation and credibility in criminal court. The earlier the certification is provided, the less it looks like a quid pro quo for testifying against the perpetrator.

Build Trust

This means being clear about where you share common ground and where your priorities differ. Try to understand and respect law enforcement's priorities (keeping our communities safe, for instance), while explaining that your job is to help the client get status, if possible. They will respect your honesty and find it much easier to trust that you are not trying to manipulate them and that you do not have a hidden agenda.

You don't work for them; they don't work for you, but that doesn't mean you can't work together on ensuring to noncitizen victims of crimes access to the safety and justice they need and deserve. This, in turn, helps them find and hold responsible the criminals who prey on immigrant communities. As you work together, you may find that you are a good team (including your advocate allies) for training others.

Reaching Out

Peers are the best trainers. If you find an ally in law enforcement who is sympathetic to noncitizen victims, use her or him to train others in their discipline. They are much better messengers for their peers than lawyers or advocates.

Help law enforcement connect with immigrant communities. Speaking on a radio show that reaches undocumented communities can be particularly helpful, as can speaking at churches or other places immigrant communities feel safe. The basic principle behind this approach is to find a place and messenger trusted by undocumented immigrants; ask that messenger to make the connection between the immigrant community and the criminal system that the community may fear.

Be Patient and Persevere

Building collaborations with law enforcement is challenging, but will pay off for your clients in the long run. It also helps us build understanding and support for fixing our laws that penalize and harm those who lack secure immigration documents. Creating social change takes time; in the meantime, you will know you are helping your crime-victim clients in the best way possible.

Resources

Check the ASISTA website[68] for samples, red flags for inadmissibility, other guidance, and Q&A's with USCIS and ICE. Join the free VAWA updates list serve,[69] where ASISTA sends out the latest practice pointers, suggestions, and guidance from the VAWA unit, legislative updates, and strategies that have worked in the field.

T VISAS

There is significant overlap, in population, procedure, and substantive law when dealing with the T and U visas. Broadly speaking, both visas are designed to protect immigrant victims:

- by ensuring access to the U.S. civil and criminal justice systems;

- by safeguarding the victims' availability so they can assist the state and their civil advocates; and

- by providing a path to legal permanent residence regardless of the victim's manner of entry in the United States.

The T, like the U, was created by the Victims of Trafficking and Violence Protection Act of 2000

(VTVPA).[70] It is significant that the original VTVPA did not enable a civil remedy. However, the Trafficking Victims Protection Reauthorization Acts of 2003 and 2005[71] remedied that oversight, opening up an opportunity to hit the traffickers where it hurts—in their wallets. The allowance of a civil remedy allows the victims of trafficking to sue for money damages and perhaps recognizes the deterrent value of civil liability. However, civil suits have barely cracked the courthouse doors, due to real-world considerations and unforeseen obstacles, discussed below.

The T visa application is submitted with Form I-914. Supporting evidence is similar to what would be gathered in an asylum claim, VAWA self-petition, or U visa application. If an immigration attorney has been contacted to assist, the primary and most helpful document will be the law enforcement agency (LEA) endorsement, which can be executed by federal, state, or local agents.[72] Unlike the U visa application, the T visa application does not *mandate* an LEA endorsement, but without it, the T applicant faces an uphill battle.

Secondary evidence might include victim and witness affidavits, payroll records (if any), travel records, photographs, and, if an LEA is not willing to commit to an endorsement, e-mails and correspondence with officers confirming an open investigation.

For remedies other than immigration, it is difficult for trafficking victims to find representation or pursue a civil action for two reasons: first, many of the defendants in these types of cases have ties to organized crime, and second, the likelihood of collecting a judgment is often distant. As this area develops, however, it may be easier to find attorneys willing and able to seek compensation for the victims and/or put the traffickers out of business via significant judgments, verdicts, or simple exposure to the light of a courthouse door.[73]

---

68 *www.asistaonline.org.*

69 Contact Joanne Picray, *Joanne@asistaonline.org*, or Ana Manigat, *ana@nationalimmigrationproject.org.*

70 *See* Trafficking Victims Protection Act of 2000, Pub. L. No. 106-386, §107(e)(1), 114 Stat. 1464, 1477–78, part of the VTVPA.

71 Trafficking Victims Protection Reauthorization Act of 2003, Pub. L. No. 108-193, 117 Stat. 2875; Trafficking Victims Protection Reauthorization Act of 2005, Pub. L. No. 109-164, 119 Stat. 3558 (2006).

72 8 CFR §214.11(f)(1).

73 The Freedom Network website, *www.freedomnetwork usa.org/members.htm*, is a good resource for information and referrals.

Elements

To qualify for a T visa, the individual must provide evidence that he or she:[74]

- is a victim of a "severe form of human trafficking of persons,"

- is physically present in the United States or its territories as a consequence of this trafficking,

- has cooperated with law enforcement in an investigation or prosecution of the trafficking, or is younger than 15 years of age; and

- would suffer extreme, severe, and unusual hardship if removed from the United States.

What Is a *Severe* Form of Human Trafficking?

A "severe form of human trafficking" is defined in the regulations as:[75]

- sex trafficking in which a commercial sex act is induced by force, fraud, or coercion, or in which the person induced to perform such act has not attained 18 years of age; or the recruitment, harboring, transportation, provision,

  or

- obtaining of a person for labor or services, through the use of force, fraud, or coercion for the purpose of subjection to involuntary servitude, peonage, debt bondage, or slavery.

Egregious Sex Trafficking Cases

Cases involving sex trafficking are easy, in the sense that these cases are sometimes "classic" and were foremost in the legislative mind when the VTVPA was enacted. Stories of persons brought to the United States as "nannies" (or any number of other gateway jobs) had became daily fare in the media as those "nannies" began showing up in brothels—brutalized beyond a normal person's imagination. In these cases (which continue to be found), the "severe" aspect and the "force" aspect are beyond (reasonable) argument, and law enforcement agencies are often unequivocal in assisting the victims in obtaining a T visa. The investigation and prosecution of these classic cases is the primary domain of criminal prosecutors. However, immigration attorneys can and should assist in preparing the T visa application, are often first responders, and are almost always better able to handle the immigration aspects of the case than is law enforcement.

The Majority of Trafficking Cases

The challenge of convincing law enforcement and prosecutors not to treat the victims as perpetrators is frequently overwhelming. The bad news for these types of cases is that: (1) an LEA endorsement can be very hard or impossible to get, and (2) the Vermont Service Center adjudicates each application individually, so the applicant must provide the context of the larger victimization scheme. The good news is that these harder cases are precisely the type Congress envisioned when they enabled civil actions against human traffickers. Further good news is that these types of cases are not beyond any lawyer or nongovernmental organization possessing the desire to help others and the tenacity and humility to keep fighting until the definition of "severe form of human trafficking" comes into alignment with global economics and reality.

Global Economics

Today, in the United States, Canada, and much of Western Europe there is a severe shortage of labor in agriculture, construction, manufacturing, and service industries. In the United States this shortage has been alleviated by immigration (documented and undocumented) from Mexico and Central America. The political and social impact of this migration is beyond the scope of this article. However, it is indisputable that the shortage of labor has created an added incentive to exploit, smuggle, and traffic human beings. As the borders get tighter and caps are reached, the value of workers goes up and employers, legitimate labor recruiters, and immigration lawyers may be less inclined to ask hard questions, as business survival becomes tantamount. On the flip side, in developing (or source) countries, potential workers do not ask hard questions, because to do so would eliminate them from consideration.[76]

Avoiding Trafficking in Persons: The Hard Questions for Attorneys Preparing Employment-Based Applications

In easy cases, the crime is obvious, the victim is obvious, and the perpetrator is obvious. In the harder cases, practitioners have to stop and ask some of the following questions:

---

[74] INA §101(a)(15)(T); 8 USC §1101(a)(15)(T).

[75] 8 CFR §214.11(a).

---

[76] *See* K. Bales, *Disposable People: New Slavery in the Global Economy* (2000). Dr. Bales' book provides the economic context that has birthed human trafficking, contrasts "old" slavery with "new" slavery, and offers concrete suggestions and action points to stop the new slavery.

Who are you dealing with? If you or your clients are drawing workers from a developing nation, you are probably using labor recruiters. If so, *do you know what the labor recruiter is promising as your agent*? For instance, is the recruiter promising "green cards" when your client's need is only temporary and more suitable to H-2 visas? These promises may be imputed to you and your client.

Are the workers your client is sponsoring relying on false promises? For instance, in India, the "price" for an H-2B visa to the United States has gone from about $3,000 in "recruiting fees" to $20,000 or more. Very few persons have these fees in a savings account. They borrow money, generally at usurious rates, not from a bank. They cannot hope to pay these loans back when they may only net minimum wage after living expenses. These workers are extremely vulnerable and easily controlled, and often have been transported to the United States via fraud. They may be in debt bondage to third parties you do not know. They will suffer severe and unusual hardship if they are required to go back to their home country; they will be humiliated, hounded, and physically injured or killed if they do not pay the loans back. For example, no one in Cochin, India—especially those who lend money—believes that any person could spend 10 months in the United States and not come back rich. Beyond that, the families of the recruiters are left behind and vulnerable to the terror tactics.

Is the person sponsored really qualified or able to do the job? If the employer is relying on a person who is charging unconscionable fees, it is highly likely that some of the workers who arrive in the United States will have been selected on the basis of their willingness to pay the fee, not on their experience or necessary skills. Again, ask yourself *who* you are dealing with and insist on reputable testing and reliable interviewers. Those testers and interviewers should be independent—not connected to the recruiter. The best practice is to send trusted "in house" personnel to test and interview. Many endline employers are faced with persons who cannot do the work they were hired to do and are therefore terminated. Those persons are tied to the sponsor (most notably in the H-2B context) and cannot simply "go down the road" and get another job. In one case, the employer had no idea that a man had gone into extreme debt to buy a visa. All the employer

knew is that the man could not do the work.[77] That employer is now a target for litigation and/or criminal prosecution.

A Severe Case of Trafficking or a Busted Contract?

The answer to the question above is very subjective. Currently, on the facts noted above, you might prevail on a civil action, but will likely be denied a T visa. The employer's agent may have lied and the employees may owe money in their home country than they can ever pay back. But many in the criminal and civil systems may say "isn't that just a 'busted contract'?" There must be more, which is the LEA endorsement. Many U.S. Attorneys may believe, however, that if they certify cooperation of the victim, they are committing to prosecute.

In a human trafficking/labor exploitation scheme there are generally dozens—if not hundreds—of victims. Often the victims do not speak English, meaning that the trial will be presented through translators and thus very long. The traffickers, on the other hand, are always well represented and well financed and can put pressure on the families of the victims. The manpower and money it takes to prosecute may not, in such situations, be worth it in the eyes of the government. The U.S. Attorney may keep an FBI agent on the periphery in case someone is actually killed, and may drop a line to ICE or confirm an investigation by e-mail, but very seldom will they go to war on these cases. They view the issue as just a "busted contract."

On the one hand, unless you can show how the victim attempted to comply with law enforcement requests despite the lack of an LEA endorsement, USCIS may not issue a T visa. The victims may not be able to work, and the case may die for lack of funding and witnesses. On the other hand, if you have more than "a hell of a fraud case," as a recent case involving 215 Indian citizens was characterized,[78] you may be able to move the case from "busted contract" to "severe form of human trafficking."

Pushing the Envelope

Imagine the same scenario as above—in which persons have been lied to, have borrowed huge

---

[77] *See* C. Helman, "Labor Unrest," *Forbes* (June 4, 2007), *available at www.forbes.com/business/global/2007/0604/058.html*, for a recent example of all that can go wrong in an H-2B program.

[78] *Abraham v. Singh*, 480 F.3d 351 (5th Cir. 2007).

sums, have come to the United States relying on promises that have been broken, and have fallen into debt bondage—then add some elements of cruelty and control by the end-line employer, or collusion with the recruiter. At that point, you are pushing the envelope beyond a bad contract to trafficking, both for getting T visas and for success in civil litigation.

For instance, you should question situations in which employees came to the United States via a training program, especially if the employees are doing work, putting products into the stream of commerce, displacing the native workforce, or otherwise appear to be acting as regular employees. Is there a real trainee program? Do the workers consider themselves trainees? You may, instead, be dealing with an employer who knows it isn't a real trainee program and simply wants to cut labor costs and compete unfairly. This is immigration fraud.

Find out how much the victim is actually making an hour. Smarter traffickers will make sure they pay at least minimum wage. Nevertheless, if you have a minimum wage violation you may have the beginning of a human trafficking case.

Ask who arranged the documents and paperwork, and how. Generally, in these types of cases, the initial promises are verbal, the worker pays the recruiter, the recruiter divides the fee as previously agreed (with the employer), the recruiter walks the worker through the consular interview, the recruiter collects the stamped passport at the embassy gates, the recruiter increases the fee, the worker pays the new/additional fee, the recruiter meets the workers at the airport (usually in a large group), and the recruiter presents the workers with documents to sign. The documents state that the worker never paid anything to anybody. By this time, the worker is in deep debt and has no way out and no way back. He or she signs the papers, is given his or her passport back, and gets on an airplane.

The next phase is crucial in terms of obtaining a T visa.

Cruelty and Control

If you are confronted with a story that tracks the one above, it is critical to ask the victim how he or she was treated upon arrival in the United States. The tell-tale sign of a trafficking scheme occurs when the passport and I-94 are collected on arrival, either by the end-line employer or by a "buffer-level subcontractor." The confiscation of travel documents is the beginning of the end of the victim's sense of freedom. It is usually done immediately upon arrival, while the victim is sleepy or disoriented from travel.

If the end-line employer is aware of the vulnerability of the worker via close contact with the labor recruiter, that employer knows there are almost no limits to the amount of abuse the employee will endure to keep the job. The only true limit is the greed of the employer or sense of humanity the employer may have retained.

For instance, in one case, the employer placed 52 Indian citizens in a small cinder block warehouse on the factory grounds. He dubbed the facility "The Cram-a-lot Inn." He ordered enough food for 25 men, ensuring that they would have half rations during their stay. He told them not to leave the facility without an escort, and set an armed guard at the gate. He discouraged church attendance during Christmas, telling the devout among the workers to "watch the Playboy Channel." He paid less than minimum wage and assigned dissenters to menial, humiliating tasks. (All the workers were skilled welders and steelworkers.) He monitored e-mail transmissions and tapped phone lines. He called the sheriff to come and get a small group he considered troublemakers. The sheriff escorted these men to the airport and put them on an airplane, as SWAT teams stood by and regular citizens watched. Fortunately, one concerned citizen intervened with legacy INS and the men were freed before they boarded their connecting flight back to India.[79]

All of the plaintiffs were granted T visa status as victims of human trafficking. They were further supported in their cause when the EEOC, via a courageous regional attorney, joined the fight, providing invaluable assistance.[80] Department of Justice (DOJ) personnel later stated that this case was about as far as DOJ/USCIS was willing to go. In other words, these plaintiffs were *barely* certified as victims of a "severe" form of human trafficking.

---

[79] *Chellen v. John Pickle Co.*, 344 F. Supp. 2d 1278, 446 F. Supp 2d 1247 (N.D. Okla. 2004, N.D. Okla. 2006). *See also* J. Bowe, *Nobodies: Modern American Slave Labor and the Dark Side of the New Global Economy* (2007). Mr. Bowe's book contains four cases studies detailing the variations of "new slavery." The *John Pickle* case is included as a case study.

[80] The EEOC is an agency that is often overlooked as a source in human trafficking cases – most of which present national origin or race discrimination claims.

Extreme Hardship

For all practical purposes, once a person shows that she or he is a victim of a severe form of human trafficking and present in the United States, the remaining elements are assumed. It is necessary, however, to be aware of the "extreme hardship" element. Extreme hardship (if removed to the home country) is not simply the absence of economic opportunity. It is defined in terms of:[81]

- the age and personal circumstances of the applicant;

- serious physical or mental illness that can only be treated in the United States;

- the nature and extent of the physical and psychological damage done by the trafficking;

- the impact of lack of access to the United States justice system—criminal and civil;

- the likelihood the victim will be punished in the home country via laws, social customs, and practices;

- the likelihood of revictimization;

- the likelihood the trafficker will punish the victim; and

- the applicant's safety if returned the to home country, based on the existence of civil unrest or armed conflict.

As a practical matter, after the initial celebration, the lawyer representing a person who has been granted a T visa will have to brace that person for the fact that he or she likely will never return to the home country safely. This is generally not a big issue at first, in light of the fact that spouses, children, parents, and siblings under 18 can be granted derivative status and may join the primary beneficiary. It is not, however, unusual for the victim to risk a return in the case of a family emergency. In that case, permission must be sought from USCIS, inasmuch as the T visa is not a multiple-entry visa. The best practice is to counsel the client not to return until lawful permanent resident (LPR) status is sought and granted.[82] If the T

visa recipient insists on a return to the home country, he or she should budget for a bodyguard, and get in and out as quickly as possible with a minimum of fanfare. Traffickers do not look generously on victims that cost them millions of dollars in civil fines or time in jail for criminal conduct. The traffickers are unlikely to forgive or forget these "debts."

Gatekeepers

Change brings opportunity. Presently, skilled and unskilled labor is abundant in certain parts of the world—parts we call "developing" and that we used to call "third world." In other parts of the world, most notably the United States, Western Europe, and Canada, skilled and unskilled labor is in short supply. It is inevitable that people will move or migrate to achieve dreams or better their living conditions. This is a wondrous process.

But change brings pain. In the United States, there is currently a strong desire in the population at large to bring order to the immigration process. It is apparent to all that the system is broken. A broken system always provides opportunity to the unscrupulous and cruel.

There are two groups of persons who are in a position to hinder the flow of trafficked persons. First, governmental agencies we charge with bringing order to the flow must step up their efforts to identify trafficking and improve communication among related agencies. The Department of State must better train consular officers to recognize trafficking schemes. DOL must talk to DHS. Because of lack of communication, some persons who have been exposed as traffickers continue to file for and sponsor immigrant and nonimmigrant visas with DOL approvals in hand. New slavery is subtle, but not so subtle that it cannot be recognized within the new global economy.[83] Control and cruelty do not come only in the form of an iron ball and chain.

The second critical group of persons is immigration lawyers. In addition to being vigilant against fraudulent immigration practice by those who prey on immigrants who wish to work, we also must examine our own practices that may facilitate human trafficking. Usually this is unwitting: sometimes we

---

[81] 8 CFR §214.11(i). *See also* M. Kramer, *Immigration Consequences of Criminal Activity* 409–12 (3d Ed. 2008); R. Germain, *AILA's Asylum Primer* 328–29 (5th Ed. 2007). Both books are available from AILA Publications, *www.ailapubs.org*, (800) 982-2839.

[82] The T visa is a three-year visa. 8 CFR §214.11(p)(1). Within 90 days of the end of that period, the client can self-petition to adjust to LPR status. 8 CFR §214.11(p)(2). Once LPR status is granted, the client can travel freely. A problem has arisen, however, in the adjustment of status for T visa
continued

recipients. Regulations for the adjustment from T to LPR have not yet been issued, and the Vermont Service Center is holding T adjustments until regulations are issued. It continues to renew employment authorization documents for those eligible to adjust.

[83] *See* K. Bales, *supra* note 76.

fall into situations in which we are purposefully kept in the dark by others. Sometimes deals do "go south" and there is no evil intent. Sometimes we are purposefully misrepresented by others in what seemed like a legitimate business opportunity. Sometimes, we are purposefully blind.

It is unlikely that anyone reading this article would facilitate the most grotesque forms of human trafficking. To avoid abetting trafficking in any way, however, all attorneys should ask the hard questions noted above. That way, we may prevent or at least hinder much of the more subtle exploitation and trafficking. This is the kind of exploitation and trafficking that may not be featured in movies, but it is severe, nevertheless, to those who suffer it.

For further guidance in working with victims of trafficking in persons or on trafficking cases, contact:

- The Freedom Network (nongovernmental) *www.freedomnetworkusa.org/members.htm*

- The Rescue and Restore Coalition member in your area (governmental) *www.acf.hhs.gov/trafficking* (list of grantees)

- ASISTA Immigration Technical Assistance

- *www.asistaonline.org* (materials and referrals to experts)

FIGHTING FOR FAMILIES:
HOW THE CHILD STATUS PROTECTION ACT LETS KIDS STAY KIDS

by Royal F. Berg and Ronald H. Ng[*]

The Child Status Protection Act (CSPA),[1] which became effective on August 6, 2002, the date that it was signed into law, provides very important, tangible benefits to certain children seeking to become lawful permanent residents through an immigrant visa petition filed by or on behalf of a parent. It also contains special provisions for children of asylum and diversity visa applicants. CSPA protects those children who are covered under its provisions from "aging out," establishing a set of rules that are used, instead of a child's chronological age, to determine and lock in the age of a child for immigration purposes.

Prior to the enactment of CSPA, a person seeking to immigrate to the United States as a "child" of a U.S. citizen or lawful permanent resident or as a derivative child on a family preference or employment-based petition had to be unmarried and under 21 years old, not only when the visa petition was filed, but on the date of his or her adjustment of status or admission to the United States as an immigrant. Since Immigration and Nationality Act (INA) §101(b) defines a "child" as an unmarried person under age 21, a child could be transferred into a different preference category or completely lose the eligibility to immigrate or adjust status as an accompanying or following-to-join child on reaching the age of 21, if the processing of his or her permanent residence could not be completed in time. Under pre-CSPA law, delays by legacy Immigration and Naturalization Service (INS) in the processing of visa petitions and applications for adjustment of status, difficulties in the gathering of the required documentation to apply for an immigrant visa at the U.S. embassy, delays in the scheduling of a visa interview at the U.S. embassy, and the inability of a child to immediately travel to the United States after being issued an immigrant visa could have a very harsh and unfortunate impact on beneficiaries.

For this reason, a client turning 21 before the completion of immigrant processing was an immigration lawyer's worst nightmare. Lawyers had to beg, cajole, sue, and seek congressional or divine intervention in an effort to get the government apparatus to complete the process in time.

CSPA ameliorates many of the harsh consequences of reaching age 21 for children who are beneficiaries of visa petitions in the immediate relative and family second-preference categories and derivative beneficiaries of family and employment preference petitions, diversity visa applications, and asylum applications. Although CSPA leaves the statutory definition of a child in INA §101(b) unchanged, it substantially alters how a person's age is determined for purposes of

[*] This article is an update of the authors' "Save the Children: How to Stop Time with the Child Status Protection Act," *Immigration & Nationality Law Handbook* 563 (AILA 2007–08 Ed.), and "Stopping Time and Ignoring the Reality of Aging—The Simple Beauty of the Child Status Protection Act," *Immigration & Nationality Law Handbook* 323 (AILA 2006–07 Ed.). This year's article includes discussion of statements relating to the Child Status Protection Act (CSPA) made by officials of U.S. Citizenship & Immigration Services (USCIS) and the Department of State (DOS) at meetings and conferences in 2007; the processing of applications covered by CSPA; and the provisions of the Violence Against Women and Department of Justice Reauthorization Act of 2005, P.L. 109-162, 119 Stat. 2960 (Jan. 5, 2006) (VAWA II or VAWA 2005) which extend CSPA's age-out protections to children who are principal or derivative beneficiaries of VAWA self-petitions.

Royal F. Berg is an elected director of the American Immigration Lawyers Association's (AILA) Board of Governors. He served as chair of the Greater Chicago Chapter of AILA and chair of the Immigration and Naturalization Law Committee of the Chicago Bar Association. Mr. Berg also served for three years as chair of AILA's Executive Office for Immigration Review Liaison Committee. He is a recipient of the AILA Chicago Chapter's Joseph Minsky Beacon of Light Award and the Chicago Bar Association's Edward Lewis Award, honoring him for his pro bono work.

Ronald H. Ng is an attorney with the Law Offices of Kenneth Y. Geman & Associates in Chicago.

[1] Pub. L. No. 107-208, 116 Stat. 927 (2002).

determining his or her eligibility for classification as a child.[2]

CSPA establishes a set of new rules of varying complexity, which fix the age of a child at an earlier point in time, enabling certain children to continue to qualify for classification for immigration purposes as a "child" under the age of 21, irrespective of the child's actual age on the date that he or she is granted adjustment of status or admitted for permanent residence as an immigrant. The rule that applies in a particular case depends on whether the child's parent is a U.S. citizen, lawful permanent resident, asylum applicant, refugee, or diversity visa applicant. A child's CSPA age, as determined by the applicable rule, is used, rather than his or her actual chronological age, in determining whether he or she is a "child" under INA §101(b).

In addition, as discussed below, INA §203(h)(3) contains special provisions for certain individuals who are determined to be over age 21 under INA §203(h)(1). INA §203(h)(3) automatically converts the petition for these individuals into the appropriate category, while permitting the priority date of the petition to be retained.

STATUS OF RULEMAKING

Although close to six years have passed since it was enacted, regulations relating to CSPA have not been promulgated yet by either the Department of Homeland Security (DHS) or the Department of State (DOS).

In its Spring 2007 semiannual regulatory agenda,[3] DHS indicated that a proposed rule on the implementation of the age-out protections afforded by the Child Status Protection Act was under review. Publication of the notice of proposed rulemaking was anticipated to occur in March 2008, with the comment period ending in May 2008.[4] The abstract to the proposed rulemaking

stated with respect to the purpose and effect of CSPA:

> The CSPA amends the Immigration and Nationality Act (the Act) by permitting an applicant for certain benefits to retain classification as a "child" under the Act, even if he or she has reached the age of 21 years. The CSPA also addresses automatic conversions for certain aliens classified as unmarried sons or daughters of lawful permanent residents (LPRs).[5]

The abstract also indicated the urgency for regulations to be published:

> The CSPA has generated litigation and much confusion among the public. While USCIS has worked tirelessly to communicate a coherent CSPA policy by way of guidance to the field, courts have consistently noted the absence of regulations addressing the issues raised by CSPA. If USCIS is to enjoy deference by the courts it must publish regulations codifying its interpretation of the CSPA before the issues are decided in binding court decisions.[6]

It is not certain when these regulations will be published.[7]

Previously, DHS had indicated that an interim final rule on the implementation of the age-out protections under CSPA, which would amend certain subsections of the regulations in 8 CFR Parts 204 and 205, would be published in April 2007.[8] DHS also indicated that a proposed rule of amendments to regulatory provisions regarding refugee and asylee relative petitions, which, among other purposes, would amend current regulations "to reflect the changes in derivative eligibility following enactment of the Child Status Protection Act," was pending.[9] Neither rule has yet been published, however.

---

[2] *See* Child Status Protection Act of 2002: ALDAC #1, State 163054 (Aug. 2002), *published on* AILA InfoNet at Doc. No. 02090940 (*posted* Sept. 9, 2002): "The new law radically changes the process for determining whether a child has 'aged out' for the purpose of the issuance of visas and the adjustment of status of aliens in most immigration categories."

[3] 72 Fed. Reg. 22574 (Apr. 30, 2007).

[4] *See id.* at 22593.

[5] *Id.*

[6] *Id.*

[7] At an USCIS-AILA Liaison Committee meeting held on April 2, 2008, USCIS indicated that the CSPA regulation is currently in the USCIS clearance process. *See* USCIS-AILA Liaison Committee Meeting Agenda, *published on* AILA InfoNet at Doc 08040235 (*posted* April 2, 2008).

[8] 71 Fed. Reg. 73278, 73306 (Dec. 11, 2006) (DHS semiannual regulatory agenda).

[9] *Id.* at 73300.

DOS had earlier indicated in a semiannual regulatory agenda that it was working on a proposed rule on CSPA beneficiaries, which "sets forth the specific formulas for calculating an alien's age for immigration purposes."[10] In its next semiannual regulatory agenda, DOS stated that this rulemaking had been completed, but was withdrawn on Feb. 28, 2007.[11]

In the absence of regulations, practitioners must turn to USCIS policy memoranda, DOS cables, BIA and federal court decisions, and informal statements by USCIS and DOS officials for guidance on interpreting the provisions of CSPA. The most important of such sources are discussed below and listed in the appendix.

NONRETROACTIVITY

CSPA applies to all children who turn 21 after its August 6, 2002, effective date, provided the requirements for a child's age to be fixed according to the applicable subsection of CSPA are met. The provisions of CSPA are not generally retroactive, however. As discussed below, CSPA does not cover anyone who turned 21 before August 6, 2002, unless he or she comes under one of the exceptions in CSPA §§8(1)–8(3).[12]

WHAT DOES CSPA NOT DO?

1. CSPA does not increase or create exceptions to the annual worldwide or per-country limits on the number of immigrant visas available in the family or employment preference categories or under the diversity visa program.

2. CSPA does not exempt a beneficiary or derivative beneficiary from the requirement of being unmarried for classification as a "child." CSPA only protects a person against "aging out" of the child definition. Marrying prior to adjustment of status or admission as an immigrant has the same adverse effect on immigration eligibility as under previous law.[13]

3. In the case of a child of a lawful permanent resident or a derivative child of the beneficiary of a family or employment preference visa petition, CSPA §3 does not provide automatic protection against "aging out," but requires action to be taken by the beneficiary, a parent, or their attorney. Specifically, the statute provides that a person is entitled to have his or her age calculated according to the formula established in CSPA §3 only if he or she "has sought to acquire the status of an alien lawfully admitted for permanent residence within one year of" the date on which an immigrant visa number became available in his or her visa category. The age of a beneficiary who fails to take the necessary action within the one-year period is determined according to the pre-CSPA rule, which is according to his or her actual age.

4. CSPA does not adequately eliminate the problem of "aging out" in the case of children of lawful permanent residents or derivative children in the family or employment preference categories with substantial waiting periods for visa availability.[14] Due to the length of time

---

[10] 71 Fed. Reg. 73576, 73577 (Dec. 11, 2006).

[11] 72 Fed. Reg. 22873, 22880 (Apr. 30, 2007).

[12] *See Matter of Avila-Perez*, 24 I&N Dec. 78 (BIA 2007), discussed *infra*. *Matter of Avila-Perez* specifically rejected USCIS's previous interpretation of the effective date provisions in CSPA §8. This interpretation required a beneficiary of a petition that was approved prior to the enactment of CSPA to have filed an adjustment of status application on or after August 6, 2002, in order to be covered by CSPA. USCIS subsequently rescinded this interpretation in a recent memorandum from D. Neufeld, "Revised Guidance for the Child Status Protection Act (CSPA)" (May 6, 2008), *published on* AILA InfoNet at Doc. No. 08050669 (*posted* May 6, 2008). *See also* USCIS Update, "USCIS Issues Revised Guidance on Child Status Protection Act (CSPA)" (May 6, 2008), *published on* AILA InfoNet at Doc. No. 08050671 (*posted* May 6, 2008); USCIS Press Release, "USCIS Issues Revised Guidance on the Applicability of the Child Status Protection Act (CSPA)" (May 6, 2008), *published on* AILA InfoNet at Doc. No. 08050672 (*posted* May 6, 2008).

[13] *See* Child Status Protection Act of 2002: ALDAC #2, State 015049 ¶14 (Jan. 2003), *published on* AILA InfoNet at Doc. No. 03020550 (*posted* Feb. 5, 2003):

While the CSPA may prevent the alien's age from changing, the alien must of course still meet the other criteria for "child" status, including being unmarried, and therefore if the alien marries, the alien will lose "child" status, even though the alien's age, for immigration purposes, may be under 21 as a result of the CSPA.

[14] *See Matter of Garcia*, A79 001 587 (BIA June 16, 2006). In *Matter of Garcia*, the BIA found that the "period during which the applicable petition … was pending" could not be interpreted, consistent with the congressional intent in enacting CSPA, to include the time spent waiting for a visa number to become available, because this delay "was not attributable to unnecessary administrative processing delays at the
continued

that the child must wait for a visa number to become available and backlog reduction initiatives by USCIS that (at least until the recent upsurge in filings around July 2007) have reduced the processing times for many immigrant visa petitions, the formula in CSPA §3 in many cases results in the child being determined to be over the age of 21.

5. CSPA does not provide age-out protection for dependents applying for adjustment of status under the Haitian Refugee Immigration Fairness Act of 1998 (HRIFA).[15] It also does not apply to K nonimmigrants, dependent children under the Nicaraguan Adjustment and Central American Relief Act of 1997 (NACARA), special immigrant juvenile applicants, or Family Unity beneficiaries.[16]

---

former INS, but was instead a function of the fact that the respondent's mother had been approved for classification as an immigrant in an oversubscribed preference category that was (and remains) subject to restrictive annual numerical limits." The BIA stated: "The CSPA was not intended to override these numerical limits or otherwise alter the preference allocation system for family-sponsored immigrants, which are set by statute."

[15] *See* USCIS Nebraska Service Center Flash #7-2005, "I-131 and I-485 Applications Under the Haitian Refugee Immigration Fairness Act (HRIFA): Important Notice Regarding Potential Age-Outs" (Dec. 29, 2004), *published on* AILA InfoNet at Doc. No. 05010360 (*posted* Jan. 3, 2005).

[16] INS Memorandum, J. Williams, "The Child Status Protection Act—Memorandum Number 2" (Feb. 14, 2003), at 2, *published on* AILA InfoNet at Doc. No. 03031040 (*posted* Mar. 10, 2003).

This memorandum also stated that CSPA does not apply to V nonimmigrants. Age-out protection has been effectively extended to V-2 and V-3 nonimmigrants, however, through USCIS's decision to apply the U.S. Court of Appeals for the Ninth Circuit's ruling in *Akhtar v. Burzinski*, 384 F. 3d 1193 (9th Cir. 2004), on a nationwide basis. *See* USCIS Memorandum, T. O'Reilly, "Adjudication of Form I-539 for V-2 and V-3 Extension" (Jan. 10, 2005), *published on* AILA InfoNet at Doc. No. 05020460 (*posted* Feb. 4, 2005); USCIS Interoffice Memorandum, M. Aytes, "Clarification of Aging Out Provisions as They Affect Preference Relatives and Immediate Family Members Under the Child Status Protection Act Section 6 and Form I-539 Adjudications for V Status" §2 (June 14, 2006), *published on* AILA InfoNet at Doc. No. 06062870 (*posted* June 28, 2006).

In *Akhtar*, the Ninth Circuit invalidated the regulation in 8 CFR §214.15(g), which had provided for the termination of the status of V-2 and V-3 nonimmigrants on the day before they turned 21, concluding that the regulation violated the congressional intent of reuniting families through the enact-
continued

DETERMINING "AGE" UNDER CSPA

CSPA establishes a series of different rules for determining the "age" of a child for immigration purposes. The rule that applies in a particular case depends on whether a person is a child of a U.S. citizen, a child of a lawful permanent resident, a child of a refugee, a child of an asylum applicant, or a child of a diversity visa applicant.

A person whose age is determined to be under 21 according to the applicable rule is entitled to continued eligibility for classification as a "child" under INA §101(b), though his or her actual age may be over 21 on the date of adjustment of status or admission as an immigrant.

Child of a U.S. Citizen

Children of U.S. citizens are covered by section 2 of CSPA, which amended the INA by adding section 201(f). Under INA §201(f)(1), the age of a child of a U.S. citizen is locked in, using the child's age on the date that the petition for classification as an immediate relative under INA section 201(b)(2)(A)(i) was first filed by the child's U.S. citizen parent. INA §201(f)(1) states:

AGE ON PETITION FILING DATE—Except as provided in [INA §§201(f)(2) and (3)], for

---

ment of the Legal Immigration Family Equity Act (LIFE Act), Pub. L. No. 106-553, §1(a)(2) (appx. B, H.R. 5548, §§1101–04), 114 Stat. 2762, 2762A-142 to 2762A-149 (2000). The O'Reilly memorandum stated:

If the only reason for potentially denying an I-539 filed for V-2 or V-3 extension is that the alien has turned 21, the application shall be approved and the period of admission shall be in accordance with 8 CFR 214.15(g)(1) (granted a period of admission not to exceed two years). The alien shall continue in such status until such status is terminated pursuant to 8 CFR 214.15(j).

In a recent memorandum, USCIS clarified that there may be "limited CSPA coverage" for certain K-4 and K-2 aliens. Neufeld Memorandum, *supra* note 12. Chapter 21.2(e)(2)(i) of the *Adjudicator's Field Manual* (AFM), as revised by the Neufeld memorandum, states that a K-4 nonimmigrant who is a child of a spouse of a U.S. citizen "may utilize the CSPA upon seeking adjustment of status because a K4 alien seeks to adjust as an IR on the basis of an approved Form I-130." The age of the K-4 nonimmigrant is fixed on the date that the I-130 petition on his or her behalf was filed by the U.S. citizen parent. In contrast, a K-2 nonimmigrant is not covered by CSPA and cannot utilize it in adjusting status, unless the U.S. citizen parent files a visa petition on his or her behalf, and only if the U.S. citizen petitioner married the K-1 when the K-2 was not yet 18 years old.

purposes of [INA §201(b)(2)(A)(i)], a determination of whether an alien satisfies the age requirement in the matter preceding [INA §101(b)(1)(A)] shall be made using the age of the alien on the date on which the petition is filed with the Attorney General under [INA §204] to classify the alien as an immediate relative under [INA §201(b)(2)(A)(i)].

The child remains eligible as an immediate relative, even if his or her adjustment of status or admission as an immigrant does not occur until after reaching age 21.

A different rule applies if the parent was a lawful permanent resident when the immigrant visa petition was filed, but subsequently naturalizes prior to the child's adjustment of status or admission as an immigrant. Instead of the age of the child on the date that the petition was filed, INA §201(f)(2) provides that the age of the child on the date that his or her parent naturalizes will be used to determine the child's age for immigration purposes under these circumstances.[17]

INA §201(f)(3) contains special provisions for certain persons who are the beneficiaries of immigrant visa petitions initially filed in the family third-preference category for a married son or daughter of a U.S. citizen. Regardless of what their age is at the time of filing, these individuals do not qualify as immediate relative children because they are married. INA §201(f)(3) provides that, if a legal termination of the marriage occurs while the son or daughter of a U.S. citizen is under age 21, the petition will convert into an immediate relative petition, with the beneficiary's age being locked in for immigration purposes at his or her age on the date of the legal termination of the marriage.

Child of a Lawful Permanent Resident

Determining the "age" of a child who is the beneficiary of a petition filed in the family second-preference category by a lawful permanent resident parent is a much more complex undertaking than it is to determine the age of a child of a U.S. citizen under CSPA §2. A child of a lawful

permanent resident is covered by CSPA §3, which amends the INA by adding §203(h). This section also applies to derivative children on family and employment preference petitions and diversity visa applications.

INA §203(h)(1) establishes a mathematical formula that is used to calculate the age of a child. Under this mathematical formula, the time spent in waiting for the visa petition to be decided is subtracted from the chronological age of the child on the date that the visa priority date of the child or the child's parent becomes current. INA §203(h)(1) states:

[A] determination of whether an alien satisfies the age requirement in the matter preceding [INA §101(b)(1)(A)] shall be made using—

(A) the age of the alien on the date on which an immigrant visa number becomes available for such alien (or, in the case of [INA§203(d)], the date on which an immigrant visa number became available for the alien's parent), but only if the alien has sought to acquire the status of an alien lawfully admitted for permanent residence within one year of such availability; reduced by

(B) the number of days in the period during which the applicable petition described in [INA §203(h)(2)] was pending.

The meaning of "the date on which an immigrant visa number becomes available," when a person is considered to have "sought to acquire the status of an alien lawfully admitted for permanent residence," and "the number of days in the period during which the applicable petition … was pending" are not defined in the statute. As discussed below, USCIS, DOS, the BIA, and the federal courts have differing interpretations for some of these terms.

The locking in of a child's age according to the mathematical formula in CSPA §3 does not occur automatically. Rather, §3 requires a child to have "sought to acquire the status of an alien lawfully admitted for permanent residence" within one year of a visa becoming available to the child or the child's parent. A child who fails to take sufficient steps to be considered to have "sought to acquire the status of an alien lawfully admitted for permanent residence" within one year of visa availability is not covered by CSPA and is not en-

---

[17] INS Memorandum, J. Williams, "The Child Status Protection Act" (Sept. 20, 2002), *published on* AILA InfoNet at Doc. No. 02092732 (*posted* Sept. 27, 2002).

titled to have his or her age determined according to the mathematical formula in INA §203(h)(1).

"Date on which an immigrant visa number becomes available"

The February 14, 2003, Williams memorandum interprets the "date on which an immigrant visa number becomes available" to the child or the child's parent to mean the first day of the month that DOS's *Visa Bulletin* indicates availability of a visa number in that preference category.[18] If a visa is available when the petition is approved, USCIS will consider the visa availability date to be the date that the petition is approved.[19]

DOS's interpretation mirrors USCIS's. DOS considers the date that a visa first becomes available to be "the date on which the priority date became current and the petition was approved, whichever came later."[20]

Due to the movement of priority dates and the common occurrence of regression in some categories, it may not be immediately clear or very easy to determine whether a child's priority date may have become current previously. Close review of earlier DOS visa bulletins is required.

"The number of days in the period during which the applicable petition … was pending"

The February 14, 2003, Williams memorandum states that "the period that a petition is pending" is considered to be the period from the receipt date of the petition to the date that the petition is adjudicated by USCIS:

> The "period that a petition is pending" is the date that it is properly filed (receipt date) until the date an approval is issued on the petition.[21]

DOS's interpretation of the meaning of this term in INA 203(h)(1) is the same as USCIS's.[22]

"Has sought to acquire the status of an alien lawfully admitted for permanent residence" within one year of visa availability

The meaning of this clause in particular has been the subject of varying interpretation.

USCIS

USCIS interprets the clause restrictively, requiring a child who is present in the United States to file an I-485 Application to Adjust Status or Register Permanent Residence within one year of eligibility. The February 14, 2003, Williams memorandum states, at footnote 3:

> An alien may benefit from section 3 of the CSPA if the alien "sought to acquire" the status of a LPR within one year of visa number availability. The filing of the Form I-485 within one year of the immigration petition approval date (or visa becoming available subsequent to petition approval date, whichever is later) has been determined to meet that definition.

It is ambiguous from the comments in the memorandum whether there could be any other circumstances, short of actually filing an I-485 application, that would satisfy for USCIS the requirement of having "sought to acquire" lawful permanent residence within one year.

Subsequent unofficial statements by USCIS seemingly suggest that the filing of an I-485 application is required.[23]

DOS

With respect to someone who is outside the United States, DOS initially took the position that an immigrant visa application had to be filed in order for a child to be considered to have sought to acquire the status of an alien lawfully admitted for permanent residence within one year of visa

[18] Feb. 14, 2003, Williams memorandum, *supra* note 16.

[19] "The date that a visa number becomes available is the approval date of the immigrant petition if, according to the DOS Visa Bulletin, a visa number was already available for that preference category on that date of approval." *Id.*

[20] DOS Cable, ALDAC #2, *supra* note 13.

[21] Feb. 14, 2003, Williams memorandum, *supra* note 16.

[22] DOS Cable, ALDAC #1, *supra* note 2: "The number of days a petition has been pending is calculated from the date the petition was filed to the date the petition is adjudicated."

[23] At an AILA/USCIS Chicago District Office liaison meeting, USCIS stated in response to a question whether there are any particular actions that the Chicago District Office will require for an applicant to show that he or she has "sought to acquire" permanent resident status within one year of visa availability: "We look at the date the visa became available and the date the I-485 was filed." AILA/USCIS Chicago District Office Liaison Questions (July 26, 2007), *published on* AILA InfoNet at Doc. 07073050 (*posted* July 30, 2007).

availability.[24] DOS subsequently revised this interpretation to require that a DS-230, Part I Application for Immigrant Visa and Alien Registration, be submitted within one year of visa availability in order for a child to be considered to have "sought to acquire" lawful permanent resident status:

> [The] Department has reconsidered its preliminary interpretation and has decided that, in cases where the principal applicant's case goes through visa processing rather than adjustment of status, a better interpretation would be to measure the date on which the applicant first seeks to acquire LPR status as the date on which the applicant submits the completed DS-230, Part I. Therefore, if a preference or DV visa applicant submits the DS-230, Part I within one year of visa availability, then the applicant would be eligible for CSPA benefits, assuming the CSPA otherwise applies to the case.[25]

A child who is a derivative on a petition filed for a parent must complete and submit a DS-230, Part I for him- or herself, as DOS does not consider a DS-230, Part I filed by the principal to be sufficient:

> In cases involving derivatives, it is not enough that the principal may have taken the required steps within the one-year time frame—the derivative him/herself must have taken those steps (or the principal must have taken the required step specifically for the derivative, acting as the derivative's agent). Therefore, if the applicant seeking CSPA benefits is a derivative, then the determining factor is the submission of a completed DS-230, Part I, that specifically covers the derivative. The submission of a DS-230 Part I that covers the principal will not serve to meet the requirement.[26]

When the parent has already adjusted status in the United States, the date that the parent files an I-824 Application for Action on an Approved Application or Petition for the child to follow-to-join will be considered by DOS to be the date that the child seeks to acquire lawful permanent residence for purposes of CSPA §3.[27] In light of this guidance, it might be advisable, in those cases in which the principal will be applying for adjustment of status in the United States while derivative children will be applying for an immigrant visa at a consulate, for the I-824 applications to be filed together with the I-485 application or very soon thereafter. This will minimize the risk of inadvertently forgetting to file timely, and thus failing to meet the requirement of having "sought to acquire" permanent residence within one year of visa availability.

Also, the lengthening of I-485 processing times could make it impossible to wait until the I-485 application of the principal is approved before filing the I-824 applications for derivative children. USCIS has confirmed that a previously filed I-824 that was denied because the principal applicant's adjustment of status application had not yet been approved can serve as evidence of having "sought to acquire" LPR status.[28]

DOS recognizes, however, that there may be cases in which "some other concrete step" may have been taken, besides the filing of an I-824, that will meet the requirement of having "sought to acquire" the status of a lawfully admitted permanent resident within one year of visa availability.[29] DOS does not provide further clarification, but merely advises that "posts should submit such

---

[24] DOS Cable, ALDAC #1, *supra* note 2: "'Seeks to acquire the status of an LPR' will be defined to mean apply for an immigrant visa, *i.e.*, the date of visa application."

[25] DOS Cable, ALDAC #2, *supra* note 13, at ¶17.

[26] *Id.* at ¶18.

[27] *Id.* at ¶22:

> The requirement that the preference or DV applicant submit the DS-230, Part I within one year of visa availability shall apply only in cases where the principal applicant was processed for a visa at a consular post abroad. If the principal applicant adjusted status in the U.S. and a derivative is applying for a visa abroad to follow-to-join, then the date on which the derivative will be considered to have sought LPR status for purposes of satisfying CSPA Section 3 will generally be the date on which the principal (acting as the derivative beneficiary's agent) filed the Form I-824 that is used to process the derivative's following to join application. Therefore, in cases involving a derivative seeking to follow to join a principal who adjusted in the U.S., the derivative can benefit from the CSPA if the principal filed a Form I-824 for the beneficiary within one year of a visa becoming available (*i.e.*, within one year of the case becoming current or petition approval, whichever is later).

[28] Neufeld Memorandum, *supra* note 12.

[29] DOS Cable, ALDAC #2, *supra* note 13, at ¶23.

cases to the Department (CA/VO/L/A) for an advisory opinion."[30]

The BIA

The February 14, 2003, Williams memorandum's requirement to file an I-485 application within one year of a visa becoming available has been specifically rejected by the BIA. In its non-precedent decision in *Matter of Kim*,[31] the BIA put forth its own, less restrictive interpretation of having "sought to acquire" lawful permanent resident status. The case involved a derivative beneficiary of an employment-based visa petition whose application for adjustment of status was denied by the immigration judge. The immigration judge found that Ms. Kim did not qualify as a "child" under INA §203(h)(1) because her adjustment of status application was filed more than 12 months after the priority date the employment preference petition had become current.

Ms. Kim's parents had consulted an attorney regarding the filing of an adjustment of status application for her within the one-year period, but the attorney did not file the adjustment of status application until 17 months after the visa number had become available. The immigration judge reasoned that because she did not file her application to adjust status within one year of visa availability, Ms. Kim was not covered by INA §203(h)(1).

The BIA determined, based on the rules of statutory construction and analysis of the legislative history and purpose of CSPA, that "sought to acquire" had to be given a broader meaning than merely "to file":

[W]e conclude that Congress intended the term "sought to acquire" lawful permanent residence at [INA] section 203(h)(1)(A) to be broadly interpreted within the context of the statute, and not limited to the filing of the application. Under the facts of this case, where the record demonstrates that the alien's parents had hired counsel to prepare the application for adjustment of status within a year of the approval of the employment based visa petition, the application for adjustment of status to lawful permanent residence was actually filed

within a reasonable time thereafter, and the alien child was still under the age of 21 at the time the application for adjustment was filed, we find that the respondent "sought to acquire" lawful permanent residence within a year of her eligibility for such status. To conclude otherwise would undermine the very purpose and intent of the statute, which was to protect an alien child from "aging out" due to "no fault of her own."[32]

The interpretation of the BIA in *Matter of Kim* is significantly broader and more generous than the one found in the February 14, 2003, Williams memorandum or the DOS cables. Although a non-precedent decision, the same arguments regarding statutory construction and the congressional intent behind the enactment of CSPA can be used before the DOS and DHS, and the Executive Office for Immigration Review (EOIR).

Whether the BIA's ruling in *Matter of Kim* can be extended to other factual situations is uncertain. Does CSPA cover a derivative beneficiary of a second-preference petition who is grandfathered under INA §245(i) and who did not apply for adjustment of status at the same time as her father when a visa number became available in 2004 because her family lacked the financial resources to pay the USCIS filing fees and the penalty fee under §245(i)? Does consulting an attorney and completing drafts of the I-485 and I-485 Supplement within one year of visa availability meet the requirement of having "sought to acquire" permanent residence within one year of visa availability?

The answers to these and other questions are unresolved.

Child of an Asylee or Refugee

INA §208(b)(3), as amended by section 4 of CSPA, provides for the continued classification as a "child" of a person seeking to accompany or follow-to-join a parent granted asylum in the United States, if he or she was under 21 years old on the date that the parent applied for asylum. Similarly, section 5 of CSPA amends INA §207(c)(2) to use the age of a person on the date that his or her par-

---

[30] *Id.*

[31] A77 828 503 (BIA Dec. 20, 2004).

[32] *Id.* at 4.

ent applied for refugee status in order to determine eligibility for derivative refugee status.

These provisions lock in the age of a "child" as of the date that the Form I-589 Application for Asylum and Withholding of Removal or the Form I-590 Registration for Classification as Refugee is filed during the period that the application is considered "pending."

USCIS interprets the period that an application is "pending" for purposes of sections 4 and 5 of CSPA to include "all related eligibility determinations."[33] The age of a derivative child of an asylee or refugee is locked on the date that the asylum or refugee application was filed by his or her parent from the date of filing until the child's adjustment of status under INA §209.[34] The derivative child must be named on the parent's Form I-589 or Form I-590 prior to a final decision or adjudication.[35]

A child who aged out before the August 6, 2002, effective date of CSPA is entitled to the benefit of section 4 or 5 of the CSPA, if a "petition or application for one of the covered benefits was pending on August 6, 2002."[36] An August 17, 2004, USCIS memorandum by William Yates states, regarding the application of CSPA in these cases:

> [I]f all necessary steps for issuing travel documents to the derivative child or following to join child (such as approval of the Form I-730, the overseas interview, or completion of all security checks) were not completed on or before August 6, 2002, the case is considered to be "pending."[37]

A person who loses his or her eligibility for classification as a derivative child due to marriage must file for asylum in his or her own right *nunc pro tunc* in order to adjust status. Such an application must be filed as soon as the practitioner becomes aware of this necessity. At a USCIS National Stakeholder Meeting on December 4, 2007, USCIS stated:

> It is strongly advised that derivative asylees who no longer qualify under the statute or will soon no longer qualify gain asylum status as principal applicants either prior to filing an I-485 or soon after the filing of the I-485 application. USCIS will no longer hold I-485 applications pending the adjudication of nunc pro tunc asylum applications with the local asylum offices.[38]

Neither the Yates memo nor any other USCIS guidance of which we are aware as this article goes to print specifically discusses the situation of a child not present in the United States or named on a parent's asylum application, who was under 21 on the date of filing, for whom an I-730 Refugee/Asylee Relative Petition is filed within two years of the grant of asylum to the parent. EOIR provides the following guidance with respect to the children of persons granted asylum based on the People's Republic of China's coercive population control policy: If the child was under 21 years old at the time the asylum application was filed by a parent and the parent was granted asylum on or after August 6, 2002, the child's eligibility for derivative asylee status is protected under CSPA if the parent complies with the requirements for filing an I-730 Refugee/Asylee Relative Petition.[39] If the parent was granted asylum prior to the effective date of CSPA, however, CSPA would protect a child who turned 21 before August 6, 2002, only if the I-730 Refugee/Asylee Relative Petition was filed before August 6, 2002, and remained pending as of that date.[40]

[33] USCIS Memorandum, W. Yates, "The Child Status Protection Act—Children of Asylees and Refugees" (Aug. 17, 2004), at 1, *published on* AILA InfoNet at Doc. No. 04091561 (*posted* Sept. 15, 2004).

[34] *Id.* at 2, stating that a derivative child "will retain classification as a child for purposes of the initial asylum or refugee determination, for any subsequent Form I-730 Refugee/Asylee Relative Petition, and/or for the Section 209 adjustment."

[35] *Id.*

[36] *Id.*

[37] *Id.*

[38] USCIS National Stakeholder Meeting Question & Answer (Dec. 4, 2007), *published on* AILA InfoNet at Doc. No. 07120670 (*posted* Dec. 6, 2007).

[39] EOIR Fact Sheet, "Conditional Grants of Asylum Based on Coercive Population Control Policies (Sept. 30, 2003), *published on* AILA InfoNet at Doc. No. 03100642 (*posted* Oct. 6, 2003).

[40] *Id.*

Child of a Diversity Immigrant

The same calculation in INA §203(h)(1) also applies to the derivative child of a diversity visa applicant. However, since there is no immigrant visa petition filed in the case of a diversity visa (DV) applicant, the period of time that a "petition is pending" is interpreted by USCIS to mean the period "between the first day of the DV mail-in application period for the program year in which the principal applicant has qualified and the date on the letter notifying the principal alien that his/her application has been selected (the congratulatory letter)."[41] This period is subtracted from the derivative child's age on the date the visa became available to his or her parent.[42]

DOS interprets the period that a "petition is pending" in the same manner.[43]

RETENTION OF PRIORITY DATE UNDER INA §203(H)(3)

INA §203(h)(3) is a very interesting provision that potentially has broad application in the cases of derivative children and beneficiaries of petitions under INA §203(a)(2)(A) who are determined to be over the age of 21 under the mathematical formula in INA §203(h)(1).[44] INA §203(h)(3) is technically not an age-out protection provision, but one that mitigates the effect when a child is determined to have "aged out" under CSPA.

INA §203(h)(3) states:

> RETENTION OF PRIORITY DATE—If the age of an alien is determined under [INA §203(h)(1)] to be 21 years of age or older for the purposes of [INA §§203(a)(2)(A) and (d)], the alien's petition shall automatically be converted to the appropriate category and the alien shall retain the original priority date issued upon receipt of the original petition.

INA §203(h)(3) applies in those cases in which a person is determined according to the calculation in INA §203(h)(1) not to be a "child." It provides for the retention of the priority date of the original petition and that the petition will "automatically be converted to the appropriate category."

The implementation of the provision is unclear. How is the "appropriate category" determined? Does a petition in the new category have to be filed for a beneficiary to retain and use the priority date of the original petition? Is there a time limit for utilizing the prospective benefits of INA §203(h)(3)?

INA §203(h)(3) was recently interpreted by the BIA in *Matter of Garcia*.[45] This nonprecedent, single-member decision was written by BIA member Roger A. Pauley. Although a nonprecedent decision, the decision is based on sound legal reasoning and firmly grounded in the language of the statutory provision and the purpose and legislative history of CSPA.

Matter of Garcia involved a 32-year-old national of Mexico whose application for adjustment of status under INA §245(i) was denied by an immigration judge on February 11, 2005. Previously, Ms. Garcia was the derivative beneficiary of a family fourth-preference petition that was filed for her by her mother's U.S. citizen sister on January 13, 1983, when Ms. Garcia was 9 years old. Due to the lengthy waiting period in the family fourth-preference category, she was 22 years old and had "aged out" under pre-CSPA law by the time that a visa number became available. Her mother obtained an immigrant visa in June 1996 and filed an I-130 petition for her in 1997 in the category of an unmarried daughter of a lawful permanent resident.

After first determining Ms. Garcia to be over 21 years old under the formula in INA §203(h)(1), the BIA proceeded to analyze her case under the retention and conversion clause in INA §203(h)(3). The BIA found this analysis to be required by the statute. The BIA determined that, in the case of a derivative beneficiary, "the appropriate category for purposes of section 203(h)(3) is

---

[41] Feb. 14, 2003, Williams memorandum, *supra* note 16.
[42] *Id.*
[43] *See* DOS Cable, ALDAC #2, *supra* note 13, at ¶15.
[44] The authors express gratitude and credit distinguished immigration attorney and author Pravinchandra J. Patel for writing to emphasize the significance of INA §203(h)(3). Mr. Patel strongly recommended that this section be discussed in an updated article on CSPA.

[45] A79 001 587 (BIA June 16, 2006).

that which applies to the 'aged out' derivative vis-à-vis the principal beneficiary of the original petition." The appropriate category in the case of a person who is the principal beneficiary of the original petition, on the other hand, "is that which applies to the beneficiary vis-à-vis the original petitioner."[46]

The BIA found that Ms. Garcia retained the January 13, 1983, priority date of the family fourth-preference petition that had been filed for her mother. The BIA also found that the "appropriate category" to which Ms. Garcia was converted under §203(h)(3) was the family second-preference category for unmarried sons and daughters of a lawful permanent resident, and that she had an immigrant visa number immediately available to her in that category because the January 13, 1983, priority date that she retained from the family fourth-preference petition filed by her aunt was current. The BIA appeared to suggest that a petition in the new category does not have to be filed:

> [T]he respondent's entitlement to a visa number under section 203(h)(3) does not derive from the 1997 visa petition, but rather from the original 1983 petition, which is 'automatically … converted' to a second-preference petition upon an administrative determination that she is 21 years old or older for purposes of section 203(h)(1).

The BIA remanded the case to the immigration judge for further consideration of Ms. Garcia's application for adjustment of status under §245(i).

At an AILA-USCIS Chicago District Office liaison meeting on June 26, 2007, the Chicago District Office indicated that it had not decided whether it will follow the BIA's decision in *Matter of Garcia*.[47]

---

[46] *Id.* at n.1.

[47] The Chicago District Office stated:

The case you cite is an unpublished BIA decision from Houston and as I'm sure you are aware, we are not bound by it. This District has not decided whether or not it will follow the reasoning of this case and will address the issue should it come up in the context of an actual case.

AILA/USCIS Chicago District Office Liaison Questions, *published on* AILA InfoNet at Doc. No. 07062550 (*posted* June 25, 2007).

SECTION 6 AUTOMATIC CONVERSION OR "OPT OUT"

CSPA §6 provides for the automatic conversion of a petition filed for an unmarried son or daughter of a lawful permanent resident parent into a petition for an unmarried son or daughter of a U.S. citizen upon the naturalization of the petitioning parent. INA §204(k)(1), as added by section 6 of CSPA, states:

> Except as provided in [INA §204(k)(2)], in the case of a petition under this section initially filed for an alien unmarried son or daughter's classification as a family-sponsored immigrant under [INA §203(a)(2)(B)], based on a parent of the son or daughter being an alien lawfully admitted for permanent residence, if such parent subsequently becomes a naturalized citizen of the United States, such petition shall be converted to a petition to classify the unmarried son or daughter as a family-sponsored immigrant under section [INA §203(a)(1)].

The automatic conversion of a petition from the family second-preference category in INA §203(a)(2)(B) into a petition in the family first-preference category in INA §203(a)(1) generally results in a shorter waiting period for an immigrant visa number to become available.

However, as the movement in visa numbers in the different preference categories cannot be predicted, INA §204(k)(2) permits unmarried sons and daughters to "opt out" of automatic conversion of their petitions into the family first-preference category and instead remain in the family second-preference category in INA §203(a)(2)(B). Section 204(k)(2) states:

> [INA §204(k)(1)] does not apply if the son or daughter files with the Attorney General a written statement that he or she elects not to have such conversion occur (or if it has occurred, to have such conversion revoked). Where such an election has been made, any determination with respect to the son or daughter's eligibility for admission as a family-sponsored immigrant shall be made as if such naturalization had not taken place.

Guidance on the opt-out provision in CSPA §6 can be found in a March 23, 2004, USCIS memorandum by Joe Cuddihy, Director of International Affairs,[48] and a June 14, 2006, USCIS memorandum by Michael Aytes, Associate Director, Domestic Operations.[49] The Cuddihy memorandum states that beneficiaries outside the United States who wish to opt out of automatic conversion must file a request in writing, addressed to the officer in charge of the appropriate U.S. embassy. The officer in charge will provide notification of a decision on the request to the beneficiary and DOS's visa issuance unit. The Cuddihy memorandum states: "If the beneficiary's request is approved, then the beneficiary's eligibility for family-based immigration will be determined as if his or her parent never naturalized and they will remain a second preference alien."

Similarly, the February 14, 2003, Williams memorandum stated with respect to the "opt-out" provision:

> If an unmarried son or daughter does not want such automatic transfer of preference categories to occur upon his or her parent's naturalization, the Service shall accept such request in the form of a letter signed by the beneficiary. If the beneficiary does make this written request to the Service, then the beneficiary's eligibility for family-based immigration will be determined as if his or her parent had never naturalized.[50]

The Aytes memorandum also modified USCIS's earlier position in the Cuddihy memorandum that a beneficiary whose I-130 petition was initially filed for a child under 21 of a lawful permanent resident under INA §203(a)(2)(A), but who was moved into the category of unmarried son or daughter in INA §203(a)(2)(B) when he or she reached the age of 21, could not utilize the opt-out provision in section 204(k)(2). That is, under the previous interpretation, the naturalization of a parent converted such a bene-

ficiary into the family first-preference category, even if remaining in the §203(a)(2)(B) category might be to his or her advantage. The rule was based on interpretation of statutory language in CSPA §6 referring to "a petition … initially filed for an alien unmarried son or daughter classified as a family-sponsored immigrant under section 203(a)(2)(B)." The Aytes memorandum adopted the alternative reading of this phrase to refer to a petition initially filed for a noncitizen who is *now* in the unmarried son or daughter classification.

The Aytes memorandum also clarifies that the age of a visa beneficiary "has no bearing on eligibility for CSPA section 6 opt-out." A person seeking to opt out under CSPA §6 can be any age at the time of the request.

Individuals seeking to utilize the "opt out" provisions in CSPA §6 "should file a request in writing with the District Office having jurisdiction over the beneficiary's residence."[51]

EFFECTIVE DATE OF THE CSPA

As noted above, CSPA is not a generally retroactive statute, but became effective on August 6, 2002, the date of its enactment. The first step of any CSPA analysis is to determine whether a visa beneficiary is entitled to have his or her age determined according to the effective date provisions in CSPA §8.

Under §8(1), CSPA applies to persons whose visa petitions were approved before August 6, 2002, "but only if a final determination has not been made on the beneficiary's application for an immigrant visa or adjustment of status to lawful permanent residence pursuant to such approved petition." Section 8(2) makes the provisions of CSPA applicable to a person who is the principal or derivative beneficiary of a petition for classification as a family or employment preference immigrant pending on or after August 6, 2002.[52] Fi-

---

[48] USCIS Memorandum, J. Cuddihy, "Section 6 of the Child Status Protection Act" (Mar. 3, 2004), *published on* AILA InfoNet at Doc. No. 04032615 (*posted* Mar. 26, 2004).

[49] USCIS Memorandum, M. Aytes, "Clarification of Aging Out Provisions as They Affect Preference Relatives and Immediate Family Members Under the Child Status Protection Act Section 6 and Form I-539 Adjudications for V Status" (June 14, 2006), *published on* AILA InfoNet at Doc. No. 06062870 (*posted* June 28, 2006).

[50] Feb. 14, 2003, Williams memorandum, *supra* note 16, at 5.

[51] *See* AFM ch. 21.2(e)(3), as revised by the Neufeld Memorandum, *supra* note 12.

[52] In last year's article by the authors, "Save the Children: How to Stop Time with the Child Status Protection Act," *Immigration & Nationality Law Handbook* 563 (AILA 2007–08 Ed.), this sentence incorrectly stated, as a result of a typographical error relating to the date:

> Section 8(2) makes the provisions of the CSPA applicable to a person who is the principal or derivative benefi-
> *continued*

nally, section 8(3) makes CSPA applicable to a person who has "an application pending before the Department of Justice or the Department of State on or after such date."

LEGACY INS/USCIS INTERPRETATION

The February 14, 2003, Williams memorandum interprets CSPA as generally applying only to persons who age out after the enactment of CSPA on August 6, 2002, with the exceptions indicated in CSPA §8.[53]

The Williams memorandum interprets the exception in CSPA §8(1) as requiring a beneficiary of a visa petition that was approved before August 6, 2002, who aged out before that date, to have *filed* an adjustment of status application in which no final determination has been made as of August 6, 2002, for that person to be covered by the provisions of CSPA:

> [I]f an alien aged out prior to August 6, 2002, the petition must have been filed on or before August 6, 2002, and either: 1) remained pending on August 6, 2002, or; 2) been approved before August 6, 2002, *with an adjustment application filed on or before August 6, 2002*, and no final determination made prior to August 6, 2002.[54]

The Williams memorandum proceeds to clarify that a visa petition is considered by USCIS to be "pending" for purposes of CSPA §8 if there is "agency action on the petition, including an appeal or motion to reopen filed with the Administrative Appeals Office (AAO) or the Board of Immigration Appeals, if such appeal or motion was filed and/or pending on August 6, 2002."[55]

As discussed below, the BIA has specifically rejected the Williams memorandum's interpretation of CSPA §8(1) as requiring the filing of an adjustment of status application.

DOS Interpretation

DOS's rules relating to CSPA §8 are complex and have undergone modification. Its general position is that CSPA applies to immigrant visa cases initiated after CSPA went into effect on August 6, 2002, with "a somewhat more limited applicability to cases that were already in progress on the date that the law went into effect."[56] DOS interprets CSPA §8 to mean that, in addition to applying to petitions filed after August 6, 2002, CSPA applies to petitions filed before August 6, 2002, that were still pending on that date, and petitions approved before August 6, 2002, but only if a final determination had not been made on the beneficiary's application before that date.[57]

DOS previously indicated that, if a petition was approved before August 6, 2002, CSPA did not apply unless the beneficiary aged out on or after August 6, 2002, or aged out before August 6, 2002, but prior to aging out had applied for an immigrant visa and was refused under INA §221(g).[58] It stated: "If the petition was approved before 8-6-02 and the alien aged out before that date and either failed to apply for a visa or applied after aging out

---

ciary of a petition for classification as a family or employment preference immigrant that is pending on or after Aug. 6, 2006.

The last part of the sentence should have stated: "pending on or after Aug. 6, 2002."

[53] Feb. 14, 2003, Williams memorandum, *supra* note 16.

[54] *Id.* at 2. As footnote 1 of the Williams memorandum advises, the grace period in section 424 of the Uniting and Strengthening America by Providing Appropriate Tools Required to Intercept and Obstruct Terrorism Act of 2001, P.L. 107-56, 115 Stat. 272 (the USA Patriot Act) must be taken into account in determining whether a child "aged out" prior to August 6, 2002. Section 424 of the USA Patriot Act states:

> For purposes of the administration of the Immigration and Nationality Act (8 USC 1101 *et seq.*), in the case of an alien—

> (1) whose 21st birthday occurs in September 2001, and who is the beneficiary of a petition or application filed under such Act on or before September 11, 2001, the alien shall be considered to be a child for 90 days after the alien's 21st birthday for purposes of adjudicating such petition or application; and

---

> (2) whose 21st birthday occurs after September 2001, and who is the beneficiary of a petition or application filed under such Act on or before September 11, 2001, the alien shall be considered to be a child for 45 days after the alien's 21st birthday for purposes of adjudicating such petition or application.

[55] Feb. 14, 2003, Williams memorandum, *supra* note 16, at 2.

[56] DOS Cable, ALDAC #2, *supra* note 13, at ¶6.

[57] *Id.*

[58] *Id.* at ¶8.

continued

and was refused on that ground, then the CSPA will not apply."[59]

DOS subsequently modified its position relating to pre-August 6, 2002 age-outs.[60] Under DOS's current interpretation, visa application refusals that occurred between August 6, 2001, and August 5, 2002, are not considered to be "final determinations" for the purposes of CSPA §8(1) because the regulations in 22 CFR §42.8(e) permit a visa applicant to overcome any refusal within a one-year period.[61] If a visa was refused prior to August 6, 2001, for a ground other than INA §221(g), the refusal will generally be considered a final determination, unless the beneficiary applied for a waiver and the waiver application was still pending as of August 6, 2002.[62] An INA §221(g) denial is generally not considered to be a final determination, regardless of when it occurred.[63]

---

[59] Id. This statement makes it clear that DOS interprets CSPA §8(1) to require an application for an immigration visa to have been filed before August 6, 2002, in the same manner that the Feb. 14, 2003, Williams memorandum interprets the provision to require the filing of an application for adjustment of status before August 6, 2002.

[60] See Child Status Protection Act of 2002: ALDAC #4—What Constitutes a "Final Determination" on an Application Adjudicated Prior to the Effective Date of CSPA, State 131625 (May 2003), published on AILA InfoNet at Doc. No. 03060243 (posted June 2, 2003).

[61] Id. at ¶3:

Department regulations at 22 CFR 42.81(e) provide that an alien has a one-year window within which to overcome any refusal without the need to file a new application. As such, in Department's view, a refusal that is less than one year old should not be considered a "final determination", even if the refusal involves a permanent, nonwaivable ineligibility. Therefore, if an alien seeking CSPA benefits was refused a visa in the one-year period prior to the August 6, 2002 effective date of the CSPA (i.e., between August 6, 2001 and August 5, 2002), the refusal will not be considered a "final determination", regardless of the ground of refusal, and the CSPA may be applied to the case.

[62] Id. at ¶4.

[63] Id. at ¶5:

A 221(g) refusal will not be considered a "final determination," regardless of whether it occurred within a year of August 6, 2002 or earlier. (The only exception to this would be if the alien's case was ultimately terminated under INA 203(g) for failure to make reasonable efforts to overcome to 221(g) refusal. A 203(g) termination will be considered a "final determination.")

The BIA and the Federal Courts

Is the filing of an application for adjustment of status on or before August 6, 2002, required in CSPA §8(1)?

The BIA specifically addressed the meaning of the requirements of the effective date provision in CSPA §8(1) in Matter of Avila-Perez.[64] This precedent decision was issued on February 9, 2007. The principal issue in the case was whether CSPA §8(1) required a person with a visa petition that was approved before August 6, 2002, to have filed an application for adjustment of status before that date in order to benefit from the provisions of CSPA. The BIA held that the filing of an adjustment of status application that remained pending on August 6, 2002, is not a prerequisite under §8(1).

Avila-Perez involved a beneficiary of an I-130 Petition for Alien Relative in the immediate relative classification. The petition was filed by the beneficiary's U.S. citizen mother on August 30, 1996, and approved by legacy INS on November 1, 1996. Mr. Avila-Perez turned 21 on April 4, 1997, more than five years before the enactment of CSPA.[65] Under the pre-CSPA INA, he was moved from the immediate relative classification into the first-preference classification for an unmarried son or daughter of a U.S. citizen. At some point not indicated in the BIA's decision, he entered the United States on a nonimmigrant visa and overstayed.

Mr. Avila-Perez filed an application for adjustment of status as an immediate relative on Oc-

---

[64] 24 I&N Dec. 78 (BIA 2007).

[65] It is not clear why Mr. Avila-Perez did not apply for adjustment of status or an immigrant visa between November 1, 1996, and April 4, 1997. As the BIA noted in footnote 2 of its opinion, the record is contradictory on this point. Mr. Avila-Perez contended on appeal to the BIA that he had applied for an immigrant visa in Ciudad Juarez, Mexico in 1996. He had asserted earlier, however, in opposition to USCIS's decision to reject his adjustment application, that the adjustment application that he submitted on October 15, 2003, represented the first time that he was seeking lawful permanent residence based on the visa petition filed by his mother that was approved on November 1, 1996.

tober 15, 2003, when he was 27 years old.[66] USCIS rejected his application and placed him in removal proceedings. USCIS contended that he was not eligible to be classified as an immediate relative under the age-out protection in CSPA §2 because he did not file an application for adjustment of status before August 6, 2002, on which no final determination was made as of August 6, 2002.

Examining the legislative history of CSPA, the BIA found that there was no indication that Congress had intended to withhold CSPA's benefits from individuals, such as Mr. Avila-Perez, whose immigrant visa petitions were approved before August 6, 2002, but who did not apply for adjustment of status or an immigrant visa before that date.[67] The BIA concluded that Mr. Avila-Perez was covered by CSPA §2, and remanded so that his application for adjustment of status as an immediate relative child could be considered by the immigration judge.

It appeared until recently that *Avila-Perez* did not provide any benefits to derivative children of lawful permanent residents who are covered by CSPA §3, rather than CSPA §2, who did not file an application for adjustment of status or an application for an immigrant visa on or before August 6, 2002. The reason is that derivative children of lawful permanent residents are specifically required by

the statute to have "sought to acquire" the status of a lawful permanent resident within one year of visa availability to have their age determined according to the formula in CSPA. As discussed below, revised guidance by USCIS appears to permit certain beneficiaries of preference petitions whose visas became available on or after August 7, 2001, but who did not file applications to adjust status due to USCIS's previous interpretation of the CSPA retroactivity provisions to require filing before August 6, 2002, to now apply for permanent residence, with their ages determined under the CSPA §3 formula, even though more than one year has elapsed since visa availability.[68]

Prior to *Avila-Perez*, the U.S. District Court for the Central District of California reached the same conclusion with respect to whether CSPA §8(1) requires the filing of an application for adjustment of status or an immigrant visa on or before August 6, 2002.[69] As in *Avila-Perez*, USCIS argued that §8(1) did not cover the plaintiff's son because he had aged out before August 6, 2002, and had not filed an application for adjustment of status or an immigrant visa before August 6, 2002, on which a final determination had not been made.

Noting that §8(1) does not contain an express requirement that an application for adjustment of

---

[66] The October 2003 *Visa Bulletin* showed the family third-preference category for nationals of Mexico as being current only for beneficiaries with visa priority dates of October 1, 1994, or earlier.

[67] *Avila-Perez* has an interesting discussion of the legislative history of the CSPA, specifically the different versions of section 8 which were previously considered before it was enacted in its final form. The original bill that was introduced in the House of Representatives was retroactive, but subsequently amended so that the provisions would apply only to petitions and applications pending before DOJ or DOS on or after the date of enactment. The effective date provisions in CSPA §8 were subsequently added in the Senate. The BIA commented regarding the changes to the effective date provision: "It is reasonable to conclude … that by including section 8(1) in the CSPA, the Senate intended to expand the coverage of the statute beyond those individuals whose visa petitions and applications were pending on the date of the CSPA to also protect those individuals whose visa petitions were approved before the effective date, but only if their applications had not already been finally adjudicated." 24 I&N Dec. 78, 83–85 (BIA 2007).

[68] Neufeld Memorandum, *supra* note 12.

[69] *Rodriguez v. Gonzales*, No. CV 04-8671 (C.D. Cal. May 31, 2006). Florentina Rodriguez filed a petition for classification as an immediate relative for her son on January 8, 1999. Her son, who was born on January 13, 1979, was 19 years old when the petition was filed, but the petition was not approved by legacy INS until nearly three years later, on October 23, 2001, when he was 22 years old. In January 2004, Mrs. Rodriguez's attorney wrote a letter to the DOS National Visa Center, advising that the petition be sent to the U.S. embassy in Manila for immigrant visa processing because Mrs. Rodriguez's son had become eligible for classification as an immediate relative under CSPA. The consular officer returned the petition to the National Visa Center, however, contending that CSPA did not apply. Mrs. Rodriguez then filed a petition in U.S. district court, seeking a writ of mandamus compelling the National Visa Center to again forward the petition to the U.S. embassy and a declaratory judgment that CSPA covered her son. After the parties cross-motioned for summary judgment, the district court grant Mrs. Rodriguez's motion. *See* American Immigration Law Foundation, Legal Action Center, 1 *Litigation Clearinghouse Newsletter* (Oct. 13, 2006), *available at www.ailf.org/lac/ litclearinghouse/litclr_newsletter_101306.pdf.* The newsletter also contains a hypertext link to the *Rodriguez* decision.

status or an immigrant visa must have been filed, the court examined the legislative history and purpose of CSPA. The court determined that CSPA had been enacted in large part to protect visa petition beneficiaries from delays by legacy INS, and concluded that the filing of an application for adjustment of status prior to Aug. 6, 2002, is not required under §8(1):

> No filing requirement is evident on the face of the statute or from the legislative history. A broad reading of the statute is consistent with its plain language and furthers the congressional objective of providing expansive relief and promoting family reunification.[70]

Regarding USCIS's position, the court stated:

> Defendants' interpretation is neither expansive nor logical. [The plaintiff's son] did not file an application for an immigrant visa—not because of any delay on his part, but because he had been rendered ineligible to do so by his conversion from immediate relative to first preference alien during the INS processing. Thus he falls outside of section 8(1) of the CSPA, as interpreted by Defendants, in whole—or at least in large part—because of the INS delays that Congress sought to remedy.[71]

The court ruled that the plaintiff's son was covered by CSPA §8(1) and that a writ of mandamus was an appropriate remedy in the case.

With respect to a beneficiary of an immediate relative petition who was under 21 when the petition was filed, newly revised chapter 21.2(e)(1)(i) of the AFM states:

> If the alien beneficiary is under the age of 21 on the date of that event, the alien will not age out and continue to be eligible for permanent residence as an IR. It does not matter whether the alien reaches the age of 21 before or after the enactment date of the CSPA, when the petition was filed, or how long the alien took after petition approval to apply for permanent residence provided the alien did not have a final decision prior to August 6, 2002 on an application for permanent residence based on the im-

migrant visa petition upon which the alien claims to be a child.

Similarly, chapter 21.2(e)(1)(ii) states with respect to a child who is the beneficiary of a petition in a preference category:

> It does not matter if the alien aged out before or after the enactment date of the CSPA, so long as the petition is filed before the child reaches the age of 21 provided the alien did not have a final decision prior to August 6, 2002 on an application for permanent residence based on the immigrant visa petition upon which the alien claims to be a child.

A person whose adjustment of status application filed after August 6, 2002, was denied may file a motion to reopen or reconsider without filing fee, if "(a) the alien would have been considered under the age of 21 under applicable CSPA rules; (b) the alien applied for permanent residence within one year of visa availability; and (c) the alien received a denial solely because he or she aged out."[72] USCIS indicates that the motion should be filed at the local USCIS field office.[73]

One of the most significant changes in USCIS's revised guidance relates to preference beneficiaries to whom a visa became available in the 364-day period before CSPA was enacted, but who did not file an application for permanent residence before or on August 6, 2002. Under USCIS's prior guidance, they were not covered by CSPA because they did not apply for adjustment of status before or on August 6, 2002. The change recognizes that some beneficiaries of preference petitions whose immigrant visa numbers became current prior to August 6, 2002, may have been deterred from subsequently filing adjustment of status applications within one year of visa availability due to USCIS's prior interpretation of the statute to require them to have filed applications for adjustment of status before August 6, 2002, to be protected under CSPA. Chapter 21.2(e)(2)(iv) of the AFM now states:

> An alien whose visa became available … on or after August 7, 2001 who did not apply for permanent residence within one year of the peti-

---

[70] *Rodriguez v. Gonzales*, *supra* note 69, at 32.

[71] *Id.* at 23–24.

[72] AFM ch. 21.2(e)(ii)(3).

[73] USCIS Update, *supra* note 12.

tion approval and visa availability, but would have qualified for CSPA coverage had he or she applied but for prior policy guidance concerning the CSPA effective date, may apply for permanent residence.

This change in effect suspends or tolls the requirement of having sought to acquire permanent residence within one year of visa availability for those preference beneficiaries who meet the specified conditions.

When is there a "final determination" for purposes of section 8(1)?

In the nonprecedent decision in *Matter of Ki Na Kim*,[74] the BIA ruled that there was no final adjudication for purposes of CSPA §8(1) where an adjustment application that was denied by the district director prior to August 6, 2002, is renewed before the immigration judge.

Ms. Kim was the derivative beneficiary of an employment preference petition, filed for her mother, which had a priority date of October 19, 1999. The petition was filed on February 11, 2000, and was approved, 166 days later, on July 26, 2000. Ms. Kim filed her application for adjustment of status on September 19, 2000, when she was approximately 19 years and 7 months old. On April 19, 2002, the district director denied Ms. Kim's application for adjustment of status on the grounds that she had "aged out" under pre-CSPA law because she had turned 21 on February 1, 2002. Ms. Kim renewed her adjustment of status application in removal proceedings. Unfortunately, the immigration judge also determined that CSPA did not apply, and denied Ms. Kim's adjustment of status application.

The BIA reversed, agreeing with Ms. Kim that the April 19, 2002, decision of the district director was not a "final determination" for purposes of CSPA §8(1) because USCIS regulations at 8 CFR §245.2(a)(5) specifically provide that a person who is not an arriving alien may renew before the immigration judge an application for adjustment of status previously denied by the district director. Ms. Kim therefore qualified for age-out protection under CSPA §3 pursuant to §8(1). The BIA determined that Ms. Kim was eligible to adjust

status as a derivative child because she was 18 years and 260 days old for immigration purposes under the formula in CSPA §3.[75]

In *Padash v. Ashcroft*,[76] the U.S. Court of Appeals for the Ninth Circuit expanded the interpretation of the period in which no "final determination" has been made to include the period that an adjustment of status applicant is seeking judicial review in the federal courts. Mr. Padash was the derivative beneficiary of a family fourth-preference petition filed in September 1984 by his uncle. A visa number became available in March 1996, while his appeal of the denial of his applications for asylum and withholding of deportation was pending before the BIA. The BIA granted his motion to expedite and reopen for adjustment of status in a timely manner on April 3, 1996, but the immigration court did not schedule a hearing until

---

[75] The result in *Kim*, that Ms. Kim qualified under CSPA for adjustment of status as a derivative child on the employment preference petition filed for her parent, was clearly correct. Interestingly, however, the formula in CSPA §3 was interpreted and applied in a manner different from that required by the February 14, 2003, Williams memorandum and other sources discussed above. The BIA interpreted "the date on which an immigrant visa number becomes available" to a beneficiary in an employment preference category that is current as the date that the priority date was established by the filing of the labor certification. The BIA stated: "[T]he operative date for determining the respondent's age for CSPA purposes is October 19, 1999, at which time the respondent was 18 years and 260 days of age." The Williams memorandum, on the other hand, interprets "the date on which an immigrant visa number becomes available" to a derivative child to be the date of the approval of the petition, if a visa number is already available on the date of approval. The Williams memorandum on page 3 states, regarding derivative beneficiaries of I-130 and I-140 petitions: "The date that a visa number becomes available is the approval date of the immigrant petition if, according to the DOS Visa Bulletin, a visa number was already available for that preference category on that date of approval." Under this interpretation, Ms. Kim would have been approximately 280 days older, but still well under the age of 21 years old.

Although the use of the filing date of the labor certification would fix a child's age at an earlier date and result in a lower age for immigration purposes under CSPA §3, it should be noted that this interpretation had the effect of nearly causing Ms. Kim to be determined to have missed the one-year filing deadline in CSPA §3. As measured from her priority date, the deadline required her to apply for adjustment of status by October 19, 2000. Under the Williams memorandum, she had until July 26, 2001.

[76] 358 F.3d 1161 (9th Cir. 2004).

---

[74] A78 706 954 (BIA June 7, 2006).

June 24, 1997. At the hearing, the immigration judge entered an order denying adjustment of status because Mr. Padash had aged out while waiting for his hearing date.

Based on the rules of statutory construction and the legislative objective of CSPA, the Ninth Circuit interpreted the term "final determination" in CSPA §8(1) to mean a "final determination of the matter" or "a decision from which no appeal or writ of error can be taken."[77] It then held that there was "no final determination" that had been made prior to August 6, 2002, on Mr. Padash's eligibility for adjustment of status because he had a petition for review pending in federal court on that date, and determined that CSPA applied to Mr. Padash.

EFFECT OF RETROGRESSION OF PRIORITY DATES

The February 14, 2003, Williams memorandum discusses what happens when visa availability retrogresses in a case that is covered by CSPA. Handling of such cases depends on whether the beneficiary has filed an I-485 adjustment application that is pending when retrogression occurs.

When visa availability retrogresses after a child applies for adjustment of status, USCIS will note the earlier visa availability date and use that date to calculate the child's age under CSPA §3 when the priority date again becomes current:

> If a visa availability date regresses, and an alien has already filed a Form I-485 based on an approved Form I-130 or Form I-140, the Service should retain the Form I-485 and note the visa availability date at the time the Form I-485 was filed. Once the visa number again becomes available for that preference category, determine

whether the beneficiary is a "child" using the visa availability date marked on the Form I-485.[78]

If visa availability retrogresses before a child files an I-485 application, the age of a beneficiary will not be calculated using the earlier date that a visa number was available. USCIS will use the later date when the priority date becomes current:

> If … an alien has not filed a Form I-485 prior to the visa availability date regressing, and then files a Form I-485 when the visa availability date again becomes current, the alien's age should be determined using the subsequent visa availability date.[79]

These excerpts from the Williams memorandum raise the possibility of a novel interpretation of CSPA §3, under which a beneficiary, who failed to seek to acquire lawful permanent residence within one year of a visa number becoming available, but for whom the category subsequently retrogresses, can qualify to have his or her age determined according to the formula in CSPA §3 if an application for adjustment of status is submitted within one year of his or her priority date again becoming current. The statutory language does not appear to require the date that a visa number becomes available to be the very first date that the beneficiary's priority date became current.

Neither the Williams memorandum nor the recent Neufeld memorandum[80] specifically addresses the issue of subsequent visa regression in the context of the concurrent filing of an I-140 petition and an I-485 application. It appears that USCIS may be applying the same rule as when an I-485 application is filed based on an approved I-130 or I-140 petition before regression of visa availability occurs.[81] Although it is uncertain at

---

[77] The Ninth Circuit stated:

> Because the legislative history makes it clear that [CSPA] was intended to address the often harsh and arbitrary effects of the age-out provisions under the previously existing statute, our interpretation of the term "final determination" also adheres to the general canon of construction that a rule intended to extend benefits should be "interpreted and applied in an ameliorative fashion." This rule of construction applies with additional force in the immigration context "where doubts are to be resolved in favor of the alien."

> *Id.* (citations omitted).

[78] Feb. 14, 2003, Williams memorandum, *supra* note 16, at 3; AFM ch. 21.2(e)(4).

[79] Feb. 14, 2003, Williams memorandum, *supra* note 16, at 3.

[80] *Supra* note 12.

[81] This conclusion is based on anecdotal evidence, including a March 31, 2008, letter from the USCIS Nebraska Service Center to Attorney Elizabeth A. Thompson, in which USCIS determined that a child who is the beneficiary of a concurrently filed I-140 petition and I-485 application is covered by CSPA, with the child's age "preserved at the point that the visa became available and then reduced by the number of days that the visa petition was pending."

that point whether the beneficiary will in fact be entitled to CSPA protection —since the I-140 petition has not yet been approved and the subsequent approval might not occur until after regression—it appears that USCIS will use the age of a derivative child beneficiary on the date of the filing of the I-140 petition and then subtract the number of days that the I-140 petition took to be approved. This approach seems to be a reasonable interpretation of the formula for age calculation under CSPA §3.[82]

The waiting periods for visa availability in the family preference and many of the employment preference categories make the formula that is use to calculate age in CSPA §3 completely inadequate in many cases to preserve the eligibility of a child to adjust status or obtain an immigrant visa as a child or derivative child on a family or employment preference petition filed on behalf of the child's parent. Under CSPA §3, the age of a derivative child is determined as the actual age of the child on the date that an immigrant visa becomes available, with the number of days that the petition was pending subtracted, provided that the child has "sought to acquire" lawful permanent residence within one year of eligibility. The wait for the priority date to become current takes several years in many cases, while the case backlog reduction initiatives implemented by USCIS have reduced processing times on petitions to less than 12 months, and less than six months in many categories.

VAWA

Section 805(b) of the Violence Against Women and Department of Justice Reauthorization Act of 2005 (VAWA 2005 or VAWA II)[83] added INA §§201(f)(4) and 203(h)(4), which explicitly state that the CSPA rules for determining the age for immigration purposes of a child of a U.S. citizen, the child of a lawful permanent resident who subsequently becomes a naturalized U.S. citizen, certain children of lawful permanent residents, and certain children who are derivative beneficiaries of petitions "shall apply to self-petitioners and derivatives of self-petitioners."

In addition, section INA §204(a)(1)(D)(v), as added by VAWA II §805(c), authorizes a person who is now over the age of 21, but under 25 years old, who had been qualified to file a VAWA self-petition before he or she reached the age of 21, but did not file due in part to the abuse, to file a VAWA self-petition:

> For purposes of this paragraph, an individual who is not less than 21 years of age, who qualified to file a petition under [INA §§204(a)(1)(A)(iv) or (B)(iii)] as of the day before the date on which the individual attained 21 years of age, and who did not file such a petition before such day, shall be treated as having filed a petition under such subparagraph as of such day if a petition is filed for the status described in such subparagraph before the individual attains 25 years of age and the individual shows that the abuse was at least one central reason for the filing delay.

The VAWA self-petition will be treated as though it was filed while the applicant was under 21.

IDENTIFYING CSPA CASES

At a National Benefits Center/AILA Liaison Committee meeting held on November 1, 2007, USCIS provided important guidance on how to complete a I-485 application when visa eligibility is based on CSPA. The National Benefits Center advised that "for unusual cases, such as those filed under the Child Status Protection Act (CSPA), Western Hemisphere, or cases where the priority date might not be clear according to the normal business rules applied by the Lockbox," practitioners should (1.) place the document that is to be used to establish the correct priority date directly under the I-485 application (2.) and marking box "h" in Part 2. of the first page of the I-485 application and "clearly indicate the basis for which the applicant is applying in the space provided (*i.e.,*

---

[82] For a good argument in support of this position, *see* T. Fox-Isicoff & R. Klasko, "The Child Status Protection Act—Is Your Child Protected," 80 *Interpreter Releases* 973 (July 21, 2003).

[83] Pub. L. No. 109-162, §805(b), 119 Stat. 2960, 3056 (2006).

Western Hemisphere, CSPA, Battered Spouse/Child, etc."[84]

For immigrant visa applications, the attorney will need to communicate with the U.S. embassy or consulate.[85] The National Visa Center often does not determine whether a derivative who has reached the age of 21 might be protected under CSPA. Continued eligibility as a derivative under CSPA is determined by the adjudicating officer at the time of the visa application.[86]

PROFESSIONAL RESPONSIBILITY ISSUES

CSPA is complex legislation that creates complicated questions of professional responsibility, case management and file review, and client notification. As the February 14, 2003, Williams memorandum and an earlier Williams memorandum note, "it is impossible to anticipate and address every possible scenario" in which CSPA could apply.[87] Due to the exceptions in §8, CSPA could be applicable in many cases that have been closed or marked as inactive due to the aging out of a child under the pre-CSPA INA.

The CSPA §3 formula is dependent on at least two major variables that the practitioner cannot predict or control, unless he or she is precognitive. A practitioner cannot predict with any level of certainty when an immigrant visa number will be available or how much processing time a petition will take.

Adding to the complexity of CSPA is that regulations have not yet been published by USCIS, DOS, or the EOIR. Grey areas exist. As the DOS cables in particular illustrate, interpreta-

tions of the effective date and terms in the statute are evolving.

The practitioner must have a basic understanding of CSPA in order to be able to identify those cases in which the client or the client's child may be covered. In ongoing cases, the applicability of CSPA can be determined as one proceeds with different aspects of the case. The potential problems in identifying older "inactive" cases that may be covered by CSPA are significant and could be insurmountable. The client's file may have been moved into storage, disposed of after a certain period of time, or no longer in the possession of the attorney. There is unlikely a system in place that will enable all cases possibly affected by CSPA to be readily identifiable without error. Even if potential cases can be identified, the client may have moved without providing a new address, and changed his or her telephone number, leaving the attorney without any means of contacting him or her.

WHEN DOES LEGAL REPRESENTATION END?

Under CSPA, an attorney's representation of a client conceivably could last for a very long period.

Although CSPA is not generally retroactive and does not apply to a person who turned 21 before August 6, 2002, unless he or she falls within an exception in CSPA §8, there may be cases involving petitions filed years before CSPA was enacted in which a beneficiary who had "aged out" prior to the enactment of CSPA is still covered by it. This is illustrated by the facts in both *Avila-Perez* and *Garcia*. As in *Garcia*, a beneficiary whose age is determined to be more than 21 under INA §203(h)(1) may qualify for retention of the original priority date and conversion into the appropriate category under INA §203(h)(3). The respondent in *Garcia*, who was 9 years old when a family fourth-preference petition was filed for her mother, was 32 years old when her adjustment of status application was denied by the immigration judge in the decision that the BIA overturned.

If a client retained an attorney five or 10 years ago to assist in the permanent residence of his family, but two of his children could not immigrate because they subsequently aged out, is there an obligation to conduct a new analysis and notify that client, if there is a possibility that the children could benefit through INA §203(h)(3) or another provision of CSPA?

The simplest answer is that it depends on the client's understanding of the scope of the representation. In the hypothetical presented above, the client reasonably would have believed when all legal work relating to the processing of the family members who were eligible under the previously existing law had been finished that the representation was complete. If earlier cases that were believed to have been completed are recalled or identified through file review, it may be appropriate to send a letter to the client's last known address, advising the client in general terms about the enactment of CSPA and asking the client to schedule a consultation or retain the practitioner for a thorough analysis of the possible applicability of CSPA.

THE ATTORNEY AS AN OPPONENT OF MARRIAGE

Whether a child is planning to marry is also beyond the control of a practitioner. As the statutory definition of a "child" is an unmarried person, marriage prior to adjustment of status or admission as an immigrant may have severe consequences for a person who otherwise qualifies for classification as a child for immigration purposes, including the loss of the eligibility to immigrate. CSPA extends the period when remaining unmarried may provide immigration benefits that would not be available if a person has married. This is illustrated by *Garcia*, where a visa number would not have been available to Ms. Garcia, had she previously married, as there is no "appropriate category" for a married child or married son or daughter of a lawful permanent resident.

In the case of a child of a U.S. citizen, marriage means being moved into the family third-preference from the immediate relative category. Persuading him or her to remain unmarried until the completion of processing of lawful permanent residence or admission as an immigrant would preserve classification as an immediate relative who is not subject to numerical restrictions on visa availability. In some cases, he or she may want to wait for a visa number in the third preference instead, since the third preference category

permits derivative immigration benefits for a spouse or child.

The consequences are much more substantial in the case of a child of a lawful permanent resident. Such a person becomes ineligible for family-sponsored immigration if he or she marries, since there is no family preference category for a married child or married son or daughter of a lawful permanent resident. The parent would need to naturalize. Due to this situation, the practitioner must make certain that the child of a client understands this potential consequence of marrying, or at least advise the client to contact the practitioner if a child is planning to marry. The practitioner will have to try to persuade the child of the need to postpone the wedding plans until adjustment of status or until his or her parent naturalizes in order to preserve immigration benefits! This highly anomalous result calls for an amendment or modification to the definition of a child to permit marriage while a child is covered by CSPA.

VISA AVAILABILITY AND THE ONE-YEAR FILING DEADLINE; NOTIFICATION RESPONSIBILITIES OF THE LEGAL REPRESENTATIVE

The child of a lawful permanent resident or a derivative child is entitled to have his or her age determined according to the calculation in INA §203(h)(1) only if he or she "sought to acquire" lawful permanent resident status within one year of eligibility. This highlights the need to notify the client on a timely basis in all ongoing cases in which CSPA could be applicable.

It is necessary for the practitioner to track the priority dates of clients, or at least those clients who could benefit from the formula in CSPA §3. This requires accurate paper or computer records of the priority dates, preference categories, and countries of chargeability of clients (or an extraordinary memory). The DOS *Visa Bulletin* must be reviewed on a regular basis for changes in the visa number cut-off dates of each preference category.

Clients covered by CSPA §3 whose priority dates have or are about to become current must be contacted to advise them of their present or impending eligibility to apply for adjustment of status so that they may complete the necessary forms and obtain the required documentation for filing to avoid missing the one-year deadline imposed by CSPA §3.

Fortunately, almost all practitioners have case management software or other procedures for tracking priority dates and notifying a client when his or her priority date has been reached or could be reached in the near future.

The issues in the preceding paragraph are, of course, more applicable when the client will be applying for adjustment of status. If the client or the client's children will be applying at the U.S. embassy, there will be notification from the DOS National Visa Center regarding visa number availability. In consular processing cases, however, it is still necessary to notify the client on a timely basis and ensure that the DS-230 Part I and other paperwork is properly completed and forwarded to the National Visa Center or the appropriate location as determined by the rules for immigrant visa processing of the U.S. embassy where the client will be applying for an immigrant visa. As discussed above, DOS generally will require that a DS-230 Part I be submitted by the beneficiary for the beneficiary to be considered to have "sought to acquire" lawful permanent residence within one year of visa availability, as INA §203(h)(1) requires. Delaying the submission of the DS-230 Part I for more than one year after visa availability will cause the beneficiary to lose the benefit of having his or her age or eligibility for immigration determined according to the rules in CSPA §3.

If the client does not respond or delays in responding to the initial notification, the circumstances may require additional attempts beyond the normal case. As in the case of the respondent in *Garcia*, the benefits of the CSPA could be substantial. Ms. Garcia would have had to wait years for the priority date established by the second-preference petition filed by her mother in 1997 to become current, if she could not have retained the priority date of the earlier fourth-preference petition.

Planning for Strategic Delays

Under the calculation in CSPA §3, a child actually benefits when there is a delay in the adjudication of a I-140 or I-130 petition. The more days the application is pending, the more days are subtracted from the age of the child. Since the number of days that an application is pending is sub-

tracted from the child's age on the date that an immigrant visa number becomes available, delays in processing might not make much of a difference in many cases. However, there are likely to be cases in which a child is several years away from turning 21, but will reach that age several months before the priority date of the child or the child's parent is expected to become current. In such cases, each day might matter.

What should a practitioner do when a longer adjudication could benefit the client? Should a letter be submitted with the I-140 or I-130 petition, asking USCIS to place the case at the end of the queue, if possible, and take a long time to adjudicate it? The best answer in most cases may be to proceed without regard to CSPA. The principal reason is that movements in the priority date cannot be estimated or projected with any certainty. If the priority date becomes current sooner than expected, the delay was not necessary. If it does not become current for a substantially longer amount of time than anticipated, then the delay provides no benefit.

What about when USCIS issues a request for evidence asking for photographs or other documentation that may have been submitted with the initial filing, but was overlooked or somehow separated from the petition? In this situation, there may be good reason to think about delaying the approval of the petition by waiting to submit the requested documents. However, due to the uncertainty of whether delay would benefit the client, as the date that a visa will become available cannot be predicted and the number of days that are subtracted from a child's age on that date is too few to make a meaningful difference in most cases, strategic delays of this nature are unlikely, in general, to benefit a client.

Rush to File

In the case of a child who is nearing the age of 21, but whose age will be fixed on the date of filing under INA §201(f)(1) because he or she is the child of a U.S. citizen, there is a responsibility on the part of the practitioner to have the I-130 petition filed as soon as possible to ensure that the child's age will be locked in. While the age-out protection in INA §201(f)(1) is automatic, a child's age is not locked in until a petition is filed by a U.S. citizen parent.

This issue also exists with respect to derivative children in employment preference categories that are current. When a category is current, as all of the employment preference categories were prior to October 1, 2005, the application of the formula in INA §203(h)(1) essentially results in the age of a child being fixed on the date of the filing of the I-140 petition minus the number of days that the I-140 petition was pending before being approved by USCIS. The prompt filing of the I-140 petition, when the principal beneficiary has a child who was nearing the age of 21, thus preserves child classification.

The issue might become complicated if premium processing for I-140 petitions is reinstated for I-140 petitions. An attorney seeking to maximize the number of days to be deducted from the age of a derivative child on the date of visa availability under the INA §203(h)(1) formula would probably not want to use premium processing. However, a delay in the approval of the I-140 petition could have adverse consequences of the principal beneficiary, including the possibility that the petitioning employer might decide to withdraw the I-140 petition before it is approved. The attorney must evaluate these considerations against the potential benefits under CSPA and explain them to the client, who must make the ultimate decision.

In the case of a child with a lawful permanent resident parent who presently meets the requirements for naturalization under INA §316, there is a responsibility to advise the parent to apply and to prepare the naturalization application as soon as possible. Under INA §201(f)(2), the age of the child locks in on the date of the parent's naturalization.

CONCLUSION

Although not perfect, and with no regulations and some of its provisions still to be interpreted by the courts, CSPA is a vast improvement over what we had before. In contrast to the "stop-time" provisions in INA §240A(d)(1), which were enacted in 1996, CSPA actually helps keep families together. It is an acknowledgement by Congress that we are "a nation that was built by immigrants and continues to be enriched by a flow of immigration."[88]

APPENDIX

Legacy INS and USCIS memoranda

- INS Memorandum, J. Williams, "The Child Status Protection Act" (Sept. 20, 2002), *published on* AILA InfoNet at Doc. No. 02092732 (*posted* Sept. 27, 2002), providing preliminary guidance on the CSPA amendments.

- INS Memorandum, J. Langlois, "H.R. 1209—Child Status Protection Act" (Aug. 7, 2002), *published on* AILA InfoNet at Doc. No. 02090531 (*posted* Sept. 5, 2002).

- INS Memorandum, J. Williams, "The Child Status Protection Act—Memorandum Number 2" (Feb. 14, 2003), *published on* AILA InfoNet at Doc. No. 03031040 (*posted* Mar. 10, 2003).

The additional guidance in this memorandum is an especially good source of information on how USCIS interprets the effective date provisions in CSPA §8 and how the age of a beneficiary or derivative beneficiary is determined under the calculation in CSPA §3. The memorandum also discusses how cases in which there is regression in the visa availability date will be handled.

- USCIS Interoffice Memorandum, J. Cuddihy, "Section 6 of the Child Status Protection Act" (Mar. 3, 2004), *published on* AILA InfoNet at Doc. No. 04032615 (*posted* Mar. 26, 2004).

- USCIS Interoffice Memorandum, W. Yates, "The Child Status Protection Act—Children of Asylees and Refugees" (Aug. 17, 2004), *published on* AILA InfoNet at Doc. No. 04091561 (*posted* Sept. 15, 2004).

- USCIS Interoffice Memorandum, M. Aytes, "Clarification of Aging Out Provisions as They Affect Preference Relatives and Immediate Family Members Under the Child Status Protection Act Section 6 and Form I-539 Adjudications for V Status" (June 14, 2006), *published on* AILA InfoNet at Doc. No. 06062870 (*posted* June 28, 2006).

---

[88] *Salameda v. INS*, 70 F.3d 447, 449 (7th Cir. 1995).

- USCIS Memorandum, D. Neufeld, "Revised Guidance for the Child Status Protection Act (CSPA)" (May 6, 2008), *published on* AILA InfoNet at Doc. No. 08050669 (*posted* May 6, 2008).

DOS cables

- Child Status Protection Act of 2002: ALDAC #1, State 163054 (Aug. 2002), *published on* AILA InfoNet at Doc. No. 02090940 (*posted* Sept. 9, 2002), which contains the text of the CSPA and initial interpretive guidance regarding the CSPA and its implementation.

- Child Status Protection Act of 2002: ALDAC #2, State 015049 (Jan. 2003), *published on* AILA InfoNet at Doc. No. 03020550 (*posted* Feb. 5, 2003).

- CSPA ALDAC No. 3—Procedural Instructions on Issuing Immigrant Visas to Aliens Qualifying for Age-Out Relief under the CSPA or Section 424 of the Patriot Act, State 144246 (May 2003), *published on* AILA InfoNet at Doc. No. 03060242 (*posted* June 2, 2003).

- Child Status Protection Act of 2002: ALDAC #4—What Constitutes a "Final Determination" on an Application Adjudicated Prior to the Effective Date of CSPA, State 131625 (May 2003), *published on* AILA InfoNet at Doc. No. 03060243 (*posted* June 2, 2003).

BIA precedent and nonprecedent decisions

- *Matter of Avila-Perez*, 24 I&N Dec. 78 (BIA 2007).

- *Matter of Garcia*, A79 001 587 (BIA June 16, 2006).

- *Matter of Kim*, A77 828 503 (BIA Dec. 20, 2004).

- *Matter of Ki Na Kim*, A78 706 954 (BIA June 7, 2006) (finding that CSPA covers a respondent who had aged out prior to August 6, 2002, because there is no "final determination" for the purposes of section 8(1) where an adjustment of status application denied by the district director prior to August 6, 2002 is renewed before the immigration judge after that date).

Federal court decisions

- *Padash v. INS*, 358 F.3d 1161 (9th Cir. 2004), in which the Ninth Circuit stated that CSPA should be interpreted expansively.

- *Akhtar v. Burzinski*, 384 F.3d 1193 (9th Cir. 2004), invalidating the regulation in 8 CFR 214.15(g) that had provided for the aging out of V-2 and V-3 nonimmigrants on the day before they turned 21.

- *Rodriguez v. Gonzales*, No. CV 04-8671 (C.D. Cal. May 31, 2006), in which the U.S. District Court for the Central Division of California addressed the effective date and legislative purpose of CSPA in eliminating the harm to beneficiaries of visa petitions due to delays by legacy INS and USCIS.

- *Dandan v. Ashcroft*, 339 F.3d 567 (7th Cir. 2003), discussing, in footnote 2, eligibility for derivative asylum benefits under INA §208(b)(3)(B), as amended by CSPA §4:

> The government contends that the two oldest children, Souzy and Raja, who turned 21 years old during the course of this proceeding, have "aged out," so that they could no longer derivatively claim asylum based on their father's claim under 8 USC 1158(b)(3). We disagree. 8 USC 1158(b)(3)(B) says
>
>> An unmarried alien who seeks to accompany, or follow to join, a parent granted asylum under this subsection, and who was under 21 years of age on the date on which such parent applied for asylum under this section, shall continue to be classified as a child for purposes of this paragraph and section 209(b)(3), if the alien attained 21 years of age after such application was filed but while it was pending.
>
> Souzy and Raja are unmarried and therefore still qualify for derivative asylum benefits.

FIANCÉ(E) PETITIONS AND K-3S: THE GOOD, THE BAD, AND THE UGLY

by Jan H. Brown, Scott D. Devore, and Gloria A. Goldman[*]

INTRODUCTION: THE GOOD

On December 21, 2000, President Bill Clinton signed into law the Legal Immigration Family Equity Act (LIFE Act).[1] The LIFE Act amended the Immigration and Nationality Act of 1952 (INA)[2] by adding §101(a)(15)(K)(ii) regarding nonimmigrant "K" classification for spouses of U.S. citizens and their children.[3] The LIFE Act made K status available to spouses and children who are the beneficiaries of pending or approved Form I-130 immigrant relative petitions filed prior to its enactment, and prospectively thereafter.[4]

Legacy Immigration and Naturalization Service (now U.S. Citizenship and Immigration Services (USCIS)) amended its regulations implementing §1103 of the LIFE Act in an interim rule effective August 14, 2001.[5] The LIFE Act and the subsequent interim rule expanded the K category to include spouses and spouses' children of U.S. citizens who are waiting outside the United States after the filing of an immigrant relative petition. The spouses of U.S. citizens under K status are now classified as "K-3," and the children of such spouses as "K-4." K-3 and K-4 visas have specific requirements for filing due to the different nature of the petitions, as is detailed below.

K-1 and K-2 Status

A fiancé(e) of a U.S. citizen may receive a K-1 visa to enter the country for the purpose of getting married to a U.S. citizen within 90 days of his or her arrival. Application is made on form I-129F. If the marriage does not occur within this 90-day window, the K-1 alien must depart the country. The child of a K-1 status alien may be granted a K-2 visa. The Department of State (DOS) clarified in the *Foreign Affairs Manual* (FAM) that the cut-off date for receiving a K-2 visa is one year after the K-1 visa has been issued to the nonimmigrant parent.[6] After this cut-off date, the alien would have to be sponsored as an immediate relative by the U.S. citizen stepparent, or as a second-preference immigrant by the lawful permanent resident parent instead (after the marriage, of course).[7]

K-3 and K-4 Classifications

K-3 Status

When it comes to K-3 visas, lawmakers have sought to make immigration law responsive to the real world needs of alien spouses and children of U.S. citizens. Previously, it was difficult for these persons, if they were living abroad, to enter the United States on a nonimmigrant visitor's visa to reunite with their U.S. family members, since immigrant intent would be presumed and the visa denied. These spouses and children of U.S. citizens had to obtain an immigrant visa outside of the United States, before being admitted as immediate relative immigrants. Consequently, family members could

---

[*] **Jan. H. Brown** is a principal in the Law Offices of Jan H. Brown, P.C., centered in New York. He has been practicing immigration and nationality law since 1979. Mr. Brown has frequently lectured and written on the subject of U.S. immigration law. He is the co-chair of the Immigration and Nationality Law Committee of the New York State Bar Association's International Law and Practice Section and the vice-chair of the AILA New York Chapter.

Scott D. Devore is a Florida Bar board-certified attorney specializing in immigration and nationality law. He is a shareholder with the law firm of Devore & Devore, P.A., with offices in West Palm Beach (Palm Beach Gardens) and Fort Lauderdale (Plantation). He is the immediate past chapter chair of AILA's South Florida Chapter. Mr. Devore is a graduate of University of Maryland (B.A.) and Thomas M. Cooley Law School (J.D.).

Gloria A. Goldman has practiced immigration and nationality law in Tucson since 1991. She practices with her son, Maurice (Mo) Goldman in the Goldman and Goldman firm. Ms. Goldman represents clients in the area of business immigration, family immigration, citizenship, as well as complicated deportation matters. She currently serves on the AILA Board of Governors.

[1] Pub. L. No. 106-553, §1(a)(2) (appx. B, H.R. 5548, §§1101–04), 114 Stat. 2762, 2762A-142 to 2762A-149 (2000).

[2] Pub. L. No. 82-414, 66 Stat. 163.

[3] Pub. L. No. 106-553, §1(a)(2) (appx. B, H.R. 5548, §1103), 114 Stat. 2762, 2762A-144 to 2762A-146 (2000).

[4] *Id.* §1103(d).

[5] 66 Fed. Reg. 42587 (Aug. 14, 2001).

---

[6] 9 *Foreign Affairs Manual* (FAM) 41.81 N12.

[7] New Nonimmigrant 41.81(k) Notes, State 190928 (Nov. 2001), *published on* AILA InfoNet at Doc. No. 01110534 (*posted* Nov. 5, 2001).

be separated for a considerable period, often longer than a year, while waiting for their U.S. citizen spouses' immigrant petitions to be approved and for their permanent resident visas to be processed. The K-3 visa category can alleviate such problems, making it a good option for many U.S. citizens and their future spouses seeking unification.

To qualify for K-3 status, the spouse of a U.S. citizen must meet the following criteria:

1. The spouse must be the beneficiary of a previously filed Form I-130 immigrant relative petition.

2. The spouse must be outside of the United States.

3. The U.S. citizen spouse must have filed Form I-129F for a K-3 visa on behalf of the alien.

The I-130 is usually filed at the USCIS service center where the U.S. citizen lives. However, if the U.S. citizen has been living abroad for at least six months, he or she may file the I-130 at the U.S. embassy or consulate assigned to that area.[8] To find out whether you can file a petition at a specific post abroad, you must ask that post.[9]

Only one Form I-129F needs to be filed for all K-3 and K-4 beneficiaries in a family. The K-3 visa is valid for two years[10] and can be extended, as discussed below.

K-4 Status

K-4 is a derivative nonimmigrant classification for the children of those who are eligible for K-3 classification. A child cannot qualify for a K-4 visa unless the U.S. citizen parent or step-parent files a K-3 petition for the child's alien parent. K-4 aliens must be under 21 years of age and unmarried to meet the definition of "child" under INA §101(b)(1). Because K-4 status depends on the filing of the parent, an I-130 need not be filed on behalf of the child.[11] However, the law does not restrict U.S. citizens from filing a Form I-130 for a child, and USCIS has encouraged that they do so as soon as

possible.[12] This would prove beneficial to the child, since the child's age at the time of filing an I-130 on his or her behalf determines the child's eligibility as an "immediate relative."[13]

The K-4 visa is valid for two years.[14] Although K-4 status was once subject to "age out" upon the alien's 21st birthday, the Child Status Protection Act[15] (CSPA) now prevents this from happening.[16] K-4 nonimmigrants may extend their status in two-year increments, as discussed below.

Application Procedures for K-3 and K-4 Visas

The LIFE Act created INA §214(r)(1), which provides that to receive K-3 or K-4 status, spouses of U.S. citizens and their children must first have a petition approved by USCIS.

An application for a nonimmigrant visa for the spouse (K-3) who married a U.S. citizen must be filed and the visa must be issued in the country where the marriage took place.[17] After the nonimmigrant visa is issued, the spouse can travel to the U.S. to await processing of his or her immigrant case.

When the beneficiary goes to the consulate to obtain a K-3 visa, he or she is required to bring:

- Two copies of the DS-156 application form
- One DS-156K, Nonimmigrant Fiancé(e) Visa Application form
- Local police certificate (called a "good conduct certificate" in some countries)
- Birth certificates for each K-3 and K-4 visa applicant
- Local marriage certificate for the principal applicant
- Divorce/death certificates (for cases involving a previous divorce)
- Standard immigrant visa medical examination, except vaccinations
- Valid passport
- Proof of financial support (Form I-134 Affidavit of Support may be requested.)

---

[8] DOS Media Note, "Consular Offices Abroad Resume Accepting I-130 Immigrant Visa Petitions" (Mar. 21, 2007), *available at www.state.gov/r/pa/prs/ps/2007/mar/82030.htm.*

[9] For information on how to contact the post, follow the link for the appropriate U.S. embassy or consulate abroad at *www.usembassy.gov.*

[10] 8 CFR §214.2(k)(8).

[11] 9 FAM 41.81 N5.3.

[12] *See* 66 Fed. Reg. 42587, 42588–90 (Aug. 14, 2001).

[13] *See infra* under the heading K-4 and Children.

[14] 8 CFR §214.2(k)(8).

[15] Pub. L. No. 107-208, 116 Stat. 927 (2002).

[16] *See infra* under the heading K-4 and Children.

[17] *http://travel.state.gov/visa/immigrants/types/types_1315.html.*

- Payment of fees[18]

As noted above, K-4 children have derivative status, so they do not need separate I-130 petitions. The petitioner must take care to name all his or her children on the I-129F petition.[19]

Changing to or from K-3/K-4 Nonimmigrant Status

Nonimmigrants already in the United States cannot change from a current nonimmigrant status *into* the K status, or *from* K status into another nonimmigrant status.[20] USCIS interprets the purpose of the K status to be family reunification, and an alien family member currently residing within the country under another status does not need the benefits of the law.[21] Of course, K-3 and K-4 aliens in the United States are not precluded from applying for adjustment of status. Note that a K-3 spouse cannot adjust status except on the basis of the marriage to the same U.S. citizen who petitioned for the K-3 status.[22]

Travel While in K-3/K-4 Status

Once admitted, aliens with valid K-3 and K-4 visas may travel outside the United States as long as they maintain their status in the United States. They are not required to maintain a foreign residence because it is assumed that they have entered the United States in order to pursue permanent residence. K-1/K-2 visa holders do not have this freedom because K-1 nonimmigrants must be married to the U.S. citizen within 90 days of entry, or they must depart and resume their foreign residence.

K-3 and K-4 classifications do not exempt beneficiaries from the three– and ten-year bars of INA§212(a)(9)(B). Beneficiaries with this problem will have to qualify for a waiver based on extreme hardship to the U.S. citizen petitioner.

Extension of K-3 and K-4 Status

Even though K-3 and K-4 nonimmigrant status is issued initially for a two-year period,[23] those in K-3/K-4 status may remain in the United States while their U.S. citizen relative's Form I-130 remains pending or valid. K-3/K-4 nonimmigrants must also file Form I-485, Application for Adjust-

ment to Permanent Residence, or consular process (per the specifications, below). They may obtain work authorization while awaiting adjudication. If permanent residence is denied, K-3 or K-4 status expires within 30 days of the date of denial.[24] Remember that a K-4 nonimmigrant need not be the beneficiary of an I-130 petition, nor file an application for adjustment of status; such a person, however, cannot renew K-4 status once the alien parent's adjustment of status application is completed.

To apply for an extension of status after the two-year initial admission, K-3/K-4 nonimmigrants must file Form I-539, Application for Extension of Stay, to gain an additional period of up to two years.[25] The alien must show proof of a pending Form I-485 or a pending application for an immigrant visa.[26] If one of these has not been filed, the alien must be the beneficiary of a pending I-130.[27] This requirement was added to discourage marriage fraud, and to support Congress' intent in creating K-3/K-4 status to unite family members while they pursue permanent residence. If the beneficiary is not awaiting adjudication of either of these applications, the nonimmigrant must prove "good cause" as to why he or she has not filed.[28] Otherwise, he or she is not "awaiting approval" of any petition or application supporting permanent residence and therefore does not satisfy the requirements of INA §101(a)(15)(K)(ii).

Employment Authorization While in K-3/K-4 Status

In order to obtain employment authorization, persons in K-3/K-4 status must file Form I-765, Application of Employment Authorization.[29] To renew employment authorization, K-3/K-4 nonimmigrants must show proof of Form I-130 filing or, if the I-130 on their behalf has been approved, that they have filed for consular processing with DOS.[30] An application for employment authorization for K-3/K-4

---

[18] *http://travel.state.gov/visa/immigrants/types/types_2993.html.* This webpage also has information on current DOS fees.

[19] *Id.*

[20] 8 CFR §248.1(a).

[21] *See* 66 Fed. Reg. 42587, 42590 (Aug. 14, 2001).

[22] *See* 8 CFR §245.1(c)(6)(ii).

[23] 8 CFR §214.2(k)(8).

---

[24] 8 CFR §214.2(k)(11).

[25] 8 CFR §214.2(k)(10)(i).

[26] *Id.*

[27] *Id.*

[28] *See* 8 CFR §214.2(k)(10)(ii) (giving the applicant the right to rebut a notice of intent to deny based on evidence not submitted by the applicant).

[29] 8 CFR §214.2(k)(9).

[30] *Id.*

nonimmigrants may be filed concurrently with an application for extension of stay.[31]

Termination of K-3/K-4 Status

When there insufficient evidence that a K-3/K-4 applicant is entitled to an extension, USCIS may send a notice of intent to deny an application, and allow the applicant 30 days to submit additional evidence.[32] K-3/K-4 status will be terminated 30 days after:[33]

1. The filed Form I-130 of which the alien is a beneficiary is denied or revoked

2. The alien's immigrant visa application is denied or revoked

3. The alien's application for adjustment of status to lawful permanent resident is denied or revoked

4. The K-3 alien's divorce to the petitioning U.S. citizen becomes final

5. An alien in K-4 status gets married.[34]

If the alien does not leave the country within 30 days of termination of status, he or she is deportable pursuant to INA §§212(a)(9)(B) and (C).[35] The alien loses employment authorization.[36] A child's K-4 status is terminated once the parent's K-3 status is terminated.[37]

K-4 and Children

On August 6, 2002, CSPA became law.[38] Before this date, a person could not immigrate as a "child" if he or she reached the age of 21 before the application for adjustment of status or an immigrant visa on his or her behalf was adjudicated and the status obtained. A person was no longer considered to be a "derivative child" upon the person's 21st birthday, and was ineligible for an immediate relative visa.[39] Consequently, the petition for the former child was either automatically moved to a lower preference category or the former child was required to submit de novo, resulting in years of delays and possible ineligibility.[40]

CSPA added §201(f)(1) to the INA. This section provides that the child's standing as an "immediate relative child" will be based upon the child's age at the time of filing of the I-130 and not upon the child's age at the time of approval.

Thus, it is advisable, albeit not required, for a U.S. citizen to file an I-130 on behalf of an unmarried alien child in K-4 status while the child is unmarried and below the age of 21. This protects the child from "age out"—that is, from becoming ineligible for an immediate relative benefit should he or she turns 21 before the I-130 is filed. A K-4 person seeking adjustment can utilize CSPA. Loss of such a benefit could result in additional years of waiting for permanent residence and loss of legal status in the United States.

Please note that a step-parent relationship is not created unless the qualifying marriage occurs on or before the alien child's 18th birthday.[41] However, the child still may enter on a K-4 visa before his or her 21st birthday if accompanying or following the K-3 parent.

THE BAD

The Adam Walsh Child Protection and Safety Act of 2006

Signed into law and effective on July 27, 2006, the Adam Walsh Child Protection and Safety Act of 2006[42] was designed to protect children from sexual exploitation and violent crime, to prevent child abuse and child pornography, to promote internet safety, and to honor the memory of Adam Walsh and other child crime victims. For the immigration practitioner, the Adam Walsh Act changed the landscape of family immigration as well as made the failure to register as a sexual offender a deportable offense.[43]

The Adam Walsh Act amended the INA to prohibit U.S. citizens and lawful permanent residents who have been convicted of any "specified offense against a minor" from filing a family-based immigrant petition (I-130, I-600, I-600A) on behalf of any beneficiary, unless the secretary of homeland

[31] 66 Fed. Reg. 42587, 42590 (Aug. 14, 2001).

[32] 8 CFR §214.2(k)(10)(ii).

[33] 8 CFR §214.2(k)(11).

[34] For important information relating to this clause, see section IV, infra.

[35] 66 Fed. Reg. 42587, 42591 (Aug. 14, 2001).

[36] Id.

[37] Id.

[38] Child Status Protection Act, Pub. L. No. 107-208, 116 Stat. 927 (2002).

[39] Summary of the "Child Status Protection Act" (H.R. 1209, Pub. L. No. 107-208), published on AILA InfoNet at Doc. No. 02080940 (posted Aug. 9, 2002).

[40] Id.

[41] INA §101(b)(1)(B).

[42] Pub. L. No. 109-248, 120 Stat. 587.

[43] INA §237(a)(2)(A)(v).

security determines in his or her *sole and unreviewable* discretion that the petitioner (U.S. citizen or lawful permanent resident) poses no risk to the beneficiary.[44] The Act also amended the INA to prohibit U.S. citizens convicted of a "specified offense" from filing K nonimmigrant visa petitions to classify their fiancé(e)s, spouses, or minor children as eligible for K nonimmigrant status unless a waiver is obtained.[45]

The million dollar question, then, is what is a "specified offense against a minor"? The term "specified offense against a minor" is defined in the Act[46] to mean an offense against a minor that involves any of the following:[47]

- An offense (unless committed by a parent or guardian) involving kidnapping;
- An offense (unless committed by a parent or guardian) involving false imprisonment;
- Solicitation to engage in sexual conduct;
- Use in a sexual performance;
- Solicitation to practice prostitution;
- Video voyeurism as described in 18 USC §1801;
- Possession, production, or distribution of child pornography;
- Criminal sexual conduct involving a minor, or the use of the Internet to facilitate or attempt such conduct; or
- Any conduct that by its nature is a sex offense against a minor.

A "minor" is an individual who has not attained the age of 18 years.[48]

Applying for a Waiver Under the Adam Walsh Child Protection and Safety Act

A petitioner who has been convicted of a "specified offense" must apply for a waiver in conjunction with his or her visa petition. As of this writing there is no specific form that a petitioner uses to apply for the waiver. A petitioner need only ask for and provide documentation for the waiver when filing the petition. USCIS has provided guidance to its officers

for the adjudication of the waiver.[49] The granting of a waiver is a long and cumbersome process with multiple levels of review.

A petitioner seeking a waiver must submit evidence of rehabilitation *and* any other evidence that "clearly demonstrates, beyond any reasonable doubt, that he or she poses no risk to the safety and well-being of his or her intended beneficiary(ies)."[50] Notice that the petitioner's burden of proof is the extremely lofty standard of *beyond a reasonable doubt*. With such a high burden of proof to satisfy, petitioners should submit as many of the following items as possible when seeking a waiver. Please note that submissions are not limited to this list and any relevant document should be submitted.

- Certified records indicating successful completion of counseling or rehabilitation programs;
- Certified evaluations conducted by licensed professionals, such as psychiatrist, clinical psychologists, or clinical social workers, that attest to the degree of a petitioner's rehabilitation or behavior modification;
- Evidence demonstrating intervening good and exemplary service to the community or in the uniformed services;
- Certified copies of police reports and court records relating to the offense;[51] and
- News accounts and trial transcripts describing the nature and circumstances surrounding the petitioner's specified offense(s) against a minor and any other criminal, violent, or abusive behavior incidents, arrests, and convictions.

USCIS Considerations in Deciding a Waiver

In its field guidance, USCIS has advised its officers that the following factors should be considered when adjudicating a waiver.[52] Again, this is not an exhaustive list and officers are not limited to considering only these factors:

---

[44] INA §§204(a)(1)(A)(viii), (B)(i)(II) (emphasis added).

[45] INA §101(a)(15)(K).

[46] INA §204(a)(1)(A)(viii)(II).

[47] Pub. L. No. 109-248, §111(a)(7), 120 Stat. 587, 592 (2006).

[48] *Id.* §111(a)(14).

[49] USCIS Memorandum, M. Aytes, "Guidance for Adjudication of Family Based-Petitions and I-129F Petition for Alien Fiancé(e) Under the Adam Walsh Child Protection and Safety Act of 2006" (Feb. 8, 2007), *published on* AILA InfoNet at Doc. No. 07030669 (*posted* Mar. 5, 2007).

[50] *Id.*

[51] The court records must include the original indictment or other charging document, any superseding charging document, any presentencing report, and the conviction judgment.

[52] USCIS Memorandum, *supra* note 49.

- The nature and severity of the petitioner's specified offense(s) against a minor, including all facts and circumstances underlying the offense(s);

- The petitioner's criminal history;

- The nature, severity and mitigating circumstances of any arrest(s), conviction(s), or history of alcohol or substance abuse, sexual or child abuse, domestic violence, or other violent or criminal behavior that may pose a risk to the safety or well-being of the principal beneficiary or any derivative beneficiary;

- The relationship of the petitioner to the principal beneficiary and any derivative beneficiary;

- The age, and if relevant, the gender of the beneficiary;

- Whether the petitioner and beneficiary will be residing either in the same household or within close proximity to one another; and

- The degree of rehabilitation or behavior modification that may alleviate any risk posed by the petitioner to the beneficiary, evidenced by the successful completion of appropriate counseling or rehabilitation programs and the significant passage of time between incidence of violent, criminal, or abusive behavior and the submission of the petition.

An important note is that USCIS takes the position that the risk to the safety and well-being of a child beneficiary *exists in all cases* and it is the burden of the petitioner to rebut and overcome the presumption of risk by providing credible and persuasive evidence of rehabilitation and any other relevant evidence that proves beyond a reasonable doubt that the petitioner poses no risk to the intended child beneficiary.[53]

Convincing the first-line adjudicator of a petitioner's worthiness for the waiver is but one step to a successful waiver request. Adjudicators must then seek consent to approve the waiver from the Regulations and Product Management Division of USCIS headquarters before exercising favorable discretion.[54] Absent headquarters' consent, a waiver application will be denied.[55] As the secretary of homeland security has the sole and unreviewable discretion to approve or deny an Adam Walsh waiver, the tradi-

tional methods of appealing the denial of a visa petition to either the Administrative Appeals Office (AAO) or the Board of Immigration Appeals (BIA) are now in question. It would appear that a denial of an I-130 on Adam Walsh grounds would not be reviewable since the BIA is part of the Department of Justice. On the other hand, a denial of an I-600, I-600A, or an I-129F would not affect the AAO's jurisdiction, since that appellate body is governed by the Department of Homeland Security.

In the end, a practitioner must now not only inquire about a potential beneficiary's admissibility into the United States but also whether the petitioner is affected by the Adam Walsh Act, and if so, whether the petitioner has substantial equities to overcome the lofty burden of proof that USCIS has established in order to obtain a waiver and be able to petition for his or her alien relative.

THE UGLY

Like most engagements and marriages, processing K-1 and K-3 applications can sometimes result in a good or bad situation. However, sometimes things can get ugly. Sometimes they can get *really* ugly. Often, unexpected situations can occur when the beneficiary finally gets to the consulate. Therefore, it's essential that a practitioner be aware of the worst case scenarios and what sort of red flags to spot when filing these applications. This will ultimately aid with determining what legal strategies can be employed, if any, or whether it's just a lost cause for the clients.

Grounds of Inadmissibility and Waivers

Getting an approval on an I-129F is only the beginning of a process that can sometimes hit a snag at the consulate. In order to qualify for either the K-1 or K-3 visa, the applicant must also demonstrate that he or she would be otherwise eligible for an immigrant visa.[56] The applicant must undergo the standard immigrant visa medical examination by a panel physician.[57] A name check through the National Crime Information Center (NCIC) must also be completed by the National Visa Center (NVC).[58] If required by the consulate, the applicant must present police certificates.[59] The applicant must also present

---

[53] *Id.*

[54] *Id.*

[55] *Id.*

[56] *See* 22 CFR §41.81(d).

[57] 9 FAM 41.81 N4(a)(1).

[58] 9 FAM 41.81 N4(a)(2).

[59] 9 FAM 41.81 N4(a)(3).

proof of the relationship to the petitioner at the time of the interview.[60]

The K-1 or K-3 applicant must also demonstrate to the consular officer's satisfaction that he or she will not become a public charge.[61] The applicant may submit a letter from the petitioner's employer or evidence that they will be self-supporting.[62] In addition, Form I-134, Affidavit of Support, will likely be required by the consular officer.[63] If this is required, the applicant will need to show that his or her sponsor's income is 100 percent of federal poverty guidelines.[64]

If the consular officer determines that the applicant would be inadmissible on any of the above grounds or certain others, he or she can waive the inadmissibility under INA §212(d)(3)(A).[65] However, in making such a determination, the officer must also consider whether the applicant would ultimately be eligible for a waiver when the K visa holder applies for adjustment of status.[66] If the officer determines that the K visa applicant is ineligible for the visa on an INA §212(a) ground for which no immigrant waiver is or would be possible after marriage to the petitioner, then the visa will be refused.[67] In the alternative, if the officer determines that a waiver would be available to the applicant once married, he or she may return the petition to the DHS for reconsideration.[68] In the case of an ineligible K-1 applicant, before commencing the waiver process the consular officer will first contact the petitioner and confirm that he or she was or is aware of the

applicant's ineligibility, and that the petitioner still wants to pursue the marriage.[69]

If the consular officer does indeed determine that a waiver is possible, he or she will assist the applicant in completing the Form I-601 and submit it simultaneously with Form OF-221, Two-Way Visa Action Request and Response, to the appropriate DHS office.[70] Unfortunately, the I-601 waiver cannot be submitted prior to the officer making an inadmissibility determination. Therefore, a delay may result due to this extra step in the process.[71]

Ugly if Identified: Factual Discrepancies in K-1 Cases

In some instances there may be unidentified problems that could raise questions in the mind of the consular officer. If the foreign beneficiary of a K-1 fiancé(e) petition has not provided a complete and accurate application, consular officers may catch certain discrepancies between the petition and the foreign beneficiary's answers. If this occurs, the officer in his or her discretion can stop the visa interview and return the petition to DHS for reconsideration.[72] "Red flags" that might lead the consular officer to question whether the relationship is bona fide or that might cause the petitioner to choose not to go forward with the marriage include having children not named in the petition, a prior undisclosed marriage (even if it has been annulled or ended by divorce or death), or, in the case of a fiancée, a current pregnancy.[73]

If this sort of situation arises, the consular officer will use his or her discretion in determining whether to return the K-1 petition to the DHS.[74] In fact, the FAM requires that the officer confirm that the petitioner is aware of the particular circumstance(s) and that he or she still wishes to proceed with the proposed marriage.[75] If the officer is satisfied by the

[60] 9 FAM 41.81 N4(a)(4).

[61] 9 FAM 41.81 N4(b). K-1 and K-3 applicants are subject to INA §212(a)(4).

[62] 9 FAM 41.81 N4(b).

[63] *Id.* Form I-864 cannot be required when applying for a K-1 nonimmigrant visa. Form I-134 must be used. Form I-864 will be required for the filing of adjustment of status once the K-1 fiancé(e) has been admitted to the United States and has filed the form I-485.

[64] INA §212(a)(4).

[65] 9 FAM 41.81 N9.1.

[66] *Id.* To determine whether a waiver is available for a K applicant, the consular officer must first examine whether the particular INA §212(a) ineligibility is waivable for immigrant spouses of U.S. citizens under either INA §212(a)(9)(B)(v), (d)(11), (d)(12), (g), (h), (i), or similar provisions. INA §212(d)(3)(A). *Id.; see* 22 CFR §40.301.

[67] 9 FAM 41.81 N9.2.

[68] 9 FAM 41.81 N9.3(a).

[69] *Id.*

[70] *Id.*

[71] DHS has made a concerted effort to expedite the adjudications of I-601 waivers. For example, in March 2007, the USCIS Ciudad Juárez Office, in conjunction with DOS, implemented a pilot program to provide same-day adjudication of many I-601 waivers. *See* USCIS Update, "New Pilot I-601 Waiver Adjudication Program—Ciudad Juarez, Mexico—American Consulate" (revised Apr. 3, 2007), *published on* AILA InfoNet at Doc. No. 07042666 (*posted* Apr. 26, 2007).

[72] 9 FAM 41.81 N6.7(d).

[73] 9 FAM 41.81 N6.7(a).

[74] 9 FAM 41.81 N6.7(c).

[75] *Id.*

petitioner's answers, he or she need not return the petition to DHS.[76]

Multiplying the Ugly: Multiple Petitions Approved for Same K-1 Beneficiary

Another red flag for a consular officer is the filing of multiple fiancé(e) petitions by different U.S. citizen fiancé(e)s on behalf of the same foreign beneficiary. If more than one K-1 visa petition has been approved for the same beneficiary, the consular officer must suspend action and return all petitions with a covering memorandum to the DHS district director who approved the last I-129F petition.[77] DHS will then be required to review the petition and interview the parties to determine how to proceed with the application.[78]

Occasionally Ugly: Proving Bona Fides

A consular officer also is responsible for confirming that the fiancé(e) or marital relationship is a bona fide one.[79] If the officer determines that the fiancé(e) or marital relationship is a sham entered into solely for immigration benefits, the officer should return the K-1 or K-3 petition with a recommendation for revocation to the NVC.[80] The returned petition must include specific, objective facts giving rise to the officer's conclusion.[81]

Almost Always Ugly: When the Petition Is Sent Back for Revocation

Once the petition is returned to DHS it can be daunting to rebut the findings of the consulate. However, depending on the service center, the attorney may have the opportunity to rebut the adverse findings. If DHS ultimately reaffirms the petition it will be returned to the consulate.[82] The consul must then determine whether it has additional derogatory factual evidence to support the belief that the applicant is not entitled to the status.[83] If the consul has no additional evidence it is required to process the case to conclusion.[84] This will likely require another interview.

In some rare instances, the consul may again disagree with the DHS decision to uphold the validity of the petition. When that occurs, the consul can either have no new evidence or additional evidence to present to DHS.[85] If the consul does not have new evidence, he or she is required to send the entire case to DOS for review and discussion with USCIS headquarters.[86] USCIS will again bear a high burden of proof in revoking the petition.[87] In the case where the consul discovers substantial new evidence not originally considered by USCIS, the consul may return the petition to USCIS through the NVC and it does not need to be referred to DOS for an advisory opinion.[88]

Appealing the Ugly: What To Do When Things Go Bad

The following are some practice pointers that an attorney can consider if a petition is going to be returned to the service center for revocation, or if the petition is ultimately revoked:

- If the K-1 or K-3 petition has not yet been returned to DHS, it is sometimes possible to reach out to an authority figure at the consulate. Try to contact either the chief of the immigrant visa section or the nonimmigrant visa section, or even the consul general. It's possible that you can stop the petition from being returned to DHS and get them to reconsider the petition.

- If you feel that the consulate is not following the relevant FAM provisions or the proper procedures, you can contact the Visa Office in Washington, D.C., at *legalnet@state.gov*. Utilize this option after you have exhausted your options at the consulate. Remember, the Visa Office cannot force a consular officer to issue a visa, as they only provide legal or procedural guidance and advisory opinions.

- The client can always refile the I-129F, but with full knowledge that he or she may come across a similar problem at the consulate.

- The client could decide to drop the plans for a K-1 or K-3 and just process the immigrant visa through an I-130 petition at the consulate.

---

[76] *Id.*

[77] 9 FAM 41.81 N6.8.

[78] *Id.*

[79] *See* 9 FAM 41.81 N6.5.

[80] *Id.*

[81] *Id.* 9 FAM 42.43 N3.

[82] 9 FAM 42.43 N4.

[83] *Id.*

[84] *Id.*

---

[85] 9 FAM 42.43 N4.1(a).

[86] *Id.*

[87] *Id.* The FAM defines the high burden of proof as "good and sufficient cause." 9 FAM 42.43 N4.1(b).

[88] 9 FAM 42.43 N4.2.

If you receive an adverse decision from the service center, you can always file an appeal to the Administrative Appeals Office in Washington, D.C.

CONFLICT OF LAW IN INTERCOUNTRY ADOPTIONS: THE INDIAN PERSPECTIVE, WITH SPECIAL REFERENCE TO THE POSITION AFTER INDIA RATIFYING THE HAGUE CONVENTION ON ADOPTIONS

*by Ranjit Malhotra and Anil Malhotra** *

INTRODUCTION

This article analyzes conflict-of-law issues relating to intercountry adoption law and procedure in the Indian jurisdiction. It also looks at the relevant legislation to be complied with by foreigners and persons of Indian origin residing abroad permanently who seek to adopt children from India. At the outset, it is important to emphasize that at present there is no exclusive general law on adoption of children governing non-Hindus and foreigners. Adoption is permitted by statute among Hindus, and by custom among some other communities. In India, in the last few years a new dimension has also arisen on account of tedious and complicated intercountry adoption laws and procedures. This is giving rise to surrogacy arrangements, preferred especially by the nonresident Indian (NRI) community overseas.

At present, non-Hindus and foreigners can only be guardians of Indian children under the Guardian and Wards Act 1890. In actual practice, foreign nationals and persons of Indian origin domiciled overseas wishing to adopt children from India first obtain guardianship orders from the District Court or the High Court, as the case may be, within whose territorial jurisdiction the child is residing. This is with a view to adopt formally under the legal system of the country of their habitual residence.

The Indian Ministry of Welfare, pursuant to certain guidelines issued by the Supreme Court of India in a public interest litigation petition, *Laxmi Kant Pandey v. Union of India*,[1] framed guidelines governing intercountry adoptions. This case was monitored by the Supreme Court from time to time until 1991, when the court scrupulously reviewed the existing procedure and practices followed in intercountry adoptions. The main objective was to prevent trafficking of children and to protect the welfare of adopted children.

In a further supplemental judgment,[2] the apex court pointed out that ordinarily the court, entertaining an application on behalf of a foreigner seeking to be appointed guardian of a child with a view to eventual adoption, should not insist on the foreigner making a deposit by way of security for due performance of the obligations undertaken by him. However, in appropriate cases, the court may pass an order requiring him or her to make such a deposit. The court also has observed that the execution of a bond would ordinarily be sufficient.

The apex court in the second supplemental judgment[3] once again, among other issues, clarified this aspect of the matter. The apex court held that the guardian judge need not insist on security or a cash deposit or bank guarantee, and it should be enough if a bond is taken from the recognized Indian placement agency that is processing the application. This

* **Ranjit Malhotra** was the first Indian lawyer to be awarded the prestigious Felix Scholarship to read for the LL.M. degree at the School of Oriental and African Studies (SOAS), University of London, which he obtained with merit in 1993. Mr. Malhotra is a member of the International Bar Association (IBA); the International Association of Youth and Family Judges; the Immigration Law Practitioners' Association (UK); AILA; Indian Council of Arbitration; the Inter-Pacific Bar Association; the Commonwealth Lawyers Association; and the International Law Association (ILA). He is a specialist in private international law, appears as an expert witness on Indian family law issues in English courts, renders expert analysis and testimony for family law and immigration cases, advises foreign lawyers, and conducts trust and probate litigation and international family law work.

Anil Malhotra is a practicing advocate in India since 1983. He obtained his B.Sc. and LL.B. from Punjab University, Chandigarh, and his LL.M. from the University of London in 1985, where he studied Comparative Family Law at the London School of Economics and Law & Society at SOAS. Mr. Malhotra has been a part-time lecturer in civil procedural law and matrimonial remedies for six years at Punjab University. Besides handling a domestic law practice for over 24 years, he handles overseas civil, criminal, and matrimonial litigation for nonresident Indians. Mr. Malhotra is a member of the International Academy of Matrimonial Lawyers, ILA, IBA, and the Indian Society of International Law.

---

[1] AIR 1984 SC 469.

[2] *Laxmi Kant Pandey v. Union of India* (AIR 1986 SC 272).

[3] *Laxmi Kant Pandey v. Union of India* (AIR 1987 SC 232).

agency may in turn take a corresponding bond from the sponsoring social or child welfare agency in the foreign country. Some directions issued in the previous judgments were also modified.

More importantly, Justice Bhagwati incorporated a vital note of clarification, as follows:[4]

We would, therefore, direct that in the case of a foreigner who has been living in India for one year or more, the home-study report and other connected documents may be allowed to be prepared by the recognized placement agency which is processing the application of such foreigner for guardianship of a child with a view to its eventual adoption and that in such a case the Court should not insist on sponsoring of such foreigner by a social or child welfare agency based in the country to which such foreigner belongs nor should a home-study report in respect of such foreigner be required to be obtained from any such foreign social or child welfare agency, the home study report and other connected documents prepared by the recognized placement agency should be regarded as sufficient.

It may, however, be pertinent to point out that the apex court in *Anokha v. State of Rajasthan*[5] has held that the above guidelines would not be applicable where the child is living with his or her biological parent(s) who have agreed that he or she is to be given in adoption to a known couple who may be of foreign origin. The court in such cases has to deal with the application under section 7 of the Guardian and Wards Act 1890 and dispose of the same after being satisfied that the child is being given in adoption voluntarily with the parents being aware of the implications of adoption—*i.e.,* that the child would legally belong to the adoptive parents' family; that the adoption is not induced by any extraneous reasons such as the receipt of money etc.; that the adoptive parents have produced evidence in support of their suitability; and that the arrangement would be in the best interest of the child.

Much more recently, the Supreme Court of India has reiterated the guidelines in case of adoption of children by foreign parents, as originally laid down in *Lakshmi Kant Pandey v. Union of India*. While emphatically following these guidelines, the apex Court pointed out: "While making the requisite and pre-

scribed exercise it has to be kept in mind that the child is a precious gift and merely because he or she for various reasons is abandoned by the parents that cannot be a reason for further neglect by the society …."[6]

PRESENT PROCEDURE TO BE FOLLOWED IN INTERCOUNTRY ADOPTIONS UNDER 2006 GUIDELINES FOR ADOPTION FROM INDIA

Central Adoption Resource Agency (CARA) guidelines stipulate that every application from a foreigner wishing to adopt a child must be sponsored by a social or child welfare agency recognized or licensed by the government of the country in which the foreigner is resident. Furthermore, the agency should be recognized by CARA, set up under the aegis of the Indian Ministry of Welfare. CARA is the principal monitoring agency of the Indian government handling all affairs connected with national and intercountry adoptions.

No application by a foreigner to adopt a child should be entertained directly by any social or child welfare agency in India working in the areas of intercountry adoption or by any institution or centre to which the children are committed by the Juvenile Court. The reasons behind this directive have been summed up by MN Das in his book *Guardians and Wards Act*:[7]

Firstly, it will help to reduce, if not eliminate altogether, the possibility of profiteering and trafficking in children, because if a foreigner were allowed to contact directly agencies or individuals in India for the purpose of obtaining a child in adoption, he might, in his anxiety to secure a child for adoption, be induced or persuaded to pay any unconscionable or unreasonable amount which might be demanded by the agency or individual procuring the child. Secondly, it would be almost impossible for the court to satisfy itself that the foreigner who wishes to take the child in adoption would be suitable as a parent for the child and whether he would be able to provide a stable and secured family life to the child and would be able to handle trans-racial, transcultural and trans-national problems likely to arise from such adoption, because, where the application for adopting a child has not been sponsored by a so-

---

[4] AIR 1987 SC 232, at 240 ¶12.

[5] (2004) 1 Hindu Law Reporter 351.

---

[6] *St. Theresa's Tender Loving Care Home et al. v. States of Andhra Pradesh*, 2006(1) Hindu Law Reporter 122, 128 ¶10.

[7] Eastern Law House, 14th ed., 1995, at 80–81.

cial or child welfare agency in the country of the foreigner, there would be no proper and satisfactory home study report on which the court can rely. Thirdly, in such a case, where the application of a foreigner for taking a child in adoption is made directly without the intervention of social or child welfare agency, there would be no authority or agency in the country of the foreigner who could be made responsible for supervising the progress of the child and ensuring that the child is adopted at the earliest in accordance with law and grows up in an atmosphere of warmth and affection with moral and material security assured to it.

ABOUT THE CENTRAL ADOPTION RESOURCE AUTHORITY

CARA is an autonomous body under the Ministry of Women and Child Development, Government of India. Its mandate is to find a loving and caring family for every orphan/destitute/surrendered child in the country. CARA was set up in 1990 under the aegis of the Ministry of Welfare in pursuance of Cabinet decision dated 9 May 1990. Pursuant to a decision of the Union Cabinet dated 2 July 1998, the then Ministry of Social Justice and Empowerment conferred the autonomous status on CARA with effect from 18 March 1999 by registering it as a Society under the Societies Registration Act, 1860. It was designated as the Central Authority by the Ministry of Social Justice and Empowerment on 17 July 2003 for the implementation of the Hague Convention on Protection of Children and Cooperation in Respect of Intercountry Adoption.[8]

In-country adoption of Indian children is governed by In-country Guidelines—2004, while intercountry adoption procedure is governed by a set of guidelines last issued on 14 February 2006. These guidelines are a follow-up to various directions given by the Supreme Court of India in *L.K. Pandey v. Union of India*.[9] These guidelines have been amended and updated from time to time. While CARA is engaged in clearing intercountry adoption of Indian children, its principal aim is to promote in-country adoption. In fact, CARA ensures that no Indian child is given for intercountry adoption without him or her having been considered by Indian

families residing in India. CARA also provides financial assistance to various nongovernmental organizations and government-run homes to promote quality child care to such children and place them in domestic adoption.

PROCEDURE TO BE FOLLOWED IN INTERCOUNTRY ADOPTIONS UNDER GUIDELINES FOR ADOPTION FROM INDIA 2006

Step 1: Enlisted Foreign Adoption Agency

- The applicants will have to contact or register with an Enlisted Foreign Adoption Agency (EFAA)/ Central Authority/government department in their country, in which they are resident, which will prepare the Home Study Report (HSR) etc. HSRs are valid for two years. HSRs prepared before two years will be updated at referral.

- The applicants should obtain the permission of the competent authority for adopting a child from India. Where such Central Authorities or government departments are not available, the applications may be sent by the enlisted agency with requisite documents, including documentary proof that the applicant is permitted to adopt from India

- The adoption application dossier should contain all documents prescribed in Annexure-2. All documents are to be notarized. The signature of the notary is either to be attested by the Indian Embassy/High Commission or the appropriate government department of the receiving country. If the documents are in any language other than English, then the originals must be accompanied by attested translations. A copy of the application of the prospective adoptive parents along with the copies of the HSR and other documents will have to be forwarded to the Recognized Indian Placement Agency (RIPA) by the EFAA or Central Authority of that country.

Step 2: Role of Recognized Indian Placement Agency

- On receipt of the documents, the RIPA will make efforts to match a child who is legally free for intercountry adoption with the applicant.

- If no suitable match is possible within three months, the RIPA will inform the EFAA and CARA with the reasons therefor.

---

[8] May 29, 1993, 1870 U.N.T.S. 167 (Reg. No. 31922 (1993)), 32 I.L.M. 1134 (1993).

[9] Writ Petition Number 1171 of 1982 and other cases.

Step 3: Child being declared free for inter-country adoption—Clearance by Adoption Coordinating Agency

- Before a RIPA proposes to place a child for intercountry adoption, it must apply to an Adoption Coordinating Agency (ACA) for assistance for Indian placement.

- The child should be legally free for adoption. The ACA will find a suitable Indian prospective adoptive parent within 30 days, failing which it will issue a clearance certificate for intercountry adoption.

- The ACA will issue clearance for intercountry adoption within 10 days in case of children more than 6 years old, siblings or twins, and special needs children as per the additional guidelines issued in this regard.

- In case the ACA cannot find suitable Indian parent/parents within 30 days, it will be incumbent upon the ACA to issue a clearance certificate on the 31st day.

- If ACA clearance is not given on the 31st day, the clearance of ACA will be assumed unless the ACA has sought clarification within the stipulation period of 30 days.

- NRI parent(s) (at least one parent) holding an Indian passport will be exempted from ACA clearance, but they have to follow all other procedures in the guidelines.

Step 4: Matching of the Child Study Report with Home Study Report of Foreign Prospective Adoptive Parent/s by RIPA

- After a successful matching, the RIPA will forward the complete dossier as per Annexure 3 to CARA for issuance of a "No Objection Certificate" (NOC).

Step 5: Issue of No Objection Certificate by CARA

- The RIPA must apply for a CARA NOC in case of foreign or persons of Indian origin (PIO) parents only after the ACA clearance certificate is obtained.

- CARA will issue the NOC within 15 days from the date of receipt of the adoption dossier if it is complete in all respects.

- If any query or clarification is sought by CARA, it must be replied to by the RIPA within 10 days.

- No RIPA can file an application in the competent court for intercountry adoption without an NOC from CARA.

Step 6: Filing of Petition in the Court

- On receipt of the NOC from CARA, the RIPA must file a petition for adoption/guardianship in the competent court within 15 days.

- The competent court may issue an appropriate order for the placement of the child with foreign prospective adoptive parent(s).

- Per Supreme Court directions, the concerned court may dispose of the case within two months.

Step 7: Passport and Visa

- RIPA has to apply in the Regional Passport Office for an Indian passport for the child.

- The concerned Regional Passport Officer may issue the passport within 10 days.

- Thereafter, the visa entry permit may be issued by the consulate/embassy/high commission of the concerned country for the child.

Step 8: Child travels to adoptive country

- The adoptive parent(s) will have to come to India and accompany the child back to their country.

As of now, all intercountry adoptions are governed by the 2006 Guidelines. The authors have learned from official sources that the draft 2007 Guidelines are likely to be finalized very soon. Nonetheless, the importance of the basic documentation cannot be undermined in intercountry adoptions. The starting point of course is the HSR.

The importance of the HSR is paramount. In fact, it is like a clear-cut balance sheet of the prospective adoptive parents. It is a very handy document at the entire stage of the adoption process, especially when guardianship proceedings are instituted in the Court of the Guardian Judge, within whose jurisdiction the minor child is residing. It also is useful at the time of the visa interview at the embassy or consulate, to impress on the visa/consular officer the positive aspects of the application, with a view to enhancing the chances of the success of the application.

HOME STUDY REPORT

Paragraph 2.14 of the earlier 1995 Guidelines categorically and emphatically enumerates the required contents of the HSR, which should include the information listed below. Although this is the list of documentation stipulated in the earlier guidelines of 1995, based on the experience of the authors in handling family migration issues, we would still recommend submitting these documents, for the reasons mentioned in the preceding paragraph.

(1) social status and family background;

(2) description of the home;

(3) standard of living as it appears in the home;

(4) current relationship between the husband and wife;

(5) current relationship between the parents and children (if there are any children);

(6) development of any already adopted children;

(7) current relationship between the couple and the members of each other's family;

(8) employment status of the couple;

(9) health details, such as clinical tests, hearing condition, past illness, etc. (medical certificate etc.);

(10) economic status of the couple;

(11) accommodation for the child;

(12) schooling facilities;

(13) amenities in the home;

(14) reasons for wanting to adopt an Indian child;

(15) attitude of grandparents and relatives towards the adoption;

(16) anticipated plans for the adoptive child;

(17) legal status of the prospective adoptive parents.

PREFERENCE FOR PARENTS OF INDIAN ORIGIN

Another significant issue in intercountry adoptions is locating prospective adoptive parents, preferably of Indian origin. The Supreme Court of India, in *Karnataka State Council for Child Welfare v. Society of Sisters of Charity St Gerosa Convent*,[10] held that the rationale behind finding Indian parents or parents of Indian origin is to ensure that the children should grow up in Indian surroundings so that they retain their culture and heritage. This is definitely an issue that has a bearing on the question of the welfare of the children. The best interest of the children is the main and prime consideration.

The Gujarat High Court, in a progressive judgment, *Jayantilal v. Asha*,[11] upheld the validity of guardianship orders in favor of two Norwegian cou-

ples who were appointed as guardians of Hindu children. The court held:[12]

[I]f the biological parents have died rendering the child an orphan then the society owes a duty to the child that at least a semblance of comfort and care which the biological parents could have provided will be provided to the child, if some people from howsoever distant a corner of this planet, come forth to do so. In such a case a petty contention like the change of religion or culture of the child can hardly stand in the way of the court in sanctioning inter-country adoption. Unfounded and imaginary apprehensions also are of little consequence and once the court is assured that there is no possibility of the child being abused which assurance can flow from the independent agencies which are ordained for the purpose then nothing can and need prevent the court from sanctioning an inter-country adoption.

Thus, the procedure described above and the supervisory role of the court serve as a double check on intercountry adoptions. Not only does this dual process ensure a check against suspected child abuse, but at the same time it also removes hypertechnical objections to facilitate the conclusion of the adoption process and to enable the adopted child to leave the country with his or her adoptive parents without further bureaucratic delays.

The Allahabad High Court in *Jagdish Chander Gupta v. Dr Ku Vimla Gupta*[13] held that under section 9 of the Guardian and Wards Act 1890, the application for guardianship of a minor must be made to the district court having jurisdiction in the place where the minor ordinarily resides. The supervisory role of the court in placing the welfare of the minor as the primary consideration is best reflected in the following words of the court:[14]

It should not be lost sight of and must be emphasized that in custody cases, a child has not to be treated as a chattel in which its parents have a proprietary interest. It is a human being to whom the parents owe serious obligations. One's own self interest sometimes clouds his perception of what is the best for those for whom he or she is responsible. It takes a very high degree of selflessness and maturity – which is for most of the

---

[10] AIR 1994 SC 658.

[11] AIR 1989 Gujarat 152.

[12] *Id.* at 156, ¶12.

[13] (2004) 1 Hindu Law Reporter 282.

[14] *Id.* at p 285, ¶16.

people probably unattainable degree—for a parent/proposed guardian to acknowledge that it might be better for the child to be brought up by someone else.

RATIFICATION OF THE HAGUE CONVENTION ON INTERCOUNTRY ADOPTION BY THE GOVERNMENT OF INDIA ON 6 JUNE 2003

The Government of India ratified the Hague Convention on Intercountry Adoption[15] on 6 June 2003. Although the Government of India has ratified the Hague Convention, in actual practice it has not been publicized. From the practical point of view, not many tangible benefits are forthcoming to people residing abroad seeking to adopt children from India. In fact, one of the authors of this article, at the Annual National Meet on Adoption organized in New Delhi on 3-4 May 2007, by CARA, strongly advocated the emergent need for setting up a committee or a task force to commission a comprehensive report to look at the potential benefits of India having signed the Hague Convention. If such a report is prepared, it can well be officially circulated to the foreign embassies and missions in India. This is, of course, with a view to creating awareness and publicizing the advantages of India signing the Hague Convention to prospective adoptive parents of foreign origin and PIOs domiciled overseas.

DOCUMENTS REQUIRED FROM FOREIGN ADOPTIVE PARENTS AND OVERSEAS SOCIAL OR CHILD WELFARE AGENCY FOR INTERCOUNTRY ADOPTION APPLICATION

Experience in dealing with CARA and/or the concerned ministry suggests that the documentation should be compiled meticulously in order to avoid bureaucratic delays. The following documents must be submitted by the foreign adoptive parents. Note that the Indian requirements are quite similar to those prescribed in various appendices of RON 117 issued by the British Home Office.

(1) home study report;

(2) recent photographs of the adoptive family;

(3) marriage certificate of the foreign adoptive parents;

---

[15] Convention on Protection of Children and Co-operation in Respect of Intercountry Adoption, May 29, 1993, 1870 U.N.T.S. 167 (Reg. No. 31922 (1993)), 32 I.L.M. 1134 (1993).

(4) declaration concerning the health of the foreign adoptive parents;

(5) certificate of medical fitness of the foreign adoptive parents duly certified by a medical doctor;

(6) declaration regarding financial status, together with supporting documents, including employer's certificate, wherever applicable;

(7) employment certificate of the foreign adoptive parents, if applicable;

(8) income tax assessment order(s) of the foreign adoptive parents;

(9) bank references for the foreign adoptive parents;

(10) particulars of properties owned by the prospective adoptive parents;

(11) joint declaration tendered by the foreign adoptive parents stating willingness to be appointed guardians of the child;

(12) undertaking from the social or child welfare enlisted agency sponsoring the foreigner to the effect that the child would be legally adopted by the foreign adoptive parents according to the law of the country within a period not exceeding two years from the time of arrival of the child;

(13) undertaking from the foreign adoptive parents to the effect that the child would be provided with the necessary education and upbringing according to status of the adoptive parents;

(14) undertaking from the recognized foreign social or child welfare agency that the report relating to the progress of the child along with his/her recent photograph would be sent quarterly during first two years and half-yearly for the next three years in the prescribed proforma through the relevant Indian diplomatic post;

(15) power of attorney conferred by the intending parents in favor of the social or the child welfare agency in India, which will be required to process the case. Such power of attorney should also authorize the lawyer in India to handle the case on behalf of the foreign adoptee parents, if they are not in a position to come to India;

(16) certificate from the recognized foreign social or child welfare agency sponsoring the application to the effect that the adoptive parents are permitted to adopt a child according to the laws of their country;

(17) undertaking from the recognized foreign social or child welfare agency to the effect that, in case of disruption of the adoptive family before

the legal adoption has been effected, it will take care of child and find a suitable alternative placement for the child with prior approval of CARA;

(18) undertaking from the recognized foreign social or child welfare agency that it will reimburse all expenses to the concerned Indian social or child welfare agency as fixed by the competent court towards maintenance of the child and the processing charge fees.

It is important to reiterate that all the above certificates, declarations, and documents in support of the application should be duly notarized by a notary public, whose signature should be duly attested either by an officer of the ministry of external affairs, the ministry of justice, or the ministry of social welfare of the country of the foreign adoptive parents or by an officer of the Indian embassy or the high commission or consulate in that country.

DOMESTIC LAW

Having elaborated the law and procedure relating to intercountry adoptions, brief reference is now made to the domestic law governing adoptions by Hindus.

The principal law relating to adoption in India by Hindus only is contained in the Hindu Adoptions and Maintenance Act 1956 (HAMA 1956).

Requisites of a Valid Adoption

Section 6 of HAMA 1956 stipulates four conditions for a valid adoption, namely:

(1) the person adopting has the capacity, and also the right, to take in adoption;

(2) the person giving the child in adoption has the capacity to do so;

(3) the person adopted is capable of being taken in adoption; and

(4) the adoption is made in compliance with the other conditions mentioned in chapter 2 of HAMA 1956.

The other conditions mentioned in chapter 2 of HAMA 1956 require compliance with the provisions of sections 7 to 11. Section 7 deals with the capacity of a male Hindu to take in adoption, and section 8 with the capacity of a female Hindu to take in adoption. Section 9 qualifies persons capable of giving children in adoption, section 10 categorizes those persons who may be adopted, and section 11 enumerates other conditions for a valid adoption.

Other Conditions for a Valid Adoption

Section 11 of HAMA 1956 stipulates other vital conditions for a valid adoption, and is reproduced below.

11. Other conditions for a valid adoption

In every adoption, the following conditions must be complied with:—

(i) if the adoption is of a son, the adoptive father or mother by whom the adoption is made must not have a Hindu son, son's son or son's son's son (whether by legitimate blood relationship or by adoption) living at the time of adoption;

(ii) if the adoption is of a daughter, the adoptive father or mother by whom the adoption is made must not have a Hindu daughter or son's daughter (whether by legitimate blood relationship or by adoption) living at the time of adoption;

(iii) if the adoption is by a male and the person to be adopted is a female, the adoptive father is at least twenty-one years older than the person to be adopted;

(iv) if the adoption is by a female and the person to be adopted is a male, the adoptive mother is at least twenty-one years older than the person to be adopted;

(v) the same child may not be adopted simultaneously by two or more persons;

(vi) the child to be adopted must be actually given and taken in adoption by the parents or guardian concerned or under their authority with intent to transfer the child from the family of its birth [or in the case of an abandoned child or child whose parentage is not known, from the place or family where it has been brought up] to the family of its adoption:

Provided that the performance of datta homam (Hindu ceremonial procedure) shall not be essential to the validity of adoption.

Effects of a Valid Adoption

Section 12 of HAMA 1956 specifically deals with the legal effects of an adoption made in accordance with the provisions of HAMA 1956. It can be pointed out that section 12 satisfies the requirements of cl. ix of para. 310 of HC 395 of the current British Immigration Rules governing adoption. This clause in very harsh terms states that the adopted child "has lost or broken his ties with his family of origin."

As to the legal effects of a valid adoption, it is important to cite certain decisions of the Supreme

Court of India. It was held by the Supreme Court in *Smt Sitabai v. Ramchandra*:[16]

> The true effect and interpretation of ss 11 and 12 of Act No 78 of 1956 therefore is that when either of the spouses adopts a child, all the ties of the child in the family of his or her birth become completely severed and these are all replaced by those created by the adoption in the adoptive family …

Similarly, it was held by the Supreme Court in *Kartar Singh v. Surjan Singh*:[17]

> The words in section 11(vi) "with intent to transfer the child from the family of its birth to the family of its adoption" are merely indicative of the result of the actual giving and taking by the parents or guardians concerned referred to in the earlier part of the clause. Where an adoption ceremony is gone through and the giving and taking takes place, there cannot be any other intention … .

And, the Supreme Court in Chandan Bilasini v. Aftabuddin Khan[18] held:

> Section 12 of the Hindu Adoptions and Maintenance Act clearly provides that an adopted child shall be deemed to be the child of his adoptive father or mother for all purposes with effect from the date of the adoption and from such date all ties of the child in the family of his or her birth shall be deemed to be severed and replaced by those created by the adoption in the adoptive family … .

Finally, section 15 of HAMA 1956 underlines the irrevocability of the validly performed adoption by stating that it cannot be cancelled or renounced. Therefore, under Indian law, once a legitimate adoption is obtained in accordance with the procedure established by law, the margin for interference is minimal, except in certain exceptional circumstances.

Registered Adoption Can Be Challenged

Section 16 of HAMA 1956 reads as follows:

> 16. Presumption as to registered documents relating to adoption

> Whenever any document registered under any law for the time being in force is produced before any court purporting to record an adoption made and is signed by the person giving and the person taking the child in adoption, the court shall pre-sume that the adoption has been made in compliance with the provisions of this Act unless and until it is disproved.

In an important ruling concerning adoption by Hindus, *Jai Singh v. Shakuntala*,[19] the Supreme Court of India has recently held that although a document registering an adoption should be treated as final proof of adoption, it could still be challenged in a court of law if evidence to the contrary was put forward.

The apex court, in interpreting the statutory intent of section 16 of the HAMA 1956, said that the presumption about the registered document relating to adoption "cannot be … irrebuttable." Justices Umesh C Banerjee and Brijesh Kumar held:[20]

> The section thus envisages a statutory presumption that in the event of there being a registered document pertaining to adoption there would be a presumption that adoption has been made in accordance with law. Mandate of the statute is rather definite since the legislature has used "shall" instead of any other word of lesser significance. Incidentally, however, the inclusion of the words "unless and until it is disproved" appearing at the end of the statutory provision has made the situation not that rigid but flexible enough to depend upon the evidence available on record in support of adoption. It is a matter of grave significance by reason of the factum of adoption and displacement of the person adopted from the natural succession—thus onus of proof is rather heavy. Statute has allowed some amount of flexibility, lest it turns out to be solely dependent on a registered adoption deed. The reason for inclusion of the words "unless and until it is disproved" shall have to be ascertained in its proper perspective and as such the presumption cannot but be said to be a rebuttable presumption. Statutory intent thus stands out to be rather expressive depicting therein that the presumption cannot be an irrebuttable presumption by reason of the inclusion of the words just noticed above … .

In the above-mentioned ruling, the Supreme Court also concurred with the similar tenor of law laid down by the Punjab and Haryana High Court in *Modan Singh v. Sham Kaur*.[21]

---

[16] AIR 1970 SC 343, 348 ¶6.

[17] AIR 1974 SC 2161, 2163, ¶7.

[18] (1996) 1 Hindu Law Reporter 79, 81, ¶6.

[19] (2002) 3 SCC 634.

[20] *Id.* at 636–37, ¶2.

[21] AIR 1973 P&H 122.

Clearly, the ruling in *Jai Singh* will be of immense help to immigration officers of foreign missions/consulates/embassies in India in weeding out suspect adoption immigration applications lodged from within the applicant's own family designed to circumvent immigration controls.

PROBLEMS FACED IN INTERCOUNTRY ADOPTION

This is an issue of immense significance. At present non-Hindus and foreign nationals can only be guardians of children under the Guardian and Wards Act 1890. They cannot adopt children. The child loses out by being deprived of the benefits of a valid adoption. There have been disturbing press reports about "greedy social activists." Sharma Vinod, in his article "Indian Child Losing out in Adoption Mart,"[22] pointed out that at the root of the problem is certain placement agencies' desire for financial gain and their propensity to extort money from childless foreigners. In the same report, it was pointed out that in practice the paperwork is complex. The system is not working because of long delays at the different levels of scrutiny.

Additionally, according to in-vitro fertilization experts in New Delhi, the number of infertile couples from foreign countries opting for in-vitro fertilization is increasing. Low-cost and hi-tech treatment in India is helping NRI couples to realize their dreams of natural parenthood. NRI couples are reluctant to opt for adoption for two major reasons. First, religious and social factors are a major issue. Secondly, it has been highlighted that cumbersome adoption and immigration laws make it very difficult to take the child to the United Kingdom or the United States, after the adoptive child is chosen from the homeland.[23]

In a hard-hitting editorial opinion titled "Maternity for Hire,"[24] it has been noticed that India is emerging as a sought-after destination for surrogate mothers. Desperate childless NRI couples are rushing to India to rent a womb. Anand, in Gujarat, has

seen as many as 14 commercial in-vitro fertilization surrogacy cases in the last two years.

This article—we believe rightly so—laments:

It is a disturbing trend. ...

It is particularly sad because there are over 12 million orphaned children in India who need parents. And another 44 million destitute children who are denied the warmth of a family. If only people could transcend the desire to have a baby that is genetically theirs, India would be the logical place where childless couples could seek parental happiness through adoption. Research shows that parental love has less to do with biological ties and more with shared experiences, and that adoptive parents love their children as much as biological parents. But our adoption figures don't go beyond a few thousand per year. Playing spoilsport is a 115-year-old Act—the Guardians and Wards Act—which does not allow Muslims, Christians, Jews, and Parsis to become a child's adoptive parents. They can only be a 'guardian.' Even the more liberal Hindu Adoption and Maintenance Act, 1956, does not allow non-Hindus to adopt a Hindu child. The adoption process is tedious and hemmed in by all sorts of unnecessary restrictions. It is ironical that in a country with so many children without a home, there's a long waiting list of couples wanting to adopt.

NEW DIMENSION: THE JUVENILE JUSTICE (CARE AND PROTECTION OF CHILDREN) AMENDMENT ACT, 2006

The Ministry of Women and Child Development has of late been mandated to look after the subject matters "Adoption" and "Juvenile Justice (Care & Protection of Children) Act, 2000" pursuant to 16 February 2006 notification of Government of India regarding reallocation of the Business.

Also, the government enacted the Juvenile Justice (Care & Protection of Children) Act, 2000 (JJ Act), and further amended it in the year 2006 to ensure adequate protection and rehabilitation measures for children in need of care and protection.

The Juvenile Justice (Care and Protection of Children) Amendment Act, 2006, applies to all children, as well as parents, irrespective of their religion and gender. All adoptable children under the category "children in need of care and protection" (as defined under the Act) must be processed under this specific legislation by district courts, city civil courts, family court, and other appropriate courts as may be defined

---

[22] *The Hindustan Times*, Sept. 9, 1997.

[23] For details, *see* S. Jyoti, "'How Egg-citing! NRIs Eye Desi Donors," The Times of India, Aug. 28, 2003, *available at* http://timesofindia.indiatimes.com/articleshow/151907.cms.

[24] *The Times of India*, New Delhi/Chandigarh Ed., Feb. 24, 2006, *available at* http://timesofindia.indiatimes.com/Opinion/Editorial/Maternity_for_Hire/articleshow/msid-1426379, curpg-2.cms.

under state juvenile justice rules to be framed based on the Act. The legislation being child-focused legislation, guarantees all rights to an adopted child and it is also recognized under international obligations by all Hague Convention member countries.

On implementation of the Juvenile Justice Amendment Act, 2006 and its state rules, all cases of orphaned, abandoned, and surrendered children have to be processed under the Act so that unrelated children have adequate safeguards in their placement.

In an editorial article published in *The Hindustan Times*,[25] it has been analyzed:

In a bid to put adoptive parents of all faiths on the same platform, amendments to the Juvenile Justice (Care and Protection of Children) Act (JJ) have now been notified and guidelines framed. One of the most important amendments to the Act made clear that adoption under this legislation would allow an adopted child to become the "legitimate child of his adoptive parents, with the rights, privileges and responsibilities attached to the relationship". This is a significant move considering till now, adoption by non-Hindus has been guided by the Guardian and Wards Act (Gawa), 1890, which gives them the status of "guardians," a relationship that becomes void when the child entered adulthood. Conversely, it doesn't give the 'ward' legal rights due to a biological child.

In effect, non-Hindu parents can now claim full parenthood instead of just the interim "guardian" status that they were allowed until recently. Prior to the enactment of the JJ Act 2006, only Hindu couples who adopted children could claim to be parents; non-Hindus were just guardians to their adopted children. This, of course, also led to children being denied rights to inherited property, besides creating day-to-day problems for parents at the time of school admissions and in other matters.

Another major upshot of the JJ Act 2006 is that it makes intercountry adoptions permissible. But how would the embassies and foreign missions in India view adoption orders granted to Hindus and non-Hindus, as well as foreigners?

All opinions are not positive. The JJ Act has drawn some amount of criticism. In an article titled "Time to Unscramble the Adoption Tangle,"[26] Swati Deshpande has come out with some very valid criticisms as follows.

Activists emphasi(z)e that there is no clarity on the provisions for adoption in the Juvenile Justice (Care and Protection) Act. "There is a lot of confusion on the issue of adoption under the Juvenile Justice (JJ) Act," said child-rights activist Sangeeta Punalekar. She noted that adoption was provided for under the JJ Act in 2000 itself to aid the rehabilitation and social integration of orphaned, abandoned or neglected children. "But even then it met with hardly any response," Punalekar said. To date, there are no known cases of adoption under the JJ Act in Maharashtra, though there have been a few cases in Delhi. Punalekar said the law stipulates that instead of getting the approval of higher courts—like district courts and high courts (in the case of inter-country adoption)—adoption should be done locally by child welfare committees and juvenile justice boards. However, she and other activists said there seem to be no rules or infrastructure in place nor is there clarity on related issues, like if the law will apply to Muslims. As it stands, the amendment to the JJ Act defines adoption as the "process through which the adopted child is permanently separated from his biological parents and becomes the legitimate child of his adoptive parents with all the rights, privileges and responsibilities attached to the relationship" In other words, the Act would apply to all Indians. ….It is not clear how this law would override the provisions of other personal laws. The Muslim personal law, for instance, does not permit adoption, he noted. The government can't try and plug loopholes in one Act by amending another … .

Surrogacy has indeed arrived in India. In our day-to-day practice; we are confronted with queries from foreign lawyers as to the legal position relating to surrogacy arrangements. Here, it would be pertinent to briefly elaborate as to the legal position in this regard.

---

[25] "Adopting New Guidelines," *The Hindustan Times*, Nov. 18, 2007, *available at* www.hindustantimes.com/StoryPage/StoryPage.aspx?id=6ec539df-9cef-4622-a03d-a3b6c3b7beab.

[26] *The Times of India*, Nov. 20, 2007.

THE LAW APPLICABLE IN INDIA AS TO THE LEGAL PARENTAGE OF CHILDREN BORN IN THAT JURISDICTION AS A RESULT OF A SURROGACY ARRANGEMENT

In India at the moment, we do not have any legislation on legal parentage as a result of surrogacy arrangements. In India, we have the Registration of the Births and Deaths Act, 1969, which does not contain any provision regarding parentage as a result of a surrogacy arrangement. That enactment, laid down by the Parliament of India, came into force on 31 May 1969. Surrogacy parentage was not an issue at that time. There have not been any amendments or additions with regard to any surrogacy issues since the enactment.

As far as legislation on surrogacy is concerned, draft surrogacy proposals were going through the Parliament at some stage. The current position in this regard is not very clear. Guidelines dealing with artificial reproductive technologies (ART) have been prepared by an expert committee of the Indian Council of Medical Research in association with the National Academy of Medical Sciences (India), which could in the future become a part of the final draft of a proposed legislation. The preface to the guidelines as circulated in March 2004 specifically points out that "There are no guidelines for the practice of ART, accreditation of infertility clinics and supervision of their performance in India. This document aims to fill this lacuna and also provide a means of maintaining a national registry of ART clinics in India . . . ."

For this purpose, the National Guidelines for Accreditation, Supervision and Regulation of ART Clinics in India have been framed. These guidelines provide a foundation for the proposed legislation relating to this field of law. They state that the surrogate mother under no circumstances is considered to be the legal mother.

Para 3.5.4 of the guidelines provides that when the surrogate mother is biologically unrelated to the child, the birth certificate must have the name of the genetic parents. Therefore, if the commissioning parents have contributed their genetic material for the unborn child, they will be recorded automatically as the legal parents, if DNA tests prove the same. No adoption procedure needs to be followed by the genetic parents under such circumstances. Para 3.5.4 of the guidelines reads:

3.5.4—A surrogate mother carrying a child biologically unrelated to her must register as a patient in her own name. While registering she must mention that she is a surrogate mother and provide all the necessary information about the genetic parents such as names, addresses, etc. She must not use/register in the name of the person for whom she is carrying the child, as this would pose legal issues, particularly in the untoward event of maternal death (in whose names will the hospital certify this death?). **The birth certificate shall be in the name of the genetic parents.** The clinic, however, must also provide a certificate to the genetic parents giving the name and address of the surrogate mother. All the expenses of the surrogate mother during the period of pregnancy and post-natal care relating to pregnancy should be borne by the couple seeking surrogacy. The surrogate mother would also be entitled to a monetary compensation from the couple for agreeing to act as a surrogate; the exact value of this compensation should be decided by discussion between the couple and the proposed surrogate mother. An oocyte donor can also act as a surrogate mother.

However, in terms of the above mentioned guidelines, when the surrogate mother also donates her egg, the commissioning parents/infertile couple will have to legally adopt the child, and it is only after this legal procedure has been complied with that the infertile couple become the legal parents of the child born through such an arrangement. This fact will also have to be recorded in the birth certificate issued to such a child.

Furthermore, when the genetic material is supplied by third-party donors, the birth certificate issued to the child initially will have the names of the genetic parents. Here, it would become mandatory for the infertile couple to legally adopt the child so born, before they can be referred to as the legal parents of the child.

To avoid conflicts at a later stage, the guidelines categorically state that once the child has been legally adopted by the infertile couple, the third-party donor and the surrogate mother must relinquish all parental rights connected with the child.

However, it is submitted that the law relating to surrogacy in India is in its prenatal stage, and unfortunately at the moment there is no legislation prescribing a code of practice governing the moral, ethical, and legal aspects of such surrogate arrangements. Hence, the guidelines currently have persuasive value only.

CONFLICT OF LAWS IN INTERCOUNTRY ADOPTIONS

During our time as counsel dealing with adoption applications at the British High Commission and other major embassies at New Delhi, we have quite frequently encountered a conflict-of-laws situation in which NRIs who have been residing abroad for several decades adopt children from within their own family. The preference for adoption by immediate blood relatives is a common South Asian phenomenon.

The unsuspecting adoptive parents duly comply with the requirements of HAMA 1956 for taking the child in adoption. The adoption deed is proudly presented to the immigration authorities; however, the American embassy and numerous European embassies at New Delhi refuse to accept the adoption deeds under the provisions of HAMA 1956 because of a conflict-of-law issue. Hence, only guardianship orders are acceptable. These can be obtained only by lodging guardianship petitions under the provisions of the Hindu Minority and Guardianship Act, 1956, in the court of the guardian judge in whose jurisdiction the minor child is residing. It is like a full-blown trial. It is very difficult to obtain guardianship orders. These petitions have to be supported by exhaustive documentation as to the background and standing of the proposed overseas adoptive parents. Sometimes, it can be a time-consuming exercise, and it is very difficult in such a situation for the foreign couple to spend long periods of time in India awaiting custody orders. With these custody orders, the adoption ultimately takes place in the foreign country of habitual residence of the adoptive parents. In India, we have no exclusive law of adoption for foreigners or NRIs.

Furthermore, adoptions within the family fold are not encouraged, while adoption applications by foreigners seeking to adopt children from orphanages and welfare homes are likely to receive positive treatment.

CONCLUSION

There has been a growing demand for a general law of adoption enabling any person, irrespective of his or her religion, race, or caste, to adopt a child. There is now a clear case for overhauling the existing adoption law in India.

As far as the mechanics of intercountry adoption are concerned, all the major embassies in India are

more than stringent in dealing with adoption applications. The refusal rates are very high. There is no room at all for compassion. The hurdles are almost insurmountable, causing lot of hardship to childless NRI couples.

The question that now remains to be answered is how successful the revised 2006 guidelines discussed in this article have been. Sadly, the answer can be found in a very recent Andhra Pradesh High Court judgment, *John Clements v. All Concerned.*[27] The court lamented:[28]

59. Para 2.14 of the guidelines envisages that no application by foreigner for taking a child in adoption should be entertained directly by any social child welfare agency in India working in the areas of inter-country adoption or by any institution or centre or Home to which children are committed by the Juvenile Court. The very next paragraph says "the original application along with original documents as prescribed by the Supreme Court of India would be forwarded by the foreign enlisted agency to a recognized placement agency in India".

60. Taking advantage of the inconsistency in the guidelines and ignoring the judgment of the Supreme Court the foreign enlisted agencies started directly approaching the placement agencies in India and are trying to take the Indian children in adoption with their connivance and active support of VCA and CARA officials, who are simply putting their seal of approval on these adoptions without bothering whether the procedure prescribed for intercountry adoption of a child is followed or not. With the result, trafficking in female children is going on unabated in violation of the guidelines given by the Supreme Court.

61. After the present scam came to light, the Government of Andhra Pradesh issued the Andhra Pradesh Orphanages and other Charitable Homes (Supervision and Control) Rules in GO Ms No 16, dated 18.04.2001. In para 11 (VII) of the said GO it is stated that "relinquishment" of child by "biological parents" on family grounds of poverty, number of children, unwanted girl child will not be permitted. Such children should not be admitted in Homes or "Orphanages" and,

[27] (2003) 2 Hindu Law Reporter 331 (AP).

[28] *Id.* at 331, ¶¶59–61.

it admitted, the license and recognition of Home or Orphanage shall be cancelled or withdrawn.'

Therefore, it can be concluded that, although there is no doubt that CARA is doing good work in its policing role, the negative media feedback has definitely not escaped judicial notice.

The finalization of the 2007 guidelines is eagerly awaited. Hopefully, the consolidated comprehensive guidelines will carve out clear-cut and precise uniformity in areas and legal issues addressed in this article and not provide piecemeal reforms and solutions.

While the government has been grappling on an ad-hoc basis with lacunas arising out of the guidelines, which have been revised from time to time, in the interim, new issues have cropped up. Firstly, there are legal issues connected with surrogacy. There is no legislation in India pertaining to surrogacy as yet. Secondly, no practical tangible useful benefits are forthcoming at all to prospective NRI adoptive parents and persons of foreign origin arising out of India's signing of the Hague Convention. Thirdly, the proposed revised guidelines of 2007 should also categorically attempt to provide a clear-cut direction in no uncertain terms to all major embassies, high commissions, and consulates in India that all adoptions under the provision of The JJ Act of 2006, by NRIs, persons of Indian origin, and foreigners should be duly acknowledged and their validity accepted, to facilitate movement of the adopted children in the country of the habitual residence of the adopting parents. This of course has to be hedged with safeguards and compliance with due process of law, both in India and abroad. But the core issue is the recognition of adoption orders handed down by the designated courts in India under the provisions of the amended provisions of the JJ Act of 2006. It is very important that these three new major issues also receive the due attention they warrant in the present day and age.

Lastly, the authors' experience reveals that guardian judges, especially in small towns and cities in India, who deal with such cases are not particularly conversant with the interpretation of the intercountry adoption guidelines discussed in this article. Therefore, in sum and substance it can be stated that a uniform but strict procedure must be evolved that can be easily followed and adhered to both in letter and spirit.

INTERCOUNTRY ADOPTIONS: PROCEDURES AND POTENTIAL ISSUES AFTER RATIFICATION OF THE HAGUE ADOPTION CONVENTION

*by Cynthia Hemphill, Karen Stoutamyer Law, and Carine Rosalia-Marion**

The United States' ratification of the Hague Convention on Protection of Children and Co-operation in Respect of Intercountry Adoption (Hague Convention)[1] on December 12, 2007, has changed the playing field for immigration attorneys assisting clients in obtaining immigration benefits following an intercountry adoption. The amendments to the regulations on intercountry adoptions,[2] which came into effect April 1, 2008, have introduced a new procedure that will apply to all adoptions by U.S. citizens of children habitually resident of a Convention country. Although the regulations governing Convention adoptions bear some resemblance to the regulations applicable to the adoption of an orphan, the determination of the eligibility of the child, the prohibition of any contact with the birth parents, and the role played by the U.S. Department of State (DOS) (designated Central Authority[3] for the United States) and the sending country's Central Authority make this new procedure substantially different from the immigration procedures already in place. It is also significant that prospective adoptive parents with nonimmigrant status or legal permanent resident status will not be able to petition for immigration benefits of a child adopted in a Convention case.[4]

Among the approximately 20,000 children adopted internationally in recent years,[5] almost half would have been affected by the new procedure introduced by the Hague Convention, and it is likely that this number will keep growing as other countries ratify the Hague Convention. Attorneys working on adoption cases will need to determine first whether the child sought to be adopted is a habitual resident of one of the numerous countries where the Hague Convention is already in force.[6] The list of countries party to the Convention is continuously updated by the Hague Conference on Private International Law and is reprinted by DOS.[7] It is recommended that attorneys regularly check the list to determine whether the sending country has ratified the Hague Convention. As for adoptions from countries that have not yet ratified the Hague Convention, such as main sending countries like Russia, South Korea, Ethiopia, or Kazakhstan, the family petition

---

* **Cynthia Hemphill** is a shareholder at Trow & Rahal, P.C. in Washington, D.C. She has practiced immigration and nationality law for over eight years, specializing in international business immigration. She also handles family-based immigration cases, including naturalization and international adoptions, and has represented professional sports figures, entertainers, and performing artists. Ms. Hemphill received her J.D. from Howard University School of Law. She is a member of AILA and the D.C. bar.

Karen Stoutamyer Law, of the Law Firm of Karen S. Law, PLC, practices law in Northern Virginia. Her practice is limited to adoption and immigration law, with a special emphasis on independent international adoptions. She graduated from the University of Pennsylvania School of Law in 1985. She is a member of AILA, the Virginia Women Attorneys Association, and the Loudoun Bar Association. Ms. Law frequently speaks on adoption and immigration at local and national conferences.

Carine Rosalia-Marion is an associate attorney with Steffas & Associates, P.C., in Georgia, where she practices immigration law, with a focus on intercountry adoptions. Ms. Rosalia-Marion recently presented the topic of adoption practices before a delegation of the French Central Authority, and her article on consular relations was recently published in the *Georgia Bar Journal*. She received her J.D. from Tulane University Law School, and also holds law degrees from France and England.

[1] The Hague Conference on Private International Law is a global intergovernmental organization working for the "progressive unification" of private international laws. The Hague Conference on Private International Law had generated 39 conventions as of November 2007. The only convention discussed in this article is Convention 33, Convention on Protection of Children and Co-operation in Respect of Intercountry Adoption, May 29, 1993, S. Treaty Doc. 105-51 (1998).

[2] 72 Fed. Reg. 56831 (Oct. 4, 2007).

[3] 8 CFR §204.301 (definition of Central Authority).

[4] *See* 8 CFR §204.307.

[5] Statistics of children adopted internationally are available at *http://travel.state.gov/family/adoption/stats/stats_451.html*.

These statistics show that 20,679 children were adopted in 2006; 22,728 in 2005; and 22,884 in 2004.

[6] *See* appx. A.

[7] The list of countries party to the Hague Convention is available at *http://travel.state.gov/family/adoption/convention/convention_4197.html*.

and orphan petition will remain available routes for the immigration of the child.

The following article presents the different routes that a U.S. petitioner may follow to adopt a child living outside of the United States (incoming cases), explaining the main requirements for the two procedures in place for adoptions that are not governed by the Hague Adoption Convention, and emphasizing the requirements and issues of adoptions governed by the Hague Adoption Convention. The article will then briefly discuss the steps involved in the adoption of a child habitually resident in the United States who emigrates to a foreign country (outgoing cases).[8]

NONCONVENTION INCOMING CASES

Prior to the ratification of the Hague Convention by the United States, intercountry adoptions occurred under the Immigration and Nationality Act (INA) by one of two procedures: either the "adopted child" provisions of INA §101(b)(1)(E), or the "orphan" provisions of INA §101(b)(1)(F). The requirements and procedures of these sections are distinct, but are often confused by practitioners. After April 1, 2008, procedures and rules contained in these sections will continue to apply to cases in which the child is not a habitual resident of a Convention country.

Petition for an Adopted Child

An "adopted child" under INA §101(b)(1)(E) is defined as one who is adopted before his or her 16th birthday, and who has been in the joint legal custody of, and has resided with, the qualifying adopting parents or parent for at least two years.[9] The provisions of INA §101(b)(1)(E) apply to children who have already been adopted, provided that the adoption was finalized prior to the child's 16th birthday.

When both the legal custody and residence requirements have been satisfied, the adoptive parent(s) can file an I-130 visa petition and supporting documentation with U.S. Citizenship and Immigration Services (USCIS). If the adoptive parent wishes to file for more than one child, a separate I-130 petition must be filed for the other child. If the child is physically present in the United States and otherwise eligible to adjust status,[10] then Forms I-485 and I-130 can be filed concurrently.

Although the two-year legal custody and two-year joint residency prerequisites may run concurrently, such is not a requirement of INA §101(b)(1)(E). The required custody and residency may take place before or after the adoption, as long as the two years for both have accrued before the filing of the I-130.[11] It is also important to note that the joint residency may be interrupted, provided that the aggregate period of time amounts to two years or more.[12]

Age Requirement

The adoption must have been finalized before the child turns 16 for the child to be eligible under INA §101(b)(1)(E). In other words, the adoption decree granted to the petitioners must predate the child's 16th birthday. It is important to note that, contrary to the provisions of INA §101(b)(1)(F), the cut-off age for the child relates to the time that the adoption must be finalized, and not the time that the petition must be filed with USCIS. There is no cut-off date to file a petition under INA §101(b)(1)(E).

INA §101(b)(1)(E) provides an exception when a child between the age of 16 and 18 is still eligible as the beneficiary of a petition for an adopted child and his or her natural sibling is adopted before the age of 16.[13] Traditionally, an adoption of an older sibling takes place concurrently with, or after, the adoption of the younger sibling.[14] However, in a recent deci-

---

[8] Please note that this article was written prior to the end of the second comment period for the DHS interim rule published at 72 Fed. Reg. 56832, which addresses the procedures for the implementation of the Hague Convention. This interim rule was implemented on April 1, 2008. However, additional comments on the interim rule were accepted through May 27, 2008. 73 Fed. Reg. 15635. Accordingly, the final rule may contain provisions that vary from those discussed in this article.

[9] INA §101(b)(1)(E)(i); *See* D. Marcus & I. Steffas, with contributions from B. Campbell, "International Adoption—A Basic Guide to the Three Visa Categories," *Immigration & Nationality Law Handbook* 364 (AILA 2006–07 Ed.); K. Sullivan, "Intercountry Adoption: A Step-by-Step Guide for the Practitioner," 95-9 *Immigration Briefings* (Sept. 1995).

[10] *See* eligibility requirements under INA §245.

[11] 9 *Foreign Affairs Manual* (FAM) 42.21 N12.5.

[12] *Id.*

[13] Such an exception is also provided under INA §101(b)(1)(F).

[14] *See* INS Memorandum, M. Cronin, "Adopted Alien Children Less Than 18 Years of Age Considered a 'Child' Under the Immigration and Nationality Act per Legislative Action" (Dec. 28, 1999), *published on* AILA InfoNet at Doc. No. 00032804 (*posted* Mar. 28, 2000).

sion, the Board of Immigration Appeals (BIA) held that the adoption of the older sibling may precede that of the younger sibling.[15]

If the adoption is not finalized before the child's 16th birthday, the court may, under limited circumstances, amend the adoption decree to reflect that the adoption should have been finalized prior to the child's 16th birthday. This procedure is referred to as *nunc pro tunc* adoption. In *Messina v. USCIS*, the district court held that USCIS must recognize an adoption *nunc pro tunc* to a date prior to child's 16th birthday.[16]

Documenting the Two-Year Joint Residency and Legal Custody Requirements

"Legal custody" refers to the "assumption of responsibility for a minor by an adult under the laws of the state and under the approval of a court of law or other appropriate government entity."[17] The two-year legal custody requirement can accrue before the adoption if a court granted legal custody of the child to the petitioner.[18] If the petitioner did not obtain legal custody before the adoption, then the date of the adoption decree is considered to be the commencement of the two-year legal custody period.[19] As emphasized in the regulations and the *Foreign Affairs Manual*, legal custody must be granted by a court or an official body; a sworn affidavit is insufficient to document legal custody.[20] The BIA has recognized completion of the required two years' legal custody based on customary adoption—where the petitioner established that the child was considered adopted under the laws and customs of the country of the child.[21]

Petitioners also must prove that they have resided with the child in a parent/child ("familial") relationship for at least two years. Evidentiary support for joint residency is often at issue in petitions for adopted children. The regulations provide some guidance on admissible evidence, indicating that school records, medical records and religious documents, as well as affidavits, can be accepted to support the claim that the petitioner has lived with the child.[22] U.S. tax returns showing the child as a dependent[23] and proof of insurance also may be provided as evidence. The evidence should provide information relating to the physical living arrangements of the child, where the petitioners resided, and where the birth parents resided for the two-year period.[24] If the child resided with the birth parents during the two-year period, the burden of proof falls on the petitioner to show that the petitioner, and not the birth parents, exercised primary parental control.[25]

When both the legal custody and joint residency requirements have been met, the adoptive parent can file an I-130 petition for an immediate relative and supporting documentation with USCIS. Note that the regulations do not require that the petition for an adopted child immediately follow completion of the two-year joint residency and legal custody requirements. However, if the I-130 petition is filed after the child's 21st birthday, the child will not be considered an immediate relative and will be subject to the first, second, or third family-preference classifi-

---

[15] *Matter of Anifowoshe*, 24 I&N Dec. 442 (BIA 2008).

[16] *Messina v. USCIS*, 2006 WL 374564 (E.D. Mich. Feb. 16, 2006), which rejected *Matter of Cariaga*, 15 I&N Dec. 716 (BIA 1976), and stated that USCIS must recognize a *nunc pro tunc* adoption.

[17] 8 CFR §204.2(d)(2)(vii)(A); 9 FAM 42.21 N12.3.

[18] 8 CFR §204.2(d)(2)(vii)(A); 9 FAM 42.21 N12.3.

[19] 8 CFR §204.2(d)(2)(vii)(A); 9 FAM 42.21 N12.3.

[20] 8 CFR §204.2(d)(2)(vii)(A); 9 FAM 42.21 N12.3.

[21] *Matter of Fakalata*, 18 I&N Dec. 213 (BIA 1982); *Matter of Mendoza*, 18 I&N Dec. 66 (BIA 1981); *Matter of Lee*, 16 I&N Dec. 511 (BIA 1978); *Matter of Yue*, 12 I&N Dec. 747 (BIA 1968). The burden of proof falls on the petitioner to show that the adoption was conformed to the laws of the country where the child was adopted. The petitioner must prove that the adoption created a legal status or relationship that is recognized by the government of the place where it occurred as carrying with it substantial legal rights and obligations. The BIA has recognized customary adoption under
continued

Chinese law (*e.g.*, *Matter of Rodriguez*, 14 I&N Dec. 335 (BIA 1973); *Matter of Poon*, 14 I&N Dec. 155 (BIA 1972); *Matter of Ng*, 14 I&N Dec. 135 (BIA 1972); *Matter of Yue*, 12 I&N Dec. 747 (BIA, 1968)). However, the BIA has refused to recognize customary adoption under the laws of Tonga (*e.g.*, *Fakalata, supra; Matter of Palelei*, 16 I&N Dec. 716 (BIA 1979)).

[22] 8 CFR §204.2(d)(2)(vii).

[23] The child will need a taxpayer identification or Social Security number.

[24] 8 CFR §204.2(d)(2)(vii)(B); 9 FAM 42.21 N12.4. Note that providing sufficient evidence to prove the custody and residency requirements at the filing of the I-130 *may* lead to a waiver of the interview requirement for younger children.

[25] "Evidence of parental control may include, but is not limited to, evidence that the adoptive parent provided financial support and day-to-day supervision of the child, and owned or maintained the property where the child resided." 9 FAM 42.21 N12.4.

cations, depending on whether the petitioner is a U.S. citizen and whether the child is married.[26]

No Effect of Unlawful Presence for a Child Adopted Pursuant to INA §101(b)(1)(E)

A child adopted under INA §101(b)(1)(E), who was legally admitted into the United States in nonimmigrant visa status but overstayed, or who entered without inspection, nevertheless may be eligible to obtain permanent resident status through the adoptive parent, unlike a child adopted under INA §§101(b)(1)(F) or (G). Indeed, a child under 18 does not accrue unlawful presence (ULP),[27] so it is possible for the child present in the United States to adjust status without the imposition of any three– or ten-year bar.

For example, a petitioner can file an I-130 petition for a child who has entered the United States without inspection. Although ULP will not accumulate, in the absence of proof of inspection, the petitioner must resort to consular processing, and the beneficiary child must return to the sending country before he or she can obtain legal permanent residency in the United States.

When a child was admitted into the United States on a B-2 visa and subsequently stayed in the United States beyond the period of authorized stay indicated on the I-94 card, the child is considered to be out of status. Since ULP will not accrue, on satisfying the requirements of INA §101(b)(1)(E), the petitioner can concurrently file an I-130 petition and I-485 application to obtain lawful permanent resident (LPR) status for the child.

Priority Date Not Yet Current

INA §101(b)(1)(E) allows an LPR to petition for an adopted child, unlike INA §§101(b)(1)(F) and (G), which require the petitioner to be a U.S. citizen. If the petitioner is an LPR and not a U.S. citizen, the child will be classified as family-sponsored second preference, and an immigrant visa number may not be immediately available. Attorneys should refer to the DOS *Visa Bulletin*[28] to verify when the priority date will become current and when the petitioner can

file Form I-485. Special care must be given to this issue, as the child can turn 18 before a visa becomes available, and thereafter can start accruing ULP.

A child is eligible to follow-to-join the principal noncitizen adoptive parent if the child is (1) adopted and (2) part of the principal's household before entry into the United States.[29]

Petition for an Orphan Child

A U.S. citizen can petition for an orphan to classify the child as an immediate relative, provided that the petition is filed prior to the child's 16th birthday and the child meets the strict definition of orphan under INA §101(b)(1)(F).[30] The process can involve two or three steps: (1) the petitioners may establish their suitability and ability to provide proper care to the child using Form I-600A, Application for Advance Processing of Orphan Petition;[31] (2) once the adoption decree is issued by the court, the petitioners must file Form I-600, Petition to Classify Orphan as an Immediate Relative, and provide supporting evidence that the child is an "orphan";[32] and (3) the petitioners must obtain an immigrant visa from the U.S. consulate for the child to enter the United States and acquire U.S. citizenship. Form I-600 cannot be filed if the child is physically present in the United States unless the child was paroled into the United States.[33]

Advance Processing

The filing of Form I-600A will generally expedite the part of the processing relating to the qualifications of the prospective adoptive parent petitioner(s). Filing Form I-600A is not a prerequisite to the filing of the I-600 petition. Form I-600A may be filed before identifying a specific child. This form is valid for 18 months, and if the orphan petition is not filed within this period, Form I-600A will be deemed abandoned and a new form must be filed.[34]

---

[26] INA §201(b)(2)(A)(i). Priority dates for the family-based preference categories can be found in DOS's *Visa Bulletin*. See *http://travel.state.gov/visa/frvi/bulletin/bulletin_1360.html*.

[27] INA §212(a)(9)(B)(iii)(I).

[28] The *Visa Bulletin* is regularly updated and is available at *http://travel.state.gov/visa/frvi/bulletin/bulletin_1360.html* and *www.aila.org/content/default.aspx?docid=8431*.

---

[29] 9 FAM 40.1 N7.2-4; Letter from H. Edward Odom, Chief, Advisory Opinions for Visa Services, to Rebecca P. Burdette (May 19, 1993), *reprinted in* 70 *Interpreter Releases* 1014, 1022–23 (Aug. 2, 1993).

[30] *See* authors cited *supra*, note 9.

[31] *See* 8 CFR §204.3(c). Filing of Form I-600A is optional.

[32] *See* 8 CFR §204.3(d). Petitioners must file one Form I-600 per child.

[33] If the child is in the United States on a nonimmigrant visa or without inspection, then filing an I-130 under INA §101(b)(1)(E) should be pursued unless the Hague Convention provisions are applicable.

[34] 9 FAM 42.21.

Form I-600 may be filed either concurrently with the I-600A, while the I-600A is pending, or after the I-600A has been approved.[35]

Age Requirement

Form I-600 must be filed before the child turns 16.[36] Filing Form I-600A before age 16, however, is insufficient alone to retain the age at the I-600 file date. The cut-off date to file the I-600 orphan petition should be distinguished from the cut-off date of INA §101(b)(1)(E), which in nonorphan cases requires the adoption to take place before the child turns 16. The provisions of INA §101(b)(1)(F) regarding adoption of orphans do not address the time that the adoption decree must be issued and relate strictly to the time that the I-600 petition must be filed.[37] There is also an exception in the provisions of INA §101(b)(1)(F) allowing the filing of the petition until the orphan turns 18 if the petitioners have adopted a sibling.[38]

Strict Interpretation of "Orphan"

Under INA §101(b)(1)(F), a child is determined to be an "orphan" due to (1) the death or disappearance of, abandonment or desertion of, or separation or loss from both parents, or (2) the fact that the sole or surviving parent is incapable of providing proper care for the child and has irrevocably released parental rights to the child in writing for emigration and adoption.[39] The regulations provide specific definitions for the terms "abandonment," "desertion," "separation from both parents," "sole parent," and "surviving parent" to determine whether the child should be considered an orphan.[40]

When both biological parents are alive, the child may be considered to be an orphan if both biological parents abandoned the child to a child-placement entity, such as an orphanage recognized by the home country and authorized to place the child for adoption.[41] The child will not qualify as an orphan if the biological parents have directed the placement by specifying who will adopt the child, as this action

does not constitute abandonment.[42] "Separation from both parents" is defined as the involuntary severance of a child from the birth parents by action of a competent authority for good cause and in accordance with the laws of the local country.[43] The termination of all parental rights and obligations must be permanent and unconditional. The term "loss from both parents," on the other hand, means the involuntary severance or detachment of the child from the parents in a permanent manner, such as that caused by a natural disaster, civil unrest, or other event beyond the control of the parents.[44]

For a sole or surviving parent, the petitioner must prove that the biological parent is "incapable of providing proper care" to the child."[45] The fact that the parent is impoverished and unemployed is insufficient to show that the biological parent is incapable of providing care unless a showing can be made that the poverty level in the sending country falls below the national average.[46] Examples of inability to support a child include a parent with a terminal illness, who is incarcerated, or experiencing an overwhelming financial burden.

Adoptive Parent Requirements

In addition to proving that the child satisfies the definition of an orphan, the child must be adopted jointly by a U.S. citizen and spouse in lawful immigrant status,[47] or a single U.S. citizen 25 years or older.[48] The adoption may take place abroad or in the United States. If adopting abroad, the parent(s) must have personally seen and observed the child

---

[35] 8 CFR §§204.3(d)(2), (3).

[36] *See* INA §101(b)(1)(F)(i).

[37] Appendix B highlights the distinction between the cut-off date of INA §§101(b)(1)(E) and (F).

[38] INA §101(b)(1)(F)(ii).

[39] INA §101(b)(1)(F)(i).

[40] 8 CFR §204.3(b).

[41] *See* 8 CFR §204.3(b) (definition of abandonment by both parents); 9 FAM 42.21 N13.2-5(3)(b).

[42] 8 CFR §204.3(b) (definition of abandonment by both parents). *See* N. Elkind, "Immigration of Orphans to the United States," 2 *Immigration & Nationality Law Handbook* 150, 153 (AILA 1995–96 Ed).

[43] 8 CFR §204.3(b) (definition of separation from both parents).

[44] *Id.* (definition of loss from both parents).

[45] "Incapable of providing proper care" is defined at 8 CFR §204.3(b). *See Rogan v. Reno*, 75 F. Supp. 2d 63 (E.D.N.Y. 1999).

[46] *Id. See also* D. Seligman, "Problematic Issues in Obtaining Immigration Benefits for the Orphan Adopted Child," 2 *Immigration & Nationality Law Handbook* 418, 423–25 (AILA 1994–95 Ed.).

[47] The spouse need not be a U.S. citizen. It is only required that the spouse be in "lawful permanent status."

[48] The unmarried adoptive parent must be at least 24 at the time of filing Form I-600A and at least 25 when Form I-600 is filed. 8 CFR §204.3(b) (definition of petitioner).

before or during the adoption proceedings. The U.S. consulate will issue an immediate relative third-preference (IR-3) visa to a child who has received a final decree of adoption from the sending country.[49] A child who is properly admitted into the United States with an IR-3 while under the age 18 will automatically acquire U.S. citizenship.[50] On the other hand, a child who is to be adopted on entering the United States, or whose foreign adoption is not valid for U.S. immigration purposes, will be considered an immediate relative fourth preference (IR-4), and U.S. citizenship will only be conferred when a U.S. state court has issued a final decree of adoption.[51] A legal foreign adoption that would not be considered a valid adoption for U.S. immigration purposes would occur if neither parent, or only one of two parents, actually saw the child before or during the foreign adoption process. A child will also be classified as an IR-4 when the sending country does not routinely grant final adoption decrees and the child is placed with the adoptive parents under a guardianship or legal custody decree.

Where to File the I-600A and I-600

The I-600A is filed with the USCIS district office having jurisdiction over the residence of the prospective adoptive parents.[52] If the I-600A has already been approved, prospective adoptive parents who are not traveling abroad to locate and adopt the child should file the I-600 with that USCIS district office having jurisdiction over the place of residence of the prospective adoptive parents.[53] When the prospective adoptive parents are traveling to the foreign country to locate and/or adopt the child, the adoptive parents may choose to file the I-600 with the USCIS district office having jurisdiction over their residence or with the U.S. consulate overseas.[54] It is recommended whenever possible that the I-600 be filed directly with the U.S. consulate, which will be able to perform investigations in that country and adjudicate the petition.[55] However, the petitioner can only file the I-600 with the U.S. consulate while physically present in the foreign country and, in the case of a married couple where one member of the

couple is an alien, the petitioner traveling abroad must be the U.S. citizen.[56] If the I-600A is still pending, the I-600 must be filed at the USCIS office where the I-600A is pending.[57]

Domestication of the Adoption

Domestication refers to a process by which a U.S. state court in the state of the adoptive parents' (or sole adoptive parent's) residence reviews the details of the adoption abroad and issues a new adoption decree, independent from the foreign decree, stating that the child has been adopted in conformity with the adoption law of the applicable state. This process is not a mandatory step when the child traveled on an IR-3, and the procedures and benefits of the domestication process vary from state to state. However, it is important to advise the adoptive parents of the possibility to domesticate the adoption decree, because the domestication will allow the child to obtain a U.S. birth certificate and may render further administrative steps such a obtaining a passport or a driver's license easier. It may also be reassuring for the adoptive parents to allow a U.S. court to have records of the adoption should a situation arise in which the child would need another certified copy of the decree.

A different procedure applies when the child is coming to the United States for purposes of adoption and there have been no adoption proceedings abroad, the adoption was not completed abroad, or the adoption is not considered final by the foreign country. Such may be the case with children from Korea or India when only a guardianship or custodial relationship between the child and the agency, or the child and the parents, is established. In this situation, the child travels on an IR-4 visa as opposed to an IR-3 visa, and the adoption is finalized in the United States according to the law of the state of the parents' residence. When the child traveled on an IR-4 visa, attorneys should advise the adoptive parents to finalize the adoption in the state of residence of the adoptive parents and obtain a certificate of adoption in that state so that the child may apply for a certificate of citizenship and a U.S. passport.

Convention Incoming Cases

The first consideration in a Convention case is whether the Convention actually applies to the case. The attorney must discern whether the Convention is

---

[49] 9 FAM 42.21 N13.2-9.

[50] Id.

[51] Id.

[52] 8 CFR §204.3(g)(1)(i).

[53] 8 CFR §204.3(g)(2)(i).

[54] 8 CFR §204.3(g)(2)(ii).

[55] Id.

---

[56] Id.

[57] 8 CFR §204.3(g)(3).

in force between the two countries. As previously discussed, a helpful starting point is the DOS Hague Convention partner countries webpage.[58] However, attorneys should verify that the foreign country has completed all the necessary steps to bring the Convention into force between the United States and that country to ensure that the sending country is not merely a signatory member. As more countries become fully compliant, it is paramount that attorneys regularly check the status table of the Hague Conference on Private International Law.

Second, the attorney must inquire as to whether the prospective adoptive parents are "habitually resident" in the United States or another Convention country, and whether the child is "habitually resident" in a different Convention country. For the prospective adoptive parents, the regulations define "habitually resident" in terms broader than domiciled; those habitually resident include citizens living abroad temporarily or living abroad but intending to establish a domicile in the United States on or before the date of the child's admission to the United States for permanent residence as a Convention adoptee.[59] The child generally is "habitually resident" in his or country of citizenship."[60] However, if a child is living in another country and the Central Authority[61] determines that the child's status in that country is sufficiently stable for it to exercise jurisdiction, the child may be considered "habitually resident" in that country.[62] The regulations caution against children being sent to another country as a prelude to adoption,[63] perhaps to avoid complying with Convention requirements.

If the case is in fact a Convention case, the family is not permitted to choose between the orphan petition process under INA §101(b)(1)(F) and Convention provisions of INA §101(b)(1)(G). The adoption *must* be done in compliance with the Convention.[64] Families that filed the I-600A or I-600 before the date on which the Convention entered into force in the United

States (April 1, 2008) are grandfathered in as "orphan" cases.[65] Also, as discussed below, a habitually resident U.S. family that meets the requirements for §101(b)(1)(E) adoption may not file a Form I-130, Petition for an Immediate Relative, if the adoption was not finalized prior to the Hague Adoption Convention effective date of April 1, 2008, if the child's last habitual residence before entry to the United States was a Convention country.[66]

The procedure in a Convention adoption tracks the orphan petition process, with some very important differences. The case will proceed in a step-by-step manner, and if a step is done out of sequence, the child may not obtain a visa. Some of the major differences are discussed below.

Use of Different Forms

Instead of the I-600A, the family files the I-800A, Application for Determination of Suitability to Adopt a Child from a Convention Country. No longer may the initial form, establishing the eligibility and suitability of the prospective adoptive parents, be filed at the same time as the form that establishes the child's eligibility to be adopted. In addition, a home study must be filed with the I-800A; it cannot be submitted later.[67] Further, the home study must have been conducted by an approved or accredited home study preparer,[68] which means that the agency has been authorized under 22 CFR §96 to conduct home studies for Convention adoption cases and is licensed in the state of the prospective adoptive parents.[69] The form that establishes that the child is eligible to be adopted is the I-800, Petition to Classify Convention Adoptee as an Immediate Relative. The filing fees for the I-800A and I-800 parallel the fees for the I-600A and I-600.[70] The I-800A is valid for 15 months from the date of the first member of the household's fingerprint expiration, instead of 18 months, as in orphan cases.[71] This is intended to alleviate the confusion in orphan cases, in which the fingerprints expire after 15 months, but the I-600A is valid for 18 months. Fi-

[58] http://travel.state.gov/family/adoption/convention/convention_4197.html.

[59] 8 CFR §204.303(a). *See* appx. A.

[60] 8 CFR §204.303(b). *See* appx. A.

[61] *See* 8 CFR §204.301 (defining Central Authority; it is the entity designated as such by a Convention country to discharge the duties imposed on it by the Convention).

[62] *Id.*

[63] *Id.*

[64] 8 CFR §§204.3(a)(2), 204.300(b).

[65] *See* 8 CFR §204.3(a)(2).

[66] 8 CFR §§204.2(d)(2)(vii)(D), (F).

[67] 8 CFR §204.310(a)(3)(viii).

[68] 8 CFR §204.311(b).

[69] 8 CFR §204.302(a); *see* 8 CFR §204.301 (definition of home study preparer).

[70] 8 CFR §103.7(b)(1).

[71] 8 CFR §204.312(e)(1).

nally, the I-800A has several supplements. Supplement 3, which is used for an extension of the I-800A approval if the applicant has not yet filed an I-800, may prove particularly useful in today's climate of longer time frames between the family's approval and the filing of the I-800. The first time the family files for an extension, the filing fee is waived, as long as it filed on or before the dated that the original I-800A approval expires.[72]

Role of the Central Authority in the Foreign Country

In orphan cases, power over the case in the foreign country is often not centralized. Rather, the foreign court decree of adoption or guardianship for purposes of adoption, along with the child's birth certificate and passport, are the primary documentation that the adoption has been completed in compliance with the laws of that country. In a Convention case, it is impossible for the case to proceed without the Central Authority's involvement. In the typical case, after the Central Authority receives the I-800A approval, home study, and other supporting evidence, it refers the child to the family.[73] This function can be performed by a designee of the Central Authority, i.e., a licensed agency in that country.[74] The Central Authority must prepare a medical and social report for the child who is referred, and make certain required findings for the submission of the I-800:[75]

(1) the child is eligible to be adopted

(2) it is in the child's best interest to be adopted internationally

(3) all consents have been given freely and in writing, after counseling, including the consent of the child, if required.

(4) no payment or inducement of any kinds has been given to obtain the consents

Later in the process, the consular officer notifies the Central Authority of "Article Five Determination," and the Central Authority then authorizes the family to obtain the guardianship or adoption decree.

Due to this high level of involvement by the Central Authority, it will be essential for the prospective adoptive parents, their adoption agencies, and legal counsel to work well with the Central Authority of the foreign country. Past experience demonstrates that when adoption is centralized in a country, the number of intercountry adoptions from that country often decreases. It remains to be seen whether this intricate, centralized process will decrease the number of intercountry adoptions from Convention countries.

Changes in the Order of the Case

It is common in orphan cases for clients to walk into an attorney's office *after* obtaining an adoption decree in a foreign country and request assistance with the orphan visa. In a Convention case, the I-800 must be provisionally approved *before* the adoption or guardianship decree is obtained or the I-800 will be denied.[76] If the family has obtained the decree too early, the regulations allow for the court decree to be voided or vacated, and the family may begin the process over.[77] Obviously, this is expensive and causes delay, so care should be taken to avoid this situation if at all possible.

USCIS has prepared a helpful flowchart of the process.[78] In summary, the prospective adoptive family first obtains a home study from an authorized home study provider, and then files the I-800A. After the I-800A is approved, the approval notice, home study, and other supporting documentation is forwarded to the Central Authority. The Central Authority, or its designee, then refers an eligible child to the family, providing a report on the medical and social background of the child and making certain required findings. If the family accepts the referral, they then file the I-800 with supporting evidence either in the United States with the USCIS office that has jurisdiction over their residence, or abroad at the USCIS office or consulate in the child's country of habitual residence.[79] The I-800 is then provisionally approved

---

[72] 8 CFR §204.312(e)(3)(i).

[73] 8 CFR §204.313(a).

[74] The definition of Central Authority includes an individual or entity that has been authorized to perform services by the Convention and the laws of that country. 8 CFR §204.301. Thus, it is envisioned that authorized adoption agencies within a country may refer children for placement if the country permits this.

[75] 8 CFR §204.313(d)(3).

---

[76] 8 CFR §204.309(b)(1).

[77] 8 CFR §204.309(b)(2)(ii).

[78] *See* appx. B.

[79] 8 CFR §204.308(b). As in orphan cases, the I-800 may be filed directly with the visa-issuing post that would have jurisdiction to adjudicate a visa application filed by the Convention adoptee or at a CIS office abroad with jurisdiction over the child. Alternatively, the form I-800 may be filed with the appropriate U.S. CIS office. The decision of where to file is a strategy decision based on processing times, travel conditions, and the necessity of the petitioners traveling to the foreign country for purposes of the foreign adoption.

and forwarded to the DOS officer at the visa issuing post. The family then files a visa application for the child with that post and the consular officer adjudicates the application. If the consular officer finds that "the child would not be ineligible to receive an immigrant visa," the visa application is annotated with this conclusion. The consular officer also must take note that there are no grounds of inadmissibility that would preclude the child's admission to the United States following the adoption or grant of custody. The consular officer then notifies the Central Authority with an "Article Five letter" that the prospective adoptive parents may proceed with the adoption or custody decree. At this point, the family obtains the adoption or custody decree. They then take the adoption decree or custody decree back to the consular officer, who takes a final look at the case and certifies it as Convention compliant.

Under the Child Citizenship Act of 2000,[80] if the family has obtained a final order of adoption, the child will become a U.S. citizen on admission to the United States as an LPR.[81] If the family has obtained a guardianship decree, the child will become a U.S. citizen once the adoption is finalized in their home state as long as the child is under the age of 18.[82]

Definition of adoptable child is broader than "orphan" definition

The definition of an eligible child in a Convention adoption can be found in INA §101(b)(1)(G):

A child, under the age of sixteen at the time a petition is filed on the child's behalf to accord a classification as an immediate relative under Section 201(b), who has been adopted in a foreign state that is a party to the Convention on Protection of Children and Co-operation in Respect of Intercountry Adoption done at The Hague on May 29, 1993, or who is emigrating from such a foreign state to be adopted in the United States, by a United States citizen and spouse jointly, or by an unmarried United State citizen at least 25 years of age—

(i) if—

(I) the Attorney General is satisfied that proper care will be furnished the child if admitted to the United States;

(II) the child's natural parents (or parent in the case of a child who has one sole or surviving parent because of the death or disappearance of, abandonment or desertion by, the other parent), or other persons or institutions that retain legal custody of the child, have freely given their written irrevocable consent to the termination of their legal relationship with the child, and to the child's emigration and adoption;

(III) In the case of a child having two living natural parents, the natural parents are incapable of providing proper care for the child;

(IV) The Attorney General is satisfied that the purpose of the adoption is to form a bona fide parent-child relationship, and the parent-child relationship of the child and the natural parents has been terminated (and in carrying out both obligations under this sub clause the Attorney General may consider whether there is a petition pending to confer immigration status on one or both of such natural parents); and

(V) In the case of a child who has not been adopted—

(aa) the competent authority of the foreign state has approved the child's emigration to the United States for the purpose of adoption by the prospective adoptive parents or parent; and

(bb) the prospective adoptive parent or parents has or have complied with any pre-adoption requirements of the child's proposed residence; and

(ii) Except that no natural parent or prior adoptive parent of any such child shall thereafter, by virtue of such parentage, be accorded any right, privilege or status under this act.

There are three key differences between an "orphan" and the "adoptable child" in a Convention case. First, unlike in orphan cases, it is possible for two birth parents to release a child for adoption as long as they are incapable of providing proper care according to the standards of the country. Currently, it is impossible to obtain an orphan visa in many non-Convention cases because the child has two living birth parents. Hence, the Convention provides an important broadening of the category of children who can be placed for international adoption. Moreover, under orphan cases, only an unmarried birth mother may be considered a "sole parent" with the ability to release her child for adoption and emigration. Thus, if an unmarried birth father wishes to

---

[80] Pub. L. No. 106-395, 114 Stat. 1631.

[81] INA §320.

[82] Id.

release the child for adoption and emigration when the birth mother has abandoned the child, that child will not qualify for an orphan visa. In Convention adoptions, the sole parent may be *either* a mother or father. A child will be eligible for adoption as the child of a sole parent if the child has only one legal parent, based on the competent authority's determination that the other legal parent has either abandoned or deserted the child, or has disappeared from the child's life.

In one regard, the regulations covering Convention cases narrow the category of children eligible to emigrate to the United States. In orphan and (non-Convention) adopted child cases, a child must be adopted under the age of 16 to qualify. However, as discussed above, the 1999 amendment to the INA expanded the definition of orphan and adopted child to include the natural sibling of a previously adopted child, when the sibling has been adopted abroad or is coming to the United State for adoption by the same U.S. citizen parent(s) or prospective parents(s) if the child is under the age of 18 when the petition to accord a classification as an immediate relative is filed on his or her behalf.[83]

However, there is no provision in Convention cases for older siblings to obtain visas. Hopefully, Congress will address this situation in the near future to allow older siblings to obtain visas from Convention countries, as well as from non-Convention countries.

Prohibited contact between birth parents, orphanage, or legal custodian and adopted parents

The Convention maintains the prohibitions against illegal payments to obtain an adoptive placement found in the laws applicable to non-Convention adoptions.[84] However, the regulations impose additional restrictions in terms of contact between the adoptive family and birth parents, orphanage directors, or legal custodians early in the adoption process. An I-800 must be denied if "the petitioner, or any additional adult member of the household had met with, or had any other form of contact with, the child's parents, legal custodian, or other individual or entity who was responsible for the child's care when the contact occurred."[85] Adop-

tion agencies are permitted to provide general information about a possible child under this rule. Contact can begin after the I-800-A has been approved, the child is deemed eligible for intercountry adoption, and the consents have been given.[86]

The prohibition on contact is problematic for many clients, such as the family that establishes a relationship with a destitute child while traveling abroad or the family that wishes to adopt the child of a close family friend. An exception may arise in such a situation if the Central Authority finds that the contact was not prohibited.[87] However, this will be a case-specific determination. Another exception is provided in the case of relative adoptions,[88] in which the prospective adoptive parents would usually have had prior contact with the child. The qualifying relative relationships are detailed in the regulations.[89]

No Requirement for Both Parents to Travel

In orphan cases, if both parents do not personally see and observe the child prior to or during the adoption, the family is required to readopt the child when returning to the United States for the child to qualify for U.S. citizenship under INA §320. They must also comply with state preadoption requirements and demonstrate that readoption is possible in their home state.[90] In Convention adoptions, there is no requirement that both parents personally see or observe the child prior to or during the adoption. However, it is still necessary for both parents to be listed on the adoption decree. Hopefully, the Convention law will increase adoptions by families who find it difficult for both parents to travel abroad due to work concerns or the need to care for other children. Of course, the particular country may still require both parents to travel in order to obtain the adoption or guardianship decree.

Prohibited Attorney Activities in Convention Cases

Attorneys must be careful not to provide clients "adoption services" that would require them to be approved as an adoption service provider, unless they have in fact been approved.[91] Sections

---

[83] *See* INA §§101(b)(1)(E), (F).

[84] Compare the description of prohibited payments contained in orphan cases, 8 CFR §204.3(i), and the more specific list in Convention cases, 8 CFR §204.304.

[85] 8 CFR §204.309(b)(2).

---

[86] 8 CFR §204.309(b)(2)(i).

[87] 8 CFR §204.309(b)(2)(ii).

[88] 8 CFR §204.309(b)(2)(iii).

[89] *Id.*

[90] *See* 8 CFR §§204.3(c)(1)(iv), (d)(1)(iv)(B)(3), (B)(4).

[91] A list of accredited agencies and approved providers was released on February 29, 2008, and is available at

continued

404(a)(1) and (c) of the Intercountry Adoption Act of 2000[92] provide *civil and criminal* penalties for anyone who provides, or facilitates the provision of, adoption services without authorization. Hence, attorneys may not engage in any of the following without first having been approved by the Council on Accreditation:[93]

(1) Identifying a child for adoption and arranging an adoption

(2) Securing necessary consent to termination of parental rights and to adoption

(3) Performing a background study on a child or a home study on a prospective adoptive parent and reporting on such a study;

(4) Making determinations of the best interests of a child and the appropriateness of adoptive placement for the child;

(5) Post-placement monitoring of a case until final adoption;

(6) Where made necessary by disruption before final adoption, assuming custody and providing child care or any other social service pending an alternative placement.

The approval and accreditation process are beyond the scope of this article.[94] The regulations do not prohibit attorneys from assisting clients in the preparation of immigration forms to be filed with USCIS, providing legal advice, and representing adoptive parents before USCIS. But if a lawyer is providing (or facilitating) any of the above six adoption services, the lawyer must obtain approval.[95]

It should be a small consolation that social workers, who routinely assist clients in completing I-600A and I-600 forms in orphan cases, even though they are not licensed attorneys, are prohibited in Convention adoptions from providing these and other legal services.[96]

Non-Convention filing procedures when the child was last habitually resident in a Convention country

As discussed above, U.S. families sometimes adopt children who enter the United States as non-immigrants or without inspection. Then, after meeting the requirements of INA §101(b)(1)(E) for an adopted child, the family files the I-130 to seek approval for the child as an immediate relative. In some instances, the child will be eligible for adjustment of status, and in others, the child will have to depart in order to consular process. This procedure allows the child who is already present in the United States to obtain LPR status without leaving the United States in most cases.

Under the Convention, the regulations state that this route cannot be used for children who were last "habitually resident" in a Convention country if the adoption is "completed" on or after the Convention effective date:[97]

On or after the Convention effective date, as defined in 8 CFR §204.301, a United States citizen who is habitually resident in the United States, as determined under 8 CFR §204.303, may not file a Form I-130 under this section on behalf of a child who was habitually resident in a Convention country, as determined under 8 CFR §204.303, unless the adoption was completed before the Convention effective date.

Instead, the family must complete the process as a Convention adoption. This may involve vacating a state adoption decree if it has already been obtained and seeking the permission of the foreign Convention administrator to process the case while the child remains in the United States. In some instances, the child will have to return to his or her country of origin. The underlying intent of the regulations is to preclude families from circumventing the Convention procedures when the child is already present in the United States.

OUTGOING CASES

In addition to being a large receiving country, the United States also acts as a sending country. The few adopted children who emigrate from the United

---

http://travel.state.gov/family/adoption/convention/convention_4169.html.

[92] Pub. L. No. 106-279, 114 Stat. 825.

[93] 22 CFR §96.2 (definition of adoption service). The Council on Accreditation has been designated an accrediting entity. 71 Fed. Reg. 40771 (July 18, 2006). It performs the tasks of accrediting agencies and approving persons, monitoring compliance of such agencies and persons with applicable requirements, and other related duties set forth in section 202(b) of the Intercountry Adoption Act.

[94] *See generally* 22 CFR Part 96.

[95] *See* 8 CFR §204.302(a).

[96] 8 CFR §204.302(b); *see* 8 CFR §292.1 (authorized representatives).

[97] 8 CFR §204.2(d)(2)(vii)(D).

States are primarily going to families in Canada, and to some Europeans countries such as France or Germany, but few statistics were available on outgoing cases before ratification of the Convention. New requirements introduced in 22 CFR Part 99 will lead to better reporting and tracking of such outgoing cases. The regulations apply to Convention cases *and* non-Convention cases, and mandate that DOS be informed of:[98]

(1) the name, date of birth and place of birth of the child,

(2) the U.S. state from which the child is emigrating,

(3) the country to which the child is immigrating,

(4) the U.S. state where the finalization is taking place, or the U.S. state where legal custody for the purpose of adoption is granted and the country where the final adoption is taking place, and

(5) the name and contact information of the reporting entity.

Such reporting obligations will be imposed on Convention outgoing cases as well as non-Convention outgoing cases. However, placement of the child and finalization of the adoption in Convention also must comply with new rules introduced in 22 CFR Parts 96 and 97.

In a Convention outgoing case, whether the child is in the care or custody of a public domestic authority or not, a U.S. agency accredited by the Council on Accreditation, an exempt provider, or a public domestic authority participating in the placement of the child will need to observe the following steps:

(1) complete a background study on the child, including information on child's identity, adoptability, background, social environment, family history, medical history, and any special needs of the child[99]

(2) ensure that the consent of the birth parents, guardian, or institution was informed,[100] freely given and expressed or evidenced in writing without any inducement by compensation[101]

(3) ensure that the child has given his or her informed consent[102]

(4) receive the home study of the prospective adoptive parents, prepared in accordance with the laws of the receiving country, under the responsibility of the foreign Central Authority or its accredited bodies or public authorities, and obtain a criminal background check on the prospective adoptive parents[103]

(5) conclude that the child is eligible for adoption and, without revealing the identity of the birth mother or the birth father if these identities may not be disclosed under applicable state laws, transmit to the foreign authorized entity the background study, proof that the necessary consents have been obtained, and the reason for its determination that the proposed placement is in the best interest of the child[104]

Once placement of the child has taken place, the adoptive parents will need to comply with the requirements of 22 CFR Part 97 and obtain from their state court a final decree of adoption or order of custody for purpose of adoption with findings that the child is eligible for adoption, that the adoption is in the child's best interest, and that reasonable efforts have been made to find a domestic placement for the child. The adoptive parents will then apply with the DOS Office of Children's Issues for a Hague Adoption Certificate (HAC)[105] if the adoption has already been finalized, or a Hague Custody Declaration (HCD)[106] if the U.S. state court issued an order of

---

[98] 22 CFR §99.2(c).

[99] 22 CFR §97.3(a).

[100] Informed means that the person giving the consent for adoption was properly counseled on the effects of the consent on the legal relationship with the child. *See* 22 CFR §97.3(g).

[101] 22 CFR §97.3(g).

[102] 22 CFR §97.3(h). The child's consent is necessary only if appropriate in light of his or her age and maturity. *See id.*

[103] 22 CFR §97.3(d).

[104] 22 CFR §97.3(b).

[105] 22 CFR §97.1(d) defines an HAC as "a certificate issued by the Secretary in an outgoing case (where the child is emigrating from the United States to another Convention country) certifying that a child has been adopted in the United States in accordance with the Convention and, except as provided in [22 CFR] §97.4(b), the [Intercountry Adoption Act of 2000]."

[106] 22 CFR §97.1(e) defines an HCD as "a declaration issued by the Secretary in an outgoing case (where the child is emigrating from the United States to another Convention country) declaring that custody of a child for purpose of adoption has been granted in the United States in accordance with the Convention and, except as provided in [22 CFR] §97.4(b), the [Intercountry Adoption Act of 2000]."

custody for purposes of adoption.[107] The HAC certifies that the U.S. adoption has been completed in accordance with the Convention and entitles the adoption to recognition in the United States as well as in any other Convention country. The HCD certifies that the U.S. state court has granted an order of custody for purposes of adoption; the adoption may then be finalized in the receiving country and entitled to recognition in any Convention country (including the United States). When the HAC or HCD is issued and travel documents have been obtained, the child is then permitted to emigrate to the receiving country with the adoptive parents. The child may maintain his or her U.S. citizenship if the receiving country so permits.

The main issues involved in outgoing cases relate to the following:

Prohibited contact between the prospective adoptive parents and birth parents

Contact between the birth parents and the prospective adoptive parents is prohibited unless the adoption takes place within a family, or if the contact is in compliance with state laws.[108]

Reasonable efforts in finding a domestic placement

The Central Authority must be satisfied that reasonable efforts have been made to find a domestic placement for the child. Reasonable efforts may encompass (1) dissemination of information on the child and his or her availability for adoption through print, media, and Internet resources designed to communicate with potential prospective adoptive parents in the United States; (2) listing of information about the child on a national or state adoption exchange or registry for at least 60 calendar days after the birth of the child; (3) responding to inquiries about a copy of the child background study to potential U.S. prospective adoptive parents.

Consent of the birth parents

The consent of the birth parents must be (1) freely given, (2) after counseling on the effects of the consent on the legal rights to the child, (3) expressed or evidenced in writing, (4) not withdrawn, (5) not made in exchange of compensation, and (6) given after the birth of the child when the birth mother is consenting.[109]

CONCLUSION

The Hague Adoption Convention has imposed a new structure for the immigration of children adopted from a Convention country, and has set more rigorous tracking for children emigrating out of the United States. While some attorneys will find the new regulations more restrictive and may fear a negative impact on intercountry adoptions, others will recognize the new possibilities that the Convention introduces by broadening the orphan category and providing more flexibility for adoptive parents who do not always have the possibility to travel to complete the adoption abroad.

Some of the issues revolve around the absence of clarification on some key elements, such as the definition of habitual residency and the breadth of the exception to the no-contact rule in the case of a family adoption. Guidance on the notion of habitual residency indeed should have been a priority, given that whether the adoptive parents and the child are habitual residents of Convention countries determines whether or not the provisions of INA §101(b)(1)(G) apply. Instead, attorneys are left with only a vague notion of what habitual residency encompasses, and will be anxious for new case law to set the parameters.[110]

---

[107] Applicants for a HAC or HCD must submit a completed application form and provide *official copies* of the state court order and findings, and any additional documentation and information as the secretary of state may request. 22 CFR §97.2(b).

[108] 22 CFR §97.3(j) permits contact when a "relevant State or public domestic authority has established conditions under which such contact occurred in accordance with such conditions." Contact must be expressly permitted under state laws.

[109] 22 CFR §97.3(g).

[110] The 1980 Hague Convention on the Civil Aspects of International Child Abduction similarly failed to define the term "habitual residency." The official reporter of the Hague Conference on Private International Law, E. Perez-Vera, issued an explanatory report that provides some guidance on the notion of "habitual residency." The explanatory report was accepted by all contracting parties as the official interpretation of the Convention. The report specifies that, for a residence to be habitual, there should be the establishment of a household or the carrying on of an occupation at the place of residence. The stability may be reflected in the length of stay or in a particularly close tie between the person and the place. Actes et Documents de la Quatorzieme session, vol. III, 1980, 25, *available at http://hcch.e-vision.nl/upload/expl28.pdf.* Moreover, some cases out of U.S. federal courts have addressed the issue of habitual residency, holding that courts should first look to the parents' last shared intention but should also consider whether the evidence points unequivocally to the conclusion that the child has become acclimatized to his or her new surroundings. *Gitter v. Gitter,*
continued

In addition to learning about the provisions of INA §101(b)(1)(G), attorneys will need to continue to perfect their knowledge of the INA §§101(b)(1)(E) and (F) regulations. Indeed, petitions for adopted children and orphaned children are not obsolete and will still apply to cases in which the Convention does not apply, or where the case is grandfathered in because the adoption was finalized or the petition filed prior to April 1, 2008. It is also important that immigration practitioners be aware of other remedies for children who have not acquired legal status in the United States, such as special immigrant juvenile (SIJ) status[111] and remedies under the Violence Against Women Act (VAWA).[112] Such remedies may be an alternative procedure for children sought to be adopted but who do not qualify under the regulations, but also they should be considered before taking any further steps toward the adoption. Adoption might place the child in a position of no return, foreclosing the possibility of qualifying as an SIJ or under VAWA.[113]

Hence, the role of attorneys has certainly become further complicated by the introduction of new rules and anticipation of new case law, but it is also possible that the Hague Adoption Convention has opened up new doors for children immigrating to the United States.

---

396 F.3d 124 (2d Cir. 2005) and *e.g. Whiting v. Krassner*, 391 F.3d 540 (3d Cir. 2004).

[111] A child who is deemed eligible for long-term foster care due to abuse, neglect, or abandonment may apply for legal permanent residence using Form I-360. INA §101(a)(27)(J); 8 CFR §204.11.

[112] A child who is subject to extreme cruelty or is battered by a U.S. citizen or LPR may apply for legal permanent residency using Form I-360. INA §§204(a)(1)(A)(iv), (B)(iii); 8 CFR §204.2(e).

[113] A child will no longer be considered "eligible for long-term foster care" under INA §101(a)(27)(J) once he or she is adopted by a suitable family and, hence, will not be able to apply for SIJ status. Similarly, a child will no longer have any parental relationship with the U.S. citizen or LPR abuser once the child is adopted by a suitable family and, hence, will not meet the requirements of 8 CFR §204.2(e) to apply for legal permanent residency under VAWA.

Appendix A
Definition of Habitual Residency Chart[114]

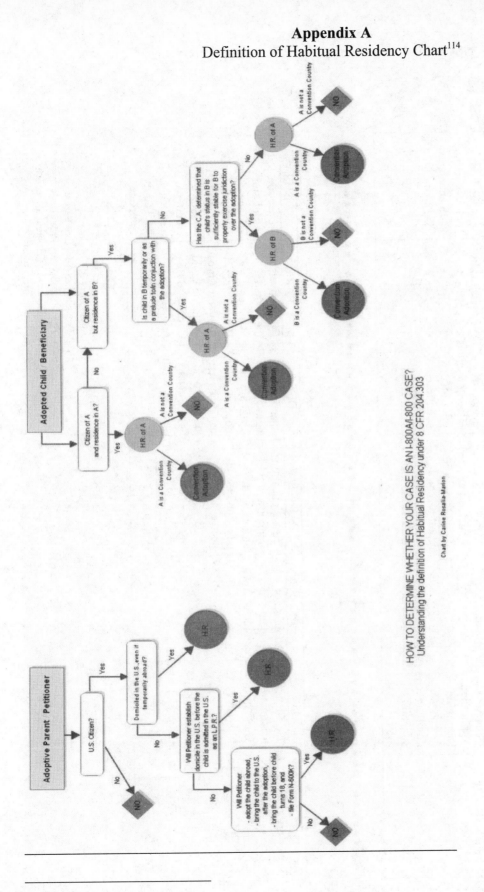

_____

[114] The chart was drafted by Irene Steffas and Carine Rosalia-Marion.

Appendix B
USCIS Flow Chart for Convention Adoptions

CONVENTION ADOPTION PROCESS
UNDER DHS REGULATION DOCKET NO. USCIS-2007-0008

Actors	PAP	DHS	PAP/ASP/ C of O	PAP	DHS/DOS	DOS
Description	After obtaining a Home Study, PAP files Home Study with DHS with a Form I-800A Application to Determine Parent(s)' Eligibility and Suitability to Adopt	Adjudicates application to determine eligibility and suitability of PAP.	-PAP gets notice of approval -ASP transmits approval to C of O -C of O accepts PAP -Match established -C of O transmits report on child-	Files I-800 Hague child petition in behalf of child Includes evidence relating to child, prior to adoption or legal custody	Initial Hague Child petition review for classification I-800- Provisionally Approved	IV application submitted for child. Initial review of visa application for visa eligibility If child eligible, DOS annotates visa application

Actors	DOS	C of O/ PAP	PAP/Child	DOS	PAP	DHS
Description	"Article 5 letter": Notification to C of O of Art. 5 Determination (parental suitability, counseling, ability to enter/reside)	Adoption or legal custody completed in C of O.	Visa application interview at post abroad, with adoption/custody decree	Issuance of Hague Certificate to Adoption or Custody order; Final approval of petition and visa application; visa issuance	Child travels to the United States as a Hague Child Adopted Abroad or Hague Child Coming to Be Adopted	Inspection and Admission -Hague child adopted abroad auto. Citizen -Hague Child coming to be adopted LPR until adoption complete

Index
C of O-Country of Origin
PAP-Prospective Adoptive Parent
ASP-Adoption Service Provider
DHS-Department of Homeland Security
DOS- Department of State

Appendix C
"E–F–G" Chart

	Family Petition	Orphan Petition	Convention Adoption
INA Definition	INA §101(b)(1)(E)	INA §101(b)(1)(F)	INA §101(b)(1)(G)
Forms	I-130	I-600A optional I-600	I-800A *and* I-800
Cut-off age for child	Child must be under 16 at time of *adoption*, or under 18 if sibling under 16.	Child must be under 16 at time of *filing*, or under 18 if sibling under 16.	Child must be under 16 at time of *filing*. (No sibling exception.)
Must the child be an orphan?	No, the child's birth parents may still be alive and able to care for the child if they consent to the termination of their parental rights toward the child.	Yes, "orphan" is defined as a child who has suffered the "death or disappearance of, abandonment or desertion by, or separation or loss from, both parents, or for whom the sole or surviving parent is incapable of providing the proper care and has in writing irrevocably released the child for emigration and adoption."	No, the child's birth parents may still be alive, although they must be incapable of providing care and must give consent to the termination of their parental rights toward the child and to the emigration of the child.
U.S. citizenship of petitioner?	Not necessarily: a lawful permanent resident may petition for the adopted child.	Yes, the petitioner must be a U.S. citizen, and the spouse must be in lawful permanent status.	Yes, the petitioner must be a U.S. citizen, and the spouse must be in lawful permanent status.
Can a single parent adopt?	Yes. (No restriction on age).	Yes, if 25 years old or older.	Yes, if 25 years old or older.
24 months' legal custody of the child	Required.	Not required.	Not required.
24 months' joint residency with the child	Required.	Not required.	Not required.
Entry without inspection of the child	Possible.	Not possible.	Not possible.
Contact with biological parents, orphanage, or legal custodian and adopted parents prior to the adoption	Possible.	Possible.	Prohibited.
Involvement of the Central Authority	Not applicable.	Not applicable.	Required.

REPRESENTING TRANSSEXUAL CLIENTS IN MARRIAGE-BASED IMMIGRATION MATTERS

by Sharon Dulberg[*]

INTRODUCTION

In a 2005 landmark decision, the Board of Immigration Appeals (BIA) finally brought to an end the U.S. Citizenship and Immigration Services' (USCIS) floundering in the area of whether USCIS will recognize a marriage where one of the spouses is transsexual.[1] After three memoranda over a two-year period in which USCIS's contorted rationale led to the denial of marriage cases where one spouse is transsexual, and three unpublished BIA decisions reversing USCIS, the BIA finally published a decision reiterating well-established case law that in determining the legality of a marriage, USCIS must look to the laws of the place of inception of the marriage. Under the BIA decision in *Matter of Lovo-Lara*,[2] a marriage where one of the spouses is transsexual will be recognized for immigration purposes if the marriage was legal in the place of inception. Despite the BIA decision in *Lovo*, there are several unanswered questions that arise in the circumstances discussed below.

HISTORY—THE USCIS MEMORANDA

Prior to 2004, USCIS and legacy Immigration and Naturalization Service (INS) had no settled policy regarding the recognition of post-operative gender. Anecdotally, USCIS and legacy INS, would grant in some instances, fiancé petitions in marriage-based cases where one of the parties was transsexual. Because there was no formal policy, adjudica-tion was inconsistent and examination of the applicants would tend toward a discussion of anatomy. In 2004, out of the blue, the Department of State and USCIS started to deny fiancé visas and petitions where one of the parties was transsexual.

USCIS issued three memoranda in 2004 interpreting marriage where one person is transsexual and found that birth gender governs.[3] USCIS based this erroneous conclusion on the Defense of Marriage Act (DOMA).[4] USCIS's argument, as expounded in these three memos and before the BIA, has been that DOMA controls. They reasoned that because DOMA does not explicitly recognize transsexual marriage or define gender, USCIS cannot recognize a transsexual marriage. This reasoning was rejected by the BIA in *Lovo*.

THE *LOVO-LARA* DECISION

In *Matter of Lovo-Lara*,[5] the petitioner, a male to female transsexual woman, petitioned for her male spouse from El Salvador.[6] The Nebraska Service Center (NSC) denied the visa petition on the ground that under DOMA, the marriage would be considered a same-sex marriage.[7] NSC reasoned that Congress had not officially recognized a marriage where one of

[*] **Sharon Dulberg** is a partner with McVey Mullery Dulberg & Cho, an immigration law firm in San Francisco. She is a certified specialist in immigration and nationality law by the California Board of Legal Specialization. Ms. Dulberg previously served as chair of the Northern California Chapter of AILA.

This article was prepared with the assistance of Ariana Zeno, a paralegal with McVey Mullery Dulberg & Cho.

[1] *Transsexual* is used in this article to refer to a person who has transitioned from his or her birth gender to the opposite gender. *See* Harper Jean Tobin, "Against The Surgical Requirement For Change Of Legal Sex," 38 *Case W. Res. J. Int'l L* 393.

[2] *Matter of Lovo-Lara*, 23 I&N Dec. 746 (BIA 2005).

[3] INS Memorandum, W. Yates, "Spousal Immigrant Visa Petitions (*AFM* Update AD 02-16)" (Mar. 20, 2003), *published on* AILA InfoNet at Doc. No. 03072915 (*posted* July 29, 2003); January 21, 2004, memo from Eduardo Aguirre to Tom Ridge laying out three options: Option 1—to recognize marriages where one spouse is transsexual, Option 2—to not recognize transsexual marriage because of the political implications, Option 3—to recognize gender transition in certain circumstances but not others including marriage; USCIS Memorandum, W. Yates, "Adjudication of Petitions and Applications Filed by or on Behalf of, or Document Requests by, Transsexual Individuals" (Apr. 16, 2004), *published on* AILA InfoNet at Doc. No. 04080367 (*posted* Aug. 3, 2004), implementing Aguirre's option 2, finalizing the USCIS position that transsexual marriage would not be recognized for immigration purposes.

[4] Pub. L. No. 104-199, 100 Stat. 2419 (Sept. 21, 1996).

[5] *Matter of Lovo-Lara*, 23 I&N Dec. 746 (BIA 2005).

[6] *Id.*

[7] *Id.* at 747.

the spouses is transsexual, so NSC would consider the marriage a same-sex marriage.[8]

The BIA wholeheartedly rejected the USCIS and government arguments. The BIA firmly reiterated its long-standing rule that in order to determine whether a marriage is valid for immigration purposes the USCIS must look first to state law to determine whether the marriage is legal at the place of inception.[9] If legal where the marriage occurred, the USCIS must then determine whether the marriage is valid under immigration laws.[10] In this case, the BIA determined that there was no question that the marriage was valid under North Carolina laws.[11] The determination was based on the North Carolina statute that allows one to petition to change their gender on their birth certificate upon certification from a licensed physician that the person has undergone sex reassignment surgery.[12]

The only issue then was whether the marriage was valid for immigration purposes.[13] The BIA found that it was valid for immigration purposes. The BIA examined DOMA and determined that DOMA's sole purpose was to prevent the recognition of same-sex marriages.[14] At the time DOMA was contemplated and passed, a number of states recognized a person's post-operative sex and marriage to a person of the opposite sex.[15] The BIA reasoned that Congress was aware of such laws and recent court rulings recognizing a marriage between a transsexual person and someone of the opposite sex.[16] As DOMA did not specifically ban marriage between a post-operative transsexual person and someone of the opposite sex and the congressional record establishes that Congress' primary concern was to prevent the recognition of same-sex marriages, the BIA found that USCIS's argument that

DOMA prevented the recognition of a marriage where one of the parties is transsexual fails.[17]

The BIA held that aside from same-sex marriages, nothing had changed in terms of the state's rights over marriage matters.[18] Therefore, affirmative legislation by Congress is not necessary before USCIS can recognize a marriage that is recognized by the state in which it occurred.[19]

In this case, the petitioner presented a birth certificate showing her gender as female, a letter from the surgeon who performed the sex reassignment surgery, a court order changing her name, her marriage certificate, and driver's license showing that her gender is female.[20]

The BIA concluded that an individual's gender should be determined based on the gender designation appearing on a current birth certificate issued to the person by the state in which he or she was born.[21] The BIA did not address the situation in which a person's birth state or country does not have a law recognizing a sex change but the person now resides in a state which does recognize the sex reassignment.

HOW TO PREPARE A MARRIAGE CASE WHEN ONE OF YOUR CLIENTS IS TRANSSEXUAL

If your client is from a state or country where he or she can obtain a birth certificate in his/her transitioned gender, under *Lovo* the USCIS should recognize the marriage, as long as the couple marries in a state where the marriage is recognized. It is not sufficient to have a birth certificate with the correct gender; the couple must also marry in a state where the marriage would be recognized. To avoid public policy arguments, the couple should also apply for benefits in a state that recognizes the marriage.[22] Marriage law in most states does not explicitly address whether a post-operative transgender person

---

[8] *Id.*

[9] *Id.* at 748.

[10] *Id.* at 751.

[11] *Id.* at 748.

[12] *Id.*

[13] *Id.* at 748 ("[T]he dispositive issue in this case, therefore, is whether the marriage of the petitioner and beneficiary qualifies as a valid marriage under the Act.").

[14] *Id.* at 749, 751.

[15] *Id.*

[16] *Id.*

[17] *Id.* at 751.

[18] *Id.* at 751.

[19] *Id.* at 752.

[20] *Id.* at 747.

[21] *Id.* at 753.

[22] In an unpublished decision, the BIA addressed whether a marriage that was legal in the state of its inception would violate the public policy of the state in which the couple lived given that the state in which they lived did not allow for a change of sex on the birth certificate. The case was remanded for such a determination. *Matter of Esperanza Martinez Widener*, 2004 WL 2375065 (BIA 2004).

can legally marry. In most instances, if a state allows for and recognizes a change in gender on the birth certificate, under *Lovo* marriage in that state should be considered legal. When preparing such a case, an attorney should obtain the birth certificate statute for the state in which the couple will or has married, as well as any published and unpublished case law on the matter.

In preparing your case, your strategy will differ according to whether:

- The U.S. citizen petitioner is the transsexual person; or

- The foreign-born beneficiary is transsexual and his/her home country does not permit the amending of birth certificates to reflect the correct gender.

These two scenarios are discussed below, along with some general tips.

A. Case Strategy Where the U.S. Citizen Petitioner is the Transsexual Person

1. Obtain as many documents with the post-operative gender as possible:

   a. U.S. passport

   b. U.S. driver's license

   c. Birth certificate— original and amended[23]

   d. Court-ordered name change

   e. Court-ordered gender change

   f. Doctor's letter indicating hormone treatment and/or surgical procedures

2. Research and obtain evidence that the state in which the couple intends to marry will recognize the gender change and marriage. This may include a copy of the birth certificate statute and case law regarding the recognition of post-operative gender for marriage purposes.

3. Should you submit the above documentation?

   a. You may not want to submit all of the above documentation immediately. If the U.S. citizen spouse can obtain a U.S. birth certificate in the post-operative gender, submit only this document but have all the others available at the time of the interview. If the birth certificate is not avail-

able, submit the client's U.S. passport listing the post-operative gender. The gender change may not even come up at the interview.

   b. If USCIS does not raise the issue of the validity of your client's marriage, do not raise it. Ethically, I believe there is no obligation on the part of the attorney or the individual to raise this issue. Alternatively, if the attorney raises the issue against the client's wishes, this can be a violation of the attorney's ethical obligations to confidentiality and zealous representation. As long as your client answers all questions on the forms truthfully, there is no fraud or misrepresentation in not raising the issue. However, there may be a strategic reason to raise or not raise the transgender issue that you should discuss with your client. You should explain to your client that if he or she does not present the issue initially and it comes up at the interview, the officer may think that the client was attempting to mislead USCIS.

   c. If the issue should arise during the interview, be prepared with the documentation listed above.

4. How will the issue arise?

   a. The transsexual client's birth name is generally a dead give away. The I-130 requests prior names used and therefore, if your client's birth name was clearly of the birth gender, USCIS may have questions regarding gender. But do not assume that it will automatically trigger an inquiry. Anecdotally, there have been cases where the "other names used" clearly indicated a female name, and the petitioner was clearly male. The officer did not inquire as to the petitioner's gender, and the case was approved.

   b. Depending on the state, the birth certificate may indicate that it has been amended or may show name changes. USCIS is generally interested in seeing the original birth certificate in addition to the amended birth certificate.

5. Prevent inquiry into client's anatomy.

   An immigration officer is not qualified to make the determination of someone's gen-

---

[23] For updated information regarding ability to change birth certificates, see *www.drbecky.com/birthcert.html*.

der.[24] Your client's doctor and the USCIS doctor will make the medical determination of your client's gender. If possible, you will have a court order and/or birth certificate demonstrating the legal recognition of the post-operative gender. It is therefore beyond the scope of the officer's expertise to question your client regarding anatomy. The role of the officer is to review the documentation to determine whether there has been a medical gender change and whether the state recognizes the gender change for purposes of marriage. If so, the marriage is legal for immigration purposes.

6. What if the US citizen spouse is from a state where he or she cannot change his or her birth certificate?

Although *Lovo* did not specifically address the situation where the transsexual spouse cannot obtain a birth certificate, the BIA made several findings that suggest that the issuance of an amended birth certificate is not controlling. The BIA made clear that "we are not persuaded by the assertions of the Department of Homeland Security (DHS) counsel that we should rely on a person's chromosomal pattern or the original birth record's gender designation in determining whether a marriage is between persons of the opposite sex." *Id.* at 753.

Although the BIA decision states that "we find it appropriate to determine an individual's gender based on the designation appearing on the current birth certificate issued to that person by the State in which he or she was born," the tenor of the BIA decision was not to limit the determination of gender to one piece of evidence, *i.e.,* the reissued birth certificate.[25] The BIA makes it clear that if the state recognizes the gender change, *i.e.,* has a birth certificate law, and the state recognizes the marriage, the marriage is valid for immigration purposes.[26]

If the BIA had meant to limit the legitimacy of marriages to only those who can obtain a new birth certificate, the anomalous result that the BIA was trying to avoid would still occur. That is, a person who is post-operative male but has a female birth certificate could marry a male and that marriage would be recognized for immigration purposes.[27] Since the BIA indicated that this was an anomaly that would result from the failure to recognize post-operative gender, the reliance solely on the birth certificate would not be logical.[28]

In an unpublished decision[29] dated September 26, 2007, the BIA overturned the denial of a visa petition where the foreign-born person was a transsexual woman from Singapore. The BIA stated that although Singapore would not issue a new birth record, her passport indicated that she was female, which demonstrated that Singapore recognized her as female. This decision suggests that other documentation of gender change would be sufficient to demonstrate post-operative gender if the birth record is not available.

B. Case Strategy Where the Foreign Born Beneficiary is Transsexual and His/Her Home Country Does Not Permit the Amending of Birth Certificates to Reflect the Correct Gender

1. What documents should be obtained?

   a. If the person can obtain a birth certificate in their post-operative gender, obtain the birth certificate. Be aware, however, that many foreign birth certificates that have been amended will indicate that they have been changed or delayed in some form or another. Make sure to obtain the original birth certificate as well, as USCIS will want to see both.

   b. If the person cannot obtain a new birth certificate, obtain as many legal documents as possible

      • U.S. court order changing name and gender

---

[24] *Yepes Prado v. INS*, 10 F.3d 1363, 1368 (9th Cir. 1993) (impermissible for the legacy INS to inquire into private sexual matters in determining §212(c) relief); *Matter of Peterson*, 12 I&N Dec. 663 (BIA 1968) (consummation is not the test for bona fide marriage.)

[25] *Id.*

[26] *Id.*

---

[27] *Id.* at 753.

[28] *Id.*

[29] *Matter of Norashikin Ahmad*, 2007 WL 3301748 (BIA Sept. 26, 2007).

- U.S. driver's license
- Passport with correct gender if possible
- Doctor's letter indicating hormone treatments and/or surgical procedures
- Other documentation from home country with post-operative gender. As mentioned above, in the unpublished decision involving a transsexual woman from Singapore, the BIA accepted her female passport as proof that Singapore accepted her change in gender.
- Letter from authorities or attorney of home country indicating that it is not possible to obtain an amended birth certificate

   c. Determine whether couple can legally marry in the state in which they reside. As discussed above, this will require obtaining a copy of the birth certificate statute and any published or unpublished decisions on the matter in the state in which the couple intends to or has married.

2. Should you submit the above documentation?

In any case where the birth record of the foreign born spouse does not contain the correct gender, you will need to submit all of the above documentation with a cover letter explaining that your client is transsexual and that the marriage is recognized by the state in which it was entered.

3. Should your clients file the petition?

You will need to advise your clients that if they cannot obtain a birth certificate or other legal document from their home country recognizing their gender change, the petition may not be granted. Does this mean that your clients should not file? I would suggest that your clients file, for there are petitions that are granted under such circumstances. In a case where the beneficiary was a transsexual woman from Thailand who could not get her birth certificate or passport changed, she obtained a name-change document from Thailand, an order for change of gender from the Judicial Council of California, a letter from her physician indicating the surgery she had undergone, a California driver's license indicating female, and a USCIS medical exam in-

dicating that she is female. Her post-operative gender was accepted, despite the lack of an amended birth certificate or passport from her home country. As long as your clients understand the risks of filing (if there are any) they should not be discouraged from filing.

C. General Tips

1. Your own comfort with issues of gender identity.

You can only effectively represent your transsexual client if you are comfortable with the issue of sexual identity and transsexual identity. Many transgender people face incredible discrimination on a daily basis and often receive sub-par treatment at hospitals and government agencies. If you do not feel comfortable representing a transgender client, please refer them to another attorney who can better represent them.

2. When should clients marry?

   a. A couple should not get married until all of the transsexual client's documents have been changed. Even if the client presents "convincingly" as the post-operative gender at their marriage and are not asked to present identification indicating their gender, the USCIS may not consider the marriage to be legal until the legal documents have been changed.

   b. If your clients cannot change any legal documents, the marriage may still be recognized by USCIS if the couple married in a state that recognizes the marriage. In a decision in the Superior Court of the State of California, the female petitioner sought to annul her marriage to her transsexual husband based on DOMA. The court upheld the validity of the marriage despite the husband's failure to apply for a new birth certificate in California, stating, "[T]he Court finds that it is the public policy of the State of California as enumerated in *Health & Safety Code* §103425 et seq. to recognize the post-operative gender of transsexuals. Accordingly . . . , who the court finds was born a female and has gone through the transsexual surgery, is for all marital purposes a male and the nullity requested based on same-sex marriage is denied."[30]

3. What if the clients are applying in a state that does not recognize the marriage even if married in a state that does?

According to *Lovo*, a marriage is valid if it is a legal marriage in the state in which it was performed and it is not against public policy. If the couple marries in a state which recognizes gender change, the BIA reasoned, it would not be against public policy. However, if the couple were to move to a state that did not recognize their marriage, it could be found that the marriage is against public policy and the visa petition denied.

4. How concerned should I be about the USCIS medical exam?

   a. You may want to have a client call the doctor's office prior to making an appointment to make sure that the doctor is willing to indicate the correct gender.

   b. Some doctors will not be willing to confirm what they would indicate without seeing the client. It may be worthwhile asking whether they would put the post-operative gender if shown the supporting documentation. It can also be helpful to ask how extensive the examination is, in order to prepare your client for possible uncomfortable invasions of privacy.

   c. In many cases the doctor will put the post-operative gender. In some cases, the doctor will put an asterisk indicating transsexual.

5. What should clients put on forms? Do you put transsexual male/female or just male or female?

There is no case law or statute governing this issue. You should discuss with your client how he or she wants to complete the forms. Options include, male, female, transgender/transsexual male/female, post-operative male/female.

6. Should you include a cover letter?

A cover letter should be included at your discretion. However, a cover letter explaining your client's situation with relevant case law included can be helpful. A letter outlining existing BIA case law and attesting to the legal

validity of your client's marriage for immigration purposes gives the interviewing officer time to understand the situation and can prevent the officer from incorrectly determining that your clients' marriage is invalid.

7. How much surgery is sufficient?

If your client's birth certificate has been changed, the USCIS should not inquire further into the surgery your client has undergone. The USCIS is not determining whether your client is legally or medically male or female. The USCIS is determining whether your client has the evidence to demonstrate a medical and legal transition. In the same way that a USCIS officer would not question a USCIS determination that a person has tuberculosis or not, the USCIS should not look behind the documentation submitted by the transsexual person. If your client cannot obtain the birth certificate but can obtain a court order changing his or her gender, the same argument applies.

8. Do not lose sight of the other eligibility factors required in your case.

Once you are over the hump of the legality of the marriage, you will still need to demonstrate that the marriage is bona fide, and then overcome any other eligibility issues.

CONCLUSION

Although *Lovo* is a great decision, it is not smooth sailing. There are still consular posts[31] and USCIS offices that are either not familiar with *Lovo* or not willing to apply the ruling. In addition, the USCIS will deny the case if the state does not recognize the marriage.[32] If your case does not fit the mold of *Lovo*, you will need to advise your clients that there is no certainty that the USCIS will grant their petition. Nevertheless, if your clients will not be worse off for having applied, and you have a legitimate basis for arguing that your clients' marriage should be recognized under the immigration laws, you should not be discouraged.

---

[30] Superior Court of California, Orange County, 1998.

[31] Apparently the consulate in Laos is unaware of *Lovo*.

[32] Unpublished case in Florida denying a visa petition where one spouse was transsexual on the basis that Florida does not recognize postoperative gender.

RESOURCES

Organizations

Immigration Equality
350 West 31st Street, Suite 505
New York, NY 10001
(212)714-2904
www.immigrationequality.org

Transgender Law Center
870 Market Street, Room 823
San Francisco, CA 94102
(415) 865-0176
www.transgenderlawcenter.org

"California Transgender Law 101," a reference
guide published by the Transgender Law Center,
*available at http://transgenderlawcenter.org/pdf/
ca_trans_law_101.pdf*

National Immigrant Justice Center
Asylum Documentation Project
P.O. Box 558
San Francisco, CA 94104
E-mail: *daraujo@heartlandalliance.org*
www.immigrantjustice.org

World Professional Association for Transgender
Health (formerly the Harry Benjamin International
Gender Dysphoria Association)
www.wpath.org

Reading

P. Currah, R.M. Juang, & S.P. Minter, *Transgender
Rights* (U 2006)

P. Randolph Frye & K. Rose, "Responsible Representation of Your First Transgender Client," 66 *Tx.
B.J.* 558 (2003)

*When is a Man a Man, and When is Woman a
Woman*, Julie Greenberg, 52 *Fla. L. Rev.* 745 (Sept.
2000)

H. Tobin, "Against The Surgical Requirement For
Change Of Legal Sex," 38 *Case W. Res. J. Int'l L.*
393

T Flynn, "Transforming the Debate: Why We Need
to Include Transgender rights in the Struggles for
Sex and Sexual Orientation Equality," 101 *Columbia Law Review 2* (Mar. 2001)

G. O. MacKenzie, *Transgender Nation* (1994)

EVERY ROSE HAS ITS THORN: ISSUES IN DIFFICULT MARRIAGE ADJUSTMENT CASES

by Jonathan S. Greene, Thipphavone Ark, and Brent Renison[*]

INTRODUCTION

Love is supposed to be a bed of roses, but difficult marriage adjustment cases can sting everyone with their thorns. Attorneys handling adjustment cases need to be aware of potential problems at the outset of these cases and take appropriate steps to protect themselves and their clients if the petals fall off the flower. Attorneys should also be prepared for complicated interviews with U.S. Citizenship and Immigration Services (USCIS) and potential denials or requests to withdraw these cases.

ROSES COME IN DIFFERENT COLORS

While the fundamental test for determining the bona fide nature of a marriage is validity at inception,[1] numerous facts can make it substantially harder to establish such proof. Hopefully, most marriage cases will feature spouses who live together in the same residence, but occasionally, the spouses are not cohabitating. This can happen when one spouse is a student taking classes at a university in a distant location, or when one spouse has been transferred to another place by an employer. Such circumstances may lend themselves to logical explanation, especially when the spouses have evidence of frequent travel to visit each other.

Not all cases of spouses living apart can be resolved satisfactorily. Separate cohabitation cannot be the sole basis for denial, but it can be relevant to determining whether the parties intended to enter into a bona fide marriage.[2] Even spouses who have separated with the intention of ending a marriage can still proceed with an adjustment case as long as the parties are still married at the time of adjudication. Insofar as the burden of proof rests with the applicant to prove the validity of the marriage, permanent separation of the parties can make the challenge of proof harder.

When the parties have a large disparity in age, USCIS can also engage in deeper questioning as to the validity of the marriage.[3] An 18-year-old high school senior will probably be received with skepticism if she is sponsoring a senior citizen spouse. Age differences that are normal in certain cultures may require supplementary research to assuage doubts of USCIS adjudicators.

What happens if the parties don't speak the same language? Failure to share a common language is not a basis for denial of a marriage petition.[4] However, vast differences in the cultural and ethnic backgrounds of the parties will likely result in more questioning from USCIS adjudicators.[5]

Marriages between close relatives, such as cousins, can also present challenges to the standard marriage-based adjustment case. The validity of a marriage is determined by the law of the state where the marriage occurred,[6] and thus cousins may proceed with a marriage-based petition if their marriage was

---

[*] **Jonathan S. Greene** is the owner of The Greene Law Firm, LLC in Columbia, MD. He is a past chair of the AILA Washington DC Chapter. He practices both immigration and family law and is an adjunct professor at Villa Julie College.

Thipphavone "Thip" Ark is a sole practitioner in San Francisco. She practices in family-based immigration, asylum, and removal defense.

Brent Renison is a partner with Parrilli Renison LLC in Lake Oswego, OR. He is the recipient of an AILA President's Award for Outstanding Achievement in Mentoring and Litigation and the AILA Oregon Chapter Gerald H. Robinson Excellence in Advocacy Award. He previously served as an adjunct professor at University of Oregon School of Law. Jonathan Greene would like to thank AILA member Jeffrey Erickson for invaluable research assistance.

[1] *Matter of McKee*, 17 I&N Dec. 322 (BIA 1980); *Matter of Boromand*, 17 I&N Dec. 450, 454 (BIA 1980); *Chan v. Bell*, 464 F. Supp 125 (D.D.C. 1978); *Dabaghian v. Civiletti*, 607 F.2d 868 (9th Cir. 1979).

[2] *Adjudicator's Field Manual* (AFM) ch. 1.3(a)(2)(G); *see also McKee, supra* note 1, at 334; *Matter of Adalatkhah*, 17 I&N Dec. 404 (BIA 1980).

[3] AFM ch. 21.3(a)(2)(H).

[4] *Damon v. Ashcroft*, 360 F.3d 1084 (9th Cir. 2004) (reversing a denial of removal of conditional residence for lack of substantial evidence). The court found that the immigration judge made an impermissible finding of marriage invalidity when the husband and wife did not share a common language.

[5] AFM ch. 21.3(a)(2)(H).

[6] *See Matter of Lovo-Lara*, 23 I&N Dec. 746 (BIA 2005).

valid in the state where they got married.[7] USCIS looks more closely at the issue by also examining whether the marriage might "offend the laws of the state where the parties reside."[8] Most states, however, offer recognition of the validity of marriages occurring in other states, even if the parties could not have contracted a marriage in the state of residence (although some exceptions may exist under particular state laws, such as for same-sex marriage). Practitioners should be prepared to address the validity of the marriage in the state where it occurred and why the state of residence of the parties would accept the validity of the marriage.

Even if a marriage is voidable, the parties may still pursue a marriage-based petition with USCIS. When either or both of the petitioner and beneficiary are minors, the marriage may be voidable under state law but still valid for immigration purposes.[9] The key for validity is that the marriage is merely voidable and not void in and of itself under state law. Underage spouses may find their marriage voidable but not usually void as a matter of law.

Multiple prior marriages can create multiple headaches for the petitioner and beneficiary. When a lawful permanent resident obtained status through a prior marriage, he or she must wait five years to sponsor a new spouse for permanent residence,[10] unless he or she can establish by clear and convincing evidence that the prior marriage was not entered into with the purpose of evading the immigration laws, or that the prior marriage ended through death.[11]

In addition, multiple prior marriages may mean multiple divorces. The petitioner is required to show that all prior marriages were previously terminated in order for the marriage on which the petition is based to be found valid.[12] This requires attorneys to review divorce decrees to make sure they are valid and that they were obtained prior to the commencement of newer marriages to avoid potential bigamy and void-marriage findings that could bar approval of the marriage-based petition.

ARRANGING THE FLOWERS

When it's time for the adjustment interview in a difficult marriage case, thoroughly preparing the clients is essential. A good starting point is to review the documents needed for the interview to prove the bona fide nature of the marriage. Such documents typically include evidence of a shared life together, combined finances, joint ownership of property, and common residence. Shared life documents can include birth certificates of children, receipts for trips taken together, church membership records, and documents that show joint activities (such as theater or concert ticket purchase documents). Combined finance documents can include joint income tax returns, bank account statements, credit card account statements, and insurance policies (health, automobile, life, dental, vision). Property documents can include rental, lease, or purchase agreements, deeds, mortgage statements, real property closing documents (such as HUD-1 statements), timeshare and vacation property ownership, and rental property ownership papers. Common residence documents typically include utility and telephone bills, ownership of personal property documents such as car titles or furniture purchase receipts, and documents evidencing joint gym memberships and joint shopping club memberships (such as Costco, BJ's, or Sam's Club). Photographs are also essential, and they should show the parties over a period of time, including dating, the wedding ceremony, the honeymoon, at their residence, and on trips.

In difficult cases with little of the above documentation available, the parties should produce numerous affidavits attesting to the validity of the marriage by describing the parties' courtship, wedding ceremony, shared residence, and experiences.[13] The affidavits can come from relatives and friends, but they carry more weight if provided from slightly less biased sources, such as clergy, neighbors, and coworkers. It is helpful to have enough affidavits to describe interactions with the parties while they were dating, at their wedding, and afterward.

If there is a limited amount of documentary material and affidavits seem hard to come by, the parties should produce letters or cards addressed to them, including the envelopes. If there is a paucity of jointly addressed envelopes, the parties should provide envelopes or even junk mail addressed to

---

[7] *See Adams v. Howerton*, 673 F.2d 1036 (9th Cir. 1992).

[8] AFM ch. 21.3(a)(2)(C).

[9] *Matter of G*, 9 I&N Dec. 89 (BIA 1960) (featuring a 16-year-old petitioner and a 19-year-old beneficiary).

[10] INA §204(a)(2)(A).

[11] *Matter of Patel*, 19 I&N Dec. 774 (BIA 1988).

[12] *Matter of Hann*, 18 I&N Dec. 196 (BIA 1982).

[13] *Matter of Laureano*, 19 I&N Dec. 1 (BIA 1983); *see also Matter of Jara Riero*, 24 I&N Dec. 267 (BIA 2007).

them individually but at the same residential address. The parties can also gather letters, cards, and e-mail they wrote to each other to show their intentions of establishing a life together.

Attorneys should pay careful attention to the documents being furnished by the parties. Do the documents look bona fide or manufactured on a home computer? Are the affidavits all written in hand by the same person or are they unsigned? Do the documents contradict each other or undermine key facts in the case? The last thing an attorney wants to provide is a credit card statement that is the joint responsibility of one party and a former spouse.

Practitioners should also practice a mock interview with the parties so they know what the experience will be like when they are in front of a USCIS adjudicator. It's always a good idea to do both a joint interview for a standard adjustment case and a separate mock interview with each spouse to prepare them for the possibility of a marriage fraud interview. After completing the separate interviews, go over any discrepancies with the parties so they can refresh their memories about things they cannot remember or otherwise don't know. Inconsistency on statements made by the parties may be and frequently are the basis for denial.[14] A list of sample questions is attached as an appendix to this article.

As part of preparing the case, attorneys should consider that couples in bona fide marriages sometimes will give materially inconsistent answers because they do not want to reveal certain things about their personal life or lifestyle. When questioning clients, attorneys should try to ascertain whether clients are trying to conceal drug use, alcoholism, or psychological problems that may affect memory; crimes or fraud unrelated to marriage fraud (*e.g.,* tax fraud, public benefit housing fraud); or embarrassing facts they do not want to reveal (*e.g.,* sexual dysfunction, meeting through an escort service, unkempt dwelling). Sometimes the parties want to hide that they are not currently living together, or that one person sleeps in the main bedroom and the other in a separate bedroom. Occasionally the parties are embarrassed that they are not currently having marital relations, or one spouse is trying to hide prior marriages, past crimes, financial troubles, or health issues from the other spouse. Additionally, the parties may be trying to hide their marriage from friends or family members (due to differences in age, culture,

or religion), or they don't want to disclose an unusual or unconventional lifestyle. It's imperative for attorneys to convey to the clients that they must be candid during the preparation stage. With advance knowledge, many challenging issues can be placed in a proper context for USCIS and adequate documentation obtained. Surprises at the adjustment interview can be much harder to manage.

Attorneys also should make sure that the parties are able to fully communicate in English and understand the language, or else an interpreter should be arranged to attend the adjustment interview. The attorney should never be utilized as an interpreter. Practitioners also should remember that all documents in a foreign language must be translated into English, with a certification from a translator that the translation is complete and accurate and the translator is competent to translate from the foreign language into English.[15]

EXAMINING THE BLOOMS

The source of the modern marriage fraud procedure is the federal district court decision in *Stokes v. INS.*[16] The *Stokes* case resulted in the creation of a set of procedures for marriage fraud interviews for the New York District Office of the legacy Immigration and Naturalization Service. In such cases, the petitioner is given a written notice describing the rights involved, a separate attachment of the list of rights is sent out with the interview appointment letter, and a list of the documents to be submitted at the time of interview is mailed to the petitioner.[17] The interview may be conducted with both spouses present, or they may be separated and questioned in the presence of a video camera. Although an interview under the *Stokes* decision is only required in New York, USCIS has applied the basic concept to all marriage cases across the country.

In cases involving suspected marriage fraud, the parties will be interviewed separately and often videotaped. Attorneys should be aware that videotapes may be erased by USCIS within 10 days, unless the information contained on the tape is considered evidence and the benefit is likely to be de-

---

[14] *Nikrodhanondha v. Reno*, 202 F.3d 922 (7th Cir. 2000).

[15] 8 CFR §103.2(b)(3).

[16] 393 F. Supp 24 (S.D.N.Y. 1975). After the *Stokes* decision was issued, procedures were codified in an intra-agency memorandum.

[17] AFM ch. 15.5.

nied, or an incident occurs during the examination.[18] In such cases, the tapes are supposed to be retained for three years or longer.

The purpose of the separate interviews is to test for discrepancies in the answers of the two parties.[19] An officer conducting the examination may recall the first party interviewed after the examination of the second party to clarify discrepancies. Adjudications officers are supposed to conduct interviews in such a manner that gives the person interviewed the opportunity to address any inconsistencies in the person's own testimony and against other known information, which could include the other person's testimony.[20] Attorneys representing parties during interviews may wish to suggest to adjudications officers that they are supposed to give each party an opportunity to address any discrepancies raised by the other party's testimony.

Interviews usually will feature questions concerning the personal living arrangements and marital situation of the spouses. The adjudicator will be asking personal questions relevant to the relationship of which both parties should have personal knowledge and that other people would not generally know. The adjudicator will try to make the questions diverse enough to preclude the parties from preparing coordinated responses before the interview.[21] Questioning is supposed to be focused on the validity of the marriage, not the viability of the marriage.

The questions asked during the interview can be categorized into five broad areas: biographical, past history, recent history, residence, and lifestyle/personal. Biographical inquiries deal with information contained on the forms submitted. Past history includes the development of the relationship and courtship, such as where and how the parties met, where they lived and worked when they first met, and questions about their wedding celebration. Recent history deals with more immediate activities, which may include recent trips, how the parties celebrate major holidays, and immediate activities at the time of the interview. Inquiries about residence involve the couple's living quarters, such as the layout and detail of their dwelling. Lifestyle and personal questions involve how the couple lives on a

day-to-day basis and things unique to each spouse. The areas of inquiry might include information about the other spouse's friends, hobbies, favorite food, banking habits, and the health of the other spouse. The questions may also include whether the other spouse has scars, birthmarks, or tattoos. USCIS adjudicators are limited in how personal the questions can be.[22] While they are allowed to ask about sexual relations, they are supposed to avoid inappropriate questions that can be construed solely as prurient or prying. The appendix at the end of this article contains a list of sample questions from separate interviews.

Attorneys are allowed to be present during the interviews of the parties, but their role is limited to ensuring that the clients' legal rights are protected.[23] The attorney can advise the clients on points of law but should not respond to questions the adjudications officer directed to the parties and should not engage in personal conversations with the officer during the course of the interview. An interview can be terminated by the USCIS officer if the attorney insists on responding to questions or coaches the parties during their interviews.[24]

WHEN THE PETALS START TO FALL OFF THE FLOWER

When an examination starts to go wrong, a number of increasingly bad things can happen. First, USCIS can conclude the interview and follow up with a notice of intent to deny the marriage petition, adjustment application, or both. When numerous discrepancies are evident from the interviews, they will often be identified in detail in the notice. It may be difficult for the parties to address all of the discrepancies in a manner that will result in approval of the benefits.

Marriage fraud cases can be referred to an officer or specialist in the Fraud Detection and National Security Unit. Such officers can carry out extensive investigations that include data mining, checks in law enforcement databases, and field inquiries featuring in-person interviews at residences, places of employment, and other locations in the community.[25]

---

[18] AFM ch. 11.2.

[19] AFM ch. 15.4.

[20] AFM appx. 15.2.

[21] See INS Examination Handbook (rev. Oct. 1, 1988), reprinted in 15 Immigration Law and Procedure 216 (2003).

[22] See AFM ch. 15.3(b).

[23] AFM ch. 15.8.

[24] AFM ch. 15.4(b).

[25] AFM appx. 4-18.

Even more troubling is when USCIS has already determined that the case appears fraudulent before the conclusion of the examination. USCIS adjudicators can offer the opportunity to the petitioner to withdraw the petition for permanent residence. Although the withdrawal is not supposed to be coerced by the adjudicator, it can be suggested as an alternative to a formal denial.[26] The attorney should ask the adjudications officer for an opportunity to confer with both clients and to provide counsel to the petitioner. In difficult cases, the attorney should confer with the clients about this potential scenario in advance of the examination to determine what the clients wish to do in the event that it occurs. However, the attorney will need to confirm with both clients at the examination that they still want to follow the same course of action. Attorneys should remember that the withdrawal cannot be retracted.[27] The impact of a withdrawal can be severe for the success of trying to petition again. Although the withdrawal is not necessarily deemed to be an indication of fraud, the facts surrounding any prior withdrawal are supposed to be considered in the event a subsequent petition is filed by the same petitioner.[28] Even worse, if the withdrawal occurs after immigration fraud has been admitted, the petitioner and beneficiary will have a heavy burden to prove the bona fide nature of the marriage.[29]

Perhaps the most difficult situation can occur when the beneficiary is issued a notice to appear in immigration court, or even worse, actually arrested. Generally, USCIS will not arrest a beneficiary at an interview, even if the beneficiary is not in lawful status.[30] However, USCIS has the right to arrest the beneficiary if it discovers that there is an outstanding arrest warrant for criminal violations.[31] Arrest also can occur if a deportation/removal warrant was previously issued for the beneficiary, unless there is a specific provision of law that allows an application for benefit despite the existence of a deportation or removal order[32] (such as the Nicaraguan Adjustment and Central American Relief Act[33] or the Haitian

Refugee Immigration Fairness Act of 1998[34]). There can also be an arrest if a person being examined assaults a government official or another person being interviewed (such as a spouse or child) or destroys government property.[35]

Attorneys must counsel clients thoroughly about potentially bad scenarios when preparing them for an interview. Clients are paying the attorneys to find out what they need to know, not just want they want to hear.

ETHICAL ISSUES IN FLOWER ARRANGING

Attorneys in marriage cases typically represents both spouses, although there is no reason aside from expense why the parties could not have separate, independent lawyers. Dual representation can be a tricky spot for the attorneys and the clients when conflicts arise.[36] Difficult marriage cases are full of potential land mines for such conflicts.

The most likely source of conflict is when the spouses are not in agreement as to whether to pursue the immigration case. This conflict can occur at the beginning of a case, in preparation for the interview, at the interview itself, or afterward. It is not clear whether such a conflict can be waived, but any such determination depends on the professional responsibility rules of the particular jurisdiction. The American Bar Association Model Rules of Professional Conduct have been adopted in relevant part in many state rules. Under the Model Rules, when a conflict of interest occurs in which the representation of one client is directly adverse to the other client, the conflict can be waived if the lawyer reasonably believes that competent and diligent representation can be provided to each client and the clients provide signed, written, informed consent.[37] Informed consent requires an "agreement by a person to a proposed course of conduct after the lawyer has communicated adequate information and explanation

[26] AFM ch. 20.4.

[27] 8 CFR §103.2(b)(6).

[28] *See Matter of Isber,* 20 I&N Dec. 676 (BIA 1993).

[29] *See Matter of Laureano, supra* note 13.

[30] AFM ch. 15.1(c).

[31] *Id.*

[32] *Id.*

[33] Pub. L. No. 105-100, tit. II, 111 Stat. 2160, 2193–201 (1997).

[34] Pub. L. No. 105-277, div. A, §101(h), tit. IX (secs. 901–04), 112 Stat. 2681, 2681-538 to 2681-542.

[35] AFM ch. 15.1(c).

[36] For a thoughtful discussion of dual representation issues, *see* B. Hake, "Dual Representation in Immigration Practice," *Ethics in a Brave New World: Professional Responsibility, Personal Accountability, and Risk Management for Immigration Practitioners* 29 (2004), *available from* AILA Publications, *www.ailapubs.org*, (800) 982-2839.

[37] *Model Rules of Prof'l Conduct* R. 1.7.

about the material risks of and reasonably available alternatives to the proposed course of conduct."[38]

If the petitioner wants to abandon or withdraw the case and the beneficiary wants to move forward, it is difficult to envision how the conflict can be waived, insofar as the goals of each client are directly adverse and the attorney cannot achieve both clients' objectives. If the petitioner is unsure whether to proceed with the case and does not realize that the case could be withdrawn, the attorney must communicate "adequate information and explanation about the material risks" of going forward.[39] The lawyer must also communicate "reasonably available alternatives" to proceeding with the case, which includes a discussion about withdrawing the petition and the consequences of doing so.[40]

Attorneys should be mindful that the conflict exists at the instant the parties' interests diverge, and it is not acceptable in states that have adopted the relevant Model Rules merely to try to talk to the clients about the conflict to see if the parties can agree on a joint course of conduct. Once the conflict arises, only a signed, written, informed consent can waive a conflict.

If the parties are deadlocked on their divergent goals and cannot agree on a single course of action, the attorney should discuss the possibility for each spouse to obtain a separate, independent attorney. If a conflict exists, the attorney cannot take unilateral action to benefit one client, such as withdrawing the petition, if the other client disagrees with the action and is adversely affected by the action.

To reduce the difficulty of dealing with a conflict in these circumstances, attorneys should have all clients sign written engagement letters that acknowledge the potential conflict inherent in dual representation and allow the attorney to withdraw from representation in the event a conflict cannot be waived.

Sample language from such an engagement letter might include the following:

> Because our office is being engaged to represent both of you in the same case, it is important to recognize that you may develop differing, and sometimes conflicting, interests and objectives regarding this legal matter or other legal matters. There is the potential for disagreement on mat-

ters. If each of you had a separate lawyer, you would each have an "advocate" for your position and receive totally independent advice. When one firm advises both of you, we cannot be an advocate for one of you against the other. If a conflict arises as a result of this immigration matter, it may be possible that the conflict could be waived. However, if the conflict is fundamental to either of your legal rights and it cannot be resolved, this firm would likely have to be excused from representing either or both of you in these matters. **By signing this engagement letter, you are indicating you understand the possibility of termination of representation in the event of conflicting interests.** If representation must be terminated, any legal fees determined to be unearned would be returned to you.

Attorneys may also wish to have the clients sign an acknowledgment that they understand the conflict provisions contained in the engagement letter.

Communication issues can also be problematic with dual representation. Attorneys should expressly indicate in the engagement letter that all communications made by one client to the attorney may be shared with the other client.

Dual representation isn't the only ethical problem faced by attorneys in the marriage case. When one or both parties disclose to the attorney that they are engaging in marriage fraud, the attorney cannot represent the parties before USCIS. If evidence has already been filed with USCIS and one or both parties disclose that the evidence is false, the attorney must take appropriate remedial measures with USCIS. Failure to do so exposes the attorney to bar discipline under federal regulation.[41] This obligation may put the attorney in a difficult position if the state rules require maintaining attorney-client privilege or confidentiality of information and the clients do not want disclosure. The Model Rules do permit an attorney to disclose information to the extent the lawyer reasonably believes necessary to comply with other law, and thus the jurisdiction's rules may permit the disclosures.[42] To avoid problems with the clients down the road, attorneys should be clear about their disclosure policy at the outset of the attorney-client relationship.

---

[38] *Model Rules of Prof'l Conduct* R. 1.0 (definition of "informed consent").

[39] *See Model Rules of Prof'l Conduct* R. 1.4.

[40] *Id.*

[41] 8 CFR §1003.102(c).

[42] *Model Rules of Prof'l Conduct* R. 1.6.

A FEW WILD ROSES

Sometimes clients have engaged in prior collateral activities that can have a dramatic and negative impact on their cases. While the use of false Social Security cards or fictitious numbers is widespread, and clients can risk criminal prosecution for use of another person's Social Security number, the use of a false card is not usually grounds for denial.[43] Unlawful employment can also cause problems for some beneficiaries, especially beneficiaries of preference petitions, insofar as INA §245(c) bars adjustment for those who work unlawfully. An exception exists for certain employment-based adjustment of status applicants when the unlawful employment has not exceeded 180 days.[44] Immediate relatives, however, are entirely exempt from this bar.[45]

Unlawful presence creates more complicated problems, and attorneys should carefully review a beneficiary's immigration status and trips to and from the United States to spot potential issues. The failure to review this history can prove devastating to a client, especially if the filing of an application for adjustment of status leads to denial and institution of removal proceedings before other possible avenues of relief become available, such as cancellation of removal for nonpermanent residents under INA §240.

The three-year bar for unlawful presence applies to those who are unlawfully present in the United States for over 180 days but less than one year, and who subsequently depart the United States voluntarily prior to the commencement of removal proceedings.[46] Therefore, if a beneficiary accrues 180 days or more (but less than one year) of unlawful presence, and then departs the country voluntarily, the bar prevents admission for three years from the date of departure. Paradoxically, if the alien is in removal proceedings and receives voluntary departure between 180 days and one year, the bar does not apply. The 10-year bar for unlawful presence applies to those who were unlawfully present in the United States for one year or more, and who subsequently depart the country at any time.[47]

It may be possible to avoid the bars altogether if the presence is not actually unlawful. Unlawful presence covers those who enter without inspection, those who overstay the date on their I-94 cards, and anyone else who is determined by USCIS or an immigration judge to be out of status. For the latter situation, the unlawful presence does not begin to accrue until the finding is made, and it does not date back to the actual violation. Other situations in which unlawful presence does not accrue include time while a minor, the time during which a bona fide asylum application is pending, time for certain beneficiaries of family unity, and Violence Against Women Act cases.[48]

If an unlawful presence bar applies, some waivers are available. The spouse, son, or daughter (but not parent) of a U.S. citizen or lawful permanent resident may apply for a waiver by showing extreme hardship to the qualifying relative or relatives.[49] Additionally, if only seeking a nonimmigrant visa, some applicants who are otherwise statutorily ineligible for an immigrant waiver may apply at a U.S. consulate abroad for a nonimmigrant waiver.[50] Because such a nonimmigrant obviously has departed the country and invoked the bar, there is no reason that the bar cannot be fulfilled while lawfully in the United States under such a waiver combined with nonimmigrant status.

A major problem for adjustment applicants is the unlawful presence bar that has been termed either the "big bar" or the "permanent bar."[51] Any foreign national who was unlawfully present in the United States for more than one year *in the aggregate*, and who then seeks entry *without inspection* is subject to an indefinite bar to admission. A waiver exists, but it may not be sought until 10 years after the foreign national's last departure from the United States.[52] The bar would not apply to someone who invoked the 10-year bar, but who entered with inspection (even erroneously, or with a false document).

A false claim to U.S. citizenship puts an end forever to most applicants for lawful permanent residence or other immigration benefits. No waiver exists for the ground of inadmissibility if the false

[43] *See* C. Wheeler, "The Immigration Consequences of Using a False Social Security Card," 8 *Bender's Immigr. Bull.* 952 (June 1, 2003).

[44] INA §245(k).

[45] *See* 8 CFR §245.1(b)(4)(i).

[46] INA §212(a)(9)(B)(i)(I).

[47] INA §212(a)(9)(B)(i)(II).

[48] *See* INA §§212(a)(9)(B)(iii)(II)–(IV).

[49] INA §212(a)(9)(B)(v).

[50] INA §212(d)(3)(A).

[51] INA §212(a)(9)(C)(i).

[52] INA §212(a)(9)(C)(ii).

claim occurred on or after September 30, 1996. For false claims before that date, a fraud waiver is available for the spouse, son, or daughter (but not parent) of a U.S. citizen or lawful permanent resident.[53]

The death of the petitioner also can create tremendous difficulty for a beneficiary to proceed with adjustment of status. Generally, USCIS will terminate a Form I-130 Petition for Alien Relative automatically on the death of the petitioner.[54] However, if a U.S. citizen spouse filed an I-130 petition, the beneficiary will remain eligible for immigrant status if he or she was a spouse of the petitioner for two years prior to the death. In such limited cases, the surviving spouse can file a self-petition on Form I-360 within two years of the death, and can include his or her minor children on the application.[55]

USCIS and a federal court have expanded slightly the opportunity for widows and widowers, but only for states within the jurisdiction of the U.S. Court of Appeals for the Ninth Circuit. In 2006, the court in *Freeman v. Gonzales* found that "an alien widow whose citizen spouse filed the necessary immediate relative petition form but died within two years of the qualifying marriage nonetheless remains a spouse for purposes of 8 USC §1151(b)(2)(A)(i), and is entitled to be treated as such when DHS adjudicates her adjustment of status application."[56] Following the *Freeman* decision, USCIS issued a special memorandum implementing the ruling only in the Ninth Circuit, but only when a Form I-485 Application for Adjustment of Status also had been filed before the death of the petitioner.[57] The memorandum also requires that the beneficiary present "a

request under 8 CFR 205.1(a)(3)(i)(C)(2) for humanitarian reinstatement, supported by a properly completed Form I-864 from an individual who qualifies under section 213A(f)(5)(B) of the Act as a qualifying substitute sponsor," or the petition will automatically be revoked.[58]

CONCLUSION

Love, like roses, can be a beautiful thing in full bloom under perfect conditions. When love fades or faces difficult conditions for parties in immigration cases, the attorney plays a necessary role. Proper preparation for USCIS interviews with difficult marriage cases can be the difference between success and destruction to the very roots of the case.

APPENDIX

The following questions may be asked in a suspected marriage fraud examination. This is not an exhaustive list, but merely a representative sample.

What is your date of birth?

Where were you born?

Do you have any prior marriages?

Did your prior marriage end in divorce or death?

When were you divorced?

Who filed for divorce?

Where does your prior spouse live now?

Do you have any children from your first marriage?

What are your children's names?

How old are they?

Where do they live?

Has your current spouse ever met your children? When?

What is your current spouse's name?

What is your spouse's date of birth?

Where was he/she born?

Does your spouse have any prior marriages? How many?

Who is your spouse's first wife/husband?

When were they divorced?

Who is your spouse's second wife/husband?

---

[53] INA §212(i).

[54] *Matter of Varela,* 13 I&N Dec. 453 (BIA 1970), *modified by Matter of Sano,* 19 I&N Dec. 299 (BIA 1985).

[55] *See* INA §204(a)(1)(A)(iii).

[56] *Freeman v. Gonzales,* 444 F.3d 1031 (9th Cir. 2006). A number of courts have followed *Freeman. See Robinson v. Chertoff,* 2007 WL 1412284 (D.N.J. May 14, 2007), *appeal docketed,* No. 07-2977 (3d Cir. July 5, 2007); *Taing v. Chertoff,* 2007 U.S. Dist. LEXIS 911411 (D. Mass 2007), *appeal docketed,* No. 08-1179 (1st Cir. Feb. 11, 2008); *Lockhart v. Chertoff,* 2008 U.S. Dist. LEXIS 889 (D. Ohio 2008), *appeal docketed,* (6th Cir. Mar. 7, 2008). *But see Burger v. McElroy,* 97 Civ. 8775 (RPP), 1999 U.S. Dist. LEXIS 4854 (S.D.N.Y. Apr. 12, 1999); *Turek v. DHS,* 450 F. Supp. 2d 736 (E.D. Mich. 2006).

[57] USCIS Memorandum, M. Aytes, "Effect of Form I-130 Petitioner's Death on Authority to Approve the Form I-130" (Nov. 8, 2007), *published on* AILA InfoNet at Doc. No. 07110969 (*posted* Nov. 9, 2007).

[58] *Id.,* adding AFM ch. 21.2(a)(4)(B)(2). These requirements are being challenged in a class action lawsuit. *Hootkins v. Chertoff,* CV07-05696 (CAS) (C.D. Cal., Aug. 30, 2007).

When were they divorced?

Does your spouse have any children from prior marriages?

What are their names?

How old are they?

Where do they live?

When did your spouse last see his/her children?

What is the date of your marriage?

Where were you married?

On the day of your wedding, where did you wake up?

On the day of your wedding, where did your spouse wake up?

Where was your wedding?

How did you get to the wedding?

How did your spouse get to the wedding?

Who was present at your wedding?

What did you do after the wedding? Where did you go?

Do you have any children together?

What are their names? When were they born?

What hospital were your children born in?

(In wife's interview) Was your husband present at the births?

What is your current address?

When did you start living there?

When did your spouse start living there?

How many floors are in your house/apartment building?

Is there a basement in your house?

What floor do you live on in your apartment building?

How many elevators are in your apartment building?

How many cars can your garage hold?

What is the name of your subdivision/apartment complex?

Who is on the deed/lease?

Who lives in your house/apartment?

How much is your current rent/mortgage payment?

Who paid the rent/mortgage the last time?

Did you have to pay a security deposit? How much?

How many bedrooms are in your house/apartment?

How many bathrooms?

What company provides electricity? Who is on the bill?

Do you have cable or satellite TV?

Who is the cable/satellite provider? Who is on the bill?

How many televisions do you have in your house/apartment?

Where are the televisions located?

Do you have a home telephone?

How many telephones are in your house?

Where are the telephones located?

What is the color of the walls in your kitchen?

What is the color of the floors in your kitchen?

If you are standing at and facing your kitchen sink, where is the stove?

Is your stove electric or gas?

Do you have a dishwasher?

If you are standing at and facing your kitchen sink, where is the dishwasher?

If you are standing at and facing your kitchen sink, where is the refrigerator?

Where is the freezer on your refrigerator?

Do you have a microwave oven?

If you are standing at and facing your kitchen sink, where is the microwave oven?

Is the microwave stationary or does it have a revolving plate?

Where are you currently employed?

When did you start working there?

What is your job title?

What do you do at your job?

Are you paid weekly, every two weeks, twice a month or monthly?

Are you paid in cash, is a paycheck handed to you, or do you have direct deposit?

How much money did you receive in your last paycheck/deposit?

Do you have health insurance through your employer?

What day did you last work?

How did you get to work?

Where is your spouse currently employed?

What is your spouse's job title?

What does he/she do there?

When did he/she start working there?

Is your spouse paid weekly, every two weeks, twice a month, or monthly?

Is he/she paid in cash, is a paycheck handed to him/her, or does he/she have direct deposit?

How much money did your spouse receive in his/her last paycheck/deposit?

Does he/she have health insurance through his/her employer?

What day did your spouse last work?

How did he/she get to work?

Does your spouse have any other jobs?

What day did he/she last work?

How did he/she get to work?

Do you have a joint bank account? What bank?

Where is the bank branch closest to your house/apartment?

Do you have a checking or savings account or both?

Do you have any other joint accounts?

Do you have any bank accounts in your name only?

What bank? What kind of account?

Does your spouse have any bank accounts in his/her name only?

What bank? What kind of account?

Where did you and your spouse first meet? When was it?

Who first spoke to whom?

Why were you there?

Were you with any other people there? Who?

Why was your spouse there?

Was your spouse with any other people there? Who?

When did you first starting dating?

When did you move in together?

Do you have any tattoos? Where? What does it look like?

Does your spouse have any tattoos? Where? What does it look like?

If you are laying in bed, which side does your spouse sleep on?

When is the last time you went to the doctor? What for?

When is the last time your spouse went to the doctor? What for?

Do you have carpet in your bedroom? What color is it?

What color is your bedspread?

What furniture do you have in your bedroom?

How many windows are in your bedroom?

What, if anything, do you have on the walls in your bedroom?

How is your bedroom closet split up?

Where do you keep your clean underwear?

Where does your spouse keep his/her underwear?

Where do you keep your dirty clothes?

Where does your spouse keep his/her dirty clothes?

Do you have a ceiling fan in the bedroom?

Do you have a bathroom attached to your bedroom?

Does the bathroom have windows? How many?

Do you have a medicine cabinet in the bathroom?

Is there a mirror on the medicine cabinet?

Does the medicine cabinet open?

What color is your toothbrush?

What color is your spouse's toothbrush?

Do you have a shower stall or bathtub?

What is your spouse's favorite food?

Where in the house do you eat?

When is the last time you and your spouse went out to eat?

Where did you go?

What was the last movie you went out to see together?

Where did you go for your honeymoon?

What did you do for your last anniversary?

What did you do for New Year's Eve?

Do you attend church?

When did you last go to church?

How many brothers/sisters does your spouse have?

What are their names?

What are the names of your spouse's parents?

Have you met them?

Do you have an answering machine at home?

Whose voice is on the message?

What did you do last night after work?

What did you have for dinner last night?

Did you and your spouse eat together?

What is the name of your spouse's manager at work?

What are the names of your spouse's coworkers?

Do you visit your spouse at work?

When was the last time you visited your spouse at work?

What if any car do you drive?

What color is it?

Does it have any problems?

What car does your spouse drive?

What color is it?

Does it have any problems?

Who is your best friend?

Who is your spouse's best friend?

What day is trash picked up at your house?

Do you recycle?

THE ETERNAL ADJUSTMENT APPLICANT—
FREQUENTLY ASKED QUESTIONS

*by Tammy Fox-Isicoff and H. Ronald Klasko**

MAINTENANCE OF NONIMMIGRANT STATUS

1) Does a principal lose O-1 status upon applying for adjustment?

Not necessarily. If the O-1 continues to work in a manner commensurate with the O-1 status, then the O-1 maintains O-1 status. On the other hand, if the O-1 works other than for the O-1 petitioner, the O-1 will lose O-1 status.

2) Does this also hold true for an F or an H-3 who maintains status while the adjustment application is pending?

Yes, although the F or H-3 may not be able to extend status, the filing of the adjustment application does not terminate lawful nonimmigrant status.[1] If the adjustment is denied, the alien likely would be unable to obtain an F-1 or H-3 visa, and would possibly encounter problems seeking readmission because of lack of nonimmigrant intent.

TRAVEL

3) Does an alien have to be in the United States when an advance parole is filed? When approved?

The applicant must have been granted advance parole, unless present in the United States on an H-1B or L, *before* leaving the United States.[2]

4) Does it make a difference if the alien departs the United States with a valid advance parole, that advance parole expires, and a new advance parole is issued when the alien is abroad?

Although the regulatory language (8 CFR §245.2(a)(4)(ii)(B) is not completely clear, there is a good argument under the regulations that as long as the alien left the country after one advance parole had been approved, he or she should be able to return to the country with a second advance parole document. However, the instructions to Form I-131 (which are in many respects outdated) state that the application is deemed abandoned by the alien's departure.

5) When should an advance parole extension be filed?

The USCIS website allows filing up to 120 days in advance of the expiration of the parole.

6) What if an alien is working in the United States with employment authorization and not maintaining H-1B status? He now needs to travel on an emergency basis. He will not be able to obtain advance parole before he travels. Can his employer file a premium processing H-1B petition and have the employee obtain an H-1B visa overseas in order to return to the United States without abandoning the adjustment of status application?

This is a very risky strategy. Logically, the alien should be able to return to the United States with the H-1B visa. However, the alien risks a determination by an astute immigration examiner at the time of adjudication of the adjustment of

---

* **Tammy Fox-Isicoff** is a former trial attorney and special assistant U.S. Attorney for legacy Immigration and Naturalization Service. She is past chair of the AILA South Florida Chapter and currently serves on AILA Board of Governors. She has represented AILA on the American Bar Association's Immigration Coordinating Committee. Tammy serves on the board of directors of Catholic Charities Legal Services and has served on the Florida Bar's Certification Committee. She has been the recipient of three AILA Presidential Awards.

H. Ronald Klasko is the Philadelphia-based managing partner of Klasko, Rulon, Stock & Seltzer, LLP. An AILA past president, Mr. Klasko served as AILA general counsel for three presidents and has been a member of the Board of Governors since 1980. He has litigated mandamus cases in federal courts throughout the country and has lectured extensively on the subject. Mr. Klasko has been selected annually for inclusion in *Best Lawyers in America* since 1991, and was recently selected for inclusion in the *International Who's Who of Business Lawyers* (2007). He has received AILA's Founders Award.

[1] *Matter of Hosseinpour*, 15 I&N Dec. 191 (BIA 1975), *aff'd on other grounds*, *Hosseinpour v. INS*, 520 F.2d 941 (5th Cir. 1975).

[2] 8 CFR §245.2(a)(4)(ii)(B).

status application that the adjustment was abandoned. The reason for this is that the regulation[3] does not just require that the alien return with the H-1B. Rather the regulation requires that the alien be in lawful H (or L) status at the time of traveling outside the United States.

7) What if the employee was maintaining H-1B status but changed employers using H-1B portability. Can she leave the United States and re-enter using a previously issued H-1B visa without abandoning her adjustment of status?

The answer should be yes. The reason it is less than completely clear is that the regulatory language requires the alien to be returning to the United States "to resume with the same employer for whom he or she had previously been authorized to work as an H-1B or L-1 nonimmigrant. ..."[4] The issue is whether the employment with the new employer was "previously authorized." Although it would be far better if this were clarified, it would appear that the best reading of the regulation is that employment with the new employer was "authorized" by statute, even though not expressly authorized by any U.S. Citizenship and Immigration Services (USCIS) adjudication.

8) Does an adjustment applicant need employment authorization to work if the adjustment applicant re-enters the United States on advance parole and remains the beneficiary of an unexpired, valid H-1B or L-1A visa?

An adjustment applicant's otherwise valid and unexpired nonimmigrant employment authorization is not terminated by his or her temporary departure from the United States, *if prior to such departure the applicant obtained advance parole* in accordance with 8 CFR §245.2(a)(4)(ii). If the alien's H-1 or L-1 employment authorization would not have expired had the alien not left and returned under advance parole, the applicant's failure to obtain a separate employment authorization document will not negate the alien's ability to work. It is important to note that this rule only applies to those who have not

been employed outside the terms of their H or L.[5]

EMPLOYMENT

9) When should an Employment Authorization Document (EAD) extension be filed?

USCIS allows filing up to four months in advance of expiration. We suggest filing as close as possible to four months in advance.

10) What happens if an adjustment applicant works without an EAD and without valid nonimmigrant status after the filing of the adjustment application?

The USCIS position, as evidenced in its training materials, is that unauthorized employment after the filing of the adjustment application can bar adjustment. USCIS will accumulate any unauthorized employment prior to the filing of the adjustment and unauthorized employment after the filing of the adjustment, and, if the total exceeds 180 days since the last entry, the applicant will be considered ineligible to adjust and not protected by INA §245(k).[6]

11) What if the adjustment applicant fails to maintain any nonimmigrant status after the filing of the adjustment, but does not work without authorization?

The USCIS position is that, as long as any violation of status was less than 180 days after last entry and before the filing of the adjustment application, INA §245(k) protects the alien's eligibility for adjustment of status.

12) What if an alien has worked without authorization after the filing of the adjustment application, travels using advance parole, returns to the United States, and continues to engage in unauthorized employment? If the total, in-

---

[3] 8 CFR §245.2(a)(4)(ii)(C).

[4] *Id.*

[5] INS Memorandum, M. Cronin, "AFM Update: Revision of March 14, 2000 Dual Intent Memorandum" (May 25, 2000), *published on* AILA InfoNet at Doc. No. 00052603 (*posted* May 26, 2000).

[6] It should be noted that the position of USCIS that the filing of the adjustment application does not stop the counting of days of unauthorized employment for purposes of INA §245(k) represents a reversal of a previous position of legacy INS. AILA-USCIS liaison meeting minutes (Oct. 28, 2004), *published on* AILA InfoNet at Doc. No. 05012163 (*posted* Jan. 21, 2005). *See* "INS General Counsel List of Resolved Issues," at #17 (Dec. 10, 1999), *published on* AILA InfoNet at Doc. No. 99122271 (*posted* Dec. 22, 1999).

cluding the time before and after travel, exceeds 180 days, is the alien ineligible to adjust?

The prevailing USCIS position appears to be that the alien is ineligible to adjust. INA §245(k) allows an employment-based alien to adjust status as long as the period of unauthorized employment does not exceed 180 days "subsequent to such lawful admission." Unfortunately, the parole entry was not an admission. As such, the unauthorized employment continues to aggregate. Once it exceeds 180 days, the alien is ineligible to adjust.

EXTENSIONS OF NONIMMIGRANT STATUS

13) Can an alien who enters on advance parole extend H-1B or L status?

An alien who held an unexpired, valid H-1 or L-1 nonimmigrant visa, but who was paroled into the United States, may apply for an extension of H-1 or L-1 status if there is a valid and approved petition, as long as the alien has not worked outside the H-1 or L-1. If USCIS approves the application for an extension, the alien's parole is terminated.[7]

14) Is it wise to extend H or L status if an adjustment is pending?

This depends on a number of factors:

a) Cost

b) It is easier to travel with an H or L as opposed to advance parole (so long as the individual has a valid visa), and there is no need for annual extensions of these documents.

c) There is a limit to the period of stay in H or L; an applicant might reach this limit while the adjustment is pending, negating any possibility of using the visa if the adjustment is denied.

d) The sponsor employer's H-1B dependency

e) If the adjustment application is denied, the applicant will still have H or L status.

f) Employment authorization is automatically extended on the filing of an H or L extension; this is not the case with employment and advance parole extensions.

g) Employment authorization and advance parole extensions require name checks that can take a long time.

h) Advance parole and employment authorization must be renewed four months before expiration to be safe; the failure to calendar this will result in the loss of these benefits.

i) Maintenance of the H or L by the principal will enable a spouse or child who did not file for adjustment, or missed the priority date cut-off, to continue to remain in the United States with the principal. It will also protect the after-acquired spouse by according status as an H-4 or L-2.

15) What period of time can an H-1B obtain when filing for an extension?

The H-1B can be approved for any period of time remaining on the H-1B, plus recover any time spent outside the United States. Moreover, the H-1B can be approved for an additional three years if the I-140 has been approved and the priority date is not current when the H-1B extension is filed, or one year if 365 days have elapsed since the filing of the labor certification or I-140. The I-140 or labor certification must have been pending at least 365 days from the requested start date on the extension.[8]

16) Is an alien still eligible for the extension if the I-140 has been denied, but an appeal has been filed?

Yes.[9]

---

[7] INS Memorandum, *supra* note 5.

[8] USCIS Memorandum, M. Aytes, "Interim Guidance for Processing I-140 Employment-Based Immigrant Petitions and I-485 and H-1B Petitions Affected by the American Competitiveness in the Twenty-First Century Act of 2000 (AC21) (Public Law 106-313) (Dec. 27, 2005), *published on* AILA InfoNet at Doc. No. 06092763 (*posted* Sept. 27, 2006), *amending* USCIS Interoffice Memorandum, W. Yates, "Interim Guidance for Processing Form I-140 Employment-Based Immigrant Petitions and Form I-485 and H-1B Petitions Affected by the American Competitiveness in the Twenty-First Century Act of 2000 (AC21) (Public Law 106-313)" (May 12, 2005), *published on* AILA InfoNet at Doc. No. 05051810 (*posted* May 18, 2005). *See also* USCIS Frequently Asked Questions (July 23, 2007), *available at* www.uscis.gov/files/pressrelease/EBFAQ1.pdf.

[9] *Id.*

PORTABILITY

17) Can a principal be the beneficiary of a non-immigrant visa petition filed by a different sponsor while the principal's adjustment is pending?

Yes. There is no requirement that the alien be employed by the sponsor on a permanent residence petition. Nevertheless, there is a requirement that the alien have the intention to be employed by the sponsor. This intention can change once the visa petition is approved and the adjustment application has been pending 180 days. [10]

CONSULAR PROCESSING

18) Can an adjustment applicant change to consular processing?

Yes, but both cannot be pending at the same time. The I-824 is treated as a request to withdraw the I-485. [11]

19) What is the procedure for doing this?

File Form I-824. Some posts will create an immigrant visa application with a copy of the receipt notice for Form I-824; however, they will not adjudicate the visa application until they receive the petition from the National Visa Center. A Department of State cable encourages posts to process cases utilizing the I-797 approval notice of an I-140, a copy of the I-140, a receipt for the I-824, and evidence that the applicant was last resident in the consular post. [12]

20) Can an adjustment applicant port if the adjustment applicant decides to consular process?

Yes. As long as the visa petition is approved and the adjustment application was pending for 180 days. [13]

I-485 TRANSFERS AND MULTIPLE APPLICATIONS

21) Can an I-485 application be transferred from one I-140 to another I-140?

Yes, with a few caveats.

Generally, if an I-140 is filed seeking to classify a foreign national as an alien of extraordinary ability and a separate I-140 is filed requesting a national interest waiver for the same foreign national, he or she may submit, at the same time or subsequently, an I-485 with one of the I-140 petitions. If more than one I-485 is pending, USCIS may request that one of the I-485s be withdrawn. [14]

The first caveat is that if the I-485 accompanies the extraordinary ability I-140, but the national interest waiver I-140 is approved first, USCIS will not transfer the I-485 to the approved I-140 until the extraordinary ability I-140 has been adjudicated. [15]

If the extraordinary ability I-140 is denied, and the priority date for the national interest waiver I-140 is current, USCIS will usually, but not always, match the pending I-485 to the approved petition. If the extraordinary ability I-140 is denied, and the priority date for the national interest waiver I-140 is *not* current, USCIS *will not* transfer the I-485 to the national interest I-140. USCIS can only transfer the I-485 if a visa number is available for that I-140 petition. Therefore, when the extraordinary ability I-140 is denied, and the national interest I-140 is approved but the priority date is not current, the I-485 will be denied.

The second caveat is that if the I-485 accompanies the national interest I-140, and the extraordinary ability I-140 is approved first, again, USCIS will not transfer the I-485 until the national interest I-140 is adjudicated. If the national interest I-140 retrogresses, meaning the priority date is no longer current, USCIS can still transfer the I-485 to the extraordinary abil-

---

[10] *Matter of* [name deleted], (AAO Jan. 12, 2005) (USCIS adopted decision), *published on* AILA InfoNet at Doc. No. 05102761 (*posted* Oct. 27, 2005).

[11] *See* INS Memorandum, M. Cronin, "Prohibition on Concurrent Pursuit of Adjustment of Status and Consular Processing" (Aug. 8, 2000), *published on* AILA InfoNet at Doc. No. 00101803 (*posted* Oct. 18, 2000).

[12] *See* Processing I-140 Petitions for Applicants Residing in the US, 00 State 180792 (Sept. 2000), *published on* AILA InfoNet at Doc. No. 00092773 (*posted* Sept. 28, 2000).

[13] *See* Questions for AILA-Visa Office Liaison Meeting (Mar. 22, 2001), *published on* AILA InfoNet at Doc. No. 01041804 (*posted* Apr. 23, 2001).

---

[14] AILA Liaison/SCOPS Q&A's (July 2, 2007), *published on* AILA InfoNet at Doc. No. 07071764 (*posted* July 17, 2007).

[15] *See* USCIS Memorandum, M. Pearson, "Transferring Section 245 Adjustment Applications to New or Subsequent Family or Employment-Based Immigrant Visa Petitions" (May 9, 2000), *published on* AILA InfoNet at Doc. No. 00062110 (*posted* June 21, 2000).

ity I-140 as long as the extraordinary ability I-140 remains current.

Finally, if the I-485 accompanies one or the other of the I-140s, and that I-140 is denied, and the other I-140 remains pending, USCIS may match the I-485 to the pending I-140 as long as the pending I-140 remains current. If this is missed by USCIS, and the I-485 is denied, it may be necessary to file a motion to reopen.[16]

22) If concurrent filing is used, and the I-485 is eligible for transfer from one I-140 to another I-140, is there a process to do so?

No. There is no established process to transfer the I-485 from one I-140 to another. If there is a request for evidence (RFE) on the I-140 filed concurrently with the I-485, and another I-140 has been approved and is current, we can request that in the context of the response to the RFE. However, if there is no RFE, it is often extremely difficult and entangling to request such a transfer. While it is possible to make a request, it may take a long time, and may go unheeded by USCIS.

23) Can an alien have more than one adjustment of status application pending at the same time? For example, what if two spouses have approved I-140s and both spouses file I-485s with their approved I-140s and separate I-485s as derivatives of their spouse's I-140 adjustments?

Although USCIS discourages such duplicate filings, they are not violative of any law or regulation. However, as a practical matter, multiple adjustment filings may result in confusion regarding multiple biometrics, multiple security clearances, multiple RFEs and possible USCIS withdrawal or denial of one of the two adjustment applications.[17]

SPOUSES

24) If the principal H-1B enters the United States on advance parole, can the spouse continue to enter the United States on an H-4?

There are two schools of thought on this. One is that the H-4's status depends on the principal's status; and if the principal is on advance parole, the spouse must also enter on advance parole. The other is that if the spouse has not violated the essential terms of his or her H status, a legal fiction is

created that the H status is still valid, and thus the H-4 can continue to travel on the H-4.

25) Does an H-4 lose status as an H-4 if granted an EAD?

Only if the H-4 uses the EAD. If the H-4 has the EAD and does not use it, the H-4 maintains H-4 status.[18]

26) Does this same analysis apply to the L-2?

No. Since the L-2 has employment authorization, employment on the L-2 will not disrupt L-2 status.

27) If an adjustment application is filed for the principal, and a child or spouse is outside of the United States, can the child or spouse re-enter the United States on an H or L visa?

Yes, if the principal is maintaining status on an H-1B or L.[19]

28) If the principal filed for adjustment when his or her priority date was current, can a spouse or child later file for adjustment, even if the priority date is not current?

No. The priority date must be current at the time of the filing of the adjustment.

29) Can an H-4 who has employment authorization travel and re-enter on an H-4?

Yes, unless the H-4 has actually taken up employment. The holding of the employment authorization document does not in and of itself alter the H-4's status.[20]

30) What if the principal has entered the United States on advance parole?

The answer appears to be that the spouse or child is not entitled to issuance of a derivative nonimmigrant visa unless the principal holds nonimmigrant status in the United States.[21]

---

[16] *Id.*

[17] *See* AILA/SCOPS Q&A's, *supra* note 14.

---

[18] *Id.*

[19] 9 *Foreign Affairs Manual* (FAM) 41.53 N18.2.

[20] INS Memorandum, *supra* note 11.

[21] Since a parolee is not in nonimmigrant status (but rather parolee status), the derivative apparently is not entitled to nonimmigrant status. Although one could argue that the Cronin memo, *supra* note 11, creates a fictional nonimmigrant status that should entitle the derivatives to obtain derivative visas, a close reading of that memo reveals that the fiction that is created allows an extension of status even though the alien is not in nonimmigrant status. Apparently this fiction has not been extended to allow issuance of derivative visas where the principal is a parolee. *See* 9 FAM 41.11 N6;
continued

31) If the principal H-1B is in the United States and working outside the parameters of the H-1B with an employment authorization document, can the spouse use the H-4 to travel?

No. If the principal is present in the United States and has not maintained H-1B status, the H-4 is not entitled to that status.[22]

CHILDREN

32) What can be done to protect the children of the principal adjustment applicant from aging out if they are abroad and will visa process?

File an I-824 with the adjustment application. This will constitute the child's application for the visa.[23]

33) Will concurrent filing of the adjustment application and visa petition freeze a child's age?

If the principal files an I-140 and I-485 concurrently and the beneficiary "child" is in the United States and wishes to adjust with the principal, the filing of an I-485 by the child contemporaneous with the parent's concurrent filing should protect the child. The child's I-485 will be pending when the parent's I-140 is approved; and, assuming the priority date is current, the child's age will be frozen at the time the I-140 is filed. However, if the priority date is not current when the I-140 is approved, the Child Status Protection Act (CSPA), which did not anticipate concurrent filing, is rather ambiguous. We believe that the better argument is that the child's age is protected on the date of filing of the concurrent I-485 irrespective of subsequent quota retrogression.[24]

34) What if the child was 21 when the adjustment was filed for the principal, is the child eligible to adjust?

Assuming the priority date is current, the child may still be eligible to adjust. Deduct the period

of time the I-140 that was filed on behalf of the principal was pending, and subtract this period of time from the child's age to determine the child's filing age. The child must still seek to procure residence within one year of the approval of the parent's I-140.[25]

35) Does the child have an argument that he is protected by CSPA if he failed to file for adjustment when his priority date became current, and subsequently the priority date retrogressed for more than a year?

CSPA itself does not take into account the possibility that a priority date might be current for a one-month period and then subsequently retrogress for over a year. The statute contemplates giving the child a one-year period to make an application for the visa or adjustment. Thus, one could argue that the period of time that the child could not apply because the priority date retrogressed tolls the year by the period of time that the priority date was unavailable. One would argue that there was impossibility of performance within the one-year filing deadline.

"AILA's Questions and the Visa Office's Responses for the AILA-VO Liaison Meeting" (Mar. 17, 2005), #14, *published on* AILA InfoNet at Doc. No. 05062117 (*posted* June 21, 2005).

[22] 9 FAM 41.53 N18.2.

[23] *See* Child Status Protection Act of 2002: ALDAC #2, State 015049 (Jan. 2003), *published on* AILA InfoNet at Doc. No. 03020550 (*posted* Feb. 5, 2003).

[24] *See* Tammy Fox-Isicoff & H. Ronald Klasko, "The Child Status Protection Act—Is Your Child Protected?" 80 *Interpreter Releases* 973 (July 21, 2003).

[25] *Id.*

HOME IS WHERE THE CARD IS: HOW TO PRESERVE LAWFUL PERMANENT RESIDENT STATUS IN A GLOBAL ECONOMY

by Gary Endelman and Cyrus D. Mehta[*]

INTRODUCTION

After working hard to obtain lawful permanent residency for a client, immigration practitioners are often confounded by their client's willingness to jeopardize this hard-won status by wishing to remain outside the United States. This is becoming increasingly common today with attractive career opportunities outside the country. As these opportunities multiply, the tension between national immigration laws and a global economy will continue to grow, posing new and unanticipated challenges for immigrants and their counsel. While the Immigration and Nationality Act (INA), like all national schemes, judges the integrity of lawful permanent resident (LPR) status by the frequency, depth, and extent of the alien's contacts with the United States, the global economy, like all great movements of capital, does not recognize or respect national boundaries, flowing across them in search of profit and potential. The job of the skilled lawyer is to recognize the inherent tension in this ever-changing relationship, understand its logic, and, to the extent possible, attempt to shape legal strategy to fit the contours of its evolving dynamic.

This article provides practitioners with practice pointers on how to preserve LPR status for their clients. In today's global economy, in which attractive opportunities abound outside the United States, a practitioner is often asked by an LPR client about his or her ability to take up employment, or an assignment, in a foreign country and still preserve permanent residence. Furthermore, this client will also be interested in preserving the ability to naturalize in the future. Despite wanting to reside outside the United States, the LPR continues to have a strong bond to this country and desires to return. Indeed, in the global economy, establishing a business organization overseas, with deep ties to the United States, could result in the LPR continuing to have strong affiliations with this country and benefiting it in immeasurable ways. Gone are the days when immigrants came to the United States in sailboats and steamships, destined never to return home. In today's globalized world, with access to cheap airfares and direct flights, broadband Internet, Blackberries, webcams, and video conferencing, an immigrant can continue to maintain deep ties and bonds even if absent from this country.

While the article will focus on the obvious pitfalls—abandonment of permanent residence and the inability to naturalize—if the LPR opts for a career overseas, it also explores ways for the client to minimize these pitfalls. The article also advocates for a reappraisal of abandonment in light of changing mores in an increasingly interconnected and interdependent world.

[*] **Gary Endelman** obtained a B.A. in History from the University of Virginia, a Ph.D. in U.S. History from the University of Delaware (1978), and a J.D. from the University of Houston (1984). He has practiced immigration and nationality law in Houston in private practice (1985–95) and as the in-house immigration counsel for BP America Inc., handling all U.S. immigration law for the BP Group of Companies throughout the world since March 1995. Dr. Endelman is board certified by Texas in immigration and nationality law. He is a frequent speaker and writer on immigration-related topics. He served as a senior editor of the *Immigration & Nationality Law Handbook* for a decade. In July 2005, Dr. Endelman testified before the U.S. Senate Judiciary Committee on comprehensive immigration reform. Dr. Endelman is the author of *Solidarity Forever: Rose Schneiderman and the Women's Trade Union Movement* (1978).

Cyrus D. Mehta, a graduate of Cambridge University and Columbia Law School, is the managing member of Cyrus D. Mehta & Associates, PLLC, in New York City. The firm represents corporations and individuals from around the world in a variety of areas, such as business and employment immigration, family immigration, consular matters, naturalization, federal court litigation, and asylum. Mr. Mehta has received an AV rating from Martindale-Hubbell and is listed in *Chambers USA*, *The International Who's Who of Corporate Immigration Lawyers*, *The Best Lawyers in America*, and *Super Lawyers*. Mr. Mehta is a former chairman of the board of trustees of the American Immigration Law Foundation (2004–06). He was also the chair of the Committee on Immigration and Nationality Law of the New York City Bar (2000–03), and later secretary and member of that bar's executive committee (2003–07). He is a frequent speaker and writer on various immigration-related issues, and will teach a course on "immigration and work" at Brooklyn Law School in Fall 2008.

TRENDS AND FACT PATTERNS

With the rise in the economies of China and India, a permanent resident is often offered a plumb position overseas.[1] A common fact pattern encountered by an immigration practitioner is as follows:

Client A, an LPR and a citizen of Brazil, is employed in a high-level capacity for a U.S. financial services institution in the United States, which is a subsidiary of a French bank. He is offered an even better position with the subsidiary of the U.S. financial institution in Shanghai, to establish and bolster its business there. He is also offered a fancy expatriate U.S.-dollar salary, and is often required to come to the U.S. entity's offices in New York for meetings and intense strategy sessions. The U.S. firm has explicitly indicated that he will resume a position in the United States after the successful accomplishment of business operations in Shanghai. It is anticipated that this assignment in China will take two years to complete. Client A opts to continue to maintain a home in the United States, and his spouse continues to hold a part-time job at the local preschool. The children also continue their schooling in the United States.

Or:

Client B, also an LPR and a citizen of India, encouraged by expanding opportunities in her country of origin, chooses to quit her job as a financial analyst with a U.S.-based investment bank. She is in the process of establishing a business in Bangalore to provide back-office support operations to U.S. companies in the area of financial analysis and related services. She cannot bear to see her family separated, and her spouse and children have accompanied her to Bangalore. The children have enrolled in an international school there. Although Client B has moved her employment and family overseas, she still harbors the hope of returning to the United States and intends to travel frequently to the United States. She believes that her start-up business in India will allow her to continue to have contacts with the United States, and once her business takes off, she will also establish a branch in the United States to further liaise with her U.S. client base.

Both Client A and Client B wish to preserve their green card,[2] as they continue to have substantial business connections with the United States. They ideally would like to naturalize, but only received permanent residency.[3] They have also heard that U.S. Customs and Border Protection (CBP) officers at airports have become increasingly probing about abandonment, and wish to ensure that they can enter the United States without intrusive questioning at a port of entry. Finally, both Client A and Client B have parents in the home country who are not in good health, and it is possible that an unforeseen medical emergency could prolong their stay outside the United States.

The careful and thorough practitioner must use the basic analytical tools provided by the statute, regulations, and case law to evaluate each client's situation and provide the appropriate legal advice.[4]

---

[1] *See* A. Saxenian, *Local and Global Networks of Immigrant Professionals in Silicon Valley (2002), available at www.ppic.org/content/pubs/report/R_502ASR.pdf.* This study reveals extensive evidence of brain circulation, or two-way flows of highly skilled professionals, between California and fast-growing regions in India and Greater China. Many immigrants have established business operations in emerging technology regions—especially Bangalore, Bombay, Taiwan, Beijing, and Shanghai—and frequently travel between these regions and Silicon Valley. *See also* J. Trumpbour, *Circular Migration, S&E Returnees and the Advance of R&D in India and China* (seminar report, Sloan West Coast Program on Science and Engineering Workers, "The H-1B Program and Labor Certification: Attestation and PERM," University of Davis, CA, Jan. 18, 2008), *available at http://migration .ucdavis.edu/wcpsew/files/J_Trumpbour.pdf.*

[2] The term "green card" is used colloquially for LPR status, since at one time the resident alien card was green in color. It is officially called the Alien Registration Receipt Card, Form I-551. INA §101(a)(20) defines LPR as "the status of having been lawfully accorded the privilege of residing permanently in the United States as an immigrant in accordance with the immigration laws, such status not having changed."

[3] INA §316(a) makes an alien eligible for naturalization five years from the date of issuance of LPR status. If the naturalization applicant is married to a U.S. citizen, the residency requirement is reduced to three years if the spouse has been a U.S. citizen for three years and the parties have been living in "marital union" at the time of filing the application for three years. INA §319(a). We assume that neither Client A nor Client B is married to a U.S. citizen.

[4] For an in-depth and scholarly treatment on this subject, see G. Endelman, "You Can Go Home Again—How to Prevent Abandonment of Lawful Permanent Resident Status," 91-04 *Immigration Briefings* 1 (Apr. 1991). Portions of this article are taken directly from that article, and are reprinted with permission.

LAW ON ABANDONMENT OF PERMANENT RESIDENCE

Most clients labor under the enticing, false, and frequently fatal illusion that, as long as they return to the United States within a certain period of time, they will not be at risk of losing permanent residence.

It is true that the green card can be presented at a port of entry only after a temporary absence abroad not exceeding one year.[5] If, however, an LPR remains outside the United States for over a year, and even if the green card cannot be used any longer, it does not mean that he or she ceases to be an LPR. There is a critical, but often overlooked, difference between the validity of the green card as a travel document and the continued viability of one's claim to resident alien status. Whether one has abandoned LPR status turns on intent rather than the length of time spent abroad.[6] While the green card may be valid so long as the client enters the United States within a year from the prior departure, he or she could be still found to have abandoned LPR status.

Many are also confused by the language in INA §101(a)(13)(C), which states the various grounds under which an LPR would be regarded as seeking admission in the United States. An LPR will be regarded as seeking admission if he or she has been absent from the United States for a continuous period in excess of 180 days.[7] This has led many to believe that if an LPR returns to the United States within 180 days he or she will not be regarded as having sought admission. Yet, another provision under INA §101(a)(13) considers an LPR as seeking admission if he or she "has abandoned or relinquished that status,"[8] regardless of the time spent abroad.

In analyzing whether one has abandoned LPR status, the practitioner must look to the client's intent rather than specific time frames. Essentially, an LPR who returns to the United States is a "special immigrant," among whom, according to the INA, is "an immigrant, lawfully admitted for permanent residence, who is returning from a temporary visit abroad."[9]

The term "temporary visit abroad" has recently been subject to interpretation by the federal circuit courts of appeals. The U.S. Court of Appeals for the Ninth Circuit's interpretation is generally followed:

A trip is a "temporary visit abroad" if (a) it is for a relatively short period, fixed by some early event; or (b) the trip will terminate upon the occurrence of an event that has a reasonable possibility of occurring within a relatively short period of time." If as in (b) "the length of the visit is contingent upon the occurrence of an event and is not fixed in time and if the event does not occur within a relatively short period of time, the visit will be considered a "temporary visit abroad" only if the alien has a continuous, uninterrupted intention to return to the United States during the visit.[10]

Moreover, the Ninth Circuit has added:

Some of the factors that could be used to determine whether an alien harbored a continuous, uninterrupted intention to return in addition to the alien's testimony include the alien's family ties, property holdings, and business affiliations within the United States, the duration of the alien's residence in the United States, and the alien's family, property and business ties in the foreign country.[11]

---

[5] 8 CFR §211.1(a)(2).

[6] For an update on recent developments in the federal circuit courts of appeals, see J. Apa & S. Feal, "Not Just a Matter of Time: The Concept of Abandonment of Permanent Residency Under Immigration and Nationality Law," 12 *Bender's Immigr. Bull.* 614 (Mar. 15, 2007).

[7] INA §101(a)(13)(C)(ii).

[8] INA §101(a)(13)(C)(i).

[9] INA §101(a)(27)(A).

[10] *Singh v. Reno*, 113 F.3d 1512, 1514 (9th Cir. 1997); *Chavez- Ramirez v. INS*, 792 F.2d 932 (9th Cir. 1985). The term "temporary" is not subject to inflexible definition; its meaning has to change in alignment with the facts and circumstances of each particular case. *See Gamero v. INS*, 367 F.2d 123 (9th Cir. 1966). The temporary nature of a visit cannot be defined solely in terms of elapsed time. *See U.S. ex rel. Polymeris v. Trudell*, 49 F.2d 730 (2d Cir. 1931), aff'd, 284 U.S. 279 (1932). Rather, the intention of the alien, when it can be determined with reliable and reasonable precision, will control. *Matter of Kane*, 15 I&N Dec. 258 (BIA 1975); *see also U.S. ex rel. Alther v. McCandless*, 46 F.2d 288 (3d Cir. 1931).

[11] *Chavez-Ramirez, supra* note 10, at 937. A diligent researcher with an inquiring mind and strong constitution can find a treasure trove of legal support in precedential decisions by the Board of Immigration Appeals (BIA). Much as the circuit courts of appeals have done most recently, the BIA has previously focused on the location of the alien's family ties, property holdings, and job, and the intention of the alien with respect to both the location of his or her actual home and the anticipated length of his or her excursion. *Matter of Muller*, 16 I&N Dec. 637 (BIA 1978); *Matter of*
continued

The U.S. Court of Appeals for the Second Circuit, with respect to the second prong, has further clarified that when the visit "relies upon an event with a reasonable possibility of occurring within a short period to time … the intention of the visitor must still be to return within a period relatively short, fixed by some early event."[12] Finally, the U.S. Court of Appeals for the Sixth Circuit, while following the two-prong analysis, has added that the "totality of the alien's circumstances" must be taken into account in addition to the usual factors such as the alien's family, property, and job, and the length of the alien's trip(s) abroad.[13]

Although a circuit court of appeals will review the Board of Immigration Appeal's (BIA) decision under a substantial evidence standard,[14] when an applicant for admission has a colorable claim to LPR status, the burden is on U.S. Citizenship and Immigration Services (USCIS) to show that he or she is not entitled to that status by clear, unequivocal, and convincing evidence.[15] The Illegal Immigration Re-

form and Immigrant Responsibility Act of 1996 (IIRAIRA)[16] introduced the notion of "admission" in INA §101(a)(13)(C).[17] Generally, an LPR will not be regarded as seeking admission unless he or she meets six specific criteria, which include the LPR abandoning or relinquishing that status or having been absent for a continuous period in excess of 180 days.[18] IIRAIRA, furthermore, introduced INA §240(c)(2), which requires the applicant for admission to demonstrate by "clear and convincing evidence" that he or she is "lawfully present in the United States pursuant to a prior admission." Despite these statutory changes, the authors strongly urge attorneys to vigorously endeavor to convince judges to retain the old burden, which rests on the government, in the context of an allegation of abandonment.[19] Post-IIRAIRA circuit court decisions on

---

Quijencio, 15 I&N Dec. 95 (BIA 1974). Also, a good lawyer should consider the client's purpose in departing from the United States, whether the visit abroad can be expected to conclude soon, or relatively soon, and whether the termination date can be fixed by some early event. *Matter of Kane*, 15 I&N Dec. 258 (BIA 1975). *See also Matter of Castro*, 14 I&N Dec. 492 (BIA 1973), and the cases cited therein. "The intention of the departing immigrant must be to return within a period relatively short, fixed by some early event." *U.S. ex. rel. Lesto v. Day*, 21 F.2d 307 (2d Cir. 1927). *See also Matter of Kane, supra; Matter of Montero*, 14 I&N Dec. 399 (BIA 1973). Sometimes, the agile advocate can turn to the law on naturalization to help preserve his or her client's green card. In *Matter of Wu*, 14 I&N Dec. 290 (R.C. 1973), it was held that an alien whose absences were caused by his employment abroad for an American firm did not lose his status as an LPR, because such a finding would have contradicted and frustrated the objectives of INA §316(b), relating to naturalization.

[12] *See Ahmed v. Ashcroft*, 286 F.3d 611, 613 (2d Cir. 2002).

[13] *See Hana v. Gonzales*, 400 F.3d 472 (6th Cir. 2005).

[14] Under this standard, the evidence must be so compelling that no reasonable factfinder could fail to find the facts were as the alien alleged. *INS v. Elias-Zacarias*, 502 U.S. 478, 483 (1992).

[15] *See Singh v. Reno*, 113 F.3d 1512 (9th Cir. 1997) (citing *Woodby v. INS*, 385 U.S. 276, 277 (1966)). Where an applicant for admission has a colorable claim to LPR status, the burden is on U.S. Citizenship and Immigration Services (USCIS) to show that he or she is not entitled to that status. *Matter of Salazar*, 17 I&N Dec. 167 (BIA 1979); *Matter of Kane*, 15 I&N Dec. 258 (BIA 1975). An alien who has been previously admitted for permanent residence and in possession of a valid, unexpired resident alien card has a "colorable

claim to returning resident status," and is therefore entitled to a presumption of eligibility for an INA §211(b) waiver. *See Matter of Huang*, 19 I&N Dec. 749, 754 (BIA 1988). However, USCIS can turn aside this presumption if it demonstrates by clear, unequivocal, and convincing evidence that the person abandoned his or her LPR status. *See id.; Matter of Kane, supra*, at 262–63.

[16] Pub. L. No. 104-208, div. C, 110 Stat. 3009, 3009-546 to 3009-724.

[17] "Admission" replaced the pre-IIRAIRA "entry" doctrine as enunciated in *Rosenberg v. Fleuti*, 374 U.S. 449 (1963), which held that an LPR was not considered making an entry into the United States if his or her departure was "brief, innocent or casual." *See Matter of Collado-Munoz*, 21 I&N Dec. 1061 (BIA 1997) (holding that *Fleuti* was no longer applicable to a returning LPR who had been charged with inadmissibility under INA §212(a)(2)).

[18] INA §101(a)(13)(C). This section also deems LPRs to be seeking admission, *inter alia*, if they have engaged in illegal activity after departing the United States or committed an offense identified in INA §212(a)(2), unless they have been granted a waiver under INA §212(h) or INA §240A(a).

[19] *But see* L. Rosenberg, "Ask Lory: Clash of Intentions," 8 *Bender's Immigr. Bull.* 1881 (Dec. 15, 2003) ("[D]icta in *Matter of Rosas* [22 I&N Dec. 616 (BIA 1999)] creates some cause for concern about the way in which the BIA might interpret INA § 240(c)(2)."). But *Rosas* was not a case involving abandonment; rather, it involved whether an alien who was convicted of an aggravated felony was deemed admitted through adjustment of status even though he was not initially admitted under INA §101(a)(13). Nor was *Sandoval-Loffredo v. Gonzales*, 414 F.3d 892 (8th Cir. 2005), which did not clarify who had the burden that an LPR was inadmissible, although the court still found that the government had proved by clear, convincing, and unequivocal evidence that the LPR engaged in unlawful activity under INA §101(a)(13)(C)(ii).

continued

abandonment continue to affirm that when an alien presents a colorable claim to returning resident status, the burden is on the Department of Homeland Security (DHS) to establish that he or she is not entitled to that status.[20] Even recent unpublished BIA decisions continue to affirm the tradition of the burden being on the government.[21]

Thus, attorneys must continue to remind judges of the well-established principle that a returning lawful permanent resident's status is assimilated to that of an alien continuously residing and physically present in the United States.[22] Although exclusion hearings have been abolished after IIRAIRA, the U.S. Supreme Court's holding in *Landon v. Plasencia*[23]—that a returning resident be accorded due process in exclusion proceedings—should apply with equal vigor to a returning resident who has been deemed inadmissible by virtue of abandonment of his or her status in post-IIRAIRA removal proceedings. Finally, as enunciated by the BIA in *Matter of Huang*,[24] "Given what the alien may have at stake, it has been held, as noted above, that a returning resident may only be deprived of that status in proceedings in which the Service bears the burden of proof. The Board similarly concludes that the deprivation that may follow also requires that the Service establish that such status has changed by clear, unequivocal, and convincing evidence."[25]

Applying this analysis to our fact pattern, Client A is less at risk of a finding of abandonment on his LPR status. Client A's objective to go overseas is fixed by the occurrence of an event, which is the successful completion of the establishment of business operations for the U.S. firm overseas. Upon that

occurrence, Client A intends to return to the United States. The only hitch is that Client A plans to spend at least two years to accomplish the U.S. company's objective overseas, and that may not be construed as a "relatively short period of time." On the other hand, Client A can clearly document that his conduct is consistent with the fact that he harbors the hope of returning to the United States. His family will stay in the United States, he will continue to own his own home here, and he will frequently visit the United States for important business and strategy meetings with the U.S. firm during this two-year period overseas.

Client B, on the other hand, faces more of a risk of losing LPR status. Although she too will maintain contacts with the United States and harbors an intention to return to the United States, her return is not predicated on the occurrence of an event that has a reasonable possibility of occurring with a relatively short period of time. Moreover, her conduct is not consistent with her intent, as she has moved her home and family. On the other hand, she will continue to have business ties with the United States, as the purpose of her overseas start-up is to provide back-office financial services to U.S. investment banks and credit rating agencies.

Despite the fact that USCIS needs to show abandonment by clear, unequivocal, and convincing evidence, many LPRs have had mixed results in circuit courts. To provide a better assessment for Clients A and B, it is important for the practitioner to know the case law on abandonment. Although the case law is fact intensive and not always consistent, this article provides a brief analysis of some of the more recent developments.

In *Singh v. Reno*,[26] Singh obtained lawful permanent residence through the special agricultural worker program on December 1, 1990. From that date until the initiation of the proceedings on July 8, 1993, Singh spent less than one-third of his time in the United States. He spent time the majority of his time in the UK with his wife and daughter, who were waiting for their family-based immigrant visa petition to materialize. During the time Singh spent in the United States, he worked sporadically for a restaurant in California, and lived in temporary housing provided by the employer. Singh also applied for a visitor visa at the U.S. consulate in London and entered the United States four times on that

---

[20] *See, e.g., Singh v. Reno*, 113 F.3d 1512 (9th Cir. 1997); *Hana v. Gonzales*, 400 F.3d 472 (6th Cir. 2005); *Khodagholian v. Ashcroft*, 335 F.3d 1003 (9th Cir. 2003). Although one could argue that *Singh v. Reno* and *Hana v. Gonzales* involved LPRs who were placed in pre-IIRAIRA exclusion proceedings, where the existing standard was obviously applicable, *Khodagholian v. Ashcroft* involved an LPR who was put into post-IIRAIRA removal proceedings as an inadmissible alien.

[21] *E.g., Matter of Heydarzadeh*, A42 545 157 (BIA Feb. 11, 2003); *Matter of Rubio*, A74 317 521 (BIA May 24, 2000).

[22] *See Kwong Hai Chew v. Colding*, 344 U.S. 276 (1966).

[23] 459 U.S. 21 (1982).

[24] 19 I&N Dec. 749 (BIA 1988).

[25] *Id.* at 754; *see Singh v. Reno*, 113 F.3d 1512 (9th Cir. 1997).

[26] 113 F.3d 1512 (9th Cir. 1997).

visa after he obtained permanent residency in the UK. The Ninth Circuit held that Singh's long visits to the UK did not qualify as temporary visits, even though he was never out of the United States for more than a year, and upheld the BIA's decision affirming his abandonment of LPR.

In a scathing dissent, Judge Reinhardt criticized the majority for failing to consider that Singh's motive for spending time abroad was due to the wait for his wife and daughter to gain immigration status. Moreover, Reinhardt disagreed with the majority that the wife and spouse were free to reside in the United States while waiting for their immigration status.

Although the facts in *Hana v. Gonzales*[27] are similar to *Singh*, the Sixth Circuit found that Hana, an Iraqi national, did not abandon her status. On May 22, 1992, Hana was granted LPR status, after which she immediately filed immigrant visa petitions for her husband and four children. A few weeks later, on July 19, 1992, Hana returned to Iraq, and to her job as an inspector at the Central Bank of Iraq under the Saddam Hussein regime. Hana was compelled to return to Iraq to work because she was afraid that the government would hurt her family. Upon obtaining a re-entry permit, Hana spent the next two years in Iraq with her family, caring for her terminally ill mother-in-law. Two weeks prior to the expiration of her re-entry permit in December 1996, Hana returned to the United States but was detained and charged with inadmissibility as an immigrant without a valid visa. Hana admitted that she had never paid income tax in the United States and had no property in this country, but had initially entered with $10,000 in jewelry and money, which she gave to her brother so that she could ultimately purchase a home and car and provide for her children when they arrived in the United States.[28]

While ruling in Hana's favor, the Sixth Circuit emphasized that it must take into account the totality of the alien's circumstances. Thus, while Hana did not possess family, property, or job in the United States, the court held that she still had an intent to return to the United States upon the materialization of her family members' immigration visa petitions. It appears that the Sixth Circuit was influenced by

Hana's decision to remain in Iraq with her family to ensure that they were not harmed by a brutal regime's henchmen and for caring for her terminally ill mother-in-law. The Sixth Circuit distinguished *Singh v. Reno* by observing that Singh's family, even though not free to reside in the United States, could freely travel between the two countries, which were relatively safe democratic nations, although the court acknowledged that *Singh* was a "close case."[29] Clearly, *Hana* is a better decision, as it recognizes an LPR's need to remain with family overseas, and is also more understanding of the realities of the backlogs in family-based immigration, along with the difficulty that sponsored family members may have in obtaining visitor visas to the United States as well as the political and economic realities that might hinder one's ability to return to the United States quickly.[30]

Another decision that was decided in favor of the LPR is *Khodagholian v. Ashcroft*.[31] Khodagholian, an Iranian national, and his wife and two children were admitted as LPRs on July 5, 1993. Between that date and September 1998, his wife and children lived in the United States. He left the United States to Iran on three trips. The first was about four months to sell items and gather documents needed for the children's schools. The second was five to six months in order to take care of his dying mother and his recently orphaned nephews. The third trip, from June 1997 to September 1998, was for 15

---

[27] 400 F.3d 472 (6th Cir. 2005).

[28] As will be discussed *infra*, an alien is considered a resident if he or she meets the "green card test" and will be taxed on worldwide income. *See* Internal Revenue Service Publication 519, *U.S. Tax Guide for Aliens.*

[29] If an LPR takes up permanent residency or citizenship in another country, it would be considered a very unfavorable factor. *See, e.g., Katebi v. Ashcroft*, 396 F.3d 463 (1st Cir. 2005) (LPR status was found abandoned when petitioner stayed in Canada for three years with his girlfriend, after being in the United States for only three months, and became a Canadian citizen).

[30] For a policy argument that LPRs should enjoy the same presumption of retention of LPR status, like citizens who cannot be deprived of their status without informed consent, see G. Endelman, *supra* note 4, at 8 ("Although not co-equal in rights, citizens and LPRs share the bedrock rights of unrestricted private sector employment and travel within the U.S. Clearly, an LPR has just as much at stake in the preservation of his or her status as a citizen does in avoiding expatriation."). To the extent that the loss of status in U.S. immigration law, whether as a citizen or resident alien, depends, in large measure, upon the matrix of one's demonstrated attachments to, and professed loyalty for, the United States, there is simply no reason in law or logic to believe that naturalized citizens trump lawful permanent residents, who frequently have superior credentials in all of the key metrics.

[31] 335 F.3d 1003 (9th Cir. 2003).

months. The initial purpose for the third trip was to sell the family house in Iran, but he was stopped by the police at the airport when he arrived in Iran, as he had an unpaid tax bill from a partnership he had sold before he first came to the United States as an LPR. Although Khodagholian was cleared by the Iranian government in April 1998, he was unable to leave Iran until September 4, 1998, as he had borrowed money to pay the tax bill and needed to stay to pay back the debt. The Ninth Circuit reversed the BIA on the ground that Khodagholian had spent a substantial amount of time in the United States prior to being put into proceedings in September 1998, and that his son was attending college and his daughter was attending high school in the United States. The court further observed that his first two trips had a reasonable possibility of being terminated within a relatively short period of time. With respect to the third trip, the court observed that he had initially gone to sell his house and then stayed on to resolve his tax problems, without ever working in Iran. This did not show that he lacked a continuous, uninterrupted intention to return. Even though Khodagholian had a spotty employment record in the United States, and like Singh and Hana, never paid taxes, given the totality of other factors, the Ninth Circuit held that there was insufficient evidence to conclude that he abandoned his residence in the United States.

Contrast *Khodagholian* with *Chavez-Ramirez v. INS*,[32] in which petitioner Chavez, a nun who had been in the United States as an LPR for five years, left for Mexico on three months' leave from her convent to look after her ailing mother. She looked after her mother for two years, and resigned from the convent. After her sick mother no longer needed Chavez to look after her, she married, gave birth to a child in Mexico, and took up employment. The Ninth Circuit supported the BIA's conclusion of abandonment not because Chavez had no family ties or property holdings in the United States—she was after all a nun. What tipped the scales was that after her mother no longer needed her care, Chavez married and stayed in Mexico for an extended period of time, and she thus did not harbor a continuous, uninterrupted intention to return to the United States. The Ninth Circuit also noted that the BIA found her reason for remaining in Mexico—to help pay for her mother's medical expenses—unconvincing.

LPRs who have taken up employment or been long-term students have not fared well. In *Matter of Huang*,[33] the BIA held that a continuous uninterrupted intent was not shown were the applicant's husband's five-year Ph.D. program was extended to seven years, with no clear end in sight, and the couple's children resided with them in Japan. This outweighed the few equities in the Huangs' favor; namely, a sister-in-law in California, investment property and a house, payment of investment and property taxes, and a bank account.[34] Similarly, in *Aleem v. Perryman*,[35] the petitioner left for Bahrain, taking his wife and children with him, but the contract kept getting extended, cutting against the petitioner's firm intent to return, even though he was a member of professional associations in the United States, paid taxes and had a U.S. citizen child. Finally, in *Ezenwafor v. Ashcroft*,[36] an unpublished Sixth Circuit decision, the petitioner remained in the United States for 11 years after becoming an LPR. In 1991 he traveled to Nigeria with the intent to incorporate a distribution company to which he would export vitamin supplements from the United States. He had also incorporated a business in the United States to serve as the export firm, which got dissolved in 1993. He stayed on in Nigeria until 1997

---

[33] 19 I&N Dec. 749 (BIA 1988).

[34] *Cf. Saxbe v. Bustos*, 419 U.S. 65, 73 (1974) ("But the Act does not declare or suggest that the status will be denied him, if he did not intend to reside permanently here. As we read the Act, the 'status' acquired carries several important privileges: He may remain in the United States indefinitely; he is free to work in this country; he may return to this country after a temporary absence abroad; and he has the privilege of establishing a permanent residence in the United States."). *Saxbe v. Bustos*, if taken on its own terms, is a rather astonishing decision, standing as it does for the novel proposition that green card status does not require an intent to stay permanently in the United States. Given the subsequent deification of intent as the supreme arbiter of abandonment, it is very hard to imagine that the U.S. Supreme Court would arrive at a similar conclusion today. Unfortunately, *Saxbe v. Bustos*, even as a Supreme Court decision, has never had the force to bind other courts, because it involved alien commuters who lived abroad but would return to the United States to work on a daily or a seasonal basis. *Cf. Moin v. Ashcroft*, 335 F.3d 415 (5th Cir. 2003) ("Unlike Moin, they [commuter aliens] were returning regularly to the United States after short visits abroad, with their return triggered by some identifiable event, i.e. the need to return to work at some determinable time.").

[35] 114 F.3d 672 (7th Cir. 1997).

[36] 97 Fed. Appx. 29, 2004 U.S. App. LEXIS 8289.

---

[32] 792 F.2d 932 (9th Cir. 1985).

as he became seriously ill. Even though Ezenwafor always had an intention to return, which he did as soon as his health permitted, his intent was not backed up with any evidence of family, employment, or property ties, according to the immigration judge, whom the Sixth Circuit affirmed.[37]

Applying all these facts to Clients A and B's situations, the cautious practitioner ought to warn them that they risk abandonment, although Client A may be more able to escape this predicament because of his extensive ties with this country, and a more definitive intent to return to the United States. Both clients must be advised that they must demonstrate their ties with the United States to the CBP official at the port of entry, if challenged, as well as the fact that they intend to return to the United States.[38] Documentation of extensive ties will corroborate that they have always had an intent to return within a relatively short period by some early fixed event or by an event with a reasonable possibility of occurring within a relatively short period.[39] And if the event does not occur within a relatively short period of time, the client still must have demonstrated a continuous uninterrupted intent to return to the United States.[40]

In the worst-case scenario, if the CBP official finds that he or she has abandoned LPR status, the client likely will be charged under INA §212(a)(7)(A)(i)(I) as an immigrant who at the time of admission is not in possession of a valid entry document. The client will be issued a notice to appear and will then have to pre-

sent a colorable claim to the immigration judge that he or she is an LPR. The government would then have the burden of establishing by clear and convincing evidence that he or she abandoned this status.[41]

VIABILITY OF RE-ENTRY PERMITS

Clients are also generally under a misconception that a re-entry permit will completely immunize them from a finding of abandonment. Often times, clients have reported that they have been aggressively questioned by CBP officials during inspection, and have been warned that if they do not produce the re-entry permit on their next entry, they will be found to have abandoned status. It appears that, at times, CBP creates the impression of the infallibility of the re-entry permit.

INA §223 provides DHS with the authority to issue a re-entry permit for a period of not more than two years.[42] The application must be filed by the LPR while in the United States.[43] The LPR does not need to wait in the United States until its approval.[44]

---

[37] See also Matter of Kane, 15 I&N Dec. 258 (BIA 1975), in which the BIA found that a Jamaican citizen, who operated an eight-room lodging house there, and who visited the United States one month each year to preserve permanent residence, had been living in Jamaica indefinitely, so her absence was not deemed to be temporary.

[38] In Matter of Manion, 11 I&N Dec. 261, an LPR, who was working indefinitely for a subsidiary of an American company in South Africa, was found still to have been a permanent resident. Note that his sons, one of whom had applied for citizenship, were residing in the United States with his sister. In Matter of Wu, 14 I&N Dec. 290 (BIA 1973), it was held that an LPR never lost his status since he also had an approved application for preserving continuity of residence for naturalization purposes based on his employment abroad for an American firm.

[39] See Hana v. Gonzales, 400 F.3d 472 (6th Cir. 2005); Singh v. Reno, 113 F.3d 1512 (9th Cir. 1997); Ahmed v. Ashcroft, 286 F.3d 611 (2d Cir. 2002).

[40] See also Chavez Ramirez v. INS, 792 F.2d 932 (9th Cir. 1985).

---

[41] See notes 15–25, supra. Interestingly, a finding of abandonment was also made in a nonimmigration context. In U.S. v. Yakou, 428 F.3d 241 (D.C. Cir. 2005), a criminal defendant was found to have unintentionally abandoned LPR status, and was able to escape prosecution under the Arms Export Control Act, which applied only to "[a]ny U.S. persons," including an LPR. Since 1993, he lived overseas and visited his family on fewer than 10 occasions. On his last three visits, he was admitted on his British passport as a nonimmigrant visitor. For an excellent commentary on this case and the consequences of finding unintentional abandonment at an earlier time, see S. Mailman & S. Yale-Loehr, "Losing 'Green Card' Status: Who's To Decide?" 11 Bender's Immigr. Bull. 257 (Mar. 15, 2006).

[42] See also 8 CFR §223.3(a).

[43] 8 CFR §223.2(b). According to the revised instructions to Form I-131, and confirmed by a USCIS press release dated March 5, 2008, all applicants who have filed I-131 applications requesting either a re-entry permit or refugee travel document on or after that date will be scheduled for biometric appointments. The new I-131 instructions state that "[d]eparture from the United States before a decision is made on the application for a Re-entry Permit usually does not affect the application. **However, where biometric collection is required and the applicant departs the United States before the biometrics are collected, the application may be denied.**" [Bold in original.] In a teleconference between the American Immigration Lawyers Association (AILA) and USCIS Service Center Operations (SCOPS) on March 19, 2008, USCIS recommended that applicants remain in the United States until biometrics can be taken, and indicated that it anticipated three weeks to schedule such an appointment. AILA has requested further clarification on this issue

continued

Although the re-entry permit does not prevent a CBP official from finding abandonment, it only prevents the official from relying "solely on the duration of an absence or absences while the permit is valid" to determine abandonment."[45] On the other hand, a CBP official may still investigate a lengthy absence, not as a reflection of intent, but to find out whether activities outside the United States (such as time spent in a foreign prison) could have any bearing on admissibility.[46] An official can also determine whether the permit was procured by fraud or misrepresentation.[47]

While a client who is departing the United States and plans to return after one year must be advised to apply for a re-entry permit, many practitioners advise clients to apply for re-entry permits even if the departure is not expected to exceed one year. Such a strategy could minimize the risk of an aggressive inspection. It might also allow the client to remain outside the United States for longer than the one year even if the initial intent was to re-enter the United States in less than one year. Both Client A and Client B in the examples above have parents who could face unforeseen medical emergencies, thus necessitating a stay outside the United States for over one year.

Finally, the prudent practitioner must warn the client that there have been numerous instances of LPRs being found to have abandoned status even though they attempted entry on a re-entry permit. In *Moin v. Ashcroft*,[48] the petitioner Moin, after obtaining LPR status, left for Pakistan to marry, and spent the majority of the next several years with her husband and children in Pakistan. Even though Moin had a sick child who died after barely one year and had a re-entry permit, the fact that she spent most of the time in Pakistan without an intent to return within a relatively short period caused the U.S. Court of Appeals for the Fifth Circuit to affirm a finding of abandonment of her LPR status. The Fifth Circuit observed that "a reentry permit, in and of itself, does not prevent a finding that an alien has abandoned her permanent residency status."[49] *Moin* appears to have cut against earlier BIA precedent, which held that in the absence of fraud or misrepresentation, "the permit shows that the alien to whom it is issued is returning from a temporary trip abroad."[50] None of this means that obtaining a re-entry permit is without meaning or value; nothing could be more wrong. The resident alien who does not obtain a re-entry permit does so very much at his or her own peril. What it does suggest, however, is that the re-entry permit should be part of a much wider and more diversified plan to retain ties with the United States. It is a strong indication of the departing resident alien's intent to return to the United States on a permanent basis. As such, it functions more like an insurance policy than an indemnification against possible abandonment. Remedial in nature, it does not cancel out damage, but serves to minimize its punitive or long-lasting effect. Much as winning the green card case in the first place requires careful planning, preserving the fruits of victory in a global economy requires the same high measure of strategic oversight.

TAX IMPLICATIONS

Failure to file a tax return as an LPR, or filing as a nonresident, can have an adverse impact on not just the LPR's present status but also with respect to the ability to naturalize in the future. 8 CFR

---

and the USCIS has acknowledged that it will issue guidance as some of the new instructions may be inconsistent. "AILA Liaison/SCOPS Q & As (3/19/08)," *published on* AILA InfoNet at Doc. No. 08032435 (*posted* Mar. 24, 2008). The authors are of the opinion that it is wholly impractical to wait in the United States for weeks or months at a time before taking biometrics and returning to a job and life abroad. It ignores the reality of a global economy and, in a very real sense, defeats the purpose of having a re-entry permit.

[44] 8 CFR §223.2(c)(2). If the applicant has been outside for more than four years in the aggregate during the preceding five years, or since becoming an LPR, whichever is less, the re-entry permit's validity is limited to one year, except for certain categories of permanent residents.

[45] 8 CFR §223.3(d)(1).

[46] Letter, Weinig, Field Manual Project Director, INS (Aug. 17, 1997), *reprinted in* 74 *Interpreter Releases* 1256, 1274–76 (Aug. 18, 1997).

[47] *Id.*

[48] 335 F.3d 415 (5th Cir. 2003).

[49] *Id.* at 419. The court also cited 3 C. Gordon & S. Mailman, *Immigration Law and Procedure*, §35.02[1]: "A reentry permit does not guarantee [an alien's] return if he or she is found inadmissible on seeking reentry." 335 F.3d at 419.

[50] *Matter of V*, 4 I&N Dec. 143 (BIA 1950); *see also U.S. ex rel. Iodice v. Wixon*, 56 F.2d 824 (2d Cir. 1932); *see also Matter of Wu*, 14 I&N Dec. 290 (BIA 1973) (denial of re-entry permit was incorrect since the LPR was employed for an American firm overseas and had successfully applied for preservation of continuity of residence for purposes of naturalization).

§316.5(c)(2) provides, with respect to naturalization applicants:

> An applicant who is a lawfully admitted permanent resident of the United States, but who voluntarily claims nonresident alien status to qualify for special exemptions from income tax liability, or fails to file either federal or state income tax returns because he or she considers himself or herself to be a nonresident alien, raises a rebuttable presumption that the applicant has relinquished the privileges of permanent resident status in the United States.[51]

An LPR is considered a resident for tax purposes, if he or she meets the "green card test" or the "substantial presence test."[52] Even if an LPR does not earn any income in the United States, but has earnings from overseas sources, the LPR is generally required to report his or her worldwide income on a U.S. tax return as a resident.[53]

While 8 CFR §316.5(c)(2) creates a rebuttable presumption of abandonment, a legacy INS general counsel memorandum[54] provides that rebuttal may be impossible unless the LPR shows that his or her claim to nonresident alien resident status was fraudulent. The memo categorically states, "It may be the case, however, that the alien will rarely, if ever, be able to rebut the presumption. And even if the alien could do so, he or she may not wish to do so."[55] The memo further states that an LPR is a resi-

dent alien for income taxation and cites 26 USC §7701(b)(1)(A)(i). According to the memo, "Under Internal Revenue Service ("IRS") regulations, an alien who has been admitted as an LPR, and who wishes to file income tax returns as a nonresident alien, must show that the alien's LPR status has been 'rescinded or administratively or judicially determined to have been abandoned.'" The memo goes on to state, "If the alien has not lost LPR status through exclusion or deportation proceedings, the IRS will consider the alien a nonresident alien for income taxation only if the alien has filed a formal abandonment of LPR status with an immigration or consular officer, and returned his or her alien registration receipt card."

Double taxation treaties allows a noncitizen to be treated as a resident of the foreign country rather than the United States, allowing the foreign country to tax him or her. Under the tie breaker provisions of recent treaties, if an alien may be considered a resident of both the United States and the foreign country for purposes of income tax, the alien is considered a resident of the country where he or she has a permanent home available.[56] If the LPR has designated the foreign country as his or her country of residence, the LPR, according to the legacy INS memo, would be considered to have abandoned LPR status.[57] Even an Internal Revenue Service (IRS) regulation gratuitously states that a foreign national's election to be treated as a nonresident under a tie-breaker provision in a treaty may affect the determination by USCIS and DOS as to whether the alien qualifies to maintain the permanent resident visa.[58]

Tax law uses many of the same terms as immigration, but the same words or concepts can have dramatically different meanings. In one area of taxation, U.S. income tax rules and regulations do contemplate a resident alien qualifying for IRC §911 exclusion of foreign-source earned income. There is no incompatibility between claiming §911 tax benefits and preservation of green card status; the U.S. government accepts the reality that a non-U.S. national can be con-

---

[51] A literal reading of this regulation can put into jeopardy people who filed nonresident state tax returns because they lived in a neighboring state. Surely, the regulation was not intended to penalize applicants who source income from one state and live in another state, such as working in New York but living in New Jersey.

[52] *See* Internal Revenue Service Publication 519, *U.S. Tax Guide for Aliens.*

[53] It behooves a person in this situation to consult with a tax advisor to ensure that he or she is not taxed in both countries.

[54] INS Memorandum, D. Martin, "The Effect of Filing Nonresident Income Tax Returns on an Alien's Status as a Lawful Permanent Resident Alien" (May 7, 1996), *reprinted in* 73 *Interpreter Releases* 948 (July 15, 1996).

[55] Those who have unwittingly filed nonresident tax returns can take some solace in USCIS Interpretation 318.4, which allows them to file a correct Form 1040 tax return. Such an alien would be "considered as having acted upon a mistake of fact and of law, and therefore, as not having terminated his status as a lawful permanent resident under the immigration laws through the prior claim to nonresident alien status for tax purposes."

[56] INS Memorandum, *supra* note 54. The memo cites the United States–Italy and the United States–Canada treaties as examples.

[57] *Id.*, *citing Matter of Huang*, 19 I&N Dec. 749, 754 (BIA 1988) and *Matter of Kane*, 15 I&N Dec. 258 (BIA 1975).

[58] 26 CFR §301.7701(b)-7(b); *see also* KPMG, *U.S. Taxation of Foreign Citizens* ch. 6, *available at www.us.kpmg.com/ microsite/ies/tfc/content/chapter6.htm.*

sidered both a resident of the United States (for immigration purposes) and a bona fide resident of a foreign country (for income tax purposes), as odd as it may seem. The authors have not found any reported decisions in which U.S. immigration authorities challenged the green card status of any individual because he or she claimed the benefits of §911 under a bona fide residence theory or tax home requirement. In those instances in which the green card did come under attack, it was primarily because the individual did not visit the United States often enough; the tax return was not a factor.[59]

Notwithstanding the strong presumption of abandonment for failure to file resident tax returns, the recent circuit court decisions have not considered it as the prime reason to either affirm the abandonment finding or reverse it. In *Hana v. Gonzales*,[60] although the Sixth Circuit observed in several instances that Hana never paid income taxes in the United States, it considered the "totality of the alien's circumstances" in holding that she did not abandon LPR status.[61] Even in *Khodagholian v. Ashcroft*,[62] the Ninth Circuit noted that "[e]ven though Khodagholian did not file a United States tax return, given the totality of other factors, this fact is insufficient to conclude that he abandoned his residence in the United States."[63] Conversely, in *Aleem v. Perryman*,[64] Aleem filed tax returns with the IRS reporting his foreign earnings

even though he incurred no tax liability for those earnings. The following observation from the U.S. Court of Appeals for the Seventh Circuit's decision is worth extracting:

> Finally, the Aleems urge that their filing of United States income tax returns while they were abroad reveals their intent to not abandon their lawful resident status. In this regard, Mr. Aleem testified that he filed the returns because he felt it was his obligation as a permanent resident alien. There can be little doubt that the Aleems faithfully complied with what they perceived to be the minimum requirements for retaining their lawful permanent resident status . . . . The determinative inquiry, however, is not whether the Aleems desired to retain their permanent resident status, rather it is whether their status was lost because their stay was not temporary. [Citation omitted.] In other words, it is not whether the Aleems sought to maintain their status but whether they held a continuous, uninterrupted intention to return to the United States. On this latter score . . . substantial evidence supported the Board's determination that they did not.[65]

PRESERVING CONTINUOUS RESIDENCE FOR NATURALIZATION

The ultimate objective of the LPR client usually is to naturalize and become a citizen of the United States. Upon naturalization, none of the issues linked to abandonment of LPR status exists.[66] Un-

---

[59] *See* Rev. Rul. 91-58 (1991-2 C.B. 340), which discusses green card holders who qualify for §911 treatment under the bona fide residence test:

> The 1984 Act added new section 7701(b) of the Code to provide a statutory definition of a resident alien. Pursuant to section 7701(b), an alien individual shall be treated as a resident of the United States if the individual is a lawful permanent resident of the United States at any time during the calendar year, the individual meets the substantial presence test set forth in section 7701(b)(3), or the individual makes the election provided in section 7701(b)(4). The new rules do not apply for purposes of determining whether a person is a bona fide resident of a foreign country for purposes of section 911. As a result, it now is possible to be both a resident of the United States pursuant to section 7701(b) and a bona fide resident of a foreign country under section 1.871-2(b) of the regulations for purposes of section 911.

[60] 400 F.3d 472 (6th Cir. 2005).

[61] *Id.* at 475.

[62] 335 F.3d 1003 (9th Cir. 2003).

[63] *Id.* at 1009.

[64] 114 F.3d 672 (7th Cir. 1997).

[65] *Id.* at 678–79; *cf. Matter of Wu,* 14 I&N Dec. 290 (BIA 1973) (the fact that the LPR had filed resident tax returns from 1968 through 1971 even though it would have been to his pecuniary advantage to file as a nonresident alien was a favorable factor in finding that he had not abandoned that status).

[66] While the permanent resident outside the United States can never really sleep soundly at night, naturalized citizens need not be so concerned. No matter how long they stay away from these golden shores, or for whatever reason, their citizenship can not be questioned. It remains pristine; they never have to come back and, indeed, can sever all ties to the United States but still avail themselves of all rights and privileges that U.S. citizens enjoy.

It is instructive to compare the degree of risk that LPRs who take international assignments, or who stay away due to family obligation, must assume against the impunity that protects the naturalized citizen who does precisely the same thing and who actually may demonstrate a far greater degree of attachment to the United States.

This was not always the case. As early as the Naturalization Act of 1906, and again in the Nationality Act of 1940, a

continued

fortunately, an LPR client who is embarking on a career or assignment overseas runs the risk of a finding of abandonment of LPR status, and he or she could be disqualified from naturalization. Thus, the prudent attorney must advise the client on both the rules relating to abandonment of LPR status as well eligibility for naturalization. Unfortunately, this may be quite a challenge, since what helps to keep the green card might injure the case for naturalization. Why? Take a peek at INA §316(b), and you will learn that once your clients apply for naturalization, they had best stay home. They cannot change their residence until they take the final oath of allegiance and pick up their shiny new passport. That is where things start to get sticky. If you file for a re-entry permit to protect your client's green card against abandonment, that prudential act can be used by an eagle-eyed naturalization examiner to prove that your client is no longer eligible for naturalization because he or she has a new residence abroad—after all, is not that the very reason why your client wanted the re-entry permit in the first place? If you do not take out this insurance policy, and your client flies away without the warm feeling of a re-entry permit in his or her breast pocket, then the underlying green card might be placed in jeopardy and, if that is lost, good bye to the N-400 application for naturalization! Tough spot, huh? Take comfort in the *Foreign Affairs Manual* (FAM), which happily reminds us that "failure to obtain a re-entry permit should not be viewed automatically as intent to abandon residence and LPR status."[67] However, you

are not completely off the hook, so perhaps the moment of celebration is a bit premature. Even if your client has a re-entry permit, this has no impact of preserving the continuity of residence for naturalization. A client who remains away from Uncle Sam for 12 continuous months disrupts the continuity of residence for naturalization and has to wait four years and one day after returning home as a permanent resident before he or she can file the N-400.[68] Very few clients understand that having a re-entry permit will not help them here. If there is one thing any conscientious lawyer should teach their green card client who wants to become an American citizen before they board the plane, it is this: keeping the green card and preserving eligibility for naturalization are two very different things with different rules and very different requirements. Don't confuse them!

While an in-depth treatment of eligibility for naturalization is outside the scope of this article,[69] to be eligible for naturalization, an applicant must reside in the United States continuously for five years immediately preceding the date of filing the application.[70] Under INA §101(a)(33), residence is defined as a place of abode; meaning the actual dwelling place in fact, without regard to intent. Note that the concept of domicile, which considers the applicant's intent rather than the place where he or she actually lives, is not relevant in determining whether the applicant for naturalization has resided continuously in the United States. During the five-year period of continuous residence, the applicant must have been physically present in the United States for periods totaling at least one half of that time. If an applicant needs to establish only three years of continuous residence based on marriage to a citizen, the applicant must have been physically present in the United States for periods totaling at least one half of that time.[71]

---

naturalized citizen who established permanent residence in another country within five years of becoming a U.S. citizen risked loss of citizenship on grounds of fraudulent procurement; unless the fraud presumption could be refuted, denaturalization followed. See Act of June 29, 1906, §15, 34 Stat. 601; Nationality Act of 1940, §338(c), 54 Stat. 1158. Section 340(d) of the Immigration and Nationality of 1952 incorporated this same punishment. Pub. L. No. 82-414, §340(d), 66 Stat. 1158. Indeed, it was not until 1986 that Congress reduced the "no departure" time period after naturalization to one year. Immigration and Nationality Act Amendments of 1986, Pub. L. No. 99-653. Not until the Immigration and Nationality Technical Corrections Act of 1994 did Congress allow naturalized citizens the leisure of moving away when they wanted to do so, and repealed §340(d) outright. Pub. L. No. 103-416, §104, 108 Stat. 4305, 4308. A cogent summary of this whole issue, and how the law in this area evolved and gradually become more relaxed before disappearing entirely, can be found in 7 C. Gordon, S. Mailman, & S. Yale-Loehr, *Immigration Law and Procedure* §96.10(4) (2007 Ed.).

[67] 9 FAM 42.22 N2.2.

[68] INA §316(b); 8 CFR §316.5(c)(2).

[69] For a comprehensive overview of eligibility requirements for naturalization, see C. Mehta (revised and updated by R. Gottfried), "Criteria for Naturalization and Selected Problem Areas," *Basic Immigration Law 2008* (2008) (Practising Law Institute course handbook). This article is also available at *www.cyrusmehta.com*.

[70] INA §316(a). If the applicant is married to a U.S. citizen, the residency requirement is reduced to three years if the spouse has been a citizen for three years and the parties have been living in "marital union" at the time of filing the application for three years.

[71] INA §319(a).

In the sample fact patterns presented earlier, both Client A and Client B can demonstrate that they have resided continuously for at least four years since the grant of LPR status. They still have one more year to go, although the regulations permit applications to be filed four years and nine months after acquiring LPR status, and two years and nine months in the case of a spouse of a U.S. citizen.[72] Unfortunately, they are unable to wait until they naturalize, as they need to take advantage of their overseas opportunities while the iron is still hot. Even after filing the N-400, the applicant should have resided continuously within the United States from the date of the application up to the time of admission for citizenship.[73] If Client A and Client B are no longer deemed to be resident in the United States, it could thwart their eligibility to naturalize and, if they continue to live outside the United States, they would forever be at risk of being found to have abandoned LPR status.[74] At some point, they may no longer be able to establish that they were physically present for half of the time during either the five-year or three-year period of continuous residence needed prior to filing the N-400.

Fortunately, continuous residence does not mean that the client cannot be absent from the United States. 8 CFR §316.5(c)(1)(i) provides that an absence of more than six months and less than one year will disrupt continuity of residence for purposes of naturalization. This presumption can be rebutted if the applicant can demonstrate that he or she did not terminate employment in the United States, the applicant's immediate family remained in the United States, the applicant retained full access to his or her U.S. abode, or the applicant did not obtain employment while abroad. Under these criteria, Client A may be in a better position to rebut the presumption of disrupting continuity of residence, because his immediate family remained in the United States and

he continued to retain full access to his U.S. abode. He can also argue that he did not terminate employment in the United States because his U.S. employer seconded him to Shanghai for a two-year assignment. Client B, on the other hand, will be in a far more difficult position to rebut the presumption, because her family moved with her to Bangalore, she terminated employment in the United States, she did not retained full access to an abode in the United States, and she sought employment while abroad through her own start-up business.

One can argue, however, that the presumption of disruption of continuity of residence only triggers, pursuant to 8 CFR §316.5(c)(1)(i), if the absence from the United States has been more than 180 days. Thus, if Client A and Client B return to the United States within 180 days, they can argue that they never triggered the presumption. While time periods away from the United States are not relevant for purposes of determining abandonment of LPR status, it could be argued that for purposes of preserving one's ability to naturalize, an absence of less than 180 days ought not result in an invocation of §316.5(c)(1)(i). Yet, the authors have known of naturalization examiners improperly clubbing two back-to-back lengthy trips out of the United States, each one of them being less than 180 days.

As noted, an absence from the United States for over one year would not just disrupt continuity of residence but also wipe the slate clean.[75] The applicant can next apply for naturalization four years and one day following the date of his or her return to the United States to resume residency, or two years and one day, if the statutory period is three years.[76] If the applicant did not apply for a re-entry permit prior to the absence of over one year, he or she would not be able to use the green card to travel back to the United States.[77] Certain exemptions to

---

[72] INA §332(a); 8 CFR §310.2.

[73] INA §316(a). Moreover, there is a good possibility that there will be delays in the processing of the N-400, as USCIS has been unable to cope with the spike in filings prior to the fee increase on July 30, 2007. Also, there have been delays in the FBI name check security clearance in recent times.

[74] Moreover, as noted *supra*, an applicant who has filed a nonresident federal or state tax return, or failed to file a return because the applicant considered himself or herself to be a nonresident alien, raises a further rebuttable presumption that the applicant has relinquished the privileges of permanent residence. 8 CFR §316.5(c)(2).

[75] INA §316; 8 CFR §316.5(c)(1)(ii).

[76] 8 CFR §316.5(c)(1)(ii).

[77] If an applicant managed to be admitted into the United States in the recent past on the green card, after being absent for over one year, and if this fact is discovered on the N-400, query whether the applicant could be placed in removal proceedings for being inadmissible at the time of entry pursuant to INA §237(a)(1)(a), or in the worst case scenario, abandoned LPR status. Prior to filing Form N-400, one creative strategy, if the client was inadmissible at the time of entry, is to attempt to file a waiver of the immigrant visa requirement under INA §211(b) on a *nunc pro tunc* basis.

the one-year absence rule exist, the most frequently used of which are as follows:

- Employees working abroad who obtain approval to preserve their residency (by filing Form N-470) are exempt.[78] To be eligible for the exemption, the applicant must demonstrate one year of actual unbroken physical presence in the United States after acquiring LPR status.[79] The applicant must be working abroad for the U.S. government; a recognized U.S. institution of research; a U.S. firm or corporation engaged in whole or part in the development of foreign trade and commerce of the United States or a subsidiary in which a majority of the stock is owned by the U.S. entity; or a public international organization of which the United States is a member by treaty or statute (where employment commenced after the applicant's admission as an LPR).[80]

- Spouses of U.S. citizens working abroad can obtain expedited citizenship. The citizen spouse must be "regularly stationed abroad" in the employment of the U.S. government, a U.S. institution of research recognized by the attorney general,[81] or a U.S. corporation (or subsidiary) in the development of foreign trade, or must be performing ministerial or missionary functions on behalf of a bona fide U.S. religious organization.[82] Thus, the citizen spouse need not be permanently assigned abroad, but at the same time the assignment cannot be short or casual. The citizen spouse can still be in the United States at the time of naturalization if he or she is proceeding abroad for not less than one year pursuant to

an employment contract or orders.[83] The alien spouse also has to be an LPR.[84]

- Military service abroad based on periods aggregating one year and if the alien is separated under honorable conditions.[85]

If an applicant for naturalization can successful invoke these exceptions and is able to naturalize, it would certainly obviate the perpetual anxiety faced by an LPR who is living outside the United States about the risk of a finding of abandonment of LPR status.

STRATEGIES FOR REPRESENTING THE CLIENT IN DIRE SITUATIONS

Suppose either Client A or Client B in the fact patterns set forth above has stayed outside the United States for over one year and does not have a re-entry permit. Or, suppose he or she obtained a re-entry permit but has stayed outside the United States beyond the two-year validity period of the permit due to an unforeseen medical emergency concerning a parent.

The best advice to the client is to apply for a special immigrant visa (SB-1) at a U.S. consulate.[86] Specifically, regulations provide:[87]

An alien shall be classifiable as a special immigrant under INA 101(a)(27)(A) if the consular officer is satisfied that:

(1) The alien had the status of an alien lawfully admitted for permanent residence at the time of departure from the United States;

(2) The alien departed from the United States with the intention of returning and has not abandoned that intention; and

(3) The alien is returning to the United States from a temporary visit abroad and, if the stay abroad was protracted, this was caused by reasons beyond the alien's control and for which the alien was not responsible.

---

[78] INA §316(b).

[79] It must indeed be one year of continuous unbroken physical presence. Even a brief trip to Canada during that 365-day period will disqualify the applicant from filing an N-470 application to preserve continuity of residence.

[80] If the N-470 application is approved, the LPR also must seek a re-entry permit in order to use the green card to travel back to the United States. The successful filing of an N-470 application can also serve as a defense to a finding of abandonment of LPR status. *See Matter of Wu*, 14 I&N Dec. 290 (BIA 1973).

[81] For a list of organizations that have been determined to be American institutions of research recognized by the attorney general, see 8 CFR §316.20(a).

[82] INA §319(b).

[83] 8 CFR §319.2(a)(1).

[84] 8 CFR §319.2(a)(2).

[85] INA §328.

[86] The specific application is DS-117, Application to Determine Returning Resident Status.

[87] 22 CFR §42.22.

The practitioner is also advised to consult with the FAM, which contains very insightful interpretations on continued U.S. residence and abandonment of residence.[88] For example, the FAM indicates that evidence of continued U.S. residence includes documentation that the "extended visit abroad was caused by unforeseen circumstances"[89] or that there is "a predetermined termination date, *i.e.,* graduation, employment contract expiration, etc."[90] Moreover, the FAM also indicates that "the term 'temporary' cannot be defined in terms of elapsed time alone,"[91] and cites to *Matter of Kane,*[92] which examines the following elements:

(1) Reason for Absence: Traveler should have a definite reason for traveling abroad temporarily;

(2) Termination Date: The visit abroad should be expected to terminate within a relatively short period, fixed by some early event;

(3) Place of Home or Employment: The applicant must expect to return to the United States as an actual home or place of employment. He or she must possess the requisite intent to do so at the time of their departure, and maintain it during the course of their sojourn.[93]

The FAM provides other invaluable insights. It indicates that "an alien employed outside the United States by a U.S. employer would not likely be considered to have abandoned U.S. residence."[94] With respect to students, the FAM helpfully states that "[e]ven prolonged absences from the United States may be considered temporary if the LPR can present evidence of a receipt of a degree within a definitive time."[95] Consular officers are further advised to consider whether students returned to the United States after each academic term, whether they had family living in the United States, and whether the student owns property or bank accounts in the United States

evidencing an intent to return upon completion of studies.[96] Finally, returning to the United States on a visitor's visa from abroad does not necessarily serve as evidence of abandonment or relinquishment of status.[97]

What if your client is returning to the United States on the green card without having obtained an SB-1 visa? Or rather, if the SB-1 visa is refused at a U.S. consulate, can a client still take a chance and arrive in the United States? While this is extremely risky, if your client truly insists, he or she can attempt to file Form I-193, Application for Waiver of Passport and/or Visa.[98] To qualify for such a waiver, the LPR must not have abandoned status and would have to submit the same type of evidence that has been discussed in this article. If the waiver is not approved, the client will most likely be placed in removal proceedings under INA §212(a)(7)(A)(i)(I), and he or she will have another opportunity to have a hearing before an immigration judge. It will be USCIS's burden to establish by clear and convincing evidence that the LPR abandoned status.[99]

At times, it may be worth abandoning LPR status by executing and filing Form I-407 at the U.S. consulate. Form I-407 can also be filed at a port of entry, and the client may be waived in as a visitor rather than as a returning resident. It might be good strategy to do so if the client can imminently be the beneficiary of an immigrant visa petition, which might enable him or her to obtain LPR status in the future when the client is more able to reside in the United States. For example, both Client A and Client B have the potential of being sponsored as multinational executives or managers under the employment-based first preference.[100] Or the spouse may be able to naturalize more quickly than the client, and the newly naturalized spouse could sponsor the cli-

---

[88] *See* 9 FAM 42.22 N1.2, N1.3.

[89] 9 FAM 42.22 N1.2(4).

[90] 9 FAM 42.22 N1.2(5).

[91] 9 FAM 42.22 N1.4.

[92] 15 I&N Dec. 258 (BIA 1975).

[93] 9 FAM 42.22 N1.4.

[94] 9 FAM 42.22 N3.3.

[95] 9 FAM 42.22 N3.5.

[96] *Id.*

[97] 9 FAM 41.31 N12.

[98] INA §211(b) provides for readmission of returning resident immigrants without "a passport, immigrant visa, reentry permit or other documentation," so long as they are otherwise admissible. *See also* 8 CFR §211.1(b)(3) (waiver of failure to present green card or re-entry permit, for good cause).

[99] *See* note 15, *supra.* With respect to children, the BIA has imputed the abandonment of LPR status by the parent to the child. *See Matter of Zamora,* 17 I&N Dec. 395 (BIA 1980); *cf. Singh v.* Gonzales, 451 F.3d 400 (6th Cir. 2006) (holding that fraudulent conduct of parent cannot be imputed to the child).

[100] INA §203(b)(1)(C).

ent as an immediate relative.[101] In the event that Client A or Client B is placed in removal proceedings, and either of them is eligible to be sponsored as an immediate relative, they can file adjustment of status applications with the USCIS district office and seek to terminate proceedings.[102]

PRESUMPTION AGAINST ABANDONMENT

We end by offering a modest proposal that, if adopted, will change the law on preservation of lawful permanent resident status in a really big way: green card holders, like U.S. citizens, should not be presumed to abandon their status without a tangible manifestation or expression of informed consent. The significance of LPR status would be greatly enhanced if a presumption existed in favor of retention of status, notwithstanding the commission of certain acts that might suggest a contrary intent. U.S. citizens now enjoy this same presumption, and there is no reason why resident aliens should not as well. It is neither sound nor sensible to assume that naturalized Americans have a stronger or more meaningful attachment to this country than lawful permanent residents; indeed, there are numerous anecdotal reasons to commend the opposite conclusion. Extended absence from the United States, without more, should never serve as the basis for abandonment; in a global economy, where international relocations are the price of career advancement or even job retention, the law should and must provide that no LPR can be stripped of a green card on the basis of abandonment unless he or she clearly states an unmistakable intention to give it up. No inference from proven conduct would be possible absent clear evidence that such was the desired and intended consequence. Application of this presumption would properly reflect the profound importance of lawful resident alien status while serving as symbolic recognition of the vast contributions that such permanent residents have made to their adopted home.

It is striking and instructive to compare the attitude U.S. law takes towards green card holders who work and live internationally with U.S. citizens who do the same. The latter have no problem. It used to be that establishing a permanent residence in a foreign country within five years of naturalization could lead to denaturalization. Then it was lowered to one year, and finally eliminated altogether so that someone could literally pick up his or her certificate of naturalization and never come back without any impact.[103] Look at the difference with LPRs! Look at how much more suspicious the law is, how many more hoops we make LPRs jump through. Re-entry permits after the first two are limited to a year's duration,[104] and now there is a biometrics requirement clearly designed to limit the flexibility of the re-entry permit for global citizens.[105] We recognize that naturalized citizens can be part of the global economy, but not LPRs—who, if they involuntarily abandon their status, will never get to file an N-400. Why the difference?[106]

How is the nation well served when we presume that a citizen does not intend the consequences of a potentially expatriating act while denying the LPR his or her right to rely on the very same presumption? Under INA §349, the law presumes that the listed expatriating acts were done voluntarily, unless rebutted, but the presumption does not extend to intent to give up citizenship itself. In fact, just the opposite is the case. The regulations contain a presumption that certain expatriating acts, such as taking a routine oath of allegiance, are done with the intent to retain U.S. nationality.[107] Why is the LPR treated less favorably? Why does the presumption of abandonment extend not only to the filing of the tax return but to the intent to give up the green card? The idea of this being rebuttable is an illusion – who would confess to tax fraud?[108] There is no nexus between such an act and status for the naturalized citizen, but we insist on an

---

[101] INA §201(b)(2)(A)(i).

[102] We assume that they will be charged as "arriving aliens." Pursuant to 8 CFR §245.2(a)(2), USCIS has jurisdiction to adjudicate adjustment of status applications filed by arriving aliens in removal proceedings. Even if the person is an LPR, it can be argued that he or she is eligible to file an application for adjustment of status under another basis. *See Matter of Stockwell*, 20 I&N Dec. 309 (BIA 1991) (if conditional LPR status was terminated, the alien may thereafter adjust if there is a legal basis of doing so).

---

[103] *See* note 66, *supra*.

[104] *See* note 44, *supra*.

[105] *See* note 43, *supra*.

[106] Compare the fact that an N-400 can be filed from outside the United States but not an I-131 for a Reentry permit. What public policy or national interest is served by forcing the LPR to come back to the United States? If the issue is that we want to make sure that the LPR still intends to reside permanently in the United States, would not this same rationale require the applicant for naturalization to return?

[107] 22 CFR §50.40.

[108] See text accompanying notes 54 and 55, *supra*.

onerous connection for the LPR, whose attachment to the United States remains suspect and subject to review. This sense of alienation and reservation stems from the fundamental nature of the status of an LPR, namely someone who gets to stay here permanently but is still not really part of us, someone who continues to owe ultimate loyalty and self-definition to a foreign state or sovereign. So long as green-card holders have not violated our laws, or otherwise subjected themselves to justifiable removal, no public interest is advanced when the law refuses to shield them from involuntary loss of status. Our liberties are not made more secure, our federal coffers do not swell with more tax dollars, our enemies are not emboldened, nor are our friends reassured by such an anomalous state of affairs.[109]

Most significantly, if the purpose of our employment immigration laws is to make the American economy more competitive in the global marketplace—it is hard to imagine what other purpose it could possibly have—then the law should work the way the market works. It is simply beyond reason to have market forces operate in the real world but outlawed in the cordon sanitaire of the INA. When U.S. immigration policies are set without reference to global realities, mature industries lose jobs and emerging industries lose something equally precious but harder to spot: the possibility for jobs. These jobs are lost to the U.S. economy even before they are created. The rejection of the global economy inevitably leads to a rejection of immigration itself and fosters the pernicious delusion that ideas and capital, but not people, can cross national boundaries. We cannot do business with the world if we tell its people to stay home or prevent our own from ever leaving. Nothing less than this is at stake. We ask only that the law on abandonment of LPR status not penalize the very patterns of commercial activity that sustain the economy in which we all work and on which we all depend. We call for the adoption of a new view that moves away from the static, formalistic paradigm that we are all familiar with towards a more subtly nuanced world view in which texture and shade now provide context against which intent and the evaluation of its consequences assumes a more complete and robust meaning.

The authors neither contemplate nor endorse the adoption of a rule under which presumption of an intent to retain LPR status would always and forever mandate green card retention. We only decry the involuntary loss of status when the LPR has done nothing other than be a part of the global economy. Nothing would inhibit or restrict immigration authorities from successfully rebutting this presumption through the presentation of significant evidence of abandonment. The presumption is not conclusive—it does not end the inquiry—but it does reflect a bias in favor of LPR retention as a matter of law and policy. Such a presumption derives its principal justification and sustaining rationale from the unremarkable but true realization that, absent contrary facts, permanent residency should mean precisely what it says.

---

[109] Hiroshi Motomura makes an eloquent argument for giving permanent residents the same rights and protections as citizens in *Americans in Waiting—The Lost Story of Immigration and Citizenship in the United States* (2006). Since the late 1700s, immigrants who landed on America's shores were put on a track to citizenship and were treated on an equal footing with citizens. These immigrants, which Motomura terms "Americans in waiting," could vote and were also given diplomatic protection. The concept faded away after it became irrelevant to declare one's intention to become a citizen. He advocates for its revival today.

CHILD CITIZENSHIP ACT OF 2000: WHOLESALE CHANGES TO DERIVATION AND NATURALIZATION FOR CHILDREN

by Kerry E. Doyle and Mary L. Mucha[*]

INTRODUCTION

Children and the treatment of children under the citizenship and naturalization laws of the United States require special consideration, particularly when the children are now adults. It is easy to overlook that even adults who had a family member naturalize when they were young may be the unknowing beneficiaries of an enormous benefit—citizenship in the United States. The value and hidden nature of derivation is no clearer, however, then when one is faced with a person who may be removed or who seeks to naturalize, but is ineligible to do so as a result of criminal convictions or other factors. Although unknowing citizens are not ubiquitous, the enormous pay-off in discovering a client's claim to citizenship makes any immigration attorney remiss without acquiring familiarity with the laws of acquisition, derivation, and §322 of the Immigration and Nationality Act (INA) regarding naturalization for children.

THE SCOPE OF CHANGE UNDER THE CHILD CITIZENSHIP ACT[1]

A significant and important change to the U.S. nationality law was introduced with the passage of the Child Citizenship Act (CCA).[2] Daniel Levy cited the CCA as "the most radical amendment of derivative citizenship since the provision was introduced in 1790.[3] The CCA did indeed dramatically alter the law relating to derivation for the children of naturalized and native-born citizens and of children adopted by U.S. citizens. Smaller but significant changes also were made to §322 naturalization, which provides for the naturalization of children living abroad. The CCA amended INA §§320 and 322, combining some of the provisions of the former §321 into §320 and repealing the remainder.[4] The CCA took effect on February 27, 2001, with interim regulations published and coming into effect on June 13, 2001.[5] Final regulations still have not been issued as of this writing. Finally, the CCA also addressed cases where certain adopted lawful permanent residents (LPR) had voted or made false claims to U.S. citizenship.

Section 320: Derivation of Citizenship

The CCA greatly expands the category of children eligible for derivation of citizenship. Under this new legal formulation, foreign-born children adopted by U.S. citizens who meet the definition of child under the INA, will automatically acquire U.S. citizenship.[6] Formerly, children adopted by U.S.

---

[*] **Kerry E. Doyle** is a partner with the Boston immigration firm of Graves & Doyle. Prior to forming Graves & Doyle with William E. Graves Jr. in August 2001, Ms. Doyle worked in the nonprofit sector representing immigrants, asylum-seekers, and refugees in Boston, Miami, and Hong Kong, and taught a seminar on asylum and refugee law at the University of Miami School of Law in 1997 and 1998. She is currently vice-chair of AILA's New England Chapter and a frequent speaker on immigration and nationality issues. She graduated cum laude from The American University, Washington College of Law with her J.D. in 1993 and George Washington University with her B.A. in 1988.

Mary L. Mucha is the directing attorney of the Los Angeles County Bar Association (LACBA) Immigration Legal Assistance Project. The Immigration Legal Assistance Project provides immigration legal assistance and counseling to all categories of low-income persons. She is a graduate of UCLA and the University of Washington School of Law. She is admitted to practice law in California. Ms. Mucha is an active member of the LACBA Immigration Section Executive Committee, the Southern California Chapter of AILA, and the AILA National Pro Bono Committee. Much of her practice focuses on family-based immigration issues and she frequently speaks on immigration and nationality law issues.

---

[1] AILA Publications is developing a much-needed handbook on children's issues in immigration and nationality law that is scheduled to come out in the near future. Attorneys should e-mail *pubs@aila.org* for further details.

[2] Child Citizenship Act of 2000, Pub. L. No. 106-395, 114 Stat. 1631.

[3] D. Levy, "The Child Citizenship Act of 2000," 6 *Bender's Immigr. Bull.* 293 (Mar. 15, 2001).

[4] 8 USC §§1431, 1432, 1433.

[5] 66 Fed. Reg. 32137 (to be codified at 8 CFR §§103, 310, 320, 322, 334, 337, 338, and 341) (proposed June 13, 2001).

[6] INS Fact Sheet, "How to Get a Certificate of Citizenship for Your Child" (Feb. 27, 2001), *published on* AILA InfoNet at Doc. No. 01030204 (*posted* Mar. 2, 2001).

citizens needed to complete the naturalization process before obtaining citizenship. Many were negatively impacted by the harsh effects of the Illegal Immigration Reform and Immigrant Responsibility Act of 1996 (IIRAIRA)[7] when children adopted as infants or very young children discovered later in life that they were subject to deportation due to, for example, criminal convictions or prior false claims to U.S. citizenship. Congress's stated goal of passing the CCA was an attempt to protect this particular population completely from future deportation by conferring citizenship at the time of immigration.[8]

For adopted children to derive citizenship under the CCA, at least one adoptive parent must be a U.S. citizen, a full and final adoption of the child must take place that meets the requirements of INA §101(b)(l),[9] and the child must be residing in the United States after having been admitted as an immigrant.[10] Derivation occurs once the final qualifying event takes place, so long as the child is under the age of 18 at that time.[11] Derivation benefits under the CCA extend to both adopted children who are not classified as orphans, but who meet the immigration definition of child, and to children adopted as orphans. The definitions of both are found in INA §101(b)(1) under subsections (E) and (F).[12] As with any situation in which derivation occurs, an application for a U.S. passport or citizenship certificate is merely requesting physical proof of what the law already has done automatically, but without visible effect. As such, the application for documentation may be made at any time, regardless of the child's age so long as the requisite conditions were met before the applicant's 18th birthday.

Nonadoptive children also have benefited under the CCA's loosening of requirements for derivation. In many instances in the past, both parents needed to naturalize for a child to derive status. Now, only one parent need naturalize, even when the parents are married and living together.[13] In another important change, a child born abroad whose parent was a citizen at birth also may potentially derive citizenship later on, where previously only children of parents who naturalize after the birth of the child could derive.[14] As with prior versions of this law, and parallel to the requirement for adopted children, biological children must be residing in the legal and physical custody of the citizen parent through whom he or she is deriving citizenship pursuant to a lawful admission for permanent residence.[15] Similarly, all qualifying events must take place while the child is under the age of 18 for derivation to occur.[16]

As in other areas of immigration law, the U.S. Citizenship and Immigration Services (USCIS) will look to the law of the state or country of residence under which the divorce, separation, or adoption took place in determining whether these actions are legally recognized.[17]

Practice Pointer: Acquiring citizenship automatically means citizenship is acquired by operation of law, without the need to apply for citizenship. Thus, a person might be a U.S. citizen without having the proper documents evidencing U.S. citizenship—such as, Certificate of Citizenship or a valid U.S. passport.

Issues of U.S. citizenship often arise during removal proceedings. If respondent has a claim of U.S. citizenship, then do not concede removability. Respondent can present prima facie eligibility of U.S. citizenship before the immigration judge.

Legal Custody

Establishing legal custody in derivation cases often creates problems. Legal separation agreements

---

[7] Pub. L. No. 104-208, div. C, 110 Stat. 3009, 3009-546 to 3009-724.

[8] H.R. 2883, 106th Cong. 2d Sess., Cong. Rec. H7, 774–78 (daily ed. Sept. 19, 2000), S1049I (daily ed. Oct. 12, 2000). S. 1485, 106th Cong. 1st Sess., Cong. Rec. S 13,19I (daily ed. Oct. 26, 1999).

[9] INA §101(b)(1).

[10] INA §321, 8 USC 1431, Amended by Sec. 101(a), Title I, Child Citizenship Act of 2000, Pub. L. No. 106-395, Act of Oct. 30, 2000, 114 Stat. 1631. The adoption, in accordance with INA §101(6)(1), must generally take place prior to the child's 16th birthday, but a narrow exception exists for an older natural sibling of adopted children who may be adopted up to age 18 and still meet the definition of child.

[11] *Id.*

[12] 8 USC §§1101(b)(I)(E), (F).

---

[13] INA §320, *as amended* by Child Citizenship Act of 2000, §101.

[14] INA §320(a)(3), 8 USC §1431(a)(3) as amended by Child Citizenship Act of 2000, §101; *Trop v. Dulles,* 356 U.S. 86 (1957).

[15] *Id.*

[16] *Id.*

[17] 66 Fed. Reg. 32139–40 (introducing regulations and discussing requirements for establishing residence) (proposed June 13, 2001).

and court-ordered custody are required in cases where the child's parents are no longer married. The CCA does not offer any specific relief for this problem, although the interim regulations provide some guidance on USCIS's approach under the new law. The regulations require a final adoption decree to confer legal custody in the case of an adopted child.[18] For derivation of biological children, USCIS will assume that legal custody exists in three specific instances. Contrary evidence may undermine such a finding, however.

Legal custody will be found:

- If the child is living with both biological parents and the parents are married, living in marital union and not separated.

- If a child resides with a surviving biological parent, the other parent having passed away.

- If a biological child is born out of wedlock and who has been legitimated and currently resides with the natural parent.[19]

Although the CCA itself does not specifically mention legitimation,[20] under its predecessor statutes, legacy INS had consistently demanded a showing of legitimation in derivation cases by incorporating this requirement through the definition of child from INA §101(c).[21] Therefore, it is not a surprise to find that USCIS has signaled its clear intention to continue this approach.

For legitimated children whose parents have never been married, however, establishing legal custody by only one parent as required by the CCA would have been impossible using legal interpretations developed prior to the passage of the CCA.[22]

The CCA, however, no longer contains the explicit language regarding legal separation found in the former INA §321(a)(3),[23] and the regulations use a definition of legal custody that incorporates legitimated biological child born out of wedlock "currently residing with the natural parent."[24] Despite the ability of parents with legitimated children born out of wedlock to establish legal custody, USCIS continues to demand a legal separation or divorce for children whose parents were married, combined with an order of sole or joint custody granted to the parent through whom derivation is claimed.[25]

Practice Pointer: Although the parents of legitimated children have additional options under the CCA, the proposed regulations seem to preclude illegitimate children from deriving citizenship in any circumstances whatsoever. Even illegitimate children attempting to derive through his or her mother seem to be precluded from the benefit. Under the previous derivation law, illegitimate children were explicitly permitted to derive when their mothers naturalized,[26] but the CCA has removed this language.[27] Nonetheless, the legislative history of the CCA does not indicate any specific intent to bar illegitimate children from its scope, with Congress focusing instead on the benefits under the CCA for adopted children?'[28]

---

possible, however, if the parents have never been initially married. Therefore, both parents needed to naturalize to avoid the requirement of establishing legal custody. Even the subsequent awarding of legal custody by a court to one parent did not cure the problem or result in derivation on account of the lack of underlying legal separation or divorce. *Id.*

[23] The naturalization of the parent having legal custody of the child when there has been a legal separation of the parents or the naturalization of the mother if the child was born out of wedlock and the paternity of the child has not been established by legitimation. 8 USC §1432 *as amended* by §§4, 5, Act of Oct. 5, 1978, Pub. L. No. 95-417, 92 Stat. 917.

[24] 66 Fed. Reg. 32144 (to be codified at 8 CFR §320.1(1)(iii) (proposed June 13, 2001).

[25] 66 Fed. Reg. 32144 (to be codified at 8 CFR §320.2) (proposed June 13, 2001).

[26] INA §321(a)(3) (repealed), 8 USC §1432(a)(3), *as amended* by §§4, 5, Act of Oct. 5, 1978, Pub. L. 95-417, 92 Stat. 917.

[27] Child Citizenship Act of 2000, Pub. L. No. 106-395, 114 Stat. 1631.

[28] H.R. 2883, 106th Cong. 2d Sess., Cong. Rec. H7,774-78 (daily ed. Sept. 19, 2000), S10491 (daily ed. Oct. 12, 2000).

continued

---

[18] 66 Fed. Reg. 32144 (to be codified as 8 CFR §320.1(2)) (proposed June 13, 2001).

[19] 66 Fed. Reg. 32139 (introducing the regulations establishing parameters for legal custody) (proposed June 13, 2001); 66 Fed. Reg. 32144 (to be codified as 8 CFR §320.1(1)(iii)) (proposed June 13, 2001).

[20] INA §320, 8 USC §1431, as amended by Child Citizenship Act of 2000, §101.

[21] INA §101(c); 8 USC §1101(c). *See* D. Levy, *U.S. Citizenship and Naturalization Handbook* 246 (2001 Ed.).

[22] *D. Levy, supra* note 21, at 239, *citing Matter of H–,* 3 I&N Dec. 742 (BIA 1949); INS Interpretations 320.1(a)(6). *See also Matter of M–,* 3 I&N Dec. 850 (BIA 1950); INS Interp. 320.1(b). Previously, the children of unmarried parents could derive only with the naturalization of both parents because "legal custody" could only be recognized where a "legal separation" had occurred. A "legal separation" is im-

continued

In fact, the CCA seems to explicitly contemplate derivation for single parent children by removing any language relating to derivation through both parents.[29] Therefore, there may be some grounds to challenge USCIS's implementing regulations, particularly in light of the fact that children from countries with strict legitimation laws will be especially impacted.

A separate requirement for establishing the legal custody requirement for children of a legally separated or divorced U.S. citizen parent has been established through regulation.[30] The parent must have custody pursuant to a court order or through "other appropriate government entit[ies]."[31] The award of primary care, control, and maintenance of a minor child or even joint custody will suffice to meet USCIS's requirements. For divorces or separation agreements that lack an explicit determination regarding custody, the law of the state or country of residence at the time of the divorce or separation will be the basis for determining whether legal custody for derivation purposes has occurred.[32] In support of this approach, the Board of Immigration Appeals has found legal custody in derivation cases in the past even without an explicit court order.[33] Presumably, this standard will survive the change in the law, particularly with support of this interpretation by USCIS through its regulations.[34]

Residence

In addition to proving legal custody, the CCA also requires that a child be admitted as a lawful permanent resident and reside in the United States. The introduction to the interim regulations set out the legacy INS interpretation, particularly as it relates to children outside the United States who may still "reside" in the United States for purposes of derivation.[35] The issue of residence is not addressed directly in the body of the regulations, however, leaving beneficiaries to rely upon existing interpretations of the law.

The introduction to the proposed regulations explain that USCIS and the Department of State (DOS) will consider (for now) only two categories of children to have met the residence requirement for derivation. First, a child admitted on or after February 27, 2002, as an LPR who is actually living in the United States will meet the residence requirement. Second, a child who was previously admitted as an LPR, but was abroad on the CCA effective date, but who has returned to the United States and been readmitted as an LPR will also meet the residence requirements.[36]

This latter requirement clearly prevents a child from deriving until his or her readmission as a LPR occurs. This approach is contrary to existing INS interpretations and BIA precedent. In *Matter of D–N–*,[37] the BIA recognized that temporary absences from the United States, even if lengthy, will not "be considered an abandonment of that residence.[38] Moreover, constructive residence in the United States permits the transfer of the benefit of derivation at the time the final qualifying act occurs, without regard to the physical location of the child.[39] Legacy INS had even supported this interpretation under prior derivation laws.[40]

Practice Pointer: This narrower interpretation of residence will be followed by USCIS and DOS without regulatory authority and in relation to a statutory requirement that did not change from previous law. Therefore, the old standard still should be argued because existing USCIS Interpretations and BIA precedent are more authoritative than a policy established through regulatory introduction only.

S. 1485, 106th Cong. 1st Sess., Cong. Rec. S13,191 (daily ed. Oct. 26, 1999).

[29] Child Citizenship Act of 2000, Pub. L. No. 106-395, 114 Stat. 1631.

[30] *Id.*

[31] 66 Fed. Reg. 32144 (to be codified as 8 CFR §320.1(2)) (proposed June 13, 2001).

[32] 66 Fed. Reg. 32139-40 (introducing the regulations establishing parameters for legal custody) (proposed June 13, 2001); 66 Fed. Reg. 32144 (to be codified as 8 CFR §320.1(2)) (proposed June 13, 2001).

[33] *Matter of M–,* 3 I&N Dec. 850 (BIA 1950).

[34] 66 Fed. Reg. 32144 (to be codified as 8 CFR §320.1(2)) (pro posed June 13, 2001).

[35] 66 Fed. Reg. 32139 (proposed June 13, 2001) (introducing the regulations).

[36] *Id.*

[37] 4 I&N Dec. 692 (BIA 1952).

[38] *Id.*

[39] INS Interp. 320.1(f).

[40] INS Interp. 320.1(f). See *U.S. Citizenship and Naturalization Handbook* 232–33 (2001 Ed.) for additional discussion of the required residence of the child in derivation cases.

Retroactive Effect

The CCA came into effect on February 27, 2001, 120 days after the date of enactment.[41] As of that day, all children, including adopted children, who met the new requirements under INA §320 derived citizenship. Legacy INS had taken the position through regulation that the CCA is not retroactive for persons who reached their 18th birthday prior to February 27, 2001.[42]

In addition, recent cases have supported legacy INS's interpretation,[43] rejecting arguments that the CCA has retroactive effect.[44] *See Drakes v. Ashcroft*, 323 F.3d 189, 191 (2d Cir. 2003).

Practice Pointer: CCA applies to a child born on or after February 28, 1983. Check the birth certificate of the child along with any other government issued documents to confirm the birth date of the child. Thus, children over the age of 18 as of February 27, 2001, must meet the generally more restrictive requirements of the law as it stood prior to the CCA.

Section 322: Naturalization of Foreign-Born Children

In addition to altering the landscape of derivation of citizenship, the CCA concomitantly impacted the naturalization of children residing abroad under INA §322. Section 322 permits the naturalization of a child through an application lodged by a citizen parent. It permits naturalization for those children who did not acquire citizenship at birth and for those residing abroad who, therefore, are ineligible for derivation under the CCA. Unlike acquisition and derivation, however, citizenship is not automatically obtained and a naturalization process is required.

The law currently requires: (1) that at least one of the parents of the child is a U.S. citizen, whether by birth or naturalization; (2) that the child resides outside the United States; (3) that the child is temporarily present in the United States pursuant to lawful admission; (4) that the child is maintaining lawful status in the United States; (5) that the child is under the age of 18 years; and (6) that the child is in the legal and physical custody of the citizen parent.[45] There also is a physical presence requirement that may be fulfilled by either the citizen parent or grandparent of the child. This requirement states generally that either the U.S. citizen parent or the citizen parent of the citizen parent must have been physically present in the United States for a period or periods totaling not less than five years. At least two of those five years must be after attaining the age of 14.[46]

Practice Pointer: A child acquires U.S. citizenship automatically under §320. Under §322, children acquire citizenship by "application" to USCIS and must go through the naturalization process.

Although much of the new §322 mirrors its previous incantation,[47] most significantly, the law now requires the beneficiary child to reside outside the United States. Additionally, the child must be in the legal and physical custody of the citizen parent.[48] Unless constructive residence outside the United States may be argued,[49] both the child and the parent must therefore be physically living outside the United States.[50] A child also needs to be temporarily present in the United States pursuant to a lawful admission and must maintain such lawful status until the time of adjudication of the §322 application for naturalization.[51]

The impact of this change under the CCA has been felt by persons who filed under §322 for the naturalization of their child while their child was residing in the United States in a lawful status other than lawful permanent residence. As a non–LPR, the child will not be eligible for As a non–LPR, the child will not be eligible for immediate derivative under the CCA, but he or she will likewise be ineligible to naturalize under §322 because of the new residence re-

---

[41] Section 104, Title I, Child Citizenship Act of 2000, Pub. L. No. 106-395, Act of October 30, 2000, 114 Stat. 1631.

[42] 66 Fed. Reg. 32137 (to be codified at 8 CFR §§103, 310, 320,322, 334, 337, 338 and 341) (proposed June 13, 2001); *Matter of Rodriguez-Tejedor*, 23 I&N Dec. 153 (BIA 2001), citing 66 Fed. Reg. at 32,139; 8 CFR §320.2(a)(2).

[43] *Matter of Rodriguez-Tejedor*, 23 I&N Dec. 153 (BIA 2001).

[44] *Nehme v. INS*, 252 F.3d 415 (5th Cir. 2001); *Hughes v. Ashcroft*, No. 99-70565, 2001 WL 699357 (9th Cir. June 22, 2001).

[45] INA §322(a), 8 USC §1433(a), as amended by Child Citizenship Act of 2000, §102.

[46] INA §322(a)(2), 8 USC §1433(a)(2), as amended by Child Citizenship Act of 2000, §102.

[47] See D. Levy, *supra* note 3, at 295, for additional discussion of the requirements of §322.

[48] INA §322(a)(4), 8 USC §1433(a)(4), as amended by Child Citizenship Act of 2000, §102.

[49] *See, supra,* footnotes 36–40 and related discussion.

[50] INA §322(a)(4), 8 USC §1433(a)(4), as amended by Child Citizenship Act of 2000, §102.

[51] *Id.*

quirements. Additionally, even if an argument can be made that the child's and parent's residence remains in a foreign country, despite their physical presence in the United States, failure of the child to maintain lawful status will also bar the child from §322 under the CCA. In addition, the INS began applying the new requirements of §322 as of February 27, 2001, even for cases pending at that time.[52] As a result, the Service has been denying cases for failure to meet the new overseas residence requirements or for failure of the child to maintain lawful status.

Application for naturalization under §322 also may be made for an adopted child of a U.S. citizen. All the general elements of the section must be fulfilled, as with natural children, but the requirements of INA §101(b)(1) for adoption must also be met for naturalization to be granted.[53] Similar issues with legal custody arise under §322 as they did under §320, as the proposed regulations utilize the same definition of legal custody.[54]

Although §322 requires the child to complete a naturalization process, neither the good moral character nor English and civics requirements apply. Other bars to naturalization such as ongoing removal proceedings that exist for adult applicants are also not found under §322.[55] The interim regulations mirror the statute and do not currently require any additional elements other than those outlined in the statute for a child to naturalize under §322.[56] However, the requirement for an oath of allegiance continues.[57] Under current law, anyone unable to under-stand the meaning of the oath of allegiance may be exempted

from the requirement by the attorney general.[58] The CCA amendment of §322 should not alter the on-going availability of the oath waiver. Previous legacy INS interpretations of the law permitted the waiver of the oath regardless of whether the child was too young to understand the oath or there was a developmental reason that inhibited the child's understanding.[59] Nothing in the current regulations or in the introduction to the regulations makes any indication that this interpretation and application of the law will change.

Practice Pointer: The child must be residing abroad and coming temporarily to the United States to pursue the naturalization process. The child cannot naturalize and remain in the United States permanently. The child must go back to their residency abroad.

THE IMPACT OF THE HAGUE CONVENTION ON ADOPTED CHILDREN

The Hague Convention entered into force with respect to the United States on April 1, 2008. The Convention establishes procedures to be followed in these intercountry adoption cases and imposes safeguards to protect the best interests of children. The Hague Convention provides a framework for the adoption of children habitually resident in one country that is a party to the Convention by persons habitually resident in another country that is also a party to the Convention. DOS published a final rule on October 30, 2007,[60] establishing the new procedure that consular officers will follow in adjudicating cases of children whose cases are covered by the Convention.

Keep in mind that the Convention on the Intercountry Adoption Act of 2000 (IAA) makes significant changes to the INA. It creates a new definition of "child" applicable in Convention adoption cases, found at INA §101(b)(1)(G). It also amends the affidavit of support to treat the Hague adopted child as deriving citizenship, allows the filing of the I-864W, and amends the provisions of allowance of the N-600K. The regulations also create new categories for the processing of immigrant visas under the Convention. Under the IH-3: A Hague child adopted abroad is an automatic citizen for the child when entering

---

[52] 66 Fed. Reg. 32141 (introducing the regulations) (proposed June 13, 2001)

[53] 66 Fed. Reg. 32145-46 (to be codified at 8 CFR §322.2(b)) (proposed June 13, 2001).

[54] 66 Fed. Reg. 32145 (to be codified at 8 CFR §322.1(1)) (proposed June 13, 2001). *See also* E. Anderson & D. Berger, "Adopted Children and the Child Citizenship Act of 2000," 20 *Immigration Law Today* 1 (Jan./Feb. 2001).

[55] Compare INA §322(a), 8 USC §1433(a) *as amended by* Child Citizenship Act of 2000, §102 and 66 Fed. Reg. 32145-46 (to be codified at 8 CFR §322) (proposed June 13, 2001) to INA §321(a)(3), 8 USC §1432(a)(3) as amended by §§4, 5, Act of Oct. 5, 1978, Pub. L. No. 95-417, 92 Stat. 917 and 8 CFR §322.

[56] *See* 66 Fed. Reg. 32145–47 (to be codified as 8 CFR §322.1–322.5) (proposed June 13, 2001).

[57] INA §322(b); 8 USC §1433(b) as amended by the Child Citizenship Act of 2000, §102.

[58] INA §337(a), 8 USC §1448(a).

[59] D. Levy, *supra* note 3, at 298 nn. 83, 84, *citing* INS Interp. 322.3(b)(3) and (4).

[60] 72 Fed. Reg. 61301 (Oct. 30, 2007).

the United States. An IH-4 Hague child coming to be adopted in the United States is a lawful permanent resident until the adoption is complete.

Ancillary Impacts of the CCA

In addition to the specific changes made by the CCA to the derivation requirements and the naturalization of children living abroad, the CCA has changed other areas of immigration law. The CCA impacted requirements for affidavits of support in certain cases. Applicants eligible for lawful permanent residence through a family petition must obtain an affidavit of support (I-864) from their sponsors. The financial obligation of the sponsor continues until the beneficiary becomes a U.S. citizen or completes 40 quarters of work.[61] As a result of the CCA, certain children of U.S. citizens will derive citizenship the instant after having been granted permanent residence, thus rendering the affidavit of support irrelevant in these cases.

In recognition of this reality, legacy INS issued a memorandum indicating that it will no longer require an affidavit of support for children applying for lawful permanent residence who are eligible for derivation.[62] This change is particularly important for low-income families who may otherwise be incapable of meeting the income requirements for an affidavit of support. It also releases all families petitioning children from some paperwork, and, if consular processing, from the processing fee now required by the consulates with affidavits of support reviewed in the United States.[63]

Practice Pointer: An I-864W is filed for children not needing an affidavit of support because of derivation of citizenship through one citizen parent. However, stepchildren are not covered by this new change in the law.

The CCA also provides protection for certain people who made false claims to citizenship or who voted unlawfully from findings of inadmissibility, deportability, lack of good moral character, and criminal prosecution.[64] Although helpful, the scope of the change is very limited because only those persons who believed themselves to be a citizen, whose parents are both citizens, and who were granted lawful permanent residence prior to the age of 16 are protected under this amendment.[65]

Finally, the changes made to INA §§322 and 320 by the CCA have created an untenable situation for some children living outside the United States whose parents are separated or divorced. If the U.S. citizen parent lives in the United States, but the child resides mainly with his or her other parent outside the United States, the child will not be able to derivation under §320, or naturalize under §322. This occurs because a child who merely visits his or her U.S. citizen mother or father during school vacations may not have the requisite intent to receive permanent residence in the United States. Without LPR status, a child cannot derive citizenship.

Likewise, a child can no longer qualify under §322 when his or her U.S. citizen parent resides in the United States. Perhaps USCIS can address the negative consequence of the CCA for children in these circumstances through regulation to permit children to receive permanent residence, and thus derive, even when the child's residence in the United States may be temporary or short-lived. Alternatively, when joint custody exists, an argument may be made that the child resides with both parents and that the child, therefore, has the requisite intent to reside in the United States, despite the length of time the child actually spends physically in the United States.

CONCLUSION

The broadening of derivation under the CCA heightens the need for attorneys to review their client's history because larger numbers of people will be deriving citizenship. As derivation acts silently and without obvious effect, however, beneficiaries must rely even more upon competent legal representation to protect their interests. Although the proposed regulations indicate a narrowing of eligibility for derivation under the CCA for illegitimate children and have restricted the interpretation of legal custody and residence under the CCA, the overall

---

[61] INA §213A(a)(2); 8 CFR §213a.2(e)(1)(i)(A).

[62] INS Memorandum, M. Pearson, "Effect of Enactment of the Child Citizenship Act of 2000 On the Affidavit of Support Requirements under INA §§212(a)(4) and 213A," (May 17, 2001), *published on* AILA InfoNet at Doc. No. 01060821 (*posted* June 8, 2001).

[63] 22 CFR §22.1; 60 Fed. Reg. 14901 (to be codified at 22 CFR §22.1) (proposed Mar. 28, 2002); 66 Fed. Reg. 16483–84 (proposed Apr. 5, 2002).

---

[64] D. Levy, *supra* note 3, at 301 n. 128, *citing* Child Citizenship Act of 2000, Pub. L. No. 106-395, §201(a)(1), 114 Stat. 1631 (Oct. 30, 2000).

[65] *Id.*

impact of the CCA has been positive for many young people in the United States.

The CCA's changes to childhood naturalization under §322 restricted access to naturalization for some children, but, nonetheless, many children will continue to qualify for important benefits under §322. Fortunately, USCIS has not narrowed the statute with the very restrictive regulations published prior to the passage of the CCA.[66] Section 322 also should be utilized whenever possible, as it is an important tool in protecting young people from future deportation if they move back to the United States—particularly given the increasing number of deportable offenses and grounds of inadmissibility, even for LPRs. Section 322 should be utilized for children while they are as young as possible so they may receive U.S. citizenship and guaranteed unfettered access to the United States as well as to the full range of constitutional rights only U.S. citizens enjoy.

ADVANCED ISSUES IN NATURALIZATION: PRACTICAL PROBLEMS AND SOLUTIONS

by Margaret D. Stock[*]

Naturalization applications were once considered to be a relatively easy area of immigration practice. Yet with record numbers of immigrants filing for citizenship,[1] new fee increases, large backlogs,[2] increased scrutiny and denial of applications by U.S. Citizenship and Immigration Services (USCIS) examiners,[3] and an upcoming election focusing attention on voter qualifications, immigration practitioners are more likely than ever to face complicated naturalization issues. This article will look at some of the more common "advanced" naturalization scenarios and suggest solutions for handling similar cases. This article assumes that the reader has a basic understanding of the mechanics of filing a naturalization application and the *prima facie* requirements for U.S. citizenship.

INTRODUCTION

This article will explore some common "advanced" naturalization issues by using examples based on real cases, some of which have been published and others that this author has advised on or handled.[4] Where applicable, footnotes will refer to the published cases on which these scenarios are based. Readers are urged to consult the actual cases for more details regarding the scenarios.

SUBSTANTIVE PROBLEMS IN QUALIFYING FOR NATURALIZATION

Citizens Trying to Naturalize

Facts. Bamidele came to the United States from Nigeria on an immigrant visa at the age of 12 after her father was granted an employment-based green card and she followed to join him along with her mother and siblings. Her father became a naturalized U.S. citizen (USC) in 2003, when Bamidele was 16 and living at home with him in New York, but he did not file anything to obtain Bamidele's U.S. citizenship. Her parents always told Bamidele that it should be her "choice" whether or not to become an American, and she could decide when she turned 18. Bamidele was busy with school, however, and never got around to filing for citizenship when she reached the age of majority. She is now about to graduate from college and has been offered a job with the federal government—but U.S. citizenship is a requirement of the job. Bamidele filed an N-400 application, but has been told that slow processing times make it unlikely that her application will be approved for more than a year, and her job starts in a few months. What can Bamidele do?

Legal Analysis. Bamidele is already an American citizen, and can file for a passport to obtain proof of citizenship. If she desires, she can request expedited issuance of the passport by paying an extra fee. Under the Child Citizenship Act of 2000,[5] there are three requirements, which, if met, result in automatic U.S. citizenship for a child born outside the United States. The child must: (1) have a parent who is a citizen of the United States, whether by birth or naturalization; (2) be under the age of 18;

[*] **Margaret D. Stock** is an attorney admitted in Alaska and a Lieutenant Colonel, Military Police Corps, U.S. Army Reserve. Ms. Stock earned her undergraduate (A.B. 1985) degree in government at Harvard-Radcliffe; her law degree at Harvard Law School (J.D. 1992); and a master's degree (M.P.A. 2001) at the John F. Kennedy School of Government at Harvard University. Ms. Stock currently serves as a Drilling Individual Mobilization Augmentee (DIMA) (Associate Professor) in the Department of Social Sciences, United States Military Academy, West Point, New York. The opinions expressed in this article are her own, and not necessarily the opinions of any government agency.

[1] C. Strohm, "Citizenship Applications Backlog May Deny Voting Eligibility," *Congress Daily* (Apr. 2, 2008), *available at www.govexec.com/dailyfed/0308/040208cdpm2.htm.*

[2] Migration Policy Institute, "Immigration Facts: Behind the Naturalization Backlog: Causes, Context, and Concerns" (Feb. 2008), *available at http://www.migrationpolicy.org/pubs/FS21_NaturalizationBacklog_022608.pdf.*

[3] J. Preston, "Perfectly Legal Immigrants, Until They Applied for Citizenship," *N.Y. Times*, Apr. 12, 2008 ("In 2007, 89,683 applications for naturalization were denied, about 12 percent of those presented. In the last 12 years, denial rates have been consistently higher than at any time since the 1920s.").

[4] My thanks to Kathrin S. Mautino for suggesting this format.

[5] Child Citizenship Act of 2000, Pub. L. No. 106-395, 114 Stat. 1631 (Oct. 30, 2000).

and (3) be residing in the United States in the legal and physical custody of the citizen parent pursuant to a lawful admission for permanent residence.[6] Bamidele met all three of these conditions at the point in time when her father naturalized, and so despite her lack of proof of her U.S. citizenship, Bamidele has been a USC since the date of her father's naturalization. Bamidele is not required to file an N-600 to obtain proof of her citizenship; instead, she can file directly for a U.S. passport.[7] Many experts would encourage Bamidele to file an N-600 later, after she has the passport, so that the Department of Homeland Security (DHS) will update its records to reflect her U.S. citizenship. DHS does not currently update its immigration files automatically when someone receives a U.S. passport, so failure to file an N-600 may lead to problems with employment verification systems such as eVerify. In some cases, DHS also has wrongly arrested USCs who derived citizenship automatically; filing an N-600 can put DHS on notice that a person has a claim to U.S. citizenship so as to prevent such wrongful arrests and/or buttress a claim for damages for wrongful detention if DHS should wrongly arrest or detain the derivative USC. Bamidele's N-400 application should be denied by DHS because she is already a citizen; unfortunately, DHS will not readily refund the N-400 filing fee, and will require her to pay a new filing fee when she files her N-600. This case reflects a common fact scenario that this author has encountered and demonstrates why practitioners should always screen naturalization applicants to be sure that they are not already (unbeknownst to themselves) American citizens.

Good Moral Character Issues

Good moral character issues can be a major stumbling block to approval of a naturalization application. Applicants for U.S. citizenship are required to demonstrate that they have good moral character for the required statutory period described in the statute under which they are applying for naturalization; this period may vary from no specific time[8] to five years.[9] Before filing a naturalization

application for a client, practitioners should ask: (1) Is the applicant statutorily barred from establishing good moral character during the required period?[10] (2) Are there other reasons why USCIS might determine that the applicant lacks good moral character during the statutory period? (3) Has the applicant done something outside any required statutory period that may show lack of good moral character?[11] The following scenarios illustrate the range of current "good moral character" issues that practitioners may encounter.

Probation or Parole

Facts. Angel is a lawful permanent resident (LPR) who filed an application for naturalization. While the application was pending, he pled guilty to the offense of failing to file a monetary and currency report when entering the United States with a large amount of cash.[12] He was fined and sentenced to three years probation. USCIS has denied his naturalization application, citing 8 CFR §316.10(c)(1), which prohibits USCIS from approving a petition for naturalization while the petitioner remains on probation or parole. Can Angel overcome this denial?

Legal Analysis. Yes, Angel can argue that serving a sentence of probation does not preclude a finding that he is of good moral character, but is just one factor to be considered in determining whether he is of good moral character. Angel should file an appeal of the naturalization denial, and if that does not succeed, an action in federal district court under INA §310(c), requesting de novo review of his denied naturalization application. Angel's attorney should check to be sure that the offense for which he is serving probation

---

[6] INA §320.

[7] At the time of this writing, passport applications were also less expensive and were being processed much more quickly than N-600 applications.

[8] For example, under INA §329, the wartime military naturalization statute, there is no specific time period of good moral character required.

[9] *See, e.g.,* INA §§316(a)(1), (2), and (3), stating that the statutory period under which good moral character is assessed is "five years immediately preceding the date of filing his application … up to the time of admission to citizenship."

[10] *See* INA §101(f) (listing statutory bars to establishing good moral character).

[11] Under INA §316(e), the government is not limited to the statutory period "[i]n determining whether the applicant has sustained the burden of establishing good moral character …;" the government "shall not be limited to the applicant's conduct during the five years preceding the filing of the application, but may take into consideration as a basis for such determination the applicant's conduct and acts at any time prior to that period." 8 CFR §316.10(a)(2) provides that conduct prior to the five-year statutory period should be considered to the extent it may "appear relevant to a determination of the applicant's present moral conduct."

[12] This hypothetical is based on the facts of *Angel v. Chertoff*, 2007 U.S. Dist. LEXIS 78084 (S.D. Ill. 2007).

is not an offense that renders him statutorily ineligible for naturalization.[13] Because it is not, he can argue that the regulation purports to add a new category of applicants who are *per se* ineligible to naturalize, and that USCIS has exceeded its authority by adopting such a regulation. Thus, the fact that Angel is on probation is one factor among many in the determination that he possesses good moral character, but it cannot bar Angel *per se*.

Failure to Pay or File Tax Returns

Facts. Monica is an LPR who travels frequently in and out of the United States, and maintains homes in both the U.S. and her home country. On the advice of her accountant, Monica has been claiming non-resident tax status in the United States in order to minimize her U.S. taxes. What effect, if any, does this have on her naturalization eligibility?

Legal Analysis. In some USCIS offices, naturalization applicants are asked to provide proof that they have filed their taxes; unless an applicant is exempt from filing taxes, failure to file income tax returns can be evidence of a lack of good moral character that can be used to deny a citizenship application. Failure to file can also lead to a criminal conviction that may result in deportation. Monica has filed taxes, but she has filed as a non-resident. While it may be legally permissible[14] for her to file as a non-resident under tax laws, DHS has taken the position that filing as a non-resident is evidence that an LPR has abandoned his or her lawful permanent residence.[15] If Monica files for naturalization without resolving this issue (perhaps by filing amended returns and paying whatever taxes are owed), her application could be denied and she may face difficulty entering the United States as an LPR upon returning from a future trip abroad. Practitioners with clients in this situation should consult a tax expert for assistance with resolving problems involving

back taxes; often these problems can be resolved by filing amended returns or late returns and paying the required penalty fees and back taxes. In some cases, and where an alien's income is low enough to qualify for assistance, it may make sense to use the free Internal Revenue Service (IRS) Taxpayer Assistance Centers to prepare and file returns.[16] Once the amended returns are filed, the alien may be able proceed with a naturalization application. Some USCIS offices require all past taxes to be paid in full before approving a naturalization application; others will only require that the applicant have made payment arrangements—such as a payment plan—with the IRS. A practitioner with a client such as Monica will also want to analyze the case fully to determine whether abandonment of lawful permanent residence is at issue, perhaps due to long residence abroad.

Failure to Pay Child Support

Facts. Leah is an LPR who has been in the United States for ten years and wants to naturalize. Leah and her USC husband divorced a year ago, and the husband received physical custody of the couple's two children, with Leah receiving joint legal custody. Leah was ordered by the divorce court to pay child support of $500 per month. Leah has been irritated at her husband because of the divorce, and has not been paying the child support on time. She now has arrears of about $2,000. Her husband has been hinting that he will go back to court to force her to pay the arrearage; he also threatened to tell DHS that she hasn't been paying her support obligation. What problems might the child support arrearage pose for approval of Leah's naturalization application?

Legal Analysis. DHS takes the position that deliberate or willful failure to pay child support can constitute a lack of good moral character;[17] such failure can also be a federal or state crime. Leah's irritation at her husband does not excuse her from complying with a court-ordered child support order. Leah's failure to pay her child support obligation can potentially lead to criminal penalties that might

---

[13] *See, e.g.*, INA §101(f) and INA §§313–315.

[14] Most LPRs are required to file taxes as "residents" under U.S. tax law, regardless of how much time they spend in the United States, *but see* Paula N. Singer, "Practice Advisory: The U.S. Tax Obligations of Foreign-Born Persons: Debunking the Myths," *Immigration Law Today* (Mar. 2002).

[15] Filing Tax Return as Nonresident—Filing income tax return as a nonresident alien raises rebuttable presumption that person has abandoned Lawful Permanent Resident status. Legacy Immigration and Naturalization Service (INS) Memorandum, David Martin, General Counsel, INS, HQ 70/11-P, 70/33-P (May 7, 1996), *reprinted in* 73 *Interpreter Releases* 929, 948–50 (July 15, 1996); 8 CFR §316.5(c)(2).

[16] Whether to use an Internal Revenue Service (IRS) Taxpayer Assistance Center to prepare and file returns is a judgment call by the attorney and client, but these Centers do provide their services for free to eligible taxpayers, so this is an option when the high cost of hiring an outside accountant or tax expert is deterring a client from complying with U.S. tax laws. The staff of these Centers will prepare federal tax returns and arrange for payment plans.

[17] 8 CFR §316.10(c)(1); *see also* INS Interpretation 316.1(f)(5).

result in removal proceedings. Under the Child Support Recovery Act of 1992,[18] it is a federal criminal offense to: (1) willfully fail to pay a support obligation with respect to a child who resides in another state, if such obligation has remained unpaid for a period longer than one year, or is greater than $5,000; (2) to travel in interstate or foreign commerce with the intent to evade a support obligation, if such obligation has remained unpaid for a period longer than one year, or is greater than $5,000; or (3) to willfully fail to pay a support obligation with respect to a child who resides in another state, if such obligation has remained unpaid for a period longer than two years, or is greater than $10,000. Leah may also be in violation of state criminal law. Were Leah's failure to pay due to financial difficulties, the result might be different; if this is the case, however, Leah should show that she has gone to state court to try to get the obligation reduced. If an applicant can demonstrate that he or she is unemployed or otherwise financially unable to pay the child support, he or she can still be naturalized, notwithstanding a child support obligation that has not been paid. Practitioners should also note that failure to pay child support can also lead the State Department to refuse to issue a U.S. passport, once the applicant has naturalized.[19] Leah should pay her child support arrearage before applying for naturalization.

Drunk Driving

Facts. José is an LPR who has been in the United States for more than 40 years and wants to become a USC.[20] He has five driving while intoxicated (DWI or DUI) offenses, but only one of them occurred in the past five years. For this latest offense, he was found sitting in the driver's seat of a parked but running car while he was intoxicated; he was sentenced to pay a fine and serve five years of probation, which he will complete in a few months. Is he eligible to naturalize? What problems might he expect in trying to naturalize?

Legal Analysis. José can expect a vigorous examination centering on whether he has the good moral character necessary for citizenship. Drunk driving offenses can affect whether an applicant for

naturalization is deemed to be of good moral character.[21] Drunk driving offenses may be considered crimes involving moral turpitude (CIMT), and a CIMT committed during the five years preceding an application for naturalization can preclude a finding of good moral character.[22] If a particular drunk driving offense is deemed to be an aggravated felony, it can bar an applicant entirely from naturalizing (and lead to deportation or removal).[23] In this case, the facts indicate that the particular drunk driving offense at issue is not a crime of moral turpitude or an aggravated felony, so the CIMT and aggravated felony bars do not apply. José must still show good moral character for the five years prior to filing his application and up until he becomes a citizen;[24] a USCIS examiner may also take into account his behavior prior to the five years if this behavior is relevant.[25] It is possible for José to show that he has good moral character despite his drunk driving conviction, but he must be prepared for a rigorous interview. If he admits responsibility for his past behavior, shows that he has been rehabilitated, and is honest in his answers during the interview, his chances are improved. An examiner may also consider his

---

[21] INS regulations preclude a finding of good moral character where an applicant has "committed unlawful acts that adversely reflect upon the applicant's moral character" during the five year statutory period, except where extenuating circumstances exist, even if such acts do not constitute crimes of moral turpitude pursuant to INA §101(f)(3); *see* 8 CFR §§316.10(b)(1) and (3)(iii).

[22] *See* INA §101(f)(3) (precluding a finding of good moral character where an applicant, during the five year statutory period preceding his application for naturalization, has committed a crime of moral turpitude).

[23] In *Leocal v. Ashcroft*, 543 U.S. 1 (2004), a unanimous Supreme Court held that state drunk driving offenses with a mens rea of negligence or less are not crimes of violence, as defined under 18 USC §16, and, therefore, are not aggravated felonies under INA §101(a)(43)(F). Other drunk driving offenses may still be aggravated felonies, however, so practitioners are urged to analyze the particular facts and statutes carefully in any given case.

[24] *See* INA §§316(a)(1), (2), and (3).

[25] INA §316(e) further provides that "in determining whether the applicant has sustained the burden of establishing good moral character ... the Attorney General shall not be limited to the applicant's conduct during the five years preceding the filing of the application, but may take into consideration as a basis for such determination the applicant's conduct and acts at any time prior to that period." 8 CFR §316.10(a)(2) provides that conduct prior to the five-year statutory period should be considered to the extent it may "appear relevant to a determination of the applicant's present moral conduct."

---

[18] 18 USC §228.

[19] *See* U.S. Dep't of State, Child Support Payments and Getting a U.S. Passport, *available at www.travel.state.gov/ passport/ppi/family/family_863.html*.

[20] This scenario is based loosely on the facts of *Rico v. INS*, 262 F. Supp. 2d 6 (E.D.N.Y. 2003).

drunk driving offenses to be evidence that José is a habitual drunkard who is barred from establishing good moral character.[26] José's likelihood of success is greater if he has stopped driving, given up his driver's license, completed formal alcohol treatment, attended alcohol counseling classes, or stopped drinking altogether.

Unlawful Voting

Facts. Ellen is an LPR who applied to renew her state driver's license and also registered to vote at the same time by checking the box on the license application indicating that she was a USC.[27] Later, her state mailed her a Notice of Voter Registration in the mail, confirming that she was registered to vote. Ellen then voted in the upcoming primary and general election, believing that it was her civic duty to do so. Now Ellen wants to apply for naturalization; is she barred from naturalizing because she has voted?

Legal Analysis. Ellen should review carefully the state law at issue, and determine what *mens rea* is required to violate the statute. Ellen may be able to argue that she did not violate the law because she did not possess the requisite intent; for example, if the law requires her to vote "knowingly," perhaps she did not realize that she was not eligible to vote. If she applies for naturalization, it is possible that she will be placed into removal proceedings and charged with removability under INA §237(a)(6)(A) for voting in violation of state law. Ellen will likely be required to testify about her intent in registering to vote. If she does not have the *mens rea* required to violate the law, she may be able to defend against the removability charge. It is also possible that USCIS will allow her to naturalize despite her past voting; to determine when this may be the case, Ellen should review carefully the DHS Memorandum on this subject.[28] According to this Memorandum, USCIS examiners will follow a six-step checklist in determining how to handle cases where an alien has registered to vote or voted unlawfully. A false claim to U.S. citizenship is also a ground of

inadmissibility,[29] but a naturalization applicant is not required to prove that he or she is admissible—and thus can still potentially naturalize, notwithstanding having made a false claim to U.S. citizenship.

Alien Smuggling

Facts. Gloria has been an LPR for five years and wants to apply for citizenship so she can sponsor her minor children for lawful permanent residence; the children are currently on the waiting list in the Family 2A category due to visa petitions that Gloria filed previously. The children are in the United States right now, however, because Gloria sent money to a coyote who smuggled the children into the United States about four years ago, after Gloria obtained her LPR status. Gloria has not been convicted of any smuggling offense. Is Gloria barred from becoming a U.S. citizen?

Legal analysis. A conviction for alien smuggling is an aggravated felony unless it was a first offense for smuggling an immediate family member.[30] An aggravated felony conviction can bar an applicant entirely from naturalization. Although this bar does not apply to Gloria because she has not been convicted of anything, anyone who commits alien smuggling—even if the person has not been convicted of any offenses—is removable.[31] The definition of alien smuggling is broad and covers anyone who has "encouraged, induced, assisted, abetted, or aided" anyone to enter the United States illegally.[32] Gloria will have difficulty establishing that she is of good moral character because the smuggling took place within the five-year period of required good moral character. If she is placed into proceedings as a result of admitting to the offense of alien smuggling, there is a discretionary waiver available from the immigration judge under INA §237(a)(1)(E)(iii). There is also an exemption from deportation avail-

---

[26] INA §101(f)(1).

[27] This hypothetical is based loosely on the facts described in the case *McDonald v. Gonzales*, 400 F.3d 684 (9th Cir. 2005), ably handled by AILA member Stuart Folinsky.

[28] U.S. Citizenship and Immigration Services (USCIS) Memorandum, W. Yates, "Procedures for Handling Naturalization Applications of Aliens Who Voted Unlawfully or Falsely Represented Themselves as U.S. Citizens by Voting or Registering to Vote" (May 7, 2002), *published on* AILA InfoNet at Doc. No. 05030768 (*posted* Mar. 7, 2005).

---

[29] INA §212(a)(6)(C)(ii)(I) ("Any alien who falsely represents, or has falsely represented, himself or herself to be a citizen of the United States for any purpose or benefit under this Act (including section 274A) or any other Federal or State law is inadmissible.").

[30] INA §101(a)(43)(N).

[31] INA §237(a)(1)(E).

[32] For a full discussion of what constitutes "smuggling," *see Covarrubias v. Gonzales*, 487 F.3d 742 (9th Cir. 2007) (upholding agency determination of lack of good moral character for alien who gave money to a smuggler to bring his brother into the United States unlawfully).

able to certain aliens who immigrated through the Family Unity program.[33]

Lack of Ability to Speak English

Facts. Maria came to the United States as the mother of a USC in 1995 and is now 75 years old. She wants to become a citizen, but she never learned to read and write in her home country, where she spoke an indigenous language. She has been attending citizenship classes at an adult learning center for the past year, but has only learned a few basic English sentences, and she cannot read or write anything in English except her name and address. Can Maria become a U.S. citizen despite her inability to speak, read, or write English?

Legal Analysis. INA §312(b) provides that naturalization applicants who are 50 years of age or older and who have had LPR status for many years can be automatically exempted from the English reading, writing, and speaking requirements. A person age 50 or older who has been an LPR for 20 years or more qualifies for such an automatic exemption; a person age 55 or older who has been an LPR for 15 years or more also qualifies. A person age 65 or older who has been an LPR for 20 years is automatically exempt from the English requirement, and also qualifies to take an easier history and civics test, based on a list of only 25 questions.[34] Unfortunately, Maria has not had her LPR status for the requisite time period for either of these automatic exemptions; accordingly, she will be required to take the English test and the regular history and civics test. All is not lost, however—under 8 CFR §312.2(c)(2), USCIS officers in their discretion are directed to give "due consideration … to the applicant's education, background, age, length of residence in the U.S., opportunities available and efforts made to acquire the requisite knowledge, and any other elements or factors relevant to an appraisal of the applicant's knowledge and understanding." There is no formal process to apply for "due consideration," but it is a good idea for the applicant to file a letter asking for due consideration, and explaining circumstances such as a lack of formal education, advanced age, long residence in the United States, attendance at citizenship classes, and other factors that bear on the applicant's fitness and ability to become an American citizen.

Disabilities

Facts. Marcus is a 60-year-old LPR who has been diagnosed with Alzheimer's disease, a form of dementia that affects thought, memory, and language. Marcus has only had his LPR status for five years, and thus is not automatically exempt from the English reading, writing, and speaking requirements for naturalization. Marcus was able to speak a little English before being diagnosed with Alzheimer's, but his English ability has deteriorated recently. He cannot read and write English at all, and has trouble remembering the answers to the history and government questions. Can Marcus become a U.S. citizen, despite being unable to speak, read, and write English, or pass the required history and government test?

Legal Analysis. Yes, Marcus can become a citizen, if he can obtain the proper certification from a physician on DHS Form N-648, Medical Certification for Disability Exemptions, and if necessary, obtain a waiver of the oath requirement. In 2007, after years of controversy over the process for granting disability exemptions from the naturalization requirements, DHS issued a new memorandum explaining how N-648s would be adjudicated.[35] Marcus should file Form N-648 along with his N-400. Marcus must find a medical professional to complete the form; this person must be a medical doctor, doctor of osteopathy, or clinical psychologist licensed to practice in the United States.[36] The medical professional must certify under penalty of perjury that his or her statements are true and correct and agree to the release of all pertinent medical records upon consent of the applicant and as requested by USCIS. He or she also must have general experience in the area of Marcus's disability and must be qualified to diagnose Marcus's disability and/or impairment(s). A doctor who is a general practitioner and not a specialist may complete the form if his or her experience or other qualifications permit him or her to make the disability and/or impairment(s) assessment. The medical professional who completes the N-648 must explain "the origin, nature, and extent of" Marcus's dementia; how the diagnosis of Alzheimer's was made through "medically acceptable clinical or laboratory diagnostic techniques;"

---

[33] INA §237(a)(1)(E)(ii).

[34] These questions are *available at www.uscis.gov/files/article/6520q.pdf.*

---

[35] USCIS Memorandum, D. Neufeld, "Guidance Clarifying the Adjudication of Form N-648, Medical Certification for Disability Exceptions" (Sept. 18, 2007), *published on* AILA InfoNet at Doc. No. 07092061 (*posted* Sept. 20, 2007).

[36] 8 CFR §312.2.

how Marcus's condition "so severely affects [him] that it renders [Marcus] unable to learn or demonstrate English proficiency and/or knowledge of United States history and government;" that Marcus's disability is expected to last 12 months or longer; and that Marcus's disability was not caused by the use of illegal drugs. The N-648 does not exempt the applicant from the oath requirement, which is separate from the English and history/civics requirements. If Marcus's dementia is so severe that he cannot take the oath, then he should request a waiver of the oath requirement. The procedures for waiving the oath are outlined in a 2003 USCIS Memorandum.[37]

Receipt of Public Benefits

Facts. Anthony came to the United States as a refugee and later adjusted status and became an LPR. He wants to apply for U.S. citizenship because he is worried about losing his Supplemental Security Income (SSI) benefits.[38] He has been receiving SSI for the past six years. How will receipt of SSI affect his ability to naturalize?

Legal Analysis. Anthony's receipt of SSI or other public benefits should not affect his ability to naturalize as long as he did not commit fraud or otherwise engage in misconduct to obtain the benefits. DHS can use the receipt of public benefits as the basis for finding a lack of good moral character when an applicant for benefits engaged in misconduct, such as failing to disclose his assets, income, or support payments from a former spouse or failing to disclose his true marital status.[39] Anthony should also be aware that DHS recently announced a settlement in a class action lawsuit filed by noncitizens who have been receiving SSI; under the terms of the settlement, Anthony may be entitled to expedited processing of his naturalization application.[40]

Failure To Register for Selective Service

Facts. Keith is a citizen of the United Kingdom who came to the United States on an F-1 visa in 2005, when he was a 22-year-old graduate student. He married a USC and adjusted status to Conditional Lawful Permanent Resident (CPR) three months ago. He has just turned 25, and at his adjustment interview, the USCIS examiner warned him that he must register for Selective Service or he could be barred from naturalizing as a USC three years later. The examiner said that Keith could register right then and there at the adjustment interview, but Keith was asking so many questions that the examiner was in a hurry to conclude the interview and told Keith to register on his own at a later time. Keith is opposed to the war and doesn't want to register. Must Keith register? What could happen if he fails to register? Can DHS later deny Keith's citizenship application if he has failed to register for Selective Service?

Legal Analysis. Since 1980, all male residents of the United States born after 1959 are required to register for Selective Service upon reaching the age of 18—unless they are in lawful nonimmigrant status, such as F-1 status. The obligation to register exists until the man has either registered or reached the age of 26.[41] Keith was not obligated to register while he was maintaining F-1 status; as soon as he stopped maintaining F-1 status, or became a CPR, he was required to register. Once he turns 26, he can no longer register. If Keith were to apply for naturalization while under the age of 26,[42] his naturalization application would be denied by USCIS if he failed to register. Assuming that he remains married to and living with his USC wife, Keith is most likely to be applying for naturalization in about three years, when he will be 28. USCIS takes the position that failure to register is not a permanent bar to naturalization, but such failure can bar naturalization if the failure was

---

[37] USCIS Memorandum, "Procedures for Implementing the Waiving of the Oath of Renunciation and Allegiance for the Naturalization of Aliens having Certain Disabilities" (June 30, 2003), *available at http://uscis.gov/graphics/lawsregs/handbook/PolMem96Pub.pdf*. While INA §312 and §337 require that the applicant have a "developmental or physical disability or mental impairment," the assessment of a person's ability to meet the oath requirement is different from the assessment of the applicant's ability to learn English and Civics." *See* Revisions to *Adjudicator's Field Manual (AFM)* Chapter 72.2(d)(5) and Appendix 72-13 (*AFM* Update AD06-09) at 8, *available at http://www.uscis.gov/files/pressrelease/AdjN648051006PUB.pdf*.

[38] *See* 8 USC §1612(a)(2)(A).

[39] INS Interpretation 316.1(f)(8).

[40] USCIS Update, "USCIS Settles *Kaplan* Class Action" (May 6, 2008), *published on* AILA InfoNet at Doc. No. 08050533 (*posted* May 5, 2008) (notice of settlement agreement in class action for noncitizens who have received or are receiving supplemental security income (SSI), *Kaplan v. Chertoff*, 06-5304, (E.D. Pa.)).

[41] 50 USC App. 456(a).

[42] This could happen if his wife were to take up a job overseas, perhaps as an employee of the U.S. government or a U.S. corporation.

knowing and willful and occurred during the period when the applicant for naturalization is required to establish his or her good moral character. Thus, if Keith applies for naturalization when he is 28, and he never registered for Selective Service, he could be barred from naturalizing for failure to show good moral character during the three years for which he is required to demonstrate good moral character under INA §319(a). To naturalize when he is 28, he must provide evidence that his failure to register was not knowing and willful, and based on the facts presented here, he cannot do this. An important memo on this issue was authored by William R. Yates in 1999, and practitioners are urged to consult this memo for more details.[43]

Desertion from the Military

Facts. Amelio became an LPR in June 2003 and joined the Army for a six-year enlistment shortly thereafter. After basic training, he filed an application for naturalization under the special military wartime naturalization statute.[44] While the application was pending, Amelio was deployed to Iraq, where he served in an infantry unit. Amelio was sent home for two weeks of leave in the middle of his deployment; upon the end of his two-week leave, he decided not to return to Iraq. After he was absent without leave for 30 days, the Army classified him as a deserter. Several months later, Amelio was stopped for a traffic violation and the police discovered that he was listed as a deserter in the National Crime Information Center database. Amelio was arrested and returned to the Army's control. When he went back to his unit, his commander advised him that he could accept an administrative discharge for "alienage," or be court-martialed and face a potential federal conviction and more serious "bad conduct" or "dishonorable" discharge. Amelio accepted the "alienage" discharge in 2006. Is Amelio barred from becoming a United States citizen?

Legal Analysis. Amelio is likely ineligible to be naturalized under the wartime military naturalization statute, but may be able to obtain citizenship through a regular application, if he is otherwise eligible. The wartime military naturalization statute prohibits the naturalization of anyone who is discharged on ac-

count of alienage.[45] While Amelio will be unable to naturalize under this statute, Amelio is an LPR who may be able to naturalize under INA §316.[46] Amelio is not necessarily barred from naturalizing because of desertion. Although the law bars the naturalization of anyone who "at any time during which the United States has been or shall be at war, deserted or shall desert the military, air, or naval forces of the United States,"[47] this bar to naturalization does not apply unless the person has been convicted by a court martial or other court of competent jurisdiction. Amelio's listing on official military records as a deserter does not in itself bar him from naturalizing.[48] On the other hand, the administrative discharge on account of alienage may be problematical because of INA §315(a), which makes permanently ineligible for citizenship "any alien who applies or has applied for exemption or discharge from training or service in the Armed Forces … on the ground that he is an alien …."[49] Not all noncitizens who are discharged from the military on account of alienage are permanently barred, however—if an alien did not know the consequences of the discharge, he may not be barred from citizenship.[50] Finally, the U.S. Court of Appeals for the Ninth Circuit recently ruled that the "ineligible to citizenship" provisions only apply where there is a draft in place,[51] and there is no draft in place today. Amelio may be able to file a regular naturalization application and obtain U.S. citizenship despite his failure to complete his enlistment contract.

EXTRAORDINARY NATURALIZATION CASES

Expedited Naturalization

Facts. Silvia is married to Douglas, a USC who is employed by an American-owned oil company. Silvia obtained her CPR based on her marriage a few months ago, and her daughter Lydia (Douglas's stepdaughter) was also granted CPR status. Douglas has now been transferred to Indonesia by his American employer, and the company will allow Silvia and Lydia to accompany him. They will be in Indo-

---

[43] Legacy INS Memorandum, W. Yates, "INS Advises on Effect of Failure to Register for Selective Service on Eligibility for Naturalization" (June 18, 1999), *published on* AILA InfoNet at Doc. No. 99010740 (*posted* July 1, 1999).

[44] INA §329.

[45] INA §329(a), 8 CFR §329.1.

[46] INA §316(a).

[47] INA §314.

[48] INS Interpretation 314.1.

[49] INA §315(a).

[50] 8 CFR §315.2(b)(4).

[51] *Gallarde v. INS*, 486 F.3d 1136 (9th Cir. 2007).

nesia, living and working, for three years. Can Silvia naturalize immediately? What about Lydia?

Legal Analysis. INA §319(b) allows for the expedited naturalization of LPRs who are married to USCs when the USC is regularly stationed abroad as an employee of the U.S. government; with certain American institutions of research; with certain American firms or corporations or their subsidiaries; with certain public international organizations; or as a religious practitioner or missionary with a denomination having a bona fide organization in the United States.[52] This statute applies when the LPR spouse plans to accompany the USC on the overseas assignment. Sylvia can file an N-400 application immediately, even if she does not meet the normal residency and physical presence requirements. Sylvia must be in the United States at the time of naturalization. Lydia may derive U.S. citizenship when Sylvia naturalizes if Lydia meets the requirements for derivative U.S. citizenship under INA §320 or §322.

Military Wartime Naturalization

Facts. Juan is serving on active duty in the United States Army. He has completed a tour of duty in Iraq. He enlisted after September 11, 2001. Juan has heard a " street rumor" that he can become a naturalized U.S. citizen despite the fact that he enlisted in the Army using a false "green card." Juan is an "undocumented immigrant" from Mexico and has never had lawful permanent residence. Can Juan become a citizen, even if he has never had lawful permanent residence?

Legal Analysis. Yes, Juan can naturalize, despite his lack of lawful status. Any person serving honorably on active duty during wartime—whether or not he has been lawfully admitted for permanent residence—can naturalize without paying a fee, as long as he enlisted inside the United States.[53] Juan need not have LPR status to apply. Moreover, he is exempt from any residency or physical presence requirements. Juan can avoid being fingerprinted again by signing a form giving USCIS permission to use his military enlistment fingerprints for naturalization purposes. Juan's interview and ceremony can also be completed overseas, if he is deployed overseas when it is time for his interview. Juan can naturalize as a military member even if he is in removal proceedings. The catch is that once he is naturalized,

the government can take away Juan's citizenship if Juan fails to complete five years of honorable service after naturalizing.[54]

PROCEDURAL PROBLEMS IN NATURALIZATION CASES

Naturalization in Removal Proceedings

Facts. Dorothy is an LPR who has been placed in removal proceedings. Prior to being placed in removal proceedings, however, she had filed a naturalization application. She appears to be *prima facie* eligible to naturalize. Dorothy has filed a regular naturalization application, not a military naturalization application. Can she go forward on her naturalization application despite being in removal proceedings?

Legal Analysis. Dorothy can go forward with her naturalization application if the immigration judge terminates proceedings. Under INA §318, an alien cannot naturalize while in removal proceedings unless the alien has filed a military naturalization application under INA §328 or §329. Under 8 CFR §1239.2(f), however, an immigration judge may terminate proceedings to permit an alien to pursue a naturalization application before DHS. To terminate proceedings, the immigration judge must find that (1) the alien has established *prima facie* eligibility for naturalization, and (2) the case involves exceptionally appealing or humanitarian factors. In *Matter of Acosta-Hidalgo*,[55] the Board of Immigration Appeals (BIA) held that immigration judges have no jurisdiction to determine whether the first element is met; only DHS may make this assessment. Thus, to obtain termination, Dorothy must first convince DHS to advise the immigration judge that she is *prima facie* eligible to naturalize. If DHS is willing to so advise the immigration judge, then the immigration judge may determine whether exceptionally appealing or humanitarian factors apply, and may terminate proceedings to allow her to go forward with her naturalization application.[56]

---

[52] INA §319(b).

[53] INA §329(a).

---

[54] INA §329(c).

[55] *Matter of Acosta-Hidalgo*, 24 I&N Dec. 103, 106 (BIA 2007).

[56] At the time that this article went to press, the American Immigration Law Foundation (AILF) was pursuing litigation on this issue. Practitioners who have clients with this issue should consult M. Kenney & T. Realmuto, AILF Practice Advisory, "Terminating Removal Proceedings to Pursue Naturalization Before DHS: Strategies for Challenging *Matter of Acosta Hidalgo*"

continued

No Interview After Filing

Facts. Torsten is an LPR who properly filed his N-400 application and had his fingerprints taken about two years ago, but has never been scheduled for a naturalization interview because his "FBI name check" has not been completed.[57] Torsten suspects that the delay may be caused by the fact that he has an FBI file. Torsten has an FBI file because he is a research scientist who has access to certain dangerous toxins and, as a result, he has already undergone a special work-related FBI background check and clearance process. What, if anything, can Torsten do to get USCIS to schedule an interview on his naturalization application?

Legal Analysis. The delay in scheduling Torsten for an interview has likely been caused by the fact that his name appears in FBI records, and so his name has received a "hit" in FBI records. Michael A. Cannon, an FBI official testifying in the case *Atabani v. Gonzalez*[58] by Affidavit, explained in detail how the FBI name check process works, and his Affidavit is essential reading for immigration practitioners handling these cases.[59] According to the Affidavit, a "hit" in FBI files can cause a substantial delay in processing an FBI name check, even if the person was a crime victim, witness or interviewee, and not a suspect or criminal. Torsten's attorney should try the following methods to get his interview scheduled: (1) check to see if DHS has Torsten's correct mailing address on file; (2) try to ascertain where Torsten's naturalization file his located, and write a letter to the office that has the file, requesting an interview; (3) write to Torsten's congressional Representative or Senator for assistance; (4) use the AILA Liaison process to attempt to find out the status of Torsten's case. If all these methods fail to result in the scheduling of an interview, Torsten can file a Petition for a Writ of Mandamus to compel adjudication of his N-400. Practice Advisories for filing such a lawsuit are available on the website of the American Immigration Law Foundation

(AILF).[60] Practitioners can also find sample pleadings on PACER, the federal court electronic filing system, or in various AILA publications.[61] In his petition, Torsten should explain the steps that he has taken to try to get USCIS to act on his application. Torsten should try to show that USCIS's failure to adjudicate his application is unreasonable and unwarranted, citing USCIS's estimated processing times for naturalization applications. Practitioners should check the USCIS website for the latest press releases regarding the status of USCIS processing times for naturalization applications.[62]

No Decision After Interview

Facts. Giuseppe is an LPR who filed his naturalization application in 2005 and was interviewed early in 2006.[63] After his interview, when no decision had been made on his case, Giuseppe contacted USCIS to find out the status of his application Shortly thereafter, he received a letter from USCIS stating that his application could not be adjudicated due to an issue with a "security clearance." What can Giuseppe do to get USCIS to make a decision on his case?

Legal Analysis. Because Giuseppe has been interviewed on his naturalization application, he can take advantage of a special provision of the naturalization statutes that allows him to file a federal lawsuit when more than 120 days have passed since the interview but no decision has been made.[64] He can

---

(Mar. 18, 2008), *available at www.ailf.org/lac/pa/Acosta_Hidalgo_lac_pa_031808.pdf.*

[57] This scenario is based loosely on the facts of *Eckstein v. Mukasey*, Case No. 08-CV-00098-LTB (D. Colo.), ably handled by AILA member Daniel M. Kowalski.

[58] *Atabani v. Gonzales*, Case No. 05-CV-457 (D. N.H.).

[59] *Available at www.bibdaily.com/pdfs/Cannon%20FBI%20name%20check.pdf.*

[60] *See* AILF Practice Advisory, "Mandamus Actions: Avoiding Dismissal and Proving the Case" (Aug. 15, 2005), *available at www.ailf.org/lac/pa/lac_pa_081505.pdf; see also* AILF Practice Advisory, "Mandamus Jurisdiction Over Delayed Applications: Responding to the Government's Motion to Dismiss" (Apr. 8, 2008), *available at www.ailf.org/lac/pa/mandamus-jurisdiction 9-24-07%20PA.pdf.*

[61] *See, e.g.,* R. Pauw, *Litigating Immigration Cases in Federal Court* (AILA 2007), App. C (Petition for a Writ of Mandamus).

[62] *See, e.g.,* USCIS Update, "USCIS Releases Projected Naturalization Processing Times for Local Offices" (Apr. 22, 2008), *available at www.uscis.gov/files/article/processing_update_042208.pdf.*

[63] This scenario is based loosely on the facts reported by one of the plaintiffs in *Mocanu v. Mueller*, 2008 U.S. Dist. LEXIS 10122 (E.D. Pa. 2008).

[64] INA §336(b) ("If there is a failure to make a determination under section 335 before the end of the 120-day period after the date on which the examination is conducted under such section, the applicant may apply to the United States district court for the district in which the applicant resides for a hearing on the matter. Such court has jurisdiction over the matter and may either

continued

file a Petition for a Hearing on Naturalization Application in the U.S. District Court. An excellent guide to filing such lawsuits is available on the AILF website.[65] Given that Giuseppe's case involves an apparent FBI name check problem, his attorney may be able to prevail on the argument that the FBI name check is unlawful, as the plaintiffs successfully argued in the *Mocanu* litigation.[66] Giuseppe should also check whether similar suits have been filed in his district, and whether any of them are class actions. As this article was going to press, a federal court had certified such a class action for such plaintiffs who reside in Washington State.[67]

After Filing a Lawsuit, Accepting a Remand, or Seeking Federal Court Adjudication

Facts. Tony filed his naturalization application, was interviewed, and more than four months passed after the interview but without a decision from USCIS. In fact, several years passed—at which point Tony hired an attorney to file suit in U.S. District Court under INA §336(b). The government has answered the complaint, but has now moved to remand the case to USCIS for a decision, rather than allowing the U.S. District Court to determine the merits of the application, which the Court is permitted to do under INA §336(b). What should Tony do—agree to the remand, or press for a federal judge to decide the merits?

Legal Analysis. Tony may want to press for the federal judge to decide the merits of his naturalization petition. The government has been asking for remands lately because it has been filing and losing motions to dismiss. It is possible that on remand, USCIS will approve the case—but sometimes when USCIS asks for a remand, USCIS will deny the case and commence removal proceedings. Once USCIS does this, Tony will be in a *Matter of Acosta-Hidalgo*[68] situation, where the immigration judge can

only terminate proceedings with a *prima facie* communication that Tony is eligible to naturalize from USCIS or a federal judge. Tony may also be forced to exhaust his administrative remedies before being naturalized, a process that could take years. Tony's lawyer should also carefully check the current law in the applicable Circuit, as there has been some difference of opinion among federal appellate courts as to whether the federal courts have exclusive or concurrent jurisdiction over naturalization petitions under INA §336(b), with the majority now holding that jurisdiction is exclusive.[69] Even where jurisdiction is exclusive, however, federal courts have sometimes been reluctant to decide naturalization cases on the merits, preferring to remand to the agency. Tony should consider whether to file an opposition to the motion to remand, requesting that the federal court take jurisdiction and decide whether his naturalization application should be granted—but also argue, as a fallback position, that should the case be remanded, the court give specific instructions to USCIS on remand, including a time limit for adjudication.[70]

CONCLUSION

This article is intended to give practitioners some insight into an array of common problems that may derail a naturalization application, and suggest possible solutions. This area of law is a fascinating and worthwhile one that can tax the creative abilities of any immigration attorney. An attorney with the ability to resolve these complex naturalization problems can earn the undying gratitude of many newly-naturalized USCs.

---

determine the matter or remand the matter, with appropriate instructions, to the Service to determine the matter.").

[65] L. Rose & M. Kenney, AILF Practice Advisory, "Circumventing Naturalization Delays: How to Get Judicial Relief Under 8 USC §1447(b) for a Stalled Naturalization Application" (Oct. 6, 2005), *available at* www.ailf.org/lac/pa/lac_pa_100605.pdf.

[66] *Mocanu v. Mueller*, 2008 U.S. Dist. LEXIS 10122 (E.D. Pa. 2008).

[67] *See Roshandel v. Chertoff*, Case. No. 07-CV-01739-MJP (W.D. Wash.), Order Granting Plaintiff's Motion for Class Certification, Apr. 25, 2008.

[68] *Matter of Acosta-Hidalgo*, 24 I&N Dec. at 103.

[69] At the time that this article was going to press, some of the leading cases on this issue included *Etape v. Chertoff*, 497 F.3d 379 (4th Cir. 2007) (holding that U.S. district courts have exclusive jurisdiction over naturalization applications under INA §336(b)); *Walji v. Gonzales*, 500 F.3d 432 (5th Cir. 2007) (reversing earlier decision and holding that there is exclusive jurisdiction); *Hovsepian v. United States*, 359 F.3d 1144 (9th Cir. 2004) (en banc) (holding that U.S. district courts have exclusive jurisdiction).

[70] For an example of the type of instructions that a court might give on remand, *see Abusadeh v. Chertoff*, 2007 U.S. Dist. LEXIS 94428 (Dec. 27, 2007) (holding that remand is more appropriate than having the federal court decide the merits of the naturalization claim, but setting deadlines for USCIS to act).

ACQUISITION OF CITIZENSHIP: PRACTICAL PROBLEMS AND SOLUTIONS

*by Kathrin S. Mautino**

Anti-immigrant sentiment in the United States always has meant that American citizens who do not have primary documentation (U.S. birth certificate or passport) are suspect. There is an increasing trend to require proof of U.S. citizenship prior to the release of benefits ranging from driver's licenses to employment to state health benefits. In addition, the world is a scarier place; U.S. Immigration and Customs Enforcement (ICE) may raid your place of work; or E-Verify may claim that you are not legally entitled to work in the United States. Many citizens are unpleasantly surprised to learn that benefits or rights can be withheld until proof of citizenship is established, especially when they have not had to establish their citizenship before. Individuals may come to your office requesting instant action in order to establish their claim to U.S. citizenship. In other more pleasant situations, you may find individuals who believe themselves to be foreigners and yet turn out to be U.S. citizens.

INTRODUCTION

This article will look at how one establishes U.S. citizenship and explore some of the changes that have occurred over the past few years. It will take an anecdotal approach, exploring issues raised by real cases seen in our office.

BASIC LAW

An individual may be a citizen of the United States under any of several different laws or principals. The most common way is by birth in the United States. This principal of *jus solis* applies to all those born in the United States or certain territories and subject to U.S. jurisdiction.[1] An individual

fulfilling certain requirements may apply for naturalization and become a U.S. citizen and the children of certain naturalized parents may automatically become citizens as well.[2] However, the situation most likely to appear in a practitioner's office is that of an individual born outside of the United States, but who nonetheless is a U.S. citizen due to the citizenship of his or her ancestors. This principal of *jus sanguinis* has long existed in the statutes of this country[3] but has never been guaranteed by the U.S. Constitution. In fact, over the years Congress has changed the requirements for citizenship by descent, adding layers of confusion to the issue.

Adoption

Facts. Rodrigo is from Mexico. Rodrigo was born in Texas in 1971 and adopted by Mexican citizens. His adoptive parents obtained a birth certificate showing that Rodrigo was born in Guadalajara and all of his official Mexican documents (marriage certificate, baptismal certificate, school records, etc.) show Guadalajara as his birth place.

Legal Analysis. Adoption by foreign citizens does not affect U.S. citizenship of the child. The child is a citizen at the moment of his or her birth in this country, and under present law cannot lose his or her citizenship unless he or she later voluntarily and with the intention to relinquish U.S. citizenship does some expatriating act.[4] That Rodrigo is recognized as a Mexican citizen does not change this. Even if Rodrigo became a Mexican citizen through a form of naturalization in Mexico, since that act occurred before he was 18, it would not be considered an expatriating act resulting in a loss of U.S. citizenship.

Similarly, adoption of foreign-born children by U.S. citizen parents does not result in automatic U.S.

---

* **Kathrin S. Mautino** is a partner in the San Diego firm of Mautino and Mautino. She is certified as a specialist in immigration and nationality law by the State Bar of California. Ms. Mautino writes and speaks frequently on various immigration related topics for local, regional, and national groups.

This article updates the version appearing in *20th Annual California Chapters Handbook* 107 (AILA 2007).

[1] U.S. Const. Amend. XIV, §1; INA§301(a), 8 USC §1401(a). Note that not all persons physically within the United States are subject to its jurisdiction. Some high-level

diplomats avoid U.S. jurisdiction and hence their children may not be U.S. citizens. *See generally* 8 CFR §101.3(a)(1).

[2] INA §§320, 321, 8 USC §§1431, 1432.

[3] *See* INA §301(g).

[4] INA §349. The law has not always required that expatriation be voluntary. For a more in-depth discussion of involuntary expatriation and the possibilities of resumption of U.S. citizenship, *see Nationality and Citizenship Handbook* (R. Mautino and G. Endelman, eds.) (AILA 1996).

continued

citizenship. In many instances, such children entered the United States as permanent residents and were later naturalized on a petition by their parents. In 1994, the statute was changed, eliminating the need for admission as a lawful permanent resident and substituting a mere lawful admission.[5]

Practical Analysis. Rodrigo's U.S. birth certificate listed his adoptive parents as his birth parents. We submitted a passport application with the birth certificate. However, given the high incidence of individuals obtaining false birth certificates in order to get U.S. passports, the Passport Agency requested school transcripts and other documents to show that Rodrigo was the child listed on the birth certificate. This presented a problem because Rodrigo's parents had used the Mexican birth certificate to obtain benefits for him. Since the issue was Rodrigo's identity, we were able to satisfy the Passport Agency by submitting grammar school and high school diplomas as well as the original court adoption order.

Children Born Out of Wedlock

Facts. Jose was born in Mexico in 1970. His mother was born in Texas in 1949 and died last year. Jose tells you that his mother was not married when he was born, although some years later, she married a man not Jose's biological father. Jose and his stepfather do not get along and the stepfather refuses to give Jose any documents relating to his mother. Jose knows nothing about his biological father.

Legal Analysis. Children whose parents were not married on the day they were born are U.S. citizens if their mothers were U.S. citizens with one year continuous physical presence in the United States or its outlying possessions prior to the child's birth.[6] Children of U.S. citizen fathers have a more difficult time under these facts. For children born after November 15, 1968, the father must legitimate or acknowledge the child prior to the child's 18th birthday, or paternity must be established by a competent court, and the father must fulfill the residence requirements listed in the statute.[7]

Practical Analysis. We submitted a passport application with Jose's birth certificate and baptismal certificate, both of which indicated that Jose's mother was unmarried when he was born. The Passport Agency requested evidence that Jose's mother had the required residence in the United States. Since we could not get personal documents from the stepfather, we filed a request for a detailed Social Security earnings information report and census records from 1950 and 1960.[8] Since these are private records, Jose had to submit his birth certificate and his mother's death certificate in order to obtain them. The Social Security records showed that Jose's mother worked in 1967 and 1968 in El Paso, Texas, and in 1969 in New York City, and thus met the physical presence requirement.

Children Born in Wedlock

Facts. Gilbert is in jail for conspiracy to sell cocaine. He was born in Mexico in 1973 and became a U.S. legal permanent resident under the amnesty program. His mother is a permanent resident of the United States and a citizen of Mexico. His father was born and raised in the Southern California area. Gilbert's parents were married but separated when he was born, and they went through a very bitter divorce before Gilbert's first birthday. Gilbert's father refuses to acknowledge or in any way help Gilbert. Gilbert is in deportation proceedings.

Legal Analysis. Gilbert is the legitimate son of a U.S. citizen father. Thus, if Gilbert's father lived in the United States for 10 years, at least five after the age of 14 prior to Gilbert's birth, Gilbert is a U.S. citizen.[9] Unlike the previous example, Gilbert does

---

knowledging father would need 10 years physical presence, at least 5 after the age of 14. For births after November 14, 1986, the father needs only five years of physical presence, at least two after the age of 14. *See generally* 4 C. Gordon, S. Mailman & S. Yale-Loehr, *Immigration Law and Procedure* §93.04 (rev. ed. 1996) (hereinafter *Immigration Law and Procedure*).

[8] Information on how to obtain Social Security records and census data can be found on their respective websites: *www.ssa.gov* and *www.census.gov*. Note that both agencies have restrictions on to whom such records may be released. Generally, children of deceased persons are able to access these records but an unrelated party cannot.

[9] 4 *Immigration Law and Procedure* §93.02. INA §301(g), 8 USC §1401(g) was modified in 1986 to require only five years physical presence, at least two after the age of 14. In 1988, the INA was amended to make clear that this applied only to children born on or after November 14, 1986. Immigration Technical Corrections Act of 1988, Pub. L. No. 100-525, §8(r), 102 Stat. 2609.

---

[5] INA §322; 8 USC §1433, As amended by §102 of the Immigration and Nationality Technical Corrections Act of 1994, Act of Oct. 25, 1994, Pub. L. No. 103-416, 108 Stat. 4305.

[6] INA §309(c); 8 USC §1409(c).

[7] INA §309(a); 8 USC §1409(a). As mentioned in the introduction, the laws regarding transmission of citizenship have been changed over time. Generally, the law in effect at the time the child was born controls. Thus, for illegitimate children born between December 24, 1952 and November 13, 1986, the ac-
continued

not have to prove the relationship beyond providing a birth certificate.[10] If Gilbert's parents had divorced prior to his birth, he would need to establish the relationship with his father as discussed in the previous example even though in many jurisdictions he would not be considered "illegitimate."

Practical Analysis. Most of the documents needed to show that Gilbert's father was born in the United States and that the father resided in the United States are not available without the consent of the individual concerned. However, the immigration judge has authority to issue subpoenas for persons and documents.[11] After getting as much information from Gilbert's mother, cousins and other relatives, we intended to subpoena the father's school records, Social Security records and the father. Unfortunately, Gilbert decided he preferred other counsel and this author is unable to say how the case was resolved.

Birth in the Philippines

Facts. Ruth was born in the Philippines on April 1, 1946. Her father was born in Texas in 1925 and went to the Philippines as part of the U.S. Army during World War II. Ruth's mother was born in the Philippines in 1927. They married about two years before Ruth was born. When Ruth was about 6 months old, she and her mother were sent to San Diego as military dependents. Ruth's mother naturalized a few years later.

Legal Analysis. There are three possible ways Ruth could be a U.S. citizen. As the daughter of one U.S. citizen and one alien who naturalized prior to her 18th birthday, Ruth could have automatically become a citizen if she was admitted to the United States as a permanent resident.[12] Additionally, as the legitimate daughter of a U.S. citizen father, Ruth could be a citizen if her father lived in the United States for 10 years, five after the age of 12.[13]

However, Ruth was born at a time that the Philippine Islands were a territory of the United States.[14] At that time, birth in the Philippines did not confer automatic U.S. citizenship. Those born in the Philippines who did not derive citizenship through their parents were "nationals" of the United States, not citizens. On the day she was born, Ruth's mother was a national (but not a citizen) of the United States.[15] Under the Nationality Act of 1940,[16] a child born with one U.S. citizen parent and one U.S. national parent was a citizen at birth.

Practical Analysis. Ruth's parents were both alive and had saved virtually all of the documents relating to their stay in the Philippines, including military records. Ruth's birth certificate listed her as a U.S. citizen. Ruth and her mother came to the United States on a military ship, but there is no evidence that Ruth was ever admitted as a permanent resident. Although her father had many documents showing his activities since joining the military, there were very few verifying his presence in the United States prior to that time. We decided to file a passport application based on the 1940 Act, understanding that we could also file based on the father's citizenship and U.S. residence if necessary. As often happens with citizenship claims brought under old laws, the clerk at the Passport Agency did not understand the claim and instructed Ruth to show that she had been residing in the United States since entry. After several telephone calls, a more senior officer reviewed and approved the application.

Marriage as a Form of Naturalization

Facts. Josephine was born in Canada in 1897. About 1899, her father moved the family to Massachusetts. The family history suggests that her father naturalized about 1904. In 1917, Josephine married Oscar, who was born in Massachusetts in 1895. About 1919, Josephine and Oscar moved to San Diego. Josephine divorced Oscar in 1925. Josephine resides in a nursing home and needs to prove lawful status in order to continue receiving federal assistance in paying for her care. Her son, Fred, is Josephine's legal guardian.

Legal Analysis. Josephine could have automatically become a citizen upon the naturalization of

---

[10] INA §309; 8 USC §1409.

[11] 8 CFR §287.4.

[12] INA §320; 8 USC §1431. Note that the requirements under this section were modified and liberalized by the Child Citizenship Act of 2000, discussed later in this article.

[13] Because her father served in the U.S. military between December 7, 1941, and December 31, 1946, the normal requirement of 10 years, five after the age of 14 discussed *supra*, note 8 was modified. *See* R. Mautino, "Acquisition of Citizenship," 90-4 *Immigration Briefings* 5 (Apr. 1990).

[14] The Philippines gained their independence on July 4, 1946. 60 Stat. 1352.

[15] *See Matter of Hermosa,* 14 I&N Dec. 447 (BIA 1973).

[16] §201(d), 54 Stat. 1138.

either parent if she was admitted as a permanent resident and was under the age of 21.[17] There was no requirement that she be unmarried at the time of her father's naturalization. Additionally, marriage to a U.S. citizen man was an act of naturalization for qualified foreign women.[18]

Practical Analysis. In the early part of this century, there were no central records kept on the naturalization of individuals. Records were kept at the court where the naturalization took place. Josephine was unable to tell us in which court in Massachusetts her father naturalized, and we were unable to locate the naturalization certificate of her father. The state of Massachusetts had centralized its birth records, but was unable to locate one for Josephine's husband, Oscar. Josephine and Oscar's marriage certificate stated that Oscar was born in Massachusetts. We then turned to a professional genealogist who searched the 1900, 1910, and 1920 census records.[19] Those records listed Oscar's place of birth as Massachusetts, and one census record showed Josephine's father as a naturalized citizen. With those records and the letter from the state of Massachusetts that it could not locate Oscar's birth certificate, we were able to convince legacy INS that Oscar was a U.S. citizen, and thus that Josephine "naturalized" when she married Oscar. INS issued a Certificate of Citizenship establishing her date of acquisition of citizenship as 1920.

Although applicants for Certificates of Citizenship are required to attend interviews, Josephine's presence was waived when we presented a letter from her doctor stating that it was impossible for her to leave the nursing home. Fred did appear for the interview and presented the California court documents appointing him as his mother's guardian.

This case came to my office in 1993, when Josephine was 96 years old. The chances that another direct beneficiary of this law appearing are slim and getting slimmer. However, it is quite possible that children or other descendants of someone who bene-

fited from this law will appear, as can be seen in the example below.

Early Law Regarding Transmission Through the Mother

Facts: Jenny was born in New York in 1850. She married Randolph, a citizen of Great Britain, and moved to London. In 1874, their son, Winston, was born in England. During the 1890s and early 1900s, Winston traveled extensively in the United States and in 1908, he married Clementine. Winston and Clementine had four daughters and one son, Randolph, all born in the United Kingdom.

Legal Analysis: Up until May 24, 1934, only American citizen males could transmit citizenship to their children born outside the United States.[20] Thus, a preliminary analysis would say that Winston was not a U.S. citizen, since his father was not an American. However, in 1994, Congress retroactively changed these provisions to allow women to transmit American citizenship to their children on the same basis as men.[21] Thus, in 1994, Winston retroactively became a U.S. citizen as of the date of his birth. In the same manner, Clementine retroactively became a U.S. citizen based on her marriage to Winston.[22] Their children, including son Randolph, automatically became American citizens as of their date of birth, as each had two U.S. citizen parents, one of whom had resided (although temporarily) in the United States.[23]

Practical Analysis: This case is not one that has been handled by our office. It is, in fact, the family history of Sir Winston Churchill. The facts and analysis are provided to show that seemingly dead citizenship cases occasionally can rise from the grave and that it is important to keep the old laws in the back of your head. Thus, all of Sir Winston's children are American citizens, and it is quite possible that some of his grandchildren and great-grandchildren are also American citizens.

Parents Naturalize

Facts: Paul was born in Canada in 1955. In 1964, he and his parents immigrated to the United States. In 1969, Paul's parents become naturalized American citizens. Paul's parents had marital problems

---

[17] Immigration Briefings, *supra*, note 13.

[18] Act of Feb. 10, 1855, §2, 10 Stat. 604, codified as Rev. Stat. §1994 (1874). Oriental women were not eligible to naturalize and could not utilize this section.

[19] The 1920 census record is the latest census records available to the public. Later census record information regarding specific individuals is protected unless its release is authorized by the person whose records you are seeking. *See* the discussion in example 2.

---

[20] *Id.*

[21] Immigration and Nationality Technical Corrections Act of 1994, Pub. L. No. 103-416, 108 Stat. 4305.

[22] *Supra* note 17 and accompanying text.

[23] INA §301(c).

and divorced in 1971. Paul returned to Canada with his mother, who renounced her American citizenship in 1973. Paul now wants to live in the United States and wonders if there is a way to reactivate his permanent resident status.

Legal Analysis: Paul became an American citizen when his parents naturalized. The law prior to the enactment of the Child Citizenship Act of 2000 required that both parents naturalize while the child was under age 18,[24] and that the child be residing in the United States pursuant to an admission as a lawful permanent resident.

Practical Analysis: Paul still had his old permanent resident card, but he had very limited access to documents from his parents. His mother did have her certificate of loss of nationality, which recorded her date of naturalization. Paul's father had died and a search of his documents turned up old passports but not a copy of the father's naturalization certificate. Paul was able to get a transcript from the junior high school showing that he was living in the United States at the time his parents naturalized. We filed for a U.S. passport and submitted the mother's certificate of loss of nationality and the father's old passports along with Paul's permanent resident card and school records. We explained to Paul that the passport office might request additional evidence of the dates of naturalization of his parents and that we would have to work with legacy INS to get that evidence. However, because the Department of State had files on both Paul's mother and father, they issued Paul a passport. Note that Paul's citizenship, once acquired, was not affected by his mother's later renunciation.

THE CHILD CITIZENSHIP ACT OF 2000[25]

Since this article was first written in 1996, Congress passed the Child Citizenship Act of 2000, greatly liberalizing the requirements for obtaining citizenship on behalf of children. Unfortunately, some of the provisions are complicated and cause much confusion among immigration practitioners and the public.

Child Immigrates and Resides With U.S. Citizen Parent

Facts: George was born in Arizona, but has lived since age 2 in Mexico. His wife, Rosa, and 10 year-old daughter, Violeta, are Mexican citizens. Five years ago, George decided to move the family to the United States and he filed I-130s for Rosa and Violeta. Four years ago, both Rosa and Violeta attended an interview at the American Consulate General in Ciudad Juarez, Mexico, and were admitted as permanent residents.

Legal Analysis: Under the Child Citizenship Act, Violeta is a U.S. citizen. INA §320 now says that a child becomes a U.S. citizen automatically if he or she is (1) admitted as a permanent resident and (2) is residing in the United States in the legal and physical custody of one U.S. citizen parent. Both of these events must occur while the child is under age 18.

Practical Analysis: Violeta does not have any evidence of her status as an American citizen. In most cases, it is easiest to apply for a U.S. passport, but that requires the submission of original documents, including Violeta's permanent resident card, leaving her without any proof that she is in the country legally. George and Rosa were hesitant to do this, so an application for a Certificate of Citizenship was filed with copies of George's birth certificate, Violeta's permanent resident card, Violeta's school records (showing her address), Violeta's birth certificate (showing her relationship to George), and George's driver's license and pay stub, as evidence that he lived at the same address as Violeta. At the interview, U.S. citizenship and Immigration Services (USCIS) compared the original documents to the copies, retained Violeta's permanent resident card, and issued her a Certificate of Citizenship, showing the date she acquired American citizenship as the date of her entry as a permanent resident.

Child Residing Overseas Acquiring Citizenship Through Parents

Facts: Fredrika is a naturalized U.S. citizen. Her son, Harry, died of a drug overdose in Mexico three years ago. Harry's son, Walter, was adopted by Fredrika two years ago. Fredrika moved to Mexicali, Mexico, 10 years ago to take care of Walter, as Walter's biological parents were both drug addicts and subject to irrational behavior. Fredrika has tried to get a visa for Walter to enter the United States, but has not been successful. Walter is now 13 years old. Walter's biological mother is still alive, but disappears for long periods of time.

---

[24] INA§320 (modified by the Child Citizenship Act of 2000).

[25] Pub. L. No. 106-395, Act of Oct. 30, 2000, 114 Stat. 1631.

Legal Analysis: For immigration purposes, Walter is Fredrika's child.[26] It is not clear if Walter would fit the definition of an orphan,[27] which would have allowed Fredrika to bring Walter to the United States immediately after his adoption. However, because Walter has lived in the legal and physical custody of Fredrika for two years, the issue is moot.[28] As discussed earlier, adopted children do not automatically acquire American citizenship. One option is for Fredrika to apply to immigrate Walter to the United States as described in the example above. Fredrika also can apply to have Walter acquire U.S. citizenship under INA §322. This section requires an affirmative application be filed by a U.S. citizen parent with USCIS and that the parent have five years' residence in the United States, two of which are after age 14. Note that the residence need not be as a U.S. citizen, nor need it be before the birth of the child. INA §322 also requires that the child receive his or her status as a U.S. citizen prior to age 18. Merely filing the application before the child's 18th birthday is not sufficient.

Practical Analysis: Because Fredrika was a naturalized U.S. citizen who immigrated through employment, in theory, USCIS had evidence that she had resided in the United States for five years.[29] However, it is never a good idea to rely on USCIS requesting and ordering additional files, since at a minimum, it results in considerable delay. Additionally, some files are more complete than others and if there was not evidence of five years' residence in Fredrika's immigration file, USCIS could investigate if Fredrika properly received U.S. citizenship. Although unlikely, such an investigation could lead to rescission of citizenship proceedings against Fredrika.

However, Fredrika had worked in the United States for 15 years before she retired and moved to Mexicali to take care of Walter. She had copies of her W-2 forms and tax returns for the last seven years she had been working, along with miscellaneous other documents showing her residence in the United States; and she had both a current U.S. passport and her certificate of naturalization. We filed an

---

[26] INA §§101(a)(50)(b)(1)(E), (F).

[27] INA §101(a)(50)(b)(1)(F).

[28] A child adopted by a relative who resides for two years in the legal custody and control of the adopting parent meets the definition of child contained in INA §101(a)(50)(b)(1)(E).

[29] INA §316(a).

N-643 with the San Diego district[30] and Walter was scheduled for an interview six months later.

When we received the USCIS appointment letter, we immediately scheduled Walter for an appointment at the American Consulate in Tijuana, Mexico. The Department of State's policy is to issue B-2 visas to children so that they may attend citizenship interviews in the United States.[31] Walter entered the United States a few days before his interview, with an I-94 card valid for six months.[32] At the interview, Walter's B-2 visa was cancelled and he was issued a certificate of citizenship.

Child Residing Overseas Acquiring Citizenship Through Grandparents Residence

Facts: Alexander and Susan were born in the United States in the 1930s. Their daughter, Debi, was born in Oregon in 1963. When Debi was 4, Alexander and Susan moved the family to Israel. Debi has visited her cousins in the United States, but has not resided here since 1967. Debi married an Israeli citizen and has three children, Rebecca, age 19, David, age 16, and Daniel, age 14. Alexander died a few years ago. Susan lives in a nursing home in Israel and cannot travel long distances.

Legal Analysis: Rebecca, David, and Daniel did not acquire U.S. citizenship at birth because Debi did not reside in the United States sufficient time prior to their birth to transmit American citizenship.[33] As the minor child of a U.S. citizen, Rebecca is eligible to immigrate to the United States but she will not acquire U.S. citizenship because she is over age 18.[34]

---

[30] The N-643 can be filed at any USCIS district office. 8 CFR §322.3.

[31] *Foreign Affairs Manual* (FAM) 41.31 N14.6. Note that the child must meet the requirements of INA 214(b). Some parents have had success presenting the appointment notice to CBP officers at a port of entry and receiving a humanitarian parole for their children to attend their interviews.

[32] In 2002, INA §322 was amended to require that a child maintain lawful temporary status in the United States through the citizenship interview. 21st Century Department of Justice Appropriations Authorization Act §11030B(5), Act of Nov. 2, 2002, Pub. L. No. 107-273, 116 Stat. 1758. Prior to that date, children who entered the United States lawfully but had overstayed were eligible for naturalization under this provision.

[33] *See* discussion, *supra* note 7 and accompanying text.

[34] *See* discussion, *supra* note 21 and accompanying text. Note that while the I-130 may be filed by a parent residing outside the United States, the I-864 affidavit of support requires that the petitioner reside in the United States. Assuming that Debi had no intention of living in the United States,

continued

Debi could apply to immigrate David and Daniel, and they would acquire American citizenship if they reside with Debi in the United States.[35] Debi can also use INA §322 to apply for citizenship on behalf of David and Daniel.

Debi did not live in the United States for five years, two after the age of 14, so she cannot base a citizenship application upon her own residence. However, because her parents were U.S. citizens, both of whom resided in the United States from birth until their mid-30s, she can file for David and Daniel based on her parent's residence. Note that INA §322 requires that, in order to use the residence of the grandparent, there must be a direct ancestral link between the child and the grandparent. In other words, the U.S. citizen grandparent must be the parent of the U.S. citizen parent.[36]

Practical Analysis: Both Alexander and Susan resided in the United States more than enough time for our needs and the application could be based on either person. Alexander and Susan had a traditional marriage, where Alexander worked and Susan remained at home, so documentation of residence was easier to obtain for Alexander. We filed two N-600s[37] (one for David and one for Daniel) with a supplement describing Alexander's residence as well as copies of supporting documentation. Note that there is no requirement that the grandparent be alive at the time of the interview or be present at the interview.[38] By the

time the packets were prepared and filed, David was 17 and 5 months' old. We used local district liaison procedures to ensure that David's interview was scheduled before his 18th birthday. David and Daniel had multiple entry B-2 visas, so they did not need to make an appointment at the American Embassy in Tel Aviv.[39] Because Debi and her children resided in Israel, we also requested advance notice of the appointment so that they could have enough time to arrange transportation. David and Daniel arrived the day before their interview. After receiving their Certificates of Citizenship, they returned to Israel to continue their education.[40]

THE TWISTS AND TURNS OF TREATIES, PRESUMPTIONS, NATURALIZATION, AND DENATURALIZATION

The following is a complex set of circumstances, provided to show that final decisions of district courts, consular officers, and others from time to time may be overcome and U.S. citizenship "restored" to those who have lost it.

Facts. Bertil was born in Sweden in 1957. In 1955, his father and mother, Nils and Marianne, became naturalized U.S. citizens. A short time later, Nils and Marianne returned to Sweden for experimental medical treatment for a progressive hearing loss suffered by Marianne. A FOIA search of Nils' file reveals the following: In 1958, Nils signed an Affidavit of Expatriated Persons, stating that he did not intend to reside in the United States at that time. In 1959, the U.S. Consul issued a Report of Expatriation, finding that Nils lost his citizenship automatically on the date that he left the United States pursuant to a treaty between the United States and Sweden.

In 1961, the district court that issued the Certificate of Naturalization canceled it ab initio based on the government's assertion of presumptive fraud[41]

---

she would be unlikely to succeed in immigrating her children under present law.

[35] *Id.* The children would have to enter the United States as permanent residents before age 18.

[36] The descendant requirement is one of two areas where people become confused with the grandparent provisions. (The other being the mistaken belief that acquisition is somehow automatic and/or that it can be applied for after age 18.) Another way of describing the descendant requirement is that if the mother is the U.S. citizen, only the residence of her parents can be considered. If the mother's parents were not US citizens, then §322 does not apply. Similarly, if the mother was the U.S. citizen, but the father's parents were U.S. citizens with sufficient residence, then §322 does not apply.

[37] Recently, USCIS created a new form for using the residence of a grandparent, the N-600K.

[38] The U.S. citizen parent must apply for—and thus consent to—the children's acquisition of American citizenship. INA §322(a)(4) as amended by 21st Century Department of Justice Appropriations Authorization Act §11030B(4), Act of Nov. 2, 2002, Pub. L. No. 107-273, 116 Stat. 1758. Thus, the U.S. citizen parent generally must be at the interview.

---

[39] Presumably, children who have passports from visa waiver countries would not need to obtain a B-2 visa.

[40] It is interesting to note that INA §322 is designed to grant citizenship to children who reside abroad and presumably have no present intention to return to the United States. Note as well that David and Daniel's children would not benefit from INA §322 unless they or their mother returns to the United States for a sufficient amount of time.

[41] A naturalized U.S. citizen who resumed a residence within the country of previous citizenship within five years of naturalization was presumed to have obtained his or her U.S. citizenship by fraud. The period in which fraud could be presumed was shortened to one year in 1986 and eventually

continued

and the submission of Nils' "form of consent and waiver."

Legal Analysis

Cancellation of the Certificate of Naturalization

Generally, when a certificate of naturalization is canceled due to presumptive fraud, its cancellation is considered to be ab initio, and children born prior to its cancellation receive no benefit.[42] However, at least one court has held that the revocation of naturalization based on a "form of consent and waiver" (which contains language virtually identical to the Affidavit mentioned above) results in a *prospective* loss of citizenship, not an *ab initio* loss.[43]

Automatic Loss of Citizenship

The loss of citizenship pursuant to the treaty was a matter of law, effective on the date the expatriating act (*i.e.,* leaving the United States for Sweden) was committed.[44] As a matter of law, expatriation pursuant to the treaty did not require an intent to relinquish U.S. citizenship. Hence, if Nils lost his U.S. citizenship automatically when he returned to Sweden, then on the day Nils voluntarily surrendered his U.S. citizenship, he was not a U.S. citizen. Nils' action in renouncing something he does not have is a legal nullity.[45] However, *Afroym v. Rusk*[46] held that an individual cannot lose U.S. citizenship unless he or she intended to give it up. The State Department has interpreted *Afroym* and similar cases broadly. Individuals who were found to have lost U.S. citizenship can petition to have those determinations overturned if they can show that they did not intend to lose U.S. citizenship at the time of the expatriating act.[47] Current law goes even farther: an individual cannot give up U.S. citizenship unless he or she voluntarily and with the intent to relinquish does an expatriating act.[48]

The District Court Order

A court order may be relied on unless it is overturned or otherwise reversed. Thus, the government may continue to hold that Nils is not a U.S. citizen. However, if the district court can be convinced that its decision was based on a faulty premise; *i.e.,* that Nils was a U.S. citizen at the time he consented to have his petition for naturalization revoked, grounds for reopening and vacating the court's earlier order exist.

Practical Analysis. This case is an example of how FOIA and other research tools can turn up interesting information that may help your client. Prior to the FOIA response, the only information we had was some letters from the State Department indicating that Nils had lost his U.S. citizenship in 1961 due to his abandonment of U.S. residence. Without more information, we had no basis to challenge this holding. Nils came to the United States for a vacation and so we were able to file the FOIA request immediately.[49] We also filed a FOIA request on Marianne, who was living in Sweden. A review of that FOIA showed that Marianne's history paralleled that of Nils and thus Bertil is a U.S. citizen. His parents "consented" to the revocation of their naturalization, thus meaning that they lost it in a prospective manner, not ab initio. Thus, when Bertil was born in 1957, he had two U.S. citizen parents, one with prior residence since Nils and Marianne did not lose their citizenship until 1961. The district court papers include the affidavit where Nils "consented" to the loss of his U.S. citizenship. Since the U.S. government position was that Nils lost his citizenship due to presumptive fraud and his "consent" to its loss, Bertil should be able to rely on that information in his own application for a citizenship document. As Bertil travels to the United States several times a year on business, a passport application would seem to be the best choice.

What effect does the treaty between the United States and Sweden have? As mentioned above, if the treaty provisions were met, it resulted in an automatic loss of U.S. citizenship. If Nils fell under the provisions of the treaty, then he lost his U.S. citizenship when he returned to Sweden in 1955, before Bertil's birth. The situation would look pretty grim for Bertil, but for *Afroym*. This case and the policies discussed above serve to vacate automatic losses of

---

eliminated in 1994. *See generally,* 4 *Immigration Law and Procedure* §100.02[3][d].

[42] INA §340, 8 USC §1451. For a more complete discussion, *see* 4 *Immigration Law and Procedure* §100.02[5].

[43] *Petition of Berger*, 83 F. Supp. 720 (S.D.N.Y. 1949).

[44] *Haaland v. Attorney General*, 42 F. Supp. 13 (D.C. Md. 1941).

[45] *Matter of J–A–W,* (BAR Oct. 3, 1989) and *Matter of M–L– J–,* (BAR Apr. 12, 1984).

[46] 387 U.S. 253 (1967).

[47] 8 FAM §220; INS OI §349.3.

[48] INA §349(a), 8 USC §1481(a).

---

[49] FOIA requests can be filed by individuals overseas, but communications are slower due to delays in international mails.

U.S. citizenship, thus restoring U.S. citizenship to Nils and Marianne—at least until 1958 when the affidavit "consenting" to the loss of citizenship was signed. Again, Bertil is the son of two U.S. citizen parents, one with prior residency.

What effect does the treaty have on Nils and Marianne? Normally, an individual cannot give up what he or she does not have. If Nils was not a U.S. citizen when he consented to its loss, his consent is a legal nullity. If in light of *Afroym* the automatic loss is reversed, is the later, formal "consent" now revived and made valid? It is this author's opinion that a nullity cannot be "fixed" by subsequent changes in the law, but there are those who differ.

If the "consent" to loss of citizenship and the subsequent court decision are nullities, then Nils and Marianne are likely still U.S. citizens, as well as the parents of a U.S. citizen. Nils, now divorced from Marianne, would like to retire in the United States. To show that Nils and Marianne are still U.S. citizens, we would need to reopen the district court proceeding and revoke the previous order. Once the court decision—which is *prima facie* evidence of their loss of citizenship—is revoked, we are free to file for a passport application.

After this article was first published in 1996, the author prepared a letter laying out the legal argument above for Nils, who sent a copy to Bertil in Sweden. On his own, Bertil took this letter and appropriate documentation to the American Embassy in Stockholm, Sweden. The consul agreed with the author's analysis and issued Bertil a U.S. passport. Nils decided that the cost of district court action to reverse the earlier cancellation of his certificate of naturalization was beyond his reach. Instead, he applied to reimmigrate as the father of an American citizen.

CONCLUSION

Citizenship cases are fascinating and present both legal and practical challenges. However, with an imaginative use of sources, most of the practical problems can be overcome. The author hopes that this article has provided you with some useful ideas as well as a taste for some of the common and exotic issues that arise.

A DISCUSSION ON BORDER BASICS

*by Reginald A. Pacis**

This article will provide practitioners with basic information concerning border practices available through AILA liaison efforts with U.S. Customs and Border Protection (CBP) and through the experiences of AILA members who work in jurisdictions that permit attorney representation at land ports of entry (POEs).[1] Immigration practitioners should be well versed regarding the adjudication process at the POEs in order to best advise, prepare, and represent their clients' interests, whether they be individuals or employers wishing to have a foreign national employee or business associate enter the United States.

INSPECTION SITES

Generally, there are two points of CBP inspection, "primary" and "secondary," at each POE. Primary inspection takes place at the initial place of inspection with a CBP officer. It might be the booth at the land border, where the officer interviews the persons in a vehicle attempting to ascertain each individual's nationality and purpose for entering the United States, or the pre-flight inspection location at an international airport, or the booth at a U.S. airport for the inspection of passengers arriving from outside the United States. It is the place where foreign nationals with visas are photographed and fingerprinted[2] as mandated by the US VISIT program.

The secondary inspection site allows the CBP officer to conduct a more detailed interview and review the foreign national's documents. During secondary inspection, CBP also is able to review re-

cords within Department of Homeland Security DHS databases regarding the immigration history of the foreign national. National Security Entry-Exit Registration System (NSEERS) registration typically occurs at secondary inspection. During secondary inspection CBP officers may contact persons listed in documents presented by the foreign national to evidence his or her reasons for temporary entry to the United States for business purposes. Both inspection sites are present at all POEs.

There are generally three types of POEs where foreign nationals may be interviewed regarding their purpose for entering the United States. Land POEs located on the northern border shared with Canada and the southern border shared with Mexico conduct countless interviews of persons entering the United States. Air POEs exist in two places, within the territorial boundaries of the United States, where passengers are inspected after exiting the airplane, and preflight inspection areas located at airports outside the United States, where passengers are interviewed prior to boarding a flight to the United States.[3] Addresses and contact information for all POE CBP offices may be found on CBP's website.[4]

Inspections generally are conducted differently at air POEs versus land POEs. One example of the difference in processing involves I-94s issued at a land POE and I-94s issued at an air POE. The regulations provide that the "master" or "commanding officer" of a commercial vessel or aircraft must present to the CBP officer a departure portion of Form I-94 for each foreign national departing the United States.[5] The regulations provide, however, that I-94 cards issued at land POEs—for TN or L-1 status, for example—will be considered for multiple entries unless otherwise specifically annotated.[6] Finally, the regulations add:

> A nonimmigrant alien departing on an aircraft proceeding directly to Canada on a flight terminating in that country must surrender any Form I-

---

* **Reginald A. Pacis** is a shareholder practicing in Butzel Long's immigration group in Detroit. He is a graduate of Detroit College of Law at Michigan State University. Mr. Pacis served as chair of AILA's Michigan Chapter and is currently a member of its Advocacy Committee. He is presently serving as a member of AILA's CBP Liaison Committee. He is a frequent presenter and author for AILA's annual conferences. He has been appointed by Governor Jennifer Granholm of Michigan to serve on the Advisory Committee for Asian Pacific American Affairs.

[1] The author of this article practices in Detroit. Michigan permits "limited" attorney representation. This point will be discussed later in the article.

[2] Some airports require only the right and left index fingers' prints be captured into the US VISIT system. The growing trend is for all 10 fingers' prints to be captured.

[3] There are preflight inspection sites at Toronto and Nassau, Bahamas, for example.

[4] *See http://cbp.customs.gov/xp/cgov/toolbox/ports/.*

[5] 8 CFR §231.2(b)(1).

[6] 8 CFR §1235.1(f)(1).

94 in his/her possession to the airline agent at the port of departure.[7]

Based on a reading of this interplay within the regulations, I-94 cards should not be collected from the nonimmigrant when exiting the United States via land (unless it is their final departure in that nonimmigrant classification). However, the I-94 must be collected when the foreign national exits the United States by air or sea. Should an I-94 card not be collected prior to the foreign national's departure via air or sea, a new I-94 card must be issued to the foreign national on return to the United States.

The general "chain of command" at POEs consists of the following hierarchical structure. CBP officers report to a CBP supervisor who is in charge of traveler inspections during the duty shift. Each POE has a port director responsible for overall traveler inspections at the port. Generally, a director of field operations governs each state with a POE within its boundaries. Each of these directors reports to a supervisor at CBP headquarters in Washington, D.C.

When confronted with an admissibility issue, many practitioners believe that the first point of contact is either the director of field operations or CBP headquarters. However, the first point of contact *always* should be with the original POE, and if possible, with the CBP officer who conducted the inspection at issue. Should a dialogue between the original CBP inspecting officer continue to yield an unfavorable result, the practitioner then may engage in a discussion with the officer's immediate supervisor, and move up the chain of CBP command until a natural conclusion. Practitioners should be aware that great deference will be given to the initial inspecting officer's judgment.

An attorney's presence at inspection interviews is generally not permitted. The pertinent regulations state:[8]

Nothing in this paragraph shall be construed to provide any applicant for admission in either primary or secondary inspection the right to representation, unless the applicant for admission has become the focus of a criminal investigation and has been taken into custody.

Citing security concerns as the primary reason for prohibiting attorney presence at inspection interviews,

CBP enforces this regulation, but adds that attorneys may assist their clients at secondary inspection sites at the request of an inspecting officer.[9] Some land POEs permit attorney presence at TN, L-1, or other applications for entry interviews, provided the attorney does not interfere with the inspecting officer's interview of the foreign national.[10]

THE MIDNIGHT CALL: WHAT TO DO IN AN "EMERGENCY"

Although attorneys generally are not permitted to participate in secondary inspection interviews, there are a few practice pointers an attorney may apply in emergency border situations, or when an attorney receives a call from a concerned relative of a person who is having problems entering the United States.

Clearly, the best way to avoid issues when entering the United States is for the person who plans to enter the United States to contact immigration counsel and discuss admissibility issues in advance. However, this does not happen often. While it sounds less appealing, the best solution for a foreign national facing admissibility issues at the POE, whether the incident occurs at a land, sea, or air POE, is often a withdrawal of application for entry, requiring that the foreign national pay for his or her return trip to the home country. This solution, while not attractive, may avoid an expedited removal order by the CBP officer and the five-year inadmissibility bar.

Regardless of whether the foreign national is permitted to withdraw his or her application for entry or if an expedited removal order is issued, practitioners should inform the foreign national of a few items that may be of assistance in a future claim for immigration benefits. The first item is to make sure the foreign national is provided Form I-831, the "Q&A." When a negative determination is made regarding a person's admissibility, the CBP officer must make a record of that determination and the facts leading to the determination. The Q&A will contain important details about the exchange between the foreign national and

---

[7] 8 CFR §231.2(b)(1).

[8] 8 CFR §292.5(b).

[9] Memorandum from Michael D'Ambrosio to Mark Kenmore, AILA Chapter Chair in Buffalo (Aug. 28, 2003), File INS-1-OFO BFO CPF.

[10] For a more detailed discussion regarding the right of representation at POEs, see G. Boos & R. Pauw, "Reasserting the Right to Representation in Immigration Matters Arising at Ports of Entry," in *Travel for Work and Business: Application, Admission, and Re-entry After 9/11* 65 (AILA Rev. Ed. 2004).

the CBP officer. It will also contain the specific grounds of inadmissibility found by the CBP officer in denying the admission of the foreign national.

A second tip for practitioners is to make sure that the name of the interviewing officer and duty supervisor are provided. While this might seem like a common sense item, most applicants for entry to the United States, particularly those faced with the possibility of experiencing an inadmissibility issue, are nervous and afraid, which often results in their not noticing names. A third practice recommendation is that the immigration attorney attempt to contact the port officer[11] of the day or supervisory officer on duty to investigate any additional information that may be available. Practitioners should be mindful that the CBP officer will also be using information learned from the attorney in making an admissibility or inadmissibility determination regarding the foreign national's case. Also, if Form G-28 indicating representation by the immigration attorney has not been filed at the time of the foreign national's application for entry, the CBP officer may not discuss the specifics of the case until one has been filed.

In most cases, the immigration attorney is contacted after the inadmissibility determination has been made. It is important that in all cases, an immigration attorney file a Freedom of Information Act (FOIA) request to gather as much information about the case as possible. As of October 1, 2007, all FOIA requests concerning CBP admissibility determinations should be made to the following address:

U.S. Customs and Border Protection
1300 Pennsylvania Ave., NW,
Attn: Mint Annex Building, FOIA Division
Washington, DC 20229

Practitioners should be aware of the DHS Traveler Redress Inquiry Program (DHS TRIP).[12] This program is designed to address misidentification issues, help travelers address screening problems at POEs, and attempt to correct situations in which travelers believe they were unfairly or incorrectly delayed when reaching connecting flights, denied boarding, or identified for additional inspection when traveling to the United States. This program is not designed to replace the FOIA process, and will not provide a comprehensive report of the informa-

tion sought, but may provide useful information for foreign nationals confronting admissibility issues. The projected response time for a DHS TRIP inquiry is 30 days.[13] If the response from the DHS TRIP inquiry indicates that the information has changed, it may mean that there was an erroneous record in the system regarding the subject of the inquiry, which hopefully will be removed from CBP's database. If CBP determines that a record in the system is valid, but does not pertain to the subject of the DHS TRIP inquiry, the record will remain in the system and CBP will ensure that the subject of the DHS TRIP inquiry will not experience future issues with respect to the item in the record. Bear in mind that a foreign national may still be placed in secondary inspection for reasons other than the subject of the DHS TRIP inquiry. If the DHS TRIP inquiry does not result in a response within 30 days, either re-submit the inquiry or file a FOIA request.

PRACTICAL POINTERS FOR IMMIGRATION BENEFITS

Processing at U.S. Ports of Entry (TN and L-1 Applications for Canadian Nationals at the Port of Entry)

Whether the POE permits attorney presence during secondary inspection interview or not, there are some basic practice pointers that many immigration lawyers should follow when assisting a client prepare a TN or L-1 employer support letter in anticipation of an interview by a CBP officer of the foreign national employee candidate.

TN

The TN employer letter always should be signed by a person affiliated with the company, such as a human resources specialist, a member of the company's legal department, or an officer of the sponsoring employer. In addition to the required information in the TN letter, such as the title of the position and job duties of the TN candidate, the TN letter should briefly provide background regarding the person signing on behalf of the company, including the author's role with sponsoring employer and the person's ability to influence personnel decisions.

The letter also should include the author's phone number and contact information. CBP officers have been known to contact the sponsoring employer to

---

[11] See *http://cbp.customs.gov/xp/cgov/toolbox/ports/* for a list of all POE contact information.

[12] See *www.dhs.gov/xtrvlsec/programs/gc_1169676919316 .shtm* for information concerning DHS TRIP.

[13] AILA/CBP meeting, December 20, 2007. Meeting minutes were not posted to AILA InfoNet at the time of drafting this article.

confirm issues regarding the TN case. When this contact information is not available, the CBP officer relies on the phone number that appears on the TN employer support letter's letterhead. This number is often a general number connecting the CBP officer to a receptionist or company operator, who might not be familiar with the fact that the sponsoring employer seeks to employ the TN applicant.

During the interview and adjudication process of a TN case, the CBP officer must enter information related to the application into the agency's database. It is important that TN employer letter specify within the body of the letter the physical location where the TN applicant will be working. While often the sponsoring employer's address and the worksite location are the same place, there are situations in which the worksite may be different than the sponsoring employer's address. The TN applicant should be aware of his or her employment location as described in the letter, to ensure consistent testimony and documentation between the TN applicant and the TN employer support letter.

The TN employer support letter also should clearly indicate the job title and description of the position the foreign national will fill with the sponsoring employer. A TN application will be challenged if the job title is not on the list of TN categories in the regulations. If the person is coming to the United States to work as a TN engineer, the TN employer should indicate that the TN applicant would work in the United States as an "engineer." Should the TN letter indicate that the person's title is "project manager," although working as a mechanical engineer for a particular project, this inconsistency between job title (project manager) and the enumerated category (engineer) in the regulations will pose a problem and could lead to a misunderstanding during the TN interview. Similarly, descriptions of job duties should contain language that logically pertains to the TN position. Ambiguity and inconsistency should be avoided to ensure the successful adjudication of the TN application.

Occasionally, the foreign national applying for TN status may be an employee of a Canadian company or a company owned by the foreign national. The TN applicant must be engaging in activity permitted under the North American Free Trade Agreement (NAFTA)[14] categories for the Canadian

company's U.S. customer at a worksite located in the United States. Immigration practitioners must present evidence in the form of invoices or contracts and evidence of payment to the Canadian company by the U.S. customer linking the U.S. and Canadian entities in this fact situation. A carefully prepared TN application package must be presented to the CBP officer carefully describing the chain linking the Canadian entity and U.S. customer. For example, a Canadian company sending one of its engineers to the United States to engage in productive activity benefiting the U.S. customer must demonstrate the contract between Canadian and U.S. entities for providing the engineering personnel in servicing the contract between the two parties. Invoices and any other evidence outlining the chain of payment from U.S. customer to Canadian company to Canadian employee working at the U.S. customer's site must be available to be examined by the CBP officer.

Occasionally, Canadians applying for TN classification were not educated in Canada or the United States. Unlike in the H-1B classification context, credentials and educational evaluations are generally not persuasive in a TN context. While there is no clear guidance regarding the issue of acceptance of evaluations, CBP officers often rely on their discretion in adjudicating TN cases when the applicant was educated in a country other than the United States or Canada. Generally, evaluations of a TN candidate's education, not credentials and experience, performed by either a U.S. or Canadian university are recognized. When an immigration attorney is confronted with a TN applicant who was educated in a country other than the United States (*i.e.,* a computer systems analyst with a degree from India in computer science), the wise immigration attorney first obtains an evaluation of the degree from either a U.S. or Canadian university.

A Few Tips Regarding the Scientific Technician/Technologist and Management Consultant

The rules pertaining to NAFTA provide little guidance regarding the scientific technician/technologist ("scientific technician") category. The regulations merely require that a person applying for a TN under this category possess:

> (a) theoretical knowledge of any of the following disciplines: agricultural sciences, astronomy, biology, chemistry, engineering, forestry, geology, geophysics, meteorology, or physics; and (b) the ability to solve practical problems in any of those

---

[14] U.S.-Can.-Mex., Dec. 17, 1992, 32 I.L.M. 296, 612 (entered into force Jan. 1, 1994).

disciplines, or the ability to apply principles of any of those disciplines to basic or applied research.[15]

The regulatory definition of a scientific technician is very broad, allowing a variety of interpretations by CBP officers as to what type of TN applicant qualifies under this category. The challenge with the scientific technician involves how to prove that a TN applicant possesses the requisite "theoretical knowledge" of one of the required fields described in the rules.

To provide guidance to the field regarding the processing of scientific technician TN applications, legacy Immigration and Nationality Service (INS) revised the *Inspector's Field Manual*.[16] This guidance provides that scientific technicians must work in "direct support" of persons who are professionals in their own right, with bachelor's degrees or equivalent in agricultural sciences, astronomy, biology, chemistry, engineering, forestry, geology, geophysics, meteorology, or physics. The educational background of the scientific technician must be related to that of the supervising professional. For instance, a scientific technician whose educational focus is in the engineering field must be working in direct support of a degreed engineer. The TN applicant under this category also must have completed two years of training in a relevant educational program.

Such training may be documented by presentation of a diploma, a certificate, or a transcript accompanied by evidence of relevant work experience.[17]

Relevant work experience may be demonstrated by reference letters from past employers confirming the scientific technician candidate's credentials in the appropriate area of theoretical knowledge as required by the regulations. This guidance instructs inspecting officers to consult with the *Occupational Outlook Handbook* when issues of job duties related to the particular field of expertise are of concern. [The guidance usefully adds that welders, boilermakers, carpenters, and electricians are not appropriate occupations for the scientific technician category.]

A second TN category that has been challenging, due to the lack of definition in the regulations, is the management consultant. Persons applying for this occupational classification should not be "managers." They would not directly manage employees of the company sponsoring the TN application, but must consult directly with the leadership/management of the company. The regulations mandate that applicants possess a baccalaureate or licenciatura degree, or equivalent professional experience as established by statement or professional credential attesting to five years' experience as a management consultant, or five years' experience in a field of specialty related to the consulting agreement.[18]

A foreign national applying for a TN under the management consultant classification must either have a bachelor's degree or at least five years' experience as a management consultant or five years' experience in the area in which he or she is consulting.

If the candidate possesses a bachelor's degree, that degree must be "closely related" to the field in which the TN applicant is consulting. When there is a degree requirement for TN categories, legacy INS found that the "degree should be in the field or in a closely related field."[19] Even though legacy INS was demonstrating this conclusion within the context of discussing the TN application of a software engineer, a CBP officer could make the argument that the degree be closely related to the field for which the TN applicant is consulting, by drawing on the following point from legacy INS:

> Returning to the "software engineer" example, it is reasonable to require the TN applicant to provide evidence of a degree in engineering just as it is reasonable to require an engineering degree for admission as a TN to perform professional level duties as a civil engineer.[20]

---

[15] 8 CFR §214.6(c).

[16] INS Memorandum, J. Williams, "Field Guidance on the Admission of Scientific Technician/Technologists under the North American Free Trade Agreement (IN 03-01)" (Nov. 7, 2002), *published on* AILA InfoNet at Doc. No. 02121331 (*posted* Dec. 13, 2002).

[17] *Id.* at 2.

---

[18] 8 CFR §214.6(c).

[19] INS Memorandum, M. Cronin, "Guidance for Processing Applicants under the North American Free Trade Agreement (NAFTA)" (July 24, 2000), *published on* AILA InfoNet at Doc. No. 00101705 (*posted* Oct. 17, 2000).

[20] *Id.* at 2. Practitioners should also be aware that the only TN category that requires a specific specialty degree is hotel manager. The regulations require that TN applicants for the hotel manager occupation possess the specific degree and field of study of baccalaureate or licenciatura degree in hotel/restaurant management or postsecondary diploma/certificate in hotel/restaurant management plus three years' experience in hotel/ restaurant management.

Generally, there are two types of management consultants. The "short-term" management consultant would be sponsored by a company to consult with its management staff because of his or her expertise in a particular field. The intention is that this person will consult with the management staff for a limited time and then move on to another project. The longer this management consultant remains with the sponsoring TN employer, the more likely that CBP could conclude that the management consultant is engaged in activities beyond "consulting," which could pose admissibility problems.

The second type of management consultant works for a consulting company as an employee to perform services for its clients. The duration of this employment relationship is less of a concern than for the short-term management consultant.

CBP officers may require a consulting agreement in adjudicating either type of management consultant case. The short-term consultant should have a consulting agreement with his or client outlining the services, payment arrangements, and other contractual arrangements between consultant and client. If the consulting company is the employer, it should provide a sample contract with its clients.

L-1

Under NAFTA, L-1 petitions for Canadians may be processed at the U.S. POE.[21] Immigration forms and supporting documentation to be submitted for consideration should be prepared as if they are being filed with the appropriate service center of U.S. Citizenship and Immigration Services (USCIS). An additional item recommended when processing an L-1 case for a Canadian citizen is copies (with originals readily available) of the T-4 document from the Canadian employer. The L-1 applicant must demonstrate that he or she worked for the foreign entity for at least one year of the last three years before the date of the L-1 application for entry. The T-4 document, like the U.S. W-2 form, is issued by employers in Canada for tax purposes and is the best evidence that the foreign national worked for the Canadian employer for the required time.

If the L-1 petition is approved, the CBP officer completes the adjudication at the POE and forwards the adjudication and the case to the appropriate USCIS service center. USCIS then forwards a re-ceipt and approval notice to the L-1 candidate's employer and the employer's attorney of record.

While L-1 classification affords limited periods of U.S. employment,[22] the regulations allow extensions beyond the statutory time limitations for L-1 employees who "do not reside continually in the United States and whose employment in the United States is seasonal, intermittent, or consists of an aggregate of six months or less per year."[23] Similarly, "the limitations will not apply to aliens who reside abroad and regularly commute to the United States to engage in part-time employment."[24] However, the petitioner company and the foreign national "must provide clear and convincing proof that the alien qualifies for an exception. Clear and convincing proof shall consist of evidence such as arrival and departure records, copies of tax returns, and records of employment abroad."[25]

I-94 CORRECTION

CBP processes countless applications by foreign nationals, lawful permanent residents, and U.S. citizens every day. With such a high volume of applications for entry, there are bound to be times when mistakes are made on the I-94 cards. While such instances are anomalous, they do happen and must be dealt with appropriately. Errors such as admitting a foreign national under the wrong nonimmigrant classification may have drastic consequences. Fortunately, mistakes may be corrected, so long as immigration practitioners provide the appropriate evidence demonstrating that the error was made by CBP.

Corrections of documents issued at the air POE generally may be addressed by contacting the air POE at issue—or, if distance presents a concern, the nearest CBP POE office—to arrange a meeting at which the appropriate evidence may be presented. For land POEs, contact the land POE before taking any action to address an incorrect entry document. Foreign nationals seeking to correct a document when the error was not caused by CBP will generally be required to exit the United States and present themselves for inspection at the POE on return. If the error was made by CBP, it will be more conven-

---

[21] 8 CFR §214.2(*l*)(17).

[22] Five years for L-1B and seven years for L-1A; one year for new office L-1 cases. 8 CFR §214.2(*l*)(12).

[23] 8 CFR §214.2(*l*)(12)(ii).

[24] *Id.*

[25] *Id.*

ient to arrange an InfoPass appointment with the CBP duty officer at a local USCIS field office.[26]

E CLASSIFICATION AND VISA WAIVER

The "turnaround option" is helpful for holders of E visas. E visas usually are issued for five years. Foreign nationals with E visas should be given an I-94 valid for two years at each entry to the United States.[27] For example, a French national holding an E visa issued in 2005 valid until 2010 may obtain a new I-94 card by simply driving into Canada,[28] turning around, and entering the United States. The French national in this situation would have to present himself to secondary inspection for processing of the new I-94 card. The new I-94 would be valid for two years.

The turnaround option, however, is not available for individuals who enter under the Visa Waiver Program. Unlike E visa holders, a visa waiver foreign national may not take advantage of the turn-around technique to obtain another 90 days of authorized stay. The foreign national must have made a "meaningful departure" from the United States to obtain another 90 days under the Visa Waiver Program. Individuals re-entering from a contiguous territory such as Canada or Mexico will be issued an I-94 only for the balance of their original visa waiver admission.[29] Determinations concerning the definition of a "meaningful departure" are made on a case-by-case basis. Travel requiring that an ocean be crossed has been traditionally considered a "meaningful departure" from the United States. A drive into Canada and turn around back to the United States generally has been found not to be a meaningful departure.

REVALIDATION

Revalidation permits foreign nationals who qualify to use expired visas or visas that expire on a date prior to the most current nonimmigrant employer-based petition.

The first type of revalidation involves the automatic extension of validity at POEs ("automatic revalidation").[30] A foreign national with a valid pass-port who intends to maintain nonimmigrant status, and is applying for readmission within an authorized period of stay from a contiguous territory to the United States after an absence less than 30 days and who has not applied for a new visa abroad [and is not a national from countries identified as supporting terrorism][31] may be readmitted into the United States for the duration of his or her underlying grant of status.

For instance, a German national who entered the United States as an F-1 student, holds an expired F-1 visa, changed his status from F-1 to H-1B (but never applied for an H-1B visa), and travels to Canada or Mexico for a one-day business meeting, may use the expired F-1 visa in conjunction with his H-1B I-94 to be readmitted to the United States as an H-1B nonimmigrant, provided that he did not apply for a new visa while in Mexico. If the person in this example applied for a visa while in Canada, he may not use automatic revalidation to re-enter the United States. It is important that persons in this situation document that their stay outside the United States was less than 30 days. Hotel receipts, travel itinerary, and gas receipts are good illustrations of evidence to support an automatic revalidation re-entry request.

The second type of revalidation involves a visa with an expiration date earlier than the most current approved nonimmigrant petition. To explain the principle, it is best to refer to legacy INS correspondence:[32]

> The issue arises where, for example, an alien enters the United States as an H-1B nonimmigrant on the basis of a petition filed by "Company A." After commencing employment, the alien receives a more attractive job offer from "Company B." Company B files a new H-1B petition in the alien's behalf which is approved by the INS. The alien then begins employment with Company B. The alien subsequently leaves the United States and then applies for admission as an H-1B nonimmigrant alien to work for Company B present-

---

[26] *See http://infopass.uscis.gov/.*

[27] 8 CFR §214.2(e)(19).

[28] French nationals may enter Canada as a visitor. *See www.cic.gc.ca/english/visit/visas.asp.*

[29] 8 CFR §217.3(b).

[30] 22 CFR §41.112(d).

[31] *See* Department of State, *Country Reports on Terrorism 2007* (2008). The report includes the following countries that support terrorism: Cuba, Iran, North Korea, Sudan, and Syria.

[32] INS Memorandum, M. Aytes, "Validity of Certain Nonimmigrant Visas" (July 8, 1997), *published on* AILA InfoNet at Doc. No. 97071690 (*posted* July 16, 1997).

ing the H-1B visa issued to him based on Company A's petition.

Be advised that the current USCIS and Department of State policy is that, in the case of an H, L, O, or P nonimmigrant visa, the visa remains valid during its validity period regardless of a change in the beneficiary's employer. As long as the alien remains in the same nonimmigrant classification, the visa is considered to be valid until the date of its expiration. An H, L, O, or P nonimmigrant alien who changes employers in the United States, but remains in the same nonimmigrant classification, may use the previously issued visa to apply for admission to the United States if it is still valid.[33]

The legacy INS directive concludes by stating, "Officers should not arbitrarily limit the admission period of an H-1B or L-1 nonimmigrant alien."[34] This instruction remains in force and is followed by the CBP currently.

LAPTOP SEARCHES

Recent case law has made searches of laptops an issue. In *U.S. v. Romm,*[35] Stuart Romm, a U.S. citizen, had visited websites containing explicit material involving child pornography, which was downloaded by his laptop into the device's Internet cache. During the course of an inspection for entry into Canada, the Canadian immigration officer discovered that Mr. Romm had a criminal history, and asked Mr. Romm to turn on his laptop so that he could briefly examine the device. On finding the pornographic material, Canadian immigration officials refused admission to Mr. Romm. Mr. Romm withdrew his application for entry into Canada and returned to the United States. CBP had been informed by the Canadian immigration officials that Mr. Romm was refused admission into Canada due to illegal images contained in his laptop. CBP took possession of the laptop and found the images of child pornography. Mr. Romm was ultimately convicted of possession of knowingly possessing child pornography. While the court engaged in a thorough examination of the pertinent legal issues, the conviction was upheld. AILA members have since reported laptop searches by CBP officers. Although search and seizure of laptops for applicants for admission to the United States is not commonplace, immigration

practitioners should be aware of this case, as many clients often travel internationally with laptops and similar computer devices.

CONCLUSION

With increased security provisions and the heightened technological capabilities available to CBP officers in processing admission requests, immigration practitioners should make every effort to be aware of the most current border processing practices of CBP so as to better serve their clients and ensure an efficient and successful adjudication process.

---

[33] *Id.*

[34] *Id.*

[35] 455 F.3d 990 (9th Cir. 2006).

HOT ISSUES IN THE "WILD WEST" OF TN BORDER APPLICATIONS

by William Z. Reich and Brian D. Zuccaro[*]

INTRODUCTION

Ever since 9/11 and the creation of the Department of Homeland Security (DHS), applications for Trade NAFTA (TN) status under NAFTA filed at the border have become increasingly difficult and subject to heightened (and often misguided) standards.

U.S. Customs and Border Protection (CBP), the border enforcement branch of DHS, is now called on to adjudicate TNs. With holsters at their hips, CBP officers have created an environment akin to the Wild West, where officers are quick to deny first, and ask questions later. Our office has observed a litany of problems surrounding the adjudication of TNs in this new environment with the following five issues emerging most frequently:

HOT ISSUES

Requirement of a Specific Degree in the Occupational Category

We find that CBP officers are increasingly requiring that an applicant for a TN possess a specific degree in the NAFTA TN occupational category. There is no basis for this interpretation under the TN regulations. Except for the Hotel Manager category, the regulations do not require a specific degree in the occupational category.[1]

As provided in a legacy INS memorandum by Michael Cronin,[2] the Hotel Manager is the only TN category that requires a specific degree or post-

secondary diploma under the NAFTA TN regulations. No other TN category requires a specific degree. According to the Cronin memo, all that is required is that "[t]he degree should be in the field or in a closely related field. Officers should use good judgment in determining whether a degree in an allied field may be appropriate."[3]

The occupational category where this problem emerges most often is the Computer Systems Analyst category. CBP officers routinely deny applications when the applicant does not possess a specific degree in Computer Science. Again, there is no basis for this requirement under the regulations. To qualify for a TN in the Computer Systems Analyst category, an applicant must possess a "Baccalaureate or Licenciatura Degree; or Post-Secondary Diploma or Post Secondary Certificate and three years' experience." No specific degree is mentioned.

When we refer to the *Occupational Outlook Handbook* (OOH) for further guidance on the qualifications for a Computer Systems Analyst, we find that a wide variety of degrees is suitable for this profession. For jobs in a technical or scientific environment, "employers often seek applicants who have at least a bachelor's degree in a technical field, such as computer science, information science, applied mathematics, engineering, or the physical sciences."[4] For jobs in a business environment, "employers often seek applicants with at least a bachelor's degree in a business-related field such as management information systems (MIS) [or] who have a master's degree in business administration (MBA) with a concentration in information systems."[5] The OOH also provides that individuals with non–computer-science degrees will qualify for Computer Systems Analyst positions provided they have completed related coursework.[6]

We maintain in our applications that the reason for requiring a degree is similar to the H-1B context, in that it is to establish the applicant as a profes-

---

[*] **William Z. Reich** is senior partner of the immigration law firm, Serotte Reich Wilson, LLP based in Buffalo, NY. A frequent publisher, lecturer, mentor and panelist at seminars and AILA conferences, Mr. Reich maintains an extensive practice in NAFTA business applications and border-problem cases.

Brian D. Zuccaro is a senior associate attorney at Serotte Reich Wilson, LLP and practices employment-based immigration law focusing specifically on NAFTA TN applications. Mr. Zuccaro writes exclusively on TN issues on his blog located at *www.naftatnlawyer.com*.

[1] *See* 8 CFR §214.6(c).

[2] INS Memorandum, M. Cronin, "Guidance for Processing Applicants under the North American Free Trade Agreement (NAFTA)" (July 24, 2000), *published on* AILA InfoNet at Doc. No. 00101705 (*posted* Oct. 17, 2000).

[3] Cronin memo, *supra* note 2.

[4] Bureau of Labor Statistics, U.S. Department of Labor, *Occupational Outlook Handbook*, 2008–09 Edition, Computer Systems Analysts, *available at www.bls.gov/oco/ocos287.htm*.

[5] *Id.*

[6] OOH, *supra* note 4.

sional. Often it is the applicant's post-education experience that becomes most relevant in determining his or her eligibility for a position. Frequently, we find applicants with nonrelated degrees who possess substantial experience in the field can make strong cases for a TN. This is especially true for the Computer Systems Analyst category, which, as provided in the OOH, does not always require a computer-related degree. For example, we have successfully argued that an individual with a degree in music, who has worked for many years as director of Information Technology for a major corporation, was eligible for a TN under the Computer Systems Analyst category. By referencing favorable language from the OOH, we have been able to reverse many denials based on the lack of a specific degree.

Unwarranted Limitations Imposed on the Number of Years as a TN

CBP officers routinely question applicants on the number of years they have worked in the United States under TN status. Without consideration of any other factors, officers have denied applications under the INA §212(a)(7)(A)(i)(I) intending immigrant provisions simply because the applicant has held TN status for several years.

In most cases, these denials are without merit and reflect overzealous enforcement of the immigrant intent provisions. Our office has successfully argued that an individual may work under TN status indefinitely as long as he or she otherwise overcomes the presumption of immigrant intent. Without additional, concrete signs of immigrant intent, an application should not be denied merely because the applicant has held TN status for several years. Unlike H-1B or L-1 status, the regulations do not place a limit on the total period of time an individual may remain in TN status.[7] The only limitation is that the admission is temporary, has a finite end, and does not equate to permanent residence.[8] As long as there is no immediate intent to immigrate, multiple years under TN status may still be considered temporary.[9]

Provided the applicant maintains that the purpose of his or her entry is to undertake a temporary job assignment, and does intend to establish permanent residence, the application should not be denied solely due to an extended period of time in TN status.

The Effect of the Filing of a Labor Certification and I-140 Petition or I-130 Petition

As with extended periods of TN status, CBP frequently considers the mere filing of a labor certification application or an immigrant petition as dispositive of an applicant's intent and will deny the TN application on the grounds of immigrant intent.

Our office maintains that the filing a labor certification, I-140 or I-130 petition in and of itself should not warrant the denial of a TN application. The requirement to maintain nonimmigrant intent does not mean that an applicant cannot possess an intent to immigrate in the future: "An intent to immigrate in the future which is in no way connected to the proposed immediate trip need not in itself result in a finding that the immediate trip is not temporary."[10] Each application for entry should be viewed as a new entry and as long as the applicant can establish that at the time of application his or her intent is solely to undertake or continue temporary employment, the mere filing of an immigrant petition should not result in a denial based on immigrant intent.

Our office recommends TN applicants pursue permanent residency through immigrant visa processing. Under this procedure, the applicant is in a better position to argue bona fide nonimmigrant intent. The argument is that, since the applicant must depart the United States to attend processing at a U.S. consulate, the applicant's admission to the United States is temporary. As long as the applicant is only seeking to enter for temporary employment and not for the purpose of adjustment of status, his or her temporary intent for the TN should still be recognized.

Requiring a Formal Education from Sci/Techs

Based on a legacy INS memorandum by Johnny N. Williams, CBP officers have taken the position that an applicant for a TN under the Scientific Technician/Technologist (Sci/Tech) category *must* possess at least two years of educational training.[11] Not only is this requirement absent in the regulations, but this position is also contrary to the actual language provided in Williams' memo.

---

[7] 8 CFR §214.6(h)(1).

[8] 8 CFR §§214.6(a) and (b).

[9] 9 *Foreign Affairs Manual* (FAM) 41.59 N5.

---

[10] 9 FAM 41.59 N5.

[11] INS Memorandum, J. Williams, "Field Guidance on the Admission of Scientific Technician/Technologists under the North American Free Trade Agreement (IN 03-01)" (Nov. 7, 2002), *published on* AILA InfoNet at Doc. No. 02121331 (*posted* Dec. 13, 2002).

Under the regulations, in order to qualify for a TN under the Scientific Technician/Technologist category, an applicant must possess "(a) theoretical knowledge of any of the following disciplines: agricultural sciences, astronomy, biology, chemistry, engineering, forestry, geology, geophysics, meteorology, or physics; and (b) the ability to solve practical problems in any of those disciplines, or the ability to apply principles of any of those disciplines to basic or applied research."[12] In addition, the applicant must "work in direct support of professionals in agricultural sciences, astronomy, biology, chemistry, engineering, forestry, geology, geophysics, meteorology or physics."[13] The regulations are clear that there is no specific educational credential required.

The Williams memo was issued to provide "additional guidance" and outlines five principles for immigration officers to use in their evaluation of Sci/Tech applications. The third principle states that an applicant's "theoretical knowledge **should** have been acquired through the successful completion of at least two years of training in a relevant educational program."[14] A close reading of the memo indicates that a Sci/Tech applicant *should*, not must, have at least two years of educational training.

The educational requirement is therefore not absolute, and CBP should not interpret it as such. By bringing this reading to CBP's attention, we have successfully obtained Sci/Tech approvals (and reversed denials) where an applicant possessed little or no education, but substantial experience in one of the listed disciplines.

CBP Officers Providing Unsolicited Legal Advice to Applicants

We have seen applicants who were refused a TN visa told by CBP officers that they should apply for either H-1B or L-1 or any other nonimmigrant visa when they apply for a TN. This is totally inappropriate. The only concern the inspecting officer should have is whether the applicant has the requisite eligibility for the position—not to render legal advice.

PRACTICE POINTERS

As noted in the introduction, when filing a TN application at the port-of-entry, you are dealing with CBP inspectors who are not benefit-oriented, and frequently not sufficiently trained to undertake the analysis required to adjudicate TN applications.

The role of the attorney is to anticipate the difficult issues in advance and guide the decision maker to the desired result. For difficult TNs, we provide a supplemental memorandum or extended cover letter to alert the officer to the unusual issues and to provide them with a road map that fully sets forth our theory of the case. It also should be kept in mind that even if the first line officer is going to deny the case, you can ask for review by a supervisor or even a port chief (formerly port director) to advocate for the case.

The key to a successful application is advanced fact gathering, theory preparation for the case, and alignment of everyone's expectations before finalizing the application. The final step is the preparation of the client in a way that educates the client about the dynamics of the case so that the client can be part of the advocacy at the time of application.

CONCLUSION

In approaching a difficult TN case, we try to demystify the application and present the case in a straightforward manner. If you have good facts and everyone's expectations are clearly understood, then the application should be successful despite misconceptions or suspicions by the adjudicating officer. In today's environment, the key to avoiding the O.K. Corral over a TN application is to clearly present the case theory to the inspector and to establish a comfort level so that he or she does not feel that it is easier to deny an application rather than to approve.

---

[12] 8 CFR §214.6(c).

[13] 8 CFR §214.6(c) n.6.

[14] Williams memo, *supra* note 11.

TRICKY TNS: HINTS AND HAZARDS

*by Norka M. Zagazeta and Leigh A. Lampert**

INTRODUCTION

Among the various professional occupations specifically designated under NAFTA as qualifying for TN nonimmigrant status are Computer Systems Analysts, Management Consultants, and Scientific Technicians/Technologists. These three categories are among the most misunderstood and they therefore seem to generate much confusion among clients, immigration officers, and—although we sometimes do not like to admit it—attorneys. In addition, because of many common misunderstandings relating to these three professions, immigration officers' decisions are often unpredictable and inconsistent.

In an effort to clarify some of these common misperceptions and to reduce the instances of unpredictability and inconsistency, this article will provide a general overview on how to file TN applications and will further discuss these three particularly "tricky" categories. Attempts will be made to clarify the meanings of "computer systems analyst," management consultant" and scientific technician/technologist" in the context of immigration law, and to provide practical suggestions for attorneys preparing these types of TN applications. The discussion will include practical tips as to what types of supporting documents, information, and other evidence applicants should be prepared to present when applying for TN nonimmigrant status, as well as some alternative options, should applicants in one of these three occupations ultimately be denied TN status.

TN PROFESSIONALS IN GENERAL

In General

A citizen of Canada or Mexico can apply for admission under the TN classification if he or she is a business person who will engage in business activities at a professional level in accordance with the North American Free Trade Agreement (NAFTA),[1] and if he or she possesses the relevant education, or background, and/or work experience listed in Appendix 1603.D.1 of the NAFTA.[2]

Where Can Citizens of Canada Apply?

A Canadian citizen seeking entry under the TN classification can apply for admission at any United States Class A port-of-entry, at a U.S. airport handling international traffic, or at a U.S. preclearance/preflight station.[3] Canadian citizens are visa-exempt and do not require consular visa issuance for TN status.[4]

Where Can Citizens of Mexico Apply?

Mexican citizens seeking TN status must apply through a U.S. embassy or consulate for a TN visa,[5] and these applications are adjudicated by consular officers.[6] Once a Mexican applicant is issued a TN nonimmigrant visa, he or she may apply for admission to the United States at a port of entry.[7]

Documentation Required

Those seeking TN nonimmigrant status will be required to present documentary evidence of their eligibility. Such will include—at a minimum—proof of citizenship; a supporting letter from the prospective U.S. employer describing the nature of the employment and confirming that this is a *temporary* assignment; and evidence that the applicant meets the minimum education and/or work experi-

---

* **Norka M. Zagazeta** is an associate with Guberman, Garson, Bush Immigration Lawyers in Toronto. Ms. Zagazeta received her B.Sc. from the University of Toronto, and her J.D. from Thomas M. Cooley Law School. She is a member of the State Bar of Florida and practices in the area of U.S. cross-border and Canadian immigration.

Leigh A. Lampert is an associate with Guberman, Garson, Bush, Immigration Lawyers in Toronto. Mr. Lampert practices exclusively in the area of immigration law. He provides legal representation to prominent institutional and multinational corporate clients, as well as to smaller corporate and individual clients. He advises the firm's clients on an ongoing basis in matters pertaining to U.S. cross-border matters and Canadian immigration.

---

[1] *See* 8 CFR §214.6(c).

[2] *See* 8 CFR §214.6(a).

[3] *See* 8 CFR §214.6(d)(2).

[4] *See* 9 *Foreign Affairs Manual* (FAM) 41.59 N4.1.

[5] *See* 9 FAM 41.59 N4.2.

[6] *Id.*

[7] *See* 8 CFR §214.6(d)(1).

ence requirements set out in Appendix 1603.D.1 of the NAFTA.[8]

The employer's supporting letter should clearly specify the applicable professional occupation for which the status is being sought. It also should describe the proposed employment roles and responsibilities and should link the applicant's educational qualifications or professional qualifications/credentials with the proposed employment and with the applicable professional occupation for which the nonimmigrant status is being sought. The employer's letter also should specify the proposed term of the temporary assignment and the remuneration to be paid.[9] The length of the temporary assignment cannot exceed one year, but proposed changes were recently announced, which—if implemented—will allow for initial temporary terms of three years, with the possibility of future extensions in three-year increments.[10]

Once admitted in TN nonimmigrant status, an applicant will receive Form I-94, Arrival/Departure Record confirming his or her status.[11] The I-94 card should bear the "multiple entry" notation, thus allowing the applicant to enter and exit the United States as many times within the prescribed period of stay.[12]

Extensions of Stay

In General

A person with TN status can live and work in the United States for up to one year at a time (and if the aforementioned proposed changes are implemented, three years) and can renew the status for additional periods in one-year increments (to be increased to three years if the proposed amendments are implemented).[13] There is no limit to the number of renewals, but at some point an officer may question whether the applicant's intent remains *temporary*.[14] Temporary entry is defined in NAFTA as entry without the intent to establish permanent resident.[15] The applicant must satisfy the inspecting immigration officer that his or her work assignment in the United States will end at a predictable time and that he or she will depart upon completion of the assignment.[16]

Readmission at the Port-of-Entry

A Canadian with TN nonimmigrant status can reapply for admission (*i.e.,* a renewal) at a port-of-entry. The new application must include the same documentation and evidence as the initial application because each application for TN status made at a port-of-entry is adjudicated as if it were a new one.[17]

A Mexican citizen wishing to renew/extend his or her TN visa will have return to the United States consulate and apply for a new visa. Once the visa is issued, a Mexican applicant will have to present it at a U.S. port-of-entry along with a valid passport.

Extending TN Status from Within the United States

Canadian and Mexican citizens who hold TN status may apply for an extension of stay by requesting their U.S. employer file Form I-129 with the Vermont Service Center, along with supporting documentation and the prescribed fee.[18] The beneficiary must be physically present in the United States at the time of the filing of the extension of stay.[19] If the beneficiary is required to leave the United States for any reason while the extension request in pending at the service center, the U.S. petitioner, in the case of a Canadian TN beneficiary, may request the director to transmit notification of approval of the application to the port-of-entry where the Canadian TN beneficiary will apply for admission to the United States.[20] In the case of a Mexican citizen, the U.S. petitioner may request the director to transmit notification of approval to the appropriate U.S. embassy or consulate abroad where the Mexican TN beneficiary will seek visa endorsement.[21]

COMPUTER SYSTEMS ANALYSTS

General Requirements

Persons seeking entry to the United States under NAFTA as computer systems analysts must possess either: (1) a bachelor's or *licenciatura* degree; *or* (2)

---

[8] 9 FAM 41.59 N4.3.

[9] *See* 8 CFR §214.6(d)(3).

[10] 73 Fed. Reg. 26349 (May 9, 2008).

[11] *See* 8 CFR §214.6(e).

[12] *Id.*

[13] *See* 8 CFR §214.6(h).

[14] *See* 8 CFR §214.6(a).

[15] *See* 8 CFR §214.6(b).

[16] *Id.*

[17] *See* 8 CFR §214.6(h)(2).

[18] *See* 8 CFR §214.6(h)(1).

[19] *Id.*

[20] *Id.*

[21] *Id.*

a post-secondary diploma or certificate *and* three years of experience.[22]

Because the term "computer systems analyst" is broad, ambiguous and vague, with multiple meanings in various contexts, inspecting officers rely on a number of different sources in determining whether an applicant qualifies as such. Three of the more commonly-used sources are the *Occupational Outlook Handbook* (OOH), published by the U.S. Department of Labor; the legacy INS *NAFTA Handbook*; and memoranda sent by regional directors to ports of entries.

Factors to Consider when Evaluating Eligibility

Whether the prospective job duties are consistent with the job duties generally performed by Computer Systems Analysts in the field.

Reference to the OOH, the *NAFTA Handbook*, and various memoranda suggests that, generally speaking, computer systems analysts' duties should involve solving computer problems and using computer technology to meet an organization's needs. Computer systems analysts often work with specific types of computer systems such as in the areas of business, accounting, or financial systems or scientific and engineering systems that vary with the kind of organization.[23] They often use techniques such as structured analysis, data modeling, information engineering, mathematical model building, sampling, and cost accounting to make sure their plans are efficient and complete.[24]

These analysts often can prepare cost-benefit and return-on-investment analyses to help management decide whether implementing the proposed technology would be financially feasible.[25] Other common duties include: coordinating tests and observing the initial use of the system to ensure that it performs as planned;[26] and selecting the appropriate computer hardware and software for an organization as it acquires a new system.[27] As a rule, systems analysts are not programmers, even though a small portion of their overall work may involve some programming. Thus far, this TN category does *not* include programmers, *per se*.[28]

Does the applicant possess the required degree and/or experience?

As mentioned, the computer system analyst occupation requires either a bachelor's or *licenciatura* degree; *or* a post-secondary diploma or certificate *and* three years of experience. In an "ideal" case, the applicant will hold a bachelor's degree in computer science or an appropriate diploma with the required three years of experience. However, there are other programs of study that conform to the minimum education requirement under NAFTA. For example, the OOH lists degrees such as computer science, information science, applied mathematics, engineering, management information systems (MIS), and master's degree in business administration (MBA) with a concentration in information systems as possible alternatives to the aforementioned bachelor's in computer science.[29] Notwithstanding this, there are many cases that are denied under this category because the TN applicant does not possess a degree "specifically" in computer science. These discrepancies are due, largely, to officers' discretion.

It is often helpful to preempt this mistaken interpretation by directing the U.S. Customs and Border Protection (CBP) officers to the July 24, 2000, Cronin memorandum relating to the adjudication of NAFTA applications, in which it is stressed that the only TN category that requires a specific degree is the Hotel Manager category.[30] The educational requirement for the remaining TN categories is that the degree "should be in the field or in a closely related field." Presenting an application with the required supporting evidence and a copy of this memorandum will obviously not guarantee success, but will certainly be helpful.

---

[22] *See* 8 CFR §214.6(c).

[23] *Id.*

[24] *Id.*

[25] *Id.*

[26] *Id.*

[27] *Id.*

[28] U.S. Immigration and Naturalization Service Headquarters, Office of Inspections North American Free Trade Agreement, *NAFTA Handbook*, November 1999, "Canadian TN Nonimmigrant pursuant to NAFTA," section five, part H, p. 137.

[29] Bureau of Labor Statistics, U.S. Department of Labor, *Occupational Outlook Handbook*, 2008–09 Edition, Computer Systems Analysts, on the Internet at *www.bls.gov/oco/ocos287.htm* (last visited Feb. 14, 2008).

[30] INS Memorandum, M. Cronin, "Guidance for Processing Applicants under the North American Free Trade Agreement (NAFTA)" (July 24, 2000), *published on* AILA InfoNet at Doc. No. 00101705 (*posted* Oct. 17, 2000).

Notwithstanding the potential misunderstandings in the context of educational requirements and educational credential equivalencies, as well as the unpredictable and disparate outcomes from one officer to the next, most problems in the context of computer systems analyst applications relate *not* to the required educational component, but rather to the proposed job duties. While the meaning of "computer systems analyst" is often misunderstood and is vague and ambiguous, this can work *for* or *against* an applicant. It can work *for* him or her in that since it is so broad, one can attempt to argue that many proposed jobs fit into this category. Likewise, and specifically because it is undefined, an officer that is inclined to interpret this narrowly could deny the application. In short, while this specific NAFTA profession can be robust and all-encompassing, for the same reasons, these applications also can be extremely tricky, and in preparing them, attorneys should pay close attention to the three aforementioned sources that CBP officers rely on.

MANAGEMENT CONSULTANTS

The management consultant TN category is very often scrutinized—perhaps more so than any other category. This is largely because it is one of only two occupations under which one may qualify *without* any formal degree. Nevertheless, the category is very popular, widely used, and favorable adjudications are commonplace.

A person seeking to enter the United States under NAFTA as a management consultant must possess either a bachelor's or *licenciatura* degree *or* equivalent professional experience as established by statement or professional credential attesting to five years' experience as a management consultant; or five years of experience in a field of specialty related to the consulting agreement.[31] In addition to proof of one's education or the required experience rather than the formal education, an applicant also should present a detailed résumé documenting the required experience, skills, and knowledge. This should relate to the problems or issues upon which the applicant is being asked to consult while in the United States.

A management consultant is commonly understood to be an "outside expert" who is hired to help solve certain problems or to address specific concerns, and/or to help an organization with things such as its long-term vision and strategy. Management consultants typically provide services that are directed toward improving the managerial, operating, and economic performance of public and private entities by analyzing and resolving strategic and operating problems and thereby improving the entity's goals, objectives, policies, strategies, administration, organization, and operation.[32]

Management consultants are usually independent contractors or employees of consulting firms under contract to U.S. entities.[33] They may be salaried employees of the U.S. entities to which they are providing services only when they are not assuming existing positions or filling newly created positions.[34] As a salaried employee of such a U.S. entity, they may only fill supernumerary temporary positions.[35] On the other hand, if the employer is a U.S. management-consulting firm, the employee may be coming temporarily to fill a permanent position.[36] Management consultants typically do not have authority to make decisions, but rather, they *recommend* changes to management who must then implement or reject their advice. Likewise, management consultants are not actively engaged in the management of an organization.

Management consultant applications are often refused when an officer believes that the applicant is actually an employee of the sponsoring company, or that the applicant is assuming a permanent position within the regular structure of the company, rather than a temporary position as an outsider. In order to preempt this type of refusal, a written agreement confirming the applicant will work as an independent contractor is often submitted with the application for TN status.

One of the main factors considered in assessing whether an applicant is an employee or an independent contractor is the extent to which he or she has the ability to control how, when, and where he or she performs his or her services. Generally, if the sponsoring entity has a substantial amount of control over how, when, and where the applicant will perform services, then it is more likely that an employer-employee relationship exists.

---

[31] *See* 8 CFR §214.6(c).

[32] *NAFTA Handbook, supra* note 28, p. 136.

[33] *Id.*

[34] *Id.*

[35] *Id.*

[36] *Id.*

In determining whether an applicant's prospective job duties are consistent with those generally performed by management consultants, once again, reference to the OOH, the *NAFTA Handbook* and various memoranda can be helpful. A management consultant's role typically includes *recommending* ways to improve an organization, and thus, a TN application under this category may describe how the applicant's services will help to improve the company's goals and objectives, as well as its policies, strategies, operations, and administration.

In a typical case, a management consultant's role might be limited to learning about the organization, and then providing strategic advice and recommendations.

SCIENTIFIC TECHNICIAN/TECHNOLOGIST
General Requirements

Those applying for TN nonimmigrant status as scientific technicians and/or technologists often encounter intense scrutiny by U.S. officials. This is often because the terms "scientific technician" and "scientific technologist" lack clear definitions or meanings in the context of U.S. immigration law. To qualify as a scientific technician/technologist, an applicant must possess theoretical knowledge of one of the following disciplines: agricultural sciences, astronomy, biology, chemistry, engineering, forestry, geology, geophysics, meteorology, or physics. In addition, he or she must have the ability to solve practical problems in one or more of these disciplines, or the ability to apply principles of any those disciplines to basic or applied research.[37]

Scientific technicians/technologists typically use the principles and theories of science and mathematics to solve problems in research and development and to help invent and improve products and processes.[38] They are distinct from scientists in that their duties are more practical and "hands-on," whereas scientists are often involved in more theoretical work.[39]

Popular duties among scientific technicians/technologists include but are not limited to: setting-up, operating and maintaining laboratory instruments; monitoring experiments; making observations; calculating and recording results; and developing conclusions.[40] In addition, those who perform production work monitor manufacturing processes and may ensure quality by testing products for proper proportions of ingredients, for purity, or for strength and durability.[41]

Applicants under this category do *not* need a degree or a diploma. However, they must have acquired theoretical knowledge in one of the aforementioned disciplines through the completion of at lease two years of training in a relevant educational program.[42] "Proof" of this theoretical knowledge can be in the form of a certificate, diploma, or school transcript accompanied by evidence of relevant work experience.[43] The *Immigration Inspectors Field Manual* also provides useful guidance in this regard, stating that "supporting documents could be an attestation from the prospective U.S. employer or the Canadian employer ..."[44]

The work of the scientific technician or technologist must be managed, coordinated, and reviewed by the professional supervisor, and must also provide input to the supervisory professional's own work.[45] Thus, a TN applicant must be working in direct support of a supervising professional in agricultural sciences, astronomy, biology, chemistry, engineering, forestry, geology, geophysics, meteorology or physics. Further, the supervising professional should have a degree in one of these fields.[46] Although some officers may approve an application by a scientific technician case where he or she will be working in direct support of a professional having a degree in a related area, many will not.

Finally, the offer of employment should show that the applicant's work will be related to that of the supervising professional. A general offer of employment by the supervisory professional will not be sufficient, by itself, to qualify for admission as a

---

[37] *See* 8 CFR §214.6(c).

[38] *Occupational Outlook Handbook, supra* note 29.

[39] *Id.*

[40] *Id.*

[41] *Id.*

[42] INS Memorandum, J. Williams, "Field Guidance on the Admission of Scientific Technician/Technologists under the North American Free Trade Agreement (IN 03-01)" (Nov. 7, 2002), *published on* AILA InfoNet at Doc. No. 02121331 (*posted* Dec. 13, 2002).

[43] *Id.*

[44] *See* INS Inspector's Field Manual (IFM) section on NAFTA TN admissions.

[45] Williams memo, *supra* note 42.

[46] *Id.*

scientific technician or technologist.[47] The offer must demonstrate that the work of the technician or technologist will be inter-related with that of the supervisory professional.[48]

CONCLUSION

There is often a perception that TN nonimmigrant status is "easy to get," especially when compared to the other types of visas available to Canadians and Mexicans seeking to work in the United States. However, while TN applications are plentiful and while positive adjudications often result, there are potential pitfalls to be avoided by applicants and their attorneys. This is especially true in the context of some of the "trickier" categories, such as the three discussed in this article.

---

[47] *Id.*

[48] *Id.*

OBTAINING CANADIAN WORK PERMITS FOR THE BUSINESS PROFESSIONAL

by David H. Davis*

INTRODUCTION

The options available to a business professional for entry into Canada are many, but it is important to choose the right one that fits the needs and expectations of both the worker and the employer. The employer almost always has an urgent need for the employee to commence work as soon as possible. The employee, on the other hand, will be interested in knowing what options are available to him or her to convert a temporary work permit to a landed immigrant visa. What follows is a summary of the various categories under which business professionals may enter Canada, and means of obtaining permanent resident status.[1]

BUSINESS VISITORS

A business visitor typically is a person who is entering Canada for the sole purpose of attending meetings or conferences, or negotiating contracts on behalf of a company.[2] If the individual is approved for entry, the examining officer issues a visitor record, which usually remains valid for a short period of time. No work permit is required.[3]

Business visitors include those who are purchasing Canadian goods or services for a foreign business or government.[4] A business visitor, however, cannot complete any hands-on tasks, and should be prepared to prove that his or her income is derived from a foreign employer.[5]

EXEMPTIONS FROM OBTAINING WORK PERMITS OR LABOR MARKET OPINION

The federal government of Canada has a list of occupations that do not require either work permits or labor market opinions (LMO). Some examples are religious clergy and entertainment groups.[6]

This category is for persons who fit into very specific job categories that the federal government has determined do not require labor market analysis due to their very specialized knowledge and occupational standing. In fact, they do not even require a work permit. The list of applicable occupations is brief. Reference to this list is always a good idea, to determine if your client is qualified to fit within this category.

INTRACOMPANY TRANSFERS: C12

The category C12 covers work permits for persons who are employed by multinational corporations with offices in Canada and a foreign country. This category is for a person who is being transferred from a foreign company to a Canadian company. It is important to identify the corporate structure to demonstrate the requisite relationship between branches and affiliates or subsidiary and parent. The business enterprise must be doing business in Canada and the foreign country concurrently or within a reasonable period of time, such as within the first 12 months of opening a new office.

If the applicant is opening a new office that is related to the foreign company, C12 status is also possible, as long as proof is shown that the company

---

* **David H. Davis** is currently chair of AILA's Canada Chapter and has been practicing immigration law for over 18 years. He is currently writing a book on Canadian immigration law practice and has lectured on Canadian immigration issues for the Canadian Bar Association, AILA, and throughout North America. He is a sole practitioner with offices in Winnipeg and Manila.

[1] All foreign nationals (aliens, non-Canadian citizens and nonpermanent residents) entering Canada are subject to examination of their request for visitor or work permit documents by Canadian Customs and Border officers. Some immigration officers will examine individuals who are referred for secondary inspection. The arrangement in Canada has similarities to the way individuals are examined on entry into the United States. For a list of countries whose nationals may apply for visitor records or work permits at the port of entry instead of having to apply at a Canadian consulate in their country of origin, see Immigration and Refugee Protection Regulations (SOR/2002-227) (IRPR) ¶190(1).

[2] IRPR ¶186(a).

[3] IRPR ¶187.

[4] IRPR ¶187(2)(a).

[5] IRPR ¶187(3).

[6] *See* Citizenship and Immigration Canada, *FW 1 Foreign Worker Manual* §§5.8, 5.13, *available at www.cic.gc.ca/ english/resources/manuals/fw/fw01e.pdf.*

official coming into Canada will be financially supported by the Canadian company. Thus, proof of capitalization or a business plan is necessary.

The worker either must be an executive/manager or possess specialized knowledge. Specialized knowledge is that which is uncommon in the workplace, but it need not be unique. Others in the work environment can possess the same knowledge. Additionally, the applicant must be able to demonstrate that at least 25 percent of his or her time will be spent in Canada.

The maximum time that the worker may remain employed in this category is three years. If the person qualifies, the work permit will issue at a cost of $150 (Canadian). Individuals may pay the processing fee in cash or with a major credit card at most ports of entry.[7]

NAFTA

The North American Free Trade Agreement (NAFTA) contains a list of occupations that make individuals eligible to apply for a work permit in Canada if they are citizens of the United States or Mexico.[8] Individuals entering Canada under NAFTA can pay for and obtain their work permit at a port of entry. These persons do not require an LMO prior to applying for their work permit at a port of entry in Canada.

Some of the more controversial occupation categories under NAFTA are computer systems analyst, management consultant, and scientific technician. The definitions of these three occupational categories in the treaty are very broad in scope. The tendency of most officials is to give them a narrow interpretation. Therefore, one should be aware of who is in charge at a given port of entry. It is advisable to fax supporting documents that support your position ahead of time. Following up delivery of your fax with a phone call to the port in question is recommended.[9]

In addition to qualifying for entry under NAFTA on the basis of a profession, individuals can enter as

a business visitor if, for example, they are providing after-sales service[10] or attending general meetings.

The work permit can be issued in one-year intervals only. Renewal can be filed inland by delivery to the Vegreville Case Processing Centre or at the port of entry of choice, either land or airport terminal, by departing Canada and then seeking re-entry.

GATS

The General Agreement on Trade in Services (GATS)[11] is one of more than 20 trade agreements administered by the World Trade Organization. The goal of GATS is to remove barriers to competition in the services sector, although individual governments may choose the degree to which GATS obligations apply to any particular service sector. Canada is a signatory to this international treaty.

GATS is useful for individuals who seek a work permit to engage, as part of a services contract between a Canadian company and a company in another signatory nation, in an activity at a professional level in certain occupations. It should be noted that GATS professionals do not require an LMO prior to obtaining their work permit at a Canadian port of entry. The worker must possess the necessary academic credentials and professional qualifications.[12] The worker must meet entry requirements as a temporary resident visitor.

The maximum length of time for which the work permit may be issued is three months or 90 days within any given 12-month period. The worker then must depart Canada and perhaps seek re-entry under GATS or seek a work permit in a different category completely.

SIGNIFICANT BENEFIT: C10

The federal immigration department created a very useful provision that allows an individual who does not fit into the above-mentioned categories to obtain a work permit. An applicant who can demonstrate that his or her employment will constitute a "significant benefit" to Canada may enter under a category designated C10. The problem with obtaining this classification is that examining officers narrowly interpret "significant benefit."

---

[7] For more information on the C12 category, *see id.* §5.31.

[8] North American Free Trade Agreement, U.S.-Can.-Mex., Dec. 17, 1992, 32 I.L.M. 289 (entered into force Jan. 1, 1994) (NAFTA), Appendix 1603.D.1, *reproduced in FW 1 Foreign Worker Manual, supra* note 6, at appx. G.

[9] For a listing of all ports of entry, see *http://cbsa-asfc.gc.ca/contact/listing/indexpages/index-e.html.*

[10] NAFTA, Appendix 1603.A.1.

[11] General Agreement on Trade in Services (GATS), Apr. 15, 1994, 33 I.L.M. 1167 (1994).

[12] *FW 1 Foreign Worker Manual, supra* note 6, at appx. D.

The C10 category is especially useful in urgent situations when no other option is available. It is vital to establish direct and immediate benefits for allowing entry of the applicant into Canada.[13] Persons can establish benefits to Canada if they include documents from the inviting company that demonstrate Canadians will be employed, business opportunities will prosper in the area they are moving to, and that the industry they are in is extremely important to the jurisdiction in which they intend to reside.

WORK PERMITS THAT REQUIRE LMO APPROVAL

Certain applications for a work permit require an LMO from Service Canada (formerly known as Human Resources Skills Development Canada), which is the federal government department responsible for labor market analysis and approvals of job offers for foreign workers. The application for an LMO is a four-page document submitted by the employer. It has many similarities to the labor certification process in U.S. immigration. The application requires proof of advertising and a description of the duties and responsibilities for the position to be filled and efforts made to hire local talent. The application must be submitted to a Service Canada office, of which there is one designated location in each province or territory across Canada. The waiting times are anywhere from 10 weeks to 15 weeks, depending on where the particular employer is situated.

It is vital to success in obtaining an LMO that the advertising for the position to be filled describes well the duties, salary, and minimum job requirements. The correct wage rate and applicable benefits must be outlined clearly, along with all minimum criteria for the job position.

The application for an LMO is usually necessary for high-demand, low-skilled occupations like long-haul truck drivers and welders. If the applicant is a highly skilled and well-educated professional it is unlikely that an LMO would need to be filed in order to obtain a work permit, since the applicant could take advantage of NAFTA, GATS, C12, or C10, as described above. If however, an LMO is going to be required, please know the processing time can be lengthy. (In some places such as Alberta, the wait time can be as long as six months or more.) One must take careful time to advertise properly and consistently in various media and all details of job position must be delineated clearly.

SPOUSES OF PRINCIPAL FOREIGN NATIONAL WORKERS

Many are not aware that spouses of the principal applicant can obtain a work permit if the principal applicant is in a skill level within certain categories of the national occupational classification (NOC) system and has worked for a minimum of six months in Canada. The principal applicant must be on a work permit of at least six months in length or, if the principal applicant is working under circumstances not requiring a work permit, can demonstrate je or she has worked in the qualifying occupation for a minimum of six months, usually by way of a supporting letter.

Spouses are eligible if their principal applicant spouse works in an occupation that falls within NOC classification 0 (management), A (professional), or B (technical or skilled trades persons). The same does not hold true for principals in lower-skilled categories (C and D).

A principal applicant's spouse is also eligible if he or she has been nominated by a provincial nominee program, discussed below, irrespective of the skill level of the principal applicant's occupation.

The work permit to which the dependent spouse is entitled is an open work permit and is valid only for as long as the principal spouse's permit is valid.

TEMPORARY FOREIGN WORKER UNITS

If counsel is going to consider assisting a foreign national in obtaining a work permit, it is critical for counsel to become familiar with the federal government website dealing with Temporary Foreign Worker Units (TFWUs).[14] These units were created to assist at certain airports with identifying whether a worker needs an LMO. Established on a pilot project basis, the units are designed to:

- guide employers or their representatives seeking to employ foreign workers;

- facilitate the entry of temporary foreign workers who are exempted from the LMO process; and

---

[13] For more on this topic, see *id.* at §5.29.

[14] *www.cic.gc.ca/EnGLIsh/work/employers/tfw-units.asp.*

- prescreen supporting documents from employers to streamline the application process and provide an opinion for officers at the port of entry.[15]

The TFWU offers guidance to employers and/or their authorized representatives seeking to employ foreign workers. Please note that the TFWU *will not respond* to enquiries coming from other sources or foreign workers themselves.

It is recommended that the applicant make contact with one of the following service units at least two weeks in advance of arrival at a Canadian port of entry, due to backlogs. The applicant needs to be well equipped with a job offer letter and all supporting information to establish the credibility of the work permit request.

Vancouver (serving British Columbia/Yukon Region)

Vancouver Temporary Foreign Worker Unit
Telephone: (604) 666-7509
Fax: (604) 666-7548
E-mail: *TFWU-Vancouver-UTET@cic.gc.ca*

Calgary (serving Prairies/Northern Territories Region, including Alberta, Saskatchewan, Manitoba, Northwest Territories, and Nunavut)

Calgary Temporary Foreign Worker Unit
Telephone: (403) 292-4183
Fax: (403) 292-6843
E-mail: *TFWU-Calgary-UTET@cic.gc.ca*

Toronto (serving Ontario region)

Toronto Temporary Foreign Worker Unit
Telephone: (416) 954-7954
Fax: (416) 973-9768
E-mail: *TFWU-Toronto-UTET@cic.gc.ca*

Montreal (serving Quebec region)

Montreal Temporary Foreign Worker Unit
Telephone: (514) 283-1061
Fax: (514) 283-1877
E-mail: *CIC-QUE-SRTE@cic.gc.ca*

Moncton (serving Atlantic Region, including Nova Scotia, Prince Edward Island, New Brunswick, and Newfoundland and Labrador)

Moncton Temporary Foreign Worker Unit
Telephone: (506) 851-2664
Fax: (506) 851-3238
E-mail: *TFWU-Atlantic-UTET@cic.gc.ca*

CONVERTING TEMPORARY FOREIGN WORKERS TO PERMANENT RESIDENT STATUS

The landscape of immigration options has changed dramatically over the past 10 years. In the past, an applicant who was a skilled professional had only one type of application to pursue: the federal skilled worker program, which was based on a set of points criteria. There are now essentially two main options for seeking permanent resident status in Canada.

One is the points system that applies to federal skilled workers.[16] The federal skilled worker selection procedure works on the basis of awarding points for individuals on the basis of their education, work experience, having a spouse who also is educated, having relatives in Canada, knowledge of English or French, and previous work or study permits in Canada. The threshold pass mark currently is 67 points. The difficulty does not lie in achieving the points but rather the lengthy processing line that exist for various regions in the world. For natives of India, China, and the Philippines, the processing time is typically five or more years.

There are alternatives to the federal points system. Over 10 years ago the federal government in Ottawa and the Province of Manitoba signed the first of many agreements known as Provincial Nominee Programs.[17] Most jurisdictions across Canada now have their own special agreements with the federal government establishing Provincial Nominee Programs.

Under the Provincial Nominee Programs, the responsibility for selection of permanent residents to Canada is basically passed over to the provincial jurisdictions. In each case the province decides what key factors will demonstrate that the skilled workers they nominate will become successfully established in that particular jurisdiction.

Each immigrant worker becomes a nominee by first completing and submitting the application form for that jurisdiction[18] identifying a category such as Employer Direct (have a job offer from a particular sponsor company), Family Stream (close blood-relative sponsor), International Student Stream (the applicant has attended university or college in the

---

[15] *www.cic.gc.ca/english/work/index.asp.*

[16] IRPR ¶¶78–83.

[17] IRPR ¶87. For more information, see *www.cic.gc.ca/english/immigrate/provincial/index.asp.*

[18] See *www.gov.mb.ca/labour/immigrate/index.html?* for examples of a provincial application form.

province and has a permanent job offer obtained as a result of applying for a postgraduate work permit that is good for a maximum of two years[19]), General Stream (usually points are given for age, work experience, education, etc.) or Community Supported (an ethnic or religious organization signs an agreement that it will support the applicant).

Next, the program officer with the provincial or territorial government reviews and determines if a Nomination Certificate ought to issue in favor of the applicant and his or her immediate family members, if any. The decision to nominate is reviewed by another officer, and then a senior officer within the program is authorized to sign the government-issued document.

The applicant then submits his or her documents to a Canadian consulate visa office outside of Canada, where all medical, criminality, and security certificates are requested and reviewed by a federal immigration official. The final step is for the Canadian government to issue immigrant visas to the principal applicant and his or her dependents.

This method of choosing permanent residents has become quite attractive, due to the fact that processing times are typically much shorter when compared to the federal skilled worker process. The target processing date for most applications is six to nine months from date of submission. The process can be expedited, especially when the individual has been employed in the jurisdiction for at least six months prior to submission of the application for nomination.

The attraction of the provincial nomination system is undoubtedly the fast processing time. In addition, immigrants who may not have a detailed education history but have good work experience can find success with the nomination program, since the federal skilled worker program may not be as generous.

The various provincial nomination programs have their own uniquely designed application forms, but in general they are all seeking immigrants who demonstrate a real desire to live and work in their jurisdiction, especially if they have relatives residing in their area or the applicant is currently working on a work permit in that jurisdiction. Although there is no requirement for the individual to live in the province for a certain minimum time, there is an understanding by each jurisdiction that the immigrant and his or her family will settle for at least one to two years.

If the principal applicant and his or family do not settle in the province that selected them, there is the possibility of a follow-up investigation by Canada Border Services Agency that could result in loss of permanent resident status on the basis that the individual did not fulfill his or her stated intention of residing in the jurisdiction.

The Provincial Nominee Program can be attractive to immigrants who have precarious status in the United States and who wish to resolve their predicament by filing an application for Canadian permanent resident status. Canada may be an option, but the applicant must have been lawfully admitted to the country in which he or she is currently residing for a period of at least one year.[20] This can be an obstacle for some, and there is no exception for asylum seekers.

At the present time all provincial jurisdictions in Canada have a nominee program in place for the selection of permanent residents. Each jurisdiction has its own application form and procedure, all of which can be reviewed by visiting the main federal government web site at *www.cic.gc.ca*. Currently the federal government is tabling new proposed legislation in Bill C50 to deal with backlog and selecting and processing quickly the right candidate. Immigration in Canada is quickly becoming a job-offer business. The process has developed into a system in which the person who has the job offer will obtain landed immigrant status in the quickest manner.

The U.S. immigration practitioner should discuss with his or her client the alternatives offered by Canada if it appears that the client may have more likelihood of success to the north.

APPENDIX: IMPORTANT WEBSITES

- Human Resources and Social Development Canada: *www.hrsdc.gc.ca/en/home.shtml*. To be read in conjunction with the Service Canada website: *www.servicecanada.gc.ca/en/home.shtml* (for LMO information).

- Citizenship and Immigration Canada: *www.cic.gc.ca* (for information on all immigration applications, both temporary and permanent).

- *http://laws.justice.gc.ca/en/showtdm/cs/I-2.5* (for the Immigration and Refugee Protection Act).

---

[19] For a description of these work permits, known as C43, see *FW 1 Foreign Worker Manual, supra* note 6, §5.38C.

[20] IRPR ¶11.

- *http://laws.justice.gc.ca/en/showtdm/cr/SOR-2002-227* (for the Immigration and Refugee Protection Regulations).

- *www.cbsa-asfc.gc.ca/menu-eng.html* (Canada Border Services Agency website, for information on criminality and other possible restrictions on getting into Canada).

- *www.wto.org* (for info on GATS).

CORPORATE COMPLIANCE PROGRAMS

by Gabrielle M. Buckley[*]

U.S. Immigration and Customs Enforcement (ICE) has initiated a strategic shift in the way it approaches enforcement of the immigration laws. Rather than relying on the traditional use of administrative fines for I-9 violations, ICE is bringing criminal charges against employers and seizing their "illegally derived" assets. Last fiscal year, this new approach resulted in 863 employers arrested on criminal charges and over 4,000 administrative workplace arrests. More employers also are being charged with money laundering, harboring, and violations of the Racketeer Influenced and Corrupt Organizations Act (RICO).[1] Convictions on these charges can result in prison sentences of up to 20 years.[2] Last year, ICE enforcement actions resulted in forfeitures and fines of over $30 million.[3] The U.S. Sentencing Commission's federal sentencing guidelines for organizations provide judges with a basis to determine the extent of the criminal sentences imposed on employers for violations of immigration laws. As a result, it is critical that employers understand, implement, execute—and document their execution of—internal immigration compliance programs that encourage due diligence at all levels in the organization.

A corporation acts through its "agents" and is liable criminally for actions of employees or corporate executives or officers who conduct illegal acts.[4] This is true provided that the actions of corporate agents were within the scope of their duties and were intended, at least in part, to benefit the corporation.[5]

Whether a corporation will be indicted will depend on a number of factors listed in the Department of Justice's "McNulty memorandum,[6] including:

1. How widespread the activity was;

2. The complicity or condonation of the wrongdoing by corporate management;

3. How high up and how extensive the complicity of management was;

4. Timely and voluntary disclosure of wrongdoing and cooperation in investigation;

5. The existence of a *preexisting* compliance program; and

6. Remedial actions—including an effective compliance program, replacing responsible management, and termination of wrongdoers.

In brief, the government has been utilizing criminal statutes to prosecute employers for violation of the U.S. immigration laws. One of the most serious statutes being applied relates to "harboring" persons unlawfully in the country.[7]

The statute makes it a crime for any person (including a corporation) to:

a. Knowingly or in reckless disregard of the fact that an alien has come to or remains in the United States in violation of the law;

b. Conceal, harbor, or shield that person from detection, or facilitate the alien remaining in the United States illegally or conspire to do so.

An appeals court that recently sustained a conviction of an employer for "harboring" found that Immigration and Nationality Act (INA) §274, regarding harboring an illegal alien, could be applied to an employer, because where there is knowledge or

---

Gabrielle M. Buckley is a shareholder with the Chicago office of Vedder Price P.C. Ms. Buckley heads the firm's business immigration practice and co-chairs the firm's international practice group. She presently serves as co-chair of the International Bar Association's Immigration & Nationality Committee, and sits on the Advisory Committee to the American Bar Association's Commission on Immigration Policy. Ms. Buckley is an adjunct professor of law at The John Marshall Law School, and is a fellow of the American Bar Foundation.

[1] 18 USC §1961 *et seq.*

[2] 18 USC §1963.

[3] "U.S. Immigration and Customs Enforcement FY07 Accomplishments" (Jan. 2008), *available at www.ice.gov/doclib/pi/news/factsheets/fy07accmplshmntsweb.pdf.*

[4] U.S. Sentencing Guidelines Manual, ch. 8, introductory cmt. (2004).

[5] *Id.*

[6] Department of Justice Memorandum, P. McNulty, "Principles of Federal Prosecution of Business Organizations" (Dec. 12, 2006), *available at www.usdoj.gov/dag/speeches/2006/mcnulty_memo.pdf.*

[7] INA §274; 8 USC §1324.

reckless disregard of the alien's unlawful status, the defendant's conduct tended to substantially facilitate the alien's remaining in the United States illegally.[8] The court also found that the employer's conduct constituted "harboring" within the meaning of the statute, because the employer knowingly or recklessly disregarded the employee's status as an alien who was not authorized to work or remain in the United States, and took steps designed to help her remain in his employ, undetected by legacy Immigration and Naturalization Service.[9]

Another criminal statute being utilized directly prohibits an employer from engaging in a pattern or practice of hiring or continuing the employment of an unauthorized alien.[10] The criminal penalties for this offense are less severe than violation of the "harboring" statute—an employer can be sentenced to six months imprisonment and fined up to $3,000.[11] In addition, there are corresponding civil remedies, and the U.S. attorney general can obtain an injunction restraining the illegal activity.[12]

A number of cases have been filed against employers under the RICO laws. These can be filed as either criminal or civil actions. An example of a recent civil action that has been permitted to proceed was filed by a competitor against a company for engaging in a pattern of violations of criminal conduct involving either harboring or hiring or continuing the employment of illegal aliens. The case alleged that the plaintiff company lost business because a competitor hired illegal alien labor, in violation of INA §274(a), and the plaintiff company suffered a direct injury.[13] The injured company had to show that violation of the harboring statute was the proximate legal cause of the defendant's ability to underbid the plaintiffs and take business away from them.[14]

Another civil RICO action was permitted by properly documented employees against their employer for hiring undocumented employees. The complaint, alleging that fruit growers had knowl-

edge of illegal harboring and/or smuggling of undocumented workers, sufficiently alleged a violation of the INA predicated on knowingly hiring undocumented workers, as required to state a RICO claim.[15] The documented laborers were found to have statutory standing to sue under RICO because they were direct victims of the fruit growers' alleged scheme to leverage hiring of undocumented immigrants in order to depress wages.[16]

What triggers governmental interest in conducting an investigation into your client's worksite that could result in criminal or civil action? Governmental investigations often arise in strange and unassuming situations. For instance, a disgruntled former employee or a competitor may relate information to ICE. This might include information and allegations pertaining to the knowing hire of unauthorized individuals or the actions of recruiters in explicitly or implicitly acknowledging the existence and procurement of fraudulent documents.

Once ICE decides to commence an investigation, there are various methods that it relies on to build its case, including:

- Investigations by ICE

- Confidential informants

- Cooperating witnesses

- Consensual electronic surveillance

- Data from government agencies: Social Security Administration (SSA), the Department of Labor's Wage and Hour Division; Office of the Inspector General; ICE; Office of Federal Contract Compliance Programs

- Visits to the worksite or homes of company representatives and officers

- An arrested employee who gives information regarding lax compliance policies or intentional conduct by the employer

Federal judges may look to the U.S. sentencing guidelines in determining how to sentence an individual/organization that is convicted of a federal crime. The guidelines set forth large fines and terms of imprisonment as punishment in order to serve as a deterrent to business crimes.[17] The 2004 amendments to chapter 8 of the guidelines, covering sen-

---

[8] *U.S. v. Kim*, 193 F.3d 567 (2d Cir. 1999).

[9] *Id.*

[10] 8 USC §1324a.

[11] 8 USC §1324b.

[12] *See* 8 USC §1324a(f).

[13] *Commercial Cleaning Servs., LLC v. Colin Serv. Sys., Inc.*, 271 F.3d 374 (2d Cir. 2001).

[14] *Id.*

[15] *Mendoza v. Zirkle Fruit Co.*, 301 F.3d 1163 (9th Cir. 2002).

[16] *Id.*

[17] U.S. Sentencing Guidelines Manual, ch. 8, introductory cmt. (2004).

tencing of organizations, were enacted for the express purpose of encouraging employers to implement structural policies and reporting procedures that prevent and detect criminal conduct.[18]

Moreover, under §8C2.5(g) of the guidelines (culpability score), an effective compliance and ethics program is one of the mitigating factors that can reduce an organization's punishment for immigration violations.[19] If the organization has an effective compliance and ethics program and makes efforts to self-report, cooperate with authorities, and/or accept responsibilities, the severity of any penalty may be mitigated. The recent amendments to the guidelines, which became effective November 1, 2004, provide updated (and more rigorous) standards for an "effective compliance and ethics program."[20]

The amended guidelines require (1) due diligence by the organization to detect/prevent criminal conduct, and (2) promotion by the organization of a culture that "encourages ethical conduct and compliance with law."[21] There are seven minimum requirements for an effective compliance and ethics program required under the amended sentencing guidelines, which create additional responsibilities for directors:

- Establishment of standards and procedures to detect/prevent criminal conduct

- Board (or committee) and senior management oversight

- Screening of management personnel for past illegal conduct

- Training/dissemination of information regarding compliance and ethics for directors and employees

- Monitoring compliance with and auditing effectiveness of program

- Promotion and enforcement of program

- Appropriate response to violations of program

Organizations that incorporate these standards and seek to self-report can achieve up to a 95 percent reduction in federal fines, and companies that do not can be subject to a 400 percent increase.[22] In light of the amended guidelines and heightened director responsibilities, many companies are reevaluating their codes of conduct/compliance programs to ensure compliance with these standards.

Clearly, it behooves employers to ensure that they have a "preexisting" immigration compliance policy in place to benefit from the provisions of the federal sentencing guidelines. To maximize such benefits, the policy should be in writing, and clearly state that the goal of the organization is to comply with all federal, state, and local immigration laws.

What are the key elements to include in a corporate immigration compliance policy?

1. The policy language should be clear and understandable, and should plainly state that all employees are to comply with relevant federal, state, and local immigration laws, and behave at all times in an ethical manner.

2. The policy should require that a compliance officer be selected. This should be an employee who is ultimately responsible for ensuring that the company and its employees and agents understand the laws and comply with the policy.

3.. The policy should require regular training programs for all levels of employees—from senior management down to the receptionists.

4. A monitoring system should be established to measure compliance with the policy and its effectiveness.

5. Ramifications for violation of the policy should be spelled out clearly and applied uniformly.

6. In consultation with litigation counsel, a procedure should be established for dealing with government visits, audits, investigations, and raids. This procedure should be communicated to "front-line" employees, including security guards, receptionists, etc. Ensure that the company provides post-audit and post-raid training for all involved individuals to further protect the company from follow-up actions by the government.

7. The policy should include clear guidelines regarding I-9 compliance:

---

[18] U.S. Sentencing Commission News Release, "Sentencing Commission Toughens Requirements for Corporate Compliance and Ethics Programs" (Apr. 13, 2004), *available at* www.ussc.gov/PRESS/rel0404.htm.

[19] U.S. Sentencing Guidelines Manual, ch. 8, introductory cmt. (2004).

[20] *Id.*

[21] U.S. Sentencing Guidelines Manual §8B2.1 (2004).

[22] D. Hess, *et al.*, "The 2004 Amendments to the Federal Sentencing Guidelines and Their Implicit Call for a Symbiotic Integration of Business Ethics," 11 *Fordham J. Corp. & Fin. L.* 725 (2006).

- Identify the level of employee permitted to complete Form I-9 on behalf of the company to ensure that the employee is knowledgeable and responsible.

- Ensure that these employees have been trained to review I-9 documents and complete the I-9 without violating discrimination laws. Periodically review and update I-9 training materials, being sure to document such review and all efforts to provide training to hiring managers.

- Determine how I-9 records should be maintained and seek to ensure uniformity in completion and maintenance of the I-9s—hard copy or electronically. If the decision is made to maintain copies of the documents presented to verify employment eligibility, copy both sides of the document and ensure that copies are maintained for all employees going forward from the date of implementation. Maintaining copies of the documents is generally recommended.

- Ensure that I-9 records are not kept with personnel files, but in a separate I-9 file, whether hard copy or electronic.

- Confirm that the company has a "tickler system" in place to reverify work authorization for employees with temporary status or work authorization. The employer will want to ensure that its software system captures expiration dates from section 1 of the I-9 for temporary work authorizations—for example, employment authorization documents, visas, and I-94 forms.

- Make sure that I-9 documents are included in the company's document retention schedules, as employers are permitted to destroy I-9 Forms and supporting documents after the statutory period of time. Employers may destroy I-9 records for former employees either one year after termination or three years after the date of hire, whichever is later.

- Set forth a schedule for conducting internal I-9 audits on a regular basis. This is one of the most important provisions of a compliance policy. The employer can analyze potential risks and possibly mitigate fines and damages by conducting internal audits prior to any government action.

8. The policy should contain a process for handling Social Security no-match letters. The Department of Homeland Security (DHS) recently issued regulations relating to Social Security no-match letters and a new definition of "constructive knowledge" that an employee does not have work authorization.[23] [These regulations are currently on hold due to a lawsuit. Although DHS announced that it planned to revise the regulations, on March 26, 2008, DHS repromulgated the regulations with nominal changes.[24] As of this writing, the regulations are not in effect.]

The policy should include the following provisions:

- Management should not disregard no-match letters.

- Employees should not assume the workforce is "illegal" based on receipt of the no-match letter.

- Employees identified in the Social Security correspondence should be advised in writing of the no-match letter.

- All employees subject to no-match letters should be treated in a consistent manner. The company should develop a standard time period within which the employee may address the discrepancy with the employer's records and the SSA records.

9. Develop an internal mechanism to address post-hire and initial I-9 completion issues, including instances in which third parties (for instance, clients or subcontractors) provide information indicating that an employee is not authorized to work.

10. Remember Wal-Mart![25] Ensure that the legal department or outside counsel reviews subcontractor agreements involving provision of temporary labor or services performed on company property. These agreements should include representations and warranties that the subcontractor(s) will comply with all federal, state, and local immigration laws. Employers may also desire to include a provision that subcontractors will indemnify the company for any damages

---

[23] 72 Fed. Reg. 45611 (Aug. 15, 2007).

[24] 73 Fed. Reg. 15944 (Mar. 26, 2008).

[25] ICE News Release, "Wal-Mart Stores, Inc. Agrees to Pay a Record $11 Million to ICE to Settle Nationwide Worksite Enforcement Investigation" (Mar. 18, 2005), *available at* *www.ice.gov/pi/news/newsreleases/articles/walmart031805. htm.*

and legal fees the company incurs should they fail to comply with applicable immigration laws.

11. Determine a decision-making process through which the company determines whether it will sponsor employees for lawful permanent residence or require the employee to bear immigration-related costs (when legally permitted). Avoid the appearance of discrimination or disparate impact by setting up a process that treats employees consistently, regardless of their national origin.

12. Establish a global immigration plan. Before transfer of employees, determine which costs the company will pay, such as whether family members/significant others will be included. Consider providing tax and estate planning advice to help make decisions regarding immigration status that can affect taxation and education issues.

Clearly, in light of increased enforcement of both civil and criminal immigration laws, as well as the amended sentencing guidelines and heightened executive responsibilities, employers should ensure that their codes of conduct and immigration compliance policies are capable of providing maximum protection for their organizations.

THE EMPLOYMENT RIGHTS AND LIABILITIES OF THE UNDOCUMENTED WORKER AFTER AN ICE RAID

*by Eileen Scofield**

Undocumented workers who lose their employment as the result of an enforcement raid by U.S. Immigration and Customs Enforcement do not lose all of their employment-related rights and benefits. The rights and benefits of which these workers may seek to avail themselves fall into two general categories: (1) the right to receive entitlements or other benefits normally associated with employment, and (2) the right to redress grievances that occurred prior to the undocumented worker's loss of employment. This article will examine the rights and benefits, within each of those two categories, that undocumented workers will be able to assert after losing their employment due to a raid.

ENTITLEMENTS AND OTHER BENEFITS NORMALLY ASSOCIATED WITH EMPLOYMENT

Social Security Benefits

Under the current state of the law, undocumented workers are not entitled to collect Social Security benefits, even if they have made contributions to the system through taxes on their earnings. However, on achieving legal status, the workers become entitled to Social Security benefits based on the contributions that they made to the system while undocumented.[1] Therefore, undocumented workers who lose their positions after an enforcement raid would not be eligible to receive Social Security benefits until they achieve legal status, but, on achieving legal status, they may collect benefits based on contributions made during any periods of unauthorized employment.

In recent years, however, Congress has considered altering this policy and preventing newly legalized workers from collecting Social Security benefits based on contributions made while those workers were undocumented.[2] Currently, House Bill 5515, a bill that would prevent undocumented workers from receiving credit for contributions made while undocumented, is under consideration in the House of Representatives.

Unemployment Benefits

In most states, one must have a valid Social Security number to receive unemployment benefits. Undocumented workers, therefore, cannot receive those benefits.

Payments at Termination for Time Worked and Accrued Vacation Pay

Undocumented workers have the same entitlement under the Fair Labor Standards Act[3] to pay for time worked and accrued vacation on termination as legal workers.[4] Therefore, undocumented workers who lose their jobs in an enforcement raid are entitled to a final paycheck and to the same payout for accrued vacation time as legal workers.

Workers' Compensation

Although workers' compensation schemes vary widely from state to state, it appears that, as a general rule, "illegal immigration status does not bar an employee from receiving workers' compensation benefits."[5] However, if a raid leads to a worker's imminent deportation or renders him or her unable to accept alternative light-duty employment because, for example, the worker loses the ability to drive, the worker may not be able to continue receiving work-

* **Eileen Scofield** is a frequent international and national public speaker and published author of numerous articles primarily on business related immigration. She has held numerous positions over her 22 years of practice with the bar associations and AILA. She is also a member of numerous organizations that advise Congress on business and immigration issues. She heads a national practice with Alston & Bird, a 700-plus attorney firm with offices in D.C., New York, Atlanta, Charlotte, Dallas, and Raleigh.

[1] J. Blazer & J. Bernstein, "Confiscating Contributions," 21 *Immigrants' Rights Update* (May 10, 2007), *available at* www.nilc.org/pubs/iru/iru2007-05-10.htm.

[2] *Id.*

[3] 29 USC §§201–19.

[4] *Flores v. Albertsons, Inc.*, No. CV0100515AHM (SHX), 2002 WL 1163623, at *5 (C.D. Cal. Apr. 9, 2002) ("Federal courts are clear that the protections of the FLSA are available to citizens and undocumented workers alike.").

[5] *Martines v. Worley & Sons Constr.*, 628 S.E.2d 113, 116 (Ga. Ct. App. 2006).

ers' compensation benefits that he or she may have been receiving before the raid.[6]

Continuing Health Insurance and COBRA

There is surprisingly little authority on whether undocumented workers are entitled to coverage under the Consolidated Omnibus Budget Reconciliation Act (COBRA)[7] and what effect a worker's undocumented status would have on any rights granted by a private insurance policy.

RIGHT TO REDRESS GRIEVANCES THAT OCCURRED PRIOR TO THE UNDOCUMENTED WORKER'S LOSS OF EMPLOYMENT

In general, undocumented workers enjoy coverage under employment laws that protect employees from discrimination along prohibited bases, retribution for attempts to assert workplace rights, and unsafe working conditions.[8] However, an undocumented worker's immigration status frequently will affect the damages to which he or she is entitled after prevailing in a lawsuit against a former employer. Therefore, if an undocumented worker loses his or her position in an enforcement raid, the worker will be able to maintain an action against the employer for discriminatory, retaliatory, or otherwise illegal treatment that occurred before the raid, but the revelation of the worker's undocumented status may reduce or eliminate the damages to which the worker is entitled.[9]

The first way in which the worker's immigration status may affect the damages calculation is by preventing the worker from collecting back pay for a period of time during which the worker was not working as a result of conduct by his or her employer that violates an employment statute. In *Hoffman Plastic Compounds, Inc. v. NLRB*,[10] the U.S. Supreme Court held that undocumented workers terminated in violation of the National Labor Relations Act's (NLRA) antiretaliation provision[11] are not entitled to back pay for the time that they did not work. Though some courts have expressed doubt as to whether *Hoffman* prohibits back pay in lawsuits brought under other employment statutes,[12] the Equal Employment Opportunity commission is of the opinion that *Hoffman* does preclude back pay for time not worked by undocumented workers regardless of which employment statute the worker relies on.[13] Therefore, if an undocumented worker seeks to redress the violation of employment laws that occurred before an enforcement raid caused him or her to be terminated, his or her immigration status should not affect the ability to maintain the lawsuit, but it may prevent an award of back pay.

If an undocumented worker who lost his or her job in an enforcement raid were successful in arguing that *Hoffman* applies only to NLRA claims and that he or she is entitled to back pay for violations of other statutes, the worker's immigration status still could come into play. The "after-acquired evidence" rule allows employers to cut off back pay as of the

---

[6] *See id.* at 117. *Cf. Asgar-Ali*, No. 114451/02, 2004 WL 2127230, at *2 (N.Y. Sup. Ct. Aug. 6, 2004) (explaining that risk of deportation was not enough to disqualify worker from receiving benefits, but implying that an imminent deportation may disqualify worker from receiving benefits).

[7] Consolidated Omnibus Budget Reconciliation Act of 1985, Pub. L. No. 99-272, 100 Stat. 82.

[8] *Pineda v. Bath Unlimited, Inc.*, No. 06-cv-2328(PGS), 2007 WL 2705150, at *1 n.1 (D.N.J. Sep. 14, 2007) ("It has been held that a plaintiff's citizenship status is not relevant for liability questions under federal labor and discrimination statutes."); National Immigration Law Center (NILC), "Overview of Key Issues Facing Low-Wage Immigrant Workers," at 5.2 (December 2007), *available at* www.nilc.org/immsemplymnt/emp_issues_ovrvw_2007-11-20.pdf ("All workers, regardless of their immigration status, are protected by federal and state labor and employment laws.").

[9] It should be made clear that an employee's termination as the result of an enforcement raid will almost definitely not create a cause of action under any labor or employment statute. The focus of this section of the article is on causes of

continued

action based on violations of labor or employment statutes that occurred before the worker was discovered to be undocumented in an enforcement raid.

[10] *Hoffman Plastic Compounds, Inc. v. NLRB*, 535 U.S. 137, 151–52 (2002).

[11] 29 USC §158(a)(4).

[12] *See De La Rosa v. N. Harvest Furniture*, 210 F.R.D. 237, 238 (C.D. Ill. 2002) (*Hoffman* is "not dispositive" on Title VII and FLSA claims).

[13] www.eeoc.gov/policy/docs/undoc-rescind.html ("Because the Commission's 1999 Enforcement Guidance relied on NLRA cases to conclude that undocumented workers are entitled to all forms of monetary relief—including post-discharge backpay—under the federal employment discrimination statutes, the Commission has decided to rescind that Guidance. The Commission will evaluate the effect *Hoffman* may have on the availability of monetary remedies to undocumented workers under the federal employment discrimination statutes."); *NILC, supra* note 8, at 5.3 ("The [EEOC], however, states that *Hoffman* precludes back pay remedies under [labor and employment] statutes.").

date the employer discovers evidence that would have led to the employee's termination.[14] At least one circuit court of appeals has indicated that, by virtue of the after-acquired evidence rule, an employer has no back-pay liability to a former worker for any time period after the employer learns of the worker's illegal status, provided that the employer can prove that "it would actually have fired the employee[] had it known that [he or she was] undocumented."[15] Therefore, if, after *Hoffman*, an undocumented worker may obtain any back pay damages in suits against his or her former employer, those damages would likely be cut off as of the date of a raid that revealed the worker's illegal status to the employer, provided that the employer could show that knowledge of a worker's illegal status would have led to the worker's termination.

CONCLUSION

Undocumented workers who lose their positions in enforcement raids remain entitled to many of the same benefits that any employee would enjoy after losing his or her job. Although they likely cannot collect unemployment, and while they must obtain legal status to collect Social Security benefits, they possess many of the same rights as legal employees under the workers' compensation statutes and wage and hour laws. Similarly, undocumented workers possess the ability to bring suit under labor and employment laws for activities that occurred prior to their termination, although they do face significant hurdles in obtaining back pay.

---

[14] *McKennon v. Nashville Banner Publ'g. Co.*, 513 U.S. 352, 362 (1995).

[15] *Rivera v. Nibco*, 364 F.3d 1057, 1072 (9th Cir. 2004).

Preparing for and Responding to Raids: The "Why" and "How" of Working with Community-Based Organizations—The Iowa Experience

*by Lori Chesser**

Increased worksite enforcement is a nightmare come true. For years we have been advising clients about I-9 compliance, how to respond to "no-match" letters, and what to do if U.S. Immigration and Customs Enforcement (ICE) comes calling; but the chances of it actually happening were so small that real preparation rarely occurred. Now that raids are a reality, the task of preparing our clients can seem overwhelming. We can handle the legal side, but what about the collateral consequences? Especially in a small town, an employer and its workforce are integral to the fabric of the community: a raid tears this fabric, and many parts begin to unravel. As lawyers, it is hard to watch and do nothing—but it is equally difficult to respond and know how to prepare your clients and the community for all the eventualities.

This article is meant to help us take heart and find resources outside our normal law-related channels to better serve our clients and the immigrant community. The way to do this is working with community-based organizations (CBOs) to develop relationships that will be mutually beneficial in preparing for, and responding to raids—and beyond.

WHY WORK WITH CBOs?

Today, immigration lawyers are a hot commodity, and we all have more than we can possibly do. Why add another task—and not a billable one at that—to our already overflowing "to do" list?

Building relationships with CBOs will truly help us respond to a raid. Even if we represent the employer, it is in our client's best interest that the affected employees' and their families' immediate needs are met. Detained employees must be released as soon as possible, not only for humanitarian rea-

sons, but to alleviate the temptation to turn against the employer in response to ICE interrogation techniques. Families that are provided with social services and assistance are less likely to blame the employer and create a public relations problem. Reducing the trauma to remaining workers (many of whom may be family and friends of those detained) is critical to keeping the employer in business. However, the employer often cannot make these things happen directly. CBOs can help.

If we represent employees who are detained, we need to focus on the legal issues, and not become a social service agency. We simply do not have time. Children whose parents, or single parent, are detained need to be cared for. If there is no power of attorney, caring for children is further complicated. Families need to know if their loved ones are detained, and if so, where. Detainees must be identified to be represented. Testimony from people who witnessed the raid must be preserved. CBOs can act as our extra eyes, ears, and hands in accomplishing these and other tasks. ICE's policy is now to contact CBOs on the date of a raid.[1] We need to be able to connect to CBOs too.

A raid can be less devastating if both the employer and the employees are prepared for it. Lawyers for the employer should provide "know your rights" (KYR) training for management and frontline staff. But it would put an employer in an awkward position, to say the least, to have its attorney conduct KYR training for employees (*i.e.,* "Exhibit A for the prosecution"). Still, if the employees do know their rights, they will be less likely to incriminate themselves or the company, and will have arrangements with family and friends regarding how to care for their children and property. CBOs can provide this valuable service.

* **Lori Chesser** is a senior shareholder in Davis, Brown, Koehn, Shors & Roberts, P.C. in Des Moines, and chairs its immigration department. She is a member of the AILA ICE Liaison and Interior Enforcement Committees, and former chair of the AILA Immigration Reform (Essential Workers) Committee. She is a cofounder of Iowa Allies for Immigration Reform, a grassroots immigration advocacy organization.

[1] AILA/ICE Liaison Committee Minutes (Dec. 12, 2007), *published on* AILA InfoNet at Doc. No. 08030662 (*posted* Mar. 6, 2008). Note that the minutes refer to CBOs and "NGOs" (nongovernmental organizations).

CBOs know the immigrants on a different level than lawyers. They can provide insight about what is being said in the community, what needs are not being met, and what employers are doing or are rumored to be doing. They can also provide referrals. However, as will be discussed below, involvement intended to drum up business is quickly seen for what it is, and is not appreciated.

CBOs can reach out to the immigrant community in ways that lawyers cannot. For example, it is important for undocumented immigrants to be represented before they are detained; getting a G-28 signed can be difficult or impossible while the person is in detention. CBOs should advise in their KYR training that workers make an appointment with a lawyer and get a G-28 signed in advance. This advice could be seen as self-serving coming from a lawyer.

CBOs also know the media. Community activists are "go to" people for reporters because they are knowledgeable and are seen as unbiased in a raid situation, and because they do not represent the employer or the government. They can shape how a story is reported or whom the press calls. If we represent the employer, we do not want our client portrayed as the "bad guy" in a story creating sympathy for the detained workers. Avoiding this frequently false perception is critical; and such perceptions impede immigration reform. Working with CBOs in advance to decide what should and should not be said to the press can help to educate the public and provide a more accurate picture of the immigration system when a raid happens.

Often, CBOs have strong relationships with government offices. They may have better access to a congressional office, the governor, or state human and civil rights agencies than do lawyers. Enlisting the help of these and other government offices can be instrumental in ameliorating trauma in a raid. For example, in the Marshalltown, IA, Swift and Co. raid,[2] a nursing mother was released only after a congressional office and the governor intervened.[3]

---

[2] This raid was part of "Operation Wagon Train," which occurred Dec. 12, 2006, at Swift and Co. plants in several states. *www.ice.gov/pi/news/factsheets/wse_ou_070301.htm.*

[3] Department of Homeland Security (DHS) field guidance now directs humanitarian needs assessment when making detention decisions. *See* "DHS Guidelines for Identifying Humanitarian Concerns in Worksite Enforcement Operations" (Nov. 16, 2007) *published on* AILA InfoNet at Doc. No. 07111632 (*posted* Nov. 16, 2007).

Even ICE is sometimes more open to liaise with CBOs than with lawyers, and information gained from these meetings can help us represent clients.

Finally, the presence of a lawyer changes the environment and outcome of a situation. ICE and other law enforcement officers may be more careful to follow protocol. A manager or union representative may refrain from making certain statements. The presence of CBO representatives often does not have the same effect, and they may see behavior that lawyers never will. Gleaning this information can be invaluable for many purposes.

In short, CBOs are critical to raid preparation and response. Working with them to prepare for a raid makes lawyers more effective when a raid comes.

HOW TO WORK WITH CBOs

The first step is to identifying CBOs in your area. Typical CBOs include faith-based groups, human rights and civil rights groups, community-organizing groups, and groups developed specifically to serve immigrants. As an example, central Iowa CBOs include Catholic Charities, American Friends Service Committee, Justice for our Neighbors (funded by the Methodist church), Iowa Citizens for Community Improvement, Iowa Allies for Immigration Reform (a grassroots coordinating organization), and the American Civil Liberties Union. The Iowa Civil Rights Commission and the Iowa Division of Latino Affairs, although technically governmental entities, also have assisted in raid response like a CBO.

The second step is gaining credibility and trust. CBOs may view immigration lawyers with some suspicion. They know that we are necessary, but they hear stories of lawyers who take advantage of a vulnerable population, charge high fees, and often do not get results. They may view a lawyer's approach as a way to get more clients or to gain access to the community. It is up to us to prove that we are committed to helping the community and helping the CBOs do their job.

One way to do this is to be a resource for CBOs when legal questions arise. Being available to answer questions (yes, without charge) can go a long way to alleviating distrust and to developing an ongoing relationship. Volunteering to speak at KYR trainings or other seminars is also appreciated. Although many CBOs have attorneys on staff, and many nonlawyers are knowledgeable about immigration law, most appreciate the perspective a practicing immigration lawyer can bring. Other volunteer opportunities include participating in naturalization clinics, providing *pro bono* legal services, and working with the CBO in immigration reform advocacy.

The third step is to become involved in organizing raid preparation. This does not mean that you have to do all the work, or even much work. It does mean that you need to be present when decisions about how to prepare for and respond to raids are made. CBOs need to understand what role lawyers can or will play in raid response. For example, our ethical considerations may not be obvious to them. (The CBO may think, "We can call the attorney representing the employer and she can help get the employees released.") Similarly, lawyers need to understand what CBOs can do.

An example of a sample raid response plan prepared by CBOs in central Iowa is attached. This plan was prepared after experience with a large-scale raid and some smaller law enforcement operations, and was refined in meetings that included CBOs and lawyers.

CBOs need help in thinking about other areas of law that come into play in a raid. For example, Iowa's state-wide immigration advocates listserv had a valuable discussion about whether law enforcement could make an immigrant self-identify in various situations. We identified a law professor from the AILA listserv, the professor contacted a former student who is a criminal lawyer, and the criminal lawyer gave us a tutorial.

This example highlights the final step in working with CBOs in raid preparation: establishing lines of communication. Effective raid response is time-sensitive. Having a means of fast and thorough communication is critical. Most CBOs will have their own networks or listservs, but they are often not willing or able to directly share these with another group. Informal coalitions often develop in which e-mails are forwarded from one contact to another among the CBOs and lawyers. This method

can be cumbersome and can result in many cross-postings; it will fail if critical people are unavailable (on vacation, for example). Another option is to develop a common listserv (easily arranged through Google or other service providers) that will reach all interested people at once. In Iowa we have a statewide general listserv for action alerts, two separate regional listservs for more targeted information, and a "strategy" listserv for those who are more involved on a daily basis in planning or discussion. One e-mail to the statewide listserv reaches several hundred people, and cross-postings have been reduced dramatically. We also have started a list of cell phone numbers, because raid response needs may not conform to normal work hours.

BEYOND RAIDS TO REAL REFORM

Working with CBOs not only can help us through the raid nightmare, but could lead to the ultimate raid response: the dawn of a better immigration system. Developing these relationships can provide avenues to educate more people about the reasons behind the raids and the need for reform. It can help us become better advocates by working more directly with laypeople and seeing the immigration world through their eyes. It can provide connections to influential people who might not otherwise be involved in the immigration issue but are connected to a CBO. It can give us legitimacy with media and government officials so we can more effectively communicate the reality of our broken immigration system. In Iowa, we have seen a marked difference between approaching legislators and governmental agencies as immigration lawyers, who are presumed to be self-interested, and approaching them with CBOs, who are seen as charitable. The same is often true with members of the media and the general public.

If the goal is serving our clients, the new day in worksite enforcement must be a call for lawyers to wake up to the advantages of working with CBOs.

ISNET Raid Action Plan[4]

What is ISNET? ISNET is the acronym for Immigrant Safety Network. This network is composed of individuals and representatives from churches, community based organizations, and unions committed to provide assistance in the case of an ICE raid at one of two levels: as a primary support network or as a secondary support network, during the first 72 hours.

Primary support will be provided when an ICE raid takes place in Central Iowa (Des Moines area and surrounding counties—as far as 50 miles around).

Secondary support will be provided when an ICE raid takes place somewhere in Iowa, and the affected community requests assistance from ISNET (either from its Legal Team, Action Team or both) because ICE brought detainees to this area (Des Moines Metro).

What is an ICE Raid? It is difficult to define an ICE raid because ICE operatives sometimes involve a large or small workplace operation; sometimes involve an apartment building or a trailer park; other times they involve an area or neighborhood where immigrants gather; and sometimes involve individuals in transit (while driving). Whenever immigration authorities (ICE) interrogate and/or arrest more than a few persons to verify their nationality or immigration status, it can be an ICE raid.

What's the Raid's Action Plan? The action plan includes activities that may vary from raid to raid. Two ISNET Coordinators with assistance of the Legal Team will help determine the degree, scope and length of action from ISNET.

The Legal Team is a small group led by experienced immigration attorneys that will be able to keep in communication with ICE and other law enforcement or governmental authorities to: a) confirm the raid, and b) provide immediate legal assistance to the detainees. This team will keep in touch with the Action Team to provide accurate information and general evaluation regarding the whereabouts and wellbeing of the detainees. Usually, the Legal Team is limited to its scope of practice.

The Action Team is a small group led by experienced community leaders and immigration advocates composed of: the **Legal Team & ISNET Coordinators,** the **Community Team,** which may include: churches, unions, community based organizations, etc., the **Government Liaison(s)** and **Media Liaison(s).** Coordination among them will limit confusion and avoid duplicity of efforts, freeing the Legal Team to do the critical job of assisting those in detention.

What is a G-28? It is a form that a BIA-accredited representative or an immigration attorney needs to have signed by the immigrant arrested or his family member in order to represent him/her, even to gain access to the detention facility where he/she is.

---

[4] Prepared by: Sandra Sánchez, American Friends Service Committee Immigrants Voice Program Director, in collaboration with Sonia Parras-Konrad, MUNA Legal Clinic Director, and Alex Orozco, co-organizer of United for the Dignity and Safety of Immigrants (UDSI).

Initial Steps

ISNET's COORDINATION

- Legal Team & ISNET Coordinators evaluate if reported raid is an ICE operation; if so:

- Legal Team starts its own action and ISNET Coordinators activate ISNET Plan (either in a primary or secondary mode).

Legal Team:

- Confirms raid has taken place

- Determines with CT ISNET activation and level of legal assistance to detainees

- Proceeds with legal activities (i.e. KYR presentation, intake, etc.)

ISNET Coordinators:

- Gets call either from community or from legal team that a raid is/has taking place

- Activates ISNET after raid confirmation (determines primary or secondary activation)

- Supports coordination among immigrant allies (entire Action Team)

Legal Team (LT) Activities

Primary Support:

- Confirms with ICE or other reliable source a raid is taking or has taken place

- Gets approximate number of immigrants involved/arrested

- Finds out location(s) of detainees

- Communicates key information to Coordination Team for community dissemination and ISNET activation (either primary or secondary)

- Makes assessment of the legal needs & communicates other needs to CT

- Activates its team members to provide basic legal assistance to detainees (intake and legal representation as possible)

- Activates G-28s previously or currently signed by detainees or a family member if they are available

- Updates Coordination Team twice a day

Secondary Support (if ICE brings detainees to Central Iowa):

- Gets help request from raided community (from a local comm. leader)

- Confirms with ICE that a raid is taking or has taken place

- Gets approximate number of immigrants involved/arrested & finds out location of detainees (LT may get a list of detainees from data collected either from community based organizations, unions, employers, and/or consulates)

- Communicates key information to raided community (list of immigration attorneys in the area, local ISNET members, etc.)

- Informs Coordination Team (as a courtesy)

- Activates its team members to provide basic legal assistance to detainees

- If requested by local community, activates G-28s previously signed by detainees or a family member

- Provides update to raided community leader once or twice a day (as it sees fit) & to Coordination Team once a day

ISNET Coordinators (IC) Activities

Primary Support:

- Get information from raided community (either by a worker, family member, consulate representative or religious leader) that a raid is taking/has taken place, and

- Inform Legal Team (LT) to obtain confirmation, or

- Get confirmation from LT that a Raid is taking/has taken place

- After confirmation from LT, activate community support by alerting:

  ➤ Community Team: churches, ministries, charities, social services agencies, service providers, community centers, nonprofits, and unions (when existing and appropriate), local/state agencies, etc.

  ➤ Governmental Liaison(s), providing accurate data

  ➤ Media Liaison(s)

- Refers callers from raided community to appropriate assistance sites/entities in their local community and/or:

  ➤ Provides them with required legal information as instructed by Legal Team

  ➤ Solicits from them information that will assist Legal Team or ISNET members

  ➤ Makes requests for help from ISNET as necessary

  ➤ Supports media contacts with pertinent & accurate information

  ➤ Provides ISNET team leaders and wider community with daily update

Secondary Support:

- Gets request for help from raided community liaison and informs LT

- Gets raid confirmation from LT, and requests its legal report ASAP

- Informs ISNET members (it's an ALERT without activating any action)

- After getting evaluation from LT, it determines activation level of ISNET and acts accordingly

ISNET (Primary) Activation

COORDINATION TEAM

- **Acts as Information Center for all teams/liaisons**

- **Coordinates & supports ISNET members in assisting raided families & community**

- **Supports advocacy efforts: community & government**

Community Team (churches, nonprofits, service providers & unions):

- Gather data from raided families or communities

- Organize humanitarian assistance to raided families or community

- Obtain signed G-28s

- Open safe spaces for immigrants and/or community meetings

Governmental Liaison(s)

- Gathers/coordinates governmental support as requested by Legal Team or Coordination Team

- Supports advocacy efforts (local, state)

- Opens lines of communication with gov. agencies & consulate(s)

Media Liaison(s)

- Provides raided community with unified message against raids

- Prepares public statement or press release

- Follows up w/media or community contacts willing to speak with the media

Community Team (CT) Activities

Churches, Nonprofits, Service Providers & Unions
Suggested Actions:

What Role can Churches Play?

- **Identify CT/LT liaison(s)** (crucial for effective coordination)

- **Assign 2 phone lines** and keep one open for your key contacts (lawyers/advocates who help you), and the other for your community contacts (those you help)

- **Gather accurate information** about those missing (at least complete names, and birthdates, A # if available); find out if there are detainees with special needs or family members of the detainees with special needs (health care, sole provider, etc.)

- **Supplement child care** for minors without parental supervision (single mothers, both parents arrested, babysitters unable to extend their care, support older siblings caring for the younger ones, support efforts to keep minors within families & in the community, etc.)

- **Keep G-28s** of your immigrant parishioners

- **Coordinate fundraising** and other needed cash assistance for raided families

- **Provide pertinent information** to Action Team

- **Help CT** to distribute accurate information to raided families/communities

- **Provide bilingual liaison between raided families & LT or CT, help raided families to post bond for their detainees, etc.** (often, families of the detainees cannot visit their loved ones in detention, do not speak English, or cannot access interpreters for other related governmental issues).

- **Open a safe space** for immigrants to get information or to hold community meetings

- **Offer hospitality** if able and requested

What Role can Nonprofits or Community Based Organizations Play?

- **Identify CT/LT liaison(s)** (crucial for effective coordination)

- **Gather accurate** information about those missing (at least complete names, and birthdates; Alien # if available is very helpful), provide this information to LT & AT

- **Supplement child care** for minors without parental supervision (single mothers, both parents arrested, baby-sitters unable to extend their care, support older siblings caring for the younger ones, support efforts to keep minors within families & in the community, etc.)

- **Coordinate fundraising** and other needed cash assistance for raided families

- **Provide pertinent information** to Action Team

- **Help AT** to distribute accurate information to raided families/communities

- **Provide bilingual liaison between raided families & LT or CT, help raided families to post bond for their detainees, etc.** (often, families of the detainees cannot visit their loved ones in detention, do not speak English, or cannot access interpreters for other related governmental issues)

- **Open a safe space for immigrants** and/or community meetings

What Role can unions play?

- Form teams of Raid Observers and ask them to:

  ➤ Call someone outside of the workplace to send the alert about the raid (please, do not play practical jokes!). Ask them to contact a trustworthy community leader.

Document:

- Time & date of the raid

- Behavior of law enforcement officials

- Conditions of the facilities where people were interrogated

- Actions that could be human/civil rights violations

- Share the gathered information with the LT and/or AT

- Negotiate with employer **not** to allow **human rights/workers' rights violations**

- Negotiate with law enforcement to provide **on-site Know Your Rights** presentation

- **Gather list of workers missing**, and provide it immediately to LT & CT

- If able, hire legal representation for arrested workers

- Make sure that your coworkers or their representative will receive their last paycheck

- Demand that ICE authorities tell you where are they taking the detainees

- Collaborate with Media Team on any vigil, public demonstration and/or other event with potential to get media coverage (a united front gets more done!)

- Help churches/community based organization with fundraising activities

- Offer interpreter assistance to the families of the detainees

- **Open a safe space** for immigrant families or service providers to hold comm. meetings

GOVERNMENTAL LIAISON(S)

Suggested Actions:

- If you learn of the Raid first, contact the LT immediately

- Wait for Coordination Team or LT to activate ISNET

- Once CT activates you, follow their suggestions for help: i.e., advocating with governmental entities such as: governor's office, senators' offices, city officials, mayor's office, DHS and/or Child Protective Services, sheriff's department, detention facilities, Latino Affairs Office, ICE, etc.

- Encourage officials of these entities to issue a public statement asking for a raids moratorium and support for comprehensive immigration reform

- Ask from higher officials (i.e., governor's office, city officials, local law enforcement, etc.) to put a policy in place indicating that constitutional, civil, and human rights violations will not be tolerated

- Open lines of communication with local agencies or service providers as needed

- Keep the CT informed about your progress twice a day

- Attend the vigil or press conference in response to the raid

MEDIA LIAISON(S)

Suggested Actions:

- Have ready your media messages (sound bites; press release templates, etc.) and share them with the raided community (church or community leaders)

- Ask leaders from the raided community if they have identified media contacts; if they have, ask for their names. If they haven't, ask them to do so very soon

- Follow up media calls for help to interview members of the raided community (always make sure that you have approval from your community contact—you won't want to lose their trust ever!)

- Prepare the press release and send it to local and state media outlets (vigil or press conference organized in response to the raid) based on CT info

- Keep in close contact with the Coordination Team so you can be updated about any irregularities or progress made that you should report in your media communications

- Compile news reports (print media, TV & radio), and if it is fair send a thank you note, if it is unfair/unbalance coverage, contact them and ask them for corrections or to run a new story that reflects immigrants' side of the story

- Follow up media calls for help to interview members of the raided community

- Share your observations and news compilation with CT/LT

ACCURATE COMMUNICATION (all team members):

When communicating information to anyone about a raid or a law enforcement operative, please, try to speak as if you were answering the following questions:

- **What happened?** Describe what you saw or heard happened as accurately as possible.

- **When did it happen?** Describe the time and day of the occurrence if you know it.

- **Where did it happen?** Give the name of workplace, neighborhood, store, etc. and location.

- **Who did it?** If you know for sure it was ICE, say so. If you don't know, try to describe the officers involved: describe any possible identifiers such as uniforms, patrol cars, vans, etc.

- **How many people are/were involved?** Give approximate number of people affected.

TROLLINGER V. TYSON FOODS, INC.: CAN THE PLAINTIFFS' BAR CONVERT IMMIGRATION CASES INTO THE NEXT AREA OF BIG-MONEY, CONTINGENCY-FEE LITIGATION?

by Jay T. Jorgensen and Matthew J. Warren[*]

In recent years there has been a new development in immigration law: the attempt to devise a private civil remedy predicated on the alleged employment of unauthorized aliens. Private plaintiffs' lawyers have been searching for a theory that would allow them to turn Immigration and Customs Enforcement (ICE) raids, criminal enforcement, and general public sentiment against illegal immigration into big-money, private-contingency-fee cases. The theory of choice has been the Racketeer Influenced and Corrupt Organizations Act (RICO), which was amended in 1996 to permit certain immigration offenses to be used as predicate acts for a RICO violation.[1] The plaintiffs' bar has seized on that provision as the vehicle to bring civil RICO suits against employers for the alleged damages caused by illegal immigration. These suits have primarily been brought on behalf of allegedly authorized workers suing their employers for damages caused by the alleged employment of illegal aliens.[2] Other suits have been brought by businesses against other businesses for damages caused by the alleged unfair competitive advantage of employing illegal workers[3] and on behalf of local governments suing for the alleged increased costs of providing services to illegal aliens.[4]

One of the leading test cases has been *Trollinger v. Tyson Foods*, in which the plaintiffs alleged that Tyson Foods, Inc. (Tyson) intentionally hired unauthorized aliens and thereby depressed the wages of workers who were authorized to work in the United States. After nearly six years of pretrial litigation, the U.S. District Court for the Eastern District of Tennessee recently granted summary judgment for Tyson.[5] The *Trollinger* opinion illustrates a number of legal and practical problems of "illegal hiring" RICO claims and has important implications for the viability of civil RICO as a mechanism for private enforcement of the immigration laws.

This article first describes the background of the *Trollinger* litigation, including the 2003 criminal case against Tyson, the initial dismissal of the *Trollinger* complaint and reversal by the Sixth Circuit, and the crystallization of the *Trollinger* plaintiffs' claims in their Second Amended Complaint. The article next discusses plaintiffs' efforts to prove the elements of an 8 USC §1324a(3) offense, which is the only illegal hiring offense that is a RICO predicate act. Those efforts included an ultimately unsuccessful attempt to access Department of Homeland Security (DHS) files for evidence on the immigration status of various workers. The article then discusses the district court's opinion granting summary judgment and the implications of the summary judgment opinion for future litigation.

---

[*] **Jay T. Jorgensen** and **Matthew J. Warren** are attorneys in the Washington, D.C. office of Sidley Austin, LLP. Both have represented clients in major criminal and civil immigration litigation, including *Trollinger v. Tyson Foods*, No. 4:02-CV-23 (E.D. Tenn. Feb. 13, 2008), and the criminal investigation and trial that preceded that litigation. All opinions expressed in this article are those of the authors and do not necessarily represent the opinions of Sidley Austin LLP.

[1] *See* Antiterrorism and Effective Death Penalty Act, §433, Pub. L. No. 104-132, 110 Stat. 1214, 1274 (Apr. 24, 1996), *codified at* 18 USC §1961(1)(F). Section 1961(1)(F) adds the following immigration offenses to the definition of "racketeering activity": "any act which is indictable under the Immigration and Nationality Act, section 274 (relating to bringing in and harboring certain aliens), section 277 (relating to aiding or assisting certain aliens to enter the United States), or section 278 (relating to importation of alien for immoral purpose) if the act indictable under such section of such Act was committed for the purpose of financial gain."

[2] *See, e.g.*, *Williams v. Mohawk Industries, Inc.*, 465 F.3d 1277 (11th Cir. 2006); *Mendoza v. Zirkle Fruit Co.*, 301 F.3d 1163 (9th Cir. 2002).

[3] *See Commercial Cleaning Servs., LLC v. Colin Serv. Sys., Inc.*, 271 F.3d 374 (2d Cir. 2001).

[4] *Canyon Cty. v. Syngenta Seeds, Inc.*, __ F.3d __, 2008 WL 746986 (9th Cir. Mar. 21, 2008).

[5] *See* Memorandum Opinion, *Trollinger v. Tyson Foods*, No. 4:02-CV-23, 2008 WL 413635 (E.D. Tenn. Feb. 13, 2008).

BACKGROUND OF PROCEEDINGS

The INS Case Against Tyson

The first *Trollinger* Complaint was filed in April 2002, on the heels of a criminal indictment of Tyson and several Tyson managers for alleged immigration violations. The criminal case against Tyson was the result of a multiyear undercover investigation and sting operation by the Immigration and Naturalization Service (INS) that targeted certain Tyson poultry processing plants. Posing as smugglers of illegal aliens, INS agents attempted to transport a number of aliens to Tyson plants and elsewhere. On December 11, 2001, a 36-count indictment was handed down against Tyson and six Tyson managers (several of whom already had been terminated by Tyson for misconduct). The indictment accused Tyson of one count of conspiracy to violate the immigration laws;[6] one count of conspiracy to defraud and obstruct INS enforcement of the immigration laws;[7] seven counts of causing illegal aliens to be brought into the United States;[8] 10 counts of causing illegal aliens to be transported within the United States;[9] nine counts of causing the use of illegal documents;[10] and eight counts of causing the possession of fraudulent documents by illegal aliens.[11]

The government's primary evidence at the criminal trial was the fact that four Tyson employees targeted by the INS sting had conspired with undercover INS agents to transport illegal aliens and provide illegal aliens with false documents. Those employees pled guilty and testified for the government. The question at the criminal trial was whether those employees were acting in accordance with Tyson policy, or whether instead they were contravening company policy. In 2003, Tyson was acquitted of all charges. After the district court dismissed 24 of the 36 counts of the indictment, the jury took less than a day to acquit Tyson and the other individual defendants of the remaining 12 counts.

The *Trollinger* Complaint

The original *Trollinger* complaint was brought on behalf of a putative class of hourly employees at 15 Tyson poultry processing plants. The complaint borrowed heavily from the claims made in the indictment (which Plaintiffs appended to their complaint).[12] Mirroring the government's allegations, Plaintiffs asserted that Tyson had used a "network of recruiters and temporary employment agencies" to "knowingly hir[e] a workforce substantially comprised of illegal immigrants for the express purpose of depressing wages."[13]

Although many of the factual allegations in the initial *Trollinger* Complaint paralleled those made in the criminal case, the legal theories of the two cases differed in important ways. For example, the *Trollinger* plaintiffs did not base their claim on any of the counts in the indictment. Instead, they claimed that Tyson violated 8 USC §1324(a)(3)(A), which prohibits the hiring of 10 or more unauthorized aliens within a 12-month period while having actual knowledge that the employees were unauthorized and had been brought into the United States in violation of 8 USC §1324(a).[14]

Moreover, as a civil RICO action, the *Trollinger* plaintiffs' claims required proof of more than simply illegal hiring: they had to prove that Tyson conducted or participated in the conduct of an enterprise through a pattern of racketeering activity[15] and that this pattern of racketeering activity injured plaintiffs in their business or property.[16] Importantly, under §1962(c), a RICO "enterprise" must be distinct from the RICO defendant.[17] While this "distinctness" requirement rarely poses difficulty in criminal RICO cases where the individual criminal defendant will

---

[6] 18 USC §371.

[7] *Id.*

[8] 8 USC §1324(a)(2)(B)(ii).

[9] 8 USC §1324(a)(1)(A)(ii).

[10] 18 USC §1546(b).

[11] 18 USC §1546(a).

[12] *See* Compl., *Trollinger v. Tyson Foods* (Docket No. 1) (Apr. 2, 2002).

[13] *Id.* §1.

[14] Section 1324(a)(3) provides:

> (A) Any person who, during any 12-month period, knowingly hires for employment at least 10 individuals with actual knowledge that the individuals are aliens described in subparagraph (B) shall be fined under title 18 or imprisoned for not more than 5 years, or both.
>
> (B) An alien described in this subparagraph is an alien who—
>
> (i) is an unauthorized alien (as defined in section 1324a (h)(3) of this title), and
>
> (ii) has been brought into the United States in violation of this subsection.

[15] *See* 18 USC §1962(c).

[16] 18 USC §1962(d).

[17] *See Cedric Kushner Promotions, Ltd. v. King*, 533 U.S. 158, 160 (2001).

naturally be distinct from the organization he conducts as an enterprise, civil RICO cases brought against corporate defendants often require creative pleading to identify an "enterprise" distinct from the defendant itself. Here, plaintiffs alleged that Tyson had associations with a "network of recruiters and temporary employment agencies" that functioned as an "association-in-fact enterprise" that Tyson was conducting in violation of RICO.[18] Plaintiffs further claimed that they suffered a cognizable injury to their "business and property" because Tyson's hiring of illegal immigrants allowed it to depress wages paid to its legal employees. Plaintiffs claimed that Tyson paid less than market wages at its facilities as a direct result of its hiring of illegal immigrants willing to work for low wages.

This latter assertion has been a key development in the efforts of the plaintiffs' bar to find a damages theory with the potential for significant awards. At bottom, plaintiffs asserted that the hiring of illegal aliens allows an employer to pay its legal workforce less than it "should have," and that the difference between the wages that were paid and the wages that "should have" been paid are forfeitable.

The district court granted Tyson's motion to dismiss, holding that Plaintiffs' theory of causation violated "the basic rules of economics."[19] The court concluded that because each of Tyson's plants operated in markets where Tyson competed for labor with other employers, and because the majority of the plants at issue actually negotiated their wages with labor unions, there could be no direct causal connection between Tyson's hiring practices and the wages Tyson paid.[20]

In 2004 the Sixth Circuit reversed, holding that dismissal on proximate cause grounds was premature "at this preliminary stage of the proceeding."[21] The Sixth Circuit acknowledged that "Tyson's proximate-cause argument may well carry the day at the summary-judgment stage," but held that Plaintiffs' general causation allegations were sufficient to survive a motion to dismiss.[22]

The Second Amended Complaint

After remand (which occurred after Tyson had been acquitted in the criminal proceedings), the *Trollinger* plaintiffs changed tactics. Rather than pursue a copycat of the government's unsuccessful criminal case, Plaintiffs amended their complaint to add new defendants, new enterprises, and a new theory of liability centered on the fact that Tyson hired individuals who did not speak English fluently.[23] Abandoning their original claims that Tyson had formed an "enterprise" by conspiring with recruiters to violate the immigration laws, Plaintiffs alleged three new "enterprises." The first, the so-called "Temporary Employment Services Enterprise," alleged that Tyson formed ongoing associations with temporary employment agencies that Tyson knew were providing it with illegal aliens.[24] Plaintiffs dropped their claim that a "network of recruiters" was part of an enterprise with temporary employment agencies, and instead claimed that Tyson formed a separate "enterprise" with each temporary employment agency that provided it with workers.[25]

One significant practical limitation of this claimed enterprise was the fact that in 2001 Tyson largely stopped using temporary agencies. Plaintiffs therefore pled two new enterprises. First, plaintiffs alleged that Tyson itself was an enterprise that had been conducted in violation of RICO by senior Tyson management who knowingly authorized a scheme to hire illegal immigrants.[26] Plaintiffs named eight senior Tyson officers—including Tyson's President, its Chief Executive Officer, and its Chief Operating Officer—as individual defendants and claimed that they had conspired to conduct Tyson in violation of RICO, primarily by adopting and implementing a "Willful Blindness Policy."[27] Plaintiffs defined the "Willful Blindness Policy" as:

> Prohibiting hiring personnel from taking into account obvious facts which indicate that documents do not relate to the persons tendering them, particularly the inability to speak English. As Tyson knows, persons who do not speak Eng-

---

[18] Compl. §1.

[19] *Trollinger v. Tyson Foods, Inc.*, 214 F. Supp. 2d 840, 843 (E.D. Tenn. 2002).

[20] *Id.*

[21] *Trollinger v. Tyson Foods*, 370 F.3d 602, 619 (6th Cir. 2004).

[22] *Id.*

---

[23] *See* Second Am. Compl., *Trollinger*, (filed June 24, 2005). The Second Amended Complaint also narrowed the scope of the case to a putative class of hourly workers at eight of Tyson poultry processing plants.

[24] *See id.* ¶¶39–43.

[25] *See id.*

[26] *See id.* ¶¶46–48.

[27] *Id.* ¶46.

lish cannot, as a practical matter be U.S. citizens or lawful permanent residents.[28]

Plaintiffs also alleged that Tyson was conducting a "Hispanic Groups Association-in-Fact Enterprise." Plaintiffs claimed that Tyson had formed "long-term partnerships" with the League of Latin American Citizens (LULAC) and the National Council of La Raza (NCLR)[29] and that it had adopted the Willful Blindness Policy at LULAC's and NCLR's behest.[30]

In addition to new defendants and new enterprises, Plaintiffs also added a new alleged RICO predicate act to their complaint: that Tyson had harbored illegal aliens in violation of 8 USC §1324(a)(1)(A)(iii). Plaintiffs claimed both that "Tyson's employment of each illegal immigrant constitutes 'harboring'" and that "Tyson has shielded illegal immigrants from detection by federal immigration officials by warning them of possible raids and providing them with housing."[31]

After the Second Amended Complaint, therefore, the Trollinger plaintiffs' claims encompassed nine defendants, three RICO enterprises, and two alleged predicate acts for a putative class of nearly 50,000 current and former hourly workers at eight Tyson plants. Plaintiffs moved for class certification shortly after filing their Second Amended Complaint. Despite defendants' objections that plaintiffs' unwieldy claim would require detailed individualized proof on liability, injury, and damages and was unsuitable for class treatment, the district court certified the class on October 10, 2006.[32]

The Trollinger Plaintiffs' Efforts to Prove an Illegal Hiring Claim

A civil RICO claim predicated on "illegal hiring" is difficult to prove, both because of the high standards required to demonstrate a hiring violation under §1324(a)(3)(A) and because of the complex elements of a civil RICO claim. To make out a RICO claim based on "illegal hiring," the Trollinger plaintiffs had to prove: (1) the hiring of large numbers of illegal aliens (at least 10 per year); (2) that the hiring was with "actual knowledge" that the aliens were unauthorized and had been brought into the United States

in violation of §1324(a); (3) that there was a pattern of hiring violations; (4) that the hiring violation was committed through an enterprise separate from the defendant itself; (5) that the defendant conducted or participated in the conduct of the enterprise's affairs through the pattern of hiring violations; and (6) that the pattern of hiring violations directly caused an injury to plaintiffs' business or property.[33]

Of particular interest are plaintiffs' attempts to prove an illegal hiring racketeering act under §1324(a)(3), a relatively new and rarely used immigration crime. The infrequency of §1324(a)(3) prosecutions is likely attributable to the high standards required for conviction: both proof of hiring a significant number of illegal aliens and proof that the hiring was done with actual knowledge that the aliens were unauthorized and had been illegally brought into the United States. In Trollinger, the plaintiffs attempted to prove these elements with shortcuts. To prove the number of alleged illegal workers, plaintiffs offered to develop a percentage from a sample that supposedly could be extrapolated to Tyson's workforce as a whole. And as proof of actual knowledge, they attempted to prove that Tyson had an illegal policy of hiring workers without considering their language skills. Each of these gambits ultimately was rejected by the court on summary judgment.

Plaintiffs' Attempts to Prove Evidence of Illegal Aliens in Tyson's Workforce

Most fundamentally, the Trollinger plaintiffs needed to elicit evidence that the eight Tyson plants in issue employed individuals who were not authorized to work in the United States. The plaintiffs attempted to do so by proving that a certain percentage from a "sample" of Tyson workers was illegal, and then extrapolating those percentages to Tyson's workforce. They tried at least three major avenues to prove that workers from their sample were illegal. Each of these is instructive on the likely course of civil immigration litigation after Trollinger.

Expert Testimony

First, plaintiffs attempted to prove the illegality of Tyson workers with the testimony of a putative expert, Michael Cutler. Mr. Cutler, a former INS

[28] Id. ¶24(b).

[29] Id. ¶50.

[30] See id. ¶53.

[31] Id. ¶37.

[32] See Trollinger v. Tyson Foods, Inc., 2006 WL 2924938 (E.D. Tenn. Oct. 10, 2006).

[33] A claim predicated on "harboring" would require similarly complex proof that there was a pattern of harboring violations, that the pattern had been used to conduct the affairs of a distinct enterprise, and that the pattern had directly caused an injury to plaintiffs.

agent, offered two primary opinions. First, he opined that in his experience, most citizens and lawful permanent residents "more often than not will demonstrate at least some familiarity with the English language." Second, he reviewed I-9s and employment applications for 497 Tyson workers and identified 91 whom he believed to be illegal aliens based on certain criteria. Mr. Cutler's identification of these individuals was based primarily on his opinion that persons who claim to be lawfully in the United States for several years but who lack familiarity with English are likely to be illegal aliens. Thus, most of the claimed illegal aliens were named because they had used a preparer/translator to complete an I-9 form, or because they filled out a Spanish-language employment application.

After Defendants moved to exclude Mr. Cutler's testimony, Plaintiffs withdrew his second opinion, stating that "Plaintiffs have decided not to use Mr. Cutler to offer any opinion as to whether any particular Tyson employee or former employee is unauthorized."[34]

Depositions of Suspected Illegal Aliens

Plaintiffs' second gambit was to depose the alleged illegal aliens Mr. Cutler identified. Plaintiffs deposed 31 of the 91 employees Mr. Cutler identified as potential illegal aliens, examining them about their immigration status, work history, and identification documents in an apparent attempt to find inconsistencies that would prove that the workers were using false identities. At the depositions all thirty-one workers strenuously maintained that they were legally in the United States, and most produced documents to demonstrate their legal status. The fruitlessness of plaintiffs' attempt to prove illegal status through these depositions is demonstrated by the fact that they did not cite a single one in their summary judgment motion as evidence that any of the workers were unauthorized.

Unsuccessful Attempt to Obtain DHS Files

Finally, plaintiffs subpoenaed DHS records for the claimed illegal aliens. Plaintiffs subpoenaed these records on September 24, 2007—after Mr. Cutler's deposition, after the depositions of many of the alleged illegal aliens, several months after the close of document discovery, and less than two months before the deadline for filing summary

judgment motions. The timing of the subpoena suggests that plaintiffs' request may have been a last-ditch effort to find evidence of illegal aliens on the eve of summary judgment.

The United States refused to comply with the subpoena on the ground that any alien files for these individuals were protected from indiscriminate disclosures pursuant to the Privacy Act, 5 USC §552a. Plaintiffs moved to compel compliance with the subpoena in the U.S. District Court for the District of Columbia, claiming that the alien files were "essential" to proving that the aliens were unauthorized.[35] The United States opposed the motion on Privacy Act grounds, arguing that plaintiffs had not satisfied any of the exceptions to the Act: they did not have written consent from any of the individuals whose files they sought; release of the records would not be a "routine use" under §552(e)(4)(D); release was not required by the Freedom of Information Act (FOIA), and plaintiffs' subpoena was not an "order of the court" requiring disclosure.[36]

Importantly, however, the United States did not oppose the subpoena on relevance grounds. The omission was particularly significant because in the same filing, the United States did oppose the subpoena of the alien file of a Tyson officer on relevance grounds.[37] Thus, while the United States objected to complying with a subpoena of an alien file on the grounds that the subpoena was not a court order, it did not appear to object to producing an alien file if the court ordered it to do so (*e.g.,* if the court granted a motion compelling production). Tyson submitted its own opposition to the motion to compel, which advanced several objections to the subpoena not raised by the United States, including the fact that the subpoena had been served after the close of discovery, that after the withdrawal of Mr. Cutler there was no factual predicate for plaintiffs' claim that these 91 individuals were illegal aliens, and that alien files that Tyson could not have lawfully checked when hiring employees were ir-

---

[34] Pls.' Resp. to Mot. to Exclude Test. of Cutler at 4 (*Trollinger*, Docket No. 435).

[35] *See* Amended Mot. to Compel USCIS to Comply With Plaintiffs' Subpoena, *Trollinger v. Tyson Foods, Inc.*, No. 1:07-MC-341 (D.D.C. filed Oct. 25, 2007).

[36] 5 USC §552a(b)(11). *See* USCIS Mem. in Opp'n to Mot. to Compel, *Trollinger* (D.D.C. filed Dec. 4, 2007).

[37] *See id.*

relevant to whether Tyson had hired illegal aliens with actual knowledge.[38]

After extensive briefing and oral argument, the district court denied Plaintiffs' motion to compel in a one-sentence minute order.[39] The court did not indicate the grounds for its denial in the order.

The Willful Blindness Theory

Perhaps the most serious hurdle plaintiffs faced in proving a "hiring" predicate act was the scienter requirement. To prevail under RICO, plaintiffs had to prove "actual knowledge" of hiring illegal aliens.

The primary federal immigration statute preventing illegal hiring is 8 USC §1324a, which forbids employers from hiring any alien "knowing the alien is an unauthorized alien."[40] Congress did *not* authorize the use of §1324a as a RICO predicate offense.[41] The only RICO predicate act that relates to illegal hiring is 8 USC §1324(a)(3)(A). Unlike §1324a, which can be satisfied by proving that an employer hired an alien "knowing" that the alien was unauthorized to work in the United States, §1324(a)(3)(A) requires both *actual knowledge* that the employee was unauthorized and *actual knowledge* that the unauthorized employee *had been brought into the United States in violation of 8 USC §1324(a)*.

To satisfy this high standard of actual knowledge, plaintiffs asserted Tyson had a corporate policy of "willful blindness" to factors that plaintiffs claimed provide proof that applicants are illegal aliens, including most prominently English language skills. This "willful blindness" theory had three fundamental flaws. First, willful blindness is not "actual knowledge." Second, English language skills are not a proxy for employment eligibility, since millions of authorized workers are not fluent in English. And third, employers are forbidden from using such a language requirement as a basis for not hiring an applicant who presents documents that appear to be reasonably genuine and to relate to the applicant.

Willful Blindness Is Not Actual Knowledge

The first flaw with using "willful blindness" to prove scienter for a §1324(a)(3) offense is the fact that willful blindness is a different, and lesser, mental state than actual knowledge. The "actual knowledge" requirement for a §1324(a)(3)(A) violation is stricter than the scienter standard for the "ordinary" hiring offense under §1324a ("knowing[ly]") and even is higher than the scienter standard for smuggling aliens under §1324(a)(1)(A) ("knowing or in reckless disregard"). Because the different criminal provisions of §1324(a) have different *mens rea* standards, Congress intended a higher standard for hiring violations.[42]

"Actual knowledge" is one of the most demanding mental states known to the law. It requires proof that the employer had "express information of [the] fact" that the applicant in question was both unauthorized and brought into the United States in violation of §1324(a).[43] Courts have treated actual knowledge and willful blindness (sometimes known as "deliberate ignorance") as distinct concepts of *mens rea* that are both subsumed in the broader concept of "knowledge."[44] In short, "willful blindness" and "actual knowledge" are not the same thing, and willful blindness is not sufficient to prove actual knowledge.

Hiring Non-English Speakers is Not Willful Blindness

Moreover, the *Trollinger* plaintiffs' assertion that "persons who do not speak English cannot, as a practical matter, be U.S. citizens or lawful permanent residents" was factually wrong. All persons born in the United States are citizens, including citizens born in predominantly Spanish-speaking Puerto Rico or in one of the millions of American households that speak a language other than English at

---

[38] *See* Tyson Mem. in Opp'n to Mot. to Compel, *Trollinger* (D.D.C. filed Nov. 20, 2007).

[39] *See* Order on Mot. to Compel, 1:07-MC-341, (D.D.C. Jan. 11, 2008).

[40] §1324a(a)(1).

[41] *See* 18 USC §1961(1)(F) (not listing INA §324A offenses as RICO predicate acts).

[42] *See Russello v. United States*, 464 U.S. 16, 23 (1983) ("[W]here Congress includes particular language in one section of a statute but omits it in another section of the same Act, it is generally presumed that Congress acts intentionally and purposely in the disparate inclusion or exclusion.'" (alteration in original)).

[43] *Attorneys Title Guar. Fund v. Goodman*, 179 F. Supp. 2d 1268, 1275 (D. Utah 2001); *see also* Black's Law Dictionary 888 (8th ed. 2004) ("actual knowledge" is "[d]irect and clear knowledge, as opposed to constructive knowledge").

[44] *See, e.g., United States v. One 1973 Rolls Royce*, 43 F.3d 794, 813 (3d Cir. 1994) ("'[K]nowledge' comprises both actual knowledge—a subjective belief that something is true—and willful blindness—a subjective belief that it is highly probabl[e] that something is true."); *United States v. Ebert*, 178 F.3d 1287, 1999 WL 261590, at *10 (4th Cir. May 3, 1999) (table case) ("'Deliberate ignorance' (or 'willful blindness') is a mental state distinct from actual knowledge.").

home.[45] So too are many persons born outside the United States to parents who are U.S. citizens.[46] And, there is no requirement that a lawful permanent resident be able to speak English. Indeed, the U.S. government publishes a handbook for new permanent residents in several languages, including Spanish, French and Tagalog.[47]

The *Trollinger* plaintiffs' argument that citizens must speak English was based on the fact that naturalization ordinarily requires English proficiency.[48] They simply ignored the fact that citizens by birth might not be proficient in English and that not all naturalized citizens need to speak English.[49] As for their argument that lawful permanent residents speak English, the *Trollinger* plaintiffs relied exclusively on Mr. Cutler's opinion that in his experience as an INS agent most lawful permanent residents had some familiarity with English.

The Federal Government Forbids Language Discrimination During I-9 Verification

Even if it were logical to assume that prospective employees with limited English skills were illegal aliens (which it is not), the federal government prohibits employers from making that assumption. When Congress first criminalized the knowing employment of unauthorized workers in the Immigration Reform and Control Act of 1986 (IRCA), Congress also imposed on employers a corollary obligation not to discriminate based on national origin or immigration status in the hiring process.[50] Rejecting identification documents that reasonably appear to

be genuine or basing hiring decisions on assumptions or suspicions about an employee's immigration status is prohibited and constitutes an unlawful "unfair immigration-related employment practice."[51]

In fact, federal law specifically provides that employers who continue to question an applicant's eligibility to work after being presented with documents that reasonably appear to be genuine are engaged in an illegal employment practice.[52] Such practices may form the basis for discrimination lawsuits by rejected applicants or by the Department of Justice's Office of Special Counsel for Immigration-Related and Unfair Employment Practices (Office of Special Counsel or OSC).[53]

The Office of Special Counsel has admonished employers to base decisions on the documents presented to them—not on their suspicions about whether employees "look" or "sound" legal. In other words, employers are told to "Look at the Facts Not the Faces."[54] Employers are told to "protect workers against discrimination on the basis of immigration status, nationality, accent, or appearance."[55] This means that employers simply cannot treat workers differently because they "look[] or sound[] foreign,"[56] or make hiring decisions based on an employee's "appearance, accent, name, or citizenship status."[57]

---

[45] According to the 2000 census, over 37 million Americans over the age of 5 speak a language other than English at home and over 21 million of those Americans do not speak English fluently. *See* U.S. Census Report, Language Use and English-Speaking Ability, 2000 at 5. These 21 million Americans comprise over eight percent of the population of the United States. *Id.* Over 5.6 million of these non-fluent English speakers were born in the United States. *See* Census Table 6: Language Spoken at Home and Ability to Speak English by Nativity at 1. *See* U.S. Const., amend XIV; 8 USC §1401(a).

[46] *See* 8 USC §1401(c–e).

[47] *See* Welcome to the United States: A Guide for New Immigrants (French, Spanish, and Tagalog versions), *available at* www.uscis.gov/files/nativedocuments/M-618_fr.pdf, /M-618_sp.pdf, and /M-618_t.pdf.

[48] 8 CFR §312.1.

[49] *See id.* §312.1(b) (detailing exceptions from English proficiency requirement).

[50] *See* 8 USC §1324b(a)(1).

[51] *See id.* §1324b(a)(6).

[52] *See* 28 CFR §44.200(a)(3) ("A person or other entity's ... refusing to honor documents tendered that on their face reasonably appear to be genuine and to relate to the individual shall be treated as an unfair immigration-related employment practice relating to the hiring of individuals."); *see also* 8 CFR §274a.1(i)(2).

[53] For example, the Office of Special Counsel imposed a civil penalty of over $174,000 against Swift & Company for subjecting individuals "who were believed to look or sound 'foreign' ... to greater scrutiny during the employment verification process than individuals who appeared to be U.S. citizens." Press Release, Department of Justice, "Department of Justice Announces Settlement Agreement With Swift & Company Regarding Workplace Discrimination Claims" (Nov. 4, 2002), *available at* www.usdoj.gov/opa/pr/2002/November/02_crt_6 30.htm. *See* 8 USC §§1324b(b)–(k).

[54] *See* Civil Rights Division, Department of Justice, "Look At The Facts. Not At The Faces. Your Guide to Fair Employment," *available at* www.usdoj.gov/crt/osc/pdf/en_guide.pdf.

[55] *Id.* at 2.

[56] *Id.* at 3.

[57] *Id.* at 6; *see* Office of Special Counsel, Overview of OSC: What Constitutes Discrimination Under §1324b, *available at* http://www.usdoj.gov/crt/osc/pdf/oscupdate_nov_06.pdf ("Employers may not treat individuals differently because of
continued

8 USC §1324(a)(3) Requires Actual Knowledge that Aliens Were Illegally Brought Into the United States

In addition, the *Trollinger* plaintiffs were required to prove actual knowledge of hiring aliens who were "brought into the United States in violation of this subsection."[58] Thus, a §1324(a)(3) violation only applies to a specific subset of unauthorized workers—those who were assisted by a person who could have been convicted of one of the two offenses in §1324(a) that criminalize "bringing" illegal aliens into the United States: §1324(a)(1)(A)(i) and §1324(a)(2). It does not apply to the hiring of aliens who have overstayed their visas.[59] Indeed, because the statute only refers to those aliens who "ha[ve] been brought" into the United States, it does not apply to those aliens who manage to enter the United States illegally without the assistance of someone to "bring" them.[60]

Legislative history confirms that Congress intended to limit the reach of §1324(a)(3) to employers with actual knowledge that their employees were smuggled illegally into the country.[61] Congress's limitation makes perfect sense. Section 1324a al-

ready provides penalties for employers who knowingly hire unauthorized workers. Section 1324(a)(3) was intended to reach a different, more culpable group of employers who effectively facilitate the smuggling of illegal aliens by employing such aliens with actual knowledge that they were smuggled into the United States.[62]

THE SUMMARY JUDGMENT RULING

The district court granted summary judgment on February 12, 2008, less than three weeks before the scheduled start of trial.[63] The court concluded that plaintiffs had failed to present evidence of an illegal hiring offense and that, while they had sufficient evidence to survive summary judgment for one harboring offense, they had no proof of causation for that offense.[64]

On the hiring predicate act, the court held that plaintiffs failed to present evidence that Tyson had hired a sufficient number of illegal aliens. The court concluded that plaintiffs were offering "mere allegation [of illegality] without factual basis," for two reasons.[65] First, the court noted that Mr. Cutler's proffered testimony that authorized workers *generally* have proficiency with English did not support a conclusion that *all* authorized workers are proficient in English.[66] Second, even if lack of English fluency could create a valid suspicion of illegality, that does not mean "that all of the suspicious applicants are illegal."[67] The court went on to reject other evidence that plaintiffs offered as proof that certain Tyson employees were illegal. Most of these documents reflected investigations that Tyson had made into employees' legal status after receiving a no-match letter from the Social Security Administration or a report that a Tyson employee was using a false identity. The court held that these other pieces of evidence were hearsay and not based on personal knowledge, and noted that they fell far short of

---

their place of birth, country of origin, ancestry, native language, accent, or because they are perceived as looking or sounding 'foreign.'").

The EEOC also prohibits employers from treating applicants differently when they are not proficient in English. Employers may not base employment actions on a lack of English fluency unless fluency "is required for the effective performance of the position for which it is imposed." EEOC Compliance Manual §13.V.B.1. Indeed, the EEOC has stated that an employer's "[f]luency-in-English requirements, such as denying employment opportunities because of an individual's foreign accent, or inability to communicate well in English," are a potentially discriminatory procedure and that it will "carefully investigate" charges that an employer requires English fluency. 29 CFR §1601.6(b) (2006).

[58] 8 USC §1324(a)(3)(B)(ii).

[59] The Government Accounting Office has estimated that one-third or more of the illegal alien population in the United States are visa overstays. *See* U.S. General Accounting Office, "Overstay Tracking: A Key Component of Homeland Security" at 10–11 (May 2004).

[60] *See Webster's Third New International Dictionary* 278 (1993) ("bring" means "to convey, lead, carry or cause to come along from one place to another").

[61] H.R. Rep. No. 104-828, at 204 (1996) (Conf. Rep.) ("In order to be liable under this provision, the employer must have actual knowledge *both* of the alien's unauthorized status *and* of the fact that the alien was brought into the United States illegally." (emphasis added)).

---

[62] *See Commercial Cleaning Servs., LLC v. Colin Serv. Sys., Inc.,* 271 F.3d 374, 387 (2d Cir. 2001) (holding that knowledge that the aliens in question had been illegally brought into the United States was essential element of a §1324(a)(3)(A) violation); *System Mgmt., Inc. v. Loiselle,* 91 F. Supp. 2d 401, 408–09 (D. Mass. 2001) (same).

[63] *Trollinger,* 2008 WL 413635 at *14.

[64] The court did not reach defendants' arguments that plaintiffs had failed to present proof of RICO's enterprise elements.

[65] *Id.* at 3–4.

[66] *See id.* at 4.

[67] *Id.*

plaintiffs' burden to identify at least 10 illegal hires per year.[68]

While the district court devoted most of its opinion to the insufficiency of plaintiffs' evidence that a sufficient number of Tyson hourly workers were unauthorized, it also resoundingly rejected the idea that "willful blindness" was a sufficient scienter for a hiring violation. While noting that "the 'actual knowledge' requirement[69] is … difficult to interpret," the court held that it requires "actual knowledge" of two facts: that "the individual was unauthorized to work in the United States" and that "the individual was brought into the United States illegally for the purposes of illegal employment."[70] The court held that plaintiffs had failed to satisfy either of these two scienter elements. It noted that plaintiffs "made no effort" to produce evidence of actual knowledge of "bringing," and that their allegations of a "willful blindness policy" did not satisfy the "actual knowledge" requirement.[71] The court rejected plaintiffs' argument that "willful blindness" was sufficient under §1324(a)(3) because willful blindness was a sufficient scienter for other immigration crimes. The court noted that other immigration statutes only required proof of "knowledge," which was a lesser mental state than actual knowledge.[72]

The court's holding that plaintiffs could not prove a hiring offense did not dispose of the case, however, because plaintiffs also alleged a harboring predicate act. The court dismissed most of plaintiffs' claimed evidence of harboring for the reasons it cited in disposing of its evidence of illegal hiring—plaintiffs produced evidence predicated on hearsay or on bald assertions unsupported by personal knowledge.[73] The court concluded that only one item of plaintiffs' cited evidence could sustain a harboring claim—a declaration from one of the class representatives who claimed she had personally observed Tyson management warning illegal alien employees to leave before a raid by immigration authorities at Tyson's Corydon, Indiana facility.[74] The court held that, if this testimony were credited by the jury, it was sufficient evidence of a harboring violation at the Corydon facility.

However, the court held that this harboring violation could not support a RICO claim because Plaintiffs could not show that it caused them any injuries. Citing the Sixth Circuit's 2004 *Trollinger* opinion and the Supreme Court's recent RICO causation decision in *Anza v. Ideal Steel Supply Corp.*,[75] the district court held that plaintiffs had to prove "a direct causal link" between the alleged harboring violation and their supposedly depressed wages.[76] The court held that even if the jury were to believe that Tyson harbored workers at the Corydon facility, and that Tyson paid below-market wages, plaintiffs had no evidence that Tyson's retention of these workers caused such lower wages. Plaintiffs' claimed causation was "wholly speculative":

> If the jury accepts Plaintiffs' claim that Tyson paid less than the going-market wage, Plaintiffs have provided no evidence the retention of illegal alien employees permitted Tyson to do so. Tyson may have been able to pay lower wages because people were willing to work for Tyson for a lower wage due to Tyson providing better benefits, more job security, or a more convenient location; or, because the worker's union was out-negotiated when wages were set, or pursued other interests at the negotiation more vigorously than the hourly wage rate. Plaintiffs have made no effort to address these potentially-material intervening causes, and there are likely others.[77]

CONCLUSION

The *Trollinger* decision reaffirmed the critical elements of §1324(a)(3), and rejected plaintiffs' attempts to make end-runs around the requirement that they demonstrate actual knowledge of hiring unauthorized aliens who were illegally brought into the United States. While the court's decision does not preclude the possibility of a viable civil RICO action predicated on illegal hiring, it does reaffirm that such actions will be limited to situations where a plaintiff can produce both evidence that an employer

---

[68] *See id.* at 4–8.

[69] 8 USC §1324(a)(3)(a).

[70] *Id.* at *2 n.2.

[71] *Id.* at *8 & n.10.

[72] *Id.* at *8 n.10 ("'Actual knowledge,' requiring subjective belief that something is true, is a higher standard than 'knowledge,' which can be shown by willful blindness, a subjective belief that it is highly probable that something if true.").

[73] *Id.* at *9–11.

[74] *Id.* at 11. Tyson presented evidence that there were no raids at the Corydon facility during the relevant time period.

[75] *Anza v. Ideal Steel Supply Corp.*, 547 U.S. 451, 457 (2006).

[76] *Trollinger*, 2008 WL 413635, at *13.

[77] *Id.* at *14.

actually knew that it was hiring illegal aliens who had been smuggled into the United States and evidence that those illegal hires directly caused damages to the plaintiffs.

Trollinger suggests a few important limitations on the ability of private plaintiffs to recover on "illegal hiring" RICO claims. First, the "actual knowledge" requirement is a significant obstacle to proving an illegal-hiring-based RICO claim. The court soundly rejected Plaintiffs' attempt to substitute "willful blindness" for "actual knowledge." While the court's holding rested on the legal ground that willful blindness is not actual knowledge, the court's opinion also suggests some skepticism toward Plaintiffs' underlying theory that an applicant who cannot speak English must be illegal.[78] And, the simple fact that millions of citizens and lawful permanent residents are authorized to work in the United States suggests that any attempt to revive the "willful blindness theory" in future cases is unlikely to succeed. Second, *Trollinger* demonstrates that proof of illegality will be a fundamental difficulty in an illegal hiring case. In the absence of firm proof such as a prior conviction for employing a particular illegal alien, some other judicial determination indicating illegality, or an admission by the suspected illegal alien, finding definitive proof that an individual worker is illegal is a substantial hurdle. As difficult as it is for a particular hiring employer to determine whether an applicant has presented legitimate employment documents, it is doubly difficult years later to prove based on the paper record whether that applicant was legal or illegal. These problems are multiplied for a putative class action, where any theory of "wage depression" will depend on proving the illegality of hundreds, if not thousands, of prior employees. Finally, *Trollinger* suggests that in all cases RICO's direct causation requirement will pose problems for private plaintiffs claiming that the hiring of illegal immigrants somehow caused them damages.

In short, *Trollinger* demonstrates serious flaws in the newly-minted "illegal hiring" civil RICO class action. Although plaintiffs generally have been successful in surviving motions to dismiss in these suits, the practical difficulties of proving actual knowledge, illegality, and causation are serious obstacles to plaintiffs' ability to survive summary judgment and prove these claims at trial.

---

[78] *See id.* at 4.

"DRIVING" US CRAZY—THE LOCALIZATION OF IMMIGRATION LAW: STATE AND LOCAL REGULATIONS

by Joan Friedland[*]

Issuance of driver's licenses—traditionally a state prerogative—became a federal matter with passage of the REAL ID Act of 2005.[1] Similarly, immigration policy—a federal issue—has played an increased role in the state driver's license debate since the terror attacks of September 11, 2001.

The interplay between driver's licenses and immigration policy has led to restrictions that affect immigrants—both documented and undocumented—and citizens alike. The contentious debate about licenses rarely has included a rational look at issues of public safety or national security and often has relied on a skewed, misguided, and superficial treatment of the complexities of immigration law. Most recently, driver's licenses and driving violations have become a critical point in the issue of whether and when police can enforce immigration law.

DRIVER'S LICENSE RESTRICTIONS DIRECTED AT IMMIGRANTS

Restrictions directed at immigrants are now an established feature of state driver's license laws.[2]

- Thirty states have "lawful presence" requirements in their statutes.

- Fifteen states have lawful presence requirements created by state agency policy or the combination of documents required of driver's license applicants to prove identity.

- Six states do not have lawful presence requirements. One of those states offers a "driving privilege card."

- Forty-nine states plus the District of Columbia require a Social Security Number (SSN) for a license but have exceptions to the rule (only one state does not have this exception).

- Five states accept an Individual Tax Identification Number (ITIN) as an alternative to the SSN.

- Seven states accept the *matrícula consular* or other foreign ID card as a form of identification.

- Thirty-four states require that the driver's license expire with an immigrant's visa.

States that do not require proof of lawful presence face considerable pressure to do so. Several have ceded to this pressure in the past few months alone. Federal legislation to force states to require proof and to verify lawful presence was introduced recently in the form of threats to withhold highway construction funds.[3]

But superimposing immigration law onto driver's license laws is not a simple proposition, and states frequently stumble in the process. Michigan is a recent example. On December 27, 2007, Michigan Attorney General Mike Cox issued an opinion concluding that "a person in this country illegally, who has not secured permanent alien status from the federal government," could not be considered a permanent resident in Michigan and was therefore ineligible for a Michigan driver's license.[4] This was a reversal of a 1995 attorney general's opinion, which concluded that undocumented immigrants were eligible for a license.[5]

---

[*] **Joan Friedland** is the immigration policy director for the National Immigration Law Center (NILC). Ms. Friedland focuses on post-9/11 documentation, database, and information-sharing policy issues affecting low-income immigrants. Before joining NILC in 2002, she had a long career as a lawyer for nonprofit organizations and in private practice in New Mexico and Florida, and has litigated many civil rights and immigration cases. Ms. Friedland holds a J.D. from Harvard Law School.

[1] Pub. L. No. 109-13, 119 Stat. 231 (May 11, 2005).

[2] For a chart outlining which states have which restrictions, see "Overview of States' Driver's License Requirements," *available at www.nilc.org/immspbs/DLs/state_dl_rqrmts_ ovrvw_2008-02-19.pdf.*

[3] *See, e.g.,* S. 2718, 110th Cong. (2008), which would withhold 10 percent of highway construction funds from states that did not require and verify evidence of lawful presence in the United States of U.S. citizens and individuals in certain immigration categories.

[4] *See http://222.ag.state.mi.us/opinion/datafiles/2000s/op10286 .htm.*

[5] Office of the Attorney General, 1995-1996, No. 6883, p. 120 (Dec. 14, 1996) (OAG No. 6883), *available at www.ag.state. mi.us/opinion/datafiles/1990s/op06883.htm.*

The Michigan opinion stated that driver's licenses were available only to Michigan residents whose stay in Michigan was "permanent and not temporary or transient." The attorney general supported his conclusion with a meandering discussion of Congress's plenary control over immigration, the REAL ID Act, references to the alien status of "lawfully admitted for permanent residence," and cases dealing with the establishment of lawful domicile for purposes of relief from deportation.

Zeroing in on the concept of permanent legal status as a requirement for establishing state residence, Michigan Secretary of State Terri Lynn Land concluded that proof of "legal and permanent presence" in the United States was required, and that individuals in the country in temporary status or on student visas were ineligible for Michigan licenses.[6] This peculiar result was widely condemned as denying licenses to a broad class of lawfully present foreign nationals in Michigan.[7] Land concluded that foreign nationals would be eligible for an "enhanced" license that could be used for border crossings, or they could drive using the licenses of their home countries. She did not explain why a foreign national ineligible for a regular license because he or she did not have permanent legal status would somehow be eligible for an "upgraded standard license."

The ACLU of Michigan filed suit challenging Land's decree.[8] The plaintiffs were a Canadian nurse, an Indian doctor, a University of Michigan language assessment specialist, and an asylee. The Michigan legislature immediately responded with a modification to the state driver's license law, making drivers who are lawfully present in the United States eligible for a state license. The new law defined this category as including, but not limited to:

a person authorized by the United States government for employment in the United States, a person with nonimmigrant status authorized under federal law, and a person who is the benefici-

ary of an approved immigrant visa petition or an approved labor certification.

By its very terms, this definition would include the beneficiary of an approved I-130 who has not yet filed for adjustment of status.[9] While the revisions gave lawfully present non-U.S. citizens access to licenses, it did not restore the status quo ante, in which undocumented immigrants were eligible for licenses.

Driver's license laws are also overtaken by political considerations that overwhelm considerations of public safety or protection of national security. The New York debate is a prime example. On September 21, 2007, Governor Eliot Spitzer and Department of Motor Vehicles Commissioner David Swarts announced an administrative policy under which New York would issue one license to all New Yorkers, regardless of immigration status. This change would be accomplished by not requiring license applicants to provide an SSN, reversing a policy initiated by former governor George Pataki to require SSNs (which in turn had been a reversal of a prior policy in which SSNs were not required).

Spitzer justified the new policy as recognizing the reality that hundreds of thousands of undocumented immigrants live in New York. He explained that making licenses available would enhance public safety, since unlicensed drivers are more likely to be involved in fatal crashes. It would also lower insurance rates and "bolster homeland security by bringing more individuals into the system and, when necessary, assisting law enforcement efforts to locate those who present a real security threat."[10] The governor simultaneously announced plans to increase the security of the licensing system.

The governor's announcement was lauded by national security experts.[11] But it also met with a storm of protest, which included a vote by 30 county clerks opposing the policy.[12] By October 27, 2007, Spitzer

---

[6] See www.michigan.gov/sos/0,1607,7-127--183894--,00.html.

[7] See, e.g., letter from the Michigan Chapter of the American Immigration Lawyers Association, Jan. 25, 2008, available at www.bibdaily.com/pdfs/AILA%20Mich%20DL%201-25-08.pdf.

[8] Gates, et al. v. Land, Circuit Court for the County of Ingham, State of Michigan, Case No. 08-186-CZ (Feb. 13, 2008). Complaint is available at www.aclumich.org/pdf/licensecomplaint.pdf.

[9] This definition of lawful presence does not comport with the categories of persons eligible for driver's licenses under the REAL ID Act. See below.

[10] See www.ny.gov/governor/press/0921071_print.html.

[11] See www.ny.gov/governor/press/1102071.html. See also M. D. Stock, "Giving Immigrants Licenses May Help Security," Newsday, Oct. 2, 2007, reprinted in part at www.aamva.org/About/PressRoom/RecentMediaCoverage/License+policy+a+win+for+security.htm. For more information about driver's licenses and national security, see M. D. Stock, "Driver Licenses and National Security," Jan. 8, 2008, available at http://drivers.com/article/971/.

[12] See www.ny.gov/governor/press/1004072.html.

had abandoned his new policy. In a press conference with Secretary of Homeland Security Michael Chertoff, he announced that New York would instead have a three-tier system: an "enhanced drivers license" for crossing the New York-Canadian border, a federally approved license under the REAL ID Act for boarding airplanes, and a New York State license for driving and identification purposes. The third license would be available to both undocumented immigrants and lawful residents who decided not to obtain one of the other licenses.[13] His about-face was in turn condemned by immigrant advocates, opponents of the REAL ID Act, and those who oppose providing any kind of license to undocumented immigrants. On November 15, 2007, the governor announced that the third license would not be available to undocumented immigrants and that the state would put compliance with the REAL ID Act on hold.[14]

HOW DRIVER'S LICENSE AND DRIVING LAWS INTERSECT WITH LOCAL POLICE ENFORCEMENT OF IMMIGRATION LAW

Driver's licenses play a critical role in the enforcement of immigration law by state and local police. Driving violations are a frequent point of contact with the police and are often used as a pretext for stopping drivers who "look" or "sound" foreign. That initial stop is often the gateway for inquiries about immigration status, which, though not authorized by law, can lead to devastating immigration consequences.

Considerable attention has focused recently on enforcement of immigration law by states and localities under §287(g) of the Immigration and Nationality Act. That section authorizes state and local enforcement agencies to enter into a memorandum of agreement (MOA) with U.S. Immigration and Customs Enforcement (ICE) that allows state or local police to be trained in enforcing immigration laws and to carry out certain designated immigration functions under the supervision of an immigration agent.[15] MOAs are viewed as providing little or nothing in the way of monitoring or compliance measurement and having minimal or ineffectual complaint procedures.

In fact, most police participation in immigration enforcement likely occurs outside §287(g) agreements and is subject to little supervision or monitoring, particularly with respect to racial profiling and the use of driving offenses as a pretext to inquire about immigration status and then turn noncitizens over to ICE.[16] The initial stop by police is often not challenged: noncitizens required to appear in immigration court often do not have a lawyer; immigration lawyers often do not take on the issue of whether the initial stop was illegal; noncitizens themselves do not necessarily know which agency the officer who arrested them belongs to or how they ended up in immigration custody; and the standard for challenging an arrest in immigration proceedings is high.

An example of racial profiling was demonstrated in the enforcement of a Louisiana law that prohibits driving without lawful presence (DWLP). In 2002 Louisiana enacted LSA-R.S. 14:100.13, making it a felony for "alien students" and "nonresident aliens" to drive a vehicle without documentation demonstrating that their presence in the United States is lawful. The defendant in *State of Louisiana v. Juan Herrera*[17] challenged his arrest under the statute, arguing that it was based on racial profiling. The officer testified that he had attended a one-day seminar in immigration law. The judge summarized the officer's testimony:

Officer Finneman has arrested 4 or 5 Latino drivers pursuant to LSA-R.S. 14:100.13 and he believes other officers have arrested Latino drivers pursuant to LSA-R.S. 14:100.13.

Officer Finneman also stated he did not know how many, if any, White, Black, Asian, Middle Eastern, Indian, or Pakistani drivers he arrested pursuant to LSA-R.S. 14:100.13.

Officer Finneman also stated he could not determine if a White, Black, Asian, Middle Eastern, Indian, or Pakistani driver was an illegal alien, but yet could not explain why he would ask a Latino driver if he was an illegal alien.

The court concluded that "the defendant's arrest pursuant to LSA-R.S. 14:100.13 was made without probable cause, because it was the result of a selec-

---

[13] See www.ny.gov/governor/press/1027071_print.html.

[14] D. Hakim, "NY: Spitzer Dropping His License Plan," *The N.Y. Times,* Nov. 14, 2007.

[15] See www.ice.gov/partners/287g/Section287_g.htm.

---

[16] *See, e.g.,* D. Gonzalez, "Racial Profiling by Police Must Be Stopped, Panel Says," *Arizona Republic,* Mar. 7, 2008, *available at www.azcentral.com/news/articles/0307profiling forum0307.html.*

[17] No. 467-763 "K" (La. Crim. Dist. Ct. Orleans Parish Feb. 1, 2007).

tive enforcement policy profiling, targeting and arresting Latino drivers."[18]

The trial court's decision confirmed anecdotal evidence that police in Louisiana used driving violations as a pretext for inquiries about immigration status. But the Louisiana statute also illustrates the complexity of grafting immigration law onto driving regulations. On December 20, 2006, the Fourth Circuit Court of Appeals (covering much of the Greater New Orleans area) quashed DWLP charges in *State of Louisiana v. Neri Lopez*.[19] The court concluded that the DWLP statute "places a burden on both legal and non-legal aliens which exceeds any standard contemplated by federal immigration law." The court held that the state statute was pre-empted by federal law because it, in effect, imposed a requirement regarding who must carry documents that goes beyond federal requirements and imposes harsher penalties than federal penalties. The Louisiana Supreme Court subsequently decided not to hear the case.

But recently, in *State of Louisiana v. Reyes*,[20] the Louisiana First Circuit Court of Appeal ruled to the contrary. The decision illustrates the disturbing results when courts make simplistic interpretations of complex immigration law. This court ignored the variance between the statute's immigration category of "non-resident alien" and federal immigration categories, treating "non-resident alien" as a term that describes all immigration categories. And the court ignored the fact that police officers were required to make an independent determination—not bound by federal determinations—about whether drivers fit within the state-created immigration categories.

The court expanded a requirement that lawful permanent residents carry proof of their status into a requirement that all noncitizens carry proof of their status, apparently assuming that all noncitizens have a card that establishes their immigration status. The court grounded its decision on the REAL ID Act, concluding that REAL ID, which actually lists categories of immigrants who may obtain licenses, allows states to issue licenses that do not conform to its requirements. The court held that "neither the REAL ID Act nor any other federal law conflicts with the Louisiana statute. La. R.S. 14:100.13 com-

plements and augments federal law by reporting to the INS [*sic*] anyone caught without evidence of legal status."

The Louisiana First Circuit decision incorporates the state's offhand connection between the presence of undocumented immigrants and national security, accepting the state's argument that it could criminalize conduct that it believed to be a legitimate terror threat. Now that there are conflicting courts of appeal decisions in Louisiana, the state supreme court may well agree to consider the issue. But a genuine threat exists that the casual misinterpretation of federal immigration law by the state may be enshrined into law.

ROLE OF THE NATIONAL CRIME INFORMATION CENTER DATABASE IN STATE AND LOCAL POLICE ENFORCEMENT

The ability of state and local police to enforce immigration law when they stop a driver for a driving infraction has been facilitated by the Bush Administration's policy of entering *civil* immigration information into the National Crime Information Center (NCIC) criminal database.[21]

The NCIC is the nation's largest collection of "actionable" crime information—the system that police officers check to find out whether the person they have just stopped or arrested is on any wanted list of ordinary criminals or terrorists. Hundreds of thousands of federal, state, and local officers have access to the system, which is administered by the FBI. In 2001, Immigration and Naturalization Service (INS) Commissioner James Ziglar announced that INS had begun sending the names of more than 300,000 noncitizens to the NCIC for inclusion in its database. These were individuals who had remained in the United States despite having a deportation or removal order issued against them. This new INS program was named the Absconder Apprehension Initiative. In June 2002, Attorney General John Ashcroft announced that violators of the National Security Entry Exit Registration System (NSEERS) would be entered into the NCIC.[22]

---

[18] Decision *available at www.nilc.org/immlawpolicy/LocalLaw/herrera_decision_2007-02-01.pdf*.

[19] 948 So. 2d 1121 (La. Ct. App. 4th Cir. 2006).

[20] 2008 La. App. LEXIS 270.

---

[21] The statutory authorization for the NCIC is found at 28 USC §534 (2003) (amended 2006).

[22] Hannah Gladstein, Annie Lai, Jennifer Wagner, and Michael Wishnie, "Blurring the Lines: A Profile of State and Local Police Enforcement of Immigration Law Using the
continued

The inclusion of civil immigration information into the NCIC reflects the Bush Administration's argument that state and local police have inherent authority to enforce immigration law. This view was first propounded in a December 2001 legal opinion issued by the Office of Legal Counsel in the Department of Justice (DOJ). That opinion conflicted with the long-held policy that treated the enforcement of civil immigration laws as strictly a federal responsibility, as reflected in a 1996 DOJ Office of Legal Counsel opinion holding that state and local police lack recognized legal authority to enforce the civil provisions of immigration law.[23]

This was followed by a little-noticed order published on March 24, 2003, in the *Federal Register*.[24] In it, DOJ ruled that data from the NCIC do not have to be accurate. The DOJ order exempts the NCIC from a longstanding legal requirement that information in major law enforcement databases be "accurate, relevant, timely and complete." It justifies the change on the curious basis that requiring accurate information would interfere with law enforcement.[25]

This policy was challenged in a lawsuit filed in a federal district court in New York several years ago. After an inordinate delay, the judge dismissed the case, ruling that the immigration organizations that had filed the lawsuit did not have standing to do so.[26] That case is on appeal to the U.S. Court of Appeals for the Second Circuit.

The upshot is that even without §287(g) MOAs, police have the tools at their command to inquire about and check immigration status, leaving noncitizens—or anyone who "looks" or "sounds" foreign—with few mechanisms to challenge the process.

HOW THE REAL ID ACT AFFECTS STATE ISSUANCE OF DRIVER'S LICENSES

The REAL ID Act, passed in 2005 as part of the Emergency Supplemental Appropriations Act for Defense, the Global War on Terror, and Tsunami Relief, will affect driver's license issuance for immigrants—both documented and undocumented—and citizens alike.[27]

The act provides specific and burdensome limitations on noncitizens' access to licenses. States that attempt to comply with the immigration-specific portions of the REAL ID Act will find that the statute's rigidity will prevent many lawful immigrants from obtaining licenses and that the flexibility they previously enjoyed in issuing licenses to qualified applicants is diminished.

The act provides that beginning three years after REAL ID's enactment (May 2008), state-issued driver's licenses cannot be accepted by federal agencies for any "official" purpose unless they meet requirements covering eligibility for a license (including eligibility of immigrants for licenses), the process for obtaining a license (including verification of documents), duration of licenses, sharing of driver's license information among the states, and the operation of motor vehicle departments.[28]

Despite the May 11, 2008, deadline for states to implement the statute, the Department of Homeland Security (DHS) did not issue final REAL ID regulations until January 29, 2008.[29] These regulations substantially extended the deadline for states to comply with the act's requirements and gave states considerable flexibility in how they would carry out the act's ostensibly strict requirements. However, the regulations did not mitigate deficiencies in the act with respect to the immigrant-specific requirements, and allowed little flexibility in implementation of the aspect of the act pertaining to immigrants. The ACLU has issued a scorecard on the regulations, giving DHS a failing grade in their impact on individuals, privacy, the states, and constitutional rights.[30]

National Crime Information Center Database, 2002–2004" (Migration Policy Institute, December 2005).

[23] "Assistance by State and Local Police in Apprehending Illegal Aliens," Department of Justice, Feb. 1996, a*vailable at www.usdoj.gov/olc/immstopo1a.htm.*

[24] 68 Fed. Reg. 14140 (Mar. 24, 2003) (codified as 28 CFR pt. 16).

[25] See *http://frwebgate.access.gpo.gov/cgi-bin/getpage.cgi? dbname=2003_register&position=all&page=14140.*

[26] *National Council of la Raza v. Gonzalez,* 468 F. Supp. 2d 429 (E.D.N.Y. 2007).

[27] For a summary of the REAL ID Act's driver's license requirements, see *www.nilc.org/immspbs/DLs/real_id_dl_ tbl_051905.pdf.*

[28] The REAL ID Act also included provisions pertaining to asylum, judicial review, material support of terrorism, and a fence on the United States–Mexico border.

[29] 6 CFR §§37.1—37.71. For an analysis of the immigrant-specific portion of the regulations, see *www.nilc.org/immspbs/ DLs/QA_re_DLs_post-regs_2008-02-27.pdf.*

[30] See *http://realnightmare.org/images/File/Real%20ID%20 Scorecard%20-%20Fed%20Reg%20page%20numbers.pdf.*

Under the act, only U.S. citizens and noncitizens with certain immigration statuses are eligible for licenses that comply with REAL ID. Citizens, lawful permanent residents, asylees, and refugees are eligible for a "regular" license, while noncitizens with a nonimmigrant visa, pending application for asylum, pending or approved application for temporary protected status, deferred action status, or a pending application for permanent residence or conditional permanent residence may receive only a "temporary" license. A temporary license may be valid only for the period of the applicant's authorized stay in the United States or one year if there is no definite end to the period of authorized stay, must clearly indicate that it is temporary and shall state the date on which it expires, and may be renewed upon proof that the person's immigration status has been extended by DHS.

States may issue a license that does not satisfy REAL ID's requirements, but the document must clearly state on its face that it may not be accepted by any federal agency for any official purpose, and it must have a unique design or color indicator to alert federal agencies and other law enforcement personnel that it is not a REAL ID document.

For example, the list of noneligible individuals does not include persons granted withholding of removal or withholding of deportation, individuals paroled into the United States; applicants for nonimmigrant visas (including as victims of trafficking or other crimes), Cuban/Haitian entrants (the subcategory of those paroled into the United States, at least until they have been in the country for one year and can apply for adjustment), battered spouses and their children, and battered children and their parents (unless and until they can apply for adjustment of status or unless they are granted deferred action), individuals granted family unity status, individuals granted deferred enforced departure (DED) status, applicants for suspension of deportation or cancellation of removal, and individuals under an order of supervision. The regulations make no attempt to analogize the missing categories to the listed categories.

The regulations also set forth a narrow list of immigration documents that prove a noncitizen's identity: an unexpired permanent resident card (I-551), unexpired employment authorization document (EAD), or unexpired passport accompanied by a valid U.S. visa.[31] Clearly, not every immigrant in the listed statuses will have one of these documents. In contrast, the regulations recognize that immigration status may be proved by a variety of documents because immigration status must be verified through the Systematic Alien Verification for Entitlements (SAVE) system.[32]

However, the reliability and efficacy of SAVE—the automated system for federal, state, and local government agencies to verify the immigration status of noncitizens—are simply assumed. The act and its pursuant regulations provide no due process protections for noncitizen and naturalized citizen license applicants whose immigration status must be verified through SAVE. They do not set time limits for the verification process or require that the applicant be issued a provisional driver's license valid until the verification process is competed. Nor is there a mandated process for access to immigration records to review them for errors, a mechanism to correct immigration records, access to an appeal if verification is wrongly denied by DHS, or an appeals process for errors in immigration determinations by the state department of motor vehicles (DMV). Finally, the act and regulations do not ensure that Social Security Administration (SSA) and DHS actions that delay issuance of an SSN do not also cause denial or delay issuance of a license.

There is good reason to question the accuracy of immigration records and the reliability of immigration processes. In a survey conducted by the American Association of Motor Vehicle Administrators, applicants at state DMVs criticized delays, the need for staff to make additional contacts with U.S. Citizenship and Immigration Services, and unavailability and unreliability of data.[33] The SSA itself, which must verify immigration status before issuing an SSN to a noncitizen, has complained that it often experiences significant delays in verifying immigration status through SAVE and sometimes receives no response at all.

Under the act, the only foreign document that may be used to meet its documentation requirements (including full legal name, date of birth, or gender) is a foreign passport. But many immigrants eligible for a driver's license (such as applicants for asylum or temporary protected status) may not have a for-

---

[31] 6 CFR §37.11(c).

[32] 6 CFR §37.11(g).

[33] Survey results are available at *www.realnightmare.org/images/File/AAMVA_survey_all.pdf* and *www.realnightmare.org/states/13/*.

eign passport and will not yet have one of the listed documents. They will not be able to use other foreign documents, such as a birth certificate, marriage certificate, school record, or the like, that are used to prove identity in immigration processes. While the regulations include an exceptions process for what appear to be core documentation requirements on nonimmigration issues,[34] they do not do the same for immigration requirements.

The act and regulations do not resolve the question of how long a temporary license is valid. Nor do they recognize or deal with the special issues presented by the requirement to provide a full legal name—a potential problem for citizens and immigrants alike who may not be able to reconcile different versions of their names in different documents. For noncitizens, the problems are more pronounced. The rules do not recognize differences in name order, name changes to conform to the U.S. system, differences introduced by transliteration, the fact that names may have been changed or shortened to make them easier to pronounce, or that a family name may be hyphenated or dropped to avoid confusion.

In 2007, 17 states passed laws or resolutions rejecting the REAL ID Act, arguing that it imposes a huge unfunded mandate and burdensome requirements.[35] Immigrants themselves, both before and after the law passed, have been engaged in an ongoing struggle to maintain or expand their access to licenses.[36]

Even states that already have immigration-specific provisions in their driver's license law will have to make modifications to comply with the REAL ID Act because these states make driver's licenses available to certain categories of noncitizens that REAL ID excludes, allow more flexibility with respect to proving and verifying identity and immigration status, and are less restrictive with respect to name-related requirements. State driver's license laws passed in response to the REAL ID Act that limit immigrants' access to licenses will likely ensure that the number of unlicensed and uninsured drivers will increase.

CONCLUSION

Noncitizens can expect no letup in the focus on driver's license issues, either because of changes in state laws pertaining to driving or immigration enforcement triggered by pretextual or real state driving violations. Once again, it is clear that a multitude of state laws is no substitute for real immigration reform that resolves the status of the millions of undocumented immigrants in the United States and provides a rational immigration system for the future.

---

[34] 6 CFR §§37.11 (g), (h).

[35] For information on state opposition, see *www.real nightmare.org.*

[36] For a resource guide on immigrant access to licenses, see *www.nilc.org/immspbs/DLs/resrc_guide/index.htm.*

SUBJECT-MATTER INDEX

violations of immigration laws, 653–657

Corroboration

benefit of the doubt and, 366

notice and opportunity to explain, 369

REAL ID Act and, 366–373

reasonable availability of, 368–369

CPT (Curricular practical training)

F-1 visas, 288–289

Credibility determinations

consistency, 363–364

demeanor, 365–366

REAL ID Act and, 360–366

specificity and detail, 365

Credible fear of persecution

expedited removal and, 389

Crimes

See also Aggravated felonies; Convictions; *specific crimes (e.g., firearms offenses)*

corporate compliance programs and criminal violations, 653–657

new criminal proceedings, effect on filing motions, 205

waiver of inadmissibility for criminal activity, 407

CSPA. *See* **Child Status Protection Act**

Curricular practical training (CPT)

F-1 visas, 288–289

Custodial interrogations

exclusionary rule and, 419–420

Customary international law

jus cogens and, 349–350

Customs and Border Protection (CBP)

TN visas and, 637–639

unsolicited legal advice from, 639

D

Death

of citizen or LPR spouse in I-751 waiver petition, 249

of petitioner with foreign spouse, 570

Debarment

fee-related, 121

Denial of visa

attorney's role in event of, 344

Deportability

waivers of, 400–401

Depression

as excessive hardship, 253

Detention

of arriving aliens, 190

challenging unlawful detention, 181–192

post removal detention, 187–190

of refugees, 190–191

Diplomatic assurances

Convention Against Torture (CAT) and, 349–356

Disabilities

naturalization, 612–613

Discovery

APA suits, 214–215

motions to suppress and, 422–423

Diversity visa applicants

child of, 498

Doctrine of immigrant intent

framework of, 301–303

in nonimmigrant visa classifications, 303–312

Document retention

law firms, 46–48

Documentation. See specific types of visas

DOL. *See* **Labor Department**

Domestic violence crimes

victims of, 253, 444–447

See also Battered children and spouses; Violence Against Women Act (VAWA)

Dominica

Economic Citizenship Program, 62

Driver's licenses

immigration policy and, 685–691

local police enforcement and immigration law, 687–688

REAL ID Act's effect on issuance of, 689–691

Drug use. *See* **Substance use and abuse**

Drunk driving

naturalization issues, 610–611

Dual intent

generally, 301

Dual representation

labor certification, 120–121

Due process

habeas corpus, 154–156

reinstatement of removal orders, 383–384

E

E nonimmigrant visas

E-3 visa anti-fraud rule, 117–118

intent of, 310

in London, 344–345

turnaround option for, 635

EB visa. *See* **Employment-based immigration**

EB-5 investors

generally, 53–79

benefiting U.S. economy, 67

"capital," 69–70

comparison of other countries with U.S., 57–62

creating an original business, 65

creating employment in targeted employment area, 71

creating or saving jobs, 67–68

Hindu Adoptions and
Maintenance Act
1956 (HAMA),
529–531
home study reports,
526–527
intercountry guidelines
(2006), 525–526
Juvenile Justice (Care &
Protection of
Children) Act,
2000, 531–532
preference for parents of
Indian origin,
527–528
problems in intercountry
adoption, 531–
532
ratification of Hague
Convention on
Intercountry
Adoption, 528
surrogacy arrangements,
533–534
graduate medical education
(GME) and EB-2
status, 140

**Ineffective assistance of
counsel**
motion to reopen based on,
197

Intent
See also Dual intent
adjustment of status and,
312–313
changed circumstances and,
313
doctrine of immigrant
intent, 301–303
exemption from
presumption of,
302–303
nonimmigrant visa
classifications, 303–
307
exemptions, 307–312
no intent required
(silent), 312
nonimmigrant vs.
preconceived intent,
302
preconceived intent issues,
313

Intercountry adoption. *See*
**Adoption; Hague
Convention on
Intercountry Adoption**
International media personnel
I visas, 312
Internships
J-1 visas, 293–300
Interviews
decision for naturalization
not made after, 616–
617
delay after filing for
naturalization, 616
Intracompany transfers
to Canada (C12), 647–648
intent of L-1 intracompany
transferees, 309
L-1B visas, 83–87
Investigative stops
exclusionary rule and, 415–
420
Investors. *See* **EB-5 investors**
**ISNET (Immigrant Safety
Network)**
assistance for dealing with
ICE raids, 666–673

J

J-1 visas
generally, 293–300
components of training
plans, 296
duration of trainee and
intern participation,
297
individualized plans, 295
intent and, 305–306
program exclusions, 296–
297
regulatory changes, 293
screening host companies,
297
training/intern placement
plan (T/IPP), 294,
299–300
Job descriptions
PERM requirements, 101–
102
Job orders
BALCA decisions, 123–
124
Judicial review
APA suits, 210–211

corroboration
determinations, 371
of motions to reopen, 169–
175
waiver of joint-filing
requirement, 249–
250
Jurisdiction
APA procedure, 208–209
CAT claims, 351
reinstatement of removal
orders, 377
waivers, 253
of joint-filing
requirement, 249
Jus cogens
customary international law
and, 349–350
**Juvenile Justice (Care &
Protection of Children)
Act, 2000**
adoption from India, 531–
532

K

K-1/K-2 fiancé(e) visa
generally, 513
appeals, 520–521
factual discrepancies in K-1
cases, 519–520
inadmissibility and waivers,
518–519
multiple petitions approved
for K-1 beneficiary,
520
proving bona fides, 520
revocation of petition, 520
**K-3/K-4 visa for spouse and
children**
generally, 513–521
Adam Walsh Act and, 516–
518
appeals, 520–521
application procedure, 514–
515
changing to or from status,
515
CSPA and age of children,
516
employment authorization,
515–516
extension of, 515

processing at U.S. ports of
entry, 631–634

qualification as
professional, 641

readmission at port of entry,
642

scientific
technician/technolo-
gist, 632–634, 638–
639, 641, 645–646

unsolicited legal advice
from CBP, 639

where to apply, 641

Tourists to U.S. *See* **B-2 visas**

Trafficking in persons

See also T visas

naturalization issues, 611–
612

**Trafficking Victims Protection
Reauthorization Acts
of 2003 and 2005**

purpose and scope of, 483

Trainees

J-1 visas, 293–300

Training programs

for paralegals, 1–4, 7

Transsexuals

marriage-based
immigration and,
555–561

Travel, right to

advance parole and, 575–
576

K-3/K-4 visa, 515

liberty rights and, 152–153

optional practical training
(OPT), 291

Trollinger v. Tyson Foods
(2008)

complaint, 676–677

description and implications
of, 675–684

INS case against Tyson,
676

plaintiffs' attempts to
provide evidence

actual knowledge that
aliens brought
illegally into
U.S., 682

attempt to obtain DHS
files, 679

depositions, 679

expert witness, 678–679

of illegal aliens in
Tyson's
workforce, 678–
679

of illegal hiring claim,
678

language discrimination
and I-9
verification, 681

second amended complaint,
677–678

summary judgment ruling,
682–683

willful blindness theory,
680–681

Tuberculosis

Form I-601 for waiver, 255

screening, 222–224

U

U visas

generally, 451–471

application procedure, 455–
459

declaration of applicant,
478

preparing winning
applications,
475–476

applying for LPR status,
461

checklist for, 464–469

cooperation with
investigation or
prosecution, 455

derivative beneficiaries,
456

documenting of case, 478

eligibility for, 453–455

ethical considerations, 473–
475

forms needed for, 462–463

law enforcement
certification, 480–
481

noncitizen currently in
immigration
proceedings or
previously ordered
removed, deported,
or excluded, 459–
460

noncitizen previously
granted U interim
relief, 460

purpose and scope of, 452–
453, 476, 482

qualifying crimes for, 453–
454

statutory cap, 460–461

substantial physical or
mental harm, 455,
458, 478–479

summary of requirements,
470, 476–477

Undocumented workers

accrued vacation pay, 659

civil RICO actions. *See*
Civil RICO actions

COBRA, 660

final payment for time
worked, 659

grievances prior to loss of
employment, 660–
661

Social Security benefits,
659

Trollinger v. Tyson Foods
(2008), 675–684

unemployment benefits,
659

workers' compensation,
659–660

Unemployment benefits

undocumented workers,
659

United Arab Emirates

establishments residence
permit, 60–61

Universities

immigrant eligibility
for financial aid, 450
for in-state tuition, 449–
450

Unlawful detention

challenging, 181–192

Unlawful expulsion

challenges to, 159–160

Unlawful presence

generally, 265–284

adjustment of status, 278–
280

appeals or motions to
reopen, 277–278

BIA decisions, 273–274

calculation for, 265–268

exceptions, 268–269

Hague Convention on
Intercountry
Adoption and, 540

inadmissibility caused by,
269–272

marriage and, 569

permanent 10-year bar,
271–272

10-year bar, 271

three-year bar, 269–271

waiver process, 272
application for, 274–277

USA PATRIOT Act of 2001
SEVIS under, 285, 286

USCIS
assistance from, 30

V

V visas
intent of, 309

Vaccination requirements. *See*
**Communicable
diseases**

Venue
APA procedure, 208

Victims of crimes. *See* **U visas;
Violence Against
Women Act (VAWA)**

**Victims of Trafficking and
Violence Protection
Act of 2000 (VTVPA)**
purpose and scope of, 483

**Violence Against Women Act
(VAWA)**
See also U visas
abuse, types of, 248
adoption of children, 550
CSPA applicability, 507
waiver of 10-year unlawful
presence bar, 272

Visa Waiver Program
adjustment of status and,
407

Visitors for business. *See* **B-1
visas**

Voluntary departure
appeals, 409
arriving aliens, 409
bonds, 409, 410
at conclusion of
proceedings, 409–
410

failure to depart during
period of, 411

involuntary prehearing
voluntary departure,
158–159

motions to reopen and,
411–412

overstaying period of, 408

preserving, 173–174

prior to completion of
proceedings, 409

strategy of seeking, 411–
412

tolling, 204–205

types of, 408–409

unlawful presence and, 277

Voluntary return/removal
unlawful presence and, 277

Vulnerable immigrants
welfare benefit applicants,
444–447

W

Waivers
See also Hardship waiver
abuse waiver to good-faith
marriage, 247–248
communicable disease
inadmissibility,
225–226
of criminal activity, 407
of deportability, 400–401
HIV-based, 217–220
See also HIV/AIDS
I-212 waivers, 385
I-751 waivers, 243–250
of inadmissibility, 251–263,
458–459
*See also specific grounds
under this
heading*
joint-filing requirement and
hardship waivers,
243–250
K-1/K-3 visa applications,
518–519
substance use as grounds
for inadmissibility,
237–240
unlawful presence bar, 272
vaccination inadmissibility,
226–227

Welfare benefits
affidavits of support, 442–
443, 446
federal means-tested public
benefit, 440–441
federal/state divide, 438,
445
five-year bar, 441
immigrant access to, 437–
450
immigrant eligibility for,
447–450
child care programs, 449
education, 449–450
food stamps, 448–449
Head Start, 449
housing benefits, 449
Medicaid, 448
SCHIP, 448
school breakfast and
lunch programs,
449
WIC benefits, 449
income maintenance
programs, 447–448
naturalization of recipients,
613
PRUCOL ("permanently
residing under color
of law"), 439–440,
446
public charges, 443–444,
446
"qualified alien" status,
438–439, 445
qualifying quarters, 441–
442, 446
vulnerable immigrants,
444–447

**Western Hemisphere Priority
Date (WHPD)**
determination and proof of,
281–284

**WIC (women, infants, and
children) benefits**
immigrant eligibility for,
449

Witnesses
cooperating witness and
family members,
434–435

Workers' compensation